1971

For
ILSE
and
SHARON

Copyright © 1971 by Holt, Rinehart and Winston, Inc.
All rights reserved

Library of Congress Catalog Card Number: 73–148058

SBN: 03-083380-9

Printed in the United States of America

0 1 2 3   0 3 8   9 8 7 6 5 4 3 2 1

Preface

*I*n planning *Problems in Philosophical Inquiry*, our desire was to gather a representative collection of essays, each complete in itself, which would provide the beginning student with a fair sampling of the problems, solutions, and techniques of argument and appraisal with which philosophers have been concerned for more than two millenia. The essays are arranged into sections, each deals with one central issue, most are arranged so that an essay presents a solution to a problem and is then criticized by the essay or essays that follow. The introductions trace the thread of one argument through the essays they introduce, and thus make no pretence of raising all the issues that the essays themselves raise.

It is perhaps easier to "do" philosophy than to define it. The same probably holds for science and (if we replace "do" by "believe") for religion. Rather than attempt a general definition of philosophy, which might produce a feeling of edification but not much actual illumination, it undoubtedly will be more helpful at the introductory level to discuss some of the fields of philosophy, noting the problems dealt with in those fields and clarifying why there are problems for which people have sought solutions within science and religion.

Theory of Knowledge (Epistemology). Apparently, the world is at our fingertips; it is there to be experienced and it is as we experience it. We also see, touch, taste, smell, and hear phenomena that exist independent of being seen, touched, tasted, smelled, and heard. Surely the existence of a solid, public world is something we have knowledge about, knowledge which is secure from the ravages of even the most determined skepticism. Psychologically, the belief that there are enduring three-dimensional objects which can be bought, sold, used, and reused is deeply rooted in thought and speech. It is unlikely that we shall stop believing in a world of observable objects, but once we distinguish between what we cannot help but believe and what we are rationally justified in believing, skepticism rears its head.

For instance, some of our sensory experiences are nonveridical in the sense that what they apparently present to us is not there to be presented. The wet spot that appears to remain equidistant from the front of our car on hot days, the pink rats a man sees in delirium tremens, the mirage seen by a tired and thirsty man in the desert—these experiences occur even though the pavement is dry, no rats are pink, and only sand is within miles of the traveler. It is easy to hear the wailing of a ghost in the howling of the wind when it is dark; each of us can supply our own examples.

In making the distinction between veridical and nonvericidal experience we are relying on our knowledge of a public world, so that we can appeal to illusions, hallucinations, and the like as instances in which we are likely to be "misled by our senses" only by assuming that other sensory experiences of ours do not mislead us. But such experiences may shake our confidence in any particular sensory experience, for now we must ask not only what it tells us but also whether what it tells us is true.

Veridical and nonveridical sensory experiences are often very similar in content. If they deceive us, it is because they are so like "the real thing," and even when we are not deceived by them we mark their similarity to veridical sensory experiences by the very language we use to describe them. Perhaps it is self-defeating to appeal to nonveridical sensory experiences as evidence that we have no secure knowledge of the physical world since the very distinction between nonveridical and veridical perception assumes that some of our sensory experiences are veridical; we are still left in doubt as to which ones are which. And, unless we can tell which are which—which experiences tell the truth and which do not—the fact that some perceptions are veridical will be of relatively little comfort. To call an experience nonveridical is to suppose that we have some reason to doubt the veracity of that experience; when we have no special reason to doubt our given common sense perception it is veridical.

The skeptic may question whether the conceptual scheme that all of us are taught is in fact correct. Why not ask if the sensory experience we have requires that we view its objects as public, stable, physical objects: Are there *other* accounts of our sensory experiences which also square with the content of that experience, however little they may square with "common sense?" George Berkeley and David Hume thought there were, though Berkeley added that common sense was correct enough when it was cleansed from metaphysical perversions. In contrast to Hume, he held the view that there is strictly no public world of public, physical objects— for metaphysical and theological reasons and not from skeptical reasons or motives.

Thus far we have been concerned with questions regarding our knowledge of the "external world" and with how skepticism may endeavor, perhaps with success, to attack our claims to have such knowledge. While questions concerning perception have always loomed large in the theory of knowledge, there are other matters that fall under this rubric. For example, the nature of knowledge—whether it is justified true belief or something more, whether there is a possibility of moral knowledge, and whether there is reliability in commonsense beliefs. These issues are exhibited in the essays that follow, and the introductions to these essays detail some crucial arguments and counter arguments.

Metaphysics. There is a subtle but important shift of emphasis when one turns from theory of knowledge, or epistemology, to metaphysics. Theory of knowledge is concerned with the capacities and limitations of the knower, metaphysics with the existence and character of the known. In theory of knowledge, one considers the possibility and conditions of knowledge, in metaphysics, the qualities and relations of objects of knowledge. The nature of the knower is relevant to his capacities for knowledge. Thus, when he seeks self-knowledge, man engages in an endeavor which has in part the same subject as it has object.

Traditionally, metaphysicians have been concerned with such problems as the nature of space and time, the question as to whether every event must have a cause and if so what it means for one event to cause another, whether the universe contains universals as well as particulars, and whether there must be something (substance) which exists and remains the same throughout change. But metaphysicians have also been concerned with issues more closely related to the nature and lives of human beings. One philosophical problem tends to lead into another, and it would be risky to suppose that the questions which bear no readily discernible relation to everyday affairs and basic human concerns are really unrelated. It seems wise to begin with matters which bear directly on ordinary human problems: Has man freedom of will? Is there a basis for personal identity? Are mind and body different and distinct or identical, or related intimately though in principle separable, or what? If they are distinct, do they interact? Freedom, fate, and choice; persons, minds, and bodies; each triad of concepts poses problems felt by poet and playwright as well as philosopher. It is easier for us to feel the bite of these issues, perhaps, than to feel any close relationship to or interest in questions concerning the nature of space-time or of the universal. The particular applications of these questions are dealt with in the introductions to individual sections as well as in the essays by traditional and contemporary philosophers.

There is a question, however, which should be dealt with here. Aren't these questions concerning personal identity, free will, and mind-body relationships simply scientific matters? Surely, when we have enough laboratory data to resolve them, we will know the answers. Until then, we remain in relative ignorance.

Now, views on this issue concerning the scope and limitations of science and the nature of philosophy are themselves philosophical views, but noting this does little to answer our question. Indeed, it seems inappropriate to try here to answer this question for the student, since he ought to try to answer it for himself, when he has read enough philosophy and science to deal responsibly with the matter. Further, it is a large issue and a basic one—one on which philosophers themselves differ. Nevertheless, it may be that some issues are matters to be decided by the sciences, either natural or social, whereas other issues remain recalcitrant under a scientific approach and are matters for philosophical reflection. Still, a few comments may be made which will perhaps provide a beginning for thought on the relation between science and philosophy.

Questions about freedom often link to questions concerning responsibility. Indeed, even those who have supposed that being free is irrelevant to being determined, or is perfectly compatible with being determined, make the relation. Moral responsibility is in turn related to legal responsibility. When a person is medically judged incapable of refraining from theft he may escape legal condemnation. A person who is judged permanently or temporarily insane is in a quite different position before the law than is one who is judged sane, for the insane are not responsible (presumably neither morally nor legally) for what they do, unless perhaps they willfully brought on their insanity (if that is possible). Personal identity is not unrelated to responsibility, and Immanuel Kant defined a person as one whose deeds were imputable to him. If freedom is incompatible with determinism, and if all choices are determined, then for Kant there would simply not be any persons. Some philosophers have argued that while all events are caused, and to be caused is to be determined, human choices and actions are not events. They have sometimes noted that choices are *mental* events and said only *physical* events are determined.

The cluster of issues surrounding the concepts of causality, determinism, freedom, responsibility, personality, personal identity, and the like are cross-disciplinary issues. Morality, law, social practices, scientific discoveries and their interpretation, the data of introspection, philosophical analyses of the concepts of choice and action, and a good deal more become relevant to the resolution of these issues, which continue to be challenging.

It is easy, too, fatally easy, to pack a particular conclusion into one's methods or the description of one's data, so that mental neutrality is not attained. These considerations do not prove that philosophical reflection is requisite to the settling or maintaining of a viable viewpoint concerning these issues. They do indicate that anyone who supposes that they are ultimately purely scientists' questions, issues to be decided in the laboratory, is not only taking a philosophical stance but he is also willing to defend that stance as one of many possible ones. He must enter the arena and not pretend to be a spectator. Careful consideration of the problems raised by the essays is one prerequisite to having an informed opinion on these matters.

Ethics. There is certainly no lack of material these days for moral reflection. The availability of drugs, the presence of "the pill," the problems posed by the draft, the various uses of violent or nonviolent protest and dozens of other matters supplement the traditional questions of whether lying is ever right, whether theft is ever justified, whether taking the life of another is ever permissible or even obligatory, among many others, as proper objects of moral consideration. But it is not the presence of new issues that gives rise to the considerable degree of moral perplexity and chaos that many now experience. New issues are always going to arise, and will continue to develop.

More fundamental than the presence of new and difficult issues is the lack of any common moral perspective—the absence of any agreed-upon set of moral principles to appeal to in making moral decisions. Perhaps some basic distinctions will help to sort out issues. Unless one is clear about what the issues are, he will be unlikely to think clearly or profitably about them. Moral heat without moral light is perhaps quite as unfortunate, and dangerous, as moral light without moral heat. In this sense, anyone who asks what he ought to do is (with qualifications to be noted shortly) making a moral decision—or, better, a *morally relevant* decision—whether he decides rightly or wrongly. A morally relevant decision may or may not be a *morally right* decision. Thus we should distinguish between *morally relevant* decisions—decisions on matters with respect to which moral reflection is appropriate—and *morally right* decisions. The former may be morally good or morally evil; the latter are, by definition, morally good.

There are, of course, at least two qualifications that must be made. First, there are senses of *ought* and *good* which are not in any obvious sense *moral* uses of these terms. That I ought to fly rather than walk if I want to go rapidly from Atlanta to Melbourne, and so on, are of course not moral matters. Second, how sharply the moral senses of *good* and *ought* are to be divided from nonmoral senses of these same terms is itself a matter of debate among moral philosophers. For example, there is much more in common between moral and nonmoral uses of such terms as *good* and *bad* if we accept Aristotle's moral theory than there is if we accept Kant's. But we find a good deal of agreement about when moral reflection is appropriate and when it is not. It is appropriate to reflect morally when we consider whether to fight in a war or weigh the degrees to which individual liberty should be restricted for the common good, and it is normally not appropriate when we are considering what brand of merchandise to buy.

Another important distinction is that between *moral principles* and *moral rules*. Such maxims as "It is normally wrong to lie" and the like are moral rules. Such statements as "One ought always to treat another as an end in himself and not merely as a means" are moral principles. That there are exceptions to moral rules does not entail that there are also exceptions to moral principles, and normally exceptions to moral rules are justified by implicit or explicit appeal to moral principles. It is sometimes supposed, because one can usually discover some context in which a moral rule should be violated, that this fact is itself an argument for moral relativism; it is not.

In most cases of morally relevant decisions there will be at least two considerations: What are the facts, the empirical features, of the situation to be judged? And what are the moral principles that are relevant? Sometimes "the facts" are hard or impossible to get; this is not a defect of moral principles.

There is immense diversity of acceptable conduct from one society to another and even from one subsociety to another within the same society. From the propriety of white shirt and tie to the permissibility of extramarital sexual relations, practices differ substantially. This, too, is often taken as evidence for moral relativism. But one should ask whether the diversity is in part or whole, one of interpretation of facts, or a difference of moral rules plus a difference as to what the facts are. If this is the case, there may be agreement on moral principles, which is quite compatible with great diversity of morally relevant practices. Or there may be disagreement about moral principles between societies. Two things should be kept in mind. One is that diversity of practice is easy to discover, whereas the presence or absence of agreement on principles is a much more basic and difficult matter to decide. The other is that to the extent that there is disagreement concerning principles there is genuine moral disagreement; the question then remains as to whether there is any rational way of deciding this difference.

A charge of "moral imperialism" is sometimes aimed at moral philosophers, those who raise and try to answer the issues evolved by philosophical reflection about morality. "Who are you to say that one person or action is morally right and another is wrong?" expresses this charge clearly enough. But the question, if it has any legitimacy at all, must be raised carefully. It is the purpose of moral philosophers to answer such questions as "Is there an absolute distinction between right and wrong? If so, what is the nature of that distinction? What makes right acts right?" And of course there are many other such questions a moral philosopher will deal with. But in endeavoring to answer them, he is not engaged in telling anyone what to do. He is asking if there are rationally defensible moral principles, not condemning or condoning anyone for following or not following them. When he turns to condemnation or praise, he is acting in the role of moral citizen, not moral philosopher, though what he holds as a moral philosopher will probably influence what he says in the role of moral citizen. Further, the task of making a moral appraisal of agent or action requires a knowledge of the purposes, intentions, goals of the agent and the information available to him, or of the context, likely consequences, and so on, of the action. It is possible that a man may act in a praiseworthy way, relative to his information and capacities, even though he violates, unknowingly, a moral principle.

This brings up another important distinction, that between *acting rightly relevant to our knowledge* and *acting rightly, period*. It seems clear that a man can only be responsible for the former; whether he has done the latter too may be hard to judge with certainty. The challenge "Who are you to judge that one person acts rightly and another wrongly?" might be met by another: "Who are you to say that such judgments cannot and should not be made?" The "tolerance" of the first question may well disguise a dogmatism as firm and unreasonable as any. Perhaps the thing to do is to eschew asking either question at the outset of one's study, and to see what the issues are and what some at least of those who have thought deeply about them have had to say.

Philosophy of Religion. What relation has Jerusalem (religious faith) to Athens (philosophical inquiry)? The answers have varied. Some philosophical systems are also ways of salvation. This is true of Plato's and Spinoza's answers. Other philosophical frameworks provided their originators with a way to reinterpret radically (or was it contradict?) religion, as Kant's or Hegel's. But relationship by competition or reinterpretation is not the most frequent manner in which philosophy and religion have had concourse.

Philosophers who were themselves religious believers have, not surprisingly, used the tools of philosophical argument and reflection to support their beliefs. In particular, arguments offered for the existence of God and the immortality of the human soul were most often regarded as having premises which could be known independent of divine revelation, either because they were self-evident or because they were evident to the senses. There is no necessity that an argument for the existence of God should follow this format, but in fact most have done so. It should not be thought that all religious believers accepted these arguments. The monk Gaunilon was not much impressed, for example, with Anselm's argument, and many believers—both among the ordinary and among the intellectually gifted—do not suppose that any argument has succeeded in establishing the divine existence.

Philosophers who were themselves unbelievers have also, not surprisingly, used the tools of philosophical argument and reflection to support their unbelief. It is fair to say that the problem of evil—the issue of whether one can both consistently and reasonably believe in an all-powerful, all-good creative Providence while accepting the fact that evil exists—has been the greatest source of tension for believers in the Judeo-Christian tradition and of polemics against faith for critics of that tradition. More recently, though very much with roots in past philosophy, the practice of arguing that religious beliefs are in fact not *beliefs*, but *feelings*, has gained approval among philosophers and theologians. The argument is that religious language is unintelligible or meaningless in the way that "triangles devour elephants" is unintelligible or meaningless. But meaningless language cannot express beliefs. The core of the charge of meaninglessness is that religious language cannot provide sentences which possess truth value (are *either* true *or* false). Religious belief cannot, the charge is, attain even to the dignity of falsehood. It may serve to express one's own emotions or to elicit the emotions of others, but religious beliefs cannot be true or false either. In any case, the verification principle—roughly, the thesis that a sentence is meaningful only if it is either true or false by definition or if there is some conceivable empirical, sensory observation which would render it false—has fallen into disrepute of late. Its major defect is expressed in the title of a journal article: "Indirectly Verifiable: Everything or Nothing."

We have noted some of the uses that have been made of philosophical arguments to establish or refute religious beliefs. Until recently, the fashion was to eschew offering proofs of God's existence but to discuss the issue of meaningfulness or lack thereof. Recently, new versions of the proof have been offered and with the demise of the verification principle there seems to be a bit less discussion of meaningfulness, though neither issue is likely to cease to concern philosophers of religion. Another sort of concourse between philosophy and religion is possible. While it, too, may fall short of complete neutrality, it offers an alternative or supplement to those mentioned.

Such terms as *conceptual clarification, analysis of meaning* (use), *the unpacking of concepts, the "logic" of a concept or proposition* have been heard frequently. They reflect the use of philosophical techniques to understand more clearly what is being said by a particular religious community, scientific hypothesis or theory, metaphysical system, and so on. It was Augustine's and Anselm's view that one should believe in order to understand. The consensus of opinion by one school of philosophy may be summarized by saying that by the careful study of the interrelationships between concepts within a religious tradition one can understand what that tradition maintains, whether one believes it or not. The same sort of descriptive pose is taken by those phenomenologists who purport to discern the structure of religious experience by techniques somewhat different from those used by more analytical philosophers. It is thus possible that philosophy can clarify and illuminate religious beliefs. But it is easy for description to become evaluation and analysis to become appraisal, and for these to shade off into one another at various points.

It is sometimes supposed that religious belief is trivialized by talk about "religious language." (Not that there is "religious language" in the sense that there is a French language; what is meant is the use to which a religious community puts language.) It is also sometimes supposed that the problems philosophers of religion now deal with and the techniques they use are different in kind from those they considered and used before the so-called revolution in philosophy. These views seem to reinforce one another, so that if one believes that philosophers are not dealing as of old with religion, it may also be supposed that they have trivialized religion too. No doubt one can find cases which give point to these suspicions, but the student should read carefully in both the traditional and contemporary sources to see if continuity is not at least as evident as discontinuity, if concern for religious truth (the truth of one's religious beliefs) is not as evident as it was in the past. Then he must make up his own mind.

Madison, Wisconsin
January 1971   K. E. Y.

Contents

PHILOSOPHY OF RELIGION

Theory
of
Knowledge

hat constitutes the knowledge of something? When is a reason a good reason? Do we have indubitable knowledge? If so, what is it? Is having indubitable knowledge necessary if we are to know anything positively? Is it true that sensory perception gives us reliable information concerning a world of physical objects? Are we directly aware of physical objects or must we infer their existence from what we are directly aware of? Do objects resemble our perceptions of them? Is a belief true if it is part of, or is presupposed by, common sense? Is diversity of moral opinion evidence for moral relativism? These questions, and many like them, supply the field of inquiry known as theory of knowledge or epistemology. They are not questions in learning theory or in any other area of psychology, though answers to psychological questions may be relevant to the answers to some epistemological queries. Neither do they come within the scope of the natural sciences, though the results of scientific inquiry may in some cases be relevant to their answers.

In the essays that follow, we have highlighted one extremely influential line of thought. Philosophers have often sought indubitable knowledge. Plato distinguished knowledge from opinion partly on the basis that knowledge provided certain truth and opinion did not. Descartes sought unshakable premises on which to base his conclusions as a builder might seek rock on which to build the foundations and superstructure of his home. Plato and Descartes have not been alone in their quest.

If most philosophers have agreed on the importance of seeking indubitable knowledge, they have been less in accord about where it resides. Among the candidates for the source of indubitable knowledge have been intuition of moral truths, experience of sensory qualities, awareness of an enduring self, cognition of logical laws, and acceptance of common-sense belief. Accordingly we have presented proponents and critics of each of these alternative sources of certainty.

There are a number of issues in the theory of knowledge that are in no obvious way dependent on whether we possess indubitable knowledge. Representative of such issues are these: Are there objects that exist independently of our experience? Do the causes of our sensory experiences resemble the experiences they cause? Is knowledge rightly defined as justified true belief? While some answers to these questions assume that we have indubitable knowledge, others do not. These questions thus have a degree of independence from the question of indubitable knowledge, and the methods used to deal with them are representative of the methods applied to answering other epistemological questions.

K. E. Y.

Is There Indubitable Knowledge

Is Moral Knowledge Possible?

It is widely held that ethical choices are arbitrary or at best are based only on changeable conventions. One important reason offered in support of this view is that when one learns what people in cultures other than one's own believe about moral matters, he discovers the greatest divergence of belief and practice. In the midst of such moral relativity, who can suppose that his own moral beliefs and practices are other than arbitrary? This is the line taken by Ruth Benedict in *Patterns of Culture*. She assures us that the proper conclusion of a survey of the varieties of moral opinion is that one should be tolerant of the views of others, no matter how contrary to his own convictions these views may be.

Ralph Linton qualifies Benedict's thesis. Underlying the diversity Benedict records, Linton insists that there is unity. We do some things, not for their own sake, but for the sake of something else. Men take medicine and submit to operations in order to maintain life and health. Medicine and operations are valued for what they bring about, not for what they are in themselves.

5

This distinction, as many others, is enshrined in a pair of technical terms. Something is intrinsically good if it is good in itself and extrinsically good if what it brings about is good. Medicine and operations have extrinsic value; health, perhaps, has intrinsic value. Linton argues that there is widespread agreement about what has intrinsic value (as an end in itself) though there is widespread disagreement about what has extrinsic value (as a means to something else). He offers examples of this agreement.

The philosopher Henry Veatch makes two objections to the sort of ethical relativism that Benedict embraces and Linton challenges. First, the data are utterly insufficient to the conclusion. That there is wide disagreement about moral issues does not entail either that there is no correct moral position or that there is no way to discern the correct position. The question, then, is whether there are right answers to moral issues and, if so, how they can be discerned. Nothing in the data Benedict appeals to helps us to answer this question. So it is gratuitous to infer relativism from these data.

Second, if relativism is true (that is, if every ethical choice really is arbitrary), then any one choice is as good as any other in any ethical context you name. Thus, if I have a chance to save a boy from drowning, it is equally appropriate morally for me to save his life, throw rocks at him to thwart his attempts to stay afloat, or rescue him and then throw him back into the water at a deeper and more turbulent point. If all choices are arbitrary, then all are equally permissible. As Veatch makes clear, the choice of dominating those with differing convictions is, on relativist ground, quite as acceptable as the choice of being tolerant. Benedict is simply inconsistent when she suggests that toleration is (nonarbitrarily) the *right* position. Further, it is not obvious that within any context one names, any choice *is* equally justified with every other, even if "equally justified" amounts only to "equally unjustified." Whether all choices are on a par with respect to justification is, at the very least, an open question after full account is taken of the data to which Benedict appeals.

Cultural and Ethical Relativism
RUTH BENEDICT

It is clear that culture may value and make socially available even highly unstable human types. If it chooses to treat their peculiarities as the most valued variants of human behavior, the individuals in question will rise to the occasion and perform their social rôles without reference to our usual ideas of the types who can make social adjustments and those who cannot. Those who function inadequately in any society are not those with certain fixed 'abnormal' traits, but may well be those whose responses have received no support in the institutions of their culture. The weakness of these aberrants is in great measure illusory. It springs, not from the fact that they are lacking in necessary vigour, but that they are individuals whose native responses are not reaffirmed by

FROM: *Patterns of Culture*, Ruth Benedict. (Boston: Houghton Mifflin Company, 1961), pp. 233–240. Reprinted by permission of Houghton Mifflin Company.

society. They are, as Sapir phrases it, 'alienated from an impossible world.'

The person unsupported by the standards of his time and place and left naked to the winds of ridicule has been unforgettably drawn in European literature in the figure of Don Quixote. Cervantes turned upon a tradition still honoured in the abstract the limelight of a changed set of practical standards, and his poor old man, the orthodox upholder of the romantic chivalry of another generation, became a simpleton. The windmills with which he tilted were the serious antagonists of a hardly vanished world, but to tilt with them when the world no longer called them serious was to rave. He loved his Dulcinea in the best traditional manner of chivalry, but another version of love was fashionable for the moment, and his fervour was counted to him for madness.

These contrasting worlds which, in the primitive cultures we have considered, are separated from one another in space, in modern Occidental history more often succeed one another in time. The major issue is the same in either case, but the importance of understanding the phenomenon is far greater in the modern world where we cannot escape if we would from the succession of configurations in time. When each culture is a world in itself, relatively stable like the Eskimo culture, for example, and geographically isolated from all others, the issue is academic. But our civilization must deal with cultural standards that go down under our eyes and new ones that arise from a shadow upon the horizon. We must be willing to take account of changing normalities even when the question is of the morality in which we were bred. Just as we are handicapped in dealing with ethical problems so long as we hold to an absolute definition of morality, so we are handicapped in dealing with human society so long as we identify our local normalities with the inevitable necessities of existence.

No society has yet attempted a self-conscious direction of the process by which its new normalities are created in the next generation. Dewey has pointed out how possible and yet how drastic such social engineering would be. For some traditional arrangements it is obvious that very high prices are paid, reckoned in terms of human suffering and frustration. If these arrangements presented themselves to us merely as arrangements and not as categorical imperatives, our reasonable course would be to adapt them by whatever means to rationally selected goals. What we do instead is to ridicule our Don Quixotes, the ludicrous embodiments of an outmoded tradition, and continue to regard our own as final and prescribed in the nature of things.

In the meantime the therapeutic problem of dealing with our psychopaths of this type is often misunderstood. Their alienation from the actual world can often be more intelligently handled than by insisting that they adopt the modes that are alien to them. Two other courses are always possible. In the first place, the misfit individual may cultivate a greater objective interest in his own preferences and learn how to manage with greater equanimity his deviation from the type. If he learns to recognize the extent to which his suffering has been due to his lack of support in a traditional ethos, he may gradually educate himself to accept his degree of difference with less suffering. Both the exaggerated emotional disturbances of the manic-depressive and the seclusion of the schizophrenic add certain values to existence which are not open to those differently constituted. The unsupported individual who valiantly accepts his favourite and native virtues may attain a feasible course of behaviour that makes it unnecessary for him to take refuge in a private world he has fashioned for himself. He may gradually achieve a more independent and less tortured attitude toward his deviations and upon this attitude he may be able to build an adequately functioning existence.

In the second place, an increased tolerance in society toward its less usual types must keep pace with the self-education of the patient. The possibilities in this direction are endless. Tradition is as neurotic as any patient; its overgrown fear of deviation from its fortuitous standards conforms to all the usual definitions of the psychopathic. This fear does not depend upon observation of the limits within which conformity is necessary to the social good. Much more deviation is allowed to the individual in some cultures than in others, and those in which much is allowed cannot be shown to suffer from their peculiarity. It is probable that social orders of the future will carry this tolerance and encouragement of individual difference much further than any cultures of which we have experience.

The American tendency at the present time leans so far to the opposite extreme that it is not easy for us to picture the changes that such an attitude would bring about. Middletown is a typical example of our usual urban fear of seeming in however slight an act different from our neighbours. Eccentricity is more feared than parasitism. Every sacrifice of time and tranquillity is made in order that no one in the family may have any taint of nonconformity attached to him. Children in school make their great tragedies out of not wearing a certain kind of stockings, not joining a certain dancing-class, not driving a certain car. The fear of being different is the dominating motivation recorded in Middletown.

The psychopathic toll that such a motivation exacts is evident in every institution for mental diseases in our country. In a society in which it existed only as a minor motive among many others, the psychiatric picture would be a very different one. At all events, there can be no reasonable doubt that one of the most effective ways in which to deal with the staggering burden of psychopathic tragedies in America at the present time is by means of an educational program which fosters tolerance in society and a kind of self-respect and independence that is foreign to Middletown and our urban traditions.

Not all psychopaths, of course, are individuals whose native responses are at variance with those of their civilization. Another large group are those who are merely inadequate and who are strongly enough motivated so that their failure is more than they can bear. In a society in which the will-to-power is most highly rewarded, those who fail may not be those who are differently constituted, but simply those who are insufficiently endowed. The inferiority complex takes a great toll of suffering in our society. It is not necessary that sufferers of this type have a history of frustration in the sense that strong native bents have been inhibited; their frustration is often enough only the reflection of their inability to reach a certain goal. There is a cultural implication here, too, in that the traditional goal may be accessible to large numbers or to very few, and in proportion as success is obsessive and is limited to the few, a greater and greater number will be liable to the extreme penalties of maladjustment.

To a certain extent, therefore, civilization in setting higher and possibly more worth-while goals may increase the number of its abnormals. But the point may very easily be overemphasized, for very small changes in social attitudes may far outweigh this correlation. On the whole, since the social possibilities of tolerance and recognition of individual difference are so little explored in practice, pessimism seems premature. Certainly other quite different social factors which we have just discussed are more directly responsible for the great proportion of our neurotics and psychotics, and with these other factors civilizations could, if they would, deal without necessary intrinsic loss.

We have been considering individuals from the point of view of their ability to function adequately in their society. This adequate functioning is one of the ways in which normality is clinically defined. It is also defined in terms of fixed symptoms, and the tendency is to identify normality with the statistically average. In practice this average is one arrived at in the laboratory, and deviations from it are defined as abnormal.

From the point of view of a single culture this procedure is very useful. It shows the clinical picture of the civilization and gives considerable information about its socially approved behaviour. To generalize this as an absolute normal, however, is a different matter. As we have seen, the range of normality in different cultures does not coincide. Some, like Zuñi and the Kwakiutl, are so far removed from each other that they overlap only slightly. The statistically determined normal on the Northwest Coast would be far outside the extreme boundaries of abnormality in the Pueblos. The normal Kwakiutl rivalry contest would only be understood as madness in Zuñi, and the traditional Zuñi indifference to dominance and the humiliation of others would be the fatuousness of a simpleton in a man of noble family on the Northwest Coast. Aberrant behaviour in either culture could never be determined in relation to any least common denominator of behaviour. Any society, according to its major preoccupations, may increase and intensify even hysterical, epileptic, or paranoid symptoms, at the same time relying socially in a greater and greater degree upon the very individuals who display them.

This fact is important in psychiatry because it makes clear another group of abnormals which probably exists in every culture: the abnormals who represent the extreme development of the local cultural type. This group is socially in the opposite situation from the group we have discussed, those whose responses are at variance with their cultural standards. Society, instead of exposing the former group at every point, supports them in their furthest aberrations. They have a licence which they may almost endlessly exploit. For this reason these persons almost never fall within the scope of any contemporary psychiatry. They are unlikely to be described even in the most careful manuals of the generation that fosters them. Yet from the point of view of another generation or culture they are ordinarily the most bizarre of the psychopathic types of the period.

The Puritan divines of New England in the eighteenth century were the last persons whom contemporary opinion in the colonies regarded as psychopathic. Few prestige groups in any culture have been allowed such complete intellectual and emotional dictatorship as they were. They were the voice of God. Yet to a modern observer it is they, not the confused and tormented women they put to death as witches, who were the psychoneurotics of Puritan New England. A sense of guilt as extreme as they portrayed and demanded both in their own conversion experiences and in those of their converts is found in a slightly saner civilization only in institutions for mental diseases. They admitted no salvation without a conviction of sin that prostrated the victim, sometimes for years, with remorse and terrible anguish. It was the duty of the minister to put the fear of hell into the heart of even the youngest child, and to exact of every convert emotional acceptance of his damnation if God saw fit to damn him. It does not matter where we turn among the records of New England Puritan churches of this period, whether to those dealing with witches or with unsaved children not yet in their teens or with such themes as damnation and predestination, we are faced with the fact that the group of people who carried out to the greatest extreme and in the fullest honour the cultural doctrine of the moment are by the slightly altered standards of our generation the victims of intolerable aberrations. From the point of view of a comparative psychiatry they fall in the category of the abnormal.

In our own generation extreme forms of ego-gratification are culturally supported in a similar fashion. Arrogant and unbridled egoists as family men, as officers of the law and in business, have been again and again portrayed by novelists and dramatists, and they are familiar in every community. Like the behaviour of Puritan divines, their courses of action are often more asocial than those of the inmates of penitentiaries. In terms of the suffering and frustration that they spread about them there is probably no comparison. There is very possibly at least as great a degree of mental warping. Yet they are entrusted with positions of great influence and importance and are as a rule fathers of families. Their impress both upon their own children and upon the structure of our society is indelible. They are not described in our manuals of psychiatry because they are supported by every tenet of our civilization. They are sure of themselves in real life in a way that is possible only to those who are oriented to the points of the compass laid down in their own culture. Nevertheless a future psychiatry may well ransack our novels and letters and public records for illumination upon a type of abnormality to which it would not otherwise give credence. In every society it is among this very group of the culturally encouraged and fortified that some of the most extreme types of human behaviour are fostered.

Social thinking at the present time has no more important task before it than that of taking adequate account of cultural relativity. In the fields of both sociology and psychology the implications are fundamental, and modern thought about contacts of peoples and about our changing standards is greatly in need of sane and scientific direction. The sophisticated modern temper has made of social relativity, even in the small area which it has recognized, a doctrine of despair. It has pointed out its incongruity with the orthodox dreams of permanence and ideality and with the individual's illusions of autonomy. It has argued that if human experience must give up these, the nutshell of existence is empty. But to interpret our dilemma in these terms is to be guilty of an anachronism. It is only the inevitable cultural lag that makes us insist that the old must be discovered again in the new, that there is no solution but to find the old certainty and stability in the new plasticity. The recognition of cultural relativity carries with it its own values, which need not be those of the absolutist philosophies. It challenges customary opinions and causes those who have been bred to them acute discomfort. It rouses pessimism because it throws old formulae into confusion, not because it contains anything intrinsically difficult. As soon as the new opinion is embraced as customary belief, it will be another trusted bulwark of the good life. We shall arrive then at a more realistic social faith, accepting as grounds of hope and as new bases for tolerance the coexisting and equally valid patterns of life which mankind has created for itself from the raw materials of existence.

The Problem of Universal Values
RALPH LINTON

The study of values has assumed much more than academic interest for the modern world. With the rapid improvement in means of communication which has taken place during the last century and the resulting increase in cross-cultural contacts, the potentialities for conflict have become greater than ever before. It is obvious that unless the various nations which compose the modern world can come to some sort of agreement as to what things are important and desirable, we are headed for catastrophe. Moreover, the very ease of

FROM *Method and Perspective in Anthropology*, ed. Robert F. Spencer, (Minneapolis: University of Minnesota Press, 1954), pp. 145–168. Reprinted by permission of University of Minnesota Press.

communication which may produce such a catastrophe ensures its inclusiveness. In the Dark Ages which would result from a world war of atomic bombs and bacteria there would be no region sufficiently isolated to escape destruction and carry on the torch of enlightenment. The peoples of the world must find common areas of understanding or die.

As students of human behavior in all its aspects, anthropologists might be expected to take a prominent part in solving the problems which the present situation has created. However, they have consistently avoided judgments regarding what things are universally desired or valued. Their principal contribution to date has been the development of the concept of cultural relativity. Through their comparative studies they have been able to demonstrate that different societies have successfully achieved the same ends by employing widely different means. From this they have concluded that the really scientific attitude toward cultural differences is the one summed up in the old saying: "Well, some do and some don't." While such tolerance is a necessary first step to international understanding, its contribution is essentially negative. Any sort of successful cooperation must be built on a realization that, no matter how various societies may go about it, all of them prize and desire certain things and should be willing to work together to get them.

No matter how much one may stress the right of every society to adhere to its own ways, the fact remains that some of the culturally approved practices of any society are likely to arouse strongly negative emotional reactions in the members of some other society. The European feels that the Muslim practice of eating with the fingers is repulsive, while the Muslim is equally revolted at the thought of using forks and spoons which may be ceremonially unclean. In spite of thorough training in cultural relativity, the present writer has never been able to observe the common Latin country practice of picking chickens alive with real equanimity. It is difficult to overcome such reactions and, the more of them the culture of another society arouses, the more difficult it is for the outsider to feel at home among its members. The assumption that continuous contact with the members of another society and increased familiarity with its culture will automatically result in increased liking is a victory of optimism over experience. Anyone who has had numerous cross-cultural contacts can testify that there are societies continued contact with which merely results in increasing dislike. If the world's societies are to reach a state of adjustment in which they can cooperate toward common ends, these ends must be so clearly defined that the societies' members can understand them and be willing to overcome some measure of mutual distaste in order to see them achieved. This, in turn, involves a recognition of universal values which can be used as a basis for determining which ends will be universally acceptable. Thanks to their long experience in comparative culture studies, the anthropologists should be able to make a real contribution toward this. They are in a particularly good position to recognize basic similarities as well as differences, and it is to be hoped that their current preoccupation with the latter is only a passing phase in the development of the science.

Philosophers have been involved with the problems of value for centuries, and scientists have been willing to leave these problems to them. Now that the importance of values is increasingly recognized in all the sciences which have to do with man, the philosophers' conclusions are not proving as useful as might be hoped. The philosophic approaches have leaned heavily upon supernatural sanctions or upon vaguely defined concepts such as the good, the true, and the beautiful. While their conclusions have been developed over centuries, they have been developed in the absence of the conceptual tools provided by modern social science and psychology. None of the great philosophic authorities on values were familiar with the modern concepts of culture or culture process, and none of them possessed our modern knowledge of the role of learning in personality development and in the establishment of group personality norms. Moreover, the philosophers' conclusions are often phrased in a language which the scientist finds it difficult to translate into his own. It would seem that the time is now ripe for an attack on the problem by the scientific method of cross-cultural comparison.[1]

The first requirement for a scientific approach to the problem of values in culture is some agreement as to what is meant by the term *value*. Like many other words in the English language, *value* carries multiple meanings depending upon its context. Even if we ignore its technical usages in such fields as economics, mathematics, and art, several meanings remain. The element common to these seems to be best expressed by the superficially humorous definition: "A value is anything of any value," i.e., anything regarded favorably. A value is thus anything capable of influencing the individual's decisions in choice situations or, going one step further back and as a necessary preliminary to such influence, anything capable of producing an emotional response. Under this definition there are, of course, individual values as well as those which are cultural, i.e., shared and transmitted by the members of a particular society. However, in a search for universals the individual values, insofar as they are individual, may be ignored. They are transitory, like the persons who hold them, and unless they come to be shared by other individuals, have little influence on the social-cultural continuum.

For our present purposes we will define a value as: *anything capable of producing similar choice responses in several of a society's members.* It may

[1] An excellent summary of the current anthropological views of the subject will be found in Kluckhohn's article on values in Parsons and Shils, *Toward a General Theory of Action* (Harvard University Press, 1952).

be noted that this fails to bring in the factor of favorable response implicit in the ordinary use of the term. However, any consideration of values as dynamic elements in culture soon reveals that there are, in all cultures, numerous acts, objects, and concepts toward which the members of the society have strong negative attitudes. These attitudes are frequently much stronger than one would anticipate from a mere antithesis between the thing toward which the attitude is held and its opposite. Thus in our society at the present time the hysterical opposition to communism and the persecution of individuals in which it is reflected certainly are not matched by an equally strong emotional attachment to the liberties assured by our democratic system of government or by an equally intense respect and admiration for those who are attempting to maintain them in the face of the present attack upon them.

One hesitates to employ the term *negative values*, yet in any attempt to understand the operation of cultures one must recognize the functional significance of negative as well as positive attitudes. The members of a society will work quite as hard to *avoid* certain things as to *obtain* others. In a brief discussion of the concept of cultural values for which the writer was responsible some years ago[2] he suggested that the situation might be clarified by substituting for the single term *value* the more precise term *value attitude system*. Under this terminology a value may be regarded as anything toward which the members of a society normally have a definite attitude, whether favorable or unfavorable. Since the question of positive versus negative attitudes is not particularly significant for the present discussion, we will use the single term *value* for systems of both sorts.

To understand the relation of values to the operation of a society, one must recognize that values are an inte-

[2] Ralph Linton, *Cultural Background of Personality* (New York: Appleton Century-Crofts, 1946).

gral part of any society's culture and that, with regard to their origin, transmission, and integration, they follow the same rules as other culture elements. The normal society consists of an organized, self-perpetuating group of individuals which persists far beyond the life span of any one of its component members. Its persistence is made possible by the presence of a culture, i.e., an organized series of ideas and behavior patterns which are transmitted from generation to generation within the society. The culture as a whole provides techniques by which the members of the society can both satisfy their individual needs and cooperate toward common ends. The latter involves an elaborate system of specialized activities and reciprocal behaviors which together constitute the social system. The needs of individuals and of the society are shaped and the possible ways of satisfying them delimited by the milieu in which the society operates. At any given point in time this milieu is a product of the interaction of the society's external environment, both natural and social, and the content of its current culture.

All societies and cultures are not only continuums but continuums in a constant state of change and internal readjustment. The milieu is always unstable, presenting the society with new problems, and the culture itself is always changing under the pressure of internal as well as external forces. Individuals develop new solutions to old problems and new patterns are borrowed from other societies while each new element introduced into the culture produces disharmonies which take time to adjust. The only really stable factors in the cultural-social continuum are the needs of individuals as these stem from the physical-psychological qualities of our species and the social imperatives, i.e., the problems posed by organized group living per se, problems which must be solved if the society is to survive.

In this situation of constant flux, the society's main guide in meeting new problems and in deciding which of the new behavior patterns brought to its attention shall be accepted and integrated into the culture is its system of values. It is this system which guides its members' choices among the possible alternatives which are always present. From what we now know of psychological mechanisms we may assume that any pattern of behavior which is consistently effective, i.e., rewarded, will be given preference over other less consistently effective patterns in situations involving choice. It will also acquire the emotional associations which make it a value. However, human beings constantly generalize from one situation to another, while their use of language provides them with a highly effective tool for organizing such generalizations and expressing them as abstract concepts. Both behavior patterns and concepts are transmitted from individual to individual within the society and thus come to form part of the culture and to function as elements in the milieu within which culture change takes place.

Most value concepts find expression in more than one pattern of overt behavior, while, conversely, all but the simplest patterns of overt behavior involve more than one conceptual value. However, the number and the functional importance of the behavior patterns in which different values are involved vary greatly even within a single culture. Thus in our own society such a conceptual value as national survival is related to innumerable behavior patterns, while a conceptual value such as amusement is related to a much smaller number. The relative importance of the same conceptual value may also differ profoundly in different cultures. Thus the importance of esthetic activities relative to economic production was quite different in ancient Greek culture from what it is in modern America.

From the foregoing it can be seen that the values recognized by any society fall at once into two classes: *instrumental* and *conceptual*. The distinction can best be illustrated by an example. Nearly all societies have a conceptual value of modesty which is reflected in specific patterns of coverage for various parts of the body under various circumstances. Insistence that the genitals of both sexes should be kept covered in public is as nearly universal as any culturally determined pattern of behavior.[3] The objects used for this purpose vary greatly, ranging from *tanga* and pubic tassels to robes and trousers. However, the custom of wearing a garment of a particular type is always a focus for attitudes and emotions and constitutes in itself a value of the instrumental type. Thus some years ago the head of a great Christian denomination refused to receive the late Mahatma Gandhi because the latter insisted on wearing a loin cloth instead of trousers. Both the parties involved would certainly have agreed on the conceptual value of modesty, yet for each the behavior pattern by which this was instrumented in his own culture had acquired meanings and attitudes which made it a value in its own right. To the prelate, trousers were a symbol of both respect and respectability. To Gandhi, the loin cloth was less a garment than an expression of the struggle for Indian independence. Trousers, as the garb of the politically dominant European, had acquired strong negative associations. He no doubt felt that to don them for his reception would be an act of obeisance to the British Raj.

While instrumental values are, in nearly all cases, concise and easily recognizable, conceptual values are much less so. Some of those whose influence can be detected in the greatest variety of behavior patterns may not even be conscious or verbalized. They belong to what Kluckhohn has called the implicit category of culture elements. Every culture includes a number of values which are so abstract and so generalized in their expression that they carry little emotional effect in themselves, although they lie at the base of the whole cultural structure. In general,

[3] Exceptions: African Nilotics, Amazonian Indians, and some Melanesians.

the more concrete and conscious a value, the easier it is to attach emotion to it. For this reason the instrumental values of a society tend to carry higher emotional effect than the conceptual values. They constitute a sort of sensitive surface layer highly susceptible to external influences, and interference with them brings a more rapid response from the society's members than does the less obvious contravention of deeper-lying conceptual values.

Instrumental values are also much more susceptible to change than conceptual ones. In studying the history of particular societies, one is struck again and again by the persistence of particular conceptual value systems. Such systems not only determine what elements will be accepted or rejected in situations of free choice but also serve as guides in the reinterpretation of elements forced upon the society. This process of reinterpretation is nowhere better illustrated than in the modifications which various proselytizing religions have undergone in their diffusion. Originally pacifistic, Christianity became a warrior's creed in militaristic Europe. The simple, clear-cut creed of Islam was transformed in Persia into Sufi, mysticism, while Buddhism, after its initial denial of the efficacy of worship, became the most highly ritualized of all the great religions.

It is obvious that instrumental values are exceedingly variable. They constitute the area of value study to which the concept of cultural relativity is most completely applicable. If universal values exist, they must be sought for at the level of the deepest and most generalized conceptual values, those which stand in closest relation to the individual needs and social imperatives shared by the whole of mankind. A comparative study of cultures would seem to indicate that there are a considerable number of such values, but their identification is rendered difficult by their generality. Most of them are so fundamental and are taken so completely for granted by people who accept them that they are likely to be overlooked.

In any attempt to list conceptual values, the mere order of precedence given to them in enumeration would seem to reflect judgments as to their relative importance, but the writer wishes to disown any such implications immediately. The values which seem to be universal are listed in a certain order only because it is impossible to present them in anything but a linear form.

Since in popular thinking the relation between values and religion is a particularly close one, supernatural values may be taken as the starting point in our search for universals. Practically all cultures believe in the existence of what we would call supernatural beings, entities which cannot be perceived by our senses at ordinary times, yet which are able in some way, usually undefined, to influence the course of nature and thus to aid or injure men. These entities are usually conceived of as essentially human in their motives and emotions, a quite natural projection of the worshiper's experience.

Some cultures, but by no means all, have also developed a concept of an impersonal force called variously *orenda, wakan, mana,* and so forth. This belief is frequently regarded as primitive, but it is more just to consider it as a philosophical *tour de force* by which all unusual ability for accomplishment is reduced to a single common denominator. It becomes the equivalent in the field of the supernatural of such a concept as energy in the field of mechanics. *Mana,* to use its most familiar name, must be distinguished from the concept of natural law, as held by modern mechanics and materialists, in that it is manipulatable. All peoples who hold the *mana* belief also believe in the existence of individuals, both human and supernatural, who are able to concentrate and utilize this force. The attitudes toward such wonder-workers are basically the same as that toward deities or individuals with miraculous power in societies which do not have the *mana* concept. Since attempts to acquire and manipulate *mana* have always been limited to a comparatively small number of cultures and have been the first victims of the rise of modern mechanistic concepts, we can eliminate them from further consideration.

Closely related to the belief in beings able to affect the lives of man is a belief in persistence after death. This belief is held by practically all societies and finds a rational explanation in the inability of the individual to imagine either himself or those who are closely associated with him as nonexistent. However, the concepts held by various societies regarding the after-life are fully as varied as their concepts of the supernatural in general. The future life is normally conceived of in terms of familiar experience. The formal Christian concepts of heaven can be traced to the royal courts of the Near Eastern region in which this religion originated. One may suspect that to most West European and American Christians they seem highly unreal, or, if taken seriously, disappointing. According to whether the trend of a culture is optimistic or pessimistic, the future life is thought of as either an endless bank holiday or an endless rainy Sunday. Extremes of either pleasure or pain are seldom anticipated. Ethical factors are much less frequently involved in determining the condition of individuals after death than the average Christian would anticipate. In general, the commonest punishment for antisocial behavior is exclusion from the company of ancestors or deities, based on the logical premise that if an individual makes himself a nuisance in earthly society, post-mortem society will not want to be bothered with him.

The behaviors enjoined by different societies for dealing with the supernatural are even more varied than the beliefs. It is obvious that the approach will differ according to whether the operator believes he is dealing with beings or with an impersonal force. In the former case, approaches are patterned upon the individual's experience with other individuals either more or less powerful than himself. In the latter, they are patterned upon his experience with the manipulation of familiar objects and forces and are correspondingly mechanistic.

The distinction between approaches to the supernatural based on the assumption that the operator is dealing with beings and those based on the assumption that he is dealing with forces has much in common with the long-established distinction between religion and magic, yet the two formulations are by no means identical. Tylor suggested as the essential difference between religion and magic that in religion the operator approaches the supernatural powers as a suppliant, uncertain of the outcome, while in magic he approaches them with a belief in his own ability to control the outcome. However, the attempt to control impersonal force is always fraught with danger and with all sorts of possibilities of failure. The operator may make a technical error or another operator may block his efforts. In dealing with supernatural beings the attitudes of human dependence and dominance may blend into each other in curious ways. Thus, if the worshiper is dependent upon the deity, the deity is also dependent upon him for the satisfactions which the deity derives from worship and sacrifice. In later Egypt, magicians frequently selected some obscure and long forgotten deity and worshiped him on the principle that, as the only person feeding the god, the magician could be assured of the full exercise of the god's powers on his behalf.

By no means all supernatural beings are regarded as more powerful than their human manipulators. In the belief of many societies there are minor spirits who can be captured and enslaved or otherwise compelled to perform the acts which the priest or magician demands of them. There are also a surprising number of cases in which the worshiper's patience becomes exhausted and he turns from petition to compulsion. The same being may have prayers and offerings made to him on one occasion and on another be subjected to threats and punishment. Such techniques are perfectly intelligible in view of the ordinary experience of interpersonal relations in which more powerful individuals have to be placated, less powerful ones can be coerced, and the same individual successfully subjected to one or another treatment according to the circumstances.

Even the rituals performed in those religions in which the worshipers' purpose is to placate an all-powerful deity vary greatly from one society to another. Where the Christian and Muslim deity is satisfied by prayer, reading of holy books, and attendance at formal services, Zeus demanded hecatombs of oxen, and Huitzilopochtli bleeding human hearts. Because of the high emotional effect involved in dealing with the supernatural, the techniques prescribed by any culture acquire high value in their own right. One has only to recollect the martyrs who have suffered at the hands of fellow Christians for minor behavioral deviations such as insistence on complete baptism instead of sprinkling, or for using a different position of the fingers in signing the Cross.

It should be noted that there are numerous societies in which the favor of supernatural beings is not to be gained by ethical behavior. This is not limited to those cases in which the supernatural being is dominated by the operator. Even where the being occupies a dominant position, the relation between him and his worshiper is frequently conceived of as something quite apart from the worshiper's relation with other human beings. So long as the worshiper performs the appropriate rites, and, so to speak, maintains his half of the reciprocal relation between himself and the being, his behavior in society is considered no concern of his supernatural vis-à-vis. In some cases this attitude reaches great lengths. Thus in Polynesia, in accordance with a generalized pattern of occupational specialization which extended even to supernatural beings, there were deities to whom one might appeal successfully for aid in each and every type of antisocial behavior. More familiar examples would be the classical Mercury, god of thieves, or Magdalene, the patron saint of medieval prostitutes.

It may be noted that until one reaches the level of monotheistic civilizations, the only category of supernatural beings who are uniformly insistent upon ethical behavior on the part of their worshipers is that of ancestral spirits. The individual's childhood experience of parents in their dual capacity of disciplinarians and protectors seems to carry over directly in so-called ancestor worship, and, while the shades feel a deep interest in the welfare of their descendants, they are also quick to censure and even punish deviations from good behavior.

The only universal features which can be derived from such a wide variety of beliefs are those of man's universal sense of inadequacy in the face of many situations and his belief that there are beings whose powers exceed his own and who will give him the aid which he so vitally needs, if he can learn the correct methods of approaching them. To this may be added the well-nigh universal belief that the individual's personality is not extinguished in death.

This is a slender foundation upon which to build mutual understanding, especially when the small but powerful group which now dominates much of the world's population denies the existence of supernatural beings and has atheism as an article of faith implemented by high emotional effect. This last would seem to negate what has been said previously regarding the universality of supernaturalism, but one must evoke once more the fact of the social-cultural continuum. It remains to be demonstrated that societies can exist for any length of time without deities or that the average individual can endure the innumerable frustrations and griefs of even normal life without the anticipation of post-mortem satisfactions.

The values associated with the operation and perpetuation of societies are more numerous than those associated with the supernatural and also show less variety. This is no doubt due to their more intimate connection with the physiological needs of human beings and the practical aspects of organizing groups of individuals for their mutual advantage. The problems presented by these are more numerous than those involved in dealing with the supernatural, but the possible solutions for each problem are much less numerous. Thus the possible methods for developing and controlling the exchange of products and services or for rearing children are strictly limited in number, while there seems to be no limit to the variety of beliefs and rituals which will serve to satisfy man's desire for help from supernatural powers and reassure him in time of crises.

Social values which are universally present are of the utmost interest, since societies rather than individuals are the units in the human struggle for survival. They also establish the limits within which many values are operative. Thus nearly all instrumental values which have to do with the interaction of individuals apply only to interaction with other members of the same society. At the primitive level the individual's tribe represents for him the limits of humanity and the same individual who will exert himself to any lengths in behalf of a fellow tribesman may regard the nontribesman as fair game to be exploited by any possible means, or even as a legitimate source of meat.

One of the most significant trends in the evolution of human culture has been toward the expansion of societies to include more and more individuals of increasingly diverse racial and cultural backgrounds. The great proselytizing religions, such as Christianity and Islam, have been particularly active in furthering this trend. At the same time, this extension has been accomplished largely by the inclusion and mutual adjustments of subsocieties whose members feel a closer tie with each other than with the members of the larger group. An excellent example of this would be the criminal subsocieties which function within the broader frame of all modern civilized nations and may even be international in their affiliations. Such groups have their own value systems and their own rules of behavior by which they abide in dealing with other members of the criminal subsociety. Their relation with the other subsocieties within the larger units is generally a parasitic one, yet they have a recognized position and even potentialities for social service under special circumstances. Thus gangsters performed a very real function under prohibition.

Societies normally include a number of individuals of both sexes and at all age levels. This fact provides the starting point for differentiation of activities. Even the simplest societies distinguish between men's work and women's work, while the trend toward specialization culminates in modern mechanized society with its innumerable skilled occupations. The well-being of the society thus depends upon an exchange of goods produced by specialists and of services performed by them. As a result, all societies attach high value to reciprocity and to fair dealing. The latter statement may be questioned by those who have had uncomfortable experiences in our own system. However, in all societies, shrewdness and deceit are considered as legitimate in certain areas, usually those which are of not too vital importance for social well-being. The mutual recognition that the rule of *caveat emptor* holds in such areas endows dealing in them with a certain sporting element. Thus the old-time Yankee who deceived another man in a horse trade without resorting to a direct falsehood was admired by his society, while an attempt to pass a bad check would result in social ostracism.

The existence of reciprocity between different subsocieties within the larger unit, particularly by members of different classes, may be doubted by those trained in Marxist doctrines. However, one must recognize that even such a seemingly exploitive system as the feudal actually represented reciprocity on a large scale between noble and peasant. The feudal system emerged in a period of violence and confusion, when the trained soldier who became the feudal lord protected the peasant in return for his economic contribution. Indeed, without this contribution the soldier would have been unable to purchase the expensive equipment which the current military techniques entailed or to get the long practice required for its efficient use. In the same way, during the early phases of the capitalist system, the owner, who was normally also a manager, not only provided the capital required to obtain the machines which increased the workers' output, but also organized production processes and attended to the marketing of the product. That his returns were disproportionately large relative to his services cannot be doubted, but in the social-cultural continuum such inequalities tend to right themselves. A feudal system which has been outmoded by the growth of new technology and tactics is swept away by revolution, and we can see how, in the capitalist system, ownership is passing from single individuals or families to large numbers of stockholders, management is passing from owner to trained technician, while the relation between management and organized labor is shifting increasingly from exploitation to cooperation.

Management, in the sense of leadership and direction, is probably as old as social life. The differentiated activities of a simple society's members and a more or less equitable sharing of the advantages derived from them can be carried on without any formal type of direction or conscious techniques for enforcing reciprocity. However, most group activities, such as land-clearing, drive hunts, or seine fishing, require a high degree of coordinated effort, while the whole society needs leadership in emergencies. All societies recognize and obey leaders under certain conditions, although different individuals may assume the leadership in different situations. Thus many American Indian tribes had a war chief and a peace chief, the functions of each being clearly delimited.

The rewards which go with leadership differ greatly from one society to another and frequently do not involve economic advantage. Thus the head of a Plains Indian band levied no contributions upon his followers, though at the same time he was expected to keep open house and to maintain his followers' allegiance by frequent gifts. Even in medieval Europe a king was expected to meet his expenses from his personal estates, and any attempt to levy taxes on his feudal lords was hotly resented. That individuals are still eager to become leaders under such circumstances shows the efficacy of the psychological rewards to be derived from prestige and power.

The need for leadership and the universality of the power drive, no matter how it may be culturally camouflaged, are responsible for the fact that there are no genuinely equalitarian societies. Every human group recognizes that certain individuals or categories of individuals are socially more important than others. The so-called equalitarian societies are those in which the individual is able to find his own level in the prestige series without initial handicaps. However, in aristocratic societies the value of individual mobility involved in the democratic system is replaced and to some degree compensated for by values of social responsibility and skilled performance in the aristocratic role. Where the status of aristocrat is hereditary, it uniformly carries obligations both toward inferiors and toward the group as a whole, and involves elaborate patterns of behavior. One of the least desirable features of our own system is that which accords high status to the man of wealth, no matter how acquired, while imposing no social obligations upon him.

The values just discussed relate to the functioning of the society. However, the need for the society's preservation is even more vital. If the social-cultural continuum is to be perpetuated, there must be a constant increment of new individuals to replace those who drop out and, equally important, these individuals must be trained in the behaviors and indoctrinated in the attitudes necessary for the performance of particular roles in the operation of the society as a whole. The family is unquestionably the most efficient institution for meeting these social imperatives. It not only produces children but it trains them in the way that they should go. For this reason one finds that in all societies the family has become a focus for strong emotional attitudes.

Families are essentially of two types, conjugal and consanguine: those like our own (conjugal), in which the functional group is primarily the close, biologically determined unit of parents and offspring, and those in which functional unit is primarily a group of siblings of the same sex and their offspring (consanguine), with their spouses always regarded as somewhat marginal. However, even in families of the latter type, the desirability of continuing matings, i.e., marriages, is recognized. Families of this type tend to be extensive and a constant turnover in spouses is as disconcerting and as injurious to efficiency as a constant turnover of labor in any other organized work group. Moreover, long before the days of modern psychology, it was recognized that the child needs affection and emotional security for its proper personality development. This is more likely to be provided by the child's own biological parents than by a succession of less emotionally involved caretakers.

The desire for permanence of matings has given rise to two quite distinct lines of approach, each with its own associated value system. In one of these, premarital chastity is valued, largely, it seems, from the anticipation that an individual who enters marriage without previous sex experience will be deterred by timidity from experimenting with other partners, the chance of new and disruptive attachments thus being reduced. This attitude is most frequently found in societies where marriages are arranged for the sons and daughters by the family elders. From this conceptual value has developed such rites as the tests of the bride's virginity, common in Muslim countries, or the idea held by our not very remote ancestors that a woman who had lost her virginity was permanently ruined and unfitted for marriage, even if she had been violated against her will. Where this particular configuration of values exists, it is usually supplemented by economic sanctions for marriage: such things as the dowry and the more widespread and frequently misunderstood bride-price. By giving both the partners and their affiliated kin groups an economic interest in the maintenance of the union, these sanctions act as a strong deterrent to separation.

In the other type, reliance for the continuity of the marriage rests primarily on the physical and emotional adjustment of the partners. Under these circumstances there may be strong insistence on postmarital faithfulness, but the attitude toward premarital experimentation is one of tolerance, if not actual encouragement. It is thought that partners are most likely to be faithful when they are sexually congenial and when their curiosity about other possible partners has been satisfied. Our own situation in this respect is a curious one, since our society reprehends premarital experimentation, the arrangement of marriage by elders, and economic sanctions—i.e., all the techniques for preserving marriage which have proved effective. Under the circumstances, it is not surprising that so many of our partnerships end up in the divorce courts.

The roles of individuals within the family are everywhere culturally prescribed. Parents, or in the case of strong consanguine family organization, members of the parents' generation in the kin group to which the child belongs, are expected to assume responsibility for the child's physical care and training. Conversely, the child is expected to render them respect and obedience, at least until it becomes adult, and to care for them in old age. The failure on either side to live up to these obligations is severely reprehended. Wives are, in general, expected to be submissive to husbands. In the marital relationship husbands are normally dominant, in spite of the claims made by certain earnest feminists. Needless to say, the exceptions to this rule fall into two groups: those in which a particular wife establishes dominance over a particular husband without cultural sanction, or those in which, owing to consanguine family organization, the husband is not regarded as a family member. In such cases the dominant role, both in respect to the woman and her children, is assumed by one of her brothers. The reasons for this are presumably to be found in physical factors, the male of our species being in general larger, stronger, and more active than the female, while the latter suffers from the additional disabilities connected with pregnancy and nursing. Each of the practices in which these factors of familial interaction are reflected becomes an instrumental value for the particular society, while such concepts as parental responsibility, filial obedience, and wifely submission are conceptual values which find incidental expression in great numbers of behavioral practices.

On the border line between the value systems which relate primarily to social imperatives and those which relate to individual needs lies the whole area of property concepts. It may be stated at once that no society has been able to maintain a completely communistic arrangement for more than a few generations. Moreover, the attempts to do so have not occurred among primitive peoples but among highly civilized ones where communities of disillusioned individuals have attempted to escape in this way from the conflicts and inequalities of an overinclusive system of individual ownership. The property concept probably originates in the sort of individual identification with particular places and objects which may be observed even in animals. Objects which the individual has made or which he uses consistently acquire a whole series of associations which give them values over and above those resulting from their practical potentialities. Among even the simplest and most primitive groups we find well-developed concepts of both personal and group property. Personal property is usually limited to tools and weapons, clothing, and similar objects of immediate utility. While there may be an easy-going attitude toward the loan of such objects, this in no way negates the fact of private ownership. Group property, aside from particular objects which acquire value from their function as symbols of the group, is mainly territorial. Each band or tribe has its range within which its members are free to hunt or exploit natural resources, but which is forbidden to members of other social units. This again is in line with the behavior of most gregarious animals.

Between the claims of the group as exemplified in these patterns of communal ownership and free exploitation and those of the individual as they may be extended over particular natural resources or means of production, there is an inevitable conflict which every society has had to solve. The solutions which various societies have chosen have depended upon whether priority was given to the interests of the entire group or to those of individuals. Where the groups involved are small enough and sufficiently localized so that there are frequent face-to-face contacts between members, the potential antisocial consequences of extreme extensions of individual ownership do not arise. They are neutralized by social pressures. The wealthy man finds it more rewarding to be admired and praised for his generosity than to continue hoarding, subjected to the disfavor of the group and to the spectacle of individuals suffering from want with whom he inevitably feels a considerable identification. Only the absentee landlord or slaveholder and the modern corporation manager are immune to these social pressures, and it is under them that the potential evils of private ownership have found fullest expression.

Another set of values, lying on the border line between the social and individual categories, comprises those which have to do with knowledge. Since organized social life depends upon individual learning, it is obvious that much knowledge has a primarily social function. No individual can operate successfully in any status unless he knows the associated roles. However, few people are content to cease learning at the point where their knowledge would suffice for adequate social integration. Curiosity and extreme teachability are characteristic of our species, and every individual tends to accumulate a quantity of information which is of no practical importance. The accumulation of this information and the drawing of conclusions from it become sources of emotional satisfaction not unlike that derived from skill in a game. They also may provide an escape from the immediate pressures of reality. Most readers have encountered persons who have followed some abstract line of study for sheer love of the intellectual exercise. Thus the writer has known a journeyman printer in Chicago who had taught himself to read and write the Malagasy language, an advertising man in a department store who had made himself one of the foremost American Tibetan scholars, and a bank clerk who was a nationally recognized authority on early American genealogies.

The attitudes of societies toward such accumulation of "unprofitable" knowledge vary profoundly. In general, the individuals who possess it are regarded with a mixture of admiration and contempt. The scholar is everywhere officially honored and unofficially starved. It is only in the few societies which support institutions of higher learning that he is able to use his accumulation of esoteric knowledge as a source of income. To these might perhaps be added Imperial China, where scholarship of a particular type was rewarded by official preferment and by assignment to political office. However, even here, pure scholarship brought no great financial reward. To be profitable, it had to be combined with good social connections and a considerable measure of shrewdness and political skill.

Impractical, "useless" knowledge of the sort just discussed is only one aspect of the need for escape from reality which underlies considerable areas of human behavior and which has not as yet been successfully explained by the behavioristic psychologists. There is no known society which does not have games of the sort in which the individual sets up purely artificial obstacles and gets satisfaction from overcoming them. Neither is there any known society which lacks literature, with its potentialities for emotional satisfaction through vicarious participation in the adventures of fictional characters. While this is only one of any literature's multiple functions, its importance is not to be discounted. Lastly, every known society has various forms of esthetic expression: music, the dance, and graphic arts. These serve to relieve the monotony of daily existence and to evoke pleasurable sensations, although why they should do the latter is still an unsolved problem.

The concrete expressions of the esthetic urge, if one may so term the human need to create beauty, are extraordinarily varied. In order to realize this, one need only contrast the music of different peoples, with its varied tonal scales and use of melody and rhythm, or the even more diverse expressions of graphic art. Whether there is some denominator common to all the expressions of a single type is one of the most important problems confronting the student of esthetics. It is obvious that appreciation of any particular art form is to some degree a result of learning and habituation. Thus, to a European, most African art is repulsive at first contact. It is only after he has become accustomed to the medium that he can appreciate its qualities and derive esthetic satisfaction from it. The real problem is whether behind such diverse objects as a Poro mask, the Venus de Milo, and a Peruvian jar there are common factors of form, dynamic interrelation of parts,

harmony of color, and so forth, which may appear in different combinations but are responsible for the esthetic effect. It seems that we have here an area in which modern psychological techniques could be brought to bear on a problem which philosophers have discussed for centuries without coming to agreement.

This discussion of values has been of necessity brief and incomplete. Nevertheless, the writer hopes that the existence of universal values has been demonstrated and it has been made clear that these are to be found at the conceptual rather than in the instrumental level. When one turns from the discussion of such values in the abstract to a consideration of their possible utility as a basis for mutual understanding between societies, a number of new problems present themselves. It has already been noted that the conceptual values which have widest influence within a culture are frequently unverbalized. The emotional reactions to them are thus vague and diffuse. The values whose contravention brings the sharpest and most immediate response are those at the instrumental level. Thus two societies which share the same basic conceptual value may fail to realize the fact because of their different ways of implementing it. The best answer to situations of this sort would seem to be to bring the conceptual values into consciousness, a difficult task.

An even more serious difficulty arises from the varying degrees of importance which different societies attach to the same conceptual values. All societies arrange the values to which they subscribe in a hierarchy which determines the reactions of individuals and of the society as a whole in situations involving choice. Concepts like business honesty, truth, or chastity may stand high in the value hierarchy of one society and low in that of another. Such differences not only make for misunderstanding but also for mutual recriminations on moral grounds and for feelings of contempt and hostility.

Of particular significance in the present world situation is the relative importance accorded in different societies to individuality and conformity. Numerous conflicts between the desires of individuals and what the society conceives of as the well-being of the group are inevitable. Every society must make some allowance for both, but the point at which one or the other is given systematic precedence will vary greatly. The white pioneer American and most of the Indian tribes with which he came in contact represented a climax of individualism, and the Indians were in no small degree its victims. Since discipline of any sort except self-discipline violated one of their most fundamental values, it was impossible for them to organize effective defense against white invaders. During the last century here in America, the individualism of the pioneer has been giving place steadily to a higher degree of social control and of integration of the individual into the group. Even the most enthusiastic individualist must admit that in many respects this has been advantageous. Thus few persons would question that a man suffering from smallpox should be prevented from traveling about freely, attending public assemblies, and in general distributing the virus of the disease, although in the first half of the nineteenth century quarantine was hotly resented as an invasion of individual rights. One of the most pressing problems for modern Americans is how far the trend toward increasing socialization should be allowed to continue and how far our conceptual values can be modified in adjustment to it. The conditions which made pioneer individualism possible have passed, and in a modern society the attempt to reinstate these values in their original functional vigor can only lead to confusion. At the same time these values have survived as ideal patterns of our society, and the conflict between these ideals and their frequent and inevitable negation in practice becomes a source of irritation and misunderstanding.

At a time when we have been thrown, largely without our own volition, into a position of world dominance, it is also important for us to recognize that most societies do not attach the same high value to individual initiative and freedom of choice which we accord them. The completely free individual is of necessity an insecure individual and one upon whom the necessity of choice constantly devolves. There are large sections of the world's population that have become habituated to obedience and to relying upon the presumably superior intelligence and ability of hereditary ruling groups. Whatever the deficiencies of these systems may be, they provide the individuals who live under them with a feeling of security. They believe that if they obey, they will be taken care of. It is exceedingly difficult for such groups to accept the responsibilities involved in democratic patterns of government or to accord respect and allegiance to individuals whom they themselves have selected. The attempt to "sell" such groups the democratic ideal calls for much skill, especially when, thanks to modern techniques of communication, they are constantly being reminded of the defects which it shows in operation here in the United States.

The values on which there is most complete agreement are those which have to do with the satisfaction of the primary needs of individuals. Whatever their other values may be, all men desire the three wishes of the Irish fairy tale, health, wealth, and happiness. To the people of the world's backward areas the first two are represented by an opportunity to acquire and put into effect the technological and scientific knowledge already available in America and Western Europe. That these do not necessarily produce happiness we have abundant evidence, but this is something which the backward people will have to find out for themselves.

A Critique of Benedict

HENRY VEATCH

*O*ne can still, perhaps, venture with impunity to admire examples of courage or integrity or decency, but one can hardly stand up and claim to know what is right and what is wrong without being laughed out of court, or at least out of a cocktail party.

Perhaps there are worse fates. At any rate, I must assert unequivocally that I for one think that it *is* possible for men to know what is right and what is wrong. I would even go so far as to say that to assert anything else can only lead one into a quite untenable, even if often unnoticed, inconsistency. Ethical relativism, in other words, is, I believe, not just an indefensible position in philosophy; it is untenable in life itself.

To the end, however, of bringing off a full-dress refutation of ethical relativism, we should perhaps first take time to consider briefly just what the sources are of such an attitude toward ethics. If I mistake not, these sources are two, the one involving what might be called factual considerations, the other logical or linguistic considerations.

One might reply to this that while in former times theories of the physical universe were no doubt a relative matter, being mere idle speculations, determined by the peculiar prejudices of the age, the class, the culture, or the particular astronomer or physicist, in the modern period all this has changed: scientific theories now have a truly objective basis, as witness the extraordinary unanimity of scientists the world over. That is to say, no matter what the culture or the country or the economic system in which the modern scientist lives, he can still, as a scientist, understand and appreciate the achievements of other scientists everywhere.

This fact of comparative unanimity among scientists at present might provide at least some ground for supposing that science had at last been put on an objective basis, while morals or ethics had not; but even so, such evidence is still not really conclusive. To suppose that it was would be tantamount to holding that the determination of truth in science is no more than an affair of counting noses among scientists. And one could then go on to argue that since a plebiscite among moralists would yield nothing like the impressive results of a plebiscite among scientists, the palm of knowledge would have to be accorded to science, whereas ethics could claim to be no more than a matter of opinion.

THE LOGICAL DIFFICULTIES OF CLAIMING A FACTUAL KNOWLEDGE IN MATTERS OF ETHICS

The mere fact of diversity in moral and ethical opinion does not suffice to prove the impossibility in principle of moral and ethical knowledge: the whole world might be wrong and a single individual right. However, the case for ethical relativism need not rest on mere factual considerations; on the contrary, there are any number of considerations of a very different sort that lie ready at hand for the defense of such relativism. For it has become almost a dogma of the current intellectual scene to suppose that a radical distinction must always be drawn between facts and values, between "is" and "ought," between the real and the ideal. Since ethics by definition must presumably concern itself with values, as contrasted with facts, the conclusion seems inescapable that ethics is without objective or factual basis. Indeed, given these presuppositions, ethics has nothing to do

FROM *Rational Man*, Henry Veatch. (Bloomington: Indiana University Press, 1962), pp. 32–46. Reprinted by permission of Indiana University Press.

with the real order, but only with the ideal—with what ought to be, rather than with what is.

In further confirmation of this conclusion, one has only to consider the logical difficulty, not to say impossibility, of ever establishing a normative or ethical judgment. For so far as empirical evidence goes, this is always evidence of what is so, of what actually is the case. But the ideal, or that which only *ought* to be, is in principle never observable. Even if it be supposed that in a given instance the ideal has not remained a mere ideal, but has actually been realized, it would still seem that its character of being ideal would be something quite above and apart from its actual properties.

For is it not true that scientific descriptions of actual things and events in the real world never seem to take account of whether these natural happenings are right or wrong, good or bad? Thus that water flows down hill may be taken to be a fact of the natural world. But that it is right or wrong, or good or bad, that water should behave in this way—any such consideration of a moral or ethical nature seems not only irrelevant in this connection, but downright silly.

For that matter, even the social sciences and sciences dealing with human behavior usually pride themselves on being scrupulous in their objectivity; and this is interpreted to mean that they refrain from any and all value judgments. An economist may study the phenomenon of slave labor, pointing out the various consequences of employing this means of production, and whether and under what circumstances such forced labor might or might not contribute to greater national productivity. But as to whether human slavery is right or wrong, morally defensible or indefensible—on this subject, while it might be hoped that as a human being the economist would have his private opinion, as an economist he can only protest that he has no objective knowledge one way or the other. Likewise, in anthropology, sociology,

and psychology, the distinction is constantly being made between describing human behavior in one's role as a scientist and passing judgment upon such behavior in one's role as a person or as a citizen, the former being in the nature of objectively verifiable knowledge, whereas the latter is held to be no more than mere personal, private opinion.

One may deplore this ethical neutrality of modern science and complain that it has the effect of making scientists pander alike to dictators and to democracies. Be this as it may, how is one to get round the fact that value judgments do seem to be of a very different logical type from factual judgments? There is no way in which they can be objectively tested and verified. Nor does it seem possible even to make it intelligible just how the values which are ascribed to things can actually inhere in the things to which they are ascribed. Things are what they are objectively and in fact, but the values which they are said to have, they apparently can have only in the minds of the persons who judge them to be valuable.

Little wonder, then, that the moral or ethical dimension of things is not amenable to scientific investigation or verification. Be the facts what they may, one can neither find values in them nor infer values from them. And as for what is so being tantamount to what ought to be so, the "is" never provides the slightest clue as to any kind of an "ought." The two belong to logically quite different orders, and never the twain shall meet.

THE REFUTATION OF RELATIVISM

Must all ethics, then, be written off as a hollow sham? Perhaps not. For the traditional disciplines of philosophy have a way of outdoing even old soldiers: they not only "never die"; they don't even "fade away." And so it may well prove to be with ethics.

Isn't there, indeed, some way in which the current criticisms of ethics can be met and answered, so as to rehabilitate the subject once more and make it a respectable scientific discipline? To this end, let us again remind ourselves of just what the thrust of these criticisms was. Briefly, it was to the effect that ethical judgments are ultimately without any basis in fact. Hence any and all human convictions as to what is right or wrong, good or bad, cannot possibly be other than relative and arbitrary.

Very well; but let us consider for a moment what would be the probable consequences of such a relativistic destruction of ethics. Offhand, it might be supposed that no sooner had men become convinced that morals and ethics were without foundation and that their various prohibitions and prescriptions were no longer binding, than the lid would be off and all hell would break loose. Certainly it is not hard to imagine how, at least with certain individuals, this might be the consequence of ethical relativism. For example, take a teenage youth with normal sex impulses, whose strict upbringing had led him to believe that sex relations outside marriage are evil and wrong. Comes now an up-to-date moral philosopher who succeeds in convincing the young man that all such moral restraints stem merely from his Puritan upbringing and hence are quite without justification; indeed, they are but relative to this old-fashioned and now outmoded religious culture. Is it hard to imagine what effects such new-found convictions will have upon our young friend's consequent behavior?

One has only to reflect a bit, however, to realize that an excited casting off of all restraints is not a necessary or inevitable consequence of becoming convinced of the truth of ethical relativism. If it is true that all moral norms and standards of value are relative and, in this sense, arbitrary, it follows that no one set of values is superior to any other: all are equally good, or equally worthless, however one may prefer to express it. But viewed in this light, lust begins to appear as having really no more to recommend it than chastity, nor

drunkenness than sobriety, nor prodigality than thrift. More generally, indeed, it begins to look as if a complete freedom from all the lets and hindrances of social convention would not really be any better than obedience and conformity. Accordingly, the wearied moral skeptic, who decides that it is less trouble after all simply to go along with everyone else and abide by the moral standards of the community, is being just as consistent— or inconsistent—in his ethical relativism as is the rebellious and hot-blooded youth whose impulsive reaction to relativism is to regard it as a free passport to wine, women, and song.

Nor are these the only variants on the possible consequences of ethical relativism. One has but to look at that very readable and plausible little book of the American anthropologist, Dr. Ruth Benedict. Entitled *Patterns of Culture*, the book attempts to exploit some of the wealth of modern anthropological research in support of a thesis of thoroughgoing ethical relativism. After all, Dr. Benedict argues, different human cultures, with their widely varying patterns, are to be regarded as "travelling along different roads in pursuit of different ends, and these ends and these means in one society cannot be judged in terms of those of another society, because essentially they are incommensurable."

What may we suppose to be the consequences of such a recognition of relativism in the eyes of Professor Benedict? Oddly enough, as she views the matter, ethical relativism offers to human beings neither an invitation to license nor the tired counsels of skeptical pessimism; instead, it provides an impressive object lesson in tolerance.

The truth of the matter is rather that the possible human institutions and motives are legion, on every plane of cultural simplicity or complexity, and that wisdom consists in a greatly increased tolerance toward their divergencies. No man can thoroughly participate in any culture unless he has been brought up and has lived according to its forms, but he can grant to other cultures the same significance to their participants which he recognizes in his own.

And in her final chapter Professor Benedict seems to turn moralist herself, sternly lecturing her readers that: "Just as we are handicapped in dealing with ethical problems so long as we hold to an absolute definition of morality,* so we are handicapped in dealing with human society so long as we identify our local normalities with the inevitable necessities of existence." And so on, right up to the final eloquence of her concluding sentences:

The recognition of cultural relativity carries with it its own values, which need not be those of the absolutist philosophies. It challenges customary opinions and causes those who have been bred to them acute discomfort. It rouses pessimism because it throws old formulae into confusion, not because it contains anything intrinsically difficult. As soon as the new opinion is embraced as customary belief, it will be another trusted bulwark of the good life. We shall arrive then at a more realistic social

* A remark might be made in passing on Professor Benedict's use of the word "absolute," in speaking of "absolute definition of morality." It is not unusual for ethical relativists to label their opponents "absolutists," the implication being that claims to absolutism in knowledge are about as fantastic and old-fashioned as claims to absolutism in monarchy. Nor is there any doubt that, linguistically, when one searches for a word that one can conveniently oppose to "relative," the only word that readily comes to mind is "absolute." And yet it is interesting that, so far as scientific knowledge is concerned, no one nowadays would venture to say that such knowledge was a purely relative matter. But does anyone for this reason consider that scientific knowledge is an absolute knowledge, or that scientists themselves are absolutists? And if scientists can enjoy an immunity from the dilemma of relativism or absolutism, why may not moral philosophers as well?

faith, accepting as grounds of hope and as new bases for tolerance the coexisting and equally valid patterns of life which mankind has created for itself from the raw materials of existence.

While we are still bathing in the gentle warmth of such noble anthropological sentiments, it may be instructive to turn right around and expose ourselves to some rather more hard and gusty utterances of that late great master of cynicism and bombast, Benito Mussolini. Indeed, Mussolini's words (written in 1921) might also serve as an ironic commentary on Professor Benedict's preaching of tolerance on the text of relativism:

In Germany relativism is an exceedingly daring and subversive theoretical construction (perhaps Germany's philosophical revenge which may herald the military revenge). In Italy, relativism is simply a fact. . . . Everything I have said and done in these last years is relativism by intuition. . . . If relativism signifies contempt for fixed categories and men who claim to be the bearers of an objective, immortal truth . . . then there is nothing more relativistic than Fascist attitudes and activity. . . . From the fact that all ideologies are of equal value, that all ideologies are mere fictions, the modern relativist infers that everybody has the right to create for himself his own ideology and to attempt to enforce it with all the energy of which he is capable.

But why bother with further examples? These suffice to indicate that however plausible and even unanswerable the evidence would appear to be in support of a purely relativistic attitude in ethics, yet as soon as one asks what meaning and import such an attitude would have for one's own life and conduct, the answers turn out to be perplexingly confused and ambiguous. For one person, relativism means rebellion and libertinism; for another, conservatism and conformity. For one, it implies a greater tolerance and understanding of one's fellow men; for another, it justifies the most ruthless intolerance and the arbitrary imposing of one's own will upon others.

To make matters even worse, the consequences of such relativism are not only ambiguous, but also on closer scrutiny each of them turns out to involve a curious internal inconsistency. To return for a moment to Professor Benedict, is it not strange that having begun by proclaiming the utter relativity of all standards of value, she ends by preaching the gospel of tolerance? Presumably, if Professor Benedict is to remain faithful to her own principles, she must recognize that the value of tolerance is strictly relative to the particular cultural background which happens to have been her own. But suppose someone from a different cultural background has been brought up to believe that tolerance is not a virtue, but rather a sign of folly and weakness, the wise and courageous course being one of strict intolerance toward all divergencies from one's own cultural norm. What could Miss Benedict say to this? She could hardly disagree with such an advocate of intolerance, or criticize him for being mistaken, for this would be tantamount to judging the values of one society in terms of those of another. In fact, any such criticism would reflect that very spirit of intolerance toward peoples of other societies and cultures which Miss Benedict herself has made such a point of condemning. On the other hand, Miss Benedict could no more agree with such a hypothetical advocate of intolerance than she could disagree. For to agree would mean that she was conceding the superiority of the values of intolerance over those of tolerance—a stand which would doubtless convict her not merely of inconsistency, but of hypocrisy.

The predicament in which we have sought to place Professor Benedict is really not one of her own making, but is—in part at least—an inescapable predicament of anyone and everyone who would be a relativist in matters of ethics. For we might as well come right

out now and unmask the battery from which we have been bombarding the various positions of relativism. As we see it, ethical relativism in any form is a radically inconsistent and thoroughly untenable position to try to hold in philosophy.

It is important to fix the precise nature of the inconsistency of such relativism. Unlike what might be called general relativism, or out-and-out philosophical skepticism, ethical relativism is not inconsistent in its very statement and formulation. When general philosophical skepticism is reduced to its simplest and crudest terms, the skeptic's position comes down to assertions of this sort: "I know that no one knows anything" or "The truth is that truth is unattainable." Assertions such as this are manifest self-contradictions.* That is why it may quite justly be said that any position of thorough-going relativism or skepticism in philosophy is untenable even in theory: the position cannot even be formulated and stated without contradiction.

On the other hand, when the relativism in question is simply a relativism in regard to matters of ethics and not in regard to human knowledge generally, there does not seem to be the same inconsistency. For one can perfectly well assert without any manifest contradiction such things as "I know that, when it comes to questions of ethics, no one knows anything"; or "The truth is that truth about values or about distinctions between right and wrong and good and evil, etc., is unattainable." Here, obviously, there is no logical inconsistency, i.e., no inconsistency in the very formulation of the position of ethical relativism itself.

But although there is no logical inconsistency, there is what one might call a practical inconsistency. Take the case of any convinced ethical relativist

---

* I am disregarding here the so-called type difficulties which have led some modern logicians to regard such statements as being not so much self-contradictory as improperly formed and hence are not proper statements at all.

like Professor Benedict or the teen-age youth or Mussolini. If the foregoing analysis be correct, there is no inconsistency involved in his merely holding or subscribing to a position of relativism as such. The only trouble is that no human being can stop with just having convictions, he also has to live and to act. But to act is to choose and to choose is to manifest some sort of preference for one course of action over another. However, to manifest any such human preference means that, consciously or unconsciously, implicitly or explicitly, one has made a judgment of value as to which course of action is the better or the wiser or the more suitable or preferable. But what kind of a standard of value could the ethical relativist employ in making such judgments? The whole point of his relativism lies precisely in the fact that he intends to challenge the validity of any and every standard of value. On what possible basis, then, can the relativist act and choose and manifest his preference for doing one thing rather than another?

Caught up in such a predicament, the relativist no doubt may try to reason his way out in some such manner as this. He may try to employ his very relativism and skepticism in regard to all standards of value as if it were itself a kind of standard of value. Thus we can imagine him saying to himself, in effect: "Since all standards of value are utterly without foundation, since no way of life or course of action is really superior to any other, then the sensible thing for me to do is

(1) to cultivate an attitude of greater tolerance toward the various modes of life and patterns of behavior that men have chosen for themselves (Miss Benedict), or
(2) to create my own set of values and attempt to enforce them with all the energy of which I am capable (Mussolini), or
(3) to throw off all moral standards and norms of conduct and simply follow the lead of my impulses and inclinations (the liberated youth), or

(4) to go along with the crowd and merely abide by the standards of the community of which I am a member, this being the line of least resistance and the one least likely to get me into trouble and difficulty (the cynical skeptic)."

But unhappily, assuming that the relativist does reason in some such way as this, it is obvious that the reasoning will not bear scrutiny even for an instant. For the fallacy is only too transparent in the attempted inference from the utter relativity of all moral norms and standards of value to a course of action which the relativist considers to be the wisest and most sensible for him to follow under the circumstances. For "wiser" and "more sensible" in this connection are but synonyms for "better" or "preferable." Hence, put in its baldest form, the relativist's reasoning amounts to no more than a glaring *non sequitur*: "Since no course of action is really better or superior to any other, I conclude that the better course of action for me to follow would be thus and so."

Little wonder that under these circumstances the practical consequences of ethical relativism should be as various and as conflicting as those exemplified by Miss Benedict and Signor Mussolini. Indeed, in the light of the analysis we have just carried out, we can now see that no matter what practical implications one seeks to derive from such relativism, they are bound to involve one in an inconsistency, there being no possible way in which the very denial of all standards of better and worse can itself be transformed into a kind of standard of better and worse. Nor is there any way in which the relativist can avoid the practical inconsistency of his position. For however convinced he may be of the relativity of all norms and standards of choice, he must nonetheless act and make choices himself. Indeed, even if *per impossibile* he were to try to evade ever having to make any sort of a choice, his policy of evasion would itself be the result of a kind of choice and would involve at least an implicit judgment to the effect that such a course of evasion was the best one or the least bad one for him to pursue under the circumstances.

One is almost tempted to suggest that there is no other way for an ethical relativist to escape the inconsistency of his position than by having the good fortune to be struck dead, or to be rendered *non compos mentis*, immediately upon becoming convinced of the truth of relativism, and before he has had a chance to make so much as a single choice or decision on the basis of his new-found convictions. Such, however, would seem to be a cruel fate to wish even upon an ethical relativist, and surely a high price to pay merely for consistency. Wouldn't it be easier for him to forgo his relativism altogether?

Does
Sensory Experience
Provide
Indubitable Knowledge?

In the view of John Locke, all the contents of our immediate experience can be divided into simple ideas and complex ideas. Complex ideas are composed of simple ideas, but what "simple" means in this context is not easy to define. Roughly, a simple idea is one that can, by reflection on our immediate experience, be distinguished from all other ideas. The difficulty in clarifying this characterization of simple ideas is thus tantamount to the difficulty of stating and describing the conditions of application of the criteria for one idea being distinguishable from another. A further feature of a simple idea is that it is *irreducible*; it is not composed of exactly similar ideas, nor is it composed of qualitatively different ideas. As Locke puts it, each simple idea is "in itself uncompounded" and so "contains in it[self] but *one uniform appearance, or conception in the mind*." This clarifies, I think, what Locke means by the rest of this description when he adds that a simple idea "is not distinguishable into different ideas." "Different" is to cover "distinct though qualitatively similar" as well as "distinct and qualitatively different."

What Locke intends by "idea" is indicated by his examples: motion, color, softness, warmth, coldness, hardness, sweetness (of an odor),—that is, sensory data. (Locke calls these "ideas of sensation"; there are also "ideas of reflection" such as "perception, thinking, doubting, believing, reasoning, knowing, willing and all the different actings of our own minds." We are not concerned here with ideas of reflection.) While our experience is not, in Locke's view, atomistic (for Locke we do not normally experience disparate colors, sounds, smells, and so on, but experience them in complexes or contexts), we can discern these simple sensory data in our experience. Insofar, then, as we are concerned with the fact that we have immediate sensory experience and not with the question of what such experience may or may not tell us about anything distinct from or independent of that experience, can we indubitably know the elements of which our immediate experience is composed?

At one point in his *Essay Concerning Human Understanding*, Locke speaks of our sometimes having only "obscure notions" of the "operations of our minds" (Book II, Chapter 1, Section 25); but this is presumably when we are being attentive to the objects of these operations rather than to the operations themselves. So this passage provides no evidence that Locke did *not* hold the view that we have indubitable knowledge of the sort mentioned. Further Locke assures us that "there is nothing that can be plainer to a man than the clear and distinct perception he has of those simple ideas." If we take him literally here, we must conclude that not even our perception of the necessary agreement or disagreement of two ideas is more certain than our knowledge, at least under optimum conditions, of our immediate experiences. To put the same point in non-Lockean language, we are justified in being as certain that our immediate experience is exactly as it seems to us as it is that "2 + 2 = 4" is true and that "The chair is made only of wood but is not made of wood," since self-contradictory is false of any chair you please. It is this contention that A. J. Ayer challenges.

Ayer distinguishes between verbal mistakes and factual mistakes concerning our own immediate experience. A verbal mistake concerning my immediate sensory experience is simply the use of one word (say "blue") to describe an experience that is known by its perceiver to be a case, say, of seeing a red afterimage; this is simply a verbal slip that entails no factual error. A factual mistake in such contexts can occur if one can think that, say, his afterimage is blue when it is red (whether he mistakenly describes it as blue or not). Can this sort of thing happen? Can an adult perceiver who is careful, sincere, attentive, and makes no verbal slips nonetheless make a factual error concerning his own immediate sensory experience?

Ayer's answer is affirmative. "If I am right," he says, "there is then no class of descriptive statements which are incorrigible. However strong the experiential basis on which a descriptive statement is put forward, the possibility of its falsehood is not excluded." Ayer's argument for this conclusion is: (1) Suppose I am asked which of two lines in my visual field look to me to be of the same length; in such circumstances (there are plenty of similar ones— whether one afterimage is a darker shade of orange than another, and so on) I can be uncertain as to whether they do or do not; (2) if I can be uncertain about this issue, I can decide wrongly concerning whether they do look to me to be of the same length; (3) this is not a verbal mistake—my doubt is not about what "looks longer than" means; (4) so one can be mistaken even about his present tense immediate sensory experience.

Ayer considers the objection to (2) that one is "the final authority on the way things look to him, and what criterion is there for deciding how things look to him except the way that he assesses them?" Ayer's response is to stress that in admitting (what seems obviously true) that one can be uncertain about how some aspect of immediate experience looks to him, one has admitted that it is possible for nonverbal mistakes to be made about such experience. In other words, (a) "*S* (a person) can be uncertain about *h* (a statement)" entails both (b) "*h* can be false" and (c) "*S* can believe *h* to be true when it is false, and *S* can believe *h* to be false when it is true."

One could escape this response by denying that claims about our immediate experience are either true or false—which would be to deny (b), since what is neither true nor false cannot be false. But then such claims cannot express knowledge, indubitable or dubitable; so this would be no defense of Locke's view. Or we could argue that we can be uncertain about whether a statement is true when in fact the statement in question is a necessary truth, and so could not be false; so (a) does not entail (c). But this is irrelevant to the present case, since statements about one's immediate experience are not, even if indubitable, necessary truths (that is, their denials are not contradictory).

Ayer rejects the claim that unless some statements describing our immediate experience are indubitably true, then no such statements can be true at all. The fact (if it is one) that we can be mistaken about our immediate experience does not provide any evidence, let alone entail, that I am always mistaken or never correct about it.

Another line of attack has been made on the thesis that we may possess indubitable knowledge of our own immediate sensory experience. Inspired, and perhaps sanctioned, by remarks in Wittgenstein's *Philosophical Investigations*, philosophers have argued that it is not meaningful to say of a man that he can be mistaken about the content of his immediate experience because there is no criterion for being mistaken in such circumstances. But then, the argument continues, it is also meaningless to say that one can be *right* about the content of his immediate experience, for if it *makes no sense* to say "He is wrong about *A*," it also makes no sense to say "He is right about *A*." Ayer holds that one *can* be mistaken and, in the course of his essay, he endeavors to offer conditions under which one can be mistaken in such cases. But if either of these criticisms—Ayer's or the one just discussed—succeeds, then the indubitablity thesis is false. So one could, perhaps, offer an argument against this thesis whose opening premise was "Either we can be mistaken about our immediate experience or we cannot," one prong of which will be developed along Ayer's lines and the other developed along the line of those influenced by Wittgenstein. This critique would be, at least at first look, quite powerful. Whether it succeeds in refuting the thesis is a question that anyone inclined to support Locke's position should ponder carefully. In reflecting on this issue, note that Ayer's argument concerns *comparisons* of one aspect of our immediate experience with another aspect of the same. Will his argument be equally effective concerning noncomparative reports of immediate experience?

Clear and Distinct Perception
JOHN LOCKE

The better to understand the nature, manner, and extent of our knowledge, one thing is carefully to be observed concerning the ideas we have; and that is, that some of them are *simple* and some *complex*.

Though the qualities that affect our senses are, in the things themselves, so united and blended, that there is no separation, no distance between them; yet it is plain, the ideas they produce in the mind enter by the senses simple and unmixed. For, though the sight and touch often take in from the same object, at the same time, different ideas; —as a man sees at once motion and colour; the hand feels softness and warmth in the same piece of wax: yet the simple ideas thus united in the same subject, are as perfectly distinct as those that come in by different senses. The coldness and hardness which a man feels in a piece of ice being as distinct ideas in the mind as the smell and whiteness of a lily; or as the taste of sugar, and smell of a rose. And there is nothing can be plainer to a man than the clear and distinct perception he has of those simple ideas; which, being each in itself uncompounded, contains in it nothing but *one uniform appearance, or conception in the mind*, and is not distinguishable into different ideas.

These simple ideas, the materials of all our knowledge, are suggested and furnished to the mind only by those two ways above mentioned, viz. sensation and reflection. When the understanding is once stored with these simple ideas, it has the power to repeat, compare, and unite them, even to an almost infinite variety, and so can make at pleasure new complex ideas. But it is not in the power of the most exalted wit, or enlarged understanding, by any quick-ness or variety of thought, to *invent* or *frame* one new simple idea in the mind, not taken in by the ways before mentioned: nor can any force of the understanding *destroy* those that are there. The dominion of man, in this little world of his own understanding being much-what the same as it is in the great world of visible things; wherein his power, however managed by art and skill, reaches no farther than to compound and divide the materials that are made to his hand; but can do nothing towards the making the least particle of new matter, or destroying one atom of what is already in being. The same inability will every one find in himself, who shall go about to fashion in his understanding one simple idea, not received in by his senses from external objects, or by reflection from the operations of his own mind about them. I would have any one try to fancy any taste which had never affected his palate; or frame the idea of a scent he had never smelt: and when he can do this, I will also conclude that a blind man hath ideas of colours, and a deaf man true distinct notions of sounds.

This is the reason why—though we cannot believe it impossible to God to make a creature with other organs, and more ways to convey into the understanding the notice of corporeal things than those five, as they are usually counted, which he has given to man— yet I think it is not possible for any *man* to imagine any other qualities in bodies, howsoever constituted, whereby they can be taken notice of, besides sounds, tastes, smells, visible and tangible qualities. And had mankind been made but with four senses, the qualities then which are the objects of the fifth sense had been as far from our notice, imagi-

FROM *An Essay Concerning Human Understanding*, John Locke. Book 2, Ch. 2, Sections 1–3 (originally published in 1690).

nation, and conception, as now any belonging to a sixth, seventh, or eighth sense can possibly be, which, whether yet some other creatures, in some other parts of this vast and stupendous universe, may not have, will be a great presumption to deny. He that will not set himself proudly at the top of all things, but will consider the immensity of this fabric, and the great variety that is to be found in this little and inconsiderable part of it which he has to do with, may be apt to think that, in other mansions of it, there may be other and different intelligent beings, of whose faculties he has as little knowledge or apprehension as a worm shut up in one drawer of a cabinet hath of the senses or understanding of a man; such variety and excellency being suitable to the wisdom and power of the Maker. I have here followed the common opinion of man's having but five senses; though, perhaps, there may be justly counted more;—but either supposition serves equally to my present purpose.

Are Mistakes about One's Own Immediate Experience Only Verbal?
ALFRED J. AYER

For those who have the use of language, there is an intimate connection between identifying an object and knowing what to call it. Indeed on many occasions one's recognizing whatever it may be is simply a matter of one's coming out with the appropriate word. Of course the word must be meant to designate the object in question, but there are not, or need not be, two separate processes, one of fixing the object and the other of labelling it. The intention is normally to be found in the way in which the label is put on. There is, however, a sense in which one can recognize an object without knowing how to describe it. One may be able to place the object as being of the same sort as such and such another, or as having appeared before on such and such occasions, although one forgets what it is called or even thinks that it is called something which it is not. To a certain extent this placing of the object is already a fashion of describing it: we are not now concerned with the cases where recognition, conceived in terms of adaptive behaviour, is independent of the use of any symbols at all: but our finding a description of this sort is consistent with our ignoring or infringing some relevant linguistic rule. And this can happen also when the rule is of one's own making, or at least constituted by one's own practice. When the usage which they infringe is private, such lapses can only be exceptional; for unless one's practice were generally consistent, there would be no rule to break: but it is to be envisaged that they should now and then occur.

If this is so, one can be mistaken, after all, in the characterization of one's present experience. One can at least misdescribe it in the sense that one applies the wrong word to it; wrong because it is not the word which by the rules of one's language is correlated with an 'object' of the sort in question. But the reply to this may be that one would then be making only a verbal mistake. One would be misusing words, but not falling into any error of fact. Those who maintain that statements which describe some feature of one's present experience are incorrigible need not deny that the sentences which express them may be incorrectly formulated. What they are

FROM *The Problem of Knowledge*, Alfred J. Ayer. (Middlesex, England Penguin Books, Ltd., 1956), Ch. 6, Section 2. Reprinted by permission of Penguin Books, Ltd.

trying to exclude is the possibility of one's being factually mistaken.

But what is supposed to be the difference in this context between a verbal and a factual mistake? The first thing to remark is that we are dealing with words which, though general in their application, are also ostensive: that is, they are meant to stand for features of what is directly given in experience. And with respect to words of this kind, it is plausible to argue that knowing what they mean is simply a matter of being disposed to use them on the right occasions, when these are presented. It then appears to follow that to be in doubt as to the nature of something which is given, to wonder, for example, what colour this looks to me to be, is to be in doubt about the meaning of a word. And, correspondingly, to misdescribe what is given is to misuse a word. If I am not sure whether this looks crimson, what I am doubting is whether 'crimson' is the right word to describe this colour: if I resolve this doubt wrongly I have used the word 'crimson' when I should not or failed to use it when I should. This example is made easier to accept because the word 'crimson' has a conventional use. It is harder to see how I can use a word improperly when it is I alone who set the standard of propriety: my mistake would then have to consist in the fact that I had made an involuntary departure from some consistent practice which I had previously followed. In any event, it is argued, my mistake is not factual. If I were to predict that something, not yet presented to me, was going to look crimson, I might very well be making a factual mistake. My use of the word 'crimson' may be quite correct. It properly expresses my expectation: only the expectation is not in fact fulfilled. But in such a case I venture beyond the description of my present experience: I issue a draft upon the facts which they may refuse to honour. But for them to frustrate me I must put myself in their power. And this it is alleged I fail to do when I am merely recording what is directly given to me.

My mistakes then can only be verbal. Thus we see that the reason why it is held to be impossible to make a factual error in describing a feature of one's present experience is that there is nothing in these circumstances which is allowed to count as one's being factually mistaken.

Against this, some philosophers would argue that it is impossible to describe anything, even a momentary private experience, without venturing beyond it. If I say that what I seem to see is crimson, I am saying that it bears the appropriate resemblance in colour to certain other objects. If it does not so resemble them I have classified it wrongly, and in doing so I have made a factual mistake. But the answer to this is that merely from the statement that a given thing looks crimson, it cannot be deduced that anything else is coloured or even that anything else exists. The fact, if it be a fact, that the colour of the thing in question does not resemble that of other things which are properly described as crimson does indeed prove that in calling it crimson I am making a mistake; I am breaking a rule which would not exist unless there were, or at any rate could be, other things to which the word applied. But in saying that this is crimson, I am not explicitly referring to these other things. In using a word according to a rule, whether rightly or wrongly, I am not talking about the rule. I operate it but I do not say how it operates. From the fact that I have to refer to other things in order to show that my description of something is correct, it does not follow that my description itself refers to them. We may admit that to describe is to classify; but this does not entail that in describing something one is bound to go beyond it, in the sense that one actually asserts that it is related to something else.

Let us allow, then, that there can be statements which refer only to the contents of one's present experiences. Then, if it is made a necessary condition for being factually mistaken that one should make some claim upon the facts which goes beyond the content of one's present experience, it will follow that even when these statements misdescribe what they refer to the error is not factual: and then there appears no choice but to say that it is verbal. The question is whether this ruling is to be accepted.

The assumption which lies behind it is that to understand the meaning of an ostensive word one must be able to pick out the instances to which it applies. If I pick out the wrong instances, or fail to pick out the right ones, I show that I have not learned how to use the word. If I hesitate whether to apply it to a given case, I show that I am so far uncertain of its meaning. Now there is clearly some truth in this assumption. We should certainly not say that someone knew the meaning of an ostensive word if he had no idea how to apply it; more than that, we require that his use of it should, in general, be both confident and right. But this is not to say that in every single case in which he hesitates over the application of the word, he must be in doubt about its meaning. Let us consider an example. Suppose that two lines of approximately the same length are drawn so that they both come within my field of vision and I am then asked to say whether either of them looks to me to be the longer, and if so which. I think I might very well be uncertain how to answer. But it seems very strange to say that what, in such a case, I should be uncertain about would be the meaning of the English expression 'looks longer than'. It is not at all like the case where I know which looks to me the longer, but having to reply in French, and speaking French badly, I hesitate whether to say 'plus longue' or 'plus large'. In this case I am uncertain only about the proper use of words, but in the other surely I am not. I know quite well how the words 'looks longer than' are used in English. It is just that in the present instance I am not sure whether, as a matter of fact, either of the lines does look to me to be longer than the other.

But if I can be in doubt about this

matter of fact, I can presumably also come to the wrong decision. I can judge that this line looks to me to be longer than that one, when in fact it does not. This would indeed be a curious position to be in. Many would say that it was an impossible position, on the ground that there is no way of distinguishing between the way things look to someone and the way he judges that they look. After all he is the final authority on the way things look to him, and what criterion is there for deciding how things look to him except the way that he assesses them? But in allowing that he may be uncertain how a thing looks to him, we have already admitted this distinction. We have drawn a line between the facts and his assessment, or description, of them.[1] Even so, it may be objected, there is no sense in talking of there being a mistake unless it is at least possible that the mistake should be discovered. And how could it ever be discovered that one had made a mistake in one's account of some momentary, private experience? Clearly no direct test is possible. The experience is past: it cannot be produced for reinspection. But there may still be indirect evidence which would carry weight. To return to our example, if I look at the lines again, it may seem quite clear to me that A looks longer than B, whereas I had previously been inclined to think that B looked longer than A, or that they looked the same length. This does not prove that I was wrong before: it may be that they look to me differently now from the way they did then. But I might have indirect, say physiological, evidence that their appearance, that is the appearance that they offer to me, has not changed. Or I may have reason to believe that in the relevant conditions things look the same to certain other people as they do to me: and then the fact that the report given

[1] Yes, but it may still be argued that his assessment, when he reaches it, *settles* the question. The point is whether a meaning can be given to saying that he decides wrongly. I suggest that it can.

by these other people disagrees with mine may have some tendency to show that I am making a mistake. In any event it is common ground that one can misdescribe one's experience. The question is only whether such misdescription is always to be taken as an instance of a verbal mistake. My contention is that there are cases in which it is more plausible to say that the mistake is factual.

If I am right, there is then no class of descriptive statements which are incorrigible. However strong the experiential basis on which a descriptive statement is put forward, the possibility of its falsehood is not excluded. Statements which do no more than describe the content of a momentary, private experience achieve the greatest security because they run the smallest risk. But they do run some risk, however small, and because of this they too can come to grief. Complete security is attained only by statements like 'I exist' which function as gesticulations. But the price which they pay for it is the sacrifice of descriptive content.

We are left still with the argument that some statements must be incorrigible, if any are ever to be verified. If the statements which have been taken as basic are fallible like all the rest, where does the process of verification terminate? The answer is that it terminates in someone's having some experience, and in his accepting the truth of some statement which describes it, or, more commonly, the truth of some more far-reaching statement which the occurrence of the experience supports. There is nothing fallible about the experience itself. What may be wrong is only one's identification of it. If an experience has been misidentified, one will be misled into thinking that some statement has been verified when it has not. But this does not mean that we never verify anything. There is no reason to doubt that the vast majority of our experiences are taken by us to be what they are; in which case they do verify the statements which are construed as describing them. What

we do not, and can not, have is a logical guarantee that our acceptance of a statement is not mistaken. It is chiefly the belief that we need such a guarantee that has led philosophers to hold that some at least of the statements which refer to what is immediately given to us in experience must be incorrigible. But, as I have already remarked, even if there could be such incorrigible statements, the guarantee which they provided would not be worth very much. In any given case it would operate only for a single person and only for the fleeting moment at which he was having the experience in question. It would not, therefore, be of any help to us in making lasting additions to our stock of knowledge.

In allowing that the descriptions which people give of their experiences may be factually mistaken, we are dissociating having an experience from knowing that one has it. To know that one is having whatever experience it may be, one must not only have it but also be able to identify it correctly, and there is no necessary transition from one to the other; not to speak of the cases when we do not identify our experiences at all, we may identify them wrongly. Once again, this does not mean that we never know, or never really know, what experiences we are having. On the contrary it is exceptional for us not to know. All that is required is that we should be able to give an account of our experiences which is both confident and correct; and these conditions are very frequently fulfilled. It is no rebuttal of our claim to knowledge that, in this as in other domains, it may sometimes happen that we think we know when we do not.

The upshot of our argument is that the philosopher's ideal of certainty has no application. Except in the cases where the truth of a statement is a condition of its being made, it can never in any circumstances be logically impossible that one should take a statement to be true when it is false; and this holds good whatever the statement may be, whether, for example, it is itself necessary or contingent. It would, however, be a mistake to express this conclusion by saying, lugubriously or in triumph, that nothing is really certain. There are a great many statements the truth of which we rightly do not doubt; and it is perfectly correct to say that they are certain. We should not be bullied by the sceptic into renouncing an expression for which we have a legitimate use. Not that the sceptic's argument is fallacious; as usual his logic is impeccable. But his victory is empty. He robs us of certainty only by so defining it as to make it certain that it cannot be obtained.

Does
Self-Awareness
Provide
Indubitable Knowledge?

René Descartes desired rational certainty and believed that he had found it in his assertion "I think, therefore I am." Several comments must be made in order that we understand just what he is, and is not, claiming. His words are: "I am, I exist is necessarily true each time that I pronounce it or mentally conceive it." He is certain, then, that when he says or thinks "I exist," he does exist; this certainty does not extend beyond the moment of spoken or unspoken thought. Further, there is strictly no logical contradiction in thinking or saying "I do not exist" for "I exist" is not necessarily true. What is logically necessary is this: if I think at a time that I exist, then at that time I do exist. It will not do to say "I walk, so I exist" because I cannot walk without having a body and that I have a body is not indubitably true in the way that the fact that I am now thinking is indubitably true. It is true that I have a body, but it is something that, however obvious it seems, needs proof; in contrast, that I think is in no need of any proof whatever, but is indubitably known in Descartes' view.

Not only, however, am I immediately conscious of my thinking, but I am immediately conscious of myself as a thing that thinks (in Cartesian language a mental substance). While my thinking and my existing are essentially connected, I do not *infer* that I, as thinker, exist from the fact that I think. Rather, I am aware of myself in a noninferential manner. In response to Gassendi, who wrote to Descartes that "you can perceive yourself, not indeed by a direct, but by a reflected, cognition," Descartes replied: "It is not the eye which sees the mirror rather than itself, but the mind which alone recognizes both mirror, and eyes, and itself as well." Descartes' claim, then, is that when he asserts that he exists he has a noninferential awareness of himself as a thing that thinks (a mental substance) and that he cannot be mistaken as to the existence or character of this object of awareness.

George Berkeley sides with Descartes in the dispute over whether we have direct self-awareness. We know what the word "mind" means—namely, "that which thinks, wills, and perceives." How do we gain this knowledge? Only by being aware of or acquainted with something (namely, our own mind) to which this description applies. "We know other spirits by means of our own soul," that is, by means of *knowledge* of our own mind. The intelligibility of the term "mind" or "spirit" is a product of, and guarantees, our being noninferentially aware of our own mind. Berkeley adds, then, to Descartes' claim to direct self-awareness an appeal to a principle of meaning, in terms of which we can be sure that we are aware of our own mind in that we know what the word "mind" means and could not know this in the absence of direct self-awareness.

John Locke, in the first of his essays that follow, offers an alternative to Descartes' view concerning self-knowledge. We directly perceive simple ideas (colored shapes, rough-feeling surfaces, and so on); but we cannot see "how these simple ideas can subsist by themselves" and hence "suppose some substratum wherein they do subsist." To put it as unproblematically as possible, we experience what are apparently the qualities of objects and suppose that there are objects whose qualities they are. But we are not directly aware of these objects; their existence is inferred. "The same thing happens concerning the operations of the mind"; we note the occurrence of reasoning, fearing, and so forth; and "not . . . apprehending how they can belong to body; or be produced by it, we are apt to think these the actions of some other substance, which we call spirit." Not only are we likely to do this; we *do* it. We infer that there is a mind which does the reasoning. Locke does not doubt the propriety of the reasoning. But if we *do* infer that minds exist, we are not directly aware of their existence (else, why *infer* that mind exists?).

Further, our idea of substance is "some thing, we know not what," which possesses perceivable qualities (if material) or sentient capacities (if mental). Beyond this, we have no idea of a substance, and in Locke's view this is no clear and distinct idea of substance at all. We must rely on what we *are* directly aware of (observable qualities and sentient states) in order to describe what we are *not* directly aware of (material and mental substances). It is apparently this reliance that lies at the basis of Locke's deprecation of our concept of a material or a mental substance. However this may be, it is plain that Locke teaches that our knowledge of ourselves is inferential.

In a later passage, however (in our second selection from Locke), he claims that we *are* noninferentially aware of own existence. "In every act of sensation, reasoning, or thinking, we are conscious to ourselves of our own being; and, in this matter, come not short of the highest degree of certainty." He claims: my existence is as *immediately* certain as that I reason or feel pleasure and pain—the very sort of experiences from which hitherto we were to *infer* our existence. The immediacy of our self-knowledge is stressed when Locke describes it as intuitive knowledge, contrasting it with the demonstrative knowledge we have of God. We infer the divine existence but intuit our own. Since Locke nowhere, at least to my knowledge, suggests that we are simply a set of experiences (rather, we *have* experiences), it will not do to say that Locke is immediately certain that he exists but not immediately certain that he is a substance. Since a person is not an idea (or a set of ideas) or a relation (or a set of relations), or both, the only remaining category in Locke's system in which persons can be placed is that of substance. Locke's only question on this score is not whether he is a substance but whether he may not conceivably be a material rather than a mental substance. The passages do seem incompatible, and the first does provide an alternative to Descartes' position, while nonetheless holding that we are mental substances.

Gilbert Ryle speaks of "the systematic elusiveness of 'I.'" This phrase is descriptive of the conclusion of the following argument. We can make our own thoughts the objects of still further thoughts of our own. Thus I can notice that my hand is moving, and then note that I have noticed this fact about my hand. My noticing that my hand is moving we can call a first-order thought; my taking note of my noticing will then be a second-order thought. If I wish for some reason to do so, I can reflect on the fact that I noted that I noticed that my hand was moving; in so doing, I have a thought whose object is a second-order thought. In other words, I can have third-order thoughts. Indeed, there is no limit to how long this process can continue except that of patience and talent for this sort of activity. In sum, any thought of mine can be made the object of another thought of mine.

From this apparently trivial fact it follows that I could never in principle give a complete description of myself since the very description that I gave would necessarily not include the further fact about me that I was giving that description of myself. But there is no analogous reason why I cannot in principle give a complete description of someone else (or why someone else could not give a complete description of me). We can put this difference by saying that I cannot give a complete description of someone else for reasons of ignorance (I do not know all the relevant facts), but I cannot give a complete description of myself for logical reasons (no description of myself could include the fact that I was giving that description). Of course, it is also true that I cannot give a complete description of myself for reasons of ignorance; I do not know all the facts about myself either. (There is an important assumption in this argument—namely, that no description can properly contain reference to itself. Since this assumption raises the fairly complex issue as to whether all self-referring statements are logically objectionable, we merely note that the assumption is made. Dealing with it would take us far afield.)

Ryle attempts to account for the convictions of Descartes, Locke, and Berkeley that there is "something more," so to speak, than our experiences—something that *has* these experiences—as due to their being misled by the role of the word "I." The "systematic elusiveness" of which Ryle speaks is not the elusiveness of a mental substance that must be inferred from our experience or that of a substantial self of which I am constantly or sometimes immediately (though often diaphonously) aware. It simply means that (for the logical reason noted above) I can never, at any time, give a complete description of myself. Ryle's own view is that "when we speak of a person's mind, we are . . . speaking . . . of certain ways in which some of the incidents of his life are ordered."

It is not clear that the philosophers in question were misled in any such manner as this. (The degree to which Ryle is willing to make this exact allegation is also not very clear.) But for anyone with Rylean sympathies, the allegation comes very naturally and is exemplary of many criticisms of traditional figures made by contemporary philosophers. Whether the allegation is fair and whether *all* that is involved is the role of the word '*I*' in a language or set of languages are highly debatable matters. But the student beginning his study of philosophy should be aware that such issues as these compose an important part of contemporary philosophical discussions.

I Think, Therefore I Am
RENÉ DESCARTES

So I suppose that all the things I see are false. I assume that nothing my mendacious memory represents really is the case: Thus I have no senses; body, figure, extension, and place are chimeras [fr. fictions of my mind]. What is true, then? Perhaps only that nothing is certain. . . .

But indeed, I certainly existed if I persuaded myself of anything. But, say, there is a deceiver, I know not what, very powerful and very cunning who deliberately always deceives me. Again, no doubt that therefore I am, if he deceives me; I let him decieve me as much as he can, yet he cannot bring it about that I am nothing as long as I think that I am something. So having thought through all this diligently, it must be stated that the utterence 'I am, I exist,' as often as it is pronounced or mentally conceived by me, is reasonably true.

(2) For when you say 'I could have inferred the same [sic *I am*] from any other of my actions,' you are greatly in error, because I am wholly certain of none of my actions (that is, with that metaphysical certitude about which alone there is a question here), excepting that of thinking. Nor is it permitted to infer, e.g., *I walk therefore, I am*, unless insofar as the consciousness of walking is a thought; the inference about thoughts of walking alone is certain, not about a movement of the body. For the latter sometimes does not exist, as in dreams when it still seems to me that I walk. So from the fact that I judge that I walk I may validly infer the existence of a mind which makes this judgement, I cannot infer the existence of a body which walks. The same holds for other cases.

(3) But I do not yet sufficiently know what I am, I who now necessarily am; hence care must be taken lest I imprudently take something else in place of

(1) FROM *Meditations on First Philosophy*, Meditation Two; (2) FROM *Reply to Objections*; V, J. R. Weinberg, trans. (Adam and Tannery, 24[14]–25[13] and 352, Vol. VII, originally published in 1641); (3) FROM: *Meditations*, Med. II, Adam and Tannery 25[14] and 28[20]–29[18], trans. J. R. Weinberg.

myself, and that I do not ever even in that cognition which I maintain is the most certain and most evident of all cognitions. Wherefore I shall now again meditate about what I believed that I was before I engaged in these thoughts. So I shall remove from my former views whatsoever could be contested to any extent by the reasons I have just set forth so that what remains is certain and incontestable.

What, then, did I formerly think that I was? Without doubt, a man. But what is a man? May I not say, a rational animal? No, because it would then have to be asked what is animal, what is rational, and then from one question I should be involved in many others and more difficult questions; and I should not like to use the time to fall into subtilities of this kind. I should rather attend to what thoughts occurred to me naturally when I considered what I am. Thus it occurred to me at the outset that I had a face, hands, arms, and all that machine of members such as can be seen in a corps which I call my body. Moreover, it seemed to me that I was nourished, that I walked, that I sensed and thought; which actions I referred to my soul. But what this soul was I either did not observe or if I did, I supposed it to be something like wind or fire or air which was infused through the grosser parts of myself. As to body I did not doubt about its nature, but I thought that I knew it very distinctly, and if I had wished to describe it, I would have explained it as follows: by a body I understand all that which is capable of being bounded by a figure, circumscribed by a place, filling out space so that it excluded every other body therefrom, perceived by touch, sight, hearing, taste or odor, moved in many ways not of course by itself but by another with

which it is in contrast, for I judged that the power of self-movement, of feeling, or of thinking did not belong to the nature of body; indeed I was surprised to find that such faculties existed in some other bodies.

But what, therefore, am I? A thinking thing. What is that? It is a thing which doubts, understands, affirms, denies, wishes, rejects, also imagines and feels.

These are not a little, if they belong to my nature. But do they indeed belong to my nature? Am I not he who doubts almost all things, but who understands something, who affirms one truth, who denies many others, who wishes to know many more, who does not wish to be deceived, who imagines many things, and who observes many things as if coming from the senses?

Is there nothing in all this which is not as veritable as that I exist, even though I always sleep and though he who created me always deceives me. What is it that can be distinguished from my thought? What is it that can be said to be separated from myself? For it is so evident that I who doubt, who understand, who will, exist, that there is nothing by which it can be explained more evidently. And also I am the same person who imagines; for, though it may be the case perhaps, (as I had assumed), that none of these imagined things exists, the power of imagining truly exists and forms part of my thinking. Lastly, I am the one who senses, i.e., who perceives corporal things as if by my senses: namely, I see light, I hear noise, I feel heat. But these are false, for I am asleep. Still, it is certain that I seem to see, hear, and feel heat. *This cannot be false*; this is properly what is called *feeling* in me; and this, taken precisely is nothing other than *to think*.

Knowledge of Mental Substance Is Inferential
JOHN LOCKE

The mind being, as I have declared, furnished with a great number of the simple ideas, conveyed in by the senses as they are found in exterior things, or by reflection on its own operations, takes notice also that a certain number of these simple ideas go constantly together; which being presumed to belong to one thing, and words being suited to common apprehensions, and made use of for quick dispatch, are called, so united in one subject, by one name; which, by inadvertency, we are apt afterward to talk of and consider as one simple idea, which indeed is a complication of many ideas together: because, as I have said, not imagining how these simple ideas *can* subsist by themselves, we accustom ourselves to suppose some *substratum* wherein they do subsist, and from which they do result, which therefore we call *substance*.

So that if any one will examine himself concerning his notion of pure substance in general, he will find he has no other idea of it at all, but only a supposition of he knows not what *support* of such qualities which are capable of producing simple ideas in us; which qualities are commonly called accidents. If any one should be asked, what is the subject wherein colour or weight inheres, he would have nothing to say, but the solid extended parts; and if he were demanded, what is it that solidity and extension adhere in, he would not be in a much better case than the Indian before mentioned who, saying that the world was supported by a great elephant, was asked what the elephant rested on; to which his answer was—a great tortoise: but being again pressed to know what gave support to the broad-backed tortoise, replied—*something, he knew not what*. And thus here, as in all other cases where we use words without having clear and distinct ideas, we talk like children: who, being questioned what such a thing is, which they know not, readily give this satisfactory answer, that it is *something*: which in truth signifies no more, when so used, either by children or men, but that they know not what; and that the thing they pretend to know, and talk of, is what they have no distinct idea of at all, and so are perfectly ignorant of it, and in the dark. The idea then we have, to which we give the *general* name substance, being nothing but the supposed, but unknown, support of those qualities we find existing, which we imagine cannot subsist *sine re substante*, without something to support them, we call that support *substantia*; which, according to the true import of the word, is, in plain English, standing under or upholding.

An obscure and relative idea of *substance in general* being thus made we come to have the ideas of *particular sorts of substances*, by collecting *such* combinations of simple ideas as are, by experience and observation of men's senses, taken notice of to exist together; and are therefore supposed to flow from the particular internal constitution, or unknown essence of that substance. Thus we come to have the ideas of a man, horse, gold, water, &c.; of which substances, whether any one has any other *clear* idea, further than of certain simple ideas co-existent together, I appeal to every one's own experience. It is the ordinary qualities observable in iron, or a diamond, put together, that make the true complex idea of those substances, which a smith or a jeweller commonly knows better than a philosopher; who, whatever *substantial* forms he may talk of, has no other idea of those substances,

FROM *An Essay Concerning Human Understanding*, John Locke. Book 2, Ch. 23, Sections 1–6 (originally published in 1690).

than what is framed by a collection of those simple ideas which are to be found in them: only we must take notice, that our complex ideas of substances, besides all those simple ideas they are made up of, have always the confused idea of something to which they belong, and in which they subsist: and therefore when we speak of any sort of substance, we say it is a thing having such or such qualities; as body is a thing that is extended, figured, and capable of motion; spirit, a thing capable of thinking; and so hardness, friability, and power to draw iron, we say, are qualities to be found in a loadstone. These, and the like fashions of speaking, intimate that the substance is supposed always *something besides* the extension, figure, solidity, motion, thinking, or other observable ideas, though we know not what it is.

Hence, when we talk or think of any particular sort of corporeal substances, as horse, stone, &c., though the idea we have of either of them be but the complication or collection of those several simple ideas of sensible qualities, which we used to find united in the thing called horse or stone; yet, *because we cannot conceive how they should subsist alone, nor one in another*, we suppose them existing in and supported by some common subject; which support we denote by the name substance, though it be certain we have no clear or distinct idea of that thing we suppose a support.

The same thing happens concerning the operations of the mind, viz. thinking, reasoning, fearing, &c., which we concluding not to subsist of themselves, nor apprehending how they can belong to body, or be produced by it, we are apt to think these the actions of some other *substance*, which we call *spirit*; whereby yet it is evident that, having no other idea or notion of matter, but something wherein those many sensible qualities which affect our senses do subsist; by supposing a substance wherein thinking, knowing, doubting, and a power of moving, &c., do subsist, we have as clear a notion of the substance of spirit, as we have of body; the one being sup-

posed to be (without knowing what it is) the *substratum* to those simple ideas we have from without; and the other supposed (with a like ignorance of what it is) to be the *substratum* to those operations we experiment in ourselves within. It is plain then, that the idea of *corporeal substance* in matter is as remote from our conceptions and apprehensions, as that of *spiritual substance*, or spirit: and therefore, from our not having any notion of the substance of spirit, we can no more conclude its nonexistence, than we can, for the same reason, deny the existence of body; it being as rational to affirm there is no body, because we have no clear and distinct idea of the substance of matter, as to say there is no spirit, because we have no clear and distinct idea of the substance of a spirit.

Whatever therefore be the secret abstract nature of substance in general, all the ideas we have of particular distinct sorts of substances are nothing but several combinations of simple ideas, co-existing in such, though unknown, cause of their union, as makes the whole subsist of itself. It is by such combinations of simple ideas, and nothing else, that we represent particular sorts of substances to ourselves; such are the ideas we have of their several species in our minds; and such only do we, by their specific names, signify to others, e.g. man, horse, sun, water, iron: upon hearing which words, every one who understands the language, frames in his mind a combination of those several simple ideas which he has usually observed, or fancied to exist together under that denomination; all which he supposes to rest in and be, as it were, adherent to that unknown common subject, which inheres not in anything else. Though, in the meantime, it be manifest, and every one, upon inquiry into his own thoughts, will find that he has no other idea of any substance . . . but what he has of those sensible qualities, which he supposes to inhere; with a supposition of such a *substratum* as gives, as it were, a support to those qualities or simple ideas, which he has observed to exist united together. . . .

Knowledge of Mental Substance Is Noninferential
JOHN LOCKE

Hitherto we have only considered the essences of things; which being only abstract ideas, and thereby removed in our thoughts from particular existence, (that being the proper operation of the mind, in abstraction, to consider an idea under no other existence but what it has in the understanding), gives us no knowledge of real existence at all. Where, by the way, we may take notice, that universal propositions of whose truth or falsehood we can have certain knowledge concern not existence: and further, that all particular affirmations or negations that would not be certain if they were made general, are only concerning existence; they declaring only the accidental union or separation of ideas in things existing, which, in their abstract natures, have no known necessary union or repugnancy [inconsistency].

But, leaving the nature of propositions, and different ways of predication to be considered more at large in another place, let us proceed now to inquire concerning our knowledge of the *existence of things*, and how we come by it. I say, then, that we have the knowledge of our own existence by intuition; of the existence of *God* by demonstration; and of *other things* by sensation.

As for *our own existence*, we perceive it so plainly and so certainly, that it neither needs nor is capable of any proof. For nothing can be more evident to us than our own existence. I think, I reason, I feel pleasure and pain: can any of these be more evident to me than my own existence? If I doubt of all other things, that very doubt makes me perceive my own existence, and will not suffer me to doubt of that. For if I know I feel pain, it is evident I have as certain perception of my own existence, as of the existence of the pain I feel: or if I know doubt, I have as certain perception of the existence of the thing doubting, as of that thought which I *call doubt*. Experience then convinces us, that we have an *intuitive knowledge* of our own existence, and an internal infallible perception that we are. In every act of sensation, reasoning, or thinking, we are conscious to ourselves of our own being; and, in this matter, come not short of the highest degree of certainty.

Knowledge of Our Own Mind Is Direct
GEORGE BERKELEY

Having dispatched what we intended to say concerning the knowledge of *ideas*, the method we proposed leads us in the next place to treat of *spirits*—with regard to which, perhaps, human knowledge is not so deficient as is vulgarly imagined. The great reason that is assigned for our being thought ignorant of the nature of spirits is our not having an *idea* of it. But surely it ought not to be looked on as a defect in a human understanding that it does not perceive the idea of spirit if it is manifestly impossible there should be any such idea. And this, if I mistake not, has been demonstrated in section 27; to which I shall here add that a spirit has been shown to be the only sub-

FROM *An Essay Concerning Human Understanding*, John Locke. Book 4, Ch. 9, Sections 1–3 (originally published in 1690).

FROM *A Treatise Concerning the Principles of Human Knowledge*, George Berkeley. Sections 135–140 (originally published in 1710).

stance or support wherein the unthinking beings or ideas can exist; but that this *substance* which supports or perceives ideas should itself be an idea or like an idea is evidently absurd.

It will perhaps be said that we want a sense (as some have imagined) proper to know substances withal, which, if we had, we might know our own soul as we do a triangle. To this I answer, that, in case we had a new sense bestowed upon us, we could only receive thereby some new sensations or ideas of sense. But I believe nobody will say that what he means by the terms "soul" and "substance" is only some particular sort of idea or sensation. We may therefore infer, that all things duly considered, it is not more reasonable to think our faculties defective in that they do not furnish us with an idea of spirit or active thinking substance than it would be if we should blame them for not being able to comprehend a *round square*.

From the opinion that spirits are to be known after the manner of an idea or sensation have risen many absurd and heterodox tenets, and much skepticism about the nature of the soul. It is even probable that this opinion may have produced a doubt in some whether they had any soul at all distinct from their body, since upon inquiry they could not find they had an idea of it. That an *idea* which is inactive, and the existence whereof consists in being perceived, should be the image or likeness of an agent subsisting by itself seems to need no other refutation than barely attending to what is meant by those words. But perhaps you will say that though an idea cannot resemble a spirit in its thinking, acting, or subsisting by itself, yet it may in some other respects; and it is not necessary that an idea or image be in all respects like the original.

I answer, if it [an idea] does not [resemble a spirit] in those [respects] mentioned, it is impossible it should represent it in any other thing. Do but leave out the power of willing, thinking, and perceiving ideas, and there remains nothing else wherein the idea can be like

a spirit. For by the word "spirit" we mean only that which thinks, wills, and perceives; this, and this alone, constitutes the signification of that term. If therefore it is impossible that any degree of those powers should be represented in an idea, it is evident there can be no idea of a spirit.

But it will be objected that, if there is no idea signified by the terms "soul," "spirit," and "substance," they are wholly insignificant or have no meaning in them. I answer, those words do mean or signify a real thing, which is neither an idea nor like an idea, but that which perceives ideas, and wills, and reasons about them. What I am myself, that which I denote by the term "I," is the same with what is meant by "soul," or "spiritual substance." If it be said that this is only quarreling at a word, and that, since the immediate significations of other names are by common consent called "ideas," no reason can be assigned why that which is signified by the name "spirit" or "soul" may not partake in the same appellation, I answer, all the unthinking objects of the mind agree in that they are entirely passive, and their existence consists only in being perceived; whereas a soul or spirit is an active being whose existence consists, not in being perceived, but in perceiving ideas and thinking. It is therefore necessary, in order to prevent equivocation and confounding natures perfectly disagreeing and unlike, that we distinguish between *spirit* and *idea*. See sec. 27.

In a large sense, indeed, we may be said to have an idea (or rather a notinon) of *spirit*; that is, we understand the meaning of the word, otherwise we could not affirm or deny anything of it. Moreover, as we conceive the ideas that are in the minds of other spirits by means of our own, which we suppose to be resemblances of them, so we know other spirits by means of our own soul —which in that sense is the image or idea of them; it having a like respect to other spirits that blueness or heat by me perceived has to those ideas perceived by another.

The Systematic Elusiveness of "I"
GILBERT RYLE

*W*e are now in a position to account for the systematic elusiveness of the notion of 'I', and the partial non-parallelism between it and the notion of 'you' or 'he'. To concern oneself about oneself in any way, theoretical or practical, is to perform a higher order act, just as it is to concern oneself about anybody else. To try, for example, to describe what one has just done, or is now doing, is to comment upon a step which is not itself, save *per accidens*, one of commenting. But the operation which is the commenting is not, and cannot be, the step on which that commentary is being made. Nor can an act of ridiculing be its own butt. A higher order action cannot be the action upon which it is performed. So my commentary on my performances must always be silent about one performance, namely itself, and this performance can be the target only of another commentary. Self-commentary, self-ridicule and self-admonition are logically condemned to eternal penultimacy. Yet nothing that is left out of any particular commentary or admonition is privileged thereby to escape comment or admonition for ever. On the contrary it may be the target of the very next comment or rebuke.

The point may be illustrated in this way. A singing-master might criticise the accents or notes of a pupil by mimicking with exaggerations each word that the pupil sang; and if the pupil sang slowly enough, the master could parody each word sung by the pupil before the next came to be uttered. But then, in a mood of humility, the singing-master tries to criticise his own singing in the same way, and more than that to mimic with exaggerations each word that he utters, including those that he utters in self-parody. It is at once clear, first, that he can never get beyond the very earliest word of his song and, second, that at any given moment he has uttered one noise which has yet to be mimicked— and it makes no difference how rapidly he chases his notes with mimicries of them. He can, in principle, never catch more than the coat-tails of the object of his pursuit, since a word cannot be a parody of itself. None the less, there is no word that he sings which remains unparodied; he is always a day late for the fair, but every day he reaches the place of yesterday's fair. He never succeeds in jumping on to the shadow of his own head, yet he is never more than one jump behind.

An ordinary reviewer may review a book, while a second order reviewer criticises reviews of the book. But the second order review is not a criticism of itself. It can only be criticised in a further third order review. Given complete editorial patience, any review of any order could be published, though at no stage would all the reviews have received critical notices. Nor can every act of a diarist be the topic of a record in his diary; for the last entry made in his diary still demands that the making of it should in its turn be chronicled.

This, I think, explains the feeling that my last year's self, or my yesterday's self, could in principle be exhaustively described and accounted for, and that your past or present self could be exhaustively described and accounted for by me, but that my today's self perpetually slips out of any hold of it that I try to take. It also explains the apparent non-parallelism between the notion of 'I' and that of 'you', without construing the elusive residuum as any kind of ultimate mystery.

FROM *The Concept of Mind*, Gilbert Ryle. (London: Hutchinson and Co., Ltd., 1949), pp. 195–198. Reprinted by permission of Hutchinson and Co., Ltd. and Barnes and Noble, Inc.

There is another thing which it explains. When people consider the problems of the Freedom of the Will and try to imagine their own careers as analogous to those of clocks or watercourses, they tend to boggle at the idea that their own immediate future is already unalterably fixed and predictable. It seems absurd to suppose that what I am just about to think, feel or do is already preappointed, though people are apt to find no such absurdity in the supposition that the futures of other people are so preappointed. The so-called 'feeling of spontaneity' is closely connected with this inability to imagine that what I am going to think or do can already be anticipated. On the other hand, when I consider what I thought and did yesterday, there seems to be no absurdity in supposing that that could have been forecast, before I did it. It is only while I am actually trying to predict my own next move that the task feels like that of a swimmer trying to overtake the waves that he sends ahead of himself.

The solution is as before. A prediction of a deed or a thought is a higher order operation, the performance of which cannot be among the things considered in making the prediction. Yet as the state of mind in which I am just before I do something may make some difference to what I do, it follows that I must overlook at least one of the data relevant to my prediction. Similarly, I can give you the fullest possible advice what to do, but I must omit one piece of counsel, since I cannot in the same breath advise you how to take that advice. There is therefore no paradox in saying that while normally I am not at all surprised to find myself doing or thinking what I do, yet when I try most carefully to anticipate what I shall do or think, then the outcome is likely to falsify my expectation. My process of pre-envisaging may divert the course of my ensuing behaviour in a direction and degree of which my prognosis cannot take account. One thing that I cannot prepare myself for is the next thought that I am going to think.

The fact that my immediate future is in this way systematically elusive to me has, of course, no tendency to prove that my career is in principle unpredictable to prophets other than myself, or even that it is inexplicable to myself after the heat of the action. I can point to any other thing with my index-finger, and other people can point at this finger. But it cannot be the object at which it itself is pointing. Nor can a missile be its own target, though anything else may be thrown at it.

This general conclusion that any performance can be the concern of a higher order performance, but cannot be the concern of itself, is connected with what was said earlier about the special functioning of index words, such as 'now', 'you' and 'I'. An 'I' sentence indicates whom in particular it is about by being itself uttered or written by someone in particular. 'I' indicates the person who utters it. So, when a person utters an 'I' sentence, his utterance of it may be part of a higher order performance, namely one, perhaps, of self-reporting, self-exhortation or self-commiseration, and this performance itself is not dealt with in the operation which it itself is. Even if the person is, for special speculative purposes, momentarily concentrating on the Problem of the Self, he has failed and knows that he has failed to catch more than the flying coat-tails of that which he was pursuing. His quarry was the hunter.

To conclude, there is nothing mysterious or occult about the range of higher order acts and attitudes, which are apt to be inadequately covered by the umbrella-title 'self-consciousness'. They are the same in kind as the higher order acts and attitudes exhibited in the dealings of people with one other. Indeed the former are only a special application of the latter and are learned first from them. If I perform the third order operation of commenting on a second order act of laughing at myself for a piece of manual awkwardness, I shall indeed use the first personal pronoun in two different ways. I say to myself, or to the company, 'I was laughing at myself for being butter-fingered'. But so far from this showing that there are two 'Mes' in my skin, not to speak, yet, of the third one which is still commenting on them, it shows only that I am applying the public two-pronoun idiom in which we talk of her laughing at him; and I am applying this linguistic idiom, because I am applying the method of inter-personal transaction which the idiom is ordinarily employed to describe.

Before concluding this chapter, it is worth mentioning that there is one influential difference between the first personal pronoun and all the rest. 'I', in my use of it, always indicates me and only indicates me. 'You,' 'she' and 'they' indicate different people at different times. 'I' is like my own shadow; I can never get away from it, as I can get away from your shadow. There is no mystery about this constancy, but I mention it because it seems to endow 'I' with a mystifying uniqueness and adhesiveness. 'Now' has something of the same besetting feeling.

Does
Logic
Provide
Indubitable Knowledge?

Aristotle claimed that we know indubitably that (1) it is impossible for the same thing both to be and not be, or if one prefers, (2) it is impossible that the same statement be both true and false. (1) is a special case of (2). (2) entails, where X designates any entity you please, that "X exists" and "X does not exist" are not both true. And this is just another way of putting (1). We cannot, of course, *prove* (2), for (2) is just the sort of claim that any attempt to prove itself, or anything else, must assume.

Suppose, though, we try to disprove (2). We offer an arugment which, in form, runs: since A and B are true, (2) is false. Then, what about A and B? For example, is A true? Perhaps—but even if it is true, we can not infer, without (2), from the fact that it is true to the fact that it is not also false. The same, of course, applies to B—no matter *what* statements A and B represent. Again, the inference from A and B to the denial of (2) must be correct; in other words, "granted A and B, not-(2) follows" must be true. But that it is true, if (2) is false, is no evidence that it is not also false. Hence no confidence can be placed in *A* or *B* or the inference from *A* and *B* to not-(2) if we suppose (2) to be false.

But things are worse still. For *A* must mean one thing, and not both something and the opposite too. This must be so for each word in *A* as well as for *A* as a whole, if *A* is to be intelligible (that is, not nonsense), let alone true. But if we deny (2), then we have no basis for confidence that this is so.

So Aristotle's defense of (2) is this. If anyone tries to disprove (2), or even say without proof that (2) is false, he either proves nothing and says nothing or he covertly assumes that (2) is true and hence defeats his own argument or affirmation.

John Stuart Mill is not certain that the laws of logic are true. In his view, they are only generalizations from our experience. We have never found an entity possessing incompatible properties, so *probably* there are none to be found. Mill denies that the laws of logic, so construed, are such that we cannot conceive their denials to be true, though he also holds that "inconceivability is no criterion of impossibility"; so even were it inconceivable that for instance, the law of contradiction did not hold, this would not for Mill show that it is impossible that it not hold.

This last issue is worth a passing comment. Mill cites Hamilton's argument to the effect that it is inconceivable both that matter be infinitely divisible and that divisibility at a certain point cease to be possible. But one or the other must be the case. So there is something possible (because true) but nonetheless inconceivable. In one sense of "inconceivable," this is true. If "inconceivable" means "unimaginable" in the sense that no image can be formed of infinite divisibility, then something inconceivable is impossible, but this is irrelevant to Mill's argument. In the sense revelant to Mill's argument, nothing inconceivable is possible; if "inconceivable" means "involves a contradiction," then neither of Hamilton's examples is appropriate, for neither example involves a contradiction.

Frege, whom Bertrand Russell referred to as "that great man," replied to Mill. First, Mill treats the identity statement "$1 = 1$" as if it meant (in part) or entailed "One (measured) pound is precisely the same as another (measured) pound." Since our measurements are not perfect, it is often false that one measured pound is exactly the same weight as another. So "$1 = 1$" is sometimes false. Even if our measurements were always perfect, this would be a contingent fact, and any other fact dependent on it could only be contingent. If "$1 = 1$" is true only if "All our measurements are perfect" is true, then since the latter statement is contingent, so is the former. And exactly analogous comments apply to "$5 + 2 = 7$" and "$7,482 + 9,478 = 16,960$." But *none* of these mathematical statements entails or presupposes anything whatever about our measurements. They say only that *if* we have, for example, 2 pounds and 5 pounds of peanuts, we have 7 pounds of peanuts. This claim depends in no way of anyone's measuring anything accurately. As Frege aptly puts it, "Mill always confuses the applications that can be made of an arithmetical proposition, which often are physical and do presuppose observed facts, with the pure mathematical proposition itself." (While Frege, throughout his remarks, deals with mathematical statements, his remarks apply in the same manner to the laws of logic.)

Second, if the laws of logic and the statements of mathematics are empirical generalizations (that is, general statements based on particular statements that are confirmed by particular observations), what statements will provide the basis for these generalizations? In the case of, say, "Nothing can have incompatible properties," we would presumably have to appeal to such statements as "My chair has compatible properties," "My pen has compatible properties." Several problems arise. I can see with my eyes that my pen is black, oblong, and shiny; I cannot see with my eyes that it has compatible properties. Nor can I discern this by the use of any other sense or combination of the senses. If I accept Mill's requirement that the particular statements on which the generalization is based be confirmed by observation, how am I ever to know that the particular statements in question are true? How can I ever get started? Again, assuming my pen to exist, "My pen has compatible properties" seems itself to be a necessary truth; so we have a necessary truth without generalizing. Further, the laws of logic state what *can* and *cannot* occur, as opposed to stating that something *does* occur. "No swan is orange" does not say that no swan *can* be orange but only that none *is*. What *can* without contradiction occur is not inferrable from what *does* occur. (We can, of course, infer that if *A* does occur then *A* can occur, but only by appeal to the proposition that what is actual is possible—an axiom of modal logic.) Finally, inductive generalizations are (roughly) inferences from premises of the form "All observed *A*'s are *B*'s" to a conclusion of the form "All *A*'s are *B*'s." The inference presupposes some such statement as "Nature is uniform," which is contingent but not itself the result of generalization from particular empirical premises (since it would again have to be presupposed in any attempt to infer it from particular empirical statements). Whether these considerations raise problems for inductive reasoning is not in question. The point is rather that even in Mill's view we must also appeal to a proposition ("Nature is uniform" or some substantially similar claim) that is not empirically confirmable or justifiable by induction. Nor is the proposition in question one so obviously true as "Nothing can have incompatible properties." This remains true, even if Frege overstates his case somewhat when he claims that induction "must base itself on the theory of probability."

These remarks transpose (and somewhat expand) Frege's comments concerning Mill's treatment of mathematics into comments concerning Mill's treatment of logic. Frege's basic point is that there is, so to speak, a difference in kind between the statements of logic and mathematics on the one hand (these are not justifiable by observation and/or induction, and most of them are such that their denials are contradictory) and empirical generalizations such as "All crows are black." He thus accuses Mill of confusing logical and mathematical statements with their applications.

Another alternative to Aristotle's view has been offered by some contemporary philosophers. This is that the laws of logic at any rate are based on, or in fact are "conventions of our language." This view can be found in A. J. Ayer's *Language, Truth and Logic* and Norman Malcolm's "Are Necessary Propositions Really Verbal?" (*Mind*, 1940), and a powerful critique of it is offered by Arthur Pap, *Semantics and Necessary Truth* (Chapter 7).

The Law of Contradiction Is Indubitable
ARISTOTLE

There are some who as we said, both themselves assert that it is possible for the same thing to be and not to be, and say that people can judge this to be the case. And among others many writers about nature use this language. But we have now posited that it is impossible for anything at the same time to be and not to be, and by this means have shown that this is the most indisputable of all principles.—Some indeed demand that even this shall be demonstrated, but this they do through want of education, for not to know of what things one should demand demonstration, and of what one should not, argues want of education. For it is impossible that there should be demonstration of absolutely everything (there would be an infinite regress, so that there would still be no demonstration); but if there are things of which one should not demand demonstration, these persons could not say what principle they maintain to be more self-evident than the present one.

We can, however, demonstrate negatively even that this view is impossible, if our opponent will only say something; and if he says nothing, it is absurd to seek to give an account of our views to one who cannot give an account of anything, in so far as he cannot do so. For such a man, as such, is from the start no better than a vegetable. Now negative demonstration I distinguish from demonstration proper, because in a demonstration one might be thought to be begging the question, but if another person is responsible for the assumption we shall have negative proof, not demonstration. The starting-point for all such arguments is not the demand that our opponent shall say that something either is or is not (for this one might perhaps take to be a begging of the question), but that he shall say something which is *significant* both for himself and for another; for this is necessary, if he really is to say anything. For, if he means nothing, such a man will not be capable of reasoning, either with himself or with another. But if any one grants this, demonstration will be possible; for we shall already have something definite. The person responsible for the proof, however, is not he who demonstrates but he who listens; for while disowning reason he listens to reason. And again he who admits this has admitted that something is true apart from demonstration [so that not everything will be 'so and not so'].

First then this at least is obviously true, that the word 'be' or 'not be' has a definite meaning, so that not everything will be 'so and not so'.—Again if 'man' has one meaning, let this be 'two-footed animal'; by having one meaning I understand this:—if 'man' means '*X*', then if *A* is a man '*X*' will be what 'being a man' means for him. (It makes no difference even if one were to say a word has several meanings, if only they are limited in number; for to each definition there might be assigned a different word. For instance, we might say that 'man' has not one meaning but several, one of which would have one definition, viz. 'two-footed animal', while there might be also several other definitions if only they were limited in number; for a peculiar name might be assigned to each of the definitions. If, however, they were not limited but one were to say that the word has an infinite number of meanings, obviously reasoning would be impossible; for not to have one meaning is to have no meaning, and if words have no meaning our reasoning with one

FROM "Metaphysics," W. D. Ross, trans. Book 4, Ch. 4 in *The Oxford Translation of Aristotle*, W. D. Ross, ed. (Oxford: The Clarendon Press, 1928), Vol. 8. Reprinted by permission of The Clarendon Press.

another, and indeed with ourselves, has been annihilated; for it is impossible to think of anything if we do not think of one thing; but if this *is* possible, one name might be assigned to this thing.)

Let it be assumed then, as was said at the beginning, that the name has a meaning and has one meaning; it is impossible, then, that 'being a man' should mean precisely 'not being a man', if 'man' not only signifies something about one subject but also has one significance (for we do not identify 'having one significance' with 'signifying something about one subject', since on *that* assumption even 'musical' and 'white' and 'man' would have had one significance, so that all things would have been one; for they would all have had the same significance).

And it will not be possible to be and not to be the same thing, except in virtue of an ambiguity, just as if one whom we call 'man', others were to call 'not-man'; but the point in question is not this, whether the same thing can at the same time be and not be a man in name, but whether it can in fact.—Now if 'man' and 'not-man' mean nothing different, obviously 'not being a man' will mean nothing different from 'being a man'; so that 'being a man' will be 'not being a man'; for they will be one. For being one means this—being related as 'raiment' and 'dress' are, if their definition is one. And if 'being a man' and 'being a not-man' are to be one, they must mean one thing. But it was shown earlier that they mean different things.—Therefore, if it is true to say of anything that it is a man, it must be a two-footed animal (for this was what 'man' meant); and if this is necessary, it is impossible that the same thing should not at that time be a two-footed animal; for this is what 'being necessary' means—that it is impossible for the thing not to be. It is, then, impossible that it should be at the same time true to say the same thing is a man and is not a man.

The same account holds good with regard to 'not being a man', for 'being a man' and 'being a not-man' mean different things, since even 'being white' and 'being a man' are different; for the former terms are much more opposed, so that they must *a fortiori* mean different things. And if any one says that '*white*' means one and the same thing as 'man', again we shall say the same as what was said before, that it would follow that *all* things are one, and not only opposites. But if this is impossible, then what we have maintained will follow, if our opponent will only answer our question.

And if, when one asks the question simply, he adds the contradictories, he is not answering the question. For there is nothing to prevent the same thing from being both a man and white and countless other things: but still, if one asks whether it is or is not true to say that this is a man, our opponent must give an answer which means one thing, and not add that 'it is also white and large'. For, besides other reasons, it is impossible to enumerate its accidental attributes, which are infinite in number; let him, then, enumerate either all or none. Similarly, therefore, even if the same thing is a thousand times a man and a not-man, he must not, in answering the question whether this is a man, add that it is also at the same time a not-man, unless he is bound to add also all the other accidents, all that the subject is or is not; and if he does this, he is not observing the rules of argument.

And in general those who say this do away with substance and essence. For they must say that all attributes are accidents, and that there is no such thing as 'being essentially a man' or 'an animal'. For if there is to be any such thing as 'being essentially a man' this will not be 'being a not-man' or 'not being a man' (yet these are negations of it); for there was one thing which is meant, and this was the substance of something. And denoting the substance of a thing means that the essence of the thing is nothing else. But if its being essentially a man is to be the same as either being essentially a not-man or essentially not being a man, then its essence *will* be something else. Therefore our opponents must say that there cannot be such a definition of anything, but that all attributes are accidental; for this is the distinction between substance and accident —'white' is accidental to man, because though he is white, whiteness is not his essence. But if *all* statements are accidental, there will be nothing primary about which they are made, if the accidental always implies predication about a subject. The predication, then, must go on *ad infinitum*. But this is impossible; for not even more than two terms can be combined in accidental predication. For (1) an accident is not an accident of an accident, unless it be because both are accidents of the same subject. I mean, for instance, that the white is musical and the latter is white, only because both are accidental to man. But (2) Socrates is musical, not in this sense, that both terms are accidental to something else. Since then some predicates are accidental in this and some in that sense, (*a*) those which are accidental in the latter sense, in which white is accidental to Socrates, cannot form an infinite series in the upward direction; e.g. Socrates the white has not yet another accident; for no unity can be got out of such a sum. Nor again (*b*) will 'white' have another term accidental to it, e.g. 'musical'. For this is no more accidental to that than that is to this; and at the same time we have drawn the distinction, that while some predicates are accidental in this sense, others are so in the sense in which 'musical' is accidental to Socrates; and the accident is an accident of an accident not in cases of the latter kind, but only in cases of the other kind, so that not *all* terms will be accidental. There must, then, even so be something which denotes substance. And if this is so, it has been shown that contradictories cannot be predicated at the same time.

Again, if all contradictory statements are true of the same subject at the same time, evidently all things will be one. For the same thing will be a trireme, a wall, and a man, if of everything it is possible either to affirm or to deny anything (and this premiss must be accepted by those who share the views of Protagoras). For if any one thinks that the man is not a trireme, evidently he is not a trireme; so that he also *is* a trireme, if, as they say, contradictory statements are both true. And we thus get the doctrine of Anaxagoras, that all things are mixed together; so that nothing really exists. They seem, then, to be speaking of the indeterminate, and, while fancying themselves to be speaking of being, they are speaking about non-being; for it is that which exists potentially and not in complete reality that is indeterminate. But they *must* predicate of every subject the affirmation or the negation of every attribute. For it is absurd if of each subject its own negation is to be predicable, while the negation of something else which cannot be predicated of it is not to be predicable of it; for instance, if it is true to say of a man that he is not a man, evidently it is also true to say that he is either a trireme or not a trireme. If, then, the affirmative can be predicated, the negative must be predicable too; and if the affirmative is not predicable, the negative, at least, will be more predicable than the negative of the subject itself. If, then, even the latter negative is predicable, the negative of 'trireme' will be also predicable; and, if this is predicable, the affirmative will be so too.

Those, then, who maintain this view are driven to this conclusion, and to the further conclusion that it is not necessary either to assert or to deny. For if it is true that a thing is a man and a not-man, evidently also it will be neither a man nor a not-man. For to the two assertions there answer two negations, and if the former is treated as a single proposition compounded out of two, the latter also is a single proposition opposite to the former.

Again, either the theory is true in all cases, and a thing is both white and not-white, and existent and non-existent, and all other assertions and negations are similarly compatible, or the theory is true of some statements and not of others. And if not of all, the exceptions will be contradictories of which admittedly only one is true; but if of all, again either the negation will be true wherever the assertion is, and the assertion true wherever the negation is, or the negation will be true where the assertion is, but the assertion not always true where the negation is. And (*a*) in the latter case there will be something which fixedly *is not*, and this will be an indisputable belief; and if non-being is something indisputable and knowable, the opposite assertion will be more knowable. But (*b*) if it is equally possible also to assert all that it is possible to deny, one must either be saying what is true when one separates the predicates (and says, for instance, that a thing is white, and again that it is not-white), or not. And if (i) it is not true to apply the predicates separately, our opponent is not saying what he professes to say, and also nothing at all exists, but how could non-existent things speak or walk, as he does? Also all things would on this view be one, as has been already said, and man and God and trireme and their contradictories will be the same. For if contradictories can be predicated alike of each subject, one thing will in no wise differ from another; for if it differ, this difference will be something true and peculiar to it. And (ii) if one may with truth apply the predicates separately, the above-mentioned result follows none the less, and, further, it follows that all would then be right and all would be in error, and our opponent himself confesses himself to be in error.—And at the same time our discussion with him is evidently about nothing at all; for he says nothing. For he says neither 'yes' nor 'no', but 'yes and no'; and again he denies both of these and says 'neither yes nor no'; for otherwise there would already be something definite.

Again, if when the assertion is true, the negation is false, and when this is true, the affirmation is false, it will not be possible to assert and deny the same thing truly at the same time. But perhaps they might say this was the very question at issue.

Again, is he in error who judges either that the thing is so or that it is not so, and is he right who judges both? If he is right, what can they mean by saying that the nature of existing things is of this kind? And if he is not right, but more right than he who judges in the other way, being will already be of a definite nature, and this will be true and not at the same time also not true. But if all are alike both wrong and right, one who is in this condition will not be able either to speak or to say anything intelligible; for he says at the same time both 'yes' and 'no'. And if he makes no judgement but 'thinks' and 'does not think', indifferently, what difference will there be between him and a vegetable? —Thus, then, it is in the highest degree evident that neither any one of those who maintain this view nor any one else is really in this position. For why does a man walk to Megara and not stay at home, when he thinks he ought to be walking there? Why does he not walk early some morning into a well or over a precipice, if one happens to be in his way? Why do we observe him guarding against this, evidently because he does not think that falling in is alike good and not good? Evidently, then, he judges one thing to be better and another worse. And if this is so, he must also judge one thing to be a man and another to be not-a-man, one thing to be sweet and another to be not-sweet. For he does not aim at and judge all things alike, when, thinking it desirable to drink water or to see a man, he proceeds to aim at these things; yet he *ought*, if the same thing were alike a man and not-a-man. But, as was said, there is no one who does not obviously avoid some things and not others. Therefore, as it seems, all men make unqualified judgements, if not about all things, still about what is better and worse. And if this is not knowledge but opinion, they should be all the more anxious about the truth, as a sick man should be more anxious about his health than one who is healthy; for he who has opinions is, in comparison with the man who knows, not in a healthy state as far as the truth is concerned.

Again, however much all things may be 'so and not so', still there is a more and a less in the nature of things; for we should not say that two and three are equally even, nor is he who thinks four things are five equally wrong with him who thinks they are a thousand. If then they are not equally wrong, obviously one is less wrong and therefore more right. If then that which has more of any quality is nearer the norm, there must be some truth to which the more true is nearer. And even if there is not, still there is already something better founded and liker the truth, and we shall have got rid of the unqualified doctrine which would prevent us from determining anything in our thought.

The Laws of Logic Are Empirical Generalizations
JOHN STUART MILL

Sir William Hamilton holds as I do, that inconceivability is no criterion of impossibility. "There is no ground for inferring a certain fact to be impossible, merely from our inability to conceive its possibility." "Things there are which *may*, nay *must*, be true, of which the understanding is wholly unable to construe to itself the possibility." Sir William Hamilton is, however, a firm believer in the *a priori* character of many axioms, and of the sciences deduced from them; and is so far from considering those axioms to rest on the evidence of experience, that he declares certain of them to be true even of Noumena—of the Unconditioned—of which it is one of the principal aims of his philosophy to prove that the nature of our faculties debars us from having any knowledge. The axioms to which he attributes this exceptional emancipation from the limits which confine all our other possibilities of knowledge the chinks through which, as he represents, one ray of light finds its way to us from behind the curtain which veils from us the mysterious world of Things in themselves—are the two principles, which he terms, after the schoolman, the Principle of Contradiction, and the Principle of Excluded Middle: the first, that two contradictory propositions can not both be true; the second, that they cannot both be false. Armed with these logical weapons, we may boldly face Things in themselves, and tender to them the double alternative, sure that they must absolutely elect one or the other side, though we may be forever precluded from discovering which. To take his favorite example, we can not conceive the infinite divisibility of matter, and we can not conceive a minimum, or end to divisibility: yet one or the other must be true.

As I have hitherto said nothing of the two axioms in question, those of Contradiction and of Excluded Middle, it is not unseasonable to consider them here. The former asserts that an affirmative proposition and the corresponding negative proposition can not both be true; which has generally been held to be intuitively evident. Sir William Hamilton and the Germans consider it to be the statement in words of a form or law of our thinking faculty. Other philosophers, not less deserving of consideration, deem it to be an identical proposition; an assertion involved in the meaning of terms; a mode of defining Negation, and the word Not.

FROM *A System of Logic*, John Stuart Mill. (New York: Harper and Bros., 1874), pp. 204–206.

I am able to go one step with these last. An affirmative assertion and its negative are not two independent assertions, connected with each other only as mutually incompatible. That if the negative be true, the affirmative must be false, really is a mere identical proposition; for the negative proposition asserts nothing but the falsity of the affirmative, and has no other sense or meaning whatever. The Principium Contradictionis should therefore put off the ambitious phraseology which gives it the air of a fundamental antithesis pervading nature, and should be enunciated in the simpler form, that the same proposition can not at the same time be false and true. But I can go no further with the Nominalists; for I can not look upon this last as a merely verbal proposition. I consider it to be, like other axioms, one of our first and most familiar generalizations from experience. The original foundation of it I take to be, that Belief and Disbelief are two different mental states, excluding one another. This we know by the simplest observation of our own minds. And if we carry our observation outward, we also find that light and darkness, sound and silence, motion and quiescence, equality and inequality, preceding and following, succession and simultaneousness, any positive phenomenon whatever and its negative, are distinct phenomena, pointedly contrasted, and the one always absent where the other is present. I consider the maxim in question to be a generalization from all these facts.

In like manner as the Principle of Contradiction (that one of two contradictories must be false) means that an assertion can not be *both* true and false, so the Principle of Excluded Middle, or that one of two contradictories must be true, means that an assertion must be *either* true or false: either the affirmative is true, or otherwise the negative is true, which means that the affirmative is false. I can not help thinking this principle a surprising specimen of a so-called necessity of Thought, since it is not even true, unless with a large qualification. A proposition must be either true or false, *provided* that the predicate be one which can in any intelligible sense be attributed to the subject; (and as this is always assumed to be the case in treatises on logic, the axiom is always laid down there as of absolute truth). "Abracadabra is a second intention" is neither true nor false. Between the true and the false there is a third possibility, the Unmeaning: and this alternative is fatal to Sir William Hamilton's extension of the maxim to Noumena. That Matter must either have a minimum of divisibility or be infinitely divisible, is more than we can ever know. For in the first place, Matter, in any other than the phenomenal sense of the term, may not exist: and it will scarcely be said that a nonentity must be either infinitely or finitely divisible. In the second place, though matter, considered as the occult cause of our sensations, do really exist, yet what we call divisibility may be an attribute only of our sensations of sight and touch, and not of their uncognizable cause. Divisibility may not be predicable at all, in any intelligible sense, of Things in themselves, nor therefore of Matter in itself; and the assumed necessity of being either infinitely or finitely divisible, may be an inapplicable alternative.

On this question I am happy to have the full concurrence of Mr. Herbert Spencer, from whose paper in the *Fortnightly Review* I extract the following passage. The germ of an idea identical with that of Mr. Spencer may be found in the present chapter, on a preceding page; but in Mr. Spencer it is not an undeveloped thought, but a philosophical theory.

"When remembering a certain thing as in a certain place, the place and the thing are mentally represented together; while to think of the nonexistence of the thing in that place implies a consciousness in which the place is represented, but not the thing. Similarly, if instead of thinking of an object as colorless, we think of its having color, the change consists in the addition to the concept of an element that was before absent from it—the object can not be thought of first as red and then as not red, without one component of the thought being totally expelled from the mind by another. The law of the Excluded Middle, then, is simply a generalization of the universal experience that some mental states are directly destructive of other states. It formulates a certain absolutely constant law, that the appearance of any positive mode of consciousness can not occur without excluding a correlative negative mode; and that the negative mode can not occur without excluding the correlative positive mode: the antithesis of positive and negative being, indeed, merely an expression of this experience. Hence it follows that if consciousness is not in one of the two modes it must be in the other."

A Critique of Mill
GOTTLOB FREGE

*A*re the laws of arithmetic inductive *truths?* The considerations adduced thus far make it probable that numerical formulae can be derived from the definitions of the individual numbers alone by means of a few general laws, and that these definitions neither assert observed facts nor presuppose them for their legitimacy. Our next task, therefore, must be to ascertain the nature of the laws involved.

MILL[1] proposes to make use, for his proof (referred to above) of the formula $5 + 2 = 7$, of the principle that "Whatever is made up of parts, is made up of parts of those parts." This he holds to be an expression in more characteristic language of the principle familiar elsewhere in the form "The sums of equals are equals." He calls it an inductive truth, and a law of nature of the highest order. It is typical of the inaccuracy of his exposition, that when he comes to the point in the proof at which, on his own view, this principle should be indispensable, he does not invoke it at all; however, it appears that his inductive truth is meant to do the work of LEIBNIZ's axiom that "If equals be substituted for equals, the equality remains." But in order to be able to call arithmetical truths laws of nature, MILL attributes to them a sense which they do not bear. For example,[2] he holds that the identity $1 = 1$ could be false, on the ground that one pound weight does not always weigh precisely the same as another. But the proposition $1 = 1$ is not intended in the least to state that it does.

MILL understands the symbol $+$ in such a way that it will serve to express the relation between the parts of a physical body or of a heap and the whole body or heap; but such is not the sense of that symbol. That if we pour 2 unit volumes of liquid into 5 unit volumes of liquid we shall have 7 unit volumes of liquid, is not the meaning of the proposition $5 + 2 = 7$, but an application of it, which only holds good provided that no alteration of the volume occurs as a result, say, of some chemical reaction. MILL always confuses the applications that can be made of an arithmetical proposition, which often are physical and do presuppose observed facts, with the pure mathematical propo-

[1] *A System of Logic,* Bk. III, cap. xxiv. § 5.

[2] Op. cit., Bk. II, cap. vi, § 3.

FROM *The Foundations of Arithmetic,* Gottlob Frege. J. L. Austin, trans. (Oxford: Basil Blackwell, Publishers, 1956), Sections 9–11. Reprinted by permission of Basil Blackwell, Publishers.

sition itself. The plus symbol can certainly look, in many applications, as though it corresponded to a process of heaping up; but that is not its meaning; for in other applications there can be no question of heaps or aggregates, or of the relationship between a physical body and its parts, as for example when we calculate about numbers of events. No doubt we can speak even here of "parts"; but then we are using the word not in the physical or geometrical sense, but in its logical sense, as we do when we speak of tyrannicides as a part of murder as a whole. This is a matter of logical subordination. And in the same way addition too does not in general correspond to any physical relationship. It follows that the general laws of addition cannot, for their part, be laws of nature.

§ 10. But might they not still be inductive truths nevertheless? I do not see how that is conceivable. From what particular facts are we to take our start here, in order to advance to the general? The only available candidates for the part are the numerical formulae. Assign them to it, and of course we lose once again the advantage gained by giving our definitions of the individual numbers; we should have to cast around for some other means of establishing the numerical formulae. Even if we manage to rise superior to this misgiving too, which is not exactly easy, we shall still find the ground unfavourable for induction; for here there is none of that uniformity, which in other fields can give the method a high degree of reliability. LEIBNIZ[3] recognized this already: for to his Philalèthe, who had asserted that *"the several modes of number are not capable of any other difference but more or less; which is why they are simple modes, like those of space,"** he returns the answer:

"That can be said of time and of

[3] *Die Lehren Von Zeit, Raum, und Mathematik*, Berlin, 1668.

* [Derived from Locke, *Essay*, Bk. II, xvi, §5.]

the straight line, but certainly not of the figures and still less of the numbers, which are not merely different in magnitude, but also dissimilar. An even number can be divided into two equal parts, an odd number cannot; three and six are triangular numbers, four and nine are squares, eight is a cube, and so on. And this is even more the case with the numbers than with the figures; for two unequal figures can be perfectly similar to each other, but never two numbers."

We have no doubt grown used to treating the numbers in many contexts as all of the same sort, but that is only because we know a set of general propositions which hold for all numbers. For the present purpose, however, we must put ourselves in the position that none of these has yet been discovered. The fact is that it would be difficult to find an example of an inductive inference to parallel our present case. In ordinary inductions we often make good use of the proposition that every position in space and every moment in time is as good in itself as every other. Our results must hold good for any other place and any other time, provided only that the conditions are the same. But in the case of the numbers this does not apply, since they are not in space or time. Position in the number series is not a matter of indifference like position in space.

The numbers, moreover, are related to one another quite differently from the way in which the individual specimens of, say, a species of animal are. It is in their nature to be arranged in a fixed, definite order of precedence; and each one is formed in its own special way and has its own unique peculiarities, which are specially prominent in the cases of 0, 1 and 2. Elsewhere when we establish by induction a proposition about a species, we are ordinarily in possession already, merely from the definition of the concept of the species, of a whole series of its common properties. But with the numbers we have difficulty in finding even a single common property which has not actually to be first proved common.

The following is perhaps the case with which our putative induction might most easily be compared. Suppose we have noticed that in a borehole the temperature increases regularly with the depth; and suppose we have so far encountered a wide variety of differing rock strata. Here it is obvious that we cannot, simply on the strength of the observations made at this borehole, infer anything whatever as to the nature of the strata at deeper levels, and that any answer to the question, whether the regular distribution of temperature would continue to hold good lower down, would be premature. There is, it is true, a concept, that of "whatever you come to by going on boring," under which fall both the strata so far observed and those at lower levels alike; but that is of little assistance to us here. And equally, it will be no help to us to learn in the case of the numbers that these all fall together under the concept of "whatever you get by going on increasing by one." It is possible to draw a distinction between the two cases, on the ground that the strata are things we simply encounter, whereas the numbers are literally created, and determined in their whole natures, by the process of continually increasing by one. Now this can only mean that from the way in which a number, say 8, is generated through increasing by one all its properties can be deduced. But this is in principle to grant that the properties of numbers follow from their definitions, and to open up the possibility that we might prove the general laws of numbers from the method of generation which is common to them all, while deducing the special properties of the individual numbers from the special way in which, through the process of continually increasing by one, each one is formed. In the same way in the geological case too, we can deduce everything that is determined simply and solely by the depth at which a stratum is encountered,

namely its spatial position relative to anything else, from the depth itself, without having any need of induction; but whatever is not so determined, cannot be learned by induction either.

The procedure of induction, we may surmise, can itself be justified only by means of general propositions of arithmetic—unless we understand by induction a mere process of habituation, in which case it has of course absolutely no power whatever of leading to the discovery of truth. The procedure of the sciences, with its objective standards, will at times find a high probability established by a single confirmatory instance, while at others it will dismiss a thousand as almost worthless; whereas our habits are determined by the number and strength of the impressions we receive and by subjective circumstances, which have no sort of right at all to influence our judgement. Induction [then, properly understood,] must base itself on the theory of probability, since it can never render a proposition more than probable. But how probability theory could possibly be developed without presupposing arithmetical laws is beyond comprehension.

Leibniz holds the opposite view, that the necessary truths, such as are found in arithmetic, must have principles whose proof does not depend on examples and therefore not on the evidence of the senses, though doubtless without the senses it would have occurred to no one to think of them. "The whole of arithmetic is innate and is in virtual fashion in us." What he means by the term "innate" is explained by another passage, where he denies "that *Everything we learn is not innate*. The truths of number are in us and yet we still learn them, whether it be by drawing them forth from their source when learning them by demonstration (which shows them to be innate), or whether it be [by some other manner] . . .".

Does
Common Sense
Provide
Indubitable Knowledge?

G. E. Moore scandalized philosophers by the apparently cavalier manner in which he sometimes argued. Is there a world external to our sensory experience? Do we *know* that this is the case? Descartes, Leibniz, Spinoza, Locke, Hume, Berkeley, Kant, McTaggert, Bradley, Russell, and others had discussed these and similar questions at length and with subtlety. In apparent contrast, Moore answers these questions in his "Proof of an External World" by arguing: Here is my right hand, and here my left. So of course there are physical objects. (As Moore notes, if this "proof" succeeds with this example, it would succeed with other examples, besides hands.)
Concerning this method of argument, he writes:

But did I prove just now that two human hands were then in existence? I do want to insist that I did; that the proof which I gave was a perfectly rigorous one; and that it is perhaps impossible to give a better or more rigorous proof of anything whatever.

The premises are true and known to be true, and they do entail the conclusion. What more could be asked?

Moore was also known as one of the most meticulously careful of all philosophers. Not surprisingly, the apparent simplicity of his proof is matched by its real complexity. What follows is an attempt to set out the form and intent of his presentation.

First, there is no question but what Moore intends to refute certain claims made by the idealists Berkeley and McTaggert. Thus Berkeley had held (to paraphrase his view): "When I undergo the experience ordinarily designated as seeing my hand, there is no object that is distinct from and exists independently of the particular shapes, colors, and so forth, that I see." McTaggert had affirmed that time is unreal in the sense that if we suppose that things do bear to one another the temporal relations they appear to, we find ourselves committed to the truth of contradictory statements. So no statement to the effect that one thing or event bears a temporal relation to another thing or event can be strictly true.

If these tenets are among those Moore intends to refute, how does the refutation go? Well, the first step is to state, with great care, a set of propositions—labeled (1)—which, according to Moore's (2), we know to be unqualifiedly true when they are taken in the ordinary sense. To take a single example, I know that I was born a while ago. Each of a large number of other people know the same thing of themselves. Berkeley and McTaggert knew this too. Indeed, "*all* philosophers, without exception, have agreed with me in holding this." But some philosophers (Moore maintains) have also held statements to be true that are incompatible with one or more of the set of statements from which our example was taken.

One phase, then, of Moore's argument is this: there are statements that are known to be true and if any philosophical system or statement entails that any of these statements are false, that system or statement is false.

This makes matters appear tidier than they really are. Berkeley admits—indeed, affirms—that sentences such as "I see an apple" are true. But he denies that "common sense" requires that any object distinct from our experience exist in order for a statement of this form to be true. The situation is complicated by the fact that the beliefs of ordinary men have been, in Berkeley's view, perverted by the doctrine of substance—the doctrine that we sense qualities which "belong to" or "inhere in" a quality-bearer. Insofar as ordinary belief implies the existence of objects that exist as distinct from and independent of our sensory experience, there is a distinction between ordinary belief and common sense. ("Common sense" seems to be used by Berkeley in such a way that "*B* is a common sense belief" entails "*B* is true"; with qualification Moore also holds that, "if they are features in the Common Sense view of the world . . . it follows that they are true.") As to McTaggert, there is no doubt from his perspective that we conceive, and even must conceive, that events are temporally related. We can conceive them in no other way, but the contradictions that arise when we reflect on our temporal concepts show that events only appear to us to be temporally connected—reality is veiled from us by the concepts we cannot escape using to interpret it. "*B* is a common-sense belief" will, for McTaggert, entail "*B* is true of appearance and not true of things as they really are." Insofar as a consistent follower of Berkeley or McTaggert accepts such beliefs as Moore mentions, he accepts them as purified of perversions or as qualified so as to apply only to how things appear as opposed to how they really are.

The same or closely related issues can be put in another way. One can grant "There are hands" but deny "There are objects which are distinct from and exist independent of our sensory experience" by analyzing hands in terms of seen shapes and colors, felt shapes and roughnesses or smoothnesses, and the like. Moore himself (see Section IV of his essay) is not sure as to how such statements as "Here is a human hand" are to be analyzed. And since one question at least about the analysis of a statement involves the question as to what the statement *entails*, there would seem on Moore's own account to be room for debate about whether "there are hands" entails that "there are independent objects."

What is perhaps more an extrapolation from Moore's argument than an exposition of it deserves brief mention. One might read the import of his argument in terms such as these: the concepts or categories of physical object, space, time, and so on, are such that no attempt to give an account of our sensory experience can dispense with them *and* that these concepts or categories are primitive (that is, cannot be analyzed into other concepts). Berkeley would admit only the first half of this thesis, and while McTaggert would perhaps admit it entirely, he would add that only knowledge of how things appear is given by such an account.

There are other features, of course, of Moore's discussion. He holds, for example, that it is false that every physical fact (a fact that does not include consciousness) could not exist without some mental fact (a fact that does include consciousness) or other. This is raised as a criticism of idealism and presupposes (what the idealist denies) that there are physical facts. But perhaps the discussion so far indicates the basic thrust, and the complexity, of Moore's case.

David Hume's "Of Scepticism with Regard to the Senses" raises a question of immediate relevance to Moore's essay. Hume grants that the existence of bodies distinct from and independent of our sensory experiences "is a point which we must take for granted in all our reasonings." But he adds that the skeptic (and this applies to everyone else) "cannot pretend by any arguments of his philosophy to maintain its veracity." Hence he is content to ask "What causes induce us to believe in the existence of body?" not "Whether there be body or not?" We will here follow Hume's argument only as he endeavors to show that neither the data provided by sensory experience nor rational inference from this data in any way justify our belief that bodies exist. Hume holds that it is plain enough that we cannot, by the senses alone, tell that something exists when it is no longer sensed nor that it exists in such a way as to be capable of existing unsensed.

Neither, Hume argues, contrary to what one might unreflectively suppose, do the senses give us knowledge of objects that exist external to, or at a distance from, our bodies. For one thing, what we call our "body" is simply "certain impressions, which enter by the senses." If one objects that "by the senses" implies that we have sensory organs, and so a body, the reply is that all references to sensory organs can be "translated out." *Sense* experience is, in this view, experience that differs in ways immediately evident to consciousness from, for instance, what is called "introspective" experience. "Sense" refers to experienced qualities of our experience, not to its source. Second, "sounds and tastes and smells" are unreflectively regarded as having an existence independent of and external to the body, whereas in fact they, as experienced, have no spatial properties at all. Not being extended (that is, having neither size nor shape), they can be at no distance from anything. Hence we cannot trust our unreflective tendency to regard what we experience as being in fact at a distance from our bodies. Finally, we do not simply *see* objects at a distance but *infer* that they are at a distance from us. We must correlate our present observations with our past experience in order to infer that an object is distant from us. And if one follows Berkeley here, "at a distance" is to be analysed in terms of *predictions* about the future course of experience, not *present tense claims* about the location of objects.

Nor can we infer from our sensory impressions to objects as their causes, as this would require use of the claim that every impression (or at least some impressions) are caused by objects, which *presupposes* that objects exist, or at least require appeal to the claim that impressions must have some sort of cause (a claim, in Hume's view, not rationally justifiable). We would also need an independent argument to the effect that physical objects are the most plausible candidates for being these causes. In sum neither sensory experience, nor sensory experience plus inference, justifies the belief that there are physical objects. The source of this belief is the imagination—our tendency to assimilate resembling impressions to a single object that can exist unsensed, thus sliding unreflectively to a conclusion that reflection cannot justify.

Two points are worth emphasizing here. First, what for Moore is the clearly true conviction of common sense is for Hume the inevitable but also rationally indefensible tendency of the human imagination. Second, Moore claims (at the conclusion of his "Proof of an External World") "I can know things which I cannot prove," and among these is "Here is my right hand, and here my left," *so interpreted as to entail* "There are physical objects." Hume too can grant that I know something I cannot prove (proofs must begin somewhere, make some initial assumptions), but Hume will not grant that Moore's premise is true *as he intends it*. This is relevant to Hall's remarks.

Everett Hall notes that when one considers the list of statements Moore claims to know to be true, "There seems to be no common factors in their content." What criterion, then, has Moore used to pick out just these statements? Not universal acceptance, or Moore's intuitions, or the possession of the property "being certainly true," or the propriety of placing "It is certain that . . ." in front of any statement to be included—or if one among these *is* his criterion, there are fatal objections to his procedure. These objections are different for each case and Hall's statement of them is, I think, quite clear. But then we are left with our original question. Indeed, one is left wondering (a) whether there is any criterion for common-sense statements that can be clearly stated, justified, and applied and (b) even if there is one (say, "beliefs accepted without question by English-speaking people from 1900 to the present"), whether the statements selected will be certainly true.

Suppose, however, that each statement Moore lists *is* certainly true. What then? Hall writes:

I cannot conceive that any philosopher who has questioned the existence of the external world has meant thereby to doubt the existence of any particular man's hand in the way one would if he thought the hand artificial or simply missing. Philosophical doubts, for example doubts about an external world, are questions about the whole framework of the world, about categorial features of it, not specific items in it that are subject to observational checking.

Moore's certainties are certain so long as one adopts, and remains within, the "ordinary" way of looking at things—the way men look at the world if they are men òf our age and time (or, at the *very* best, any age and time) and are burdened with concern for survival and/or technical achievement. When philosophers such as Berkeley and McTaggert challenge that conceptual perspective, their followers, or their comprehending readers, can hardly be impressed by answers offered within (and hence assuming) the framework being challenged.

It has become fashionable among some philosophers to ask, in effect, "But what way other than the ordinary one *is* there for looking at things?" If one answers "Plato's, Aristotle's, Occam's, Aquinas', Descartes', Leibniz', Spinoza's, Berkeley's, and others," the answer is often that insofar as these and other philosophers have supposed they could depart from the uses put to words in ordinary speech, they merely raise questions that require unraveling to reveal their latent confusions. Whether this is so in any given case is something to be investigated with regard to that particular case; and it is open to question whether any of the (perhaps unintentional) founders of this outlook thought that *all* philosophy arose from taking as genuine those issues that really reveal only linguistic confusion. If Moore's "Defense of Common Sense" is, historically though perhaps not intentionally, a forerunner of this outlook, Hall's challenge to Moore is also a general challenge. Many philosophers have conceived part at least of the philosopher's task to be that of asking "questions about the whole framework of the world." Is the claim that they cannot be raised different from Moore's attempt to show that the questions must be answered on the basis of common-sense belief? Don't both presuppose the framework of thought that is, in each instance, being challenged or altered? In Moore's case, it is supposed as being true; in the case of later philosophers, as being uniquely meaningful. (See page 152 and pages following in Hall's *Philosophical Systems.*) But part of knowing how to use a language is being able to use it in new ways. How new and different the ways can be is of course open to debate, but given the history of philosophy, it seems evident that there is a great deal of leeway in these matters. In any case, these comments may help to make clear one way in which Moore's views have led to other, more radical, philosophical contentions.

A Defense of Common Sense
GEORGE E. MOORE

In what follows I have merely tried to state, one by one, some of the most important points in which my philosophical position differs from positions which have been taken up by *some* other philosophers. It may be that the points which I have had room to mention are not really the most important, and possibly some of them may be points as to which no philosopher has ever really differed from me. But, to the best of my belief, each is a point as to which many have really differed; although (in most cases, at all events) each is also a point as to which many have agreed with me.

I. The first point is a point which embraces a great many other points. And it is one which I cannot state as clearly as I wish to state it, except at some length. The method I am going to use for stating it is this. I am going to begin by enunciating, under the heading (1), a whole long list of propositions, which may seem, at first sight, such obvious truisms as not to be worth stating: they are, in fact, a set of propositions, every one of which (in my opinion) I *know*, with certainty, to be true. I shall, next, under the heading (2), state a single proposition which makes an assertion about a whole set of *classes* of propositions—each class being defined, as the class consisting of all propositions which resemble *one* of the propositions in (1) in a certain respect. (2), therefore, is a proposition which could not be stated, until the list of propositions in (1), or some similar list, had already been given. (2) is itself a proposition which may seem such an obvious truism as not to be worth stating: and it is also a proposition which (in my own opinion) I *know* with certainty, to be true. But, nevertheless, it

is, to the best of my belief, a proposition with regard to which many philosophers have, for different reasons, differed from me; even if they have not directly denied (2) itself, they have held views incompatible with it. My first point, then, may be said to be that (2), together with all its implications, some of which I shall expressly mention, is true.

(1) I begin, then, with my list of truisms, every one of which (in my own opinion) I *know*, with certainty, to be true. The propositions to be included in this list are the following:

There exists at present a living human body, which is *my* body. This body was born at a certain time in the past, and has existed continuously ever since, though not without undergoing changes; it was, for instance, much smaller when it was born, and for some time afterwards, than it is now. Ever since it was born, it has been either in contact with or not far from the surface of the earth; and, at every moment since it was born, there have also existed many other things, having shape and size in three dimensions (in the same familiar sense in which it has), from which it has been *at various distances* (in the familiar sense in which it is now at a distance both from that mantel-piece and from that book-case, and at a greater distance from the book-case than it is from the mantel-piece); also there have (very often, at all events) existed some other things of this kind with which it was *in contact* (in the familiar sense in which it is now in contact with the pen I am holding in my right hand and with some of the clothes I am wearing). Among the things which have, in this sense, formed part of its environment (i.e., have been either in

FROM *Contemporary British Philosophy*, Series 2, J. H. Muirhead, ed. (London: George Allen and Unwin, Ltd., 1925), pp. 193–223. Reprinted by permission of George Allen and Unwin, Ltd.

contact with it, or at *some* distance from it, however *great*) there have, at every moment since its birth, been large numbers of other living human bodies, each of which has, like it, (a) at some time been born, (b) continued to exist for some time after birth, (c) been, at every moment of its life after birth, either in contact with or not far from the surface of the earth; and many of these bodies have already died and ceased to exist. But the earth has existed also for many years before my body was born; and for many of these years, also, large numbers of human bodies had, at every moment, been alive upon it; and many of these bodies had died and ceased to exist before it was born. Finally (to come to a different class of propositions), I am a human being, and I have, at different times since my body was born, had many different experiences, of each of many different kinds: e.g., I have often perceived both my own body and other things which formed part of its environment, including other human bodies; I have not only perceived things of this kind, but have also observed facts about them, such as, for instance, the fact which I am now observing, that that mantel-piece is at present nearer to my body than that book-case; I have been aware of other facts, which I was not at the time observing, such as, for instance, the fact, of which I am now aware, that my body existed yesterday and was then also for some time nearer to that mantel-piece than to that book-case; I have had expectations with regard to the future, and many beliefs of other kinds, both true and false; I have thought of imaginary things, and persons and incidents, in the reality of which I did not believe; I have had dreams; and I have had feelings of many different kinds. And, just as my body has been the body of a human being, namely myself, who has, during its life-time, had many experiences of each of these (and other) different kinds; so, in the case of very many of the other human bodies which have lived upon the earth, each has been

the body of a different human being, who has, during the life-time of that body, had many different experiences of each of these (and other) different kinds.

(2) I now come to the single truism which, as will be seen, could not be stated except by reference to the whole list of truisms, just given in (1). This truism also (in my opinion) I *know*, with certainty, to be true; and it is as follows:

In the case of *very many* (I do not say *all*) of the human beings belonging to the class (which includes myself) defined in the following way, i.e., as human beings who have had human bodies, that were born and lived for some time upon the earth, and who have, during the life-time of those bodies, had many different experiences of each of the kinds mentioned in (1), it is true that each has frequently, during the life of his body, known, with regard to *himself* or *his* body, and with regard to some time earlier than any of the times at which I wrote down the propositions in (1), a proposition *corresponding* to each of the propositions in (1), in the sense that it asserts with regard to *him*self or *his* body and the earlier time in question (namely, in each case, the time at which he knew it), just what the corresponding proposition in (1) asserts with regard to *me* or *my* body and the time at which I wrote that proposition down.

In other words what (2) asserts is only (what seems an obvious enough truism) that each of *us* (meaning by "us," very many human beings of the class defined) has frequently *known*, with regard to *him*self, or *his* body and the time at which he knew it, everything which, in writing down my list of propositions in (1), I was claiming to know about *my*self or *my* body and the time at which I wrote that proposition down. I.e., just as *I* knew (when I wrote it down) "There exists at present a living human body which is my body," so each of us has frequently known with regard to himself and some other time the different but corresponding proposition, which *he* could *then* have properly expressed by, "There exists *at present* a human body which is *my* body"; just as *I* know "Many human bodies other than mine have before now lived on the earth," so each of us has frequently known the different but corresponding proposition "Many human bodies other than *mine* have before *now* lived on the earth"; just as *I* know "Many human beings other than myself have before now perceived, and dreamed, and felt," so each of *us* has frequently known the different but corresponding proposition "Many human beings other than *myself* have before *now* perceived, and dreamed, and felt"; and so on, in the case of *each* of the propositions enumerated in (1).

I hope there is no difficulty in understanding, so far, what this proposition (2) asserts. I have tried to make clear by examples what I mean by "propositions *corresponding* to each of the propositions in (1)." And what (2) asserts is merely that each of us has frequently known to be true a proposition *corresponding* (in that sense) to each of the propositions in (1)—a *different* corresponding proposition, of course, at each of the times at which he knew such a proposition to be true.

But there remain two points, which, in view of the way in which some philosophers have used the English language, ought, I think, to be expressly mentioned, if I am to make quite clear exactly how much I am asserting in asserting (2).

The first point is this. Some philosophers seem to have thought it legitimate to use the word "true" in such a sense, that a proposition which is partially false may nevertheless also be true; and some of these, therefore, would perhaps say that propositions like those enumerated in (1) are, in their view, true, when all the time they believe that every such proposition is partially false. I wish, therefore, to make it quite plain that I am not using "true" in any such sense. I am using it in such a sense (and

I think this is the ordinary usage) that if a proposition is partially false, it follows that it is *not* true, though, of course, it may be *partially* true. I am maintaining, in short, that all the propositions in (1), and also many propositions corresponding to each of these, are *wholly* true; I am asserting this in asserting (2). And hence any philosopher, who does in fact believe, with regard to any or all of these classes of propositions, that every proposition of the class in question is partially false, is, in fact, disagreeing with me and holding a view incompatible with (2), even though he may think himself justified in *saying* that he believes some propositions belonging to all of these classes to be "true."

And the second point is this. Some philosophers seem to have thought it legitimate to use such expressions as, e.g., "The earth has existed for many years past," as if they expressed something which they really believed, when in fact they believe that every proposition, which such an expression would *ordinarily* be understood to express, is, at least partially, false; and all they really believe is that there is some *other* set of propositions, related in a certain way to those which such expressions do actually express, which, unlike these, really are true. That is to say, they use the expression "The earth has existed for many years past" to express, not what it would ordinarily be understood to express, but the proposition that some proposition, related to this in a certain way, is true; when all the time they believe that the proposition, which this expression would ordinarily be understood to express, is, at least partially, false. I wish, therefore, to make it quite plain that I was not using the expressions I used in (1) in any such subtle sense. I meant by each of them precisely what every reader, in reading them, will have understood me to mean. And any philosopher, therefore, who holds that any of these expressions, if understood in this popular manner, expresses a proposition which embodies some popular error, is disagreeing with me and holding a view incompatible with (2), even though he may hold that there is some *other*, true, proposition which the expression in question might be legitimately used to express.

In what I have just said, I have assumed that there is some meaning which is *the* ordinary or popular meaning of such expressions as "The earth has existed for many years past." And this, I am afraid, is an assumption which some philosophers are capable of disputing. They seem to think that the question "Do you believe that the earth has existed for many years past?" is not a plain question, such as should be met either by a plain "Yes" or "No," or by a plain "I can't make up my mind," but is the sort of question which can be properly met by: "It all depends on what you mean by 'the earth' and 'exists' and 'years': if you mean so and so, and so and so, and so and so, then I do; but if you mean so and so, and so and so, and so and so, or so and so, and so and so, and so and so, or so and so, and so and so, and so and so, then I don't, or at least I think it is extremely doubtful." It seems to me that such a view is as profoundly mistaken as any view can be. Such an expression as "The earth has existed for many years past" is the very type of an unambiguous expression, the meaning of which we all understand. Any one who takes a contrary view must, I suppose, be confusing the question whether we understand its meaning (which we all certainly do) with the entirely different question whether we *know what it means*, in the sense that we are able to *give a correct analysis* of its meaning. The question what is the correct analysis of *the* proposition meant *on any occasion* [for, of course, as I insisted in defining (2), a different proposition is meant at every different time at which the expression is used] by "The earth has existed for many years past" is, it seems to me, a profoundly difficult question, and one to which, as I shall presently urge, no one knows the answer. But to hold that we do not know what, in certain respects, is the

analysis of what we understand by such an expression, is an entirely different thing from holding that we do not understand the expression. It is obvious that we cannot even raise the question how what we do understand by it is to be analysed, unless we do understand it. So soon, therefore, as we know that a person who uses such an expression, is using it in its ordinary sense, we understand his meaning. So that in explaining that I was using the expressions used in (1) in their ordinary sense (those of them which have an ordinary sense, which is not the case with quite all of them), I have done all that is required to make my meaning clear.

But now, assuming that the expressions which I have used to express (2) are understood, I think, as I have said, that many philosophers have really held views incompatible with (2). And the philosophers who have done so may, I think, be divided into two main groups. *A*. What (2) asserts is, with regard to a whole set of *classes* of propositions, that we have, each of us, frequently *known* to be true propositions belonging to *each* of these classes. And one way of holding a view incompatible with this proposition is, of course, to hold, with regard to one or more of the classes in question, that *no* propositions of that class are true—that all of them are, at least partially, false; since if, in the case of any one of these classes, no propositions of that class *are* true, it is obvious that nobody can have *known* any propositions of that class to be true, and therefore that *we* cannot have known to be true propositions belonging to *each* of these classes. And my first group of philosophers consists of philosophers who have held views incompatible with (2) for this reason. They have held, with regard to one or more of the classes in question, simply that no propositions of that class *are* true. Some of them have held this with regard to *all* the classes in question; some only with regard to *some* of them. But, of course, whichever of these two views they have held, they have been holding a view inconsistent with (2). *B*. Some philosophers, on the other hand, have not ventured to assert, with regard to *any* of the classes in (2), that no propositions of that class *are* true, but what they have asserted is that, in the case of some of these classes, no human being has ever *known*, with certainty, that any propositions of the class in question are true. That is to say, they differ profoundly from philosophers of group *A*, in that they hold that propositions of *all* these classes *may* be true; but nevertheless they hold a view incompatible with (2) since they hold, with regard to some of these classes, that none of us has ever known a proposition of the class in question to be true.

A. I said that some philosophers, belonging to this group, have held that no propositions belonging to any of the classes in (2) are wholly true, while others have only held this with regard to *some* of the classes in (2). And I think the chief division of this kind has been the following. Some of the propositions in (1) [and, therefore, of course, all propositions belonging to the corresponding classes in (2)] are propositions which cannot be true, unless some *material things* have existed and have stood *in spatial relations* to one another; that is to say, they are propositions which, *in a certain sense*, imply *the reality of material things*, and *the reality of Space*. E.g., the proposition that my body has existed for many years past, and has, at every moment during that time been either in contact with or not far from the earth, is a proposition which implies both the *reality of material things* (provided you use "material things" in such a sense that to deny the reality of material things implies that no proposition which asserts that human bodies have existed, or that the earth has existed, is wholly true) and also the *reality of Space* [provided, again, that you use "Space" in such a sense that to deny the reality of Space implies that no proposition which asserts that anything has ever been in contact with or at a distance from another, in the familiar

senses pointed out in (1), is wholly true]. But others among the propositions in (1) [and, therefore, propositions belonging to the corresponding classes in (2)], do not (at least obviously) imply either the reality of material things or the reality of Space: e.g., the propositions that I have often had dreams, and have had many different feelings at different times. It is true that propositions of this second class do imply one thing which is also implied by all propositions of the first, namely that (*in a certain sense*) *Time is real*, and imply also one thing not implied by propositions of the first class, namely that (*in a certain sense*) at least one Self is real. But I think there are some philosophers, who, while denying that (in the senses in question) either material things or Space are real, have been willing to admit that Selves and Time are real, in the sense required. Other philosophers, on the other hand, have used the expression "Time is not real," to express some view that they held; and some, at least, of these have, I think, meant by this expression something which is incompatible with the truth of *any* of the propositions in (1)—they have meant, namely, that *every* proposition of the sort that is expressed by the use of "now" or "at present," e.g., "I am now both seeing and hearing" or "There exists at present a living human body," or by the use of a *past* tense, e.g., "I *have* had many experiences in the past," or "The earth *has* existed for many years," are, at least partially, false.

All the four expressions I have just introduced, namely "Material things are not real," "Space is not real," "Time is not real," "The Self is not real," are, I think, unlike the expressions I used in (1), really ambiguous. And it may be that, in the case of each of them, some philosopher has used the expression in question to express some view he held which was not incompatible with (2). With such philosophers, if there are any, I am not, of course, at present concerned. But it seems to me that the most natural and proper usage of each of these expressions is a usage in which it *does* express a view incompatible with (2); and, in the case of each of them, some philosophers have, I think, really used the expression in question to express such a view. All such philosophers have, therefore, been holding a view incompatible with (2).

All such views, whether incompatible with *all* of the propositions in (1), or only with *some* of them, seem to me to be quite certainly false; and I think the following points are specially deserving of notice with regard to them:

(a) If *any* of the classes of propositions in (2) is such that no proposition of that class is true, then no philosopher has ever existed, and therefore none can ever have held with regard to any such class, that no proposition belonging to it is true. In other words, the proposition that some propositions belonging to each of these classes are true is a proposition which has the peculiarity, that, if any philosopher has ever denied it, it follows from the fact that he has denied it, that he must have been wrong in denying it. For when I speak of "philosophers" I mean, of course (as we all do), exclusively philosophers who have been human beings, with human bodies that have lived upon the earth, and who have at different times had many different experiences. If, therefore, there have been any philosophers, there have been human beings of this class; and if there have been human beings of this class, all the rest of what is asserted in (1) is certainly true too. Any view, therefore, incompatible with the proposition that many propositions corresponding to each of the propositions in (1) are true, can only be true, on the hypothesis that no philosopher has ever held any such view. It follows, therefore, that, in considering whether this proposition is true, I cannot consistently regard the fact that many philosophers, whom I respect, have, to the best of my belief, held views incompatible with it, as having any weight at all against it. Since, if I know that they have held such views, I am, *ipso facto*, knowing that they were

mistaken; and, if I have no reason to believe that the proposition in question is true, I have still less reason to believe that they have held views incompatible with it; since I am more certain that they have existed and held *some* views, i.e., that the proposition in question is true, than that they have held any views incompatible with it.

(b) It is, of course, the case that all philosophers who have held such views have repeatedly, even in their philosophical works, expressed other views inconsistent with them: i.e., no philosopher has ever been able to hold such views consistently. One way in which they have betrayed this inconsistency, is by alluding to the existence of other philosophers. Another way is by alluding to the existence of the human race, and in particular by using "we" in the sense in which I have already constantly used it, in which any philosopher who asserts that "we" do so and so, e.g., that "we sometimes believe propositions that are not true," is asserting not only that he himself has done the thing in question, but that *very many other human beings, who have had bodies and lived upon the earth*, have done the same. The fact is, of course, that all philosophers have belonged to the class of human beings, which exists only if (2) be true: that is to say, to the class of human beings, who have frequently *known* propositions corresponding to each of the propositions in (1). In holding views incompatible with the proposition that propositions of all these classes are true, they have, therefore, been holding views inconsistent with propositions which they themselves *knew* to be true; and it was, therefore, only to be expected that they should sometimes betray their knowledge of such propositions. The strange thing is that philosophers should have been able to hold sincerely, as part of their philosophical creed, propositions inconsistent with what they themselves knew to be true; and yet, so far as I can make out, this has really frequently happened. My position, therefore, on this first point, differs from that of philosophers belonging to this group *A*, not in that I hold anything which they don't hold, but only in that I don't hold, as part of my philosophical creed, things which they do hold as part of theirs—that is to say propositions inconsistent with some which they and I both hold in common. But this difference seems to me to be an important one.

(c) Some of these philosophers have brought forward, in favour of their position, arguments designed to show, in the case of some or all of the propositions in (1), that no propositions of that type can possibly be wholly true, because every such proposition entails both of two incompatible propositions. And I admit, of course, that if any of the propositions in (1) did entail both of two incompatible propositions it could not be true. But it seems to me I have an absolutely conclusive argument to show that none of them does entail both of two incompatible propositions. Namely this: All of the propositions in (1) are true; no true proposition entails both of two incompatible propositions; therefore, none of the propositions in (1) entails both of two incompatible propositions.

(d) Although, as I have urged, no philosopher who has held with regard to any of these types of proposition, that no propositions of that type are true, has failed to hold also other views inconsistent with his view in this respect, yet I do not think that the view, with regard to any or all of these types, that no proposition belonging to them is true, is *in itself* a self-contradictory view, i.e., entails both of two incompatible propositions. On the contrary, it seems to me quite clear that it *might* have been the case that Time was not real, material things not real, Space not real, selves not real. And in favour of my view that none of these things, which might have been the case, *is* in fact the case, I have, I think, no better argument than simply this—namely, that all the propositions in (1) are, in fact, true.

B. This view, which is usually considered a much more modest view than

A, has, I think, the defect that, unlike *A*, it really is self-contradictory, i.e., entails both of two mutually incompatible propositions.

Most philosophers who have held this view, have held, I think, that though each of us knows propositions corresponding to *some* of the propositions in (1), namely to those which merely assert that I myself have had in the past experiences of certain kinds at many different times, yet none of us knows for certain any propositions either of the type (a) which assert the existence of *material things* or of the *other* selves, beside myself, and that *they* also have had experiences. They admit that we do in fact *believe* propositions of both these types, and that they *may* be true: some would even say that we know them to be highly probable; but they deny that we ever know them, *for certain*, to be true. Some of them have spoken of such beliefs as "beliefs of Common Sense," expressing thereby their conviction that beliefs of this kind are very commonly entertained by mankind: but they are convinced that these things are, in all cases, only *believed*, not known for certain; and some have expressed this by saying that they are matters of Faith, not of Knowledge.

Now the remarkable thing, which those who take this view have not, I think, in general duly appreciated, is that, in each case, the philosopher who takes it is making an assertion about "us"—that is to say, not merely about himself, but about *many other human beings as well*. When he says "No human being has ever *known* of the existence of other human beings," he is saying: "There have been many other human beings beside myself, and none of them (including myself) has ever known of the existence of other human beings." If he says: "*These* beliefs are beliefs of Common Sense, but they are not matters of *knowledge*," he is saying: "There have been many other human beings, beside myself, who have shared these beliefs, but neither I nor any of the rest has ever known them to be true." In other words, he asserts with confidence that these beliefs *are* beliefs of Common Sense, and seems often to fail to notice that, *if* they are, they must be true; since the proposition that they are beliefs of Common Sense, is one which logically entails propositions both of type (a) and of type (b); it logically entails the proposition that many human beings, beside the philosopher himself, have had human bodies, which lived upon the earth, and have had various experiences, including beliefs of this kind. This is why this position, as contrasted with positions of group *A*, seems to me to be self-contradictory. Its difference from *A* consists in the fact that it is making a proposition about *human knowledge* in general, and therefore is actually asserting the existence of many human beings, whereas philosophers of group *A* in stating their position are not doing this: they are only contradicting other things which they hold. It is true that a philosopher who says "There have existed many human beings beside myself, and none of us has ever known of the existence of any human beings beside himself," is only contradicting himself, if what he holds is "There have *certainly* existed many human beings beside myself" or, in other words, "I know that there have existed other human beings beside myself." But this, it seems to me, is what such philosophers have in fact been generally doing. They seem to me constantly to betray the fact that they regard the proposition that those beliefs *are* beliefs of Common Sense, or the proposition that they themselves are not the only members of the human race, as not merely true, but *certainly* true; and *certainly* true it cannot be, unless one member, at least, of the human race, namely themselves, has *known* the very things which that member is declaring that no human being has ever known.

Nevertheless, my position that I *know*, with certainty, to be true all of the propositions in (1), is certainly not a position, the denial of which entails both of two incompatible propositions. If I do *know* all these propositions to be

true, then, I think, it is quite certain that other human beings also have known corresponding propositions: that is to say (2) also *is* true, and I know it to be true. But do I really *know* all the propositions in (1) to be true? Isn't it possible that I merely believe them? or know them to be highly probable? In answer to this question, I think I have nothing better to say than that it seems to me that I *do* know them, with certainty. It is, indeed, obvious that, in the case of most of them, I do not know them *directly*: that is to say, I only know them because, in the past, I have known to be true other propositions which were evidence for them. If, for instance I do know that the earth had existed for many years before I was born, I certainly only know this because I have known other things in the past which were evidence for it. And I certainly do not know exactly what the evidence was. Yet all this seems to me to be no good reason for doubting that I do know it. We are all, I think, in this strange position that we do *know* many things, with regard to which we *know* further that we must have had evidence for them, and yet we do not know *how* we know them, i.e., we do not know what the evidence was. If there is any "we" and if we know that there is, this must be so: for, that there is a "we," is one of the things in question. And that I do know that there is a "we," that is to say, that many other human beings, with human bodies, have lived upon the earth, it seems to me that I do know, for certain.

If this first point in my philosophical position, namely my belief in (2), is to be given any name, which has actually been used by philosophers in classifying the positions of other philosophers, it would have, I think, to be expressed by saying that I am one of those philosophers who have held that the "Common Sense view of the world" is, in certain fundamental features, *wholly* true. But it must be remembered that, according to me, *all* philosophers, without exception, have agreed with me in holding this: and that the real difference, which is commonly expressed in this way is only a difference between those philosophers, who have *also* held views inconsistent with these features in "the Common Sense view of the world," and those who have not.

The features in question [namely, propositions of any of the classes defined in defining (2)] are all of them features, which have this peculiar property—namely, that *if we know that they are features in the "Common Sense view of the world," it follows that they are true*: *it is* self-contradictory to maintain that *we* know them to be features in the Common Sense view, and that yet they are not true; since to say that *we* know this, is to say that they are true. And many of them also have the further peculiar property that, *if they are features in the Common Sense view of the world (whether "we" know this or not), it follows that they are true*, since to say that there is a "Common Sense view of the world," is to say that they are true. The phrases "Common Sense view of the world" or "Common Sense beliefs" (as used by philosophers) are, of course, extraordinarily vague; and, for all I know, there may be many propositions which may be properly called features in "the Common Sense view of the world" or "Common Sense beliefs," which are not true, and which deserve to be mentioned with the contempt with which some philosophers speak of "Common Sense beliefs." But to speak with contempt of those "Common Sense beliefs" which I have mentioned is quite certainly the height of absurdity. And there are, of course, enormous numbers of other features in "the Common Sense view of the world" which, if these are true, are quite certainly true too: e.g., that there have lived upon the surface of the earth not only human beings, but also many different species of plants and animals, etc., etc.

II. What seems to me the next in importance of the points in which my philosophical position differs from posi-

tions held by *some* other philosophers, is one which I will express in the following way. I hold namely, that there is no good reason to suppose either (*A*) that *every* physical fact is *logically* dependent upon some mental fact or (*B*) that *every* physical fact is *causally* dependent upon some mental fact. In saying this, I am not, of course, saying that there *are* any physical facts which are wholly independent (i.e., both logically and causally) of mental facts: I do, in fact, believe that there are; but that is not what I am asserting. I am only asserting that there is *no good reason* to suppose the contrary; by which I mean, of course, that none of the human beings, who have had human bodies that lived upon the earth, have during the life-time of their bodies, had any good reason to suppose the contrary. Many philosophers have, I think, not only believed either that *every* physical fact is *logically* dependent upon some mental fact ("physical fact" and "mental fact" being understood in the sense in which I am using these terms) or that *every* physical fact is *causally* dependent upon some mental fact, or both, but also that they themselves had good reason for these beliefs. In this respect, therefore, I differ from them.

In the case of the term "physical fact," I can only explain how I am using it by giving examples. I mean by "physical facts," facts *like* the following: "That mantel-piece is at present nearer to this body than that book-case is," "The earth has existed for many years past," "The moon has at every moment for many years been nearer to the earth than to the sun," "That mantel-piece is of a light colour." But, when I say "facts *like* these," I mean, of course, facts like them *in a certain respect;* and what this respect is, I cannot define. The term "physical fact" is, however, in common use; and I think that I am using it in its ordinary sense. Moreover, there is no need for a definition to make my point clear; since among the examples I have given, there are some with regard to which I hold that there is no reason to suppose *them* (i.e., these particular physical facts) either logically or causally dependent upon any mental fact.

"Mental fact," on the other hand, is a much more unusual expression, and I am using it in a specially limited sense, which, though I think it is a natural one, does need to be explained. There may be many other senses in which the term can be properly used. But I am only concerned with this one; and hence it is essential that I should explain what it is.

There may, possibly, I hold, be "mental facts" of three different kinds. It is only with regard to the first kind that I am sure that there are facts of that kind; but if there were any facts of either of the other two kinds, they would be "mental facts" in my limited sense, and therefore I must explain what is meant by the hypothesis that there are facts of those two kinds.

(a) My first kind is this. I am conscious now; and also I am seeing something now. These two facts are both of them mental facts of my first kind: and my first kind consists exclusively of facts which resemble one or other of the two in a certain aspect.

(α) The fact that I am conscious now is obviously, in a certain sense, a fact, with regard to a particular individual and a particular time, to the effect that that individual is conscious at that time. And every fact which resembles this one in that respect is to be included in my first kind of mental fact. Thus the fact that I was also conscious at many different times yesterday is not itself a fact of this kind: but it entails that there *are* (or, as we should commonly say, because the times in question are past times, "were") many other facts of this kind, namely each of the facts, which, at each of the times in question, I could have properly expressed by "I am conscious *now*." *Any* fact which is, in this sense, a fact with regard to an individual and a time (whether the individual be myself or another, and whether the time be past or present), to the effect that that individual *is* conscious at that time, is to be included in my first kind of

mental fact: and I call such facts, facts of class (ß).

(ß) The second example I gave, namely the fact that I am seeing something now, is obviously related to the fact that I am conscious now in a peculiar manner. It not only *entails* the fact that I am conscious now (for from the fact that I am seeing something it follows that I am conscious: I *could* not have been seeing anything, unless I had been conscious, though I might quite well have been conscious without seeing anything) but it also is a fact, with regard to a specific way (or mode) of being conscious, to the effect that I am conscious in that way: in the same sense in which the proposition (with regard to any particular thing) "This is red" both entails the proposition (with regard to the same thing) "This is coloured," and is also a proposition, with regard to a specific way of being coloured, to the effect that that thing is coloured in that way. And any fact which is related in this peculiar manner to any fact of class (α), is also to be included in my first kind of mental fact, and is to be called a fact of class (ß). Thus the fact that I am hearing now, is, like the fact that I am seeing now, a fact of class (ß); and so is any fact, with regard to myself and a past time, which could at that time have been properly expressed by "I am dreaming now," "I am imagining now," "I am at present aware of the fact that . . ." etc., etc. In short, any fact, which is a fact with regard to a particular individual (myself or another), a particular time (past or present), and *any particular kind of experience*, to the effect that that individual is having at that time an experience of that particular kind, is a fact of class (ß): and only such facts are facts of class (ß).

My first kind of mental facts consists exclusively of facts of classes (α) and (ß), and consists of *all* facts of either of these kinds.

(b) That there are many facts of classes (α) and (ß) seems to me perfectly certain. But many philosophers seem to me to have held a certain view with regard to the *analysis* of facts of class (α), which is such that, if it were true, there would be facts of another kind, which I should wish also to call "mental facts." I don't feel at all sure that this analysis is true; but it seems to me that it *may* be true; and since we can understand what is meant by the supposition that it is true, we can also understand what is meant by the supposition that there are "mental facts" of this second kind.

Many philosophers have, I think, held the following view as to the analysis of what each of us knows, when he knows at any time "I am conscious now." They have held, namely, that there is a certain intrinsic property (with which we are all of us familiar and which might be called that of "being an experience") which is such that, at any time at which any man knows "I am conscious now," he is knowing, with regard to that property and himself and the time in question, "There is occurring now an event which has this property (i.e., "is an experience") and which is an experience of *mine*," and such that this fact is what he expresses by "I am conscious now." And if this view is true, there must be many facts of each of three kinds, each of which I should wish to call "mental facts"; viz. (1) facts with regard to some event, which has this supposed intrinsic property, and to some time, to the effect that that event is occurring at that time, (2) facts with regard to this supposed intrinsic property and some time to the effect that *some* event which has that property is occurring at that time, and (3) facts with regard to some property, which is a *specific way* of having the supposed intrinsic property (in the sense above explained in which "being red" is a specific way of "being coloured") and some time, to the effect that some event which has that specific property is occurring at that time. Of course, there not only are not, but *cannot* be, facts of any of these kinds, unless there is an intrinsic property related to what each of us (on

any occasion) expresses by "I am conscious now," in the manner defined above; and I feel very doubtful whether there is any such property; in other words, although I know for certain both that I have had many experiences, and that I have had experiences of many different kinds, I feel very doubtful whether to say the first is the same thing as to say that there have been many events, each of which was an experience and an experience of mine, and whether to say the second is the same thing as to say that there have been many events, each of which was an experience of mine, and each of which also had a different property, which was a specific way of being an experience. The proposition that I have had experiences does not necessarily entail the proposition that there have been any events which were experiences; and I cannot satisfy myself that I am acquainted with any events of the supposed kind. But yet it seems to me possible that the proposed analysis of "I am conscious now" is correct: that I am really acquainted with events of the supposed kind, though I cannot see that I am. And *if* I am, then I should wish to call the three kinds of facts defined above "mental facts." Of course, if there are "experiences" in the sense defined, it would be possible (as many have held) that there *can* be no experiences which are not *some individual's* experiences; and in that case any fact of any of these three kinds would be logically dependent on, though not necessarily identical with, some fact of class (α) and (ß). But it seems to me also a possibility that, if there are "experiences," there might be experiences which did not belong to any individual; and, in that case, there would be "mental facts" which were neither identical with nor logically dependent on any fact of class (α) or (ß).

(c) Finally some philosophers have, so far as I can make out, held that there are or may be facts, which are facts with regard to some individual, to the effect that he is conscious, or is conscious in some specific way, which differ from facts of classes (α) and (ß), in the important respect that they are not facts *with regard to any time*: they have conceived the possibility that there may be one or more individuals, who are *timelessly* conscious, and timelessly conscious in specific modes. And others, again, have, I think, conceived the hypothesis that the intrinsic property defined in (b) may be one which does not belong only to *events*, but may also belong to one or more wholes, which do *not* occur at any time: in other words, that there may be one or more *timeless* experiences, which might or might not be the experiences of some individual. It seems to me very doubtful whether any of these hypotheses are even possibly true; but I cannot see for certain that they are not possible: and, if they are possible, then I should wish to give the name "mental fact" to any fact (if there were any) of any of the five following kinds, viz. (1) to any fact which is the fact, with regard to any individual, that he is *timelessly* conscious, (2) to any fact which is the fact with regard to any individual, that he is *timelessly* conscious in any specific way, (3) to any fact which is the fact with regard to a *timeless* experience that it exists, (4) to any fact which is the fact with regard to the supposed intrinsic property "being an experience," which is the fact that something timelessly exists which has that property, and (5) to any fact which is the fact, with regard to any property, which is a specific mode of this supposed intrinsic property, that something timelessly exists which has that property.

I have then defined three different kinds of facts, each of which is such that, if there *were* any facts of that kind (as there certainly *are,* in the case of the first kind), the facts in question *would be* "mental facts" in my sense; and to complete the definition of the limited sense in which I am using "mental facts," I have only to add that I wish also to apply the name to one *fourth* class of facts: namely to any fact, which is the fact, with regard to any of these three kinds of facts, or any

kinds included in them, *that there are facts of the kind in question*; i.e., not only will each individual fact of class class (α) be, in my sense, a "mental fact," but also the general fact "that there are facts of class (α)," will itself be a "mental fact"; and similarly in all other cases: e.g., not only will the fact that I am now perceiving [which is a fact of class (ß)] be a "mental fact," but also the general fact that *there are* facts, with regard to individuals and times, to the effect that the individual in question is perceiving at the time in question, will be a "mental fact."

A. Understanding "physical fact" and "mental fact" in the senses just explained I hold, then, that there is no good reason to suppose that *every* physical fact is *logically* dependent upon some mental fact. And I use the phrase with regard to two facts, F_1 and F_2, "F_1 is *logically dependent* on F_2" wherever and only where F_1 entails F_2, either in the sense in which the proposition "I am seeing now" *entails* the proposition "I am conscious now" or the proposition (with regard to any particular thing) "This is red" entails the proposition (with regard to the same thing) "This is coloured," or else in the more strictly logical sense in which (for instance) the conjunctive proposition "All men are mortal, and Mr. Baldwin is a man" entails the proposition "Mr. Baldwin is mortal." To say, then, of two facts, F_1 and F_2, that F_1 is *not* logically dependent upon F_2, is only to say that F_1 *might* have been a fact, even if there had been no such fact as F_2; or that the conjunctive proposition "F_1 is a fact, but there is no such fact as F_2" is a proposition which is not self-contradictory, i.e., does not entail both of two mutually incompatible propositions.

I hold, then, that, in the case of *some* physical facts, there is no good reason to suppose that there is some mental fact, such that the physical fact in question could not have been a fact unless the mental fact in question had also been one. And my position is perfectly definite, since I hold that this is the case with all the four physical facts, which I have given as examples of physical facts. E.g., there is no good reason to suppose that there is any mental fact whatever, such that the fact that that mantel-piece is at present nearer to my body than that book-case could not have been a fact, unless the mental fact in question had also been a fact; and, similarly, in all the other three cases.

In holding this I am certainly differing from some philosophers. I am, for instance, differing from Berkeley, who held that that mantel-piece, that book-case, and my body are, all of them, either "ideas" or "constituted by ideas," and that no "idea" can possibly exist without being perceived. He held, that is, that this physical fact is logically dependent upon a mental fact of my fourth class: namely a fact which is the fact that there is at least one fact which is a fact with regard to an individual and the present time, to the effect that that individual is now perceiving something. He does not say that this physical fact is logically dependent upon any fact which is a fact of any of my first three classes, e.g., on any fact which is the fact, with regard to a particular individual and the present time, that *that* individual is now perceiving something: what he does say is that the physical fact couldn't have been a fact, unless it had been a fact that there was *some* mental fact of this sort. And it seems to me that many philosophers, who would perhaps disagree either with Berkeley's assumption that my body is an "idea" or "constituted by ideas," or with his assumption that "ideas" cannot exist without being perceived, or with both, nevertheless would agree with him in thinking that this physical fact is logically dependent upon *some* "mental fact"; e.g., they might say, that it could not have been a fact, unless there had been, at some time or other, or, were timelessly, *some* "experience." Many, indeed, so far as I can make out, have held that *every* fact is logically dependent on every other fact. And, of course, they have held in the case of their

opinions, as Berkeley did in the case of his, that they had good reasons for them.

B. I also hold that there is no good reason to suppose that *every* physical fact is *causally* dependent upon some mental fact. By saying that F_1 is *causally* dependent on F_2, I mean only that F_1 *wouldn't* have been a fact unless F_2 had been; *not* (which is what "logically dependent" asserts) that F_1 *couldn't conceivably* have been a fact, unless F_2 had been. And I can illustrate my meaning by reference to the example which I have just given. The fact that that mantel-piece is at present nearer to my body than that book-case, is (as I have just explained) so far as I can see, not *logically* dependent upon any mental fact; it *might* have been a fact, even if there have been no mental facts. But it certainly is *causally* dependent on many mental facts: my body *would* not have been here unless I had been conscious in various ways in the past; and the mantel-piece and the book-case certainly *would* not have existed, unless other men had been conscious too.

But with regard to two of the facts, which I gave as instances of physical facts, namely the fact that the earth has existed for many years past, and the fact that the moon has for many years past been nearer to the earth than to the sun, I hold that there is no good reason to suppose that these are causally dependent upon any mental fact. So far as I can see, there is no reason to suppose that there is any mental fact of which it could be truly said: unless this fact had been a fact, the earth would not have existed for many years past. And in holding this, again, I think I differ from some philosophers. I differ, for instance, from those who have held that all material things were created by God, and that they had good reasons for supporting this.

III. I have just explained that I differ from those philosophers who have held that there is good reason to suppose that all material things were created by God. And it is, I think, an important point in my position, which should be mentioned, that I differ also from all philosophers who have held that there is good reason to suppose that there is a God at all, whether or not they have held it likely that he created material things.

And similarly, whereas some philosophers have held that there is good reason to suppose that we, human beings, shall continue to exist and to be conscious after the death of our bodies, I hold that there is no good reason to suppose this.

IV. I now come to a point of a very different order.

As I have explained under I, I am not at all sceptical as to the *truth* of such propositions as "The earth has existed for many years past," "Many human bodies have each lived for many years upon it," i.e., propositions which assert the existence of material things: on the contrary, I hold that we all know, with certainty, many such propositions to be true. But I am very sceptical as to what, in certain respects, the correct *analysis* of such propositions is. And this is a matter as to which I think I differ from many philosophers. Many seem to hold that there is no doubt at all as to their *analysis*, nor, therefore, as to the analysis of the proposition "Material things have existed," in certain respects in which I hold that the analysis of the propositions in question is extremely doubtful; and some of them, as we have seen, while holding that there is no doubt as to their *analysis*, seem to have doubted whether any such propositions are *true*. I, on the other hand, while holding that there is no doubt whatever that many such propositions are wholly true, hold also that no philosopher, hitherto, has succeeded in suggesting an analysis of them, as regards certain important points, which comes anywhere near to being certainly true.

It seems to me quite evident that the question how propositions of the type I have just given are to be analysed, depends on the question how propositions of another and simpler type are to be analysed. I know, at present, that I

am perceiving a human hand, a pen, a sheet of paper, etc.; and it seems to me that I cannot know how the proposition "Material things exist" is to be analysed, until I know how, in certain respects, these simpler propositions are to be analysed. But even these are not simple enough. It seems to me quite evident that my knowledge that I am now perceiving a human hand is a deduction from a pair of propositions simpler still —propositions which I can only express in the form "I am perceiving *this*" and "*This* is a human hand." It is the analysis of propositions of the latter kind, which seems to me to present such great difficulties; while nevertheless the whole question as to the nature of material things obviously depends upon their analysis. It seems to me a surprising thing that so few philosophers, while saying a great deal as to what material things *are* and as to what it is to perceive them, have attempted to give a clear account as to what precisely they suppose themselves to *know* (or to *judge*, in case they have held that we don't *know* any such propositions to be true, or even that no such propositions *are* true) when they know or judge such things as "This is a hand," "That is the sun," "This is a dog," etc., etc., etc.

Two things only seem to me to be quite certain about the analysis of such propositions (and even with regard to these I am afraid some philosophers would differ from me) namely that whenever I know, or judge, such a proposition to be true, (1) there is always some *sense-datum* about which the proposition in question is a proposition— some sense-datum which is a subject (and, in a certain sense, the principal or ultimate subject) of the proposition in question, and (2) that, nevertheless, *what* I am knowing or judging to be true about this sense-datum is not (in general) that it is itself a hand, or a dog, or the sun, etc., etc., as the case may be.

Some philosophers have I think doubted whether there are any such things as other philosophers have meant by "sense-data" or "sensa." And I think it is quite possible that some philosophers (including myself, in the past) have used these terms in senses, such that it is really doubtful whether there are any such things. But there is no doubt at all that there are sense-data, in the sense in which I am now using that term. I am at present seeing a great number of them, and feeling others. And, in order to point out to the reader what sort of things I mean by sense-data, I need only ask him to look at his own right hand. If he does this he will be able to pick out something (and, unless he is seeing double, *only* one thing) with regard to which he will see that it is, at first sight, a natural view to take that that thing is identical, not, indeed, with his whole right hand, but with that part of its surface which he is actually seeing, but will also (on a little reflection) be able to see that it is doubtful whether it can be identical with the part of the surface of his hand in question. Things of *the sort* (in a certain respect) of which this thing is, which he sees in looking at his hand, and with regard to which he can understand how some philosophers should have supposed it to be the part of the surface of his hand which he is seeing, while others have supposed that it can't be, are what I mean by "sense-data." I therefore define the term in such a way that it is an open question whether the sense-datum which I now see in looking at my hand and which is a sense-datum of my hand is or is not identical with that part of its surface which I am now actually seeing.

That what I know, with regard to this sense-datum, when I know "This is a human hand," is not that it is *itself* a human hand, seems to me certain because I know that my hand has many parts (e.g., its other side, and the bones inside it), which are quite certainly *not* parts of this sense-datum.

I think it certain, therefore, that the analysis of the proposition "This is a human hand" is, roughly at least, of the form "There is a thing, and only one thing, of which it is true both that it is a human hand and that *this surface* is a part of its surface." In other words, to put my view in terms of the phrase "theory of representative perception," I hold it to be quite certain that I do not *directly* perceive *my hand*; and that when I am said (as I may be correctly said) to "perceive" it, that I "perceive" it means that I perceive (in a different and more fundamental sense) something which is (in a suitable sense) *representative* of it, namely, a certain part of its surface.

This is all that I hold to be *certain* about the analysis of the proposition "This is a human hand." We have seen that it includes in its analysis a proposition of the form "This is part of the surface of a human hand" (where "This," of course, has a different meaning from that which it has in the original proposition which has now been analysed). But this proposition also is undoubtedly a proposition about the sense-datum, which I am seeing, which is a sense-datum *of* my hand. And hence the further question arises: *What*, when I know "*This* is *part of the surface of a human hand*," am I knowing about the sense-datum in question? Am I, in this case, really knowing, about the sense-datum in question that it *itself* is part of the surface of a human hand? Or, just as we found in the case of "This is a human hand," that what I was knowing about the sense-datum was certainly not that it *itself* was a human hand, so, is it perhaps the case, with this new proposition, that even here I am not knowing, with regard to the sense-datum, that it is *itself* part of the surface of a hand? and, if so, what is it that I am knowing about the sense-datum itself?

This is the question to which, as it seems to me, no philosopher has hitherto suggested an answer which comes anywhere near to being certainly true.

There seem to me to be three, and only three, alternative types of answer possible; and to any answer yet suggested, of any of these types, there seem to me to be very grave objections.

(1) Of the first type, there is but one answer: namely, that in this case what I am knowing really is that the sense-datum *itself* is a part of the surface of a human hand. In other words that, though I don't perceive *my hand* directly, I do *directly* perceive part of its surface; that the sense-datum itself *is* this part of its surface and not merely something which (in a sense yet to be determined) "represents" this part of its surface; and that hence the sense in which I "perceive" this part of the surface of my hand, is not in its turn a sense which needs to be defined by reference to yet a third more ultimate sense of "perceive," which is the only one in which perception is direct, namely that in which I perceive the sense-datum.

If this view is true (as I think it may just possibly be), it seems to me certain that we must abandon a view which has been held to be certainly true by most philosophers, namely the view that our sense-data always really have the qualities which they sensibly appear to us to have. For I know that if another man were looking through a microscope at the same surface which I am seeing with the naked eye, the sense-datum which he saw would sensibly appear to him to have qualities very different from and incompatible with those which my sense-datum sensibly appears to me to have: and yet, if my sense-datum is identical with the surface we are both of us seeing, his must be identical with it also. My sense-datum can, therefore, be identical with this surface only on condition that it is identical with his sense-datum: and, since his sense-datum sensibly appears to him to have qualities incompatible with those which mine sensibly appears to me to have, his sense-datum can be identical with mine, only on condition that the sense-datum in question either has not got the qualities which it sensibly appears to me to have, or has not got those which it sensibly appears to him to have.

I do not, however, think that this is a fatal objection to this first type of view. A far more serious objection seems to me to be that, when we see a thing double (have what is called "a double image" of it), we certainly have *two* sense-data each of which is *of* the surface seen, and which cannot therefore both be identical with it; and that yet it seems as if, if any sense-datum is ever identical with the surface *of* which it is a sense-datum, each of these so-called "images" must be so. It looks, therefore, as if every sense-datum is, after all, only "representative" of the surface, *of* which it is a sense-datum.

(2) But, if so, what relation has it to the surface in question?

This second type of view is one which holds that when I know "This is part of the surface of a human hand," what I am knowing with regard to the sense-datum which is *of* that surface, is, *not* that it is *itself* part of the surface of a human hand, but something of the following kind. There is, it says, *some* relation, *R*, such that what I am knowing with regard to the sense-datum is either "There is one thing and only one thing, of which it is true both that it is a part of the surface of a human hand, and that it has *R* to this sense-datum," or else "There are a set of things, of which it is true both that that set, taken collectively, *are* part of the surface of a human hand, and also that each member of the set has *R* to his sense-datum, and that nothing which is not a member of the set has *R* to it."

Obviously, in the case of this second type, many different views are possible, differing according to the view they take as to what the relation *R* is. But there is only one of them, which seems to me to have any plausibility; namely that which holds that *R* is an ultimate and unanalysable relation, which might be expressed by saying that "xRy" means the same as "*y* is an appearance or manifestation of *x*." I.e., the analysis which this answer would give of "This is part of the surface of a human hand" would be "There is one and only one thing which it is true both that it is part of the surface of a human hand, and that this sense-datum is an appearance or manifestation of it."

To this view also there seem to me to be very grave objections, chiefly drawn from a consideration of the questions how we can possibly *know* with regard to any of our sense-data that there is one thing and one thing only which has to them such a supposed ultimate relation; and how, if we do, we can possibly *know* anything further about such things, e.g., of what size or shape they are.

(3) The third type of answer, which seems to me to be the only possible alternative if (1) and (2) are rejected, is the type of answer which J. S. Mill seems to have been implying to be the true one when he said that material things are "permanent possibilities of sensation." He seems to have thought that when I know such a fact as "This is part of the surface of a human hand," what I am knowing with regard to the sense-datum which is the principal subject of that fact, is not that it is itself part of the surface of a human hand, nor yet, with regard to any relation, that *the* thing which has to it that relation is part of the surface of a human hand, but a whole set of hypothetical facts each of which is a fact of the form "If *these* conditions had been fulfilled, I should have been perceiving a sense-datum intrinsically related to *this* sense-datum in *this* way," "If *these* (other) conditions had been fulfilled, I should have been perceiving a sense-datum intrinsically related to this sense-datum in *this* (other) way," etc., etc.

With regard to this third type of view as to the analysis of propositions of the kind we are considering, it seems to me, again, just *possible* that it is a true one; but to hold (as Mill himself and others seem to have held) that it is *certainly*, or nearly certainly, true, seems to me as great a mistake, as to hold with regard either to (1) or to (2), that they are *certainly*, or nearly certainly, true. There seem to me to be very grave

objections to it; in particular the three, (a) that though, in general, when I know such a fact as "This is a hand," I certainly do know some hypothetical facts of the form "If *these* conditions had been fulfilled, I should have been perceiving a sense-datum of *this* kind, which would have been a sense-datum of the same surface of which *this* is a sense-datum," it seems doubtful whether any conditions with regard to which I know this are not themselves conditions of the form "If this and that *material thing* had been in those positions and conditions . . ." (b) that it seems again very doubtful whether there is any intrinsic relation, such that my knowledge that (under these conditions) I should have been perceiving a sense-datum of *this* kind, which would have been a sense-datum of the same surface of which *this* is a sense-datum is equivalent to a knowledge, with regard to that relation, that I should, under those conditions, have been perceiving a sense-datum related by it to *this* sense-datum and (c) that, if it were true, the sense in which a material surface is "round" or "square," would necessarily be utterly different from that in which our sense-data sensibly appear to us to be "round" or "square."

V. Just as I hold that the proposition "There are and have been material things" is quite certainly true, but that the question how this proposition is to be analysed is one to which no answer that has been hitherto given is anywhere near certainly true; so I hold that the proposition "There are and have been many Selves" is quite certainly true, but that here again all the analyses of this proposition that have been suggested by philosophers are highly doubtful.

That I am now perceiving many different sense-data, and that I have at many times in the past perceived many different sense-data, I know for certain —that is to say, I know that there are mental facts of class (ß), connected in a way which it is proper to express by saying that they are all of them facts about *me;* but how this kind of connection is to be analysed, I do not know for certain, nor do I think that any other philosopher knows with any approach to certainty. Just as in the case of the proposition "This is part of the surface of a human hand," there are several extremely different views as to its analysis, each of which seems to me *possible*, but none nearly certain, so also in the case of the proposition "This, that and that sense-datum are all at present being perceived by *me*," and still more so in the case of the proposition "I am now perceiving this sense-datum, and I have in the past perceived sense-data of these other kinds." Of the *truth* of these propositions there seems to me to be no doubt, but as to what is the correct analysis of them there seems to me to be the gravest doubt—the true analysis may, for instance, *possibly* be quite as paradoxical as is the third view given above under IV as to the analysis of "This is part of the surface of a human hand"; but whether it is as paradoxical as this seems to me to be quite as doubtful as in that case. Many philosophers, on the other hand, seem to me to have assumed that there is little or no doubt as to the correct analysis of such propositions; and many of these, just reversing my position, have also held that the propositions themselves are not true.

Of Scepticism with Regard to the Senses
DAVID HUME

Thus the sceptic still continues to reason and believe, even tho' he asserts, that he cannot defend his reason by reason; and by the same rule he must assent to the principle concerning the existence of body, tho' he cannot pretend by any arguments of philosophy to maintain its veracity. Nature has not left this to his choice, and has doubtless esteem'd it an affair of too great importance to be trusted to our uncertain reasonings and speculations. We may well ask, *What causes induce us to believe in the existence of body?* but 'tis in vain to ask, *Whether there be body or not?* That is a point, which we must take for granted in all our reasonings.

The subject, then, of our present enquiry is concerning the *causes* which induce us to believe in the existence of body: And my reasonings on this head I shall begin with a distinction, which at first sight may seem superfluous, but which will contribute very much to the perfect understanding of what follows. We ought to examine apart those two questions, which are commonly con-founded together, *viz.* Why we attribute a CONTINU'D existence to objects, even when they are not present to the senses; and why we suppose them to have an existence DISTINCT from the mind and perception. Under this last head I comprehend their situation as well as relations, their *external* position as well as the *independence* of their existence and operation. These two questions concerning the continu'd and distinct existence of body are intimately connected together. For if the objects of our senses continue to exist, even when they are not perceiv'd, their existence is of course independent of and distinct from the perception; and *vice versa*, if their existence be independent of the perception and distinct from it, they must continue to exist, even tho' they be not perceiv'd. But tho' the decision of the one question decides the other; yet that we may the more easily discover the principles of human nature, from whence the decision arises, we shall carry along with us this distinction, and shall consider, whether it be the *senses, reason*, or the *imagina-*

FROM *A Treatise of Human Nature*, David Hume. Book I, Part 4, Section 2 (originally published in 1739).

tion, that produces the opinion of a *continu'd* or of a *distinct* existence. These are the only questions, that are intelligible on the present subject. For as to the notion of external existence, when taken for something specifically different from our perceptions,[1] we have already shewn its absurdity.

To begin with the SENSES, 'tis evident these faculties are incapable of giving rise to the notion of the *continu'd* existence of their objects, after they no longer appear to the senses. For that is a contradiction in terms, and supposes that the senses continue to operate, even after they have ceas'd all manner of operation. These faculties, therefore, if they have any influence in the present case, must produce the opinion of a distinct, not of a continu'd existence; and in order to that, must present their impressions either as images and representations, or as these very distinct and external existences.

That our senses offer not their impressions as the the images of something *distinct*, or *independent*, and *external*, is evident; because they convey to us nothing but a single perception, and never give us the least intimation of any thing beyond. A single perception can never produce the idea of a double existence, but by some inference either of the reason or imagination. When the mind looks farther than what immediately appears to it, its conclusions can never be put to the account of the senses; and it certainly looks farther, when from a single perception it infers a double existence, and supposes the relations of resemblance and causation betwixt them.

If our senses, therefore, suggest any idea of distinct existences, they must convey the impressions as those very existences, by a kind of fallacy and illusion. Upon this head we may observe, that all sensations are felt by the mind, such as they really are, and that when we doubt, whether they present themselves as distinct objects, or as mere impressions, the difficulty is not concerning their nature, but concerning their relations and situation. Now if the senses presented our impressions as external to, and independent of ourselves, both the objects and ourselves must be obvious to our senses, otherwise they cou'd not be compar'd by these faculties. The difficulty, then, is how far we are *ourselves* the objects of our senses.

'Tis certain there is no question in philosophy more abstruse than that concerning identity, and the nature of the uniting principle, which constitutes a person. So far from being able by our senses merely to determine this question, we must have recourse to the most profound metaphysics to give a satisfactory answer to it; and in common life 'tis evident these ideas of self and person are never very fix'd nor determinate. 'Tis absurd, therefore, to imagine the senses can ever distinguish betwixt ourselves and external objects.

Add to this, that every impression, external and internal, passions, affections, sensations, pains and pleasures, are originally on the same footing; and that whatever other differences we may observe among them, they appear, all of them, in their true colours, as impressions or perceptions. And indeed, if we consider the matter aright, 'tis scarce possible it shou'd be otherwise, nor is it conceivable that our senses shou'd be more capable of deceiving us in the situation and relations, than in the nature of our impressions. For since all actions and sensations of the mind are known to us by consciousness, they must necessarily appear in every particular what they are, and be what they appear. Every thing that enters the mind, being in *reality* as the perception, 'tis impossible any thing shou'd to *feeling* appear different. This were to suppose, that even where we are most intimately conscious, we might be mistaken.

But not to lose time in examining, whether 'tis possible for our senses to deceive us, and represent our perceptions as distinct from ourselves, that is as *external* to and *independent* of us; let us consider whether they really do so, and whether this error proceeds from

---

[1] Part II. sect. 6.

an immediate sensation, or from some other causes.

To begin with the question concerning *external* existence, it may perhaps be said, that setting aside the metaphysical question of the identity of a thinking substance, our own body evidently belongs to us; and as several impressions appear exterior to the body, we suppose them also exterior to ourselves. The paper, on which I write at present, is beyond my hand. The table is beyond the paper. The walls of the chamber beyond the table. And in casting my eye towards the window, I perceive a great extent of fields and buildings beyond my chamber. From all this it may be infer'd, that no other faculty is requir'd, beside the senses, to convince as of the external existence of body. But to prevent this inference, we need only weigh the three following considerations. *First*, That, properly speaking, 'tis not our body we perceive, when we regard our limbs and members, but certain impressions, which enter by the senses; so that the ascribing a real and corporeal existence to these impressions, or to their objects, is an act of the mind as difficult to explain, as that which we examine at present. *Secondly*, Sounds, and tastes, and smells, tho' commonly regarded by the mind as continu'd independent qualities, appear not to have any existence in extension, and consequently cannot appear to the senses as situated externally to the body. The reason, why we ascribe a place to them, shall be consider'd[1] afterwards. *Thirdly*, Even our sight informs us not of distance or outness (so to speak) immediately and without a certain reasoning and experience, as is acknowledg'd by the most rational philosophers.

As to the *independency* of our perceptions on ourselves, this can never be an object of the senses; but any opinion we form concerning it, must be deriv'd from experience and observation: And we shall see afterwards, that our conclusions from experience are far from being favourable to the doctrine of

[1] Sect. 5.

the independency of our perceptions. Mean while we may observe that when we talk of real distinct existences, we have commonly more in our eye their independency than external situation in place, and think an object has a sufficient reality, when its Being is uninterrupted, and independent of the incessant revolutions, which we are conscious of in ourselves.

Thus to resume what I have said concerning the senses; they give us no notion of continu'd existence, because they cannot operate beyond the extent, in which they really operate. They as little produce the opinion of a distinct existence, because they neither can offer it to the mind as represented, nor as original. To offer it as represented, they must present both an object and an image. To make it appear as original, they must convey a falsehood; and this falsehood must be in the relations and situation: In order to which they must be able to compare the object with ourselves; and even in that case they do not, nor is it possible they shou'd, deceive us. We may, therefore, conclude with certainty, that the opinion of a continu'd and of a distinct existence never arises from the senses.

To confirm this we may observe, that there are three different kinds of impressions convey'd by the senses. The first are those of the figure, bulk, motion and solidity of bodies. The second those of colours, tastes, smells, sounds, heat and cold. The third are the pains and pleasures, that arise from the application of objects to our bodies, as by the cutting of our flesh with steel, and such like. Both philosophers and the vulgar suppose the first of these to have a distinct continu'd existence. The vulgar only regard the second as on the same footing. Both philosophers and the vulgar, again, esteem the third to be merely perceptions; and consequently interrupted and dependent beings.

Now 'tis evident, that, whatever may be our philosophical opinion, colours, sounds, heat and cold, as far as appears to the senses, exist after the same manner with motion and solidity, and that the difference we make betwixt them in this respect, arises not from the mere perception. So strong is the prejudice for the distinct continu'd existence of the former qualities, that when the contrary opinion is advanc'd by modern philosophers, people imagine they can almost refute it from their feeling and experience, and that their very senses contradict this philosophy. 'Tis also evident, that colours, sounds, &c. are originally on the same footing with the pain that arises from steel, and pleasure that proceeds from a fire; and that the difference betwixt them is founded neither on perception nor reason, but on the imagination. For as they are confest to be, both of them, nothing but perceptions arising from the particular configurations and motions of the parts of body, wherein possibly can their difference consist? Upon the whole, then, we may conclude, that as far as the senses are judges, all perceptions are the same in the manner of their existence.

We may also observe in this instance of sounds and colours, that we can attribute a distinct continu'd existence to objects without ever consulting REASON, or weighing our opinions by any philosophical principles. And indeed, whatever convincing arguments philosophers may fancy they can produce to establish the belief of objects independent of the mind, 'tis obvious these arguments are known but to very few, and that 'tis not by them, that children,

peasants, and the greatest part of mankind are induc'd to attribute objects to some impressions, and deny them to others. Accordingly we find, that all the conclusions, which the vulgar form on this head, are directly contrary to those, which are confirm'd by philosophy. For philosophy informs us, that every thing, which appears to the mind, is nothing but a perception, and is interrupted, and dependent on the mind; whereas the vulgar confound perceptions and objects, and attribute a distinct continu'd existence to the very things they feel or see. This sentiment, then, as it is entirely unreasonable, must proceed from some other faculty than the understanding. To which we may add, that as long as we take our perceptions and objects to be the same, we can never infer the existence of the one from that of the other, nor form any argument from the relation of cause and effect; which is the only one that can assure us of matter of fact. Even after we distinguish our perceptions from our objects, 'twill appear presently, that we are still incapable of reasoning from the existence of one to that of the other: So that upon the whole our reason neither does, nor is it possible it ever shou'd, upon any supposition, give us an assurance of the continu'd and distinct existence of body. That opinion must be entirely owing to the IMAGINATION: which must now be the subject of our enquiry.

A Critique of Moore
EVERETT W. HALL

For one who prided himself on the clarity of his thought and expression, G. E. Moore must have had his moments of discouragement as he noted the variety of interpretations placed upon his writings by his most friendly ex-

positors. Although I do not cast myself in the role of an opponent, I am critical of his sort of commonsensical grounding of philosophy, so perhaps my reading of his statement should be suspect. My understanding is that what he has done

FROM *Philosophical Systems*, Everett W. Hall. (Chicago: University of Chicago Press, 1959), pp. 98–104. Reprinted by permission of the University of Chicago Press.

has been to take a number of very common expressions as they might be uttered in simple everyday situations and say of them (*a*) that they are, as used in those situations, incontestably true and (*b*) that thus in them we have a common ground of certainty for all philosophies alike—the latter diverging from one another in their analyses of these and losing their certainty in the process. He has also, I think, meant to do something further, though I am not so sure of this: he has meant to accuse many philosophers, as they have pressed on with their analyses, of thinking that they were in opposition to these commonsensical certitudes or at least were calling them in question, and to condemn them if they so thought, since no one can really question them.

Moore's examples of such everyday beliefs are too well known to require mentioning, but if we ask what, if anything, they have in common beyond their certitude, what marks them out, what criterion he uses to select them, the going is not so easy.

In the first place, there seems to be no common factor in their content. Probably his most extensive list of examples is given in his "A Defence of Common Sense" (in *Contemporary British Philosophy*). Perusing this set may leave the impression that every case has some connection with a person's body or its environment viewed from the standpoint of that person; if so, this is easily overcome by looking elsewhere, say in his essay, "Some Judgments of Perception," where the cases seem to be drawn from the region of physical things presented to direct perception. Perhaps we can say negatively that Moore (in contrast with his predecessors in the Scottish school of common-sense realism) admits no theological beliefs to be unimpeachable; on the other hand, at least some ethical ones seem to be (I have in mind some of his criticism of naturalists).

Leaving then their content to one side, let us see if something about their mode of occurrence marks out those everyday beliefs which, for Moore, are beyond question. We might expect to find a social criterion. This at first offers hope, but I believe a careful reading of Moore will dash it. On the one hand, he frequently gives the impression that a belief that possesses certainty is one held by everyone, or by every normal person of mature age. This seems indicated when he admonishes his audience that they, severally, do really know that, for example, what he shows them is a finger or a hand, clearly assuming that there are no exceptions even among philosophers who claim to doubt it. But to take such universal acceptance as a test of certitude seems prohibited to us since at least in some places (as in his Morley College lectures) he admits such agreement at certain periods in the past on beliefs we now know to be false, and surely he would concede on this point that history may repeat itself in the future as regards contemporary unanimities. Moreover, he also on occasion suggests that beliefs that lack universal acceptance may have certainty, as when he identifies the tenets of "common sense" as beliefs held by the "vast majority" of people. Moreover, as mentioned above, if his criterion were really social concurrence (whether of all or of an overwhelming majority), it would seem that his method of applying it would be so crude as to be ridiculous (it would consist in telling his audience or readers what they accept with certainty and refusing to listen to any demurrers).

This leads to another pragmatic test, namely, what strikes Moore himself very forcefully. This is indicated by a number of characteristic phrases he uses, such as "it seems to me to be very certain," "(in my own opinion) I *know*, with certainty, to be true," "how absurd it would be to suggest that I did not know it, but only believed it." Now these expressions could be construed differently, but I interpret them as an appeal by Moore to his own strong and indeed supposedly unshakable convictions. Unfortunately their reliability is subject to debate, particularly by men of other intellectual and cultural backgrounds. In fact, in some instances Moore has questioned them himself (I have in mind some admissions Moore makes in his reply to Stevenson in Schilpp's volume devoted to *The Philosophy of G. E. Moore*). Moreover, Moore has frequently underlined the distinction between having a strong and even indeflectible propensity to believe something and knowing with certainty that something is the case. Of course this does not rule our the possibility that Moore is particularly attached to his own convictions and assumes they possess some rather extraordinary reliability.

There is another construction that can be put upon Moore's characteristic phrases just now mentioned. It is to the effect that, when he finds what seem to him cases of unquestionable knowledge, he is not simply reporting states of psychological conviction on his part, nor is he using them as marks of certainty, but that he is finding certainty itself, as if this were a property open to direct inspection in the way a pain or an attitude of anxiety is. But though this is a possible reading it is not a very probable one. Moore, a fairly articulate writer, never formulates his view this way, nor faces any of the problems it involves, as he did with the comparable case of good considered as a simple, non-natural property. And there would be special problems; not only would he need to face the vast majority of us who do not find, upon introspecting our beliefs, that any of them possess this property, he would also need to note some awkward peculiarities of the property itself. It would be non-natural in that one could fully describe the belief possessing it without mentioning it (remembering that it is to be distinguished from psychological conviction); it would, moreover, entail the belief's truth and yet not be its truth, and to say that this is open to direct inspection seems rather obviously to spurn the facts of experience.

In this predicament, failing to find anything common to those everyday beliefs that possess certainty other than the fact that they are certain, Moore might well have availed himself of the help which Norman Malcolm has been eager to offer, although I do not find

that he has. He would then have said that the mark of certainty is good usage; when it is stylistically proper in colloquial language to say, "It is certain that . . .," then we may correctly assign certainty to the belief expressed in the clause following "that." Here of course one must rely upon a person's sense of the proprieties.

It is somewhat indicative of the reliability of this approach that Malcolm, who began with almost a reverential awe for "Moore's extraordinarily powerful language-sense" (*The Philosophy of G. E. Moore*), has more recently claimed ("Defending Common Sense" in *The Philosophical Review* for 1949), on this very issue we are discussing, that Moore has missed the grammar of certitude in everyday speech. This brings us up short: whose sense of linguistic propriety are we to accept? And if we cannot trust an individual's feeling for speech—whether that person be oneself or someone else—how good is this criterion?

Moreover, can we trust the vernacular itself? Is it infallible in picking out those beliefs that really are indubitable? Here Malcolm is forthright and unswerving in his statement: "ordinary language is correct language," "ordinary language must be right"; but there may be some question about his meaning. Does he intend to say merely that on the matter of linguistic usage ordinary language must be taken as our model? If so, his remarks are irrelevant to our problem, which is not about the usage of "certainty" but the certainty of a variety of common beliefs. Moreover, he frequently expresses himself in a manner indicative of a material and not merely stylistic claim, as when he asserts in general that "any philosophical statement which violates ordinary language is false."

Let us for the moment read Mr. Malcolm in this second way. The unfailing mark of commonsensical beliefs that are certain is that it is good English to say of them (putting them in the concrete situations in which they occur) that they are certain. Now this is helpful in that it furnishes a fairly definite criterion. I say "fairly" because I am not as confident of my ability to identify cases of it as Mr. Malcolm is of his. To cite one example he gives: I can imagine myself seeing a house apparently thrown into the air by a sudden gust of wind: I doubt my senses, I investigate in the way and to the extent he specifies, I even come to say, "Yes, I'm now certain the house was tossed into the air by the wind," and all seems quite proper (linguistically, that is) until a quizzical bystander asks, "Is it really beyond doubt that the wind did it? Couldn't some accumulated gas have exploded just at that moment?" Then I say, "You're right, it wasn't really certain that the gust of air did it." Now, of course it might have been certain precisely at the moment when it wasn't certain, so that I was within linguistic proprieties both when I said it was certain and later when, speaking of exactly the same belief, I said that it wasn't. But this way of saving the appearances would require our sacrificing the law of contradiction, and even if we had no other attachment to that law, our renunciation of it would hardly fit the amenities of good taste except in the Strawsonian sense (where "It is and it isn't" is allowable but only in different senses and without damage to the law).

Furthermore, one wonders about the connection between the criterion and the thing itself (which on this reading of Mr. Malcolm are distinct). Is it because it is good usage to say that a statement is indubitable that it is indubitable? This surely would not, in ordinary cases, be good usage. Imagine ourselves again in the situation just now mentioned. I say, "It is certain that the wind blew a house into the air right before me." Now someone accosts me, "Is it really certain?" It would not be within the proprieties for me to answer, "Of course it is because it is correct English to say so," even though I were to add "providing one has obtained such-and-such corroborating evidence, as I have done." The point here is not too fine: it is the corroborat-

ing evidence that bestows the certainty (if anything does), and not the agreement with good English.

Of course one can convert the connection, and say that it is proper to say that a belief is certain because (thus if but only if) it is certain. But this destroys our criterion of certainty. Moreover, it does not agree with good usage since if there is anything we can agree on at all about language it is that false sentences must be permitted, and this must surely apply to false sentences about certainty.

No, I really do not think Mr. Malcolm has helped us in our problem, though he may have contributed to our linguistic sensibilities. But if Moore is left in trouble about a criterion marking out those commonsensical beliefs that are indubitable, this, I think, is not the worst of his difficulties. In the interpretation we gave him, he was saying that philosophers do have extra-systemic certainties upon which to build, namely, a set of commonsensical beliefs. Let us grant him his everyday certitudes. Will they do the trick?

Here we may tear out a leaf from the casuist's own book. We cannot be sure that these beliefs will perform properly if taken out of their appropriate contexts. Now the original and proper context of Moore's examples ("Here is a hand," "This is an inkstand," "I have a body that was born in 1901"), as he himself quite specifically emphasizes, was in each case a practical situation of everyday life. If any philosopher were to debate the certainty of any of them in this kind of context, it would not be as a philosopher going about his business, which in my idiom is categorial analysis. But Moore's whole purpose is to use them in the philosophical context, as a premise, for example, of a proof of the existence of an external world, or as material for and a test of what Moore calls "analysis." Now have we any reason to suppose that with this shift of context they retain their incontestibility? I do not see that we have.

Moore has on several occasions

tried to meet this challenge. His response amounts to the contention that, as far as it is relevant to the claim of certainty, the philosophical context is not to be distinguished from the ordinary one of everyday life. What he actually says is that when a philosopher denies or questions the existence of an external world, he is denying or questioning the existence of Moore's hand when Moore holds it right before him, in the same way a man would who believed it the case or possibly the case that Moore's hand had been cut off and, let us say, replaced by an artificial one.

Now I must confess that this leaves me completely unmoved. I cannot conceive that any philosopher who has questioned the existence of the external world has meant thereby to doubt the existence of any particular man's hand in the way one would if he thought the hand artificial or simply missing. Philosophical doubts, for example doubts about an external world, are questions about the whole framework of the world, about categorial features of it, not specific items in it that are subject to observational checking. This is a point that has been so frequently made, in one way or another, that there is no need to dwell upon it.

Questions
Concerning
Perceptual Knowledge

Are There
Physical Objects?

René Descartes, in "Meditation Six," offers this argument for the existence of physical objects: I have experience of sensory qualities—sounds, shapes, tactual sensations, and so on. Further, I have an irresistible tendency to ascribe these qualities to physical objects, objects that are spatio-temporal and exist independent of my perceptions. Now since all that exists must have a cause, my experience of sensory qualities must have a cause. If God causes them, then He deceives me, for I have a natural tendency (given or at least permitted by Him), which I cannot resist, to ascribe these qualities to physical objects, to say that what causes me to have such experiences is that I perceive objects that have the qualities in question. (Actually Descartes held, as did Locke, that objects possess only primary qualities though they could produce experiences of secondary qualities in us.) If I am the cause of these experiences (Descartes might have added, "or if another mind is their cause"), then God allows me to be deceived when I follow a tendency natural to me. Further, and of equal importance, it is

Descartes' view that if I am mistaken in my belief that there are physical objects, I cannot discover this fact. "There are no physical objects" is not a proposition we could ever know to be true. But surely if I have an irresistible tendency to have a belief, and if I cannot discover that the belief is false even if it is in fact false, then God is a deceiver. God is all good and so is no deceiver. Hence there are things that possess the sensory qualities that I experience, and it is clearly and distinctly true that only a material substance could possess these qualities. Thus my sensory experience is to be causally accounted for on the basis of my perceiving these objects or material substances.

Leibniz challenges one of the assumptions of Descartes' argument. Why suppose that God won't deceive us? Because He is all good? This only shows that He won't deceive us unless it is good that He do so. Descartes needs, but does not provide, a proof that an all-good being could have no good reason to deceive us. It is not easy to see what such a proof might be, even if we restrict ourselves just to the one sort of belief that Descartes discusses. If we assume that we are not allowed to be deceived, we only assume, but do not prove, that there are physical objects.

Berkeley challenges another assumption of the argument. Do we really have the natural tendency that Descartes alleges we have, and if so, is it irresistible as he claims? Berkeley claims to analyze common-sense belief about our environment without discovering either the tendency to believe or the belief itself, which Descartes asserts is overpoweringly present. It must be added, of course, that Berkeley ascribes the tendency to believe, and the belief, that there are physical objects to the *perversion* of common sense by metaphysics. It is probably not easy to decide what does or does not in fact belong to unperverted common sense. In any case Berkeley has more fundamental arguments, and we will discuss two of them.

These arguments can be viewed as challenging Descartes' additional assumption that if there are no physical objects, we can never discover this fact. The first of Berkeley's arguments that we shall consider concerns the distinction between primary and secondary qualities. Primary qualities include extension, figure, motion, rest, solidity or impenetrability, and number. Secondary qualities include colors, sounds, tastes, odors, and tactual sensations. These are distinguished in two important ways, at least according to the official doctrine that Berkeley attacks.

Primary qualities are directly measurable; they themselves are quantifiable. Secondary qualities are not quantifiable. It is not red as a perceived color, but its cause, that can be defined in terms of a formula describing a particular wavelength. This provides one basis for distinguishing primary from secondary qualities. Another is provided by the fact that primary but not secondary qualities are common sensibles. Primary qualities can be experienced by more than one sense, but secondary qualities cannot be: for example, one can see or feel the shape of a red ball but can only see its color. Now, if one holds that the physically real must be capable of mathematical expression, the quantifiability of primary qualities will allow them really to belong to physical objects, but secondary qualities, being unquantifiable, are eliminated. Further, what one can test by appeal to the data of two senses is not unreasonably viewed as more reliable than what can be checked by appeal to the data of one sense only. For these reasons appeal to the primary qualities as actually belonging to objects seemed more forceful than appeal to secondary qualities as actually belonging to physical objects.

Berkeley agreed with Descartes and Locke that secondary qualities do not belong to physical objects, though for Berkeley they are not (as Locke put it) "powers in objects to cause sensations in us." Berkeley argued, in effect, "you grant that secondary qualities depend for their existence upon there being a perceiver and that they do not exist as qualities of the objects themselves, but you do not grant the same thing about primary qualities. But if this view of secondary qualities is correct, then primary qualities also do not belong to objects themselves: thus you ought to alter your view of the status of primary qualities, and if you do not do so you are inconsistent." To put the argument another way, Berkeley argues: (1) unperceived secondary qualities cannot exist; (2) no primary quality can exist independently of some secondary quality; so (3) no primary quality can exist independent of perception. In defense of (2), which in this context is the crucial premise, Berkeley argues:

I desire any one to reflect and try whether he can, by any abstraction of thought, conceive the extension and motion of a body without all sensible qualities. For my own part, I see evidently that it is not in my power to frame an idea of a body extended and moving, but I must withal give it some color of sensible quality . . . In short, extension, figure and motion, abstracted from all other qualities, are inconceivable.

Berkeley's claim, then, is this. When we say that something is extended, we say that it is a whole whose parts stand in certain relations: to the left of, above, to the right of, below, and so on. These relations are definable only ostensively by referring to visible or tactual objects actually standing in these relations to one another. But if we attempt to say that something is composed of parts that cannot be perceived at all and yet is extended in the sense that its parts bear the same relation to one another as the perceptible parts of a visual expanse or a tactual expanse bear to one another, we find upon examination that we have said nothing intelligible at all.

More formally Berkeley's point is that we cannot make sense of any statement of the form "X has relation R to Y" unless we can assign a non-relational property P (say, "is red" or "is rough") to both X and Y. If the nonrelational properties of two entities—the properties that they possess "on their own" and not by virtue of their relation to something else—are unknown, then any supposed relation in which the pretended relata stand is in fact unintelligible.

Now extension is central among the primary qualities. If anything moves from place to place, it occupies space. If it is numerable but not mind-dependent, it is extended, and so on through the primary qualities. So, if something has some primary quality other than extension, it has extension as well. But nothing can be conceived as extended unless it is also conceived as visual or tactual, or both. What cannot be conceived cannot be postulated as existing. So the hypothesis that there is an instance of extension that is not colored and that possesses no tactual qualities is literally unintelligible. So each instance of extension is also necessarily an instance of a color quality and/or a tactual quality. Since all instances of color qualities and all instances of tactual qualities are mind-dependent, so are all instances of extension, and hence all instances of primary qualities. As no object can exist distinct from all primary qualities, and no primary quality can exist distinct from all secondary qualities, and no secondary quality is mind-independent, it follows that no object is mind-independent. This is one argument, then, that Berkeley offers in criticism of the view that primary qualities exist in objects that are mind-independent.

A second argument can be mentioned briefly. Berkeley was accused by G. E. Moore, in his famed "The Refutation of Idealism," of neglecting the distinction between consciousness and the object of consciousness. Bertrand Russell, in Chapter 4 of *The Problems of Philosophy*, accuses Berkeley of ignoring the distinction between sensation and the object of sensation. Berkeley did not in fact neglect these distinctions. With respect to perception, though not with respect to self-awareness and other cognition involving notions, he denied them. He wrote that "in truth, the object and the sensation are the same thing, and cannot therefore be abstracted from one another" (*Principles*, Section 5). This claim is closely related to the ones just noted in discussing Berkeley's first argument. If we cannot distinguish between a sensation and the object of a sensation, we plainly cannot ask such questions as "Does the object cause the sensation?" or "Does the object resemble the sensation?". The problem of the existence and features of the external world cannot ever be raised. So there is of course no need to solve them.

Crucial in this regard is Berkeley's use of pain as an example of sensation. The feeling of pain and the pain that is felt are, he asserts, the same; in the case of pain, there is no sense to the distinction between a process of sensing and an object of the process or between an act of consciousness and the object of the act. Sensation is passive, not active. Pain is properly viewed as a paradigm for the analysis of sensation. The lack of a sensation-object distinction in the case of pain breaks the back of the general thesis that this distinction must always be made. If pain is the legitimate paradigm of sensation that Berkeley's use of it suggests, we ought never to make this distinction with respect to perceptual experience. Of course, the passivity of perception and the appropriateness of Berkeley's paradigm can be challenged.

Berkeley offers other arguments (but discussion and appraisal of all of Berkeley's arguments is beyond the purview of this introduction). For example, he claims that even if we waive the above objections and suppose that the claim that there are mind-independent objects is intelligible, there is nothing we can explain with this hypothesis that we cannot explain equally well without it.

Bertrand Russell offers a response to this claim, suggesting that one reason for holding that there are physical objects is that affirmation is simpler than denial. This claim is exemplary of a fairly standard move in philosophy: other things being equal, the simpler view is the more reasonable to adopt. This is also a move of debated legitimacy. Is simplicity a mark of truth? The rationale of the move is not a mere penchant for tidiness. Parsimonious views claim less, being less open to error. Nonetheless we can ask if nature always operates in the simplest manner, or is it just that thought-systems that are simpler than their competitors run less risk of error (but perhaps correlatively offer less truth, as William James contended)?

In any case, what *sort* of simplicity is in view here? Simplicity in the number of entities, the number of kinds of entities, the number of axioms or rules of inference required, or what? Russell answers:

The way in which simplicity comes in from supposing that there really are physical objects is easily seen. If the cat appears at one moment in one part of the room, and at another in another part, it is natural to suppose that it has moved from the one to the other, passing over a series of intermediate positions.

Russell is saying that it is simpler to suppose that we perceive one cat at several positions than to suppose that there are several distinct cat-experiences but no enduring animal. In one sense this is not simpler. If we follow Russell, we must assume that in addition to our experiences there is also something not an experience—namely, the cat. Here Russell may have been misled by supposing that Berkeley's ideas are sense data. About sense data the questions noted above (do they resemble physical objects? are they caused by physical objects?) are appropriate. This is false with respect to ideas. The *experience-object* model is simpler than the *experience-sense data-object* model. It is not simpler than the Berkeleyian model in which even the distinction between sensory experience and its object is denied in favor of a view in which ideas literally constitute sensory experience.

Russell suggests another criticism in these words: If the cat consists only of sense data, it cannot be *hungry*, since no hunger but my own can be a sense-datum to me.

The argument implicit here seems to be that we can say things about objects of our experience (for example, that they are hungry) that we could not say about them if they were sense data or Berkeleyian ideas. Russell's argument is that not everything we can say truly about objects can be translated into statements about ideas. Berkeley can respond that whatever resists this translation is not true as it stands. If the suggestion is that Berkeley cannot know that a cat is hungry because he cannot feel its hunger, the answer surely is that he can infer it, though a little reflection on Berkeley's doctrines will show that for Berkeley one must infer the body of the cat from his ideas as well as its hunger. (The cat's body is presumably a set of *its* ideas, not a set of Berkeley's ideas, though some of Berkeley's ideas—the ones constituting his perception of the cat—will resemble the cat's body.)

Another argument seems to be involved in Russell's comments. We cannot, he suggests, explain the behavior of a hungry animal on Berkeley's view. Russell does not explicate in exactly what sense this is inexplicable for Berkeley, but surely there are senses of "explain" in which Berkeley can explain such phenomena. There is no reason why Berkeleyian ideas cannot be classified under general laws that make prediction and retrodiction possible.

Yet another argument frequently offered in criticism of Berkeley's idealism and similar positions is that it is impossible to restate in terms of statements that refer only to ideas the statements we make, and make truly, about physical objects. A word has already been said about this argument, but it is an important one, and it may be well to pause long enough to consider it a bit more fully. It is claimed that a sentence such as "The table, from three feet away, looks tan under the present normal lighting conditions" cannot be translated into a statement whose terms refer to no physical objects. The task is indeed difficult, if not impossible. Thus reference to physical objects is essential and irreducible in sentences that we know to be true. So there are such objects.

This argument is powerful but not decisive. It does not show that (a) the sentences we take to be true about physical objects are fully true as they stand (Berkeley would argue that they are not) or that (b) there is no set of sentences compatible with an accurate description of our actual observations but incompatible with our physical-object statements, which interpret or account for our observational data as well as physical-object statements do. The argument in question is best viewed as a challenge to one who takes Berkeley's line: to provide the schema at least of the view of things that is not committed to there being physical objects but does account for our observational data. This places with Berkeley the burden of showing that his view can account for our sensory experience without supposing that physical objects exist. Whether this task can be done is something the reader must judge for himself.

W. T. Stace offers a brief, straightforward critique of realism, which he defines as entailing that "some entities exist without being experienced by any finite mind." He asserts that

there are only two ways in which it could be asserted that the existence of any sense-object can be established. One is by sense-perception, the other by inference from sense-perception.

Can a realist prove his claim in either of these ways? Not by sense perception "for that would be self-contradictory. It would amount to asserting that I can experience the unexperienced." Nor by inference from sense perception, for any such inference must be deductive or inductive and neither will do.

To see why Stace makes the claim that neither will do, consider the premise (1) I see a gray pen. The realist will need (2) The gray pen exists when I don't perceive it. Now (1) alone does not entail (2), for (1) can be true but (2) false without contradiction. Further, for any other proposition I add to (1) that reports still further sensory experiences, it will be possible without contradiction to accept (1) plus that further proposition and to deny (2). So (1), by itself or supplemented with other propositions reporting my sensory experience, will not deductively lead to (2).

Well, what about inductive inference from (1) to (2)? According to Stace:

Inductive reasoning proceeds always upon the basis that what has been found in certain observed cases to be true will also be true in unobserved cases. But there is no single case in which it has been observed to be true that an experienced object continues to exist when it is not being experienced; for, by hypothesis, its existence when it is not being experienced cannot be observed.

So we cannot move inductively from a premise like (1) to a conclusion like (2).

Stace's argument puts concisely the difficulty we face if we take "the way of ideas," supposing that what we perceive is not itself a physical object but is rather an intermediary between objects and ourselves. As the history of philosophy makes plain, when we allow only indirect perception of physical objects, it is hard indeed to defend ourselves against the claim that we can quite reasonably drop these objects altogther.

A Proof That There Are Physical Objects
RENÉ DESCARTES

Now there is indeed in me a certain passive faculty of sensing or receiving and cognizing ideas of sensible things, but I would be able to make no use of this unless there were also in me or in another, a certain active faculty of producing or bringing about these ideas. But surely this cannot exist in me* because it obviously presupposes no intellection, and without my cooperation, and often indeed against my will, these ideas are produced. Hence it remains that this faculty is in some substance different from me in which all the reality which exists by representation in the ideas produced by this faculty must exist formally or eminently. Either this other substance is in a body (i.e., a corporeal

* fr. version adds here "insofar as I am a thing which thinks."

nature) in which all the things are formally contained which is contained by representation in my ideas or it is God or some creature nobler than a body in which these things exist eminently. Since God is not a deceiver, it is completely clear that He does not put these ideas in me directly nor even by the intermediation of some creature in which the representative reality of these things is contained not formally but merely eminently. For since He plainly has given me no faculty for knowing this* but on the contrary, has given me a great propensity for believing that these ideas are put in me by corporeal things, I do not see how it could be supposed that He is not deceptive, if the ideas were produced other than by corporeal things. Hence, corporeal things exist.

A Critique of Descartes
GOTTFRIED W. LEIBNIZ

The argument by which Descartes attempts to demonstrate that material things exist is weak. Better not to have tried. The thrust of the argument is

this: The reason why we sense material things outside ourselves is either from God or from another or from material things themselves. Not from God, for if

FROM *Meditations on First Philosophy*, Meditation Six; J. R. Weinberg, trans. (Adam and Tannery, VII, 79^5–80^{30}, originally published in 1641.)

FROM *Critical Remarks Concerning Descartes' Principles*, Gottfried W. Leibniz. Part II, Article One; J. R. Weinberg, trans. (originally published in 1692).

none of the material things exist, God would be a deceiver; not from another, but he forgot to prove this; hence, from the material things, so they exist. It can be replied that sensations can be from a being other than God. For just as He permits other evils for various reasons, so God could permit this deception without being called a deceiver, especially because no damage is combined with this

deception in that we would be worse off were we not deceived. Moreover, there is a fallacy here, for it could be the case that the sensations come from God or another, while the judgment that the cause is from a real object outside us and so the deception comes from us. Indeed, this happens when colors and similar sensations are taken for real objects . . .

A Proof That There Are No Physical Objects
GEORGE BERKELEY

It is evident to anyone who takes a survey of the *objects* of human knowledge that they are either ideas actually imprinted on the senses, or else such as are perceived by attending to the passions and operations of the mind, or lastly, ideas formed by help of memory and imagination—either compounding, dividing, or barely representing those originally perceived in the aforesaid ways. By sight I have the ideas of light and colors, with their several degrees and variations. By touch I perceive, for example, hard and soft, heat and cold, motion and resistance, and of all these more and less either as to quantity or degree. Smelling furnishes me with odors, the palate with tastes, and hearing conveys sounds to the mind in all their variety of tone and composition. And as several of these are observed to accompany each other, they come to be marked by one name, and so to be reputed as one thing. Thus, for example, a certain color, taste, smell, figure, and consistence having been observed to go together, are accounted one distinct thing signified by the name "apple"; other collections of ideas constitute a stone, a tree, a book, and the like sensible things—which as they are pleasing or disagreeable excite the passions of love, hatred, joy, grief, and so forth.

2. But, besides all that endless variety of ideas or objects of knowledge, there is likewise something which knows or perceives them and exercises divers operations, as willing, imagining, remembering, about them. This perceiving, active being is what I call "mind," "spirit," "soul," or "myself." By which words I do not denote any one of my ideas, but a thing entirely distinct from them, wherein they exist or, which is the same thing, whereby they are perceived —for the existence of an idea consists in being perceived.

3. That neither our thoughts, nor passions, nor ideas formed by the imagination exist without the mind is what everybody will allow. And it seems no less evident that the various sensations or ideas imprinted on the sense, however blended or combined together (that is, whatever objects they compose), cannot exist otherwise than in a mind perceiving them.—I think an intuitive knowledge may be obtained of this by anyone that shall attend to what is meant by the term "exist" when applied to sensible things. The table I write on I say exists, that is, I see and feel it; and if I were out of my study I should say it existed—meaning thereby that if I was in my study I might perceive it, or that some other spirit actu-

FROM *A Treatise Concerning the Principles of Human Knowledge*, George Berkeley, Sections 1–33, (originally published in 1710).

ally does perceive it. There was an odor, that is, it was smelled, there was a sound, that is to say, it was heard; a color or figure, and it was perceived by sight or touch. This is all that I can understand by these and the like expressions. For as to what is said of the absolute existence of unthinking things without any relation to their being perceived, that seems perfectly unintelligible. Their *esse* is *percipi*, nor is it possible they should have any existence out of the minds or thinking things which perceive them.

4. It is indeed an opinion strangely prevailing amongst men that houses, mountains, rivers, and, in a word, all sensible objects have an existence, natural or real, distinct from their being perceived by the understanding. But with how great an assurance and acquiescence soever this principle may be entertained in the world, yet whoever shall find in his heart to call it in question may, if I mistake not, perceive it to involve a manifest contradiction. For what are the forementioned objects but the things we perceive by sense? And what do we perceive besides our own ideas or sensations? And is it not plainly repugnant [contradictory] that any one of these, or any combination of them, should exist unperceived?

5. If we thoroughly examine this tenet it will, perhaps, be found at bottom to depend on the doctrine of *abstract ideas*. For can there be a nicer strain of abstraction than to distinguish the existence of sensible objects from their being perceived, so as to conceive them existing unperceived? Light and colors, heat and cold, extension and figures—in a word, the things we see and feel—what are they but so many sensations, notions, ideas, or impressions on the sense? And is it possible to separate, even in thought, any of these from perception? For my part, I might as easily divide a thing from itself. I may, indeed, divide in my thoughts, or conceive apart from each other, those things which, perhaps, I never perceived by sense so divided. Thus I imagine the trunk of a human

body without the limbs, or conceive the smell of a rose without thinking on the rose itself. So far, I will not deny, I can abstract—if that may properly be called "abstraction" which extends only to the conceiving separately such objects as it is possible may really exist or be actually perceived asunder. But my conceiving or imagining power does not extend beyond the possibility of real existence or perception. Hence, as it is impossible for me to see or feel anything without an actual sensation of that thing, so it is impossible for me to conceive in my thoughts any sensible thing or object distinct from the sensation or perception of it.

6. Some truths there are so near and obvious to the mind that a man need only open his eyes to see them. Such I take this important one to be, to wit, that all the choir of heaven and furniture of the earth, in a word, all those bodies which compose the mighty frame of the world, have not any subsistence without a mind—that their *being* is to be perceived or known, that, consequently, so long as they are not actually perceived by me or do not exist in my mind or that of any other created spirit, they must either have no existence at all or else subsist in the mind of some eternal spirit—it being perfectly unintelligible, and involving all the absurdity of abstraction, to attribute to any single part of them an existence independent of a spirit. To be convinced of which, the reader need only reflect, and try to separate in his own thoughts, the *being* of a sensible thing from its *being perceived*.

7. From what has been said it follows there is not any other substance than *spirit*, or that which perceives. But, for the fuller proof of this point, let it be considered the sensible qualities are color, figure, motion, smell, taste, and such like—that is, the ideas perceived by sense. Now, for an idea to exist in an unperceiving thing is a manifest contradiction, for to have an idea is all one as to perceive; that, therefore, wherein color, figure, and the like qualities exist

must perceive them; hence it is clear there can be no unthinking substance or *substratum* of those ideas.

8. But, say you, though the ideas themselves do not exist without the mind, yet there may be things like them, whereof they are copies or resemblances, which things exist without the mind in an unthinking substance. I answer, an idea can be like nothing but an idea; a color or figure can be like nothing but another color or figure. If we look but ever so little into our thoughts, we shall find it impossible for us to conceive a likeness except only between our ideas. Again, I ask whether those supposed originals or external things, of which our ideas are the pictures or representations, be themselves perceivable or no? If they are, then they are ideas and we have gained our point; but if you say they are not, I appeal to anyone whether it be sense to assert a color is like something which is invisible; hard or soft, like something which is intangible; and so of the rest.

9. Some there are who make a distinction betwixt *primary* and *secondary* qualities. By the former they mean extension, figure, motion, rest, solidity or impenetrability, and number; by the latter they denote all other sensible qualities, as colors, sounds, tastes, and so forth. The ideas we have of these they acknowledge not to be the resemblances of anything existing without the mind, or unperceived, but they will have our ideas of the primary qualities to be patterns or images of things which exist without the mind, in an unthinking substance which they call "matter." By "matter," therefore, we are to understand an inert, senseless substance, in which extension, figure, and motion do actually subsist. But it is evident from what we have already shown that extension, figure, and motion are only ideas existing in the mind, and that an idea can be like nothing but another idea, and that consequently neither they nor their archetypes can exist in an unperceiving substance. Hence it is plain that the very notion of what is called "matter" or

"corporeal substance" involves a contradiction in it.

10. They who assert that figure, motion, and the rest of the primary or original qualities do exist without the mind in unthinking substances do at the same time acknowledge that colors, sounds, heat, cold, and suchlike secondary qualities do not—which they tell us are sensations existing in the mind alone, that depend on and are occasioned by the different size, texture, and motion of the minute particles of matter. This they take for an undoubted truth which they can demonstrate beyond all exception. Now, if it be certain that those original qualities are inseparably united with the other sensible qualities, and not, even in thought, capable of being abstracted from them, it plainly follows that they exist only in the mind. But I desire anyone to reflect and try whether he can, by any abstraction of thought, conceive the extension and motion of a body without all other sensible qualities. For my own part, I see evidently that it is not in my power to frame an idea of a body extended and moved, but I must withal give it some color or other sensible quality which is acknowledged to exist only in the mind. In short, extension, figure, and motion, abstracted from all other qualities, are inconceivable. Where therefore the other sensible qualities are, there must these be also, to wit, in the mind and nowhere else.

11. Again, *great* and *small, swift* and *slow* are allowed to exist nowhere without the mind, being entirely relative, and exchanging as the frame or position of the organs of sense varies. The extension, therefore, which exists without the mind is neither great nor small, the motion neither swift nor slow; that is, they are nothing at all. But, say you, they are extension in general, and motion in general: thus we see how much the tenet of extended movable substances existing without the mind depends on that strange doctrine of *abstract ideas*. And here I cannot but remark how nearly the vague and indeterminate description of matter or corporeal substance, which

the modern philosophers are run into by their own principles, resembles that antiquated and so much ridiculed notion of *materia prima*, to be met with in Aristotle and his followers. Without extension, solidity cannot be conceived; since, therefore, it has been shown that extension exists not in an unthinking substance, the same must also be true of solidity.

12. That number is entirely the creature of the mind, even though the other qualities be allowed to exist without, will be evident to whoever considers that the same thing bears a different denomination of number as the mind views it with different respects. Thus the same extension is one, or three, or thirty-six, according as the mind considers it with reference to a yard, a foot, or an inch. Number is so visibly relative and dependent on men's understanding that it is strange to think how anyone should give it an absolute existence without the mind. We say one book, one page, one line; all these are equally units, though some contain several of the others. And in each instance it is plain the unit relates to some particular combination of ideas arbitrarily put together by the mind.

13. Unity I know some will have to be a simple or uncompounded idea accompanying all other ideas into the mind. That I have any such idea answering the word "unity" I do not find; and if I had, methinks I could not miss finding it; on the contrary, it should be the most familiar to my understanding, since it is said to accompany all other ideas and to be perceived by all the ways of sensation and reflection. To say no more, it is an *abstract idea.*

14. I shall further add that, after the same manner as modern philosophers prove certain sensible qualities to have no existence in matter, or without the mind, the same thing may be likewise proved of all other sensible qualities whatsoever. Thus, for instance, it is said that heat and cold are affections only of the mind, and not at all patterns of real beings existing in the corporeal

substances which excite them, for that the same body which appears cold to one hand seems warm to another. Now, why may we not as well argue that figure and extension are not patterns or resemblances of qualities existing in matter, because to the same eye at different stations, or eyes of a different texture at the same station, they appear various and cannot, therefore, be the images of anything settled and determinate without the mind? Again, it is proved that sweetness is not really in the sapid thing, because, the thing remaining unaltered, the sweetness if changed into bitter, as in case of a fever or otherwise vitiated palate. Is it not as reasonable to say that motion is not without the mind, since if the succession of ideas in the mind become swifter, the motion, it is acknowledged, shall appear slower without any alteration in any external object?

15. In short, let anyone consider those arguments which are thought manifestly to prove that colors and tastes exist only in the mind, and he shall find they may with equal force be brought to prove the same thing of extension, figure, and motion. Though it must be confessed this method of arguing does not so much prove that there is no extension of color in an outward object as that we do not know by sense which is the true extension or color of the object. But the arguments foregoing plainly show it to be impossible that any color or extension at all, or other sensible quality whatsoever, should exist in an unthinking subject without the mind, or, in truth, that there should be any such thing as an outward object.

16. But let us examine a little the received opinion.—It is said extension is a mode or accident of matter, and that matter is the *substratum* that supports it. Now I desire that you would explain what is meant by matter's "supporting" extension. Say you, I have no idea of matter and, therefore, cannot explain it. I answer, though you have no positive, yet, if you have any meaning at all, you must at least have a relative idea of matter; though you know not what it is,

yet you must be supposed to know what relation it bears to accidents, and what is meant by its supporting them. It is evident "support" cannot here be taken in its usual or literal sense—as when we say that pillars support a building; in what sense therefore must it be taken?

17. If we inquire into what the most accurate philosophers declare themselves to mean by "material substance," we shall find them acknowledge they have no other meaning annexed to those sounds but the idea of being in general together with the relative notion of its supporting accidents. The general idea of being appears to me the most abstract and incomprehensible of all other; and as for its supporting accidents, this, as we have just now observed, cannot be understood in the common sense of those words; it must, therefore, be taken in some other sense, but what that is they do not explain. So that when I consider the two parts or branches which make the signification of the words "material substance," I am convinced there is no distinct meaning annexed to them. But why should we trouble ourselves any further in discussing this material *substratum* or support of figure and motion and other sensible qualities? Does it not suppose they have an existence without the mind? And is not this a direct repugnancy [contradiction] and altogether inconceivable?

18. But, though it were possible that solid, figured, movable substances may exist without the mind, corresponding to the ideas we have of bodies, yet how it is possible for us to know this? Either we must know it by sense or by reason. As for our senses, by them we have the knowledge only of our sensations, ideas, or those things that are immediately perceived by sense, call them what you will; but they do not inform us that things exist without the mind, or unperceived, like to those which are perceived. This the materialists themselves acknowledge. It remains therefore that if we have any knowledge at all of external things, it must be by reason, inferring their existence from what is immediately perceived by sense. But what reason can induce us to believe the existence of bodies without the mind, from what we perceive, since the very patrons of matter themselves do not pretend there is any necessary connection betwixt them and our ideas? I say it is granted on all hands (and what happens in dreams, frenzies, and the like, puts it beyond dispute) that it is possible we might be affected with all the ideas we have now, though no bodies existed without resembling them. Hence it is evident the supposition of external bodies is not necessary for the producing our ideas; since it is granted they are produced sometimes, and might possibly be produced always in the same order as we see them in at present, without their concurrence.

19. But though we might possibly have all our sensations without them, yet perhaps it may be thought easier to conceive and explain the manner of their production by supposing external bodies in their likeness rather than otherwise; and so it might be at least probable there are such things as bodies that excite their ideas in our minds. But neither can this be said, for, though we give the materialists their external bodies, they by their own confession are never the nearer knowing how our ideas are produced, since they own themselves unable to comprehend in what manner body can act upon spirit, or how it is possible it should imprint any idea in the mind. Hence it is evident the production of ideas or sensations in our minds can be no reason why we should suppose matter of corporeal substances, since that is acknowledged to remain equally inexplicable with or without this supposition. If therefore it were possible for bodies to exist without the mind, yet to hold they do so must needs be a very precarious opinion, since it is to suppose, without any reason at all, that God has created innumerable beings that are entirely useless and serve to no manner of purpose.

20. In short, if there were external bodies, it is impossible we should ever

come to know it; and if there were not, we might have the very same reasons to think there were that we have now. Suppose—what no one can deny possible— an intelligence without the help of external bodies, to be affected with the same train of sensations or ideas that you are, imprinted in the same order and with like vividness in his mind: I ask whether that intelligence has not all the reason to believe the existence of corporeal substances, represented by his ideas and exciting them in his mind, that you can possibly have for believing the same thing? Of this there can be no question—which one consideration is enough to make any reasonable person suspect the strength of whatever arguments he may think himself to have for the existence of bodies without the mind.

21. Were it necessary to add any further proof against the existence of matter after what has been said, I could instance several of those errors and difficulties (not to mention impieties) which have sprung from that tenet. It has occasioned numberless controversies and disputes in philosophy, and not a few of far greater moment in religion. But I shall not enter into the detail of them in this place as well because I think arguments a posteriori are unnecessary for confirming what has been, if I mistake not, sufficiently demonstrated a priori, as because I shall hereafter find occasion to speak somewhat of them.

22. I am afraid I have given cause to think me needlessly prolix in handling this subject. For to what purpose is it to dilate on that which may be demonstrated with the utmost evidence in a line or two to anyone that is capable of the least reflection? It is but looking into your own thoughts, and so trying whether you can conceive it possible for a sound, or figure, or motion, or color to exist without the mind or unperceived. This easy trial may make you see that what you contend for is a downright contradiction. Insomuch that I am content to put the whole upon this issue: if you can but conceive it possible for one extended movable substance, or, in gen-

eral, for any one idea, or anything like an idea, to exist otherwise than in a mind perceiving it, I shall readily give up the cause. And, as for all that compages [company] of external bodies which you contend for, I shall grant you its existence, though you cannot either give me any reason why you believe it exists, or assign any use to it when it is supposed to exist. I say the bare possibility of your opinion's being true shall pass for an argument that it is so.

23. But, say you, surely there is nothing easier than to imagine trees, for instance, in a park, or books existing in a closet, and nobody by to perceive them. I answer you may so, there is no difficulty in it; but what is all this, I beseech you, more than framing in your mind certain ideas which you call books and trees, and at the same time omitting to frame the idea of anyone that may perceive them? But do not you yourself perceive or think of them all the while? This therefore is nothing to the purpose; it only shows you have the power of imagining or forming ideas in your mind; but it does not show that you can conceive it possible the objects of your thought may exist without the mind. To make out this, it is necessary that you conceive them existing unconceived or unthought of, which is a manifest repugnancy [contradiction]. When we do our utmost to conceive the existence of external bodies, we are all the while only contemplating our own ideas. But the mind, taking no notice of itself, is deluded to think it can and does conceive bodies existing unthought of or without the mind, though at the same time they are apprehended by or exist in itself. A little attention will discover to anyone the truth and evidence of what is here said, and make it unnecessary to insist on any other proofs against the existence of *material substance.*

24. It is very obvious, upon the least inquiry into our own thoughts, to know whether it be possible for us to understand what is meant by "the absolute existence of sensible objects in themselves, or without the mind." To me it is evident those words mark out

either a direct contradiction or else nothing at all. And to convince others of this, I know no readier or fairer way than to entreat they would calmly attend to their own thoughts; and if by this attention the emptiness or repugnancy of those expressions does appear, surely nothing more is requisite for their conviction. It is on this, therefore, that I insist, to wit, that "the absolute existence of unthinking things" are words without a meaning, or which include a contradiction. This is what I repeat and inculcate, and earnestly recommend to the attentive thoughts of the reader.

25. All our ideas, sensations, or the things which we perceive, by whatsoever names they may be distinguished, are visibly inactive—there is nothing of power or agency included in them. So that one idea or object of thought cannot produce or make any alteration in another. To be satisfied of the truth of this, there is nothing else requisite but a bare observation of our ideas. For since they and every part of them exist only in the mind, it follows that there is nothing in them but what is perceived; but whoever shall attend to his ideas, whether of sense or reflection, will not perceive in them any power or activity; there is, therefore, no such thing contained in them. A little attention will discover to us that the very being of an idea implies passiveness and inertness in it, insomuch that it is impossible for an idea to do anything or, strictly speaking, to be the cause of anything; neither can it be the resemblance or pattern of any active being, as is evident from sec. 8. Whence it plainly follows that extension, figure, and motion cannot be the cause of our sensations. To say, therefore, that these are the effects of powers resulting from the configuration, number, motion, and size of corpuscles must certainly be false.

26. We perceive a continual succession of ideas, some are anew excited, others are changed or totally disappear. There is, therefore, some cause of these ideas, whereon they depend and which produces and changes them. That this cause cannot be any quality or idea or combination of ideas is clear from the preceding section. It must therefore be a substance; but it has been shown that there is no corporeal or material substance: it remains, therefore, that the cause of ideas is an incorporeal, active substance or spirit.

27. A spirit is one simple, undivided, active being—as it perceives ideas it is called "the understanding," and as it produces or otherwise operates about them it is called "the will." Hence there can be no *idea* formed of a soul or spirit; for all ideas whatever, being passive and inert (*vide* sec. 25), they cannot represent unto us, by way of image or likeness, that which acts. A little attention will make it plain to anyone that to have an idea which shall be like that active principle of motion and change of ideas is absolutely impossible. Such is the nature of *spirit*, or that which acts, that it cannot be of itself perceived, but only by the effects which it produces. If any man shall doubt of the truth of what is here delivered, let him but reflect and try if he can frame the idea of any power or active being, and whether he has ideas of two principal powers marked by the names "will" and "understanding," distinct from each other as well as from a third idea of substance or being in general, with a relative notion of its supporting or being the subject of the aforesaid powers—which is signified by the name "soul" or "spirit." This is what some hold; but, so far as I can see, the words "will," "soul," "spirit" do not stand for different ideas or, in truth, for any idea at all, but for something which is very different from ideas, and which, being an agent, cannot be like unto, or represented by, any idea whatsoever. [Though it must be owned at the same time that we have some notion of soul, spirit, and the operations of the mind, such as willing, loving, hating—in as much as we know or understand the meaning of those words.

28. I find I can excite ideas in my mind at pleasure, and vary and shift the scene as oft as I think fit. It is no more than willing, and straightway this or that idea arises in my fancy; and by the same

power it is obliterated and makes way for another. This making and unmaking of ideas does very properly denominate the mind active. This much is certain and grounded on experience; but when we talk of unthinking agents or of exciting ideas exclusive of volition, we only amuse ourselves with words.

29. But, whatever power I may have over my own thoughts, I find the ideas actually perceived by sense have not a like dependence on my will. When in broad daylight I open my eyes, it is not in my power to choose whether I shall see or no, or to determine what particular objects shall present themselves to my view; and so likewise as to the hearing and other senses; the ideas imprinted on them are not creatures of my will. There is therefore some *other* will or spirit that produces them.

30. The ideas of sense are more strong, lively, and distinct than those of the imagination; they have likewise a steadiness, order, and coherence, and are not excited at random, as those which are the effects of human wills often are, but in a regular train or series, the admirable connection whereof sufficiently testifies the wisdom and benevolence of its Author. Now the set rules or established methods wherein the mind we depend on excites in us the ideas of sense are called "the laws of nature"; and these we learn by experience, which teaches us that such and such ideas are attended with such and such other ideas in the ordinary course of things.

31. This gives us a sort of foresight which enables us to regulate our actions for the benefit of life. And without this we should be eternally at a loss; we could not know how to act anything that might procure us the least pleasure or remove the least pain of sense. That food nourishes, sleep refreshes, and fire warms us; that to sow in the seedtime is the way to reap in the harvest; and in general that to obtain such or such ends, such or such means are conducive—all this we know, not by discovering any necessary connection between our ideas, but only by the observation of the set-tled laws of nature, without which we should be all in uncertainty and confusion, and a grown man no more know how to manage himself in the affairs of life than an infant just born.

32. And yet this consistent, uniform working which so evidently displays the goodness and wisdom of that Governing Spirit whose Will constitutes the laws of nature, is so far from leading our thoughts to Him that it rather sends them awandering after second causes. For when we perceive certain ideas of sense constantly followed by other ideas, and we know this is not of our own doing, we forthwith attribute power and agency to the ideas themselves and make one the cause of another, than which nothing can be more absurd and unintelligible. Thus, for example, having observed that when we perceive by sight a certain round, luminous figure, we at the same time perceive by touch the idea or sensation called "heat," we do from thence conclude the sun to be the cause of heat. And in like manner perceiving the motion and collision of bodies to be attended with sound, we are inclined to think the latter an effect of the former.

33. The ideas imprinted on the senses by the Author of Nature are called "real things"; and those excited in the imagination, being less regular, vivid, and constant, are more properly termed "ideas" or "images of things" which they copy and represent. But then our sensations, be they never so vivid and distinct, are nevertheless ideas, that is, they exist in the mind, or are perceived by it, as truly as the ideas of its own framing. The ideas of sense are allowed to have more reality in them, that is, to be more strong, orderly, and coherent than the creatures of the mind; but this is no argument that they exist without the mind. They are also less dependent on the spirit, or thinking substance which perceives them, in that they are excited by the will of another and more powerful spirit; yet still they are *ideas;* and certainly no idea, whether faint or strong, can exist otherwise than in a mind perceiving it.

A Critique of Idealism
BERTRAND RUSSELL

In this chapter we have to ask ourselves whether, in any sense at all, there is such a thing as matter. Is there a table which has a certain intrinsic nature, and continues to exist when I am not looking, or is the table merely a product of my imagination, a dream-table in a very prolonged dream? This question is of the greatest importance. For if we cannot be sure of the independent existence of objects, we cannot be sure of the independent existence of other people's bodies, and therefore still less of other people's minds, since we have no grounds for believing in their minds except such as are derived from observing their bodies. Thus if we cannot be sure of the independent existence of objects, we shall be left alone in a desert—it may be that the whole outer world is nothing but a dream, and that we alone exist. This is an uncomfortable possibility; but although it cannot be strictly *proved* to be false, there is not the slightest reason to suppose that it is true. In this chapter we have to see why this is the case.

Before we embark upon doubtful matters, let us try to find some more or less fixed point from which to start. Although we are doubting the physical existence of the table, we are not doubting the existence of the sense-data which made us think there was a table; we are not doubting that, while we look, a certain colour and shape appear to us, and while we press, a certain sensation of hardness is experienced by us. All this, which is psychological, we are not calling in question. In fact, whatever else may be doubtful, some at least of our immediate experiences seem absolutely certain.

Descartes (1596–1650), the founder of modern philosophy, invented a method which may still be used with profit—the method of systematic doubt. He determined that he would believe nothing which he did not see quite clearly and distinctly to be true. Whatever he could bring himself to doubt, he would doubt, until he saw reason for not doubting it. By applying this method he gradually became convinced that the only existence of which he could be *quite* certain was his own. He imagined a deceitful demon, who presented unreal things to his senses in a perpetual phantasmagoria; it might be very improbable that such a demon existed, but still it was possible, and therefore doubt concerning things perceived by the senses was possible.

But doubt concerning his own existence was not possible, for if he did not exist, no demon could deceive him. If he doubted, he must exist; if he had any experiences whatever, he must exist. Thus his own existence was an absolute certainty to him. 'I think, therefore I am,' he said (*Cogito, ergo sum*); and on the basis of this certainty he set to work to build up again the world of knowledge which his doubt had laid in ruins. By inventing the method of doubt, and by showing that subjective things are the most certain, Descartes performed a great service to philosophy, and one which makes him still useful to all students of the subject.

But some care is needed in using Descartes' argument. '*I* think, therefore *I* am' says rather more than is strictly certain. It might seem as though we were quite sure of being the same person to-day as we were yesterday, and this is no doubt true in some sense. But the real Self is as hard to arrive at as the real table, and does not seem to have that absolute, convincing certainty that belongs to particular experiences. When

FROM *The Problems of Philosophy*, Bertrand Russell. (New York: Oxford University Press, 1957), Chapter Three. Reprinted by permission of the Oxford University Press.

I look at my table and see a certain brown colour, what is quite certain at once is not '*I* am seeing a brown colour', but rather, 'a brown colour is being seen'. This of course involves something (or somebody) which (or who) sees the brown colour; but it does not of itself involve that more or less permanent person whom we call 'I'. So far as immediate certainty goes, it might be that the something which sees the brown colour is quite momentary, and not the same as the something which has some different experience the next moment.

Thus it is our particular thoughts and feelings that have primitive certainty. And this applies to dreams and hallucinations as well as to normal perceptions: when we dream or see a ghost, we certainly do have the sensations we think we have, but for various reasons it is held that no physical object corresponds to these sensations. Thus the certainty of our knowledge of our own experiences does not have to be limited in any way to allow for exceptional cases. Here, therefore, we have, for what it is worth, a solid basis from which to begin our pursuit of knowledge.

The problem we have to consider is this: Granted that we are certain of our own sense-data, have we any reason for regarding them as signs of the existence of something else, which we can call the physical object? When we have enumerated all the sense-data which we should naturally regard as connected with the table have we said all there is to say about the table, or is there still something else—something not a sense-datum, something which persists when we go out of the room? Common sense unhesitatingly answers that there is. What can be bought and sold and pushed about and have a cloth laid on it, and so on, cannot be a *mere* collection of sense-data. If the cloth completely hides the table, we shall derive no sense-data from the table, and therefore, if the table were merely sense-data, it would have ceased to exist, and the cloth would be suspended in empty air, resting, by a miracle, in the place where the table

formerly was. This seems plainly absurd; but whoever wishes to become a philosopher must learn not to be frightened by absurdities.

One great reason why it is felt that we must secure a physical object in addition to the sense-data, is that we want the *same* object for different people. When ten people are sitting round a dinner-table, it seems preposterous to maintain that they are not seeing the same tablecloth, the same knives and forks and spoons and glasses. But the sense-data are private to each separate person; what is immediately present to the sight of one is not immediately present to the sight of another: they all see things from slightly different points of view, and therefore see them slightly differently. Thus, if there are to be public neutral objects, which can be in some sense known to many different people, there must be something over and above the private and particular sense-data which appear to various people. What reason, then, have we for believing that there are such public neutral objects?

The first answer that naturally occurs to one is that, although different people may see the table slightly differently, still they all see more or less similar things when they look at the table, and the variations in what they see follow the laws of perspective and reflection of light, so that it is easy to arrive at a permanent object underlying all the different people's sense-data. I bought my table from the former occupant of my room; I could not buy *his* sense-data, which died when he went away, but I could and did buy the confident expectation of more or less similar sense-data. Thus it is the fact that different people have similar sense-data, and that one person in a given place at different times has similar sense-data, which makes us suppose that over and above the sense-data there is a permanent public object which underlies or causes the sense-data of various people at various times.

Now in so far as the above considerations depend upon supposing that there are other people besides ourselves, they beg the very question at issue. Other people are represented to me by certain sense-data, such as the sight of them or the sound of their voices, and if I had no reason to believe that there were physical objects independent of my sense-data, I should have no reason to believe that other people exist except as part of my dream. Thus, when we are trying to show that there must be objects independent of our own sense-data, we cannot appeal to the testimony of other people, since this testimony itself consists of sense-data, and does not reveal other people's experiences unless our own sense-data are signs of things existing independently of us. We must therefore, if possible, find, in our own purely private experiences, characteristics which show, or tend to show, that there are in the world things other than ourselves and our private experiences.

In one sense it must be admitted that we can never *prove* the existence of things other than ourselves and our experiences. No logical absurdity results from the hypothesis that the world consists of myself and my thoughts and feelings and sensations, and that everything else is mere fancy. In dreams a very complicated world may seem to be present, and yet on waking we find it was a delusion; that is to say, we find that the sense-data in the dream do not appear to have corresponded with such physical objects as we should naturally infer from our sense-data. (It is true that, when the physical world is assumed, it is possible to find physical causes for the sense-data in dreams: a door banging, for instance, may cause us to dream of a naval engagement. But although, in this case, there is a physical *cause* for the sense-data, there is not a physical object *corresponding* to the sense-data in the way in which an actual naval battle would correspond.) There is no logical impossibility in the supposition that the whole of life is a dream, in which we ourselves create all the objects that come before us. But although this

is not logically impossible, there is no reason whatever to suppose that it is true; and it is, in fact, a less simple hypothesis, viewed as a means of accounting for the facts of our own life, than the common-sense hypothesis that there really are objects independent of us, whose action on us causes our sensations.

The way in which simplicity comes in from supposing that there really are physical objects is easily seen. If the cat appears at one moment in one part of the room, and at another in another part, it is natural to suppose that it has moved from the one to the other, passing over a series of intermediate positions. But if it is merely a set of sense-data, it cannot have ever been in any place where I did not see it; thus we shall have to suppose that it did not exist at all while I was not looking, but suddenly sprang into being in a new place. If the cat exists whether I see it or not, we can understand from our own experience how it gets hungry between one meal and the next; but if it does not exist when I am not seeing it, it seems odd that appetite should grow during non-existence as fast as during existence. And if the cat consists only of sense-data, it cannot be *hungry*, since no hunger but my own can be a sense-datum to me. Thus the behaviour of the sense-data which represent the cat to me, though it seems quite natural when regarded as an expression of hunger, becomes utterly inexplicable when regarded as mere movements and changes of patches of colour, which are as incapable of hunger as a triangle is of playing football.

But the difficulty in the case of the cat is nothing compared to the difficulty in the case of human beings. When human beings speak—that is, when we hear certain noises which we associate with ideas, and simultaneously see certain motions of lips and expressions of face—it is very difficult to suppose that what we hear is not the expression of a thought, as we know it would be if we emitted the same sounds. Of course similar things happen in dreams, where we are mistaken as to the existence of other people. But dreams are more or less suggested by what we call waking life, and are capable of being more or less accounted for on scientific principles if we assume that there really is a physical world. Thus every principle of simplicity urges us to adopt the natural view, that there really are objects other than ourselves and our sense-data which have an existence not dependent upon our perceiving them.

Of course it is not by argument that we originally come by our belief in an independent external world. We find this belief ready in ourselves as soon as we begin to reflect: it is what may be called an *instinctive* belief. We should never have been led to question this belief but for the fact that, at any rate in the case of sight, it seems as if the sense-datum itself were instinctively believed to be the independent object, whereas argument shows that the object cannot be identical with the sense-datum. This discovery, however—which is not at all paradoxical in the case of taste and smell and sound, and only slightly so in the case of touch—leaves undiminished our instinctive belief that there *are* objects *corresponding* to our sense-data. Since this belief does not lead to any difficulties, but on the contrary tends to simplify and systematize our account of our experiences, there seems no good reason for rejecting it. We may therefore admit—though with a slight doubt derived from dreams—that the external world does really exist, and is not wholly dependent for its existence upon our continuing to perceive it.

The argument which has led us to this conclusion is doubtless less strong than we could wish, but it is typical of many philosophical arguments, and it is therefore worth while to consider briefly its general character and validity. All knowledge, we find, must be built up upon our instinctive beliefs, and if these are rejected, nothing is left. But among our instinctive beliefs some are much stronger than others, while many have,

by habit and association, become entangled with other beliefs, not really instinctive, but falsely supposed to be part of what is believed instinctively.

Philosophy should show us the hierarchy of our instinctive beliefs, beginning with those we hold most strongly, and presenting each as much isolated and as free from irrelevant additions as possible. It should take care to show that, in the form in which they are finally set forth, our instinctive beliefs do not clash, but form a harmonious system. There can never be any reason for rejecting one instinctive belief except that it clashes with others; thus, if they are found to harmonize, the whole system becomes worthy of acceptance.

It is of course *possible* that all or any of our beliefs may be mistaken, and therefore all ought to be held with at least some slight element of doubt. But we cannot have *reason* to reject a belief except on the ground of some other belief. Hence, by organizing our instinctive beliefs and their consequences, by considering which among them is most possible, if necessary, to modify or abandon, we can arrive, on the basis of accepting as our sole data what we instinctively believe, at an orderly systematic organization of our knowledge, in which, though the *possibility* of error remains, its likelihood is diminished by the interrelation of the parts and by the critical scrutiny which has preceded acquiescence.

This function, at least, philosophy can perform. Most philosophers, rightly or wrongly, believe that philosophy can do much more than this—that it can give us knowledge, not otherwise attainable, concerning the universe as a whole, and concerning the nature of ultimate reality. Whether this be the case or not, the more modest function we have spoken of can certainly be performed by philosophy, and certainly suffices, for those who have once begun to doubt the adequacy of common sense, to justify the arduous and difficult labours that philosophical problems involve.

The Refutation of Realism
WALTER T. STACE

More than thirty years have now elapsed since Prof. Moore published in MIND his famous article, "The Refutation of Idealism". Therewith the curtain rose upon the episode of contemporary British realism. After three decades perhaps the time is now ripe for the inauguration of another episode. And it is but fitting that "The Refutation of Realism" should appear on the same stage as its famous predecessor.

I shall not gird at realism because its exponents disagree among themselves as to what precisely their philosophy teaches. But disagreements certainly exist, and they make it difficult for a would-be refuter to know precisely what is the proposition which he ought to refute. It is far from certain that all idealists would agree that the idealism which Prof. Moore purported to refute represented adequately, or even inadequately, their views. And it may be that a similar criticism will be urged by realists against what I shall here have to say. But I must take my courage in my hands. Realists, it seems to me, agree in asserting that "some entities sometimes exist without being experienced by any finite mind". This, at any rate, is the proposition which I shall undertake to refute.

I insert the word "finite" in this formula because if I wrote "some entities exist without being experienced by any mind", it might be objected that the proposition so framed would imply that some entities exist of which God is ignorant, if there is such a being as God, and that it is not certain that all realists would wish to assert this. I think that we can very well leave God out of the discussion. In front of me is a piece of paper. I assume that the realist believes that this paper will continue to exist when it is put away in my desk for the night, and when no finite mind is experiencing it. He *may* also believe that it will continue to exist even if God is not experiencing it. But he must at *least* assert that it will exist when no finite mind is experiencing it. That, I think, is essential to his position. And therefore to refute that proposition will be to refute realism. In what follows, therefore, when I speak of minds I must be understood as referring to finite minds.

Possibly I shall be told that although realists probably do as a matter of fact believe that some entities exist unexperienced, yet this is not the essence of realism. Its essence, it may be said, is the belief that the relation between knowledge and its object is such that the knowledge makes no difference to the object, so that the object *might* exist without being known, whether as a matter of fact it does so exist or not.

But it would seem that there could be no point in asserting that entities *might* exist unexperienced, unless as a matter of fact they at least sometimes do so exist. To prove that the universe *might* have the property X, if as a matter of fact the universe has no such property, would seem to be a useless proceeding which no philosophy surely would take as its central contribution to truth. And I think that the only reason why realists are anxious to show that objects are such, and that the relation between knowledge and object is such, that objects might exist unexperienced, is that they think that this will lead on to the belief that objects actually do exist unexperienced. They have been anxious to prove that the existence of objects is not dependent on being experienced by minds because they wished to draw the conclusion that objects exist unexperienced. Hence I think that I am correct in saying that the essential proposition

FROM *Mind*, Vol. LIII, (1934), pp. 145–155. Reprinted by permission of the editor of *Mind*.

of realism, which has to be refuted, is that "some entities sometimes exist without being experienced by any finite mind".

Now, lest I should be misunderstood, I will state clearly at the outset that I cannot prove that no entities exist without being experienced by minds. For all I know completely unexperienced entities may exist, but what I shall assert is that we have not the slightest reason for believing that they do exist. And from this it will follow that the realistic position that they do exist is perfectly groundless and gratuitous, and one which ought not to be believed. It will be in exactly the same position as the proposition "there is a unicorn on the planet Mars". I cannot prove that there is no unicorn on Mars. But since there is not the slightest reason to suppose that there is one, it is a proposition which ought not to be believed.

And still further to clarify the issue, I will say that I shall not be discussing in this paper whether sense-objects are "mental". My personal opinion is that this question is a pointless one, but that if I am forced to answer it with a "yes" or "no", I should do so by saying that they are not mental; just as, if I were forced to answer the pointless question whether the mind is an elephant, I should have to answer that it is not an elephant. I will, in fact, assume for the purposes of this paper that sense-objects, whether they be colour patches or other sense-data, or objects, are not mental. My position will then be as follows: There is absolutely no reason for asserting that these non-mental, or physical, entities ever exist except when they are being experienced, and the proposition that they do so exist is utterly groundless and gratuitous, and one which ought not to be believed.

The refutation of realism will therefore be sufficiently accomplished if it can be shown that we do *not* know that any single entity exists unexperienced. And that is what I shall in this paper endeavour to show. I shall inquire how we could possibly know that unex-

perienced entities exist, even if, as a matter of fact, they do exist. And I shall show that there is no possible way in which we could know this, and that therefore we do *not* know it, and have no reason to believe it.

For the sake of clearness, let us take once again the concrete example of the piece of paper. I am at this moment experiencing it, and at this moment it exists, but how can I know that it existed last night in my desk when, so far as I know, no mind was experiencing it? How can I know that it will continue to exist to-night when there is no one in the room? The knowledge of these alleged facts is what the realists assert that they possess. And the question is, Whence could such knowledge have been obtained, and how can it be justified? What I assert is that it is absolutely impossible to have any such knowledge.

There are only two ways in which it could be asserted that the existence of any sense-object can be established. One is by sense-perception, the other by inference from sense-perception. I know of the existence of this paper *now* because I see it. I am supposed to know of the existence of the other side of the moon, which no one has ever seen, by inference from various actual astronomical observations, that is, by inference from things actually experienced. There are no other ways of proving the existence of a sense-object. Is either of them possible in the present case?

1. *Sense-perception.* I obviously cannot know by perception the existence of the paper when no one is experiencing it. For that would be self-contradictory. It would amount to asserting that I can experience the unexperienced.

2. *Inference.* Nor is it possible to prove by inference the existence of the paper when no mind is experiencing it. For how can I possibly pass by inference from the particular fact of the existence of the paper now, when I am experiencing it, to the quite different particular fact of the existence of the paper yesterday or to-morrow, when neither I nor any other mind is experiencing it?

Strictly speaking, the onus of proving that such an inference is impossible is not on me. The onus of proving that it is possible is upon anyone who asserts it, and I am entitled to sit back and wait until someone comes forward with such an alleged proof. Many realists who know their business admit that no valid inference from an experienced to an unexperienced existence is possible. Thus Mr. Russell says, 'Belief in the existence of things outside my own biography must, from the standpoint of theoretical logic, be regarded as a prejudice, not as a well-grounded theory.'[1]

I might therefore adopt the strategy of masterly inaction. But I prefer to carry the war into the enemy's camp. I propose to *prove* that no proof of the existence of unexperienced objects is possible.

It is clear in the first place that any supposed reasoning could not be inductive. Inductive reasoning proceeds always upon the basis that what has been found in certain observed cases to be true will also be true in unobserved cases. But there is no single case in which it has been observed to be true that an experienced object continues to exist when it is not being experienced; for, by hypothesis, its existence when it is not being experienced cannot be observed. Induction is generalisation from observed facts, but there is not a single case of an unexperienced existence having been observed on which could be based the generalisation that entities continue to exist when no one is experiencing them. And there is likewise not a single known instance of the existence of an unexperienced entity which could lead me to have even the slightest reason for supposing that this paper ever did exist, or will exist, when no one is experiencing it.

Since inductive reasoning is ruled out, the required inference, if there is to be an inference, must be of a formal nature. But deductive inference of all kinds depends upon the principle of con-

[1] *Analysis of Mind*, p. 133.

sistency. If P $\supset$ Q [P implies Q], then we can only prove Q, *if* P is admitted. From P $\supset$ Q, therefore, all that can be deduced is that P and not-Q are inconsistent, and that we cannot hold both P and not-Q together, though we may hold either of them separately.

Hence, if it is alleged that a deductive inference can be drawn from the existence of the paper now, when I am experiencing it, to its existence when no one is experiencing it, this can only mean that to assert together the two propositions, (1) that it exists now, and (2) that it does not exist when no one is experiencing it, is an internally inconsistent position. But there is absolutely no inconsistency between these two propositions. If I believe that nothing whatever exists or ever did or will exist, except my own personal sense-data, this may be a view of the universe which no one would ever hold, but there is absolutely nothing internally inconsistent in it. Therefore, no deductive inference can prove the existence of an unexperienced entity. Therefore, by no reasoning at all, inductive or deductive, can the existence of such an entity be proved.

Nevertheless, arguments have been put forward from time to time by realists which are apparently intended to prove this conclusion. I will deal shortly with those with which I am acquainted. I am not bound to do this, since I have already proved that no proof of the realists' conclusion is possible. And for the same reason, if there are any arguments of this kind with which I am not acquainted, I am under no obligation to disprove them. But it will be better to meet at least the most well-known arguments.

(*a*) It was Mr. Perry, I believe, who invented the phrase "egocentric predicament". The egocentric predicament was supposed to indicate where lay a fallacy committed by idealists. It consisted in arguing from the fact that it is impossible to discover anything which is not known to the conclusion that all things are known. That any competent idealist ever did use such an argument may well be doubted, but I will waive that point. Mr. Perry's comment was that the egocentric predicament, as employed by idealists, appeared to imply that from our ignorance of unexperienced entities we could conclude to their non-existence, and that to do so is a fallacy.

No doubt such a procedure would be a fallacy. But though Mr. Perry's argument may refute a supposed idealistic argument, *it does not prove anything whatever in favour of realism*. It would be a fallacy to argue that, because we have never observed a unicorn on Mars, therefore there is no unicorn there; but by pointing out this fallacy, one does not prove the existence of a unicorn there. And by pointing out that our ignorance of the existence of unexperienced entities does not prove their non-existence, one does nothing whatever towards proving that unexperienced entities do exist. As regards the unicorn on Mars, the correct position, as far as logic is concerned, is obviously that if anyone asserts that there is a unicorn there, the onus is on him to prove it; and that until he does prove it, we ought not to believe it to be true. As regards the unexperienced entities, the correct position, as far as logic is concerned, is that if realists assert their existence, the onus is on them to prove it; and that until they do prove it, we ought not to believe that they exist. Mr. Perry's argument, therefore, proves nothing whatever in favour of realism.

Possibly all this is admitted and understood by realists. But there seems, nevertheless, to have been a tendency to think that the overthrow of the supposed idealistic argument was a very important matter in forwarding the interests of realism. To point out, therefore, that it actually accomplishes nothing seems desirable.

(*b*) Mr. Lovejoy, in his recent book, *The Revolt Against Dualism*, argues that we can infer, or at least render probable, the existence of things during interperceptual intervals by means of the law of causation. He writes, "The same uniform causal sequences of natural events which may be observed within experience appear to go on in the same manner when not experienced. You build a fire in your grate of a certain quantity of coal, of a certain chemical composition. Whenever you remain in the room there occurs a typical succession of sensible phenomena according to an approximately regular schedule of clock-time; in, say, half an hour the coal is half consumed; at the end of the hour the grate contains only ashes. If you build a fire of the same quantity of the same material under the same conditions, leave the room, and return after any given time has elapsed, you get approximately the same sense-experiences as you would have had at the corresponding moment if you had remained in the room. You infer, therefore, that the fire has been burning as usual during your absence, and that being perceived is not a condition necessary for the occurrence of the process."[1]

This argument is simply a *petitio principii*. It assumes that we must believe that the law of causality continues to operate in the universe when no one is observing it. But the law of causality is one aspect of the universe, the unobserved existence of which is the very thing to be proved.

Why must we believe that causation continues to operate during interperceptual intervals? Obviously, the case as regards unexperienced processes and laws is in exactly the same position as the case regarding unexperienced *things*. Just as we cannot perceive unexperienced things, so we cannot perceive unexperienced processes and laws. Just as we cannot infer from anything which we experience the existence of unexperienced things so we cannot infer from anything we experience the existence of unexperienced processes and laws. There is absolutely no evidence (sense-experience) to show that the fire went on burning during your absence, nor is any

[1] *The Revolt against Dualism*, p. 268.

inference to that alleged fact possible. Any supposed inference will obviously be based upon our belief that the law of causation operates continuously through time whether observed or unobserved. But this is one of the very things which has to be proved. Nor is there the slightest logical inconsistency in believing that, when you first observe the phenomena, unburnt coal existed, that there followed an interval in which nothing existed, not even a law, and that at the end of the interval ashes began to exist.

No doubt this sounds very absurd and contrary to what we usually believe, but that is nothing to the point. We usually believe that things go on existing when no one is aware of them. But if we are enquiring how this can be *proved*, we must, of course, begin from the position that we do not know it, and therefore that it might not be true.

(*c*) The distinction between sense-data and our awareness of them, which was first emphasised, so far as I know, by Prof. Moore, has been made the basis of an argument in favour of realism. Green, it said, is not the same thing as awareness of green. For if we compare a green sense-datum with a blue sense-datum, we find a common element, namely awareness. The awareness must be different from the green because awareness also exists in the case of awareness of blue, and *that* awareness, at any rate, is not green. Therefore, since green is not the same thing as awareness of green, green might exist without awareness. Connected with this argument, too, is the assertion of a special kind of relationship between the awareness and the green.

Possibly this argument proves that green is not "mental" I do not know whether it proves this or not, but the point is unimportant, since I have already admitted that sense-data are not "mental". But whatever the argument proves, it certainly does *not* prove that unexperienced entities exist. For suppose that it proves that green has the predicate *x* (which may be "non-mental" or "independent of mind", or anything else

you please), it still can only prove that green has the predicate *x* during the period when green is related to the awareness in the alleged manner, that is, when some mind is aware of the green. It cannot possibly prove anything about green when no mind is aware of it. Therefore, it cannot prove that green exists when no mind is aware of it.

For the sake of clearness, I will put the same point in another way. Suppose we admit that green and awareness of green are two quite different things, and suppose we admit that the relation between them is *r*—which may stand for the special relation asserted in the argument. Now it is not in any way inconsistent with these admissions to hold that green begins to exist only when awareness of green begins to exist, and that when awareness of green ceases to exist, green ceases to exist. It may be the case that these two quite different things always co-exist, always accompany each other, and are co-terminous in the sense that they always begin and end simultaneously, and that while they co-exist, they have the relation *r*. And this will be so *whatever* the relation *r* may be. And not only is this supposition that they always co-exist not at all absurd or arbitrary. It is on the contrary precisely the conclusion to which such evidence as we possess points. For we never have evidence that green exists except when some mind is aware of green. And it will not be asserted that awareness of green exists when green does not exist.

The argument from the distinction between green and the awareness of it, therefore, does nothing whatever towards proving the realist conclusion that some entities exist unexperienced.

(*d*) It has also been argued that if we identify a green or a square sense-datum with our awareness of it, then, since awareness is admittedly a state of mind, we shall have to admit that there exist green and square states of mind.

This argument is merely intended to support the previous argument that a sense-datum is different from our awareness of it. And as it has already been shown that this proposition, even if admitted, proves nothing in favour of realism, it is not necessary to say anything further about the present argument.

I will, however, add the following. It is not by any means certain, as is here assumed, that awareness is a state of mind, or indeed that such a thing as a *state* of mind exists. For the mind is not static. It is active. And what exists in it are *acts* of mind. Now the *attention* involved in being aware of a sense-datum is certainly an act of mind. But it is certainly arguable that *bare* awareness of a sense-datum (if there is such a thing as *bare* awareness) would be identical with the sense-datum and would not be an act of mind. For such bare awareness would be purely passive. In that case, the conclusion that there must exist green or square states of mind would not follow.

Moreover, even if we admit that there exist green and square states of mind, what then? I can see no reason why we should not admit it, except that (1) it is an unusual and unexplored view, and (2) it seems to smack of materialism, although I do not believe that it does really involve materialism. This shows that the whole argument is not really a logical argument at all. It is merely an attempt to throw dust in our eyes by appealing to the popular prejudices against (1) unfamiliar views, and (2) materialism.

It is not possible in the brief space at my disposal to make plausible the suggestions contained in the last two paragraphs. A full discussion of them would be necessary and this I have endeavoured to give elsewhere. In the present place, therefore, I must rely upon the strict logical position, which is, that this argument, since it is merely intended to support argument (*c*) above, and since argument (*c*) has already been refuted, proves nothing in favour of realism.

By the preceding discussion, I claim to have proved (1) that the existence of an unexperienced entity cannot be known by perception, (2) that it cannot be known by reasoning, and (3) that the arguments commonly relied upon by realists to prove it are all fallacies.

I think it is not worth while to discuss the possible suggestion that the arguments in favour of realism, although not proving their conclusion rigorously, render that conclusion probable. For what has been shown is that no valid reasoning of *any* kind can possibly exist in favour of this conclusion. Any conceivable reasoning intended to prove that unexperienced entities exist must, it has been shown, be *totally* fallacious. It cannot, therefore, lead even to a probable conclusion. The position, therefore, is that we have not even the faintest reason for believing in the existence of unexperienced entities.

That this is the correct logical position seems to be dimly perceived by many realists themselves, for it is common among them to assert that our belief in unexperienced existences is a "primitive belief", or is founded upon "instinctive belief", or upon "animal faith". This suggestion is obviously based upon the realisation that we cannot obtain a knowledge of unexperienced existences either from perception or from reasoning. Since this is so, realists are compelled to appeal to instinctive beliefs.

Such a weak position seems hardly to require discussion. A "primitive belief" is merely a belief which we have held for a long time, and may well be false. An "instinctive belief" is in much the same case. An "instinct", so far as I know, is some kind of urge to *action*, not an urge to believe a proposition. And it is therefore questionable whether there are such things as instinctive beliefs in any strict sense, although, of course, no one will deny that we have beliefs the grounds of which are only dimly, or not at all, perceived. Certainly the psychology of such alleged instinctive beliefs has not been adequately investigated. And certainly we have no good ground for supposing that an instinctive belief (if any such exists) might not be false.

And if we have such an instinctive or primitive belief in unexperienced existences, the question must obviously be asked How, When, and Why such a belief arose in the course of our mental evolution. Will it be alleged that the amoeba has this belief? And if not, why and when did it come into existence? Or did it at some arbitrarily determined stage in our evolution descend suddenly upon us out of the blue sky, like the immortal soul itself?

Is it not obvious that to base our belief in unexperienced existences on such grounds is a mere gesture of despair, an admission of the bankruptcy of realism in its attempt to find a rational ground for our beliefs?

Strictly speaking, I have here come to the end of my argument. I have refuted realism by showing that we have absolutely no good reason for believing in its fundamental proposition that entities exist unexperienced. Nothing I have said, of course, goes any distance towards proving that entities do *not* exist unexperienced. That, in my opinion, cannot be proved. The logically correct position is as follows. We have no reason whatever to believe that unexperienced entities exist. We cannot prove that they do not exist. The onus of proof is on those who assert that they do. Therefore, as such proof is impossible, the belief ought not to be entertained, any more than the belief that there is a unicorn on Mars ought to be entertained.

It is no part of the purpose of this essay to do more than arrive at this negative result. But lest it should be thought that this thinking necessarily leads to nothing but a negative result, or to a pure scepticism, I will indicate in no more than a dozen sentences that there is is the possibility of a positive and constructive philosophy arising from it. That positive philosophy I have attempted to work out in detail in another place. Here, I will say no more than the following. Since our belief in unexperienced existences is not to be explained as either (1) a perception, or (2) an inference, or (3) an "instinctive belief", how is it to be explained? I believe that it can only be explained as a mental construction or fiction, a pure assumption which has been adopted, not because there is the slightest evidence for it, but solely because it simplifies our view of the universe. How it simplifies our view of the universe, and by what detailed steps it has arisen, I cannot discuss in this place. But the resulting conception is that, in the last analysis, nothing exists except minds and their sense-data (which are not "mental"), and that human minds have, out of these sense-data, slowly and laboriously constructed the rest of the solid universe of our knowledge. Unexperienced entities can only be said to exist in the sense that minds have chosen by means of a fiction to project them into the void of interperceptual intervals, and thus to construct or create their existence in imagination.

Do Our
Sensory Experiences
Resemble
Their Causes?

J *ohn Locke* offered an analysis of perceptual knowledge (that is, knowledge derived from sensory experience) that included the following claims: (1) all that we are immediately aware of are our own sensory and introspective experiences which are not themselves physical objects; (2) these experiences are divisible into two kinds: those that come to us through more than one sense (for example motion, which can be both seen and felt) and those that come to us through one sense alone (for example, color, which can only be seen); (3) experiences that comes to us through more than one sense are (or are experiences of) primary qualities, and those which come to us through one sense only are (or are experiences of) secondary qualities; (4) these experiences (where veridical) are caused by physical objects which they resemble; (5) all our knowledge of physical objects must be *inferred* from these experiences; (6) when an object causes experience in us of a primary quality, it *has* that quality whereas if an object causes experience in us of a secondary quality it only has the capacity to cause that experience in us; it does not *have* the quality in question. There are only a few primary qualities—extension, figure, rest, motion, number, and solidity. (Solidity would seem, however, to be knowable only by touch.)

Physical objects can rightly, in Locke's view, be asserted to have the primary qualities they are experienced as having. (This holds, of course, only when our experiences are not delusory, hallucinatory, or otherwise mistaken—a matter to be decided mainly by the degree to which a given experience coheres with other experiences). Physical objects cannot, however, be said to have the secondary qualities (colors, sounds, tastes, and so on) we experience them as having. Primary qualities actually belong to objects and secondary qualities are only the powers in the objects to produce secondary-quality sensations within us. When one experience fits into a coherent pattern with our other experiences, it is veridical, and the objects really have the primary qualities they appear to have.

Berkeley raises a simple but powerful objection to Locke's view. We are, according to Locke, immediately aware only of our own ideas or experiences. We *infer* the existence of objects and we *infer* that the objects have the properties we take them to have. Berkeley's arguments concerning the inference from ideas to objects are not our present concern; they are discussed in our previous section. Our concern is only with the inference from ideas or experiences to the properties that objects putatively possess. For Locke, if I know that "I experience object O as having primary quality Q" is true, I am entitled (on condition that my experience is not delusory or hallucinatory) to infer that "O has Q" is true, but on what grounds? I can recognize a picture of a friend because I have seen the friend and recognize that the picture resembles him. I can compare the picture and the friend. Now for Locke primary-quality experiences are like pictures of physical objects. But I am never immediately aware of objects; I only have "pictures" of them. But how can I then know that the pictures (the primary-quality experiences) properly represent the pictured (the objects)? Here, I must remain skeptical if I am consistent and if I grant Locke's premises. But the very point of Locke's account was to provide an escape from skepticism—to provide a correct theory that made perceptual knowledge possible. Hence this account is a failure.

There is, however, a passage in Berkeley (our second Berkeley selection) that obliquely suggests a way of saving something not completely unlike Locke's view. For Berkeley, there is no quality that an area which is square to the touch shares with an area which is square to the sight. We describe both by the word "square," in Berkeley's view, neither arbitrarily nor in virtue of a shared common quality, but because the relation of the tactual parts to one another is the same as, or is analogous to, the relation of the visible parts to one another. The multiplicity of the one corresponds to that of the other, that is, each is isomorphic with the other. A consequence of this account of visual shape as compared to tactual shape is that both sorts of shape are relational. To say that x is visually round is to say that the parts of x are related in a certain way; to say that y is tactually round is to say something similar about y. Finally, the justification of using "round" depends on the similarity of arrangement of their respective parts. (Berkeley would not have put it this way because he held the view that relations are mental activities or results of mental activities but this qualification is not important here.)

In this view the primary qualities are relational in character, whereas secondary qualities are not. To say of some entity x that it is red, or sour, or rough, or high-pitched is to ascribe a nonrelational property to x (though it may *also* be to place x in relation to other things). But, in the view being discussed, to say of x that x is in motion, has a specific shape, is numerable in a certain way, or has any other primary quality is to ascribe a given sort of relational property to x; that is, to say that one part of x is related to another part in a certain manner.

Now, if we consider the kind of resemblance a tactual square and a visual square possess on Berkeley's account, we have a new possibility for interpreting the thesis that a cause always resembles its effect. Instead of taking this to mean that for every nonrelational property the effect has, the cause must have had this property, we can say that for every relational property that holds between the parts of the effect there is an isomorphic relation which holds between the parts of the cause. Ignoring the still further complication that arises when we consider whether anything simple (in the sense of not having parts) can be either a cause or an effect, we note two things about the claim that every effect must be isomorphic with its cause. First, if it is false it is harder to refute than the former reading of the kind of resemblance that supposedly holds between cause and effect. Second, to know that a cause and an effect resemble one another in this manner is to know rather less about them than to know of them that they share a common property with which we are acquainted.

This second point can be clarified and reinforced as follows. Suppose we accept the view that the world we know by our senses is more accurately known by the physicist as physicist than by the physicist as ordinary perceiver. The description of my chair as a mass of particles whose movements are statistically describable and predictable will then be more accurate than the description I would give of it to someone who had never seen it and wanted an idea of what it was like, although both descriptions are in some sense concerned with the same object. (Otherwise one can hardly be more accurate than the other.) Thinking along these lines, we then hold that the secondary qualities that we perceive objects as possessing are really only due to perceiving them and do not belong to the objects in their own right. These secondary qualities will, in Locke's words, be "powers in objects to cause sensations in us." Whatever is actually "in an object" will at best be isomorphic with some aspect of the experience we have of that object.

Because of this, I am never acquainted as such with objects. I can know only their relational, structural features, and that only by inference from the data of observation. Now if I can know of an object O *only* that its parts bear some specified relation R to one another, then for all I know the elements of which O is composed may be anything whatever that can stand in the relation R. If I know only that the parts of O stand in relation R to one another, any relata that can stand in R to one another are fully viable candidates for being O's components. Berkeley's idealism and Locke's realism, plus hosts of other views, can incorporate the thesis that cause must resemble effect, and there is at least no a priori reason to suppose that Berkeleyian ideas may not serve as relata in any relation in which Locke's material substances with accidents can serve. If this is correct, then even the revamped version of the thesis that effect must resemble cause also leads to something very like skepticism concerning the world which is "known" by sensory observation.

Our Sensory Experiences Resemble Their Causes
JOHN LOCKE

To discover the nature of our *ideas* the better, and to discourse of them intelligibly, it will be convenient to distinguish them *as they are ideas or perceptions in our minds; and as they are modifications of matter in the bodies that cause such perceptions in us*: that so we may not think (as perhaps usually is done) that they are exactly the images and resemblances of something inherent in the subject; most of those of sensation being in the mind no more the likeness of something existing without us, than the names that stand for them are the likeness of our ideas, which yet upon hearing they are apt to excite in us.

Whatsoever the mind perceives *in itself*, or is the immediate object of perception, thought, or understanding, that I call *idea*; and the power to produce any idea in our mind, I call *quality* of the subject wherein that power is. Thus a snowball having the power to produce in us the ideas of white, cold, and round, —the power to produce those ideas in us, as they are in the snowball, I call qualities; and as they are sensations or perceptions in our understandings, I call them ideas; which *ideas*, if I speak of sometimes as in the things themselves, I would be understood to mean those qualities in the objects which produce them in us.

[Qualities thus considered in bodies are,

First, such as are utterly inseparable from the body, in what state soever it be;] and such as in all the alterations and changes it suffers, all the force can be used upon it, it constantly keeps; and such as sense constantly finds in every particle of matter which has bulk enough to be perceived; and the mind finds inseparable from every particle of matter, though less than to make itself singly be perceived by our senses: e.g. Take a grain of wheat, divide it into two parts; each part has still solidity, extension, figure, and mobility: divide it again, and it retains still the same qualities; and so divide it on, till the parts become insensible; they must retain still each of them all those qualities. For division (which is all that a mill, or pestle, or any other body, does upon another, in reducing it to insensible parts) can never take away either solidity, extension, figure, or mobility from any body, but only makes two or more distinct separate masses of matter, of that which was but one before; all which distinct masses, reckoned as so many distinct bodies, after division, make a certain number. [These I call *original* or *primary qualities* of body, which I think we may observe to produce simple ideas in us, viz. solidity, extension, figure, motion or rest, and number.

Secondly, such qualities which in truth are nothing in the objects themselves but powers to produce various sensations in us by their primary quali-

FROM *An Essay Concerning Human Understanding*, John Locke. Book II, Ch. 8, Sections 7–26 (originally published in 1690).

ties, i.e. by the bulk, figure, texture, and motion of their insensible parts, as colours, sounds, tastes, &c. These I call *secondary qualities*. To these might be added a *third* sort, which are allowed to be barely powers; though they are as much real qualities in the subject as those which I, to comply with the common way of speaking, call qualities, but for distinction, secondary qualities. For the power in fire to produce a new colour, or consistency, in *wax* or *clay*,—by its primary qualities, is as much a quality in fire, as the power it has to produce in *me* a new idea or sensation of warmth or burning, which I felt not before,—by the same primary qualities, viz. the bulk, texture, and motion of its insensible parts.]

[The next thing to be considered is, how bodies produce ideas in us; and that is manifestly by impulse, the only way which we can conceive bodies to operate in.]

If then external objects be not united to our minds when they produce ideas therein; and yet we perceive these *original* qualities in such of them as singly fall under our senses, it is evident that some motion must be thence continued by our nerves, or animal spirits, by some parts of our bodies, to the brains or the seat of sensation, there to produce in our minds the particular ideas we have of them. And since the extension, figure, number, and motion of bodies of an observable bigness, may be perceived at a distance by the sight, it is evident some singly imperceptible bodies must come from them to the eyes, and thereby convey to the brain some motion; which produces these ideas which we have of them in us.

After the same manner that the ideas of these original qualities are produced in us, we may conceive that the ideas of *secondary* qualities are also produced, viz. by the operation of insensible particles on our senses. For, it being manifest that there are bodies and good store of bodies, each whereof are so small, that we cannot by any of our senses discover either their bulk, figure,

or motions,—as is evident in the particles of the air and water, and others extremely smaller than those; perhaps as much smaller than the particles of air and water, as the particles of air and water are smaller than peas or hailstones;—let us suppose at present that the different motions and figures, bulk and number, of such particles, affecting the several organs of our senses, produce in us those different sensations which we have from the colours and smells of bodies; e.g. that a violet, by the impulse of such insensible particles of matter, of peculiar figures and bulks, and in different degrees and modifications of their motions, causes the ideas of the blue colour, and sweet scent of that flower to be produced in our minds. It being no more impossible to conceive that God should annex such ideas to such motions, with which they have no similitude, than that he should annex the idea of pain to the motion of a piece of steel dividing our flesh, with which that idea hath no resemblance.

What I have said concerning colours and smells may be understood also of tastes and sounds, and other the like sensible qualities; which, whatever reality we by mistake attribute to them, are in truth nothing in the objects themselves, but powers to produce various sensations in us; and depend on those primary qualities, viz. bulk, figure, texture, and motion of parts [as I have said].

From whence I think it easy to draw this observation,—that the ideas of primary qualities of bodies are resemblances of them, and their patterns do really exist in the bodies themselves, but the ideas produced in us by these secondary qualities have no resemblance of them at all. There is nothing like our ideas, existing in the bodies themselves. They are, in the bodies we denominate from them, only a power to produce those sensations in us: and what is sweet, blue, or warm in idea, is but the certain bulk, figure, and motion of the insensible parts, in the bodies themselves, which we call so.

Flame is denominated hot and light; snow, white and cold; and manna, white and sweet, from the ideas they produce in us. Which qualities are commonly thought to be the same in those bodies that those ideas are in us, the one the perfect resemblance of the other, as they are in a mirror, and it would by most men be judged very extravagant if one should say otherwise. And yet he that will consider that the same fire that, at one distance produces in us the sensation of warmth, does, at a nearer approach, produce in us the far different sensation of pain, ought to bethink himself what reason he has to say—that this idea of warmth, which was produced in him by the fire, is *actually in the fire*; and his idea of pain, which the same fire produced in him the same way, is *not* in the fire. Why are whiteness and coldness in snow, and pain not, when it produces the one and the other idea in us; and can do neither, but by the bulk, figure, number, and motion of its solid parts?

The particular bulk, number, figure, and motion of the parts of fire or snow are really in them,—whether any one's senses perceive them or no: and therefore they may be called *real* qualities, because they really exist in those bodies. But light, heat, whiteness, or coldness, are no more really in them than sickness or pain is in manna. Take away the sensation of them; let not the eyes see light or colours, nor the ears hear sounds; let the palate not taste, nor the nose smell, and all colours, tastes, odours, and sounds, *as they are such particular ideas*, vanish and cease, and are reduced to their causes, i.e. bulk, figure, and motion of parts.

A piece of manna of a sensible bulk is able to produce in us the idea of a round or square figure; and by being removed from one place to another, the idea of motion. This idea of motion represents it as it really is in manna moving: a circle or square are the same, whether in idea or existence, in the mind or in the manna. And this, both motion and figure, are really in the manna, whether we take notice of them or no: this everybody is ready to agree to. Besides, manna, by the bulk, figure, texture, and motion of its parts, has a power to produce the sensations of sickness, and sometimes of acute pains or gripings in us. That these ideas of sickness and pain are *not* in the manna, but effects of its operations on us, and are nowhere when we feel them not; this also every one readily agrees to. And yet men are hardly to be brought to think that sweetness and whiteness are not really in manna; which are but the effects of the operations of manna, by the motion, size, and figure of its particles, on the eyes and palate: as the pain and sickness caused by manna are confessedly nothing but the effects of its operations on the stomach and guts, by the size, motion, and figure of its insensible parts, (for by nothing else can a body operate, as has been proved): as if it could not operate on the eyes and palate, and thereby produce in the mind particular distinct ideas, which in itself it has not, as well as we allow it can operate on the guts and stomach, and thereby produce distinct ideas, which in itself it has not. These ideas, being all effects of the operations of manna on several parts of our bodies, by the size, figure, number, and motion of its parts;— why those produced by the eyes and palate should rather be thought to be really in the manna, than those produced by the stomach and guts; or why the pain and sickness, ideas that are the effect of manna, should be thought to be nowhere when they are not felt; and yet the sweetness and whiteness, effects of the same manna on other parts of the body, by ways equally as unknown, should be thought to exist in the manna, when they are not seen or tasted, would need some reason to explain.

Let us consider the red and white colours in porphyry. Hinder light from striking on it, and its colours vanish; it no longer produces any such ideas in us: upon the return of light it produces these appearances on us again. Can any one think any real alterations are made in the porphyry by the presence or absence of light; and that those ideas of whiteness and redness are really in porphyry in the light when it is plain *it has no colour in the dark*? It has, indeed, such a configuration of particles, both night and day, as are apt, by the rays of light rebounding from some parts of that hard stone, to produce in us the idea of redness, and from others the idea of whiteness; but whiteness or redness are not in it at any time, but such a texture that hath the power to produce such a sensation in us.

Pound an almond, and the clear white colour will be altered into a dirty one, and the sweet taste into an oily one. What real alteration can the beating of the pestle make in any body, but an alteration of the texture of it?

Ideas being thus distinguished and understood, we may be able to give an account how the same water, at the same time, may produce the idea of cold by one hand and of heat by the other: whereas it is impossible that the same water, if those ideas were really in it, should at the same time be both hot and cold. For, if we imagine *warmth*, as it is in our hands, to be nothing but a certain sort and degree of motion in the minute particles of our nerves or animal spirits, we may understand how it is possible that the same water may, at the same time, produce the sensations of heat in one hand and cold in the other; which yet *figure* never does, that never producing the idea of a square by one hand which has produced the idea of a globe by another. But if the sensation of heat and cold be nothing but the increase or diminution of the motion of the minute parts of our bodies, caused by the corpuscles of any other body, it is easy to be understood, that if that motion be greater in one hand than in the other; if a body be applied to the two hands, which has in its minute particles a greater motion than in those of one of the hands, and a less than in those of the other, it will increase the motion of the one hand and lessen it in the other; and so cause the different sensations of heat and cold that depend thereon.

I have in what just goes before been engaged in physical inquiries a little further than perhaps I intended. But, it being necessary to make the nature of sensation a little understood; and to make the difference between the *qualities* in bodies, and the *ideas* produced by them in the mind, to be distinctly conceived, without which it were impossible to discourse intelligibly of them;—I hope I shall be pardoned this little excursion into natural philosophy; it being necessary in our present inquiry to distinguish the *primary* and *real* qualities of bodies, which are always in them (viz. solidity, extension, figure, number, and motion, or rest, and are sometimes perceived by us, viz. when the bodies they are in are big enough singly to be discerned), from those *secondary* and *imputed* qualities, which are but the powers of several combinations of those primary ones, when they operate without being distinctly discerned;—whereby we may also come to know what ideas are, and what are not, resemblances of something really existing in the bodies we denominate from them.

The qualities, then, that are in bodies, rightly considered, are of three sorts:—

First, The bulk, figure, number, situation, and motion or rest of their solid parts. Those are in them, whether we perceive them or not; and when they are of that size that we can discover them, we have by these an idea of the thing as it is in itself; as is plain in artificial things. These I call *primary qualities.*

Secondly, The power that is in any body, by reason of its insensible primary qualities, to operate after a peculiar manner on any of our senses, and thereby produce in *us* the different ideas of several colours, sounds, smells, tastes, &c. These are usually called *sensible qualities.*

Thirdly, The power that is in any body, by reason of the particular constitution of its primary qualities, to make such a change in the bulk, figure, texture, and motion of *another body*, as to make it operate on our senses differently from what it did before. Thus the sun has a power to make wax white, and fire to make lead fluid. [These are usually called *powers.*]

The first of these, as has been said, I think may be properly called real, original, or primary qualities; because they are in the things themselves, whether they are perceived or not: and upon their different modifications it is that the secondary qualities depend.

The other two are only powers to act differently upon other things: which powers result from the different modifications of those primary qualities.

But, though the two latter sorts of qualities are powers barely, and nothing but powers, relating to several other bodies, and resulting from the different modifications of the original qualities, yet they are generally otherwise thought of. For the *second* sort, viz. the powers to produce several ideas in us, by our senses, are looked upon as real qualities in the things thus affecting us: but the *third* sort are called and esteemed barely powers. e.g. The idea of heat or light, which we receive by our eyes, or touch, from the sun, are commonly thought real qualities existing in the sun, and something more than mere powers in it. But when we consider the sun in reference to wax, which it melts or blanches, we look on the whiteness and softness produced in the wax, not as qualities in the sun, but effects produced by powers in it. Whereas, if rightly considered, these qualities of light and warmth, which are perceptions in me when I am warmed or enlightened by the sun, are no otherwise in the sun, than the changes made in the wax, when it is blanched or melted, are in the sun. They are all of them equally *powers in the sun, depending on its primary qualities*; whereby it is able, in the one case, so to alter the bulk, figure, texture, or motion of some of the insensible parts of my eyes or hands, as thereby to produce in me the idea of light or heat; and in the other,

it is able so to alter the bulk, figure, texture, or motion of the insensible parts of the wax, as to make them fit to produce in me the distinct ideas of white and fluid.

The reason why the one are ordinarily taken for real qualities, and the other only for bare powers, seems to be, because the ideas we have of distinct colours, sounds, &c., containing nothing at all in them of bulk, figure, or motion, we are not apt to think them the effects of these primary qualities; which appear not, to our senses, to operate in their production, and with which they have not any apparent congruity or conceivable connexion. Hence it is that we are so forward to imagine, that those ideas are the resemblances of something really existing in the objects themselves: since sensation discovers nothing of bulk, figure, or motion of parts in their production; nor can reason show how bodies, *by their bulk, figure, and motion*, should produce in the mind the ideas of blue or yellow, &c. But in the other case, in the operations of bodies changing the qualities one of another, we plainly discover that the quality produced hath commonly no resemblance with anything in the thing producing it; wherefore we look on it as a bare effect of power. For, through receiving the idea of heat or light from the sun, we are apt to think *it* is a perception and resemblance of such a quality in the sun; yet when we see wax, or a fair face, receive change of colour from the sun, we cannot imagine *that* to be the reception or resemblance of anything in the sun, because we find not those different colours in the sun itself. For, our senses being able to observe a likeness or unlikeness of sensible qualities in two different external objects, we forwardly enough conclude the production of any sensible quality in any subject to be an effect of bare power, and not the communication of any quality which was really in the efficient, when we find no such sensible quality in the thing that produced it. But our senses, not being able to discover any unlikeness between the idea produced in us, and the quality of the object producing it, we are apt to imagine that our ideas are resemblances of something in the objects, and not the effects of certain powers placed in the modification of their primary qualities, with which primary qualities the ideas produced in us have no resemblance.

To conclude. Beside those before-mentioned primary qualities in bodies, viz. bulk, figure, extension, number, and motion of their solid parts; all the rest, whereby we take notice of bodies, and distinguish them one from another, are nothing else but several powers in them, depending on those primary qualities; whereby they are fitted, either by immediately operating on our bodies to produce several different ideas in us; or else, by operating on other bodies, so to change their primary qualities as to render them capable of producing ideas in us different from what before they did. The former of these, I think, may be called secondary qualities *immediately perceivable*: the latter, secondary qualities, *mediately perceivable*.

We Cannot Know That Our Sensory Experiences Resemble Their Causes
GEORGE BERKELEY

HYL. To speak the truth, Philonous, I think there are two kinds of objects: the one perceived immediately, which are likewise called "ideas"; the other are real things or external objects, perceived by the mediation of ideas which are their images and representations. Now I own ideas do not exist without the mind, but the latter sort of objects do. I am sorry I did not think of this distinction sooner; it would probably have cut short your discourse.

PHIL. Are those external objects perceived by sense or by some other faculty?

HYL. They are perceived by sense.

PHIL. How! is there anything perceived by sense which is not immediately perceived?

HYL. Yes, Philonous, in some sort there is. For example, when I look on a picture or statue of Julius Caesar, I may be said, after a manner, to perceive him (though not immediately) by my senses.

PHIL. It seems then you will have our ideas, which alone are immediately perceived, to be pictures of external things: and that these also are perceived by sense inasmuch as they have a conformity or resemblance to our ideas?

HYL. That is my meaning.

PHIL. And in the same way that Julius Caesar, in himself invisible, is nevertheless perceived by sight, real things, in themselves inperceptible, are perceived by sense.

HYL. In the very same.

PHIL. Tell me, Hylas, when you behold the picture of Julius Caesar, do you see with your eyes any more than some colors and figures, with a certain symmetry and composition of the whole?

HYL. Nothing else.

PHIL. And would not a man who had never known anything of Julius Caesar see as much?

HYL. He would.

PHIL. Consequently, he has his sight and the use of it in as perfect a degree as you?

HYL. I agree with you.

PHIL. Whence comes it then that your thoughts are directed to the Roman emperor, and his are not? This cannot proceed from the sensations or ideas of sense by you then perceived, since you

FROM *Three Dialogues Between Hylas and Philonous*, George Berkeley. From Dialogue One (originally published in 1713).

acknowledge you have no advantage over him in that respect. It should seem therefore to proceed from reason and memory, should it not?

HYL. It should.

PHIL. Consequently, it will not follow from that instance that anything is perceived by sense which is not immediately perceived. Though I grant we may, in one acceptation, be said to perceive sensible things mediately by sense—that is, when, from a frequently perceived connection, the immediate perception of ideas by one sense suggests to the mind others, perhaps belonging to another sense, which are wont to be connected with them. For instance, when I hear a coach drive along the streets, immediately I perceive only the sound; but from the experience I have had that such a sound is connected with a coach, I am said to hear the coach. It is nevertheless evident that, in truth and strictness, nothing can be *heard* but *sound*; and the coach is not then properly perceived by sense, but suggested from experience. So likewise when we are said to see a red-hot bar of iron; the solidity and heat of the iron are not the objects of sight, but suggested to the imagination by the color and figure which are properly perceived by that sense. In short, those things alone are actually and strictly perceived by any sense which would have been perceived in case that same sense had then been first conferred on us. As for other things, it is plain they are only suggested to the mind by experience grounded on former perceptions. But, to return to your comparison of Caesar's picture, it is plain, if you keep to that, you must hold the real things or archetypes of our ideas are not perceived by sense, but by some internal faculty of the soul, as reason or memory. I would, therefore, fain know what arguments you can draw from reason for the existence of what you call "real things" or "material objects," or whether you remember to have seen them formerly as they are in themselves, or if you have heard or read of anyone that did.

HYL. I see, Philonous, you are disposed to raillery; but that will never convince me.

PHIL. My aim is only to learn from you the way to come at the knowledge of *material beings*. Whatever we perceive is perceived either immediately or mediately—by sense, or by reason and reflection. But, as you have excluded sense, pray show me what reason you have to believe their existence, or what *medium* you can possibly make use of to prove it, either to mine or your own understanding.

HYL. To deal ingenuously, Philonous, now I consider the point, I do not find I can give you any good reason for it. But this much seems pretty plain, that it is at least possible such things may really exist. And as long as there is no absurdity in supposing them, I am resolved to believe as I did, till you bring good reasons to the contrary.

PHIL. What! is it come to this, that you only believe the existence of material objects, and that your belief is founded barely on the possibility of its being true? Then you will have me bring reasons against it, though another would think it reasonable the proof should lie on him who holds the affirmative. And, after all, this very point which you are now resolved to maintain, without any reason, is in effect what you have more than once during this discourse seen good reason to give up. But to pass over all this—if I understand you rightly, you say our ideas do not exist without the mind, but that they are copies, images, or representations of certain originals that do?

HYL. You take me right.

PHIL. They are then like external things?

HYL. They are.

PHIL. Have those things a stable and permanent nature, independent of our senses, or are they in a perpetual change, upon our producing any motions in our bodies, suspending, exerting, or altering our faculties or organs of sense?

HYL. Real things, it is plain, have a fixed and real nature, which remains the same notwithstanding any change in our senses or in the posture and motion of our bodies; which indeed may affect the ideas in our minds, but it were absurd to think they had the same effect on things existing without the mind.

PHIL. How then is it possible that things perpetually fleeting and variable as our ideas should be copies or images of anything fixed and constant? Or, in other words, since all sensible qualities, as size, figure, color, etc., that is, our ideas, are continually changing upon every alteration in the distance, medium, or instruments of sensation—how can any determinate material objects be properly represented or painted forth by several distinct things each of which is so different from and unlike the rest? Or, if you say it resembles some one only of our ideas, how shall we be able to distinguish the true copy from all the false ones?

HYL. I profess, Philonous, I am at a loss. I know not what to say to this.

PHIL. But neither is this all. Which are material objects in themselves—perceptible or imperceptible?

HYL. Properly and immediately nothing can be perceived but ideas. All material things, therefore, are in themselves insensible and to be perceived only by their ideas.

PHIL. Ideas then are sensible, and their archetypes or originals insensible?

HYL. Right.

PHIL. But how can that which is sensible be like that which is insensible? Can a real thing, in itself *invisible*, be like a *color*, or a real thing which is not *audible* be like a *sound?* In a word, can anything be like a sensation or idea, but another sensation or idea?

HYL. I must own, I think not.

PHIL. Is it possible there should be any doubt on the point? Do you not perfectly know your own ideas?

HYL. I know them perfectly, since what I do not perceive or know can be no part of my idea.

PHIL. Consider, therefore, and examine them, and then tell me if there be anything in them which can exist without the mind, or if you can conceive anything like them existing without the mind?

HYL. Upon inquiry I find it is impossible for me to conceive or understand how anything but an idea can be like an idea. And it is most evident that *no idea can exist without the mind.*

PHIL. You are, therefore, by your principles forced to deny the reality of sensible things, since you made it to consist in an absolute existence exterior to the mind. That is to say, you are a downright skeptic. So I have gained my point, which was to show your principles led to skepticism.

HYL. For the present I am, if not entirely convinced, at least silenced.

PHIL. I would fain know what more you would require in order to a perfect conviction. Have you not had the liberty of explaining yourself all manner of ways? Were any little slips in discourse laid hold and insisted on? Or were you not allowed to retract or reinforce anything you had offered, as best served your purpose? Has not everything you could say been heard and examined with all the fairness imaginable? In a word, have you not in every point been convinced out of your own mouth? And, if you can at present discover any flaw in any of your former concessions, or think of any remaining subterfuge, any new distinction, color, or comment whatsoever, why do you not produce it?

HYL. A little patience, Philonous. I am at present so amazed to see myself ensnared, and as it were imprisoned in the labyrinths you have drawn me into, that on the sudden it cannot be expected I should find my way out. You must give me time to look about me and recollect myself.

PHIL. Hark; is not this the college bell?

HYL. It rings for prayers.

PHIL. We will go in then, if you please, and meet here again tomorrow morning. In the meantime, you may employ your thoughts on this morning's discourse and try if you can find any fallacy in it, or invent any new means to extricate yourself.

HYL. Agreed.

Is Knowledge
Only
Justified
True Belief?

The title question of this section was raised long ago by Plato. The issue it raises is still quite alive, as the selections from the contemporary philosophers Chisholm and Gettier reveal.

Theatetus, the namesake of the dialogue from which our Plato selection is taken, seeks to define the term "knowledge." The question is by no means merely verbal; it could be put equally well: "Under what conditions were we justified in claiming to know that a statement is true?"

Theatetus offers as a first suggestion that (1) "true judgment is knowledge." A man knows, in other words, if he makes a true judgment. If one weds this definition to the claim that (2) no one can judge falsely (a Protagorean doctrine previously mentioned in the *Theatetus* at 167A), one finds himself with the obviously false contention that whenever one judges that a given statement *P* is true, he knows that *P* is true—even if *P* is false. Any analysis of what judgment is, or of what knowledge is, plainly must make allowance for the fact that false judgments are made.

It is easy enough, perhaps, to see that one either knows *P* or he does not, and that if one person asserts that he knows that *P* and another asserts that he knows that not-*P*, both cannot be right. And if we take (1) alone, forsaking (2), we can agree with Theatetus that "There can at least be no mistake in believing what is true." Nonetheless, (1) is easily disposed of. For suppose that Otto believes, and that it is true, that the last car to win at Le Mans was a Ford. But suppose the reason that Otto believes this is because he read his tea leaves to find out which car would win at Le Mans and (luckily) he "read off" from them the information that a Ford won. He has read no papers, heard no news broadcasts, and cannot back up his claim in any way save by appeal to his tea leaves. Further, on the same basis, he believes that an Edsel won this race some time. Surely, under such circumstances, though his belief is true, Otto does not *know* that a Ford won. He has true belief, but not knowledge. So (1) is false.

Well, that seems easy enough to repair. Suppose Otto was there and watched the Ford win, heard the driver of the Ford shout "I won," saw him receive the winner's check and be carried off in triumph on the shoulders of his admirers. Then Otto will know that the Ford really won. More formally, person *S* knows *P* if, and only if, (a) *P* is true, (b) *S* believes *P*, (c) *S* has good reasons for believing *P*. As Theatetus puts it, knowledge is "true belief with the addition of an account." In a passage not here included, however, Socrates raises an objection to this analysis of knowledge.

This objection can be stated clearly if we note that, for all of his satisfying (a), (b) and (c), Otto may still accept *P*, not because of what he sees, but because of his tea leaves and the prediction he made from them. He is, let us say, a skeptic about sense perception but an adamant believer in the efficacy of tea-leaf reading. So he accepts the claim that the Ford won for "reasons" which in fact do not support that claim. He believes truly but not for the right reasons though those reasons are available to him. Well, again we can repair this by adding (d) *S* believes *P* is virtue of his having adequate reasons for *P*. But (and here we turn to Socrate's objection of 209E and following) (d) can be true only if (e) is true: (e) *S* knows that reasons he possesses are relevant to, and adequate for, *P*. But now our definition is circular, for we started out analyizng "*S* knows *P*" and now "*S* knows . . ." appears all over again in (e). Chisholm's and Gettier's remarks are relevant to this issue.

We should mention another question that Socrates raises. A man, he notes (at 197B), can possess a coat that he is not wearing and never has worn. What about the sense in which we "possess" knowledge? I need not "have in mind" *P* in order to know *P*; I knew a moment ago that Abraham Lincoln had a beard even though I was not then thinking about this fact. But can I also be correctly said to know things that I have never thought of? For example, never before in my life have I considered the sentence "The first time I shaved occurred some time after the last dinosaur died." But I know that this is so (or at least think that I know propositions that are true and entail this one). Did I know this before I ever considered it? How, to put it formally, are "*S* has thought of *P*" and "*S* knows *P*" related?

Roderick Chisholm offers and defends an analysis of (1) "*S* (a person) knows that *h* (a statement) is true" in which this sentence means the same thing as these sentences: (2) "*S* accepts *h*"; (3) "*S* has adequate evidence for *h*"; (4) "*h* is true." He illustrates as follows:

If a man knows, say, that the hall has been painted, then, according to our definition, he accepts the hypothesis that it has been painted, he has adequate evidence for this hypothesis, and, finally, the hall has *been painted.*

Chisholm notes that a further element is required before we have (in one sense of "know" at least) an adequate analysis of (1). It is: (5) "*S* accepts *h* because of the adequate evidence for *h* that he has." For as we have seen, a man could possess sufficient evidence for a statement but in fact accept that statement for inadequate or irrelevant reasons. If we hold that reasons are not causes and wish to escape the *causal* implications of (5), we could replace (5) by (5a) "The reason that *S* accepts *h* is that *S* has adequate evidence for *h*" or (5b) "*S*'s reason for accepting *h* is the adequate evidence for *h* that he possesses."

Now Chisholm grants that in one sense—the sense in which to believe is simply to accept—"*S* knows *h*" entails that "*S* believes *h*," and so to know is to have justified true belief (that is, to accept a true statement for the reason that one has adequate evidence for it). But in no sense, Chisholm contends, is knowledge a *species* of belief. Knowledge is not related to belief as being blue to being colored. His defense of this contention is an instance of a standard method of philosophical argumentation: one can ask questions (and, correspondingly, make assertions) about cases of belief that cannot sensibly be asked (or made) about cases of knowledge, and conversely. Further that *A* entails *B* does not show that *B* is a species of *A*; that *x* has arrived entails that *x* has traveled, but this does not show that arriving is a species of traveling. In sum, then, Chisholm holds that whenever a statement of the form of (1) is true, there will also be corresponding statements of forms (2), (3), (4) and, sometimes, (5) that are true, and conversely. Nonetheless knowledge is not justified true belief, for if it were it would be a species of belief, which it is not.

Edmund Gettier denies that this type of analysis of (1) is successful. He endeavors to show this by offering instances in which a sentence of form (1) is false but the corresponding sentences of forms (2), (3), (4), and (5) are true. Again, this exhibits a standard method of philosophic argumentation. A general thesis is offered—say, necessarily, every *A* that is *B* is also *C*. Then a counterexample is offered: here is an *A* that is *B* but not *C*. Then, perhaps, the original thesis will be qualified or abandoned, or perhaps there will be a reply to the effect that the *A* in question is not really a *B*, or is a *B* but is also really a *C*, or is in fact not an *A* at all. The classic illustration is the refutation of "Man is a featherless biped" by producing a plucked fowl. The method, as Gettier's use of it exhibits, has more serious applications. The question as to whether Gettier's counterexamples do refute Chisholm's analysis is left as an exercise for the reader.

True Belief, False Belief, and Knowledge

PLATO

SOC. But the original aim of our discussion was to find out rather what knowledge is than what it is not; at the same time we have made some progress, for we no longer seek for knowledge in perception at all, but in that other process, however called, in which the mind is alone and engaged with being.

THEAET. And that, Socrates, if I am not mistaken, is called thinking or opining.

SOC. You conceive truly. And now, my friend, please to begin again at this point; and having wiped out of your memory all that has preceded, see if you have arrived at any clearer view, and once more say what is knowledge.

THEAET. I cannot say, Socrates, that all opinion is knowledge, because there may be a false opinion; but I will venture to assert that knowledge is true opinion: let this then be my reply; and if this is hereafter disproved, we must try to find another.

SOC. That is the way in which you ought to answer, Theaetetus, and not in your former hesitating strain, for if we are bold we shall gain one of two advantages; either we shall find what we seek, or we shall be less likely to think that we know what we do not know—in either case we shall be richly rewarded. And now, what are you saying?—Are there two sorts of opinion, one true and the other false; and do you define knowledge to be the true?

THEAET. Yes, according to my present view.

SOC. Is it still worth our while to resume the discussion touching opinion?

THEAET. To what are you alluding?

SOC. There is a point which troubles me, as it has often done before; my discussion with myself or with others has left me in great perplexity about the nature or origin of the mental experience to which I refer.

THEAET. Pray what is it?

SOC. How can a man form a false opinion—that difficulty still troubles the eye but I am even now in doubt whether we ought to leave this question, or examine it by another method that we used a short time ago.

THEAET. Begin again, Socrates,— at least if you think that there is the slightest necessity for doing so. Were not you and Theodorus just now remarking very truly, that in discussions of this kind we may take our own time?

SOC. You are quite right, and perhaps there will be no harm in retracing our steps and beginning again. Better a little which is well done, than a great deal imperfectly.

THEAET. Certainly.

SOC. Well, and what is the difficulty? Do we not speak of false opinion, and say that one man holds a false and another a true opinion, as though there were some natural distinction between them?

THEAET. We certainly say so.

SOC. And we can at least say that all things and each thing severally are either known or not known. I leave out of view the intermediate conceptions of learning and forgetting, because they have nothing to do with our present question.

THEAET. There can be no doubt, Socrates, if you exclude these, that there is no other alternative but knowing or not knowing a thing.

SOC. That point being now determined, must we not say that he who has

FROM "Theatetus" (187A–202C) from *The Dialogues of Plato*, trans. Benjamin Jowett. 4th ed., Vol. 3 (Oxford, England: The Clarendon Press, 1953), pp. 288–308. Reprinted by permission of The Clarendon Press, Oxford.

an opinion, must either know or not know that to which his opinion refers?

THEAET. He must.

SOC. Moreover, he who knows, cannot not know; and he who does not know, cannot know one and the same thing?

THEAET. Of course.

SOC. What shall we say then? When a man has a false opinion does he think that which he knows to be some other thing which he knows, and knowing both, is he at the same time ignorant of both?

THEAET. That, Socrates, is impossible.

SOC. But perhaps he thinks of something which he does not know as some other thing which he does not know; for example, he knows neither Theaetetus nor Socrates, and yet he fancies that Theaetetus is Socrates, or Socrates Theaetetus?

THEAET. How can he?

SOC. But surely he cannot suppose something which he knows to be a thing which he does not know, or what he does not know to be what he knows?

THEAET. That would be monstrous.

SOC. How, then, is false opinion formed? For if all things are either known or unknown, there can be no opinion which is not comprehended under this alternative, and within it we can find no scope for false opinion.

THEAET. Most true.

SOC. Suppose that we remove the question out of the sphere of knowing or not knowing, into that of being and not-being.

THEAET. What do you mean?

SOC. May we not suspect the simple truth to be that he who thinks on any subject, that which is not, will necessarily think what is false, whatever in other respects may be the state of his mind?

THEAET. That, again, is not unlikely, Socrates.

SOC. Then suppose some one to say to us, Theaetetus:—Is it possible for any man to think as you now say that which is not, either as a self-existent sub-

stance or as a predicate of something else? And suppose, that we answer, 'Yes, he can, when in thinking he thinks what is not true.'—That will be our answer?

THEAET. Yes.

SOC. But is there any parallel to this?

THEAET. What do you mean?

SOC. Can a man see something and yet see nothing?

THEAET. Impossible.

SOC. But if he sees any one thing, he sees something that exists. Do you suppose that what is one is ever to be found among non-existing things?

THEAET. I do not.

SOC. He then who sees some one thing, sees something which is?

THEAET. Apparently.

SOC. And he who hears anything, hears some one thing, a thing which is?

THEAET. Yes.

SOC. And he who touches any-thing, touches something which is one and therefore is?

THEAET That again is true.

SOC. And does not he who thinks, think some one thing?

THEAET. Certainly.

SOC. And does not he who thinks some one thing, think something which is?

THEAET. I agree.

SOC. Then he who thinks of that which is not, thinks of nothing?

THEAET. Apparently not.

SOC. And he who thinks of that which is not thinks of nothing, does not think at all?

THEAET. That seems clear.

SOC. Then no one can think that which is not, either as a self-existent substance or as a predicate of something else?

THEAET. Apparently not.

SOC. Then to think falsely is different from thinking that which is not?

THEAET. It would seem so.

SOC. Then false opinion has no existence in us, either in this way or in that which we took a short time before?

THEAET. Certainly not.

SOC. But may not the following be

the description of what we express by this name?

THEAET. What?

SOC. May we not suppose that false opinion or thought is a sort of heterodoxy; a person may make an exchange in his mind, and say that one real object is another real object. For thus he always thinks that which is, but he puts one thing in place of another, and missing the aim of his thoughts, he may be truly said to have false opinion.

THEAET. Now you appear to me to have spoken the exact truth: when a man puts the base in the place of the noble, or the noble in the place of the base, then he has truly false opinion.

SOC. I see, Theaetetus, that your fear has disappeared, and that you are beginning to despise me.

THEAET. What makes you say so?

SOC. You think, if I am not mistaken, that your 'truly false' is safe from censure, and that I shall never ask whether there can be a swift which is slow, or a heavy which is light, or any other self-contradictory thing, which works, not according to its own nature, but according to that of its opposite. But I will not insist upon this, for I do not wish needlessly to discourage you. And so you are satisfied that false opinion is heterodoxy, or the thought of something else?

THEAET. I am.

SOC. It is possible then upon your view for the mind to conceive of one thing as another?

THEAET. True.

SOC. But must not the mind, or thinking power, which misplaces them, have a conception either of both objects or of one of them?

THEAET. Certainly.

SOC. Either together or in succession?

THEAET. Very good.

SOC. And do you mean by conceiving, the same which I mean?

THEAET. What is that?

SOC. I mean the conversation which the soul holds with herself in considering of anything. I speak of what I scarcely understand; but the soul when thinking appears to me to be just talking —asking questions of herself and answering them, affirming and denying. And when she has arrived at a decision, either gradually or by a sudden impulse, and has at last agreed, and does not doubt, this is called her opinion. I say, then, that to form an opinion is to speak, and opinion is a word spoken,—I mean, to oneself and in silence, not aloud or to another: What think you?

THEAET. I agree.

SOC. Then when any one thinks of one thing as another, he is saying to himself that one thing is another?

THEAET. Yes.

SOC. But do you ever remember saying to yourself that the noble is certainly base, or the unjust just; or, in a word have you ever attempted to convince yourself that one thing is another? Nay, not even in sleep, did you ever venture to say to yourself that odd is undoubtedly even, or anything of the kind?

THEAET. Never.

SOC. And do you suppose that any other man, either in his senses or out of them, ever seriously tried to persuade himself that an ox is a horse, or that two are one?

THEAET. Certainly not.

SOC. But if thinking is talking to oneself, no one speaking and thinking of two objects, and apprehending them both in his soul, will say and think that the one is the other of them, and I must add that you too, had better let the word "other" alone [i.e. not insist that 'one' and 'other' are the same[1]], I mean to say, that no one thinks the noble to be base, or anything of the kind.

THEAET. I will pass the word 'other,' Socrates; and I agree to what you say.

SOC. If a man has both of them in his thoughts, he cannot think that the one of them is the other?

---

[1] Both words in Greek are called ἕτερον: cp. Parmen. 147 C; Euthyd. 301 A.

THEAET. So it seems.

SOC. Neither, if he has one of them only in his mind and not the other, will he ever think that one is the other?

THEAET. True; for we should have to suppose that he apprehends that which is not in his thoughts at all.

SOC. Then no one who has either both or only one of the two objects in his mind can think that the one is the other. And therefore he who maintains that false opinion is heterodoxy is talking nonsense; for neither in this, any more than in the two previous ways, can false opinion exist in us.

THEAET. No.

SOC. But if, Theaetetus, this experience is not shown to be real, we shall be driven into many absurdities.

THEAET. What are they?

SOC. I will not tell you until I have endeavoured to consider the matter from every point of view. For I should be ashamed of us if we were driven in our perplexity to admit the absurd consequences of which I speak. But if we find the solution, and get away from them, we may regard them only as the difficulties of others, and the ridicule will not attach to us. On the other hand, if we utterly fail, I suppose that we must be humble, and allow the argument to trample us under foot, as the sea-sick passenger is trampled upon by the sailor, and to do anything to us. Listen, then, while I tell you how I hope to find a way out of our difficulty.

THEAET. Let me hear.

SOC. I think that we were wrong in denying that a man could think what he knew to be what he did not know; and that there is a way in which such a deception is possible.

THEAET. You mean to say, as I suspected at the time when we made that denial, that I may know Socrates, and at a distance see some one who is unknown to me, and suppose him to be Socrates whom I know—then the deception will occur?

SOC. But has not that position been relinquished by us, because involving the absurdity that we should know and not know the things which we know?

THEAET. True.

SOC. Let us make the assertion in another form, which may or may not have a favourable issue; but as we are in a great strait, every argument should be turned over and tested. Tell me, then, whether I am right in saying that you may learn a thing which at one time you did not know?

THEAET. Certainly you may.

SOC. And another and another?

THEAET. Yes.

SOC. I would have you imagine, then, that there exists in the mind of man a block of wax, which is of different sizes in different men; harder, moister, and having more or less of purity in one than another, and in some of an intermediate quality.

THEAET. I see.

SOC. Let us say that this tablet is a gift of Memory, the mother of the Muses; and that when we wish to remember anything which we have seen, or heard, or thought in our own minds, we hold the wax to the perceptions and thoughts, and in that material receive the impression of them as from the seal of a ring; and that we remember and know what is imprinted as long as the image lasts; but when the image is effaced, or cannot be taken, then we forget and do not know.

THEAET. Very good.

SOC. Now, when a person has this knowledge, and is considering something which he sees or hears, may not false opinion arise in the following manner?

THEAET. In what manner?

SOC. When he thinks what he knows, sometimes to be what he knows, and sometimes to be what he does not know. We were wrong before in denying the possibility of this.

THEAET. And how would you amend the former statement?

SOC. I should begin by making a list of the impossible cases which must be excluded. (1) No one can think one thing to be another when he does not perceive either of them, but has the memorial or seal of both of them in his mind; nor can any mistaking of one thing for another occur, when he only knows one, and does not know, and has no impression of the other; nor can he think that one thing which he does not know is another thing which he does not know, or that what he does not know is what he knows; nor (2) that one thing which he perceives, is another thing which he perceives, or that something which he perceives is something which he does not perceive; or that something which he does not perceive is something else which he does not perceive; or that something which he does not perceive is something which he perceives; nor again (3) can he think that something which he knows and perceives, and of which he has the impression coinciding with sense, is something else which he knows and perceives, and of which he has the impression coinciding with sense;—this last case, if possible, is still more inconceivable than the others; nor (4) can he think that something which he knows and perceives, and of which he has the memorial in good order is something else which he knows; nor if his mind is thus furnished, can he think that a thing which he knows and perceives is another thing which he perceives; or that a thing which he does not know and does not perceive, is the same as another thing which he does not know and does not perceive;—nor again, can he suppose that a thing which he does not know and does not perceive is the same as another thing which he does not know; or that a thing which he does not know and does not perceive is another thing which he does not perceive:—All these utterly and absolutely exclude the possibility of false opinion. The only cases, if any, which remain, are the following.

THEAET. What are they? If you tell me, I may perhaps understand you better; but at the present I am unable to follow you.

SOC. A person may think that some things which he knows, or which he perceives and does not know, are some other things which he knows and perceives; or that some things which he knows and perceives, are other things which he knows and perceives.

THEAET. I understand you less than ever now.

SOC. Hear me once more, then:—I, knowing Theodorus, and remembering in my own mind what sort of person he is, and also what sort of person Theaetetus is, at one time see them, and at another time do not see them, and sometimes I touch them, and at another time not, or at one time I may hear them or perceive them in some other way, and at another time not perceive you, but still I remember you, and know you in my own mind.

THEAET. Very true.

SOC. Then, first of all, I want you to understand that a man may or may not perceive sensibly that which he knows.

THEAET. True.

SOC. And that which he does not know will sometimes not be perceived by him and sometimes will be perceived and only perceived?

THEAET. That is also true.

SOC. See whether you can follow me better now: Socrates can recognize Theodorus and Theaetetus, but he sees neither of them, nor does he perceive them in any other way; he cannot then by any possibility imagine in his own mind that Theaetetus is Theodorus. Am I not right?

THEAET. You are quite right.

SOC. Then that was the first case of which I spoke.

THEAET. Yes.

SOC. The second case was, that I, knowing one of you and not knowing the other, and perceiving neither, can never think him whom I know to be him whom I do not know.

THEAET. True.

SOC. In the third case, not knowing and not perceiving either of you, I cannot think that one of you whom I do not know is the other whom I do not know. I need not again go over the catalogue of excluded cases, in which I cannot form a false opinion about you and Theodorus, either when I know both or when I am in ignorance of both, or when I know one and not the other. And the same of perceiving: do you understand me?

THEAET. I do.

SOC. The only possibility of erroneous opinion is, when knowing you and Theodorus, and having on the waxen block the impression of both of you given as by a seal, but seeing you imperfectly and at a distance, I am eager to assign the right impression of memory to the right visual impression, and to fit this into its own print in order that recognition may take place; but if I fail and transpose them, putting the foot into the wrong shoe—that is to say, putting the vision of either of you on to the wrong impression, or if my mind, like the sight in a mirror, which is transferred from right to left, err by reason of some similar affection, then 'heterodoxy' and false opinion ensues.

THEAET. Yes, Socrates, you have described the nature of opinion with wonderful exactness.

SOC. Or again, when I know both of you, and perceive as well as know one of you, but not the other, and my knowledge of him does not accord with perception—that was the case put by me just now which you did not understand.

THEAET. No, I did not.

SOC. I meant to say, that when a person knows and perceives one of you, and his knowledge coincides with his perception, he will never think him to be some other person, whom he knows and perceives, and the knowledge of whom coincides with his perception—for that also was a case supposed.

THEAET. True.

SOC. But there was an omission of the further case, in which, as we now say, false opinion may arise, when knowing both, and seeing, or having some other sensible perception of both, I fail in holding the seal over against the corresponding sensation; like a bad archer, I miss and fall wide of the mark—and this is called falsehood.

THEAET. Yes; it is rightly so called.

SOC. When, therefore, perception is present to one of the seals or impressions but not to the other, and the mind fits the seal of the absent perception on the one which is present, in any case of this sort the mind is deceived; in a word, if our view is sound, there can be no error or deception about things which a man does not know and has never perceived, but only in things which are known and perceived; in these alone opinion turns and twists about, and becomes alternately true and false;—true when the seals and impressions of sense meet straight and opposite—false when they go awry and are crooked.

THEAET. And is not that, Socrates, nobly said?

SOC. Nobly! yes; but wait a little and hear the explanation, and then you will say so with more reason; for to think truly is noble and to be deceived is base.

THEAET. Undoubtedly.

SOC. And the origin of truth and error, men say, is as follows:—When the wax in the soul of any one is deep and abundant, and smooth and perfectly tempered, then the impressions which pass through the senses and sink into the heart of the soul, as Homer says in a parable, meaning to indicate the likeness of the soul to wax ($\chi\tilde{\eta}\rho$ $\chi\eta\rho\dot{o}s$); these, I say, being pure and clear, and having a sufficient depth of wax, are also lasting, and minds, such as these, easily learn and easily retain, and are not liable to confuse the imprints of sensations, but have true thoughts, for having clear impressions well spaced out, they can quickly say what they are;—that is, distribute them into their proper places on the block. And such men are called wise. Do you agree?

THEAET. Entirely.

SOC. But when the heart of any one is shaggy—a quality which the all-wise poet commends, or muddy and of impure wax, or very soft, or very hard, then there is a corresponding defect in the mind—the soft are good at learning, but apt to forget; and the hard are the reverse; the shaggy and rugged and gritty, or those who have an admixture of earth or dung in their composition, have the impressions indistinct, as also the hard, for there is no depth in them; and the soft too are indistinct, for their impressions are easily confused and effaced. Yet greater is the indistinctness when they are all jostled together in a little soul, which has no room. These are the natures which are prone to false opinion; for when they see or hear or think of anything, they are slow in assigning the right objects to the right impressions— in their stupidity they confuse them, and are apt to see and hear and think amiss —and such men are said to be deceived in their knowledge of objects, and ignorant.

THEAET. No man, Socratees, can say anything truer than that.

SOC. Then now we may admit the existence of false opinion in us?

THEAET. Certainly.

SOC. And of true opinion also?

THEAET. Yes.

SOC. We have at length satisfactorily proven that beyond a doubt there are these two sorts of opinion?

THEAET. Undoubtedly.

SOC. Alas, Theaetetus, what a tiresome creature is a man who is fond of talking!

THEAET. What makes you say so?

SOC. Because I am disheartened at my own stupidity and tiresome garrulity; for what other term will describe the habit of a man who is always arguing on all sides of a question; whose dulness cannot be convinced, and who will never leave off?

THEAET. But what puts you out of heart?

SOC. I am not only out of heart, but in positive despair; for I do not know what to answer if any one were to ask me:—O Socrates, have you indeed discovered that false opinion arises neither in the comparison of perceptions with one another nor yet in thought, but in the linking of thought with perception? Yes, I shall say, with the complacence of one who thinks that he has made a noble discovery.

THEAET. I see no reason why we should be ashamed of our demonstration, Socrates.

SOC. He will say: You mean to argue that the man whom we only think of and do not see, cannot be confused with the horse which we do not see or touch, but only think of and do not perceive? That I believe to be my meaning, I shall reply.

THEAET. Quite right.

SOC. Well, then, he will say, according to that argument, the number eleven, which is only thought, can never be mistaken for twelve, which is only thought: How would you answer him?

THEAET. I should say that a mistake may very likely arise between the eleven or twelve which are seen or handled, but that no similar mistake can arise between the eleven and twelve which are in the mind.

SOC. Well, but do you think that no one ever put before his own mind five and seven,—I do not mean five or seven men or other such objects, but five or seven in the abstract, which, as we say, are recorded on the waxen block, and in which false opinion is held to be impossible;—did no man ever ask himself how many these numbers make when added together, and answer that they are eleven, while another thinks that they are twelve, or would all agree in thinking and saying that they are twelve?

THEAET. Certainly not; many would think that they are eleven, and in the higher numbers the chance of error is greater still; for I assume you to be speaking of numbers in general.

SOC. Exactly; and I want you to consider whether this does not imply that the twelve in the waxen block are supposed to be eleven?

THEAET. Yes, that seems to be the case.

SOC. Then do we not come back to

the old difficulty? For he who makes such a mistake does think one thing which he knows to be another thing which he knows; but this, as we said, was impossible, and afforded an irresistible proof of the non-existence of false opinion, because otherwise the same person would inevitably know and not know the same thing at the same time.

THEAET. Most true.

SOC. Then false opinion cannot be explained as a confusion of thought and sense, for in that case we could not have been mistaken about pure conceptions of thought; and thus we are obliged to say, either that false opinion does not exist, or that a man may not know that which he knows;—which alternative do you prefer?

THEAET. It is hard to determine, Socrates.

SOC. And yet the argument will scarcely admit of both. But, as we are at our wits' end, suppose that we do a shameless thing?

THEAET. What is it?

SOC. Let us attempt to explain what it is like 'to know.'

THEAET. And why should that be shameless?

SOC. You seem not to be aware that the whole of our discussion from the very beginning has been a search after knowledge, of which we are assumed not to know the nature.

THEAET. Nay, but I am well aware.

SOC. And is it not shameless when we do not know what knowledge is, to be explaining the verb 'to know'? The truth is, Theaetetus, that we have long been infected with logical impurity. Thousands of times have we repeated the words 'we know,' and 'do not know,' and 'we have or have not science or knowledge,' as if we could understand what we are saying to one another, even while we remain ignorant about knowledge; and at this moment we are using the words 'we understand,' 'we are ignorant,' as though we could still employ them when deprived of knowledge or science.

THEAET. But if you avoid these expressions, Socrates, how will you ever argue at all?

SOC. I could not, being the man I am. The case would be different if I were a true hero of dialectic: and O that such an one were present! for he would have told us to avoid the use of these terms; at the same time he would not have spared in you and me the faults which I have noted. But, seeing that we are no great wits, shall I venture to say what knowing is? for I think that the attempt may be worth making.

THEAET. Then by all means venture, and no one shall find fault with you for using the forbidden terms.

SOC. You have heard the common explanation of the verb 'to know'?

THEAET. I think so, but I do not remember it at the moment.

SOC. They explain the word 'to know' as meaning 'to have knowledge.'

THEAET. True.

SOC. I propose that we make a slight change, and say 'to possess' knowledge.

THEAET. How do the two expressions differ?

SOC. Perhaps there may be no difference; but still I should like you to hear my view, that you may help me to test it.

THEAET. I will, if I can.

SOC. I should distinguish 'having' from 'possessing': for example, a man may buy and keep under his control a garment which he does not wear; and then we should say, not that he has, but that he possesses the garment.

THEAET. It would be the correct expression.

SOC. Well, may not a man 'possess' and yet not 'have' knowledge in the sense of which I am speaking? As you may suppose a man to have caught wild birds —doves or any other birds—and to be keeping them in an aviary which he has constructed at home; we might say of him in one sense, that he always has them because he possesses them, might we not?

THEAET. Yes.

SOC. And yet, in another sense, he has none of them; but they are in his power, and he has got them under his hand in an enclosure of his own, and can take and have them whenever he likes;—he can catch any which he likes, and let the bird go again, and he may do so as often as he pleases.

THEAET. True.

SOC. Once more, then, as in what preceded we made a sort of waxen tablet in the mind, so let us now suppose that in the mind of each man there is an aviary of all sorts of birds—some flocking together apart from the rest, others in small groups, others solitary, flying anywhere and everywhere.

THEAET. Let us imagine such an aviary—and what is to follow?

SOC. We may suppose that the birds are kinds of knowledge, and that when we were children, this receptacle was empty; whenever a man has gotten and detained in the enclosure a kind of knowledge, he may be said to have learned or discovered the thing which is the subject of the knowledge: and this is to know.

THEAET. Granted.

SOC. And further, when any one wishes to catch any of these knowledges or sciences, and having taken, to hold it, and again to let them go, how will he express himself?—will he describe the 'catching' of them and the original 'possession' in the same words? I will make my meaning clearer by an example:— You admit that there is an art of arithmetic?

THEAET. To be sure.

SOC. Conceive this as an attempt to capture knowledge of every species of the odd and even in general.

THEAET. I follow.

SOC. Having the use of the art, the arithmetician, if I am not mistaken, has the conceptions of number under his hand, and can transmit them to another.

THEAET. Yes.

SOC. And when transmitting them he may be said to teach them, and when receiving to learn them, and when having them in possession in the aforesaid aviary he may be said to know them.

THEAET. Exactly.

SOC. Attend to what follows: must not the perfect arithmetician know all numbers, for he has the science of all numbers in his mind?

THEAET. True.

SOC. And he can reckon abstract numbers in his head, or things about him which are numerable?

THEAET. Of course he can.

SOC. And to reckon is simply to consider how much such and such a number amounts to?

THEAET. Very true.

SOC. And so he appears to be searching into something which he knows, as if he did not know it, for we have already admitted that he knows all numbers;—you have heard these perplexing questions raised?

THEAET. I have.

SOC. May we not pursue the image of the doves, and say that the chase after knowledge is of two kinds? one kind is prior to possession and for the sake of possession, and the other for the sake of taking and holding in the hands that which is possessed already. And thus, when a man has learned and known something long ago, he may resume and get hold of the knowledge which he has long possessed, but has not at hand in his mind.

THEAET. True.

SOC. That was my reason for asking how we ought to speak when an arithmetician sets about numbering, or a grammarian about reading? Shall we say, that although he knows, he comes back to himself on such an occasion to learn what he already knows?

THEAET. It would be too absurd, Socrates.

SOC. Shall we say then that he is going to read or number what he does not know, although we have admitted that he knows all letters and all numbers?

THEAET. That, again, would be an absurdity.

SOC. Then shall we say that we care nothing about the mere names?—any one may twist and turn the words 'knowing' and 'learning' in any way which he likes, but that since we have made a clear distinction between the possession of knowledge and the having or using it, we do assert that a man cannot possess that which he possesses; and, therefore, in no case can a man not know that which he knows, but he may get a false opinion about it; for he may have the knowledge, not of this particular thing, but of some other;—when the various numbers and forms of knowledge are flying about in the aviary and wishing to capture a certain sort of knowledge out of the general store, he may take the wrong one by mistake, thus it is that he may think eleven to be twelve, getting hold as it were of the ring-dove which he had in his mind, when he wanted the pigeon.

THEAET. A very rational explanation.

SOC. But when he catches the one which he wants, then he is not deceived, and has an opinion of what is, and thus both false and true opinion may exist, and the difficulties which were previously raised disappear. I dare say that you agree with me, do you not?

THEAET. Yes.

SOC. And so we are rid of the difficulty of a man's not knowing what he knows, for we are not driven to the inference that he does not possess what he possesses, whether he be or be not deceived. And yet I fear that a greater difficulty is looking in at the window.

THEAET. What is it?

SOC. How can the exchange of one knowledge for another ever become false opinion?

THEAET. What do you mean?

SOC. In the first place, how can a man who has the knowledge of anything be ignorant of that which he knows, not by reason of ignorance, but by reason of his own knowledge? And, again, is it not an extreme absurdity that he should suppose another thing to be this, and this to be another thing;—that, having knowledge present with him in his mind, he should still know nothing and be ignorant of all things?—you might as well argue that ignorance may make a man know, and blindness make him see, as that knowledge can make him ignorant.

THEAET. Perhaps, Socrates, we may have been wrong in making only forms of knowledge our birds: whereas there ought to have been forms of ignorance as well, flying about together in the mind, and then he who sought to take one of them might sometimes catch a form of knowledge, and sometimes a form of ignorance; and thus he would have a false opinion from ignorance, but a true one from knowledge, about the same thing.

SOC. I cannot help praising you, Theaetetus, and yet I must beg you to reconsider your words. Let us grant what you say—then, according to you, he who takes ignorance will have a false opinion—am I right?

THEAET. Yes.

SOC. He will certainly not think that he has a false opinion?

THEAET. Of course not.

SOC. He will think that his opinion is true, and he will fancy that he knows the things about which he has been deceived?

THEAET. Certainly.

SOC. Then he will think that he has captured a knowledge and not an ignorance?

THEAET. Clearly.

SOC. And thus, after going a long way round, we are once more face to face with our original difficulty. The hero of dialectic will retort upon us:— 'O my excellent friends, he will say, laughing, if a man knows both the specimen of ignorance and also that of knowledge, can he think that one of them which he knows is the other which he knows? or, if he knows neither of them, can he think that the one which he knows not is another which he knows not? or, if he knows one and not the other, can he think the one which he knows to be the one which he does not know? or the one which he does not know to be the one which he knows? or will you proceed to tell me that there are other knowledges which know the types of knowledge and ignorance, and which the owner keeps in some other aviaries or graven on waxen blocks according to your foolish images, and which he may be said to know while he possesses them, even though he have them not at hand in his mind? And thus, in a perpetual circle, you will be compelled to go round and round, and you will make no progress.' What are we to say in reply, Theaetetus?

THEAET. Indeed, Socrates, I do not know what we are to say.

SOC. Are not his reproaches just, and does not the argument truly show that we are wrong in seeking for false opinion until we know what knowledge is; that must be first ascertained; then, the nature of false opinion?

THEAET. I cannot but agree with you, Socrates, so far as we have yet gone.

SOC. Then, once more, what shall we say that knowledge is?—for we are not going to lose heart as yet.

THEAET. Certainly, I shall not lose heart, if you do not.

SOC. What definition will be most consistent with our former views?

THEAET. I cannot think of any but our old one, Socrates.

SOC. What was it?

THEAET. Knowledge was said by us to be true opinion; and true opinion is surely unerring, and the results which follow from it are all noble and good.

SOC. He who led the way into the river, Theaetetus, said 'The experiment will show;' and perhaps if we go forward in the search we may stumble upon the thing which we are looking for; but if we stay where we are, nothing will come to light.

THEAET. Very true; let us go forward and try.

SOC. The trail soon comes to an end, for a whole profession is against us.

THEAET. How is that, and what profession do you mean?

SOC. The profession of the great wise ones who are called orators and lawyers; for these persuade men by their art and make them think whatever they like, but they do not teach them. Do you imagine that there are any teachers in the world so clever as to be able to impart the full truth about past acts of robbery or violence to men who were not eye-witnesses, while a little water is flowing in the clepsydra?

THEAET. Certainly not, they can only persuade them.

SOC. And would you not say that persuading them is making them have an opinion?

THEAET. To be sure.

SOC. When, therefore, judges are justly persuaded about matters which you can know only by seeing them, and not in any other way, and when thus judging of them from report they attain a true opinion about them, they judge without knowledge and yet are rightly persuaded, if they have judged well.

THEAET. Certainly.

SOC. And yet, O my friend, if true opinion in law courts[1] and knowledge are the same, the perfect judge could not have judged rightly without knowledge; and therefore I must infer that they are not the same.

---

[1] Reading $\kappa\alpha\tau\grave{\alpha}$ $\delta\iota\kappa\alpha\sigma\tau\acute{\eta}\rho\iota\alpha$: an emendation suggested by Professor Campbell.

Knowledge Is Justified True Belief
RODERICK M. CHISHOLM

*I*f *a man* looks toward the roof and sees that his cat is there, he is not likely to *say*, "I have adequate evidence for the proposition or hypothesis that that is a cat," "I take that to be a cat," or "There is something which is appearing to me in a certain way." But, I suggest, if he does see that his cat is there, then he has adequate evidence for the proposition that a cat is there; moreover, there is something—his cat—which he *takes* to be his cat and which *is* appearing to him in a certain way. And I would suggest, more generally, that the locution "S perceives something to have such and such a characteristic," in one of its most important uses, may be defined as follows:

(1) "There is something that S *perceives* to be *f*" means: there is an *x* which is *f* and which appears in some way to S; S takes *x* to be *f*; and S has adequate evidence for the proposition that *x* is *f*.

By adding qualifications about sense organs, we could formulate similar definitions of important uses of "see" and of "hear."

Such definitions are not interesting or significant unless we can say what is meant by "appear," "take," and "adequate evidence" without using "see," "hear," or "perceive." I will begin, then, with "adequate evidence." In trying to understand this term, we will find ourselves involved in a number of philosophical problems.

"Adequate evidence"—like "acceptable," "unreasonable," "indifferent," "certain," "probable," and "improbable" —is a term we use in appraising the epistemic, or cognitive, worth of propositions, hypotheses, and beliefs. The statements in which we express such appraisal—for example, "We do not have adequate evidence for believing that acquired characteristics are inherited," "The astronomy of Ptolemy is unreasonable," and "In all probability, the accused is innocent"—are similar in significant respects to "Stealing is wicked," "We ought to forgive our enemies," and other statements expressing our ethical or moral appraisals. Many of the characteristics which philosophers and others have thought peculiar to ethical statements also hold of epistemic statements. And when we consider the application of "evident" and our other epistemic terms, we meet with problems very much like those traditionally associated with "right," "good," and "duty."

I shall propose definitions of several important epistemic terms. The definitions are intended to be adequate only to some of the epistemic uses of the terms defined. Many of the terms I shall define have other, nonepistemic uses I shall not mention. And there are many terms having important epistemic uses which I shall not attempt to define; the epistemic uses of such terms, I believe, can be defined by means of the epistemic vocabulary presented here. The definitions make use of one undefined epistemic locution. This is the locution: "*h* is more worthy of S's belief than *i*," where "S" may be replaced by the name of a person and "*h*" and "*i*" by names of propositions, statements, or hypotheses. An alternative reading is "*h* is more acceptable than *i* for S." In subsequent chapters I shall discuss the application of our epistemic vocabulary, and in

FROM *Perceiving: A Philosophical Study*, Roderick M. Chisholm. (Ithaca: Cornell University Press, 1957), pp. 3–18. Reprinted by permission of the Cornell University Press.

Chapter Seven I shall discuss the meaning of our undefined locution.

A proposition, statement, or hypothesis is *unreasonable* if it is less worthy of belief than is its denial or contradictory. Let us say, then:

> (2) "It would be *unreasonable* for S to accept *h*" means that non-*h* is more worthy of S's belief than *h*.

If S *does* accept *h*, we may say, of course, that it *is* unreasonable of him to do so. When it is clear from the general context what subject S is intended, we may say, elliptically, that a proposition, statement, or hypothesis is unreasonable.

"Absurd" and "preposterous" are sometimes synonyms of "unreasonable" in its present sense. And the belief—or feeling—that a proposition is unreasonable may also be expressed by means of imperatives. If I say to you, "Don't count on seeing me before Thursday," I may mean that it would be unreasonable of you to believe that you will see me before Thursday.

Whenever it would be unreasonable for a man to accept a certain proposition, then he may be said to have *adequate evidence* for its contradictory. Our next definition is:

> (3) "S has *adequate evidence* for *h*" means that it would be unreasonable for S to accept non-*h*.

When it is clear what subject S is intended, then we may speak elliptically, once again, and say that a proposition, statement, or hypothesis is *evident*. The expression "adequate evidence" as it is used in this definition should be thought of as a single term; I use it because it seems to be ordinarily used in such contexts. An alternative locution which I shall also use is "*h* is evident for S."

As examples of propositions which are evident, we could cite what a man knows or perceives to be true. But we are not defining "adequate evidence" in terms "known" or "perceive." In definition (1) we have defined "perceive" in terms of "adequate evidence." And in definition (6) we shall define "know" in terms of "adequate evidence." There are, moreover, propositions for which a man may have adequate evidence without knowing or perceiving them to be true. For there are times when, as we would ordinarily say, the available evidence may favor some proposition which is false; at such times, a false proposition is more worthy of one's belief than is a true proposition. Thus it may be true that a man is going to win a lottery and yet unreasonable for him to believe that he is. But once the drawings are announced, the belief may no longer be unreasonable.

The example indicates that our definitions should contain temporal references. For a proposition may be evident at one date and unreasonable at another. The phrase "at *t*" could be inserted in our definitions: a proposition would then be said to be evident *at a time t* provided only that its contradictory is unreasonable at *t*; and so on. But, for simplicity, I shall not make these temporal references explicit.

The *evident*, according to our definition, is more worthy of belief than is the unreasonable. But there is another sense of the phrase "worthy of belief" in which we can say, more simply, that the *true* is more worthy of belief than the false. If the evident, as I have suggested, is sometimes false, then there are hypotheses which, in the one sense, are more worthy of belief than are their contradictories but which, in the other, are less. This twofold sense of "worthy" is not peculiar to our epistemic terms, but holds of ethical terms generally. Following Richard Price, let us distinguish between the *absolute* and the *practical* senses of these terms.[1]

[1] See Richard Price, *Review of the Principal Questions of Morals* (Oxford, 1948; first published in 1787), ch. viii. Compare H. A. Prichard's "Duty and Ignorance of Fact," reprinted in his *Moral Obligation* (Oxford, 1950), and W. D. Ross, *Foundations of Ethics* (London, 1939), ch. vii.

Using the ethical term "right" in its *absolute* sense, we may say that no one can ever know what actions are right; for no one can ever know what *all* of the consequences of any action will be. In this absolute sense of "right," perhaps it would have been right for someone to have killed Hitler and Stalin when they were infants; perhaps their parents acted (absolutely) wrongly in allowing them to live.[2] But in the *practical* sense of "right" such killings would *not* have been right. It was not possible, when Hitler and Stalin were infants, for anyone to foresee the harm they would do and, I think we may assume, there is no motive which would have justified putting them to death. If we try, as some philosophers do, to restrict "right" and "wrong" and other ethical terms to their absolute use, then other terms must take over their practical use. We might then say of the killings we have been discussing that, although they might have been right, they would hardly have been *praiseworthy*—or that, although they would not have been wrong, they would certainly have been *blameworthy*.

We cannot know, of any action, whether it is right or wrong in the absolute senses of these terms unless we know what all of its consequences are going to be. But, I believe, we can know, of any contemplated act of our own, whether it is right or wrong in the practical senses of these terms; we can know of any act we contemplate whether that act would be praiseworthy or blameworthy.

When it is said, then, that people ought to believe what is evident and that they ought not to believe what is unreasonable, "ought" has its practical use. But when it is said that they ought to believe what is true and that they ought not to believe what is false, "ought" has its absolute use.[3] Our locution "*h* is

more worthy of belief than *i*" is to be taken in its practical sense. And all of the other epistemic terms to be used here are, similarly, to be taken in a practical and not in an absolute sense.

I shall return to this distinction in Chapter Two.

Let us say that a proposition, statement, or hypothesis is acceptable provided only that it is not unreasonable.

> (4) "*h* is *acceptable* for S" means: it is false that it would be unreasonable for S to accept *h*.

In other words, if the contradictory of a proposition is not evident, then the proposition is acceptable. "Justifiable," "reasonable," or "credible" might be used in place of "acceptable" here; I have avoided them, however, because in their ordinary use in such contexts they are often taken as synonymous with "evident." The modal term "*possible*" sometimes used as a synonym of "acceptable"; when a man says, "It is possible that we will have good news tomorrow," he may mean it is not unreasonable of us to believe that we will have good news tomorrow.

In his lecture "The Ethics of Belief," W. K. Clifford said, "It is wrong to believe upon insufficient evidence."[4] His ethics was somewhat more rigid

---

[2] Compare Bertrand Russell, *Human Knowledge* (New York, 1948), pt. v, ch. vi.

[3] There is a useful discussion of this distinction in R. B. Braithwaite, *Scientific Explanation* (Cambridge, 1953), pp. 279 ff.

In *The Orgin of the Knowledge of Right and Wrong* (London, 1902), sec. 23, Franz Brentano says in effect that we ought to believe only what is true. In a colloquium entitled "The Normative in the Descriptive," Konstantin Kolenda and Abraham Edel say we ought to believe only what is true, while Alan Ross Anderson, Max Black, and Irving Copi say there are times when we need not believe what is true (*Review of Metaphysics*, X [1956], 106–121).

[4] W. K. Clifford, *Lectures and Essays*, vol. II (London, 1879). It should be noted that our definitions, as they now stand, have this limitation: they do not enable us to formulate Clifford's position, for we cannot consistently say that a hypothesis and its contradictory are *both* unreasonable.

than that suggested here, for he held that, for each of us, there is a large class of propositions concerning which we ought to withhold both assent and denial. But I have suggested, in effect, that a proposition should be treated as innocent until proven guilty. It is only when we have adequate evidence for the contradictory of a proposition that it is unreasonable for us to accept the proposition. We have adequate evidence for the proposition that Eisenhower was President in 1956; hence it is unreasonable for us to accept the proposition that he was *not* President in 1956. We do not now have adequate evidence for the proposition that a Republican will be President in 1975; Clifford would say, therefore, that we ought not to believe that a Republican will be President in 1975. I suggest that we *may* believe this, that the proposition is "acceptable" in the sense defined above.[5] But to say that we have a right to believe it is not to say that we have a right to bet our savings on it.

We may say that a hypothesis is acceptable for someone without implying that it is always reasonable for him to *act upon* it; indeed, we may say that he has *adequate evidence* for a hypothesis without implying that it is always reasonable for him to act upon it. And in saying that in a certain instance it may be reasonable for a man to act upon a hypothesis, we do not imply that the hypothesis is one for which he has adequate evidence. A man may have adequate evidence for believing he will win if he plays Russian roulette; he may also have adequate evidence for believing he will be paid $10 if he does win. But it would be foolish of him to play, despite the fact that, in so doing, he would be acting upon hypotheses for which he has

adequate evidence. On the other hand, a swimmer may have adequate evidence for the hypothesis that he cannot swim ashore and yet be in a position wherein it would be unreasonable of him *not* to act upon it. And often, when we take precautionary measures—when we buy insurance, for example—we are justified in acting on hypotheses which are unreasonable and which we believe to be false. In deciding whether to act upon a hypothesis we must consider, not only the evidence that bears upon the hypothesis itself, but also the evidence that bears upon the "utility" or "moral gain" of acting upon it. We should try to decide, for example, what the value of acting upon the hypothesis would be if the hypothesis were true, what the "disvalue" of acting upon the hypothesis would be if the hypothesis were false, and we must try to compare these values and disvalues.[6] And we should also consider whether we ought to inquire further—whether we ought to seek out *additional* evidence. I have adequate evidence for the hypothesis that this is a piece of paper and in setting out to write I may be satisfied with the evidence at hand; but before betting my savings on the hypothesis I should make a more thorough investigation.

The question whether to *accept* a certain hypothesis—whether to *believe* it—is thus easier to answer than the question of whether to act upon it.[7] In deciding whether to accept it, we need not consider the "utility" or "moral gain"

---

[5] Compare this dialogue from Sheridan's *The Rivals*: "Absolute: 'Sure, Sir, this is not very reasonable, to summon my affection for a lady I know nothing of.' Sir Anthony: I am sure, Sir, 'tis more unreasonable in you to object to a lady you know nothing of" (quoted by J. M. Keynes in *A Treatise on Probability* [London, 1921], p. 41).

[6] These concepts are discussed with more exactness in writings on probability. See, for example, Rudolph Carnap, *Logical Foundations of Probability* (Chicago, 1950), pp. 226–279.

[7] I suggest that the concept of *acting upon* a hypothesis must be defined by reference to *action, purpose,* and *belief* in some such way as this. "In acting A, S is *acting upon* h" means: in acting A, S is trying to produce E; and he is acting as he would act if, further, (i) he believed h and (ii) he believed that A will result in E if and only if h is true. I shall not discuss the concepts of *purpose* and *action* in this book.

that would result from acting upon it. And we need not consider whether we ought to make further inquiry and investigation.

If a proposition, statement, or hypothesis is acceptable but not evident, then its contradictory is also acceptable but not evident. Such a proposition might be called epistemically indifferent. We may add, then, the following definition:

> (5) "*h* is *indifferent* for S" means: (i) it is false that S has adequate evidence for *h* and (ii) it is also false that S has adequate evidence for non-*h*.

The hypothesis that it will rain in London a year from today is, for most of us, epistemically indifferent; we do not have adequate evidence either for it or for its contradictory. If a proposition or hypothesis is indifferent, its contradictory is also indifferent. An indifferent proposition is thus one which is neither evident nor unreasonable. According to Clifford, no proposition is epistemically indifferent. According to the "absolute skeptic," all propositions are epistemically indifferent.[8]

If we were to need the term "dubitable," meaning fit to be disbelieved, we could define "*h* is *dubitable* for S" as "non-*h* is acceptable for S." We could then say that an epistemically indifferent proposition is one that is both acceptable and dubitable.

Without attempting to formulate an exact logic of epistemic terms, let us note certain principles which have been assumed in the foregoing. The expressions "*h* is more worthy of S's belief than non-*H*" and "non-*h* is more worthy of S's belief than *h*" are contraries; they may both be false but they cannot both be true. (We should suppose that these expressions contain the temporal reference

"at *t*.") Hence, for any hypothesis *h* and any subject S, either *h* is acceptable for S or non-*h* is acceptable for S. This principle is not incompatible with saying that some hypotheses are epistemically indifferent; for, although it says, of any hypothesis and its contradictory, that at least one is acceptable, it does not preclude the possibility of both being acceptable.

In an important series of studies, G. H. von Wright has pointed out the logical analogy which holds between the *ethical* terms "wrong," "obligatory," "permitted," and "indifferent," respectively, and the *modal* terms "impossible," "necessary," "possible," and "contingent."[9] The analogy also holds between each of these sets of terms and our *epistemic* terms "unreasonable," "evident," "acceptable," and "indifferent." ("Dubitable" would correspond to the terms "unrequired" and "unnecessary.") The assumptions discussed below have their analogues in ethics and in modal logic.

We should assume that the conjunction "*h* is acceptable for S and *i* is acceptable for S" does *not* imply "The conjunction of *h* and *i* is acceptable for S." The hypothesis that a certain object is a dog may be acceptable; the hypothesis that it is a stone may also be acceptable; but the hypothesis that it is both a dog and a stone is unreasonable. On the other hand, the conjunction "*h* is evident for S and *i* is evident for S" is equivalent to "The conjunction, *h* and *i*, is evident

---

[8] See Sextus Empiricus, *Outlines of Pyrrhonism*, bk. I, especially pp. 9, 112, and 123 of vol. I of *Sextus Empiricus* (Loeb Classical Library, London, 1933).

[9] Compare G. H. von Wright, *An Essay in Modal Logic* (Amsterdam, 1951); "Deontic Logic," *Mind*, LX (1951), 1–13; and "On the Logic of Some Axiological and Epistemological Concepts," *Ajatus* (Helsinki), XVII (1952), 213–234. Although Von Wright does not discuss the epistemic concepts listed above, much of what I have said about the first four concepts is suggested by his work. In the *Ajatus* article, he introduces the epistemological concepts "falsified," "verified," "not-falsified," and "undecided." Compare Alan Ross Anderson, *The Formal Analysis of Normative Systems* (Technical Report, no. 2, Interaction Laboratory, Sociology Department, Yale University, 1956).

for S." If it is evident that the thief worked alone and also evident that he came at night, then it is evident that he worked alone and came at night. We should assume, further, that the disjunction "Either h is acceptable for S or i is acceptable for S" is equivalent to "The disjunction, h or i, is acceptable for S." But "The disjunction, h or i, is *evident* for S is *not* equivalent to "Either h is evident for S or i is evident for S." It is now evident, for example, that the next man to be elected President of the United States will be either a Democrat or a Republican, but it is not now evident that he will be a Democrat and it is not now evident that he will be a Republican.

Note that we may form a logical square, whose upper right and left corners are, respectively, "evident" and "unreasonable," and whose lower right and left corners are "acceptable" and "dubitable." For "h is evident" implies "h is acceptable" and contradicts "h is dubitable," and "h is unreasonable" implies "h is dubitable" and contradicts "h is acceptable."

I have been assuming that, if it is unreasonable for S to accept h, then S ought to *refrain* from accepting h. If we wish to avoid a rigid ethics of belief, we may confine our principles to what one ought to *refrain* from believing. In such a case, we may say that a man fulfills his epistemic obligations provided only that he doesn't believe what he ought not to believe. A more rigid ethics would be concerned, more positively, with what we *ought* to believe. It might tell us, for example, that, if a proposition is unreasonable and therefore one which ought *not* to be accepted, then its contradictory, which is evident, is a proposition which *ought* to be accepted. For our present purposes, it is not necessary to make a decision concerning these two types of ethics.[10]

An adequate epistemology would also include such principles as this: if it is evident that h implies i and if i is unreasonable, then h is unreasonable. It may be evident, for example, that if the Senator votes, he will vote against his party. If it is unreasonable to believe that he will vote against his party, then it is also unreasonable to believe that he will vote. But if, on the other hand, the hypothesis that he will vote is acceptable, then so, too, is the hypothesis that he will vote against his party.

There are other epistemic principles whose status is more difficult to determine. Suppose, for example, that h is evident, that h entails i, but that it is not evident that h entails i. Should we say, in such a case, that i is evident? R. B. Braithwaite, in *Scientific Explanation*, discusses similar questions in some detail, noting that the issues which they involve are very much like those involved in distinguishing between what we have called the "practical" and "absolute" senses of the ethical terms "right" and "duty."[11]

Let us now consider the epistemic uses of "know"—its uses in such statements as "He knows the earth to be round" and "The speaker knows that the hall is filled."

A number of authors have tried to reduce this epistemic sense of know —*knowing that*—to a kind of verbal *knowing how*. "Knowing that some fact is the case is to know how to tell the truth about matters of a certain kind."[12]

contexts such as the above should not be interpreted in this way; I shall consider their interpretation in Chapter Seven.

10 Some ought-statements—for example, "If you want to be happy, you ought to believe in God"—are concerned only with telling how to bring about certain ends, ends which can be described without ethical or epistemic terms. But ought-statements in

11 R. B. Braithwaite, *Scientific Explanation*, pp. 279 ff. Compare C. S. Peirce, *Collected Papers* (Cambridge, Mass., 1931), I, 311 ff.; C. I. Lewis, "Right Believing and Concluding," in *The Ground and Nature of the Right* (New York, 1955), ch. ii; and G. Polya, *Patterns of Plausible Inference* (Princeton, 1954), *passim*.

12 John Watling, "Inferences from the Known to the Unknown," *Proceedings of the Aristotelian Society*, LV (1954–1955), 58.

Knowing that the earth is round, according to this conception, differs from knowing how to swim only in that a different kind of skill or aptness is involved, namely, "the capacity to state correctly what is the case."[13] If, by "the capacity to state correctly what is the case," we were to mean merely "the capacity to utter words truly describing what is the case," then this capacity, like the ability to swim, *would* be a kind of aptness of the body. But if we define "knowing that the earth is round" in terms of *this* capacity—the capacity to utter the sentence "The earth is round" (or some other sentence having the same meaning)—then we must say, of most of those people who believe that the earth is *flat*, that they *know* that it is round. For most of those people are capable of uttering the sentence "The earth is round." Hence a qualification must be introduced in the phrase "the capacity of uttering words truly describing what is the case" if this phrase is to provide us with an adequate definition of *knowing that*.[14]

A definition of *knowing that* should be adequate, moreover, to the distinction between *knowing* and *believing truly*. If I now predict the winner on the basis of what the tea leaves say, then, even though my prediction may be true, I cannot now be said to *know* that it is true.

"Knowing that," I suggest, has at least two epistemic senses. In what follows, I shall confine "know" to the broader of these senses and use "certain" for the narrower sense. The following, then, will be our definition of "know":

(6) "S *knows* that *h* is true" means: (i) S accepts *h*; (ii) S has ade-

quate evidence for *h*; and (iii) *h* is true.

If we wish to avoid the term "true," we may substitute this formulation:

"S knows that . . ." means: (i) S accepts the hypothesis (or proposition) that . . .; (ii) S has adequate evidence for the hypothesis (or proposition) that . . .; and (iii). . . .

Or we may use the locution of definition (1) and speak of S knowing "that *x* is *f*."

The term "accepts" which appears in (6) has not been previously defined; I shall discuss it in detail in Chapter Eleven. "Assumes" is an alternative: for "S accepts *h*" is replaceable by "S assumes that *h* is true"; and "S accepts the proposition or hypothesis that *x* is *f*" is replaceable by "S assumes that *x* is *f*."

If a man knows, say, that the hall has been painted, then, according to our definition, he accepts the hypothesis that it has been painted, he has adequate evidence for this hypothesis, and, finally, the hall *has* been painted. On the other hand, if he accepts the hypothesis, has adequate evidence for it, but does not *know* that it is true, then the hall has not been painted.

Should we say that, if S knows *h* to be true, then S *believes* that *h* is true? (It should be noted that *believing* a proposition is not the same as asserting, proclaiming, or announcing that one believes it. When we *assert* a proposition and when we *say* that we believe it, then, unless we are lying, we are *acting upon* the proposition. I shall return to this distinction in Chapter Eleven.) There is a sense of "believe," in its ordinary use, which is such that "S believes that *h* is true" entails "S does *not* know that *h* is true." If I *know* that La Paz is in Bolivia, I'm not likely to say, "I believe that La Paz is in Bolivia," for "I *believe* that La Paz is in Bolivia" suggests I don't know that it is. In this use, "S believes that *h* is true" means that S

[13] John Hartland-Swann, "The Logical Status of 'Knowing That,' " *Analysis*, XVI (1956), 114.

[14] Still other complications which this "verbal aptitude" definition of *knowing that* involves are discussed in Chapter Eleven, Section 3.

accepts *h* but does not know that *h* is true. Hence, if we interpret "believe" in this way, we cannot say that *knowing* entails *believing*. There is still another use of "believe" which is such that the expression "*I* believe"—an expression in the first person—entails "I know," or at least entails "I have adequate evidence." If a man says, "His policy, I believe, will not succeed," the parenthetical expression may be intended to express the claim to know or the claim to have adequate evidence that the policy will not succeed.[15]

But "believe" is also used to mean the same as "accept," in the sense in which "accept" is meant above, and in this use *knowing* does entail *believing*. I may believe that *x* is *f,* in this third sense of "believe," and yet not *say*, "I believe that *x* is *f*"; for, as we have noted, when "I believe" is used in this construction (in contrast with its parenthetical use) it is ordinarily intended to express doubt or hesitation. *You* may say of me, however, "He believes that *x* is *f* and, for all I know, he *knows* that *x* is *f*."

But even if there is a sense of "believe," or "accept," in which *knowing* entails *believing*, or *accepting*, we must not think of knowing as being, in any sense, a "species of" believing, or accepting. A man can be said to believe firmly, or reluctantly, or hesitatingly, but no one can be said to know firmly, or reluctantly, or hesitatingly. Professor Austin has noted that, although we may ask, "*How* do you know?" and "*Why* do you believe?" we may not ask, "*Why* do you know?" or "*How* do you believe?"[16] The relation of knowing to

believing, in the present sense of "believe," is not that of falcon to bird or of airedale to dog; it is more like that of arriving to traveling. *Arriving* entails *traveling*—a man cannot arrive unless he has traveled—but arriving is not a species of traveling.[17]

When we exhort people epistemically, we say, not "You ought to *believe h*," but "You ought to *know h*." If I say to my friend, "You ought to know *h*," it is likely that I accept *h* and believe that he has adequate evidence for *h*; hence the only additional condition I'm exhorting him to meet is that of believing *h*. Or it may be that I claim to know *h* myself and am suggesting that he ought to make further inquiry or investigation (see Section 4 of the present chapter) and that when he does he will then have adequate evidence for *h*. Similar remarks hold of such statements as "You ought to have *known h*."

A second sense of "know" may be obtained by stipulating that the subject *know*, in the first sense, that he has adequate evidence. The statement "S knows that he has adequate evidence" raises important philosophical questions, comparable to certain controversial questions about ethics, which I shall consider in Chapter Seven. If, as many philosophers believe, there is reason to say that people cannot *know* what they ought to do, then there is also reason to say that people cannot know which of their beliefs are evident.

Still another sense of "know" may be obtained by stipulating that (ii), in definition (6), describe a *causal* condition of (i). Using "know" in this sense, we cannot say that a man knows a proposition to be true unless we can also say that he believes it *because* he has adequate evidence for it.[18]

---

[15] Compare J. O. Urmson, "Parenthetical Verbs," *Mind*, vol. LXI (1952), reprinted in Antony Flew, ed., *Essays in Conceptual Analysis* (London, 1956).

[16] J. L. Austin, "Other Minds," *Proceedings of the Aristotelian Society*, suppl. vol. XX (1946), reprinted in Antony Flew, ed., *Logic and Language*, 2d ser. (Oxford, 1953).

[17] Professor Gilbert Ryle has used this example in another connection, which I discuss in Chapter Ten, Section 7.

[18] In Chapter Six I shall discuss what is sometimes called—misleadingly, I think—"knowledge by acquaintance."

The term "certain," like "know," is used in many ways. Sometimes it is a synonym for the modal term "necessary"; sometimes one is said to be certain of a proposition only if one is unable to doubt it or if one accepts it with a "maximum degree of confidence"; and sometimes one is said to be certain only if one *knows* that one knows. But the sense of "certain" which is of most importance epistemically, I think, is this:

(7) "S is *certain* that *h* is true" means: (i) S knows that *h* is true and (ii) there is no hypothesis *i* such that *i* is more worthy of S's belief than *h*.

We could avoid "true," if we chose, in the manner suggested in connection with the definition of "know" above.

Sometimes the locution "S is certain" is used to mean merely that S *feels sure*. And in this use, of course, "S is certain" does not imply that S knows. I felt sure that my candidate would win the election, but since he did not, I could not have known that he would.

Knowledge Is Not Justified True Belief
EDMUND L. GETTIER

V arious attempts have been made in recent years to state necessary and sufficient conditions for someone's knowing a given proposition. The attempts have often been such that they can be stated in a form similar to the following:[1]

  (a) S knows that P *IFF**
     (i) P is true,
     (ii) S believes that P, and
     (iii) S is justified in believing that P.

For example, Chisholm has held that the following gives the necessary and sufficient conditions for knowledge:[2]

  (b) S knows that P *IFF*
     (i) S accepts P,
     (ii) S has adequate evidence for P, and
     (iii) P is true.

Ayer has stated the necessary and sufficient conditions for knowledge as follows:[3]

  (c) S knows that P *IFF*
     (i) P is true,
     (ii) S is sure that P is true, and
     (iii) S has the right to be sure that P is true.

I shall argue that (a) is false in that the conditions stated therein do not constitute a *sufficient* condition for the truth of the proposition that S knows

[1] Plato seems to be considering some such definition at *Theaetetus* 201, and perhaps accepting one at *Meno* 98.

* Gettier uses IFF for "if and only if." Ed.

[2] Roderick M. Chisholm, *Perceiving: a Philosophical Study*, Cornell University Press (Ithaca, New York, 1957), p. 16.

[3] A. J. Ayer, *The Problem of Knowledge*, Macmillan (London, 1956), p. 34.

FROM *Analysis*, Vol. 26 (June 1963), 121–123. Reprinted by permission of the editor and author.

that P. The same argument will show that (b) and (c) fail if 'has adequate evidence for' or 'has the right to be sure that' is substituted for 'is justified in believing that' throughout.

I shall begin by noting two points. First, in that sense of 'justified' in which S's being justified in believing P is a necessary condition of S's knowing that P, it is possible for a person to be justified in believing a proposition that is in fact false. Secondly, for any proposition P, if S is justified in believing P, and P entails Q, and S deduces Q from P and accepts Q as a result of this deduction, then S is justified in believing Q. Keeping these two points in mind, I shall now present two cases in which the conditions stated in (a) are true for some proposition, though it is at the same time false that the person in question knows that proposition.

Case I:

Suppose that Smith and Jones have applied for a certain job. And suppose that Smith has strong evidence for the following conjunctive proposition:

(d) Jones is the man who will get the job, and Jones has ten coins in his pocket.

Smith's evidence for (d) might be that the president of the company assured him that Jones would in the end be selected, and that he, Smith, had counted the coins in Jones's pocket ten minutes ago. Proposition (d) entails:

(e) The man who will get the job has ten coins in his pocket. Let us suppose that Smith sees the entailment from (d) to (e), and accepts (e) on the grounds of (d), for which he has strong evidence. In this case, Smith is clearly justified in believing that (e) is true.

But imagine, further, that unknown to Smith, he himself, not Jones, will get the job. And, also, unknown to Smith, he himself has ten coins in his pocket. Proposition (e) is then true, though proposition (d), from which Smith inferred (e), is false. In our example, then, all of the following are

true: *(i)* (e) is true, *(ii)* Smith believes that (e) is true, and *(iii)* Smith is justified in believing that (e) is true. But it is equally clear that Smith does not *know* that (e) is true; for (e) is true in virtue of the number of coins in Smith's pocket, while Smith does not know how many coins are in Smith's pocket, and bases his belief in (e) on a count of the coins in Jones's pocket, whom he falsely believes to be the man who will get the job.

Case II:

Let us suppose that Smith has strong evidence for the following proposition:

(f) Jones owns a Ford.

Smith's evidence might be that Jones has at all times in the past within Smith's memory owned a car, and always a Ford, and that Jones has just offered Smith a ride while driving a Ford. Let us imagine, now, that Smith has another friend, Brown, of whose whereabouts he is totally ignorant. Smith selects three place-names quite at random, and constructs the following three propositions:

(g) Either Jones owns a Ford, or Brown is in Boston;

(h) Either Jones owns a Ford, or Brown is in Barcelona;

(i) Either Jones owns a Ford, or Brown is in Brest-Litovsk.

Each of these propositions is entailed (f). Imagine that Smith realizes the entailment of each of these propositions he has constructed by (f), and proceeds to accept (g), (h), and (i) on the basis of (f). Smith has correctly inferred (g), (h), and (i) from a proposition for which he has strong evidence. Smith is therefore completely justified in believing each of these three propositions. Smith, of course, has no idea where Brown is.

But imagine now that two further conditions hold. First, Jones does *not* own a Ford, but is at present driving a rented car. And secondly, by the sheerest coincidence, and entirely unknown to Smith, the place mentioned in proposition (h) happens really to be the place where Brown is. If these two conditions hold then Smith does *not* know that (h) is true, even though *(i)* (h) *is* true, *(ii)* Smith does believe that (h) is true, and

(iii) Smith is justified in believing that (h) is true.

These two examples show that definition (a) does not state a *sufficient* condition for someone's knowing a given proposition. The same cases, with appropriate changes, will suffice to show that neither definition (b) nor definition (c) do so either.

Metaphysics

The essays that follow are concerned with causality, personal identity, freedom of the will, and mind and body. The causal principle affirms that everything that has a beginning has a cause. Few if any principles have played a larger role in the systems and debates of philosophers from the beginning of philosophy to the present.

Many of the issues concerning the causal principle cluster around two questions. First, is it self-evident? That is, is the denial of the causal principle self-contradictory? John Locke thought it contradictory to deny the causal principle, but David Hume powerfully challenged Locke's view. It is fair to say that almost all contemporary philosophers follow Hume in this matter.

Second, how is the causal principle related to experience? Is Kant right in maintaining that sensory experience is possible only because the causal principle applies without exception to everything we sense? Or is Mill right when he suggests that we can justify the causal principle by inductive reasoning? For Kant the principle is "necessary" in a sense we attempt to explain in our introduction to his essay. For Mill the principle is not necessary in any sense but is simply an empirical generalization. Who is right here? Or are both men mistaken?

Two questions concerning persons come next. One asks: "Do men have free will?" If we answer in the affirmative, we should probably say that there is a self that is distinct from its states and that is the choosing agent. That there is an agent or self does not of course, entail, that the agent is free. Let us say that an agent S is free with respect to an action A at time T if and only if, given all that is the case at T, S can perform A or not perform A. Whether he does or not is up to him. He may act for a given justifying reason, but he may also act without a justifying reason or against justifying reasons. Is this concept of freedom intelligible? Is it compatible with what we know about the physical universe? If God exists, can men be free? Is freedom of this kind required if men are to be morally responsible for what they do? Is a sense of being free enough to guarantee that we are free? What does the contrary view—that men are determined—amount to? These questions raise issues central to the resolution of the umbrella question "Do men have free will?"

A second question, "What is a person," can be approached through another, slightly more restricted, question: "What makes a person the same at one time as at another?" Or, to reduce the number of assumptions, we can ask "Is there a basis for personal identity?" Is personal identity only a continuity of processes and states? Is a person only a bundle of thoughts and deeds related merely by temporal succession? Or is there something that *has* the states and undergoes the processes but remains distinct from them? How is memory related to personal identity? Can a person exist distinct from his body? Answering these questions would provide a substantial beginning toward an understanding of what it is to be a person.

Turning to topics concerning mind, the first question would be: "Are mind and body distinct?" A negative answer has the advantage of simplicity; instead of two kinds of things—minds and bodies—we will have only one. But which one? Bodies, because we can see and touch them, whereas we can treat minds simply as capacities of bodies to behave intelligently? Or minds, because we are self-conscious, directly and reflexively aware of our own consciousness, whereas we can treat the objects of sight and touch as dependent for their existence on the self that experiences them? Does the fact, or at least the apparent fact, that we can say some things about bodies that we cannot sensibly say about minds and say other things about minds that we cannot sensibly say about bodies entail that minds and bodies, however closely related, are quite distinct and not to be identified? Is there any empirically established data that requires us to answer our questions in one way rather than another? If mind-body dualism is the common-sense view, does this count in its favor? To answer our initial question involves providing answers to these others as well.

Suppose that mind and body are distinct. Do they interact? Do states of minds cause bodily states, and do states of bodies cause mental states? If we say such interaction does not take place then how do we account for the apparent correlation between choice and bodily movement, worry and ulcers, pains and cuts, and depression and drug intake? Choices, pains, worry, and depression are, or involve, mental states, whereas bodily movements, cuts, ulcers and drug intakes are, or involve, bodily states. They appear to be causally related. If we answer our question in the affirmative, how is the interaction possible? Minds are temporal but nonspatial; bodies are temporal and spatial. How can one kind of entity affect the other?

These questions about causality, persons, and minds and bodies by no means exhaust the traditional topics of metaphysics. But the questions we have chosen are representative, interrelated, and central. The methods of argument and appraisal illustrated in the topics discussed will be appropriate for the other questions as well.

K. E. Y.

The Causal Principle

The Causal Principle and Self-Evidence

*J*ohn *Locke* claims that "Everything that has a beginning must have a cause" is "a proposition certainly true." His defense of this claim is simply this: "the idea of beginning to be is necessarily connected with the idea of some operation; and the idea of operation [is identical] with the idea of something operating which we call a cause." Put in contemporary language, Locke's claim is that the statement "Something came into existence but was not caused to do so by something else" is a flat contradiction. So for Locke the question "Must every event have a cause?" is exactly analogous to "Must every triangle have three angles?" Anyone who has the concepts in question clearly in mind can see that the answers are plainly and irrevocably in the affirmative, and necessarily so.

David Hume radically challenges the confidence of much of the philosophic tradition that "Whatever begins to exist must have a cause of existence." According to a widely accepted doctrine, the closest that anyone can come to denying that this is so is to utter its verbal denial: no one can *believe,* though one can *say,* "Some event comes into existence without being caused to do so."

Hume's concern is not to show that the causal principle is false. Rather, he is interested in discovering whether it is the patent and obvious truth that it is supposed to be and in discerning (in case it is not a self-evident truth) just what its status is.

His critique of the claim that the causal principle is "intuitively certain" consists of two arguments. They are: (1) a statement that can be denied without contradiction is not intuitively certain; the causal principle can be denied without contradiction; hence the causal principle is not intuitively certain. (This states the essence of the second paragraph of Hume's essay.) (2) For any two distinct things we choose, there is no contradiction in supposing that the one exists without the other. ("Distinct" indicates that we are not concerned with the relation between a thing and a *part* of that thing.) In fact, fish cannot exist without water, but there is no self-contradiction in supposing that a fish exists without there being any water: finding such an entity is not inconceivable, however unlikely it may be. But if, for any two things we choose, either could exist without the other, then either could exist without being *caused* by the other.

We can put this argument schematically. Suppose, for the sake of simplicity, that only three distinct things exist—namely *A*, *B*, and *C*. *A* could (without contradiction) exist without *B* or *C* existing. So *A* could exist without being caused to exist by *B* or *C*. Precisely analogous comments apply with respect to *B* and *C*. And no matter how many things exist, exactly similar comments will be true of each of them. Still another way of putting this argument is this. For any two things *A* and *B*, the statement that "*A* causes *B*" is true does not entail that the existence of *B* can be *deduced* from the existence of *A* alone.

The force of Hume's critique is this: Anyone who holds (as did Locke) that the causal principle is true must *show* that it is, and he cannot do so by saying that the denial of this principle is contradictory, for it is not contradictory to deny the causal principle.

The remainder of Hume's essay contains his replies to arguments offered by Hobbes, Clarke, and Locke to prove the causal principle. Each of these arguments is shown simply to beg the question—in order to prove the principle, they assume it by using as a premise in their proof a statement identical to the principle itself. Hume adds the comment that the fact that "Every *effect* has cause" *is* necessarily true (its denial being plainly contradictory) is of no help to Locke. For it leaves open the question "Is every thing that exists an effect?" which is the same question as "Does everything have a cause?" Hume's conclusion (not included in the selection that follows) is that belief in the causal principle is a "natural belief"—a belief that we can neither justify nor escape adopting.

The Causal Principle Is Self-Evident
JOHN LOCKE

" *E*verything must have a cause" is not a true principle of reason, nor a true proposition, but the contrary. The certainty whereof we attain by the contemplation of our ideas, and by perceiving that the idea of eternity and the idea of the existence of something do agree; and the idea of existence from eternity and of having a cause do not agree or are inconsistent within the same thing. But "everything that has a beginning must have a cause" is a true principle of reason or a proposition certainly true; which we come to know by the same way, i.e. by contemplating our ideas and perceiving that the idea of beginning to be is necessarily connected with the idea of some operation; and the idea of operation with the idea of something operating which we call a cause. And so the beginning to be is perceived to agree with the idea of a cause, as is expressed in the proposition, and thus it comes to be a certain proposition, and so may be called a principle of reason, as every true proposition is to him that perceives the certainty of it.

The Causal Principle Is Not Self-Evident
DAVID HUME

*T*o begin with the first question concerning the necessity of a cause: 'Tis a general maxim in philosophy, that *whatever begins to exist, must have a cause of existence.* This is commonly taken for granted in all reasonings, without any proof given or demanded. 'Tis suppos'd to be founded on intuition, and to be one of those maxims, which tho' they may be deny'd with the lips, 'tis impossible for men in their hearts really to doubt of. But if we examine this maxim by the idea of knowledge above-explain'd, we shall discover in it no mark of any such intuitive certainty; but on the contrary shall find, that 'tis of a nature quite foreign to that species of conviction.

All certainty arises from the comparison of ideas, and from the discovery of such relations as are unalterable, so long as the ideas continue the same. These relations are *resemblance, proportions in quantity and number, degrees of any quality, and contrariety*; none of which are imply'd in this proposition, *Whatever has a beginning has also a cause of existence.* That proposition therefore is not intuitively certain. At least any one, who wou'd assert it to be intuitively certain, must deny those to be the only infallible relations, and must find some other relation of that kind to be imply'd in it; which it will then be time enough to examine.

But here is an argument, which proves at once, that the foregoing proposition is neither intuitively nor demonstrably certain. We can never demonstrate the necessity of a cause to every new existence, or new modification of existence, without shewing at the same time the impossibility there is, that any thing can ever begin to exist without

FROM John Locke's first *Letter* to Bishop Stillingfleet (1697).

FROM: Section III "Why A Cause Is Always Necessary?" and Section IV "The Component Parts of Our Reasonings Concerning Causes and Effects" in *A Treatise of Human Nature,* David Hume. Book I, Part III (originally published in 1739).

some productive principle; and where the latter proposition cannot be prov'd, we must despair of ever being able to prove the former. Now that the latter proposition is utterly incapable of a demonstrative proof, we may satisfy ourselves by considering, that as all distinct ideas are separable from each other, and as the ideas of cause and effect are evidently distinct, 'twill be easy for us to conceive any object to be non-existent this moment, and existent the next, without conjoining to it the distinct idea of a cause or productive principle. The separation, therefore, of the idea of a cause from that of a beginning of existence, is plainly possible for the imagination; and consequently the actual separation of these objects is so far possible, that it implies no contradiction nor absurdity; and is therefore incapable of being refuted by any reasoning from mere ideas; without which 'tis impossible to demonstrate the necessity of a cause.

Accordingly we shall find upon examination, that every demonstration, which has been produc'd for the necessity of a cause, is fallacious and sophistical. All the points of time and place,[1] say some philosophers, in which we can suppose any object to begin to exist, are in themselves equal; and unless there be some cause, which is peculiar to one time and to one place, and which by that means determines and fixes the existence, it must remain in eternal suspence; and the object can never begin to be, for want of something to fix its beginning. But I ask; Is there any more difficulty in supposing the time and place to be fix'd without a cause, than to suppose the existence to be determin'd in that manner? The first question that occurs on this subject is always, *whether* the object shall exist or not: The next, *when* and *where* it shall begin to exist. If the removal of a cause be intuitively absurd in the one case, it must be so in the other: And if that absurdity be not clear without a proof in the one case, it will

equally require one in the other. The absurdity, then, of the one supposition can never be a proof of that of the other; since they are both upon the same footing, and must stand or fall by the same reasoning.

The second argument,[2] which I find us'd on this head, labours under an equal difficulty. Every thing, 'tis said, must have a cause; for if any thing wanted a cause, *it* wou'd produce *itself*; that is, exist before it existed; which is impossible. But this reasoning is plainly inconclusive; because it supposes, that in our denial of a cause we still grant what we expressly deny, *viz.* that there must be a cause; which therefore is taken to be the object itself; and *that*, no doubt, is an evident contradiction. But to say that any thing is produc'd, or to express myself more properly; comes into existence, without a cause, is not to affirm, that 'tis itself its own cause; but on the contrary in excluding all external causes, excludes *a fortiori* the thing itself which is created. An object, that exists absolutely without any cause, certainly is not its own cause; and when you assert, that the one follows from the other, you suppose the very point in question, and take it for granted, that 'tis utterly impossible any thing can ever begin to exist without a cause, but that upon the exclusion of one productive principle, we must still have recourse to another.

'Tis exactly the same case with the[3] third argument, which has been employ'd to demonstrate the necessity of a cause. Whatever is produc'd without any cause, is produc'd by *nothing*; or in other words, has nothing for its cause. But nothing can never be a cause, no more than it can be something, or equal to two right angles. By the same intuition, that we perceive nothing not to be equal to two right angles, or not to be something, we perceive, that it can never be a cause; and consequently must perceive, that every object has a real cause of its existence.

[2] Dr. *Clarke* and others.

[3] Mr. *Locke*.

[1] Mr. *Hobbes*.

I believe it will not be necessary to employ many words in shewing the weakness of this argument, after what I have said of the foregoing. They are all of them founded on the same fallacy, and are deriv'd from the same turn of thought. 'Tis sufficient only to observe, that when we exclude all causes we really do exclude them, and neither suppose nothing nor the object itself to be the causes of the existence; and consequently can draw no argument from the absurdity of these suppositions to prove the absurdity of that exclusion. If every thing must have a cause, it follows, that upon the exclusion of other causes we must accept of the object itself or of nothing as causes. But 'tis the very point in question, whether every thing must have a cause or not; and therefore, according to all just reasoning, it ought never to be taken for granted.

They are still more frivolous, who say, that every effect must have a cause, because 'tis imply'd in the very idea of effect. Every effect necessarily pre-supposes a cause; effect being a relative term, of which cause is the correlative. But this does not prove, that every being must be preceded by a cause; no more than it follows, because every husband must have a wife, that therefore every man must be marry'd. The true state of the question is, whether every object, which begins to exist, must owe its existence to a cause; and this I assert neither to be intuitively nor demonstratively certain, and hope to have prov'd it sufficiently by the foregoing arguments.

Since it is not from knowledge or any scientific reasoning, that we derive the opinion of the necessity of a cause to every new production, that opinion must necessarily arise from observation and experience. The next question, then, shou'd naturally be, *how experience gives rise to such a principle?* But as I find it will be more convenient to sink this question in the following, *Why we conclude, that such particular causes must necessarily have such particular effects, and why we form an inference from one to another?* we shall make that the subject of our future enquiry. 'Twill, perhaps, be found in the end, that the same answer will serve for both questions.

SECTION IV
OF THE COMPONENT PARTS OF OUR REASONINGS CONCERNING CAUSE AND EFFECT

THO' the mind in its reasonings from causes or effects carries its view beyond those objects, which it sees or remembers, it must never lose sight of them entirely, nor reason merely upon its own ideas, without some mixture of impressions, or at least of ideas of the memory, which are equivalent to impressions. When we infer effects from causes, we must establish the existence of these causes; which we have only two ways of doing, either by an immediate perception of our memory or senses, or by an inference from other causes; which causes again we must ascertain in the same manner, either by a present impression, or by an inference from *their* causes, and so on, till we arrive at some object, which we see or remember. 'Tis impossible for us to carry on our inference *in infinitum*; and the only thing, that can stop them, is an impression of the memory or senses, beyond which there is no room for doubt or enquiry.

To give an instance of this, we may chuse any point of history, and consider for what reason we either believe or reject it. Thus we believe that CAESAR was kill'd in the senate-house on the *ides* of *March*; and that because this fact is establish'd on the unanimous testimony of historians, who agree to assign this precise time and place to that event. Here are certain characters and letters present either to our memory or senses; which characters we likewise remember to have been used as the signs of certain ideas; and these ideas were either in the minds of such as were immediately present at that action, and received the ideas directly from its existence; or they were derived from the testimony of others, and that again from another testimony, by a visible gradation, 'till we arrive at those who were eye-witnesses and spectators of the event. 'Tis obvious all this chain of argument or connexion of causes and effects, is at first founded on those characters or letters, which are seen or remembered, and that without the authority either of the memory or senses our whole reasoning would be chimerical and without foundation. Every link of the chain would in that case hang upon another; but there would not be any thing fixed to one end of it, capable of sustaining the whole; and consequently there would be no belief nor evidence. And this actually is the case with all *hypothetical* arguments, or reasonings upon a supposition; there being in them, neither any present impression, nor belief of a real existence.

I need not observe, that 'tis not just objection to the present doctrine, that we can reason upon our past conclusions or principles, without having recourse to those impressions, from which they first arose. For even supposing these impressions shou'd be entirely effaced from the memory, the conviction they produc'd may still remain; and 'tis equally true, that all reasonings concerning causes and effects are originally derived from some impression; in the same manner, as the assurance of a demonstration proceeds always from a comparison of ideas, tho' it may continue after the comparison is forgot.

The
Causal Principle
and
Experience

I *mmanuel Kant* accepted Hume's critique of Locke's view, but he believed
that "Every event has a cause" is necessarily true in an intelligible sense
of "necessary" other than "logical necessary." He held that its necessary truth
is sufficient to provide a basis for knowledge beyond that which Hume's system
could allow. Kant's concern is with "not the origin of experience but of that
which lies in experience." In other words, his question is "What is the origin
of the order and connection of our sensory data?" not "What is the origin of
the content of sensory experience?" The difference involved here is roughly like
that between the man who wants to know why the stars have the orbits they do
versus the man who wants to know why there are any stars. The latter is concerned with the *content* of space, the former with *ordering* of the content of space.

Kant sharply distinguishes "experience from a mere aggregate of perceptions." For we relate our perceptions to one another by virtue of certain key
concepts, or categories. Among these are causality ("the reference of the
existence of one thing to the existence of another, which is necessitated by

the former"), subsistence or substance ("a subject which cannot itself be a predicate of any other thing"), and community ("substances which have each their own separate existence should depend on one another necessarily" so as to make possible "from the state of one thing an inference to the state of another thing beyond it").

Thus a priori *principles form the basis of objectively valid, though empirical judgments, that is, of the possibility of experience so far as it must connect objects as existing in nature. These principles are the proper laws of nature.*

The categories provide, as Josiah Royce once said, a sort of outline plan of the natural universe. Awareness of the plan is awakened by sensory experience, and the sounds, colored shapes, tastes, tactile sensations, and odors fill in the outline. The overall outline is determined by our possession of the categories. What the particular details are is determined by the particular content of sensory experience. The experiences are united by being the experiences of one subject of experience. Every experience can be accompanied by an "I think," that is, by an actual or potential awareness on the part of the experiencer that the experience is his. Any sensory experience we conceive of must be conceived of as someone's experience and as subject to, or manifesting, the categories; otherwise it is not conceived of at all.

We have seen that there are, according to Kant, certain basic concepts that underlie our thought and speech about sensory phenomena. The relation of these concepts to sensory experience is no mere contingent but universal fact, as it is a contingent but universal fact that decapitated men die. Possession of these concepts is a logically necessary condition of our thinking and speaking about the physical world in the way that we do. Indeed, what we call "laws of nature" are in part the products of our possession and application of these fundamental concepts.

What we call experience has roughly two elements: a formal element and a material element, or an a priori element versus an a posteriori one, or a *contributed* factor plus a *given* factor. The material, a posteriori, given element in our experience is simply the colored areas, the sounds, the odors, the tastes, the felt areas, the pressures, heat sensations, cold sensations, and so forth—all the elements that can, by abstraction or isolation from the pattern of our experience, be held up for individual consideration. What Kant calls "the faculty of sensibility" is simply our receptive capacity for such items of awareness as these; together they constitute our "sensory manifold."

The formal, a priori, contributed element is the key concepts mentioned above. In this attempt to make Kant's views intelligible and plausible, I shall waive the question as to how many key concepts, or categories, there are and the related question of how they are related to formal logic. Kant thought that there were exactly twelve and that these could be shown to form four groups of triads of properties such that every assertion could be shown to possess exactly one property from each triad.

Plainly, we do not experience isolated colored patches, tactile shapes and pressures, odors, and the like. Sensory data come to us in rather orderly bundles—we correlate the sweet taste, the shiny red surface, the crunching sound, the smooth feel, and the distinct and pleasant aroma that occur simultaneously into one experience by relating them all under the one concept "apple." We correlate the successive series of visual sensory phenomena of first a round red surface, then a concave red-and-white surface, and finally a mainly white, thin, oblong surface into the concept of one event—"the eating of an apple." And we correlate two "objects" together as being causally related when we treat the visual phenomena just noted (plus their taste, odor, and so forth) as the event of eating an apple.

When we correlate a set of sensory phenomena by regarding them as an experience of one thing (for example, an apple), perhaps unknowingly, we apply the concept of substance. When we regard the visual phenomena noted as belonging together in one process (such as the eating of an apple), we treat the various phenomena as presenting to us succeeding states of one substance (and so as an event). But in almost any kind of event, one stage follows upon another in a particular order. When we eat an apple, it gets smaller; the biting sensation is followed by a sweet taste; in sum, to classify a series of sensory phenomena under the rubric of a particular event-concept (such as, "eating an apple," "playing a record," "writing a letter"), we put the phenomena in question in a concrete order. We separate one set of phenomena from others and relate the members of that set in a nonarbitrary manner.

From the concept "substance" (or "object") we descend to particular object-concepts—apple, ball, pen, and so forth. The latter, as it were, "fill in" the former—give specific content and concrete application. We can, in Kant's view, "fill in" the concept of an object or a substance in various ways, but unless this general concept were part of our conceptual apparatus, we could not interpret sensory experience as we do. The concept of cause and effect plays a similar role to that of substance.

The notion of cause-effect Kant describes as applying "so far as a succession is found among phenomena, that is, an event." When successive states of a single object are in question, or when correlation and mutual affect of the states of two or more objects are in view, the concept of cause and effect (and, in the latter case, the concept of community) are applicable. Of course the general categories of cause and effect and community also need to be filled in by means of particular event-concepts—the eating of an apple, the melting of an ice cube, the clash of billard balls, or my raising my arm. Again, there are various ways of filling in these basic concepts or categories. But unless they were available to be filled in, we could not interpret sensory phenomena as we do. Similar remarks will hold about the other Kantian categories. Perhaps, then, we can now allow Kant to state his contention in a more general way.

. . . appearances [sensory phenomena] must be subsumed under the concept of Substance, which is the foundation of all determination of existence, as a concept of the thing itself; or secondly—so far as succession is found among phenomena, that is an event—under the concept of an effect with reference to

Cause; or lastly—so far as co-existence is to be known objectively . . . under the concept of Community (action and reaction). Thus a priori *principles form the basis of . . . the possibility of experience.*

If Kant's program is accepted, by comparison with Hume's empiricism there is gain. One can know a priori that the causal principle holds for every possible object of human sensory experience. There is also, by comparison with the rationalism of Descartes, Leibniz, or Spinoza, loss; one cannot know that the causal principle applies to anything that is not a possible object of sensory experience.

There are three claims, each somewhat more specific than its predecessor, that can usefully be appealed to in order to make clear what Kant, at least on the present account of his views, is maintaining.

(1)   There is a set of concepts common to all human interpretation of sensory experience without which this interpretation could not be made.

(2)   There is a set of concepts—namely, substance, cause and effect, community, and so forth—common to all human interpretation of sensory experience, without which this interpretation could not be made.

(3)   There is a set of concepts—namely, substance, cause and effect, community, and so forth—common to all human interpretation of sensory experience, and another set—namely, apple, pen, finger, and so forth—and without both of these sets this interpretation could not be made.

Now we could accept (1) but not (2) or (3). That is, we could agree that some set of concepts was basic to interpreting sense experience in the way that all men do, but deny that Kant has stated that set correctly. Or we could, as Kant does, hold (1) and (2) but deny (3); for Kant allows, apparently, for various systems of particular physical-object concepts and various systems of particular event-concepts that could serve equally well to "fill in" the categories he contends he has discovered to be essential to our interpretation of our sensory experience.

We can further expound Kant's view by contrasting it with alternative accounts of our interpretation of sensory experience. Kant rejects the view held by Aristotle and Locke that we abstract categories from sensory experience. He denies the view represented by Plato that the categories correspond to, or stand for, eternal, unchanging objects independent of all experience. He will not allow the view offered by Leibniz that God has established a harmony between the knower's mind and the object known. Insofar as the contributed, formal, a priori aspect of experience is concerned, we *make* experience—not consciously but still inevitably. He denies the claim of, for example, Descartes, Leibniz, and Spinoza, that we can unproblematically infer the nature of reality from the concepts basic to our interpretation of it. Kant does allow a certain analogue of traditional metaphysical reasoning, but this is not based on our interpretation of sensory phenomena but on moral experience and the concepts relevant to its analysis. (*See* Kant, "The Moral Argument, *Philosophy of Religion*.)

By way of putting Kant's view in contemporary terms, then, and contrasting it with competing philosophies, we have attempted to clarify what the Koenigsberg genius was saying. There are of course other ways of understanding his contentions.

We should note that attempts have been made by contemporary philosophers (especially C.D. Broad) to state the causal principle more precisely. Thus it has been suggested that the causal principle means that:

> (CP1) For everything that beings to exist, there is a sufficient condition of its existence and for every property that anything has there is a sufficient condition of its having that property.

A "sufficient condition" of *A* is any state of affairs *B* such that if *B* exists, then *A* exists. This, however, leaves open an ambiguity in "sufficient condition," for the fact that the number of planets is 3 $\times$ 3 is a sufficient condition of the fact that their number is 9, and the fact that there are 7 chairs in a room is a sufficient condition of the fact that the room contains at least 6 chairs, and the fact that a man is decapitated is a sufficient condition of the fact that the man is dead. Even if we rule out allowing that anything can be its own sufficient condition (thus ruling out our first example, since the "two" facts amount to exactly the same thing), we are left with our other two examples. The first of these is a case of entailment—that there are 7 chairs entails that there are at least 6 in the sense that the denial of this is contradictory. Causes are not generally held to be related to their effects in this way; if *A* was caused by *B*, this does not mean that *B* occurring is logically impossible without *A* occurring. That there are 7 chairs in a room would not normally be taken as causing it to be so that there are 6. Since, normally, that a cause occurs does not entail in this strict sense that its effect does, our final example is the only genuinely causal relation among the three instances mentioned. Further, the notion of causation is a *temporal* notion, whereas the notion of "sufficient condition" is an atemporal notion. For these reasons, it is perhaps wise to replace (CP1) by:

> (CP2) Everything that comes to exist has its sufficient precursor, and for every property that anything has, there is a sufficient precursor of its having that property.

The crucial concept in (CP2) can be defined in this manner: *a* is a sufficient precursor of *b* if *a* temporally precedes *b*, and if the occurrence of *a* at time *t* is always followed by the existence of *b* at time *t + 1*. (CP2), then, provides us with a statement of the causal principle in which the causal relation is treated as amounting simply to a relation of invariable temporal sequence of one member of a class of states of affairs upon a member of another class of states of affairs with temporal precedence belonging always to the member of the same class.

(CP2) may seem even *temporally* insufficient, as it allows that the cause may not exist at the same time as does the effect. At least if *efficacy* is to be salvaged as well as temporal precedence of cause to effect, we must restate (CP2) as:

> (CP3) Everything that comes to exist has its sufficient precursor, and for every property that anything has, there is a sufficient precursor of its having that property, and every sufficient precursor coexists for at least one moment with that to which it is a sufficient precursor.

It may, of course, be necessary to complicate (CP3) still further by requiring spatial contiguity between the relata in a relationship of sufficient precursorship (as did Hume) and/or by specifying (as did Kant) that if *a* is genuinely a sufficient precursor of *b*, then it is inconceivable that *b* is a sufficient precursor of *a*. Still other refinements may be necessary. For now, however, let us consider how any of these versions of the causal principle might conceivably be appraised. Is there any way to tell whether such claims are true?

A moment's reflection on (CP2) or (CP3) will show that it is not possible to confirm or disconfirm either in any simple empirical manner. Consider any property P^1. There is, according to (CP2) and (CP3), a sufficient precursor to P^1—say, P^2. But, again according to our causal principles, P^2 also has a sufficient precursor—say, P^3. And by now it will be evident that for any sufficient precursor P^n there will be another sufficient precursor—that of P^n—which may appropriately be dubbed P^{n+1}. In short, there will be an infinite number of sufficient precursors. This is tantamount to there being an infinite number of entities with a finite number of properties or a finite number of entities with an infinite number of properties or an infinite number of entities with an infinite number of properties. It needs no argument to see that no simple observation could possibly justify this staggeringly complex claim, which may conveniently be called "the infinity thesis."

We have seen that both (CP2) and (CP3)—and the same is true of (CP1) for that matter—entail the infinity thesis. Now if *A* entails *B*, then *B*'s truth is a logically necessary condition of *A*'s truth. If, then, *B* cannot be confirmed by simple observation, neither can *A* be confirmed by simple observation, as a necessary condition of *A*'s being confirmed is that *B* be confirmed. So neither (CP2) nor (CP3) can be confirmed by simple observation. Nor, more importantly, it is possible to conceive any of our versions of the causal principle as a mere summary of reports of simple observations; for no such summary of reports could, as does the causal principle, entail the infinity thesis.

Still further, none of these versions could ever be justified inductively. Suppose we know of events E^1, E^2 . . . E_n that each of these events has a cause. We might then infer quite plausibly that the next event will have a cause. But from such information nothing whatever will follow about the *cardinality* of the universe—that is, about whether there is or is not an infinite number of events to be taken account of. Exactly the same considerations follow if we speak of things and their properties—in line with (CP1), (CP2), and (CP3)—instead of speaking in terms of events. Once the causal principle is stated with a higher degree of precision, it can be seen, I think, that Mill's account of it as an inductive generalization will not do.

Still it is conceivable that an adaptation of Mill's view is defensible. Strictly none of our versions of the causal principle entail that there will be an infinitely long series of *future* conditions, for the simple reason that they entail nothing whatever about the future. More carefully, taking (CP2) as an example, they entail that *if* there is a future existent or property, it will have a sufficient precursor. But there is no claim that there *will be* such an existent or property. So the infinity thesis covers *past* events only; it entails that there have been an infinite number of past events. Now, if there were to be found a theory *T* which, better than any other, covers a set of sensory observations, and if *T* entails, or includes as an essential element, the infinity thesis, then this thesis could be said to be (in a wide sense) empirically confirmed. On one theory of the origin of our region of the universe, there was a "big bang" in which intensely dense matter exploded in a catastrophic beginning of our universe. According to another theory there is a constant flux over the millenia of millenia in stellar history from relative chaos to relative order and back and forth again *ad infinitum*. The latter theory entails the infinity thesis or something very like it. The former theory is not incompatible with this thesis unless it is so stated that the state preceding the "bang" was uncaused, but apparently it does not entail it. If, then, the theory of fluctuations covers the data better than the "big bang" theory, and if no other theory covers the relevant data as well, then it—and the infinity thesis that it entails—is tentatively confirmed.

It is obvious, however, that all this is a far cry from any ordinary version of inductive confirmation. Among the questions that arise are those concerning such matters as whether one theory does explain a set of data (taken as correct) with greater accuracy and simplicity than another theory, and whether one theory is more fruitful with respect to predictive power than another. The more complex a theory is, in terms of requiring appeal to various levels of hypotheses that are not mere reports of observed phenomena, (roughly) the more appeal is necessary to formal criteria (for example, coherence, simplicity, and elegance) in appraising the theory. At these rarified levels, the distinction between science and speculative metaphysics becomes less and less easy to make. It may be too strong to say, with Quine, that philosophers' questions differ from scientists' questions only in the level of their generality; the former's questions are for Quine simply more general than the latter's, and both are to be decided on ultimately pragmatic grounds. Nonethless, when a theory complex and powerful enough to entail the infinity thesis is under review, the barrier between science and speculative philosophy is likely to become very thin indeed.

If, then, the infinity thesis is in even an oblique way empirically confirmable, it is presumably in some such sense as that outlined above. But even if the infinity thesis were shown to be true, this would of course not establish any version of the causal principle. It would only show that the causal principle was not *false* because it entailed the infinity thesis. The important point in this context is that only by stretching Mill's view almost beyond recognition can it be made defensible with respect to a fairly precise formulation of the causal principle.

There might, of course, be a way of justifying some formulation of the causal principle by means of justifying a scientific or metaphysical system that entailed it or included it as an essential element. But this would involve appeal to the appraisal of one or more systems in terms of simplicity, coherence, consistency, and perhaps other formal considerations, and appeal to such criteria necessitates both their precise statement and their defense as guides to truth.

We can perhaps best sum up this rather complex discussion as follows: (1) the causal principle is not, in any of its formulations, such that to deny it is self-contradictory; (2) in no very precise formulation is the causal principle an empirical statement in the sense that it can be seen by simple observation to be true or considered to be merely a summary statement of reports of particular simple observations or to be the conclusion of an inductive argument; (3) appeal to a scientific (or metaphysical) system may provide some means of rationally deciding, pro or con, with respect to the truth or falsity of this principle, but if so, (a) that the system in question entails the infinity thesis will be no proof of any version of the causal principle, and (b) the criteria appealed to in appraising any system of the requisite power and complexity will likely themselves be open to some dispute.

The Causal Principle Is Presupposed in Experience
IMMANUEL KANT

In order to comprise the whole matter in one idea, it is first necessary to remind the reader that we are discussing, not the origin of experience, but that which lies in experience. The former pertains to empirical psychology and would even then never be adequately explained without the latter, which belongs to the critique of knowledge, and particularly of the understanding.

Experience consists of intuitions, which belong to the sensibility, and of judgments, which are entirely a work of the understanding. But the judgments which the understanding forms solely from sensuous intuitions are far from being judgments of experience. For in the one case the judgment connects only the perceptions as they are given in sensuous intuition, while in the other the judgments must express what experience in general and not what the mere perception (which possesses only subjective validity) contains. The judgment of experience must therefore add to the sensuous intuition and its logical connection in a judgment (after it has been rendered universal by comparison) something that determines the synthetical judgment as necessary and therefore as universally valid. This can be nothing else than that concept which represents the intuition as determined in itself with regard to one form of judgment rather than another, namely, a concept of that synthetical unity of intuitions which can only be represented by a given logical function of judgments.

The sum of the matter is this: the business of the senses is to intuit, that of the understanding is to think. But thinking is uniting representations in one consciousness. This union originates either merely relative to the subject and is accidental and subjective, or takes place absolutely and is necessary or objective. The union of representations in one consciousness is judgment. Thinking, therefore, is the same as judging or referring representations to judgments in general. Hence judgments are either merely subjective, when representations are referred to a consciousness in one subject only and united in it, or objective, when

FROM: *A Prolegomena to Any Future Metaphysics*, Immanuel Kant, P. Carus, trans. Sections 21a–30. Reprinted by permission of the Open Court Publishing Co. (originally published in 1783).

they are united in consciousness in general, that is, necessarily. The logical functions of all judgments are but various modes of uniting representations in consciousness. But if they serve for concepts, they are concepts of the necessary union of representations in [any] consciousness, and so are principles of objectively valid judgments. This union in consciousness is either analytical, by identity, or synthetical, by the combination and addition of various representations one to another. Experience consists in the synthetical connection of phenomena (perceptions) in consciousness, so far as this connection is necessary. Hence the pure concepts of the understanding are those under which all perceptions must be subsumed ere they can serve for judgments of experience, in which the synthetical unity of the perceptions is represented as necessary and universally valid.[1]

Judgments, when considered merely as the condition of the union of given representations in a consciousness, are rules. These rules, so far as they represent the union as necessary, are rules *a priori*, and, insofar as they cannot be deduced from higher rules, are principles. But in regard to the possibility of all experience, merely in relation to

the form of thinking in it, no conditions of judgments of experience are higher than those which bring the appearances, according to the various form of their intuition, under pure concepts of the understanding, which render the empirical judgment objectively valid. These are therefore the *a priori* principles of possible experience.

The principles of possible experience are then at the same time universal laws of nature, which can be known *a priori*. And thus the problem of our second question, "How is the pure science of nature possible?" is solved. For the system which is required for the form of a science is to be met with in perfection here, because, beyond the above-mentioned formal conditions of all judgments in general (and hence of all rules in general) offered in logic, no others are possible, and these constitute a logical system. The concepts grounded thereupon, which contain the *a priori* conditions of all synthetical and necessary judgments, accordingly constitute a transcendental system. Finally the principles, by means of which all phenomena are subsumed under these concepts, constitute a physical system, that is, a system of nature, which precedes all empirical knowledge of nature, and makes it possible. It may in strictness be denominated the universal and pure science of nature.

The first of the physical principles subsumes all phenomena, as intuitions in space and time, under the concept of quantity, and is thus a principle of the application of mathematics to experience. The second one subsumes the strictly empirical element, namely, sensation, which denotes the real in intuitions, not indeed directly under the concept of quantity, because sensation is not an intuition that *contains* either space or time, though it places the respective object corresponding to it in both. But still there is between reality (sense-representation) and the zero, or total void of intuition in time, a difference which has a quantity. For between every given degree of light and of darkness, between every degree of heat and of absolute cold, between every degree

[1] But how does the proposition that judgments of experience contain necessity in the synthesis of perceptions agree with my statement so often before inculcated that experience as cognition *a posteriori* can afford contingent judgments only? When I say that experience teaches me something, I mean only the perception that lies in experience—for example, that heat always follows the shining of the sun on a stone; consequently the proposition of experience is always so far accidental. That this heat necessarily follows the shining of the sun is contained indeed in the judgment of experience (by means of the concept of cause), yet is a fact not learned by experience; for conversely, experience is first of all generated by this addition of the concept of the understanding (of cause) to perception. How perception attains this addition may be seen by referring in the *Critique* itself to the [first] section of the "Transcendental Faculty of Judgment."

of weight and of absolute lightness, between every degree of occupancy space and of totally void space, diminishing degrees can be conceived, in the same manner as between consciousness and total unconsciousness (psychological darkness) ever-diminishing degrees obtain. Hence there is no perception that can prove an absolute absence; for instance, no psychological darkness that cannot be considered as consciousness which is only outbalanced by a stronger consciousness. This occurs in all cases of sensation, and so the understanding can anticipate even sensations, which constitute the peculiar quality of empirical representations (appearances), by means of the principle that they all have degree (and consequently that what is real in all appearance has degree). Here is the second application of mathematics (*mathesis intensorum*) to the science of nature.

Anent the relation of appearances merely with a view to their existence, the determination of the relation is not mathematical but dynamical, and can never be objectively valid, consequently never fit for experience, if it does not come under *a priori* principles by which the empirical knowledge relative to appearances first becomes possible. Hence appearances must be subsumed under the concept of substance, which as a concept of a thing is the foundation of all determination of existence; or, secondly—so far as a succession is found among appearances, that is, an event—under the concept of an effect with reference to cause; or lastly—so far as coexistence is to be known objectively, that is, by a judgment of experience—under the concept of community (action and reaction). Thus *a priori* principles form the basis of objectively valid, though empirical, judgments—that is, of the possibility of experience so far as it must connect objects as existing in nature. These principles are the real laws of nature, which may be termed "dynamical."

Finally knowledge of the agreement and connection, not only of appear-

ances among themselves in experience, but of their relation to experience in general, belongs to the judgments of experience. This relation contains either their agreement with the formal conditions, which the understanding recognizes, or their coherence with the materials of the senses and of perception, or combines both into one concept. Consequently, their relation to experience in general entails possibility, actuality, and necessity, according to universal laws of nature. This would constitute the physical doctrine of method for distinguishing truth from hypotheses and for determining the limits of certainty of the latter.

The third table of principles drawn by the critical method from the nature of the understanding itself shows an inherent perfection, which raises it far above every other table which has hitherto, though in vain, been tried or may yet be tried by analyzing the objects themselves dogmatically. It exhibits all synthetical *a priori* principles completely and according to one principle, namely, the faculty of judging in general, constituting the essence of experience as regards the understanding; so that we can be certain that there are no more such principles. This affords a satisfaction which can never be attained by the dogmatic method. Yet this is not all; there is a still greater merit in it.

We must carefully bear in mind the premise which shows the possibility of this cognition *a priori* and, at the same time, limits all such principles to a condition which must never be lost sight of if we desire it not to be misunderstood and extended in use beyond the original sense which the understanding attaches to it. This limit is that they contain nothing but the conditions of possible experience in general so far as it is subjected to laws *a priori*. Consequently, I do not say that things *in themselves* possess a magnitude; that their reality possesses a degree, their existence a connection of accidents in a substance, etc. This nobody can prove, because such a synthetical connection from mere concepts, without any reference to sensuous intuition on the one side or connection of it in a possible experience on the other, is absolutely impossible. The essential limitation of the concepts in these principles then is that all things *as objects of experience only* stand necessarily *a priori* under the aforementioned conditions.

Hence there follows, secondly, a specifically peculiar mode of proof of these principles; they are not directly referred to appearances and to their relation, but to the possibility of experience, of which appearances constitute the matter only, not the form. Thus they are referred to objectively and universally valid synthetical propositions, in which we distinguish judgments of experience from those of perception. This takes place because appearances, as mere intuitions *occupying a part of space and time*, come under the concept of quantity, which synthetically unites their multiplicity *a priori* according to rules. Again, insofar as the perception contains, besides intuition, sensation, and between the latter and nothing (that is, the total disappearance of sensation), there is an ever-decreasing transition, it is apparent that the real within appearances must have a degree, so far as it (namely, the sensation) *does not itself occupy any part of space or of time.*[2] Still the transition to this real from

[2] Heat and light are in a small space just as large, as to degree, as in a large one; in like manner the internal representations, pain, consciousness generally, whether they last a short or a long time, need not vary as to the degree. Hence the quantity is here in a point and in a moment just as great as in any space or time, however great. Degrees are quantities not in intuition, but in mere sensation (or the quantity of the content [*Grundes*] of an intuition). Hence they can only be estimated quantitatively by the relation of 1 to 0, namely, by their capability of decreasing by infinite intermediate degrees to disappearance, or of increasing from naught through infinite gradations to a determine sensation in a certain time. *Quantitas qualitatis est gradus.* "The quantity of quality is degree."

empty time or empty space is possible only in time. Consequently, although sensation, as the quality of empirical intuition specifically differentiating it from other sensations, can never be known *a priori,* yet it can, in a possible experience in general, as quantity of perception be intensively distinguished from every other similar perception. Hence the application of mathematics to nature, as regards the sensuous intuition by which nature is given to us, thus becomes possible and definite.

Above all, the reader must pay attention to the mode of proof of the principles which occur under the title of "analogies of experience." For these do not refer to the genesis of intuitions, as do the principles of applying mathematics to natural science in general, but to the connection of their existence in an experience; and this can be nothing but the determination of their existence in time according to necessary laws, under which alone the connection is objectively valid and thus becomes experience. The proof, therefore, does not turn on the synthetical unity in the connection of things in themselves, but merely of perceptions; and of these, not in regard to their matter, but to the determination of time and of the relation of their existence in it according to universal laws. If the empirical determination in relative time is indeed to be objectively valid (that is, to be experience), these universal laws must contain the necessary determination of existence in time generally (namely, according to a rule of the understanding *a priori*).

As these are prolegomena I cannot here further descant on the subject, but my reader (who has probably been long accustomed to consider experience a mere empirical synthesis of perceptions, and hence has not considered that it goes much beyond them since it imparts to empirical judgments universal validity, and for that purpose requires a pure and *a priori* unity of the understanding) is recommended to pay special attention to this distinction of experience from a mere aggregate of perceptions and to judge the mode of proof from this point of view.

Now we are prepared to remove Hume's doubt. He justly maintains that we cannot comprehend by reason the possibility of causality, that is, of the reference of the existence of one thing to the existence of another which is necessitated by the former. I add that we comprehend just as little the concept of subsistence, that is, the necessity that at the foundation of the existence of things there lies a subject which cannot itself be a predicate of any other thing; nay, we cannot even form a notion of the possibility of such a thing (though we can point out examples of its use in experience). The very same incomprehensibility affects the community of things, as we cannot comprehend how from the state of one thing an inference to the state of quite another thing beyond it, and *vice versa,* can be drawn, and how substances which have each their own separate existence should depend upon one another necessarily. But I am very far from holding these concepts to be derived merely from experience, and the necessity represented in them to be imaginary and a mere illusion produced in us by long habit. On the contrary, I have amply shown that they and the principles derived from them are firmly established *a priori* before all experience and have their undoubted objective value, though only with regard to experience.

Although I have no notion of such a connection of things in themselves, how they can either exist as substances, or act as causes, or stand in community with others (as parts of a real whole), and I can just as little conceive such properties in appearances as such (because those concepts contain nothing that lies in the appearances, but only what the understanding alone must think), we have yet a concept of such a connection of representations in our understanding and in judgments generally. This concept is: that representations appear, in one sort of judgments, as subject in relation to predicates; in another, as ground in relation to consequent; and, in a third, as parts which constitute together a total possible cognition. Furthermore, we know *a priori* that without considering the representation of an object as determined in one or the other of these respects, we can have no valid knowledge of the object; and, if we should occupy ourselves about the object in itself, there is not a single possible attribute by which I could know that it is determined under any of these aspects, that is, under the concept either of substance, or of cause, or (in relation to other substances) of community, for I have no concept of the possibility of such a connection of existence. But the question is not how things in themselves but how the empirical knowledge of things is determined, as regards the above aspects of judgments in general; that is, how things, as objects of experience, can and must be subsumed under these concepts of the understanding. And then it is clear that I completely comprehend, not only the possibility, but also the necessity, of subsuming all appearances under these concepts—that is, of using them for principles of the possibility of experience.

In order to test Hume's problematical concept (his *crux metaphysicorum*), the concept of cause, we are first given *a priori*, by means of logic, the form of a conditional judgment in general; that is, we have one cognition given as antecedent and another as consequent. But it is possible that in perception we may meet with a rule of relation which runs thus: that a certain appearance is constantly followed by another (though not conversely); and this is a case for me to use the hypothetical judgment and, for instance, to say if the sun shines long enough upon a body it grows warm. Here there is indeed as yet no necessity of connection or concept of cause. But I proceed and say that, if this proposition, which is merely a subjective connection of perceptions, is to be a proposition of experience, it must be seen as necessary and universally valid. Such a proposition would be that the sun is by its light the cause of heat. The empirical rule is now considered as a law, and as valid, not merely of appearances but valid of them for the purposes of a possible experience which requires universal and therefore necessarily valid rules. I therefore easily comprehend the concept of cause, as a concept necessarily belonging to the mere form of experience, and its possibility as a synthetical union of perceptions in consciousness in general; but I do not at all comprehend the possibility of a thing in general as a cause, because the concept of cause denotes a condition not at all belonging to things, but to experience. For experience can be nothing but objectively valid knowledge of appearances and of their succession, only so far as the earlier can be conjoined with the later according to the rule of hypothetical judgments.

Hence if even the pure concepts of the understanding are thought to go beyond objects of experience to things in themselves (*noumena*), they have no meaning whatever. They serve, as it were, only to decipher appearances, that we may be able to read them as experience. The principles which arise from their reference to the sensible world only serve our understanding for empirical use. Beyond this they are arbitrary combinations without objective reality, and we can neither know their possibility *a priori* nor verify—or even render intelligible by any example—their reference to objects; because examples can only be borrowed from some possible experience, and consequently the objects of these concepts can be found nowhere but in a possible experience.

This complete (though to its originator unexpected) solution of Hume's problem rescues for the pure concepts of the understanding their *a priori* origin and for the universal laws of nature their validity as laws of the understanding, yet in such a way as to limit their use to experience, because their possibility depends solely on the reference of the understanding to experience, but with a completely reversed mode of connection which never occurred to Hume—they do not derive from experience, but experience derives from them.

This is, therefore, the result of all our foregoing inquiries: "All synthetical principles *a priori* are nothing more than principles of possible experience" and can never be referred to things in themselves, but to appearances as objects of experience. And hence pure mathematics as well as a pure science of nature can never be referred to anything more than mere appearances, and can only represent either that which makes experience in general possible, or else that which, as it is derived from these principles, must always be capable of being represented in some possible experience.

The Causal Principle Is an Empirical Generalization
JOHN STUART MILL

The notion of Cause being the root of the whole theory of Induction, it is indispensable that this idea should, at the very outset of our inquiry, be, with the utmost practicable degree of precision, fixed and determined. If, indeed, it were necessary for the purposes of inductive logic that the strife should be quelled, which has so long raged among the different schools of metaphysicians, respecting the origin and analysis of our idea of causation; the promulgation, or at least the general reception, of a true theory of induction, might be considered

FROM: *A System of Logic*, John Stuart Mill. 10*th* Ed., Vol. I, p. 376–378 (originally published in 1843).

desperate, for a long time to come. But in this as in most other respects, the science of the Investigation of Truth by means of Evidence, has no need to borrow any premises from the science of the ultimate constitution of the human mind, except such as have at last, though often after long controversy, been incorporated into all the existing systems of mental philosophy, or all but such as may be regarded as essentially effete.

I premise, then, that when in the course of this inquiry I speak of the cause of any phenomenon, I do not mean a cause which is not itself a phenomenon; I make no research into the ultimate, or ontological cause of anything. To adopt a distinction familiar in the writings of the Scotch metaphysicians, and especially of Reid, the causes with which I concern myself are not *efficient*, but *physical* causes. They are causes in that sense alone, in which one physical fact may be said to be the cause of another. Of the efficient causes of phenomena, or whether any such causes exist at all, I am not called upon to give an opinion. The notion of causation is deemed, by the schools of metaphysics most in vogue at the present moment, to imply a mysterious and most powerful tie, such as cannot, or at least does not, exist between any physical fact and that other physical fact upon which it is invariably consequent, and which is popularly termed its cause: and thence is deduced the supposed necessity of ascending higher, into the essences and inherent constitution of things, to find the true cause, the cause which is not only followed by, but actually *produces*, the effect. No such necessity exists for the purposes of the present inquiry, nor will any such doctrine be found in the following pages. But neither will there be found anything incompatible with it. We are in no way concerned in the question. The only notion of a cause, which the theory of induction requires, is such a notion as can be gained from experience. The Law of

Causation, the recognition of which is the main pillar of inductive philosophy, is but the familiar truth, that invariability of succession is found by observation to obtain between every fact in nature and some other fact which has preceded it; independently of all consideration respecting the ultimate mode of production of phenomena, and of every other question regarding the nature of "Things in themselves."

Between the phenomena, then, which exist at any instant, and the phenomena which exist at the succeeding instant, there is an invariable order of succession; and, as we said in speaking of the general uniformity of the course of nature, this web is composed of separate fibres; this collective order is made up of particular sequences, obtaining invariably among the separate parts. To certain facts, certain facts always do, and, as we believe, always will, succeed. The invariable antecedent is termed the cause; the invariable consequent, the effect. And the universality of the law of causation consists in this, that every consequent is connected in this manner with some particular antecedent, or set of antecedents. Let the fact be what it may, if it has begun to exist, it was preceded by some fact or facts, with which it is invariably connected. For every event, there exists some combination of objects or events, some given concurrence of circumstances, positive and negative, the occurrence of which will always be followed by that phenomenon. We may not have found out what this concurrence of circumstances may be; but we never doubt that there is such a one, and that it never occurs without having the phenomenon in question as its effect or consequence. Upon the universality of this truth depends the possibility of reducing the inductive process to rules. The undoubted assurance we have that there is a law to be found if we only knew how to find it, [is] . . . the source from which the canons of the Inductive Logic derive their validity.

Freedom
and
Personal Identity

Do Men
Have
Free Will?

The libertarian, or defender of the view that man has free will, maintains a thesis that contrasts with both determinism and indeterminism. For an event not to be determined is for it to have no cause. If a hydrogen atom should pop into existence with nothing having caused it to do so, it would be a counterexample to determinism. But a libertarian could take no comfort from that fact. If human choices just popped into existence—if to make a choice were simply for a decision to be formed willy-nilly within one's consciousness—then indeterminism would be right about human choices, but libertarianism would be wrong. For a choice to be free is not for it not to be caused; it is for it to be caused by a person, by the agent who makes that choice.

How, then, can the libertarian disagree with the determinist? An event is determined when given its predecessors, it is inevitable. Given decapitation, death is inevitable. Decapitating a man determines that he will die. Of course many causes do not appear to lead inevitably to their effects as decapitation does. Drinking iodine need not be fatal; there are antidotes. But, a determinist will suggest, this way of speaking is due to our ignorance. If we examine the case carefully, we will see that, given the antidote in the prevailing conditions, recovery is inevitable; given iodine in sufficient quantity without antidote, death is inevitable. Any cause determines that its effect shall follow; any impression we may have to the contrary is due to an incomplete description of cause or effect or to ignorance about causal connections.

The libertarian claims that while a person may be said to cause his choices (after all, he makes them), it would be clearer to speak of a person's making a choice as not determined by any cause. Unlike the hydrogen atom, choices are made in the context of reasons, purposes, intentions, deliberation, and the like. A person's making a choice is not fortuitous in the sense of not fitting any sort of explanatory pattern. Explanation of choices in terms of intentions or purposes—*teleological* explanation, to use the traditional terminology—is appropriate with respect to choices. But not explanation vis-a-vis determining causes. Unlike our example of death following decapitation, nothing makes it inevitable that a man who chooses freely choose the way he does; when he chooses freely, he is responsible for his choice and responsible for his course of conduct.

Some philosophers have doubted that sense can be made of the notion of an agent who is himself not causally determined but who nonetheless is able to interact effectively with the course of events in space-time. It is true that one task facing a libertarian is to offer a theory of agency—a view of what it is to be a person—that is both intelligible and consistent with libertarianism. Of course, any alternative view about choices has analogous responsibilities. But our concern here is not with theories of agency, which are discussed, at least by implication, in other sections.

Having attempted to make clear in an initial way what the alternative positions are, it is appropriate to highlight some of the central issues and arguments discussed in the essays that follow.

Augustine wrestles with the question, "Does divine foreknowledge entail determinism?" If God knows before I ask Mary to be my wife that I will choose her for my wife, is my choice of a wife determined and unfree? Augustine acknowledges that some philosophers, Cicero for example—have taken:

(1)   God knows the future, knows what will happen before it happens,

to entail:

(2)   whatever happens is fated to happen—that is, no choice, any more than any other event, occurs undetermined or freely.

Augustine denies this. For suppose, as Augustine, who is a Christian, supposes, that God exists and is omniscient. Suppose that God knows the future perfectly. Then suppose also that I freely choose to ask Mary for her hand. Given these suppositions, what follows is not that I was unfree or determined in asking Mary for her hand, but only that from eternity God, in his ominiscience, has known what choice I would make as He knows the free choices that all individuals make. God knows that these choices will be made, but He does not cause them to be made.

Augustine recounts an argument for the opposite conclusion. It runs: if all events are foreknown, then their order is known. If their order is known before they occur, then they must occur in that order. If events occur in a certain order, there is a cause for their doing so. Hence there is a cause for events occurring in the order in which they do occur. If there is such an order, events occur by fate, not by free choice. If events occur by fate but not by free choice, then of course we are not free agents. But if God exists, then all events are foreknown. So if God exists, we are not free agents. But we must accept our own free moral agency; and thus we must deny that God exists.

Augustine suggests the fallacy in this argument: that one important factor in determining the order of events is in fact the choices that men freely make. God can know that a choice will be made freely in advance of the choice's being made, and "our wills themselves have a very important place in the order of causes." If we accept this line of reasoning, foreknowledge and freedom are compatible. But the question remains: Are men free?

Thomas Aquinas offers the following defense of the claim that men have free will: Men deliberate, make judgments, wonder about what they will do, decide what they ought to do, and sometimes decide to do what they ought. To act from deliberation rather than instinct or compulsion is to act from free choice. As Aquinas puts it,

man acts from judgment . . . For reason in contingent matters may follow opposite courses . . . Now particular operations [actions] are contingent and therefore in such matters the judgment of reason may follow opposite courses, and is not determinate to one. And in that man is rational, it is necessary that he have free choice.

Deliberation about what I shall do assumes that what I shall do is up to me. Of course deliberation may never occur; what appears to be genuine deliberation about what is up to me may be in fact simply a process of reasoning that is itself determined and whose product—namely, a particular course of action—is no more free than a rock blown off a cliff. But apparently we do deliberate—genuinely and not only in unknown but inexorable obedience to causes that we cannot escape. If so, then we are free.

At this point Spinoza's objections become relevant. Spinoza grants that we appear to be free but explains this by saying that apparent freedom is due to ignorance of the determining causes. So long as I do not know what causes me to choose as I do, I can suppose that I choose freely. But for everything that happens there is a cause. This is as true for choices as for falling apples. My ignorance of what caused my choice does not in any way justify my denying that my choice had a cause or that I was caused to make my choice in the way that I did. Hence freedom is an illusion based on ignorance. "Consequently, those who believe that they . . . do anything from a free decree of the mind dream with their eyes open."

We now have a dilemma. Apparently we do deliberate, and I can genuinely deliberate only about what is in fact up to me. But we are also inclined to assign causes to whatever occurs—or at least to say that nothing (including choices) happens without some cause for its happening. One way out of the dilemma would be to treat choices as unique—to say, for example, that choices are not events and that the causal principle ranges over events only. But if we could retain our belief in our freedom and not sacrifice our belief that the causal principle applies universally, this would be preferable to restricting the causal principle or giving up our belief that we are free. Thus there is a good deal of promise, at least initially, in John Stuart Mill's suggestion that freedom and determinism are compatible after all.

What do we mean, or at least what should we mean, when we say that our choice is free? We mean that the choice was made from whatever motives, dispositions, intentions, or purposes we had, that our character and disposition gave rise to the choice, that it was not compelled by causes external to us. And what do we mean, at least what should we mean, when we say that a choice is caused? We mean that it had precedents without which it would not occur. To say of an event *A* that it caused another event *B* is to say that *A* occurred prior to *B* (and also temporally overlapped *B*); that whenever an event like *B* occurs, there is an event like *A* that precedes it (and partially temporally overlaps it); and that there is thus a true generalization to the effect that *A*-like events precede (and partially overlap) *B*-like events. There is no necessary connection, no "mysterious tie," between *A* and *B*. This is the character of causality with respect to choices and actions but equally with respect to any instance of causal connection. In Mill's words, "It would be more correct to say that matter is not bound by necessity, than that mind is so."

Where then is the dilemma? Free choices arise from the character of the agent. Determined choices are choices that have precedents—a determined choice *B* is simply a choice preceded by an event *A* such that *B*-type choices and *A*-type events have the temporal relations just noted. A choice may perfectly well be both determined and free. Deliberation and universal causation are saved together. So, at least, Mill claims.

This solution has its difficulties. For one thing, it is not clear that when we hold a man responsible for what he does, we are simply saying that his action arose from his character. We seem also to be saying that given his character, he could still have refrained from performing the action for which he is blamed. (Praise, too, seems to be appropriate only when the one praised could have refrained from the act for which he is praised, and could have done so under the existing conditions.) Mill's proposal has thus been attacked by philosophers who regard it as not allowing for moral responsibility. (On this issue, see the selection from Immanuel Kant's *Ethics*, "Must an Action Right for One Be Right for All?").

Mill has also been attacked by determinists. They have argued, as does D'Holbach, that:

Man's mode of thinking is necessarily determined by his manner of being; it must therefore depend on his natural organization, and the modification his system receives independently of his will. From this, we are obliged to conclude that his thoughts, his reflections, his manner of viewing things, of feeling, of judging, of combining ideas, is neither voluntary nor free.

For if my character arises without my forming it in whole or in part, and if my choices arise from my character—they are caused by purposes and intentions and dispositions that are mine—then it is false that I could in fact have chosen in some other way than I did (though it is true that if my character had been different, so would my choice). My character is mine as my liver is mine; they both grew in me without my knowledge or consent; as well hold me accountable for one as for the other. On such a basis Clarence Darrow argued eloquently that criminals ought not to be punished for what they could not help doing—for what they "did" only in the sense that it occurred to, or through, them. The man who murders "acts" in murdering only in the sense that the man who bleeds when cut "acts" in bleeding; which is to say that neither acts at all. Thus in the interest of defending genuine moral responsibility, some philosophers have suggested that Mill's account of free will is too weak. In the interest of denying that men are morally responsible for anything they do, other philosophers have suggested that Mill waters down the sense in which men are determined, that he does not face fully the consequences of all human action falling under the principle "Everything that has a beginning has a cause."

In the essay that concludes this section, William James poses what he calls "the dilemma of determinism," which is this: There are things we regret having done or not having done—we regret having left unsaid a word of thanks or unread a book that would have saved us much useless inquiry or unasked a question that would have prompted the answer we wanted above all else had we only possessed the courage to ask it. But regret is pointless in a deterministic world. What is, is; what will be, will be. What is not, cannot be; what will not happen is something that cannot occur. Still we do regret things; we cannot help but do so sometimes. And so we are in an awkward position—that of being unable not to regret what could not have been avoided:

. . . determinism leads us to call our judgments of regret wrong, because they are pessimistic in implying that what is impossible yet ought to be. But how then about the judgments of regret themselves? . . . as they are necessitated, nothing else can *be in their place . . . so something must be fatally unreasonable, absurd and wrong in the world.*

But if we join James and take as axioms for appraising philosophical views the contentions that "if there be two conceptions, and the one seems to us, on the whole, more rational than the other, we are entitled to suppose that the more reasonable one is the truer of the two" and that "we make theories about the world . . . in order to attain a conception of things which shall give us subjective satisfaction," perhaps this dilemma will lead us to reject determinism.

Freedom and Divine Foreknowledge
AURELIUS AUGUSTINE

CONCERNING
THE FOREKNOWLEDGE OF GOD
AND THE FREE WILL OF MAN,
IN OPPOSITION TO
THE DEFINITION OF CICERO

*T*he *manner* in which Cicero addresses himself to the task of refuting the Stoics, shows that he did not think he could effect anything against them in argument unless he had first demolished divination.[1] And this he attempts to accomplish by denying that there is any knowledge of future things, and maintains with all his might that there is no such knowledge either in God or man, and that there is no prediction of events. Thus he both denies the foreknowledge of God, and attempts by vain arguments, and by opposing to himself certain oracles very easy to be refuted, to overthrow all prophecy, even such as is clearer than the light (though even these oracles are not refuted by him).

But, in refuting these conjectures of the mathematicians, his argument is triumphant, because truly these are such as destroy and refute themselves. Nevertheless, they are far more tolerable who assert the fatal influence of the stars than they who deny the foreknowledge of future events. For, to confess that God exists, and at the same time to deny that He has foreknowledge of future things, is the most manifest folly. This Cicero himself saw, and therefore attempted to assert the doctrine embodied in the words of Scripture, "The fool hath said in his heart, There is no God."[2] That, however, he did not do in his own

person, for he saw how odious and offensive such an opinion would be; and therefore in his book on the nature of the gods,[3] he makes Cotta dispute concerning this against the Stoics, and preferred to give his own opinion in favour of Lucilius Balbus, to whom he assigned the defence of the Stoical position, rather than in favour of Cotta, who maintained that no divinity exists. However, in his book on divination, he in his own person most openly opposes the doctrine of the prescience of future things. But all this he seems to do in order that he may not grant the doctrine of fate, and by so doing destroy free will. For he thinks that, the knowledge of future things being once conceded, fate follows as so necessary a consequence that it cannot be denied.

But, let these perplexing debatings and disputations of the philosophers go on as they may, we, in order that we may confess the most high and true God Himself, do confess His will, supreme power, and prescience. Neither let us be afraid lest, after all, we do not do by will that which we do by will, because He, whose foreknowledge is infallible, foreknew that we would do it. It was this which Cicero was afraid of, and therefore opposed foreknowledge. The Stoics also maintained that all things do not come to pass by necessity, although they contended that all things happen according to destiny. What is it, then, that Cicero feared in the prescience of future things? Doubtless it was this— that if all future things have been foreknown, they will happen in the order in which they have been foreknown; and if they come to pass in this order, there

[1] *De Divinat,* ii.

[2] Ps. xiv. 1.

[3] Book iii.

FROM: *The City of God*, Aurelius Augustine. J. J. Smith, trans. Book V, Sections 9–11. *Basic Writings of St. Augustine*, Vol. II, Whitney J. Oates, ed. (New York: Random House, Inc., 1948). Reprinted by permission of Random House, Inc.

is a certain order of things foreknown by God; and if a certain order of things, then a certain order of causes, for nothing can happen which is not preceded by some efficient cause. But if there is a certain order of causes according to which everything happens which does happen, then by fate, says he, all things happen which do happen. But if this be so, then is there nothing in our own power, and there is no such thing as freedom of will; and if we grant that, says he, the whole economy of human life is subverted. In vain are laws enacted. In vain are reproaches, praises, chidings, exhortations had recourse to; and there is no justice whatever in the appointment of rewards for the good, and punishments for the wicked. And that consequences so disgraceful, and absurd, and pernicious to humanity may not follow, Cicero chooses to reject the foreknowledge of future things, and shuts up the religious mind to this alternative, to make choice between two things, either that something is in our own power, or that there is foreknowledge—both of which cannot be true; but if the one is affirmed, the other is thereby denied. He therefore, like a truly great and wise man, and one who consulted very much and very skillfully for the good of humanity, of those two chose the freedom of the will, to confirm which he denied the foreknowledge of future things; and thus, wishing to make men free, he makes them sacrilegious. But the religious mind chooses both, confesses both, and maintains both by the faith of piety. But how so? says Cicero; for the knowledge of future things being granted, there follows a chain of consequences which ends in this, that there can be nothing depending on our own free wills. And further, if there is anything depending on our wills, we must go backwards by the same steps of reasoning till we arrive at the conclusion that there is no foreknowledge of future things. For we go backwards through all the steps in the following order:—If there is free will, all things do not happen according to fate; if all

things do not happen according to fate, there is not a certain order of causes; and if there is not a certain order of causes, neither is there a certain order of things foreknown by God—for things cannot come to pass except they are preceded by efficient causes—but, if there is no fixed and certain order of causes foreknown by God, all things cannot be said to happen according as He foreknew that they would happen. And further, if it is not true that all things happen just as they have been foreknown by Him, there is not, says he, in God any foreknowledge of future events.

Now, against the sacrilegious and impious darings of reason, we assert both that God knows all things before they come to pass, and that we do by our free will whatsoever we know and feel to be done by us only because we will it. But that all things come to pass by fate, we do not say; nay we affirm that nothing comes to pass by fate; for we demonstrate that the name of fate, as it is wont to be used by those who speak of fate, meaning thereby the position of the stars at the time of each one's conception or birth, is an unmeaning word, for astrology itself is a delusion. But an order of causes in which the highest efficiency is attributed to the will of God, we neither deny nor do we designate it by the name of fate, unless, perhaps, we may understand fate to mean that which is spoken, deriving it from *fari*, to speak; for we cannot deny that it is written in the sacred Scriptures, "God hath spoken once; these two things have I heard, that power belongeth unto God. Also unto Thee, O God, belongeth mercy: for Thou wilt render unto every man according to his works."[4] Now the expression, "Once hath He spoken," is to be understood as meaning "*immovably*," that is, unchangeably hath He spoken, inasmuch as He knows unchangeably all things which shall be, and all things which He will do. We might, then, use the word fate in the sense it bears when derived from *fari*, to speak, had it not

[4] Ps. lxii. 11, 12.

already come to be understood in another sense, into which I am unwilling that the hearts of men should unconsciously slide. But it does not follow that, though there is for God a certain order of all causes, there must therefore be nothing depending on the free exercise of our own wills, for our wills themselves are included in that order of causes which is certain to God, and is embraced by His foreknowledge for human wills are also causes of human actions; and He who foreknew all the causes of things would certainly among those causes not have been ignorant of our wills. For even that very concession which Cicero himself makes is enough to refute him in this argument. For what does it help him to say that nothing takes place without a cause, but that every cause is not fatal, there being a fortuitous cause, a natural cause, and a voluntary cause? It is sufficient that he confesses that whatever happens must be preceded by a cause. For we say that those causes which are called fortuitous are not a mere name for the absence of causes, but are only latent, and we attribute them either to the will of the true God, or to that of spirits of some kind or other. And as to natural causes, we by no means separate them from the will of Him who is the author and framer of all nature. But now as to voluntary causes. They are referable either to God, or to angels, or to men, or to animals of whatever description, if indeed those instinctive movements of animals devoid of reason, by which, in accordance with their own nature, they seek or shun various things, are to be called wills. And when I speak of the wills of angels, I mean either the wills of good angels, whom we call the angels of God, or of the wicked angels, whom we call the angels of the devil, or demons. Also by the wills of men I mean the wills either of the good or of the wicked. And from this we conclude that there are no efficient causes of all things which come to pass unless voluntary causes, that is, such as belong to that nature, which

is the spirit of life. For the air or wind is called spirit, but, inasmuch as it is a body, it is not the spirit of life. The spirit of life, therefore, which quickens all things, and is the creator of every body, and of every created spirit, is God Himself, the uncreated spirit. In His supreme will resides the power which acts on the wills of all created spirits, helping the good, judging the evil, controlling all, granting power to some, not granting it to others. For, as He is the creator of all natures, so also is He the bestower of all powers, not of all wills; for wicked wills are not from Him, being contrary to nature, which is from Him. As to bodies, they are more subject to wills; some to our wills, by which I mean the wills of all living mortal creatures, but more to the wills of men than of beasts. But all of them are most of all subject to the will of God, to whom all wills also are subject, since they have no power except what He has bestowed upon them. The cause of things, therefore, which makes but is not made, is God; but all other causes both make and are made. Such are all created spirits, and especially the rational. Material causes, therefore, which may rather be said to be made than to make, are not to be reckoned among efficient causes, because they can only do what the wills of spirits do by them. How, then, does an order of causes which is certain to the foreknowledge of God necessitate that there should be nothing which is dependent on our wills, when our wills themselves have a very important place in the order of causes? Cicero, then, contends with those who call this order of causes fatal, or rather designate this order itself by the name of fate; to which we have an abhorrence, especially on account of the word, which men have become accustomed to understand as meaning what is not true. But, whereas he denies that the order of all causes is most certain, and perfectly clear to the prescience of God, we detest his opinion more than the Stoics do. For he either denies that God exists—which, indeed, in an assumed personage, he has laboured to do, in his book *De Natura Deorum*—or if he confesses that He exists, but denies that He is prescient of future things, what is that but just "the fool saying in his heart there is no God?" For one who is not prescient of all future things is not God. Wherefore our wills also have just so much power as God willed and foreknew that they should have; and therefore whatever power they have, they have it within most certain limits; and whatever they are to do, they are most assuredly to do, for He whose foreknowledge is infallible foreknew that they would have the power to do it, and would do it. Wherefore, if I should choose to apply the name of fate to anything at all, I should rather say that fate belongs to the weaker of two parties, will to the stronger, who has the other in his power, than that the freedom of our will is excluded by that order of causes, which, by an unusual application of the word peculiar to themselves, the Stoics call *Fate*.

WHETHER OUR WILLS ARE RULED BY NECESSITY

Wherefore, neither is that necessity to be feared, for dread of which the Stoics laboured to make such distinctions among the causes of things as should enable them to rescue certain things from the dominion of necessity, and to subject others to it. Among those things which they wished not to be subject to necessity they placed our wills, knowing that they would not be free if subjected to necessity. For if that is to be called *our necessity* which is not in our power, but even though we be unwilling effects what it can effect—as, for instance, the necessity of death—it is manifest that our wills by which we live uprightly or wickedly are not under such a necessity; for we do many things which, if we were not willing, we should certainly not do. This is primarily true of the act of willing itself—for if we will, it *is*; if we will not, it *is* not—for we should not will if we were unwilling.

But if we define necessity to be that according to which we say that it is necessary that anything be of such or such a nature, or be done in such and such a manner, I know not why we should have any dread of that necessity taking away the freedom of our will. For we do not put the life of God or the foreknowledge of God under necessity if we should say that it is necessary that God should live for ever, and foreknow all things; as neither is His power diminished when we say that He cannot die or fall into error—for this is in such a way impossible to Him, that if it were possible for Him, He would be of less power. But assuredly He is rightly called omnipotent, though He can neither die nor fall into error. For He is called omnipotent on account of His doing what He wills, not on account of His suffering what He wills not; for if that should befall Him, He would by no means be omnipotent. Wherefore, He cannot do some things for the very reason that He is omnipotent. So also, when we say that it is necessary that, when we will, we will by free choice, in so saying we both affirm what is true beyond doubt, and do not still subject our wills thereby to a necessity which destroys liberty. Our wills, therefore, *exist* as *wills*, and do themselves whatever we do by willing, and which would not be done if we were unwilling. But when any one suffers anything, being unwilling, by the will of another, even in that case will retains its essential validity—we do not mean the will of the party who inflicts the suffering, for we resolve it into the power of God. For if a will should simply exist, but not be able to do what it wills, it would be overborne by a more powerful will. Nor would this be the case unless there had existed will, and that not the will of the other party, but the will of him who willed, but was not able to accomplish what he willed. Therefore, whatsoever a man suffers contrary to his own will, he ought not to attribute to the will of men, or of angels, or of any created spirit, but rather to His will who gives power to wills. It is not the case, therefore, that because God foreknew what would be in the power of our wills, there is for that reason nothing in the power of our wills. For he who foreknew this did not foreknow nothing. Moreover, if He who foreknew what would be in the power of our wills did not foreknow nothing, but something, assuredly, even though He did foreknow, there is something in the power of our wills. Therefore we are by no means compelled, either, retaining the prescience of God, to take away the freedom of the will, or, retaining the freedom of the will, to deny that He is prescient of future things, which is impious. But we embrace both. We faithfully and sincerely confess both. The former, that we may believe well; the latter, that we may live well. For he lives ill who does not believe well concerning God. Wherefore, be it far from us, in order to maintain our freedom, to deny the prescience of Him by whose help we are or shall be free. Consequently, it is not in vain that laws are enacted, and that reproaches, exhortations, praises, and vituperations are had recourse to; for these also He foreknew, and they are of great avail, even as great as He foreknew that they would be of. Prayers, also, are of avail to procure those things which He foreknew that He would grant to those who offered them; and with justice have rewards been appointed for good deeds, and punishments for sins. For a man does not therefore sin because God foreknew that he would sin. Nay, it cannot be doubted but that it is the man himself who sins when he does sin, because He, whose foreknowledge is infallible, foreknew not that fate, or fortune, or something else would sin, but that the man himself would sin, who, if he wills not, sins not. But if he shall not will to sin, even this did God foreknow.

CONCERNING
THE UNIVERSAL PROVIDENCE OF
GOD IN THE LAWS OF WHICH
ALL THINGS ARE COMPREHENDED

Therefore God supreme and true, with His Word and Holy Spirit (which three are one), one God omnipotent, creator and maker of every soul and of every body; by whose gift all are happy who are happy through verity and not through vanity; who made man a rational animal consisting of soul and body, who, when he sinned, neither permitted him to go unpunished, nor left him without mercy; who has given to the good and to the evil, being in common with stones, vegetable life in common with tress, sensuous life in common with brutes, intellectual life in common with angels alone; from whom is every mode, every species, every order; from whom are measure, number, weight; from whom is everything which has an existence in nature, of whatever kind it be, of whatever value; from whom are the seeds of forms and the forms of seeds, and the motion of seeds and of forms; who gave also to flesh its origin, beauty, health, reproductive fecundity, disposition of members, and the salutary concord of its parts; who also to the irrational soul has given memory, sense, appetite, but to the rational soul, in addition to these, has given intelligence and will; who has not left, not to speak of heaven and earth, angels and men, but not even the entrails of the smallest and most contemptible animal, or the feather of a bird, or the little flower of a plant, or the leaf of a tree, without an harmony, and, as it were, a mutual peace among all its parts;—that God can never be believed to have left the kingdoms of men, their dominations and servitudes, outside of the laws of His providence.

Free Choice
ST. THOMAS AQUINAS

*W*e now inquire concerning free choice. Under this head there are four points of inquiry: (1) Whether man has free choice? (2) What is free choice—a power, an act, or a habit? (3) If it is a power, is it appetitive or cognitive? (4) If if is appetitive, is it the same power as the will, or distinct?

First Article

WHETHER MAN HAS FREE CHOICE?
We proceed thus to the First Article:—

OBJECTION 1. It would seem that man has not free choice. For whoever has free choice does what he wills. But man does not what he wills, for it is written (*Rom.* vii. 19): *For the good which I will I do not, but the evil which I will not, that I do.* Therefore man has not free choice.

OBJ. 2. Further, whoever has free choice has in his power to will or not to will, to do or not to do. But this is not in man's power, for it is written (*Rom.* ix. 16); *It is not of him that willeth—* namely, to will—*nor of him that runneth* —namely, to run. Therefore man has not free choice.

OBJ. 3. Further, he is free who is his own master, as the Philosopher says.[1] Therefore what is moved by another is not free. But God moves the will, for it is written (*Prov.* xxi. 1): *The heart of the king is in the hand of the Lord; whithersoever He will He shall turn it;* and (*Phil.* ii. 13): *It is God Who worketh in you both to will and to accomplish.* Therefore man has not free choice.

OBJ. 4. Further, whoever has free choice is master of his own actions. But man is not master of his own actions,

for it is written (*Jer.* x 23): *The way of a man is not his, neither is it in a man to walk.* Therefore man has not free choice.

OBJ. 5. Further, the Philosopher says: *According as each one is, such does the end seem to him.*[2] But it is not in our power to be such as we are, for this comes to us from nature therefore it is natural to us to follow some particular end, and therefore we are not free in so doing.

On the contrary, It is written (*Ecclus.* xv. 14): *God made man from the beginning, and left him in the hand of his own counsel;* and the *Gloss* adds: *That is, in the liberty of choice.*[3]

I answer that, Man has free choice, or otherwise counsels, exhortations, commands, prohibitions, rewards and punishments would be in vain. In order to make this evident, we must observe that some things act without judgment, as a stone moves downwards; and in like manner all things which lack knowledge. And some act from judgment, but not a free judgment; as brute animals. For the sheep, seeing the wolf, judges it a thing to be shunned, from a natural and not a free judgment; because it judges, not from deliberation, but from natural instinct. And the same thing is to be said of any judgment in brute animals. But man acts from judgment, because by his apprehensive power he judges that something should be avoided or sought. But because this judgment, in the case of some particular act, is not from a natural instinct, but from some act of comparison

[1] Aristotle, *Metaph.*, I, 2 (982b 26).

[2] *Eth.*, III, 5 (1114a 32).

[3] *Glossa interl.* (III, 401v); cf. *Glossa ordin.* (III, 401E).

FROM: the *Summa Theologica*, St. Thomas Aquinas, Part I, Question 83, Articles 1–4. *Basic Writings of St. Thomas Aquinas*, Anton C. Pegis, ed. (New York: Random House, Inc., 1945). Reprinted by permission of Random House, Inc., and Burns and Oates, Ltd.

in the reason, therefore he acts from free judgment and retains the power of being inclined to various things. For reason in contingent matters may follow opposite courses, as we see in dialectical syllogisms and rhetorical arguments. Now particular operations are contingent, and therefore in such matters the judgment of reason may follow opposite courses, and is not determinate to one. And in that man is rational, it is necessary that he have free choice.

REPLY OBJ. 1. As we have said above, the sensitive appetite, though it obeys the reason, yet in a given case can resist by desiring what the reason forbids.[4] This is therefore the good which man does not when he wishes—namely, *not to desire against reason*, as Augustine says.[5]

REPLY OBJ. 2. Those words of the Apostle are not to be taken as though man does not wish or does not run of his free choice, but because free choice is not sufficient thereto unless it be moved and helped by God.

REPLY OBJ. 3. Free choice is the cause of its own movement, because by his free choice man moves himself to act. But it does not of necessity belong to liberty that what is free should be the first cause of itself, as neither for one thing to be cause of another need it be the first cause. God, therefore, is the first cause, Who moves causes both natural and voluntary. And just as by moving natural causes He does not prevent their actions from being natural, so by moving voluntary causes He does not deprive their actions of being voluntary; but rather is He the cause of this very thing in them, for He operates in each thing according to its own nature.

REPLY OBJ. 4. *Man's way* is said *not to be his* in the execution of his choice, wherein he may be impeded, whether he will or not. The choice itself,

however, is in us, but presupposes the help of God.

REPLY OBJ. 5. Quality in man is of two kinds: natural and adventitious. Now the natural quality may be in the intellectual part, or in the body and its powers. From the very fact, therefore, that man is such by virtue of a natural quality which is in the intellectual part, he naturally desires his last end, which is happiness. This desire is, indeed, a natural desire, and is not subject to free choice, as is clear from what we have said above.[6] But on the part of the body and its powers, man may be such by virtue of a natural quality, inasmuch as he is of such a temperament or disposition due to any impression whatever produced by corporeal causes, which cannot affect the intellectual part, since it is not the act of a corporeal organ. And such as a man is by virtue of a corporeal quality, such also does his end seem to him, because from such a disposition a man is inclined to choose or reject something. But these inclinations are subject to the judgment of reason, which the lower appetite obeys, as we have said.[7] Therefore this is in no way prejudicial to free choice.

The adventitious qualities are habits and passions, by virtue of which a man is inclined to one thing rather than to another. And yet even these inclinations are subject to the judgment of reason. Such qualities, too, are subject to reason, as it is in our power either to acquire them, whether by causing them or disposing ourselves to them, or to reject them. And so there is nothing in this that is repugnant to free choice.

Second Article

WHETHER FREE CHOICE
IS A POWER?

We proceed thus to the Second Article:—
OBJECTION 1. It would seem that free choice is not a power. For free

[4] Q. 81, a. 3, ad 2.

[5] *Glossa interl.*, super *Rom.*, VII, 19 (VI, 17r).—Cf. St. Augustine, *Serm. ad Popul.*, serm. CLIV, 3 (PL 38, 834).

[6] Q. 82, a. 1 and 2.

[7] Q. 81, a. 3.

choice is nothing but a free judgment. But judgment denominates an act, not a power. Therefore free choice is not a power.

OBJ. 2. Further, free choice is defined as *the faculty of the will and reason*.[8] But faculty denominates the facility of power, which is due to a habit. Therefore free choice is a habit. Moreover Bernard says that free choice is *the soul's habit of disposing of itself*.[9] Therefore it is not a power.

OBJ. 3. Further, no natural power is forfeited through sin. But free choice is forfeited through sin, for Augustine says that *man, by abusing free choice, loses both it and himself*.[10] Therefore free choice is not a power.

On the contrary, Nothing but a power, seemingly, is the subject of a habit. But free choice is the subject of grace, by the help of which it chooses what is good. Therefore free choice is a power.

I answer that, Although *free choice,* in its strict sense, denotes an act, in the common manner of speaking we call free choice that which is the principle of the act by which man judges freely. Now in us the principle of an act is both power and habit; for we say that we know something both by science and by the intellectual power. Therefore free choice must be either a power,[11] or a habit,[12] or a power with a habit.[13] That it is neither a habit nor a power together with a habit can be clearly proved in two ways. First of all, because, if it is a habit, it must be a natural habit; for it is natural to man to have free choice. But

there is no natural habit in us with respect to those things which come under free choice, for we are naturally inclined to those things of which we have natural habits, for instance, to assent to first principles. Now those things to which we are naturally inclined are not subject to free choice, as we have said in the case of the desire of happiness.[14] Therefore it is against the very notion of free choice that it should be a natural habit; and that it should be a non-natural habit is against its nature. Therefore in no sense is it a habit.

Second, this is clear because habits are defined as that *by reason of which we are well or ill disposed with regard to actions and passions*.[15] For by temperance we are well-disposed as regards concupiscences, and by intemperance ill-disposed; and by science we are well-disposed to the act of the intellect when we know the truth, and by the contrary habit ill-disposed. But free choice is indifferent to choosing well or ill, and therefore it is impossible that it be a habit. Therefore it is a power.

REPLY OBJ. 1. It is not unusual for a power to be named from its act. And so from this act, which is a free judgment, is named the power which is the principle of this act. Otherwise, if free choice denominated an act, it would not always remain in man.

REPLY OBJ. 2. *Faculty* sometimes denominates a power ready for operation, and in this sense faculty is used in the definition of free choice. But Bernard takes habit, not as divided against power, but as signifying any aptitude by which a man is somehow disposed to an act.[16] This may be both by a power and by a habit, for by a power man is, as it were, empowered to do the action, and by the habit he is apt to act well or ill.

REPLY OBJ. 3. Man is said to have lost free choice by falling into sin, not

[8] Peter Lombard, *Sent.*, II, xxiv, 3 (I, 421).

[9] St. Bernard, *De Gratia et Libero Arbitrio,* I (PL 182, 1002).

[10] *Enchir.*, XXX (PL 40, 246).

[11] St. Albert, *Summa de Creatur.*, II, q. 70, a. 2 (XXXV, 505).

[12] St. Bonaventure, *In II Cent.*, d. xxv, pt. I, a. 1, q. 4 (II. 601).

[13] Alex. of Hales, *Summa Theol.*, II, I, no. 390 (11, 486).

[14] Q. 82, a. 1 and 2.

[15] Aristotle, *Eth.,* II, 5 (1105b 25).

[16] *De Grat. et Lib. Arb.*, I (PL 182, 1002).

as to natural liberty, which is freedom from coercion, but as regards freedom from fault and unhappiness. Of this we shall treat later in the treatise on Morals in the second part of this work.[17]

Third Article

WHETHER FREE CHOICE IS AN APPETITIVE POWER?

We proceed thus to the Third Article:—

OBJECTION 1. It would seem that free choice is not an appetitive, but a cognitive power. For Damascene says that *free choice straightway accompanies the rational power.*[18] But reason is a cognitive power. Therefore free choice is a cognitive power.

OBJ. 2. Further, free choice is so called as though it were a free judgment. But to judge is an act of a cognitive power. Therefore free choice is a cognitive power.

OBJ. 3. Further, the principal function of free choice is election. But election seems to belong to knowledge, because it implies a certain comparison of one thing to another; which belongs to the cognitive power. Therefore free choice is a cognitive power.

On the contrary, The Philosopher says that election is *the desire of those things which are in our power.*[19] But desire is an act of the appetitive power. Therefore election is also. But free choice is that by which we elect. Therefore free choice is an appetitive power.

I answer that, The proper act of free choice is election, for we say that we have a free choice because we can take one thing while refusing another; and this is to elect. Therefore we must consider the nature of free choice by considering the nature of election. Now two things concur in election: one on the part of the cognitive power, the other on the part of the appetitive power. On

the part of the cognitive power, counsel is required, by which we judge one thing to be preferred to another: on the part of the appetitive power, it is required that the appetite should accept the judgment of counsel. Therefore Aristotle leaves it in doubt whether election belongs principally to the appetitive or the cognitive power: since he says that election is either *an appetitive intellect or an intellectual appetite.*[20] But he inclines to its being an intellectual appetite when he describes election as *a desire proceeding from counsel.*[21] And the reason of this is because the proper object of election is the means to the end. Now the means, as such, has the nature of that good which is called *useful*; and since the good, as such, is the object of the appetite, it follows that election is principally an act of an appetitive power. And thus free choice is an appetitive power.

REPLY OBJ. 1. The appetitive powers accompany the apprehensive, and in this sense Damascene says that free choice straightway accompanies the rational power.

REPLY OBJ. 2. Judgment, as it were, concludes and terminates counsel. Now counsel is terminated, first, by the judgment of reason; secondly, by the acceptation of the appetite. Hence the Philosopher says that, *having formed judgment by counsel, we desire in accordance with that counsel.*[22] And in this sense election itself is a judgment from which free choice takes its name.

REPLY OBJ. 3. This comparison which is implied in the term election belongs to the preceding counsel, which is an act of reason. For though the appetite does not make comparisons, yet inasmuch as it is moved by the apprehensive power which does compare, it has some likeness of comparison, by choosing one in preference to another.

[17] *S.T.*, I-II, q. 85; q. 109.

[18] *De Fide Orth.,* II, 27 (PG 94, 949).

[19] *Eth.*, III, 3 (1113a 11).

[20] *Op. cit.*, VII, 2 (1139b 4).

[21] *Op. cit.*, III, 3 (1113a 11).

[22] *Ibid.*

Fourth Article

WHETHER FREE CHOICE
IS A POWER
DISTINCT FROM THE WILL?

We proceed thus to the Fourth Article:—
OBJECTION 1. It would seem that free choice is a power distinct from the will.[23] For Damascene says that θέλησις is one thing and βούλησις another.[24] But θέλησις is will, while βούλησις seems to be free choice, because βούλησις, according to him, is the will as concerning an object by way of comparison between two things. Therefore it seems that free choice is a power distinct from the will.

OBJ. 2. Further, powers are known by their acts. But election, which is the act of free choice, is distinct from the will, because *the will regards the end, whereas choice regards the means to the end.*[25] Therefore free choice is a power from the will.

OBJ. 3. Further, the will is the intellectual appetite. But on the part of the intellect there are two powers—agent and possible. Therefore, also on the part of the intellectual appetite there must be another power besides the will. And this, seemingly, can be only free choice. Therefore free choice is a power distinct from the will.

On the contrary, Damascene says free choice is nothing else than the will.[26]

I answer that, The appetitive powers must be proportionate to the apprehensive powers, as we have said above.[27] Now, as on the part of intellectual apprehension we have intellect and reason, so on the part of the intellectual appetite we have will and free choice, which is nothing else but the power of election.

[23] Cf. St. Albert, *Summa de Creatur.*, II, q. 70, a. 2 (XXXV, 577).

[24] *De Fide Orth.*, XXII (PG 94, 944).

[25] Aristotle, *Eth.*, III, 2 (1111b 26).

[26] *De Fide Orth.*, XIV (PG 94, 1037).

[27] Q. 64, a. 2; q. 80, a 2.

And this is clear from their relations to their respective objects and acts. For the act of *understanding* implies the simple acceptation of something, and hence we say that we understand first principles, which are known of themselves without any comparison. But to *reason*, properly speaking, is to come from one thing to the knowledge of another, and so, properly speaking, we reason about conclusions, which are known from the principles. In like manner, on the part of the appetite, to *will* implies the simple appetite for something, and so the will is said to regard the end, which is desired for itself. But to *elect* is to desire something for the sake of obtaining something else, and so, properly speaking, it regards the means to the end. Now in appetitive matters, the end is related to the means, which is desired for the end, in the same way as, in knowledge, principles are related to the conclusion to which we assent because of the principles. Therefore it is evident that as *intellect* is to *reason*, so *will* is to the *elective power*, which is free choice. But it has been shown above that it belongs to the same power both to understand and to reason,[28] even as it belongs to the same power to be at rest and to be in movement. Hence it belongs also to the same power to will and to elect. And on this account will and the free choice are not two powers, but one.

REPLY OBJ. 1. βούλησις is distinct from θέλησις because of a distinction, not of powers, but of acts.

REPLY OBJ. 2. Election and will— that is, the act of willing—are different acts, yet they belong to the same power, as do *to understand* and *to reason*, as we have said.

REPLY OBJ. 3. The intellect is compared to the will as moving the will. And therefore there is no need to distinguish in the will an *agent* and a *possible* will.

[28] Q. 79, a. 8.

Free Will An Illusion
BENEDICT SPINOZA

M ost persons who have written about the affects and man's conduct of life seem to discuss, not the natural things which follow the common laws of nature, but things which are outside her. They seem indeed to consider man in nature as a kingdom within a kingdom. For they believe that man disturbs rather than follows her order; that he has an absolute power over his own actions; and that he is altogether self-determined. They then proceed to attribute the cause of human weakness and changeableness, not to the common power of nature, but to some vice of human nature, which they therefore bewail, laugh at, mock, or, as is more generally the case, detest; whilst he who knows to revile most eloquently or subtilly the weakness of the mind is looked upon as divine. It is true that very eminent men have not been wanting, to whose labour and industry we confess ourselves much indebted, who have written many excellent things about the right conduct of life, and who have given to mortals counsels full of prudence, but no one so far as I know has determined the nature and strength of the effects, and what the mind is able to do towards controlling them. I remember, indeed, that the celebrated Descartes, although he believed that the mind is absolute master over its own actions, tried nevertheless to explain by their first causes human affects, and at the same time to show the way by which the mind could obtain absolute power over them; but in my opinion he has shown nothing but the acuteness of his great intellect, as I shall make evident in the proper place, for I wish to return to those who prefer to detest and scoff at human affects and actions than understand them. To such as these it will doubtless seem a marvellous thing for me to endeavour to treat by a geometrical method the vices and follies of men, and to desire by a sure method to demonstrate those things which these people cry out against as being opposed to reason, or as being vanities, absurdities, and monstrosities. The following is my reason for so doing. Nothing happens in nature which can be attributed to any vice of nature, for she is always the same and everywhere one. Her virtue is the same, and her power of acting; that is to say, her laws and rules, according to which all things are and are changed from form to form, are everywhere and always the same; so that there must also be one and the same method of understanding the nature of all things whatsoever, that is to say, by the universal laws and rules of nature. The affects, therefore, of hatred, anger, envy, considered in themselves, follow from the same necessity and virtue of nature as other individual things; they have therefore certain causes through which they are to be understood, and certain properties which are just as worthy of being known as the properties of any other thing in the contemplation alone of which we delight. I shall, therefore, pursue the same method in considering the nature and strength of the affect and the power of the mind over them which I pursued in our previous discussion of God and the mind, and I shall consider human actions and appetites just as if I were considering lines, planes, or bodies.

DEF. I. I call that an adequate cause whose effect can be clearly and distinctly perceived by means of the cause. I call that an inadequate or partial cause whose effect cannot be understood by means of the cause alone.

DEF. II. I say that we act when

FROM: the *Ethics*, Benedict Spinoza. Elwes, trans. Part III, Preface and Definitions, plus Propositions 1 and 2 (originally published in 1677).

anything is done, either within us or without us, of which we are the adequate cause, that is to say (by the preceding Def.), when from our nature anything follows, either within us or without us, which by that nature alone can be clearly and distinctly understood. On the other hand, I say that we suffer when anything is done within us, or when anything follows from our nature, of which we are not the cause excepting partially.

DEF. III. By affect I understand the affections of the body, by which the power of acting of the body itself is increased, diminished, helped, or hindered, together with the ideas of these affections.

If, therefore, we can be the adequate cause of any of these affections, I understand the affect to be an action, otherwise it is a passion.

Postulate 1. The human body can be affected in many ways by which its power of acting is increased or diminished, and also in other ways which make its power of acting neither greater nor less.

This postulate or axiom is based upon Post. 1 and Lems. 5 and 7, following Prop. 13, pt. 2.

Postulate 2. The human body is capable of suffering many changes, and, nevertheless, can retain the impressions or traces of objects (Post. 5, pt. 2), and consequently the same images of things. (For the definition of images see Schol. Prop. 17, pt. 2.)

PROP. I. *Our mind acts at times and at times suffers: in so far as it has adequate ideas, it necessarily acts; and in so far as it has inadequate ideas, it necessarily suffers.*

Demonst. In every human mind some ideas are adequate, and others mutilated and confused (Schol. Prop. 40, pt. 2). But the ideas which in any mind are adequate are adequate in God in so far as He forms the essence of that mind (Corol. Prop. 11, pt. 2), while those again which are inadequate in the mind are also adequate in God (by the same Corol.), not in so far as He contains the essence of that mind only, but in so far as He contains the ideas of other things at the same time in Himself. Again, from any given idea some effect must necessarily follow (Prop. 36, pt. 1), of which God is the adequate cause (Def. 1, pt. 3), not in so far as He is infinite, but in so far as He is considered as affected with the given idea (Prop. 9, pt. 2). But of that effect of which God is the cause, in so far as He is affected by an idea which is adequate in any mind, that same mind is the adequate cause (Corol. Prop. 11, pt. 2). Our mind, therefore (Def. 2, pt. 3), in so far as it has adequate ideas, necessarily at times acts, which is the first thing we had to prove. Again, if there be anything which necessarily follows from an idea which is adequate in God, not in so far as He contains within Himself the mind of one man only, but also, together with this, the ideas of other things, then the mind of that man (Corol. Prop. 11, pt. 2) is not the adequate cause of that thing, but is only its partial cause, and therefore (Def. 2, pt. 3), in so far as the mind has inadequate ideas, it necessarily at times suffers. This was the second thing to be proved. Therefore our mind, &c.— Q.E.D.

Corol. Hence it follows that the mind is subject to passions in proportion to the number of inadequate ideas which it has, and that it acts in proportion to the number of adequate ideas which it has.

PROP. II. *The body cannot determine the mind to thought, neither can the mind determine the body to motion nor rest, nor to anything else, if there be anything else.*

Demonst. All modes of thought have God for a cause in so far as He is a thinking thing, and not in so far as He is manifested by any other attribute (Prop. 6, pt. 2). That which determines the mind to thought, therefore, is a mode of thought and not of extension, that is to say (Def. 1, pt. 2), it is not the body. This is the first thing which was to be proved. Again, the motion and rest of the body must be derived from some other body, which has also been determined to motion or rest by another, and, absolutely, whatever arises in the body must arise from God, in so far as He is considered as affected by some mode of extension, and not in so far as He is considered as affected by any mode of thought (Prop. 6, pt. 2), that is to say, whatever arises in the body cannot arise from the mind, which is a mode of thought (Prop. 11, pt. 2). This is the second thing which was to be proved. Therefore, the body cannot determine, &c.—Q.E.D.

Schol. This proposition will be better understood from what has been said in the scholium of Prop. 7, pt. 2, that is to say, that the mind and the body are one and the same thing, conceived at one time under the attribute of thought, and at another under that of extension. For this reason, the order or concatenation of things is one, whether nature be conceived under this or under that attribute, and consequently the order of the actions and passions of our body is coincident in nature with the order of the actions and passions of the mind. This is also plain from the manner in which we have demonstrated Prop. 12, pt. 2.

Although these things are so, and no ground for doubting remains, I scarcely believe, nevertheless, that, without a proof derived from experience, men will be induced calmly to weigh what has been said, so firmly are they persuaded that, solely at the bidding of the mind, the body moves or rests, and does a number of things which depend upon the will of the mind alone, and upon the power of thought. For what the body can do no one has hitherto determined, that is to say, experience has taught no one hitherto what the body, without being determined by the mind, can do and what it cannot do from the laws of nature alone, in so far as nature is considered merely as corporeal. For no one as yet has understood the structure of the body so accurately as to be able to explain all its functions, not to mention the fact that many things are observed in brutes which far surpass human sagacity, and that sleep-walkers in their sleep do very many things which they dare not do when awake; all this showing that the body itself can do many things from the laws of its own nature alone at which the mind belonging to that body is amazed. Again, nobody knows by what means or by what method the mind moves the body, nor how many degrees of motion it can communicate to the body, nor with what speed it can move the body. So that it follows that when men say that this or that action of the body springs from the mind which has command over the body, they do not know what they say, and they do nothing but confess with pretentious words that they know nothing about the cause of the action, and see nothing in it to wonder at. But they will say, that whether they know or do not know by what means the mind moves the body, it is nevertheless in their experience that if the mind were not fit for thinking the body would be inert. They say, again, it is in their experience that the mind alone has power both to speak and be silent, and to do many other things which they therefore think to be dependent on a decree of the mind. But with regard to the first assertion, I ask them if experience does not also teach that if the body be sluggish the mind at the same time is not fit for thinking? When the body is asleep, the mind slumbers with it, and has not the power to think, as it has when the body is awake. Again, I believe that all have discovered that the mind is not always equally fitted for thinking about the same subject, but in proportion to the fitness of the body for this or that image to be excited in it will the mind be better fitted to contemplate this or that object. But my opponents will say, that from the laws of nature alone, in so far as it is considered to be corporeal merely, it cannot be that the causes of architecture, painting, and things of this sort, which are the results of human art alone, could be deduced, and that the human body, unless it were determined and guided by the mind, would not be able to build a temple. I have already shown, however, that they do not know what the body can do, nor what can be deduced from the consideration of its nature alone, and that they find that many things are done merely by the laws of nature which they would never have believed to be possible without the direction of the mind, as, for example, those things which sleep-walkers do in their sleep, and at which they themselves are astonished when they wake. I adduce also here the structure itself of the human body, which so greatly surpasses in workmanship all those things which are constructed by human art, not to mention what I have already proved, that an infinitude of things follows from nature under whatever attribute it may be considered.

With regard to the second point, I should say that human affairs would be much more happily conducted if it were equally in the power of men to be silent and to speak; but experience shows over and over again that there is nothing which men have less power over than the tongue, and that there is nothing which they are less able to do than to govern their appetites, so that many persons believe that we do those things only with freedom which we seek indifferently; as the desire for such things can easily be lessened by the recollection of another thing which we frequently call to mind; it being impossible, on the other hand, to do those things with freedom which we seek with such ardour that the recollection of another thing is unable to mitigate it. But if, however, we had not found out that we do many things which we afterwards repent, and that when agitated by conflicting affects we see that which is better and follow that which is worse, nothing would hinder us from believing that we do everything with freedom. Thus the infant

believes that it is by free will that it seeks the breast; the angry boy believes that by free will he wishes vengeance; the timid man thinks it is with free will he seeks flight; the drunkard believes that by a free command of his mind he speaks the things which when sober he wishes he had left unsaid. Thus the madman, the chatterer, the boy, and others of the same kind, all believe that they speak by a free command of the mind, whilst, in truth, they have no power to restrain the impulse which they have to speak, so that experience itself, no less than reason, clearly teaches that men believe themselves to be free simply because they are conscious of their own actions, knowing nothing of the causes by which they are determined: it teaches, too, that the decrees of the mind are nothing but the appetites themselves, which differ, therefore, according to the different temper of the body. For every man determines all things from his affect; those who are agitated by contrary affects do not know what they want, whilst those who are agitated by no affect are easily driven hither and thither. All this plainly shows that the decree of the mind, the appetite, and determination of the body are coincident in nature, or rather that they are one and the same thing, which, when it is considered under the attribute of thought and manifested by that, is called a decree, and when it is considered under the attribute of extension and is deduced from the laws of motion and rest, is called a determination. This, however, will be better understood as we go on, for there is another thing which I wish to be observed here—that we cannot by a mental decree do a thing unless we recollect it. We cannot speak a word, for instance, unless we recollect it. But it is not in the free power of the mind either to recollect a thing or to forget it. It is believed, therefore, that the power of the mind extends only thus far—that from a mental decree we can speak or be silent about a thing only when we recollect it. But when we dream that we speak, we believe that we do so from a free decree of the mind; and yet we do not speak, or, if we do, it is the result of a spontaneous motion of the body. We dream, again, that we are concealing things, and that we do this by virtue of a decree of the mind like that by which, when awake, we are silent about things we know. We dream, again, that, from a decree of the mind, we do some things which we should not dare to do when awake. And I should like to know, therefore, whether there are two kinds of decrees in the mind—one belonging to dreams and the other free. If this be too great nonsense, we must necessarily grant that this decree of the mind, which is believed to be free, is not distinguishable from the imagination or memory, and is nothing but the affirmation which the idea necessarily involves in so far as it is an idea (Prop. 49, pt. 2). These decrees of the mind, therefore, arise in the mind by the same necessity as the ideas of things actually existing. Consequently, those who believe that they speak, or are silent, or do anything else from a free decree of the mind, dream with their eyes open.

Free Will and Determinism Are Compatible
JOHN STUART MILL

The question whether the law of causality applies in the same strict sense to human actions as to other phenomena, is the celebrated controversy concerning the freedom of the will, which, from at least as far back as the time of Pelagius, has divided both the philosophical and the religious world. The affirmative opinion is commonly called the doctrine of Necessity, as asserting human volitions and actions to be necessary and inevitable. The negative maintains that the will is not determined, like other phenomena, by antecedents, but determines itself; that our volitions are not, properly speaking, the effects of causes, or at least have no causes which they uniformly and implicitly obey.

I have already made it sufficiently apparent that the former of these opinions is that which I consider the true one; but the misleading terms in which it is often expressed, and the indistinct manner in which it is usually apprehended, have both obstructed its reception and perverted its influence when received. The metaphysical theory of free-will, as held by philosophers (for the practical feeling of it, common in a greater or less degree to all mankind, is in no way inconsistent with the contrary theory), was invented because the supposed alternative of admitting human actions to be *necessary* was deemed inconsistent with everyone's instinctive consciousness, as well as humiliating to the pride, even degrading to the moral nature of man. Nor do I deny that the doctrine, as sometimes held, is open to these imputations; for the misapprehension in which I shall be able to show that they originate unfortunately is not confined to the opponents of the doctrine, but is participated in by many, perhaps we might say by most, of its supporters.

Correctly conceived, the doctrine entitled Philosophical Necessity is simply this: that, given the motives which are present to an individual's mind, and given likewise the character and disposition of the individual, the manner in which he will act might be unerringly inferred; that if we knew the person thoroughly, and knew all the inducements which are acting upon him, we could foretell his conduct with as much

FROM: *A System of Logic*, John Stuart Mill. Book VI, Ch. 2 (originally published in 1843).

certainty as we can predict any physical event. This proposition I take to be a mere interpretation of universal experience, a statement in words of what everyone is internally convinced of. No one who believed that he knew thoroughly the circumstances of any case, and the characters of the different persons concerned, would hesitate to foretell how all of them would act. Whatever degree of doubt he may in fact feel arises from the uncertainty whether he really knows the circumstances, or the character of someone or other of the persons, with the degree of accuracy required; but by no means from thinking that if he did know these things, there could be any uncertainty what the conduct should be. Nor does this full assurance conflict in the smallest degree with what is called our feeling of freedom. We do not feel ourselves the less free because those to whom we are intimately known are well assured how we shall will to act in a particular case. We often, on the contrary, regard the doubt of what our conduct will be as a mark of ignorance of our characters, and sometimes even resent it as an imputation. The religious metaphysicians who have asserted the freedom of the will have always maintained it to be consistent with divine foreknowledge of our actions; and if with divine, then with any other foreknowledge. We may be free, and yet another may have reason to be perfectly certain what use we shall make of our freedom. It is not, therefore, the doctrine that our volitions and actions are invariable consequents of our antecedent states of mind, that is either contradicted by our consciousness or felt to be degrading.

But the doctrine of causation, when considered as obtaining between our volitions and their antecedents, is almost universally conceived as involving more than this. Many do not believe, and very few practically feel, that there is nothing in causation but invariable, certain, and unconditional sequence. There are few to whom mere constancy of succession appears a sufficiently strin-

gent bond of union for so peculiar a relation as that of cause and effect. Even if the reason repudiates, the imagination retains, the feeling of some more intimate connection, of some peculiar tie or mysterious constraint exercised by the antecedent over the consequent. Now this it is which, considered as applying to the human will, conflicts with our consciousness and revolts our feelings. We are certain that, in the case of our volitions, there is not this mysterious constraint. We know that we are not compelled, as by a magical spell, to obey any particular motives. We feel that if we wished to prove that we have the power of resisting the motive, we could do so, (that wish being, it needs scarcely be observed, a *new antecedent*); and it would be humiliating to our pride, and (what is of more importance) paralyzing to our desire of excellence, if we thought otherwise. But neither is any such mysterious compulsion now supposed, by the best philosophical authorities, to be exercised by any other such cause over its effect. Those who think that causes draw their effects after them by a mystical tie are right in believing that the relation between volitions and their antecedents is of another nature. But they should go farther, and admit that this is also true of all other effects and their antecedents. If such a tie is considered to be involved in the word necessity, the doctrine is not true of human actions; but neither is it then true of inanimate objects. It would be more correct to say that matter is not bound by necessity, than that mind is so.

That the free-will metaphysicians, being mostly of the school which rejects Hume's and Brown's analysis of Cause and Effect, should miss their way for want of the light which that analysis affords, cannot surprise us. The wonder is, that the Necessitarians, who usually admit that philosophical theory, should in practice equally lose sight of it. The very same misconception of the doctrine called Philosophical Necessity which prevents the opposite party from recognising its truth, I believe to exist more or less obscurely in the minds of most Necessitarians, however they may in words disavow it. I am much mistaken if they habitually feel that the necessity which they recognise in actions is but uniformity of order, and capability of being predicted. They have a feeling as if there were at bottom a stronger tie between the volitions and their causes: as if, when they asserted that the will is governed by the balance of motives, they meant something more cogent than if they had only said, that whoever knew the motives, and our habitual susceptibilities to them, could predict how we should will to act. They commit, in opposition to their own scientific system, the very same mistake which their adversaries commit in obedience to theirs; and in consequence do really in some instances suffer those depressing consequences which their opponents erroneously impute to the doctrine itself.

I am inclined to think that this error is almost wholly an effect of the associations with a word, and that it would be prevented by forebearing to employ, for the expression of the simple fact of causation, so extremely inappropriate a term as Necessity. That word, in its other acceptations, involves much more than mere uniformity of sequence: it implies irresistibleness. Applied to the will, it only means that the given cause will be followed by the effect, subject to all possibilities of counteraction by other causes; but in common use it stands for the operation of those causes exclusively, which are supposed too powerful to be counteracted at all. When we say that all human actions take place of necessity, we only mean that they will certainly happen if nothing prevents:— when we say that dying of want, to those who cannot get food, is a necessity, we mean that it will certainly happen, whatever may be done to prevent it. The application of the same term to the agencies on which human actions depend as is used to express those agencies of nature which are really uncontrollable, cannot fail, when habitual, to create a feeling of uncontrollableness in the former also. This, however, is a mere illusion. There are physical sequences which we call necessary as death for want of food or air; there are others which, though as much cases of causation as the former, are not said to be necessary, as death from poison, which an antidote, or the use of the stomach pump, will sometimes avert. It is apt to be forgotten by people's feelings, even if remembered by their understandings, that human actions are in this last predicament: they are never (except in some cases of mania) ruled by any one motive with such absolute sway that there is no room for the influence of any other. The causes, therefore, on which action depends are never uncontrollable, and any given effect is only necessary provided that the causes tending to produce it are not controlled. That whatever happens could not have happened otherwise unless something had taken place which was capable of preventing it, no one surely needs hesitate to admit. But to call this by the name necessity is to use the term in a sense so different from its primitive and familiar meaning, from that which it bears in the common occasions of life, as to amount almost to a play upon words. The associations derived from the ordinary sense of the term will adhere to it in spite of all we can do; and though the doctrine of Necessity, as stated by most who hold it, is very remote from fatalism, it is probable that most Necessitarians are Fatalists, more or less, in their feelings.

A Fatalist believes, or half believes (for nobody is a consistent Fatalist), not only that whatever is about to happen will be the infallible result of the causes which produce it (which is the true Necessitarian doctrine), but, moreover, that there is no use in struggling against it; that it will happen however we may strive to prevent it. Now, a Necessitarian, believing that our actions follow from our characters, and that our characters follow from our organisation, our education, and our circumstances, is apt to be, with more or less of consciousness on his part, a Fatalist as to his own actions, and to believe that his nature is such, or that his education and circumstances have so moulded his character, that nothing can now prevent him from feeling and acting in a particular way, or at least that no effort of his own can hinder it. In the words of the sect which in our own day has most perseveringly inculcated and most perversely misunderstood this great doctrine, his character is formed *for* him, and not *by* him; therefore his wishing that it had been formed differently is of no use; he has no power to alter it. But this is a grand error. He has, to a certain extent, a power to alter his character. Its being, in the ultimate resort, formed for him, is not inconsistent with its being, in part, formed *by* him as one of the intermediate agents. His character is formed by his circumstances (including among these his particular organisation), but his own desire to mould it in a particular way is one of these circumstances, and by no means one of the least influential. We cannot, indeed, directly will to be different from what we are; but neither did those who are supposed to have formed our characters directly will that we should be what we are. Their will had no direct power except over their own actions. They made us what they did make us by willing, not the end, but the requisite means; and we, when our habits are not too inveterate, can, by similarly willing the requisite means, make ourselves different. If they could place us under the influence of certain circumstances, we in like manner can place ourselves under the influence of other circumstances. We are exactly as capable of making our own character, *if we will*, as others are of making it for us.

Yes (answers the Owenite), but these words, "if we will," surrender the whole point, since the will to alter our own character is given us, not by any efforts of ours, but by circumstances which we cannot help; it comes to us either from external causes or not at all. Most true: if the Owenite stop here, he is in a position from which nothing can expel him. Our character is formed by us as well as for us; but the wish which induces us to attempt to form it is

formed for us; and how? Not, in general, by our organisation, nor wholly by our education, but by our experience—experience of the painful consequences of the character we previously had, or by some strong feeling of admiration or aspiration accidentally aroused. But to think that we have no power of altering our character, and to think that we shall not use our power unless we desire to use it, are very different things, and have a very different effect on the mind. A person who does not wish to alter his character cannot be the person who is supposed to feel discouraged or paralysed by thinking himself unable to do it. The depressing effect of the Fatalist doctrine can only be felt where there *is* a wish to do what the doctrine represents as impossible. It is of no consequence what we think forms our character, when we have no desire of our own about forming it, but it is of great consequence that we should not be prevented from forming such a desire by thinking the attainment impracticable, and that if we have the desire we should know that the work is not so irrevocably done as to be incapable of being altered.

And, indeed, if we examine closely, we shall find that this feeling, of our being able to modify our own character *if we wish*, is itself the feeling of moral freedom which we are conscious of. A person feels morally free who feels that his habits or his temptations are not his masters, but he theirs: who even in yielding to them knows that he could resist; that were he desirous of altogether throwing them off, there would not be required for that purpose a stronger desire than he knows himself to be capable of feeling. It is of course necessary, to render our consciousness of freedom complete, that we should have succeeded in making our character all we have hitherto attempted to make it; for if we have wished and not attained, we have, to that extent, not power over our own character—we are not free. Or at least, we must feel that our wish, if not strong enough to alter our character, is strong enough to conquer our character when the two are brought into conflict in any particular case of conduct. And hence it is said with truth, that none but a person of confirmed virtue is completely free.

The application of so improper a term as Necessity to the doctrine of cause and effect in the matter of human character seems to me one of the most signal instances in philosophy of the abuse of terms, and its practical consequences one of the most striking examples of the power of language over our associations. The subject will never be generally understood until that objectionable term is dropped. The free-will doctrine, by keeping in view precisely that portion of the truth which the word Necessity puts out of sight, namely, the power of the mind to cooperate in the formation of its own character, has given to its adherents a practical feeling much nearer to the truth than has generally (I believe) existed in the minds of Necessitarians. The latter may have had a stronger sense of the importance of what human beings can do to shape the characters of one another; but the free-will doctrine has, I believe, fostered in its supporters a much stronger spirit of self-culture.

There is still one fact which requires to be noticed (in addition to the existence of a power of self-formation) before the doctrine of the causation of human actions can be freed from the confusion and misapprehensions which surround it in many minds. When the will is said to be determined by motives, a motive does not mean always, or solely, the anticipation of a pleasure or of a pain. I shall not here inquire whether it be true that, in the commencements, all our voluntary actions are mere means consciously employed to obtain some pleasure or avoid some pain. It is at least certain that we gradually, through the influence of association, come to desire the means without thinking of the end: the action itself becomes an object of desire, and is performed without reference to any motive beyond itself. Thus far, it may still be objected, that the action having through

association become pleasurable, we are, as much as before, moved to act by the anticipation of a pleasure, namely, the pleasure of the action itself. But granting this, the matter does not end here. As we proceed in the formation of habits, and become accustomed to will a particular act or a particular course of conduct because it is pleasurable, we at last continue to will it without any reference to its being pleasurable. Although, from some change in us or in our circumstances, we have ceased to find any pleasure in the action, or perhaps to anticipate any pleasure as the consequence of it, we still continue to desire the action, and consequently to do it. In this manner it is that habits of hurtful excess continue to be practised although they have ceased to be pleasurable; and in this manner also it is that the habit of willing to persevere in the course which he has chosen does not desert the moral hero, even when the reward, however real, which he doubtless receives from the consciousness of well-doing, is anything but an equivalent for the sufferings he undergoes or the wishes he may have to renounce.

A habit of willing is commonly called a purpose; and among the causes of our volitions, and of the actions which flow from them, must be reckoned not only likings and aversions, but also purposes. It is only when our purposes have become independent of the feelings of pain or pleasure from which they originally took their rise that we are said to have a confirmed character. "A character," says Novalis, "is a completely fashioned will"; and the will, once so fashioned, may be steady and constant, when the passive susceptibilities of pleasure and pain are greatly weakened or materially changed.

With the corrections and explanations now given, the doctrine of the causation of our volitions by motives, and of motives by the desirable objects offered to us, combined without particular susceptibilities of desire, may be considered, I hope, as sufficiently established for the purposes of this treatise.

Determinism Is True
BARON D'HOLBACH

*T*hose who have pretended that the soul is distinguished from the body, is immaterial, draws its ideas from its own peculiar source, acts by its own energies, without the aid of any exterior object, have, by a consequence of their own system, enfranchised it from those physical laws according to which all beings of which we have a knowledge are obliged to act. They have believed that the soul is mistress of its own conduct, is able to regulate its own peculiar operations, has the faculty to determine its will by its own natural energy; in a word, they have pretended that man is a *free agent*.

It has been already sufficiently proved that the soul is nothing more than the body considered relatively to some of its functions more concealed than others: it has been shown that this soul, even when it shall be supposed immaterial, is continually modified conjointly with the body, is submitted to all its motion, and that without this it would remain inert and dead: that, consequently, it is subjected to the influence of those material and physical causes which give impulse to the body; of which the mode of existence, whether habitual or transitory, depends upon the material elements by which it is surrounded, that form its texture, constitute its temperament, enter into it by means of the aliments, and penetrate it by their subtility. The faculties which are called *intellectual*, and those qualities which are styled *moral*, have been explained in a manner purely physical and natural. In the last place it has been demonstrated that all the ideas, all the systems, all the affections, all the opinions, whether true or false, which man forms to himself, are to be attributed to his physical and material senses. Thus man is a being purely physical; in whatever manner he is considered, he is connected to universal nature, and submitted to the necessary and immutable laws that she imposes on all the beings she contains, according to their peculiar essences or to the respective properties with which, without consulting them, she endows each particular species. Man's life is a line that nature commands him to describe upon the surface of the earth, without his ever being able to swerve from it, even for an instant. He is born without his own consent; his organization does in nowise depend upon himself; his ideas come to him involuntarily; his habits are in the power of those who cause him to contract them; he is unceasingly modified by causes, whether visible or concealed, over which he has no control, which necessarily regulate his mode of existence, give the hue to his way of thinking, and determine his manner of acting. He is good or bad, happy or miserable, wise or foolish, reasonable or irrational, without his will being for any thing in these various states. Nevertheless, in despite of the shackles by which he is bound, it is pretended he is a free agent, or that independent of the causes by which he is moved, he determines his own will, and regulates his own condition.

However slender the foundation of this opinion, of which every thing ought to point out to him the errour, it is current at this day and passes for an incontestable truth with a great number of people, otherwise extremely enlightened; it is the basis of religion, which, supposing relations between man and the unknown being she has placed above nature, has been incapable of imagining how man could either merit reward or deserve punishment from this being, if

FROM: *The System of Nature*, Baron D'Holbach. H. D. Robinson, trans. Ch. 11 (originally published in 1770).

he was not a free agent. Society has been believed interested in this system; because an idea has gone abroad, that if all the actions of man were to be contemplated as necessary, the right of punishing those who injure their associates would no longer exist. At length human vanity accommodated itself to a hypothesis which, unquestionably, appears to distinguish man from all other physical beings, by assigning to him the special privilege of a total independence of all other causes, but of which a very little reflection would have shown him the impossibility.

The will, as we have elsewhere said, is a modification of the brain, by which it is disposed to action, or prepared to give play to the organs. This will is necessarily determined by the qualities, good or bad, agreeable or painful, of the object or the motive that acts upon his senses, or of which the idea remains with him, and is resuscitated by his memory. In consequence, he acts necessarily, his action is the result of the impulse he receives either from the motive, from the object, or from the idea which has modified his brain, or disposed his will. When he does not act according to this impulse, it is because there comes some new cause, some new motive, some new idea, which modifies his brain in a different manner, gives him a new impulse, determines his will in another way, by which the action of the former impulse is suspended: thus, the sight of an agreeable object, or its idea, determines his will to set him in action to procure it; but if a new object or a new idea more powerfully attracts him, it gives a new direction to his will, annihilates the effect of the former, and prevents the action by which it was to be procured. This is the mode in which reflection, experience, reason, necessarily arrests or suspends the action of man's will: without this he would of necessity have followed the anterior impulse which carried him towards a then desirable object. In all this he always acts according to necessary laws, from which

he has no means of emancipating himself.

If when tormented with violent thirst, he figures to himself in idea, or really perceives a fountain, whose limpid streams might cool his feverish want, is he sufficient master of himself to desire or not to desire the object competent to satisfy so lively a want? It will no doubt be conceded, that it is impossible he should not be desirous to satisfy it; but it will be said—if at this moment it is announced to him that the water he so ardently desires is poisoned, he will, notwithstanding his vehement thirst, abstain from drinking it: and it has, therefore, been falsely concluded that he is a free agent. The fact, however, is, that the motive in either case is exactly the same: his own conservation. The same necessity that determined him to drink before he knew the water was deleterious, upon this new discovery equally determines him not to drink; the desire of conserving himself either annihilates or suspends the former impulse; the second motive becomes stronger than the preceding, that is, the fear of death, or the desire of preserving himself, necessarily prevails over the painful sensation caused by his eagerness to drink: but, it will be said, if the thirst is very parching, an inconsiderate man without regarding the danger will risk swallowing the water. Nothing is gained by this remark: in this case the anterior impulse only regains the ascendency; he is persuaded that life may possibly be longer preserved, or that he shall derive a greater good by drinking the poisoned water than by enduring the torment, which, to his mind, threatens instant dissolution: thus the first becomes the strongest and necessarily urges him on to action. Nevertheless, in either case, whether he partakes of the water, or whether he does not, the two actions will be equally necessary; they will be the effect of that motive which finds itself most puissant; which consequently acts in the most coercive manner upon his will.

This example will serve to explain

the whole phenomena of the human will. This will, or rather the brain, finds itself in the same situation as a bowl, which, although it has received an impulse that drives it forward in a straight line, is deranged in its course whenever a force superior to the first obliges it to change its direction. The man who drinks the poisoned water appears a madman; but the actions of fools are as necessary as those of the most prudent individuals. The motives that determine the voluptuary and the debauchee to risk their health, are as powerful, and their actions are as necessary, as those which decide the wise man to manage his. But, it will be insisted, the debauchee may be prevailed on to change his conduct: this does not imply that he is a free agent; but that motives may be found sufficiently powerful to annihilate the effect of those that previously acted upon him; then these new motives determine his will to the new mode of conduct he may adopt as necessarily as the former did to the old mode.

Man is said to *deliberate*, when the action of the will is suspended; this happens when two opposite motives act alternately upon him. To *deliberate*, is to hate and to love in succession; it is to be alternately attracted and repelled; it is to be moved, sometimes by one motive, sometimes by another. Man only deliberates when he does not distinctly understand the quality of the objects from which he receives impulse, or when experience has not sufficiently apprised him of the effects, more or less remote, which his actions will produce. He would take the air, but the weather is uncertain; he deliberates in consequence; he weighs the various motives that urge his will to go out or to stay at home; he is at length determined by that motive which is most probable; this removes his indecision, which necessarily settles his will, either to remain within or to go abroad: his motive is always either the immediate or ultimate advantage he finds, or thinks he finds, in the action to which he is persuaded.

Man's will frequently fluctuates between two objects, of which either the presence or the ideas move him alternately: he waits until he has contemplated the objects, or the ideas they have left in his brain which solicit him to different actions; he then compares these objects or ideas; but even in the time of deliberation, during the comparison, pending these alternatives of love and hatred which succeed each other, sometimes with the utmost rapidity, he is not a free agent for a single instant; the good or the evil which he believes he finds successively in the objects, are the necessary motives of these momentary wills; of the rapid motion of desire or fear, that he experiences as long as his uncertainty continues. From this it will be obvious that deliberation is necessary; that uncertainty is necessary; that whatever part he takes, in consequence of this deliberation, it will always necessarily be that which he has judged, whether well or ill, is most probable to turn to his advantage.

When the soul is assailed by two motives that act alternately upon it, or modify it successively, it deliberates; the brain is in a sort of equilibrium, accompanied with perpetual oscillations, sometimes towards one object, sometimes towards the other, until the most forcible carries the point, and thereby extricates it from this state of suspense, in which consists the indecision of his will. But when the brain is simultaneously assailed by causes equally strong that move it in opposite directions, agreeable to the general law of all bodies when they are struck equally by contrary powers, it stops, it is in *nisu*; it is neither capable to will nor to act; it waits until one of the two causes has obtained sufficient force to overpower the other; to determine its will; to attract it in such a manner that it may prevail over the efforts of the other cause.

This mechanism, so simple, so natural, suffices to demonstrate why uncertainty is painful, and why suspense is always a violent state for man. The brain, an organ so delicate and so mobile, experiences such rapid modifications that it is fatigued; or when it is urged in contrary directions, by causes equally powerful, it suffers a kind of compression, that prevents the activity which is suitable to the preservation of the whole, and which is necessary to procure what is advantageous to its existence. This mechanism will also explain the irregularity, the indecision, the inconstancy of man, and account for that conduct which frequently appears an inexplicable mystery, and which is, indeed, the effect of the received systems. In consulting experience, it will be found that the soul is submitted to precisely the same physical laws as the material body. If the will of each individual, during a given time, was only moved by a single cause or passion, nothing would be more easy than to foresee his actions; but his heart is frequently assailed by contrary powers, by adverse motives, which either act on him simultaneously or in succession; then his brain, attracted in opposite directions, is either fatigued, or else tormented by a state of compression, which deprives it of activity. Sometimes it is in a state of incommodious inaction; sometimes it is the sport of the alternate shocks it undergoes. Such, no doubt, is the state in which man finds himself when a lively passion solicits him to the commission of crime, whilst fear points out to him the danger by which it is attended: such, also, is the condition of him whom remorse, by the continued labour of his distracted soul, prevents from enjoying the objects he has criminally obtained.

Choice by no means proves the free agency of man: he only deliberates when he does not yet know which to choose of the many objects that move him, he is then in an embarrassment, which does not terminate until his will is decided by the greater advantage he believes he shall find in the object he chooses, or the action he undertakes. From whence it may be seen, that choice is necessary, because he would not determine for an object, or for an action, if he did not believe that he should find in it some direct advantage. That man should have free agency it were needful that he should be able to will or choose without motive, or that he could prevent motives coercing his will. Action always being the effect of his will once determined, and as his will cannot be determined but by a motive which is not in his own power, it follows that he is never the master of the determination of his own peculiar will; that consequently he never acts as a free agent. It has been believed that man was a free agent because he had a will with the power of choosing; but attention has not been paid to the fact that even his will is moved by causes independent of himself; is owing to that which is inherent in his own organization, or which belongs to the nature of the beings acting on him.† Is he the master of willing not to withdraw his hand from the fire when he fears it will be burnt? Or has he the power to take away from fire the property which makes him fear it? Is he the master of not choosing a dish of meat, which he knows to be agreeable or analogous to his palate; of not preferring it to that which he knows to be disagreeable or dangerous? It is always according to his sensations, to his own peculiar experience, or to his suppositions, that he judges of things, either well or ill; but whatever may be his judgment, it depends necessarily on his mode of feeling, whether habitual or accidental, and

† Man passes a great portion of his life without even willing. His will depends on the motive by which he is determined. If he were to render an exact account of every thing he does in the course of each day—from rising in the morning to lying down at night—he would find that not one of his actions have been in the least voluntary; that they have been mechanical, habitual, determined by causes he was not able to foresee; to which he was either obliged to yield, or with which he was allured to acquiesce: he would discover, that all the motives of his labours, of his amusements, of his discourses, of his thoughts, have been necessary; that they have evidently either seduced him or drawn him along.

the qualities he finds in the causes that move him, which exist in despite of himself.

It has been believed that man was a free agent, because it has been imagined that his soul could at will recall ideas which sometimes suffice to check his most unruly desires. Thus, the idea of a remote evil, frequently prevents him from enjoying a present and actual good: thus remembrance, which is an almost insensible or slight modification of his brain, annihilates, at each instant, the real objects that act upon his will. But he is not master of recalling to himself his ideas at pleasure; their association is independent of him; they are arranged in his brain in despite of him and without his own knowledge, where they have made an impression more or less profound; his memory itself depends upon his organization; its fidelity depends upon the habitual or momentary state in which he finds himself; when his will is vigorously determined to some object or idea that excites a very lively passion in him, those objects or ideas that would be able to arrest his action, no longer present themselves to his mind; in those moments his eyes are shut to the dangers that menace him; of which the idea ought to make him forbear; he marches forwards headlong towards the object by whose image he is hurried on; reflection cannot operate upon him in any way; he sees nothing but the object of his desires; the salutary ideas which might be able to arrest his progress disappear, or else display themselves either too faintly or too late to prevent his acting. Such is the case with all those who, blinded by some strong passion, are not in a condition to recall to themselves those motives, of which the idea alone, in cooler moments, would be sufficient to deter them from proceeding the disorder in which they are, prevents their judging soundly; renders them incapable of foreseeing the consequences of their actions; precludes them from applying to their experience; from making use of their reason; natural operations which suppose a justness in the manner of

associating their ideas, but to which their brain is then not more competent, in consequence of the momentary delirium it suffers, than their hand is to write whilst they are taking violent exercise.

Man's mode of thinking is necessarily determined by his manner of being; it must therefore depend on his natural organization, and the modification his system receives independently of his will. From this, we are obliged to conclude, that his thoughts, his reflections, his manner of viewing things, of feeling, of judging, of combining ideas, is neither voluntary nor free. In a word, that his soul is neither mistress of the motion excited in it, nor of representing to itself, when wanted, those images or ideas that are capable of counterbalancing the impulse it receives. This is the reason, why man, when in a passion, ceases to reason; at that moment reason is as impossible to be heard, as it is during an ecstacy, or in a fit of drunkenness. The wicked are never more than men who are either drunk or mad; if they reason, it is not until tranquillity is re-established in their machine; then, and not till then, the tardy ideas that present themselves to their mind enable them to see the consequence of their actions, and give birth to ideas that bring on them that trouble, which is designated *shame, regret, remorse.*

The errours of philosophers on the free agency of man, have arisen from their regarding his will as the *primum mobile,* the original motive of his actions; for want of recurring back, they have not perceived the multiplied, the complicated causes which, independently of him, give motion to the will itself; or which dispose and modify his brain, whilst he himself is purely passive in the motion he receives. Is he the master of desiring or not desiring an object that appears desirable to him? Without doubt it will be answered, no: but he is the master of resisting his desire, if he reflects on the consequences. But, I ask, is he capable of reflecting on these consequences, when his soul is hurried along by a very lively passion, which entirely depends upon his natural organization, and the causes by which he is modified? Is it in his power to add to these consequences all the weight necessary to counterbalance his desire? Is he the master of preventing the qualities which render an object desirable from residing in it? I shall be told: he ought to have learned to resist his passions; to contract a habit of putting a curb on his desires. I agree to it without any difficulty. But in reply, I again ask, is his nature susceptible of this modification? Does his boiling blood, his unruly imagination, the igneous fluid that circulates in his veins, permit him to make, enable him to apply true experience in the moment when it is wanted? And even when his temperament has capacitated him, has his education, the examples set before him, the ideas with which he has been inspired in early life, been suitable to make him contract this habit of repressing his desires? Have not all these things rather contributed to induce him to seek with advidity, to make him actually desire those objects which you say he ought to resist.

In despite of these proofs of the want of free agency in man, so clear to unprejudiced minds, it will, perhaps, be insisted upon with no small feeling of triumph, that if it be proposed to any one, to move or not to move his hand, an action in the number of those called *indifferent,* he evidently appears to be the master of choosing; from which it is concluded that evidence has been offered of his free agency. The reply is, this example is perfectly simple; man in performing some action which he is resolved on doing, does not by any means prove his free agency: the very desire of displaying this quality, excited by the dispute, becomes a necessary motive, which decides his will either for the one or the other of these actions: what deludes him in this instance, or that which persuades him he is a free agent at this moment, is, that he does not discern the true motive which sets him in action, namely, the desire of convincing his op-

ponent: if in the heat of the dispute he insists and asks, "Am I not the master of throwing myself out of the window?" I shall answer him, no; that whilst he preserves his reason there is no probability that the desire of proving his free agency, will become a motive sufficiently powerful to make him sacrifice his life to the attempt: if, notwithstanding this, to prove he is a free agent, he should actually precipitate himself from the window, it would not be a sufficient warranty to conclude he acted freely, but rather that it was the violence of his temperament which spurred him on to this folly. Madness is a state, that depends upon the heat of the blood, not upon the will. A fanatic or a hero, braves death as necessarily as a more phlegmatic man or a coward flies from it.*

It is said that free agency is the absence of those obstacles competent to oppose themselves to the actions of man, or to the exercise of his faculties: it is pretended that he is a free agent whenever, making use of these faculties, he produces the effect he has proposed to himself. In reply to this reasoning, it is

---

* There is, in point of fact, no difference between the man that is cast out of the window by another, and the man who throws himself out of it, except that the impulse in the first instance comes immediately from without, whilst that which determines the fall in the second case, springs from within his own peculiar machine, having its more remote cause also exterior. When Mutius Scaevola held his hand in the fire, he was as much acting under the influence of necessity (caused by interior motives) that urged him to this strange action, as if his arm had been held by strong men: pride, despair, the desire of braving his enemy, a wish to astonish him, an anxiety to intimidate him, &c., were the invisible chains that held his hand bound to the fire. The love of glory, enthusiasm for their country, in like manner caused Codrus and Decius to devote themselves for their fellow-citizens. The Indian Colanus and the philosopher Peregrinus were equally obliged to burn themselves, by desire of exciting the astonishment of the Grecian assembly.

sufficient to consider that it in nowise depends upon himself to place or remove the obstacles that either determine or resist him; the motive that causes his action is no more in his own power than the obstacle that impedes him, whether this obstacle or motive be within his own machine or exterior of his person: he is not master of the thought presented to his mind, which determines his will; this thought is excited by some cause independent of himself.

To be undeceived on the system of his free agency, man has simply to recur to the motive by which his will is determined; he will always find this motive is out of his own control. It is said: that in consequence of an idea to which the mind gives birth, man acts freely if he encounters no obstacle. But the question is, what gives birth to this idea in his brain? was he the master either to prevent it from presenting itself, or from renewing itself in his brain? Does not this idea depend either upon objects that strike him exteriorly and in despite of himself, or upon causes, that without his knowledge, act within himself and modify his brain? Can he prevent his eyes, cast without design upon any object whatever, from giving him an idea of this object, and from moving his brain? He is not more master of the obstacles; they are the necessary effects of either interior or exterior causes, which always act according to their given properties. A man insults a coward, this necessarily irritates him against his insulter, but his will cannot vanquish the obstacle that cowardice places to the object of his desire, because his natural conformation, which does not depend upon himself, prevents his having courage. In this case, the coward is insulted in despite of himself; and against his will is obliged patiently to brook the insult he has received.

The partisans of the system of free agency appear ever to have confounded constraint with necessity. Man believes he acts as a free agent, every time he does not see any thing that places obstacles to his actions; he does not perceive that the motive which causes him to will, is always necessary and independent of himself. A prisoner loaded with chains is compelled to remain in prison; but he is not a free agent in the desire to emancipate himself; his chains prevent him from acting, but they do not prevent him from willing; he would save himself if they would loose his fetters; but he would not save himself as a free agent; fear or the idea of punishment would be sufficient motives for his action.

Man may, therefore, cease to be restrained, without, for that reason, becoming a free agent: in whatever manner he acts, he will act necessarily, according to motives by which he shall be determined. He may be compared to a heavy body that finds itself arrested in its descent by any obstacle whatever: take away this obstacle, it will gravitate or continue to fall; but who shall say this dense body is free to fall or not? Is not its descent the necessary effect of its own specific gravity? The virtuous Socrates submitted to the laws of his country, although they were unjust; and though the doors of his jail were left open to him, he would not save himself; but in this he did not act as a free agent: the invisible chains of opinion, the secret love of decorum, the inward respect for the laws, even when they are iniquitous, the fear of tarnishing his glory, kept him in his prison; they were motives sufficiently powerful with this enthusiast for virtue, to induce him to wait death with tranquillity; it was not in his power to save himself, because he could find no potential motive to bring him to depart, even for an instant, from those principles to which his mind was accustomed.

Man, it is said, frequently acts against his inclination, from whence it is falsely concluded he is a free agent; but when he appears to act contrary to his inclination, he is always determined to it by some motive sufficiently efficacious to vanquish this inclination. A sick man, with a view to his cure, arrives at conquering his repugnance to the most disgusting remedies: the fear of pain, or the dread of death, then become necessary motives; consequently this sick man cannot be said to act freely.

When it is said, that man is not a free agent, it is not pretended to compare him to a body moved by a simple impulsive cause: he contains within himself causes inherent to his existence; he is moved by an interior organ, which has its own peculiar laws, and is itself necessarily determined in consequence of ideas formed from perceptions resulting from sensations which it receives from exterior objects. As the mechanism of these sensations, of these perceptions, and the manner they engrave ideas on the brain of man, are not known to him; because he is unable to unravel all these motions; because he cannot perceive the chain of operations in his soul, or the motive principle that acts within him, he supposes himself a free agent; which, literally translated, signifies, that he moves himself by himself; that he determines himself without cause: when he rather ought to say, that he is ignorant how or for why he acts in the manner he does. It is true the soul enjoys an activity peculiar to itself; but it is equally certain that this activity would never be displayed, if some motive or some cause did not put it in a condition to exercise itself: at least it will not be pretended that the soul is able either to love or to hate without being moved, without knowing the objects, without having some idea of their qualities. Gunpowder has unquestionably a particular activity, but this activity will never display itself, unless fire be applied to it; this, however, immediately sets it in motion.

It is the great complication of motion in man, it is the variety of his action, it is the multiplicity of causes that move him, whether simultaneously or in continual succession, that persuades him he is a free agent: if all his motions were simple, if the causes that move him did not confound themselves with each other, if they were distinct, if his machine were less complicated, he would perceive that all his actions were necessary, because he would be enabled to recur instantly to the cause that made him act. A man who should be always obliged to go towards the west, would always go on that side; but he would feel that, in so going, he was not a free agent: if he had another sense, as his actions or his motion, augmented by a sixth, would be still more varied and much more complicated, he would believe himself still more a free agent than he does with his five senses.

It is, then, for want of recurring to the causes that move him; for want of being able to analyze, from not being competent to decompose the complicated motion of his machine, that man believes himself a free agent; it is only upon his own ignorance that he founds the profound yet deceitful notion he has of his free agency; that he builds those opinions which he brings forward as a striking proof of his pretended freedom of action. If, for a short time, each man was willing to examine his own peculiar actions, search out their true motives to discover their concatenation, he would remain convinced that the sentiment he has of his natural free agency, is a chimera that must speedily be destroyed by experience.

Nevertheless it must be acknowledged that the multiplicity and diversity of the causes which continually act upon man, frequently without even his knowledge, render it impossible, or at least extremely difficult for him to recur to the true principles of his own peculiar actions, much less the actions of others: they frequently depend upon causes so fugitive, so remote from their effects, and which, superficially examined, appear to have so little analogy, so slender a relation with them, that it requires singular sagacity to bring them into light. This is what renders the study of the moral man a task of such difficulty; this is the reason why his heart is an abyss, of which it is frequently impossible for him to fathom the depth. He is then obliged to content himself with a knowledge of the general and necessary laws by which the human heart is regulated: for the individuals of his own species these laws are pretty nearly the same; they vary only in consequence of the organization that is peculiar to each, and of the modification it undergoes: this, however, cannot be rigorously the same in any two. It suffices to know, that by his essence, man tends to conserve himself, and to render his existence happy: this granted, whatever may be his actions, if he recur back to this first principle, to this general, this necessary tendency of his will, he never can be deceived with regard to his motives.

The Dilemma of Determinism
WILLIAM JAMES

A common opinion prevails that the juice has ages been pressed out of the free-will controversy, and that no new champion can do more than warm up stale arguments which every one has heard. This is a radical mistake. I know of no subject less worn out, or in which inventive genius has a better chance of breaking open new ground,—not, perhaps, of forcing a conclusion or of coercing assent, but of deepening our sense of what the issue between the two parties really is, of what the ideas of fate and of free-will imply. At our very side almost, in the past few years, we have seen falling in rapid succession from the press works that present the alternative in entirely novel lights. Not to speak of the English disciples of Hegel, such as Green and Bradley; not to speak of Hinton and Hodgson, nor of Hazard here,—we see in the writings of Renouvier, Fouillée, and Delbœuf[1] how completely changed and refreshed is the form of all the old disputes. I cannot pretend to vie in originality with any of the masters I have named, and my ambition limits itself to just one little point. If I can make two of the necessarily implied corollaries of determinism clearer to you than they have been made before, I shall have made it possible for you to decide for or against that doctrine with a better understanding of what you are about. And if you prefer not to decide at all, but to remain doubters, you will at least see more plainly what the subject of your hesitation is. I thus disclaim openly on the threshold all pretension to prove to you that the freedom of the will is true. The most I hope is to induce some of you to follow my own example in assuming it true, and acting as if it were true. If it be true, it seems to me that this is involved in the strict logic of the case. Its truth ought not to be forced willy-nilly down our indifferent throats. It ought to be freely espoused by men who can equally well turn their backs upon it. In other words, our first act of freedom, if we are free, ought in all inward propriety to be to affirm that we are free. This should exclude, it seems to me, from the free-will side of the question all hope of a coercive demonstration,—a demonstration which I, for one, am perfectly contented to go without.

With thus much understood at the outset, we can advance. But not without one more point understood as well. The arguments I am about to urge all proceed on two suppositions: first, when we make theories about the world and

[1] And I may now say Charles S. Peirce,— see the Monist, for 1892–93.

FROM: *The Will to Believe and Other Essays* (originally published in 1897). An Address by William James to the Harvard Divinity Students, originally published in the Unitarian Review for September, 1884.

discuss them with one another, we do so in order to attain a conception of things which shall give us subjective satisfaction; and, second, if there be two conceptions, and the one seems to us, on the whole, more rational than the other, we are entitled to suppose that the more rational one is the truer of the two. I hope that you are all willing to make these suppositions with me; for I am afraid that if there be any of you here who are not, they will find little edification in the rest of what I have to say. I cannot stop to argue the point; but I myself believe that all the magnificent achievements of mathematical and physical science—our doctrines of evolution, of uniformity of law, and the rest—proceed from our indomitable desire to cast the world into a more rational shape in our minds than the shape into which it is thrown there by the crude order of our experience. The world has shown itself, to a great extent, plastic to this demand of ours for rationality. How much farther it will show itself plastic no one can say. Our only means of finding out is to try; and I, for one, feel as free to try conceptions of moral as of mechanical or of logical rationality. If a certain formula for expressing the nature of the world violates my moral demand, I shall feel as free to throw it overboard, or at least to doubt it, as if it disappointed my demand for uniformity of sequence, for example; the one demand being, so far as I can see, quite as subjective and emotional as the other is. The principle of causality, for example, —what is it but a postulate, an empty name covering simply a demand that the sequence of events shall some day manifest a deeper kind of belonging of one thing with another than the mere arbitrary juxtaposition which now phenomenally appears? It is as much an altar to an unknown god as the one that Saint Paul found at Athens. All our scientific and philosophic ideals are altars to unknown gods. Uniformity is as much so as is free-will. If this be admitted, we can debate on even terms. But if any one pretends that while freedom and variety are, in the first instance, subjec-

tive demands, necessity and uniformity are something altogether different, I do not see how we can debate at all.[2]

To begin, then, I must suppose you acquainted with all the usual arguments on the subject. I cannot stop to take up the old proofs from causation, from statistics, from the certainty with which we can foretell one another's conduct, from the fixity of character, and

---

[2] "The whole history of popular beliefs about Nature refutes the notion that the thought of a universal physical order can possibly have arisen from the purely passive reception and association of particular perceptions. Indubitable as it is that men infer from known cases to unknown, it is equally certain that this procedure, if restricted to the phenomenal materials that spontaneously offer themselves, would never have led to the belief in a general uniformity, but only to the belief that law and lawlessness rule the world in motley alternation. From the point of view of strict experience, nothing exists but the sum of particular perceptions, with their coincidences on the one hand, their contradictions on the other.

"That there is more order in the world than appears at first sight is not discovered *till the order is looked for*. The first impulse to look for it proceeds from practical needs: where ends must be attained, we must know trustworthy means which infallibly possess a property, or produce a result. But the practical need is only the first occasion for our reflection on the conditions of true knowledge; and even were there no such need, motives would still be present for carrying us beyond the stage of mere association. For not with an equal interest, or rather with an equal lack of interest, does man contemplate those natural processes in which a thing is linked with its former mate, and those in which it is linked to something else. *The former processes harmonize with the conditions of his own thinking*: the latter do not. In the former, his *concepts, general judgments,* and *inferences* apply to reality: in the latter, they have no such application. And thus the intellectual satisfaction which at first comes to him without reflection, at last excites in him the conscious wish to find realized throughout the entire phenomenal world those rational continuities, uniformities, and necessities which are the fundamental element and guiding principle of his own thought." (Sigwart, Logik, bd. 2, s. 382.)

all the rest. But there are two *words* which usually encumber these classical arguments, and which we must immediately dispose of if we are to make any progress. One is the eulogistic word *freedom*, and the other is the opprobrious word *chance*. The word 'chance' I wish to keep, but I wish to get rid of the word 'freedom.' Its eulogistic associations have so far overshadowed all the rest of its meaning that both parties claim the sole right to use it, and determinists to-day insist that they alone are freedom's champions. Old-fashioned determinism was what we may call *hard* determinism. It did not shrink from such words as fatality, bondage of the will, necessitation, and the like. Nowadays, we have a *soft* determinism which abhors harsh words, and, repudiating fatality, necessity, and even predetermination, says that its real name is freedom; for freedom is only necessity understood, and bondage to the highest is identical with true freedom. Even a writer as little used to making capital out of soft words as Mr. Hodgson hesitates not to call himself a 'free-will determinist.'

Now, all this is a quagmire of evasion under which the real issue of fact has been entirely smothered. Freedom in all these senses presents simply no problem at all. No matter what the soft determinist mean by it,—whether he mean the acting without external constraint; whether he mean the acting rightly, or whether he mean the acquiescing in the law of the whole,—who cannot answer him that sometimes we are free and sometimes we are not? But there *is* a problem, an issue of fact and not of words, an issue of the most momentous importance, which is often decided without discussion in one sentence, —nay, in one clause of a sentence,—by those very writers who spin out whole chapters in their efforts to show what 'true' freedom is; and that is the question of determinism, about which we are to talk to-night.

Fortunately, no ambiguities hang about this word or about its opposite, indeterminism. Both designate an outward way in which things may happen, and their cold and mathematical sound has no sentimental associations that can bribe our partiality either way in advance. Now, evidence of an external kind to decide between determinism and indeterminism is, as I intimated a while back, strictly impossible to find. Let us look at the difference between them and see for ourselves. What does determinism profess?

It professes that those parts of the universe already laid down absolutely appoint and decree what the other parts shall be. The future has no ambiguous possibilities hidden in its womb: the part we call the present is compatible with only one totality. Any other future complement than the one fixed from eternity is impossible. The whole is in each and every part, and welds it with the rest into an absolute unity, an iron block, in which there can be no equivocation or shadow of turning.

With earth's first clay they did the
    last man knead,
And there of the last harvest
    sowed the seed.
And the first morning of creation
    wrote
What the last dawn of reckoning
    shall read.

Indeterminism, on the contrary, says that the parts have a certain amount of loose play on one another, so that the laying down of one of them does not necessarily determine what the others shall be. It admits that possibilities may be in excess of actualities, and that things not yet revealed to our knowledge may really in themselves be ambiguous. Of two alternative futures which we conceive, both may now be really possible; and the one become impossible only at the very moment when the other excludes it by becoming real itself. Indeterminism thus denies the world to be one unbending unit of fact. It says there is a certain ultimate pluralism in it; and, so saying, it corroborates our ordinary unsophisticated view of things. To that view, actualities seem to float in a wider sea of possibilities from out of which they are chosen; and, *somewhere*, indeterminism says, such possibilities exist, and form a part of truth.

Determinism, on the contrary, says they exist *nowhere*, and that necessity on the one hand and impossibility on the other are the sole categories of the real. Possibilities that fail to get realized are, for determinism, pure illusions: they never were possibilities at all. There is nothing inchoate, it says, about this universe of ours, all that was or is or shall be actual in it having been from eternity virtually there. The cloud of alternatives our minds escort this mass of actuality withal is a cloud of sheer deceptions, to which 'impossibilities' is the only name that rightfully belongs.

The issue, it will be seen, is a perfectly sharp one, which no eulogistic terminology can smear over or wipe out. The truth *must* lie with one side or the other, and its lying with one side makes the other false.

The question relates solely to the existence of possibilities, in the strict sense of the term, as things that may, but need not, be. Both sides admit that a volition, for instance, has occurred. The indeterminists say another volition might have occurred in its place: the determinists swear that nothing could possibly have occurred in its place. Now, can science be called in to tell us which of these two point-blank contradicters of each other is right? Science professes to draw no conclusions but such as are based on matters of fact, things that have actually happened; but how can any amount of assurance that something actually happened give us the least grain of information as to whether another thing might or might not have happened in its place? Only facts can be proved by other facts. With things that are possibilities and not facts, facts have no concern. If we have no other evidence than the evidence of existing facts, the possibility-question must remain a mystery never to be cleared up.

And the truth is that facts practically have hardly anything to do with making us either determinists or indeterminists. Sure enough, we make a flourish of quoting facts this way or that; and if we are determinists, we talk about the infallibility with which we can predict one another's conduct; while if we are indeterminists, we lay great stress on the fact that it is just because we cannot foretell one another's conduct, either in war or statecraft or in any of the great and small intrigues and businesses of men, that life is so intensely anxious and hazardous a game. But who does not see the wretched insufficiency of this so-called objective testimony on both sides? What fills up the gaps in our minds is something not objective, not external. What divides us into possibility men and anti-possibility men is different faiths or postulates,— postulates of rationality. To this man the world seems more rational with possibilities in it,—to that man more rational with possibilities excluded; and talk as we will about having to yield to evidence, what makes us monists or pluralists, determinists or indeterminists, is at bottom always some sentiment like this.

The stronghold of the deterministic sentiment is the antipathy to the idea of chance. As soon as we begin to talk indeterminism to our friends, we find a number of them shaking their heads. This notion of alternative possibility, they say, this admission that any one of several things may come to pass, is, after all, only a roundabout name for chance; and chance is something the notion of which no sane mind can for an instant tolerate in the world. What is it, they ask, but barefaced crazy unreason, the negation of intelligibility and law? And if the slightest particle of it exist anywhere, what is to prevent the whole fabric from falling together, the stars from going out, and chaos from recommencing her topsy-turvy reign?

Remarks of this sort about chance will put an end to discussion as quickly as anything one can find. I have already told you that 'chance' was a word I wished to keep and use. Let us then examine exactly what it means, and see whether it ought to be such a terrible bugbear to us. I fancy that squeezing the thistle boldly will rob it of its sting.

The sting of the word 'chance' seems to lie in the assumption that it means something positive, and that if anything happens by chance, it must needs be something of an intrinsically irrational and preposterous sort. Now, chance means nothing of the kind. It is a purely negative and relative term,[3] giving us no information about that of which it is predicated, except that it happens to be disconnected with something else,—not controlled, secured, or necessitated by other things in advance of its own actual presence. As this point is the most subtile one of the whole lecture, and at the same time the point on which all the rest hinges, I beg you to pay particular attention to it. What I say is that it tells us nothing about what a thing may be in itself to call it 'chance.' It may be a bad thing, it may be a good thing. It may be lucidity, transparency, fitness incarnate, matching the whole system of other things, when it has once befallen, in an unimaginabley perfect way. All you mean by calling it 'chance' is that this is not guaranteed, that it may also fall out otherwise. For the system of other things has no positive hold on the chance-thing. Its origin is in a certain fashion negative: it escapes, and says, Hands off! coming, when it comes, as a free gift, or not at all.

This negativeness, however, and this opacity of the chance-thing when thus considered *ab extra*, or from the point of view of previous things or distant things, do not preclude its having any amount of positiveness and luminosity from within, and at its own place and moment. All that its chance-character asserts about it is that there is something in it really of its own, something that is not the unconditional property

[3] Speaking technically, it is a word with a positive denotation, but a connotation that is negative. Other things must be silent about *what it is*: it alone can decide that point at the moment in which it reveals itself.

of the whole. If the whole wants this property, the whole must wait till it can get it, if it be a matter of chance. That the universe may actually be a sort of joint-stock society of this sort, in which the sharers have both limited liabilities and limited powers, is of course a simple and conceivable notion.

Nevertheless, many persons talk as if the minutest dose of disconnectedness of one part with another, the smallest modicum of independence, the faintest tremor of ambiguity about the future, for example, would ruin everything, and turn this goodly universe into a sort of insane sand-heap or nulliverse, no universe at all. Since future human volitions are as a matter of fact the only ambiguous things we are tempted to believe in, let us stop for a moment to make ourselves sure whether their independent and accidental character need be fraught with such direful consequences to the universe as these.

What is meant by saying that my choice of which way to walk home after the lecture is ambiguous and matter of chance as far as the present moment is concerned? It means that both Divinity Avenue and Oxford Street are called; but that only one, and that one *either* one, shall be chosen. Now, I ask you seriously to suppose that this ambiguity of my choice is real; and then to make the impossible hypothesis that the choice is made twice over, and each time falls on a different street. In other words, imagine that I first walk through Divinity Avenue, and then imagine that the powers governing the universe annihilate ten minutes of time with all that it contained, and set me back at the door of this hall just as I was before the choice was made. Imagine then that, everything else being the same, I now make a different choice and traverse Oxford Street. You, as passive spectators, look on and see the two alternative universes, —one of them with me walking through Divinity Avenue in it, the other with the same me walking through Oxford Street. Now, if you are determinists you believe one of these universes to have been from eternity impossible: you believe it to have been impossible because of the intrinsic irrationality or accidentality somewhere involved in it. But looking outwardly at these universes, can you say which is the impossible and accidental one, and which the rational and necessary one? I doubt if the most ironclad determinist among you could have the slightest glimmer of light on this point. In other words, either universe *after the fact* and once there would, to our means of observation and understanding, appear just as rational as the other. There would be absolutely no criterion by which we might judge one necessary and the other matter of chance. Suppose now we relieve the gods of their hypothetical task and assume my choice, once made, to be made forever. I go through Divinity Avenue for good and all. If, as good determinists, you now begin to affirm, what all good determinists punctually do affirm, that in the nature of things I *couldn't* have gone through Oxford Street,—had I done so it would have been chance, irrationality, insanity, a horrid gap in nature,—I simply call your attention to this, that your affirmation is what the Germans call a *Machtspruch*, a mere conception fulminated as a dogma and based on no insight into details. Before my choice, either street seemed as natural to you as to me. Had I happened to take Oxford Street, Divinity Avenue would have figured in your philosophy as the gap in nature; and you would have so proclaimed it with the best deterministic conscience in the world.

But what a hollow outcry, then, is this against a chance which, if it were present to us, we could by no character whatever distinguish from a rational necessity! I have taken the most trivial of examples, but no possible example could lead to any different result. For what are the alternatives which, in point of fact, offer themselves to human volition? What are those futures that now seem matters of chance? Are they not one and all like the Divinity Avenue and Oxford Street of our example? Are they not all of them *kinds* of things already

here and based in the existing frame of nature? Is any one ever tempted to produce an *absolute* accident, something utterly irrelevant to the rest of the world? Do not all the motives that assail us, all the futures that offer themselves to our choice, spring equally from the soil of the past; and would not either one of them, whether realized through chance or through necessity, the moment it was realized, seem to us to fit that past, and in the completest and most continuous manner to interdigitate with the phenomena already there?[4]

The more one thinks of the matter, the more one wonders that so empty and gratuitous a hubbub as this outcry against chance should have found so great an echo in the hearts of men. It is a word which tells us absolutely nothing about what chances, or about the *modus operandi* of the chancing; and the use of it as a war-cry shows only a temper of intellectual absolutism, a demand that the world shall be a solid block, subject to one control,—which temper, which demand, the world may not be bound to gratify at all. In every outwardly verifiable and practical respect, a world in which the alternatives that now actually distract *your* choice were decided by pure chance would be by *me* absolutely undistinguished from the world in which I now live. I am, therefore, entirely willing to call it, so far as your

---

[4] A favorite argument against free-will is that if it be true, a man's murderer may as probably be his best friend as his worst enemy, a mother be as likely to strangle as to suckle her first-born, and all of us be as ready to jump from fourth-story windows as to go out of front doors, etc. Users of this argument should properly be excluded from debate till they learn what the real question is. 'Free-will' does not say that everything that is physically conceivable is also morally possible. It merely says that of alternatives that really *tempt* our will more than one is really possible. Of course, the alternatives that do thus tempt our will are vastly fewer than the physical possibilities we can coldly fancy. Persons really tempted often do murder their best friends, mothers do strangle their first-born, people do jump out of fourth-story windows, etc.

choices go, a world of chance for me. To *yourselves*, it is true, those very acts of choice, which to me are so blind, opaque, and external, are the opposites of this, for you are within them and effect them. To you they appear as decisions; and decisions, for him who makes them, are altogether peculiar psychic facts. Self-luminous and self-justifying at the living moment at which they occur, they appeal to no outside moment to put its stamp upon them or make them continuous with the rest of nature. Themselves it is rather who seem to make nature continuous; and in their strange and intense function of granting consent to one possibility and withholding it from another, to transform an equivocal and double future into an inalterable and simple past.

But with the psychology of the matter we have no concern this evening. The quarrel which determinism has with chance fortunately has nothing to do with this or that psychological detail. It is a quarrel altogether metaphysical. Determinism denies the ambiguity of future volitions, because it affirms that nothing future can be ambiguous. But we have said enough to meet the issue. Indeterminate future volitions *do* mean chance. Let us not fear to shout it from the house-tops if need be; for we now know that the idea of chance is, at bottom, exactly the same thing as the idea of gift,—the one simply being a disparaging, and the other a eulogistic, name for anything on which we have no effective *claim*. And whether the world be the better or the worse for having either chances or gifts in it will depend altogether on *what* these uncertain and unclaimable things turn out to be.

And this at last brings us within sight of our subject. We have seen what determinism means: we have seen that indeterminism is rightly described as meaning chance; and we have seen that chance, the very name of which we are urged to shrink from as from a metaphysical pestilence, means only the negative fact that no part of the world, however big, can claim to control absolutely the destinies of the whole. But although,

in discussing the word 'chance,' I may at moments have seemed to be arguing for its real existence, I have not meant to do so yet. We have not yet ascertained whether this be a world of chance or no; at most, we have agreed that it seems so. And I now repeat what I said at the outset, that, from any strict theoretical point of view, the question is insoluble. To deepen our theoretic sense of the *difference* between a world with chances in it and a deterministic world is the most I can hope to do; and this I may now at last begin upon, after all our tedious clearing of the way.

I wish first of all to show you just what the notion that this is a deterministic world implies. The implications I call your attention to are all bound up with the fact that it is a world in which we constantly have to make what I shall, with your permission, call judgments of regret. Hardly an hour passes in which we do not wish that something might be otherwise; and happy indeed are those of us whose hearts have never echoed the wish of Omar Khayam—

That we might clasp, ere closed, the book of fate,
    And make the writer on a fairer leaf
Inscribe our names, or quite obliterate.

Ah! Love, could you and I with fate conspire
To mend this sorry scheme of things entire,
    Would we not shatter it to bits, and then
Remould it nearer to the heart's desire?"

Now, it is undeniable that most of these regrets are foolish, and quite on a par in point of philosophic value with the criticisms on the universe of that friend of our infancy, the hero of the fable The Atheist and the Acorn,—

"Fool! had that bough a pumpkin bore,
Thy whimsies would have worked no more," etc.

Even from the point of view of our own ends, we should probably make a botch of remodelling the universe. How much more then from the point of view of ends we cannot see! Wise men therefore regret as little as they can. But still some regrets are pretty obstinate and hard to stifle,—regrets for acts of wanton cruelty or treachery, for example, whether performed by others or by ourselves. Hardly any one can remain *entirely* optimistic after reading the confession of the murderer at Brockton the other day: how, to get rid of the wife whose continued existence bored him, he inveigled her into a desert spot, shot her four times, and then, as she lay on the ground and said to him, "You didn't do it on purpose, did you, dear?" replied, "No, I didn't do it on purpose," as he raised a rock and smashed her skull. Such an occurrence, with the mild sentence and self-satisfaction of the prisoner, is a field for a crop of regrets, which one need not take up in detail. We feel that, although a perfect mechanical fit to the rest of the universe, it is a bad moral fit, and that something else would really have been better in its place.

But for the deterministic philosophy the murder, the sentence, and the prisoner's optimism were all necessary from eternity; and nothing else for a moment had a ghost of a chance of being put into their place. To admit such a chance, the determinists tell us, would be to make a suicide of reason; so we must steel our hearts against the thought. And here our plot thickens, for we see the first of those difficult implications of determinism and monism which it is my purpose to make you feel. If this Brockton murder was called for by the rest of the universe, if it had to come at its preappointed hour, and if nothing else would have been consistent with the sense of the whole, what are we to think of the universe? Are we stubbornly to stick to our judgment of regret, and say, though it *couldn't* be, yet it *would* have been a better universe with something different from this Brockton murder in

it? That, of course, seems the natural and spontaneous thing for us to do; and yet it is nothing short of deliberately espousing a kind of pessimism. The judgment of regret calls the murder bad. Calling a thing bad means, if it mean anything at all, that the thing ought not to be, that something else ought to be in its stead. Determinism, in denying that anything else can be in its stead, virtually defines the universe as a place in which what ought to be is impossible,— in other words, as an organism whose constitution is afflicted with an incurable taint, an irremediable flaw. The pessimism of a Schopenhauer says no more than this,—that the murder is a symptom; and that it is a vicious symptom because it belongs to a vicious whole, which can express its nature no otherwise than by bringing forth just such a symptom as that at this particular spot. Regret for the murder must transform itself, if we are determinists and wise, into a larger regret. It is absurd to regret the murder alone. Other things being what they are, *it* could not be different. What we should regret is that whole frame of things of which the murder is one member. I see no escape whatever from this pessimistic conclusion, if, being determinists, our judgment of regret is to be allowed to stand at all.

The only deterministic escape from pessimism is everywhere to abandon the judgment of regret. That this can be done, history shows to be not impossible. The devil, *quoad existentiam*, may be good. That is, although he be a *principle* of evil, yet the universe, with such a principle in it, may practically be a better universe than it could have been without. On every hand, in a small way, we find that a certain amount of evil is a condition by which a higher form of good is bought. There is nothing to prevent anybody from generalizing this view, and trusting that if we could but see things in the largest of all ways, even such matters as this Brockton murder would appear to be paid for by the uses that follow in their train. An optimism *quand même*, a systematic and infatuated optimism like that ridiculed by Voltaire in his Candide, is one of the possible ideal ways in which a man may train himself to look on life. Bereft of dogmatic hardness and lit up with the expression of a tender and pathetic hope, such an optimism has been the grace of some of the most religious characters that ever lived.

> *"Throb thine with Nature's*
> *throbbing breast,*
> *And all is clear from east to west."*

Even cruelty and treachery may be among the absolutely blessed fruits of time, and to quarrel with any of their details may be blasphemy. The only real blasphemy, in short, may be that pessimistic temper of the soul which lets it give way to such things as regrets, remorse, and grief.

Thus, our deterministic pessimism may become a deterministic optimism at the price of extinguishing our judgments of regret.

But does not this immediately bring us into a curious logical predicament? Our determinism leads us to call our judgments of regret wrong, because they are pessimistic in implying that what is impossible yet ought to be. But how then about the judgments of regret themselves? If they are wrong, other judgments, judgments of approval presumably, ought to be in their place. But as they are necessitated, nothing else *can* be in their place; and the universe is just what it was before,—namely, a place in which what ought to be appears impossible. We have got one foot out of the pessimistic bog, but the other one sinks all the deeper. We have rescued our actions from the bonds of evil, but our judgments are now held fast. When murders and treacheries cease to be sins, regrets are theoretic absurdities and errors. The theoretic and the active life thus play a kind of seesaw with each other on the ground of evil. The rise of either sends the other down. Murder and treachery cannot be good without

regret being bad: regret cannot be good without treachery and murder being bad. Both, however, are supposed to have been foredoomed; so something must be fatally unreasonable, absurd, and wrong in the world. It must be a place of which either sin or error forms a necessary part. From this dilemma there seems at first sight no escape. Are we then so soon to fall back into the pessimism from which we thought we had emerged? And is there no possible way by which we may, with good intellectual consciences, call the cruelties and the treacheries, the reluctances and the regrets, *all* good together?

Certainly there is such a way, and you are probably most of you ready to formulate it yourselves. But, before doing so, remark how inevitably the question of determinism and indeterminism slides us into the question of optimism and pessimism, or, as our fathers called it, 'the question of evil.' The theological form of all these disputes is the simplest and the deepest, the form from which there is the least escape,—not because, as some have sarcastically said, remorse and regret are clung to with a morbid fondness by the theologians as spiritual luxuries, but because they are existing facts of the world, and as such must be taken into account in the deterministic interpretation of all that is fated to be. If they are fated to be error, does not the bat's wing of irrationality still cast its shadow over the world?

The refuge from the quandary lies, as I said, not far off. The necessary acts we erroneously regret may be good, and yet our error in so regretting them may be also good, on one simple condition; and that condition is this: The world must not be regarded as a machine whose final purpose is the making real of any outward good, but rather as a contrivance for deepening the theoretic consciousness of what goodness and evil in their intrinsic natures are. Not the doing either of good or of evil is what nature cares for, but the knowing of them. Life is one long eating of the fruit of the tree of *knowledge*. I am in the habit, in thinking to myself, of calling this point of view the *gnostical* point of view. According to it, the world is neither an optimism nor a pessimism, but a *gnosticism*. But as this term may perhaps lead to some misunderstandings, I will use it as little as possible here, and speak rather of *subjectivism*, and the *subjectivistic* point of view.

Subjectivism has three great branches,—we may call them scientificism, sentimentalism, and sensualism, respectively. They all agree essentially about the universe, in deeming that what happens there is subsidiary to what we think or feel about it. Crime justifies its criminality by awakening our intelligence of that criminality, and eventually our remorses and regrets; and the error included in remorses and regrets, the error of supposing that the past could have been different, justifies itself by its use. Its use is to quicken our sense of *what* the irretrievably lost is. When we think of it as that which might have been ('the saddest words of tongue or pen'), the quality of its worth speaks to us with a wilder sweetness; and, conversely, the dissatisfaction wherewith we think of what seems to have driven it from its natural place gives us the severer pang. Admirable artifice of nature! we might be tempted to exclaim, —deceiving us in order the better to enlighten us, and leaving nothing undone to accentuate to our consciousness the yawning distance of those opposite poles of good and evil between which creation swings.

We have thus clearly revealed to our view what may be called the dilemma of determinism, so far as determinism pretends to think things out at all. A merely mechanical determinism, it is true, rather rejoices in not thinking them out. It is very sure that the universe must satisfy its postulate of a physical continuity and coherence, but it smiles at any one who comes forward with a postulate of moral coherence as well. I may suppose, however, that the number of purely mechanical or hard determinists among you this evening is

small. The determinism to whose seductions you are most exposed is what I have called soft determinism,—the determinism which allows considerations of good and bad to mingle with those of cause and effect in deciding what sort of a universe this may rationally be held to be. The dilemma of this determinism is one whose left horn is pessimism and whose right horn is subjectivism. In other words, if determinism is to escape pessimism, it must leave off looking at the goods and ills of life in a simple objective way, and regard them as materials, indifferent in themselves, for the production of consciousness, scientific and ethical, in us.

To escape pessimism is, as we all know, no easy task. Your own studies have sufficiently shown you the almost desperate difficulty of making the notion that there is a single principle of things, and that principle absolute perfection, rhyme together with our daily vision of the facts of life. If perfection be the principle, how comes there any imperfection here? If God be good, how come he to create—or, if he did not create, how comes he to permit—the devil? The evil facts must be explained as seeming: the devil must be whitewashed, the universe must be disinfected, if neither God's goodness nor his unity and power are to remain impugned. And of all the various ways of operating the disinfection, and making bad seem less bad, the way of subjectivism appears by far the best.[5]

For, after all, is there not something rather absurd in our ordinary

[5] To a reader who says he is satisfied with a pessimism, and has no objection to thinking the whole bad, I have no more to say: he makes fewer demands on the world than I, who, making them, wish to look a little further before I give all hope of having them satisfied. If, however, all he means is that the badness of some parts does not prevent his acceptance of a universe whose *other* parts give him satisfaction, I welcome him as an ally. He has abandoned the notion of the *Whole*, which is the essence of deterministic monism, and views things as a pluralism, just as I do in this paper.

notion of external things being good or bad in themselves? Can murders and treacheries, considered as mere outward happenings, or motions of matter, be bad without any one to feel their badness? And could paradise properly be good in the absence of a sentient principle by which the goodness was perceived? Outward goods and evils seem practically indistinguishable except in so far as they result in getting moral judgments made about them. But then the moral judgments seem the main thing, and the outward facts mere perishing instruments for their production. This is subjectivism. Every one must at some time have wondered at that strange paradox of our moral nature, that, though the pursuit of outward good is the breath of its nostrils, the attainment of outward good would seem to be its suffocation and death. Why does the painting of any paradise or utopia, in heaven or on earth, awaken such yawnings for nirvana and escape? The white-robed hard-playing heaven of our sabbath-schools, and the ladylike tea-table elysium represented in Mr. Spencer's Data of Ethics, as the final consummation of progress, are exactly on a par in this respect,—lubberlands, pure and simple, one and all.[6] We look upon them from this delicious mess of insanities and realities, strivings and deadnesses, hopes and fears, agonies and exultations, which forms our present state, and *tedium vitæ* is the only sentiment they awaken in our breasts. To our crepuscular natures, born for the conflict, the Rembrandtesque moral chiaroscuro, the shifting struggle of the sunbeam in the gloom, such pictures of light upon light are vacuous and expressionless, and neither to be enjoyed nor understood. If *this* be the whole fruit of the victory, we say; if the generations of mankind suffered and laid down their lives; if prophets confessed and martyrs sang in the fire, and all the sacred tears were shed for no other end than that a race of creatures of such unexampled

insipidity should succeed, and protract *in saecula saeculorum* their contented and inoffensive lives,—why, at such a rate, better lose than win the battle, or at all events better ring down the curtain before the last act of the play, so that a business that began so importantly may be saved from so singularly flat a winding-up.

All this is what I should instantly say, were I called on to plead for gnosticism; and its real friends, of whom you will presently perceive I am not one, would say without difficulty a great deal more. Regarded as a stable finality, every outward good becomes a mere weariness to the flesh. It must be menaced, be occasionally lost, for its goodness to be fully felt as such. Nay, more than occasionally lost. No one knows the worth of innocence till he knows it is gone forever, and that money cannot buy it back. Not the saint, but the sinner that repenteth, is he to whom the full length and breadth, and height and depth, of life's meaning is revealed. Not the absence of vice, but vice there, and virtue holding her by the throat, seems the ideal human state. And there seems no reason to suppose it not a permanent human state. There is a deep truth in what the school of Schopenhauer insists on,—the illusoriness of the notion of moral progress. The more brutal forms of evil that go are replaced by others more subtle and more poisonous. Our moral horizon moves with us as we move, and never do we draw nearer to the far-off line where the black waves and the azure meet. The final purpose of our creation seems most plausibly to be the greatest possible enrichment of our ethical consciousness, through the intensest play of contrasts and the widest diversity of characters. This of course obliges some of us to be vessels of wrath, while it calls others to be vessels of honor. But the subjectivist point of view reduces all these outward distinctions to a common denominator. The wretch languishing in the felon's cell may be drinking draughts of the wine of truth that will never pass the lips of the so-called favorite of fortune. And the

---

[6] Compare Sir James Stephen's Essays by a Barrister, London, 1862, pp. 138, 318.

peculiar consciousness of each of them is an indispensable note in the great ethical concert which the centuries as they roll are grinding out of the living heart of man.

So much for subjectivism! If the dilemma of determinism be to choose between it and pessimism, I see little room for hesitation from the strictly theoretical point of view. Subjectivism seems the more rational scheme. And the world may, possibly, for aught I know, be nothing else. When the healthy love of life is on one, and all its forms and its appetites seem so unutterably real; when the most brutal and the most spiritual things are lit by the same sun, and each is an integral part of the total richness,—why, then it seems a grudging and sickly way of meeting so robust a universe to shrink from any of its facts and wish them not to be. Rather take the strictly dramatic point of view, and treat the whole thing as a great unending romance which the spirit of the universe, striving to realize its own content, is eternally thinking out and representing itself.[7]

No one, I hope, will accuse me, after I have said all this, of underrating the reasons in favor of subjectivism. And now that I proceed to say why those reasons, strong as they are, fail to convince my own mind, I trust the presumption may be that my objections are stronger still.

I frankly confess that they are of a practical order. If we practically take up subjectivism in a sincere and radical manner and follow its consequences, we meet with some that make us pause. Let a subjectivism begin in never so severe and intellectual a way, it is forced by the law of its nature to develop another side of itself and end with the corruptest curiosity. Once dismiss the notion that certain duties are good in themselves, and that we are here to do them, no

matter how we feel about them; once consecrate the opposite notion that our performances and our violations of duty are for a common purpose, the attainment of subjective knowledge and feeling, and that the deepening of these is the chief end of our lives,—and at what point on the downward slope are we to stop? In theology, subjectivism develops as its 'left wing' antinomianism. In literature, its left wing is romanticism. And in practical life it is either a nerveless sentimentality or a sensualism without bounds.

Everywhere it fosters the fatalistic mood of mind. It makes those who are already too inert more passive still; it renders wholly reckless those whose energy is already in excess. All through history we find how subjectivism, as soon as it has a free career, exhausts itself in every sort of spiritual, moral, and practical license. Its optimism turns to an ethical indifference, which infallibly brings dissolution in its train. It is perfectly safe to say now that if the Hegelian gnosticism, which has begun to show itself here and in Great Britain, were to become a popular philosophy, as it once was in Germany, it would certainly develop its left wing here as there, and produce a reaction of disgust. Already I have heard a graduate of this very school express in the pulpit his willingness to sin like David, if only he might repent like David. You may tell me he was only sowing his wild, or rather his tame, oats; and perhaps he was. But the point is that in the subjectivistic or gnostical philosophy oat-sowing, wild or tame, becomes a systematic necessity and the chief function of life. After the pure and classic truths, the exciting and rancid ones must be experienced; and if the stupid virtues of the philistine herd do not then come in and save society from the influence of the children of light, a sort of inward putrefaction becomes its inevitable doom.

Look at the last runnings of the romantic school, as we see them in that strange contemporary Parisian literature, with which we of the less clever countries are so often driven to rinse out our

[7] Cet univers est un spectacle que Dieu se donne à lui-même. Servons les intentions du grand chorège en contribuant à rendre le spectacle aussi brillant, aussi varié que possible.—RENAN.

minds after they have become clogged with the dulness and heaviness of our native pursuits. The romantic school began with the worship of subjective sensibility and the revolt against legality of which Rousseau was the first great prophet: and through various fluxes and refluxes, right wings and left wings, it stands to-day with two men of genius, M. Renan and M. Zola, as its principal exponents,—one speaking with its masculine, and the other with what might be called its feminine, voice. I prefer not to think now of less noble members of the school, and the Renan I have in mind is of course the Renan of latest dates. As I have used the term gnostic, both he and Zola are gnostics of the most pronounced sort. Both are athirst for the facts of life, and both think the facts of human sensibility to be of all facts the most worthy of attention. Both agree, moreover, that sensibility seems to be there for no higher purpose,—certainly not, as the Philistines say, for the sake of bringing mere outward rights to pass and frustrating outward wrongs. One dwells on the sensibilities for their energy, the other for their sweetness; one speaks with a voice of bronze, the other with that of an Æolian harp; one ruggedly ignores the distinction of good and evil, the other plays the coquette between the craven unmanliness of his Philosophic Dialogues and the butterfly optimism of his Souvenirs de Jeunesse. But under the pages of both there sounds incessantly the hoarse bass of *vanitas vanitatum, omnia vanitas*, which the reader may hear, whenever he will, between the lines. No writer of this French romantic school has a word of rescue from the hour of satiety with the things of life,—the hour in which we say, "I take no pleasure in them,"—or from the hour of terror at the world's vast meaningless grinding, if perchance such hours should come. For terror and satiety are facts of sensibility like any others; and at their own hour they reign in their own right. The heart of the romantic utterances, whether poetical, critical, or historical, is this inward remedilessness, what Carlyle calls this far-off whimpering of

wail and woe. And from this romantic state of mind there is absolutely no possible *theoretic* escape. Whether, like Renan, we look upon life in a more refined way, as a romance of the spirit; or whether, like the friends of M. Zola, we pique ourselves on our 'scientific' and 'analytic' character, and prefer to be cynical, and call the world a 'roman expérimental' on an infinite scale,—in either case the world appears to us potentially as what the same Carlyle once called it, a vast, gloomy, solitary Golgotha and mill of death.

The only escape is by the practical way. And since I have mentioned the nowadays much-reviled name of Carlyle, let me mention it once more, and say it is the way of his teaching. No matter for Carlyle's life, no matter for a great deal of his writing. What was the most important thing he said to us? He said: "Hang your sensibilities! Stop your snivelling complaints, and your equally snivelling raptures! Leave off your general emotional tomfoolery, and get to WORK like men!" But this means a complete rupture with the subjectivist philosophy of things. It says conduct, and not sensibility, is the ultimate fact for our recognition. With the vision of certain works to be done, of certain outward changes to be wrought or resisted, it says our intellectual horizon terminates. No matter how we succeed in doing these outward duties, whether gladly and spontaneously, or heavily and unwillingly, do them we somehow must; for the leaving of them undone is perdition. No matter how we feel; if we are only faithful in the outward act and refuse to do wrong, the world will in so far be safe, and we quit of our debt toward it. Take, then, the yoke upon our shoulders; bend our neck beneath the heavy legality of its weight; regard something else than our feeling as our limit, our master, and our law; be willing to live and die in its service,—and, at a stroke, we have passed from the subjective into the objective philosophy of things, much as one awakens from some feverish dream, full of bad lights and noises, to find one's self bathed in the sacred coolness and quiet of the air of the night.

But what is the essence of this philosophy of objective conduct, so old-fashioned and finite, but so chaste and sane and strong, when compared with its romantic rival? It is the recognition of limits, foreign and opaque to our understanding. It is the willingness, after bringing about some external good, to feel at peace; for our responsibility ends with the performance of that duty, and the burden of the rest we may lay on higher powers.[8]

"Look to thyself, O Universe,
Thou art better and not worse,"

we may say in that philosophy, the moment we have done our stroke of conduct, however small. For in the view of that philosophy the universe belongs to a plurality of semi-independent forces, each one of which may help or hinder, and be helped or hindered by, the operations of the rest.

But this brings us right back, after such a long détour, to the question of indeterminism and to the conclusion of all I came here to say to-night. For the only consistent way of representing a pluralism and a world whose parts may affect one another through their conduct being either good or bad is the indeterministic way. What interest, zest, or excitement can there be in achieving the right way, unless we are enabled to feel that the wrong way is also a possible and a natural way,—nay, more, a menacing and an imminent way? And what sense can there be in condemning ourselves for taking the wrong way, unless we need have done nothing of the sort, unless the right way was open to us as well? I cannot understand the willingness to act, no matter how we feel, without the belief that acts are really good and bad. I cannot understand the belief that an act is bad, without regret at its happening. I cannot understand regret without the admission of real, genuine

---

[8] The burden for example, of seeing to it that the *end* of all our righteousness be some positive universal gain.

possibilities in the world. Only *then* is it other than a mockery to feel, after we have failed to do our best, that an irreparable opportunity is gone from the universe, the loss of which it must forever after mourn.

If you insist that this is all superstition, that possibility is in the eye of science and reason impossibility, and that if I act badly 't is that the universe was foredoomed to suffer this defect, you fall right back into the dilemma, the labyrinth, of pessimism and subjectivism, from out of whose toils we have just wound our way.

Now, we are of course free to fall back, if we please. For my own part, though, whatever difficulties may beset the philosophy of objective right and wrong, and the indeterminism it seems to imply, determinism, with its alternative of pessimism or romanticism, contains difficulties that are greater still. But you will remember that I expressly repudiated awhile ago the pretension to offer any arguments which could be coercive in a so-called scientific fashion in this matter. And I consequently find myself, at the end of this long talk, obliged to state my conclusions in an altogether personal way. This personal method of appeal seems to be among the very conditions of the problem; and the most any one can do is to confess as candidly as he can the grounds for the faith that is in him, and leave his example to work on others as it may.

Let me, then, without circumlocution say just this. The world is enigmatical enough in all conscience, whatever theory we may take up toward it. The indeterminism I defend, the free-will theory of popular sense based on the judgment of regret, represents that world as vulnerable, and liable to be injured by certain of its parts if they act wrong. And it represents their acting wrong as a matter of possibility or accident, neither inevitable nor yet to be infallibly warded off. In all this, it is a theory devoid either of transparency or of stability. It gives us a pluralistic, restless universe, in which no single point of view can ever take in the whole scene;

and to a mind possessed of the love of unity at any cost, it will, no doubt, remain forever inacceptable. A friend with such a mind once told me that the thought of my universe made him sick, like the sight of the horrible motion of a mass of maggots in their carrion bed.

But while I freely admit that the pluralism and the restlessness are repugnant and irrational in a certain way, I find that every alternative to them is irrational in a deeper way. The indeterminism with its maggots, if you please to speak so about it, offends only the native absolutism of my intellect,—an absolutism which, after all, perhaps, deserves to be snubbed and kept in check. But the determinism with its necessary carrion, to continue the figure of speech, and with no possible maggots to eat the latter up, violates my sense of moral reality through and through. When, for example, I imagine such carrion as the Brockton murder, I cannot conceive it as an act by which the universe, as a whole, logically and necessarily expresses its nature without shrinking from complicity with such a whole. And I deliberately refuse to keep on terms of loyalty with the universe by saying blankly that the murder, since it does flow from the nature of the whole, is not carrion. There are *some* instinctive reactions which I, for one, will not tamper with. The only remaining alternative, the attitude of gnostical romanticism, wrenches my personal instincts in quite as violent a way. It falsifies the simple objectivity of their deliverance. It makes the goose-flesh the murder excites in me a sufficient reason for the perpetration of the crime. It transforms life from a tragic reality into an insincere melodramatic exhibition, as foul or as tawdry as any one's diseased curiosity pleases to carry it out. And with its consecration of the 'roman naturaliste' state of mind, and its enthronement of the baser crew of Parisian *littérateurs* among the eternally indispensable organs by which the infinite spirit of things attains to that subjective illumination which is the task of its life, it leaves me in presence of a sort of subjective carrion considerably more

noisome than the objective carrion I called it in to take away.

No! better a thousand times, than such systematic corruption of our moral sanity, the plainest pessimism, so that it be straightforward; but better far than that the world of chance. Make as great an uproar about chance as you please, I know that chance means pluralism and nothing more. If some of the members of the pluralism are bad, the philosophy of pluralism, whatever broad views it may deny me, permits me, at least, to turn to the other members with a clean breast of affection and an unsophisticated moral sense. And if I still wish to think of the world as a totality, it lets me feel that a world with a *chance* in it of being altogether good, even if the chance never come to pass, is better than a world with no such chance at all. That 'chance' whose very notion I am exhorted and conjured to banish from my view of the future as the suicide of reason concerning it, that 'chance' is— what? Just this,—the chance that in moral respects the future may be other and better than the past has been. This is the only chance we have any motive for supposing to exist. Shame, rather, on its repudiation and its denial! For its presence is the vital air which lets the world live, the salt which keeps it sweet.

And here I might legitimately stop, having expressed all I care to see admitted by others to-night. But I know that if I do stop here, misapprehensions will remain in the minds of some of you, and keep all I have said from having its effect; so I judge it best to add a few more words.

In the first place, in spite of all my explanations, the word 'chance' will still be giving trouble. Though you may yourselves be adverse to the deterministic doctrine, you wish a pleasanter word than 'chance' to name the opposite doctrine by; and you very likely consider my preference for such a word a perverse sort of a partiality on my part. It certainly *is* a bad word to make converts with; and you wish I had not thrust it so butt-foremost at you,—you wish to use a milder term.

Well, I admit there may be just a dash of perversity in its choice. The spectacle of the mere word-grabbing game played by the soft determinists has perhaps driven me too violently the other way; and, rather than be found wrangling with them for the good words, I am willing to take the first bad one which comes along, provided it be unequivocal. The question is of things, not of eulogistic names for them; and the best word is the one that enables men to know the quickest whether they disagree or not about the things. But the word 'chance,' with its singular negativity, is just the word for this purpose. Whoever uses it instead of 'freedom,' squarely and resolutely gives up all pretence to control the things he says are free. For *him*, he confesses that they are no better than mere chance would be. It is a word of *impotence*, and is therefore the only sincere word we can use, if, in granting freedom to certain things, we grant it honestly, and really risk the game. "Who chooses me must give and forfeit all he hath." Any other word permits of quibbling, and lets us, after the fashion of the soft determinists, make a pretence of restoring the caged bird to liberty with one hand, while with the other we anxiously tie a string to its leg to make sure it does not get beyond our sight.

But now you will bring up your final doubt. Does not the admission of such an unguaranteed chance or freedom preclude utterly the notion of a Providence governing the world? Does it not leave the fate of the universe at the mercy of the chance-possibilities, and so far insecure? Does it not, in short, deny the craving of our nature for an ultimate peace behind all tempests, for a blue zenith above all clouds?

To this my answer must be very brief. The belief in free-will is not in the least incompatible with the belief in Providence, provided you do not restrict the Providence to fulminating nothing but *fatal* decrees. If you allow him to provide possibilities as well as actualities to the universe, and to carry on his own

thinking in those two categories just as we do ours, chances may be there, uncontrolled even by him, and the course of the universe be really ambiguous; and yet the end of all things may be just what he intended it to be from all eternity.

An analogy will make the meaning of this clear. Suppose two men before a chessboard,—the one a novice, the other an expert player of the game. The expert intends to beat. But he cannot foresee exactly what any one actual move of his adversary may be. He knows, however, all the *possible* moves of the latter; and he knows in advance how to meet each of them by a move of his own which leads in the direction of victory. And the victory infallibly arrives, after no matter how devious a course, in the one predestined form of check-mate to the novice's king.

Let now the novice stand for us finite free agents, and the expert for the infinite mind in which the universe lies. Suppose the latter to be thinking out his universe before he actually creates it. Suppose him to say, I will lead things to a certain end, but I will not *now*[9] decide on all the steps thereto. At various

[9] This of course leaves the creative mind subject to the law of time. And to any one who insists on the timelessness of that mind I have no reply to make. A mind to whom all time is simultaneously present must see all things under the form of actuality, or under some form to us unknown. If he thinks certain moments as ambiguous in their content while future, he must simultaneously know how the ambiguity will have been decided when they are past. So that none of his mental judgments can possibly be called hypothetical, and his world is one from which chance is excluded. Is not, however, the timeless mind rather a gratuitous fiction? And is not the notion of eternity being given at a stroke to omniscience only just another way of whacking upon us the block-universe, and of denying that possibilities exist?—just the point to be proved. To say that time is an illusory appearance is only a roundabout manner of saying there is no real plurality, and that the frame of things is an absolute unit. Admit plurality, and time may be its form.

points, ambiguous possibilities shall be left open, *either* of which, at a given instant, may become actual. But whichever branch of these bifurcations become real, I know what I shall do at the *next* bifurcation to keep things from drifting away from the final result I intend.[10]

The creator's plan of the universe would thus be left blank as to many of its actual details, but all possibilities would be marked down. The realization of some of these would be left absolutely to chance; that is, would only be determined when the moment of realization came. Other possibilities would be *contingently* determined; that is, their decision would have to wait till it was seen how the matters of absolute chance fell out. But the rest of the plan, including its final upshot, would be rigorously determined once for all. So the creator himself would not need to know *all* the details of actuality until they came; and at any time his own view of the world would be a view partly of facts and partly of possibilities, exactly as ours is

now. Of one thing, however, he might be certain; and that is that his world was safe, and that no matter how much it might zigzag he could surely bring it home at last.

Now, it is entirely immaterial, in this scheme, whether the creator leave the absolute chance-possibilities to be decided by himself, each when its proper moment arrives, or whether, on the contrary, he alienate this power from himself, and leave the decision out and out to finite creatures such as we men are. The great point is that the possibilities are really *here*. Whether it be we who solve them, or he working through us, at those soul-trying moments when fate's scales seem to quiver, and good snatches the victory from evil or shrinks nerveless from the fight, is of small account, so long as we admit that the issue is decided nowhere else than *here* and *now*. *That* is what gives the palpitating reality to our moral life and makes it tingle, as Mr. Mallock says, with so strange and elaborate an excitement. This reality, this excitement, are what the determinisms, hard and soft alike, suppress by their denial that *anything* is decided here and now, and their dogma that all things were foredoomed and settled long ago. If it be so, may you and I then have been foredoomed to the error of continuing to believe in liberty.[11] It is fortunate for the winding up of controversy that in every discussion with determinism this *argumentum ad hominem* can be its adversary's last word.

---

[10] And this of course means 'miraculous' interposition, but not necessarily of the gross sort our fathers took such delight in representing, and which has so lost its magic for us. Emerson quotes some Eastern sage as saying that if evil were really done under the sun, the sky would incontinently shrivel to a snakeskin and cast it out in spasms. But, says Emerson, the spasms of Nature are years and centuries; and it will tax man's patience to wait so long. We may think of the reserved possibilities God keeps in his own hand, under as invisible and molecular and slowly self-summating a form as we please. We may think of them as counteracting human agencies which he inspires *ad hoc*. In short, signs and wonders and convulsions of the earth and sky are not the only neutralizers of obstruction to a god's plans of which it is possible to think.

[11] As long as languages contain a future perfect tense, determinists, following the bent of laziness or passion, the lines of least resistance, can reply in that tense, saying, "It will have been fated," to the still small voice which urges an opposite course; and thus excuse themselves from effort in a quite unanswerable way.

Is There
a Basis
for
Personal Identity?

*D*avid Hume summarized the claims of many philosophers when he wrote of our knowledge of mental substance that:

we are every moment intimately conscious of what we call our self; that we feel its existence and its continuance in existence; and are certain, beyond the evidence of a demonstration, both of its perfect identity and simplicity . . . nor is there any thing of which we can be certain, if we doubt of this.

Nonetheless, he assures us, "These positive assertions are contrary to that very experience, which is pleaded for them." Indeed, it is not merely that the claim "There is a self" is not supported by empirical evidence; we do not even have the *idea* of a self "after the manner it is here explained." A self must be distinct from all our experiences, being something that *has* experiences. Hence it must remain the same through our experiences. For two reasons, Hume suggests, we can have no idea of such a self.

First, our experience is composed of impressions and ideas. The self is not an impression or an idea. So we do not experience a self distinct from (and the possessor of) our experience. "Self, or person, is not any one impression, but that to which our several impressions and ideas are supposed to have a reference."

Second, waiving the first objection and concentrating on the continuity rather than the distinctness of self, there is no impression that remains "invariably the same, through the whole course of our lives." But "since self is supposed to exist after that manner," it follows that there is no impression from which the idea of a self can be derived. Formally Hume's argument is: (1) "It must be some one impression that gives rise to every idea." (2) If an idea B is derived from an impression A, B cannot have any property not possessed by A (3) "There is no impression constant and invariable"; hence (4) there is no idea that is constant and invariable. But (5) any idea representing a self would have to be constant and invariable; so (6) There is no idea representing a self.

Two remarks should be made about these arguments. One is that Hume reports no awareness or experience of anything other than impressions and ideas, whereas Descartes and Berkeley reported awareness or experience of a substantial self. These divergent reports by first-rate philosophers as to what can be known by "direct awareness" or noninferential experience raises a question concerning the philosophical value of appeals to direct awareness as a way of settling philosophical disputes. But whether this question can be answered in such a way as to show that appeal to noninferential experience is sometimes philosophically decisive, it is clear that Hume's basic epistemological principles make impossible the sort of self-awareness that Descartes and Berkeley claim. Either the latter's claim or the former's principles are mistaken.

Second, there is something peculiar about the way Hume handles this topic. Consider the form of his argument: (a) If we had the idea of a self, it would have to have properties P_1 and P_2; but (b) we have no impression with these properties; so (c) we have no idea with these properties. How could we make any *sense* of (a) if (c) were true? How could we say what the idea of a self is in order to say that we do not have it? Indeed, since no impression has the property "being distinct from all impressions and ideas" or the property "being invariable throughout our experience," how can I (on Hume's terms) use the locutions in quotes so as to convey Hume's meaning?

Hume raises the question "What gives us so great a propension to ascribe an identity to these successive perceptions and to suppose ourselves possessed of an invariable and uninterrupted existence through the whole course of our lives?" We can regard his answer to this question also as an attempt to answer another one: "How can we have the concept (idea) of a self at all?"

The answer is complex and we can deal with it only briefly. We experience sets of closely resembling impressions. This experience activates a propensity to take resembling perceptions as one perception. But we know that strictly there has been variation among the closely resembling perceptions. We must make this knowledge consistent with the belief toward which the above-mentioned propensity leads us. In order to do so, we unconsciously posit an object distinct from all impressions but *represented* to us by impressions, which closely resemble one another. Belief in a single entity that has a set of impressions but is not identical with any or all of these impressions both eliminates the contradictions and satisfies (realizes) the propensity we have mentioned. Still, this—even if it explains in some sense *belief* in a self—gives us no answer to the question as to how on Hume's principles the concept crucial to the belief could ever arise. For all of this, Hume knows that I believe I am the same person as the one born to my parents on a specifiable date, that a man sentenced for a crime is the same man who serves the sentence, and that a man and woman who celebrate their golden wedding anniversary are the same man and woman who were married half a century prior to their celebration. Is there any way, in Hume's view, in which these beliefs can be both intelligible and true?

Well, there is more than one sense in which identity may be ascribed to something or someone—a ship is the same after massive repair (involving replacement of parts of the ship) for the repaired vessel is historically continuous with the defective one and serves the same end. An oak in full bloom is the oak latent in a particular acorn by virtue of historical continuity plus a chain of causal connections reaching from one to the other. There has been but one United States Congress, which has met numerous times, even though no member of its first meeting attended its most recent one. Identity thus need not be identity of *a continuing substance*, and it is to these other senses of identity (especially the last) that Hume invites us to turn when "unpacking" the beliefs noted above. The issue as to whether the other senses of identity are satisfactory with respect to identity of a self, or *personal* identity, is of course debatable. Hume is aware of the problem of saying what, in his view, our ordinary beliefs about identity can amount to, and he offers the senses of "identity" we have specified as relevant and adequate to this task.

Locke's theory of personal identity is also complex. In his view we must distinguish personal identity from the identity of a man. The latter is determined by the continuity of "one fitly organized body, taken in any one instant, and from thence continued, under one organization of life." It is possible that one spiritual substance "be united to different bodies" or that various persons consecutively be associated with the same body. "The idea in our minds, of which the sound *man* in our mouths is the sign, is nothing else but [the idea] of an animal of such a certain form," and "an animal identity is preserved in identity of life and not of substance."

To see, then, "wherein personal identity consists, we must consider what *person* stands for," namely (in Locke's analysis) "a thinking, intelligent being, that has reason and reflection, and can consider itself as itself, the same thinking thing, in different times and places; which it does only by that consciousness which is inseparable from thinking." Locke adds:

Since consciousness always accompanies thinking, and it thereby distinguishes himself from all other thinking beings, in this alone consists personal identity, i.e., the sameness of a rational being: and as far as this consciousness can be extended backwards to any past action or thought, so far reaches the identity of that person; it is the same self now it was then; and it is by the same self with this present one that now reflects on it, that that action was done.

An objection comes immediately to mind: Locke's view entails that if I have forgotten performing an action, I am not the man who performed it. But surely I have done many things I have forgotten, and this does not count against its being I who did them? Locke reiterates and clarifies his claim in this fashion:

> . . . *as far as any intelligent being* can *repeat the idea of any past action with the same consciousness it had of it at first, and with the same consciousness it has of any present action; so far it is the same personal self.*

Locke rightly stresses the word "can"; and it seems likely that when he asks whether one substance can at one time be conscious of having performed an action and at another time not be conscious of it, he elucidates the latter possibility as tantamount to the substance finding itself

> *wholly stripped of all the consciousness of its past existence, . . . beyond the power of ever retrieving it again: and so as it were beginning a new account from a new period, . . . a consciousness that* cannot *reach* [*backward*] *beyond this new state.*

If a man cannot, under any circumstances remember doing A, he is not to be considered the same person as the one who did A. In part this should perhaps be taken as a thesis concerning moral culpability. One *could* defend the thesis that if a man really cannot, in Locke's sense, remember doing A, it would be morally wrong to punish him for doing A—because his inability to remember doing A argues that he is suffering a psychological disorder or because it could not under the circumstances prevent him from doing A again or for some other reason. But suppose, for the sake of argument, that this thesis is true. Still it seems paradoxical that even if one cannot retrieve a memory to the effect "I did A," this is by itself sufficient for his not having done A. There is no contradiction in my saying "I did A, but I am completely unable to remember doing it." Indeed, given the testimony of witnesses, or evidence that A was done and that only I had opportunity to do it, I can have strong reasons to believe "I did A" is true. While Locke can deal with this objection by claiming that the "I" in "I did A" must, under the circumstances mentioned, mean "I am the same man" or "I am the same substance" but not "I am the same person," it is not obvious that this is so.

A brief mention of Locke's comments contrasting "same person" with "same substance" are in order. If "same substance" means "same immaterial substance," we can conceive of one consciousness acting through several substances or several distinct consciousnesses being associated with a single substance. (And the same things can, for Locke, be said concerning *material* substances.)

It should come as no surprise, given the above, that Locke should comment late in his discussion that *person* "is a forensic term, appropriating actions and their merit." But apparently it is also an ontological term—his analysis appears to be intended to be factually correct as well as juridically sound.

Thomas Reid finds much to object to in the views of Hume and Locke. He takes it as evident that:

(1) Every man has the conviction "of his identity, as far back as his memory reaches."
(2) This conviction is indubitably correct.
(3) "Identity supposes an uninterrupted continuance of existence."
(4) Personality, which has no parts, cannot be partitioned.
(5) I am not action, feeling, thought; I am something that thinks, and acts, and feels.
(6) "The self . . . is permanent, and has the same relation to all succeeding thoughts, actions and feelings which I call mine."
(7) Personal identity admits of no degrees.

The primary evidence that there is such a permanent self is memory. Reid writes:

I remember that twenty years ago I conversed with such a person; I remember several things that passed in that conversation: my memory testifies, not only that this was done, but that it was done by me who now remembers it. If it was done by me, I must have existed at that time, and [by (3)] continued to exist from that time to the present.

Still, "it is not my remembering any action of mine that *makes* me to be the person who did it . . . that relation to me, which is expressed by saying that *I did it*, would be the same, though I had not the least remembrance of it." And Reid adds that were one to suppose that my (apparently) remembering to have done *A* makes me to have done *A* "appears to me as great an absurdity as it would be to say that my belief that the world was created made it to be created."

In addition to some "strange consequences" that Locke noticed (that as the same consciousness "can be transferred from one intelligent being to another" in Locke's view, "two or twenty beings may be [associated with] the same person"; that if an intelligent being remembered at t that he did A but could not remember at $t+1$ that he did A, the intelligent being would be two different persons), Reid claims that there was one he did not note. This consequence is more damaging than the others, involving (in Reid's account of the matter) the contradiction "that a man may be, and at the same time not be, the person that did a particular action."

We can put Reid's argument schematically as follows. Let A, B, and C be events occurring to (or, if one prefers, actions performed by) the same man, whom we shall call "Maxmillian." Surely it is possible that: (1) at time t, Maxmillian remembers A and B, whereas C has not occurred; (2) at *time $t+1$*, Maxmillian remembers B and C, but cannot at all remember A (A is irretrievably lost). Now Locke's view entails that if Maxmillian at both t and $t+1$ remembers B, Maxmillian is the same *person* (not merely the same *man*) at t

and *t+1*. But equally, in Locke's view, if Maxmillian can remember *A* at *t* but cannot (in the relevant sense) remember *A* at *t+1*, then he is a different *person* at *t* than at *t+1* (though he may be the same *man* throughout). So for Locke, Maxmillian is, but is not, the same person at *t+1* as he was at *t*.

Against Hume, Reid maintains in particular (6), namely, that the self is permanent and has the same relation to all its states. Admitting that he cannot prove (6), Reid adds that "there is evidence in the proposition itself which I am unable to resist."

I would wish to be further instructed, whether the impressions remember and are conscious of the ideas, or the ideas remember and are conscious of the impressions, or if both remember and are conscious of both? . . . These are questions naturally arising from this system [Hume's], that have not yet been explained.

Reid holds that we must appeal to something besides the occurrence of impressions and ideas in order to give an account of personal identity. Whether we can do so or not, short of accepting Reid's contentions—*see* (1)–(7) above—is a topic still debated among philosophers.

Gilbert Ryle argues that when we speak of a person's mind, we speak "of certain ways in which some of the incidents of his . . . life are ordered." The phrase "my mind" signifies "my ability and proneness to do certain things and not some piece of personal apparatus without which I could or would not do them." For Ryle minds are not mental substances, nor are they sets of Humean impressions. In Ryle's opinion talk about minds is misleading, for in talking of minds we are led to ask about the relations between mind and body, about knowledge of minds other than our own, and so on.

In part Ryle rejects a mental-substance view of mind because "in real life we are quite familiar with the techniques of assessing persons and accounting for their actions, though according to the standard theory no such techniques could exist." The standard theory is that of Descartes and Reid, for whom minds are mental substances, not merely a group of capacities and tendencies. If we say that minds are substances, then (according to a common assumption) we can know that minds exist only by direct acquaintance or by inference. While some philosophers have claimed direct accquaintance with mental substances—at least with their own minds—other philosophers have reported complete lack of such acquaintance. Whereas some philosophers have claimed to discover arguments by which we can show that minds other than our own exist, other philosophers have found these arguments unsatisfactory. Thus skepticism—at a theoretical level at least—seems imminent. But theoretical skepticism about the existence of minds—ours or others'—is at odds with our practical action and belief. Hence we are wise to escape skepticism by taking some other view about minds than that they are mental substances.

Ryle's suspicion that viewing minds as mental substances leads to skepticism arises from the connection between substance theories of mind and the doctrine of privileged access. Descartes claimed that (1) minds are mental substances, and (2) each person is directly acquainted with his own mind. Descartes believed that our knowledge of other minds depended on our being able to infer their existence from the observation of other people's bodies. To make things worse, the existence of bodies—my own or another's—was itself known only by inference. Thus my knowledge of my own mind was secure, gained by access available only to me, whereas my knowledge of other minds was shaky at best.

Ryle disagrees:

The superiority of the speaker's knowledge of what he is doing over that of the listener does not indicate that he has Privileged Access to facts of a type inevitably inaccessible to the listener, but only that he is in a good position to know what the listener is often in a very poor position to know.

In the above paragraphs we have traced only one aspect of Ryle's reasoning. In what follows we will notice a response to Ryle in one portion of John Wisdom's essay.

The phrase "Privileged Access" might be used to describe either of two doctrines:

(a) Each man is aware of his own mind and mental states in a way in which no one else is aware of them.

(b) Each man is aware of facts about his own mind and mental states that no one else can know.

Ryle's own use of "Privileged Access" suggests (b). But Descartes and Wisdom hold (a). If I hold that minds are mental substances, and adopt (a), am I led to skepticism about knowledge of minds other than my own? The answer is "no," for I may grant that everything that I know about my mind and mental states can also be known by another person. All that (a) says is that, for example, no one can know that I am in pain by having my pains, although that is how I know that I am in pain. More formally (a) is compatible with (c) Anyone else can know every fact about my mind and mental states that I can know about them. Indeed, even (b) is compatible with (c) if we replace "every fact" in (c) by "most facts." So (a) alone does not lead to the skepticism Ryle wishes to escape.

Wisdom describes a path leading from (a) to skepticism: "no one who makes a statement about the mind of another *ever* has the right to make it which that other has, . . . therefore he never has all the reason one could have for the statement he makes." If I assume that no one can know that a statement is true unless he can have all the reasons he might have for accepting that statement, I must—given (a)—also suppose that I have no knowledge of the mind of others, for I cannot know the mind of another by direct acquaintance. Hence he will have a reason for believing that he has a mind that I can never have.

Wisdom argues that this path does not really lead from (a) to skepticism. I can escape skepticism both by rejecting (a) and by rejecting the assumption just mentioned. The assumption has little or nothing to recommend it; it is doubtful that I ever have every possible reason that I might have for accepting any statement. It is also dubious that there is any reason for accepting the assumption. Accepting the assumption will involve my ceasing to claim to know most of what I suppose I know. Since rejecting the assumption allows me to retain (a) without being led to skepticism, a philosopher who accepts (a) has an answer to Ryle's critique.

Dealing with another issue related to the topic of personal identity, Peter Geach denies that we can even conceive of a being that lacks a body but has feelings, sensations, and emotions. He claims that "our concept of sight has its life only in connection with a whole set of other concepts, some of them relating to the physical characteristics of visible objects, others relating to the behavior of people who see things." Necessarily, then, only living organisms can have sensory experience. A consequence of this is that if having sensory experience is essential to being a human person, human persons either do not survive death or they survive in some bodily form. Geach himself believes in the resurrection of the body.

It is not possible to evaluate Geach's claim without investigating the conceptual connections that "having sensory experience" has with other concepts such as "being or possessing a living organism." This task is left to the reader.

Of Personal Identity
DAVID HUME

*T*here are some philosophers, who imagine we are every moment intimately conscious of what we call our SELF; that we feel its existence and its continuance in existence; and are certain, beyond the evidence of a demonstration, both of its perfect identity and simplicity. The strongest sensation, the most violent passion, say they, instead of distracting us from this view, only fix it the more intensely, and make us consider their influence on *self* either by their pain or pleasure. To attempt a farther proof of this were to weaken its evidence; since no proof can be deriv'd from any fact, of which we are so intimately conscious; nor is there any thing, of which we can be certain, if we doubt of this.

Unluckily all these positive assertions are contrary to that very experience, which is pleaded for them, nor have we any idea of *self*, after the man-

ner it is here explain'd. For from what impression cou'd this idea be deriv'd? This question 'tis impossible to answer without a manifest contradiction and absurdity; and yet 'tis a question, which must necessarily be answer'd, if we wou'd have the idea of self pass for clear and intelligible. It must be some one impression, that gives rise to every real idea. But self or person is not any one impression, but that to which our several impressions and ideas are suppos'd to have a reference. If any impression gives rise to the idea of self, that impression must continue invariably the same, thro' the whole course of our lives; since self is suppos'd to exist after that manner. But there is no impression constant and invariable. Pain and pleasure, grief and joy, passions and sensations succeed each other, and never all exist at the same time. It cannot, therefore, be from any of these impressions, or

FROM: *A Treatise of Human Nature*, David Hume. Book I, Part IV, Section 6 (originally published in 1739).

from any other, that the idea of self is deriv'd; and consequently there is no such idea.

But farther, what must become of all our particular perceptions upon this hypothesis? All these are different, and distinguishable, and separable from each other, and may be separately consider'd, and may exist separately, and have no need of any thing to support their existence. After what manner, therefore, do they belong to self; and how are they connected with it? For my part, when I enter most intimately into what I call *myself*, I always stumble on some particular perception or other, of heat or cold, light or shade, love or hatred, pain or pleasure. I never can catch *myself* at any time without a perception, and never can observe any thing but the perception. When my perceptions are remov'd for any time, as by sound sleep; so long am I insensible of *myself*, and may truly be said not to exist. And were all my perceptions remov'd by death, and cou'd I neither think, nor feel, nor see, nor love, nor hate after the dissolution of my body, I shou'd be entirely annihilated, nor do I conceive what is farther requisite to make me a perfect nonentity. If any one upon serious and unprejudic'd reflexion, thinks he has a different notion of *himself*, I must confess I can reason no longer with him. All I can allow him is, that he may be in the right as well as I, and that we are essentially different in this particular. He may, perhaps, perceive something simple and continu'd, which he calls *himself*; tho' I am certain there is no such principle in me.

But setting aside some metaphysicians of this kind, I may venture to affirm of the rest of mankind, that they are nothing but a bundle or collection of different perceptions, which succeed each other with an inconceivable rapidity, and are in a perpetual flux and movement. Our eyes cannot turn in their sockets without varying our perceptions. Our thought is still more variable than our sight; and all our other senses and faculties contribute to this change;

nor is there any single power of the soul, which remains unalterably the same, perhaps for one moment. The mind is a kind of theatre, where several perceptions successively make their appearance; pass, re-pass, glide away, and mingle in an infinite variety of postures and situations. There is properly no *simplicity* in it at one time, nor *identity* in different; whatever natural propension we may have to imagine that simplicity and identity. The comparison of the theatre must not mislead us. They are the successive perceptions only, that constitute the mind; nor have we the most distant notion of the place, where these scenes are represented, or of the materials, of which it is compos'd.

What then gives us so great a propension to ascribe an identity to these successive perceptions, and to suppose ourselves possest of an invariable and uninterrupted existence thro' the whole course of our lives? In order to answer this question, we must distinguish betwixt personal identity, as it regards our thought or imagination, and as it regards our passions or the concern we take in ourselves. The first is our present subject; and to explain it perfectly we must take the matter pretty deep, and account for that identity, which we attribute to plants and animals; there being a great analogy betwixt it, and the identity of a self or person.

We have a distinct idea of an object, that remains invariable and uninterrupted thro' a suppos'd variation of time; and this idea we call that of *identity* or *sameness*. We have also a distinct idea of several different objects existing in succession, and connected together by a close relation; and this to an accurate view affords as perfect a notion of *diversity*, as if there was no manner of relation among the objects. But tho' these two ideas of identity, and a succession of related objects be in themselves perfectly distinct, and even contrary, yet 'tis certain, that in our common way of thinking they are generally confounded with each other. That action of the imagination, by which we consider the uninterrupted and invariable object, and that by which we reflect on the succession of related objects, are almost the same to the feeling, nor is there much more effort of thought requir'd in the latter case than in the former. The relation facilitates the transition of the mind from one object to another, and renders its passage as smooth as if it contemplated one continu'd object. This resemblance is the cause of the confusion and mistake, and makes us substitute the notion of identity, instead of that of related objects. However at one instant we may consider the related succession as variable or interrupted, we are sure the next to ascribe to it a perfect identity, and regard it as invariable and uninterrupted. Our propensity to this mistake is so great from the resemblance above-mention'd, that we fall into it before we are aware; and tho' we incessantly correct ourselves by reflexion, and return to a more accurate method of thinking, yet we cannot long sustain our philosophy, or take off this biass from the imagination. Our last resource is to yield to it, and boldly assert that these different related objects are in effect the same, however, interrupted and variable. In order to justify to ourselves this absurdity, we often feign some new and unintelligible principle, that connects the objects together, and prevents their interruption or variation. Thus we feign the continu'd existence of the perceptions of our senses, to remove the interruption; and run into the notion of a *soul*, and *self*, and *substance*, to disguise the variation. But we may farther observe, that where we do not give rise to such a fiction, our propension to confound identity with relation is so great, that we are apt to imagine[1] something unknown and mys-

[1] If the reader is desirous to see how a great genius may be influenc'd by these seemingly trivial principles of the imagination, as well as the mere vulgar, let him read my Lord *Shaftsbury's* reasonings concerning the uniting principle of the universe, and the identity of plants and animals. See his *Moralists* or, *Philosophical rhapsody*.

terious, connecting the parts, beside their relation; and this I take to be the case with regard to the identity we ascribe to plants and vegetables. And even when this does not take place, we still feel a propensity to confound these ideas, tho' we are not able fully to satisfy ourselves in that particular, nor find any thing invariable and uninterrupted to justify our notion of identity.

Thus the controversy concerning identity is not merely a dispute of words. For when we attribute identity, in an improper sense, to variable or interrupted objects, our mistake is not confin'd to the expression, but is commonly attended with a fiction, either of something invariable and uninterrupted, or of something mysterious and inexplicable, or at least with a propensity to such fictions. What will suffice to prove this hypothesis to the satisfaction of every fair enquirer, is to shew from daily experience and observation, that the objects, which are variable or interrupted, and yet are suppos'd to continue the same, are such only as consist of a succession of parts, connected together by resemblance, contiguity, or causation. For as such a succession answers evidently to our notion of diversity, it can only be by mistake we ascribe to it an identity; and as the relation of parts, which leads us into this mistake, is really nothing but a quality, which produces an association of ideas, and an easy transition of the imagination from one to another, it can only be from the resemblance, which this act of the mind bears to that, by which we contemplate one continu'd object, that the error arises. Our chief business, then, must be to prove, that all objects, to which we ascribe identity, without observing their invariableness and uninterruptedness, are such as consist of a succession of related objects.

In order to this, suppose any mass of matter, of which the parts are contiguous and connected, to be plac'd before us; 'tis plain we must attribute a perfect identity to this mass, provided all the parts continue uninterruptedly and invariably the same, whatever motion or change of place we may observe either in the whole or in any of the parts. But supposing some very *small* or *inconsiderable* part to be added to the mass, or substracted from it; tho' this absolutely destroys the identity of the whole, strictly speaking; yet as we seldom think so accurately, we scruple not to pronounce a mass of matter the same, where we find so trivial an alteration. The passage of the thought from the object before the change to the object after it, is so smooth and easy, that we scarce perceive the transition, and are apt to imagine that 'tis nothing but a continu'd survey of the same object.

There is a very remarkable circumstance, that attends this experiment; which is, that tho' the change of any considerable part in a mass of matter destroys the identity of the whole, yet we must measure the greatness of the part, not absolutely, but by its *proportion* to the whole. The addition or diminution of a mountain wou'd not be sufficient to produce a diversity in a planet; tho' the change of a very few inches wou'd be able to destroy the identity of some bodies. 'Twill be impossible to account for this, but by reflecting that objects operate upon the mind, and break or interrupt the continuity of its actions not according to their real greatness, but according to their proportion to each other: And therefore, since this interruption makes an object cease to appear the same, it must be the uninterrupted progress of the thought, which constitutes the identity.

This may be confirm'd by another phænomenon. A change in any considerable part of a body destroys its identity; but 'tis remarkable, that where the change is produc'd *gradually* and *insensibly* we are less apt to ascribe to it the same effect. The reason can plainly be no other, than that the mind, in following the successive changes of the body, feels an easy passage from the surveying its condition in one moment to the viewing of it in another, and at no particular time perceives any interruption in its actions. From which continu'd perception, it ascribes a continu'd existence and identity to the object.

But whatever precaution we may use in introducing the changes gradually, and making them proportionable to the whole, 'tis certain, that where the changes are at last observ'd to become considerable, we make a scruple of ascribing identity to such different objects. There is, however, another artifice, by which we may induce the imagination to advance a step farther; and that is, by producing a reference of the parts to each other, and a combination to some *common end* or purpose. A ship, of which a considerable part has been chang'd by frequent reparations, is still consider'd as the same; nor does the difference of the materials hinder us from ascribing an identity to it. The common end, in which the parts conspire, is the same under all their variations, and affords an easy transition of the imagination from one situation of the body to another.

But this is still more remarkable, when we add a *sympathy* of parts to their *common end*, and suppose that they bear to each other, the reciprocal relation of cause and effect in all their actions and operations. This is the case with all animals and vegetables; where not only the several parts have a reference to some general purpose, but also a mutual dependance on, and connexion with each other. The effect of so strong a relation is, that tho' every one must allow, that in a very few years both vegetables and animals endure a *total* change, yet we still attribute identity to them, while their form, size, and substance are entirely alter'd. An oak, that grows from a small plant to a large tree, is still the same oak; tho' there be not one particle of matter, or figure of its parts the same. An infant becomes a man, and is sometimes fat, sometimes lean, without any change in his identity.

We may also consider the two following phænomena, which are remarkable in their kind. The first is, that tho' we commonly be able to distinguish pretty exactly betwixt numerical and specific identity, yet it sometimes happens, that we confound them, and in our thinking and reasoning employ the one for the other. Thus a man, who hears a noise, that is frequently interrupted and renew'd, says, it is still the same noise; tho' 'tis evident the sounds have only a specific identity or resemblance, and there is nothing numerically the same, but the cause, which produc'd them. In like manner it may be said without breach of the propriety of language, that such a church, which was formerly of brick, fell to ruin, and that the parish rebuilt the same church of free-stone, and according to modern architecture. Here neither the form nor materials are the same, nor is there any thing common to the two objects, but their relation to the inhabitants of the parish; and yet this alone is sufficient to make us denominate them the same. But we must observe, that in these cases the first object is in a manner annihilated before the second comes into existence; by which means, we are never presented in any one point of time with the idea of difference and multiplicity; and for that reason are less scrupulous in calling them the same.

Secondly, We may remark, that tho' in a succession of related objects, it be in a manner requisite, that the change of parts be not sudden nor entire, in order to preserve the identity, yet where the objects are in their nature changeable and inconstant, we admit of a more sudden transition, than wou'd otherwise be consistent with that relation. Thus as the nature of a river consists in the motion and change of parts; tho' in less than four and twenty hours these be totally alter'd; this hinders not the river from continuing the same during several ages. What is natural and essential to any thing is, in a manner, expected; and what is expected makes less impression, and appears of less moment, than what is unusual and extraordinary. A considerable change of the former kind seems really less to the imagination, than the most trivial

alteration of the latter; and by breaking less the continuity of the thought, has less influence in destroying the identity.

We now proceed to explain the nature of *personal identity*, which has become so great a question in philosophy, especially of late years in *England*, where all the abstruser sciences are study'd with a peculiar ardour and application. And here 'tis evident, the same method of reasoning must be continu'd, which has so successfully explain'd the identity of plants, and animals, and ships, and houses, and of all the compounded and changeable productions either of art or nature. The identity, which we ascribe to the mind of man, is only a fictitious one, and of a like kind with that which we ascribe to vegetables and animal bodies. It cannot, therefore, have a different origin, but must proceed from a like operation of the imagination upon like objects.

But lest this argument shou'd not convince the reader; tho' in my opinion perfectly decisive; let him weigh the following reasoning, which is still closer and more immediate. 'Tis evident, that the identity, which we attribute to the human mind, however perfect we may imagine it to be, is not able to run the several different perceptions into one, and make them lose their characters of distinction and difference, which are essential to them. 'Tis still true, that every distinct perception, which enters into the composition of the mind, is a distinct existence, and is different, and distinguishable, and separable from every other perception, either contemporary or successive. But, as, notwithstanding this distinction and separability, we suppose the whole train of perceptions to be united by identity, a question naturally arises concerning this relation of identity; whether it be something that really binds our several perceptions together, or only associates their ideas in the imagination. That is, in other words, whether in pronouncing concerning the identity of a person, we observe some real bond among his perceptions, or only feel one among the ideas we form of them. This question we might easily decide, if we wou'd recollect what has been already prov'd at large, that the understanding never observes any real connexion among objects, and that even the union of cause and effect, when strictly examin'd, resolves itself into a customary association of ideas. For from thence it evidently follows, that identity is nothing really belonging to these different perceptions, and uniting them together; but is merely a quality, which we attribute to them, because of the union of their ideas in the imagination, when we reflect upon them. Now the only qualities, which can give ideas an union in the imagination, are these three relations above-mention'd. These are the uniting principles in the ideal world, and without them every distinct object is separable by the mind, and may be separately consider'd, and appears not to have any more connexion with any other object, than if disjoin'd by the greatest difference and remoteness. 'Tis, therefore, on some of these three relations of resemblance, contiguity and causation, that identity depends; and as the very essence of these relations consists in their producing an easy transition of ideas; it follows, that our notions of personal identity, proceed entirely from the smooth and uninterrupted progress of the thought along a train of connected ideas, according to the principles above-explain'd.

The only question, therefore, which remains, is, by what relations this uninterrupted progress of our thought is produc'd, when we consider the successive existence of a mind or thinking person. And here 'tis evident we must confine ourselves to resemblance and causation, and must drop contiguity, which has little or no influence in the present case.

To begin with *resemblance*; suppose we cou'd see clearly into the breast of another, and observe that succession of perceptions, which constitutes his mind or thinking principle, and suppose that he always preserves the memory of a considerable part of past perceptions; 'tis evident that nothing cou'd more contribute to the bestowing a relation on this succession amidst all its variations. For what is the memory but a faculty, by which we raise up the images of past perceptions? And as an image necessarily resembles its objects, must not the frequent placing of these resembling perceptions in the chain of thought, convey the imagination more easily from one link to another, and make the whole seem like the continuance of one object? In this particular, then, the memory not only discovers the identity, but also contributes to its production, by producing the relation of resemblance among the perceptions. The case is the same whether we consider ourselves or others.

As to *causation*; we may observe, that the true idea of the human mind, is to consider it as a system of different perceptions or different existences, which are link'd together by the relation of cause and effect, and mutually produce, destroy, influence, and modify each other. Our impressions give rise to their correspondent ideas; and these ideas in their turn produce other impressions. One thought chaces another, and draws after it a third, by which it is expell'd in its turn. In this respect, I cannot compare the soul more properly to any thing than to a republic or commonwealth, in which the several members are united by the reciprocal ties of government and subordination, and give rise to other persons, who propagate the same republic in the incessant changes of its parts. And as the same individual republic may not only change its members, but also its laws and constitutions; in like manner the same person may vary his character and disposition, as well as his impressions and ideas, without losing his identity. Whatever changes he endures, his several parts are still connected by the relation of causation. And in this view our identity with regard to the passions serves to corroborate that with regard to the imagination, by the making our distant perceptions influence each other, and by giving us a present concern for our past or future pains or pleasures.

As memory alone acquaints us with the continuance and extent of this succession of perceptions, 'tis to be consider'd, upon that account chiefly, as the source of personal identity Had we no memory, we never shou'd have any notion of causation, nor consequently of that chain of causes and effects, which constitute our self or person. But having once acquir'd this notion of causation from the memory, we can extend the same chain of causes, and consequently the identity of our persons beyond our memory, and can comprehend times, and circumstances, and actions, which we have entirely forgot, but suppose in general to have existed. For how few of our past actions are there, of which we have any memory? Who can tell me, for instance, what were his thoughts and actions on the first of *January* 1715, the 11th of *March* 1719, and the 3d of *August* 1733? Or will he affirm, because he has entirely forgot the incidents of these days, that the present self is not the same person with the self of that time; and by that means overturn all the most establish'd notions of personal identity? In this view, therefore, memory does not so much *produce* as *discover* personal identity, by shewing us the relation of cause and effect among our different perceptions. 'Twill be incumbent on those, who affirm that memory produces entirely our personal identity, to give a reason why we can thus extend our identity beyond our memory.

The whole of this doctrine leads us to a conclusion, which is of great importance in the present affair, *viz.* that all the nice and subtle questions concerning personal identity can never possibly be decided, and are to be regarded rather as grammatical than as philosophical difficulties. Identity depends on the relations of ideas; and these relations produce identity, by means of that easy transition they occasion. But as the relations, and the easiness of the transition may diminish by insensible degrees, we have no just standard, by which we can decide any dispute concerning the time, when they acquire or lose a title to the name of identity. All the disputes concerning the identity of connected objects are merely verbal, except so far as the relation of parts gives rise to some fiction or imaginary principle of union, as we have already observ'd.

What I have said concerning the first origin and uncertainty of our notion of identity, as apply'd to the human mind, may be extended with little or no variation to that of *simplicity*. An object, whose different co-existent parts are bound together by a close relation, operates upon the imagination after much the same manner as one perfectly simple and indivisible, and requires not a much greater stretch of thought in order to its conception. From this similarity of operation we attribute a simplicity to it, and feign a principle of union as the support of this simplicity, and the center of all the different parts and qualities of the object.

Thus we have finish'd our examination of the several systems of philosophy, both of the intellectual and natural world; and in our miscellaneous way of reasoning have been led into several topics; which will either illustrate and confirm some preceding part of this discourse, or prepare the way for our following opinions. 'Tis now time to return to a more close examination of our subject, and to proceed in the accurate anatomy of human nature, having fully explain'd the nature of our judgment and understanding.

Memory and Personal Identity
JOHN LOCKE

*A*nother *occasion* the mind often takes of comparing, is the very being of things, when, considering *anything as existing at any determined time and place*, we compare it with *itself existing at another time*, and thereon form the ideas of *identity* and *diversity*. When we see anything to be in any place in any instant of time, we are sure (be it what it will) that it is that very thing, and not another which at that same time exists in another place, how like and undistinguishable soever it may be in all other respects: and in this consists *identity*, when the ideas it is attributed to vary not at all from what they were that moment wherein we consider their former existence, and to which we compare the present. For we never finding, nor conceiving it possible, that two things of the same kind should exist in the same place at the same time, we rightly conclude, that, whatever exists anywhere at any time, excludes all of the same kind, and is there itself alone. When therefore we demand whether anything be the *same* or no, it refers always to something that existed such a time in such a place, which it was certain, at that instant was the same with itself, and no other. From whence it follows, that one thing cannot have two beginnings of existence, nor two things one beginning; it being impossible for two things of the same kind to be or exist in the same instant, in the very same place; or one and the same thing in different places. That, therefore, that had one beginning, is the same thing; and that which had a different beginning in time and place from that, is not the same, but diverse. That which has made the difficulty about this relation has been the little care and attention used in having precise notions of the things to which it is attributed.

We have the ideas but of three sorts of substances: 1. *God.* 2. *Finite intelligences.* 3. *Bodies.*

First, *God* is without beginning, eternal, unalterable, and everywhere, and therefore concerning his identity there can be no doubt.

Secondly, *Finite spirits* having had each its determinate time and place of beginning to exist, the relation to that time and place will always determine to each of them its identity, as long as it exists.

Thirdly, The same will hold of every *particle of matter*, to which no addition or subtraction of matter being made, it is the same. For, though these three sorts of substances, as we term them, do not exclude one another out of the same place, yet we cannot conceive but that they must necessarily each of them exclude any of the same kind out of the same place: or else the notions and names of identity and diversity would be in vain, and there could be no such distinctions of substances, or anything else one from another. For example: could two bodies be in the same place at the same time; then those two parcels of matter must be one and the same, take them great or little; nay, all bodies must be one and the same. For, by the same reason that two particles of matter may be in one place, all bodies may be in one place: which, when it can be supposed, takes away the distinction of identity and diversity of one and more, and renders it ridiculous. But it being a contradiction that two or more should be one, identity and diversity are relations and ways of comparing well founded, and of use to the understanding.

All other things being but modes or relations ultimately terminated in substances, the identity and diversity of each particular existence of them too

FROM: "Of Our Ideas of Identity and Diversity" in *An Essay Concerning Human Understanding*, John Locke. Book II, Ch. 27, (originally published in 1690).

will be by the same way determined: only as to things whose existence is in succession, such as are the actions of finite beings, e.g. *motion* and *thought*, both which consist in a continued train of succession, concerning *their* diversity there can be no question: because each perishing the moment it begins, they cannot exist in different times, or in different places, as permanent beings can at different times exist in distant places; and therefore no motion or thought, considered as at different times, can be the same, each part thereof having a different beginning of existence.

From what has been said, it is easy to discover what is so much inquired after, the *principium individuationis* [principle of individuation]; and that, it is plain, is existence itself; which determines a being of any sort to a particular time and place, incommunicable to two beings of the same kind. This, though it seems easier to conceive in simple substances or modes; yet, when reflected on, is not more difficult in compound ones, if care be taken to what it is applied: e.g. let us suppose an atom, i.e. a continued body under one immutable superficies, existing in a determined time and place; it is evident, that, considered in any instant of its existence, it is in that instant the same with itself. For, being at that instant what it is, and nothing else, it is the same, and so must continue as long as its existence is continued; for so long it will be the same, and no other. In like manner, if two or more atoms be joined together into the same mass, every one of those atoms will be the same, by the foregoing rule: and whilst they exist united together, the mass, consisting of the same atoms, must be the same mass, or the same body, let the parts be ever so differently jumbled. But if one of these atoms be taken away, or one new one added, it is no longer the same mass or the same body. In the state of living creatures, their identity depends not on a mass of the same particles, but on something else. For in them the variation of great parcels of matter alters not the identity: an oak growing from a plant to a great tree, and then lopped, is still the same oak; and a colt grown up to a horse, sometimes fat, sometimes lean, is all the while the same horse: though, in both these cases, there may be a manifest change of the parts; so that truly they are not either of them the same masses of matter, though they be truly one of them the same oak, and the other the same horse. The reason whereof is, that, in these two cases—a *mass of matter* and a *living body*—identity is not applied to the same thing.

We must therefore consider wherein an oak differs from a mass of matter, and that seems to me to be in this, that the one is only the cohesion of particles of matter any how united, the other such a disposition of them as constitutes the parts of an oak; and such an organization of those parts as is fit to receive and distribute nourishment, so as to continue and frame the wood, bark, and leaves, &c., of an oak, in which consists the vegetable life. That being then one plant which has such an organization of parts in one coherent body, partaking of one common life, it continues to be the same plant as long as it partakes of the same life, though that life be communicated to new particles of matter vitally united to the living plant, in a like continued organization conformable to that sort of plants. For this organization, being at any one instant in any one collection of matter, is in that particular concrete distinguished from all other, and *is* that individual life, which existing constantly from that moment both forwards and backwards, in the same continuity of insensibly succeeding parts united to the living body of the plant, it has that identity which makes the same plant, and all the parts of it, parts of the same plant, during all the time that they exist united in that continued organization, which is fit to convey that common life to all the parts so united.

The case is not so much different in *brutes* but that any one may hence see what makes an animal and continues it the same. Something we have like this in machines, and may serve to illustrate it. For example, what is a watch? It is plain it is nothing but a fit organization or construction of parts to a certain end, which, when a sufficient force is added to it, it is capable to attain. If we would suppose this machine one continued body, all whose organized parts were repaired, increased, or diminished by a constant addition or separation of insensible parts, with one common life, we should have something very much like the body of an animal; with this difference, That, in an animal the fitness of the organization, and the motion wherein life consists, begin together, the motion coming from within; but in machines the force coming sensibly from without, is often away when the organ is in order, and well fitted to receive it.

This also shows wherein the identity of the same *man* consists; viz. in nothing but a participation of the same continued life, by constantly fleeting particles of matter, in succession vitally united to the same organized body. He that shall place the identity of man in anything else, but, like that of other animals, in one fitly organized body, taken in any one instant, and from thence continued, under one organization of life, in several successively fleeting particles of matter united to it, will find it hard to make an embryo, one of years, mad and sober, the *same* man, by any supposition, that will not make it possible for Seth, Ismael, Socrates, Pilate, St. Austin, and Cæsar Borgia, to be the same man. For if the identity of *soul alone* makes the same *man*; and there be nothing in the nature of matter why the same indivual spirit may not be united to different bodies, it will be possible that those men, living in distant ages, and of different tempers, may have been the same man: which way of speaking must be from a very strange use of the word man, applied to an idea but of which body and shape are excluded. And that way of speaking would agree yet worse with the notions of those philosophers who allow of transmigration, and are of

opinion that the souls of men may, for their miscarriages, be detruded into the bodies of beasts, as fit habitations, with organs suited to the satisfaction of their brutal inclinations. But yet I think nobody, could he be sure that the *soul* of Heliogabalus were in one of his hogs, would yet say that hog were a *man* or *Heliogabalus.*

It is not therefore unity of substance that comprehends all sorts of identity, or will determine it in every case; but to conceive and judge of it aright, we must consider what idea the word it is applied to stands for: it being one thing to be the same *substance*, another the same *man*, and a third the same *person*, if *person*, *man*, and *substance*, are three names standing for three different ideas;—for such as is the idea belonging to that name, such must be the identity; which, if it had been a little more carefully attended to, would possibly have prevented a great deal of that confusion which often occurs about this matter, with no small seeming difficulties, especially concerning *personal* identity, which therefore we shall in the next place a little consider.

An animal is a living organized body; and consequently the same animal, as we have observed, is the same continued *life* communicated to different particles of matter, as they happen successively to be united to that organized living body. And whatever is talked of other definitions, ingenious observation puts it past doubt, that the idea in our minds, of which the sound man in our mouths is the sign, is nothing else but of an animal of such a certain form. Since I think I may be confident, that, whoever should see a creature of his own shape or make, though it had no more reason all its life than a cat or a parrot, would call him still a *man*; or whoever should hear a cat or a parrot discourse, reason, and philosophize would call or think it nothing but a *cat* or a *parrot*; and say, the one was a dull irrational man, and the other a very intelligent rational parrot. [A relation we have in an author of great note, is sufficient to countenance the supposition of a rational parrot. His words are:

'I had a mind to know, from Prince Maurice's own mouth, the account of a common, but much credited story, that I had heard so often from many others, of an old parrot he had in Brazil, during his government there, that spoke, and asked, and answered common questions, like a reasonable creature: so that those of his train there generally concluded it to be witchery or possession; and one of his chaplains, who lived long afterwards in Holland, would never from that time endure a parrot, but said they all had a devil in them. I had heard many particulars of this story, and assevered by people hard to be discredited, which made me ask Prince Maurice what there was of it. He said, with his usual plainness and dryness in talk, there was something true, but a great deal false of what had been reported. I desired to know of him what there was of the first. He told me short and coldly, that he had heard of such an old parrot when he had been at Brazil; and though he believed nothing of it, and it was a good way off, yet he had so much curiosity as to send for it: that it was a very great and a very old one; and when it came first into the room where the prince was, with a great many Dutchmen about him, it said presently, *What a company of white men are here!* They asked it, what it thought that man was, pointing to the prince. It answered, *Some General or other.* When they brought it close to him, he asked it, *D'où venez-vous?* It answered, *De Marinnan.* The Prince, *À qui estes-vous?* The Parrot, *À un Portugais.* The Prince, *Que fais-tu là?* Parrot, *Fe garde les poulles.* The Prince laughed, and said, *Vous gardez les poulles?* The parrot answered, *Oui, moi; et je sçai bien faire*; and made the chuck four or five times that people use to make to chickens when they call them. I set down the words of this worthy dialogue in French, just as Prince Mau-

rice said them to me. I asked him in what language the parrot spoke, and he said in Brazilian. I asked whether he understood Brazilian; he said No, but he had taken care to have two interpreters by him, the one a Dutchman that spoke Brazilian, and the other a Brazilian that spoke Dutch; that he asked them separately and privately, and both of them agreed in telling him just the same thing that the parrot had said. I could not but tell this odd story, because it is so much out of the way, and from the first hand, and what may pass for a good one; for I dare say this Prince at least believed himself in all he told me, having ever passed for a very honest and pious man: I leave it to naturalists to reason, and to other men to believe, as they please upon it; however, it is not, perhaps, amiss to relieve or enliven a busy scene sometimes with such digressions whether to the purpose or no.'

I have taken care that the reader should have the story at large in the author's own words, because he seems to me not to have thought it incredible; for it cannot be imagined that so able a man as he, who had sufficiency enough to warrant all the testimonies he gives of himself, should take so much pains, in a place where it had nothing to do, to pin so close, not only a man whom he mentions as his friend, but on a Prince in whom he acknowledges very great honesty and piety, a story which, if he himself thought incredible, he could not but also think ridiculous! The Prince, it is plain, who vouches this story, and our author, who relates it from him, both of them call this talker a parrot: and I ask any one else who thinks such a story fit to be told, whether, if this parrot, and all of its kind, had always talked, as we have a prince's word for it this one did, —whether, I say, they would not have passed for a race of *rational animals;* but yet, whether, for all that, they would have been allowed to be men, and not *parrots?* For I presume it is not the idea of a thinking or rational being alone that makes the *idea of a man* in most people's sense: but of a body, so and so shaped, joined to it; and if that be the idea of a man, the same successive body not shifted all at once, must, as well as the same immaterial spirit, go to the making of the same man.

This being premised, to find wherein personal identity consists, we must consider what *person* stands for;—which, I think, is a thinking intelligent being, that has reason and reflection, and can consider itself as itself, the same thinking thing, in different times and places; which it does only by that consciousness which is inseparable from thinking, and, as it seems to me, essential to it: it being impossible for any one to perceive without *perceiving* that he does perceive. When we see, hear, smell, taste, feel, meditate, or will anything, we know that we do so. Thus it is always as to our present sensations and perceptions: and by this every one is to himself that which he calls *self*:—it not being considered, in this case, whether the same self be continued in the same or divers substances. For, since consciousness always accompanies thinking, and it is that which makes every one to be what he calls self, and thereby distinguishes himself from all other thinking things, in this alone consists personal identity, i.e. the sameness of a rational being: and as far as this consciousness can be extended backwards to any past action or thought, so far reaches the identity of that person; it is the same self now it was then; and it is by the same self with this present one that now reflects on it, that that action was done.

But it is further inquired, whether it be the same identical substance. This few would think they had reason to doubt of, if these perceptions, with their consciousness, always remained present in the mind, whereby the same thinking thing would be always consciously present, and, as would be thought, evidently the same to itself. But that which seems to make the difficulty is this, that this consciousness being interrupted always by forgetfulness, there being no moment of our lives wherein we have the whole train of all our past actions before our eyes in one view, but even the best memories losing the sight of one part whilst they are viewing another; and we sometimes, and that the greatest part of our lives, not reflecting on our past selves, being intent on our present thoughts, and in sound sleep having no thoughts at all, or at least none with that consciousness which remarks our waking thoughts,—I say, in all these cases, our consciousness being interrupted, and we losing the sight of our past selves, doubts are raised whether we are the same thinking thing, i.e. the same *substance* or no. Which, however reasonable or unreasonable, concerns not *personal* identity at all. The question being what makes the same person; and not whether it be the same identical substance, which always thinks in the same person, which, in this case, matters not at all: different substances, by the same consciousness (where they do partake in it) being united into one person, as well as different bodies by the same life are united into one animal, whose identity is preserved in that change of substances by the unity of one continued life. For, it being the same consciousness that makes a man be himself to himself, personal identity depends on that only, whether it be annexed solely to one individual substance, or can be continued in a succession of several substances. For as far as any intelligent being *can* repeat the idea of any past action with the same consciousness it had of it at first, and with the same consciousness it has of any present action; so far it is the same personal self. For it is by the consciousness it has of its present thoughts and actions, that it is *self to itself* now, and so will be the same self, as far as the same consciousness can extend to actions past or to come; and would be by distance of time, or change of substance, no more two persons, than a man be two men by wearing other clothes to-day than he did yesterday, with a long or a short sleep between: the same consciousness uniting those distant actions into the same person, whatever substances contributed to their production.

That this is so, we have some kind of evidence in our very bodies, all whose particles, whilst vitally united to this same thinking conscious self, so that *we feel* when they are touched, and are affected by, and conscious of good or harm that happens to them, are a part of ourselves; i.e. of our thinking conscious self. Thus, the limbs of his body are to every one a part of himself; he sympathizes and is concerned for them. Cut off a hand, and thereby separate it from that consciousness he had of its heat, cold, and other affections, and it is then no longer a part of that which is himself, any more than the remotest part of matter. Thus, we see the *substance* whereof personal self consisted at one time may be varied at another, without the change of personal identity; there being no question about the same person, though the limbs which but now were a part of it, be cut off.

But the question is, Whether if the same substance which thinks be changed, it can be the same person; or, remaining the same, it can be different persons?

And to this I answer: First, This can be no question at all to those who place thought in a purely material animal constitution, void of an immaterial substance. For, whether their supposition be true or no, it is plain they conceive personal identity preserved in something else than identity of substance; as animal identity is preserved in identity of life, and not of substance. And therefore those who place thinking in an immaterial substance only, before they can come to deal with these men, must show why personal identity cannot be preserved in the change of immaterial substances, or variety of particular immaterial substances, as well as animal identity is preserved in the change of material substances, or variety of particular bodies: unless they will say, it is one immaterial spirit that makes the same life in brutes, as it is one immaterial spirit that makes the same person in men; which the Cartesians at least will not admit, for fear of making brutes thinking things too.

But next, as to the first part of the question, Whether, if the same thinking substance (supposing immaterial substances only to think) be changed, it can be the same person? I answer, that cannot be resolved but by those who know what kind of substances they are that do think; and whether the consciousness of past actions can be transferred from one thinking substance to another. I grant were the same consciousness the same individual action it could not: but it being a present representation of a past action, why it may not be possible, that that may be represented to the mind to have been which really never was, will remain to be shown. And therefore how far the consciousness of past actions is annexed to any individual agent, so that another cannot possibly have it, will be hard for us to determine, till we know what kind of action it is that cannot be done without a reflex act of perception accompanying it, and how performed by thinking substances, who cannot think without being conscious of it. But that which we call the same consciousness, not being the same individual act, why one intellectual substance may not have represented to it, as done by itself, what *it* never did, and was perhaps done by some other agent—why, I say, such a representation may not possibly be without reality of matter of fact, as well as several representations in dreams are, which yet whilst dreaming we take for true—will be difficult to conclude from the nature of things. And that it never is so, will by us, till we have clearer views of the nature of thinking substances, be best resolved into the goodness of God; who, as far as the happiness or misery of any of his sensible creatures is concerned in it, will not, by a fatal error of theirs, transfer from one to another that consciousness which draws reward or punishment with it. How far this may be an argument against those who would place thinking in a system of fleeting animal spirits, I leave to be considered. But yet, to return to the question before us, it must be allowed, that, if the same consciousness (which, as has been shown, is quite a different thing from the same numerical figure or motion in body) can be transferred from one thinking substance to another, it will be possible that two thinking substances may make but one person. For the same consciousness being preserved, whether in the same or different substances, the personal identity is preserved.

As to the second part of the question, Whether the same immaterial substance remaining, there may be two distinct persons; which question seems to me to be built on this,—Whether the same immaterial being, being conscious of the action of its past duration, may be wholly stripped of all the consciousness of its past existence, and lose it beyond the power of ever retrieving it again: and so as it were beginning a new account from a new period, have a consciousness that *cannot* reach beyond this new state. All those who hold pre-existence are evidently of this mind; since they allow the soul to have no remaining consciousness of what it did in that pre-existent state, either wholly separate from body, or informing any other body; and if they should not, it is plain experience would be against them. So that personal identity, reaching no further than consciousness reaches, a pre-existent spirit not having continued so many ages in a state of silence, must needs make different persons. Suppose a Christian Platonist or a Pythagorean should, upon God's having ended all his works of creation the seventh day, think his soul hath existed ever since; and should imagine it has revolved in several human bodies; as I once met with one, who was persuaded his had been the *soul* of Socrates (how reasonably I will not dispute; this I know, that in the post he filled, which was no inconsiderable one, he passed for a very rational man, and the press has shown that he wanted not parts or learning;) —would any one say, that he, being not conscious of any of Socrates's actions or thoughts, could be the same *person* with Socrates? Let any one reflect upon himself, and conclude that he has in himself an immaterial spirit, which is that which thinks in him, and, in the constant change of his body keeps him the same: and is that which he calls *himself*: let him also suppose it to be the same soul that was in Nestor or Thersites, at the siege of Troy, (for souls being, as far as we know anything of them, in their nature indifferent to any parcel of matter, the supposition has no apparent absurdity in it,) which it may have been, as well as it is now the soul of any other man: but he now having no consciousness of any of the actions either of Nestor or Thersites, does or can he conceive himself the same person with either of them? Can he be concerned in either of their actions? attribute them to himself, or think them his own, more than the actions of any other men that ever existed? So that this consciousness, not reaching to any of the actions of either of those men, he is no more one *self* with either of them than if the soul or immaterial spirit that now informs him had been created, and began to exist, when it began to inform his present body; though it were never so true, that the same *spirit* that informed Nestor's or Thersites' body were numerically the same that now informs his. For this would no more make him the same person with Nestor, than if some of the particles of matter that were once a part of Nestor were now a part of this man; the same consciousness, no more making the same person, by being united to any body, than the same particle of matter, without consciousness, united to any body, makes the same person. But let him once find himself conscious of any of the actions of Nestor, he then finds himself the same person with Nestor.

And thus may we be able, without any difficulty, to conceive the same person at the resurrection, though in a body not exactly in make or parts the same which he had here,—the same consciousness going along with the soul that inhabits it. But yet the soul alone, in the change of bodies, would scarce to any one but to him that makes the soul the man, be enough to make the same man. For should the soul of a prince, carrying with it the consciousness of the prince's past life, enter and inform the body of a cobbler, as soon as deserted by his own soul, every one sees he would be the same *person* with the prince, accountable only for the prince's actions: but who would say it was the same *man*? The body too goes to the making the man, and would, I guess, to everybody determine the man in this case, wherein the soul, with all its princely thoughts about it, would not make another man: but he would be the same cobbler to every one besides himself. I know that, in the ordinary way of speaking, the same person, and the same man, stand for one and the same thing. And indeed every one will always have a liberty to speak as he pleases, and to apply what articulate sounds to what ideas he thinks fit, and change them as often as he pleases. But yet, when we will inquire what makes the same *spirit*, *man*, or *person*, we must fix the ideas of spirit, man, or person in our minds; and having resolved with ourselves what we mean by them, it will not be hard to determine, in either of them, or the like, when it is the same, and when not.

But though the same immaterial substance or soul does not alone, wherever it be, and in whatsoever state, make the same *man*; yet it is plain, consciousness, as far as ever it can be extended—should it be to ages past—unites existences and actions very remote in time into the same *person*, as well as it does the existences and actions of the immediately preceding moment: so that whatever has the consciousness of present and past actions, is the same person to whom they both belong. Had I the same consciousness that I saw the ark and Noah's flood, as that I saw an overflowing of the Thames last winter, or as that I write now, I could no more doubt that I who write this now, that saw the Thames overflowed last winter, and that viewed the flood at the general deluge,

was the same *self*,—place that self in what *substance* you please—than that I who write this am the same *myself* now whilst I write (whether I consist of all the same substance, material or immaterial, or no) that I was yesterday. For as to this point of being the same self, it matters not whether this present self be made up of the same or other substances —I being as much concerned, and as justly accountable for any action that was done a thousand years since, appropriated to me now by this self-consciousness, as I am for what I did the last moment.

Self is that conscious thinking thing,—whatever substance made up of, (whether spiritual or material, simple or compounded, it matters not)—which is sensible or conscious of pleasure and pain, capable of happiness or misery, and so is concerned for itself, as far as that consciousness extends. Thus every one finds that, whilst comprehended under that consciousness, the little finger is as much a part of himself as what is most so. Upon separation of this little finger, should this consciousness go along with the little finger, and leave the rest of the body, it is evident the little finger would be the person, the same person; and self then would have nothing to do with the rest of the body. As in this case it is the consciousness that goes along with the substance, when one part is separate from another, which makes the same person, and constitutes this inseparable self: so it is in reference to substances remote in time. That with which the consciousness of this present thinking thing *can* join itself, makes the same person, and is one self with it, and with nothing else; and so attributes to itself, and owns all the actions of that thing, as its own, as far as that consciousness reaches, and no further; as every one who reflects will perceive.

In this personal identity is founded all the right and justice of reward and punishment; happiness and misery being that for which every one is concerned for *himself*, and not mattering what becomes of any *substance*, not joined to, or affected with that consciousness. For, as it is evident in the instance I gave but now, if the consciousness went along with the little finger when it was cut off, that would be the same self which was concerned for the whole body yesterday, as making part of itself, whose actions then it cannot but admit as its own now. Though, if the same body should still live, and immediately from the separation of the little finger have its own peculiar consciousness, whereof the little finger knew nothing, it would not at all be concerned for it, as a part of itself, or could own any of its actions, or have any of them imputed to him.

This may show us wherein personal identity consists: not in the identity of substance, but, as I have said, in the identity of consciousness, wherein if Socrates and the present mayor of Queinborough agree, they are the same person: if the same Socrates waking and sleeping do not partake of the same consciousness, Socrates waking and sleeping is not the same person. And to punish Socrates waking for what sleeping Socrates thought, and waking Socrates was never conscious of, would be no more of right, than to punish one twin for what his brother-twin did, whereof he knew nothing, because their outsides were so like, that they could not be distinguished; for such twins have been seen.

But yet possibly it will still be objected,—Suppose I wholly lose the memory of some parts of my life, beyond a possibility of retrieving them, so that perhaps I shall never be conscious of them again; yet am I not the same person that did those actions, had those thoughts that I once was conscious of, though I have now forgot them? To which I answer, that we must here take notice what the word *I* is applied to; which, in this case, is the *man* only. And the same man being presumed to be the same person, I is easily here supposed to stand also for the same person. But if it be possible for the same man to have distinct incommunicable consciousness at different times, it is past doubt the same

man would at different times make different persons; which, we see, is the sense of mankind in the solemnest declaration of their opinions, human laws not punishing the mad man for the sober man's actions, nor the sober man for what the mad man did,—thereby making them two persons: which is somewhat explained by our way of speaking in English when we say such an one is 'not himself,' or is 'beside himself'; in which phrases it is insinuated, as if those who now, or at least first used them, thought that self was changed; the self-same person was no longer in that man.

But yet it is hard to conceive that Socrates, the same individual man, should be two persons. To help us a little in this, we must consider what is meant by Socrates, or the same individual *man*.

First, it must be either the same individual, immaterial, thinking substance; in short, the same numerical soul, and nothing else.

Secondly, or the same animal, without any regard to an immaterial soul.

Thirdly, or the same immaterial spirit united to the same animal.

Now, take which of these suppositions you please, it is impossible to make personal identity to consist in anything but consciousness; or reach any further than that does.

For, by the first of them, it must be allowed possible that a man born of different women, and in distant times, may be the same man. A way of speaking which, whoever admits, must allow it possible for the same man to be two distinct persons, as any two that have lived in different ages without the knowledge of another's thoughts.

By the second and third, Socrates, in this life and after it, cannot be the same man any way, but by the same consciousness; and so making human identity to consist in the same thing wherein we place personal identity, there will be no difficulty to allow the same man to be the same person. But then they who place human identity in consciousness only, and not in something else, must consider how they will make the infant Socrates the same man with Socrates after the resurrection. But whatsoever to some men makes a man, and consequently the same individual man, wherein perhaps few are agreed, personal identity can by us be placed in nothing but consciousness, (which is that alone which makes what we call *self*,) without involving us in great absurdities.

But is not a man drunk and sober the same person? why else is he punished for the fact he commits when drunk, though he be never afterwards conscious of it? Just as much the same person as a man that walks, and does other things in his sleep, is the same person, and is answerable for any mischief he shall do in it. Human laws punish both, with a justice suitable to *their* way of knowledge;—because, in these cases, they cannot distinguish certainly what is real, what counterfeit: and so the ignorance in drunkenness or sleep is not admitted as a plea. [For, though punishment be annexed to personality, and personality to consciousness, and the drunkard perhaps be not conscious of what he did, yet human judicatures justly punish him; because the fact is proved against him, but want of consciousness cannot be proved for him.] But in the Great Day, wherein the secrets of all hearts shall be laid open, it may be reasonable to think, no one shall be made to answer for what he knows nothing of; but shall receive his doom, his conscience accusing or excusing him.

Nothing but consciousness can unite remote existences into the same person: the identity of substance will not do it; for whatever substance there is, however framed, without consciousness there is no person: and a carcass may be a person, as well as any sort of substance be so, without consciousness.

Could we suppose two distinct incommunicable consciousnesses acting the same body, the one constantly by day, the other by night; and, on the other side, the same consciousness, acting by intervals, two distinct bodies: I ask, in the first case, whether the day and the night—man would not be two as distinct persons as Socrates and Plato? And whether, in the second case, there would not be one person in two distinct bodies, as much as one man is the same in two distinct clothings? Nor is it at all material to say, that this same, and this distinct consciousness, in the cases above mentioned, is owing to the same and distinct immaterial substances, bringing it with them to those bodies; which, whether true or no, alters not the case: since it is evident the personal identity would equally be determined by the consciousness, whether that consciousness were annexed to some individual immaterial substance or no. For, granting that the thinking substance in man must be necessarily supposed immaterial, it is evident that immaterial thinking thing may sometimes part with its past consciousness, and be restored to it again: as appears in the forgetfulness men often have of their past actions; and the mind many times recovers the memory of a past consciousness, which it had lost for twenty years together. Make these intervals of memory and forgetfulness to take their turns regularly by day and night, and you have two persons with the same immaterial spirit, as much as in the former instance two persons with the same body. So that self is not determined by identity or diversity of substance, which it cannot be sure of, but only by identity of consciousness.

Indeed it may conceive the substance whereof it is now made up to have existed formerly, united in the same conscious being: but, consciousness removed, that substance is no more itself, or makes no more a part of it, than any other substance; as is evident in the instance we have already given of a limb cut off, of whose heat, or cold, or other affections, having no longer any consciousness, it is no more of a man's self than any other matter of the universe. In like manner it will be in reference to any immaterial substance, which is void of that consciousness whereby I am myself to myself: [if there be any part of its existence which] I cannot upon recollection join with that present consciousness whereby I am now myself, it is, in that part of its existence, no more *myself* than any other immaterial being. For, whatsoever any substance has thought or done, which I cannot recollect, and by my consciousness make my own thought and action, it will no more belong to me, whether a part of me thought or did it, than if it had been thought or done by any other immaterial being anywhere existing.

I agree, the more probable opinion is, that this consciousness is annexed to, and the affection of, one individual immaterial substance.

But let men, according to their diverse hypotheses, resolve of that as they please. This every intelligent being, sensible of happiness or misery, must grant—that there is something that is himself, that he is concerned for, and would have happy; that this self has existed in a continued duration more than one instant, and therefore it is possible may exist, as it has done, months and years to come, without any certain bounds to be set to its duration; and may be the same self, by the same consciousness continued on for the future. And thus, by this consciousness he finds himself to be the same self which did such and such an action some years since, by which he comes to be happy or miserable now. In all which account of self, the same numerical *substance* is not considered as making the same self; but the same continued *consciousness*, in which several substances may have been united, and again separated from it, which, whilst they continued in a vital union with that wherein this consciousness then resided, made a part of that same self. Thus any part of our bodies, vitally united to that which is conscious in us, makes a part of ourselves: but upon separation from the vital union by which that consciousness is communicated, that which a moment since was part of ourselves, is now no more so than a part of another man's self is a part of me: and it is not impossible but

in a little time may become a real part of another person. And so we have the same numerical substance become a part of two different persons; and the same person preserved under the change of various substances. Could we suppose any spirit wholly stripped of all its memory or consciousness of past actions, as we find our minds always are of a great part of ours, and sometimes of them all; the union or separation of such a spiritual substance would make no variation of personal identity, any more than that of any particle of matter does. Any substance vitally united to the present thinking being is a part of that very same self which now is; anything united to it by a consciousness of former actions, makes also a part of the same self, which is the same both then and now.

Person, as I take it, is the name for this self. Wherever a man finds what he calls himself, there, I think, another may say is the same person. It is a forensic term, appropriating actions and their merit; and so belongs only to intelligent agents, capable of a law, and happiness, and misery. This personality extends itself beyond present existence to what is past, only by consciousness,— whereby it becomes concerned and accountable; owns and imputes to itself past actions, just upon the same ground and for the same reason as it does the present. All which is founded in a concern for happiness, the unavoidable concomitant of consciousness; that which is conscious of pleasure and pain, desiring that that self that is conscious should be happy. And therefore whatever past actions it cannot reconcile or *appropriate* to that present self by consciousness, it can be no more concerned in than if they had never been done: and to receive pleasure or pain, i.e. reward or punishment, on the account of any such action, is all one as to be made happy or miserable in its first being, without any demerit at all. For, supposing a man punished now for what he had done in another life whereof he could be made to have no consciousness at all, what difference is there between that punishment and being *created* miserable? And therefore, conformable to this, the apostle tells us, that, at the great day, when every one shall 'receive according to his doings, the secrets of all hearts shall be laid open.' The sentence shall be justified by the consciousness all persons shall have, that *they themselves*, in what bodies soever they appear, or what substances soever that consciousness adheres to, are the *same* that committed those actions, and deserve that punishment for them.

I am apt enough to think I have, in treating of this subject, made some suppositions that will look strange to some readers, and possibly they are so in themselves. But yet, I think they are such as are pardonable, in this ignorance we are in of the nature of that thinking thing that is in us, and which we look on as *ourselves*. Did we know what it was; or how it was tied to a certain system of fleeting animal spirits; or whether it could or could not perform its operations of thinking and memory out of a body organized as ours is; and whether it has pleased God that no one such spirit shall ever be united to any but one such body, upon the right constitution of whose organs its memory should depend; we might see the absurdity of some of those suppositions I have made. But taking, as we ordinarily now do (in the dark concerning these matters,) the soul of a man for an immaterial substance, independent from matter, and indifferent alike to it all; there can, from the nature of things, be no absurdity at all to suppose that the same *soul* may at different times be united to different *bodies*, and with them make up for that time one *man*: as well as we suppose a part of a sheep's body yesterday should be a part of a man's body to-morrow, and in that union make a vital part of Meli-

bœus himself, as well as it did of his ram.

To conclude: Whatever substance begins to exist, it must, during its existence, necessarily be the same: whatever compositions of substances begin to exist, during the union of those substances, the concrete must be the same: whatsoever mode begins to exist, during its existence it is the same: and so if the composition be of distinct substances and different modes, the same rule holds. Whereby it will appear, that the difficulty or obscurity that has been about this matter rather rises from the names ill-used, than from any obscurity in things themselves. For whatever makes the specific idea to which the name is applied, if that idea be steadily kept to, the distinction of anything into the same and divers will easily be conceived, and there can arise no doubt about it.

For, supposing a rational spirit be the idea of a *man*, it is easy to know what is the same man, viz. the same spirit—whether separate or in a body—will be the *same man*. Supposing a rational spirit vitally united to a body of a certain conformation of parts to make a man; whilst that rational spirit, with that vital conformation of parts, though continued in a fleeting successive body, remains, it will be the *same man*. But if to any one the idea of a man be but the vital union of parts in a certain shape; as long as that vital union and shape remain in a concrete, no otherwise the same but by a continued succession of fleeting particles, it will be the *same man*. For, whatever be the composition whereof the complex idea is made, whenever existence makes it one particular thing under any denomination, *the same existence continued* preserves it the *same* individual under the same denomination.

A Critique of Hume and Locke
THOMAS REID

The conviction which every man has of his identity, as far back as his memory reaches, needs no aid of philosophy to strengthen it; and no philosophy can weaken it, without first producing some degree of insanity.

The philosopher, however, may very properly consider this conviction as a phenomenon of human nature worthy of his attention. If he can discover its cause, an addition is made to his stock of knowledge; if not, it must be held as a part of our original constitution, or an effect of that constitution produced in a manner unknown to us.

That we may form as distinct a notion as we are able of this phenomenon of the human mind, it is proper to consider what is meant by identity in general, what by our own personal identity, and how we are led into that invincible belief and conviction which every man has of his own personal identity, as far as his memory reaches.

Identity in general I take to be a relation between a thing which is known to exist at one time, and a thing which is known to have existed at another time. If you ask whether they are one and the same, or two different things, every man of common sense understands the meaning of your question perfectly. Whence we may infer with certainty, that every man of common sense has a clear and distinct notion of identity.

If you ask a definition of identity, I confess I can give none; it is too simple a notion to admit of logical definition: I can say it is a relation, but I cannot find words to express the specific difference between this and other relations, though I am in no danger of confounding it with any other. I can say that diversity is a contrary relation, and that similitude and dissimilitude are another couple of contrary relations, which every man easily distinguishes in his conception from identity and diversity.

I see evidently that identity supposes *an uninterrupted continuance of existence*. That which has ceased to exist cannot be the same with that which afterwards begins to exist; for this would be to suppose a being to exist after it ceased to exist, and to have had existence before it was produced, which are manifest contradictions. Continued uninterrupted existence is therefore necessarily implied in identity. Hence we may infer, that identity cannot, in its proper sense, be applied to our pains, our pleasures, our thoughts, or any operation of our minds. The pain felt this day is not the same individual pain which I felt yesterday, though they may be *similar* in kind and degree, and have the same cause. The same may be said of every feeling, and of every operation of mind. They are all successive in their nature, like time itself, no two moments of which can be the same moment. It is otherwise with the parts of absolute space. They always are, and were, and will be the same. So far, I think, we proceed upon clear ground in fixing the notion of identity in general.

It is perhaps more difficult to ascertain with precision the meaning of *personality*; but it is not necessary in the present subject: it is sufficient for our purpose to observe, that all mankind place their personality in something that *cannot be divided, or consist of parts*. A part of a person is a manifest absurdity. When a man loses his estate, his health, his strength, he is still the same person, and has lost nothing of his personality. If he has a leg or an arm cut off, he is the same person he was before. The amputated member is no part of his person, otherwise it would have a right to a part of his estate, and be liable

FROM: *Essays on the Intellectual Powers of Man*, Thomas Reid, Essay III, Ch. 4 and ch. 6 (in part), and Essay VI, ch. 5 (in part) (originally published in 1785).

for a part of his engagements. It would be entitled to a share of his merit and demerit, which is manifestly absurd. A person is something indivisible, and is what Leibnitz calls a *monad*.

My personal identity, therefore, implies the continued existence of that indivisible thing which I call *myself*. Whatever this self may be, it is something which thinks, and deliberates, and resolves, and acts, and suffers. I am not thought, I am not action, I am not feeling; I am something that thinks, and acts, and suffers. My thoughts, and actions, and feelings, change every moment; they have no continued, but a successive, existence; but that *self*, or *I*, to which they belong, is permanent, and has the same relation to all the succeeding thoughts, actions, and feelings which I call mine.

Such are the notions that I have of my personal identity. But perhaps it may be said, this may all be fancy without reality. How do you know—what evidence have you—that there is such a permanent self which has a claim to all the thoughts, actions, and feelings which you call yours?

To this I answer, that the proper evidence I have of all this is *remembrance*. I remember that twenty years ago I conversed with such a person; I remember several things that passed in that conversation: my memory testifies, not only that this was done, but that it was done by me who now remembers it. If it was done by me, I must have existed at that time, and continued to exist from that time to the present: if the identical person whom I call myself had not a part in that conversation, my memory is fallacious; it gives a distinct and positive testimony of what is not true. Every man in his senses believes what he distinctly remembers, and everything he remembers convinces him that he existed at the time remembered.

Although memory gives the most irresistible evidence of my being the identical person that did such a thing, at such a time, I may have other good evidence of things which befell me, and which I do not remember: I know who bare me, and suckled me, but I do not remember these events.

It may here be observed (though the observation would have been unnecessary, if some great philosophers had not contradicted it), that it is not my remembering any action of mine that *makes* me to be the person who did it. This remembrance makes me to *know* assuredly that I did it; *but I might have done it, though I did not remember it.* That relation to me, which is expressed by saying that *I did it*, would be the same, though I had not the least remembrance of it. To say that my remembering that I did such a thing, or, as some choose to express it, my being conscious that I did it, makes me to have done it, appears to me as great an absurdity as it would be to say, that my belief that the world was created made it to be created.

When we pass judgment on the identity of other persons than ourselves, we proceed upon other grounds, and determine from a variety of circumstances, which sometimes produce the firmest assurance, and sometimes leave room for doubt. The identity of persons has often furnished matter of serious litigation before tribunals of justice. But no man of a sound mind ever doubted of his own identity, as far as he distinctly remembered.

The identity of a person is a perfect identity: wherever it is real, it admits of no degrees; and it is impossible that a person should be in part the same, and in part different; because a person is a *monad,* and is not divisible into parts. The evidence of identity in other persons than ourselves does indeed admit of all degrees, from what we account certainty, to the least degree of probability. But still it is true, that the same person is perfectly the same, and cannot be so in part or in some degree only.

For this cause, I have first considered personal identity, as that which is perfect in its kind, and the natural measure of that which is imperfect.

We probably at first derive our notion of identity from that natural conviction which every man has from the dawn of reason of *his own* identity and continued existence. The operations of our minds, are all successive, and have no continued existence. But the thinking being has a continued existence, and we have an invincible belief, that it remains the same when all its thoughts and operations change.

Our judgments of the identity of objects of sense seem to be formed much upon the same grounds as our judgments of the identity of *other persons* than ourselves. Wherever we observe great *similarity*, we are apt to presume identity, if no reason appears to the contrary. Two objects ever so like, when they are perceived at the same time, cannot be the same; but if they are presented to our senses at different times, we are apt to think them the same, merely from their similarity.

Whether this be a natural prejudice, or from whatever cause it proceeds, it certainly appears in children from infancy; and when we grow up, it is confirmed in most instances by experience: for we rarely find two individuals of the same species that are not distinguishable by obvious differences. A man challenges a thief whom he finds in possession of his horse or his watch, only on similarity. When the watchmaker swears that he sold this watch to such a person, his testimony is grounded on similarity. The testimony of witnesses to the identity of a person is commonly grounded on no other evidence.

Thus it appears, that the evidence we have of our own identity, as far back as we remember, is totally of a different kind from the evidence we have of the identity of other persons, or of objects of sense. The first is grounded on *memory*, and gives undoubted certainty. The last is grounded on *similarity*, and on other circumstances, which in many cases are not so decisive as to leave no room for doubt. It may likewise be observed, that the identity of *objects of sense* is never perfect. All bodies, as

they consist of innumerable parts that may be disjoined from them by a great variety of causes, are subject to continual changes of their own substance, increasing, diminishing, changing insensibly. When such alterations are gradual, because language could not afford a different name for every different state of such a changeable being, it retains the same name, and is considered as the same thing. Thus we say of an old regiment, that it did such a thing a century ago, though there now is not a man alive who then belonged to it. We say a tree is the same in the seed-bed and in the forest. A ship of war, which has successively changed her anchors, her tackle, her sails, her masts, her planks, and her timbers, while she keeps the same name, is the same.

The identity, therefore, which we ascribe to bodies, whether natural or artificial, is not perfect identity; it is rather something which, for the convenience of speech, we call identity. It admits of a great change of the subject, providing the change be *gradual*; sometimes, even of a total change. And the changes which in common language are made consistent with identity differ from those that are thought to destroy it, not in *kind*, but in *number* and *degree*. It has no fixed nature when applied to bodies; and questions about the identity of a body are very often questions about words. But identity, when applied to persons, has no ambiguity, and admits not of degrees, or of more and less. It is the foundation of all rights and obligations, and of all accountableness; and the notion of it is fixed and precise.

The thoughts of which I am conscious are the thoughts of a being which I call MYSELF, and MIND, my PERSON.

The thoughts and feelings of which we are conscious are continually changing, and the thought of this moment is not the thought of the last; but something which I call *myself* remains under this change of thought. This self has the same relation to all the successive thoughts I am conscious of; they are all *my* thoughts; and every thought which is not my thought must be the thought of some other person.

If any man asks a proof of this, I confess I can give none; there is an evidence in the proposition itself which I am unable to resist. Shall I think, that thought can stand by itself without a thinking being? or that ideas can feel pleasure or pain? My nature dictates to me that it is impossible. And that nature has dictated the same to all men appears from the structure of all languages: for in all languages men have expressed thinking, reasoning, willing, loving, hating, by *personal* verbs, which from their nature require a person who thinks, reasons, wills, loves, or hates. From which it appears, that men have been taught by nature to believe that thought requires a thinker, reason a reasoner, and love a lover.

Here we must leave Mr. Hume, who conceives it to be a vulgar error, that, besides the thoughts we are conscious of, there is a mind which is the subject of those thoughts. If the mind be anything else than impressions and ideas, it must be a word without a meaning. The mind, therefore, according to this philosopher, is a word which signifies a bundle of perceptions; or, when he defines it more accurately, "it is that succession of related ideas and impressions, of which we have an intimate memory and consciousness."

I am, therefore, that succession of related ideas and impressions of which I have the intimate memory and consciousness. But who is the *I* that has this memory and consciousness of a succession of ideas and impressions? Why, it is nothing but that succession itself. Hence I learn, that this succession of ideas and impressions intimately remembers, and is conscious of itself. I would wish to be further instructed, whether the impressions remember and are conscious of the ideas, or the ideas remember and are conscious of the impressions, of if both remember and are conscious

of both? and whether the ideas remember those that come after them, as well as those that were before them? These are questions naturally arising from this system, that have not yet been explained.

This, however, is clear, that this succession of ideas and impressions not only remembers and is conscious, but that it judges, reasons, affirms, denies; nay, that it eats and drinks, and is sometimes merry and sometimes sad. If these things can be ascribed to a succession of ideas and impressions, in a consistency with common sense, I should be very glad to know what is nonsense.

The scholastic philosophers have been wittily ridiculed, by representing them as disputing upon this question, *Num chimaera bombinana in vacuo possit comedere secundas intentiones?* [Roughly, whether an imaginary being can eat ideas of ideas while making noises in a void. The question (made up by Rabelais) is intended to be a nonsense question, like "How many square roots are there in a dish of coffee ice cream?" Eds.] And I believe the wit of man cannot invent a more ridiculous question. But, if Mr. Hume's philosophy be admitted, this question deserves to be treated more gravely; for if, as we learn from this philosophy, a succession of ideas and impressions may eat, and drink, and be merry, I see no good reason why a chimera, which, if not the same, is of kin to an idea, may not chew the cud upon that kind of food which the schoolmen call *second intentions*.

Mr. Locke tells us "that personal identity, that is, the sameness of a rational being, *consists in consciousness alone*, and, as far as this consciousness can be extended backwards to any past action or thought, so far reaches the identity of that person. So that whatever has the consciousness of present and past actions is the same person to whom they belong."

This doctrine has some strange consequences, which the author was aware of. (1) . . . that if the same consciousness can be transferred from one intelligent being to another, which he thinks we cannot show to be impossible, *then two or twenty intelligent beings may be the same person.* (2) And if the intelligent being may lose the consciousness of the actions done by him, which surely is possible, then he is not the person that did those actions; so that *one intelligent being may be two or twenty different persons,* if he shall so often lose the consciousness of his former actions.

(3) There is another consequence of this doctrine, which follows no less necessarily, though Mr. Locke probably did not see it. It is, *that a man may be, and at the same time not be, the person that did a particular action.* Suppose a brave officer to have been flogged when a boy at school for robbing an orchard, to have taken a standard from the enemy in his first campaign, and to have been made a general in advanced life;

suppose, also, which must be admitted to be possible, that, when he took the standard, he was conscious of his having been flogged at school, and that, when made a general, he was conscious of his taking the standard, but had absolutely lost the consciousness of his flogging. These things being supposed, it follows, from Mr. Locke's doctrine, that he who was flogged at school is the same person who took the standard, and that he who took the standard is the same person who was made a general. Whence it follows, if there be any truth in logic, that the general is the same person with him who was flogged at school. But the general's consciousness does not reach so far back as his flogging; therefore, according to Mr. Locke's doctrine, he is not the person who was flogged. Therefore the general is, and at the same time is not, the same person with him who was flogged at school. . . .

Sensory Experience and Personal Identity
PETER GEACH

*'I*nner sense' is supposed to show us, and to be the only thing that shows us, what it is like to see, hear, be afraid, etc. With this there goes a view that the connexion between such 'sensuous' experiences and a bodily organism is only a well-established empirical generalization. Such experiences are indeed dependent upon material things in the sense of being occupied with them; but they are not identifiable with any describable physiological processes in a living organism, and their connexion with such processes is only something empirically determined. There is no necessary, conceptual, connexion between the experience we call "seeing" and the processes that physiologists tell us happen in eye and brain; the statement "James can still

see, although his optic centres are destroyed" is very unlikely on inductive grounds but perfectly intelligible—after all, people used the word "see" long before they had any idea of things happening in the optic centres of the brain. It therefore appears to be clearly conceivable that seeing and other 'sensuous' experiences might go on continuously even after the death of the organism with which they are now associated, and that the inductive reasons for doubting whether this ever happens might be outweighed by the evidence of Psychical Research.

I think it is an important conceptual enquiry to consider whether *really* disembodied seeing, hearing, pain, hunger, emotion, etc., are so clearly intelligi-

FROM: "Could Sensuous Experiences Occur Apart from an Organism?" in *Mental Acts*, Peter Geach. Section 25, (New York: Humanities Press Inc., 1957). Reprinted by permission of Humanities Press Inc. and Routledge and Kegan Paul, Ltd.

ble as is supposed in this common philosophical point of view. (I stress "really disembodied". Some people believe that there is a subtle body endowed with its own sense-organs, which persists after the dissolution of the body commonly so called. This view, so far as I can see, is philosophically speaking both unobjectionable and uninteresting. It is clear offhand that the 'mind-body problem' is just the same whether the body is gross or subtle.)

"The verb 'to see' has its meaning for me because I *do* see—I have that experience!" Nonsense. As well suppose that I can come to know what a minus quantity is by setting out to lose weight. What shows a man to have the concept *seeing* is not merely that he sees, but that he can take an intelligent part in our everyday use of the word "seeing". Our concept of sight has its life only in connexion with a whole set of other concepts, some of them relating to the physical characteristics of visible objects, others relating to the behaviour of people who see things. (I express exercise of this concept in such utterances as "I can't see, it's too far off—now it's coming into view!" "He couldn't see me, he didn't look round", "I caught his eye", etc., etc.) It would be merely silly to be frightened off admitting this by the bogy of behaviourism; you can very well admit it without also thinking that "seeing" stands for a kind of behaviour.

Our investigation is put on the wrong track by an abstractionist prejudice. For an abstractionist, the possession of the concept *seeing* must be taken to be a capacity for finding and recognizing some recurrent feature—or at least to be that primarily; and I can find instances of seeing only in my own mind, by 'inner sense'; in other people I find nothing but characteristic pieces of behaviour, from which however it could justifiably be inferred (how?) that they also see.—In fact, of course, I learn to use the word "see" of others and of myself simultaneously; and if we reject the doctrine of abstractionism, we need not distinguish between exercises of the concept *seeing* as primary ones, when I catch myself in the act of seeing something, and secondary ones, when I (with great rashness, surely, on this view) form the judgment that others likewise see. To have the concept *seeing* is not even primarily a matter of being able to spot instances of a characteristic repeatedly given in my ('inner-sense') experiences; *no* concept is primarily a recognitional capacity. And the exercise of one concept is intertwined with the exercise of others; as with a spider's web, some connexions may be broken with impunity, but if you break enough the whole web collapses—the concept becomes unusable. Just such a collapse happens, I believe, when we try to think of seeing, hearing, pain, emotion, etc., going on independently of a body.

When I apply this sort of concept to a human being, I do so in connexion with a whole lot of other concepts that I apply to human beings and their natural environment. It is easy enough to extend the concepts of 'sensuous' experience to creatures fairly like human beings, such as cats, dogs, and horses; when we try to extend them to creatures extremely unlike human beings in their style of life, we feel, if we are wise, great uncertainty—not just uncertainty as to the facts, or as to the possibility of finding them out, but uncertainty as to the *meaning* of saying: "I now know how to tell when an earthworm is angry". One is of course tempted to say: "That's easy; an earthworm is angry if it is feeling the way I feel when I am angry!" But this is just like saying: "Of course I know what it is for the time on the Sun to be five o'clock; it is five o'clock on the Sun when it is the same time as when it is five o'clock here!" (WITTGENSTEIN, Part I, §350)—which clearly gets us no for'arder. There is just the same difficulty in extending the concept *the same time* as in extending the concept *five o'clock*. So in the psychological case: I know how to apply the concept *anger* to myself and to James, and I know how to apply the concept *feeling the same way* as between myself and James, or

James and Smith; I get into the same difficulties if I try applying the concept *feeling the same way* as between myself and an earthworm as I do over applying the concept *anger* to it.[1]

Even an earthworm, though, affords some handholds for the application of 'sensuous' psychological concepts; we connect its writhings when injured with our own pain-reactions. But when it comes to an automaton, or again if we are invited to apply the concepts to a supposed disembodied existence, then we may be sure that we are right in refusing to play; too many threads are broken, and the conceptual web has collapsed. An automaton, by all sorts of criteria, is not even alive; we know this, though we may be uncertain whether to call a virus (say) alive or not. (Doctors may not agree whether a patient is yet dead; but we know that Queen Anne is dead.) Between what is certainly inanimate and ourselves there is far too little similarity for us to be able to pick out anything in its behaviour corresponding to the context in which we judge that human beings are in pain, or hungry, or afraid; we know that any particular movement which might even remotely suggest similarity is performed because the designer of the automaton intended such an imitation, and we ought to be no more inclined to ascribe feelings to the

automaton than, after childhood, we think that a doll is in pain because it has been so constructed as to cry when it is smacked.—As for disembodied sensations and feelings, even more connexions are broken in this case; there is no handhold for applying 'sensuous' concepts to disembodied existence at all— we just do not know what we are doing if we try.

A good illustration, I think, of a concept's losing its applicability through connexions being broken is the following. Certain hysterics claimed to have magnetic sensations; it was discovered, however, that their claim to be having them at a given time did not go with the presence of a magnet in their neighbourhood but with their belief, true or false, that a magnet was there. It would now have been possible to say: "We must take the patients' word for it that they have these peculiar sensations, which are quite different from ordinary people's sense-modalities; it is merely the term "magnetic sensations" that has turned out to be inappropriate; they had formed a wrong hypothesis about the physical cause of their sensations". But nobody even considered saying this; it was decided that the patients had just been indulging in the sort of pointless talk that hysterics often do indulge in. This decision just to drop the idea of magnetic sensations and to ignore the patients' 'reports' of them was taken after a much smaller breakdown of the ordinary connexions than we are asked to tolerate when it is attempted to apply sensation-concepts to automata or to disembodied existence.

Denying sense to the attempt to think of feelings, sensations, emotions, etc., apart from a living organism may seem to be practically the same as denying disembodied mind altogether. Such a denial does not follow, nor has it historically always been held to follow. Aquinas, for example, believed that there were wholly disembodied intelligences, but that they were not liable to any such experiences as seeing and hearing and feeling afraid and having a

---

[1] On a point of interpretation, I think it is a mistake to read Wittgenstein as having intended to show that I cannot apply a concept like *anger* both to myself and to others, and that it is meaningless to speak of others' feeling the same way as I do (unless indeed I just mean that they behave as I do). The difficulty of transferring the concept *anger* from myself to others is a spurious one, arising from the abstractionism that Wittgenstein consistently rejected; and the solution that the term "anger" is an equivocal term, applied in my own case to a recurrent experience and in other cases to a recurrent pattern of behaviour, is plausible, I think, only on astractionist presuppositions; I do not believe, as some people I have had discussion with apparently do, that Wittgenstein really held this view and only shrank from a brash statement of it.

pain: the evil spirits in hell are tormented not by aches but by the frustration of their wicked will. (Ia q. 54 art. 6, q. 59 art. 4, q. 64 art. 3.) Sensuous experiences are possible only in connexion with a living organism (Ia q. 77 art. 8). Only since Descartes has the main problem become: "How is *cogitatio* related to bodily processes?" ("*cogitatio*" covering, for him, everything 'in the mind', from a toothache to a metaphysical meditation); the old problem was rather: "How can a being that thinks and judges and decides *also* have sensu-

ous experiences?" It was 'intellectual' acts like judgment, not just *anything* that would now be called 'consciousness', which seemed to Aquinas to be wholly incommensurable with events in the physical world; for him, the 'unbridgeable gulf' was at a different place. The usefulness of historical knowledge in philosophy, here as elsewhere, is that the prejudices of our own period may lose their grip on us if we imaginatively enter into another period, when people's prejudices were different.

Personal Identity and Bodily Capacities
GILBERT RYLE

*I*t has been argued from a number of directions that when we speak of a person's mind, we are not speaking of a second theatre of special-status incidents, but of certain ways in which some of the incidents of his one life are ordered. His life is not a double series of events taking place in two different kinds of stuff; it is one concatenation of events, the differences between some and other classes of which largely consist in the applicability or inapplicability to them of logically different types of law-propositions and law-like propositions. Assertions about a person's mind are therefore assertions of special sorts about that person. So questions about the relations between a person and his mind, like those about the relations between a person's body and his mind are improper questions. They are improper in much the same way as is the question. 'What transactions go on between the House of Commons and the British Constitution?"

It follows that it is a logical solecism to speak, as theorists often do, of someone's mind knowing this, or choos-

ing that. The person himself knows this and chooses that, though the fact that he does so can, if desired, be classified as a mental fact about that person. In partly the same way it is improper to speak of my eyes seeing this, or my nose smelling that; we should say, rather, that I see this, or I smell that, and that these assertions carry with them certain facts about my eyes and nose. But the analogy is not exact, for while my eyes and nose are organs of sense, 'my mind' does not stand for another organ. It signifies my ability and proneness to do certain sorts of things and not some piece of personal apparatus without which I could or would not do them. Similarly the British Constitution is not another British political institution functioning alongside of the Civil Service, the Judiciary, the Established Church, the Houses of Parliament and the Royal Family. Nor is it the sum of these institutions, or a liaison-staff between them. We can say that Great Britain has gone to the polls; but we cannot say that the British Constitution has gone to the polls, though the fact that Great Britain has

FROM: *The Concept of Mind*, Gilbert Ryle. (London: Hutchinson and Co., Ltd., 1949). Ch. 6, Sections 3 and 4. Used by permission of Hutchinson and Co. and Barnes and Noble, Inc.

gone to the polls might be described as a constitutional fact about Great Britain.

Actually, though it is not always convenient to avoid the practice, there is a considerable logical hazard in using the nouns 'mind' and 'minds' at all. The idiom makes it too easy to construct logically improper conjunctions, disjunctions and cause-effect propositions such as 'so and so took place not in my body but in my mind', 'my mind made my hand write', 'a person's body and mind interact upon each other' and so on. Where logical candour is required from us, we ought to follow the example set by novelists, biographers and diarists, who speak only of persons doing and undergoing things.

The questions 'What knowledge can a person get of the workings of his own mind?' and 'How does he get it?' by their very wording suggest absurd answers. They suggest that, for a person to know that he is lazy, or has done a sum carefully, he must have taken a peep into a windowless chamber, illuminated by a very peculiar sort of light, and one to which only he has access. And when the question is construed in this sort of way, the parallel questions, 'What knowledge can one person get of the workings of another mind?' and 'How does he get it?' by their very wording seem to preclude any answer at all; for they suggest that one person could only know that another person was lazy, or had done a sum carefully, by peering into another secret chamber to which, *ex hypothesi,* he has no access.

In fact the problem is not one of this sort. It is simply the methodological question, how we establish, and how we apply, certain sorts of law-like propositions about the overt and the silent behaviour of persons. I come to appreciate the skill and tactics of a chess-player by watching him and others playing chess, and I learn that a certain pupil of mine is lazy, ambitious and witty by following his work, noticing his excuses, listening to his conversation and comparing his performances with those of others. Nor does it make any important difference if I happen myself to be that

pupil. I can indeed then listen to more of his conversations, as I am the addressee of his unspoken soliloquies; I notice more of his excuses, as I am never absent, when they are made. On the other hand, my comparison of his performances with those of others is more difficult, since the examiner is himself taking the examination, which makes neutrality hard to preserve and precludes the demeanour of the candidate, when under interrogation, from being in good view.

To repeat a point previously made, the question is not the envelope-question 'How do I discover that I or you have a mind?' but the range of specific questions of the pattern, 'How do I discover that I am more unselfish than you; that I can do long division well, but differential equations only badly; that you suffer from certain phobias and tend to shirk facing certain sorts of facts; that I am more easily irritated than most people, but less subject to panic, vertigo, or morbid conscientiousness?' Besides such pure dispositional questions there is also the range of particular performance questions and occurrence questions of the patterns, 'How do I find out that I saw the joke and that you did not; that your action took more courage than mine; that the service I rendered to you was rendered from a sense of duty and not from expectation of kudos; that, though I did not fully understand what was said at the time, I did fully understand it, when I went over it in my head afterwards, while you understood it perfectly from the start; that I was feeling homesick yesterday?' Questions of these sorts offer no mysteries; we know quite well how to set to work to find out the answers to them; and though often we cannot finally solve them and may have to stop short at mere conjecture, yet, even so, we have no doubt what sorts of information would satisfy our requirements, if we could get it; and we know what it would be like to get it. For example, after listening to an argument, you aver that you understand it perfectly; but you may be deceiving yourself, or trying to deceive me. If we then part for a day or two, I am no longer in a position to test whether or not you did understand it perfectly. But still I know what tests would have settled the point. If you had put the argument into your own words, or translated it into French; if you had invented appropriate concrete illustrations of the generalisations and abstractions in the argument; if you had stood up to cross-questioning; if you had correctly drawn further consequences from different stages of the argument and indicated points where the theory was inconsistent with other theories; if you had inferred correctly from the nature of the argument to the qualities of intellect and character of its author and predicted accurately the subsequent development of his theory, then I should have required no further evidence that you understood it perfectly. And exactly the same sorts of tests would satisfy me that I had understood it perfectly; the sole differences would be that I should probably not have voiced aloud the expressions of my deductions, illustrations, etc., but told them to myself more perfunctorily in silent soliloquy; and I should probably have been more easily satisfied of the completeness of my understanding than I was of yours.

In short it is part of the *meaning* of 'you understood it' that you could have done so and so and would have done it, if such and such, and the *test* of whether you understood it is a range of performances satisfying the apodoses of these general hypothetical statements. It should be noticed, on the one hand, that there is no single nuclear performance, overt or in your head, which would determine that you had understood the argument. Even if you claimed that you had experienced a flash or click of comprehension and had actually done so, you would still withdraw your other claim to have understood the argument, if you found that you could not paraphrase it, illustrate, expand or recast it; and you would allow someone else to have understood it who could meet all examination-questions about it, but reported no click of comprehension. It

should also be noticed, on the other hand, that though there is no way of specifying how many or what sub-tests must be satisfied for a person to qualify as having perfectly understood the argument, this does not imply that no finite set of sub-tests is ever enough. To settle whether a boy can do long division, we do not require him to try out his hand on a million, a thousand, or even a hundred different problems in long division. We should not be quite satisfied after one success, but we should not remain dissatisfied after twenty, provided that they were judiciously variegated and that he had not done them before. A good teacher, who not only recorded the boy's correct and incorrect solutions, but also watched his procedure in reaching them, would be satisfied much sooner, and he would be satisfied sooner still if he got the boy to describe and justify the constituent operations that he performed, though of course many boys can do long division sums who cannot describe or justify the operations performed in doing them.

I discover my or your motives in much, though not quite the same way as I discover my or your abilities. The big practical difference is that I cannot put the subject through his paces in my inquiries into his inclinations as I can in my inquiries into his competences. To discover how conceited or patriotic you are, I must still observe your conduct, remarks, demeanour and tones of voice, but I cannot subject you to examination-tests or experiments which you recognise as such. You would have a special motive for responding to such experiments in a particular way. From mere conceit, perhaps, you would try to behave self-effacingly, or from mere modesty you might try to behave conceitedly. None the less, ordinary day to day observation normally serves swiftly to settle such questions. To be conceited is to tend to boast of one's own excellences, to pity or ridicule the deficiencies of others, to daydream about imaginary triumphs, to reminisce about actual triumphs, to weary quickly of conversations which reflect unfavourably upon oneself, to lavish one's society upon distinguished persons and to economise in association with the undistinguished. The tests of whether a person is conceited are the actions he takes and the reactions he manifests in such circumstances. Not many anecdotes, sneers or sycophancies are required from the subject for the ordinary observer to make up his mind, unless the candidate and the examiner happen to be identical.

The ascertainment of a person's mental capacities and propensities is an inductive process, an induction to lawlike propositions from observed actions and reactions. Having ascertained these long-term qualities, we explain a particular action or reaction by applying the result of such an induction to the new specimen, save where open avowals let us know the explanation without research. These inductions are not, of course, carried out under laboratory conditions, or with any statistical apparatus, any more than is the shepherd's weatherlore, or the general practitioner's understanding of a particular patient's constitution. But they are ordinarily reliable enough. It is a truism to say that the appreciations of character and the explanations of conduct given by critical, unprejudiced and humane observers, who have had a lot of experience and take a lot of interest, tend to be both swift and reliable; those of inferior judges tend to be slower and less reliable. Similarly the marks awarded by practised and keen examiners who know their subject well and are reasonably sympathetic towards the candidates tend to be about right; those of inferior examiners tend to scatter more widely from the proper order. The point of these truisms is to remind us that in real life we are quite familiar with the techniques of assessing persons and accounting for their actions, though according to the standard theory no such techniques could exist.

There is one class of persons whose qualities and frames of mind are specially difficult to appreciate, namely persons who simulate qualities which they lack and dissimulate qualities which they possess. I refer to hypocrites and charlatans, the people who pretend to motives and moods and the people who pretend to abilities; that is, to most of us in some stretches of our lives and to some of us in most stretches of our lives. It is always possible to pretend to motives and abilities other than one's real ones, or to pretend to strengths of motives and levels of ability other than their real strengths and levels. The theatre could not exist, if it was not possible to make such pretences and to make them efficiently. It is, moreover, always possible for a person to take others or himself in by acting a part (as the spectators are not taken in at the theatre, since they have paid to see people act who advertise themselves as actors). At first sight it seems, then, that no one can ever have proper knowledge of his own mind, or of the minds of others, since there is no kind of observable behaviour of which we can say, 'no one could possibly be putting that on'. Certainly we do not ordinarily feel practically embarrassed by this possibility, but some people feel a theoretical embarrassment, since if any particular action or reaction might be a piece of shamming, might not every action or reaction be a piece of shamming? Might not all our appreciations of the conduct of others and of ourselves be uniformly deluded? People sometimes feel an analogous embarrassment about sense perception, for since there is nothing to prevent any particular sensible appearance from being an illusion, there seems to be nothing to prevent all of them from being illusions.

However, the menace of universal shamming is an empty menace. We know what shamming is. It is deliberately behaving in ways in which other people behave who are not shamming. To simulate contrition is to put on gestures, accents, words and deeds like those of people who are contrite. Both the hypocrite and the people whom he deceives must therefore know what it is like for someone to be contrite and not merely to be pretending to be contrite. If we were not usually correct in sizing up contrite people as contrite, we could not be gulled into thinking that the hypocrite was really contrite. Furthermore, we know what it is like to be hypocritical, namely to try to appear actuated by a motive other than one's real motive. We know the sorts of tricks the hypocrite must use. We possess, though we cannot always apply, the criteria by which to judge whether these tricks are being used or not and whether they are being used cleverly or stupidly. So sometimes we can, and sometimes we cannot, detect hypocrisies; but even when we cannot, we know what sorts of extra clues, if we could secure them, would betray the hypocrite. We should, for example, like to see how he would act if told that the cause for which he professed devotion required half his fortune or his life. All that we need, though we often cannot get it, is an *experimentum crucis*, just as the doctor often needs but cannot get an *experimentum crucis* to decide between two diagnoses. To establish hypocrisy and charlatanry is an inductive task which differs from the ordinary inductive tasks of assessing motives and capacities only in being a second order induction. It is trying to discover whether someone is trying to model his actions on what he and we have inductively discovered to be the behaviour of people who are not shamming. When we and the hypocrite have learned how hypocrisy is exposed, we might have to cope with the second order hypocrite, the double-bluffer who has learnt how not to act like a first order hypocrite. There is no mystery about shamming, though it is a tautology to say that skilful shamming is hard to detect and that successful shamming is undetected.

So far we have been considering chiefly those brands of self-knowledge and the knowledge of others which consist in the more or less judicial assessment of long-term propensities and capacities, together with the application of those assessments in explanations of particular episodes. We have been considering how we interpret or understand courses of conduct. But there remains

another sense of 'know' in which a person is commonly said to know what he is at this moment doing, thinking, feeling, etc., a sense which is nearer to what the phosphorescence-theory of consciousness tried, but failed, to describe. To bring out the force of this sense of 'know', we should consider first certain kinds of situations in which a person admits that he did not know at the time what he was doing, although what he was doing was not an automatism but an intelligent operation. A person trying to solve a cross-word puzzle is confronted by an anagram; after a short or long pause he gets the answer, but denies that he was aware of taking any specifiable steps, or following any specifiable method, to get it. He may even say that he was thinking, and knew that he was thinking, about some other part of the puzzle. He is in some degree surprised to find that he has got the answer to the anagram, for he had not been aware of going through any shuffling and reshuffling operations, or considering any of the unsuccessful rearrangements of the letters. Yet his solution is correct and he may repeat his success several times in the course of solving the whole puzzle. Our impromptu witticisms often take us by surprise in the same sort of way.

Now usually we are not surprised to catch ourselves having whistled, planned or imagined something and we say, if asked, that we are not surprised, because we knew we were doing these things, while we were doing them. What sort of a rider are we adding when we say 'I did so and so and knew at the time that I was doing it'? The tempting reply is to say 'Well, while I was doing the thing, it must have flashed or dawned upon me that I was doing it; or, if the action was a protracted one, it must have kept on flashing or dawning on me that I was doing the thing'. Yet these metaphors of flashing and dawning leave us uneasy, for we do not ordinarily recall any such occurrences, even when we are quite sure that we knew what we were doing, while we were doing it. Moreover, if there had occurred any such flashings or dawnings, the same question would arise once more. Did you know that you were getting these lightings-up, when they were on, and that you were not getting them, when they were not on? Did it flash on you that it was flashing on you that you were whistling? Or is your knowing that something is going on not always a matter of something flashing on you?

When a person is described as not being surprised when something takes place, he can also be described as having expected it or having been prepared for it. But we use 'expect' in at least two markedly different ways. Sometimes we mean that at a particular moment he considered and accepted the proposition that the event would, or would probably, take place; in this sense, there would be an answer to the question, 'Exactly when did you make this forecast?' But sometimes we mean that whether or not he ever went through the process of making such a forecast, he was continuously prepared or ready for the thing to happen. The gardener who, in this sense, expects rain need not be repeatedly switching his attention from gardening tasks to silent or vocal prognostications of rain; he just leaves the watering-can in the tool-shed, keeps his coat handy, beds out more seedlings, and so on. He anticipates the rain not by delivering occasional or incessant verbal presages, but by gardening appropriately. All the afternoon he is ready and making ready for rain. It may be objected, 'Oh, but he must be constantly considering the proposition that it will rain. That is what makes him keep his coat handy and the watering-pot in the shed.' But the answer to this is easy. 'Tell me at which particular moments he told himself or others that it was going to rain, and then tell me whether he was or was not expecting rain in the intervals between those prognostications.' He prognosticated rain at this, that and the other moment, because he was all the time expecting rain; and he kept his coat handy and the watering-can in the shed for the same reason. In this sense 'expect' is used to signify not an occurrence but a standing condition or frame of mind. He is all the afternoon in the frame of mind to say certain things in the future tense in certain contingencies, as well as to conduct his gardening-operations in certain ways, to keep his coat handy and so on. To expect, in this sense, is to be prepared; and the giving of warnings, private or public, is only one sort of precautionary measure among others. So when we say that the gardener was not taken by surprise by the rain, or that he was sure that it was going to rain, or that he was ready for rain, we are not referring, save *per accidens*, to any internal flashes of foresight, or to any silent or vocal utterances in the future tense. All his afternoon activities, horticultural and verbal, were performed in a rain-expectant frame of mind.

This lesson can be applied to our problem. There are many tasks in which we are from time to time engaged the execution of which requires continued application; doing the second step requires having done the first step. Sometimes the earlier steps stand to the later as means to ends, as we lay the table in order to have a meal. Sometimes the earlier steps stand in some other relation to the later; we do not eat the first course in order to eat the second, or begin to hum a tune in order to finish humming it. Very often an undertaking, though it requires consecutive application, is only artificially divisible into steps or stages, but it still remains significant to say that it might be broken off short, when only about half or about three-quarters accomplished. Now if the agent is carrying out such a serial operation with any degree of heed, he must at any given stage in it have in mind, in some sense, what is to be done next and what has already been done; he must have kept track of where he has got to and he must be expecting, or even intending, to be getting on to the stages after the present stage. This is sometimes expressed by saying that, in anyhow those serial undertakings that are more or less intelligently performed, the agent must have had from the start a plan or programme of what he is to do and he must continuously consult this plan as he progresses. And this does frequently happen. But it cannot always happen, and even when it does happen, this construction and consultation of programmes is not enough to explain the consecutive and methodical prosecution of the undertaking, since constructing and consulting plans are themselves serial operations intelligently and consecutively prosecuted, and it would be absurd to suggest that an infinite series of serial operations must precede the intelligent performance of any serial operation. Nor can intermittent consultation of a plan explain how we know what to be getting on with between the consultations, how we know which items of the plan to consult at different stages in the task, or how we know that what we are now doing is in accordance with the recently consulted plan.

The prime sense in which a person engaged in a non-sudden task has it in mind what is to be done at later stages is that he is ready to perform step three when the occasion requires, namely when step two is completed; and, what goes with this, that he is ready to tell himself or the world what he would have gone on to do, if he had not been prevented. While engaged in any given step, he is prepared for what should or may follow, and when it does follow, he is not surprised. In this sense he may be alive to what he is doing all the time he is doing it, even though his attention is concentrated on his task and is not divided between the task and any contemplations or chroniclings of his prosecution of it.

In other cases, as when he suddenly makes an unpremeditated witticism, he is surprised to find what he has done and would not describe himself as having known what he was doing, while he did it, or even as having been trying to make a joke. The same thing is true of other sudden acts performed on the spur of the moment. The action may well be the right action to have performed, but the agent does not know how he came to perform it, as he was unprepared for it. His being unprepared for it

is not the effect or the cause of his not knowing what he was doing; it is the same thing, differently expressed.

Unlike the man who with surprise catches himself making a good impromptu joke, the man who pursues a new argument is ordinarily alive to what he is doing. He may be surprised by the conclusion at which he arrives, but he is not surprised to find himself arriving at a conclusion. His progressive operation of reasoning was a display of his effort to reach one. So he knew what he was then doing, not in the sense that he had to dilute his consideration of his premises with other acts of considering his consideration of them—he need not have had any such side-issues flash or dawn upon him—but in the sense that he was prepared not only for the steps in reasoning that he was to take, but also for a variety of other eventualities, most of which never occurred, such as being asked what he was doing, what justification he had for taking this rather than that line, and so forth. The phosphorescence-theory of consciousness was in part an attempt to construe concepts of frames of mind like 'prepared', 'ready', 'on the *qui vive*', 'bearing in mind', 'would not be surprised', 'expect', 'realise' and 'alive to' as concepts of special internal happenings.

The same sort of account holds good of not-forgetting. When a person engaged in conversation reaches the middle of a sentence, he has ordinarily not forgotten how his sentence began. In some sense he keeps continuous track of what he has already said. Yet it would be absurd to suggest that he accompanies every word that he utters with an internal repetition of all its predecessors. Apart from the physical impossibility of reciting the previous seventeen words in the moment when the eighteenth word is just giving place to the nineteenth, the process of repetition is itself a serial operation, the execution of the later parts of which would again require that its author had kept track of its earlier parts. Not-to-have-forgotten cannot be described in terms of the performance of actual reminiscences; on the contrary, reminiscences are only one kind of exercise of the condition of not-having-forgotten. Bearing in mind is not recalling; it is what makes recalling, among other things, possible.

Thus the intelligent conduct of serial operations does entail that the agent is throughout the progress of the operation *au fait* both with what he has completed and with what remains to do, but it does not entail that the performance of such operations is backed up by any second order performance or process of monitoring the first order performance. Of course an agent can, from time to time, if he is prompted to do so, announce to himself or the world "Hallo, here I am whistling 'Home Sweet Home'." His ability to do so is part of what is meant by saying that he is in that particular frame of mind that we call 'being alive to what he is doing'. But not only is his actually making such announcements not entailed by the fact that he is concentrating on whistling this tune, but his concentration would be broken each time he produced such a commentary.

I have so far illustrated what I mean by a serial performance by such relatively brief operations as whistling a tune, or uttering a sentence. But in a slightly looser and more elastic sense, an entire conversation may be a serial performance; and so may be the conduct of one's work and recreation during a day or a year. Eating porridge is a non-sudden performance, but so is eating breakfast; giving a lecture is a serial performance, but so is giving a course of lectures.

Now in almost the same way as a person may be, in this sense, alive to what he is doing, he may be alive to what someone else is doing. In the serial operation of listening to a sentence or a lecture delivered by someone else, the listener, like the speaker, does not altogether forget, yet nor does he have constantly to recall the earlier parts of the talk, and he is in some degree prepared for the parts still to come, though he does not have to tell himself how he ex-

pects the sentence or lecture to go on. Certainly his frame of mind is considerably different from that of the speaker, since the speaker is, sometimes, creative or inventive, while the listener is passive and receptive; the listener may be frequently surprised to find the speaker saying something, while the speaker is only seldom surprised; the listener may find it hard to keep track of the course taken by the sentences and arguments, while the speaker can do this quite easily. While the speaker intends to say certain fairly specific things, his hearer can anticipate only roughly what sorts of topics are going to be discussed.

But the differences are differences of degree, not of kind. The superiority of the speaker's knowledge of what he is doing over that of the listener does not indicate that he has Privileged Access to facts of a type inevitably inaccessible to the listener, but only that he is in a very good position to know what the listener is often in a very poor position to know. The turns taken by a man's conversation do not startle or perplex his wife as much as they had surprised and puzzled his fiancée, nor do close colleagues have to explain themselves to each other as much as they have to explain themselves to their new pupils.

I have, for expository purposes, treated as separate things the way in which an ordinary person is ordinarily alive to what, at a particular moment, he is occupied with and the ways in which judicially minded persons assess the characters and explain the actions of others and of themselves. There are undoubtedly many big differences. To appraise or examine requires special gifts, interests training, experience, powers of comparison and generalisation, and impartiality; whereas merely to be alive to what one is whistling or where one is walking, is within the capacities of an ordinary child. None the less, the most naive knowledge of what one is doing shades into the most sophisticated appreciations of particular performances, much as the child's interest in the robins on the bird table shades into ornithology. A boy working out an arithmetical problem is alive in the most primitive way to what he is doing; for while he is thinking about numbers (and not about thinking about numbers), he does not forget the earlier stages of his reckoning, he bears in mind the rules of multiplication and he is not surprised to find himself arriving at the solution. But he differs only in degree of alertness, caution and sophistication from the boy who checks his results, from the boy who tries to find out where he has made a mistake, or from the boy who spots and explains the mistakes in the calculations of someone else; this last boy, again, differs only in degree from the co-operative parent, the professional teacher, or the examiner. The boy who is just capable of working out a simple sum is probably not yet able to state precisely what he is doing, or why he takes the steps that he takes; the examiner can evaluate the actual performances of the candidates in a fairly precise and highly formalised system of marks. But here again the inarticulateness of the beginner's knowledge of what he is doing shades by a series of gradations into the examiner's numerical appraisal code.

A person's knowledge about himself and others may be distributed between many roughly distinguishable grades yielding correspondingly numerous roughly distinguishable senses of 'knowledge.' He may be aware that he is whistling 'Tipperary' and not know that

he is whistling it in order to give the appearance of a sang-froid which he does not feel. Or, again, he may be aware that he is shamming sang-froid without knowing that the tremors which he is trying to hide derive from the agitation of a guilty conscience. He may know that he has an uneasy conscience and not know that this issues from some specific repression. But in none of the senses in which we ordinarily consider whether a person does or does not know something about himself, is the postulate of a Privileged Access necessary or helpful for the explanation of how he has achieved, or might have achieved, this knowledge. There are respects in which it is easier for me to get such knowledge about myself than to get it about someone else; there are other respects in which it is harder. But these differences of facility do not derive from, or lead to, a difference in kind between a person's knowledge about himself and his knowledge about other people. No metaphysical Iron Curtain exists compelling us to be for ever absolute strangers to one another, though ordinary circumstances, together with some deliberate management, serve to maintain a reasonable aloofness. Similarly no metaphysical looking-glass exists compelling us to be for ever completely disclosed and explained to ourselves, though from the everyday conduct of our sociable and unsociable lives we learn to be reasonably conversant with ourselves.

A Critique of Ryle
JOHN WISDOM

*T*his *paper* is not a review of Professor Ryle's book *The Concept of Mind* but it is an attempt to criticize and at the same time to continue it. Before coming to the criticism, may I say how much I admire the power, the simplicity

and the grace of Ryle's work. It is an achievement and a part of the progress of philosophy.

Wittgenstein said that we have the idea that the soul is a little man within, and also that we have the idea

FROM: "The Concept of Mind," *Proceedings of the Aristotelian Society,* (June 1950). Reprinted by permission of APS editor and the author.

that within us is a mental mechanism. Ryle says (p. 22) that he will be concerned with the dogma of the ghost in the machine. He has assembled a thousand instances to illustrate the influence and demonstrate the menace of the myth, the myths, of the hidden stream, the concealed mirrors, the private pictures, the invisible incidents, the flames of passion fanned by the winds of fancy.

I am not suggesting that Wittgenstein's treatment of the metaphysics of mind is not very different from Ryle's. (He did not neglect what Ryle never adequately recognizes, the difference between the method of verification of statements about thoughts and feelings and the method of verification of statements about the movements of wheels, levers, limbs, electricity and the wind that bloweth where it listeth, visible to none though we hear the sound of it.)

To come to the ghost, Stuart Hampshire, in his excellent review in *Mind* of Ryle's book, says that Ryle has given the impression that philosophers have foisted this myth, these myths, on the masses, and that this impression is a false one. He is right, surely? Philosophers have made us aware of the myth and in such a way as to increase its power, not free us from it. But it wasn't they who impregnated our talk and thought with this myth. And this is important to the explanation of its merits and demerits.

Hampshire points out that Ryle often draws attention to the evils of the myth in a misleading way. He says: "On what grounds does Professor Ryle decide that there are no acts 'answering to such verbs as "see," "hear," "deduce" and "recall" ' ". Ryle here has put his point in the old form: "There are no such things as so and so's"—compare "There is no such thing as matter", "Belief in the causal connexion is supersition", "There are no such things as infinite numbers", "There are no such things as numbers", "Universals do not exist", "We have the idea that the meaning of a word is an object" (Wittgenstein). Russell began to put part of Ryle's point when he

wrote "Empirically I cannot discover anything corresponding to the supposed act" (*Analysis of Mind*, p. 17). No sea serpents in the depths of the ocean, no acts behind the "presentational continuum" (an old phrase from Ward's *Principles of Psychology*).

The old form for putting a metaphysical point, namely, "There are no such things as so and so's", tempts people to object in the old inappropriate but powerful way in which Moore objected to "There are no material things". Moore said: "I have two thumbs. Thumbs are material things". It also tempts people to reply in the newer inappropriate way: "The question 'Are there any so and so's?' asked metaphysically is meaningless".[1]

Moore forces those who say "There are no so and so's" to hasten to explain that they mean "There are no so and so's over and above such and such's, that so and so's are nothing but such and such's, that so and so's are logical fictions though not fictions, that they are logical myths not myths. (This is still not what they mean but it is a great improvement.) And Ryle has explained that this is what he means to say. He writes (p. 22): ("I am not, for example, denying that there are mental processes. Doing long division is a mental process and so is making a joke. But I am saying that the phrase 'there occur mental processes' does not mean the same sort of thing as 'there occur physical processes', and therefore that it makes no sense to conjoin or disjoin the two.")

To conjoin or disjoin the two is to make what Ryle would call a "category mistake" comparable to that made by a child who, having observed the passing of men and guns, asks "And has the division passed, too?"

He says (p. 22): "The 'reduction' of the material world to mental states and processes, as well as the reduction of mental states and processes to physical states and processes presupposes the

---

[1] For example Carnap, "Revue Internationale de Philosophie," 15 Jan., 1950, p. 25.

legitimacy of the disjunction 'Either there exist minds or there exist bodies (but not both)' ". This shows that he does not mean by the reduction of X's to Y's the claim that there are not X's over and above Y's but the claim that there are no X's, only Y's. Thus the average man is not reducible, in Ryle's sense, to individual men. He does, however, often use words which suggest that he does wish to say that in the sense in which the average man is reducible to individual men the mind is reducible to the body, that in the sense in which the passing of a division is reducible to the passing of men and guns, mental processes are reducible to bodily processes, that consciousness is to its manifestations as electricity to its manifestations.

And now two things emerge—one is, I submit, a confusion and the second an inadequacy in Ryle's work—a serious inadequacy.

The confusion is one which has lasted since James' exposition of his theory of emotions and of thought. He didn't make clear whether what he was concerned with was the connexion between (1) statements about emotions and (2) statements about the bodily changes associated with emotions or with the connexion between (1) statements about emotions and (2^1) statements about the feelings and sensations of the bodily manifestations associated with emotions. It is true that statements only about the bodily changes associated with an emotion are not sharply separated from those which are also about the sensations of those changes. "He is shivering", even "His breathing is harsh", usually tell not only of bodily changes but also of how he feels though not when he is plainly under an anæsthetic. "He is walking very fast" many philosophers would call a description of bodily performance and "He is thinking about the trade cycle" a description of a mental performance. And yet both are both—like the novelist's "He turned away, his eyes filled with tears". Ryle sets this fact in the light. But though

many statements which philosophers would call descriptions of bodily performance are not merely that, and there are no statements about sensations to which nothing about bodily symptoms is relevant, it remains true that a philosopher who is concerned with "How do I know I am wishing for this, fearing that, thinking of so and so, since all I know is that my heart is fluttering or feels as if it is, that I have a sinking feeling, that I hear as it were a voice? How can I from these presentations that float on the stream of mental activity know the condition of the currents in it?" is concerned with a very different problem from that which concerns the philosopher who asks "How do I know from the fluttering of Bill's heart that he has a feeling as of his heart fluttering?"

There are two myths: the myth of the stream of pure spiritual activity on which or in which float patches of oil, sensations and images, and the myth of the inner, mental, spiritual, sensual, stream which drives the bodily machine and is in its turn affected by that machine. The reduction of the spiritual to the sensual is Sensationism about mental events. It corresponds to Sensationism about material events. The two combined give Neutral Monism. The reduction of the sensual and, with it, the spiritual to the material is Materialism. In both cases only when categorical statements about that which is to be reduced are presented as involving hypothetical statements about that to which it is reduced are the doctrines not obviously utterly absurd.

This brings us to the second point —Ryle's insufficient explanation of the purpose of his demonstration of the omnipresence in our minds of the model of the hidden stream, his insufficient explanation of the purpose and merits of that model, and the consequent insufficiency of his explanation of the defects of that model.

All this begins to emerge if we ask "What is the dispute between Ryle and Hampshire? One of them says 'Our language is riddled with the myth of the ghost in the machine', the other says 'Certainly, certainly our language is riddled with the myth of the ghost in the machine' ". Only the tone of voice is different.

Plain men and philosophers have continually presented the peculiarities in the way classes of statements are known as a peculiarity in their subject matters, as a peculiarity in the sorts of things to which they refer, that is, they have presented the peculiarities of the ultimate logical characters of statements in the form of myths of other worlds— the world of legend, the universe of fiction, the womb of Time, the realms of logical space. But what's the harm? What's the harm of a myth impregnating our language? And what is the harm of developing and rendering explicit that myth?

To plain men, by and large, no harm. It is true, perhaps, that for every class of statements there are outlying areas on the manifold of discussions in which they appear where the myth in them bedevils discussion. And with some classes of statements these areas are more important to us and larger than with other classes. This is true, I think, of ethical statements and also more than we realize of statements about minds. But exactly how it is that misleading models of statements about minds mislead discussion carried on *in* these statements it is not easy to bring out, any more than it is easy for a psycho-analyst to assemble in a moment the evidence to prove that a person is dominated and harmed by a model from the past, by the idea, for example, that They are all against me.

It is easier to bring out how a myth harms discussion *about* a class of statements, that is, it is easier to bring out how the myth suggested by a language in which a class of discussions is conducted befuddles those who step back and consider the discussions themselves—in short, metaphysicians. For the befuddlement shows in curious scepticism, in talking of a class of statements as myths without realizing that speak-

ing in this way one is misleadingly employing a myth—that of proving a myth a myth, that of proving harpies fictions.

Ryle, of course, realizes that minds aren't myths like harpies or sea serpents —that it is to use a myth to call them myths. And he says so. And his proof of the prevalence of the myth or myths he speaks of is not invalidated by his sometimes expressing himself in terms of that myth. The proofs a philosopher offers of "There are no integers" are not invalidated by the fact that he puts his point in terms of the very myth he purposes to extinguish. Ryle's point is that statements about minds are not related to what in the end gives a man a right to make them, as statements about a temporarily hidden mechanism to that which makes us guess it is present.

Nevertheless, it seems to me that Hampshire is not being merely doctrinaire when he claims that Ryle's exposition is in places obscured by being put in terms of the logical model the fascination of which it is designed to destroy and does destroy. Had Ryle put his point more often in terms of a misleading pattern for the ultimate logic of a class of statements he would have said more of the purpose of exposing the inadequacy of the pattern.

He may reply "The purpose of saying that our language is riddled with this myth is to say that our language is riddled with this myth; the purpose of saying that we continually talk as if the logic of statements about thoughts and feelings were what it is not is to say just that." He may say that he doesn't wish to put his point in the form "Philosophers, metaphysicians, have got into difficulties about how we know what we claim to know about minds. These difficulties are removed by noticing how we are dominated by the idea that a mind is a hidden stream".

Again Ryle may reply that my accusation is false and that he has made it clear that he aims to give such an apprehension of the logic of the soul that one will not be troubled by such questions as "How does a man know from the images and feelings which float on the surface of the stream of spiritual activity the currents in that stream or whether it exists at all? How does a man know from the behaviour and surroundings of another the feelings of the other?" "How does a mental state explain a bodily act?"

But I submit that he has not. The peculiarity of the soul is not that it is visible to none but that it is visible only to one. Unless we understand this we cannot understand why people have so persistently clung to the model for the logic of the soul which gives rise to scepticism not only about the mental acts of others but also about their aches and pains, feelings of quickened heart beats, sensations as of voices, daggers, snakes.

Ryle rightly stresses the fact that pictures in the mind are not like pictures in a gallery, that statements about what is in or on the mirror of the mind have a different logic from those about what is in the mirror on the mantle piece and that sensation, or the "observation of the presentational continuum," has a different logic from the observation of a film, and that knowledge that one is observing the presentational continuum or this or that in it, for example knowledge that one is seeing as it were snakes, has a different logic from knowledge that one is observing a film or this or that in it. He rightly insists that if we talk of sensations as observations and then of these observations as reasons, everything fails into confusion if we expect the same of these reasons as we expect of the reasons garnered from the observation of the scenes of a show.

I don't think he explains clearly *how* things fall into confusion and how solipsism and subjectivism are born, but that is not my point. My point is that, though the sources of solipsism are also sources of doubt about the minds of others, there is also a source of this doubt other than those sources of it which also lead to solipsism. And this source lies in the facts covered by the words "The soul is visible only to one".

What are these facts? They are the facts which lead people to say that a person has a way of knowing how he feels which no one else has, has a right to say what he does about how he feels which no one else has ever had or ever will have.

But what are the facts which have led them to say this? And do these facts justify the Sceptic in saying "No one but Bill really knows how Bill feels. No one but Bill has any real reason for saying anything about how Bill feels".

First, what are the facts which have led people to say that a man can know himself in a way others can't. They are the same as those which have led people to say that other people have a peculiar difficulty in knowing how a man feels.

One might think that the special facility and the special difficulty lie in the fact that while Bill, if he is in pain, has every right to say that Bill is in pain, Arabella has not because she is in pain the right to say Bill is in pain. Bill, when he feels a choking in his throat has a reason for saying he is angry, while Arabella has not because she has a choking in her throat a reason for saying that Bill is angry.

But isn't this an accident? Suppose Arabella, having a pain or a choking feeling, says with confidence "Bill is in pain" or "Bill is angry" and suppose that she is again and again right. We should say "Extraordinary thing, she knows *from* her own feelings that Bill is in pain or angry—as if she were Bill himself". Were she never to learn of the success of her telepathy we should not say that her confidence was reasoned and hardly that it was reasonable, any more than we say this of the young antelope who instinctively knows that lions are dangerous. But we should say that she had every reason for her confidence once she had learned of the unvaried correctness of her claims, like the antelope that has been repeatedly clawed. Again, from a sensation of snakes in blue or in a monogram B, I, L, Arabella might know that Bill was having a sensation as of snakes or was in for the horrors.

Under such circumstances we would say that Arabella has an extraordinary knowledge of Bill's mind, that she can see into his mind, that while the rest of us have to guess from external signs at what is in his mind, she can know what is in his mind as well as he can himself and in the way he does himself. Like Bill, because she has a sensation as of snakes, she has a right to say "Bill sees as it were snakes"; a choking feeling in her throat, angry words coming to her mind, give her the right to say "Bill is angry" as they do Bill himself; other pictures, other feelings, give her the right to say "Bill's in love".

But the philosophical sceptic says "Do they *as* they do Bill himself?" No doubt some people do, much more than others, know how another person is feeling by "feeling themselves into" the other person, and the connexion between this and telepathy deserves attention. But the question at the moment is "Does the philosophical sceptic when he says that a person, A, never really knows how another, B, feels refer to the fact that it seldom or never happens that one person knows the mind of another as we have imagined Arabella to know Bill's mind, that is altogether from feeling as she feels Bill feels?

And the answer is No. For in so far as a person is referring to this fact, whether or not he is right is to be settled by investigation and experiment, not by philosophical reflection. If someone says philosophically "One can never really know the mind of another, only the way he lays back his ears and frowns" and we say to him "That is upon the whole true but it is said that sometimes a person knows the mind of another without at all relying upon external signs and for good or ill this sort of thing may become more common", then the philosopher will reply "I don't think you quite understand. I am not denying that there occur the most striking instances of telepathy of a person knowing from his or her own feelings the mind of another. But such a person wouldn't be really and directly knowing the mind of another. Even one with such insight as Arabella's would not because she saw as it were snakes have that right to say that Bill sees as it were snakes which Bill has because he sees as it were snakes".

It might now be thought that what the philosopher refers to is the fact that while what gives Bill the right to say that he sees as it were snakes or is in for the horrors is *his* sensation of as it were snakes, what gives a telepathic person the right to say that Bill sees as it were snakes or is in for the horrors is *her* sensation of as it were snakes. I am sure that some sceptics about the minds of others would seek to prove their point this way. But this proof proves that no one really knows there's a snake in the grass just as much as it proves that no one really knows that there's a snake in Bill's mind. And therefore let us now ignore this proof; for we are concerned with a sceptic who finds in some feature of our knowledge of the mind of others a reason for saying that we never know the minds of others, which reason does not plunge him into solipsism and make him say we can never know whether or no there's a snake in the grass.

We must now again try to say what that feature is. It is this: while one can from one's own sensation as of a snake have a right to say that there is a snake in the grass *in the way any*one can, one cannot from one's own sensation as of a snake have a right to say that there is a snake in someone else's mind *in the way he* can because of his sensation as of a snake. And the familiar but complicated facts to which this refers are the following: Suppose that a certain person, Arabella, upon seeing as it were snakes, says "Bill sees as it were snakes". Upon being asked, Bill says he sees no such thing. Arabella is impressed by this but doesn't regard it as proving her wrong; instead she asks the rest of us whether we can see snakes, and when we say "Yes, we can," she says "There you are, Bill sees them". "But," we say, "look, he has blundered into them". "Ah," she says, "he saw them all right. I can see them, you can see them, the camera can see them. That settles it." In this story we have indeed arranged that Arabella shall know as well as Bill what Bill sees and that the rest of us can do so too. And with this we have arranged too much. For if Arabella uses the words "Bill sees as it were snakes" in the way described, then with them she makes a statement of a well-known sort, a statement whose familiar features now begin to show through its disguise, the statement "Snakes, real, live, snakes".

We must tell a different story if we are to tell one of how Arabella knows as well as Bill the snakes in his mind. We must tell a story in which it doesn't turn out that what she is talking about are real snakes. And we can easily do this. Suppose that Arabella, elated by many proofs of her telepathic powers, now on a new occasion says "Bill sees snakes". We ask Bill and he says he does not see snakes. We may, because of Arabella's past successes as a telepathist, suspect that Bill is lieing and that later he will say he did see snakes. But if he does not and this happens again and again and Arabella pays no more attention to the evidence we offer against her statements than she would have done had she made them of herself, then we say "When Arabella says 'Bill sees snakes', although she uses Bill's name, what she says amounts to 'I see snakes' or 'I see snakes and have a feeling about Bill'. She has lost her power of insight into Bill's mind and conceals this from us and from herself by using still the words 'Bill sees snakes' while using them in such a way that all that counts in a dispute as to whether he does is just the same as what counts in a dispute as to whether she does".

If we talk about Bill as Arabella does and ignore or treat lightly Bill's protests, then, of course, we may say, as she, perhaps, does, that she knows better than Bill how he feels or what he fancies.

"Exactly so," says the Sceptic, "when Arabella's statement becomes really one about herself she knows bet-

ter than anyone else whether it is right, but while it is still about Bill she doesn't know it to be right like she would were it about herself, that is, like Bill does."

It is true that the circumstances which make us say of a statement, S, made by A that A has a right to make it just like B has a right to make a statement about how things seem to him, are also the circumstances which make us say that S is not about how things seem to B but about how things seem to A. It thus appears that it is perfectly true that A cannot make a statement about how things seem to B and have a right to say it just like B has.

Now it is not unnatural to express this by saying that A never has that reason for a statement about how things seem to B which B has. And it is not unnatural to express this by saying that when one person makes a statement about the mind of another then he never has all the reason one could have for such a statement.

And this leads to "No one ever knows anything about the mind of another". For though we often speak of a person knowing something even when he hasn't all the reason he could have for what he says—for example, we say that a man knows that a stream is flowing because he sees the mill wheel turning—in these cases we speak of knowledge only because, though on the particular occasion in question the person of whom we speak hasn't all those reasons one could have for what he says, on other occasions he has been better placed and has had, not only the reasons he has on this occasion, but also those which one better placed would have— seen beneath the wheel the water. Further, it is only because one who sees a mill wheel turning has on other occasions had other reason to say that the water is high to-day that we allow that now seeing the mill wheel turning, he has a right to say "The water's high to-day".

Now we have said that no one who makes a statement about the mind of another *ever* has right to make it which that other has, that therefore he never has had all the reason one could have for the statement he makes.

It is tempting to infer that no one ever knows anything about the mind of another and even that no one ever has any right to assert anything about the mind of another, since it is not true of him that on some other occasion he has been better placed and had then the reason, the ground, the data, the premiss, he now lacks.

But we must notice that if we express the facts referred to by the soul is visible only to one by saying that a person, A, never has all the right, all the reason, one could have for a statement about the mind of B, then we are using these words here very differently from the way we use them when we say of one who sees only a mill wheel that he hasn't on this occasion all the reason one could for what he says about the mill stream. One who sees only the mill wheel could have all the reason one could have for what he says about the stream and could have all the reason he could have for what he says about the stream. One, A, who has all the reason one ever has for a statement about the mind of another, B, couldn't have all the reason one could have for what he says—not in the sense of "has all the reason one could have" which requires that he should have the reason B has, in the sense which requires that, like B, he need not look to the face of another for confirmation of what he says. For such a requirement guarantees that what he says is not about another but about himself. When we say of one who sees only the mill wheel that he hasn't all the reason one could have for what he says about the stream one contrasts him with someone better placed. But if because of the facts about statements about the minds of others of which the Sceptic reminds us we say that no one ever has all the right one could have, all the reason one could have, for a statement about the mind of another, then we contrast ourselves with no one, in earth or heaven. If we use has "all the right

he could have" in the way the Sceptic does, then "A has all the right he could have for a statement about the mind of B" becomes self-contradictory. And if we wed in the usual way "has all the reason he could have" to "has all the right he could have" then "A has all the reason he could have for a statement about the mind of B" becomes self-contradictory. And if we then wed in the usual way "knowledge" to "sometimes has all the reason he could have", then "A has knowledge of the mind of B" becomes self-contradictory and the paradox that no one ever knows the mind of another a necessary truth.

It is not unnatural to describe the facts about the usage of statements about people, particularly about what is in their minds as opposed to what is in their stomachs, by saying that the person the statement is about can have a right to make it which no one else has. It is tempting then to say that the person the statement is about can have reason to make it which no one else can have. It is tempting then to say that he can know the statement to be true in a way no one else can and then to say that no one else can really know it to be true. But we do not in fact in connexion with statements about thoughts and feelings use the expression "has all the right *a* person could have" like we use "has just the sort of right some person could have, including the person it is about"; still less do we use "has all the right *one* could have" in this way; still less do we use "has all the right *he* could have" in this sense in which no one could have all the right he could have. Nor do we use "has all the reason one could have in this way". Still less do we use "one knows how he feels" in this way, that is, in such a way that one could not, because one could not without having reason for saying it in that sense in which it is senseless to say that one could. That is, we do not use these expressions in such a way that "No one has real right, real reason, to make, real knowledge of, statements about the minds of others" is a necessary truth. In other words, when in the course of life we say "Arabella knows how Bill feels, Clarissa does not" we do not mean to deny that, were Arabella to make a statement about how Bill feels according to how *she* feels just as Bill does according to how *he* feels then she would be making a statement not about Bill but about herself. So if we express the fact that it is ridiculous to speak of her doing this by saying that Arabella must always lack reason Bill could have and therefore reason one could have, for statements about the mind of Bill, we must remember that this form of words means the facts it refers to and no more, and that these are not facts from which it follows that she never knows the thoughts and feelings in Bill's mind. When we claim that someone knows the thoughts and feelings of another we do not deny any of those facts about what ultimately gives a right to make statements about thoughts and feelings to which the Sceptic draws our attention. And therefore what the Sceptic says does not show that what we claim could not be true nor that what we claim is false.

This does not show that what we claim is true, it does not settle the question whether sometimes we do know what is in the mind of another. This is a question of fact and not of philosophy. But the fact is we do.

Mind
and
Body

Are the Mind
and the Body
Distinct?

Descartes offers in "Meditation Six," two arguments for the claim that the mind is one type of substance and the body another type of substance. If this contention is true, then no mind is identical with any body (and, of course, conversely). So the fact that the body of a given person died and decayed would not entail that the person ceased to exist; his mind could continue to exist, either disembodied or associated with some other body.

One of Descartes' arguments can be stated in this fashion: (1) If *A* can be conceived without *B*, God can create *A* but not create *B*; (2) if God can create *A* without creating *B*, then *A* can exist even if *B* does not; (3) that a mind exists can be conceived without conceiving that a body exists; so (4) God can create a mind without creating a body; therefore (5) a mind can exist without a body existing—and so of course a mind can exist without a body being associated with it.

Descartes' other argument runs essentially as follows: (1) If "*A* has property *P*" is intelligible and true, whereas "*B* has property *P*" is unintelligible or self-contradictory, then *A* and *B* are different types (kinds) of things; (2) "Body *B* is divisible" is, for any body you please, both intelligible and true, whereas "Mind *A* is divisible" is unintelligible or contradictory; so: (3) minds and bodies are different types (kinds) of things. This argument provides a pattern for many others. While (2) depends on bodies being spatial and minds being nonspatial, one could argue on the same model that minds are essentially thinking entities and bodies are nonthinking, and so on.

John Locke does not deny that mind and body are distinct. He does doubt that our concepts of mind and body, or of mental substance and physical substance, are sufficiently clear for us to say with certainty that nothing can be both mental and physical.

Brand Blanshard offers a detailed critique of materialism or behaviorism. His arguments are of various sorts: one way of showing that two things are distinct is by showing that one can exist without another; and one way of showing this is by showing that one *does* exist without the other. In exactly this manner Blanshard claims that speech and thought are distinct and so the version of behaviorism that identifies them is mistaken. This portion of Blanshard's argument appeals to facts concerning language use, introspective experience, and psychological experiments.

Another position appeals to a quite different type of consideration. Thoughts can be true or false, insightful or stupid, whereas the movement of atoms or impulses can be none of these. On the other hand, atoms or impulses have velocity and location (at least *en masse*), while thoughts have neither. Two points are involved here. One is that thoughts and the motions of material things must be discussed in logically different terms. They can only receive different predicates, and they require different sorts of descriptions; so they belong to different categories. The importance of claims that one thing belongs to a different category than another and the difficulty of making these claims clear are notorious in philosophy; both importance and difficulty are illustrated in the denials by Descartes, Blanshard, and Ducasse, but affirmation by Locke and Taylor that "Bodies think" is an intelligible or nonabsurd expression. For the latter pair it is at least as clear as "Minds think"; for the former trio it (as opposed to "Minds think") is precisely as intelligible as "Triangles sing beautifully." A second point is that since things that can be said truly of thoughts cannot be said truly of movements, these necessarily cannot be the same thing. As against any attempt simply to identify thoughts and movements in such way that one can legitimately say that three-sided figures are identical to three-angled figures, these arguments of Blanshard seem quite conclusive.

There are other criticisms that Blanshard makes of materialism—for example, that if it were true, it could not account for the existence of such views as those of Descartes (and, for that matter, of Blanshard), that it is a self-defeating position, and so on. While these further criticisms will not be considered here, an interesting and important exercise for the reader would be to consider whether Blanshard's arguments are, or could be altered so as to be, refutations of every sort of materialism.

Richard Taylor, who defends materialism, responds to the type of argument that Blanshard offers and raises what he takes to be a conclusive objection to dualism. By way of reply to Blanshard, Taylor makes explicit Locke's doubts about the possibility that matter is capable of thinking. It is not, Taylor insists, conceptually absurd that matter can think. The most precise notion, he suggests, that we have of a mental substance is that it is "that which thinks." No property that material substance has prevents it from satisfying his description. Further, it is simpler to posit just one sort of substance (material) rather than two (mental and material). So materialism is superior. (Of course, idealism also has the advantage of being simpler than dualism and as simple as materialism, but Taylor devotes little time to idealism, perhaps because not many philosophers today are idealists).

Of course, the greater simplicity of materialism over dualism is a reason to accept materialism (if it is a reason at all) only if there is no reason to accept dualism rather than materialism. Taylor denies that there are any such reasons. The only plausible version of dualism, Taylor insists, is interactionism— the view that there is mutual causal commerce between minds and bodies.

Taylor raises two basic objections to this view: (a) it is unintelligible that two kinds of things so radically different as minds and bodies are conceived to be by the dualist should ever causally affect one another; (b) one can trace back a given bodily event to bodily causes in an enormously complex causal chain, the complexity of which is limited only by the present condition of our knowledge and which is so exhaustive as to rule out any necessity of, or room for, appeal to mental causes.

We have already discussed the clash between Blanshard and Taylor as to whether "Bodies think" does or does not express a possibility. The type of criticisms of (interactionistic) dualism that Taylor raises are discussed by C. J. Ducasse.

Ducasse defends dualism in these terms: (1) We do unquestionably designate some things (rocks, trees, human bodies, for example) as physical or material, other things (for instance, images, desires, moods, and memories) as psychical or mental; (2) those designated material are sensibly observable by more than the perceiver (or are conceived as elements composing such objects— as are electrons, protons, and neutrons), while those designated mental are introspectively observable only by those whose states or characteristics they are; (3) the sense in which a given mental image is private is this: it is logically impossible that anyone observe (introspectively) numerically the same image that I observe, whereas, say, the amount of digestive juices in my stomach at a given moment is in principle sensorily observable by myself or another; (4) the fact that my mental states are private to me does not mean that only I can know that I have them, for (a) I may tell others about them or (b) others may infer my mental states from my behavior and/or my physical states; (5) terms such as "anger," "fear," "remembering that . . .," particularly when one uses them about oneself, "denote . . . the particular kind of inherently private event . . . which *he* is experiencing at the time." These, Ducasse suggests, are the facts, or at least what certainly seem to be the facts, of the matter. Unless there are powerful theoretical considerations to the contrary, they should be accepted at face value.

What might such considerations be? Well, the various versions of behaviorism, Ducasse suggests, have in common the thesis that "the causes of the behavior of organisms, including human organisms, *are never other than physical.*" And this will be an eminently plausible claim if any attempt to produce a psychical cause for a physical effect produces an incoherent statement. This will be so if it is inconceivable that any psychical event be related causally to any physical event. But, Ducasse affirms, "The causality relation . . . does not presuppose at all that its cause-term and its effect-term both belong to the same ontological category [for example, physical], but only that both of them be events." Further, it will not do, Ducasse suggests, to say that it is impossible to understand how a mental event can cause a physical one (or conversely) since "the question as to the 'how' of causation of a given event by a given other event never has any other sense than *through what intermediary causal steps* does the one cause the other." If an event *A* directly causes an event *B*, the question "*How* does *A* cause *B*?" does not arise. Otherwise put, Ducasse's point is that some cases of causal connection will, on any view, necessarily be "brute facts"—that is, not to be explained in terms of other causal connections. There is no theoretical reason why mental-physical or physical-mental cause-effect relations may not be among these.

Another theoretical consideration that might cause us not to take the apparent facts noted above at face value is that the claim that mental events cause physical events seems to entail that energy enters the physical universe and the claim that physical events cause mental events seems to entail that energy leaves the physical universe. That energy either enters or leaves the physical universe violates the principle of conservation of energy widely accepted among scientists, that the total amount of energy in the physical universe is always constant.

With respect to this issue Ducasse makes three points: (a) The *status* of the principle is itself a debatable issue—is it a methodological assumption or a truth about the physical universe? It presupposes that the physical universe is a closed system, if this assumption is false, then the principle of the conservation of energy is only a heuristic principle. (b) It is possible that whenever, due to mental-physical or physical-mental causation, energy leaves or enters the physical universe, an exactly proportionate amount of energy enters or leaves. But at best this would be an *ad hoc* position; no one would, presumably, adopt the view that energy spontaneously comes and goes unless he were concerned to defend a thesis at almost any cost. (c) As "causality" is not to be defined in terms of "energy," it is possible that not all causation involves any transfer of energy, and any causation that did not involve transfer of energy would not, of course, violate the principle of conservation of energy. Ducasse closes his essay by noting some difficulties with dualism's competitors.

An Argument That Mind and Body Are Distinct
RENÉ DESCARTES

And first of all, since I know that all things which I clearly and distinctly understand can be made by God just as I understand those things, it suffices for me to be certain that one thing is different from another that I can clearly and distinctly understand one without the other because at the least, God can make one apart from the other. It makes no difference by which power God does this, that the two things be regarded as distinct. So, from the mere fact that I know that I exist and that meanwhile, I observe that nothing else obviously pertains to my nature or essence than that I am a thinking thing, I correctly conclude that my essense consists only in this one thing, that I am a thinking thing. And although *perhaps* (or rather as I shall fervently say *for certain*), I have a body, which is very closely conformed with me, still because, on the one hand I have a clear and distinct idea of myself insofar as I am merely a thinking thing and non-extended, and on the other hand, I have a distinct idea of body insofar as it is merely a non-thinking extended thing, I am certain that I am truly distinct from my body and could exist without it.

That Body Might Be Able to Think
JOHN LOCKE

Knowledge, as has been said, lying in the perception of the agreement or disagreement of any of our ideas, it follows from hence, That,

First, we can have knowledge no further than we have *ideas.*

Secondly, That we can have no knowledge further than we can have *perception* of that agreement or disagreement. Which perception being: 1. Either by *intuition*, or the immediate comparing any two ideas; or, 2. By *reason*, examining the agreement or disagreement of two ideas, by the intervention of some others; or, 3. By *sensation*, perceiving the existence of particular things: hence it also follows:

Thirdly, That we cannot have an *intuitive knowledge* that shall extend itself to all our ideas, and all that we would know about them; because we cannot examine and perceive all the relations they have one to another, by juxta-position, or an immediate comparison one with another. Thus, having the ideas of an obtuse and an acute angled triangle, both drawn from equal bases, and between parallels, I can, by intuitive knowledge, perceive the one not to be the other, but cannot that way know whether they be equal or no; because their agreement or disagreement in equality can never be perceived by an immediate comparing them: the difference of figure makes their parts incapable of an exact immediate application; and therefore there is need of some intervening qualities to measure them by, which is demonstration, or rational knowledge.

Fourthly, It follows, also, from what is above observed, that our *rational*

FROM: *Meditations on First Philosophy*, Meditation Six; J. R. Weinberg trans. (Adam and Tannery, VII, 78¹–78²⁰, originally published in 1641).

FROM: *Essays Concerning Human Understanding*, Book IV, Ch. 3 (originally published in 1960).

knowledge cannot reach to the whole extent of our ideas: because between two different ideas we would examine, we cannot always find such mediums as we can connect one to another with an intuitive knowledge in all the parts of the deduction; and wherever that fails, we come short of knowledge and demonstration.

Fifthly, *Sensitive knowledge* reaching no further than the existence of things actually present to our senses, is yet much narrower than either of the former.

Sixthly, From all which it is evident that the *extent of our knowledge* comes not only short of the reality of things, but even of the extent of our own ideas. Though our knowledge be limited to our ideas, and cannot exceed them either in extent or perfection; and though these be very narrow bounds, in respect of the extent of All-being, and far short of what we may justly imagine to be in some even created understandings, not tied down to the dull and narrow information that is to be received from some few, and not very acute, ways of perception, such as are our senses; yet it would be well with us if our knowledge were but as large as our ideas, and there were not many doubts and inquiries *concerning the ideas we have*, whereof we are not, nor I believe ever shall be in this world resolved. Nevertheless, I do not question but that human knowledge, under the present circumstances of our beings and constitutions, may be carried much further than it has hitherto been, if men would sincerely, and with freedom of mind, employ all that industry and labour of thought, in improving the means of discovering truth, which they do for the colouring or support of falsehood, to maintain a system, interest, or party they are once engaged in. But yet after all, I think I may, without injury to human perfection, be confident, that our knowledge would never reach to all we might desire to know concerning those ideas we have; nor be able to surmount all the difficulties, and resolve all the questions that might arise concerning any of them. We have the ideas of a *square*, a *circle*, and *equality*; and yet, perhaps, shall never be able to find a circle equal to a square, and certainly know that it is so. We have the ideas of *matter* and *thinking*, but possibly shall never be able to know whether [any mere material being] thinks or no; it being impossible for us, by the contemplation of our own ideas, without revelation, to discover whether Omnipotency has not given to some systems of matter, fitly disposed, a power to perceive and think, or else joined and fixed to matter, so disposed, a thinking immaterial substance: it being, in respect of our notions, not much more remote from our comprehension to conceive that GOD can, if he pleases, superadd to matter *a faculty of thinking*, than that he should superadd to it *another substance with a faculty of thinking*; since we know not wherein thinking consists, nor to what sort of substances the Almighty has been pleased to give that power, which cannot be in any created being, but merely by the good pleasure and bounty of the Creator. For [I see no contradiction in it, that the first Eternal thinking Being, or Omnipotent Spirit, should, if he pleased, give to certain systems of created senseless matter, put together as he thinks fit, some degrees of sense, perception, and thought: though, as I think I have proved, lib. iv. ch. 10, § 14, &c., it is no less than a contradiction to suppose matter (which is evidently in its own nature void of sense and thought) should be that Eternal first-thinking Being. What certainty of knowledge can any one have, that some perceptions, such as, e.g., pleasure and pain, should not be in some bodies themselves,] after a certain manner modified and moved, as well as that they should be in an immaterial substance, upon the motion of the parts of body: Body, as far as we can conceive, being able only to strike and affect body, and motion, according to the utmost reach of our ideas, being able to produce nothing but motion; so that when we allow it to produce pleasure or pain, or the idea of a colour or sound, we are fain to quit our reason, go beyond our ideas, and attribute it wholly to the good pleasure of our Maker. For, since we must allow He has annexed effects to motion which we can no way conceive motion able to produce, what reason have we to conclude that He could not order them as well to be produced in a subject we cannot conceive capable of them, as well as in a subject we cannot conceive the motion of matter can any way operate upon? I say not this, that I would any way lessen the belief of the soul's immateriality: I am not here speaking of probability, but knowledge; and I think not only that it becomes the modesty of philosophy not to pronounce magisterially, where we want that evidence that can produce knowledge; but also, that it is of use to us to discern how far our knowledge does reach; for the state we are at present in, not being that of vision, we must in many things content ourselves with faith and probability: and in the present question, about the Immateriality of the Soul, if our faculties cannot arrive at demonstrative certainty, we need not think it strange. All the great ends of morality and religion are well enough secured, without philosophical proofs of the soul's immateriality; since it is evident, that he who made us at the beginning to subsist here, sensible intelligent beings, and for several years continued us in such a state, can and will restore us to the like state of sensibility in another world, and make us capable there to receive the retribution he has designed to men, according to their doings in this life. [And therefore it is not of such mighty necessity to determine one way or the other, as some, over-zealous for or against the immateriality of the soul, have been forward to make the world believe. Who, either on the one side, indulging too much their thoughts immersed altogether in matter, can allow no existence to what is not material: or who, on the other side, finding not *cogitation* within the natural powers

of matter, examined over and over again by the utmost intention of mind, have the confidence to conclude—That Omnipotency itself cannot give perception and thought to a substance which has the modification of solidity. He that considers how hardly sensation is, in our thoughts, reconcilable to extended matter; or existence to anything that has no extension at all, will confess that he is very far from certainly knowing what his soul is. It is a point which seems to me to be put out of the reach of our knowledge: and he who will give himself leave to consider freely, and look into the dark and intricate part of each hypothesis, will scarce find his reason able to determine him fixedly for or against the soul's materiality. Since, on which side soever he views it, either as an *unextended substance*, or as a *thinking extended matter*, the difficulty to conceive either will, whilst either alone is in his thoughts, still drive him to the contrary side. An unfair way which some men take with themselves: who, because of the inconceivableness of something they find in one, throw themselves violently into the contrary hypothesis, though altogether as unintelligible to an unbiassed understanding. This serves not only to show the weakness and the scantiness of our knowledge, but the insignificant triumph of such sort of arguments; which, drawn from our own views, may satisfy us that we can find no certainty on one side of the question: but do not at all thereby help us to truth by running into the opposite opinion; which, on examination, will be found clogged with equal difficulties. For what safety, what advantage to any one is it, for the avoiding the seeming absurdities, and to him unsurmountable rubs, he meets with in one opinion, to take refuge in the contrary, which is built on something altogether as inexplicable, and as far remote from his comprehension? It is past controversy, that we have in us *something* that thinks; our very doubts about what it is, confirm the certainty of its being, though we must content ourselves in the ignorance of what *kind* of being it is: and it is in vain to go about to be sceptical in this, as it is unreasonable in most other cases to be positive against the being of anything, because we cannot comprehend its nature. For I would fain know what substance exists, that has not something in it which manifestly baffles our understandings. Other spirits, who see and know the nature and inward constitution of things, how much must they exceed us in knowledge? To which, if we add larger comprehension, which enables them at one glance to see the connexion and agreement of very many ideas, and readily supplies to them the intermediate proofs, which we by single and slow steps, and long poring in the dark, hardly at last find out, and are often ready to forget one before we have hunted out another; we may guess at some part of the happiness of superior ranks of spirits, who have a quicker and more penetrating sight, as well as a larger field of knowledge.]

The Body Is Not Able to Think
BRAND BLANSHARD

The theory that thought 'is the action of language mechanisms' may easily be shown mistaken. It has one kind of defender, however, to whom the argument that follows is not addressed. If a man insists stolidly and unwaveringly that when he speaks of pleasure or pain, reflection or emotion, all he means by these words is certain bodily changes, and that he has not the slightest notion what is meant when anyone uses them in any other sense, argument becomes unprofitable. The only way to dislodge him is to show that he sometimes speaks and acts as if he meant something else than what he claims, but if he insists that he has meant one thing all along, there is nothing more to be done. It is not that he has won the argument; he would be equally beyond dislodging if he held consistently that whenever he spoke of the moon he meant a round of green cheese. You cannot persuade a person that he is confusing two things if he fails to see, or refuses to see, that there are two things to confuse. But to the mind of average keenness and candour who has felt leanings toward behaviourism, it can easily be shown, I think, that the identification of thought with language mechanism runs flatly counter to his experience, and indeed is as strictly unthinkable as the identification of black with white.

In order to be as clear as may be, we shall set out the argument formally. We shall show briefly (1) that language may vary while thought remains the same; (2) that thought may vary while language remains the same; (3) that language may be present while thought is absent; (4) that thought may be present while language is absent. These considerations are not so much arguments as helps to the clarification of one's own meaning. They show that if behaviourism is true, we are all talking nonsense most of the time, and that if we really mean what we normally think we mean, then we cannot believe behaviourism, no matter how hard we try.

(1) First, then, language may vary while thought is the same. Suppose that an American, a German, and a Frenchman are all regarding a youthful and charming member of the opposite sex. 'Very pretty', comments the American. 'Sehr hübsch', remarks the German. 'Très jolie', exclaims the Frenchman.

FROM: *The Nature of Thought*, Brand Blanshard. (London: George Allen and Unwin, Ltd., 1939), Chapter 7, Sections 6–20. Reprinted by permission of George Allen and Unwin, Ltd.

The three sounds they have uttered and the vocal reactions involved in them have been exceedingly different. If such reaction *is* the thought, the thought should have been different. But anyone who was not defending a theory at all costs would say what the plain man would say, that they all had the same thought, but were expressing it in different ways. And if this is true, speech and thought are not the same.[1]

(2) Thought may vary while speech remains the same. We may repeat an illustration from James. One writes the French words, Pas de lieu Rhone que nous, and asks a student to read them aloud. He says something like 'Paddle your own canoe', and then with a little shock of realization, 'Why, that's "paddle your own canoe!"' How is this shock to be accounted for on behaviourist principles? So far as the language mechanism is concerned, these two utterances are the same. There should not, therefore, be anything in the way of thought involved in the second that was not involved in the first. But there obviously is. It is precisely the fact that between the first utterance and the second the words have acquired a meaning that causes the surprise and amusement. One may of course explain that the two utterances have obscure connections, neural and muscular, which differ in the two cases, and that it is this difference in what is conditioned by the two expressions that constitutes the difference in meaning. But this is merely an abandonment of the view in question, that thought is to be identified with the process of speech. Whether it is an eligible retreat will be examined later.

(3) Language mechanisms may be at work where thought is not. The case last cited shows this also, but other examples are plentiful. Is the repetition

[1] 'Let a man make to himself the idea of a figure with three angles, whereof one is a right one, and call it, if he pleases, *equilaterum* or *trapezium*, or anything else, the properties of and demonstrations about that idea will be the same as if he called it a "rectangular triangle".' Locke, *Essay*, Bk. IV, Chap. 4, sec. 9.

of nonsense syllables thinking? It may be said that such repetition is not speech, but I do not know how the case would be made out except through insistence on a differentia of speech, namely meaningfulness, that would give the case away. Is the person who talks in his sleep thinking in precisely the same sense as when he is uttering the same words awake? When the servant girl mentioned by Coleridge repeated in delirium Hebrew passages, heard many years before in a rabbi's study and registered in her memory without ever being understood, was she *thinking* in precisely the same sense as the rabbi who originally uttered them? For that matter, cannot a parrot talk? It certainly has 'language mechanisms' that come into play with all degrees of 'implicitness' and 'explicitness'. Is it therefore thinking? But the view that since thinking *is* talking it is impossible to talk without thinking is so very odd and invites such unseemly pleasantries that it is perhaps better not to pursue the matter further.

(4) Thought may be present without speech. Since this point seems at once more questionable and more interesting than the last, it may be worth while to develop it a little more amply. It can be demonstrated in more ways than one. (i) We said long ago that we must be taken to think whenever we judge, i.e. whenever we accept or affirm anything as true or false. And it has been shown that such judgement is indubitably present in perception. But not even a behaviourist would say that whenever we recognize a road or building, or identify our own hat in a collection, the process consists of *sotto voce* speech. It is useless to insist that this might be proved by further experimentation. Experimentation will never prove that when I walk into a room and recognize at a glance three or four of my friends who are present, my vocal organs are naming them all simultaneously, or that when a lecturer in midcourse perceives an acquaintance in the crowd, his vocal mechanism can perform at once two incompatible tasks. Thus, even if it were true that all

processes of explicit inference entailed the use of speech organs, it would still remain true that in perception there may be no trace of this. And since perception involves thought, thought may be present without language.

(ii) But is it true that explicit inference always does involve speech reactions? There is no good evidence for this whatever. Let us look at one of the commonest conditions under which inference is performed. A reader who follows understandingly any book on economics, philosophy, or law, is compelled to make numerous inferences; he is as truly performing an act of reasoning in following another's argument as if he had proceeded on his own initiative by a stumbling process of trial and error, though of course the process is easier. Now is it true that when I read an argument in print, I follow it invariably through sub-vocal speech? What we have seen already of the place of imagery in thinking would certainly not lead us to expect this. We saw that as we pass from mind to mind the types and amounts of imagery that serve to carry a meaning differ immensely, and that the sort of mind in which motor cues predominate, such as the sensation or image of vocal movement, is only one type among several.[2] It is possible, Galton showed, for a mind to use habitually a certain type of imagery at the start and gradually abandon it in favour of another type, or even in favour of thinking in which no imagery at all is introspectively discernible. Our present problem is very similar, though the question is not now whether the *image or sensation* of sub-vocal speech is always present when thinking occurs, but whether the act of speech itself is always so present; for if it is not, then speech and thought cannot be the same. This question is not to be settled by a priori considerations. Fortunately it has often been investigated, both through introspection and through instruments. Professor J. A. O'Brien, who has compiled a useful bibliography on the matter,[3] shows that while earlier investigators were inclined to think that all reading was attended by sub-vocal speech, later inquiry has brought to light many partial or complete exceptions. 'L'homme fait, qui lit silenceusement, accompagner chaque perception visuelle d'un mouvement secret d'articulation', wrote Ribot in 1879. Egger, two years later, writes, 'Lire, en effet, c'est traduire l'écriture en parole', and the German psychologist, Stricker, writing about the same time, agreed. Stumpf, Paulhan, and Baldwin, a few years later, 'agree with Stricker that abridged articulatory movements are usually present, but that they are necessary, or even, *de facto*, always present, they deny'.[4] Stricker had held that to think of a word, one must more or less sketchily pronounce it. Stumpf replied that if this were true, one would need to sing a note to recall it, whereas one could recall it without this; 'ohne lautes, leises oder stilles Singen kann ich verschidene Tone vorstellen'. Baldwin went further and said that while imagining a note of a given pitch, he could vocalize another of a different pitch. Pintner, in 1915, reported a similar fact about speech. He asked certain subjects to read silently, and at the same time to count aloud a series of numbers, 13, 14, 15, 16, etc.; and this proved entirely possible. Now if, as the behaviourist says, thought is speech, one would suppose the only thought concerned lay in the

[2] Graham Wallas writes: 'Some of the most completely conscious and most rational thought may be carried on entirely by the use of wordless images. A very able and rapid financial thinker, who was trained as a mathematician, told me that even when his thought is most conscious and rational he thinks, like a chess-player, in terms of seen or felt wordless "situations". The wordless images of such a "situation" may be purely "kinetic", with little or no visual element. The chess correspondent of the *Observer* (February 8, 1925) writes that the great chess-player Alekine said that "he does not see the pieces in his mind, as pictures, but as *force symbols*; that is as near as one can put it in words".' *The Art of Thought*, 72.

[3] In his *Silent Readings*, 1925. I am indebted to this book for the historical facts in this paragraph.

[4] *Silent Reading*, 104.

reciting of the numbers. But it clearly did not, since the subjects were taking the meaning of the passages while their mechanisms of language were otherwise engaged.[5]

(iii) The behaviourist view becomes still less plausible when abnormal cases are considered. In cases of motor aphasia, the articulatory movements of speech are cut off through paralysis, though the patient may continue to read and follow the thought. How could he do this if the process of thought really lapsed with the process of speech?[6]

(iv) Another line of investigation that bears on this matter may be men-

tioned both for its theoretical and its practical interest. Some persons, as everyone knows, are able to read much faster than others. Macaulay remarked in his diary that he seemed to be able to read a book as fast as most men would skim it, and to skim it as fast as most men would turn the pages. 'A university friend', writes Huey, 'a mathematician, informs me that he has read the whole of a standard novel of 320 pages in two and one-fourth hours.'[7] Titchener remarks upon this statement, 'I should not have supposed that the rate of reading mentioned by Huey was exceptional; I certainly often read at the same or a higher speed.'[8] On the other hand, there are many persons who read little if any faster than if they were using the same words in talking. How account for this disparity? There are many causes for slow reading, from deficient ocular span to deficient general intelligence; but certainly one of the commonest causes is the habit of sub-vocal speech. The reader articulates to himself as he goes along, and hence his reading is retarded to about the speed of his speaking.[9] Now since the eye can take in words much faster than the tongue can pronounce them, it occurred to some investigators that by a change from speech to reading to sight reading they might increase their rate. And this they did with marked success, both for themselves and for students whom they trained. O'Brien assigned to six grades of school children a programme of daily exercises to decrease vocalization in reading, and in thirty-nine school days increased their rate of reading 56 per cent, an advance of 31 per cent over the increase of a similar set of pupils taken as controls. And the

[5] 'We think, indeed, to a considerable extent, by means of names, but what we think of are the things called by these names; and there cannot be a greater error than to imagine that thought can be carried on with nothing in our mind but names, or that we can make the names think for us.'—J. S. Mill, *Logic*, Bk. II, Chap. 2, Sec. 2.

[6] Dr. Head, while doing careful justice to the value of words in thinking, makes it clear that his aphasic patients could still grasp a large range of ideas without them, through the aid of other symbols. Thus, 'No. 10 was able to recall spontaneously the shape and colour of his hives and to see the bees arriving at the entrance loaded with yellow pollen . . . when No. 2 attempted to give an account of a famous prize fight, he failed grossly so long as he relied on recalling what he had read. But my question, "Can you see it?" evoked so lively a series of visual images that he was able to describe many more details correctly; finally springing out of bed, he assumed the exact attitude of the triumphant Carpentier gazing down on his vanquished opponent.' 'I was able to carry on lengthy conversations with one of my patients, aided by maps, pictures, and his use of a pencil, although his wife reduced him to incomprehensible jargon, and insisted he was out of his mind.'—*Aphasia and Kindred Disorders of Speech*, I. 520–1, 531. Of such cases McDougall remarks: 'Some patients can play such a game as chess, even though their cerebral speech-organs are so destroyed that, as well as finding it impossible to utter coherent speech, they cannot understand written or spoken language.'—*Battle of Behaviourism*, 71.

[7] *Psychology and Pedagogy of Reading*, 180.

[8] *Experimental Psychology of the Thought Processes*, 203.

[9] The person who belongs to this type will not find all writers equally easy. Wilfred Lay reports of one such: 'After reading to himself a few pages of Browning, his jaws became tired!'—*Psych. Rev. Mon. Sup.*, Vol. II. 24.

point of special interest is that along with this increase in speed went, not a decrease, but a slight improvement in the comprehension of what they read, an improvement that held both absolutely and by comparison with that of the controls.[10] This result forms a significant comment on the behaviourist theory. If a thought really consisted in the process of vocal or sub-vocal speech, is it likely that this process could be reduced almost or quite to the vanishing point while the comprehension actually increased?

But to all such attacks the behaviourist has ready a well-worn reply. The account of the orthodox psychologist, that what has happened is a transfer from motor to visual cues for carrying the meaning, he declines to accept. If sub-vocal processes are no longer in evidence, he insists that they are still there; they are only buried out of sight. The language mechanism is a very complicated and far-reaching system, and if the more conspicuous parts of it are not in play, the obscurer parts still may be. The principal organ of speech, the larynx, has been frequently removed altogether, and thought has still been possible. But this does not disturb Dr. Watson. He points out that 'so long as the air can pass from the lungs to the pharynx and mouth, faint whispered speech is possible.'[11] Suppose, however, that this passage of air is cut off, that below the larynx an opening is made in the trachea through which the patient is compelled to breathe; then, as he admits, all speech, even of the whispered kind, disappears. But he is still unmoved. For the upper organs of speech, the teeth, tongue, and lips, remain, and

hence 'such individuals can and do still make all of the movements necessary for articulate speech. This is the answer to the criticisms which have been directed against the point of view that has been advocated throughout the text, namely that thought is the action of language mechanisms.'[12] But carry the assumption further. Suppose a radical motor aphasia were to paralyse those organs too. Or suppose, to take a less extreme instance, that one sits in silent meditation with no movements visible of the outward organs of speech, and suppose further (Bühler reports many such cases) that the subject, as a thought occurs, can detect no sensations of vocal movement from within; is the behaviourist troubled? Apparently not at all. He admits that such cases occur. But he insists that the thought consists in physical processes which are as yet beyond detection. 'The behaviourist's answer', says Dr. Watson, 'is that he can *at present* arrive at this conclusion only by making use of a logical inference. In those cases where the response to the stimulus is not immediate but where it finally occurs in some form of explicit verbal or manual behaviour, it is safe to say that something does go on, and that something is surely not different in essence from that which goes on when his behaviour is explicit.'[13] Now there is no catching the behaviourist while he plays this game. You no sooner show that thought is not to be identified with some particular physical process than you find him contending that it is some other and more obscure process which you, and perhaps everyone else, have as yet failed to detect, indeed that 'any and every bodily response may become a word substitute'.[14] Against such agility and elusiveness there is but one strategy that can avail. One must forsake the unending business of showing that this, that, and the other physical process is not to be identified with

[10] *Op. cit.*, Chap. VIII. Cf. the conclusion drawn by Miss M. R. Fernald from her experimental work on imagery: 'Rapid reading produces in the majority of cases a reduction and slurring of the auditory-vocal-motor [processes of sensation and imagery], and in some cases a complete elimination of it.'—'Diagnosis of Mental Imagery,' *Psych. Rev. Mon. Sup.*, Vol. XIV. 48.

[11] *Psych. from St. of a Beh.*, 347

[12] *Psych. from St. of a Beh.*, 347.

[13] *Ibid.*, 361.

[14] *Behaviourism*, 192.

thought, and, attacking the matter in principle, show that in physical responses *as such* there is something that excludes this identification.

The thesis, then, which we must examine is that a conscious process *is* the same thing as a process of physical change, and *which* physical process it shall be we may leave to the behaviourist's choice. For our contention about his proposal is this, that no matter what process of bodily change he may elect, to identify consciousness with it is strictly unthinkable.

Of course there are cases in plenty in which two things may quite legitimately be called the same. The actor on the stage and the same actor on the street present two very different appearances, but they are the same man. When I look first at the head and then at the tail of a coin, what I see is different, and yet I am seeing the same coin. And at first sight there would seem to be no more difficulty in saying that a conscious and bodily process may be the same, despite the difference of appearance, than to say so of a coin or of a man. Nevertheless, this would be a mistake. When we say that we are seeing the same coin, we do not mean that there is no difference at all between what appeared when we saw the head and what appeared when we saw the tail; we do not mean that the appearances themselves are the same, for that would be absurd; what is the same is not the appearances, but the thing that owns them. Similarly of the man. His two appearances are not the same, but he is the same in spite of their differences. Now is it open to the behaviourist to say in the same way that conscious and bodily processes are one? Clearly not. If he does say so, his programme loses its point; and if his programme is to retain any point, he is committed to an assertion of identity in the very sense which makes such an assertion nonsense. Let us get this clear.

If, when he says that mental and bodily process are the same, the behaviourist means that they are the same in the ordinary sense, the sense in which I say a man is the same or a coin is the same, what he means is that they are two aspects or appearances of something which owns both but is identical with neither. Just as the coin is not identical with one of its faces or the man with one of his appearances, so also that which is the same in bodily and mental process is not to be identified with either, but with something underlying them of which both are appearances. Is this the behaviourist's meaning? Obviously not, for it would amount to the proposal that metaphysics supersedes science, a consummation which he would most devoutly wish to avoid. It would imply that what science directly deals with is not the reality at all, but only the appearance of something else underlying it of which mind is one manifestation. This is of course a theory that has been held by respectable metaphysicians, but it is safe to say that no theory which thus exalts metaphysics at the expense of science can be what the behaviourist wishes to offer us.

What sort of identity is it, then, to which the behaviourist is committed? Unhappily it is precisely the sort which we saw in our analogies to be absurd. He is compelled to hold that the appearances themselves are identical, that a toothache *is* simply and solely a change in physical tissue, and the change in physical tissue is all we mean by a toothache. This is the only sort of identity that would leave any point in his programme. To say that mental and nervous processes are obverse sides of an underlying identity is, as we have just seen, out of the question. To reduce matter to mind by saying that the nervous process is at bottom an appearance presented by what is really mental would be the sort of thing that he describes as 'moonshine'. To reduce mind to matter in the same way, by saying that the ache is an illusion, something that is really a physical process which appears to us as mental, would be futile. For where are we to place the illusion? If it is a mistaken idea in my mind, then behaviourism is abandoned. If it is itself merely a nervous change, nothing is gained by introducing it, for it is just as difficult to see how an illusion that I am conscious can be a change in my nerves as to see this about consciousness itself. What is identical for the behaviourist is not some basic substance which is belied by one of its appearances; his programme requires him to say that the pain and the change in the nerve are literally and numerically the same, that when I speak of an ache or pain, the ache or pain I mean *is* nothing but a change in bodily tissue.

Now this view is silly. There would not be the least absurdity, although no doubt there are difficulties, in saying that the pain is *caused* by a physical change or that the two are differing *manifestations* of something that lies behind them; but to say that it *is* the pain is to say what no one can really think and what only a thoroughly muddled head could suppose he thought. If a great many otherwise sensible people do suppose that they think it, this can only be because they have confused it with some other theory of a similar sound, such as that there is an extremely close dependence of mind on body. But unfortunately, as Paulsen has pointed out, 'the absurd has this advantage in common with truth, that it cannot be refuted'. If a man insists that what he means when he speaks of having a toothache is that the molecules in nerve or brain are behaving in a certain way, I suppose he must be the final judge of what he means. But we have pointed out that there are ways of showing a candid mind that at times it does not really mean what it had supposed it meant. It is perfectly easy to be mistaken on this point. We would invite anyone who is inclined to take seriously either the present-day doctrine of behaviourism or the old-fashioned identity materialism, of which it is only the most recent form, to ask himself whether in the light of the considerations that follow such a position can really express what he means.

(1) We may note in the first place that the behaviourist's conclusion could never have been arrived at except through a process which proves it false. In lieu of each of the processes that used to be called mental he offers us a specific bodily reaction. Instead of the sensation of blue we have the visual reaction to light-waves possessing a determinate length; instead of a sensation of red, the reaction to waves of a different length; a train of thought is a series of movements in the vocal organs; an emotion a set of reactions in glands and viscera. How has the behaviourist been able to specify these processes so confidently and precisely? The difference between the nervous reaction which is to constitute one mental process and that which is to constitute another is often exceedingly fine. For example, the difference between the way my optic nerve behaves when stimulated by waves of 700 millionths and 400 millionths of a millimetre is so small that not only does it remain invisible to the naked eye, but after all attempts at instrumental observation, it remains for the most part a matter of conjecture. Why, then, the behaviourist's confidence that two different nervous processes are involved? Obviously because he has had two different sensations of the old-fashioned kind, the sensations of blue and red, and is convinced that for each there must be some physiological correlate. Is the difference between the two reactions of the optic nerve or even the difference between the auditory and the visual regions of the cerebrum so conspicuous of itself that one could mark them out from direct inspection as performing functions radically different? No one, I suppose, would say this, least of all anyone who has some acquaintance with the way in which discoveries have actually been made in the field of 'cerebral localization'.[15] The only way in which these discoveries could possibly have been made

[15] 'It (the method of introspection) has been applied in proper places by physiologists such as Johannes Müller, Helmholtz, Hering, and many others, men of the highest repute in their profession. We owe the most valuable results of sense-physiology to this method, without which the imposing and securely founded edifice of this science would never have been built.'—Semon, *The Mneme*, 41.

was for the observer to start with certain differences in consciousness as his cue, and then to search for their correlates in the nervous system and the brain. To explain these conscious differences was the motive of his search; without them he would have had no problem; and without checking their connection with physical processes through the ordinary inductive methods he would never have been able to tell when his correlation was achieved. The very process then, by which the behaviourist is enabled to identify conscious events with physical depends on the fact that they are different. If conscious differences had not been there to initiate the search and to check its conclusions, there would have been no problem at all. The history of behaviourism is thus its refutation.

(2) Not only has the conscious state, in distinction from the physical, been the indispensable clue to the latter; an elaborate knowledge of it was developed before the knowledge of its physical correlates came into existence. Now this is a very odd fact if bodily reactions are all there is to conscious life, since if this is true, anyone who was acquainted with conscious processes ought *ipso facto* to be acquainted with the bodily processes. But that the two kinds of acquaintance are not the same and do not involve each other can be illustrated almost endlessly. Since one would hesitate to charge a behaviourist like Dr. Watson with anything so frivolous, on his theory, as reading Plato, one may be permitted to point out that in the *Philebus* there is an elaborate and minute discussion of the kinds of pleasure, and the relation of pleasure to other elements of conscious life. If the behaviourist is right, Plato was either discussing the reactions of glands, viscera and the autonomic nervous system, or he was discussing nothing at all. But since Plato knew, and could have known, next to nothing about glands, viscera, and the autonomic nervous system, the inference is irresistible; he was thinking, i.e., vocalizing, 'moonshine'. This conclusion is more courageous than convincing. Once more, in the *Prior Analytics*, Aristotle dissected very minutely a common form of reasoning. The behaviourist points out that when such reasoning goes on there is a process of change in muscles, nerves and brain, and these physical events *are* the reasoning process. So far, therefore, as Aristotle analysed the reasoning process, he must have been speaking of these. The perverse logician has left his opinion on record, however, that this process, alone of all the psychical processes, had no physical basis whatever, and as for the brain, he believed its function to be the cooling of the blood. According to the behaviourist, therefore, Aristotle could not have been talking about the reasoning process at all, and was more ignorant of it than a modern school boy; what he did discuss under that head was an irrelevant mythology. Again I find this less than convincing.

(3) Indeed there is more than one respect in which the behaviourist might have profited from a perusal of the history of logic. Logicians are the connoisseurs of certainty; and it is therefore interesting to note that they have commonly found it in the very realm which the behaviourist thinks an illusion. Descartes may serve as the type of many. What gave certainty to anything for Descartes was a kind of clearness and distinctness that could not be presented to eye or ear; and the one thing he found himself unable to doubt was his own process of conscious thinking. For example, he could not doubt that he was doubting, for in so doubting he was doing the doubting he doubted about. What would this argument come to if interpreted by a behaviourist? This, I suppose, that one cannot engage in speech reaction of a certain type while simultaneously engaging in another reaction of the same type toward the first. This makes sense. But it misses altogether the cogency of the Cartesian argument. If Descartes could not doubt that he doubted, it was because there was an evident inconsistency between the fact of his judging and what he judged; if

one cannot react through speech to a simultaneous reaction through speech, it is merely because the organs are so constructed that they cannot perform the two movements at once. What gave force to the Cartesian argument was a relation of logical necessity holding between the meanings; it is only between such non-sensible meanings that this relation can obtain; and both such relations and such meanings are for the behaviourist nonexistent. But it is only in this realm of the non-sensible that the relations of implication and consistency, or indeed any of the relations of logic, can subsist; to say that two physical things, two billiard balls or two boulders, implied each other or were mutually inconsistent, would be nonsense. Such relations as physical concomitance and collision, which the behaviourist must offer as substitutes, are totally different things. Thus if he builds on the foundations he has laid, he has not title to a belief in logic or the use of it. Of course he does use it; everyone does and must. But the attempt to *prove* his case must proceed through an appeal to meanings and relations for which this theory has no room.[16]

(4) Such philosophers as we have mentioned—Plato, Aristotle, Descartes—who talked about conscious states were of course arch-dealers in mythology. Now it is instructive to consider how, on the behaviourist assumptions, all this mythology could have arisen. On these assumptions no one has ever observed an event of any kind except the movements of physical bodies; there is no other kind of event to observe. How, then, did the illusion that there were also pleasures, pains, and ideas ever grow up? Not from perceiving them in animals and other persons, for what we directly perceive in these cases is never conscious states, but only bodies reacting. Whence, then, the curious notion that there are such states? The answer one would ordinarily give is that we have known these states in ourselves, that when we have had them we have commonly acted in certain ways, and that when we have seen others acting in the same ways we assume that they feel as we do. But from this explanation the behaviourist is cut off. He cannot admit that even in ourselves we are aware of these conscious states. The result is that he is left without any explanation at all of the illusion that they exist. The illusion is universal; it is extremely strong; but it is wholly gratuitous. In spite of the fact that nothing exists but matter in motion, we have managed to conjure up a luxuriant jungle of mythology, in the way of sensations, pleasures and displeasures, emotions and ideas, which has not the least foundation in anything that anyone has ever observed. The thing is as inexplicable as it is scandalous. The only course here open to the behaviourist is suggested by the remark that he is really the fundamentalist of the natural sciences. To account for such catholic human perversity, what he needs is a good robust doctrine of original sin.

(5) The great illusion is so troublesome that the behaviourist is moved at times to deny that the illusion itself exists. These sensations, images, and ideas that people talk of—they are words only: 'I frankly do not know what they mean', says Dr. Watson.[17] This statement, it may be remarked in passing, is somewhat puzzling. For according to the same writer, 'thinking is merely talking, but talking with concealed musculature'.[18] Persons, then, who are talking about sensations and ideas must be as truly thinking as anyone else. Dr. Watson is inclined to dismiss such thinking, however, as having no meaning. But to use meaning as the criterion for dividing

[16] "The existence of universals is often denied; men are apt to imagine that if they exist one should be able to find them as one finds instances of them. Hence the remarks of Antisthenes—ιππον μεν ορω, ιπποτητα δε ουχ ορω, "I see a horse, but not horseness"; to which Plato replied, that it was because, though he had eyes, he had no intelligence'. —Joseph, *Logic*, 27.

[17] *Psych. from St. of a Beh.*, xii.

[18] *The Battle of Behaviourism*, 34–5.

the sheep from the goats is a surprising procedure. For meaning is one of the most objectionable of all the mythical entities of consciousness; and if the behaviourist is consistent (as he wants to be, though his scheme, as we have seen, has no place for such a relation) he cannot say that one way of thinking, i.e. talking, is more 'meaningful' than another. A clear physiological meaning of 'meaning' is called for, but missing. But this is only a passing remark. We were saying that the behaviourist sometimes denies that the illusion of consciousness exists. And it is worth seeing that while common sense is no great authority on scientific matters, it is quite adequate to refute a theory like this. If a dentist lays his instrument lightly alongside an exposed nerve, there happens what is ordinarily called a mild feeling of pain. If he plunges his buzzing file into the nerve and there turns and twists it, there happens what is called an excruciating pain. According to the behaviourist there is no conscious difference between the one event and the other, since neither sensation nor any other form of consciousness exists. Nevertheless, even behaviourists have been known to prefer the one type of event to the other. Why? Because they have a passionate desire that one exchange of energy among molecules rather than some other should occur? Clearly not; the sorts of energy-exchange involved in different types of pain are far too little known to make definite preference possible. But even if they were known, why should a behaviourist be interested in one rather than another? He cannot say, 'because the one is more pleasant, or less painful, or more worth while, than the other'. Pleasure, pain, and value, are not particles in the physical world; they are not movements of such particles; they are not properties or relations of such particles; they do not exist there at all, as he has uneasily seen; in a world of mere matter in motion, no event is better or worse, more or less desirable, than any other. If, then, the behaviourist does desire one event rather than another, this can only

be because it possesses, or seems to possess, some quality of pleasingness or worth that does not belong to it as a merely physical event. He cannot so much as seek to avoid a toothache without, by implication, forsaking his theory.

(6) That we really do mean something different by consciousness and bodily behaviour is made clear again by the different attributes that we assign to them.[19] We speak of an idea as clear or confused, as apposite or inapposite, as witty or dull. Are such terms intelligible when applied to those motions of electrons, atoms, molecules, or muscles, which for the behaviourist are all there is to consciousness? Can a motion be clear, or cogent, or witty? What exactly would a clear motion be like? What sort of thing is a germane or cogent reflex? Or a witty muscular reaction? These adjectives are perfectly in order when applied to ideas; they become at once absurd when applied to movements in muscle or nerve; and how account for this absurdity if we do not mean different things when we speak of ideas and movements?

On the other side, movements have attributes which are unthinkable as applied to ideas. Movements have velocity; but what is the average velocity of one's ideas on a protective tariff? Movements have direction; would there be any sense in talking of the north-easterly direction of one's thought on the morality of revenge? Finally Dr. Watson makes it plain that though there is much in the 'thinking activity' which is not yet visible to the eye, there is nothing in principle beyond the range of vision; the microscopic and concealed movements in the interior of the body need only sufficiently fine instruments to make them as apparent to the eye as gross muscular reactions.[20] Such confidence is hard to share. It means that a surgeon, if his technique were sufficiently advanced, could *see* my awareness of blue, or my opinion about

[19] Cf. Broad, *The Mind and Its Place in Nature*, 622–3.

[20] *Psych. from St. of a Beh.*, 360–4.

behaviourism, or my headache, there in the tissues before him. This is surely nonsense. One can understand what it means to feel a headache, but to *see* a headache moving about in space is as unintelligible as to hear temperature or to smell the musical scale. Nor is it easy to see how such an absurdity could arise if the only difference between a headache and a handspring lay in gross physical magnitude.

(7) The arguments we have been using consist for the most part in mere appeal to common sense and have avoided those excursions into metaphysics which the behaviourist so much distrusts. The one further consideration we shall offer is of the same kind, though to him it may look at first suspicious. It is this, that if he is right, no judgement or idea can be either true or false; truth or falsity have no place in the behaviourist universe. This is a criticism of some moment, since even one who eschews metaphysics and conceives of science in the most dogmatically fundamentalist manner values his position because he thinks it in some sense true.

But how can a reflex be true? Is there any sense in saying that the passage of air through the vocal cords, or the wagging of the tongue, or the opening and closing of the lips, are themselves true or false? It is hard to conjecture what such assertions could mean. To be sure, truth has been defined in various ways. Sometimes it has been made to consist in correspondence, sometimes in coherence, sometimes in the production of good effects. Could a bodily reaction be true in any of these senses? Not in the sense of correspondence; for that would imply that when I say 'New York has more than six million inhabitants', an incident in my throat and mouth corresponds to the population of a city; and that is meaningless. Not in the sense of coherence; for, so far as one can see,

any other incident in my body would cohere equally well with the fact, and the incident that did happen would cohere equally well with almost any other fact. Nor in the sense of producing good effects; since an apoplectic stroke, suffered immediately after judgement, might cut off all good effects, while the judgement would still have been true. The fact is that behaviourism has not offered, and cannot offer, any intelligible account of truth. Mr Russell, who has behaviourist leanings, was able to offer correspondence so far as he identified ideas with images. But of course images have no existence for a thorough-going behaviourism, and when we tried to find from Mr. Russell how words could be true, nothing was forthcoming that we could understand. And without attempting to anticipate what the future epistemologists of behaviourism may achieve, one may suspect that where the greatest of their forerunners, Hobbes,[21] so signally failed, they will not find success easy. For what they must explain is such things as these: How a motion can be an error; how the deflection of an air current through my throat can be true, while the passage of a current through the pine trees cannot; how, when questions are asked me and I go through the motions of uttering the word yes, this motion may reflect with equal faithfulness the characteristics of a thousand different situations. To carry behaviourism into the region of truth and falsity is to stir up a hornet's nest of paradoxes and absurdities, and all for one root reason, namely that 'it seems as nonsensical to call a movement true as a flavour purple or a sound avaricious'.[22]

[21] He even says explicitly, at one point, '*ratio*, now, is but *oratio*'.

[22] H. W. B. Joseph, *Some Problems in Ethics*, 14.

There Is No Distinction Between Mind and Body
RICHARD TAYLOR

In response to difficulties of the sort we have considered, many thinkers and investigators, particularly those not trained in philosophy, have been eager to maintain that human beings or persons are physical objects having, of course, psychological powers and attributes which distinguish them from other kinds of physical objects, but that such psychological powers and attributes can be understood in terms of certain bodily functions, or even identified with these.

EPIPHENOMENALISM
Many such views amount to some version of epiphenomenalism, according to which mental entities, such as thoughts, images, ideas, and feelings, never enter as causes into any physical processes, and hence never act upon the body or any part of it, yet are sometimes, if not always, the effects of bodily processes, particularly those within the nervous system. Mind and body do not, then, on this view *inter*act, for no mental state or event ever causes any bodily one. Yet the body does act upon the "mind" in this sense, that some, if not all, psychological states or events are the direct or indirect effects of occurrences within the body, especially those within the brain and nerves.

If, then, we ask our original question, concerning what a person essentially is, the answer turns out on this view to be something like this: A person is a living physical body having a mind, the mind consisting, however, of nothing but a more or less continuous series of conscious or unconscious states and events, such as feelings, thoughts, images, and ideas, which are the effects but never the causes of bodily activity.

Such a view does indeed avoid the apparent absurdities of ordinary interactionism, but it involves additional difficulties no less appalling and, when clearly conceived, appears so bizarre a description of human nature as to make almost any alternative conception more acceptable. For in the first place, whatever difficulty there is in the idea of purely mental entities entering into physical chains of causation and altering, for instance, the direction and outcome of chemical reactions and mechanical processes, there is no less difficulty in the idea that purely physical chains of causation, involving chemical reactions and the like, should have effects that could in principle never enter into the physical description of anything. That bodily processes, in other words, should have nonbodily effects is no more comprehensible than that mental processes should have nonmental effects; causation in either direction is neither more nor less difficult to comprehend than in the other.

THE ALLEGED SUPERFLUITY OF THOUGHT
To see just how odd is the conception of human behavior that results from this view, we need to note carefully just what it asserts. It asserts that all bodily processes are self-contained; that is, that no nonbodily state or event ever enters causally into any physical process. It follows, then, that all bodily behavior is caused by bodily processes alone, and that the mind, and all states and events transpiring therein, being only incidental by-products of these physical processes, are entirely superfluous so far as the understanding and explanation of human behavior is concerned. This means that it makes no difference, so far as human behavior is concerned, whether those mental states and events exist or not, that human behavior would be just

FROM: *Metaphysics*, Richard Taylor. (Englewood Cliffs, N.J.: Prentice-Hall, 1963), pp. 22–32. Reprinted by permission of Prentice-Hall, Inc.

what it is without them, since they in no way influence the direction or outcome of any state, process, or motion of the body. But this seems quite impossible to believe. We can, no doubt, suppose that the behavior of certain organisms such as plants and insects is nothing but the resultant of physical or chemical processes within them, and is entirely without conscious direction, but it is impossible to believe that a man's thoughts and ideas have no influence upon what he does. One can hardly suppose that a man's behavior would be no different even if his mental life were quite different or even nonexistent, or that even the whole of human history, with all its wars and political upheavals, would have been just what it has been even without all those thoughts and feelings which, on this theory, superfluously attended them. What a man does is sometimes quite obviously the more or less direct outcome of what he thinks, desires, plans and intends. Some allegedly mental states, such as twinges of pain and the like, may indeed be the mere accompaniments and effects of bodily processes, having themselves no direct influence on bodily behavior, but it is difficult to believe that the entire mental life of a man is the mere accompaniment and effect of bodily processes, and that those bodily processes—i.e., the whole of that man's observable behavior—are altogether unaffected by them.

Now it might be suggested, in response to this kind of *reductio ad absurdum* of epiphenomenalism, that causes are impossible without their effects. Since thoughts, ideas and feelings, then, are the regular effects of bodily changes, these latter could not occur without them. Hence (it might be claimed) whereas such thoughts, ideas, and feelings in no way act as causes of bodily behavior, that behavior would nevertheless be impossible without them, and it is therefore false to suggest that, on this theory, a man's behavior would be no different even in the absence of those mental phenomena.

This line of thought does not, however, properly represent the epiphenomenalist position. For according to epiphenomenalism, mental states are not the effects of observable bodily behavior but of certain states of the brain and nervous system, a man's observable behavior, including his voluntary acts, being likewise the effects of those same or other states of the brain and nervous system. States of the brain and nervous system, accordingly, have two entirely different *kinds* of effects, effects in two entirely different realms, the mental and the physical. Now so long as certain brain and nervous states occur, then on this theory the observable bodily behavior which is the consequence of them is guaranteed, whether the attendant mental effects occur or not, and these latter need not therefore be taken into account at all in the explanation of human conduct. They are, then, superfluous, after all, human behavior being unaffected either by their presence or their absence. Now one can indeed say that without the mental states, those particular brain and nerve states which are their normal causes could not occur, since from the nonoccurrence of the effect we can infer the nonoccurrence of its cause. But from this we cannot conclude that those mental states are necessary for the occurrence of the observable behavior of men, for that behavior might well be the effect of other bodily states, including, of course, other states of the brain and nervous system, and must in any case be the effect of *some* state of the body, according to the epiphenomenalist view.

MATERIALISM AGAIN

We have drawn no closer to an answer to our question but have, on the contrary, gotten progressively farther from it, each difficulty raising a new theory having more difficulties in it than the last. Perhaps the only sure conclusion we can draw is that human nature is mysterious. But this, however unsatisfactory, is nonetheless worth affirming, for certainly no one can hold any of the views we have outlined, or any of the numberless variations on them, entirely without embarrassment, unless he simply resolves to see no obstacles where they are nonetheless securely lodged.

One thing should by now seem quite plain, however, and that is that the difficulties of simple materialism are not overcome by any form of dualism. There is, therefore, no point in recommending dualism as an improvement over materialism. To assert that a man is both body *and* mind—that is, that he is two things rather than one—not only does not remove any problem involved in saying that he is one thing only, namely, a body, but introduces all the problems of describing the connection between those two things. We are led to conclude, then, that a metaphysical understanding of human nature must be sought within the framework of materialism, according to which a man is entirely identical with his body.

All forms of dualism arise from the alleged disparity between persons and physical objects. Men, it is rightly noted, are capable of thinking, believing, feeling, wishing, and so on; but bodies, it is claimed, are capable of none of these things, and the conclusion is drawn that men are not bodies. Yet it cannot be denied that men *have* bodies; hence, it is decided that a man, or a person, is a nonphysical entity, somehow more or less intimately related to a body. But here it is rarely noted that whatever difficulties there may be in applying personal and psychological predicates and descriptions to bodies, precisely the same difficulties are involved in applying such predicates and descriptions to *anything whatever*, including spirits or souls. If, for example, a philosopher reasons that a body cannot think, and thereby affirms that, since a person thinks, a person is a soul or spirit or mind rather than a body, we are entitled to ask how a spirit can think. For surely, if a spirit or soul can think, we can affirm that a body can do so; and if we are then asked *how* a body can think, our reply can be that it thinks in precisely the manner in which the

dualist supposes a soul thinks. The difficulty of imagining how a body thinks is not in the least lessened by asserting that something else, which is not a body, thinks. And so it is with every other personal predicate or description. Whenever faced with the dualist's challenge to explain how a body can have desires, wishes, how it can deliberate, choose, repent, how it can be intelligent or stupid, virtuous or wicked, and so on, our reply can always be: The body can do these things, and be these things, in whatever manner one imagines the soul can do these things and be these things. For to repeat, the difficulty here is in seeing how *anything at all* can deliberate, choose, repent, think, be virtuous or wicked, and so on, and *that* difficulty is not removed but simply glossed over by the invention of some new thing, henceforth to be called the "mind" or "soul."

It becomes quite obvious what is the source of dualistic metaphysics when the dualist or soul philosopher is pressed for some description of the mind or soul. The mind or soul, it turns out in such descriptions, is just whatever it is that thinks, reasons, deliberates, chooses, feels, and so on. But the fact with which we began was that *men* think, reason, deliberate, choose, feel, and so on. And we do in fact have some fairly clear notion of what we mean by a man, for we think of an individual man as a being existing in space and time, having a certain height and weight—as a being, in short, having many things in common with other objects in space and time, and particularly with those that are living, i.e., with other animals. But the dualist, noting that a man is significantly different from other beings, insofar as he, unlike most of them, is capable of thinking, deliberating, choosing, and so on, suddenly asserts that it is not a man, as previously conceived, that does these things at all, but something else, namely, a mind or soul, or something that does not exist in space and time nor have any height and weight, nor have, in fact, any material properties at all. And then when we seek some understanding of what this mind or soul is, we find it simply described as a thing that thinks, deliberates, feels, and so on. But surely the proper inferences should have been that men are like all other physical objects in some respects—e.g., in having size, mass, and location in space and time; that they are like some physical objects but unlike others in certain further respects—e.g., in being living, sentient, and so on; and like no other physical objects at all in still other respects—e.g., in being rational, deliberative, and so on. And of course none of this suggests that men are not physical objects, but rather that they are precisely physical objects, like other bodies in some ways, unlike many other bodies in other ways, and unlike any other bodies in still other respects.

The dualist or soul philosopher reasons that since men think, feel, desire, choose, and so on, and since such things cannot be asserted of bodies, then men are not bodies. Reasoning in this fashion, we are forced to the conclusion that men are not bodies—though it is a stubborn fact that men nevertheless *have* bodies. So the great problem then is to connect men, now conceived as souls or minds, to their bodies. But philosophically, it is just exactly as good to reason that, since men think, feel, desire, choose, etc., and since men are bodies—i.e., are living, animal organisms having the essential material attributes of weight, size, and so on—then *some* bodies think, feel, desire, choose, etc. This argument is just as good as the dualist's argument and does not lead us into a morass of problems concerning the connection between soul and body.

THE SOURCE
OF DUALISTIC THEORIES
Why, then, does the dualist's argument have, and this one lack, such an initial plausibility? Why have so many philosophers been led into dualistic metaphysical views, on the basis of arguments apparently no stronger than other arguments having simpler conclusions but which are rarely even considered?

Part of the answer is perhaps that, when we form an idea of a *body* or a *physical object*, what is most likely to come to mind is not some man or animal but something much simpler, such as a stone or a marble. When we are then invited to consider whether a physical object might think, deliberate, choose, and the like, we are led to contemplate the evident absurdity of supposing things like *that* do such things, and thus we readily receive the claim that bodies cannot think, deliberate, choose, and the like, and the dualist extracts his conclusion. But suppose we began somewhat differently. Suppose we began with a consideration of two quite dissimilar physical objects—a living, animal body, of the kind commonly denominated "man," on the one hand, and a simple body, of the kind denominated "stone," on the other. Now let it be asked whether there is any absurdity in supposing that one of these things might be capable of thinking, deliberating, choosing, and the like. Here there is no absurdity at all in asserting that an object of the first kind might indeed have such capacities, but evidently not one of the second kind—from which we would conclude, not that men are not physical objects, but rather that they are physical objects which are significantly different from other physical objects, such as stones. And there is, of course, nothing the least astonishing in this.

But how, one may wonder, can a "mere physical object" have feelings? But here the answer should be: Why, if it is a physical object of a certain familiar kind, should it not have feelings? Suppose, for example, that it is a living body, like a frog or mouse, equipped with a complicated and living nervous system. Where is the absurdity in asserting that a "mere physical object" of this sort can feel? Evidently there is none. Hardly anyone would want to insist that beings of this sort—frogs and mice, for instance—must have souls to enable them to feel. It seems enough that they have complicated living nervous systems.

The same type of answer can be

given if it is asked how a "mere physical object" can think. If we suppose that it is a physical object of a certain familiar kind, namely, a living body having the form and other visible attributes of a man, and possessed of an enormously complex living brain and nervous system—in short, that the object in question is a living human being—then there is no absurdity in supposing that this being thinks. Any argument purporting to show that such a being cannot think, and must therefore have a nonmaterial soul to do its thinking for it, would be just as good an argument to show that frogs and mice cannot feel, and must therefore have souls to do their feeling for them. The outcome of such philosophizing is just as good, and just as absurd, in the one case as it is in the other.

Now the materialist would, of course, like to maintain that psychological states, such as feeling, believing, desiring, and so on, are really nothing but perfectly *familiar* kinds of material states, that is, states of the body, particularly of the brain and nervous system; states that are either observable or testable by the usual methods of biology, physics, and chemistry. But this, as we have seen earlier, seems to be a vain hope, and will always be an obstacle to any simple materialism. There is always, it seems, something that can be asserted of certain psychological states which makes little if any sense when asserted of any ordinary or familiar state of matter. One can say of a belief, for instance, that it is true or false, but this can never be said, except metaphorically or derivatively, of any familiar state of matter, such as an arrangement of molecules; we could say of such a thing that it is true or false, only if we first assumed that it is identical with some belief that is such. Again, one can say of a desire that it is the desire *for* this or that—for instance, the desire for food; of a fear that it is a fear *of* something—for instance, a fear of heights; but of no familiar state of matter can it be said that it is, in the same sense, *for* or *of*

anything. It just *is* the state of matter that it is. Suppose, for example, that the materialist should say that the feeling of hunger is simply *identical* with a certain familiar state of the body; not merely that it is prompted by that state but that it *is* that state, and is describable in terms of the concepts of physics and chemistry. Thus, let us suppose him to claim that hunger just *is* the state consisting of having an empty stomach, together with a deficiency of certain salts or other substances in the blood, and a certain physical disequilibrium of the nervous system consequent upon these conditions. Now there is, of course, no doubt an intimate connection between such states as these and the desire for food, but the assertion of their *identity* with that desire will always be plagued because, unlike the desire, those bodily states can be fully described without mentioning food at all, and without saying that they are in any sense states that are *for* food. Indeed, the notion of something being *for* or *of* something else, in the sense in which a desire may be a desire *for* food, or a fear may be a fear *of* heights, is not a concept of physics or chemistry at all. And yet it can surely be said of a certain desire that it is a desire for food, or of a certain fear that it is a fear of heights. The referential character of such states seems, indeed, essential to any proper description of them. Significantly, when those substances that are physiologically associated with such states are artificially administered to someone, in the effort to create within him those states themselves, the effort fails. It is fairly well known, for example, what physiological changes a man undergoes when he is in a state of fear; but when these changes are artificially evoked in him, he does not experience fear in the usual sense. He describes his state as being vaguely *like* fear, but finds that he is not afraid *of* anything.

But while psychological states are thus evidently not identical with any familiar bodily states, it does not follow that they are identical with no state of matter at all. They may, in fact, be unfamiliar states of matter, that is, states of the body that are not observable or testable by the ordinary methods of biology, physics, and chemistry. This suggestion is not as question-begging as it appears, for it is conceded by the most resolute soul philosophers and dualists that psychological states are strange ones in this respect at least, that they are not thus observable. From the fact that some state is unobservable by the usual methods of scientific observation, nothing whatever follows with respect to the truth or falsity of materialism. From the fact that a certain state is in some respect unusual it does not follow that it is a state of an unusual thing, of a soul rather than a body, but rather, that if it is a state of the body it is an unusual one, and if it is a state of the soul it is no less unusual. Nothing is made clearer, more comprehensible, or less strange by postulating some new substance as the subject of certain states not familiar to the natural sciences, and then baptizing that new substance "the mind" or "the soul." Nor does one avoid materialism at this point by saying that by the "mind" or "soul" we just *mean* that which is the subject of psychological states; for while that might indeed be true, it is nevertheless an open question whether what we thus mean by the "mind" or "soul" might not turn out, after all, to be what we ordinarily denominate "the body." The existence of nothing whatever can be derived from any definitions of terms.

THE SOUL

This point can perhaps be borne home to the imagination by the following sort of consideration. Suppose one feels, as probably everyone more or less does, that a *person* cannot be a mere *body*, and that no increase in the physical, biological, and physiological complexity of any body can bridge the gulf between being a body, albeit a complicated and living one, and being a person. Consider then, a highly complex and living animal organism, physically and biologically

identical in every respect to a living man, but lacking that one thing that is, we are supposing, still needed in order to convert this body into a person. Now just what can this extra essential ingredient be? What do we need to *add* to convert a mere body into a person?

Let us suppose it is a *soul*. If we add a soul to this living, complicated animal organism, let us suppose, then, *lo!* it will cease to be a mere body and become a person. No one knows, however, exactly what a soul is or what properties it must possess in order to confer personality upon something. All we can say is that it is what distinguishes a person from a mere body, which of course tells us nothing here. So let us give it some definite properties. It does not matter what properties we give it, as we shall shortly see, so to make it simple and easy to grasp, let us suppose that this soul is a small round ball, about the size of a marble, transparent and indestructible. Now clearly, by implanting *that* anywhere in the living organism we get no closer to converting it from a mere body to a person. We manage only to add one further, trivial complication. But why so? Why are we now no closer to having a person than before? Is it just because the "soul" we added is itself a mere body? If that is the difficulty, then let us remove its corporeality. Let us suppose that the soul we add to this living animal organism is not a small round *physical* ball but a nonphysical one. This will permit us to retain its transparency. If, being nonphysical, it can no longer be described as a ball, then we can drop that part of the description too. Let the thing we add be, in short, anything one likes. Let it be a small hard ball, a small soft ball, an immaterial ball, or something that is neither material nor a ball. The point is, that no matter *what* it is that is added, it goes not the least way toward converting what was a mere body into a person. If a small hard ball does not bridge the gap, then we get no closer to bridging it by simply removing its properties of hardness, smallness, and sphericity—by making it, in short, something that is merely *non*physical. What we need to do is state just what positive properties this extra thing must possess, in order to elevate an animal body to the status of a person, and no positive properties suggest themselves at all. We cannot give it psychological properties—by saying, for example, that this soul thinks, desires, deliberates, wills, believes, repents, and so on; for if the thing we are adding has *those* properties, than it is *already* a person in its own right, and there is no question of *adding* it to something in order to *get* a person. We could have as easily given *those* properties to the animal organism with which we began, as to give them to something else and then superfluously amalgamate the two things. Plainly, there are no positive properties of any soul that will do the trick. The best we can do is to say that the extra something required—the soul, or the mind, or whatever we choose to call this additional thing—is that which, when added, makes up the difference between being a mere animal body and being a person. This is about as good a way as one could find for indicating that he has no idea what he is talking about.

THE "PRIVACY"
OF PSYCHOLOGICAL STATES

One final point will serve to illustrate the futility of dualistic hypotheses as solutions to difficulties admittedly inherent in any materialistic theory.

The states of the mind or soul, it is said, are simply those states that are not observable by any ordinary way but which can nevertheless be known, by an immediate awareness, to the person who has them. It is thus the *privacy* of such states that marks them as mental and, being mental, it is forthwith concluded that they are states of a mind or soul rather than of a body, and sometimes that the person who is aware of them is identical with that mind or soul. But concerning some such states—namely, pains and other simple sensations, which are most assuredly private—there is an

absurdity in asserting that they are states of the mind or soul.

Suppose, for instance, that one has a decayed tooth, or a lacerated toe. Now the dentist, it is said, can observe, perhaps in minute detail, the condition of the tooth, and the physician the condition of the toe, but neither can have any awareness of the pain associated with either, pains that are nevertheless felt by him whose tooth or toe is thus damaged. The conclusion is then drawn that the dentist and physician are aware only of states of the body, while the patient is aware of something else which, being no state of the body, must be a state of the mind or soul.

But surely all that follows from such an argument is that persons other than oneself can observe some, but not others, of one's states. It does not at all follow that those private states—pains, in this case—are states of some further thing, such as a mind or soul, that is unobservable. From the fact that some state is, in the sense described, private, it does not follow that it is a state of a private thing. The argument is, in short, a simple *non sequitur*.

The conclusion of the argument is moreover absurd; for that conclusion is that a toothache or a toe ache is a state of mind, or a condition of the soul, which they manifestly are not. A toothache is a state of the tooth, and a toe ache a state of the toe: That the dentist and physician cannot observe these states does not show that they are states of the mind or soul rather than of the tooth and toe, but only that some of a man's states are not observable to dentists and doctors, which is hardly surprising. The physician, contemplating one's lacerated toe, might reasonably ask whether *it* hurts, and in doing so he would be inquiring about the toe and nothing else. The pain that the patient feels, moreover, is felt in the toe. It would be an utter distortion to say that the pain is felt in, or by, the mind, and then somehow *referred* to the toe. And it would be not only a distortion, but an absurdity, for the patient to say that he feels pain in his mind, or that a pain is felt by his mind, this pain being occasioned by a condition of his toe. The pain is located, by the patient, in his toe, just as surely as the wound; that is where the pain is felt, nowhere else. What the patient can truly say is that *he* feels pain and that the pain he feels is in his toe. In thus referring to himself as the subject of the feeling, he is not referring to some metaphysical thing, like a soul or mind, and saying that *it* feels pain; he is referring to himself, as a man—that is, as a living, animal organism, seated here and now before the physician, an animal organism with which he identifies himself, and saying that this man, himself, feels pain. And the pain that he feels, he surely does not doubt, is in his toe. At no point in his discussion with the physician could it ever be relevant in this situation to

make any reference to his mind or his soul: it is not the soul or mind that hurts but the toe, nor is it the soul or mind that feels it, but he himself, the very man, the very animal organism, the very living, physical body that is sitting there.

Of course we cannot, by these reflections, pretend to have solved the problems of mind and matter, nor to have proved any theory of materialism. Human nature is mysterious, and remains so, no matter what one's metaphysical theory is or how simple it is. It does nevertheless seem evident that no dualistic theory of man renders human nature any less mysterious, and that whatever questions are left unanswered by the materialist are left equally unanswered, though perhaps better concealed, by his opponents.

In Defense of Dualism
CURT DUCASSE

*N*either in the section of this symposium on "The Mind-Body Problem" nor in that on "The Brain and the Machine" is much, if any, attention given to the dualist-interactionist conception of the relation between mind and brain. A summary presentation of the case for it and against its rivals may therefore be appropriate here.

The first point to which attention must be called is that, beyond question, there are things—events, substances, processes, relations, etc.—denominated "material," or "physical," that there are also certain others denominated instead "mental," or "psychical," and that no thing is denominated both "physical" and "psychical," or both "material" and "mental." Rocks, trees, water, air animal and human bodies, and the processes occurring among them or within them, are examples of the things called "ma-

terial" or "physical"; emotions, desires, moods, sensations, cravings, images, thoughts, etc., are examples of the things called "mental" or "psychical."

To question whether the first *really* are physical or the second *really* are psychical would be absurd, as it would be absurd to question whether a certain boy whom his parents named "George" really was George. For just as "George" is a name, so "physical" or "material," and "psychical" or "mental," are names; and a name is essentially a *pointer*, which does point at—designates, indicates, denotes, directs attention to—whatever it actually is employed to point at.

It is necessary, however, to ask what characteristic shared by all the things called "physical" or "material" determined their being all designated by one and the same name; and the same question arises with regard to those

FROM: *Dimensions of Mind*, S. Hook, ed. (New York: New York University Press. Reprinted by permission of New York University Press 1960), pp. 85–89.

denominated instead "psychical" or "mental." Evidently, the characteristic concerned had to be an obvious, not a recondite one, since investigation of the recondite characteristics respectively of physical and of psychical things could begin only *after* one knew which things were the physical and which the psychical ones.

In the cases of the things called "physical," the patent characteristic common to and peculiar to them, which determined their being all denoted by one and the same name, was simply that all of them were, or were capable of being, *perceptually public*—the same tree, the same thunderclaps, the same wind, the same dog, the same man, etc., can be perceived by every member of a human public suitably located in space and in time. To be material or physical, then, *basically* means to be, or to be capable of being, perceptually public. And the unperceivable, recondite things physicists discover—electrons, protons, etc., and the processes that occur among them—only have title at all to be also called physical *derivatively*—in virtue, namely, (and *only* in virtue) of their being *constituents* of the things that are perceptually public.

On the other hand, the patent characteristic which functioned as a basis for the application of one identical name to all the things called "psychical" or "mental" was their *inherently private* character, attention to them, as distinguished from attention to what they may signify, being accordingly termed "introspection," not "perception."

The events called "psychical," it must be emphasized, are private in a sense radically different from that in which the events occurring inside the body are private. The latter are private only in the sense that visual, tactual, or other exteroceptive perception of them is *difficult*—indeed, even more difficult for the person whose body is concerned than for other persons—such perception of those events being possible, perhaps, only by means of of special instruments, or perhaps only by anatomical

"introspection"(!), i.e., by opening up the body surgically and looking at the processes going on inside it. The "privacy" of intra-somatic stimuli, including so-called "covert behavior, is thus purely adventitious. The privacy of psychical events, on the other hand, is *inherent and ultimate*.

It is sometimes alleged, of course, that their privacy too is only adventitious. But this allegation rests only on failure to distinguish between being *public* and being *published*. Psychical events can be more or less adequately published. That is, perceptually public forms of behavior correlated with occurrence of them can function as *signs* that they are occurring —but *only* as signs, for correlation is not identity. Indeed, correlation presupposes non-identity.

Psychical events *themselves* are never *public* and never can be made so. That, for example, I *now remember* having dreamed of a Siamese cat last night is something which I can publish by means of perceptually public words, spoken or written. Other persons are then *informed of it*. But to be informed *that I remember* having so dreamed is one thing, and to *remember* having so dreamed is altogether another thing, and one *inherently private*. The dreaming itself was not, and the remembering itself is not, a *public* event at all and cannot possibly be made so in the way in which my *statement* that I remember that I remember that I so dreamed is or can be made public.

How then does it happen that we have names understood by all for events of inherently private kinds? The answer is, of course, that we heard those names —e.g., "anger," "desire," "remembering," etc.,—uttered by other persons when they perceived us behaving in certain more or less stereotyped manners. But the point crucial here is that although each of us acquires his vocabulary for mental events in this way, the words of it, at the times when they are applied by others to *his* behavior, denote *from him* not primarily or perhaps at all his behavior, but the particular kind of inherently private event, i.e., of physical state, which *he* is experiencing at the time. It is only in "behaviors," i.e., in the language of dogmatic behaviorism, that for example the word "anger," and the words "anger-behavior," both denote the same event, to wit, the event which ordinary language terms "behaving angrily."

There are several varieties of behaviorism, but they agree in that they attempt to account for the behavior of organisms wholly without invoking a psychical cause for any behavior—that is, wholly by reference to physical, perceptually public causes, present and/or past.

Dogmatic behaviorism is the pious belief that the causes of the behavior of organisms, including human organisms, *are never other than physical.* Nothing but this dogma dictates that even when no physical occurrences are actually found that would account for a given behavior, physical occurrences nevertheless *must* be assumed to have taken place.

Empirical or methodological behaviorism, on the other hand, is not thus fideistic. It is simply *a research program*, perfectly legitimate and often fruitful—the program, namely, of *seeking*, for all behavior, causes consisting of physical, i.e., of perceptually public stimulus events, present and past. Evidently, the fact that one undertakes to search for causes of this kind for all behavior leaves entirely open the possibility that, in many of the innumerable cases where no physical causes adequate to account for the given behavior can in fact be observed, the behavior had a psychical not a physical cause.

For, contrary to what is sometimes alleged, causation of a physical by a psychical event, or of a psychical event by stimulation of a physical sense organ, is not in the least paradoxical. The causality relation—whether defined in terms of regularity of succession, or (preferably) in terms of single antecedent difference—does not presuppose at all that its cause-term and its effect-term

both belong to the same ontological category, but only that both of them be *events*.

Moreover, the objection that we cannot understand how a psychical event could cause a physical one (or vice versa) has no basis other than blindness to the fact that the "how" of causation is capable at all of being either mysterious or understood only in cases of *remote* causation, never in cases of *proximate* causation. For the question as to the "how" of causation of a given event by a given other event never has any other sense than *through what intermediary causal steps* does the one cause the other. Hence, to ask it in a case of proximate causation is to be guilty of what Professor Ryle has called a "category mistake"—a mistake, incidentally, of which he is himself guilty when he alleges that the "how" of psycho-physical causation would be mysterious.

Again, the objection to interactionism that causation, in either direction, as between psychical and physical events is precluded by the principle of the conservation of energy (or of energy-matter) is invalid for several reasons.

(A) One reason is that the conservation which that principle asserts is not something known to be true without exception, but is, as M. T. Keeton has pointed out, only a defining-postulate of the notion of a *wholly closed* physical world, so that the question whether psycho-physical or physico-psychical causation ever occurs is (but in different words) the question whether the physical world *is* wholly closed. And that question is not answered by dignifying as a "principle" the assumption that the physical world is wholly closed.

(B) Anyway, as C. D. Broad has pointed out, it might be the case that whenever a given amount of energy vanishes from, or emerges in, the physical world at one place, then an equal amount of energy respectively emerges in, or vanishes from, that world at another place.

(C) And thirdly, if "energy" is meant to designate something experimentally measurable, then "energy" is defined in terms of causality, *not* "causality" in terms of transfer of energy. That is, it is not known that *all* causation, or, in particular, causation as between psychical and physical events, involves transfer of energy.

These various objections to interactionism—which, let it be noted, would automatically be objections also to epiphenomenalism—are thus wholly without force.

Epiphenomenalism, however, is open to the charge of being *arbitrary* in asserting that psychical events are always effects of physical events but never themselves cause other psychical events nor cause any physical events. For the experimental evidence we have—that, for instance, decision to raise one's arm causes it to rise under normal circumstances—is of exactly the same form as the experimental evidence we have that, under normal circumstances, burning one's skin causes occurrence of pain.

Psychophysical "parallelism" has widely been adopted as supposedly an alternative escaping the difficulties which —mistakenly, as we have now seen—are alleged to stand in the way of interactionism. "Parallelism," however, is really the name not of a solution but of a problem. For the parallelism itself remains to be accounted for. And the "double-aspect" explanation, or would-be explanation, of it is but an empty figure of speech unless and until the "substance," of which mind and brain are alleged to be two "aspects," has first been shown to exist. And this never yet has been done.

Interactionism, then, as presented in what precedes, though not as presented by Descartes, is a perfectly tenable conception of the relation between some mental events and some brain events, allowing as it does also that some brain events have bodily causes, and that some mental events directly cause some other mental events. It conceives minds as consisting, like material substances, of sets of systematically interrelated dispositions, i.e., of capacities, abilities, powers, and susceptibilities, each of which can be analyzed as a causal connection, more or less enduring, between any event of some particular kind—*C*, occurring in a state of affairs of some particular kind —*S*, and a sequent event in it, of some particular kind—*E*. The series of *exercises* of the different dispositions (which together define the *nature* of a given mind) constitutes the *history* of that particular mind, i.e., its *existence* as distinguished from only its *description*.

Do
Mind
and Body
Interact?

Interactionism is the thesis that the mind and the body, conceived as distinct, have mutual causal effects. If any position on this score has a right to be called "the common sense view," it is interactionism. Offering an interpretation along interactionist lines of such statements as "Worry causes ulcers" and "I'm so tired I can't think" is at least very tempting. Psychosomatic medicine is naturally analyzed along these lines.

Nonetheless not all dualists have been interactionists. Since decision, say, to rise from a chair is often correlated with rising (and hosts of other mental events are correlated with bodily events), a noninteractionist who is a dualist must explain this phenomenon. Noninteractionist dualists have attempted this in various ways: by maintaining that God established at creation a perfect harmony between the events that occur in a mind and those that occur in its associated body (Leibniz' preestablished harmony) or that He constantly arranges matters so that mental events and bodily events correspond without having direct effect on one another (Malebranche's occasionalism). Leibniz' development of preestablished harmony is included in the selections that follow. It provides one answer to the question, "What position can a dualist take if interactionism is untenable?" (Taylor briefly discusses these alternatives in the essay included under "Are Mind and Body Distinct?") Our major concern here, however, is with interactionism, which is certainly the majority view among dualists.

From these remarks two things should already be clear. First, as interactionism is a form of dualism, any critique of dualism is also at least an indirect critique of interactionism. Second, a refutation of interactionism would not by itself be a disproof of dualism. The considerations in favor of dualism might be so convincing that even were interactionism clearly false, we would feel obliged to retain a dualistic position—Leibniz's, for example.

Descartes was not only a dualist; he was also an interactionist. The short passage from a letter to Regius makes this clear. So does his remark in "Meditation Six" that he is not merely lodged in his body as a pilot in his ship, but as mental substance, is "so intimately conjoined, and intermingled" with his body that he says "with it I form a unitary whole."

Since mind and body are so different, however, the question arises as to how they can "form a unitary whole." This question troubled Descartes, and it is not at all clear that he gave a satisfactory answer to it. In particular, the question arises as to how mind and body interact, and it is this question that has received the bulk of the attention of later philosophers. Descartes conceives the mind as "co-extensive with the body" in the sense that it can "exercise its force at any point of the body." He adds that we have a "primary notion" of the union of mind and body—a basic, irreducible, and unshakable recognition that they are united. For Descartes, whether an adequate account of this union is even possible is open to doubt, for "it is by relying exclusively on the activities and concerns of ordinary life, and by abstaining from metaphysical meditation and concentrating instead on the things which exercise the imagination, that we can learn to apprehend the union of soul and body." Since, for Descartes, it is only when the mind can make use of concepts that are not representable by percepts or images that clear and distinct knowledge is available, these remarks of his are tantamount to the suggestion that (to adopt a Humean phrase) the union of mind and body is more to be *felt* than thought.

Leibniz did not, in fact, accept Descartes' claim that there are material substances, but his views concerning a preestablished harmony could easily enough be adopted by a dualist such as Descartes.

C. D. Broad discusses arguments both for and against interactionism and decides that the weight of evidence is in its favor. He takes it to be simply a fact of everyday experience (something "no one can deny") that "there is a close correlation between certain bodily events and certain mental events, and conversely." (See his first paragraph.) Why, then, should anyone deny that there are causal connections between these types of events? Because (1) it is hard to see how two types of events so dissimilar as mental and physical could ever be such as to permit an event of the one type to interact causally with an event of the other; because (2) a physical event belongs to a physical system and a mental event to a mental system (Broad's phrase is "substantial whole"), and while there are laws relating events within the physical system and there are perhaps also laws relating events within the mental system, there are no laws relating members of the one system to those of the other. A very forceful way of putting these reservations, which Broad only implies, is this. Insofar as dualism is successful in showing mind and body to belong to different types, it is successful to roughly the same degree in showing that there are genuine difficulties in maintaining that the mental and the physical are causally connected.

With respect to (1), Broad replies that very different sorts of things are causally connected (for example, drafts and colds). This is true and is perhaps sufficient reply to (1). But (2) in effect clarifies and expands the point made in (1), and (2) can be further explicated as follows. Bodily events occur at a place. When one physical event is said to cause another, we can ask "Where did the causal interaction take place?" This was a question that Descartes attempted to answer with, to be charitable, little success. But necessarily, in the dualist's view, mental events do not occur in space (though in some or all cases correlated brain-events that are spatial may occur). Now suppose that mental event *M* causes bodily event *B*. To ask "*Where* did the interactions take place?" is both appropriate and not appropriate. If a physical event is caused to occur, it is caused to occur somewhere, and so (it seems reasonable to suppose) that is also where the interaction occurred. But if a mental event causes a physical event, the mental event is *not* located somewhere and so cannot be located where the physical event was located. Similarly that cannot be where the interaction took place (nor can any *other* place). So bodily event *B* was caused to occur, occurred at place *P*, was even caused to occur at *P*, but no causal interaction occurred at *P* (since if a causal interaction occurred at *P*, both cause and effect must be at *P*). Now add to this that we can trace a causal chain of physical events of which *B* is a member, with no gap where reference to something nonphysical is required. These are, I think, the considerations against interactionism which (2) brings forth.

The obvious answer to (2) is to reply that a system of mental events and a system of bodily events, under the special condition in which (at least some) members of the one system are correlated with (at least some) members of the other, are both subsystems of a larger system (parts of a "substantial whole")— namely, a person. This is the line that Broad takes, and it seems really necessary to do more than he does by way of elucidation before any careful appraisal of it is possible. Thus it is hard to tell how convincing a criticism (2) is until the type of reply that Board outlines is filled in far more fully.

Broad believes, however, that he has a proof of interactionism that will suffice by itself. It is the thesis that "in voluntary action, and there only, we are immediately acquainted with an instance of causal connection. If this be true the controversy is of course settled at once in favor of the Interactionist." Actually, a cluster of claims are united here: That volitions occur and are mental events, that bodily motions occur and are physical events, that volitions cause physical events (perhaps that we are incorrigibly aware of volitions and of bodily events), that we are noninferentially (and incorrigibly?) aware of volitions causing bodily movements. Since we are assuming dualism to be true for the sake of the argument in this section, we will discuss only the last claim.

Broad notes that Hume is widely held to have refuted the thesis that we

are ever noninferentially aware of any causal connections. Broad believes
that Hume's contentions do not refute this thesis. He contends that Hume has
proved only this: that choosing to perform a bodily movement *B* is never by
itself sufficient for performing *B* (muscle tissue in a healthy condition, the
occurrence of neural synapses and the like are also necessary). But we can,
Broad suggests, know two things about the connection between choices and
bodily movements: (a) that a certain bodily movement is the one I chose to
perform, (b) that had I not chosen to perform a certain bodily movement,
I would not have done so, that the volition was a necessary condition of the
movement. And in knowing (b), we know that a mental event causally
interacts with a physical event.

If I choose to scratch my left ear with my right hand, and I do so, there
is no difficulty in my knowing that the movement I performed was the one I
chose to perform. But it does not follow (nor does Broad claim that it does)
that the movement was caused by my choice, that is, (a) does not entail (b).

Further, it is not easy to see how I can know, on the basis of introspective
experience, that (b) is true. Hume's claim (which Broad does not explicitly
mention) is that I can "observe" both a volition and a bodily movement, but
I observe no causal connection between them. *At best*, I must *infer* such
a connection. Otherwise stated, Hume's point is that everything I observe
in this sort of case, both introspectively and through sensory perception, is
compatible with (c) my bodily movement would have occurred even if I
had not made any choice concerning it. If (c) is false, it is not false simply on
the basis of what I observe, but on the basis of a theory concerning, or an
interpretation of, what I observe. But if (c) is compatible with what I observe,
(b) is not something I know on the basis of what I observe. Thus the proof
of interactionism by means of introspection seems to fail.

Broad also discusses "scientific arguments against two-sided interactionism," and his remarks here are relevant to objection (2) above. He also
considers difficulties we face if we deny that the body affects the mind. Central
among these is the problem of accounting for mental events that bear no
discoverable connection with the mental events preceding them. In the final
section of the selection, Broad considers, and rejects, two further arguments
for interactionism.

Mind and Body Do Interact
RENÉ DESCARTES

I can say with truth that the question
which Yr Royal Highness proposes
seems to me to be that which can most
reasonably be asked of me in the light of
my published critiques. For having these
two things in the human soul, on which
depend all the knowledge we can have
of its nature, one being that it thanks,
the other that it is united to a body with
which it can act and suffer, I said almost

FROM: René Descartes' *Letter* to Princess Elizabeth (May 31, 1643 and June 28,
1643), J. R. Weinberg, trans.

nothing about the latter, and only concerned myself with explaining the former. The reason for this was that my principal purpose was to prove the distinction between soul and body, so the former alone was able to serve my purpose, whereas the latter would have been useless. But because Yr Highness sees so clearly that one cannot conceal anything from Her, I shall try here to explain the way I conceive the unison of the soul with the body and how it has the force to move the body.

First of all, I notice that there are some primitive notions in us on the pattern of which we form all our other knowledge. There are very few of such notions. For in addition to the most general notions of *being, number, duration,* etc. which apply to whatever we can conceive, we have for body in particular only the notion of extension, from which follows the notions of figures and movement; for the soul we have only the notion of thought in which are comprised the perceptions of the understanding and the inclinations of the will. Finally, for soul and body together, we have only the notion of their union on which depends the notion of the force which the soul has to move the body and which the body has for acting on the soul and for causing its sentiments and passion. I think also that the whole knowledge of men consists only on correctly distinguishing these notions and of attributing each of them only to things to which they [properly] pertain. For when we wish to explain some difficulty by means of a notion which does not pertain to it, we cannot fail to be deceived.

This also happens when we desire to explain one of these notions by another; for, since they are primitive notions, each of them can be understood only through itself.

And especially as the exercise of our senses has reduced the notions of extension, figures, and movements, much more familiar than the others, the principal cause of our errors consists in the fact that we commonly wish to use these notions to explain things to which they do not pertain, as when we wish help from the imagination in order to conceive the nature of the soul, or again, when we want to conceive the manner in which the soul moves the body by means of that by which one body is moved by another.

LETTER TO PRINCESS ELIZABETH: (JUNE 28, 1643)

First, I notice a great difference between these three kinds of notions, in that the soul only conceives of itself by pure understanding; the body, i.e., extension, figures, and movements, can be known by the understanding helped by the imagination, and finally the things which pertain to the union of soul and body can be known only obscurely by the understanding alone or by the understanding helped by imagination, but they can be known very clearly by the senses. So it happens that those who never philosophize and who are only served by their senses do not doubt that the soul moves the body and that the body acts on the soul, but they regard body and soul as only one thing, i.e., they conceive the union which is between these things; for to conceive the union between them is to conceive them as only one. The metaphysical thoughts which exercise the pure understanding serve to make the notion of the soul familiar, and the study of mathematics which exercises the imagination in considering figures and movements, accustoms us to form the very distinct notions of body; and finally it is in using only the concerns of life and ordinary conversations and in abstaining from meditating on and studying the things which exercise the imagination that we come to conceive the union of the soul and the body.

Preestablished Harmony Between Mind and Body
GOTTFRIED W. LEIBNIZ

God produces different substances according to the different views He has of the universe, and by the intervention of God the nature proper to each substance brings it about that what happens to one of them corresponds to what happens to all the others without any one of them acting immediately on another.

After seeing to some extent in what the nature of substances consists, it is necessary to attempt to explain the dependence which substances have on one another, and their actions and passions. Now, to begin with, it is quite plain that created substances depend on God who conserves them and even produces them continually by a kind of emanation as we produce our thoughts. For God turning, so to speak, on all sides and in all ways the general system of phenomena which He finds good to produce in order to manifest His glory, and seeing all aspects of the world in all possible ways, since there is no connection which escapes His omnipotence, it results, from each view of the universe seen from a certain aspect, that there is a substance which expresses the universe conformed to this view, if God finds it good to make His thought effective and to produce this substance. And as God's view is always true, our perceptions are also, our judgement came from us, and it is these judgements which deceive us. As we have already stated, and it follows from what we are about to say, that each substance is like a separate world, independent of everything except God. Thus, all our phenomena, i.e., all that can ever happen to us, are only consequences of our being and as these phenomena preserve a certain order suitable to our nature (or to the world which is in us, so to speak),

which allows us to make useful observations for regulating our conduct which are justified by the outcome of future phenomena, and so we can often judge the future by the past with being deceived, and this would suffice for us to say that these phenomena are true without bothering whether they exist outside ourselves and whether others also perceive them.

However, it is quite true that perceptions or expressions of all substances correspond with one another such that each observing carefully the reasons or laws it has observed, encounters another which has followed these laws, as when many people, having agreed to meet together somewhere on a fixed day, can do this effectively if they so desire. Now, although all express the same phenomena, this is not because their expressions are perfectly similar, for it suffices that they are proportional, just as many specators believe that they see the same thing, and are in fact in agreement, even though each one sees it and speaks about it according to the character of his own view. Now it is God alone (from whom all individuals continually emanate and Who sees the universe not only as they see it but quite differently from them) Who is the cause of this correspondence of their phenomena, and Who brings it about that what is peculiar to one is public to all. Otherwise, there would be no connection. One could therefore say in some manner with a good sense, however far from received usage, that one particular substance never acts on another particular substance, even suffers therefrom, if one considers that what happens to each substance is only the consequence of the idea or complete notion of that substance, because this idea already con-

FROM: *Discourse on Metaphysics*, Gottfried Leibniz. Section 14; J. R. Weinberg, trans. (originally published in 1686).

tains all its predicater co-events and expresses the whole universe. In fact, nothing can happen to us save thoughts and perceptions, and all our thoughts and perceptions are but the consequences, albeit contingent consequences of our preceding thoughts and perceptions such that, if I were able to consider deliber-ately all that happens to me or appears at this time, I would be able to see all that will ever happen or appear to me at any time. This would not tend to be so and everything would happen the same if everything outside me were destroyed, provided that God and I would still exist.

Arguments Pro and Con Concerning Interaction
C. D. BROAD

PHILOSOPHICAL ARGUMENTS AGAINST TWO-SIDED INTERACTION

*N*o one can deny that there is a close correlation between certain bodily events and certain mental events, and conversely. Therefore anyone who denies that there is action of mind on body and of body on mind must presumably hold (a) that concomitant variation is not an adequate criterion of causal connexion, and (b) that the other feature which is essential for causal connexion is absent in the case of body and mind. Now the common philosophical argument is that minds and mental states are so extremely unlike bodies and bodily states that it is inconceivable that the two should be causally connected. It is certainly true that, if minds and mental events are just what they seem to be to introspection and nothing more, and if bodies and bodily events are just what enlightened common-sense thinks them to be and nothing more, the two *are* extremely unlike. And this fact is supposed to show that, however closely correlated certain pairs of events in mind and body respectively may be, they cannot be causally connected.

Evidently the assumption at the back of this argument is that concomi-tant variation, together with a high enough degree of likeness, is an adequate test for causation; but that no amount of concomitant variation can establish causation in the absence of a high enough degree of likeness. Now I am inclined to admit part of this assumption. I think it is practically certain that causation does not simply *mean* concomitant variation. (And, if it did, *cadit quæstio*.) Hence the existence of the latter is not *ipso facto* a proof of the presence of the former. Again, I think it is almost certain that concomitant variation between A and B is not in fact a sufficient sign of the presence of a *direct* causal relation between the two. (I think it may perhaps be a sufficient sign of *either* a direct causal relation between A and B *or* of several causal relations which indirectly unite A and B through the medium of other terms C, D, etc.) So far I agree with the assumptions of the argument. But I cannot see the least reason to think that the other character-istic, which must be added to concomi-tant variation before we can be sure that A and B are causally connected, is a high degree of likeness between the two. One would like to know just how unlike two events may be before it becomes impossible to admit the existence of a causal relation between them. No one hestitates to hold that draughts and colds

FROM: *The Mind and Its Place in Nature*, C. D. Broad. (London: Routledge and Kegan Paul, Ltd., 1925), pp. 97–121. Reprinted by permission of Routledge and Kegan Paul, Ltd. and the Humanities Press, Inc.

in the head are causally connected, although the two are extremely unlike each other. If the unlikeness of draughts and colds in the head does not prevent one from admitting a causal connexion between the two, why should the unlikeness of volitions and voluntary movements prevent one from holding that they are causally connected? To sum up. I am willing to admit that an adequate criterion of causal connexion needs some other relation between a pair of events beside concomitant variation; but I do not believe for a moment that this other relation is that of qualitative likeness.

This brings us to a rather more refined form of the argument against Interaction. It is said that, whenever we admit the existence of a causal relation between two events, these two events (to put it crudely) must also form parts of a single substantial whole. E.g., all physical events are spatially related and form one great extended whole. And the mental events which would commonly be admitted to be causally connected are always events in a single mind. A mind is a substantial whole of a peculiar kind too. Now it is said that between bodily events and mental events there are no relations such as those which unite physical events in different parts of the same Space or mental events in the history of the same mind. In the absence of such relations, binding mind and body into a single substantial whole, we cannot admit that bodily and mental events can be causally connected with each other, no matter how closely correlated their variations may be.

This is a much better argument than the argument about qualitative likeness and unlikeness. If we accept the premise that causal relations can subsist only between terms which form parts of a single substantial whole must we deny that mental and bodily events can be causally connected? I do not think that we need. (i) It is of course perfectly true that an organism and the mind which animates it do not form a physical whole, and that they do not form a mental

whole; and these, no doubt, are the two kinds of substantial whole with which we are most familiar. But it does not follow that a mind and its organism do not form a substantial whole of *some* kind. There, plainly, is the extraordinary intimate union between the two which I have called "animation" of the one by the other. Even if the mind be just what it seems to introspection, and the body be just what it seems to perception aided by the more precise methods of science, this seems to me to be enough to make a mind and its body a substantial whole. Even so extreme a dualist about Mind and Matter as Descartes occasionally suggests that a mind and its body together form a quasi-substance; and, although we may quarrel with the language of the very numerous philosophers who have said that the mind is "the form" of its body, we must admit that such language would never have seemed plausible unless a mind and its body together had formed something very much like a single substantial whole.

(ii) We must, moreover, admit the possibility that minds and mental events have properties and relations which do not reveal themselves to introspection, and that bodies and bodily events may have properties and relations which do not reveal themselves to perception or to physical and chemical experiment. In virtue of these properties and relations the two together may well form a single substantial whole of the kind which is alleged to be needed for causal interaction. Thus, if we accept the premise of the argument, we have no right to assert that mind and body *cannot* interact; but only the much more modest proposition that introspection and perception do not suffice to assure us that mind and body are so interrelated that they *can* interact.

(iii) We must further remember that the Two-sided Interactionist is under no obligation to hold that the *complete* conditions of any mental event are bodily or that the complete conditions of any bodily event are mental. He needs only to assert that some mental events include certain bodily events among their necessary conditions, and that some bodily events include certain mental events among their necessary conditions. If I am paralysed my volition may not move my arm; and, if I am hypnotised or intensely interested or frightened, a wound may not produce a painful sensation. Now, if the complete cause and the complete effect in all interaction include both a bodily and a mental factor, the two wholes will be related by the fact that the mental constituents belong to a single mind, that the bodily constituents belong to a single body, and that this mind animates this body. This amount of connexion should surely be enough to allow of causal interaction.

This will be the most appropriate place to deal with the contention that, in voluntary action, and there only, we are immediately acquainted with an instance of causal connexion. If this be true the controversy is of course settled at once in favour of the Interactionist. It is generally supposed that this view was refuted once and for all by Mr. Hume in his *Enquiry concerning Human Understanding* (Sect. VII, Part I). I should not care to assert that the doctrine in question is true; but I do think that it is plausible, and I am quite sure that Mr Hume's arguments do not refute it. Mr Hume uses three closely connected arguments. (1) The connexion between a successful volition and the resulting bodily movement is as mysterious and as little self-evident as the connexion between any other event and its effect. (2) We have to learn from experience which of our volitions will be effective and which will not. *E.g.*, we do not know, until we have tried, that we can voluntarily move our arms and cannot voluntarily move our livers. And again, if a man were suddenly paralysed, he would still expect to be able to move his arm voluntarily, and would be surprised when he found that it kept still in spite of his volition. (3) We have discovered that the immediate consequence of a volition is a change in our nerves and muscles, which most people know nothing about; and is not the movement of a limb, which most people believe to be its immediate and necessary consequence.

The second and third arguments are valid only against the contention that we know immediately that a volition to make a certain movement is the *sufficient* condition for the happening of that movement. They are quite irrelevant to the contention that we know immediately that the volition is a *necessary* condition for the happening of just that movement at just that time. No doubt many other conditions are also necessary, *e.g.*, that our nerves and muscles shall be in the right state; and these other necessary conditions can be discovered only by special investigation. Since our volitions to move our limbs are in fact followed in the vast majority of cases by the willed movement, and since the other necessary conditions are not very obvious, it is natural enough that we should think that we know immediately that our volition is the *sufficient* condition of the movement of our limbs. If we think so, we are certainly wrong; and Mr Hume's arguments prove that we are. But they prove nothing else. It does not follow that we are wrong in thinking that we know, without having to wait for the result, that the volition is a *necessary* condition of the movement.

It remains to consider the first argument. Is the connexion between cause and effect as mysterious and as little self-evident in the case of the voluntary production of bodily movement as in all other cases? If so, we must hold that the first time a baby wills to move its hand it is just as much surprised to find its hand moving as it would be to find its leg moving or its nurse bursting into flames. I do not profess to know anything about the infant mind; but it seems to me that this is a wildly paradoxical consequence, for which there is no evidence or likelihood. But there is no need to leave the matter there. It is perfectly plain that, in the case of volition and voluntary movement, there *is* a connexion between the cause and the effect which is not present in other cases of causation, and which does make it plausible to hold that in this one case the nature of the effect can be foreseen by merely reflecting on the nature of the cause. The peculiarity of a volition as a cause-factor is that it involves as an essential part of it the idea of the effect. To say that a person has a volition to move his arm involves saying that he has an idea of his arm (and not of his leg or his liver) and an idea of the position in which he wants his arm to be. It is simply silly in view of this fact to say that there is no closer connexion between the desire to move my arm and the movement of my arm than there is between this desire and the movement of my leg or my liver. We cannot detect any analogous connexion between cause and effect in causal transactions which we view wholly from outside, such as the movement of a billiard-ball by a cue. It is therefore by no means unreasonable to suggest that, in the one case of our own voluntary movements, we can see without waiting for the result that such and such a volition is a necessary condition of such and such a bodily movement.

It seems to me then that Mr Hume's arguments on this point are absolutely irrelevant, and that it may very well be true that in volition we positively know that our desire for such and such a bodily movement is a necessary (though not a sufficient) condition of the happening of just that movement at just that time. On the whole then I conclude that the philosophical arguments certainly do not disprove Two-sided Interaction, and that they do not even raise any strong presumption against it. And, while I am not prepared definitely to commit myself to the view that, in voluntary movement, we positively *know* that the mind acts on the body, I do think that this opinion is quite plausible when properly stated and that the arguments which have been brought against it are worthless. I pass therefore to the scientific arguments.

SCIENTIFIC ARGUMENTS AGAINST TWO-SIDED INTERACTION

There are, so far as I know, two of these. One is supposed to be based on the physical principle of the Conservation of Energy, and on certain experiments which have been made on human bodies. The other is based on the close analogy which is said to exist between the structures of the physiological mechanism of reflex action and that of voluntary action. I will take them in turn.

(1) THE ARGUMENT FROM ENERGY

It will first be needful to state clearly what is asserted by the principle of the Conservation of Energy. It is found that, if we take certain material systems, *e.g.*, a gun, a cartridge, and a bullet, there is a certain magnitude which keeps approximately constant throughout all their changes. This is called "Energy". When the gun has not been fired it and the bullet have no motion, but the explosive in the cartridge has great chemical energy. When it has been fired the bullet is moving very fast and has great energy of movement. The gun, though not moving fast in its recoil, has also great energy of movement because it is very massive. The gases produced by the explosion have some energy of movement and some heat-energy, but much less chemical energy than the unexploded charge had. These various kinds of energy can be measured in common units according to certain conventions. To an innocent mind there seems to be a good deal of "cooking" at this stage, *i.e.*, the conventions seem to be chosen and various kinds and amounts of concealed energy seem to be postulated in order to make the principle come out right at the end. I do not propose to go into this in detail, for two reasons. In the first place, I think that the conventions adopted and the postulates made, though somewhat suggestive of the fraudulent company-promoter, can be justified by their coherence with certain experimental facts, and that they are not simply made *ad hoc*. Secondly, I shall show that the Conservation of Energy is absolutely irrelevant to the question at issue, so that it would be waste of time to treat it too seriously in the present connexion. Now it is found that the total energy of all kinds in this system, when measured according to these conventions, is approximately the same in amount though very differently distributed after the explosion and before it. If we had confined our attention to a part of this system and *its* energy this would not have been true. The bullet, *e.g.*, had no energy at all before the explosion and a great deal afterwards. A system like the bullet, the gun, and the charge, is called a "Conservative System"; the bullet alone, or the gun and the charge, would be called "Non-conservative Systems". A conservative system might therefore be defined as one whose total energy is redistributed, but not altered in amount, by changes that happen within it. Of course a given system might be conservative for some kinds of change and not for others.

So far we have merely defined a "Conservative System", and admitted that there are systems which, for some kinds of changes at any rate, answer approximately to our definition. We can now state the Principle of the Conservation of Energy in terms of the conceptions just defined. The principle asserts that every material system is either itself conservative, or, if not, is part of a larger material system which is conservative. We may take it that there is good inductive evidence for this proposition.

The next thing to consider is the experiments on the human body. These tend to prove that a living body, with the air that it breathes and the food that it eats, forms a conservative system to a high degree of approximation. We can measure the chemical energy of the food given to a man, and that which enters his body in the form of Oxygen breathed in.

We can also, with suitable apparatus, collect, measure and analyse the air breathed out, and thus find its chemical energy. Similarly, we can find the energy given out in bodily movement, in heat, and in excretion. It is alleged that, on the average, whatever the man may do, the energy of his bodily movements is exactly accounted for by the energy given to him in the form of food and of Oxygen. If you take the energy put in in food and Oxygen, and subtract the energy given out in waste-products, the balance is almost exactly equal to the energy put out in bodily movements. Such slight differences as are found are as often on one side as on the other, and are therefore probably due to unavoidable experimental errors. I do not propose to criticise the interpretation of these experiments in detail, because, as I shall show soon, they are completely irrelevant to the problem of whether mind and body interact. But there is just one point that I will make before passing on. It is perfectly clear that such experiments can tell us only what happens on the average over a long time. To know whether the balance was accurately kept at every moment we should have to kill the patient at each moment and analyse his body so as to find out the energy present then in the form of stored-up products. Obviously we cannot keep on killing the patient in order to analyse him, and then reviving him in order to go on with the experiment. Thus it would seem that the results of the experiment are perfectly compatible with the presence of quite large excesses or defects in the total bodily energy at certain moments, provided that these average out over longer periods. However, I do not want to press this criticism; I am quite ready to accept for our present purpose the traditional interpretation which has been put on the experiments.

We now understand the physical principle and the experimental facts. The two together are generally supposed to prove that mind and body cannot interact. What precisely is the argument, and is it valid? I imagine that the argument, when fully stated, would run somewhat as follows: "I will to move my arm, and it moves. If the volition has anything to do with causing the movement we might expect energy to flow from my mind to my body. Thus the energy of my body ought to receive a measurable increase, not accounted for by the food that I eat and the Oxygen that I breathe. But no such physically unaccountable increases of bodily energy are found. Again, I tread on a tin-tack, and a painful sensation arises in my mind. If treading on the tack has anything to do with causing the sensation we might expect energy to flow from my body to my mind. Such energy would cease to be measurable. Thus there ought to be a noticeable decrease in my bodily energy, not balanced by increases anywhere in the physical system. But such unbalanced decreases of bodily energy are not found." So it is concluded that the volition has nothing to do with causing my arm to move, and that treading on the tack has nothing to do with causing the painful sensation.

Is this argument valid? In the first place it is important to notice that the conclusion does not follow from the Conservation of Energy and the experimental facts alone. The real premise is a tacitly assumed proposition about causation; viz., that, if a change in A has anything to do with causing a change in B, energy must leave A and flow into B. This is neither asserted nor entailed by the Conservation of Energy. What *it* says is that, *if* energy leaves A, it must appear in something else, say B; so that A and B together form a conservative system. Since the Conservation of Energy is not itself the premise for the argument against Interaction, and since it does not entail that premise, the evidence for the Conservation of Energy is not evidence against Interaction. Is there any independent evidence for the premise? We may admit that it *is* true of many, though not of all, transactions with the physical realm. But there are cases where it is not true even of purely physical transactions; and, even

if it were always true in the physical realm, it would not follow that it must also be true of trans-physical causation. Take the case of a weight swinging at the end of a string hung from a fixed point. The total energy of the weight is the same at all positions in its course. It is thus a conservative system. But at every moment the direction and velocity of the weight's motion are different, and the proportion between its kinetic and its potential energy is constantly changing. These changes are caused by the pull of the string, which acts in a different direction at each different moment. The string makes no difference to the total energy of the weight; but it makes all the difference in the world to the particular way in which the weight moves and the particular way in which the energy is distributed between the potential and the kinetic forms. This is evident when we remember that the weight would begin to move in an utterly different course if at any moment the string were cut.

Here, then, we have a clear case even in the physical realm where a system is conservative but is continually acted on by something which affects its movement and the distribution of its total energy. Why should not the mind act on the body in this way? If you say that you can see how a string can affect the movement of a weight, but cannot see how a volition could affect the movement of a material particle, you have deserted the scientific argument and have gone back to one of the philosophical arguments. Your real difficulty is either that volitions are so very unlike movements, or that the volition is in your mind whilst the movement belongs to the physical realm. And we have seen how little weight can be attached to these objections.

The fact is that, even in purely physical systems, the Conservation of Energy does not explain what changes will happen or when they will happen. It merely imposes a very general limiting condition on the changes that are possible. The fact that the system composed of bullet, charge, and gun, in our earlier example, is conservative does not tell us that the gun ever will be fired, or when it will be fired if at all, or what will cause it to go off, or what forms of energy will appear if and when it does go off. The change in this case is determined by pulling the trigger. Likewise the mere face that the human body and its neighbourhood form a conservative system does not explain any particular bodily movement; it does not explain why I ever move at all, or why I sometimes write, sometimes walk, and sometimes swim. To explain the happening of these particular movements at certain times it seems to be essential to take into account the volitions which happen from time to time in my mind; just as it is essential to take the string into account to explain the particular behaviour of the weight, and to take the trigger into account to explain the going off of the gun at a certain moment. The difference between the gun-system and the body-system is that a little energy does flow into the former when the trigger is pulled, whilst it is alleged that none does so when a volition starts a bodily movement. But there is not even this amount of difference between the body-system and the swinging weight.

Thus the argument from energy has no tendency to disprove Two-sided Interaction. It has gained a spurious authority from the august name of the Conservation of Energy. But this impressive principle proves to have nothing to do with the case. And the real premise of the argument is not self-evident, and is not universally true even in purely intraphysical transactions. In the end this scientific argument has to lean on the old philosophic arguments; and we have seen that these are but bruised reeds. Nevertheless, the facts brought forward by the argument from energy do throw some light on the *nature* of the interaction between mind and body, assuming this to happen. They do suggest that all the energy of our bodily actions comes out of and goes back into the physical world, and that minds neither

add energy to nor abstract it from the latter. What they do, if they do anything, is to determine that at a given moment so much energy shall change from the chemical form to the form of bodily movement; and they determine this, so far as we can see, without altering the total amount of energy in the physical world.

(2) THE ARGUMENT FROM THE STRUCTURE OF THE NERVOUS SYSTEM

There are purely reflex actions, like sneezing and blinking, in which there is no reason to suppose that the mind plays any essential part. Now we know the nervous structure which is used in such acts as these. A stimulus is given to the outer end of an efferent nerve; some change or other runs up this nerve, crosses a synapse between this and an afferent nerve, travels down the latter to a muscle, causes the muscle to contract, and so produces a bodily movement. There seems no reason to believe that the mind plays any essential part in this process. The process may be irreducibly vital, and not merely physicochemical; but there seems no need to assume anything more than this. Now it is said that the whole nervous system is simply an immense complication of interconnected nervous arcs. The result is that a change which travels inwards has an immense number of alternative paths by which it may travel outwards. Thus the reaction to a given stimulus is no longer one definite movement, as in the simple reflex. Almost any movement may follow any stimulus according to the path which the afferent disturbance happens to take. This path will depend on the relative resistance of the various synapses at the time. Now a variable response to the same stimulus is characteristic of deliberate as opposed to reflex action.

These are the facts. The argument based on them runs as follows. It is admitted that the mind has nothing to do with the causation of purely reflex actions. But the nervous structure and the nervous processes involved in deliberate action do not differ in kind from those involved in reflex action; they differ only in degree of complexity. The variability which characterises deliberate action is fully explained by the variety of alternative paths and the variable resistances of the synapses. So it is unreasonable to suppose that the mind has any more to do with causing deliberate actions than it has to do with causing reflex actions.

I think that this argument is invalid. In the first place I am pretty sure that the persons who use it have before their imagination a kind of picture of how mind and body must interact if they interact at all. They find that the facts do not answer to this picture, and so they conclude that there is no interaction. The picture is of the following kind. They think of the mind as sitting somewhere in a hole in the brain, surrounded by telephones. And they think of the efferent disturbances as coming to an end at one of these telephones and there affecting the mind. The mind is then supposed to respond by sending an efferent impulse down another of these telephones. As no such hole, with efferent nerves stopping at its walls and afferent nerves starting from them, can be found, they conclude that the mind can play no part in the transaction. But another alternative is that this picture of how the mind must act if it acts at all is wrong. To put it shortly, the mistake is to confuse a gap in an explanation with a spatio-temporal gap, and to argue from the absence of the latter to the absence of the former.

The Interactionist's contention is simply that there is a gap in any purely physiological explanation of deliberate action; *i.e.*, that all such explanations fail to account completely for the facts because they leave out one necessary condition. It does not follow in the least that there must be a spatio-temporal breach of continuity in the physiological conditions, and that the missing condition must fill this gap in the way in which the movement of a wire fills the spatio-temporal interval between the

pulling of a bell-handle and the ringing of a distant bell. To assume this is to make the mind a kind of physical object, and to make its action a kind of mechanical action. Really, the mind and its actions are not literally in Space at all, and the time which is occupied by the mental event is no doubt *also* occupied by some part of the physiological process. Thus I am inclined to think that much of the force which this argument actually exercises on many people is simply due to the presupposition about the *modus operandi* of interaction, and that it is greatly weakened when this presupposition is shown to be a mere prejudice due to our limited power of envisaging unfamiliar alternative possibilities.

We can, however, make more detailed objections to the argument than this. There is a clear introspective difference between the mental accompaniment of voluntary action and that of reflex action. What goes on in our minds when we decide with difficulty to get out of a hot bath on a cold morning is obviously extremely different from what goes on in our minds when we sniff pepper and sneeze. And the difference is qualitative; it is not a mere difference of complexity. This difference has to be explained somehow; and the theory under discussion gives no plausible explanation of it. The ordinary view that, in the latter case, the mind is not acting on the body at all; whilst, in the former, it is acting on the body in a specific way, does at least make the introspective difference between the two intelligible.

Again, whilst it is true that deliberate action differs from reflex action in its greater variability of response to the same stimulus, this is certainly not the whole or the most important part of the difference between them. The really important difference is that, in deliberate action, the response is varied *appropriately* to meet the special circumstances which are supposed to exist at the time or are expected to arise later; whilst reflex action is not varied in this way, but is blind and almost mechanical.

The complexity of the nervous system explains the *possibility* of variation; it does not in the least explain why the alternative which actually takes place should as a rule be appropriate and not merely haphazard. And so again it seems as if some factor were in operation in deliberate action which is not present in reflex action; and it is reasonable to suppose that this factor is the volition in the mind.

It seems to me that this second scientific argument has no tendency to disprove interaction; but that the facts which it brings forward do tend to suggest the particular form which interaction probably takes if it happens at all. They suggest that what the mind does to the body in voluntary action, if it does anything, is to lower the resistance of certain synapses and to raise that of others. The result is that the nervous current follows such a course as to produce the particular movement which the mind judges to be appropriate at the time. On such a view the difference between reflex, habitual, and deliberate actions for the present purpose becomes fairly plain. In pure reflexes the mind cannot voluntarily affect the resistance of the synapses concerned, and so the action takes place in spite of it. In habitual action it deliberately refrains from interfering with the resistance of the synapses, and so the action goes on like a complicated reflex. But it *can* affect these resistances if it wishes, though often only with difficulty; and it is ready to do so if it judges this to be expedient. Finally, it may lose the power altogether. This would be what happens when a person becomes a slave to some habit, such as drug-taking.

I conclude that, at the level of enlightened common-sense at which the ordinary discussion of Interaction moves, no good reason has been produced for doubting that the mind acts on the body in volition, and that the body acts on the mind in sensation. The philosophic arguments are quite inconclusive; and the scientific arguments, when properly understood, are quite compatible with Two-sided Interaction. At most they suggest certain conclusions as to the form which interaction probably takes if it happens at all.

DIFFICULTIES IN THE DENIAL OF INTERACTION

I propose now to consider some of the difficulties which would attend the denial of Interaction, still keeping the discussion at the same common-sense level. If a man denies the action of body on mind he is at once in trouble over the causation of new sensations. Suppose that I suddenly tread on an unsuspected tin-tack. A new sensation suddenly comes into my mind. This is an event, and it presumably has some cause. Now, however carefully I introspect and retrospect, I can find no other mental event which is adequate to account for the fact that just that sensation has arisen at just that moment. If I reject the common-sense view that treading on the tack is an essential part of the cause of the sensation, I must suppose either that it is uncaused, or that it is caused by other events in my mind which I cannot discover by introspection or retrospection, or that it is caused telepathically by other finite minds or by God. Now enquiry of my neighbours would show that it is not caused telepathically by any event in their minds which they can introspect or remember. Thus anyone who denies the action of body on mind, and admits that sensations have causes, must postulate either (*a*) immense numbers of unobservable states in his own mind; or (*b*) as many unobservable states in his neighbours' minds, together with telepathic action; or (*c*) some non-human spirit together with telepathic action. I must confess that the difficulties which have been alleged against the action of body on mind seem to be mild compared with those of the alternative hypotheses which are involved in the denial of such action.

The difficulties which are involved in the denial of the action of mind on body are at first sight equally great; but I do not think that they turn out to be so serious as those which are involved in denying the action of body on mind. The *prima facie* difficulty is this. The world contains many obviously artificial objects, such as books, bridges, clothes, etc. We know that, if we go far enough back in the history of their production, we always do in fact come on the actions of some human body. And the minds connected with these bodies did design the objects in question, did will to produce them, and did believe that they were initiating and guiding the physical process by means of these designs and volitions. If it be true that the mind does not act on the body, it follows that the designs and volitions in the agents' minds did not in fact play any part in the production of books, bridges, clothes, etc. This appears highly paradoxical. And it is an easy step from it to say that anyone who denies the action of mind on body must admit that books, bridges, and other such objects *could* have been produced even though there had been no minds, no thought of these objects and no desire for them. This consequence seems manifestly absurd to commonsense, and it might be argued that it reflects its absurdity back on the theory which entails it.

The man who denies that mind can act on body might deal with this difficulty in two ways: (1) He might deny that the conclusion *is* intrinsically absurd. He might say that human bodies are extraordinarily complex physical objects, which probably obey irreducible laws of their own, and that we really do not know enough about them to set limits to what their unaided powers could accomplish. This is the line which Spinoza took. The conclusion, it would be argued, *seems* absurd only because the state of affairs which it contemplates is so very unfamiliar. We find it difficult to imagine a body like ours without a mind like ours; but, if we could get over this defect in our powers of imagination, we might have no difficulty in admitting that such a body could do all the things which our bodies do. I think it must be admitted that the difficulty is not so

great as that which is involved in denying the action of body on mind. There we had to postulate *ad hoc* utterly unfamiliar entities and modes of action; here it is not certain that we should have to do this.

(2) The other line of argument would be to say that the alleged consequence does not necessarily follow from denying the action of mind on body. I assume that both parties admit that causation is something more than mere *de facto* regularity of sequence and concomitance. If they do not, of course the whole controversy between them becomes futile; for there will certainly be causation between mind and body and between body and mind, in the only sense in which there is causation anywhere. This being presupposed, the following kind of answer is logically possible. When I say that B could not have happened unless A had happened, there are two alternative possibilities. (*a*). A may itself be an indispensable link in any chain of causes which ends up with B. (*b*) A may not itself be a link in any chain of causation which ends up with B. But there may be an indispensable like α in any such chain of causation, and A may be a necessary accompaniment or sequent of α. These two possibilities may be illustrated by diagrams. (*a*) is represented by the figure below:—

$$\begin{array}{ccccccc} A_0 & & A & & A_1 & & A_2 & & B \\ . & \rightarrow & . & \rightarrow & . & \rightarrow & . & \rightarrow & . \end{array}$$

The two forms of (*b*) are represented by the two figures below:—

$$\begin{array}{ccccccc} & & A & & & & & \\ A_0 & & \uparrow & & A_1 & & A_2 & & B \\ . & \rightarrow & . & \rightarrow & . & \rightarrow & . & \rightarrow & . \\ & & \alpha_1 & & & & & \end{array}$$

and

$$\begin{array}{ccccccc} & & & . A & & & \\ A_0 & & \nearrow & A_1 & & A_2 & & B \\ . & \rightarrow & . & \rightarrow & . & \rightarrow & . & \rightarrow & . \\ & & \alpha_1 & & & & \end{array}$$

Evidently, if B cannot happen unless α precedes, and if α cannot happen without A accompanying or immediately following it, B will not be able to happen unless A precedes it. And yet A will have had no part in causing B. It will be noticed that, on this view, a has a complex effect AA_1, of which a certain part, viz., A_1 is sufficient by itself to produce A_2 and ultimately B. Let us apply this abstract possibility to our present problem. Suppose that B is some artificial object, like a book or a bridge. If we admit that this could not have come into existence unless a certain design and volition had existed in a certain mind, we could interpret the facts in two ways. (*a*) We could hold that the design and volition are themselves an indispensable link in the chain of causation which ends in the production of a bridge or a book. This is the common view, and it requires us to admit the action of mind on body. (*b*) We might hold that the design and the volition are not themselves a link in the chain of causation which ends in the production of the artificial object; but that they are a necessary accompaniment or sequent of something which *is* an indispensable link in this chain of causation. On this view the chain consists wholly of physical events; but one of these physical events (viz., some event in the brain) has a complex consequent. One part of this consequent is purely physical, and leads by purely physical causation to the ultimate production of a bridge or a book. The other is purely mental, and consists of a certain design and volition in the mind which animates the human body concerned. If this has any consequences they are purely mental. Each part of this complex consequent follows with equal necessity; this particular brain-state could no more have existed without such and such a mental state accompanying or following it than it could have existed without such and such a bodily movement following it. If we are willing to take some such view as this, we can admit that certain objects could not have existed unless there had been designs of them and desires for them; and yet we could consistently deny that these desires and designs have any effect on the movements of our bodies.

It seems to me then that the doctrine which I will call "One-sided Action of Body on Mind" is logically possible; *i.e.*, a theory which accepts the action of body on mind but denies the action of mind on body. But I do not see the least reason to accept it, since I see no reason to deny that mind acts on body in volition. One-sided Action has, I think, generally been held in the special form called "Epiphenomenalism." I take this doctrine to consist of the following four propositions: (1) Certain bodily events cause certain mental events. (2) No mental event plays any part in the causation of any bodily event. (3) No mental event plays any part in the causation of any other mental event. Consequently (4) all mental events are caused by bodily events and by them only. Thus Epiphenomenalism is just One-sided Action of Body on Mind, together with a special theory about the nature and structure of mind. This special theory does not call for discussion here, where I am dealing only with the relations between minds and bodies, and am not concerned with a detailed analysis of mind. In a later chapter we shall have to consider the special features of Epiphenomenalism.

ARGUMENTS IN FAVOUR OF INTERACTION

The only arguments *for* One-sided Action of Body on Mind or for Parallelism are the arguments *against* Two-sided Interaction; and these, as we have seen, are worthless. Are there any arguments in favour of Two-sided Interaction? I have incidentally given two which seem to me to have considerable weight. In favour of the action of mind on body is the fact that we seem to be immediately aware of a causal relation when we voluntarily try to produce a bodily movement, and that the arguments to show that this cannot be true are invalid. In favour of the action of body on mind are the insuperable difficulties which I have pointed out in accounting for the happening of new sensations on any other hypothesis. There are, however, two other arguments which have often been thought to prove the action of mind on body. These are (1) an evolutionary argument, first used, I believe, by William James; and (2) the famous "Telegram argument." They both seem to me to be quite obviously invalid.

(1) The evolutionary argument runs as follows: It is a fact, which is admitted by persons who deny Two-sided Interaction, that minds increase in complexity and power with the growth in complexity of the brain and nervous system. Now, if the mind makes no difference to the actions of the body, this development on the mental side is quite unintelligible from the point of view of natural selection. Let us imagine two animals whose brains and nervous systems were of the same degree of complexity; and suppose, if possible, that one had a mind and the other had none. If the mind makes no difference to the behaviour of the body the chance of survival and of leaving descendants will clearly be the same for the two animals. Therefore natural selection will have no tendency to favour the evolution of mind which has actually taken place. I do not think that there is anything in this argument. Natural selection is a purely negative process; it simply tends to eliminate individuals and species which have variations unfavourable to survival. Now, by hypothesis, the possession of a mind is not *unfavourable* to survival; it simply makes no difference. Now it may be that the existence of a mind of such and such a kind is an inevitable consequence of the existence of a brain and nervous system of such and such a degree of complexity. Indeed we have seen that some such view is essential if the opponent of Two-sided Interaction is to answer the common-sense objection that artificial objects could not have existed unless there had been a mind which designed and desired them. On this hypothesis there is no need to invoke natural selection twice over, once to explain the evolution of the brain and nervous system, and once to explain the evolution of the mind. If

natural selection will account for the evolution of the brain and nervous system, the evolution of the mind will follow inevitably, even though it adds nothing to the survival-value of the organism. The plain fact is that natural selection does not account for the origin or for the growth in complexity of anything whatever; and therefore it is no objection to any particular theory of the relations of mind and body that, if it were true, natural selection would not explain the origin and development of mind.

(2) The "telegram argument" is as follows: Suppose there were two telegrams, one saying "Our son has been killed", and the other saying: "Your son has been killed". And suppose that one or other of them was delivered to a parent whose son was away from home. As physical stimuli they are obviously extremely alike, since they differ only in the fact that the letter "Y" is present in one and absent in the other. Yet we know that the reaction of the person who received the telegram might be very different according to which one he received. This is supposed to show that the reactions of the body cannot be wholly accounted for by bodily causes, and that the mind must intervene causally in some cases. Now I have very little doubt that the mind does play a part in determining the action of the recipient of the telegram; but I do not see why this argument should prove it to a person who doubted or denied it. If two very similar stimuli are followed by two very different results, we are no doubt justified in concluding that these stimuli are not the complete causes of the reactions which follow them. But of course it would be admitted by every one that the receipt of the telegram is not the complete cause of the recipient's reaction. We all know that his brain and nervous system play an essential part in any reaction that he may make to the stimulus. The question then is whether the minute structure of his brain and nervous system, including in this the supposed traces left by past stimuli and

past reactions, is not enough to account for the great difference in his behaviour on receiving two very similar stimuli. Two keys may be very much alike, but one may fit a certain lock and the other may not. And, if the lock be connected with the trigger of a loaded gun, the results of "stimulating" the system with one or other of the two keys will be extremely different. We know that the brain and nervous system are very complex, and we commonly suppose that they contain more or less permanent traces and linkages due to past stimuli and reactions. If this be granted, it is obvious that two very similar stimuli may produce very different results, simply because one fits in with the internal structure of the brain and nervous system whilst the other does not. And I do not see how we can be sure that anything more is needed to account for the mere difference of reaction adduced by the "telegram argument."

Ethics

he question "What shall I do?" is one we all face again and again. It is, of course, an elliptical one. Given that I must want to become wealthy, or be happy, or do my duty, or save face, what shall I do? Supposing that I know or can learn what will attain my ends, what I shall do depends on what my purposes are.

What ought I to do? is another question we all face, but one that in this sense, at least, is not elliptical: What I ought morally to do does not depend on what I want to attain. I may not know what I ought to do, or I may know what I ought to do, and still not do it. But if it is true that I ought to do A, it is true whether doing A serves my purposes or not.

But that I ought to do A, whether A is or is not something that happens to serve my subjectively adopted ends, supposes that there are in fact duties that bind me in some absolute and objective sense. The existence of such duties has of course been questioned. The great diversity of moral practice within some societies and from one society to another has been used as a basis for rejecting the notion of a duty that binds men in an unconditional way and for supposing that morality is relative and society-bound. Some existentialists go even further, claiming that men can only be free and responsible beings if they are not bound by an absolute moral law. Cultural relativism and contemporary existentialism both suggest that any answer to the question "What ought I to do?" will be arbitrary, since any answer can be countered by incompatible but equally satisfactory answers. "Right" answers are right only because we live when and where we happen to live or choose as we happen to choose. We are really limited to our first question, "What shall I do?" and this question can be answered in a nonarbitrary way only about means to ends which we have arbitrarily adopted. So, at least, goes a popular interpretation of morality.

Powerful critiques of cultural and existential relativism serve notice that relativism may have to be abandoned and that it is possible that some system of ethical principles be known to be demonstrably superior to its competitors. (For a presentation and critique of cultural relativism, see *Theory of Knowledge*, Section One.) This raises the question: How can ethical viewpoints be evaluated?

Are there moral facts as well as moral theories? Do we gain insight into this issue by comparing science and morality? These and similar issues concern us in reflecting on how to appraise competing moral perspectives.

A related issue is raised by the question: "How, if at all, are fact and value connected?" It seems implausible to divorce description and evaluation entirely. That an action would cause great pain to many and bring gain only to one, or that a man cares only for himself, seems very relevant to a sane evaluation of the action or person. But it has seemed wrong to many careful philosophers to try to deduce, say, (2) "*A* is wrong," from some such premise as (1) "*A* will cause great pain to many and bring small benefit to only a few," even though they granted that (1) would indeed be a reason for accepting (2). Are (1) and (2) related by way of definition of "right" and "wrong," or are they more loosely related in terms of (1) being a good reason for (2), or is there some other alternative?

Another closely related issue concerns the role of rules and consequences in evaluating actions. We appeal to rules like "One ought not to lie," but we appeal also to consequences, as when we say "She will be hurt if you tell her what you really think." Has one sort of appeal primacy, generally at least, over the other? Are they distinct appeals after all?

If we appeal to consequences, as we often do, it may be that if I do *A*, this will bring great good consequences to a few but bad consequences to many whereas if I do *B*, there will be slightly good consequences for everyone affected by my action. Do I have to take everyone affected into account and distribute the consequences in the way that is best for all? Is justice, or equity of distribution, an overriding consideration? This too is an aspect of the question as to how rules and consequences are used in the evaluation of actions.

Still another issue is closely connected with the others we have mentioned, namely "Must an action that is right for one be right for all?" If, under a given set of circumstances, I ought to do *A*, does it follow that under the same circumstances everyone ought to do *A*?

This question, of course, raises a legitimate issue only if there are actions that are right in some nonarbitrary way for me to perform. This will be so only if the challenges to cultural relativism and contemporary existentialism discredit these views and there is a way of appraising ethical views.

Our questions cluster together, one leading to another, and an answer to one will presuppose or suggest answers to others. Such interconnecting of issues is common in philosophy; and to make this fact clear is one thing an introductory study of philosophy should do.

K. E. Y.

Are Ethical Claims Arbitrary?

Does Moral Diversity
Entail Moral Skepticism?

Sartre defends relativism by appeal to philosophical, not anthropological, considerations. Essentially he claims that (a) since God does not exist, there is no standard for right or wrong conduct; (b) none of the standard philosophical or theological accounts of ethics provides a way of deciding in concrete cases what is right; (c) were there any standard for right or wrong conduct, men would not be genuinely free, and so would not be men at all. Concerning (a), two questions arise. How does Sartre know that God does not exist? He offers no argument in support of this contention. Further, he assumes that if God does not exist, then there can be no standard to appeal to in deciding the answer to the question "Is this particular action right or wrong?" Perhaps so; but Plato and Mill, philosophers with quite diverse moral systems, would disagree. Sartre offers offers no argument for (a). So the best we can say is that if one chooses for some reason (or without reasons) to accept (a), he may then want to adopt Sartre's position.

With respect to (b), a distinction should be made between two considerations relevant to applying a criterion for distinguishing between right and wrong action. Taking a single example, suppose one maintains that an action is right only if it serves to maximize pleasure for the majority concerned. One may ask: is this criterion justified? This question is a philosophical one concerning the adequacy of a criterion for distinquishing between right and wrong. But if one accepts the criterion, then there is a further question: Will this particular action, as opposed to all others, heighten pleasure for all concerned? In the main at least, this is, a factual question, and it may in a given case be extremely hard to decide which action will in fact produce maximum pleasure. The same issue will arise for many other criteria for discerning right and wrong action. That "the facts" are relevant to deciding what one ought to do is widely recognized: but, we have noted, what the facts *are* is often not easy to decide. For this reason, among others, moral choices are often chancy endeavors. The case that Sartre poses as insoluble for various examples of philosophical and theological moral systems is one in which the facts are unavailable: What *will* the effect be if the man joins the resistance movement, and what will they be if he does not? One does not know with any certainty but must rely on whatever educated guess he can manage. But it is quite fallacious to suppose that this constitutes an objection to any moral system or to there being moral *systems* as opposed to intuitive decisions or random choices. Again, to put the point formally, "If we do not have sufficient facts the application of a moral criterion is quite difficult" does not entail "There is no adequate or correct moral criterion."

But these considerations affect only the context of Sartre's own analysis, not that analysis itself. For this, we must turn to (c). Speaking very roughly, two analyses of moral freedom have been offered in traditional philosophy. For one, to be free is to be rational and to be rational is to be determined (with respect to both moral belief and conduct) by necessary truths. He is free who is determined by reasons which are necessary truths, and no one who sees a course of conduct to be right can fail to follow it. (This assumes, of course, that some moral statements are true, and necessarily so.) For the other, to be free is to be able to accept or reject good reasons for conduct, and to know that an action is right but be able nonetheless not to do it. Only if one performs an action freely (under conditions in which he could in fact have failed to do it) can he be praiseworthy or blameworthy for doing that action.

Sartre offers a third analysis. To be free with respect to a choice is to be in a position in which there is no nonarbitrary reason (that is, no reason at all) for making the choice in one way as opposed to making it in another. In this respect. Plantinga raises some crucial questions. What can it mean to say that I am free in a context where any choice I make is purely arbitrary? How, in such contexts, can I be responsible (as Sartre, in some sense, claims that I am)? Why am I, in such contexts, to feel *anguish* over what I have done (as Sartre feels is appropriate)? I may feel anguish over there being no reasons to guide me (if I accept Sartre's view); I may (if I reject this view) feel anguish over not having acted more wisely or kindly—for not having done *better*; but no meaning can be attached to "better" in a Sartrean context (except an arbitrary one). How can I be responsible if anything I do is (except on an arbitrarily adopted standard) on the same moral level as anything else? And what sort of freedom do I have if I can only make blind stabs in the dark with respect to "freely" choosing my course of action, my life style, and my goals? After a careful combing of Sartre's perspective, Plantinga concludes that only by abandoning it and its correlative account of freedom— that is, by rejecting (c)—can Sartre retain room for any element of responsibility, anguish, or even freedom. "Sartre's doctrine seems to take crucial moral notions very seriously. But in the last analysis the doctrine of freedom undercuts the very possibility of morality." Only by covertly reintroducing an account of man's essence and restricting the scope of "absolute" freedom does Sartre appear to offer the possibility of morality. "Sartre himself finds it impossible consistently to maintain a doctrine of absolute freedom. And this is a case where his inconsistency does him credit."

Plantinga's critique of Sartre cuts deeply. If both the anthropological and the philosophical defenses of relativism are open to devastating critique, it is worth asking the questions with which traditional moral philosophy has been concerned. (For the critique of the anthropological defense, see *Theory of Knowledge*, "Is Moral Knowledge Possible?")

Existential Relativism
JEAN-PAUL SARTRE

*W*hat is *this* that we call existentialism? Most men who use this word would be quite hard-up to explain it, since as it has become the fashion today we readily declare that a musician or a painter is an existentialist. A columnist of *Clartes* signs [himself as] "The Existentialist"; and after all, the word has taken [on] today such a breadth and extension that it no longer means anything at all. It seems that, for want of an avant-garde doctrine analogous to surrealism, men [who are] eager for scandal and action appeal to this philosophy, which can supply nothing further to them in this area; actually it is the least shocking doctrine, and the most austere; it is intended strictly for technicians, and philosophers. However, it can easily be defined. What makes the matter complicated is that there are two kinds of existentialists: the first, who are Christian, and among whom I will include Jaspers and Gabriel Marcel, of the Catholic faith; and also, the atheistic existentialists among whom we must include Heidegger, and also the French existentialists, and myself. What they have in common is simply the fact that they think that existence precedes essence, or, if you wish, that we must start from subjectivity. What [do] we mean by that exactly? When we consider a manufactured object, as for example a book or a letter-opener, this object has been made by a craftsman who has been inspired by an idea; he refers to the idea of a letter-opener, and likewise to a prior technique of production which forms part of the idea, and which is, basically, a recipe. Hence, the letter-opener is at the same time an object which comes into being in a certain manner and which, moreover, has a definite function, and we cannot imagine a man who would make a letter-opener without knowing what use

FROM: *L'Esistentialism est un humanisme*, Jean-Paul Sartre, Deanna Stein McMahon, trans. Paris: Les Editions Nagel, Reprinted by permission of Les Editions Nagel and Methuen & Co., Ltd., London [publishers of the translation by Philip Mairet, *Existentialism and Humanism* (1948)].

the object will have. We will say, then, for the letter-opener, its essence—that is to say the whole of the recipes and qualities which allow it to be produced and defined—precedes its existence; and thus, the presence, before me, of this letter-opener or this book is determined. Hence we have here a technical view of the world, in which we can say that production precedes existence.

When we conceive of God as creator, this God is compared, most of the time, to a superior craftsman; and whatever doctrine we may consider, whether it concerns a doctrine like that of Descartes or the doctrine of Leibniz, we always grant that the will more or less follows the understanding, or at least accompanies it, and that God, when he creates, knows precisely what he is creating. Thus, the idea of man, in the mind of God, is comparable to the idea of the letter-opener in the mind of the manufacturer; and God makes man according to techniques and an idea, exactly as the craftsman makes a letter-opener according to a definition and a technique. Thus, the individual man is the realization of a certain idea which is in the divine understanding. In the philosophical atheism of the 18th century, the idea of God is eliminated, but not the idea that essence precedes existence. We find this idea nearly everywhere: we find it in Diderot, in Voltaire, and even in Kant. Man possesses a human nature; this human nature, which is the concept 'human', is found among all men, [and it is this concept] which signifies that every man is a particular example of a universal concept, *man*; in Kant, it follows from this universality that the man of the woods, the man of nature, like the bourgeois [man], is on the whole subject to the same definition and possesses the same qualities. Thus, there again, man's essence precedes this historical existence that we encounter in nature.

Atheistic existentialism, which I represent, is more coherent. It declares that if God does not exist, there is at least a being whose existence precedes [his] essence, a being who exists before being able to be defined by any concept, and that this being is man, or, as Heidegger says, human reality. What does it mean here that existence precedes essence? It means that man exists first, experiences himself, springs up in the world, and that he defines himself afterwards. If man, as the existentialist conceives him, is not definable, it is because he is nothing at first. He will only be [something] afterwards, and he will be as he will have made himself. So, there is no human nature, since there is no God to think it. Man simply is, not only as he conceives himself, but as he determines himself, and as he conceives himself after existing, as he determines himself after this impulse toward existence; man is nothing other than what he makes himself. This is the first principle of existentialism. It is also what we call subjectivity, and what we are reproached with under this same name. But what do we mean by that, except that man has a greater dignity than a stone or a table? For we mean that man exists first, that is to say that man is at first [something] which projects itself toward a future, and which is conscious of projecting itself into the future. Man is at first a project which lives subjectively, instead of being a moss, a decaying thing, or a cauliflower; nothing exists prior to this project; nothing is intelligible in the heavens, and man will at first be what he has planned to be. Not what he may wish to be. For what we ordinarily understand by will is a conscious decision, and which for most of us is subsequent to what we have made ourselves. I may wish to join a party, write a book, get married; all that is only a manifestation of a more original choice, [which is] more spontaneous than what we call "will." But if existence really precedes essence, man is responsible for what he is. Thus, the first step of existentialism is to show every man [to be] in control of what he is and to make him assume total responsibility for his existence. And, when we say that man is responsible for himself, we do not [only] mean that man is responsible for his precise individuality, but that he is responsible for all men. There are two senses of the word 'subjectivism', and our adversaries play on these two senses. On the one hand subjectivism means the determination of the individual subject by himself, and, on the other hand, the impossibility for man to go beyond human subjectivity. It is the second sense which is the profound meaning of existentialism. When we say that man determines himself, we understand that each of us chooses himself, but by that we mean also that in choosing himself he chooses all men. Indeed, there is not one of our actions which, in creating the man we wish to be, does not [also] create at the same time an image of the man we think we ought to be. To choose to be this or that, is to affirm at the same time the value of what we choose, for we can never choose evil; what we choose is always the good, and nothing can be good for us without [also] being [good] for all. Moreover, if existence precedes essence and if we will to exist at the same time as we shape our image, this image is valid for everyone and for our entire age. Thus, our responsibility is much greater than we had supposed it, for it involves all mankind. If I am a workman and if I choose to join a Christian trade-union rather than be a Communist, [and] if, by this membership I want to show that resignation is fundamentally the solution which suits man, that the kingdom of man is not on earth, I involve not only my own case: I want everyone to be resigned, therefore my step has completely involved all mankind. And, [to take] a more personal action, if I want to get married, to have children, even if this marriage depends only on my situation, or on my passion, or on my desire, by that [action] I commit not just myself but all mankind on the path of monogamy. Thus I am responsible for myself and for everyone, and I create a certain image of man which I choose; in choosing myself, I choose man.

This enables us to understand what some rather lofty words, like anguish, abandonment, despair mean. As you will see, it is quite simple. First, what do we mean by anguish? The existentialist readily declares that man is [in] anguish. That means this: the man who commits himself and who realizes that it is not only himself that he chooses, but [that] he is also a lawgiver choosing at the same time [for] all mankind, would not know how to escape the feeling of his total and profound responsibility. Certainly, many men are not anxious; but we claim that they are hiding their anguish, that they are fleeing from it; certainly, many men believe [that] in acting [they] commit only themselves, and when one says to them: "what if everyone acted like that?" they shrug their shoulders and reply: "everyone does not act like that." But really, one should always ask himself: "what would happen if everyone did the same?" and we cannot escape this troubling thought except by a kind of bad faith. The man who lies and who excuses himself by declaring: "everyone does not act like that", is someone who is ill at ease with his conscience, because the act of lying implies a universal value attributed to the lie. Even when it conceals itself, anguish appears. It is this anguish that Kierkegaard called the anguish of Abraham. You know the story: an angel ordered Abraham to sacrifice his son; all goes well if it is really an angel who came and said: "You are Abraham, you will sacrifice your son." But each [man] may ask himself, first, "is it really an angel, and am I really Abraham?" What [can] prove it to me? There was a madwoman who had hallucinations: people spoke to her on the telephone and gave her orders. The doctor asked her: "But who speaks to you?" She replied: "He says that he is God." And what really proved to her that it was God? If an angel comes to me, what proves that it is an angel? And if I hear voices, what proves that they come from heaven and not from hell, or from a subconscious, or from a pathological condition? Who proves that they are addressed to me?

Who proves that I am really appointed to impose my conception of man and my choice on mankind? I will never find any proof, any sign to convince me of it. If a voice addresses me, it is always I who will decide that this voice is the voice of [an] angel; if I consider that such an action is good, it is I who will decide to say that this action is good rather than bad. Nothing shows that I am Abraham, and still I am obliged at each moment to perform exemplary deeds. Everything happens as if, for every man, all mankind had its eyes fixed on what he does and takes what he does as an example. And each man should say to himself: "do I really have the right to act in such a way that mankind takes my actions as an example?" And if he does not say that to himself, it is because he is hiding his anguish from himself. It is not a question of an anguish which might lead to quietism, to inaction. It is here a question of a simple anguish, that all those who have had responsibilities are acquainted with. For example, when a military chief assumes the responsibility of an attack and sends a certain number of men to [their] death, he chooses to do it, and at bottom he chooses alone. Without doubt there are orders which come from above, but they are too broad and an interpretation is called for, which comes from him, and on this interpretation depends the life of ten or fourteen or twenty men. In the decision he makes he cannot avoid a certain anguish. All chiefs are familiar with this anxiety. That does not prevent them from acting; on the contrary, it is the very condition of their action. For it assumes that they envisage a multitude of possibilities, and when they choose one of them, they realize that it has value only because it is chosen. We will see that this kind of anguish, which is what existentialism describes, is explained, moreover, by a direct responsibility with respect to other men that it involves. It is not a screen which would separate us from action, but forms part of the action itself.

And when we speak of abandon-

ment, an expression dear to Heidegger, we mean only that God does not exist, and that we must draw out the consequences of this to the very end. The existentialist is very much opposed to a certain kind of secular morality which would be willing to abolish God with the least possible expense. When, about 1880, some French professors tried to form a secular morality, they pretty much said this: "God is a useless and costly hypothesis, we eliminate it, but it is still necessary that there be a morality, a society, a civilized world, so that certain values be taken seriously and considered as existing a priori; it must be obligatory a priori to be honest, not to lie, not to beat your wife, to have children, etc. . . . we will do a little work, then, which will enable us to show that these values exist all the same, written in an intelligible heaven, although, incidentally, God does not exist." In other words, and it is, I believe the tendency of everything that we in France call radicalism, nothing will be changed if God does not exist; we will again find the same standards of honesty, of progress, of humanism, and we will have made God an outdated hypothesis that will die peacefully and of itself. The existentialist, on the contrary, thinks that it is very troubling that God does not exist, for with him disappears every possibility of finding values in an intelligible heaven; there can no longer be any good a priori, since there is no infinite and perfect consciousness to think it; it is not written anywhere that the good exists, that we must be honest, that we must not lie, since precisely we exist in a context where there are only men. Dostoyevsky has written, "If God did not exist, everything would be allowed." This is the point of departure for existentialism. Indeed, everything is allowed if God does not exist, and consequently man is abandoned, because neither in himself nor beyond himself does he find any possibility of clinging on [to something]. At the start, he finds no excuses. If, indeed, existence precedes essence, we will never be able to give an explanation by reference to a human nature [which is] given and fixed; in other words, there is no determinism, man is free, man is freedom. Moreover, if God does not exist, we do not find before us any values or orders which will justify our conduct. So, we have neither behind us nor before us, in the luminous realm of values, any justifications or excuses. We are alone, without excuses. It is what I will express by saying that man is condemned to be free. Condemned, because he has not created himself, and nevertheless, in other respects [he is] free, because once [he is] cast into the world, he is responsible for everything that he does. The existentialist does not believe in the power of passion. He will never think that a noble passion is a devastating torrent which inevitably leads man to [perform] certain actions, and which, consequently, is an excuse. He thinks that man is responsible for his passion. Neither will the existentialist think that man can find help in a given sign on earth which will direct him; for he thinks that man deciphers the sign himself as it pleases him. He thinks, then, that man, without any support and without any help, is condemned at each moment to invent man. In an excellent article, Ponge said: "Man is the future of man." This is perfectly correct. Only, if we understand by that this future is written in heaven, that God beholds it, then it is false, for that would no longer even be a future. If we mean that, whatever man may appear, there is a future to be made, an unwrought future which awaits him, then this saying is accurate. But then, we are abandoned. To give you an example which [will] allow [you] to understand abandonment better, I will cite the case of one of my students who came to see me in the following circumstances. His father was on bad terms with his mother, and moreover, was inclined to be a collaborator. His older brother had been killed in the German offensive of 1940, and this young man, with feelings somewhat primitive but generous, wanted to avenge him. His

mother lived alone with him, quite distressed by the semi-betrayal of his father and by the death of her eldest son, and found consolation only in him. This young man had the choice, at that time, between leaving for England and enlisting in the Free French Forces—that is to say, to forsake his mother—or to stay near his mother and to help her [to] live. He fully realized that this woman lived only for him and that his disappearance—and perhaps his death—would cast her into despair. He also realized that, in reality, [and] concretely, each action that he performed with regard to his mother had its surety in the sense that he was helping her to live, whereas each action that he might perform in order to leave and fight was an ambiguous action which could be lost in the sands, to answer no purpose. For example, leaving for England, he might remain indefinitely in a Spanish camp, while passing through Spain; he might arrive in England or in Algiers and be placed in an office to keep records. Consequently, he found himself facing two very different kinds of action: one concrete, immediate, but applying only to one individual; or else an action which applied to a whole [group] infinitely vaster, a national community, but which was by that reason ambiguous, and which could be interrupted on the way. And, at the same time, he hesitated between two kinds of ethics. On the one hand, an ethic of sympathy, of individual devotion; and on the other hand a wider ethic, but whose effectiveness was more questionable. He had to choose between the two. Who could help him to choose? Christian doctrine? No. Christian doctrine says: "be charitable, love your neighbor, devote yourself to others, choose the hardest way, etc. . . ." But which is the hardest way? Whom must we love as our brother, the soldier or the mother? Which has the greatest utility, the one [which is] vague, to fight in a group, or the one [which is] definite, to help a definite individual to live? Who can decide it *a priori*? No one. No written ethic can tell him. The Kantian ethic says: "never treat others as [a] means, but as [an] end." Very well; if I remain near [with] my mother, I will treat her as an end and not as a means, but by this same action, I risk treating those who fight around me as a means; and conversely, if I go to rejoin those who are fighting I will treat them as an end, and by this action I risk treating my mother as a means.

If these values are vague, and if they are still too broad for the specific and concrete case that we are considering, it remains for us only to rely on our instincts. This is what this young man tried to do; and when I saw him, he said: "basically, what counts is the sentiment; I ought to choose that which actually pushes me in a certain direction. If I feel that I love my mother enough to sacrifice everything else for her—my desire for vengeance, my desire for action, my desire for adventures—I [will] stay near her. If, on the contrary, I feel that my love for my mother is not sufficient, I [will] leave." But how [do we] judge the weight of a feeling? What constituted the worth of his feeling for his mother? Precisely the fact that he stayed for her. I may say, I love this friend enough to sacrifice such a [a certain] sum of money for him; I can say it, only if I have done it. I may say: I love my mother enough to remain with her, if I have remained with her. I can determine the worth of this affection only if, precisely, I have performed an action which confirms and defines it. Now, as I require this affection to justify my action, I find myself caught in a vicious circle.

Further, Gide has said very well, that a feeling which is acting and a feeling which is real are two nearly indiscernable things: to decide that I love my mother by remaining near her, or to act a part which will make me stay for my mother, is nearly the same thing. In other words, the feeling is constituted by the actions that we perform; I cannot then consult it in order to guide myself according to it. What that means is that I can neither seek for in myself the authentic state which will push me

to act, nor demand from an ethic the concepts which will allow me to act. At least, you say, he went to see a professor to ask his advice. But, if you seek advice from a priest, for example, you have chosen this priest, you already knew, after all, more or less, what he was going to advise you. In other words, to choose the adviser is still to commit yourself. The proof of it is what you will say, if you are a Christian: consult a priest. But there are priests who are collaborators, priests who wait for the tide to turn, priests who belong to the resistance. Which [should you] choose? And if the young man chooses a priest who is a member of the resistance, or a priest who is a collaborator, he has already decided [on] the kind of advice he will receive. Thus, in coming to see me, he knew the reply that I was going to make to him, and I had only one reply to make: you are free, choose, that is to say, invent. No general ethic can show you what there is to do; there is no sign in the world. The Catholics will reply: "but there are signs". Let's admit it; it is myself in any case who chooses the meaning that they have. While I was a prisoner I knew a rather remarkable man who was a Jesuit; he had entered the order of Jesuits in the following way: he had undergone [experienced] a large number of rather bitter defeats. His father died [when he was a] child, leaving him poor, and he had held a scholarship in a religious institution where they made him constantly feel that he was accepted on charity; later on, he missed a number of honorary distinctions which please children; then, at about the age of 18, he failed in a sentimental experience. Finally, at age 22, a matter rather childish, but which was the drop of water that made the vase overflow, he failed his military preparation. This young man could then consider that he had completely failed; it was a sign, but a sign of what? He could take refuge in bitterness or in despair. But he judged, very skillfully for him, that it was a sign that he was not made for worldly successes, and that only the triumphs of religion, of holiness, of faith, were open to him. He then saw there a word of God, and he entered the order. Who does not perceive that the decision about the meaning of the sign had been made completely by him alone? One could have inferred something else from this series of failures: for example, that he should have been a carpenter or a revolutionary. He therefore assumes complete responsibility for the interpretation. Abandonment implies that we ourselves choose our being. Abandonment goes with anguish. As for despair, this expression has a very simple meaning. It means that we will restrict ourselves to a reliance upon that which depends on our will, or on the set of the probabilities which make our action possible. When one wills something, there are always probable elements. I may count on the arrival of a friend. This friend is coming by railway or by tram; that implies that the train will arrive at the given hour, or that the tram will not be derailed. I dwell in the sphere of possibilities; but it is a matter of counting on the possibles only in the strict degree where our action involves the whole of these possibles. From the moment when the possibilities that I am considering are not strictly involved by my action, I must take no further interest in them, because no God, no design can adjust the world and its possibilities to my will. Indeed, when Descartes said "Conquer yourself rather than the world" he meant the same thing [as] "act without hope." The Marxists with whom I have talked, answer me: "in your action, which will obviously be limited by your death, you can rely on the support of others. That means, rely at the same time on what others will do elsewhere, in China, in Russia, to help you, and at the same time on what they will do later, after your death, to resume [your] action and to carry it towards its completion which will be the revolution. You even ought to rely on that, otherwise you are immoral." I reply first, that I will always count on comrades of the struggle in so far as these comrades are committed with me in a concrete and common struggle, in the unity of a party or of a group that I can more or less control, that is to say in which I am involved as a militant and whose movements I know at each moment. At this time, to count on the unity and on the will of this party, is precisely the same thing as to count on the fact that the tram will arrive on time, or that the train will not [be] derailed. But I cannot count on men whom I do not know by placing my reliance on human kindness or on man's interest in the good of society, given that man is free, and that there is no human nature on which I can rely. I do not know what will become of the Russian revolution. I can admire it and make it an example in so far as today proves to me that the proletariat plays a role in Russia that it does not play in any other nation. But I cannot affirm that this will inevitably lead to a triumph of the proletariat; I must restrict myself to what I [can] see. I cannot be certain that [my] comrades of the struggle will resume my work after my death in order to carry it to a maximum of perfection, given that these men are free and that they will freely choose tomorrow what man will be. Tomorrow, after my death, men may decide to establish fascism, and others may be lax and crippled enough to let them do it. At that time, fascism will be human reality, and so much the worse for us. In reality, things will be as man will have decided them to be. Does that mean that I must give way to quietism? No. First, I must commit myself, then [I must] act according to the old formula: it is not necessary to hope in order to try. That does not mean that I ought not to belong to a party, but that I should be without illusion and that I should do what I can. For example, if I ask myself: "will collectivization, such as it is, succeed?" I know nothing about it, I only know that I will do everything in my power to make it succeed. Beyond that, I cannot count on anything. Quietism is the attitude of men who say: "others can do what I cannot do." The doctrine that I am presenting to you is exactly opposite to quietism, since it claims: "there is reality only in action". It goes further [than this] besides, since it adds: "man is nothing other than his project, he exists only in so far as he realizes himself, thus he is nothing other than the whole of his actions, nothing other than his life." According to this, we can understand why our doctrine horrifies a good many men. Because often they have only one way of enduring their misery. It is to think: "circumstances have been against me, I was worth much more than what I have been; to be sure, I have not had a great love, or a great friendship, but it is because I have not met a man or a woman who was worthy of it. I have not written very good books because I have not had the leisure to do it. I have not had children to whom to devote myself because I did not find a person with whom I could have made my life. [There] remains, then, in me, unused and wholly feasible a multitude of dispositions, inclinations, possibilities which give me a worth that the simple set of my actions does not allow [one] to infer. Now, in reality, for the existentialist there is no love other than that which is made, there is no possibility of love

other than that which manifests itself in a love; there is no genius other than that which expresses itself in works of art. The genius of Proust is the totality of Proust's works; the genius of Racine is the set of his tragedies, beyond that there is nothing. Why [should we] attribute to Racine the possibility of writing a new tragedy, since precisely he did not write it? In his life a man commits himself, draws his own figure, and beyond this figure there is nothing. Obviously, this thought may seem harsh to someone who has not had a successful life. But, on the other hand, it prepares men to understand that only reality counts, that the dreams, the expectations, the hopes allow [us] only to define a man as [a] disappointed dream, as miscarried hopes, as useless expectations; that is to say that that defines them negatively and not positively. However, when we say "you are nothing other than your life", that does not imply that the artist will be judged only by his art-works, for a thousand other things also contribute to define him. What we mean is that man is nothing other than a set of undertakings, that he is the sum, the organization, the whole of the relations which make up these undertakings.

An Existentialist's Ethics
ALVIN PLANTINGA

*C*ontemporary *existentialist* philosophy appears to be fundamentally ethical in its origin and motivation. Essentially concerned with man's status in the universe and its implications for behavior, the existentialist often adopts the tone of the Old Testament prophets. He extolls the virtues of authenticity and legitimate anguish; the life of bad faith, the attempted escape from freedom, warrant his scornful disapproval. The moral —and perhaps moralistic—aspect of ex-

istentialism is pervasive and unmistakable.

This is especially clear in the case of Jean Paul Sartre's philosophy of freedom. Existentialists in general and Sartre in particular argue that an analysis, not of human nature, indeed, but of, say, "the universal human condition" reveals that certain kinds of behavior are morally appropriate and others morally reprehensible. My aim in this paper is to show that Sartre's analysis of "the uni-

FROM: *The Review of Metaphysics*, Vol. XII, No. 2 (December 1958). Reprinted by permission of the editor and author.

versal human condition" is quite inconsistent with morality in anything like the ordinary sense. We might think that attempt otiose in view of Sartre's notorious rejection of "absolute values." But in spite of his claim to dispense with absolute morality, Sartre's philosophy, like other existentialist philosophies, is through-and-through ethical. A concern with the human condition and its implications for morality is the moving force behind Sartre's thought. "Bad faith," "responsibility," "anguish,"—these and other ethical notions play a central role in Sartre's philosophy of freedom. Though he has in one sense rejected "absolute values" (in rejecting any ethical system based upon an essentialist metaphysics) in another sense he accepts the absolute values of authenticity and good faith, recommends these values to others, and passes moral judgment upon those who live in "bad faith."

Sartre's ethics is grounded in his theory of freedom. I shall try to give a fairly clear if truncated account of that theory, followed by an examination of the implications of the theory for morality. In the last section I shall try to show that the arguments by which he supports this radical theory of freedom are inconclusive in that they rest at worst upon puns and at best upon ambiguities.

AN ONTOLOGY OF FREEDOM

The title of Sartre's main philosophical work is *Being and Nothingness*.[1] Since it is the doctrine of nothingness that is crucial to Sartre's account of freedom, it is best to begin by examining that doctrine. Nothingness, or negation, plays a central role in Sartre's philosophy from the start. Indeed, the very posing of the "ontological question" immediately leads to a confrontation with nothingness: "What being will be must of necessity arise on the basis of what it is not."

Whatever being is, it will allow this formulation: 'Being is *that* and outside of that, nothing.' Thus a new component of the real has just appeared to us—nonbeing" (BN 5). The posing of the ontological question, according to Sartre, reveals not-being in a triple way. In the first place, the fact that the question is asked presupposes that the questioner is ignorant; *ignorance*, as a *lack* of knowledge, is a kind of non-being. Secondly there is the possibility of a negative answer: The ontological question is as follows: "Is there any conduct which can reveal to me the relation of man with the world?" (loc. cit.). Since we do not know the answer, we face the possibility that the answer might be negative, that as a matter of fact there is no such conduct. And every negative judgment presupposes not-being.[2] Third, the existence of the question presupposes the existence of an answer and therefore of *truth*, another form of not-being.[3] Why is truth a form of not-being? Apparently for the following reasons: since truth is different from what it is the truth about, and since it is always true *of* being, truth must be not-being. If truth is always *about* being and therefore distinguished from it, it cannot *be* being and therefore must be not-being or nothing. Further, truth always involves distinction and limitation; if it is true to say that this is a table, then this must not be a chair. But being as it is in-itself is a plenum, completely opaque and full (BN 74). There are in it as it is in-itself no distinctions and no limitation. Hence truth cannot be being; it must, therefore, be not-being. If being is an absolute plenum with no limitation at all, then judgment and truth cannot be in being,

[1] Tr. Hazel Barnes (New York, 1956). I shall use the abbreviation 'BN' to refer to this work.

[2] Below pp. 352–353. I shall examine this statement and try to outline the argument by which Sartre supports it.

[3] BN lxvii-lxviii, 5. It is never clear from Sartre's account whether he thinks there are a number of different kinds of not-being, or only one kind revealing itself in different situations. But that difference is not important for my purposes here.

since in any judgment I distinguish the object of judgment from everything else, thereby introducing limitation and distinction. Hence the very existence of the ontological question reveals to us that not-being lies coiled in the heart of being—like a worm (BN 21).

We have now discovered not-being. It appears to be a "component of the real," of crucial importance for ontology. But the appearance of not-being is puzzling. Being cannot, of course, give rise to not-being, for from being, only being can come (BN 23). On the other hand, sheer "nothingness is not" (BN 22); this means among other things, says Sartre, that sheer nothing lacks the power to nihilate itself. What does *that* mean? So far as I can make out, something like the following: To *be* requires a certain power; an act of being requires an ontological force or energy. To nihilate being, to not-be, Sartre apparently thinks, requires an analogous force. And therefore sheer nothing, since it has no force at all, cannot have any power with which to nihilate itself.[4] The origin of nothingness presents a paradox. Being cannot introduce it; neither, it seems, can nothing. The introducer of nothingness into the world must have very special qualities: "The being by which Nothingness arrives in the world must nihilate Nothingness in its Being, and even so it still runs the risk of establishing Nothingness as a transcendent in the very heart of immanence unless it nihilates Nothingness in its being *in connection with its own being*. The Being by which Nothingness

arrives in the world is a being such that in its Being, the Nothingness of its Being is in question. *The being by which Nothingness comes to the world must be its own Nothingness"* (BN 23). What can this mean? There is Nothingness in the world in the peculiar sense of distinction and opposition and limitation. This could not come from being, since being is a Parmenidean whole, void of all distinction or qualification. On the other hand, this Nothingness cannot come from sheer nothing for the latter has not the power of "nihilating" anything. Mere nothing has no power at all. It is inert. Yet the act of being nothing, in the special sense of introducing limitation and distinction into a formless whole, requires a certain ontological power. Since sheer nothing does not possess this power, and since being cannot of course be the source of nothing, a third thing seems to be required—a being which can introduce Nothingness. Now this cannot be being in the sense of the in-itself. On the other hand, it must have nothingness within itself in order to be the source of Nothingness in the world. This nothingness which it has within itself cannot have come to it from some other source, since neither being nor nothing could produce it. Therefore the being by which Nothingness enters the world must be its own Nothingness.

Extraordinarily puzzling at best, this may be sheer nonsense. But the important thing to recognize is that this being which is its own nothingness is consciousness, or human reality (BN 24). Sartre's next question is this: what must man be if he is the being through which nothingness enters the world? The answer is that he must have, or rather be, *freedom.* Freedom is identical with the being of human reality, *constitutes* it. Man *is* freedom. This means that man must be able to be *distant* from the world (loc. cit.); he must be able to *detach* himself from the world; he "retires behind a nothingness" (loc. cit.). That ability to other the world, to be at a distance from it, to negate it, is freedom. Thus the fact that man is a nothingness

---

[4] The essential ambiguity of Sartre's use of the word "nothing" is what makes the above statement seem so puzzling. As a matter of fact, Sartre is implicitly distinguishing "nothing" in the sense of sheer unadulterated nothing from "nothing" in the sense of "absence of being in-itself." The latter is not, or not in every case, at any rate, *sheer* nothing, for not-being in the sense of for-itself is (1) a kind of representation, and (2) an introduction of form into being. This ambiguity is in the last analysis fatal to Sartre's philosophy, I think, and I shall deal with it below pp. 352-354.

(in Sartre's peculiar sense) constitutes his freedom; man, as the one by whom nothingness comes into the world, cannot be being. For if he were, then he could not be the source of distinction and limitation. Man is therefore a nothing, a lack of being, a hole in being (BN 617). "Freedom in its foundation coincides with the nothingness which is at the heart of man. Human reality is free because it is not enough" (BN 440).

Human reality is its own nothingness. For the for-itself, to be is to nihilate the in-itself which it is. Under these conditions, freedom can be nothing other than this nihilation. It is through this that the for-itself escapes its being as its essence; it is through this that the for-itself is always something other than what can be said of it. For in the final analysis, the for-itself is the one which escapes this very denomination, the one which is already beyond the name which is given to it, beyond the property which is recognized in it. To say that the for-itself has to be what it is, to say that it is what it is not, to say that in it existence precedes and conditions essence or inversely according to Hegel that for it "Wasen ist was gewesen ist"—all this is to say one and the same thing; to be aware that man is free. . . . I am condemned to exist forever beyond my essence, beyond the causes and motives of my act. I am condemned to be free. This means that no limits to my freedom can be found except freedom itself, or if you prefer, that we are not free to cease being free (BN 439).

This is about as clear a capsule statement of Sartre's doctrine of freedom as he gives. Freedom is logically contingent upon the fact that man is a nothingness. Man is "wholly and forever free" (BN 441). The fact that he is a lack of being, that "The for-itself is nothing but the pure nihilation of the in-itself" (BN 611), is the ground of the freedom of the for-itself. In fact the for-itself *is* this nihilation and is its freedom: therefore the freedom of the for-

itself is identical with its negative character.

SPECIFIC FREEDOM

But Sartre goes on to give a more concrete account of human freedom.

1. We have freedom from the passions. We are never determined by our passions; we freely choose to give in to them when we do. We can always decide to resist passion, to live a life in which it is not a determining factor. In the last analysis this is because insofar as the self or consciousness is a nothing, the passions cannot get a purchase on it (BN 518). Our every decision (and every action implies decision) is completely free.

2. We are free from our motives. Choice is free from motives both as psychological pushes and pulls and as rational considerations leading us to act in one way rather than another. Freedom from motives in the psychological sense is a result of the fact that there is no centrum or ego to which motives can adhere. But we are also free from motives as rational decision-making considerations. Rational deliberation is always specious since before deliberating we have already decided which sorts of reasons we will allow to have weight. Thus the choice has already been made before deliberation begins. In *Existentialism*,[5] Sartre recounts the case of the young man who has come to him for advice. In coming to him, Sartre claims, the young man had already made his decision, for he knew what sort of advice to expect. Had he wanted different advice, he would have gone to a priest or a communist. And it follows that we make our decision prior to deliberation or the rehearsing of reasons. Indeed, he holds that choice and consciousness are finally one and the same thing (BN 449-453). As Wilfrid Desan says in his excellent book *The Tragic Finale*, "For-itself, Nothingness, Human conscious-

[5] Tr. Bernard Frechtman. (New York, 1947), p. 32.

ness, Freedom, Free Choice are, in Sartre's system, one and the same thing."[6]

3. If man is free from passions and motives, he is also free from the in-itself. The latter, says Sartre, can affect only being; it cannot touch not-being. There is nothing in consciousness, which *is* a nothing, upon which the in-itself could get a purchase. Thus the for-itself, or consciousness, is outside the causal series; hence it cannot be determined by the in-itself (BN 435).

4. In the for-itself, existence precedes and formulates essence; man is therefore free from his essence. The following is Sartre's attempt to explicate this oft-repeated slogan:

What is meant by saying that existence precedes essence? It means that, first of all, man exists, turns up, appears on the scene, and only afterwards, defines himself. If man, as the existentialist conceives him, is indefinable, it is because at first he is nothing. Only afterward will he be something, and he himself will have made what he will be. Thus there is no human nature, since there is no God to conceive it. Not only is man what he conceives himself, but he is also only what he wills himself to be after this thrust towards existence. Man is nothing else but what he makes of himself. Such is the first principle of existentialism (Existentialism, *p. 13*).

The essential point here is the statement that man is only what he wills himself to be. Our essence is always in the past. The total ensemble of truths about a man are truths about his past. We can place no *a priori* limits upon his future choices; since man is a nothing (i.e., quite free) he has no nature which limits or defines him; he defines himself as he goes along. It is in *choice* that man defines himself or constitutes himself, thus giving himself an essence. And since a man's essence is always in the past, we can make an essential judgment

[6] (Cambridge, Mass., 1953), p. 101. Desan's book combines a sympathetic approach with a lucid exposition; when the subject is Sartre, this is a real achievement.

of him only after he is dead. For he is always free to choose a new essence. Hence Sartre quotes with approval the maxim of the Greek tragedians: "Never count a man happy until he is dead" (BN 510). The essential meaning of the doctrine that existence precedes essence, then, is that man has no nature or defining characteristics prior to his existence as a choosing being who *decides* what he will be.

5. Finally, man is free from antecedently fixed values. Human reality creates values; it does not discover them.

The existentialist, on the contrary [i.e., as opposed to those who believe that there are values independently of human choice] *thinks it very distressing that God does not exist, because all possibility of finding values in a heaven of ideas disappears along with Him; there can no longer be an* a priori *good, since there is no infinite and perfect consciousness to think it. Nowhere is it written that the good exists, that we must be honest, that we must not lie; because the fact is that we are on a plane where there are only men. Dostoievsky said, "If God didn't exist, everything would be possible." That is the very starting point of existentialism, and as a result man is forlorn, because neither within him nor without does he find anything to cling to. . . . If God does not exist, we find no values or commands to turn to which legitimate our conduct* (Existentialism, *p. 27*).

Hence there are no values existing prior to choice. In choosing, we define values; any choice is unjustifiable and "absurd" in the sense that it can have no rational justification or sufficient reason (BN 479). For the very standards in terms of which a choice could be justified are logically posterior to that choice (loc. cit.). There are not good choices and bad choices, for every choice as a choice defines the good (*Existentialism*, p. 20); hence denominations such as "good" and "bad" are inapplicable to choice. Human reality or the for-itself, therefore, is not bound by any system of pre-established values;

it has absolute freedom with respect to values.[7] Man is absolutely and completely free—from his essence, from the in-itself, from his passions and motives. As Desan says, "Sartres's freedom is something absolute; he rejects all determinism whatever . . . consequently he presents us with a freedom more acute than, possibly, has been seen in two thousand years of philosophy" (op. cit., p. 107). Now this doctrine of freedom, insofar as it follows from the central premisses of Sartre's ontology, is a liability as well as an asset. If the doctrine is false Sartre's ontology is refuted by modus tollens. Sartre recognizes that human reality seems to be limited by a whole host of factors. I am limited by physical laws, by my environment in the form of my nationality, social class, education, and the like, by my inherent capacities or lack of them for certain kinds of endeavor, etc. Unlike a horse, I am not free to run a mile in two minutes, and I cannot become a philosopher without a modicum of intelligence.[8] I seem to be limited by the nature of the world, by my cultural milieu, by my inherent abilities, and by many other factors. How does Sartre deal with these objections?

The whole realm of factors which seem to limit freedom is called "facticity" (BN 481). This includes five kinds of facts: my place, my past, my surroundings, my fellow brethren, and my death.[9] Sartre deals with facticity by means of two kinds of arguments.

1. An obstacle is always an obstacle *for* someone; it is constituted as an ob-

stacle by the fact that someone has chosen a goal with which it is incompatible. A mountain is an obstacle only for someone who has chosen a course which involves crossing it. *In itself*, the mountain is not an obstacle; it simply is. In general, an obstacle is an obstacle only because of choice; it becomes an obstacle only after choice, and thus in a sense freedom or the for-itself *chooses* its obstacles. How, then, can they be said to be limitations upon freedom? "In particular, the coefficient of adversity in things cannot be an argument against our freedom for it is by us—i.e., by the preliminary positing of an end—that this coefficient of adversity arises. A particular crag, which may manifest a profound resistance if I wish to displace it, will be on the contrary a valuable aid if I want to climb upon it in order to look over the countryside" (BN 482). This argument will work with any kind of obstacle. Let us suppose that I am a professional baseball player and I suddenly decide to become a concert pianist. Is not my lack of musical training an obstacle to the realization of my ambition? Certainly not, says Sartre. My lack of musical training is not in itself an obstacle. It becomes an obstacle only if I decide upon a course of action presupposing a good deal of musical training. And therefore it is my decision that constitutes the obstacle. I have *chosen* this obstacle in choosing to become a pianist; it cannot, therefore, be thought of as a restriction of my freedom. Sartre's first way of dealing with facticity is to maintain that insofar as a choice sets up or constitutes its own obstacles, they cannot be regarded as limitations upon freedom.

2. But Sartre has a second way of dealing with facticity. He distinguishes between freedom of choice and freedom of achievement. "In addition it is necessary to point out to common sense that the formula 'to be free' does not mean 'to obtain what one wishes' but rather 'by oneself to determine oneself to wish' in the broad sense of 'choosing.' The technical and philosophical concept of freedom, the only one which we are con-

---

[7] In a way this is the crux of Sartre's ethical doctrine as presented in *Being and Nothingness* and *Existentialism*. In the next section I shall try to show that this implication of his ontology makes morality in anything like the ordinary sense completely impossible.

[8] There seems to be less than universal agreement upon this point.

[9] BN 485. These are for the most part self-explanatory, and there is no need to discuss them in detail; my place, for example, is just my physical position in space and time.

sidering here, means only the autonomy of choice" (BN 483). So far so good. This seems to mean that though indeed I cannot *accomplish* anything I choose, I can nevertheless choose to accomplish it. If I am in prison, I can choose to be at liberty, though of course there is no question of my actually *being* at liberty. But in a very puzzling paragraph he goes on to *deny* that we can distinguish choice from action; this allows him to distinguish merely *longing* or *wishing* from *choosing*, avoiding the empty truism that I can always desire, or choose in the sense of desire, to do or be something which as a matter of fact is quite impossible to me. If choice involves action, then I can choose only that which as a matter of fact *is* possible for me to accomplish—at least in a sort of preliminary way (BN 484). But if this is his meaning, then of course choice is very definitely limited. Hence it is difficult to see just what Sartre means here; but insofar as this second way of dealing with facticity is an argument at all, it is an assertion that though we have not freedom of accomplishment, we do have freedom of choice. This seems to be the point of his distinction between the "philosophical, technical sense" of freedom and the common-sense or ordinary sense.

There is another puzzling thing about these ways of dealing with facticity: they seem to be inconsistent with one another. For the first presupposes what the second denies—i.e., the first argument is an argument with respect to the ordinary sense of freedom according to which freedom entails the possibility of accomplishment. Hence if the second argument is valid the first fails to make an essential distinction, and if the first is valid, the second proceeds from an improper distinction. One can try to validate absolute freedom in either one of these ways, but not in both.[10]

The doctrine of absolute freedom is crucial to Sartre's philosophic endeavor. As we might expect, it is a common theme in his novels and plays. In *The Age of Reason*, Mathieu glumly reflects about his condition as a human being:

Even if he let himself be carried off, in helplessness and despair, even if he let himself be carried off like an old sack of coal, he would have chosen his own damnation: he was free, free in every way, free to behave like a fool or a machine, free to accept or refuse, free to equivocate: to marry, to give up the game, to drag this dead weight about with him for years to come. He could do what he liked, no one had the right to advise him, there would be for him no good nor evil unless he brought them into being. All around him things were gathered in a circle, expectant, impassive, and indicative of nothing. He was alone, enveloped in this monstrous silence, free and alone, without assistance, and without excuse, condemned to decide without support from any quarter, condemned forever to be free.[11]

And in *The Reprieve*: "Half way across the Pont-Neuf he stopped and began to laugh: liberty—I sought it far away; it was so near that I couldn't touch it; it is in fact myself. I am my own freedom."[12]

ABSOLUTE FREEDOM AND MORALITY

Sartre's moral philosophy follows from his doctrine of absolute freedom. In this section I shall indicate the implication for ethics Sartre draws from this doctrine, and then try to show that it is inconsistent with any kind of morality. Sartres's ethical doctrines center about the notions of responsibility and anguish.

1. He holds that the doctrine of absolute freedom implies absolute responsibility. "But if existence really does

[10] Below (p. 354) I shall try to show that neither suffices to demonstrate an absolute freedom in a sense strong enough to support Sartre's conclusions.

[11] Tr. Eric Sutton (New York, 1952), p. 320.

[12] Tr. Eric Sutton (New York, 1951), p. 363.

precede essence, man is responsible for what he is. Thus existentialism's first move is to make every man aware of what he is and to make the full responsibility of his existence rest on him" (*Existentialism*, p. 19). Since we constitute ourselves, since we choose our own essences, whatever we are is the result of our own choice. Hence we are responsible for what we are. If I am a failure, it is only because I have chosen to fail; there is no one and nothing to blame but myself. But our responsibility extends considerably further than this. I am responsible, says Sartre, not only for myself, but for all mankind. "In fact, in creating the man that we want to be, there is not a single one of our acts which does not at the same time create an image of man as we think he ought to be. To choose to be this or that is to affirm at the same time the value of what we choose, because we can never choose evil. We always choose the good, and nothing can be good for us without being good for all" (*Existentialism*, p. 20). In choosing myself, I choose man; hence I am a kind of universal legislator: "The man who involves himself and who realizes that he is not only the person he chooses to be but also the law maker who is, at the same time, choosing all mankind as well as himself cannot help escape the feeling of his total and deep responsibility" (*Existentialism*, p. 24). A man who acts must always ask himself "Am I really the kind of man who has the right to act in such a way that humanity might guide itself by my actions?" (loc. cit.).

I am responsible for whatever I am, and, in addition, in choosing myself I act as a universal legislator who sets up standards for the whole of mankind. But even this is not the extent of my responsibility. As the for-itself, I am the being by whom nothing, and therefore truth, comes into the world. We have noted that in-itself apart from man is a pure undifferentiated whole, a Parmenidean plenum in which there are no distinctions and about which, therefore, nothing can be said. Whatever

actual structure the world has is a result of the free activity of the for-itself. A passage from *La Nausée* will make clear Sartre's view of the for-itself as it is apart from the negating activity of human reality:

And then all of a sudden, there it is, clear as day: existence had suddenly unveiled itself. It had lost the harmless look of an abstract category: it was the very paste of things, this root was kneaded into existence. Or rather the root, the park gates, the bench, the sparse grass, all that had vanished: the diversity of things, their individuality was only an appearance, a veneer. This veneer had melted, leaving soft, monstrous masses, all in disorder—naked, in a frightful obscene nakedness.[13]

Structureless and without form, the in-itself is like Aristotle's prime matter. And therefore, says Sartre, I *choose* my world. For I give to it whatever characteristics it actually has. I constitute it as a world characterized by the law and structure it exhibits. And I do this as a free individual. This is what distinguishes Sartre from any kind of Kantianism: for Sartre, the structures imposed by the for-itself upon the in-itself do not flow from any kind of inner necessity, nor are they given in the nature of reason. I freely choose them; I could have chosen others.[14] Thus:

The essential consequence of our earlier remarks is that man being concerned to be free carries the weight of the whole world on his shoulders; he is responsible for the world and for himself as a way of being. We are taking the word "responsibility" in its ordinary sense as "consciousness of being the incontestable

[13] (English title: The Diary of Antoine Roquentin), tr. Lloyd Alexander (London, 1948), pp. 170-171.

[14] This might be the "existential psychoanalytic" explanation of radical insanity. The psychotic has simply given a different structure to his world.

*author of an event or of an object." In
this sense the responsibility of the for-
itself is overwhelming, since he is the
one by whom it happens that there is
a world; since he is also the one who
makes himself be, then whatever may
be the situation in which he finds himself, the for-itself must wholly assume
this situation with its peculiar coefficient
of adversity, even though it be insup-
portable. He must assume the situation
with the proud consciousness of being
the author of it, for the very worst dis-
advantages or the worst threats which
can endanger my person have meaning
only in and through my project; and it
is on the grounds of the engagement
which I am that they appear. It is therefore senseless to think of complaining
since nothing foreign has decided what
we feel, what we live, or what we are
(BN 554).*

The point of this passage is clear: man
is absolutely and totally responsible since
he is absolutely and totally free. In his
choice he defines himself, he defines the
other, and he constitutes the world, not
by creating it or giving it being, but by
giving it whatever limitation, differentiation, form, and meaning that it has.

2. The result of this fearful responsibility is anguish. Man is anguished
because he *alone* must choose, and because he *must* choose. He is anguished
also because he has no guarantee that
he will not, at some future date, choose
a different essence for himself and
therefore cease to be as *this* man. Anguish appears when we realize that there
is nothing between us and our lives;
when we realize that we are entirely
free and therefore utterly responsible.
In *The Reprieve* Mathieu contemplates
the fact that the coming war has completely cut him off from his past. " 'I
am free,' he said suddenly. And his
joy changed, on the spot, to a crush-
ing sense of anguish."[15] Anguish is the
way our freedom reveals itself to con-

sciousness. It is the consciousness that
nothing separates me from any possibility
whatever (BN 32). We cannot escape
anguish. We may try—to try to escape
anguish [is] to adopt the attitude of "bad
faith" (BN 43), but such an attempt is
doomed to failure, for we *are* anguish
just as we are freedom. Even in bad
faith we do not escape anguish, for in
order to try to escape it, conceal it
from ourselves, we must already know
it (BN 45).

Such is Sartre's doctrine of the responsibility and anguish following from
our absolute freedom. This doctrine
seems to take crucial moral notions very
seriously. But in the last analysis the
doctrine of absolute freedom undercuts
the very possibility of morality. Sartre's
responsibility and anguish are a delusion. Every choice, he tells us, is unconditioned and completely contingent;
there is nothing to which it can appeal,
and it is therefore "absurd." "It is absurd
in this sense; that the choice is that by
which all foundations, all reasons come
into being, that by which the very notion
of the absurd receives a meaning. It is
absurd as being beyond all reasons" (BN
479). Every choice defines both value
and rationality. But if that is so, then
it is impossible to make a wrong choice.
As we have seen,[16] and as Sartre constantly repeats, my choice defines value;
prior to my choice there is no right or
wrong. But then my choice, in defining
the right, can never be mistaken. *Whatever* I choose is right by definition.
Sartre is surreptitiously holding on to
the meaning of responsibility appropriate
to a world in which there are objective
values which I may decide to realize
or to reject. But if there is no value
exterior to choice, then this notion of
responsibility is no longer appropriate or
even meaningful. If every action, every
decision, constitutes a moral Weltan-
schauung, then there is no possibility of
guilt, and no point to anguish. I am
then a being whose every decision con-

---

[15] Op. cit., p. 352.

[16] Above, pp. 346-347.

stitutes the moral standard and who by definition cannot commit a wrong.

For Sartre, *every* action, *every* choice, is necessarily right. But morality presupposes that there is a something morally at stake when I choose or act; there is the possibility of right and wrong, better or worse. For Sartre these distinctions disappear; the notion of a wrong action is for him analytically impossible. And if every actual action is right by definition, there can be no distinction between right and wrong. If the notions of *Action* and *Choice* analytically entail that the action or choice in question is right, then to say that "X is a right action" is to say no more than "X is an action." This doctrine makes negative moral judgments impossible and positive ones otiose.

And thereby the notions of responsibility and anguish lose their point. Sartre tells us of a military commander who has decided to send men on a mission that may cost them their lives. The man is anguished. But why should he be? If we think of the preservation of human life as a value prior to any choice on our part, we can understand his anguish—he is forced to choose a positive disvalue. But if his very choice constitutes value, then no matter what he chooses, he will be right. Why then be anguished?

Sartre is not unaware of the difficulty and makes an attempt to reply to it. In *Being and Nothingness* he tries to show that, appearances to the contrary, his doctrine does not mean that action and choice are merely arbitrary and capricious. His doctrine there is that every action and every choice is an expression of a more fundamental, aboriginal choice—the choice by which we define our being (BN 464). And therefore a man's actions can be guided by reference to this fundamental and original choice. But the difficulty with this, as an answer to the charge that any choice is morally arbitrary, is that it is *logically* impossible, in Sartre's system, for anyone to contradict his fundamental choice.

He is, of course, completely free to make a choice inconsistent with the aboriginal choice he has been expressing; but in so doing he simply makes a new aboriginal choice (BN 464-465). If my moral standards are defined by my fundamental choice, and if in acting inconsistently with these standards I am simply making another fundamental choice, then any action or choice is morally correct by definition. Therefore this reply to the objection I have raised seems to miss the mark completely.[17]

In *Existentialism*, he gives a different answer to this kind of objection. There he tells us that certain choices are dishonest, based upon manifest errors, and constitute a rejection of freedom. The man who denies his freedom is taking refuge in "bad faith." But it is man's nature to desire freedom; we *are* freedom. Therefore to try to escape freedom is to be either a "coward or a stinker" (*Existentialism*, p. 51). But this is obviously an inadequate answer. For if man desires freedom by his very nature,[18] how can anyone fail to desire it? If the basis of the obligation to desire freedom and to accept it is that as a matter of fact we *do* desire it, then anyone who refuses to desire it has by that very fact destroyed the basis for his obligation to desire it.

The conclusion seems to be that Sartre's theory of freedom is quite inconsistent with morality. Any choice is as good as any other; there is no possibility of making a moral mistake. And that is fatal to morality. An absolute freedom, like a through-going determi-

---

[17] As a matter of fact, there is in Sartre's philosophy no reason why a person could not oscillate between several different projects or initial choices—this might be the "existential psychoanalytic" explanation of multiple personality.

[18] Insofar as Sartre is saying that man *must* desire freedom *by his very nature*, he seems to be contradicting the doctrine of absolute freedom and the doctrine that existence precedes essence.

nism, undercuts the very possibility of morality.

THE ARGUMENT
FOR ABSOLUTE FREEDOM

Sartre's theory of freedom makes it impossible to draw a distinction between right and wrong, and therefore it cuts off the very possibility of moral endeavor or action. In this section I propose to examine some of the arguments by which he seeks to establish this theory of freedom. I hope to show that the doctrine results from a series of confusions. Sartre's nihilistic ontology, it seems to me, involves a number of puns upon the word "nothing." We remember that the doctrine of freedom followed from the fact that human reality is a Nothingness.[19] Sartre seems to mean this quite seriously; as Hazel Barnes says in the introduction to her translation of *Being and Nothingness*, ". . . when Sartre speaks of a Nothingness, he means just that and is not using the word as a misleading name for a new metaphysical substance" (BN xxi). It is because the for-itself is a Nothingness that being can have no effect upon it, that it has no ego or centrum upon which motives and passions could adhere, and that it is cut off from the past.[20] The sense of "nothing" involved in the argument for the doctrine of freedom is the ordinary sense according to which "nothing" signifies the absence of everything whatever. But this is not the only sense of "nothing" for Sartre. There are at least four important senses of "nothing" involved in *Being and Nothingness*, and as I hope to show, the argument for freedom depends upon confusing these senses.

(1) Sheer nothing. Nothing in this sense would occur if there were no being(s) anywhere of any kind. Nothing in this sense is impossible and unthinkable, according to Sartre, for nothing depends upon being. Why? Nothing is the

[19] See above, pp. 344–346.

[20] See above, p. 346.

negation of being, and if there were no being, there could be no nothing either. There is an internal relation of *otherness* between being and nothing, such that nothing could not "exist" without being; he does not hold that the relation extends the other way, for being can get on very nicely without nothing.[21]

(2) The common or garden variety of nothing: nothing as the absence of all being in the broadest coherent sense (though dependent upon the existence of being "somewhere else" so to speak). In this sense, nothing is a kind of local absence of any kind of subsistence or existence. (2) is distinguished from (1) in that (1) is impossible and inconceivable; (2) is nothing in the broadest *possible* sense. It is nothing in this sense that underlies the argument for freedom.

(3) Nothing as the presence of qualities incompatible with the in-itself and therefore as the absence of the latter. This sense includes *truth*, which is *about* and therefore other than the in-itself, *form* in the sense of differentiation, quality and individuality (since being as it is in-itself is a qualityless and formless plenum), and the *reflection* of being in (or as) consciousness. That consciousness is a nothing in sense (3) is hardly startling, since it means only that consciousness cannot be identified with its object.

(4) Nothing as the *source* of nothing in sense (3). This is the sense in which Sartre tries to show that for-itself is a Nothingness. But since the argument for freedom depends upon the assertion that the for-itself is nothing in sense (2), Sartre can make out his case only if he can show that sense (4)

[21] Sartre has apparently overlooked the fact that his analysis of sheer nothing provides an easy answer to the fairly standard existentialist question "Why is there anything at all?" If nothing cannot exist without being, then since the absence of being would be nothing, the necessary condition of the absence of being would be the presence of being. Therefore the concept of the absence of being is self-contradictory and absurd, and being is necessary.

entails sense (2). Let us see how he attempts this.

Every question (and questions emanate from consciousness) involves a triple negation. In the first place, there is *ignorance* on the part of the questioner; secondly, there is the possibility of a negative reply, and every negative judgment presupposes not-being; thirdly, every question presupposes *truth*, another form of not-being.[22]

(a) In what sense is ignorance not-being? "Thus the question is a bridge set up between two non-beings: the *non-being of knowing* in man . . ." (BN 5). Ignorance is the non-being of knowledge where knowledge is possible. And if consciousness is a necessary condition of knowledge, then ignorance presupposes and is a sign of not-being in sense (3) (as the absence of the in-itself, which by definition is not conscious). Where there is ignorance, there is consciousness and therefore an absence of the in-itself.

(b) The question also presupposes the possibility of a negative answer, and every negative judgment presupposes the existence of not-being. "The necessary condition of our saying *not* is that non-being be a perpetual presence in us and outside of us, that nothingness haunt being" (BN 16). But it is surely not nothing in sense (2) that is presupposed by a negative judgment. In judging, e.g., "this is not a table" I am surely not judging that "this" is a nothing. I am instead saying that it is *other* than a table; that it *excludes*, stands opposed to, a table. And it can do this only on the basis of *being* something else—say a chair. To take Sartre's example (BN 9), if I judge that Peter is not in the cafe, I am not attributing a kind of nothingness to Peter. I am judging either that the cafe is filled with things other than Peter, or that Peter is somewhere else. The category of otherness, of opposition, is all that is required to make a negative judgment, and the relation of otherness presupposes being on the part of both terms.

[22] See above, pp. 343-344.

Hence the negative judgment presupposes nothingness only in the sense of otherness—more specifically, otherness of some particular existent. For the only judgment which could involve otherness of everything whatever would be a judgment involving sheer nothing in Sartre's sense (1). Hence the negative judgment, like ignorance, presupposes nothingness only in sense (3) insofar as it involves differentiation and individualization which by definition are excluded from the in-itself.

(c) In what sense is *truth* not-being? Sartre has two answers to this question. In the first place, truth, insofar as it is about being, is distinguished from being and other of it. It is therefore nothing in sense (3). Secondly, truth involves limitation and distinction; in judging that x is a horse, I am distinguishing x from all non-horsy entities (BN 10). And insofar as the in-self is an undifferentiated continuum, truth is again nothingness in sense (3).

Accordingly, all three of the "negatives" implied by the question turn out to be nothingnesses only in sense (3)—nothing as the absence of being-in-itself by virtue of the presence of qualities incompatible with the latter. Now Sartre holds that consciousness is a nothingness on the grounds that it is the source of nothingness in sense (3). Consciousness is the source of differentiation, quality, and individuality—in a word, *form*. This introduction of form into the in-itself Sartre calls "nihilation." Hence, "the for-itself is nothing but the pure nihilation of the in-itself" (BN 617). "The for-itself has no reality save that of being the nihilation of being" (BN 618).

The upshot of this is that the for-itself is nothing only in the sense that it is the origin of *form* or *quality*. But this sense of "nothing" is to be sharply distinguished from "nothing" in sense (2); it would be plausible to hold that Kant's noumenal self, for example, is nothing in sense (4) though not in sense (2). The fact that consciousness is nothing in sense (4) gives us no grounds at all for holding that it is nothing in sense (2). For Sartre, consciousness clearly is an existent of *some* sort. It is a reflection of being; it is the source of form and limitation; it has the ability to know; and it is the source of truth. The fact that consciousness is a nothing in *this* sense surely does not imply that the for-itself cannot have an ego, or that it cannot be in any way determined by being; the argument for freedom depends upon the supposition that the for-itself is nothing in sense (2). And insofar as this is the case, the whole argument falls to the ground. For it involves a confusion of sense (2) with sense (4). When Sartre argues that I am free from the past because separated from it by this nothingness which I am, when he argues that since I am a nothing I cannot have an essence, and when he argues that insofar as I am a nothing, being cannot in any way affect me, he is in every case confusing these two senses of "nothing." When we realize that for Sartre the self is nothing only in the sense that it introduces form and qualification into being, the argument loses all appearance of plausibility.

The proper conclusion, then, is that Sartre's ontological argument for absolute freedom is involved in serious confusion. It Sartre really means to hold that consciousness is nothing at all, then it makes no sense to talk about its being free, anguished, the sources of truth, etc. But if he does not mean that it is nothing in the literal sense, then his arguments for freedom collapse. And if his ontological arguments for absolute freedom are unconvincing, we may expect that the way in which he tries to take care of the traditional objections to a theory of absolute freedom will also be less than adequate. As we have seen Sartre's way of dealing with facticity was as follows: an obstacle is always an obstacle *for* someone; it becomes an obstacle only by virtue of a choice with the accomplishment of which it is inconsistent.[23] A mountain is an obstacle only to someone who wants to get to the other side. In

itself, it just is. And therefore in choosing a goal, I choose as obstacles all those things which are incompatible with realizing that goal. Hence I choose my own obstacles, and they cannot possibly be thought of as limitations upon my freedom. Now Sartre is surely correct in maintaining that an obstacle is always an obstacle *for* someone, and in particular is an obstacle in that it is incompatible with the execution of a choice. Nevertheless it is a mistake to say that therefore I choose my own obstacles. For I do not choose the connection between X, my goal, and Y, the element of facticity incompatible with that goal. This incompatibility appears to be a simple given; this is just the way the world is. The fact that the law of gravity and the constitution of my muscles prevent me from leaping a ten foot wall is not a result of my choice. Sartre has not shown that obstacles do not limit my freedom.

Now Sartre has an answer to the above line of criticism. For he maintains not merely that I choose my own goals, but that I *choose* the world.[24] Consciousness is the source of whatever qualities the world has; and consciousness *freely* gives the world its form and character. Thus I really have chosen not only my goals, which may turn out to be inconsistent with some fact about the world, but also those facts and the inconsistency between them and the accomplishment of my choice. This follows from the fact that I freely give to the world whatever qualities and characters it possesses. But this doctrine is simply preposterous. And it is also self-referentially inconsistent. For if it is really the case that we individually and freely (i.e., arbitrarily) choose the truth, then the whole noetic enterprise becomes senseless and self-defeating. Sartre's ontology then becomes a merely personal expression of *his* choice; no better though no worse on its own grounds than an ontology according to which human reality completely lacks freedom. If each of us lives in a

23 See above, pp. 347-348.

24 See above, pp. 349-350.

world of his own choosing, then the world of absolute freedom which Sartre has chosen is rationally no more compelling than any other. There is an ultimate subjectivism involved in Sartre's ontology —a subjectivism which stultifies the notion of truth and makes knowledge impossible. A theory of absolute freedom, like one of absolute determinism, is self-referentially inconsistent. If Sartre is right, there is no reason to think that he's right.

While it is true that Sartre holds this extreme doctrine of absolute freedom, he does not hold it consistently. And thus in spite of repeated asseverations of absolute freedom, man, on Sartre's view, is limited to a very considerable degree. Though he insists that human reality has no antecedent essence, he nevertheless holds that the role of the for-itself in the world is limited and circumscribed by many conditions. In a sense, the whole point of Sartre's philosophy is the attempt to describe the predicament of man in a world without God (*Existentialism*, p. 211). And though Sartre does not admit that man has an essence, he does speak of "a universal human condition":

Besides, if it is impossible to find in every man some universal essence which would be human nature, yet there does exist a universal human condition. It's not by chance that today's thinkers speak more readily of man's condition than of his nature. By condition they mean, more or less definitely the a priori *limits which outline man's fundamental situation in the universe. Historical situations vary; a man may be born a slave in a pagan society or a feudal lord or a proletarian. What does not vary is the necessity for him to exist in the world, to be at work*

there, to be there in the midst of other people, and to be mortal there. (Exis-tentialism, p. 40).

Elsewhere he speaks of "an ensemble of abstract conditions which constitute the human situation." Now the difference between "an ensemble of abstract conditions" or "a universal human condition" and an essence seems to be mostly verbal. In *Being and Nothingness* Sartre provides a sort of inventory of the most significant attributes or characteristics of the for-itself. What is this but to describe its essence? Man cannot escape the desire to be in-itself-for-itself; he cannot escape anguish; and he cannot escape responsibility. He is *defined* as "the being who tries to become God" (BN 566). And these constitute very significant limitations upon him. He is not free to choose to live in a world in which it is possible to be both for-itself and in-itself. Nor is he free to escape his anguish. ". . . the original tendency of the for-itself is towards being: this project of being or desire or tendency toward being does not proceed from some psychological differentiation or contingent event; it is not distinguished from the being of the for-itself. The for-itself may be defined as the being which tries to become God. This is the fundamental structure of the for-itself" (loc. cit.). Hence it is perfectly clear that the for-itself has a fundamental structure, that it is limited by the laws of logic (since the only trouble with being for-itself-in-itself, is that this happy condition is self-contradictory) and by the actual constitution of the world. Sartre himself finds it impossible consistently to maintain a doctrine of absolute freedom. And this is a case where his inconsistency does him credit.

How Can
Ethical
Viewpoints
Be Evaluated?

An obvious way to evaluate a moral theory is by "appeal to the facts." In this manner both F. H. Bradley and John Dewey attempted to adduce evidence for their quite different moral theories; the essay by Marvin Fox demonstrates the dangers and ambiguities of such an attempt. The same sort of approach, though with a difference, is used by John Stuart Mill, and the reader will want to ask if Mill's attempt falls under the condemnation noted at the end of Fox's essay. Alan Gewirth reveals and discusses an important difference in the approach to "the facts" of science, as opposed to the approach to "the facts" of morality, and denies that this difference in approach is legitimate. Finally, William Frankena proposes, in outline form, an approach to appraising the success of an ethical theory by appeal to what Kurt Baier has called "the moral point of view." We will look briefly at the arguments of each of these essays.

In "*Moral Facts and Moral Theory*," Marvin Fox uses the writings of two widely divergent moral philosophers—F. H. Bradley and John Dewey—to illustrate his thesis that while moral philosophers often claim that "facts are indispensable to a formulation of an acceptable and defensible ethical theory," they often tailor the facts, with their own moral theory providing the pattern for alteration.

Dewey and Bradley are contemporaries and so have access to basically the same factual data. They hold very different philosophic positions, so their common approach to facts is not idiosyncratic. Both appeal to factual considerations in support of their moral contentions, and Dewey acknowledges a debt to Bradley, so that "there is enough of a relationship to make comparisons both reasonable and fruitful."

Fox's charge against Dewey and Bradley (and he adds that "It could be shown that . . . the way in which they handle matters of fact is common to many ethical theories") is this:

. . . even philosophers like Dewey and Bradley, who acknowledge the importance of facts for their theories, do not establish their facts scientifically. Instead, it can be shown that they see the facts primarily in the light of their theories.

This, he suggests, explains two phenomena. It explains why contemporaries differ as to what the facts are when, and as, their moral theories differ. It explains why, within a particular moral theory, inconsistent factual claims are made—"why their conception of what the facts are tends to change as the requirements of their theories change."

Fox considers as a test of his thesis the way Bradley and Dewey deal with the question as to whether moral judgments are universally the same. Bradley contends that all men possess "the voice of the moral consciousness" and that because of it there is an area of universal moral agreement. Thus to make virtue as a means to an ulterior end is in direct antagonism to moral consciousness. Further, all "normal, decent, and serious" men of sufficient experience have basically the same notion of happiness, and this notion is a "unity" in which particulars serve one another. Again, all men order their lives in terms of a hierarchy of ends, and "if we turn to life, we see that no man has disconnected particular ends."

Now these are not obviously true claims. What evidence does Bradley offer for them?

Bradley conceives of both knowledge and being as dialectical in character. That is to say, dialectic is not merely a method by which we acquire knowledge, but reality itself is a dialectical structure. Within that dialectical conception of reality, Bradley describes the various sub-phenomena as dialectical also. Thus morality is conceived as the process of self-realization, and this is understood by Bradley as a developmental movement in which contradictory aspects of the individual personality are brought together in a higher unity . . . (This movement) is bound up with his very nature as man and with the metaphysical structure of the world which he inhabits.

Why, then, do men putatively exhibit such unity of view concerning the value of virtue as an end, the nature of happiness, and the cohesiveness of their goals? Because of the dialectical structure of reality and their own participation in it. As microcosms in a dialectical macrocosm, they manifest features similar to those of the whole. Apparent exceptions are mere confusions; when some hedonists value pleasure but not virtue as an end in itself, this is a "misunderstanding" on their part. Their defense of hedonist ethics perverts their view of the facts. At least, so Bradley says. But, as Fox notes:

Bradley does not seem at all disturbed by the two most obvious objections that might be raised. In the first place, he, too, has a theory, but this does not seem to impede his feeling of assurance in the correctness of his own moral insights. Furthermore, if there is a common moral consciousness, the hedonists, being human, ought to share in it. But Bradley ignores these objections completely.

On the other hand, Bradley, in other contexts, insists on the fact of moral diversity. This is only in part, as Fox notes, dependent on the fact that Bradley in emphasizing difference of moral beliefs is dealing with moral art (whose object is moral *practice*) *rather than moral science* (whose object is moral *knowledge*). More basically, it reflects the requirements of his theory; since

There is a clear sense in which Bradley's dialectic requires the conclusion that there is a common moral consciousness with certain universal moral judgments. But there is another sense in which this very same dialectic requires the belief in a diversity of moral patterns. For Bradley believes that apart from the absolute whole which represents the ultimate fulfillment and the highest synthesis of every developing tendency—apart from this absolute whole whatever exists implies the existence of its contradictory . . . the very same dialectic requires him at one pole to assert that the same moral insights are possessed by all men, and at the other pole to assert that every society, even every individual, is a unique moral entity with its own special set of moral prescriptions.

Fox's conclusion: "in both cases, the facts seem to be dependent on his theory rather than the reverse."

Of course, this verdict, if just, may seem to be merely a reflection of Bradley's rather esoteric metaphysical predilections. Dewey can hardly be accused of sharing these predilections. Nonetheless, we find Dewey maintaining (in passages that Fox quotes) both that

The notion of the intuitional theory that all persons possess a uniform and equal stock of moral judgments is contrary to fact.

One cannot imagine an honest person convincing himself that a disposition of disregard for human life would have beneficial consequences.

The former claim would seem at least to be more in line with the results of the social scientists. (*See* the essays by Benedict and Linton in *Theory of Knowledge*, "Is Moral Knowledge Possible?") It is also understandable in the light of Dewey's view that "The end of all theory, including moral theory, is action,":

A moral philosophy whose end is action cannot help but take note of the peculiarities and particularities of each individual moral agent and of his situation. Within this kind of framework it is almost inevitable that Dewey . . . should be extremely sensitive to the diversity of moral fashions that occur in human society. . . . However, like Bradley, Dewey cannot let the matter rest there. Any systematic structure has to base itself on some uniformities and regularities. Without at least a minimum of uniformity and regularity there is not a systematic structure, but mere chaos.

For Dewey, the uniformities are to be found in two places. One is in the approval and disapproval that are always present in moral judgments. Dewey claims that some attitudes are shared at least by all "honest" men. Hence there are some moral judgments all men can agree upon. If not an absolute requirement of his theory, this is an element which does occur in it and in virtue of which his claim that "every kind of practice seems to have been (somewhere) tolerated or praised" is restricted.

The other is in the "framework" of morality, which is, Dewey believes, everywhere the same. Fox emphasizes this feature of Dewey's thought.

Moral theory is for him an extension of biology and psychology and thus must share certain of the characteristics of these disciplines. Like them it must be rooted in human nature, and must presume that human nature is everywhere the same. If this is the case, then it is inevitable that the phenomena of morals should be characterized by certain uniform attributes which are understood as rooted in the essential nature of man.

As Dewey puts it, "the framework of moral conception is as permanent as human life itself." Why? "Because his moral theory requires it," Fox answers; and Fox's argument is carefully developed and powerful. The conclusion that Fox invites us to draw with respect to both Bradley and Dewey is one suggested by Bradley himself.

We reflect in general not to find the facts, but to prove our theories at the expense of them. The ready-made doctrines we bring to the work color whatever we touch with them.

Such is, at any rate, a very real danger—a danger that John Stuart Mill attempted to avoid.

Among the "General Remarks" that precede the main body of *Utilitarianism* is one Mill returns to in the final chapter of that volume.

There is a larger meaning of the word "proof," in which this question is as amenable to it as any other of the disputed questions of philosophy. The subject is within the cognizance of the rational faculty, and neither does that faculty deal with it solely in the way of intuition. Considerations may be presented capable of determining the intellect either to give or withhold its assent to the doctrine, and this is equivalent to proof.

"This question" is "What proof is it possible to give that pleasure is good?" and "this subject" includes at least the issue raised in the title question of this section.

The universal hedonistic utilitarianism Mill embraces requires as an essential element that only pleasure (and absence of pain) is intrinsically good. How can one prove this? "To be incapable of proof by reasoning is common to all first principles, to the first premises of our knowledge as well as our conduct." By "reasoning" Mill evidently means "deduction from self-evident first principles or induction from observed phenomena," for he spends a chapter attempting to show that we can prove that only pleasure is good. The proof goes as follows:

(1) Moral questions about conduct (What should I do?) are in part questions about ends (What end should I seek?).

(2) Questions about ends are questions about what is desirable.

(3) The sole evidence it is possible to produce that anything is desirable is that people do actually desire it.

(4) Each person desires his own happiness.

(5) That each person be happy is desirable.

Mill could accept (4′) instead of (4), where (4′) reads: Each person desires his own and the general happiness. But he seems to believe (and not without reason) that the premise that men desire the *general* happiness in addition to their own needs proof.

This [(4)] . . . being a fact, we have . . . all the proof . . . it is possible to require that happiness is a good, that each person's happiness is a good to that person, and the general happiness, therefore, a good to the aggregate of all persons.

So Mill infers from (4) that (6) the aggregate of all persons desire the general happiness. The transition is made in some such manner as this: That mankind be happy is the same as that all men are happy. Each person desires his own happiness, so (6) the aggregate of all persons desires the general happiness. We must, then, be able to speak of the "general will" and its objects of willing, for only the general will—and not the will of any particular human being—is said to desire the general happiness. Without some such doctrine it is sheer alchemy to deduce a desire no one has from a desire everyone has. While this is not the occasion to discuss doctrines of the general will, it is by no means clear that any such doctrine will, as Mill's argument requires, be more plausible than (5). But it is a necessary condition of a claim serving as relevant evidence for (5) that it be more plausible (less in doubt) than (5) itself.

Of course, (2) is also problematic. What is desirable is (in the sense of "desirable" relevant to Mill's argument) worthy of being desired, or good. There is no contradiction in the claim that (7) all men desire x but x is evil. But this would have to be contradictory if "x is desired by all" entailed "x is desirable." Of course, Mill does not claim that an entailment holds in this context, but only that universal desire for x is completely sufficient evidence for x's worthiness to be desired. But is it?

Mill promised to prove that men *only* desire happiness, which of course does not follow from (4), as Mill knows. He claims, however, that all the other things men desire—virtue, material possessions, fame, and so on—they desire either as a means to happiness or else as an element in their total happiness. "Happiness is not an abstract idea but a concrete whole, and these [the "other" things men desire] are some of its parts." This analysis depends, of course, on the claim that it is only for its being pleasurable that knowledge, virtue, or anything else is an object of human action.

Again, Mill is aware of this, and he says that "to desire anything except in proportion as the idea of it is pleasant is a physical and metaphysical impossibility. So obvious does this appear to me that I expect it will hardly be disputed." Why is this an impossibility? Because "human nature is so constituted as to desire nothing which is not either a part of happiness or a means of happiness."

This makes it clear that Mill's views about ethics are predicated on his view of man—a view only partly empirical, for while evidence of what men actually do is relevant to it, the possibility of contrary evidence is vitiated by the flexibility of Mill's use of "pleasure" and "happiness." Apparently contrary evidence is always so interpreted as not really to be contrary. Where reasonable explanation ends and special pleading begins is not an empirical question. Whether Mill's proof is in any way successful must now, as he says, "be left to the consideration of the thoughtful reader."

In an unusual and carefully argued essay, Alan Gewirth claims that the widespread conviction that scientific issues are patently open to rational settlement while ethical issues are matters of private feeling is itself based on a prejudiced treatment of the data. We approach the science of primitive culture, such as it is, with the assumption that the norms for scientific explanation prevalent in our culture are correct, and those in any other culture, insofar as they differ, are incorrect. But we assume that the moral norms of our culture are quite on a par with those of any other, being no more correct or defensible than any discovered set of alternative moral norms. We take, in short, a "normative" view of our science (that is, it is correct) and a positive or nonnormative view of our morality (that is, any other is just as defensible). This disparity of approach is, in Gewirth's opinion, utterly indefensible; he calls it "the fallacy of disparateness."

More carefully, the fallacy of disparateness consists in comparing, as if they were on a par, disagreement over the ultimate good and disagreement over the answer to a particular scientific issue. Gewirth writes

In comparing ethics and science, or any other fields for that matter, one must be careful not to commit what I shall call the fallacy of disparateness—*the fallacy of discussing one field on one level or in one respect and the other field on a quite different level or in a quite different respect. . . . If this precept is violated, then nothing conclusive follows about the relations in question nor, to that extent, about the fields being compared.*

One commits the fallacy if, for example, he compares as on a par the questions "At what temperature does water boil?" and "What sort of life should one lead?"

A "much more fundamental and far-reaching logical disparity" is evident when philosophers and others

characterize "science" and "scientific" questions and disagreements. They always give a "normative" interpretation of the words "science" and "scientific"; but when they characterize "ethics" and "ethical" questions and disagreements, they usually give a "positive" interpretation of the words "ethics" and "ethical."

By "positive" in this quotation, Gewirth seems to mean "purely descriptive." As indicated, the net effect of this practice is to define "science" via our norms for science (for example, empirical testability, explanatory fruitfulness) but not to define "ethics" via our norms for ethics. Gewirth continues

For example, such philosophers do not regard Christian Science and neurology as examples of "science," but they do regard the discourse of both Al Capone and Albert Schweitzer as examples of "ethical" language.

A similar disparity, Gewirth suggests, infects their discussions of metaethics as compared with the philosophy of science and leaves the philosopher "powerless to distinguish between good and bad ethics."

In response to this disparity, Gewirth insists that the "principles of science are no more 'cognitive' than the principles of ethics." But they are no *less* cognitive, for, he suggests,

To decide a cognitive issue in any field requires at least two things; first, knowledge of the relevant facts, and second, agreement on criteria or norms for decision. . . . Among "ethical" men there is agreement on ethical norms, just as among "scientific" men there is agreement on scientific norms. Hence disputes among the former can be resolved by cognitive means just as can disputes among the latter.

Gewirth considers several objections to his thesis: (1) There are far more kinds of "ethical" adjustments to the world than "scientific" adjustments to it. (2) There are experts in science but not in ethics. (3) Men differ far more in their ethical beliefs than in their scientific. (4) Even if one assumes a common ethical framework, disagreements within that framework are sometimes not capable of cognitive resolution.

While conceding that "many points" made in (1)–(4) "are sound," Gewirth maintains that "they nonetheless beg the question at issue for they all proceed by way of a normative definition of "science" and a positive definition of "ethics."

As to (1), suppose we regard ethics as a necessarily impartial reconciliation of disagreements—this rules out many supposedly ethical adjustments—and suppose we regard science as necessarily a way of understanding the world or part of it. This definition will "rule in" Christian Science, phrenology, and astrology as types of scientific adjustment. As Gewirth's remarks indicate, similar responses are possible with respect to (2)–(4).

Gerwirth's conclusion from all this is not that we should abandon mathematical physics or embrace astrology, but rather "There should be a parity in the approaches which philosophers take to ethics and to science." Thus:

There can be no absolute justification of ethical norms any more than of scientific ones; for any attempt to justify the norms in either field will sooner or

later adduce criteria which assume the very norms in question. But on the other hand, just as we do not accept scepticism with regard to science, so too we need not accept scepticism in regard to ethics.

William Frankena in effect develops Gewirth's comments. Rejecting the more extreme forms of emotivism, which classify evaluative sentences as expressions or evocations of emotion or, at most, of attitude, he also refuses to join the naturalists (those who endeavor to define ethical terms via nonethical ones or to derive evaluative conclusions from purely descriptive premises) or the intuitionists (those who claim to be intuitively aware of the meaning of ethical terms or the truth of ethical claims). All these alternatives, he suggests

generally assume that if . . . judgments are not self-evident and cannot be proved inductively or deductively on the basis of empirical or non-empirical facts. . . . Then it follows that they are purely arbitrary. But it does not follow.

As anyone who so argues must, he urges that there is another mode of rational appraisal. (He here appeals to Mill's suggestion about "considerations . . . capable of determining the intellect.")

Emotions are themselves in some sense rational or irrational (appropriate or inappropriate). Further, ethical statements seem to "somehow imply a claim to be objectively and rationally justified or valid." Frankena hopes then to outline a defensible theory of justification. Central to this theory is the notion of the "moral point of view." An ethical claim is (as at least a necessary condition) justified only if one can accept it while taking the moral point of view— that is, if one is free, impartial, informed of all relevant facts, conceptually clear, willing to universalize one's principles, is doing things on principle, is considering the good of everyone alike, is not being egoistic. This list (composed by combining two of Frankena's) is redundant but characterizes what is involved in taking a moral point of view. Frankena claims then that

If one considers an item in this effective way and comes out in favor of it, one is rationally justified in judging it to be intrinsically good, even if one cannot prove one's judgment. . . . Here enters the autonomy of the moral agent—he must take the moral point of view and must claim an eventual consensus with others who do so, but he must judge for himself. He may be mistaken, but, like Luther, he cannot do otherwise.

Frankena suggests, in effect, that we are not worse, or much worse, off with respect to moral claims than we are with respect to nonmoral ones. In order to evaluate any claim, we must adopt an attitude not unlike "the moral point of view." In this respect he carries on Gewirth's reasoning.

Of course, taking a point of view of this sort is not enough: there must be tools for appraisal, criteria of some sort that correct views meet and incorrect do not—or that correct views meet at least more adequately than incorrect ones. But there is no reason in principle why such conditions cannot be stated for moral claims, and Frankena applies a number of them in the course of his book.

Of What Sort of Proof the Utility Principle Is Susceptible

JOHN STUART MILL

It has already been remarked that questions of ultimate ends do not admit of proof, in the ordinary acceptance of the term. To be incapable of proof by reasoning is common to all first principles, to the first premises of our knowledge, as well as to those of our conduct. But the former, being matters of fact, may be the subject of a direct appeal to the faculties which judge of fact—namely, our senses and our internal consciousness. Can an appeal be made to the same faculties on questions of practical ends? Or by what other faculty is cognizance taken of them?

Questions about ends are, in other words, questions what things are desirable. The utilitarian doctrine is that happiness is desirable, and the only thing desirable, as an end; all other things being only desirable as means to that end. What ought to be required of this doctrine, what conditions is it requisite that the doctrine should fulfill—to make good its claim to be believed?

The only proof capable of being given that an object is visible is that people actually see it. The only proof that a sound is audible is that people hear it; and so of the other sources of our experience. In like manner, I apprehend, the sole evidence it is possible to produce that anything is desirable is that people do actually desire it. If the end which the utilitarian doctrine proposes to itself were not, in theory and in practice, acknowledged to be an end, nothing could ever convince any person that it was so. No reason can be given why the general happiness is desirable, except that each person, so far as he believes it to be attainable, desires his own happiness. This, however, being a fact, we have not only all the proof which the case admits of, but all which

it is possible to require, that happiness is a good, that each person's happiness is a good to that person, and the general happiness, therefore, a good to the aggregate of all persons. Happiness has made out its title as *one* of the ends of conduct and, consequently, one of the criteria of morality.

But it has not, by this alone, proved itself to be the sole criterion. To do that, it would seem, by the same rule, necessary to show, not only that people desire happiness, but that they never desire anything else. Now it is palpable that they do desire things which, in common language, are decidedly distinguished from happiness. They desire, for example, virtue and the absence of vice no less really than pleasure and the absence of pain. The desire of virtue is not as universal, but it is as authentic a fact as the desire of happiness. And hence the opponents of the utilitarian standard deem that they have a right to infer that there are other ends of human action besides happiness, and that happiness is not the standard of approbation and disapprobation.

But does the utilitarian doctrine deny that people desire virtue, or maintain that virtue is not a thing to be desired? The very reverse. It maintains not only that virtue is to be desired, but that it is to be desired distinterestedly, for itself. Whatever may be the opinion of utilitarian moralists as to the original conditions by which virtue is made virtue, however they may believe (as they do) that actions and dispositions are only virtuous because they promote another end than virtue, yet this being granted, and it having been decided, from considerations of this description, what *is* virtuous, they not only place virtue at the very head of the things which are good as

FROM: *Utilitarianism*, John Stuart Mill. Ch. 4 (originally published in 1863).

means to the ultimate end, but they also recognize as a psychological fact the possibility of its being, to the individual, a good in itself, without looking to any end beyond it; and hold that the mind is not in a right state, not in a state comformable to utility, not in the state most conducive to the general happiness, unless it does love virtue in this manner—as a thing desirable in itself, even although, in the individual instance, it should not produce those other desirable consequences which it tends to produce, and on account of which it is held to be virtue. This opinion is not, in the smallest degree, a departure from the happiness principle. The ingredients of happiness are very various, and each of them is desirable in itself, and not merely when considered as swelling an aggregate. The principle of utility does not mean that any given pleasure, as music for instance, or any given exemption from pain, as for example health, is to be looked upon as means to a collective something termed happiness, and to be desired on that account. They are desired and desirable in and for themselves; besides being means, they are a part of the end. Virtue, according to the utilitarian doctrine, is not naturally and originally part of the end, but it is capable of becoming so; and in those who live it disinterestedly it has become so, and is desired and cherished, not as a means to happiness, but as a part of their happiness.

To illustrate this further, we may remember that virtue is not the only thing originally a means, and which if it were not a means to anything else would be and remain indifferent, but which by association with what it is a means to comes to be desired for itself, and that too with the utmost intensity. What, for example, shall we say of the love of money? There is nothing originally more desirable about money than about any heap of glittering pebbles. Its worth is solely that of the things which it will buy; the desires for other things than itself, which it is a means of gratifying. Yet the love of money is not only one of the strongest moving forces of human life, but money is, in many cases, desired in and for itself; the desire to possess it is often stronger than the desire to use it, and goes on increasing when all the desires which point to ends beyond it, to be compassed by it, are falling off. It may, then, be said truly that money is desired not for the sake of an end, but as part of the end. From being a means to happiness, it has come to be itself a principle ingredient of the individual's conception of happiness. The same may be said of the majority of the great objects of human life: power, for example, or fame, except that to each of these there is a certain amount of immediate pleasure annexed, which has at least the semblance of being naturally inherent in them—a thing which cannot be said of money. Still, however, the strongest natural attraction, both of power and of fame, is the immense aid they give to the attainment of our other wishes; and it is the strong association thus generated between them and all our objects of desire which gives to the direct desire of them the intensity it often assumes, so as in some characters to surpass in strength all other desires. In these cases the means have become a part of the end, and a more important part of it than any of the things which they are means to. What was once desired as an instrument for the attainment of happiness has come to be desired for its own sake. In being desired for its own sake it is, however, desired as *part* of happiness. The person is made, or thinks he would be made, happy by its mere possession; and is made unhappy by failure to obtain it. The desire of it is not a different thing from the desire of happiness any more than the love of music or the desire of health. They are included in happiness. They are some of the elements of which the desire of happiness is made up. Happiness is not an abstract idea but a concrete whole; and these are some of its parts. And the utilitarian standard sanctions and approves their being so. Life would be a poor thing, very ill provided with sources of happiness, if there were not this provision of nature by which things originally indifferent, but conductive to, or otherwise associated with, the satisfaction of our primitive desires, become in themselves sources of pleasure more valuable than the primitive pleasures, both in permanency, in the space of human existence that they are capable of covering, and even in intensity.

Virtue, according to the utilitarian conception, is a good of this description. There was no original desire of it, or motive to it, save its conduciveness to pleasure, and especially to protection from pain. But through the association thus formed it may be felt a good in itself, and desired as such with as great intensity as any other good; and with this difference between it and the love of money, of power, or of fame—that all of these may, and often do, render the individual noxious to the other members of the society to which he belongs, whereas there is nothing which makes him so much a blessing to them as the cultivation of the disinterested love of virtue. And consequently, the utilitarian standard, while it tolerates and approves those other acquired desires, up to the point beyond which they would be more injurious to the general happiness than promotive of it, enjoins and requires the cultivation of the love of virtue up to the greatest strength possible, as being above all things important to the general happiness.

It results from the preceding considerations that there is in reality nothing desired except happiness. Whatever is desired otherwise than as a means to some end beyond itself, and ultimately to happiness, is desired as itself a part of happiness, and is not desired for itself until it has become so. Those who desire virtue for its own sake desire it either because the consciousness of it is a pleasure, or because the consciousness of being without it is a pain, or for both reasons united; as in truth the pleasure and pain seldom exist separately, but almost always together—the same person feeling pleasure in the degree of virtue

attained, and pain in not having attained more. If one of these gave him no pleasure, and the other no pain, he would not love or desire virtue, or would desire it only for the other benefits which it might produce to himself or to persons whom he cared for.

We have now, then, an answer to the question, of what sort of proof the principle of utility is susceptible. If the opinion which I have now stated is psychologically true—if human nature is so constituted as to desire nothing which is not either a part of happiness or a means of happiness—we can have no other proof, and we require no other, that these are the only things desirable. If so, happiness is the sole end of human action, and the promotion of it the test by which to judge of all human conduct; from whence it necessarily follows that it must be the criterion of morality, since a part is included in the whole.

And now to decide whether this is really so, whether mankind do desire nothing for itself but that which is a pleasure to them, or of which the absence is a pain, we have evidently arrived at a question of fact and experience, dependent like all similar questions, upon evidence. It can only be determined by practiced self-consciousness and self-observation, assisted by observation of others. I believe that these sources of evidence, impartially consulted, will declare that desiring a thing and finding it pleasant, aversion to it and thinking of it as painful, are phenomena entirely inseparable or, rather, two parts of the same phenomenon—in strictness of language, two different modes of naming the same psychological fact; that to think of an object as desirable (unless for the sake of its consequences) and to think of it as pleasant are one and the same thing; and that to desire anything except in proportion as the idea of it is pleasant is a physical and metaphysical impossibility.

So obvious does this appear to me that I expect it will hardly be disputed; and the objection made will be, not that desire can possibly be directed to anything ultimately except pleasure and exemption from pain, but that the will is a different thing from desire, that a person of confirmed virtue or any other person whose purposes are fixed carries out his purposes without any thought of the pleasure he has in contemplating them or expects to derive from their fulfillment, and persists in acting on them, even though these pleasures are much diminished by changes in his character or decay of his passive sensibilities, or are outweighed by the pains which the pursuit of the purposes may bring upon him. All this I fully admit and have stated it elsewhere as positively and emphatically as anyone. Will, the active phenomenon, is a different thing from desire, the state of passive sensibility, and, though originally an offshoot from it, may in time take root and detach itself from the parent stock, so much so that in the case of a habitual purpose, instead of willing the thing because we desire it, we often desire it only because we will it. This, however, is but an instance of that familiar fact, the power of habit, and is nowise confined to the case of virtuous actions. Many different things which men originally did from a motive of some sort they continue to do from habit. Sometimes this is done unconsciously, the consciousness coming only after the action; at other times with conscious volition, but volition which has become habitual and is put in operation by the force of habit, in opposition perhaps to the deliberate preference, as often happens with those who have contracted habits of vicious or hurtful indulgence. Third and last comes the case in which the habitual act of will in the individual instance is not in contradiction to the general intention prevailing at other times, but in fulfillment of it, as in the case of the person of confirmed virtue and of all who pursue deliberately and consistently any determinate end. The distinction between will and desire thus understood is an authentic and highly important psychological fact; but the fact consists solely in this—that will, like all other parts of

our constitution, is amenable to habit, and that we may will from habit what we no longer desire for itself, or desire only because we will it. It is not the less true that will, in the beginning, is entirely produced by desire, including in that term the repelling influence of pain as well as the attractive one of pleasure. Let us take into consideration no longer the person who has a confirmed will to do right, but him in whom that virtuous will is still feeble, conquerable by temptation, and not to be fully relied on; by what means can it be strengthened? How can the will to be virtuous, where it does not exist in sufficient force, be implanted or awakened? Only by making the person *desire* virtue—by making him think of it in a pleasurable light, or of its absence in a painful one. It is by associating the doing right with pleasure, or the wrong with pain, or by eliciting and impressing and bringing home to the person's experience the pleasure naturally involved in the one or the pain in the other, that it is possible to call forth that will to be virtuous which, when confirmed, acts without any thought of either pleasure or pain. Will is the child of desire, and passes out of the dominion of its parent only to come under that of habit. That which is the result of habit affords no presumption of being intrinsically good; and there would be no reason for wishing that the purpose of virtue should become independent of pleasure and pain were it not that the influence of the pleasurable and painful associations which prompt to virtue is not sufficiently to be depended on for unerring constancy of action until it has acquired the support of habit. Both in feeling and in conduct, habit is the only thing which imparts certainty; and it is because of the importance to others of being able to rely absolutely on one's feelings and conduct, and to oneself of being able to rely on one's own, that the will to do right ought to be cultivated into this habitual independence. In other words, this state of the will is a means to good, not intrinsically a good; and does not contradict the doctrine that nothing is a good to human beings but in so far as it is either itself pleasurable or a means of attaining pleasure or averting pain.

But if this doctrine be true, the principle of utility is proved. Whether it is so or not must now be left to the consideration of the thoughtful reader.

Moral Facts and Moral Theory
MARVIN FOX

*T*he following statement, which occurs very early in *Human Nature and Conduct* is a clear expression of Dewey's belief that a moral theory cannot be formulated adequately without a knowledge of the relevant facts. Dewey asserts that:

It is impossible to say how much of the unnecessary slavery of the world is due to the conception that moral issues can be settled within conscience or human sentiment apart from consistent study of facts and application of specific knowledge in industry, law and politics.—It is not pretended that a moral theory based upon realities of human nature and a study of the specific connections of these realities with those of physical science would do away with moral struggle and defeat. . . . But morals based upon concern with facts and deriving guidance from knowledge of them would at least locate the points of effective endeavor and would focus available resources upon them.[1]

This insistence that a moral philosophy is both mistaken and useless unless it is based on a knowledge of the facts of man's nature and of the dynamics of society is characteristic of many current naturalistic and empirical theories.

But even the non-naturalistic and the non-empirical moralists feel called upon to pay homage to the importance of facts. This is hardly surprising when we remember that there is some sense in which every moralist wants his principles to be able to serve as a guide to practice. Even those philosophers who classify ethics as a theoretical science, whose proper end is knowledge and not practice, recognize that what they are aiming at is a theoretical knowledge of practical principles. But if this is the case then it seems reasonable to suppose that such principles cannot be developed in ignorance of the fundamental facts about the beings whose practice they are intended to control. Typical of this position is the attitude of a philosopher like F. H. Bradley who would not normally be thought of as a naturalist or an empiricist. Discussing one of the central problems in his *Ethical Studies* Bradley observes that:

—what we most want, more especially those of us who talk most about facts, is to stand by all the facts. It is our duty to take them without picking and choosing them to suit our views, to explain them, if we can, but not to explain them away; and to reason on them, and find the reason of them, but never to think ourselves rational when, by the shortest cut to reason we have reasoned ourselves out of them.[2]

[1] John Dewey, *Human Nature and Conduct* (New York: The Modern Library, 1930), pp. 11–12.

[2] F. H. Bradley, *Ethical Studies* (Oxford: The Clarendon Press, 1927), p. 251.

FROM: *Perspectives in Philosophy: Essays by Members of the Dept of Philosophy*, The Ohio State University. (Columbus: The Ohio State University Press, 1953). Reprinted by permission of the Department of Philosophy at Ohio State and the author.

For Bradley, as well as for the empiricists, facts are indispensable to a formulation of an acceptable and defensible ethical theory.

II

It is surprising, in the light of such statements, to find that in Dewey's and Bradley's ethical writings facts are not dealt with in the way that we might expect. Surely, if philosophers consider facts to be basically important in establishing moral principles, then they should employ the best possible techniques for determining what the facts are. One would tend to presume that such philosophers would use the most reliable scientific data, that they would be cautious and tentative where the evidence is incomplete, and that their factual statements would be rigorously consistent. Moreover, it would be reasonable to expect that there would be among such philosophers fairly general agreement as to what the facts are. These are expectations which are taken for granted in the factual statements of scientists. Ideally, philosophers who claim central importance for factual knowledge should meet these same minimal scientific standards in dealing with facts.

Yet if we read Dewey's and Bradley's ethical writings we find that their factual statements frequently lack all scientific character. Instead of the rigorous care of the scientists we are offered vague assurances, dogmatic statements, and simple appeals to common opinion. Inadequate as these would appear to be as evidence for presumed facts, the weakness of the factual statements of these philosophers is increased by internal contradictions as well as by the marked disagreements concerning matters of fact which obtain between different thinkers. It is not at all uncommon (as we shall show subsequently) to find that a particular ethical work presents us with factual statements that are internally contradictory. It is even more common to find striking differences and disagreements in the factual statements of different moral philosophers. I shall attempt to

show, in what follows, that both Dewey and Bradley deal with facts in the manner which we have discussed, that one can find in their moral philosophies factual statements which are either self-contradictory or mutually contradictory. My main purpose is to offer an analysis and possible explanation for the curious fashion in which these philosophers deal with matters of fact.

III

Dewey and Bradley have been chosen as prototypical instances for several reasons. First, they are contemporaries, and as such might certainly be expected to agree about matters of fact. A common body of information, common sources, and certain common and well established methods have been available to them. Perhaps we can countenance disagreements about facts between thinkers who are widely separated in time, but it is certainly reasonable to expect that contemporaries will agree. Factual disagreements, then, between two such contemporaries as Bradley and Dewey point up the seriousness of the issues which we are raising. For their very contemporaneity strengthens the likelihood that the differences between these philosophers are genuine and significant, that they are not merely the result of differences in the information that was available at widely separated times.

Secondly, Dewey and Bradley hold very different philosophic positions. If the thesis which is proposed here can be shown to be true of two such diverse thinkers, then we are, at least, immune from the criticism that what we are pointing out is merely the peculiarity of a certain kind of moral philosophy. Instead it becomes clear that we are examining a phenomenon which may well be characteristic of moral philosophy generally. (If space would permit it could be shown that Dewey and Bradley are in no sense unique, and that the way in which they handle matters of fact is common to many ethical theorists.) Thirdly, in spite of their differences, Dewey, in a number of places, acknowledges a very heavy debt to Bradley.[3] This means that there is enough of a relationship to make comparisons both reasonable and fruitful. Finally, as was pointed out at the beginning of this essay, both Dewey and Bradley take facts seriously. As a result we cannot discuss internal contradictions or mutual disagreements about matters of fact as mere carelessness or unconcern. We rightfully expect deliberate and conscious care in judgments about what the facts are of any writer who emphasizes as strongly as do these two the inescapable importance of facts for moral theory. Thus, the ethical works of Bradley and Dewey seem to offer us an excellent opportunity to study the way in which facts are dealt with by moral philosophers.

The central thesis of this paper is that even philosophers like Dewey and Bradley, who acknowledge the importance of facts for their theories, do not establish their facts scientifically. Instead, it can be shown that they see the facts primarily in the light of the requirements of their theories. As a result, their conceptions of what the facts are tend to change as the requirements of their theories change. We can explain their internal contradictions, as well as their mutual disagreements, in this fashion. For it turns out that, in spite of their open espousal of the need for accurate knowledge of the facts, their own statements of facts are sometimes inconsistent, and this is a result of the varying needs of their theories. It is a commonplace that sound theories must be based on accurate facts. We are proposing a consideration of the view that the facts, at least of moral philosophers, tend to be derived from their theories. Given any moral doctrine the facts must be conceived in a way that will be consistent with it. This means that frequently theory dictates what the facts must be.

[3] Cf. John Dewey, *Outlines of a Critical Theory of Ethics* (Ann Arbor: Register Publishing Co., 1891), p. vi.

IV

One of the questions regarding matters of fact which occupies the attention of both Bradley and Dewey is the following: "Are moral judgments universally the same, or do they differ greatly from one society to another? Do people everywhere have identical opinions concerning what constitutes the good and the evil, or is there a great diversity of opinion on this fundamental question?" This question involves the kind of facts which most contemporary scholars would hold to be readily ascertainable. The social sciences, and especially anthropology, should, presumably, be able to give us this kind of information. Yet neither Bradley nor Dewey, though they both wrote within the decades which have marked the ascendancy of the social sciences, attempt to substantiate their factual judgments by appeal to these authorities. Instead their views on such matters of fact as the uniformity or diversity of moral judgments are supported by nothing more than their own pronouncements, occasionally tempered by an appeal to common sense observation. It is our contention that it can be shown clearly that their particular views on these questions are, at least, a necessary corollary, if not the direct result of the positions they hold with regard to certain theoretical matters. As the most economical way of dealing with our general problem, we shall devote ourselves to an analysis of the way in which Dewey and Bradley deal with this one area of factual knowledge.

In his *Ethical Studies* Bradley offers two kinds of answers to the question of the uniformity of moral judgments. In some regards he assures us that there is complete uniformity, that all men are agreed about moral questions, while in other connections he claims that there is a great diversity of moral judgments and that different men and different societies have radically differing moral rules. The area of uniformity in moral matters arises in connection with what Bradley calls "the voice of the moral consciousness".[4] He speaks of it as a "common consciousness",[5] and it is clear that he believes that all men possess this common moral consciousness. It is a sort of intuitive moral sense that Bradley believes every man has, merely by virtue of the fact that he is a man. It follows that such a moral sense will, within the scope of its operation, lead all men to identical judgments. Bradley conceives this moral sense as concerned only with some very general principles of morality, and with regard to these he assures us that there is universal agreement.

We must remember that for Bradley the facts are supposedly given. It is the business of theory merely to explain and account for the facts. However, it appears that he has in actuality reversed this procedure. He tells us that it is a matter of fact that the common moral consciousness affirms certain things. Consequently, men everywhere, irrespective of the particular elements of their moral situation, can be expected to acknowledge these affirmations of the moral consciousness. Yet it is clear enough that there are many who have denied and still deny what Bradley tells us that the moral consciousness affirms. He himself mentions, as one instance, the hedonists. Yet in the face of this he continues to talk as if it were a fact that these are matters on which all men are agreed. It is my contention, in the light of this, that Bradley is not explaining facts that are given, but that he is instead affirming as facts items which his theory requires of him.

Before we can demonstrate this we must first examine some of the dictates of the common moral consciousness as Bradley describes them. According to him our moral sense informs us (presumably all of us) that virtue is its own end, and consequently that the only reason that I ought to be moral is because I ought to be moral. For he considers it an obvious and unquestionable fact that

"to take virtue as a mere means to an ulterior end *is* in direct antagonism to the voice of the moral consciousness."[6] It is that same moral consciousness that informs us that "to do good for its own sake is virtue, to do it for some ulterior end or object, not itself good, is never virtue."[7] In line with this view Bradley goes on to point out that morality must be accepted as a present reality, but cannot be justified by any external justification. The title of the chapter in which these reflections occur is "Why Should I be Moral?" Bradley concludes without any hesitation at all that "The question has no sense at all; it is simply unmeaning."[8]

How can we explain Bradley's insistence that these are matters of universal agreement? Bradley conceives of both knowledge and being as dialectical in character. That is to say, dialectic is not merely a method by which we acquire knowledge, but reality itself is a dialectical structure. Within that dialectical conception of reality Bradley describes the various sub-phenomena as dialectical also. Thus, morality is conceived as the process of self-realization, and this is understood by Bradley as a developmental movement in which contradictory aspects of the individual personality are brought together in a higher unity. In each case this synthesis is a movement toward the fulfillment of the true nature of the self, that is, of self-realization. This is not merely a process in which man engages casually, if and when the inclination strikes him. It is bound up with his very nature as man and with the metaphysical structure of the world which he inhabits.

Morality is an endless process, and therefore a self-contradiction; and, being such, it does not remain standing in itself, but feeds the impulse to transcend

[4] Bradley, *op. cit.*, p. 61.

[5] *Ibid.*, p. 63.

[6] *Ibid.*, p. 61.

[7] *Ibid.*, p. 62.

[8] *Ibid.*, p. 64.

its existing reality. . . . Neither in me, nor in the world, is what ought to be what is, and what is what ought to be. . . .[9]

It is, in some sense, an inevitable and inexorable process, and it is for this very reason that the question, "Why should I be moral?", is in Bradley's eyes, totally meaningless. Both metaphysical and moral reality make the process an absolutely necessary one. To ask why I should be moral is equivalent to asking why I should be a man living in this kind of world. Neither question is answerable.

If I am asked why I am to be moral, I can say no more than this, that what I can not doubt is my own being now, and that, since in that being is involved a self, which is to be here and now, and yet in this here and now is not, I therefore cannot doubt that there is an end which I am to make real; and morality, if not equivalent to, is at all events included in this making real of myself. . . . The only rational question here is not why? but what? What is the self that I know and will?[10]

To ask why I should want to realize that self is, from this point of view a total absurdity.

We can now see, why Bradley must hold that virtue is an end in itself, and that this is recognized by the moral consciousness. If the very meaning of morality is the process by which we realize the whole as a synthesis of its various parts, then it is necessarily the case that virtue is its own end. For nothing stands beyond the consummation of the striving for virtue. In the dialectical movement the realization of the whole is a finality. It makes no sense to say that one does this for still another purpose. It is self-sufficient and nothing can be postulated beyond it.

We must point out in passing that Bradley is fully aware that the realization

of the individual self is by his own principles not enough. It, too, is merely a partial realization. He goes on to require as a moral duty the social realization of the individual self. Every man must see himself as a member of society, and, as such, can find his genuine fulfillment. Self-realization is only a step on the way toward social realization. Social realization, furthermore, is also a stage in the process of realizing the absolute whole which is the ultimate reality.

We may still ask, in spite of all that has been said, why Bradley thinks that the common moral consciousness affirms that virtue is its own end. It is certainly possible for him to recognize that while his metaphysics requires this another metaphysical position may not. The answer lies in the fact that Bradley felt certain that his metaphysics was correct, and that every reasonable man must see the truth of his doctrine. In so doing one cannot help but recognize its consequences for morality. The common moral consciousness is merely an extension of the rational faculties which all men may be presumed to possess in common. Thus, we see that his statement of supposed fact is really a necessary consequence and extension of his prior theoretical commitments.

We may now return to the problem which we posed earlier, namely how Bradley, in the face of his belief in a common moral consciousness, is able to explain the existence of hedonists and others who believe that virtue is a means to another end. One would have expected that a common moral consciousness would express itself through a series of universally held judgments. As a matter of fact, Bradley suggests that this very situation obtains. For he assures us, among other things, that "never, except on a misunderstanding, has the moral consciousness in any case acquiesced in Hedonism."[11] How, then do we explain the presence of hedonists in the world? For Bradley the answer is quite simple. Hedonists are men with a theory.

[9] *Ibid.*, p. 313.

[10] *Ibid.*, p. 84.

[11] *Ibid.*, p. 89.

They have an axe to grind. As a result their perceptions and understanding are distorted in the effort to make the facts fit their theory. They are guilty of basic misunderstanding resulting from the effort to justify their own position.

Bradley does not seem at all disturbed by the two most obvious objections that might be raised. In the first place, he, too, has a theory, but this does not seem to impede his feeling of assurance in the correctness of his own moral insights. Furthermore, if there is a common moral consciousness then the hedonists, being human, ought to share in it. But Bradley ignores these objections completely. He merely insists that when "moral persons without a theory on the matter" are told that the end of virtue is pleasure, "there is no gainsaying that they repudiate such a result."[12] The hedonists, having a theory, are thus incapable of seeing what all men of unbiased insight are immediately able to grasp.

Bradley's conception of virtue as self-realization leads him to several other supposedly factual statements. He tells us, for example, that "if we turn to life, we see that no man has disconnected particular ends."[13] According to this view men plan their lives in a kind of hierarchical pattern. They conceive their immediate choices as means leading to the realization of certain ends, and of those ends as means to still further ends, and of the whole structure as controlled by some single final purpose. This purpose is, of course, the realization of the whole. "If the life of the normal man be inspected, and the ends he has in view (as exhibited in his acts) be considered, they will, roughly speaking, be embraced in one main end or whole of ends."[14] Here, again, we see the effect of Bradley's scheme of dialectic on his description of the facts. If it is true that both knowledge and being are dialectical

in character then it seems to follow, at least in Bradley's judgment, that the processes of the individual human life must also be structured dialectically. What is true of the macrocosm ought, according to such a theory, to be true of the microcosm. What is true of the world as a whole is equally true of each individual man who embodies the entire cosmic process within the limits of his being. Bradley's theory seems to require that the facts be as he describes them to us.

This same theme is further carried out in his initial comments on happiness where we can again see the dialectical pattern at work. Bradley denies that "every man has a different notion of happiness." On the contrary, here, too, there is a kind of uniformity of judgment. There may be some variations in the particular details of how happiness is conceived by various individuals, but the basic pattern is the same for all men.

. . . if you take (not of course anyone, but) the normal decent and serious man, when he has been long enough in the world to know what he wants, you will find that his notion of perfect happiness, or ideal life, is not something straggling, as it were, and discontinuous, but is brought before the mind as a unity, and, if imagined more in detail, is a system where particulars subserve one whole.[15]

One can see here, also, the same conception and the same dialectical pattern that has already been described. Happiness, according to Bradley, must be a "unity . . . where particulars subserve one whole," because both man and the universe are, in his view, similarly constructed according to this pattern.

Further more, every man must acknowledge that this is what he means by happiness. If he denies it then he is irrational, and consequently, we need not reckon seriously with his opinions. Bradley, himself, admits that what he

[12] *Ibid.*, p. 88.

[13] *Ibid.*, p. 69.

[14] *Ibid.*, p. 70.

[15] *Ibid.*

means by "every man" is "not of course anyone, but the normal decent and serious man", i.e., the man whose opinions coincide with his own. This may seem to be a somewhat strained way to achieve uniformity of judgment in moral matters, but it seems undeniable that this is Bradley's way. We need only recall that he employed an essentially similar device when he rejected the opinion of the hedonists as unimportant since it came from men with a theory to defend. In neither instance does he abide by his own statement of purpose, namely to account for acknowledged facts. On the contrary, where his theory requires it he appears to be quite ready to explain away facts that even he admits as true.

It is a matter of considerable interest, in the light of our discussion, to note that there is also an area in which Bradley acknowledges the existence of an extensive moral diversity. When we examine the practices of particular societies we find that they differ extensively and in many fundamental regards.

It is abundantly clear that the morality of one time is not that of another time, that the men considered good in one age might in another age not be thought good, and what would be right for us here might be mean and base in another country, and what would be wrong for us here might there be our bounden duty.[16]

He goes on to assure us that, "Different men, who have lived in different times and countries, judge or would judge a case in morals differently."[17] This is a curious statement from one who believes in the existence of a common moral consciousness. But these apparently contradictory factual statements can be explained in the terms of the position which we are seeking to defend here, namely that Bradley's facts are derived in many instances from the requirements of his

[16] *Ibid.,* p. 189.

[17] *Ibid.,* p. 195.

theory, rather than from an examination of the world. Our discussion and analysis will now move on two levels. First we shall try to analyze the opposing instances of the uniformity and diversity of moral judgments as necessary functions of the theoretical distinction which Bradley draws between moral science and moral art. Then we shall go on to show that at a deeper level the assertion of some uniformity and some diversity is an inevitable result of the dialectical scheme which Bradley employs to explain the nature of things.

Bradley distinguishes between what he calls moral science and moral art. Moral science is what we more usually call moral philosophy, and its end according to Bradley is knowledge. Its purpose is to "understand morals which exist." Moral art has as its end successful moral practice. It is not concerned with understanding morality, but rather with developing the techniques which are required for moral action.

When Bradley develops his theory of the common moral consciousness and its universal moral dictates, he does so in the context of his discussion of moral science. It is that part of the structure of his moral philosophy in which he is seeking to understand the nature of morality. For this purpose it is necessary to conceive moral phenomena as characterized by certain basic uniformities. He thinks that no knowledge is possible unless we can discover in a mass of apparently diverse phenomena some general patterns and structures in terms of which we can describe and organize our subject matter. Unless there is some uniformity we have utter chaos, and under these circumstances the end of moral philosophy or moral science is incapable of achievement. So long as his goal is theoretical knowledge Bradley is forced to assert that there are some basic similarities in morality, wherever and whenever it occurs. The belief in the existence of a common moral consciousness and its supposedly uniform prescriptions serves this purpose.

When, on the other hand, Bradley freely admits the existence of considerable moral diversity he is no longer concerned with moral science, but only with moral art. He is not interested in understanding moral phenomena, but rather in helping his reader decide what he, as a moral agent, must do. The passage which was quoted as an example of Bradley's belief in the diversity of moral judgments is preceded by a caution "against the common error that there is something 'right in itself' for me to do."[18] Insofar as his concern is practical rather than theoretical Bradley can allow for a great measure of diversity. In fact, when he is establishing the procedures of moral art he is almost forced to acknowledge moral diversity, since morality as an art necessarily deals with the particularities and specificities of each individual moral situation. Here the common moral consciousness can serve no good purpose, for in this situation the facts must be presented so as to emphasize the diversities, rather than the uniformities, of the moral life.

There is, however, a more deeply rooted explanation than the one we have given for the presence of elements both of uniformity and diversity in Bradley's description of the facts of the moral life. We showed earlier that there is a clear sense in which Bradley's dialectic requires the conclusion that there is a common moral consciousness with certain universal moral judgments. But there is another sense in which this very same dialectic requires the belief in a diversity of moral patterns. For Bradley believes that apart from the absolute whole which represents the ultimate fulfillment and the highest synthesis of every developing tendency—apart from this absolute whole whatever exists implies the existence of its contradictory. If there is moral uniformity then there must, in the very nature of things, be moral diversity as well. Bradley expresses this by making reference to the Kantian principles of homogeneity and specification.[19] Whatever exists must have certain universal characteristics, certain features that it shares with all other existing things, or, in a more limited respect, features that it shares with all other things of the same genus. But at the same time it must also have those qualities and characteristics that specify it as uniquely what it is. Human societies, conceived as moral entities, must share certain features. These are the features ascribed by Bradley to the common moral consciousness and its prescriptions. But at the same time each of these societies is a unique and special entity, and insofar as this is the case it must have its own special characteristics. These mark it out as a morally diverse unit.

We can see the workings of this pattern in the case both of individuals and societies. For all individuals there are, according to Bradley, certain common moral rules, as we have already shown. But one of these rules is that the good for me as for every other individual is determined by "my station and its duties." This means that each individual recognizes his moral obligations as specifically determined by the particular society in which he lives and by the particular place which he occupies in that society. The general rule is one which in its very uniformity implies endless diversity.

What is true of each individual person is also true of human societies. Bradley's doctrine is such that he is forced to represent each individual society as a separate and distinct moral unit. For in the moral process, as it has already been described, each individual strives for self-realization and each society strives for its own realization. Furthermore, the totality of social realization is a moment in the realization of the absolute unity which is the end goal of the entire cosmic process. Now unless societies were morally different, and even, in some regards, antithetical, the de-

[18] *Ibid.*, p. 189.

[19] Cf. *Ibid.*, pp. 74 ff.

velopmental movement would be stopped. Each society must first unify the diverse tendencies, within itself in order to fulfill its own special destiny. But having done so it must then merge with the stream of history in order that humanity may arrive at a higher state of development. In connection with this Bradley develops his belief that there is a process of social evolution in which each historical period is an advance over its predecessors. History is not merely blind change. It is teleological in character. It is a purposive movement of human societies from lower to higher stages.[20] And the development of the societies is measured by the degree to which they are an advance in the realization of the absolute whole toward which history inexorably is directed. All of this—the view of social evolution, as well as the moral diversity which it necessarily implies— is expressed clearly and succinctly by Bradley when he says that:

> . . . *if evolution is more than a tortured phrase, and progress to a goal no mere idea but an actual fact, then history is the working out of the true human nature through various incomplete stages toward completion, and 'my station' is the one satisfactory view of morals. Here . . . all morality is and must be 'relative', because the essence of realization is evolution through stages, and hence existence in some one stage which is not final; here, on the other hand, all morality is 'absolute', because in every stage the essence of man is realized, however imperfectly.*[21]

This, then, is the explanation of Bradley's position. The very same dialectic requires him at one pole to assert that the same moral insights are possessed by all men, and at the other pole to assert that every society, and even every individual, is a unique moral entity with its own special set of moral prescriptions. In both cases the facts seem to be de-

pendent on this theory rather than the reverse. He appears to have been guilty of the very thing against which he cautions us. For he, too, like those whom he condemns, does not merely account for the facts that are given. He relies on his theories to help decide what those facts must be.

V

Like Bradley Dewey also has more than one position with regard to the question of the uniformity and diversity of moral judgment and practice in various human societies. In some areas and concerning some matters he believes that there is very extensive diversity. In these particular regards morality, as he pictures it, is conditioned by the specific character of the moral situation in which it occurs. On the other hand, there are some aspects of the moral life which he assures us are universally the same irrespective of when or where they occur.

Particular codes and particular patterns of practice differ, according to Dewey, from culture to culture and from age to age. The ancient and the modern, the rural and the urban, the savage and the civilized, all have their own ways of doing things. "The notion of the intuitional theory that all persons possess a uniform and equal stock of moral judgments is contrary to fact."[22] Instead of this kind of uniformity as the actual pattern of moral practice Dewey informs us that, "At some place on the globe, at some time, every kind of practice seems to have been tolerated or even praised." He goes on to ask with considerable wonder, "How is this tremendous diversity of institutions (including moral codes) to be accounted for?"[23] This belief in the extensive diversity of moral codes and practices is one to which Dewey has held consistently. In the earliest of his writings on moral philoso-

---

[20] Cf. *Ibid.*, pp. 190–192.

[21] *Ibid.*, p. 192.

[22] John Dewey and James H. Tufts, *Ethics*, Revised Edition, (New York, 1932), p. 311.

[23] John Dewey, *Human Nature and Conduct*, (New York, 1930), p. 91.

phy he already comments on the fact that, "The savage and the civilized man may vary greatly in their estimate of what particular acts are right or wrong."[24] It is in similar spirit that, writing in a more recent book, he says:

The conception which looks for the end of action within the circumstances of the actual situation will not have the same measure of judgment for all cases. . . . The absurdity of applying the same standards of moral judgment to savage peoples that is used with civilized will be apparent.[25]

Thus we see that Dewey is clearly committed to the view that in matters of moral practice and judgment men differ very considerably. These are, presumably, facts which would be born out by observation. We must remember that Dewey places great emphasis on the necessity of knowing the facts before we can theorize about them adequately. He describes himself as within the empiricist-naturalist tradition and he is very respectful of scientific procedures. So far as is possible he urges that these procedures be transferred to moral and social studies. He conceives his own ethical theory as scientific in method, and we, therefore, have every reason to expect that the facts which he offers will satisfy the requirements of scientific criticism and scrutiny.

It is, therefore, a source of considerable wonder to us when we discover that, in spite of his belief in the diversity of moral practice, Dewey occasionally insists on a rather total uniformity. We find, for example, in one of his discussions of utilitarianism the following statement:

A man who trusted simply to details of external consequences might readily convince himself that the removal of a certain person by murder would contribute to general happiness. One cannot imagine an honest person convincing himself that a disposition of disregard for human life would have beneficial consequences.[26]

In a very similar spirit he asserts that, "A normal person will not witness an act of wanton cruelty without an immediate response of disfavor; resentment and indignation immediately follow."[27] These are views which seem totally out of harmony with the statements which were quoted above. If it is the case, as Dewey says, that somewhere on this earth at some time just about every conceivable practice has been approved, then with what ground and justification are we told that no honest man can ever believe that murder might have beneficial consequences? Clearly Dewey is involved in some sort of internal contradiction.

His belief that murder is universally disapproved, or more precisely that "a disposition of disregard for human life" is by honest men always considered evil is especially puzzling in the light of contemporary anthropological studies. We can presume that Dewey would almost certainly pay attention to such inquiries, and it is common knowledge that these studies consistently represent the facts in an opposite fashion. Of course, there is the possible alternative that Dewey considers all people living in cultures which approve homicide to be dishonest, but this hardly seems likely. Yet, if they are honest, then there is considerable evidence that there are honest men who do have little regard for human life. One example of what anthropologists have to say on this point will suffice for our purposes. In her well known book, *Patterns of Culture*, Ruth Benedict is very clear and forthright in her assertion that, "The diversity of cultures can be endlessly documented." As an illustration of this point she makes the following set of observations:

[24] John Dewey, *Outlines of a Critical Theory of Ethics*, (Ann Arbor, 1891), p. 183.

[25] John Dewey, *Reconstruction in Philosophy*, (New York, 1920), p. 176.

[26] *Ethics*, (revised edition), *op. cit.*, p. 256.

[27] *Ibid.*, p. 292.

We might suppose that in the matter of taking life all peoples would agree in condemnation. On the contrary, in a matter of homicide, it may be held that one is blameless if diplomatic relations have been severed between neighboring countries, or that one kills by custom his first two children, or that a husband has the right of life and death over his wife, or that it is the duty of the child to kill his parents before they are old. It may be that those are killed who steal a fowl, or who cut their upper teeth first, or who are born on a Wednesday.[28]

In the face of presumably factual reports of this sort—and they can be paralleled by many more—it is somewhat puzzling to find Dewey taking an opposite stand. It is even more puzzling when we recall that in other places he expressly recognizes the existence of the kind of diversity which Miss Benedict describes. This seems to be another instance in which our thesis can be shown to be correct. For it seems clear that, like Bradley, Dewey is forced to relate fact to theory. In any given instance his conception of the facts must be related to the particular theoretical requirements of the discussion. We shall attempt to show that this is the case in the analysis which follows.

Dewey's more usual view is that there is almost total diversity of moral judgment and practice, and this is a view which we might properly expect him to hold. Common observation, historical research, and the inquiries of contemporary social scientists all seem to lead to this conclusion. Moreover this is the view that Dewey's general theoretical position would seem to require. Unlike Bradley he does not distinguish between ethical theory whose sole end is knowledge and moral practice which is concerned only with appropriate action. For Dewey the end of all theory, including moral theory, is action. Even at the highest level of theoretical abstraction our theory is sig-

nificant and meaningful only if it leads to successful practice and it can be verified only by such practice. If this is the case, then Dewey must estimate the adequacy of any aspect of his moral philosophy in terms of its practical aims. But while theories and principles may be general all activity is particularized. Each act is done by a particular individual, at some specific time and place, and under a given set of conditions. Action, to be successful, must be cognizant of the uniquely individual character of the situation in which it occurs. A moral philosophy whose end is action cannot help but take note of the peculiarities and particularities of each individual moral agent and of his situation. Within this kind of framework it is almost inevitable that Dewey (like Bradley when he deals with moral art) should be extremely sensitive to the diversity of moral fashions that occur in human society. The various passages which we quoted as examples of his belief that there is such diversity are taken from different books and from different periods of his writing. However, they are all in agreement because all are derived from a theory whose consistently avowed aim is to make successful action possible. Given this goal Dewey's emphasis on moral differences is both necessary and understandable.

However, like Bradley, Dewey cannot let the matter rest there. Any systematic structure has to base itself on some uniformities and regularties. Without at least a minimum of uniformity and regularity there is not a systematic structure, but mere chaos. Dewey yields to this general need, just as Bradley does, and the passages which were quoted as apparent contradictions of his general position are clear cut instances of this yielding. When he tells us that no honest man could really believe that disregard for human life could have beneficial consequences, Dewey is in the midst of a discussion of hedonism. In typical fashion he is searching for those elements of hedonism that he can retain in his own theory, and has already concluded that

28 Ruth Benedict, *Patterns of Culture*, (New York, 1946), p. 41.

approval and disapproval are original facts. Every morality must recognize, says Dewey, that approval and disapproval are among the most elementary moral attitudes and that they are always present in moral judgment. In such judgment, accordingly, the character and disposition of the judger enters very strongly into the picture, for these determine to a considerable degree what he will approve and disapprove. And it is at this point that a certain amount of uniformity must be postulated. For, if we are dependent on individual judges and each of these differs from his fellows there can only be moral chaos. In such a situation no moral principles would be possible and whatever anybody approved would be good at least for the approver himself. To avoid this Dewey is forced to assert that there are certain uniform attitudes possessed by honest men. If we grant this then our difficulties are considerably lessened. If we know that all honest men have a given disposition and attitude with regard to certain matters then we also know that they will, so long as they are honest, necessarily approve or disapprove of certain kinds of acts. Given this knowledge it is then inevitable that we should conclude that in all societies there are certain areas of moral and social practice which are the same. Dewey's examples involved murder and cruelty, hence it was with regard to these that he felt compelled to assert a uniform disposition. Presumably had he chosen other illustrations he might still, within the context of his discussion, have found it necessary to believe that all men had uniform dispositions and attitudes concerning these matters. His statement that somewhere and sometime "every kind of practice seems to have been tolerated or praised" must be narrowed and restricted. For if praise is a basic element of moral judgment then it seems necessary to insist that there are some things from which men always withhold praise and some which they are always inclined to praise. Otherwise we would have total moral chaos.

There is a second kind of uniformity which Dewey conceives to be present, which is even more important than this specific uniformity of particular moral attitudes. I refer to his belief that the framework of morality is everywhere the same. No matter how particular practices may differ the general framework from which they are derived is everywhere the same. This is again significant as a device by which systematic order is brought into a subject matter which would otherwise be chaotic. The technique by which Dewey achieves this is quite simple, and it is appropriate within the context of his system. He believes in a total unity of science. Moral theory is for him an extension of biology and psychology and thus must share certain of the characteristics of these disciplines. Like them it must be rooted in human nature, and must presume that human nature is everywhere the same. If this is the case, then it is inevitable that the phenomena of morals should be characterized by certain uniform attributes which are understood as rooted in the essential nature of man. It is precisely this which Dewey has in mind when he says:

Special phenomena of morals change from time to time with change of social conditions and the level of culture. The facts of desiring, purpose, social demand and law, sympathetic approval and hostile disapproval are constant. We cannot imagine them disappearing so long as human nature remains human nature, and lives in association with others. The fundamental conceptions of morals are, therefore, neither arbitrary nor artificial. They are not imposed upon human nature from without but develop out of its own operations and needs. Particular aspects of morals are transient. . . . But the framework of moral conceptions is as permanent as human life itself.[29]

We see here how far the process of selectivity is operative in determining

[29] *Ethics,* (revised edition), *op. cit.,* pp. 343–4.

what the facts are and which facts are relevant. Because Dewey conceives morality as natural the only facts which concern him are natural facts. The artificial has no place in the framework of morality. Moreover because these facts are natural they must be everywhere the same. This introduces the uniform framework which his theory requires. Furthermore, out of the vast array of available natural facts he chooses as relevant primarily psychological and social facts. This is perfectly consistent with Dewey's conception of the subject-matter of ethics, since according to him ethics is concerned with deliberate conduct which affects the self and society. If this is the subject matter of ethics then it follows necessarily that the facts which interest us will be psychological and social facts, and that insofar as these are conceived as natural they will be described as everywhere the same.

Thus, he is certain that on the one side all morality must involve some kind of pleasure, for he believes that one of the most basic elements in man's nature is desire. "Desire belongs to the intrinsic nature of man; we cannot conceive a human being who does have wants, needs, nor one to whom fulfillment of desire does not afford satisfaction."[30] The satisfaction of desire is a natural striving, therefore, of all human activity, and morals must everywhere be judged within this general framework. For this reason Dewey is able to assert that, "There is nothing good to us which does not contain an element of enjoyment and nothing bad which does not contain an element of the disagreeable and repulsive."[31] The facts must be so if this aspect of morals is rooted in man's nature, and Dewey asserts clearly and unequivocally that it is so rooted.

On the other side Dewey can equally hold it to be a fact that morality everywhere is social. Again this is derived from man's nature as a social animal and thus must be thought of as part of the general framework of morality. Man is a social animal, according to Dewey, and his conduct is affected by, and affects, his society. There is no non-social conduct, and since morals deals with conduct its framework must be social.

These two facts, that moral judgment and moral responsibility are the work wrought in us by the social environment, signify that all morality is social. . . . Our conduct is socially conditioned whether we perceive the fact or not."[32]

Again this fact is relevant because the subject matter of ethics is defined by Dewey as involving the social situation, and it is universally the case because it is presumably rooted in human nature.

We may note the difference between Dewey's uniformities and those which Bradley claims to have found. Their conception of the facts is considerably different. Dewey derives his uniform aspects of the moral life from what he conceives to be human nature, from the biological, psychological and social disciplines. Bradley, on the other hand, derives his uniformities from the requirements of the metaphysical framework on which his ethical theory depends. Thus Bradley has no need to assert that any particular moral dispositions, such as the disapproval of murder, are universal. For he is in no way dependent for his uniformities on such simple psychological issues. He is not concerned with desire and approbation as crucial elements in the moral life. Instead he is forced by his metaphysical position to assert that virtue is always recognized as its own end. This, in turn, is a formulation which Dewey is forced to deny, since it comes into conflict with his emphasis on practice and his concern with ongoing process. In this process there are no final ends, only ends-in-view which are destined to become means to still

---

[30] *Ibid.*, p. 343.

[31] *Ibid.*, p. 210.

[32] *Human Nature and Conduct, op. cit.*, p. 316.

further ends. We see here again the way in which different theories are required, first to select different sets of facts as relevant to their purposes, and then to describe their facts differently even when they concern the same matters.

Perhaps we can best summarize the position which this paper has sought to defend and explicate by quoting another very revealing statement of Bradley's. At the beginning of his *Ethical Studies* he announces that his first task is "to enter on a question of fact." However, he goes on to caution us, "that asking is reflection, and that we reflect in general not to find the facts, but to prove our theories at the expense of them. The ready-made doctrines we bring to the work color whatever we touch with them."[33]

[33] Bradley, *op. cit.*, p. 2.

Positive "Ethics" and Normative "Science"
ALAN GEWIRTH

The relation between ethics and science has been a focal point in the arguments of many moral philosophers. The noncognitivists' doctrines of the primarily emotive or prescriptive meaning of ethical terms have derived in part from the sharp contrasts they have drawn between ethics and science. Evidence for these contrasts has been found in such considerations as the difference between moral and scientific disagreements in respect of cognitive decidability. Many of the cognitivists, on the other hand, have emphasized the similarities between ethics and science. These emphases have taken two closely related forms. Some philosophers have tried to show that ethics is "scientific" in that ethical terms, sentences, and arguments, like scientific ones, are respectively descriptive, cognitive, and rational (appealing to reasons and principles). Other philosophers have tried to show that science is "ethical" in that science, like ethics, is attitudinal (exhibited in the scientific "attitude," "respect" for the facts, and so forth), prescriptive (giving directions as to how to look at the world), evaluative (weighing evidence), purposive, pragmatic, socially structured, resting on conventions, and even "personal" in that science involves basic choices or commitments on the part of the scientist.

THE FALLACY OF DISPARATENESS

The purpose of this paper is not to participate directly in this debate, but rather to call attention to a fundamental feature of its logic. This feature consists in a disparity between the levels at which, or the respects in which, ethics and science are characterized by many participants on each side, although more particularly perhaps by the noncognitivists. I shall first briefly illustrate this disparity in a rather obvious form and shall then devote the bulk of this paper to a critical examination of a less obvious but much more far-reaching form of it.

In discussing the moral disagreement between Bentham and those who opposed his hedonism as a "pig's philosophy," Russell comments as follows:

Neither he nor his opponents could advance any argument. In a scientific question, evidence can be adduced on both sides, and in the end one side is seen to have the better case—or, if this does not happen, the question is left undecided. But in a question as to whether this or

FROM: *The Philosophical Review*, Vol. LXIX, No. 3 (July 1960). Reprinted by permission of editor and author.

that is the ultimate Good, there is no evidence either way; each disputant can only appeal to his own emotions, and employ such rhetorical devices as shall rouse similar emotions in others.[1]

It will be noticed that in this passage Russell contrasts a moral disagreement over "the ultimate Good" with a disagreement over "a scientific question" as if these were logically on a par. But obviously they are not. Questions of "ultimate" principles in any field, including science as well as ethics, are not on the same level as intermediate questions in regard to which the relevant principles are assumed; for in the former case one cannot appeal to higher principles in order to answer them. Consequently, in comparing scientific with moral disagreement, Russell should have balanced his moral example about "the ultimate Good" with a scientific example of disagreement over an ultimate scientific

---

[1] *Religion and Science* (London, 1935), p. 229. In some of his later writings Russell has recognized that the issue of the relation between moral and scientific disagreement is more complex than the above statement suggests, but he has not shifted his basic position. Cf. *Human Society in Ethics and Politics* (London, 1954), pp. 80, 81, 100–118. For essentially similar contrasts between moral and scientific disagreement, see C. L. Stevenson, *Ethics and Language* (New Haven, 1944), pp. 2 ff.; A. J. Ayer, *Language, Truth, and Logic*, 2nd ed. (London, 1948), pp. 21–22; *Philosophical Essays* (London, 1954), pp. 236–237; P. Edwards, *The Logic of Moral Discourse* (Glencoe, Ill., 1955), pp. 182–192. The same contrast is found, in principle, also in such noncognitivists as Hare, Urmson, and Nowell-Smith when they emphasize the differences between the meaning of "good" and the varying criteria of its application, or between moral and empirical predicates. For here too this difference involves the contrast between the cognitive decidability of scientific or factual disagreements as to whether an empirical predicate is to be applied to some object, and the undecidability of moral disagreements by reference to cognitive considerations alone, as to whether an ethical predicate is to be applied to an object.

principle. This would have strongly affected his contrast between the cognitive decidability of scientific disagreements and the undecidability of moral ones. It might even have led him to the suspicion that in science, too, disagreements over ultimate questions are not decidable by cognitive means alone.

While recognizing that this example from Russell might be held to involve many further issues, I intend for the present to use it only for the purpose of drawing a moral from it. The moral is this: in comparing ethics and science, or any other fields for that matter, one must be careful not to commit what I shall call the *fallacy of disparateness*— the fallacy of discussing one field on one level or in one respect and the other field on a quite different level or in a quite different respect. Or, to put it in affirmative terms, comparisons between fields or subject matters should always refer to the same level or respect in each case. If this precept is violated, then nothing conclusive follows about the relations in question nor, to that extent, about the fields being compared.[2]

THE FUNDAMENTAL DISPARITY

I now wish to call attention to a much more fundamental and far-reaching logical disparity in the approach which many moral philosophers, especially

---

[2] Political rhetoric notoriously exhibits this fallacy. When politicians "point with pride" and "view with alarm," they frequently characterize their own policies on an ideal level while portraying those of their opponents on the level of its actual manifestations or its worst possibilities. Such rhetorical devices may even contain the truth, but if so, then the truth is presented on two different levels. For example, the Soviets exalt their own system by citing the Marxist philosophy or the Soviet Constitution with its libertarian provisions (ideal level), while they denigrate the "capitalist" system by repeating newspaper reports about racial discrimination and gangsterism in the United States (level of selected actualities). Although such devices are effective in rhetoric, I take it that philosophy differs from rhetoric.

noncognitivists, take to the relation between ethics and science. This disparity involves their very use of the words "ethics" and "science," and hence the basic assumption of the contrasts they have tried to draw between ethics and science.

What I am referring to is this: when the noncognitivists, as well as other philosophers, characterize "science" and "scientific" questions and disagreements, they always give a "normative" interpretation of the words "science" and "scientific"; but when they characterize "ethics" and "ethical" questions and disagreements, they usually give a "positive" interpretation of the words "ethics" and "ethical." By "normative" interpretation of the words "science" and "scientific," I mean that the philosophers' use of these words always carries an evaluative connotation which serves to restrict the words' application, from among the various candidates for being regarded as "cognitive" or "scientific," to those which fulfill certain cognitive norms or value-criteria, such as logical consistency, empirical testability, explanatory fruitfulness. But their use of the words "ethics" and "ethical" carries no such evaluative connotation, and hence the application of these words is not restricted to those candidates for being regarded as "moral" or "ethical" which fulfill certain moral norms or value-criteria. For example, such philosophers do not regard both Christian Science and neurology as examples of "science," but they do regard the discourse of both Al Capone and Albert Schweitzer as examples of "ethical" language. Hence there is a logical disparity between the philosophers' uses of the words "science" and "ethics": they use "science" on the level of the fulfillment of certain restrictive norms, while they use "ethics" without restriction to the corresponding norms.[3]

[3] These evaluative and restrictive features of the normative as against the positive uses of words are also exhibited in many other contexts. For example, in legal theory

This disparity emerges especially clearly from the analogy drawn by many moral philosophers between their "meta-ethics" (or "analytical ethics") and the philosophy of science. They regard these two philosophic disciplines as being logically on a par in that, just as the philosophy of science does not do the work of science itself but rather analyzes the meanings of scientific concepts and the methods of scientific inference and explanation, so meta-ethics does not do the work of ethics itself; that is, it makes no ethical judgments of its own but rather analyzes the meanings of ethical terms and the methods of supporting ethical judgments.[4] However, the noncognitivists carry out the part of this analogy pertaining to ethics in a way

the word "law" is used positively when it is applied to any system of rules enforced in a community, regardless of whether the rules be just or unjust; but if the view is taken that the rules must be just ones before they can be called "laws," then the word is used normatively. Or, to take an example outside the moral sphere, if one says that Ingrid Bergman is not an actress, or not a "real" or "genuine" actress, because her character portrayals lack range and depth, then one is using the word "actress" normatively. If, on the other hand, one applies the word "actress" to any female performer on stage, screen, or other theatrical media, without restriction as to norms by which one evaluates her performance, then one is using the word positively.

[4] Cf. Stevenson, *op. cit.*, p. 1: "Such a study is related to normative (or 'evaluative') ethics in much the same way that conceptual analysis and scientific method are related to the sciences. One would not expect a book on scientific method to do the work of science itself; and one must not expect to find here any conclusions about what conduct is right and wrong." For a similar analogy of meta-ethics to philosophy of science, see J. Harrison, "Can Ethics Do Without Propositions?," *Mind*, LIX (1950), 361–362. Cf. also T. D. Weldon, "Political Principles," in *Philosophy, Politics and Society*, ed. by P. Laslett (Oxford, 1956), pp. 22 ff. I have examined the "meta-ethical" distinction in "Meta-Ethics and Normative Ethics," *Mind*, LXIX (1960).

which is logically quite disparate from the interpretation they give to the part pertaining to science. The philosophy of science as they view it always involves an initial normative commitment and restriction; when it studies the nature and methods of science, it does not try to make its theories about science fit the common denominators of the meanings of words like "science" and "know" as used by Christian Science, phrenology, and astrology as well as by neurology, physiology, and astronomy. On the contrary, it restricts its purview to the latter kind of sciences, for it deals only with those disciplines whose propositions and procedures fulfill certain methodological requirements or norms. In excluding such pretenders to the name of "science" as Christian Science from their purview, then, the philosophers of science distinguish at the outset between good and bad science, or rather between genuine science and bogus or illegitimate science, which they would say is not science at all. But the noncognitivists' approach to the philosophy of ethics, or meta-ethics, is on a quite different level. Here they make no such normative restrictions or differentiations between good or genuine ethics and bogus or counterfeit ethics; on the contrary, they try to base their theories about ethics on the common denominators of the meaning of ethical terms as used by missionaries, cannibals, democrats, and Nazis. Thus, qua meta-ethics, they insist on a strict ethical neutrality. Stevenson, for example, calls attention to the "detachment" with which he approaches ethics, and refers to his work as a "relatively neutral study";[5] Ayer similarly writes that "All moral theories . . . in so far as they are philosophical theories, are neutral as regards actual conduct."[6]

In these references to neutrality the writers do not mean merely that, just as the philosopher of science as such does not himself do science or take a stand on competing scientific theories, so the phi-

losopher of ethics does not himself do ethics or take a stand on competing ethical doctrines. For the detachment and neutrality of the meta-ethicist are far more extensive and generous than that of the philosopher of science. The latter does not himself pronounce on the scientific merits of the wave theory of light as against the corpuscular theory, but he does insist, when he discusses the nature of "science," on confirming his purview to what is common to *such* theories as against the pronouncements of astrologists and other occultists. But the meta-ethicist is far more permissive in his view of the scope of that "ethics" whose meanings and methods he studies. He imposes no such initial restrictions on what he will regard as the "ethics" or "ethical language" relevant to his concerns. Thus R. M. Hare, for example, in discussing the meaning of "good," concerns himself indifferently with the ethical language of missionaries, cannibals, and communists;[7] J. O. Urmson with the rhetorical tricks of advertisers and moral reformers;[8] and Russell with the ethical views of Nazis as well as democrats.[9]

Now this generalizing approach reflects, of course, the correct conviction of such philosophers that there are certain aspects of meaning common to the ways in which words like "good" are used not only in "moral" contexts by cannibals, missionaries, communists, and so on, but even in "non-moral" contexts by carpenters referring to good augers and ballplayers referring to good throws. But these philosophers deal only with such generic features of ethical terms, and they hold that, so far as their own philosophic interest is concerned, there is no need to look for what differentiates the morally good, or normatively ethical, from other meanings of these terms. If the philosophers of science were to oper-

[5] *Op. cit.*, p. 1.

[6] *Philosophical Essays*, p. 246.

[7] *The Language of Morals* (Oxford, 1952), pp. 148–149.

[8] "On Grading," in *Logic and Language*, II, ed. by A. Flew (Oxford, 1955), p. 182.

[9] *Human Society in Ethics and Politics*, pp. 80, 81.

ate in an analogous way, the would confine themselves to the aspects of meaning common to the ways in which such terms as "know" and "true" are used by Christian Scientists, neurologists, phrenologists, physiologists, astrologists, and astronomers; and they would refuse to show how the neurologist's "science" is different from that of the Christian Scientist, that is, what are the norms or criteria by which to distinguish genuine science from bogus science. But of course the philosophers of science do just the opposite; and this involves that they take a normative position as to what constitutes the genuinely "scientific." Thus the anomalous outcome is that while the philosophy of science is normative and prescrpitive, the philosophy of ethics has become positivistic and descriptive.

CONSEQUENCES
OF THE DISPARITY

This disparity has some serious consequences. For one thing, it leaves the philosophical ethicist, as such, powerless to distinguish between good and bad ethics. If ethics is to be viewed purely positively—in the sense that wherever there is a dispute over what should be done, the philosopher is to describe and analyze the language of the dispute but is to make no discriminations as to where the normatively ethical lies therein—then he pursues as vacuous a course as if he were to describe with complete impartiality a debate between a Christian Scientist and a neurologist, calling the debate an example of "scientific controversy" and making no attempt to differentiate between good and bad science or scientific argument.

To be sure, the philosopher may still insist on pointing out the difference between logical and illogical arguments in this connection. But his criteria of the "logical" would be of the sort which the neurologist rather than the Christian Scientist would admit, so that here already the philosopher would not, strictly speaking, be "neutral" as between them. Hence the question arises: why does the philosopher refuse to be neutral as be-

tween the "logics" of the neurologist and of the Christian Scientist, while he insists on being neutral, qua philosopher, between the "ethics" of the democrat and the Nazi? It seems to be because he regards the normative difference between the "logics" as a cognitively ascertainable one, while he holds that the normative difference between the "ethics" is not cognitively ascertainable. But it must be emphasized that *this distinction between the cognitiveness of the principles of science, including logic, and the noncognitiveness of the principles of ethics is itself a consequence of the disparate approaches to science and ethics. If science and ethics were approached on the same level, both would turn out in basic ways to be equally cognitive or equally noncognitive. I shall now try to show this, first with respect to ethical principles and then with respect to ethical disagreements and decisions.*

(1) *The cognitiveness of ethical principles.* The philosopher of science as we have seen, defines and explicates science by reference to certain methodological rquirements or norms. These norms may be of different kinds, but let us assume that ultimately they consist in the canons of inductive and deductive logic. Hence, these norms constitute the basic regulative principles of science; among other things, they provide definitions of what it is to be a "fact and evidence," "truth," "scientific explanation," and so forth. In other words, these norms define what it means to *know* and to have *scientific knowledge*. Hence, it is the at least possible conformity to these norms which defines what is to be meant when a sentence or a belief is called "cognitive." Consequently, it is circular to say that the basic principles of science are themselves cognitive; for it is these principles or norms which determine whether anything else is to be called cognitive. Moreover, these principles are a selection from among other possible principles— possible, that is, in the sense that they are espoused by people who claim to have "science" or "knowledge" by methods which are in important respects different

from those grounded in inductive and deductive logic. These other methods include those of Christian Science, astrology, phrenology, tribal medicine-men, and many others. Each of these other methods has its own way of defining what is to be meant by "fact," "knowledge," and so forth. Hence, if any of these latter is to be called "noncognitive," it will be by reference not to *its* norms of principles but to those of *some* other way of viewing "science" and "knowledge." To claim that any of those is "absolutely" noncognitive is to ignore the relativity of all claims of cognitiveness to norms or principles which define what is to be meant by "cognitive."

This does not mean, however, that the claim of cognitiveness is arbitrary. Considerations will usually be adduced in support of one or another way of defining "knowledge." But these considerations are not *proofs* that one or another definition is "correct" to the exclusion of alternative definitions; they constitute only an explication of the grounds which lead to the upholding of one definition as against another. Hence, strictly speaking, the choice among different conceptions of "knowledge" or "science" cannot itself be said to be made by cognitive means.

Now the principles of ethics have a similar logical status. These principles consist in the ultimate norms on the basis of which one way of life or kind of character is regarded as morally good as against its alternatives, whether it be ethics of Jesus, of Hitler, of the Dobuans, of Middleton, or others. Hence, it is these norms which define what is to be meant by "morally good," "ethical," and so forth. And just as it would be circular to say that one "knows" that certain norms or principles of science are the "true" ones or that they constitute "knowledge," so for a parallel but not identical reason it is circular to say that one "knows" that certain norms or principles of ethics are the "true" ones in the sense that they are the morally good ones. One cannot know this about the principles of ethics, for it is the con-

formity to these principles which constitutes the moral goodness of anything else.

In this way, then, the principles of science are no more "cognitive" than the principles of ethics. To hold the opposite is possible only if one adopts disparate approaches to science and to ethics, for example, if one approaches science by its intermediate theorems and ethics by its ultimate principles, or if one takes a normative aproach to science as against a positive approach to ethics. In the latter case, one will *assume* the definition of "cognitive" provided by the norms of science which one accepts, and will ignore the existence of rival conceptions of science and hence of the cognitive; consequently, in the absence of competitors, all of "science," including its principles, will be regarded as cognitive since the operation of the implicit "cognitive-making" definitions will be ignored. But since, on the other hand, the existence of rival conceptions of the "ethical" will be recognized, and since, as we have seen, the choice among these conceptions cannot ultimately be made by cognitive means, the principles of ethics will be regarded as noncognitive. To recognize the disparity of the noncognitivists' approaches to ethics and to science is thus to remove the grounds on which they have contrasted the principles of science and of ethics as respectively cognitive and noncognitive.

(2) *The cognitiveness of ethical disagreements to decisions.* Similarly it is this disparity which underlies the conclusions of many moral philosophers about the noncognitive character of ethical disagreements and decisions. These conclusions, far from being a consequence of logical or empirical analyses of ethical language, are in many respects rather a result of the positive, nonrestrictive approach which the philosophers in question take to ethics.

Consider again the parallel case of science. Suppose that the philosopher were to describe with complete impartiality a dispute between a Christian Scientist and a neurologist, calling the debate an example of "scientific controversy." He would then come up with the acute observation that these "scientists" are disagreeing in attitude as well as in belief; that since no *empirical* facts on whose factual character both agree remove their disagreement, their controversy must be rooted in a disagreement in attitude; and that consequently the characteristic feature and the basis of "scientific" disagreement is disagreement in attitude.

The point, in other words, is that disagreements can be primarily cognitive and not emotive wherever, as in the sciences which the noncognitivist philosophers recognize, there are already agreed-upon norms, and particularly norms as to the methods by which to solve problems and resolve controversies. To decide a cognitive issue in any field requires at least two things: first, knowledge of the relevant facts, and second, agreement on criteria or norms for decision. The reason why scientific questions can be decided solely by cognitive means is that, since we (and I here exclude the Christian Scientist, and so forth) agree on the norms or criteria of scientific method, the chief thing that remains is to determine the facts by the use of this method, and such determination is hence a purely cognitive process. But this is also true in respect of ethical and political issues. If men agree on ethical or political norms or criteria, then they can come to agreement by considering the facts in the light of these norms, and such consideration, too, is a purely cognitive process. It is at least partly because the noncognitivists take for granted men's agreement on scientific norms but not on ethical ones that they can contrast science and ethics as respectively cognitive and noncognitive. But this assumption involves taking a normative approach to science and a positive approach to ethics. Among "ethical" men there is agreement on ethical norms, just as among "scientific" men there is agreement on scientific norms. Hence disputes among the former can be resolved by cognitive means just as can disputes among the latter.

To be sure, as Aristotle pointed out, the subject matter of ethics is a contingent one in that it involves not the nature of things independent of man but the effects of human habits, volitions, and institutions; moreover, ethics, being practical, is concerned with what is to be done in the particular case. From these points it follows that ethical theorems cannot be derived from ethical principles with the same degree of probability of application to their subject matter as is the case in physics.[10] This, however, is only a difference in the modality of ethical and natural-scientific propositions and arguments; it does not make the former any less "cognitive" than the latter.

CAN THE DISPARITY BE JUSTIFIED?

It may, however, be contended that even though the noncognitivists' approaches to ethics and to science do involve the logical disparity to which I have called attention, and that it is this disparity which underlies their conclusions about ethical language, still in none of this do they commit any error, because the disparity is quite justifiable. We must hence consider this possibility. I shall refrain from the familiar kind of invidious statements to the effect that what motivates this disparity of approaches is that moral philosophers have become infected with the ethical relativism and skepticism which marks our age, and that they exhibit the "scientism" which has faith only in the norms or criteria of science. I think we can get at the grounds they would adduce in justification of their disparate approach if we focus on the analogy which I have used to bring out the disparity in question. For what I have been saying is that in basing their theories about ethics nonrestrictively on the common denominators of the meanings of ethical terms as used by missionaries,

[10] Cf. Aristotle, *Nicomachean Ethics*, I. 3. 1094b 12 ff.; I. 7. 1098a 26 ff.; II. 1. 1103a 14 ff.; V. 10. 1137b 18 ff.; VI. 5. 1140a 32 ff.

cannibals, democrats, and Nazis, the meta-ethicists have been doing the same sort of thing as if philosophers were to base their theories about science non-restrictively on the common denominators of the meaning of the words "science," "know," "true," and the like, as used by neurologists, Christian Scientists, astronomers, and astrologists. Thus I have been assuming an analogy which runs somewhat as follows: as Christian Science is to neurology, so is Nazi ethics to democratic ethics. But this analogy, it may be held, is open to attack on many grounds.

(1) *The nature and function of science and ethics.* Does Christian Science, and the like, constitute a "science" or "knowledge" in anything like the way in which Nazi ethics, and the like, constitutes an "ethics"? Is it not the case that the word "science" is used equivocally when applied to both Christian Science and neurology, whereas the word "ethics" is not used equivocally when applied to both Nazi ethics and Christian ethics? We may amplify this query as follows. What we mean by a "science" is a group of propositions and procedures which perform certain functions: they enable us to describe, explain, and predict phenomena. These achievements constitute what we may call a "scientific" adjustment to the world. But now Christian Science, astrology, and so forth, either do not claim to perform such functions at all, or else if they do claim to do so, they can be proven to be not even minimally successful in fulfilling these claims. On the first alternative, Christian Science, and so forth, are not even claiming to be "sciences" in the sense in which we use the term, so that the word is admittedly being used equivocally. On the second alternative, Christian Science, and so forth, fall so completely short of what is achieved by neurology and other sciences that, if the word "science" is applied to both kinds, then it is only in the sense in which one word applies to the two opposite extremes of what is not even a continuum.

In either case, the failure of Christian Science, and so forth, to *be* "scientific" is conclusively demonstrable. Consequently, there is clear justification for the philosopher of science's normative restriction of the word "science" to neurology, and so forth, as against Christian Science, and so forth.

Now contrast this with the situation in regard to ethics. What we mean by an "ethics" is a body of rules, ideals, and practices which enable us to get along with ourselves and with other people. An ethics, in other words, functions as a way of life, as is suggested by the etymological connection of the words "ethics" and "morality" with habits and customs. Now the fact is that there are and have been many different ethics in the sense of functioning, viable rules or ways of life. The Dobuans, the Trobriand Islanders, the Middletowners all have their own ethics, and even though we may not approve of them, they nevertheless do function as kinds of ethics in a sense in which Christian Science and astrology do not function as kinds of science. Hence there are far more kinds of "ethical" adjustments to the world than of "scientific" adjustments to the world. The reason for this is that far more latitude is possible in respect to ways of life than in respect to ways of knowing the world. As Feigl puts it, "The validating principles of deductive and inductive logic do not seem at all to have any plausible alternatives or competitors."[11] And the reason for this, in turn, is that there is a kind of cognitive compellingness found in the bases of deductive and inductive logic—consistency on the one hand, sense perception on the other—which is not similarly to be found in the basis of any ethics, To be sure, philosophers and logicians may have different theories *about* science, sense

[11] H. Feigl, "Validation and Vindication: An Analysis of the Nature and Limits of Ethical Arguments," in *Readings in Ethical Theory,* ed. by W. Sellars and J. Hospers (New York, 1952), p. 676.

perception, and logic; but logic and science themselves are basically uniform in their underlying norms in a way which is not the case in regard to the diversities of ethics. Consequently, the philosopher of science is justified in confining his purview to the norms of genuine science, while the meta-ethicist would not be similarly justified in confining his purview to just one kind of ethics and ignoring the large number of viable alternative ethics.

(2) *Knowledge of science and knowledge of ethics.* There are experts in science but not in ethics, institutes and academies for scientific research but not for ethical research. As Plato pointed out, all men consider themselves experts when it comes to moral virtue but not when it comes to scientific knowledge. Hence the meta-ethicists show both their realism and their democratic bent when they go for their materials to ethical discussions in daily life. The philosopher of science, by the same token, is justified in regarding science as a non-ordinary subject developed by experts, and in confining himself to what meets the norms in question.

(3) *Beliefs or opinions about science and ethics.* Men differ far more in their beliefs or opinions about what is ethically good or right than about what is scientifically valid or true. The Nazis and the Soviets, for all their differences from the Western democracies in their ethical beliefs, still had, and have, very largely the same faith in science, and in the same kind of science, as is found in the Western democracies. Hence, on this dialectical ground of universality of recognition, too, the philosopher of science is justified in adopting a normative approach to science, while the meta-ethicist is justified in taking account of the great diversity in ethics and not trying to single out only one ethic for favored attention.

(4) *Extent and resolubility of disagreements in science and ethics.* Even if one assumes a common ethical framework such as that of liberal democracy, ethical disagreements still occur within that framework which are not resoluble by cognitive means as they are within science. Men may uphold all the ethical values of liberal democracy and still differ sharply on such issues as capital punishment and euthanasia, for the issues are not resoluble solely by reference to those values, unless we define the latter in a question-begging way so as to include one or another of the disputed alternatives. Consequently, the model of ethical argument cannot be assimilated very closely to the model of scientific argument; the field of ethics is far more pluralistic and indeterminate than that of science, in that in ethics there are many more *kinds* of objects of argument, which cannot be subsumed under a single principle or set of principles. The meta-ethicist must take account of this pluralism.

It is now time to consider the merits of these defenses of the disparity between the normative approach to science and the positive approach to ethics. I think many points in these defenses are sound. But they nevertheless beg the question at issue. For they all proceed by the way of a normative definition of "science" and a positive definition of "ethics." Moreover, the evidence they adduce for these disparate definitions could easily be balanced or outweighed by counter-evidence for defining both "science" and "ethics" as normative, and even for defining "science" in a positive way and "ethics" in a normative way.

(1) Consider, for example, the question of the "nature and function" of science and ethics. It is true that if one defines "science" by reference to empirical description, explanation, and prediction, then a normative, restrictive approach to science is justified, and Christian Science, and so forth, are only equivocally to be called "sciences." But by the same token, if one defines "ethics" by reference to impartial reconciliation of conflicting interests and mutuality of consideration, then a normative, restrictive approach to ethics would also be justified, and Nazi ethics, and so forth,

could only equivocally be called "ethics." Moreover, one might counterbalance this normative approach to "ethics" with a positive approach to "science," such that Christian Science, phrenology, and astrology would all be kinds of "science" in a nonequivocal sense. For all of these claim to provide a scientific adjustment to the world in the sense that they enable men to understand the underlying realities of the world. All of them, that is, make cognitive claims, in that they claim to know and to present true general propositions about the world. As was indicated above, the meaning of such terms as "know" and "true" are not entirely the same in all these cases. But they have at least as much generic similarity as have words like "good" and "ought" when used by Nazis, democrats, missionaries, and cannibals. Where they differ is on the contents of the propositions which they declare to be true, and on the epistemological questions of how to validate these claims. Similarly, Nazi and other kinds of ethics claim to tell us what good men ought to be like and how they ought to act, but they differ on the content of these "goods" and "oughts," and to a certain extent at least on the ways in which one should go about ascertaining who is good and doing what one ought. Hence, whether one puts the differences between the Nazis and the democrats in terms of the specific meanings of "good," "ought," and so forth, or in terms of the criteria of application for these words, the same factors could be used to explicate the differences between the Christian Scientists and the neurologists with regard to "true," "know," and so forth. And just as the Nazis, democrats, and so forth, may be said to agree on the *generic* meanings of "good," "ought," and so forth, so the Christian Scientists, neurologists, and so forth, agree on the *generic* meanings of "true," "know," and so forth.

If the nonrestrictive approach to "ethics" be justified on the ground of the plurality of the ways of "getting along" with people, a nonrestrictive approach to "science" may be similarly justified on the ground of the plurality of the ways in which men have actually made "cognitive" adjustments to the world. The existence of tribal medicine-men and the many other superstitions in the history of mankind, as well as the many fundamental disagreements among philosophers, scientists, and others claiming to present knowledge of reality, show that the sphere of the cognitive is at least as involved in sharp contrasts of basic content and method as is the sphere of the ethical. (In this respect human nature is just as plastic, and environment and history just as productive of diversities, in the sphere of the cognitive as in the sphere of the ethical.) On the other hand, just as our language recognizes a perfectly clear sense in which some "sciences," such as Christian Science, are not scientific, so too it recognizes a clear sense in which some "ethics," such as that of the Dobuans or the Nazis, are not ethical. And just as the criteria involved in the first statement can be specified in such terms as predictive fruitfulness and empirical testability, with whose explication the philosophy of science is concerned, so the criteria involved in the second case can be specified in such terms as mutual consideration and impartiality, with whose explication the philosophy of ethics should be and traditionally has been concerned.[12]

As for the "compellingness" of basic principles of science and of ethics,

[12] This point would also be relevant against any attempt to justify the disparity of approaches to science and ethics on the ground that "science," unlike "ethics," is always an "achievement word" (cf. G. Ryle, *Concept of Mind*, London, 1949, pp. 133–134, 152, on "know"). For in phrases like "medieval science" or "Nazi racial science" we use the word "science" to refer to claims to cognitive adequacy which are not fulfilled or successful, so that "science" is not always an achievement word. Moreover, can we get a sound view of the logical relations between science and morally good ethics by concentrating only on the features which the latter shares with all other "ethics"?

this is to be interpreted either logically or empirically. If it is interpreted logically it begs the question, for what is at issue *is* the question of what is the right or cognitively cogent logic of science. And if it is interpreted empirically, as referring to what men have in fact found to be compelling, there is a good deal of evidence to suggest that ideals like the golden rule have seemed to men to be no less cogent ethically than principles like that of noncontradiction and experimentalism have seemed cogent in the logic of science.

(2) The fact that there are no recognized experts in ethics as there are in science is a consequence of the fact that ethics is a practical matter affecting everybody, whereas science is a more specialized matter. Yet this does not mean that standards of comparative value or excellence are not as possible in ethics as in science, nor does it mean that such standards cannot be recognized and explicated by philosophers and others.

(3) On the other hand, to what extent are the diversities of men's opinions about science and ethics relevant to our problem? This dialectical level provides a prime field for the disparate approach. Feigl, for example, writes that the "basic criteria" of science "have attained practically universal consent. It is only too tempting to hope for a similarly universal code of morals." But he rules this out because of such factors as "the stark realities of group and culture-centered ethical standards."[13] Now if Feigl is here making a sociological statement about the greater degree to which men all over the world "consent" to scientific as against ethical criteria, he adduces no statistical or other evidence in support of this, nor does he indicate the relevance of such sociological or rhetorical considerations to the question of the validity or logical status of scientific and ethical norms. The meaning of his statement seems rather to be that

[13] Feigl, *op. cit.*, pp. 676–677.

scientifically-minded persons all over the world accept the same scientific criteria, while men and groups without qualification accept different ethical criteria. But it could just as well be held that ethical men all over the world accept the same ethical criteria, while men and groups without qualification accept may different kinds of superstition and other unscientific criteria. Would this latter fact invalidate the universal *validity* of scientific criteria?

(4) One may grant that the field of ethics is more indeterminate and pluralistic in respect of disputed issues and principles than is science and still point out that these issues and principles may on closer scrutiny turn out to be more unified than we think. In this respect the drive toward unity of science is matched not only by the increasing communication and homogeneity of ethical standards among the peoples of the world, but also by the traditional concern of philosophers, in opposition to cultural relativism, to find unifying principles under which to organize and interrelate man's ethical ideals.

CONCLUSION:
PHILOSOPHIC ETHICS
AS A NORMATIVE DISCIPLINE

The upshot of these considerations is that, to a large extent at least, the disparity between the normative approach to science and the positive approach to ethics is not justified. I do not pretend to have exhausted every possible argument in favor of the disparity, nor do I deny that the arguments presented carry some plausibility. Yet the arguments against the disparity have by far the greater weight. What follows from this is not that ethics ought to be "scientific" in the sense of being deduced from science or of using the same methods as science. The burden of the argument has been rather that there should be a parity in the approaches which philosophers take to ethics and to science insofar as those approaches delimit or recognize the respective fields as being constituted by the norms relevant to each. Initially I have argued for this parity insofar as it has concerned the explicit or implicit comparisons between ethics and science which have been used by philosophers to deal with the cognitive-noncognitive issue about the meaning of ethical terms. But in addition I have held that even apart from this issue, the disparity with its positivist approach to ethics makes it impossible to do justice to distinctive features of ethics in the way in which the normative approach in philosophy of science does justice to science. From this it follows that the philosopher of ethics, like the philosopher of science, must begin with the recognition that the field about which he is to philosophize is constituted by certain basic norms, and that his job is to explicate their content and how they are exhibited in that field.

But which norms? And on what ground do we select some norms rather than others? Does not our insistence on beginning with ethical norms open the door to dogmatism, parochialism, and worse?

There is not space here to go into the content and logic of the normative approach to ethics that I would substitute for the positive approach; I hope to deal with this elsewhere. The following considerations are relevant. There can be no absolute justification of ethical norms any more than of scientific ones; for any attempt to justify the norms in either field will sooner or later adduce criteria which assume the very norms in question. But on the other hand, just as we do not therefore accept skepticism in regard to science, so too we need not accept skepticism in regard to ethics. The areas to which one should look for ethical norms

are multiple; I shall here indicate only one of them, which is in line with some of the illustrations used in this paper. The development of the ideas of modern liberal democracy, involving in particular certain methods of resolving conflicts of interest, is just as compelling for the field of ethics as is the development of the hypothetico-deductive-experimental methods for the field of science. The moral philosopher who attempted to reject the former ideals in favor of their contraries would be just as philosophically suspect as would the philosopher of science who insisted on treating the cognitive methods of nuclear physicists and tribal medicine-men as if these were scientifically on a par. This does not mean that the moral philosopher should accept these ideals "unquestioningly" any more than the philosopher of science unquestioningly accepts the canons of scientific method. But the philosopher in each of these fields must regard the norms in each case as providing the subject matter which he is to subject to critical analysis. Such analysis clarifies the meaning or content of the norms and thereby sometimes suggests better ways of formulating or interpreting them.

The removal of the unjustified disparity between the approaches of the philosopher of science and the moral philosopher should help to return the latter to his traditional role of clarifying and criticizing men's moral ideals within the context of ongoing moral practices and institutions. The result should be not only the avoidance of a large measure of noncognitivism, but also the reinstatement of philosophical ethics as a normative discipline.

The Moral Point of View
WILLIAM FRANKENA

The third general type of theory of the meaning or nature of ethical and value judgments has no very satisfactory label.* However, it has been called noncognitivist or nondescriptivist because, as against both definists and intuitionists, it holds that such judgments are not assertions or statements which ascribe properties to (or deny them of) actions, persons, or things; it asserts that such judgments have a very different "logic," meaning, or use. It embraces a wide variety of views, some more and others much less extreme.

1. The most extreme of these are a number of views which deny that ethical and value judgments, or at least the most basic ones, are capable of any kind of rational or objectively valid justification. On one such view—that of A. J. Ayer—they are simply expressions of emotion much like ejaculations. Saying that killing is wrong is like saying, "Killing, booh!"; it says nothing which is true or false and cannot be justified in any rational way. Rudolf Carnap once took a similar view, except that he interpreted "Killing is wrong" as a command, "Do not kill!" rather than as an ejaculation. Many existentialists likewise regard basic ethical and value judgments, particular or general, as arbitrary commitments or decisions for which no justification can be given.

I should point out here that such irrationalistic views about ethical and value judgments are not held only by atheistic positivists and existentialists.

* The other two views are the *intuitive*, on which the meaning of ethical terms or the justification of ethical claims is self-evident to intuition and the *definist*, on which the meaning of ethical terms and the justification of ethical claims derive solely, respectively, from the meaning of descriptive terms and the empirical data available.

They are also held by at least some religious existentialists and by other theologians. For example, a theologian who maintains that the basic principles of ethics are divine commands is taking a position much like Carnap's. If he adds that God's commands are arbitrary and cannot be justified rationally, then his position is no less extreme. If he holds that God's commands are, at least in principle, rationally defensible, then his position is like the less extreme ones to be described shortly.

2. C. L. Stevenson's form of the emotive theory is less extreme than Ayer's. He argues that ethical and value judgments express the speaker's attitudes and evoke, or seek to evoke, similar attitudes in the hearer. But he realizes that to a very considerable extent our attitudes are based on our beliefs, and so can be reasoned about. For example, I may favor a certain course of action because I believe it has or will have certain results. I will then advance the fact it has these results as an argument in its favor. But you may argue that it does not have these results, and if you can show this, my attitude may change and I may withdraw my judgment that the course of action in question is right or good. In a sense, you have refuted me. But, of course, this is only because of an underlying attitude on my part of being in favor of certain results rather than others. Stevenson goes on to suggest that our most basic attitudes, and the ethical or value judgments in which we express them, may not be rooted in beliefs of any kind, in which case they cannot be reasoned about in any way. He is open-minded about this, however, and allows a good deal of room for a kind of argument and reasoning.

3. More recently, especially from a number of Oxford philosophers, we

FROM: *Ethics*, William Frankena. (Englewood Cliffs, N.J.: Prentice-Hall, Inc., 1963), pp. 88–98. Reprinted by permission of Prentice-Hall, Inc.

have had still less extreme views. They refuse to regard ethical and value judgments as mere expressions or evocations of feeling or attitude, as mere commands, or as arbitrary decisions or commitments. Rather, they regard them as evaluations, recommendations, prescriptions, and the like; and they stress the fact that such judgments imply that we are willing to generalize or universalize them and are ready to reason about them, points in which we have followed them. That is, they point out that when we say of something that it is good or right, we imply that there are reasons for our judgment which are not purely private in their cogency. They are even ready to say that such a judgment may be called true or false, though it is a very different kind of judgment from "X is yellow" or "Y is to the left of Z." For them ethical and value judgments are essentially rational acts of evaluating, recommending, and prescribing.

The arguments for such theories —the open question argument against definists and the similar argument against intuitionists—we have found to be less conclusive than they are thought to be. To my mind, nevertheless, these theories, or rather the least extreme of them, are on the right track. The kind of account which they give of the meaning and nature of ethical and value judgments is in itself plausible and acceptable. Such judgments do not just say that something has or does not have a certain property. Neither are they mere expressions of emotion, will, or decision. They do more than just express or indicate the speaker's attitudes. They evaluate, instruct, recommend, prescribe, advise, and so on; and they claim or imply that what they do is rationally justified or justifiable, which mere expressions of emotion and commands do not do. The more extreme views, therefore, are mistaken as a description of the nature of ethical and value judgments. Moreover, it is not necessary to agree with them that such judgments are not capable of being justified in any important sense. They generally assume that if such judg-

ments are not self-evident and cannot be proved inductively or deductively on the basis of empirical or nonempirical facts, as we have seen to be the case, that it follows that they are purely arbitrary. But this does not follow. It may be that this conception of rational justification is too narrow. Mill may be right when he says, near the end of Chapter I of *Utilitarianism*,

We are not . . . to infer that [the acceptance or rejection of an ethical first principle] must depend on blind impulse, or arbitrary choice. There is a larger meaning of the word "proof," in which this question is . . . amenable to it . . . The subject is within the cognizance of the rational faculty; and neither does that faculty deal with it solely in the way of intuition. Considerations may be presented capable of determining the intellect either to give or withhold its assent . . .

Here, Mill is with the less extreme of the recent nondescriptive theories, as against the definists, the intuitionists, and the more extreme nondescriptivists. All of these share the conception of justification as consisting either in self-evidence or in inductive or deductive proof. Only the definists and intuitionists believe that ethical and value judgments can be justified in one or the other of these ways. Positivists and existentialists deny that ethical and value judgments can be justified at all. Mill and the less extreme recent philosophers, on the other hand, agree with intuitionists and definists, that they can be justified in some rational sense but only in some "larger meaning of the word 'proof.' "

At this point, it may help to notice that even such things as "mere" expressions of feeling and commands may be justified or unjustified, rational or irrational. Suppose that A is angry at B, believing B to have insulted him. C may be able to show A that his anger is unjustified, since B has not actually insulted him at all. If A simply goes on being angry, although he no longer has any reason, we should regard his anger as quite irrational. Again, if an officer commands a private to close the door, believing it to be open when it is not, it is reasonable for the private to answer, "But, sir, the door is closed," and it would be quite irrational if the officer were to retort, "It makes no difference. Close it!" Emotions and commands, generally at least, have a background of beliefs and are justified or unjustified, rational or irrational, depending on whether these beliefs themselves are so.

In my opinion, even the less extreme nondescriptivist theories have not gone far enough. They have been too ready to admit a kind of basic relativism after all. They insist that ethical and value judgments imply the presence of, or at least the possibility of giving, reasons which justify them. But they almost invariably allow or even insist that the validity of these reasons is ultimately relative, either to the individual or to his culture, and, therefore, conflicting basic judgments may both be justified or justifiable. Now, it may be that in the end one must agree with this view, but most recent discussions entirely neglect a fact about ethical and value judgments on which the lingering intuitionist, A. C. Ewing, has long insisted, namely, that they make or somehow imply a claim to be objectively and rationally justified or valid. In other words, an ethical or value judgment claims that it will stand up under scrutiny by oneself and others in the light of the most careful thinking and the best knowledge, and that rival judgments will not stand up under such scrutiny. David Hume makes the point nicely in Part I of his *Enquiry into the Principles of Morals* (but only for *moral* judgments):

The notion of morals implies some sentiment common to all mankind, which recommends the same object to general approbation. . . . When a man denominates another his enemy, his rival, his antagonist, his adversary, he is understood to speak the language of self-love, and to express sentiments, peculiar to

himself, and arising from his particular circumstance and situation. But when he bestows on any man the epithets of vicious or odious or depraved, he then speaks another language, and expresses sentiments, in which he expects all his audience are to concur with him. He must here . . . depart from his private and particular situation, and must choose a point of view, common to himself with others. . .

And, he must claim, Hume might have added, that anyone else who takes this point of view and from it reviews the relevant facts will come to the same conclusion. In fact, he goes on to suggest that precisely because we need or want a language in which to express, not just sentiments peculiar to ourselves but sentiments in which we expect all men are to concur with us, another language in which we may claim that our sentiments are justified and valid, we had to

. . . invent a peculiar set of terms, in order to express those universal sentiments of censure or approbation. . . . Virtue and vice become then known; morals are recognized; certain general ideas are framed of human conduct and behavior. . . .

This kind of an account of our normative discourse appears to me to be eminently wise. It is a language in which we may express our sentiments—approvals, disapprovals, evaluations, recommendations, advice, instructions, prescriptions—and put them out into the public arena for rational scrutiny and discussion, claiming that they will hold up under such scrutiny and discussion and that all our audience will concur with us if they will also choose the same common point of view. That this is so is indicated by the fact that if A makes an ethical judgment about X and then, upon being challenged by B, says, "Well, at least I'm in favor of X," we think he has backed down. He has shifted from the language of public dialogue to that of mere self-revelation. This view recognizes the claim to objective validity on which intuitionists and definists alike insist, but it also recognizes the force of recent criticisms of such views.

RELATIVISM

Against any such view it will be argued, of course, that this claim to be objectively and rationally justified or valid, in the sense of holding up against all rivals through an impartial and informed examination, is simply mistaken and must be given up. This is the contention of the relativist and we must consider it now, although we can do so only briefly.

Actually, we must distinguish at least three forms of relativism. First, there is what may be called *descriptive relativism*. It does not say merely that the ethical and value judgments of different people and societies are different. For this would be true even if people and societies agreed in their basic ethical and value judgments and differed only in their *derivative* ones. What descriptive relativism says is that the *basic* ethical beliefs and value judgments of different people and societies are different and even conflicting. I stress this because the fact that in some primitive societies children believe they should put their parents to death before they get old, whereas we do not, does not prove descriptive relativism. These primitive peoples may believe this because they think their parents will be better off in the hereafter if they enter it while they are still able-bodied; if this is the case, their ethics and ours are both alike in that they include the precept that children should do the best they can for their parents. The divergence, then, would be in factual, rather than in ethical beliefs.

Second, there is *meta-ethical relativism*, which is the view we must consider. It holds that in the case of basic ethical or value judgments, at least, there is no objectively valid rational way of justifying one against another; consequently, two conflicting basic judgments may be equally valid.

The third form of relativism is *normative relativism*. While descriptive relativism makes an anthropological or sociological assertion and meta-ethical relativism a meta-ethical one, this form of relativism puts forward a normative principle: what is right or good for one individual or society is not right or good for another, even if the situations involved are similar, meaning not merely that what is thought right or good by one is not thought right or good by another (this is just descriptive relativism over again) but that what is really right or good in the one case is not so in another. Such a normative principle seems to violate the requirements of consistency and universalization which we mentioned earlier. We need not consider it here, except to point out that it cannot be justified by appeal to either of the other forms of relativism and does not follow from them.

Our question is about the second kind of relativism. The usual argument used to establish it rests on descriptive relativism. Now, descriptive relativism has not been incontrovertibly established. Some cultural anthropologists and social psychologists have even questioned its truth, for example, Ralph Linton and S. E. Asch. However, to prove meta-ethical relativism one must prove more than descriptive relativism. One must also prove that people's basic ethical and value judgments would differ and conflict even if they were fully enlightened and shared all the same factual beliefs. It is not enough to show that people's basic ethical and value judgments are different, for such differences might all be due to differences and incompleteness in their factual beliefs, as in the example of the primitive societies used previously. In this case, it would still be possible to hold that there are basic ethical principles or value judgments which can be justified as valid to everyone, in principle at least, if not in practice.

It is, however, extremely difficult to show that people's basic ethical and value judgments would still be different even if they were fully enlightened, conceptually clear, shared the same factual beliefs, and were taking the same point of view. To show this, one would have to find clear cases in which all of these conditions are fulfilled and people still differ. Cultural anthropologists do not show us such cases; in all of their cases, there are differences in conceptual understanding and factual belief. Even when one takes two people in the same culture, one cannot be sure that all of the necessary conditions are fulfilled. I conclude, therefore, that meta-ethical relativism has not been proved and, hence, that we need not, in our ethical and value judgments, give up the claim that they are objectively valid in the sense that they will be sustained by a review by all those who are free, clear-headed, fully informed, and who take the point of view in question.

A THEORY OF JUSTIFICATION

We now have the essence of a theory of the meaning and justification of ethical and value judgments. To go any further, we must separate moral and nonmoral normative judgments and say something about the justification of each. Under moral judgments, we distinguished judgments of obligation and judgments of moral value; and under nonmoral value judgments, we distinguished judgments of intrinsic value and judgments of other kinds of value. It seems clear that if we know how to justify judgments of obligation, we will know how to justify judgments of moral value; and if we know how to justify judgments of intrinsic value, we will know how to justify judgments of nonintrinsic value. We may, then, limit ourselves to the justification of judgments of moral obligation, particular and general, and judgments of intrinsic nonmoral value, particular and general.

1. We may take the latter first. The question of the justification of judgments of intrinsic value is relevant only because, through the principle of benevolence, the question of what is good or bad (nonmorally) comes to bear on the question of what is right or wrong. It is sometimes said that judgments of intrinsic value cannot be justified, but that judgments of extrinsic value can be justified, because we can show that a thing has or does not have certain effects. The fact, however, that we cannot prove judgments of intrinsic value does not mean that we cannot justify them or reasonably claim them to be justified. Whether they are particular or general, we can still try to take the evaluative point of view to see what judgment we are led to make when we do so, considering the thing in question wholly on the basis of its intrinsic character, not its consequences, its conditions, or its moral aspects. What is it to take the nonmorally evaluative point of view? It is to be free, informed, clear-headed, impartial, willing to universalize; in general, it is to be "calm" and "cool," as Butler would say, in one's consideration of such items as pleasure, knowledge, and love. This is what we tried to do in Chapter 5. If one considers an item in this reflective way and comes out in favor of it, one is rationally justified in judging it to be intrinsically good, even if one cannot prove one's judgment. In doing so, one claims that everyone else who does likewise will concur; and one's judgment is really justified if this claim is correct, which, however, one can never know for certain. If others who also claim to be calm and cool do not concur, one must reconsider to see if both sides are really taking the evaluative point of view, considering only intrinsic features, clearly understanding one another, and so on. More one cannot do and, if disagreement persists, one may still claim to be right (i.e., that others will concur eventually if . . .); but one must be open-minded and tolerant. In fact, we saw in Chapter 5 that one may have to admit a certain relativity, at least, in the ranking of things listed as intrinsically good, although possibly not in the listing itself.

2. Already in Chapters 2 and 3 we have, in effect, said something about the justification of judgments of right, wrong, and obligation. We argued that a particular judgment essentially entails a general one, so that one cannot regard a particular judgment as justified unless

one is also willing to accept the entailed general one, and vice versa. This is true whether we are speaking of judgments of actual or of prima facie duty. We have also seen that judgments of actual duty, whether particular judgments or rules, cannot simply be deduced from the basic principles of benevolence and justice, even with the help of factual premises, since these must be taken as prima facie principles and may conflict on occasion. Thus, we have two questions: first, how can we justify judgments of actual duty, rules or particular judgments, if at all; and second, how can we justify general principles of prima facie duty, if at all? The same answer, however, will do for both.

First, we must take the moral point of view, as Hume indicated: be free, impartial, willing to universalize, conceptually clear, and informed about all possible relevant facts. Then, we are justified in judging that a certain act or kind of action is right, wrong, or obligatory, and in claiming that our judgment is objectively valid, at least as long as no one who is doing likewise disagrees. Our judgment or principle is really justified if it holds up under sustained scrutiny of this sort from the moral point of view on the part of everyone. Suppose we encounter someone who claims to be doing this but comes to a different conclusion. Then we must do our best, through reconsideration and discussion, to see if one of us is failing to meet the conditions in some way. If we can detect no failing on either side and still disagree, we may and I think still must each claim to be correct, for the conditions never are, in fact, perfectly fulfilled by both of us; consequently one of us may turn out to be mistaken after all. If what was said about relativism is true, we cannot be correct. But both of us must be open-minded and tolerant if we are to go on living within the moral institution of life and not resort to force or other nonmoral devices.

Are our own principles of benevolence and justice justified in this sense? The argument in Chapters 2 and 3 was essentially an attempt to take the moral point of view and from it to review various normative theories and arrive at one of our own. Our conclusions have not been proved, but perhaps it may be claimed that they will be concurred in by those who try to do likewise. This claim was implicitly made in presenting the conclusions. Whether the claim is true or not must wait upon the scrutiny of others.

The fact that ethical and value judgments claim a consensus on the part of others does not mean that the individual thinker must bow to the judgment of the majority in his society. He is not claiming an *actual* consensus, he is claiming that in the end—which never comes or comes only on the Day of Judgment—his position will be concurred in by those who freely and clear-headedly review the relevant facts from the moral point of view. In other words, he is claiming an *ideal* consensus which transcends majorities and actual societies. One's society and its code and institutions may be wrong. Here enters the autonomy of the moral agent—he must take the moral point of view and must claim an eventual consensus with others who do so, but he must judge for himself. He may be mistaken, but, like Luther, he cannot do otherwise.

Problems remain. What is the moral point of view? This is a crucial question for the view we have suggested. It is also one on which there has been much controversy lately, which we can hardly try to resolve. According to one theory, one is taking the moral point of view if and only if one is willing to universalize one's maxims. Kant would probably accept this if he were alive. But I pointed out that one may be willing to universalize from a prudential point of view; and also that what one is willing to universalize is not necessarily a moral rule. Other such formal characterizations of the moral point of view have been proposed. The most plausible characterization to my mind, however, is that of Kurt Baier in *The Moral Point of View*. He holds that one is taking the moral point of view if one is not being egoistic, one is doing things on principle, one is willing to universalize one's principles, and in doing so one considers the good of everyone alike.

WHY BE MORAL?

Another problem that remains has been mentioned before. Why should we be moral? Why should we take part in the moral institution of life? Why should we adopt the moral point of view? We have already seen that the question, "Why should. . . ?" is ambiguous, and may be a request either for motivation or for justification. Here, then, one may be asking for (1) the motives for doing what is morally right, (2) a justification for doing what is morally right, (3) motivation for adopting the moral point of view and otherwise subscribing to the moral institution of life, or (4) a justification of morality and the moral point of view. It is easy to see the form which an answer to a request for (1) and (3) must take; it will consist in pointing out the various prudential and non-prudential motives for doing what is right or for enrolling in the moral institution of life. Most of these are familiar or readily thought of and need not be detailed here. A request for (2) might be taken as a request for a moral justification for doing what is right. Then, the answer is that doing what is morally right does not need a justification, since the justification has already been given in showing that it is right. Under these circumstances, a request for (2) is like asking, "Why morally ought I to do what is morally right?" A request for (2) may also, however, be meant as a demand for a non-moral justification of doing what is morally right; then, the answer to it will be like the answer to a request for (4). For a request for (4), being a request for reasons for subscribing to the moral way of thinking, judging, and living, must be a request for a nonmoral justification of morality. What will this be like?

There seem to be two questions here. First, why should *society* adopt such an institution as morality? Why should it foster such a system for the guidance of conduct in addition to convention, law, and prudence? To this the answer is clear. The conditions of a satisfactory human life for people living in groups could hardly obtain otherwise. The alternatives would seem to be either a state of nature in which all or most of us would be worse off than we are, even *if* Hobbes is wrong in thinking that life in such a state would be "solitary, poor, nasty, brutish, and short;" or a leviathan civil state more totalitarian than any yet dreamed of, one in which the laws would cover all aspects of life and every possible deviation by the individual would be closed off by an effective threat of force.

The other question concerns what nonmoral reasons (not just motives) there are for an *individual's* adopting the moral way of thinking and living. To some extent, the answer has just been given, but only to some extent. For on reading the last paragraph an individual might say, "Yes. This shows that society requires morality and even that it is to my advantage to have others adopt the moral way of life. But it does not show that I should adopt it. And it is no use arguing on moral grounds that I should. I want a nonmoral justification for thinking I should." Now, if this means that he wants to be shown that it is always to his advantage—that is, that his life will invariably be better or, at least, not worse in the nonmoral sense of better —if he thoroughly adopts the moral way of life, then I doubt that his demand can always be met. Through the use of various familiar arguments, one can show that the moral way of life is pretty likely to be to his advantage, but one must admit in all honesty that one who takes the moral road may be called upon to make a sacrifice and, hence, may not have as good a life in the nonmoral sense as he would otherwise have had.

It does not follow that one cannot justify the ways of morality to an individual, although it may follow that one cannot justify morality to some individuals. For nonmoral justification is not necessarily egoistic or prudential. If A asks B why he, A, should be moral, B may reply by asking A to try to decide in a rational way what kind of a life he wishes to live or what kind of a person he wishes to be. That is, he may ask A what way of life he would choose if he were to choose rationally, or in other words, freely, impartially, and in full knowledge of what it is like to live the various alternative ways of life, including the moral one. B may then be able to convince A, when he is calm and cool in this way, that the way of life he prefers, all things considered, includes the moral way of life. If so, then he has justified the moral way of life to A.

Of course, A may refuse to be rational, calm, and cool. He may retort, "But why should I be rational?" If this was his posture in originally asking for justification, he had no business asking for it. For one can only ask for justification if one is willing to be rational. One cannot consistently ask for reasons unless one is ready to accept reasons of some sort. Even in asking, "Why should I be rational?" one is implicitly committing oneself to rationality; for such a commitment is, at least, part of the connotation of the word "should."

Perhaps A has yet one more question: "What justification has society in demanding that I adopt the moral way of life, and in punishing me if I do not?" But this is a moral question; and A can hardly expect it to be allowed that society is justified in doing this to A only if it can show that doing so is to A's advantage. However, if A is asking whether society is morally justified in requiring of him at least a certain minimal subscription to the moral institution of life, then the answer surely is that society sometimes is justified in this, as we saw before. But, as we also saw, society must be careful here. For it is itself morally required to respect the individual's autonomy and liberty, and in general to treat him justly; and it must remember that morality is made to minister to the good lives of individuals and not to interfere with them any more than is necessary. Morality is made for man, not man for morality.

*Fact
and
Value*

*How Are Fact
and Value
Related?*

If we compare such remarks as "Steel buildings generally withstand high winds better than frame ones," "Leaves change color in the autumn," and "Albino elephants are rarer than gray ones" with such statements as "It is good that a man aid his fellow men," "It is wrong to discriminate against a man on the basis of skin pigmentation," and "Willfully causing pointless pain is wrong," we might detect the difference between them as follows: the first three statements are descriptive; the last three are evaluative. We might call the first three "factual statements" and the last three "value judgments," were these not loaded terms. But "value judgment" is often so used as to be in effect a term of abuse; "*merely* a value judgment" (and so subjective) comes naturally to one's thought. And "factual judgments" is very like "true judgments," so that to contrast the former triad with the latter by allowing only the first triad to be factual would make the sort of statement represented by the second triad not a candidate for being true (or false either). Either of these consequences is undesirable, since in each case the issues involved are complex.

These matters ought not to be settled simply by using one set of terminology rather than another.

The question as to whether there is indeed a hard and sharp distinction between descriptive statements (along with what justifies them) and evaluative statements (along with what justifies them) is an important and difficult one. Two considerations in favor of making this distinction a hard and fast one have been offered by contemporary philosophers. One is that value words cannot be redefined, without remainder, into purely descriptive words. The other is that evaluative statements cannot follow deductively from descriptive statements. The former consideration looms large in the work of G. E. Moore.

Moore believed that "The most fundamental question in all Ethics" is "how 'good' is to be defined." Moore does not mean to ask simply "What does the dictionary say about the word 'good'?" Nor is he asking "To what things does the word 'good' apply?" To understand what he is asking, we must consider the model on which Moore works.

My business is solely with that object or idea, which I hold, rightly or wrongly, that the word is generally used to stand for. What I want to discover is the nature of that object or idea. . . .

To the word "good" there corresponds something—which Moore variously calls an "idea," an "object," a "notion," and a "quality"—which the word stands for. And what Moore wants is a definition that will "describe the real nature of the object or notion" denoted by the word "good." Such a definition of a word provides an *analysis* of what the word stands for, breaking it down in thought into its constituent parts. Moore's claim is that "good" is, in this crucial sense, indefinable.

Now Moore holds that "it is impossible that, 'till the answer to this question be known, anyone should know *what is the evidence* for any ethical judgment whatsoever." Thus he believes that the answer to his question determines the sort of reason one can offer for ethical statements. It is this consideration that makes Moore's use of the notion of a "naturalistic fallacy" philosophically significant. Moore believes that many thinkers have confused the quality "good" stands for with *other* qualities—for instance, the quality of being pleasant—and so identified things that were different. Moore holds that "far too many philosophers have thought that when they named those other properties they were actually defining good"—that is, giving the "real nature" of what "good" stands for. Making this misidentification is committing the naturalistic fallacy.

An argument of Moore's can serve to elucidate what committing the naturalistic fallacy amounts to. Suppose one says, "to say of an action that it is good is to say that it is pleasant," defending this claim by saying that "is good" and "is pleasant" mean the same thing.

Well, if this is so, then certain questions will be in a sense inappropriate. To ask, "Must a triangle have three angles?" is inappropriate for anyone who is clear about the concepts involved. To ask the question seriously is to reveal ignorance of important features of these concepts. Consider the claim that "this action is good" and "this action is pleasant" are identical in meaning.

If this is so, then there will be three questions that are inappropriate in the sense just indicated: (1) "Is whatever is pleasant also good?" (2) "Is whatever is good also pleasant?" and (3) "Is being pleasant itself good?" But these questions are plainly not inappropriate in the sense that to ask them reveals important confusion about the concepts involved. For some people, it is pleasant to watch others suffer. To ask if it is good that one enjoy another's suffering is not to ask a question like "Do all triangles have angles?" It is perhaps good to sacrifice something one dearly wants in order to have enough to aid someone else; and it is perhaps good to do so even if it is unpleasant. To maintain that this is so is not like maintaining that some triangles have no angles. Again, one may without logical absurdity wonder if being pleasant is itself a morally good feature. But none of this would be possible were the definition correct.

To commit the naturalistic fallacy is to identify the quality the word "good" stands for with some other quality. When one commits this fallacy, the error of his ways can be demonstrated by use of the above argument, commonly called "the open question argument." Moore believed that this argument was conclusive against each and every attempt to define "good" in the relevant sense of "define," and so he believed he had a proof of what his own introspection informed him in any case—that goodness, like yellowness, is a simple, unique, indefinable quality.

It is doubtless more profitable to stress the argument and de-emphasize Moore's introspective claims. What does the argument show? A. N. Prior claims that it does prove something but not what Moore had hoped. It proves that no one can at the same time define "A is good" in terms of "A is x" (where x indicates any definition of "good" you please—even in terms of other ethical words such as "right") and claim that "A is x" is a *reason for* saying that "A is good." For if "A is x" and "A is good" are identical in meaning, plainly one cannot be a *reason* for the other, since a reason for a claim must be some *other* claim. "A is a reason for B" entails "A is not identical with B." In Prior's view Moore's criticism actually shows the positions of some philosophers to be mistaken. But it does not refute all attempts to define "good."

Again, as Prior notes, there is an explanation other than Moore's why the "open question" argument is powerful. "Good" may be ambiguous, so that the reason why "Is x itself good?" is intelligible no matter what value we choose for x is because "good" has no *one* sense. *This* would explain the force of this argument as well as Moore's own explanation that there is only one meaning for "good," namely that derived from its standing for a unique, simple quality that all good things share in common. If "good" is in this sense ambiguous, then one could offer reasons for only using "good" in some one way, and there is no guarantee that in that way it would not turn out that "good" *is* definable. If one points to Moore's introspective awareness of a single quality of goodness, one can equally well point out that many philosophers report no such results.

It is not clear then that there can in principle be no definition of "good." Thus, in the sense that "There is a distinction between fact and value" means "There is no way of defining or analyzing 'good,'" it is not clear that there is, on Moore's grounds at least, such a distinction.

The Naturalistic Fallacy
G. E. MOORE

B ut our question 'What is good?' may have still another meaning. [The first two meanings concerned the dictionary meaning of, and the things denoted by, the word "good."] We may, in the third place, mean to ask, not what thing or things are good, but how 'good' is to be defined. This is an enquiry which belongs only to Ethics, not to Casuistry; and this is the enquiry which will occupy us first.

It is an enquiry to which most special attention should be directed; since this question, how 'good' is to be defined, is the most fundamental question in all Ethics. That which is meant by 'good' is, in fact, except its converse 'bad,' the *only* simple object of thought which is peculiar to Ethics. Its definition is, therefore, the most essential point in the definition of Ethics; and moreover a mistake with regard to it entails a far larger number of erroneous ethical judgments than any other. Unless this first question be fully understood, and its true answer clearly recognised. the rest of Ethics is as good as useless from the point of view of systematic knowledge. True ethical judgments, of the two kinds last dealt with, may indeed be made by those who do not know the answer to this question as well as by those who do; and it goes without saying that the two classes of people may lead equally good lives. But it is extremely unlikely that the *most general* ethical judgments will be equally valid, in the absence of a true answer to this question: I shall presently try to shew that the gravest errors have been largely due to beliefs in a false answer. And, in any case, it is impossible that, till the answer to this question be known, any one should know *what is the evidence* for any ethical judgment whatsoever. But the main object of Ethics, as a systematic science, is to give correct *reasons* for thinking that this or that is good; and unless this question be answered, such reasons cannot be given. Even, therefore, apart from the fact that a false answer leads to false conclusions, the present enquiry is a most necessary and important part of the science of Ethics.

What, then, is good? How is good to be defined? Now, it may be thought that this is a verbal question. A definition does indeed often mean the expressing of one word's meaning in other words. But this is not the sort of definition I am asking for. Such a definition can never be of ultimate importance in any study except lexicography. If I wanted that kind of definition I should have to consider in the first place how people generally used the word 'good'; but my business is not with its proper usage, as established by custom. I should, indeed, be foolish, if I tried to use it for something which it did not usually denote: if, for instance, I were to announce that, whenever I used the word 'good,' I must be understood to be thinking of that object which is usually denoted by the word 'table.' I shall, therefore, use the word in the sense in which I think it is ordinarily used; but at the same time I am not anxious to discuss whether I am right in thinking that it is so used. My business is solely with that object or idea, which I hold, rightly or wrongly, that the word is generally used to stand for. What I want to discover is the nature of that object or idea, and about this I am extremely anxious to arrive at an agreement.

But, if we understand the question in this sense, my answer to it may seem a very disappointing one. If I am asked

FROM: *Principia Ethica*, G. E. Moore. (New York: Cambridge University Press, 1903), Ch. I, Section B, pp. 5–21. Reprinted by permission of Cambridge University Press and Mrs. G. E. Moore.

'What is good?' my answer is that good is good, and that is the end of the matter. Or if I am asked 'How is good to be defined?' my answer is that it cannot be defined, and that is all I have to say about it. But disappointing as these answers may appear, they are of the very last importance. To readers who are familiar with philosophic terminology, I can express their importance by saying that they amount to this: That propositions about the good are all of them synthetic and never analytic; and that is plainly no trivial matter. And the same thing may be expressed more popularly, by saying that, if I am right, then nobody can foist upon us such an axiom as that 'Pleasure is the only good' or that 'The good is the desired' on the pretence that this is 'the very meaning of the word.'

Let us, then, consider this position. My point is that 'good' is a simple notion, just as 'yellow' is a simple notion; that, just as you cannot by any manner of means, explain to any one who does not already know it, what yellow is, so you cannot explain what good is. Definitions of the kind that I was asking for, definitions which describe the real nature of the object or notion denoted by a word, and which do not merely tell us what the word is used to mean, are only possible when the object or notion in question is something complex. You can give a definition of a horse, because a horse has many different properties and qualities, all of which you can enumerate. But when you have enumerated them all, when you have reduced a horse to his simplest terms, then you can no longer define those terms. They are simply something which you think of or perceive, and to any one who cannot think of or perceive them, you can never, by any definition, make their nature known. It may perhaps be objected to this that we are able to describe to others, objects which they have never seen or thought of. We can, for instance, make a man understand what a chimaera is, although he has never heard of one or seen one. You can tell him that it is an animal with a lioness's head and body,

with a goat's head growing from the middle of its back, and with a snake in place of a tail. But here the object which you are describing is a complex object; it is entirely composed of parts, with which we are all perfectly familiar—a snake, a goat, a lioness; and we know, too, the manner in which those parts are to be put together, because we know what is meant by the middle of a lioness's back, and where her tail is wont to grow. And so it is with all objects, not previously known, which we are able to define: they are all complex; all composed of parts, which may themselves, in the first instance, be capable of similar definition, but which must in the end be reducible to simplest parts, which can no longer be defined. But yellow and good, we say, are not complex: they are notions of that simple kind, out of which definitions are composed and with which the power of further defining ceases.

When we say, as Webster says, 'The definition of horse is "A hoofed quadruped of the genus Equus," ' we may, in fact, mean three different things. (1) We may mean merely: 'When I say "horse," you are to understand that I am talking about a hoofed quadruped of the genus Equus.' This might be called the arbitrary verbal definition: and I do not mean that good is indefinable in that sense. (2) We may mean, as Webster ought to mean: 'When most English people say "horse," they mean a hoofed quadruped of the genus Equus.' This may be called the verbal definition proper, and I do not say that good is indefinable in this sense either; for it is certainly possible to discover how people use a word: otherwise, we could never have known that 'good' may be translated by 'gut' in German and by 'bon' in French. But (3) we may, when we define horse, mean something much more important. We may mean that a certain object, which we all of us know, is composed in a certain manner: that it has four legs, a head, a heart, a liver, etc., etc., all of them arranged in definite relations to one another. It is in this sense that I deny good to be definable. I say that it is not composed of any parts, which we can substitute for it in our minds when we are thinking of it. We might think just as clearly and correctly about a horse, if we thought of all its parts and their arrangement instead of thinking of the whole: we could, I say, think how a horse differed from a donkey just as well, just as truly, in this way, as now we do, only not so easily; but there is nothing whatsoever which we could so substitute for good; and that is what I mean, when I say that good is indefinable.

But I am afraid I have still not removed the chief difficulty which may prevent acceptance of the proposition that good is indefinable. I do not mean to say that *the* good, that which is good, is thus indefinable; if I did think so, I should not be writing on Ethics, for my main object is to help towards discovering that definition. It is just because I think there will be less risk of error in our search for a definition of 'the good,' that I am now insisting that *good* is indefinable. I must try to explain the difference between these two. I suppose it may be granted that 'good' is an adjective. Well 'the good,' 'that which is good,' must therefore be the substantive to which the adjective 'good' will apply: it must be the whole of that to which the adjective will apply, and the adjective must *always* truly apply to it. But if it is that to which the adjective will apply, it must be something different from that adjective itself; and the whole of that something different whatever it is, will be our definition of *the* good. Now it may be that this something will have other adjectives, beside 'good,' that will apply to it. It may be full of pleasure, for example; it may be intelligent: and if these two adjectives are really part of its definition, then it will certainly be true, that pleasure and intelligence are good. And many people appear to think that, if we say 'Pleasure and intelligence are good,' or if we say 'Only pleasure and intelligence are good,' we are defining 'good.' Well, I cannot deny that propositions of this nature may sometimes be called definitions; I do not

know well enough how the word is generally used to decide upon this point. I only wish it to be understood that that is not what I mean when I say there is no possible definition of good, and that I shall not mean this if I use the word again. I do most fully believe that some true proposition of the form 'Intelligence is good and intelligence alone is good' can be found; if none could be found, our definition of *the* good would be impossible. As it is, I believe *the* good to be definable; and yet I still say that good itself is indefinable.

'Good,' then, if we mean by it that quality which we assert to belong to a thing, when we say that the thing is good, is incapable of any definition, in the most important sense of that word. The most important sense of 'definition' is that in which a definition states what are the parts which invariably compose a certain whole; and in this sense 'good' has no definition because it is simple and has no parts. It is one of those innumerable objects of thought which are themselves incapable of definition, because they are the ultimate terms by reference to which whatever *is* capable of definition must be defined. That there must be an indefinite number of such terms is obvious, on reflection; since we cannot define anything except by an analysis, which, when carried as far as it will go, refers us to something, which is simply different from anything else, and which by that ultimate explains the peculiarity of the whole which we are defining: for every whole contains some parts which are common to other wholes also. There is, therefore, no intrinsic difficulty in the contention that 'good' denotes a simple and indefinable quality. There are many other instances of such qualities.

Consider yellow, for example. We may try to define it, by describing its physical equivalent; we may state what kind of light-vibrations must stimulate the normal eye, in order that we may perceive it. But a moment's reflection is sufficient to shew that those light-vibrations are not themselves what we mean by yellow. *They* are not what we perceive. Indeed we should never have been able to discover their existence, unless we had first been struck by the patent difference of quality between the different colours. The most we can be entitled to say of those vibrations is that they are what corresponds in space to the yellow which we actually perceive.

Yet a mistake of this simple kind has commonly been made about 'good.' It may be true that all things which are good are *also* something else, just as it is true that all things which are yellow produce a certain kind of vibration in the light. And it is a fact, that Ethics aims at discovering what are those other properties belonging to all things which are good. But far too many philosophers have thought that when they named those other properties they were actually defining good; that these properties, in fact, were simply not 'other,' but absolutely and entirely the same with goodness. This view I propose to call the 'naturalistic fallacy' and of it I shall now endeavour to dispose.

Let us consider what it is such philosophers say. And first it is to be noticed that they do not agree among themselves. They not only say that they are right as to what good is, but they endeavour to prove that other people who say that it is something else, are wrong. One, for instance, will affirm that good is pleasure, another, perhaps, that good is that which is desired; and each of these will argue eagerly to prove that the other is wrong. But how is that possible? One of them says that good is nothing but the object of desire, and at the same time tries to prove that it is not pleasure. But from his first assertion, that good just means the object of desire, one of two things must follow as regards his proof:

(1) He may be trying to prove that the object of desire is not pleasure. But, if this be all, where is his Ethics? The position he is maintaining is merely a psychological one. Desire is something which occurs in our minds, and pleasure is something else which so occurs; and our would-be ethical philosopher is merely holding that the latter is not the object of the former. But what has that to do with the question in dispute? His opponent held the ethical proposition that pleasure was the good, and although he should prove a million times over the psychological proposition that pleasure is not the object of desire, he is no nearer proving his opponent to be wrong. The position is like this. One man says a triangle is a circle: another replies 'A triangle is a straight line, and I will prove to you that I am right: *for*' (this is the only argument) 'a straight line is not a circle.' 'That is quite true,' the other may reply; 'but nevertheless a triangle is a circle, and you have said nothing whatever to prove the contrary. What is proved is that one of us is wrong, for we agree that a triangle cannot be both a straight line and a circle: but which is wrong, there can be no earthly means of proving, since you define triangle as a straight line and I define it as circle.'— Well, that is one alternative which any naturalistic Ethics has to face; if good is *defined* as something else, it is then impossible either to prove that any other definition is wrong or even to deny such definition.

(2) The other alternative will scarcely be more welcome. It is that the discussion is after all a verbal one. When A says 'Good means pleasant' and B says 'Good means desired,' they may merely wish to assert that most people have used the word for what is pleasant and for what is desired respectively. And this is quite an interesting subject for discussion: only it is not a whit more an ethical discussion than the last was. Nor do I think that any exponent of naturalistic Ethics would be willing to allow that this was all he meant. They are all so anxious to persuade us that what they call the good is what we really ought to do. 'Do, pray, act so, because the word "good" is generally used to denote actions of this nature': such, on this view, would be the substance of their teaching. And in so far as they tell us how we ought to act, their teaching is truly ethical, as they mean it to be. But how perfectly absurd is the reason they would give for it! 'You

are to do this, because most people use a certain word to denote conduct such as this.' 'You are to say the thing which is not, because most people call it lying.' That is an argument just as good!—My dear sirs, what we want to know from you as ethical teachers, is not how people use a word; it is not even, what kind of actions they approve, which the use of this word 'good' may certainly imply: what we want to know is simply what *is* good. We may indeed agree that what most people do think good, is actually so; we shall at all events be glad to know their opinions: but when we say their opinions *about* what *is* good, we do mean what we say; we do not care whether they call that thing which they mean 'horse' or 'table' or 'chair,' 'gut' or 'bon' or 'ἀγαθός'; we want to know what it is that they so call. When they say 'Pleasure is good,' we cannot believe that they merely mean 'Pleasure is pleasure' and nothing more than that.

Suppose a man says 'I am pleased'; and suppose that is not a lie or a mistake but the truth. Well, if it is true, what does that mean? It means that his mind, a certain definite mind, distinguished by certain definite marks from all others, has at this moment a certain definite feeling called pleasure. 'Pleased' *means* nothing but having pleasure, and though we may be more pleased or less pleased, and even, we may admit for the present, have one or another kind of pleasure; yet in so far as it is pleasure we have, whether there be more or less of it, and whether it be of one kind or another, what we have is one definite thing, absolutely indefinable, some one thing that is the same in all the various degrees and in all the various kinds of it that there may be. We may be able to say how it is related to other things: that, for example, it is in the mind, that it causes desire, that we are conscious of it, etc., etc. We can, I say, describe its relations to other things, but define it we can *not*. And if anybody tried to define pleasure for us as being any other natural object; if anybody were to say, for instance, that pleasure *means* the sensation of red, and

were to proceed to deduce from that that pleasure is a colour, we should be entitled to laugh at him and to distrust his future statements about pleasure. Well, that would be the same fallacy which I have called the naturalistic fallacy. That 'pleased' does not mean 'having the sensation of red,' or anything else whatever, does not prevent us from understanding what it does mean. It is enough for us to know that 'pleased' does mean 'having the sensation of pleasure,' and though pleasure is absolutely indefinable, though pleasure is pleasure and nothing else whatever, yet we feel no difficulty in saying that we are pleased. The reason is, of course, that when I say 'I am pleased,' I do *not* mean that 'I' am the same thing as 'having pleasure.' And similarly no difficulty need be found in my saying that 'pleasure is good' and yet not meaning that 'pleasure' is the same thing as 'good,' that pleasure *means* good, and that good *means* pleasure. If I were to imagine that when I said 'I am pleased,' I meant that I was exactly the same thing as 'pleased,' I should not indeed call that a naturalistic fallacy, although it would be the same fallacy as I have called naturalistic with reference to Ethics. The reason of this is obvious enough. When a man confuses two natural objects with one another, defining the one by the other, if for instance, he confuses himself, who is one natural object, with 'pleased' or with 'pleasure' which are others, then there is no reason to call the fallacy naturalistic. But if he confuses 'good,' which is not in the same sense a natural object, with any natural object whatever, then there is a reason for calling that a naturalistic fallacy; its being made with regard to 'good' marks it as something quite specific, and this specific mistake deserves a name because it is so common. As for the reasons why good is not to be considered a natural object, they may be reserved for discussion in another place. But, for the present, it is sufficient to notice this: Even if it were a natural object, that would not alter the nature of the fallacy nor diminish its importance one whit. All that I have said about it would remain quite equally true: only the name which I have called it would not be so appropriate as I think it is. And I do not care about the name: what I do care about is the fallacy. It does not matter what we call it, provided we recognise it when we meet with it. It is to be met with in almost every book on Ethics; and yet it is not recognised: and that is why it is necessary to multiply illustrations of it, and convenient to give it a name. It is a very simple fallacy indeed. When we say that an orange is yellow, we do not think our statement binds us to hold that 'orange' means nothing else than 'yellow,' or that nothing can be yellow but an orange. Supposing the orange is also sweet! Does that bind us to say that 'sweet' is exactly the same thing as 'yellow,' that 'sweet' must be defined as 'yellow'? And supposing it be recognised that 'yellow' just means 'yellow' and nothing else whatever, does that make it any more difficult to hold that oranges are yellow? Most certainly it does not: on the contrary, it would be absolutely meaningless to say that oranges were yellow, unless yellow did in the end mean just 'yellow' and nothing else whatever—unless it was absolutely indefinable. We should not get any very clear notion about things, which are yellow—we should not get very far with our science, if we were bound to hold that everything which was yellow, *meant* exactly the same thing as yellow. We should find we had to hold that an orange was exactly the same thing as a stool, a piece of paper, a lemon, anything you like. We could prove any number of absurdities; but should we be the nearer to the truth? Why, then, should it be different with 'good'? Why, if good is good and indefinable, should I be held to deny that pleasure is good? Is there any difficulty in holding both to be true at once? On the contrary, there is no meaning in saying that pleasure is good, unless good is something different from pleasure. It is absolutely useless, so far as Ethics is concerned, to prove, as Mr. Spencer tries to do, that increase of pleasure coincides with increase of life, unless

good *means* something different from either life or pleasure. He might just as well try to prove that an orange is yellow by shewing that it always is wrapped up in paper.

In fact, if it is not the case that 'good' denotes something simple and indefinable, only two alternatives are possible: either it is a complex, a given whole, about the correct analysis of which there may be disagreement; or else it means nothing at all, and there is no such subject as Ethics. In general however, ethical philosophers have attempted to define good, without recognising what such an attempt must mean. They actually use arguments which involve one or both of the absurdities considered i.e. [on p. 407]. We are, therefore, justified in concluding that the attempt to define good is chiefly due to want of clearness as to the possible nature of definition. There are, in fact, only two serious alternatives to be considered, in order to establish the conclusion that 'good' does denote a simple and indefinable notion. It might possibly denote a complex, as 'horse' does; or it might have no meaning at all. Neither of these possibilities has, however, been clearly conceived and seriously maintained, as such, by those who presume to define good; and both may be dismissed by a simple appeal to facts.

(1) The hypothesis that disagreement about the meaning of good is disagreement with regard to the correct analysis of a given whole, may be most plainly seen to be incorrect by consideration of the fact that, whatever definition be offered, it may be always asked, with significance, of the complex so defined, whether it is itself good. To take, for instance, one of the more plausible, because one of the more complicated, of such proposed definitions, it may easily be thought, at first sight, that to be good may mean to be that which we desire to desire. Thus if we apply this definition to a particular instance and say 'When we think that A is good, we are thinking that A is one of the things which we desire to desire,' our proposition may seem quite

plausible. But, if we carry the investigation further, and ask ourselves 'Is it good to desire to desire A?' it is apparent, on a little reflection, that this question is itself as intelligible, as the original question 'Is A good?'—that we are in fact, now asking for exactly the same information about the desire to desire A, for which we formerly asked with regard to A itself. But it is also apparent that the meaning of this second question cannot be correctly analysed into 'Is the desire to desire A one of the things which we desire to desire?': we have not before our minds anything so complicated as the question 'Do we desire to desire to desire to desire A?' Moreover any one can easily convince himself by inspection that the predicate of this proposition—'good' —is positively different from the notion of 'desiring to desire' which enters into its subject: 'That we should desire to desire A is good' is *not* merely equivalent to 'That A should be good is good.' It may indeed be true that what we desire to desire is always also good; perhaps, even the converse may be true: but it is very doubtful whether this is the case, and the mere fact that we understand very well what is meant by doubting it, shews clearly that we have two different notions before our minds.

(2) *And* the same consideration is sufficient to dismiss the hypothesis that 'good' has no meaning whatsoever. It is very natural to make the mistake of supposing that what is universally true is of such a nature that its negation would be self-contradictory: the importance which has been assigned to analytic propositions in the history of philosophy shews how easy such a mistake is. And thus it is very easy to conclude that what seems to be a universal ethical principle is in fact an identical proposition; that, if, for example, whatever is called 'good' seems to be pleasant, the proposition 'Pleasure is the good' does not assert a connection between two different notions, but involves only one, that of pleasure, which is easily recognised as a distinct entity. But whoever will attentively consider with himself what is actually before his

mind when he asks the question 'Is pleasure (or whatever it may be) after all good?' can easily satisfy himself that he is not merely wondering whether pleasure is pleasant. And if he will try this experiment with each suggested definition in succession, he may become expert enough to recognise that in every case he has before his mind a unique object, with regard to the connection of which with any other object, a distinct question may be asked. Every one does in fact understand the question 'Is this good?' When he thinks of it, his state of mind is different from what it would be, were he asked 'Is this pleasant, or desired, or approved?' It has a distinct meaning for him, even though he may not recognise in what respect it is distinct. Whether he thinks of 'intrinsic value,' or 'intrinsic worth,' or says that a thing 'ought to exist,' he has before his mind the unique object—the unique property of things— which I mean by 'good.' Everybody is constantly aware of this notion, although he may never become aware at all that it is different from other notions of which he is also aware. But, for correct ethical reasoning, it is extremely important that he should become aware of this fact; and, as soon as the nature of the problem is clearly understood, there should be little difficulty in advancing so far in analysis.

'Good,' then, is indefinable; and yet, so far as I know, there is only one ethical writer, Prof. Henry Sidgwick, who has clearly recognised and stated this fact. We shall see, indeed, how far many of the most reputed ethical systems fall short of drawing the conclusions which follow from such a recognition. At present I will only quote one instance, which will serve to illustrate the meaning and importance of this principle that 'good' is indefinable, or, as Prof. Sidgwick says, an 'unanalysable notion.' It is an instance to which Prof. Sidgwick himself refers in a note on the passage, in which he argues that 'ought' is unanalysable[1].

'Bentham,' says Sidgwick, 'explains

---

[1] *Methods of Ethics*, Bk. 1, Chap. iii, § 1 (6th edition).

that his fundamental principle "states the greatest happiness of all those whose interest is in question as being the right and proper end of human action" '; and yet 'his language in other passages of the same chapter would seem to imply' that he *means* by the word "right" "conducive to the general happiness." Prof. Sidgwick sees that, if you take these two statements together, you get the absurd result that 'greatest happiness is the end of human action, which is conducive to the general happiness'; and so absurd does it seem to him to call this result, as Bentham calls it, 'the fundamental principle of a moral system,' that he suggests that Bentham cannot have meant it. Yet Prof. Sidgwick himself states elsewhere[2] that Psychological Hedonism is 'not seldom confounded with Egoistic Hedonism'; and that confusion, as we shall see, rests chiefly on that same fallacy, the naturalistic fallacy, which is implied in Bentham's statements. Prof. Sidgwick admits therefore that this fallacy is sometimes committed, absurd as it is; and I am inclined to think that Bentham may really have been one of those who committed it. Mill, as we shall see, certainly did commit it. In any case, whether Bentham committed it or not, his doctrine, as above quoted, will serve as a very good illustration of this fallacy, and of the importance of the contrary proposition that good is indefinable.

Let us consider this doctrine. Bentham seems to imply, so Prof. Sidgwick says, that the word 'right' *means* 'conducive to general happiness.' Now this, by itself, need not necessarily involve the naturalistic fallacy. For the word 'right' is very commonly appropriated to actions which lead to the attainment of what is good; which are regarded as *means* to the ideal and not as ends-in-themselves. This use of 'right,' as denoting what is good as a means, whether or not it be also good as an end, is indeed the use to which I shall confine the word. Had Bentham been using 'right' in this sense, it might be perfectly

consistent for him to *define* right as 'conducive to the general happiness,' *provided only* (and notice this proviso) he had already proved, or laid down as an axiom, that general happiness was *the* good, or (what is equivalent to this) that general happiness alone was good. For in that case he would have already defined *the* good as general happiness (a position perfectly consistent, as we have seen, with the contention that 'good' is indefinable), and, since right was to be defined as 'conducive to *the* good,' it would actually *mean* 'conducive to general happiness.' But this method of escape from the charge of having committed the naturalistic fallacy has been closed by Bentham himself. For his fundamental principle is, we see, that the greatest happiness of all concerned is the *right* and proper *end* of human action. He applies the word 'right,' therefore, to the end, as such, not only to the means which are conducive to it; and, that being so, right can no longer be defined as 'conducive to the general happiness,' without involving the fallacy in question. For now it is obvious that the definition of right as conducive to general happiness can be used by him in support of the fundamental principle that general happiness is the right end; instead of being itself derived from that principle. If right, by definition, means conducive to general happiness, then it is obvious that general happiness is the right end. It is not necessary now first to prove or assert that general happiness is the right end, before right is defined as conducive to general happiness —a perfectly valid procedure; but on the contrary the definition of right as conducive to general happiness proves general happiness to be the right end—a perfectly invalid procedure, since in this case the statement that 'general happiness is the right end of human action' is not an ethical principle at all, but either, as we have seen, a proposition about the meaning of words, or else a proposition about the *nature* of general happiness, not about its rightness or goodness.

Now, I do not wish the importance I assign to this fallacy to be misunder-

[2] *Methods of Ethics*, Bk. 1, Chap. iv, § 1.

stood. The discovery of it does not at all refute Bentham's contention that greatest happiness is the proper end of human action, if that be understood as an ethical proposition, as he undoubtedly intended it. That principle may be true all the same; we shall consider whether it is so in succeeding chapters. Bentham might have maintained it, as Prof. Sidgwick does, if the fallacy had been pointed out to him. What I am maintaining is that the *reasons* which he actually gives for his ethical proposition are fallacious ones so far as they consist in a definition of right. What I suggest is that he did not perceive them to be fallacious; that, if he had done so, he would have been led to seek for other reasons in support of his Utilitarianism; and that, had he sought for other reasons, he *might* have found none which he thought to be sufficient. In that case he would have changed his whole system—a most important consequence. It is undoubtedly also possible that he would have thought other reasons to be sufficient, and in that case his ethical system, in its main results, would still have stood. But, even in this latter case, his use of the fallacy would be a serious objection to him as an ethical philosopher. For it is the business of Ethics, I must insist, not only to obtain true results, but also to find valid reasons for them. The direct object of Ethics is knowledge and not practice; and any one who uses the naturalistic fallacy has certainly not fulfilled this first object, however correct his practical principles may be.

My objections to Naturalism are then, in the first place, that it offers no reason at all, far less any valid reason, for any ethical principle whatever; and in this it already fails to satisfy the requirements of Ethics, as a scientific study. But in the second place I contend that, though it gives a reason for no ethical principle, it is a *cause* of the acceptance of false principles—it deludes the mind into accepting ethical principles, which are false; and in this it ·is contrary to

every aim of Ethics. It is easy to see that if we start with a definition of right conduct as conduct conducive to general happiness; then, knowing that right conduct is universally conduct conducive to the good, we very easily arrive at the result that the good is general happiness. If, on the other hand, we once recognise that we must start our Ethics without a definition, we shall be much more apt to look about us, before we adopt any ethical principle whatever; and the more we look about us, the less likely are we to adopt a false one. It may be replied to this: Yes, but we shall look about us just as much, before we settle on our definition, and are therefore just as likely to be right. But I will try to shew that this is not the case. If we start with the conviction that a definition of good can be found, we start with the conviction that good *can mean* nothing else than some one property of things; and our only business will then be to discover what that property is. But if we recognise that, so far as the meaning of good goes, anything whatever may be good, we start with a much more open mind. Moreover, apart from the fact that, when we think we have a definition, we cannot logically defend our ethical principles in any way whatever, we shall also be much less apt to defend them well, even if illogically. For we shall start with the conviction that good must mean so and so, and shall therefore be inclined either to misunderstand our opponent's arguments or to cut them short with the reply, 'This is not an open question: the very meaning of the word decides it; no one can think otherwise except through confusion.'

Our first conclusion as to the subject-matter of Ethics is, then, that there is a simple, indefinable, unanalysable object of thought by reference to which it must be defined. By what name we call this unique object is a matter of indifference, so long as we clearly recognise what it is and that it does differ from other objects.

A Critique of Moore
ARTHUR N. PRIOR

If there is any contribution to moral philosophy which is more likely than any other to become permanently associated with the name of Professor G. E. Moore, it is the identification and refutation, in his *Principia Ethica*,[1] of what he calls the 'naturalistic fallacy'. I propose now to explain what it is to which Professor Moore gives this name, and what he considers to be involved in its fallaciousness; and I shall offer reasons for regarding his argument, not as disproving ethical naturalism itself, but as exposing an inconsistency into which some naturalists have fallen.

What Professor Moore means by the 'naturalistic fallacy' is the assumption that because some quality or combination of qualities invariably and necessarily accompanies the quality of goodness, or is invariably and necessarily accompanied by it, or both, this quality or combination of qualities is *identical* with goodness. If, for example, it is believed that whatever is pleasant is and must be good, or that whatever is good is and must be pleasant, or both, it is committing the naturalistic fallacy to infer from this that goodness and pleasantness are one and the same quality. The naturalistic fallacy is the assumption that because the words 'good' and, say, 'pleasant' necessarily describe the same objects, they must attribute the same quality to them. We might, with Mill, call the objects to which a term is applicable the denotation of the term, and the characteristics which an object must have for the term to be applicable to it, the connotation of the term.[2] What the man who commits the

naturalistic fallacy fails to realize is that 'good' and some other adjective may denote or be applicable to the same things, yet not connote the same quality, i.e. describe the things in the same way. The difference between identity of denotation and identity of connotation may be brought out, as Professor Moore shows, by the following simple consideration: if the word 'good' and, say, the word 'pleasant' apply to the same things, but do not attribute the same quality to them, then to say that what is pleasant is good, or that what is good is pleasant, is to make a significant statement, however obvious its truth may appear to many people. But if the word 'good' and the word 'pleasant' not merely have the same application but the same connotation or 'meaning'—if, that is to say, the quality of pleasantness is identical with the quality of goodness—then to say that what is good is pleasant, or that what is pleasant is good, is to utter an empty tautology, or, as Mill would call it,[3] a 'merely verbal' proposition; for both statements are on this supposition merely ways of saying that what is pleasant is pleasant.

From this consideration Professor Moore attempts to show that the term 'good' is incapable of definition. By 'definition' he means the exhibition of a quality referred to by some term as a combination of simpler qualities. And he argues that if we take any such combination of relatively simple qualities (such

---

[1] pp. 6–17.

[2] J. S. Mill, *System of Logic*, I. ii. 5. The importance of Mill's distinction in the interpretation of Professor Moore's account of the naturalistic fallacy is rightly em-

phasized in Dr. D. Daiches Raphael's *The Moral Sense*, pp. 111–14; though on p. 113 Dr. Raphael attributes to certain modern mathematicians a confusion in regard to this point, of which I do not think they are really guilty.

[3] *System of Logic*, I. vi.

FROM: *Logic and The Basis of Ethics*, A. N. Prior. (Oxford: The Clarendon Press, 1949), Chapter I. Reprinted by permission of The Clarendon Press.

as the combination 'being what we desire to desire'), the statement that what possesses this combination of qualities is good (e.g. the statement that what we desire to desire is good) will always be found on careful inspection to be a significant statement and not a mere truism (like 'What we desire to desire, we desire to desire'). But this is not all that he claims to be able to show by this method. We may use it, he thinks, to show that goodness is not only simple, i.e. incapable of analysis into simpler parts, but unique. For even if we take a *simple* quality, such as pleasantness, we can always see that it is significant, and not a mere truism, to assert that what possesses this quality is good. (Despite his definition of 'definition,' as analysis, he slips readily into calling 'Good means pleasant' a 'definition' too.)

This latter contention of Professor Moore's is exceedingly difficult to state with any precision. It plainly does not apply to the quality of goodness itself—it *is* a truism to assert that what is good is good. Nor does it apply to the quality of goodness itself when it is merely given another name, such as 'value' (which is often used as synonymous with 'goodness' by Professor Moore, as well as by many other writers). Yet if we merely say that goodness is not identical with any other quality, this is itself a truism—it merely tells us that goodness is not identical with any quality, simple or complex, with which it is not identical. It is a little ominous that Professor Moore quotes on his title-page the sentence from Bishop Butler, 'Everything is what it is, and not another thing'. For who would deny this? Even the man who identifies goodness with pleasantness, i.e. who regards 'good' as a mere synonym of 'pleasant', would not deny that it is in this sense 'unique'. For pleasantness also 'is what it is, and not another thing'; and to say that goodness is pleasantness is not, on such a view, to deny that it is what it is, or to affirm that it is another thing—it is merely to deny that pleasantness is 'another thing'.

Professor Moore's real aim, of course, is to show that goodness is not identical with any 'natural' quality. This is why he calls the kind of identification which he is opposing the 'naturalistic' fallacy. But what does he mean by a 'natural' quality? He attempts an answer to this in the *Principia,* but now says that the answer there given is 'utterly silly and preposterous,'[4] as indeed it is (there is no need to reproduce it here). And at times it looks very much as if what he means by a 'natural' quality is simply any quality other than goodness or badness, or at all events other than goodness, badness, rightness, wrongness, and obligatoriness (if the last three are taken to be distinct from goodness and badness and from one another—which, in the *Principia Ethica,* they are not), and compounds containing these. But if this is what he means, are we not back where we were?—are we not still left with the truism that 'Everything is what it is, and not another thing'?

It is worth examining this sentence in its original context. Butler's argument in the paragraph from which it is taken[5] is directed against people who were putting it about that it can never be to any man's interest to be virtuous, since disinterestedness is of the essence of virtue. Mandeville, holding that nothing is virtuous but 'self-denial', went so far as to say that virtue was not only not in a man's own interests but generally not in anyone else's either, so that 'private vices' were 'public benefits'. So Butler sets out to show that virtue and disinterestedness are not the same thing (though virtue and self-interest are not the same thing either).

Virtue and interest, are not to be opposed, but only to be distinguished from each other; in the same way as virtue and any other particular affection, love of arts, suppose, are to be distinguished. Everything is what it is, and not another

[4] *The Philosophy of G. E. Moore* [ed. P. Schilpp], p. 582.

[5] *Sermons on Human Nature*, Preface, par. 39.

thing. *The goodness or badness of actions does not arise from hence, that the epithet, interested or disinterested, may be applied to them, any more than that any other indifferent epithet, suppose inquisitive or jealous, may or may not be applied to them; not from their being attended with present or future pleasure or pain; but from their being what they are; namely, what becomes such creatures as we are, what the state of the case requires, or the contrary.*

Butler is not, I think, denying that the moral quality of an act is determined by its other qualities—he is not denying, for example, that in a given situation a certain intensity of jealousy is always wrong, i.e. 'unbecoming' to 'such creatures as we are'. But he is denying that anything of this sort—expressing jealousy of such-and-such an intensity in such-and-such a situation—is what we *mean* by calling an act good or bad. Its goodness or badness is its 'moral appropriateness' to our nature and our situation. That is, its goodness or badness is its goodness or badness; it is its 'being what it is', good or bad as the case may be. Goodness or badness cannot be identified with any 'indifferent' epithets.

But what kind of epithet is that? If we take 'indifferent' to mean merely 'non-moral'—i.e. if an 'indifferent' epithet is any one that does not mean the same as 'good' or 'bad'—is not Butler's argument open to the same objection as Professor Moore's? Certainly goodness and badness are not to be identified with any qualities that are other than goodness and badness; but how does this forbid us to identify goodness with disinterestedness? Does not the identification of goodness with disinterestedness merely remove the latter from the class of 'indifferent' epithets, i.e. from the class of the 'other things' which goodness is not (just as, on Butler's own view, what we have called 'moral appropriateness' is something that goodness is, 'and not another thing')?

I think we must take it that what Butler means by 'indifference', and Pro-

fessor Moore by 'naturalness', is something more than mere non-identity with goodness or badness. Their view seems to be that all qualities other than goodness and badness have something positive in common—something which is so near to universal that we do not notice it until we compare the qualities marked by it with goodness and badness; and then it is intuitively evident. When we compare such qualities as goodness and badness with such qualities as pleasantness, pinkness, everlastingness—to take a quite random selection—we see that the former and the latter are not only individually non-identical, as pleasantness and pinkness are, but fall into two quite different categories or 'realms', namely, those which we sometimes call the realm of value (or of duty) and the realm of fact. These terms are not perhaps quite fortunately chosen, since it may be held—it is held by Professor Moore, for example, and was by Butler—that to say that something is our duty, or possesses value, is to state a fact, albeit of a very peculiar kind. (. . . There are some writers who deny this; but such a denial seems to amount to saying that there is really only one realm—the 'natural' one—and this is not the position which we are at present trying to formulate.) But however we describe these two 'realms', their existence and distinctness is what seems to be referred to in Professor Moore's distinction between ethical predicates and all 'natural' ones, as it is in the old distinction between the 'moral' perfections of the Deity and His 'natural' ones (omnipotence, omniscience, eternity, &c.), and in Aristotle's distinction between the 'ethical', the 'natural', and the 'logical' fields of inquiry. And Aristotle notes that 'the nature of each of the aforesaid kinds of proposition is not easily rendered in a definition, but we have to try to recognize each of them by means of the familiarity attained through induction, examining them in the light' of certain 'illustrations' given previously —'ethical' questions being illustrated by 'Ought one rather to obey one's parents or the laws, if they disagree?' and 'natural' ones by 'Is the universe eternal or not?'[6] (Aristotle is here using 'induction' to mean, not a process of reasoning, but the examining of instances until their common quality 'dawns' upon one—his appeal is to intuition.) But such an intuitively perceived difference between 'moral' qualities and all others plainly goes far beyond anything that can be proved from the principle that 'Everything is what it is and not another thing,' since this principle would still apply within a single 'natural' realm even if there were no other.[7]

Professor Moore's appeal to this truism, and the little dialectical device which he bases upon it, are not, however, entirely pointless. For there are occasions when men implicitly deny logical truisms, and need to be reminded of them; namely, when they are inconsistent. It is not against the naturalist as such, but the inconsistent naturalist, the man who tries to 'have it both ways', that Professor Moore's type of argument is really effective and important. And such people are not uncommon. Professor Moore himself mentions them—the people who begin by laying down as a truth of primary importance, perhaps even as something rather revolutionary, that nothing is good but pleasure, or that nothing is good but what promotes biological survival, and who, when asked why they are so certain of this, reply that 'that is the very meaning of the word'. To such people it is certainly legitimate and necessary to reply that if pleasantness, or the promotion of survival, is what 'goodness' *means,* then the fact that only pleasure is good, or that only what promotes survival is good, is hardly worth shouting from the housetop, since nobody in his senses ever denied that what is pleasant, and only what is pleasant, is pleasant, or that what promotes survival, and only what promotes survival, promotes survival. What these people would plainly like

to hold is that goodness is both identical with pleasantness and not identical with it; and, of course, it cannot be done. They want to regard 'What is pleasant is good' as a significant assertion; and it can only be so if the pleasantness of what is pleasant is one thing, and its goodness another. On the other hand they want to make it logically impossible to contradict this assertion—they want to treat the opposing assertion that what is pleasant may not be good as not merely false but logically absurd—and this can only be done if pleasantness and goodness are taken to be identical. To represent an opponent's position in such a way as to make it not only false but self-contradictory is a dialectical triumph which can never be obtained without being duly paid for; and the price is the representation of one's position as not only true but a truism. 'If a denial is to have any value as a statement of matter of fact', as Dr. J. N. Keynes says,[8] then what it denies 'must be consistent with the meaning of the terms employed. . . . The denial of a contradiction in terms . . . yields merely what is tautologous and practically useless.'

It is sometimes pointed out by naturalists that there is never more than one ethical statement which is rendered trivial by a naturalistic definition of 'good'. If, for example, we use 'good' as synonymous with 'conducive to biological survival', then, while it is a truism to say that what is conducive to biological survival is 'good' in this sense, it is not a truism to say that pleasure is, since it is not a truism to say that pleasure is conducive to survival. We shall find shortly that there is a point at which this consideration is important; but if Professor Moore's argument is regarded as a criticism of the attempt to deduce significant assertions from definitions, this answer to it is irrelevant, since the statement which the definition makes trivial is always precisely the one which it is put forward to 'prove', in a sense in which it is not trivial but significant. A man who

---

[6] *Topics*, 105[b]21–9.

[7] This point is elaborated in an article on 'The Naturalistic Fallacy', by W. K. Frankena, in *Mind*, 1939, pp. 472 ff.

[8] *Formal Logic*, pp. 119–20.

has defined 'good' as 'conducive to biological survival', with the express purpose of establishing it as an ethical principle of primary importance that only what conduces to survival is good, will not be greatly cheered by the consideration that it is 'only' this principle which the definition renders insignificant. Confronted with Professor Moore's argument, an inconsistent ethical naturalist has two courses open to him. He may clear himself of inconsistency, on the one hand, by abandoning his naturalism—he may continue to insist that only pleasure, or conduciveness to survival, or whatever it may be, is good, but may preserve the significance of this assertion by sacrificing its certainty, admitting that its denial, though still in his opinion false, is not self-contradictory. Professor Moore writes as if this is what any naturalist who really grasps his argument will do —he seems to consider his argument a *refutation* of naturalism. But a naturalist can preserve his naturalism if he wants to, even in the face of Professor Moore's argument—he can do so by admitting that the assertion that, say, pleasure and nothing but pleasure is good, *is* for him a mere truism; and that if Ethics be the attempt to determine what is in fact good, then the statement that what is pleasant is good is not, strictly, an ethical statement, but only a way of indicating just what is to go under the name of 'Ethics'—the study of what is actually pleasant, without any pretence of maintaining that pleasure has any 'goodness' beyond its pleasantness. He might add at the same time that he is not only going to discuss goodness as a 'nonnatural' quality, but that in his belief there is no such quality, and that this is worth shouting from the housetops, as it liberates us from a transcendental notion which has haunted us too long. (He might say that this is what he really means by the assertion that 'Nothing is good but pleasure'—he means, not that what is pleasant alone possesses some other quality called 'goodness', but that there are no qualities beyond 'natural' ones such as pleasantness to which the

word 'goodness' could be applied.) Indeed, he is bound to say something of this sort if he is to justify his appropriation of the word 'good' for the purpose to which he puts it. And such a man, it seems to me, should be prepared to state his position in an alternative way, namely, as a denial that there *is* such a study as Ethics—he should be prepared, for the sake of clarity, and to further the mental 'liberation' in which he is primarily interested, to call his inquiry into the sources of pleasure, not Ethics, but some such name as 'Hedonics'; or if he defines goodness as 'conduciveness to survival', to call his substitute for Ethics 'Biological Strategy'.

But how—as Mr. E. F. Carritt pertinently asks[9]—can we be 'liberated' from a notion which we cannot ever have had? For how can we have had a 'transcendental' notion of goodness if the word which is alleged to have called it up is also alleged to have no meaning, or none beyond ones which are not 'transcendental' at all? Even this question it is not beyond the power of a consistent naturalist to answer.

'A name', as J. S. Mill points out, 'is not imposed at once and by previous purpose upon a class *of objects, but is first applied to one thing, and then extended by a series of transitions to another. By this process . . . a name not unfrequently passes by successive links of resemblance from one object to another, until it becomes applied to things having nothing in common with the first things to which the name was given; which, however, do not, for that reason, drop the name; so that it at last denotes a confused huddle of objects, having nothing whatever in common; and connotes nothing, not even a vague and general resemblance. When a name has fallen into this state, . . . it has become unfit for the purposes either of thought or of the communication of thought; and can only be made serviceable by stripping it of some part of its multifarious denotation, and confining it*

[9] *Ethical and Political Thinking*, pp. 33–4.

to objects possessed of some attributes in common, which it may be made to connote.'[10]

And this, a naturalist may say, is precisely what has happened with the word 'good', and what needs to be done about it. At present, when we call a thing good we may mean that it is pleasant, or that it is commanded by someone, or that it is customary, or that it promotes survival, or any one of a number of things; and because we use the same term to connote all these characteristics, we think there must be some other single characteristic which they all entail; but in fact there is not. When it is said that being good means promoting survival, we are dissatisfied; we feel that it is still significant to say that promoting survival is good; and the same thing happens with every identification that is suggested; but this is just because, in each case, the other meanings are still hovering in our minds —to say that promoting survival is good is significant because it means that to promote survival is what we desire; to say that what we desire is good is significant because it means that what we desire promotes survival; and so on. Once we realize this, we may either recommend and adopt a more consistent usage; or we may leave the word with its present 'flexibility', but with the misleading suggestions of that flexibility removed. The naturalist who proposes some unambiguous definition is taking the first course.[11]

This way of dealing with words

---

[10] *System of Logic*, I. viii. 7; see also IV. iv. 5, V. 2.

[11] For an answer to Professor Moore along these general lines see a dialogue by E. and M. Clark entitled 'What is Goodness?' in the *Australasian Journal of Psychology and Philosophy*, 1941.

like 'good' is characteristic of the 'therapeutic positivism' developed at Cambridge in the past few decades under the influence of Professor Wittgenstein. While this is unquestionably a useful philosophical technique, there are obvious limits to its applicability. For it is plain that in some cases in which diverse objects are called by a common name there *is* a common characteristic on account of which the name is given to them all. We need some principle enabling us to decide when such a common characteristic exists and when it does not; and what principle we use for this purpose will depend upon our general philosophical position. Analyses of the sort just given cannot therefore replace philosophical inquiry, as 'therapeutic positivists' seem at times to think they can, but both aid it and depend upon it. If we have other reasons for regarding the distinction between the 'natural' and the 'moral' realms as an illusory one, then tricks of language may explain how the illusion has come about; but it may still, as a matter of fact, be real.

It remains true, however, that a naturalist *can* extricate himself from Professor Moore's trap if he is bold enough and tough enough. And in imagining that in his refutation of what he calls the 'naturalistic fallacy' he has refuted naturalism, Professor Moore has himself fallen into a fallacy not unlike it. For if Professor Moore's own non-naturalism is a significant belief, then it must be possible to formulate the naturalism which it contradicts in a significant way; and if naturalism itself, and not merely the inadvertent combination of naturalism with something inconsistent with it, is senseless, then the denial of it is trivial. A significant non-naturalism, in other words, must comprise more than mere freedom from the 'naturalistic fallacy'.

How Are Rules
and Consequences
Related
to Actions?

J ohn Stuart Mill, in his influential *Utilitarianism*, offers a criterion for
deciding which action among various alternatives open to an agent is morally right. This is the familiar "greatest happiness" rule of the English Utilitarians. According to Mill, his criterion is easy to understand and apply and has the
advantage of being a refinement of the one we use in ordinary life; it has the
further advantage of being a single sufficient ultimate criterion—thus free from
the danger of conflicting with some other, equally ultimate criterion. Mill's
defense of this criterion will be considered in another section (*see* "How Can
Ethical Viewpoints Be Evaluated?"). Our present interest is in his statement of
it. Here is Mill's criterion:

*The creed which accepts as the foundation of morals "utility" or the "greatest
happiness principle" holds that actions are right in proportion as they tend to
promote happiness; wrong as they tend to produce the reverse of happiness.
By happiness is intended pleasure and the absence of pain; by unhappiness,
pain and the privation of pleasure.*

There are three things to be noted about this criterion as Mill interprets it. First, it is *hedonistic*: "pleasure and freedom from pain are the only things desirable as ends; and that all desirable things . . . are desirable either for pleasure inherent in themselves or as means to the promotion of pleasure and the prevention of pain." Mill regards the pleasures of the intellect as higher than those of the senses, denying that a pig satisfied is better off than a Socrates unsatisfied. But pleasure alone is good in itself. Second, the criterion is *universal*: the pleasure of all people affected by one's action must be considered, and the pleasure of the majority is determinative in deciding which act is right. In case of conflict between personal and general happiness, general happiness wins out, although it is presumed that generally there will be no very serious conflict. Third, the criterion is teleological; it counts only consequences as relevant in the appraisal of actions. Motives, intentions, purposes, and the like are relevant only to the evaluation of an agent, not an action. Hence an act's *utility* in producing pleasure is the measure of its moral worth. Mill's view, then, is that a *universal hedonistic utilitarianism* provides the one ultimate criterion for the moral appraisal of human action; that on the basis of this criterion alone a morally upright man may chart the course of his conduct.

In a discussion of act-utilitarianism, A. C. Ewing illustrates some of the considerations that have led philosophers who are utilitarians at all to abandon act-utilitarianism in favor of rule-utilitarianism (terms to be explained shortly). As against the apparent simplicity of Mill's view, there is the difficulty of measuring or accurately calculating pleasure and pain.

Suppose, to take a difficult but common case, performing action *A* will bring both pleasure and pain, and the same is true of performing *B*. Suppose further that *A* and *B* are the only actions open to an agent, that only one can be performed, and that in either action the pleasure outweighs the pain. The agent must then ask: Does the pleasure consequent upon performing *A* outweigh the pain consequent upon performing *A* more than the pleasure consequent upon performing *B* outweighs the pain consequent upon performing *B*? Waiving the obvious point that there are no precise scales to be applied to such cases, the reflection involved is difficult at best. For any two mutually exclusive actions whose performance will bring only pleasure (or only pain), it is not always easy to decide which outweighs which in this regard. When both pleasure and pain will result, the decision becomes all the more complicated.

Again, the utilitarian is committed to the thesis that only pleasure is intrinsically good (remember that we are using "utilitarian" as short for "utilitarian *hedonist*"). In order to be at all plausible, this claim must be read so that not only scratching an itch and eating good food but also understanding oneself or aiding another person are pleasures—that is, are valuable ultimately only for the pleasure they bring to oneself or others. Malice (taking pleasure in the sufferings of another) would seem to be evil, and the more pleasurable one finds the misfortune of others, the more evil a person is. (*See also* Ewing's example of the masochist.) But if there are bad pleasures, pleasure cannot be intrinsically good. Pleasure might still be the *only* thing that was good, but even this is doubtful. It is doubtful that the value of self-understanding or aiding another or friendship lies simply in the pleasure derived from them. Again, we *rank* pleasures; we do not rank them on the basis of the simple rule "the more pleasure, the higher the ranking." We rank them *qualitatively*: a little friendship is usually held to be worth a great deal more than the satisfying of a sweet tooth. Mill, in ranking pleasures as qualitatively higher or lower, went beyond the limits of a consistent hedonistic utilitarianism; the test for "qualitatively higher pleasure" cannot itself be a matter of "more pleasure," but is rather a matter of "more *valuable* pleasure" and so presupposes some criterion for value besides pleasantness itself. (This is the point of Ewing's *Brave New World* and "two communities" examples.) Bentham was more consistent when he maintained that *only* amount of pleasure mattered; but his view was correspondingly less plausible. The moral is not that consistency is undesirable but that a consistent utilitarianism is implausible.

But not even Mill's inconsistent introduction of higher-quality pleasures will save his theory. Two considerations make this clear. Suppose that ten men live in isolation (so that we need not consider the effects the behavior of these men will have on other people). Nine men torture the tenth man daily and receive more pleasure than the tenth receives pain (any problem in establishing that they do is reason for doubting the applicability of utilitarian theory). Then among these men, the daily act of torture is permissible (indeed, obligatory). But which is more plausible: that the only relevant consideration in deciding the rightness or wrongness of an action is the pleasure and/or pain it brings or that it is wrong to torture for pleasure even when one's pleasure outweighs the pain suffered by the tortured? There is something bizarre about the view that so long as we assume that the administrators at Auschwitz got a grain more pleasure from their atrocities than their victims received pain from them, their acts were permissible (indeed, obligatory), and that only the shock of outraged men who heard of the atrocities made these acts wrong. But if the administrators were pleased more than the victims were pained, utilitarianism entails their actions were permissible, and a moral theory that has this entailment is rendered implausible at best.

Again, nothing in utilitarian theory requires that pleasure, even if it is the only intrinsic good, be equitably distributed. In weighing the right action, the pleasures of all must be considered. But that all men receive, if possible, more pleasure than pain is *not* considered. If inequitable distribution makes for a greater balance of pleasure over pain, then inequitable distribution is required by utilitarianism. But that equitable distribution is (if it is possible) morally obligatory is at least as plausible as is the claim that only the greatest total happiness counts in considering what action is right. It *might* be that the greatest happiness (that is, the greatest balance of total pleasure over total pain) coincided with equitable distribution, but equally it might not be the case. That the utilitarian is morally indifferent to these considerations is a defect of utilitarianism. It won't do, of course, simply to say "when the balance of pleasure over pain is equal or almost equal—whether there is equitable distribution or not—then let there be equitable distribution of pleasure and pain"; for unless equitable distribution is a good, it is arbitrary to decide this, and if it is a good, then (its goodness not being itself reducible to a state of pleasure or pain) utilitarianism is not by itself adequate as a moral theory.

Perhaps these difficulties can be met by considering, not individual actions but classes of actions. In so doing, we move from *act* to *rule* utilitarianism.

A rule utilitarian can grant that an isolated act (or many acts) of torture or an isolated instance (or many instances) of inequitable pleasure-pain distribution will have utility *considered as isolated cases*. But he will maintain that we cannot consider isolated cases, but must consider the relevant *class* of actions. Over the long haul the class of torturing-for-pleasure actions, or the class of inequitable pleasure-pain distributions, will be seen to have this feature: more of its members will have disutility than will have utility. So to adopt the *practice* of torturing for pleasure, or the *practice* of inequitably distributing pleasure and pain, will be to adopt practices one ought not to adopt. Thus the crucial question concerning moral appraisal of human action is: would everyone adopting the practice of performing this action (in these circumstances) have utility?

This version of utilitarianism is developed by John Rawls. It may well have been intended by Mill himself (*see* the references contained in footnote 2 of Rawls' paper). Rawls claims only to be making a

logical point in that where a form of action is specified by a practice there is no justification possible of a particular action of a particular person save by reference to the practice. In such cases the action is what it is in virtue of the practice and to explain it is to refer to the practice.

Rawls uses this conception of how an action is to be justified to answer objections to utilitarianism in connection with punishment and promise-keeping. This defense, as has been suggested, can be adopted to deal with the objections we have found in Ewing. Rawls' point is that the distinction between "justifying a practice and justifying a particular action falling under it" can be used to strengthen utilitarianism, whether or not this perspective is ultimately defensible.

Andrew Oldenquist, in his provocative "Rules and Consequences," questions the adequacy of a distinction held to be basic in traditional moral disputes concerning the rightness of actions. One either holds that an action is right or wrong as it is commanded or prohibited by a rule (deontological theory) or as it has good or evil consequences (teleological theory). Appeal either to rules or to consequences, not ever to both: this was the way many moral philosophers thought (and think) about the moral evaluation of actions.

The privilege has been claimed, for both rules of action and good or bad consequences, of being the sole or primary ground of an action's rightness. But how are we to separate an action from its consequences with clarity and finality sufficient to support the importance of this distinction?

Oldenquist answers that the act-consequence distinction is not all that clear.

In general, almost any occurrence or set of occurrences, having a conscious human source, may, at the sole cost of stretching certain conventional ways of speaking, be called either as an action or the consequence of an action.

Suppose, for example, we speak of stopping the car quickly as an action and saving a life as an effect. We could equally well speak of pressing the brake pedal as the action and stopping the car and saving the life as effects. Or we could speak of the motion of a foot as action and the other factors mentioned as effects. Oldenquist admits that

When we reach activities that are simple enough . . . We cannot easily redescribe them as ends or goals because we cannot easily think of antecedent actions which would lead to these goals.

Nonetheless, we can sort out events that we take to be morally relevant effects of these simple actions and argue that these actions are obligatory either in terms of consequences or of rules. Thus if *A* is a simple action and *F* the set of all morally relevant effects of *A*, we can say either:

(1) We ought to do *A* because *F* is a consequence of *A* and *F* is good.

(2) We ought to do *A* because there is a rule to the effect that *F*-causing actions should be done.

Even the case of "simple action," then, gives no firm basis for the distinction between evaluating actions in terms of consequences and in terms of rules.

While the idea behind Oldenquist's contention is fundamentally a simple one, it is for that reason all the more powerful. Oldenquist's carefully worked-out challenge to the deontology-teleology distinction is thus a potentially revolutionary thesis; if correct, it reveals the bogus nature of what has been widely accepted as a fundamental distinction in moral philosophy.

Act-Utilitarianism
JOHN STUART MILL

A passing remark is all that needs be given to the ignorant blunder of supposing that those who stand up for utility as the test of right and wrong use the term in that restricted and merely colloquial sense in which utility is opposed to pleasure. An apology is due to the philosophical opponents of utilitarianism for even the momentary appearance of confounding them with anyone capable of so absurd a misconception; which is the more extraordinary, inasmuch as the contrary accusation, of referring everything to pleasure, and that, too, in its grossest form, is another of the common charges against utilitarianism: and, as has been pointedly remarked by an able writer, the same sort of persons, and often the very same persons, denounce the theory 'as impracticably dry when the word "utility" precedes the word "pleasure," and as too practicably voluptuous when the word "pleasure" precedes the word "utility." ' Those who know anything about the matter are aware that every writer, from Epicurus to Bentham, who maintained the theory of utility meant by it, not something to be contradistinguished from pleasure, but pleasure itself, together with exemption from pain; and instead of opposing the useful to the agreeable or the ornamental, have always declared that the useful means these, among other things. Yet the common herd, including the herd of writers, not only in newspapers and periodicals, but in books of weight and pretension, are perpetually falling into

FROM: *Utilitarianism*, John Stuart Mill. Ch. 2 (originally published in 1863).

this shallow mistake. Having caught up the word 'utilitarian,' while knowing nothing whatever about it but its sound, they habitually express by it the rejection or the neglect of pleasure in some of its forms: of beauty, of ornament, or of amusement. Nor is the term thus ignorantly misapplied solely in disparagement, but occasionally in compliment, as though it implied superiority to frivolity and the mere pleasures of the moment. And this perverted use is the only one in which the word is popularly known, and the one from which the new generation are acquiring their sole notion of its meaning. Those who introduced the word, but who had for many years discontinued it as a distinctive appellation, may well feel themselves called upon to resume it if by doing so they can hope to contribute anything toward rescuing it from this utter degradation.[1]

The creed which accepts as the foundation of morals 'utility' or the 'greatest happiness principle' holds that actions · are right in proportion as they tend to promote happiness; wrong as they tend to produce the reverse of happiness. By happiness is intended pleasure and the absence of pain; by unhappiness, pain and the privation of pleasure. To give a clear view of the moral standard set up by the theory, much more requires to be said; in particular, what things it includes in the ideas of pain and pleasure, and to what extent this is left an open question. But these supplementary explanations do not affect the theory of

[1] The author of this essay has reason for believing himself to be the first person who brought the word 'utilitarian' into use. He did not invent it, but adopted it from a passing expression in Mr. Galt's *Annals of the Parish*. After using it as a designation for several years, he and others abandoned it from a growing dislike to anything resembling a badge or watchword of sectarian distinction. But as a name for one single opinion, not a set of opinions—to denote the recognition of utility as a standard, not any particular way of applying it—the term supplies a want in the language, and offers, in many cases, a convenient mode of avoiding tiresome circumlocution.

life on which this theory of morality is grounded—namely, that pleasure and freedom from pain are the only things desirable as ends; and that all desirable things (which are as numerous in the utilitarian as in any other scheme) are desirable either for pleasure inherent in themselves or as means to the promotion of pleasure and the prevention of pain.

Now such a theory of life excites in many minds, and among them in some of the most estimable in feeling and purpose, inveterate dislike. To suppose that life has (as they express it) no higher end than pleasure—no better and nobler object of desire and pursuit—they designate as utterly mean and groveling, as a doctrine worthy only of swine, to whom the followers of Epicurus were, at a very early period, contemptuously likened; and modern holders of the doctrine are occasionally made the subject of equally polite comparisons by its German, French, and English assailants.

When thus attacked, the Epicureans have always answered that it is not they, but their accusers, who represent human nature in a degrading light, since the accusation supposes human beings to be capable of no pleasure except those of which swine are capable. If this supposition were true, the charge could not be gainsaid, but would then be no longer an imputation; for if the sources of pleasure were precisely the same to human beings and to swine, the rule of life which is good enough for the one would be good enough for the other. The comparison of the Epicurean life to that of beasts is felt as degrading, precisely because a beast's pleasures do not satisfy a human being's conceptions of happiness. Human beings have faculties more elevated than the animal appetites and, when once made conscious of them, do not regard anything as happiness which does not include their gratification. I do not, indeed, consider the Epicureans to have been by any means faultless in drawing out their scheme of consequences from the utilitarian principle. To do this in any sufficient manner, many Stoic, as well as Christian, elements require to be included. But there is no known Epicurean theory of life which does not assign to the pleasures of the intellect, of the feelings and imagination, and of the moral sentiments a much higher value as pleasures than to those of mere sensation. It must be admitted, however, that utilitarian writers in general have placed the superiority of mental over bodily pleasures chiefly in the greater permanency, safety, uncostliness, etc., of the former—that is, in their circumstantial advantages rather than in their intrinsic nature. And on all these points utilitarians have fully proved their case; but they might have taken the other and, as it may be called, higher ground with entire consistency. It is quite compatible with the principle of utility to recognize the fact that some kinds of pleasure are more desirable and more valuable than others. It would be absurd that, while in estimating all other things quality is considered as well as quantity, the estimation of pleasure should be supposed to depend on quantity alone.

If I am asked what I mean by difference of quality in pleasures, or what makes one pleasure more valuable than another, merely as a pleasure, except its being greater in amount, there is but one possible answer. Of two pleasures, if there be one to which all or almost all who have experience of both give a decided preference, irrespective of any feeling of moral obligation to prefer it, that is the more desirable pleasure. If one of the two is, by those who are competently acquainted with both, placed so far above the other that they prefer it, even though knowing it to be attended with a greater amount of discontent, and would not resign it for any quantity of the other pleasure which their nature is capable of, we are justified in ascribing to the preferred enjoyment a superiority in quality so far outweighing quantity as to render it, in comparison, of small account.

Now it is an unquestionable fact that those who are equally acquainted with and equally capable of appreciating and enjoying both do give a most marked preference to the manner of existence which employs their higher faculties. Few human creatures would consent to be changed into any of the lower animals for a promise of the fullest allowance of a beast's pleasures; no intelligent human being would consent to be a fool, no instructed person would be an ignoramus, no person of feeling and conscience would be selfish and base, even though they should be persuaded that the fool, the dunce, or the rascal is better satisfied with his lot than they are with theirs. They would not resign what they possess more than he for the most complete satisfaction of all the desires which they have in common with him. If they ever fancy they would, it is only in cases of unhappiness so extreme that to escape from it they would exchange their lot for almost any other, however undesirable in their own eyes. A being of higher faculties requires more to make him happy, is capable probably of more acute suffering, and certainly accessible to it at more points, than one of an inferior type; but in spite of these liabilities, he can never really wish to sink into what he feels to be a lower grade of existence. We may give what explanation we please of this unwillingness; we may attribute it to pride, a name which is given indiscriminately to some of the most and to some of the least estimable feelings of which mankind are capable; we may refer it to the love of liberty and personal independence, an appeal to which was with the Stoics one of the most effective means for the inculcation of it; to the love of power or to the love of excitement, both of which do really enter into and contribute to it; but its most appropriate appellation is a sense of dignity, which all human beings possess in one form or other, and in some, though by no means in exact, proportion to their higher faculties, and which is so essential a part of the happiness of those in whom it is strong that nothing which conflicts with it could be otherwise than momentarily an object of desire to them. Whoever supposes that this preference takes place at a sacrifice of happiness—that the superior being, in anything like equal circumstances, is not happier than the inferior—confounds the two very different ideas of happiness and content. It is indisputable that the being whose capacities of enjoyment are low has the greatest chance of having them fully satisfied; and a highly endowed being will always feel that any happiness which he can look for, as the world is constituted, is imperfect. But he can learn to bear its imperfections, if they are at all bearable; and they will not make him envy the being who is indeed unconscious of the imperfections, but only because he feels not at all the good which those imperfections qualify. It is better to be a human being dissatisfied than a pig satisfied; ·better to be Socrates dissatisfied than a fool satisfied. And if the fool, or the pig, are of a different opinion, it is because they only know their own side of the question. The other party to the comparison knows both sides.

It may be objected that many who are capable of the higher pleasures occasionally, under the influence of temptation, postpone them to the lower. But this is quite compatible with a full appreciation of the intrinsic superiority of the higher. Men often, from infirmity of character, make their election for the nearer good, though they know it to be the less valuable; and this no less when the choice is between two bodily pleasures than when it is between bodily and mental. They pursue sensual indulgences to the injury of health, though perfectly aware that health is the greater good. It may be further objected that many who begin with youthful enthusiasm for everything noble, as they advance in years, sink into indolence and selfishness. But I do not believe that those who undergo this very common change voluntarily choose the lower description of pleasures in preference to the higher. I believe that, before they devote themselves exclusively to the one, they have already become incapable of the other. Capacity for the nobler feelings is in most natures a very tender plant, easily killed, not only by hostile influences, but by mere want of

sustenance; and in the majority of young persons it speedily dies away if the occupations to which their position in life has devoted them, and the society into which it has thrown them, are not favorable to keeping that higher capacity in exercise. Men lose their high aspirations as they lose their intellectual tastes, because they have not time or opportunity for indulging them; and they addict themselves to inferior pleasures, not because they deliberately prefer them, but because they are either the only ones to which they have access or the only ones which they are any longer capable of enjoying. It may be questioned whether anyone who has remained equally susceptible to both classes of pleasures ever knowingly and calmly preferred the lower, though many, in all ages, have broken down in an ineffectual attempt to combine both.

From this verdict of the only competent judges, I apprehend there can be no appeal. On a question which is the best worth having of two pleasures, or which of two modes of existence is the most grateful to the feelings, apart from its moral attributes and from its consequences, the judgment of those who are qualified by knowledge of both, or, if they differ, that of the majority among them, must be admitted as final. And there needs be the less hesitation to accept this judgment respecting the quality of pleasures, since there is no other tribunal to be referred to even on the question of quantity. What means are there of determining which is the acutest of two pains, or the intensest of two pleasurable sensations, except the general suffrage of those who are familiar with both? Neither pains nor pleasures are homogeneous, and pain is always heterogeneous with pleasure. What is there to decide whether a particular pleasure is worth purchasing at the cost of a particular pain, except the feelings and judgment of the experience? When, therefore, those feelings and judgment declare the pleasures derived from the higher faculties to be preferable *in kind*, apart from the question of intensity, to those of which the animal nature, disjoined from the higher faculties, is susceptible, they are entitled on this subject to the same regard.

I have dwelt on this point as being a necessary part of a perfectly just conception of utility or happiness considered as the directive rule of human conduct. But it is by no means an indispensable condition to the acceptance of the utilitarian standard; for that standard is not the agent's own greatest happiness, but the greatest amount of happiness altogether; and if it may possibly be doubted whether a noble character is always the happier for its nobleness, there can be no doubt that it makes other people happier, and that the world in general is immensely a gainer by it. Utilitarianism, therefore, could only attain its end by the general cultivation of nobleness of character, even if each individual were only benefited by the nobleness of others, and his own, so far as happiness is concerned, were a sheer deduction from the benefit. But the bare enunciation of such an absurdity as this last renders refutation superfluous.

According to the greatest happiness principle, as above explained, the ultimate end, with reference to and for the sake of which all other things are desirable—whether we are considering our own good or that of other people— is an existence exempt as far as possible from pain, and as rich as possible in enjoyments, both in point of quantity and quality; the test of quality and the rule for measuring it against quantity being the preference felt by those who, in their opportunities of experience, to which must be added their habits of self-consciousness and self-observation, are best furnished with the means of comparison. This, being according to the utilitarian opinion the end of human action, is necessarily also the standard of morality, which may accordingly be defined 'the rules and precepts for human conduct,' by the observance of which an existence such as has been described might be, to the greatest extent possible, secured to all mankind; and not to them only, but, so far as the nature of things admits, to the whole sentient creation.

Against this doctrine, however, arises another class of objectors who say that happiness, in any form, cannot be the rational purpose of human life and action; because, in the first place, it is unattainable; and they contemptuously ask, What right hast thou to be happy? —a question which Mr. Carlyle clinches by the addition, What right, a short time ago, hadst thou even *to be?* Next they say that men can do *without* happiness; that all noble human beings have felt this, and could not have become noble but by learning the lesson of *Entsagen*, or renunciation; which lesson, thoroughly learned and submitted to, they affirm to be the beginning and necessary condition of all virtue.

The first of these objections would go to the root of the matter were it well founded; for if no happiness is to be had at all by human beings, the attainment of it cannot be the end of morality or of any rational conduct. Though, even in that case, something might still be said for the utilitarian theory, since utility includes not solely the pursuit of happiness, but the prevention or mitigation of unhappiness; and if the former aim be chimerical, there will be all the greater scope and more imperative need for the latter, so long at least as mankind think fit to live and do not take refuge in the simultaneous act of suicide recommended under certain conditions by Novalis. When, however, it is thus positively asserted to be impossible that human life should be happy, the assertion, if not something like a verbal quibble, is at least an exaggeration. If by happiness be meant a continuity of highly pleasurable excitement, it is evident enough that this is impossible. A state of exalted pleasure lasts only moments or in some cases, and with some intermissions, hours or days, and is the occasional brilliant flash of enjoyment, not its permanent and steady flame. Of this the philosophers who have taught that happiness is the end of life were as fully aware as those who taught them. The happiness which they meant was not a life of rapture, but moments of such, in an existence made up of few and transitory pains, many and various pleasures, with a decided predominance of the active over the passive, and having as the foundation of the whole not to expect more from life than it is capable of bestowing. A life thus composed, to those who have been fortunate enough to obtain it, has always appeared worthy of the name of happiness. And such an existence is even now the lot of many during some considerable portion of their lives. The present wretched education and wretched social arrangements are the only real hindrance to its being attainable by almost all.

The objectors perhaps may doubt whether human beings, if taught to consider happiness as the end of life, would be satisfied with such a moderate share of it. But great numbers of mankind have been satisfied with much less. The main constituents of a satisfied life appear to be two, either of which by itself is often found sufficient for the purpose: tranquillity and excitement. With much tranquillity, many find that they can be content with very little pleasure; with much excitement, many can reconcile themselves to a considerable quantity of pain. There is assuredly no inherent impossibility of enabling even the mass of mankind to unite both, since the two are so far from being incompatible that they are in natural alliance, the prolongation of either being a preparation for, and exciting a wish for, the other. It is only those in whom indolence amounts to a vice that do not desire excitement after an interval of repose; it is only those in whom the need of excitement is a disease that feel the tranquillity which follows excitement dull and insipid, instead of pleasurable in direct proportion to the excitement which preceded it. When people who are tolerably fortunate in their outward lot do not find in life sufficient enjoyment to make it valuable to them, the cause generally is caring for nobody but themselves. To those who have neither public nor private affections, the excitements of life are much curtailed, and in any case dwindle in value as the time approaches when all selfish interests must be terminated by death; while those who leave after them objects of personal affection, and especially those who have also cultivated a fellow-feeling with the collective interests of mankind, retain as lively an interest in life on the eve of death as in the vigor of youth and health. Next to selfishness, the principal cause which makes life unsatisfactory is want of mental cultivation. A cultivated mind—I do not mean that of a philosopher, but any mind to which the fountains of knowledge have been opened, and which has been taught, in any tolerable degree, to exercise its faculties—finds sources of inexhaustible interest in all that surrounds it: in the objects of nature, the achievements of art, the imaginations of poetry, the incidents of history, the ways of mankind, past and present, and their prospects in the future. It is possible, indeed, to become indifferent to all this, and that too without having exhausted a thousandth part of it, but only when one has had from the beginning no moral or human interest in these things and has sought in them only the gratification of curiosity.

Now there is absolutely no reason in the nature of things why an amount of mental culture sufficient to give an intelligent interest in these objects of contemplation should not be the inheritance of everyone born in a civilized country. As little is there an inherent necessity that any human being should be a selfish egotist, devoid of every feeling or care but those which center in his own miserable individuality. Something far superior to this is sufficiently common even now, to give ample earnest of what the human species may be made. Genuine private affections and a sincere interest in the public good are possible, though in unequal degrees, to every rightly brought up human being. In a world in which there is so much to interest, so much to enjoy, and so much also to correct and improve, everyone who has this moderate amount of moral and intellectual requisites is capable of an existence which may be called enviable; and unless such a person, through bad laws or subjection to the will of others, is denied the liberty to use the sources of happiness within his reach, he will not fail to find this enviable existence, if he escape the positive evils of life, the great sources of physical and mental suffering—such as indigence, disease, and the unkindness, worthlessness, or premature loss of objects of affection. The main stress of the problem lies, therefore, in the contest with these calamities from which it is a rare good fortune entirely to escape; which, as things now are, cannot be obviated, and often cannot be in any material degree mitigated. Yet no one whose opinion deserves a moment's consideration can doubt that most of the great positive evils of the world are in themselves removable, and will, if human affairs continue to improve, be in the end reduced within narrow limits. Poverty, in any sense implying suffering, may be completely extinguished by the wisdom of society combined with the good sense and providence of individuals. Even that most intractable of enemies, disease, may be indefinitely reduced in dimensions by good physical and moral education and proper control of noxious influences, while the progress of science holds out a promise for the future of still more direct conquests over this detestable foe. And every advance in that direction relieves us from some, not only of the chances which cut short our own lives, but, what concerns us still more, which deprive us of those in whom our happiness is wrapt up. As for vicissitudes of fortune and other disappointments connected with worldly circumstances, these are principally the effect either of gross imprudence, of ill-regulated desires, or of bad or imperfect social institutions. All the grand sources, in short, of human suffering are in a great degree, many of them almost entirely, conquerable by human care and effort; and though their removal is grievously slow—though a long succession of generations will perish in the breach before the conquest is completed, and this world becomes all that,

if will and knowledge were not wanting, it might easily be made—yet every mind sufficiently intelligent and generous to bear a part, however small and inconspicuous, in the endeavor will draw a noble enjoyment from the contest itself, which he would not for any bribe in the form of selfish indulgence consent to be without.

And this leads to the true estimation of what is said by the objectors concerning the possibility and the obligation of learning to do without happiness. Unquestionably it is possible to do without happiness; it is done involuntarily by nineteen-twentieths of mankind, even in those parts of our present world which are least deep in barbarism; and it often has to be done voluntarily by the hero or the martyr, for the sake of something which he prizes more than his individual happiness. But this something, what is it, unless the happiness of others or some of the requisites of happiness? It is noble to be capable of resigning entirely one's own portion of happiness, or chances of it; but, after all, this self-sacrifice must be for some end; it is not its own end; and if we are told that its end is not happiness but virtue, which is better than happiness, I ask, would the sacrifice be made if the hero or martyr did not believe that it would earn for others immunity from similar sacrifices? Would it be made if he thought that his renunciation of happiness for himself would produce no fruit for any of his fellow creatures, but to make their lot like his and place them also in the condition of persons who have renounced happiness? All honor to those who can abnegate for themselves the personal enjoyment of life when by such renunciation they contribute worthily to increase the amount of happiness in the world; but he who does it or professes to do it for any other purpose is no more deserving of admiration than the ascetic mounted on his pillar. He may be an inspiring proof of what men *can* do, but assuredly not an example of what they *should*.

Though it is only in a very imperfect state of the world's arrangements that anyone can best serve the happiness of others by the absolute sacrifice of his own, yet, so long as the world is in that imperfect state, I fully acknowledge that the readiness to make such a sacrifice is the highest virtue which can be found in man. I will add that in this condition of the world, paradoxical as the assertion may be, the conscious ability to do without happiness gives the best prospect of realizing such happiness as is attainable. For nothing except that consciousness can raise a person above the chances of life by making him feel that, let fate and fortune do their worst, they have not power to subdue him; which, once felt, frees him from excess of anxiety concerning the evils of life and enables him, like many a Stoic in the worst times of the Roman Empire, to cultivate in tranquillity the sources of satisfaction accessible to him, without concerning himself about the uncertainty of their duration any more than about their inevitable end.

Meanwhile, let utilitarians never cease to claim the morality of self-devotion as a possession which belongs by as good a right to them as either to the Stoic or to the Transcendentalist. The utilitarian morality does recognize in human beings the power of sacrificing their own greatest good for the good of others. It only refuses to admit that the sacrifice is itself a good. A sacrifice which does not increase or tend to increase the sum total of happiness, it considers as wasted. The only self-renunciation which it applauds is devotion to the happiness, or to some of the means of happiness, of others, either of mankind collectively or of individuals within the limits imposed by the collective interests of mankind.

I must again repeat what the assailants of utilitarianism seldom have the justice to acknowledge, that the happiness which forms the utilitarian standard of what is right in conduct is not the agent's own happiness but that of all concerned. As between his own happiness and that of others, utilitarianism requires him to be as strictly impartial as a disinterested and benevolent spectator. In the golden rule of Jesus of Nazareth, we read the complete spirit of the ethics of utility. 'To do as you would be done by,' and 'to love your neighbor as yourself,' constitute the ideal perfection of utilitarian morality. As the means of making the nearest approach to this ideal, utility would enjoin, first, that laws and social arrangements should place the happiness or (as, speaking practically, it may be called) the interest of every individual as nearly as possible in harmony with the interest of the whole; and secondly, that education and opinion, which have so vast a power over human character, should so use that power as to establish in the mind of every individual an indissoluble association between his own happiness and the good of the whole, especially between his own happiness and the practice of such modes of conduct, negative and positive, as regard for the universal happiness prescribes; so that not only he may be unable to conceive the possibility of happiness to himself, consistently with conduct opposed to the general good, but also that a direct impulse to promote the general good may be in every individual one of the habitual motives of action, and the sentiments connected therewith may fill a large and prominent place in every human being's sentient existence. If the impugners of the utilitarian morality represented it to their own minds in this its true character, I know not what recommendation possessed by any other morality they could possibly affirm to be wanting to it; what more beautiful or more exalted developments of human nature any other ethical system can be supposed to foster, or what springs of action, not accessible to the utilitarian, such systems rely on for giving effect to their mandates.

The objectors to utilitarianism cannot always be charged with representing it in a discreditable light. On the contrary, those among them who entertain anything like a just idea of its disinterested character sometimes find fault with its standard as being too high for humanity. They say it is exacting too much to require that people shall always act from the inducement of promoting the general interests of society. But this is to mistake the very meaning of a standard of morals and confound the rule of action with the motive of it. It is the business of ethics to tell us what are our duties, or by what test we may know them; but no system of ethics requires that the sole motive of all we do shall be a feeling of duty; on the contrary, ninety-nine hundredths of all our actions are done from other motives, and rightly so done if the rule of duty does not condemn them. It is the more unjust to utilitarianism that this particular misapprehension should be made a ground of objection to it, inasmuch as utilitarian moralists have gone beyond almost all others in affirming that the motive has nothing to do with the morality of the action, though much with the worth of the agent. He who saves a fellow creature from drowning does what is morally right, whether his motive be duty or the hope of being paid for his trouble; he who betrays the friend that trusts him is guilty of a crime, even if his object be to serve another friend to whom he is under greater obligations. But to speak only of actions done from the motive of duty, and in direct obedience to principle: it is a misapprehension of the utilitarian mode of thought to conceive it as implying that people should fix their minds upon so wide a generality as the world, or society at large. The great majority of good actions are intended not for the benefit of the world, but for that of individuals, of which the good of the world is made up; and the thoughts of the most virtuous man need not on these occasions travel beyond the particular persons concerned, except so far as is necessary to assure himself that in benefiting them he is not violating the rights, that is, the legitimate and authorized expectations, of anyone else. The multiplication of happiness is, according to the utilitarian ethics, the object of virtue: the occasions on which any person (except one in a thousand) has it in his power to do this on an extended scale—in other

words, to be a public benefactor—are but exceptional; and on these occasions alone is he called on to consider public utility; in every other case, private utility, the interest or happiness of some few persons, is all he has to attend to. Those alone the influence of whose actions extends to society in general need concern themselves habitually about so large an object. In the case of abstinences indeed —of things which people forbear to do from moral considerations, though the consequences in the particular case might be beneficial—it would be unworthy of an intelligent agent not to be consciously aware that the action is of a class which, if practiced generally, would be generally injurious, and that this is the ground of the obligation to abstain from it. The amount of regard for the public interest implied in this recognition is no greater than is demanded by every system of morals, for they all enjoin to abstain from whatever is manifestly pernicious to society.

The same considerations dispose of another reproach against the doctrine of utility, founded on a still grosser misconception of the purpose of a standard of morality and of the very meaning of the words 'right' and 'wrong.' It is often affirmed that utilitarianism renders men cold and unsympathizing; that it chills their moral feelings toward individuals; that it makes them regard only the dry and hard consideration of the consequences of actions, not taking into their moral estimate the qualities from which those actions emanate. If the assertion means that they do not allow their judgment respecting the rightness or wrongness of an action to be influenced by their opinion of the qualities of the person who does it, this is a complaint not against utilitarianism, but against any standard of morality at all; for certainly no known ethical standard decides an action to be good or bad because it is done by a good or a bad man, still less because done by an amiable, a brave, or a benevolent man, or the contrary. These considerations are relevant, not to the estimation of actions, but of persons;

and there is nothing in the utilitarian theory inconsistent with the fact that there are other things which interest us in persons besides the rightness and wrongness of their actions. The Stoics, indeed, with the paradoxical misuse of language which was part of their system, and by which they strove to raise themselves above all concern about anything but virtue, were fond of saying that he who has that has everything; that he, and only he, is rich, is beautiful, is a king. But no claim of this description is made for the virtuous man by the utilitarian doctrine. Utilitarians are quite aware that there are other desirable possessions and qualities besides virtue, and are perfectly willing to allow to all of them their full worth. They are also aware that a right action does not necessarily indicate a virtuous character, and that actions which are blamable often proceed from qualities entitled to praise. When this is apparent in any particular case, it modifies their estimation, not certainly of the act, but of the agent. I grant that they are, notwithstanding, of opinion that in the long run the best proof of a good character is good actions; and resolutely refuse to consider any mental disposition as good of which the predominant tendency is to produce bad conduct. This makes them unpopular with many people, but it is an unpopularity which they must share with everyone who regards the distinction between right and wrong in a serious light; and the reproach is not one which a conscientious utilitarian need be anxious to repel.

If no more be meant by the objection than that many utilitarians look on the morality of actions, as measured by the utilitarian standards, with too exclusive a regard, and do not lay sufficient stress upon the other beauties of character which go toward making a human being lovable or admirable, this may be admitted. Utilitarians who have cultivated their moral feelings, but not their sympathies, nor their artistic perceptions, do fall into this mistake; and so do all other moralists under the same conditions. What can be said in excuse for other moralists is equally available for them, namely, that, if there is to be any error, it is better that it should be on that side. As a matter of fact, we may affirm that among utilitarians, as among adherents of other systems, there is every imaginable degree of rigidity and of laxity in the application of their standard; some are even puritanically rigorous, while others are as indulgent as can possibly be desired by sinner or by sentimentalist. But on the whole, a doctrine which brings prominently forward the interest that mankind have in the repression and prevention of conduct which violates the moral law is likely to be inferior to no other in turning the sanctions of opinion against such violations. It is true, the question 'What does violate the moral law?' is one on which those who recognize different standards of morality are likely now and then to differ. But difference of opinion on moral questions was not first introduced into the world by utilitarianism, while that doctrine does supply, if not always an easy, at all events a tangible and intelligible, mode of deciding such differences.

It may not be superfluous to notice a few more of the common misapprehensions of utilitarian ethics, even those which are so obvious and gross that it might appear impossible for any person of candor and intelligence to fall into them; since persons, even of considerable mental endowment, often give themselves so little trouble to understand the bearings of any opinion against which they entertain a prejudice, and men are in general so little conscious of this voluntary ignorance as a defect that the vulgarest misunderstandings of ethical doctrines are continually met with in the deliberate writings of persons of the greatest pretensions both to high principle and to philosophy. We not uncommonly hear the doctrine of utility inveighed against as *godless* doctrine. If it be necessary to say anything at all against so mere an assumption, we may say that the question depends upon what idea we have formed of the moral character of the Deity. If it be a true belief that God desires, above all things, the happiness of his creatures, and that this was his purpose in their creation, utility is not only not a godless doctrine, but more profoundly religious than any other. If it be meant that utilitarianism does not recognize the revealed will of God as the supreme law of morals, I answer that a utilitarian who believes in the perfect goodness and wisdom of *God* necessarily believes that whatever God has thought fit to reveal on the subject of morals must fulfill the requirements of utility in a supreme degree. But others besides utilitarians have been of opinion that the Christian revelation was intended, and is fitted, to inform the hearts and minds of mankind with a spirit which should enable them to find for themselves what is right, and incline them to do it when found rather than to tell them except in a very general way, what it is; and that we need a doctrine of ethics, carefully followed out, to *interpret* to us the will of God. Whether this opinion is correct or not, it is superfluous here to discuss; since whatever aid religion, either natural or revealed, can afford to ethical investigation is as open to the utilitarian moralist as to any other. He can use it as the testimony of God to the usefulness or hurtfulness of any given course of action by as good a right as others can use it for the indication of a transcendental law having no connection with usefulness or with happiness.

Again, utility is often summarily stigmatized as an immoral doctrine by giving it the name of 'expediency,' and taking advantage of the popular use of that term to contrast it with principle. But the expedient, in the sense in which it is opposed to the right, generally means that which is expedient for the particular interest of the agent himself; as when a minister sacrifices the interests of his country to keep himself in place. When it means anything better than this, it means that which is expedient for some immediate object, some temporary purpose, but which violates a rule whose observance is expedient in a much higher degree. The expedient, in this sense, instead of being the same thing with the useful, is a branch of the hurtful. Thus it would often be expedient, for the purpose of getting over some momentary embarrassment, or attaining some object immediately useful to ourselves or others, to tell a lie. But inasmuch as the cultivation in ourselves of a sensitive feeling on the subject of veracity is one of the most useful, and the enfeeblement of that feeling one of the most hurtful, things to which our conduct can be instrumental; and inasmuch as any, even unintentional, deviation from truth does that much toward weakening the trustworthiness of human assertion, which is not only the principal support of all present social well-being, but the insufficiency of which does more than any one thing that can be named to keep back civilization, virtue, everything on which human happiness on the largest scale depends—we feel that the violation, for a present advantage, of a rule of such transcendent expediency is not expedient, and that he who, for the sake of convenience to himself or to some other individual, does what depends on him to deprive mankind of the good, and inflict upon them the evil, involved in the greater or less reliance which they can place in each other's word, acts the part of one of their worst enemies. Yet that even this rule, sacred as it is, admits of possible exceptions is acknowledged by all moralists; the chief of which is when the withholding of some fact (as of information from a malefactor, or of bad news from a person dangerously ill) would save an individual (especially an individual other than oneself) from great and unmerited evil, and when the withholding can only be effected by denial. But in order that the exception may not extend itself beyond the need, and may have the least possible effect in weakening reliance on veracity, it ought to be recognized, and, if possible, its limits defined; and, if the principle of utility is good for anything, it must be good for weighing these conflicting utilities against one another and marking out the region within which one or the other preponderates.

Again, defenders of utility often find themselves called upon to reply to such objections as this—that there is not time, previous to action, for calculating and weighing the effects of any line of conduct on the general happiness. This is exactly as if anyone were to say that it is impossible to guide our conduct by Christianity because there is not time, on every occasion on which anything has to be done, to read through the Old and New Testaments. The answer to the objection is that there has been ample time, namely, the whole past duration of the human species. During all that time mankind have been learning by experience the tendencies of actions; on which experience all the prudence as well as all the morality of life are dependent. People talk as if the commencement of this course of experience had hitherto been put off, and as if, at the moment when some man feels tempted to meddle with the property or life of another, he had to begin considering for the first time whether murder and theft are injurious to human happiness. Even then I do not think he would find the question very puzzling; but, at all events, the matter is now done to his hand. It is truly a whimsical supposition that, if mankind were agreed in considering utility to be the test of morality, they would remain without any agreement as to what *is* useful, and would take no measures for having their notions on the subject taught to the young and enforced by law and opinion. There is no difficulty in proving any ethical standard whatever to work ill if we suppose universal idiocy to be conjoined with it; but on any hypothesis short of that, mankind must by this time have acquired positive beliefs as to the effects of some actions on their happiness; and the beliefs which have thus come down are the rules of morality for the multitude, and for the philosopher until he has succeeded in finding better. That philosophers might easily do this, even now, on many subjects; that the received code of ethics is by no means of divine right; and that mankind have still much to learn as to the effects of

actions on the general happiness, I admit or rather earnestly maintain. The corollaries from the principle of utility, like the precepts of every practical art, admit of indefinite improvement, and, in a progressive state of the human mind, their improvement is perpetually going on. But to consider the rules of morality as improvable is one thing; to pass over the intermediate generalization entirely and endeavor to test each individual action directly by the first principle is another. It is a strange notion that the acknowledgement of a first principle is inconsistent with the admission of secondary ones. To inform a traveler respecting the place of his ultimate destination is not to forbid the use of landmarks and direction-posts on the way. The proposition that happiness is the end and aim of morality does not mean that no road ought to be laid down to that goal, or that persons going thither should not be advised to take one direction rather than another. Men really ought to leave off talking a kind of nonsense on this subject, which they would neither talk nor listen to on other matters of practical concernment. Nobody argues that the art of navigation is not founded on astronomy because sailors cannot wait to calculate the Nautical Almanac. Being rational creatures, they go to sea with it ready calculated; and all rational creatures go out upon the sea of life with their minds made up on the common questions of right and wrong, as well as on many of the far more difficult questions of wise and foolish. And this, as long as foresight is a human quality, it is to be presumed they will continue to do. Whatever we adopt as the fundamental principle of morality, we require subordinate principles to apply it by; the impossibility of doing without them, being common to all systems, can afford no argument against any one in particular; but gravely to argue as if no such secondary principles could be had, and as if mankind had remained till now, and always must remain, without drawing any general conclusions from the experience of human life is as high a pitch, I think, as absurdity has ever reached in philosophical controversy.

The remainder of the stock arguments against utilitarianism mostly consist in laying to its charge the common infirmities of human nature, and the general difficulties which embarrass conscientious persons in shaping their course through life. We are told that a utilitarian will be apt to make his own particular case an exception to moral rules, and, when under temptation, will see a utility in the breach of a rule, greater than he will see in its observance. But is utility the only creed which is able to furnish us with excuses for evil-doing and means of cheating our own conscience? They are afforded in abundance by all doctrines which recognize as a fact in morals the existence of conflicting considerations, which all doctrines do that have been believed by sane persons. It is not the fault of any creed, but of the complicated nature of human affairs, that rules of conduct cannot be so framed as to require no exceptions, and that hardly any kind of action can safely be laid down as either always obligatory or always condemnable. There is no ethical creed which does not temper the rigidity of its laws by giving a certain latitude, under the moral responsibility of the agent, for accommodation to peculiarities of circumstances; and under every creed, at the opening thus made, self-deception and dishonest casuistry get in. There exists no moral system under which there do not arise unequivocal cases of con-

flicting obligation. These are the real difficulties, the knotty points both in the theory of ethics and in the conscientious guidance of personal conduct. They are overcome practically, with greater or with less success, according to the intellect and virtue of the individual; but it can hardly be pretended that anyone will be the less qualified for dealing with them, from possessing an ultimate standard to which conflicting rights and duties can be referred. If utility is the ultimate source of moral obligations, utility may be invoked to decide between them when their demands are incompatible. Though the application of the standard may be difficult, it is better than none at all; while in other systems, the moral laws all claiming independent authority, there is no common umpire entitled to interfere between them; their claims to precedence one over another rest on little better than sophistry, and, unless determined, as they generally are, by the unacknowledged influence of consideration of utility, afford a free scope for the action of personal desires and partialities. We must remember that only in these cases of conflict between secondary principles is it requisite that first principles should be appealed to. There is no case of moral obligation in which some secondary principle is not involved; and if only one, there can seldom be any real doubt which one it is, in the mind of any person by whom the principle itself is recognized.

A Critique of Act-Utilitarianism
ARTHUR C. EWING

*I*f *pleasure or* happiness is the only thing good-in-itself—and it is certainly the only thing about the *intrinsic* goodness of which there is anything like universal agreement—it seems irrational to hold that it makes any difference to its goodness who enjoys the happiness. And it seems reasonable to hold that it is

FROM: *Teach Yourself Ethics*, Arthur C. Ewing. (London: The English Universities Press, Ltd., 1953), pp. 35–50. Reprinted by permission of The English Universities Press, Ltd., and Dover Publications.

our duty to produce as much good as possible and that it is wrong to neglect any opportunities to do so. From these assumptions we get a form of hedonism which differs from the egoistic form and seems to approach much more closely to what we ordinarily believe about ethical matters. The theory is most commonly known by the name of *Utilitarianism*. It is also sometimes called *Universalistic Hedonism,* "universalistic" because it considers everybody's good, and "hedonism" because it holds pleasure to be the only good. It maintains that our sole duty is to produce as much pleasure as possible, counting for this purpose a diminution of pain as equivalent to an increase in pleasure, and holds that in doing so we should count every man's pleasure as of equal worth to that of any other man. (It makes no distinction, any more than does egoistic hedonism, between happiness and pleasure, happiness being regarded as prolonged pleasure.) It thus agrees with egoistic hedonism as to what is good, but not as to what are the ultimate principles of ethical action. Both theories hold that pleasure is the only good, but while egoistic hedonism thinks we are under no obligation to further the happiness of anybody else except as a means to our own, the theory I am now going to discuss maintains that we are under a direct obligation to pursue happiness as such, to whomever the happiness belongs. The theory is now held by very few moral philosophers, but it was extremely important in the nineteenth and in a less fully thought-out form in the eighteenth century, and is no doubt approximately the working theory of vast numbers of people to-day in so far as they can be said to have an ethical theory at all. Its most important exponents in this country were John Stuart Mill[1] and Sidgwick.[2]

Now it is quite obvious that the amount of happiness or pain produced by our actions should be at least one of the chief criteria for deciding which actions

[1] *Utilitarianism* (1863).

[2] *The Methods of Ethics* (1874).

we ought to perform. There are vast numbers of actions which are wrong for no other reason than that they tend to produce pain or unhappiness in other people, and if it can be shown that an act will lead to suffering, this is, usually at least, quite a sufficient reason why we ought not to perform it. Further, a utilitarian can deal with most of the relatively rare cases where it is right to inflict pain by contending that the infliction of pain now is necessary to avoid greater pain in the future or as a means to gain in happiness which is worth the cost. We must remember, as with egoistic hedonism, that under "pleasure" are meant to be comprised all satisfactions and joys and not only the relatively "lower" ones to which the term pleasure is most commonly applied in ordinary speech. We must further realize that the utilitarian is not bound to suppose that in practice we ought always to settle what we are to do by a direct calculation of the amount of pleasure likely to be produced. He usually insists on the contrary that there are certain rules of behaviour such as those against lying and stealing whose violation human experience has adequately shown to be productive of unhappiness, and that in consequence we do not need to calculate afresh each time the amount of happiness or unhappiness likely to be produced before deciding to obey one of these laws. The ultimate ground for their validity lies in the general happiness, but we need not go back to this ultimate ground each time, any more than we need before applying an established mathematical law go back each time to the axioms on which it is based. Nor can utilitarianism possibly be dismissed as selfish, for it bids us treat the happiness or pain of any other man as no less important than our own. And utilitarianism has the great attraction of being a relatively simple theory and one in close relation to verifiable empirical facts. For an Ethics which admits only one good will obviously be simpler to apply than one which admits several that may on occasion conflict, and pleasure and pain are after all feelings the occurrence of which we can easily verify in a straightforward empirical way. All this does not however prove it to be the true theory.

As compared to common-sense morality a consistent utilitarianism would be in some respects stricter and in others less strict. Ordinarily we consider that we are much more under an obligation to some people than to others. We admit indeed that we are under some obligation to help anyone in need, but we feel a very much stronger obligation to promote the happiness of our own family, as is shown by the general attitude to appeals for charity. It is clear that the money spent by a man in order to provide his son with a university education could save the lives of many people who were perishing of hunger in a famine, yet most people would rather blame than praise a man who should deprive his son of a university education on this account. Further, while the obligation to contribute something to charity if one can afford it is generally recognized, only a very small minority of people have felt it their duty to curtail their comforts and luxuries very seriously on that account, and still less the comforts and luxuries of those dependent on them. Yet there can hardly be any doubt that, even if we allow for any indirect evil effects which might accrue, in most cases money given to any even tolerably well managed charity will do much more good by relieving the suffering of those in distress than would be done by using the same money to increase the pleasure of a person who is at all tolerably comfortable by enabling him to have a more pleasant house, better furniture, more tobacco, more holiday travel, etc. This does not, however, straightway prove the utilitarian wrong. He may reply that all but the very poor ought to give much more money to charity than on the average they do, and in view of the very small proportion of the national income that is spent on this and the vast amount of suffering in the world which calls for help, it seems to me plain that he is so far right. But, even if we grant this, it still seems plain

to me, and I am sure would seem so to almost everybody else that, if a man were to deprive his wife and children against their will of all comforts and purchasable pleasures, leaving them only bare necessaries, on the ground that he could use the money thus saved to preserve several families from a greater pain or loss of happiness than he inflicted on his own by giving it to a charitable organization he would be acting wrongly not rightly. Again, suppose he obtained the money to give to the charity by stealing it from a man very much richer than himself. He might argue that the victim of his theft would lose little in happiness by being a few pounds worse off, while the people to whom he gave the money would be saved from great misery. Even if he kept the money himself, he might indeed argue that, being much poorer,[3] he would gain more in happiness from it than the other man lost. These reflections seem to disclose a sharp conflict between utilitarianism and even enlightened common-sense morality. According to the former there is an equal obligation to further the happiness of everybody, according to the latter we have special obligations to some people much stronger than those we have to others; according to the former what produces most happiness is always right, according to the latter it is wrong to produce happiness by stealing and lying.

The utilitarian however will contend that the conflict is not a real but only an apparent one. He will argue that, if we take a more far-sighted view, we can see that greater happiness is produced by recognizing and insisting on special obligations. Family life is a great source of happiness, and family life as we know it would be impossible if we did not look on ourselves as having much

---

[3] Note that I am referring to theft by a man who is comparatively poor, not by one who is starving, still less one whose family is starving. I am not prepared to say that it is wrong for such people to steal in a community where there are no other means such as poor relief available to save them from their desperate condition.

stronger obligations to members of our family than to perfect strangers. And, if we admitted the principle that the poor were ethically entitled to steal from the rich, the result would be a social confusion which would be far worse than the present system. But it seems to me that what the utilitarian has done here is to point out that a whole class of acts or system of recognized obligations produces good results in the way of happiness, not that each particular act does so. We may admit that it would be a bad thing if the poorer generally and indiscriminately tried to steal from the richer, but does it necessarily follow from this that to do so in any one instance is wrong? A poor man who is prepared to cheat a richer may say—It would be a bad thing if everybody acted like me, but why should not I do so, when it is certain that my action will not result in everybody acting like me? It seems only possible to answer such a question adequately if we say that it is *unfair* to profit by the rules governing society and yet refuse yourself to obey them. But if we appeal to fairness, we are introducing another consideration besides happiness. It may therefore be doubted whether we can give an adequate account of our obligations without abandoning utilitarianism and admitting that there are other obligations which we should not ignore even in order to produce greater happiness and that it is bad to acquire happiness by unfair means whether for ourselves or others. It is indeed difficult to maintain that it cannot under any circumstances be right to lie, etc., on utilitarian grounds, e.g. to save life, but it seems to me pretty clear that utilitarian principles, logically carried out, would result in far more cheating, lying and unfair action than any good man would tolerate. This is not of course the same thing as saying that utilitarians are more likely to cheat and lie than other people, but only that if they carried out their theory consistently they would be so.

We may add that utilitarianism is far from being so simple a theory to apply as has been claimed by its advocates.

How are we going to measure against each other quite different kinds of pleasure and say how many times more pleasure seeing *Hamlet* will give a particular man than will a good dinner? And it becomes still more complicated when we introduce different agents who cannot be expected all to take the same amount of enjoyment in the same pleasures. Yet such calculations are necessary if we are to apply the utilitarian criterion consistently to all practical questions. Similar difficulties will no doubt arise with any ethical theory that takes account of consequences, as we surely must, but at least this shows that utilitarianism has less cause than might be thought to pride itself on its simplicity. It is about as difficult to estimate the relative pleasantness of different pleasures as it would be on a non-hedonistic view to estimate their relative goodness.

It is however very hard to give any conclusive disproof of utilitarianism by considering the kind of actions to which it would logically lead. For suppose I argue that utilitarianism is a mistaken theory because, if carried out consistently, it would require me in a given situation to do something which is wrong. Now in any actual instance of a kind that could provide a ground for dispute the effects will be very complicated and uncertain, so that will always leave a loophole for the utilitarian to argue that I am wrong in my views as to their bearing on general happiness and that the act which seems right to common sense is really after all on a long view that most productive of happiness. And even if there are some instances where this is very unplausible (as indeed I think there are), he may reply by amending common-sense ethics here and saying that the act we ordinarily think right in this case is not really so. We are not bound to and indeed cannot accept the common sense view (where there is one) about every action. The utilitarian view could only be shaken by a very considerable series of such instances. As I have suggested already, I think that it can be shaken by citing a series of instances of cheating and lying where what a good man could not help regarding as a "dirty trick" seemed to add to the general happiness, but it is easier to attack utilitarianism by considering its bearing not on the question what we ought to do but rather on the question what is good in itself.

Now the answer of utilitarianism to this question is very simple. The only thing good in itself, it maintains, is pleasure. But there are all kinds of pleasures, and it is very difficult to regard them as all of equal value. To take an instance given by G. E. Moore,[4] a man who is watching a Shakespearian tragedy with full understanding and aesthetic appreciation at its highest pitch may be enjoying no more pleasure quantitatively than a drunkard who is amusing himself by smashing crockery, yet it is surely obvious that the former's pleasure is worth more than the latter's. But, if it is, there must be other factors besides pleasure on which the goodness of an experience depends, since the pleasure is *ex hypothesi* not greater in the former case than it is in the latter but only qualitatively better. Mill[5] tried indeed to reconcile his utilitarianism with the admission that a lesser pleasure might rationally be preferred to a greater on the ground of the superior quality of the former, but it is generally, and I think rightly, agreed among philosophers that he failed to escape inconsistency. To say that pleasure is the only good and yet admit that a lesser pleasure may be preferable to a greater is like saying that money is the only thing which counts and then adding that money earned by public work is better than the same amount of money earned by business. If pleasure is the only good, the more pleasure always the better.

In order to decide whether one pleasure can be qualitatively better than another let us consider the following instances. Let us suppose that you were offered 50 more years, each equal in quantity of pleasure to the most pleasant

year you have ever spent, but that the pleasure was to be derived entirely from eating, drinking, playing childish games and lying in the sun. Imagine this proposed life shorn of every element of intelligence above that of an imbecile, of all aesthetic experience, of all love of other men. Now suppose that you were offered as an alternative 49 years of equal pleasure, but that in this case the pleasure was no longer to be derived exclusively from these sources but also from the exercise of intelligence, of love, and of a developed capacity to appreciate the best in art and literature, and suppose also that the effect of the two alternative lives on the general happiness would be equal, the superior advantages for other men that one would expect to accrue from the second life being neutralized and only just neutralized by some evil influence that would intervene if you chose the second and not if you chose the first. Can we doubt that it would be better to choose the second? Yet, if utilitarianism were true, it would certainly be better to choose the first since you would thereby obtain a year's more pleasure. The utilitarian may reply that you would soon get bored by the first life and not enjoy it, but suppose some drug or conditioning process were invented that would prevent you getting bored so that you really got the pleasure promised? It is not inconceivable that a drug might be invented which had these properties. To take a slightly less fanciful illustration, I think Huxley's *Brave New World* is a good refutation of hedonism because it shows us an imaginary state of society which is hedonistically most satisfactory and yet ethically revolting.

Suppose again two communities in which an equal amount of pleasure was enjoyed and an equal amount of pain suffered. But suppose that in one community the citizens were selfish, unjust and capable only of pleasures which did not involve considerable intelligence, aesthetic appreciation, goodness or love, and that in the other community they derived their pleasures chiefly from those sources which I have just excluded from

[4] *Ethics*, p. 147.

[5] *Utilitarianism*, Chap. II.

the first. Surely it is plain that the state of the second community would be much better than the state of the first. Yet, if utilitarianism were true, the two states should be equal in value. Two objections may be made against this example. First, it may be objected that the qualities possessed by the members of the second community would of their inherent nature necessarily lead to a greater happiness than any possessed by the first. But we can meet this by supposing the second community to be much less advantageously situated than the first as regards wealth, health and external circumstances. These factors might quite conceivably counteract the advantages in respect of happiness which would otherwise accrue to them from their superior character. Secondly, it may be objected that we cannot measure happiness as exactly as these examples presuppose. To this we may reply by substituting "approximately equal" or "equal as far as we can tell" for "exactly equal." If we are not able to compare experiences in respect of pleasure, utilitarianism cannot be applied at all; and if we can compare them, there is a good sense in saying that two lives or two communities are "equal in happiness as far as we can tell," meaning that we have no reason to think either happier than the other. That is all that is needed for my illustrations, and this negative condition certainly may be fulfilled.

Thirdly, let us suppose a man revelling in the infliction of tortures on his enemy. Of course this will be very painful for his victim and may have other less direct detrimental consequences in the future for the general welfare, but we are not now asking whether this state of affairs is conducive to the general good, we are asking about its value or disvalue in itself. Let us just consider the state of mind of the man inflicting the suffering. He is enjoying himself, yet can we say that his state of mind is good in itself? Surely it is on the contrary very bad indeed, and the more so the greater the pleasure. As a matter of fact his state of mind would still be very bad if he

were not really inflicting the pain but only thought he was, like a witch-doctor who believed he could make his enemy suffer by roasting his effigy over a slow fire, yet in this case his victim would suffer no pain at all. But, if utilitarianism were true, the state should be good in itself because pleasurable, however deplorable its effects. Still less could it be the case on the utilitarian view that the state was made worse, not better, by increasing the pleasure.

Let us now take other instances which show up the defects of the utilitarian theory. Suppose a shipwreck in which two men are left clinging to a raft unable to support more than one. Let us call them A and B. Now suppose A to be a person whose life is of much less value to society or other individuals than that of B. Under these circumstances we should hold it a very meritorious act of A to surrender his place to B, but we should hold it the reverse of meritorious on the part of B to push off A. Yet the effect of the two acts would be almost the same: by either the life of A is sacrificed and that of B preserved. The only important difference in the effects seems to be that in the second case B will, if he is fundamentally good, be troubled by remorse, and if he is not so troubled, will probably deteriorate in character still further as the result of his action. But this cannot possibly be cited as a reason for the different estimate of the two actions, since unless it is already admitted that the second act is wrong there is no point in the remorse. Of course the utilitarian may argue that we are mistaken in thinking the second act wrong, if B is entitled to be certain that his life is really more important, and that the only reason why we think it wrong is because it would be a dangerous principle in general to allow a man to be judge whether his life was or was not more useful than that of another man. But the very most the utilitarian could maintain with the least show of plausibility would be that the action of B was excusable or not blameworthy, he could not possibly maintain that it was positively admirable, yet we should all admit that the action of A which had practically the same effects was not just excusable but positively admirable. Utilitarianism cannot account for this difference. The latter cannot be explained by effects on happiness but only by something intrinsically good in the nature of the one action. It is not a matter of pleasurable feelings—A probably did not enjoy drowning—but of something quite different from pleasure.

Finally, utilitarianism may be condemned as irreconcilable with the dictates of justice. The principle of utilitarianism tells us only to produce as much happiness as possible, thus implying that the way in which it is distributed does not matter. But justice requires that of two distributions which produce equal happiness we ought to prefer the fairer to the less fair, and that we ought to do this even if slightly less happiness is yielded by the former than by the latter. To take an extreme instance, suppose we could slightly increase the collective happiness of ten men by taking away all happiness from one of them, would it be right to do so? It is perhaps arguable that it would if the difference in happiness of the nine was very large, but not if it was very slight. And if the happiness of the nine were purchased by the actual torture of the one, the injustice of it would seem to poison the happiness and render it worse than valueless even if they were callous enough to enjoy it. Yet on the utilitarian view any distribution of good, however unfair, ought to be preferred to any other, however just, if it would yield *the slightest* additional happiness. Again, ought an innocent man to be punished, if it would on the balance cause less pain with an equal deterrent effect to punish him than it would to punish the guilty? In view of these difficulties it is not surprising that to-day very few philosophers could be found to accept utilitarianism.

What modifications must be made in utilitarianism in order to deal with these examples satisfactorily? In the first place we must admit that not only the quantity but the quality of a pleasure is relevant, so that a lesser pleasure of a higher kind may rightly be preferred to a greater pleasure of a kind which is lower. But what makes one pleasure higher than another? It is not a difference in the nature of the pleasurable feeling as such. It is rather a difference in the activity of the mind with which it is connected or in its object. Some pleasures are regarded as higher than others, because they are connected with thinking, aesthetic experiences, love, moral action, and we regard these activities as higher than eating and drinking and as having an intrinsic value which must be added to any intrinsic value possessed by the pleasures they give as pleasure. Now, if we classify pleasures and activities according to their object, we value specially those concerned with the pursuit of truth, beauty and goodness. As regards the last, my example of the shipwreck has brought out the point that certain morally good acts of self-sacrifice have an intrinsic value not dependent on any pleasant feelings they produce, and my example of the man torturing his enemy has brought out the point that moral badness and not only pain is intrinsically evil. Most people who have thought about the subject have attributed an ultimate value to these three—truth, beauty and goodness (or rather the search for and attainment of them), as well as to love between human beings and (with the religious) to what they call contemplation of or communion with God.

Finally, the point that of two distributions of the same amount of happiness the fairer should be preferred to the unfair seems to show that not only the amount of good distributed but the way in which it is distributed can be intrinsically good (or evil). It is not possible indeed to *prove* that any of these things are good-in-themselves, but neither is it possible to prove that this is so with pleasure. As I have said, the utilitarian has to admit that he can know without proof that pleasure is good-in-itself. Cannot we equally see that these other things are so? Pleasure is only the good of one side of our nature, the feeling side; but we are not only feeling, we are also thinking and acting beings. If so, why should the good of our feeling side be the only one that is of value as an end in itself and not merely as a means to something else?

The utilitarian is indeed right in holding that whatever is good is pleasant. Even painful acts of self-sacrifice done because they are right or out of love give a certain amount of satisfaction to the person who does them, though this may easily be quite outweighed for him at the time by the suffering involved. But the utilitarian is still wrong in holding that what is good is so only because it is pleasurable. Although all good things are pleasant, their goodness is not in proportion to their pleasantness, and more often something is pleasant because it is good than good because it is pleasant. Yet a very large proportion of the ethical questions with which we are confronted can legitimately be answered by applying the utilitarian criterion. And this for two reasons. In the first place there are many cases of action where there simply are no relevant considerations but the pleasure or pain produced, since other values do not come in question in these particular cases. A sick man's virtue may be more important than his freedom from pain, but since he may just as well be virtuous if he is healthy, a doctor may usually freely prescribe for the latter without considering the former. A vast number of wrong actions are pronounced wrong simply because they give pain, and probably a large majority of actions pronounced good are so because they give pleasure or alleviate pain and are done on that account. Secondly, it is plain that actions which promote the other values, knowledge, beauty, love, virtue, justice, will also on the whole make for happiness. This explains why the utilitarian criterion is not so wildly off the mark that it is impossible for intelligent men to be deceived into accepting it as the only ultimate criterion in ethics.

It is of interest that utilitarianism made its mark especially in the field of political and large scale social reform. In these matters I think utilitarianism comes very much nearer to providing a completely satisfactory criterion than in the sphere of individual ethics. For here we are concerned rather with the removal of causes of unhappiness than with the direct promotion of positive good. You cannot produce high morality or fine art or science by law or make people love each other, and you had much better not try, but you can ameliorate their physical state and remove many causes of avoidable suffering. We must not regard it as an argument for utilitarianism that, if it were universally adopted and consistently carried out by everybody, we should be secure from war and soon end acute poverty throughout the world, for the same would be true of any at all plausible ethical theory, of which there are a great variety. But I wish for more straightforward utilitarian argument in politics, not less. I should like to emphasize this point strongly because, whatever is the ultimate truth about utilitarianism, it is plain at least that we have no right to increase greatly human unhappiness or subtract greatly from human happiness, unless this grave disadvantage be outweighed by a very important gain in respect of other goods, or could only be avoided by action that for some other reason was immoral (contingencies which do not seem to me at all likely). Now I shall not go into this point at length because I am not writing a book on Politics, but I am convinced that a careful survey of either Communism, Fascism, Nazism or *Laissez-faire* Individualism would show that they have made enormous sacrifices of human happiness which were not necessary to further any good that could rationally be approved by a sane man or to avoid action that could be called immoral. Hence they must be condemned even apart from the fact that they are of the greatest detriment also to goods other than happiness.

Rule-Utilitarianism

JOHN RAWLS

In this paper I want to show the importance of the distinction between justifying a practice[1] and justifying a particular action falling under it, and I want to explain the logical basis of this distinction and how it is possible to miss its significance. While the distinction has frequently been made,[2] and is now becoming commonplace, there remains the task of explaining the tendency either to overlook it altogether, or to fail to appreciate its importance.

To show the importance of the distinction I am going to defend utilitarianism against those objections which have traditionally been made against it in connection with punishment and the obligation to keep promises. I hope to show that if one uses the distinction in question then one can state utilitarianism in a way which makes it a much better explication of our considered moral judgments than these traditional objections would seem to admit.[3] Thus the importance of the distinction is shown by the way it strengthens the utilitarian view regardless of whether that view is completely defensible or not.

To explain how the significance of the distinction may be overlooked, I am going to discuss two conceptions of rules. One of these conceptions conceals the importance of distinguishing between the justification of a rule or practice and the justification of a particular action falling under it. The other conception makes it clear why this distinction must be made and what is its logical basis.

I

The subject of punishment, in the sense of attaching legal penalties to the violation of legal rules, has always been

---

[1] I use the word "practice" throughout as a sort of technical term meaning any form of activity specified by a system of rules which defines offices, roles, moves, penalties, defenses, and so on, and which gives the activity its structure. As examples one may think of games and rituals, trials and parliaments.

[2] The distinction is central to Hume's discussion of justice in *A Treatise of Human Nature*, bk. III, p. II, esp. secs. 2–4. It is clearly stated by John Austin in the second lecture of *Lectures on Jurisprudence* (4th ed.; London, 1873), I, 116ff. (1st ed., 1832). Also it may be argued that J. S. Mill took it for granted in *Utilitarianism*; on this point cf. J. O. Urmson, "The Interpretation of the Moral Philosophy of J. S. Mill," *Philosophical Quarterly*, vol. III (1953). In addition to the arguments given by Urmson there are several clear statements of the distinction in *A System of Logic* (8th ed.; London, 1872), bk. VI, ch. xii pars. 2, 3, 7. The distinction is fundamental to J. D. Mabbott's important paper, "Punishment," *Mind*, n.s., vol. XLVIII (April, 1939). More recently the distinction has been stated with particular emphasis by S. E. Toulmin in *The Place of Reason in Ethics* (Cambridge, 1950), see esp. ch. xi, where it plays a major part in his account of moral reasoning. Toulmin doesn't explain the basis of the distinction, nor how one might overlook its importance, as I try to in this paper, and in my review of his book (*Philosophical Review*, vol. LK [October, 1951]), as some of my criticisms show, I failed to understand the force of it. See also H. D. Aiken, "The Levels of Moral Discourse," *Ethics*, vol. LXII (1952), A. M. Quinton, "Punishment," *Analysis*, vol. XIV (June, 1954), and P. H. Nowell-Smith, *Ethics* (London, 1954), pp. 236–239. 271–273.

[3] On the concept of explication see the author's paper *Philosophical Review*, vol. LX (April, 1951).

FROM: "Two Concepts of Rules" (complete), *The Philosophical Review*, Vol. LXIV (January 1955). Reprinted by permission of editor and author. This is a revision of a paper given at the Harvard Philosophy Club on April 30, 1954.

a troubling moral question.[4] The trouble about it has not been that people disagree as to whether or not punishment is justifiable. Most people have held that, freed from certain abuses, it is an acceptable institution. Only a few have rejected punishment entirely, which is rather surprising when one considers all that can be said against it. The difficulty is with the justification of punishment: various arguments for it have been given by moral philosophers, but so far none of them has won any sort of general acceptance; no justification is without those who detest it. I hope to show that the use of the aforementioned distinction enables one to state the utilitarian view in a way which allows for the sound points of its critics.

For our purposes we may say that there are two justifications of punishment. What we may call the retributive view is that punishment is justified on the grounds that wrongdoing merits punishment. It is morally fitting that a person who does wrong should suffer in proportion to his wrongdoing. That a criminal should be punished follows from his guilt, and the severity of the appropriate punishment depends on the depravity of his act. The state of affairs where a wrongdoer suffers punishment is morally better than the state of affairs where he does not; and it is better irrespective of any of the consequences of punishing him.

What we may call the utilitarian view holds on the principle that bygones are bygones and that only future consequences are material to present decisions, punishment is justifiable only by reference to the probable consequences of maintaining it as one of the devices of the social order. Wrongs committed

[4] While this paper was being revised, Quinton's appeared; footnote 2 supra. There are several respects in which my remarks are similar to his. Yet as I consider some further questions and rely on somewhat different arguments, I have retained the discussion of punishment and promises together as two test cases for utilitarianism.

in the past are, as such, not relevant considerations for deciding what to do. If punishment can be shown to promote effectively the interest of society it is justifiable, otherwise it is not.

I have stated these two competing views very roughly to make one feel the conflict between them: one feels the force of *both* arguments and one wonders how they can be reconciled. From my introductory remarks it is obvious that the resolution which I am going to propose is that in this case one must distinguish between justifying a practice as a system of rules to be applied and enforced, and justifying a particular action which falls under these rules; utilitarian arguments are appropriate with regard to questions about practices, while retributive arguments fit the application of particular rules to particular cases.

We might try to get clear about this distinction by imagining how a father might answer the question of his son. Suppose the son asks. "Why was *J* put in jail yesterday?" The father answers, "Because he robbed the bank at *B*. He was duly tried and found guilty. That's why he was put in jail yesterday." But suppose the son had asked a different question, namely, "Why do people put other people in jail?" Then the father might answer, "To protect good people from bad people" or "To stop people from doing things that would make it uneasy for all of us; for otherwise we wouldn't be able to go to bed at night and sleep in peace." There are two very different questions here. One question emphasizes the proper name: it asks why *J* was punished rather than someone else, or it asks what he was punished for. The other question asks why we have the institution of punishment: why do people punish one another rather than, say, always forgiving one another?

Thus the father says in effect that a particular man is punished, rather than some other man, because he is guilty, and he is guilty because he broke the law (past tense). In his case the law looks back, the judge looks back, the jury looks back, and a penalty is visited upon him for something he did. That a man is to be punished, and what his punishment is to be, is settled by its being shown that he broke the law and that the law assigns that penalty for the violation of it.

On the other hand we have the institution of punishment itself, and recommend and accept various changes in it, because it is thought by the (ideal) legislator and by those to whom the law applies that, as a part of a system of law impartially applied from case to case arising under it, it will have the consequence, in the long run, of furthering the interests of society.

One can say, then, that the judge and the legislator stand in different positions and look in different directions: one to the past, the other to the future. The justification of what the judge does, *qua* judge, sounds like the retributive view; the justification of what the (ideal) legislator does, *qua* legislator, sounds like the utilitarian view. Thus both views have a point (this is as it should be since intelligent and sensitive persons have been on both sides of the argument); and one's initial confusion disappears once one sees that these views apply to persons holding different offices with different duties, and situated differently with respect to the system of rules that make up the criminal law.[5]

One might say, however, that the utilitarian view is more fundamental since it applies to a more fundamental office, for the judge carries out the legislator's will so far as he can determine it. Once the legislator decides to have laws and to assign penalties for their violation (as things are there must be both the law and the penalty) an institution is set up which involves a retributive conception of particular cases. It is part of the concept of the criminal law as a system of rules that the application and enforcement of these rules in particular cases should be justifiable by arguments of a retributive character. The decision whether or not to use law rather than some other mechanism of social control, and the decision as to what laws to have and what penalties to assign, may be settled by utilitarian arguments; but if one decides to have laws then one has decided on something whose working in particular cases is retributive in form.[6]

The answer, then, to the confusion engendered by the two views of punishment is quite simple: one distinguishes two offices, that of the judge and that of the legislator, and one distinguishes their different stations with respect to the system of rules which make up the law; and then one notes that the different sorts of considerations which would usually be offered as reasons for what is done under the cover of these offices can be paired off with the competing justifications of punishment. One reconciles the two views by the time-honored device of making them apply to different situations.

But can it really be this simple? Well, this answer allows for the apparent intent of each side. Does a person who advocates the retributive view necessarily advocate, as an *institution,* legal machinery whose essential purpose is to set up and preserve a correspondence between moral turpitude and suffering? Surely not.[7] What retributionists have rightly insisted upon is that no man can be punished unless he is guilty, that is, unless he has broken the law. Their fundamental criticism of the utilitarian account is that, as they interpret it, it sanctions an innocent person's being punished (if one may call it that) for the benefit of society.

On the other hand, utilitarians agree that punishment is to be inflicted only for the violation of law. They re-

---

[5] Note the fact that different sorts of arguments are suited to different offices. One way of taking the differences between ethical theories is to regard them as accounts of the reasons expected in different offices.

[6] In this connection see Mabbott, *op. cit.,* pp. 163–164.

[7] On this point Sir David Ross, *The Right and the Good* (Oxford, 1930), pp. 57–60.

gard this much as understood from the concept of punishment itself.[8] The point of the utilitarian account concerns the institution as a system of rules: utilitarianism seeks to limit its use by declaring it justifiable only if it can be shown to foster effectively the good of society. Historically it is a protest against the indiscriminate and ineffective use of the criminal law.[9] It seeks to dissuade us from assigning to penal institutions the improper, if not sacrilegious, task of matching suffering with moral turpitude. Like others, utilitarians want penal institutions designed so that, as far as humanly possible, only those who break the law run afoul of it. They hold that no official should have discretionary power to inflict penalties whenever he thinks it for the benefit of society; for on utilitarian grounds an institution granting such power could not be justified.[10]

[8] See Hobbes's definition of punishment in *Leviathan*, ch. xxviii; and Bentham's definition in *The Principle of Morals and Legislation*, ch. xii, par. 36, ch. xv, par. 28, and in *The Rationale of Punishment*, (London, 1830), bk. I, ch. i. They could agree with Bradley that: "Punishment is punishment only when it is deserved. We pay the penalty, because we owe it, and for no other reason; and if punishment is inflicted for any other reason whatever than because it is merited by wrong, it is a gross immorality, a crying injustice, an abominable crime, and not what it pretends to be." *Ethical Studies* (2nd ed.; Oxford, 1927), pp. 26–27. Certainly by definition it isn't what it pretends to be. The innocent can only be punished by mistake; deliberate "punishment" of the innocent necessarily involves fraud.

[9] Cf. Leon Radzinowicz, *A History of English Criminal Law: The Movement for Reform 1750–1833* (London, 1948), esp. ch. xi on Bentham.

[10] Bentham discusses how corresponding to a punitory provision of a criminal law there is another provision which stands to it as an antagonist and which needs a name as much as the punitory. He calls it, as one might expect, the *anaetiosostic*, and of it

The suggested way of reconciling the retributive and the utilitarian justifications of punishment seems to account for what both sides have wanted to say. There are, however, two further questions which arise, and I shall devote the remainder of this section to them.

First, will not a difference of opinion as to the proper criterion of just law make the proposed reconciliation unacceptable to retributionists? Will they not question whether, if the utilitarian principle is used as the criterion, it follows that those who have broken the law are guilty in a way which satisfies their demand that those punished deserve to be punished? To answer this difficulty, suppose that the rules of the criminal law are justified on utilitarian grounds (it is only for laws that meet his criterion that the utilitarian can be held responsible). Then it follows that the actions which the criminal law specifies as offenses are such that, if they were tolerated, terror and alarm would spread in society. Consequently, retributionists can only deny that those who are punished deserve to be punished if they deny that such actions are wrong. This they will not want to do.

The second question is whether utilitarianism doesn't justify too much. One pictures it as an engine of justification which, if consistently adopted, could be used to justify cruel and arbitrary institutions. Retributionists may be supposed to concede that utilitarians *intend*

he says: "The punishment of guilt is the object of the former one: the preservation of innocence that of the latter." In the same connection he asserts that it is never thought fit to give the judge the option of deciding whether a thief (that is, a person whom he believes to be a thief, for the judge's belief is what the question must always turn upon) should hang or not, and so the law writes the provision: "The judge shall not cause a thief to be hanged unless he have been duly convicted and sentenced in course of law" (*The Limits of Jurisprudence Defined*, ed. C. W. Everett [New York, 1945], pp. 238–239).

to reform the law and to make it more humane; that utilitarians do not *wish* to justify any such thing as punishment of the innocent; and that utilitarians may appeal to the fact that punishment presupposes guilt in the sense that by punishment one understands an institution attaching penalties to the infraction of legal rules, and therefore that it is logically absurd to suppose that utilitarians in justifying *punishment* might also have justified punishment (if we may call it that) of the innocent. The real question, however, is whether the utilitarian, in justifying punishment, hasn't used arguments which commit him to accepting the infliction of suffering on innocent persons if it is for the good of society (whether or not one calls this punishment). More generally, isn't the utilitarian committed in principle to accepting many practices which he, as a morally sensitive person, wouldn't want to accept? Retributionists are inclined to hold that there is no way to stop the utilitarian principle from justifying too much except by adding to it a principle which distributes certain rights to individuals. Then the amended criterion is not the greatest benefit of society *simpliciter*, but the greatest benefit of society subject to the constraint that no one's rights may be violated. Now while I think that the classical utilitarians proposed a criterion of this more complicated sort, I do not want to argue that point here.[11] What I want to show is that there is *another* way of preventing the utilitarian principle from justifying too much, or at least of making it much less likely to do so: namely, by stating utilitarianism in a way which accounts for the distinction between the justification of an institution and the justification of a particular action falling under it.

I begin by defining the institution of punishment as follows: a person is said to suffer punishment whenever he is legally deprived of some of the normal rights of a citizen on the ground that he has violated a rule of law, the violation having been established by trial according to the due process of law, provided that the deprivation is carried out by the recognized legal authorities of the state, that the rule of law clearly specifies both the offense and the attached penalty, that the courts construe statutes strictly, and that the statute was on the books prior to the time of the offense.[12] This definition specifies what I shall understand by punishment. The question is whether utilitarian arguments may be found to justify institutions widely different from this and such as one would find cruel and arbitrary.

This quesion is best answered, I think, by taking up a particular accusation. Consider the following from Carritt:

. . . the utilitarian must hold that we are justified in inflicting pain always and only to prevent worse pain or bring about greater happiness. This, then, is all we need to consider in so-called punishment, which must be purely preventive. But if some kind of very cruel crime becomes common, and none of the criminals can be caught, it might be highly expedient, as an example, to hang an innocent man, if a charge against him could be so framed that he were universally thought guilty; indeed this would only fail to be an ideal instance of utilitarian 'punishment' because the victim himself would not have been so likely as a real felon to commit such a crime in the future; in all other respects it would be perfectly deterrent and therefore felicific.[13]

Carritt is trying to show that there are occasions when a utilitarian argument would justify an action which would be generally condemned; and thus that utili-

---

[11] By the classical utilitarians I understand Hobbes, Hume, Bentham, J. S. Mill, and Sidgwick.

[12] All these features of punishment are mentioned by Hobbes; cf. *Leviathan*, ch. xxviii.

[13] *Ethical and Political Thinking* (Oxford, 1947), p. 65.

tarianism justifies too much. But the failure of Carritt's argument lies in the fact that he makes no distinction between the justification of the general system of rules which constitutes penal institutions and the justification of particular applications of these rules to particular cases by the various officials whose job it is to administer them. This becomes perfectly clear when one asks who the "we" are of whom Carritt speaks. Who is this who has a sort of absolute authority on particular occasions to decide that an innocent man shall be "punished" if everyone can be convinced that he is guilty? Is this person the legislator, or the judge, or the body of private citizens, or what? It is utterly crucial to know who is to decide such matters, and by what authority, for all of this must be written into the rules of the institution. Until one knows these things one doesn't know what the institution is whose justification is being challenged; and as the utilitarian principle applies to the institution one doesn't know whether it is justifiable on utilitarian grounds or not.

Once this is understood it is clear what the countermove to Carritt's argument is. One must describe more carefully what the *institution* is which his example suggests, and then ask oneself whether or not it is likely that having this institution would be for the benefit of society in the long run. One must not content oneself with the vague thought that, when it's a question of *this* case, it would be a good thing if *somebody* did something even if an innocent person were to suffer.

Try to imagine, then, an institution (which we may call "telishment") which is such that the officials set up by it have authority to arrange a trial for the condemnation of an innocent man whenever they are of the opinion that doing so would be in the best interests of society. The discretion of officials is limited, however, by the rule that they may not condemn an innocent man to undergo such an ordeal unless there is,

at the time, a wave of offenses similar to that with which they charge him and telish him for. We may imagine that the officials having the discretionary authority are the judges of the higher courts in consultation with the chief of police, the minister of justice, and a committee of the legislature.

Once one realizes that one is involved in setting up an *institution,* one sees that the hazards are very great. For example, what check is there on the officials? How is one to tell whether or not their actions are authorized? How is one to limit the risks involved in allowing such systematic deception? How is one to avoid giving anything short of complete discretion to the authorities to telish anyone they like? In addition to these considerations, it is obvious that people will come to have a very different attitude towards their penal system when telishment is adjoined to it. They will be uncertain as to whether a convicted man has been punished or telished. They will wonder whether or not they should feel sorry for him. They will wonder whether the same fate won't at any time fall on them. If one pictures how such an institution would actually work, and the enormous risks involved in it, it seems clear that it would serve no useful purpose. A utilitarian justification for this institution is most unlikely.

It happens in general that as one drops off the defining features of punishment one ends up with an institution whose utilitarian justification is highly doubtful. One reason for this is that punishment works like a kind of price system: by altering the prices one has to pay for the performance of actions it supplies a motive for avoiding some actions and doing others. The defining features are essential if punishment is to work in this way; so that an institution which lacks these features, e.g., an institution which is set up to "punish" the innocent, is likely to have about as much point as a price system (if one may call it that) where the prices of things change at random from day to day and one learns the price of something after one has agreed to buy it.[14]

If one is careful to apply the utilitarian principle to the institution which is to authorize particular actions, then there is *less* danger of its justifying too much. Carritt's example gains plausibility by its indefiniteness and by its concentration on the particular case. His argument will only hold if it can be shown that there are utilitarian arguments which justify an institution whose publicly ascertainable offices and powers are such as to permit officials to exercise that kind of discretion in particular cases. But the requirement of having to build the arbitrary features of the particular decision into the institutional practice makes the justification much less likely to go through.

[14] The analogy with the price system suggests an answer to the question how utilitarian considerations insure that punishment is proportional to the offense. It is interesting to note that Sir David Ross, after making the distinction between justifying a penal law and justifying a particular application of it, and after stating that utilitarian considerations have a large place in determining the former, still holds back from accepting the utilitarian justification of punishment on the grounds that justice requires that punishment be proportional to the offense, and that utilitarianism is unable to account for this. Cf. *The Right and the Good*, pp. 61–62. I do not claim that utilitarianism can account for this requirement as Sir David might wish, but it happens, nevertheless, that if utilitarian considerations are followed penalties will be proportional to offenses in this sense: the order of offenses according to seriousness can be paired off with the order of penalties according to severity. Also the absolute level of penalties will be as low as possible. This follows from the assumption that people are rational (i.e., that they are able to take into account the "prices" the state puts on actions), the utilitarian rule that a penal system should provide a motive for preferring the less serious offense, and the principle that punishment as such is an evil. All this was carefully worked out by Bentham in *The Principles of Morals and Legislation*, chs. xii–xv.

II

I shall now consider the question of promises. The objection to utilitarianism in connection with promises seems to be this: it is believed that on the utilitarian view when a person makes a promise the only ground upon which he should keep it, if he should keep it, is that by keeping it he will realize the most good on the whole. So that if one asks the question "Why should I keep *my* promise?" the utilitarian answer is understood to be that doing so in *this* case will have the best consequences. And this answer is said, quite rightly, to conflict with the way in which the obligation to keep promises is regarded.

Now of course critics of utilitarianism are not unaware that one defense sometimes attributed to utilitarians is the consideration involving the practice of promise-keeping.[15] In this connection they are supposed to argue something like this: it must be admitted that we feel strictly about keeping promises, more strictly than it might seem our view can account for. But when we consider the matter carefully it is always necessary to take into account the effect which our action will have on the practice of making promises. The promisor must weigh, not only the effects of breaking his promise on the particular case, but also the effect which his breaking his promise will have on the practice itself. Since the practice is of great utilitarian value, and since breaking one's promise always seriously damages it, one will seldom be justified in breaking one's promise. If we view our individual promises in the wider

[15] Ross, *The Right and the Good*, pp. 37–39, and *Foundations of Ethics* (Oxford, 1939), pp. 92–94. I know of no utilitarian who has used this argument except W. A. Pickard-Cambridge in "Two Problems about Duty," *Mind*, n.s., XLI (April, 1932), 153–157, although the argument goes with G. E. Moore's version of utilitarianism in *Principia Ethica* (Cambridge, 1903). To my knowledge it does not appear in the classical utilitarians; and if one interprets their view correctly this is no accident.

context of the practice of promising itself we can account for the strictness of the obligation to keep promises. There is always one very strong utilitarian consideration in favor of keeping them, and this will insure that when the question arises as to whether or not to keep a promise it will usually turn out that one should, even where the facts of the particular case taken by itself would seem to justify one's breaking it. In this way the strictness with which we view the obligation to keep promises is accounted for.

Ross has criticized this defense as follows:[16] however great the value of the practice of promising, on utilitarian grounds, there must be some value which is greater, and one can imagine it to be obtainable by breaking a promise. Therefore there might be a case where the promisor could argue that breaking his promise was justified as leading to a better state of affairs on the whole. And the promisor could argue in this way no matter how slight the advantage won by breaking the promise. If one were to challenge the promisor his defense would be that what he did was best on the whole in view of all the utilitarian considerations, which in this case *include* the importance of the practice. Ross feels that such a defense would be unacceptable. I think he is right insofar as he is protesting against the appeal to consequences in general and without further explanation. Yet it is extremely difficult to weigh the force of Ross's argument. The kind of case imagined seems unrealistic and one feels that it needs to be described. One is inclined to think that it would either turn out that such a case came under an exception defined by the practice itself, in which case there would not be an appeal to consequences in general on the particular case, or it would happen that the circumstances were so peculiar that the conditions which the practice presupposes no longer obtained. But certainly Ross is right in thinking that it strikes us as wrong for a person to defend

breaking a promise by a general appeal to consequences. For a general utilitarian defense is not open to the promisor: it is not one of the defenses allowed by the practice of making promises.

Ross gives two further counterarguments:[17] First, he holds that it overestimates the damage done to the practice of promising by a failure to keep a promise. One who breaks a promise harms his own name certainly, but it isn't clear that a broken promise always damages the practice itself sufficiently to account for the strictness of the obligation. Second, and more important, I think, he raises the question of what one is to say of a promise which isn't known to have been made except to the promisor and the promisee, as in the case of a promise a son makes to his dying father concerning the handling of the estate.[18] In this sort of case the consideration relating to the practice doesn't weigh on the promisor at all, and yet one feels that this sort of promise is as binding as other promises. The question of the effect which breaking it has on the practice seems irrelevant. The only consequence seems to be that one can break the promise without running any risk of being censured; but the obligation itself seems not the least weakened. Hence it is doubtful whether

[16] Ross, *The Right and the Good*, pp. 38–39.

[17] Ross, *ibid.*, p. 39. The case of the non-public promise is discussed again in *Foundations of Ethics*, pp. 95–96, 104–105. It occurs also in Mabbott, "Punishment," *op. cit.*, pp. 155–157, and in A. I. Melden, "Two Comments on Utilitarianism," *Philosophical Review*, LX (October, 1951), 519–523, which discusses Carritt's example in *Ethical and Political Thinking*, p. 64.

[18] Ross's example is described simply as that of two men dying alone where one makes a promise to the other. Carritt's example (cf. n. 17 supra) is that of two men at the North Pole. The example in the text is more realistic and is similar to Mabbott's. Another example is that of being told something in confidence by one who subsequently dies. Such cases need not be "desert-island arguments" as Nowell-Smith seems to believe (cf. his *Ethics*, pp. 239–244).

the effect on the practice ever weighs in the particular case; certainly it cannot account for the strictness of the obligation where it fails to obtain. It seems to follow that a utilitarian account of the obligation to keep promises cannot be successfully carried out.

From what I have said in connection with punishment, one can foresee what I am going to say about these arguments and counterarguments. They fail to make the distinction between the justification of a practice and the justification of a particular action falling under it, and therefore they fall into the mistake of taking it for granted that the promisor, like Carritt's official, is entitled without restriction to bring utilitarian considerations to bear in deciding whether to keep *his* promise. But if one considers what the practice of promising is one will see, I think, that it is such as not to allow this sort of general discretion to the promisor. Indeed, the point of the practice is to abdicate one's title to act in accordance with utilitarian and prudential considerations in order that the future may be tied down and plans coordinated in advance. There are obvious utilitarian advantages in having a practice which denies to the promisor, as a defense, any general appeal to the utilitarian principle in accordance with which the practice itself may be justified. There is nothing contradictory, or surprising, in this: utilitarian (or aesthetic) reasons might properly be given in arguing that the game of chess, or baseball, is satisfactory just as it is, or in arguing that it should be changed in various respects, but a player in a game cannot properly appeal to such considerations as reasons for his making one move rather than another. It is a mistake to think that if the practice is justified on utilitarian grounds then the promisor must have complete liberty to use utilitarian arguments to decide whether or not to keep his promise. The practice forbids this general defense; and it is a purpose of the practice to do this. Therefore what the above arguments presuppose—the idea that if the utilitarian view is ac-

cepted then the promisor is bound if, and only if, the application of the utilitarian principle to his own case shows that keeping it is best on the whole—is false. The promisor is bound because he promised: weighing the case on its merits is not open to him.[19]

Is this to say that in particular cases one cannot deliberate whether or not to keep one's promise? Of course not. But to do so is to deliberate whether the various excuses, exceptions and defenses, which are understood by, and which constitute an important part of, the practice, apply to one's own case.[20] Various defenses for not keeping one's promise are allowed, but among them there isn't the one that, on general utilitarian grounds, the promisor (truly) thought his action best on the whole, even though there may be the defense that the consequences of keeping one's promise would have been *extremely* severe. While there are too many complexities here to consider all the necessary details, one can see that the general defense isn't allowed if one asks the following question: what would one say of someone who, when asked why he broke his promise, replied simply that breaking it was best on the whole? Assuming that his reply is sincere, and that his belief was reasonable (i.e., one need not consider the possibility that he was mistaken), I think that one would question whether or not he knows what it means to say "I promise" (in the appropriate circumstances). It would be said of someone who used this excuse without further explanation that he didn't understand what defenses the practice, which defines a promise, allows to him. If a child were to use this excuse one would correct him; for it is part of the way one is taught the concept of a promise to be corrected if one uses this excuse.

[19] What I have said in this paragraph seems to me to coincide with Hume's important discussion in the *Treatise of Human Nature,* bk. III, pt. II, sec. 5; and also sec. 6, par. 8.

[20] For a discussion of these, see H. Sidgwick, *The Methods of Ethics* (6th ed.; London, 1901), bk. III, ch. vi.

The point of having the practice would be lost if the practice did allow this excuse.

It is no doubt part of the utilitarian view that every practice should admit the defense that the consequences of abiding by it would have been extremely severe; and utilitarians would be inclined to hold that some reliance on people's good sense and some concession to hard cases is necessary. They would hold that a practice is justified by serving the interests of those who take part in it; and as with any set of rules there is understood a background of circumstances under which it is expected to be applied and which need not—indeed which cannot—be fully stated. Should these circumstances change, then even if there is no rule which provides for the case, it may still be in accordance with the practice that one be released from one's obligation. But this sort of defense allowed by a practice must not be confused with the general option to weigh each particular case on utilitarian grounds which critics of utilitarianism have thought it necessarily to involve.

The concern which utilitarianism raises by its justification of punishment is that it may justify too much. The question in connection with promises is different: it is how utilitarianism can account for the obligation to keep promises at all. One feels that the recognized obligation to keep one's promise and utilitarianism are incompatible. And to be sure, they are incompatible if one interprets the utilitarian view as necessarily holding that each person has complete liberty to weigh every particular action on general utilitarian grounds. But must one interpret utilitarianism in this way? I hope to show that, in the sorts of cases I have discussed, one cannot interpret it in this way.

III

So far I have tried to show the importance of the distinction between the justification of a practice and the justification of a particular action falling under it by indicating how this distinction might be used to defend utilitarianism against two long-standing objections. One might be tempted to close the discussion at this point by saying that utilitarian considerations should be understood as applying to practices in the first instance and not to particular actions falling under them except insofar as the practices admit of it. One might say that in this modified form it is a better account of our considered moral opinions and let it go at that. But to stop here would be to neglect the interesting question as to how one can fail to appreciate the significance of this rather obvious distinction and can take it for granted that utilitarianism has the consequence that particular cases may always be decided on general utilitarian grounds.[21] I want to argue that this mistake may be connected with misconceiving the logical status of the rules of practices; and to show this I am going to examine two conceptions of rules, two ways of placing them within the utilitarian theory.

The conception which conceals

[21] So far as I can see it is not until Moore that the doctrine is expressly stated in this way. See, for example, *Principia Ethica*, p. 147, where it is said that the statement "I am morally bound to perform this action" is identical with the statement "*This* action will produce the greatest possible amount of good in the Universe" (my italics). It is important to remember that those whom I have called the classical utilitarians were largely interested in social institutions. They were among the leading economists and political theorists of their day, and they were not infrequently reformers interested in practical affairs. Utilitarianism historically goes together with a coherent view of society, and is not simply an ethical theory, much less an attempt at philosophical analysis in the modern sense. The utilitarian principle was quite naturally thought of, and used, as a criterion for judging social institutions (practices) and as a basis for urging reforms. It is not clear, therefore, how far it is necessary to amend utilitarianism in its classical form. For a discussion of utilitarianism as an integral part of a theory of society, see L. Robbins, *The Theory of Economic Policy in English Classical Political Economy* (London, 1952).

from us the significance of the distinction I am going to call the summary view. It regards rules in the following way: one supposes that each person decides what he shall do in particular cases by applying the utilitarian principle; one supposes further that different people will decide the same particular case in the same way and that there will be recurrences of cases similar to those previously decided. Thus it will happen that in cases of certain kinds the same decision will be made either by the same person at different times or by different persons at the same time. If a case occurs frequently enough one supposes that a rule is formulated to cover that sort of case. I have called this conception the summary view because rules are pictured as summaries of past decisions arrived at by the *direct* application of the utilitarian principle to particular cases. Rules are regarded as reports that cases of a certain sort have been found on *other* grounds to be properly decided in a certain way (although, of course, they do not *say* this).

There are several things to notice about this way of placing rules within the utilitarian theory.[22]

[22] This footnote should be read after sec. 3 and presupposes what I have said there. It provides a few references to statements by leading utilitarians of the summary conception. In general it appears that when they discussed the logical features of rules the summary conception prevailed and that it was typical of the way they talked about moral rules. I cite a rather lengthy group of passages from Austin as a full illustration. John Austin in his *Lectures on Jurisprudence* meets the objection that deciding in accordance with the utilitarian principle case by case is impractical by saying that this is a misinterpretation of utilitarianism. According to the utilitarian view ". . . our conduct would conform to *rules* inferred from the tendencies of actions, but would not be determined by a direct resort to the principle of general utility. Utility would be the test of our conduct, ultimately, but not immediately: the immediate test of the rules to which our conduct would conform, but not the immediate test of specific or individual actions. Our rules would be

1. The point of having rules derives from the fact that similar cases tend to recur and that one can decide cases more quickly if one records past decisions in the form of rules. If similar cases didn't recur, one would be required to apply the utilitarian principle directly, case by case, and rules reporting past decisions would be of no use.

fashioned on utility; our conduct, on our rules" (vol. I, p. 116). As to how one decides on the tendency of an action he says: "If we would try the tendency of a specific or individual act, we must not contemplate the act as if it were single and insulated, but must look at the class of acts to which it belongs. We must suppose that acts of the class were generally done or omitted, and consider the probable effect upon the general happiness or good. We must guess the consequences which would follow, if the class of acts were general; and also the consequences which would follow, if they were generally omitted. We must then compare the consequences on the positive and negative sides, and determine on which of the two the *balance* of advantage lies. . . . If we truly try the tendency of a specific or individual act, we try the tendency of the class to which that act belongs. The *particular* conclusion which we draw, with regard to the single act, implies a *general* conclusion embracing all similar acts. . . . To the rules thus inferred, and lodged in the memory, our conduct would conform *immediately* if it were truly adjusted to utility" (*ibid.*, p. 117). One might think that Austin meets the objection by stating the practice conception of rules; and perhaps he did intend to. But it is not clear that he has stated this conception. Is the generality he refers to of the statistical sort? This is suggested by the notion of tendency. Or does he refer to the utility of setting up a practice? I don't know; but what suggests the summary view is his subsequent remarks. He says: "To consider the specific consequences of single or individual acts, would *seldom* [my italics] consist with that ultimate principle" (*ibid.*, p. 117). But would one ever do this? He continues: ". . . this being admitted, the necessity of pausing and calculating, which the objection in question supposes, is an imagined necessity. To preface each act or forebearance by a conjecture and comparison of consequences, were clearly *superfluous* [my italics] and mis-

2. The decisions made on particular cases are logically prior to rules. Since rules gain their point from the need to apply the utilitarian principle to many cases, it follows that a particular case (or several cases similar to it) may exist whether or not there is a rule covering that case. We are pictured as recognizing particular cases prior to there being a rule which covers them, for it is only if we meet with a number of cases of a certain sort that we formulate a rule. Thus we are able to describe a particular case as a particular case of the requisite sort whether there is a rule regarding *that* sort of case or not. Put another way: what the *A*'s and the *B*'s refer to in rules of the form 'Whenever *A* do *B*' may be described as *A*'s and *B*'s whether or not there is the rule 'Whenever *A* do *B*', or whether or not there is any body of rules which make up a practice of which that rule is a part.

To illustrate this consider a rule, or maxim, which could arise in this way: suppose that a person is trying to decide

---

chievous. It were clearly superfluous, inasmuch as the *result of that process* [my italics] would be embodied in a known *rule*. It were clearly mischievous, inasmuch as the *true* result would be expressed by that rule, whilst the process would probably be faulty, if it were done on the spur of the occasion" (*ibid.*, pp. 117–118). He goes on: "If our experience and observation of particulars were not *generalized*, our experience and observation of particulars would seldom avail us in *practice*. . . . The inferences suggested to our minds by repeated experience and observation are, therefore, drawn into *principles*, or compressed into *maxims*. These we carry about us ready for use, and apply to individual cases promptly . . . without reverting to the process by which they were obtained; or without recalling, and arraying before our minds, the numerous and intricate considerations of which they are *handy abridgments* [my italics]. . . . True theory is a *compendium* of particular truths. . . . Speaking then, generally, human conduct is inevitably *guided* [my italics] by *rules*, or by *principles or maxims*" (*ibid.*, pp. 117–118). I need not trouble to show all these remarks incline to the summary view. Further, when Austin comes to deal with cases "of comparatively rare occurrence" he holds that specific considerations may outweigh the general. "Looking at the reasons from which we had inferred the rule, it were absurd to think it inflexible. We should therefore dismiss the *rule*; resort directly to the *principle* upon which our rules were fashioned; and calculate *specific* consequences to the best of our knowledge and ability" (*ibid.*, pp. 120–121). Austin's view is interesting because it shows how one may come close to the practice conception and then slide away from it.

In *A System of Logic*, bk. VI, ch. xii, par. 2, Mill distinguishes clearly between the position of judge and legislator and in doing so suggests the distinction between the two concepts of rules. However, he distinguishes the two positions to illustrate the difference between cases where one is to apply a rule already established and cases where one must formulate a rule to govern subsequent conduct. It's the latter case that interests him and he takes the "maxim of policy" of a legislator as typical of rules. In par. 3 the summary conception is very clearly stated. For example, he says of rules of conduct that they should be taken provisionally, as they are made for the most numerous cases. He says that they "point out" the manner in which it is least perilous to act; they serve as an "admonition" that a certain mode of conduct has been found suited to the most common occurrences. In *Utilitarianism*, ch. ii, par. 24, the summary conception appears in Mill's answer to the same objection Austin considered. Here he speaks of rules as "corollaries" from the principle of utility; these "secondary" rules are compared to "landmarks" and "direction-posts." They are based on long experience and so make it unnecessary to apply the utilitarian principle to each case. In par. 25 Mill refers to the task of the utilitarian principle in adjudicating between competing moral rules. He talks here as if one then applies the utilitarian principle directly to the particular case. On the practice view one would rather use the principle to decide which of the ways that make the practice consistent is the best. It should be noted that while in par. 10 Mill's definition of utilitarianism makes the utilitarian principle apply to morality, i.e., to the rules and precepts of human conduct, the definition in par. 2 uses the phrase "actions are right in *proportion* as they *tend* to promote happiness" [my italics] and this inclines towards whether to tell someone who is fatally ill what his illness is when he has been asked to do so. Suppose the person to reflect and then decide, on utilitarian grounds, that he should not answer truthfully; and suppose that on the basis of this and other like occasions he formulates a rule to the effect that when asked by someone fatally ill what his illness is, one should not tell him. The point to notice is that someone's being fatally ill and asking what his illness is, and someone's telling him, are things that can be described as such whether or not there is this rule. The performance of the action to which the rule refers doesn't

---

the summary view. In the last paragraph of the essay "On the Definition of Political Economy," *Westminster Review* (October, 1836), Mill says that it is only in art, as distinguished from science, that one can properly speak of exceptions. In a question of practice, if something is fit to be done "in the majority of cases" then it is made the rule. "We may . . . in talking of art *unobjectionably* speak of the *rule* and the *exception*, meaning by the rule the cases in which there exists a preponderance . . . of inducements for acting in a particular way; and by the exception, the cases in which the preponderance is on the contrary side." These remarks, too, suggest the summary view.

In Moore's *Principia Ethica*, ch. v, there is a complicated and difficult discussion of moral rules. I will not examine it here except to express my suspicion that the summary conception prevails. To be sure, Moore speaks frequently of the utility of rules as generally followed, and of actions as generally practiced, but it is possible that these passages fit the statistical notion of generality which the summary conception allows. This conception is suggested by Moore's taking the utilitarian principle as applying directly to particular actions (pp. 147–148) and by his notion of a rule as something indicating which of the few alternatives likely to occur to anyone will generally produce a greater total good in the immediate future (p. 154). He talks of an "ethical law" as a prediction, and as a generalization (pp. 146, 155). The summary conception is also suggested by his discussion of exceptions (pp. 162–163) and of the force of examples of breaching a rule (pp. 163–164).

require the stage-setting of a practice of which this rule is a part. This is what is meant by saying that on the summary view particular cases are logically prior to rules.

3. Each person is in principle always entitled to reconsider the correctness of a rule and to question whether or not it is proper to follow it in a particular case. As rules are guides and aids, one may ask whether in past decisions there might not have been a mistake in applying the utilitarian principle to get the rule in question, and wonder whether or not it is best in this case. The reason for rules is that people are not able to apply the utilitarian principle effortlessly and flawlessly; there is need to save time and to post a guide. On this view a society of rational utilitarians would be a society without rules in which each person applied the utilitarian principle directly and smoothly, and without error, case by case. On the other hand, ours is a society in which rules are formulated to serve as aids in reaching these ideally rational decisions on particular cases, guides which have been built up and tested by the experience of generations. If one applies this view to rules, one is interpreting them as maxims, as "rules of thumb"; and it is doubtful that anything to which the summary conception did apply would be called a *rule*. Arguing as if one regarded rules in this way is a mistake one makes while doing philosophy.

4. The concept of a *general* rule takes the following form. One is pictured as estimating on what percentage of the cases likely to arise a given rule may be relied upon to express the correct decision, that is, the decision that would be arrived at if one were to correctly apply the utilitarian principle case by case. If one estimates that by and large the rule will give the correct decision, or if one estimates that the likelihood of making a mistake by applying the utilitarian principle directly on one's own is greater than the likelihood of making a mistake by following the rule, and if these considerations held of persons generally, then one would be justified in

urging its adoption as a general rule. In this way *general* rules might be accounted for on the summary view. It will still make sense, however, to speak of applying the utilitarian principle case by case, for it was by trying to foresee the results of doing this that one got the initial estimates upon which acceptance of the rule depends. That one is taking a rule in accordance with the summary conception will show itself in the naturalness with which one speaks of the rule as a guide, or as a maxim, or as a generalization from experience, and as something to be laid aside in extraordinary cases where there is no assurance that the generalization will hold and the case must therefore be treated on its merits. Thus there goes with this conception the notion of a particular exception which renders a rule suspect on a particular occasion.

The other conception of rules I will call the practice conception. On this view rules are pictured as defining a practice. Practices are set up for various reasons, but one of them is that in many areas of conduct each person's deciding what to do on utilitarian grounds case by case leads to confusion, and that the attempt to coordinate behavior by trying to foresee how others will act is bound to fail. As an alternative one realizes that what is required is the establishment of a practice, the specification of a new form of activity; and from this one sees that a practice necessarily involves the abdication of full liberty to act on utilitarian and prudential grounds. It is the mark of a practice that being taught how to engage in it involves being instructed in the rules which define it, and that appeal is made to those rules to correct the behavior of those engaged in it. Those engaged in a practice recognize the rules as defining it. The rules cannot be taken as simply describing how those engaged in the practice in fact behave: it is not simply that they act as if they were obeying the rules. Thus it is essential to the notion of a practice that the rules are publicly known and understood as definitive; and it is essential also that the rules of a practice can be taught and

can be acted upon to yield a coherent practice. On this conception, then, rules are not generalizations from the decisions of individuals applying the utilitarian principle directly and independently to recurrent particular cases. On the contrary, rules define a practice and are themselves the subject of the utilitarian principle.

To show the important differences between this way of fitting rules into the utilitarian theory and the previous way, I shall consider the differences between the two conceptions on the points previously discussed.

1. In contrast with the summary view, the rules of practices are logically prior to particular cases. This is so because there cannot be a particular case of an action falling under a rule of a practice unless there is the practice. This can be made clearer as follows: in a practice there are rules setting up offices, specifying certain forms of action appropriate to various offices, establishing penalties for the breach of rules, and so on. We may think of the rules of a practice as defining offices, moves, and offenses. Now what is meant by saying that the practice is logically prior to particular cases is this: given any rule which specifies a form of action (a move), a particular action which would be taken as falling under this rule given that there is the practice would not be *described as* that sort of action unless there was the practice. In the case of actions specified by practices it is logically impossible to perform them outside the stage-setting provided by those practices, for unless there is the practice, and unless the requisite proprieties are fulfilled, whatever one does, whatever movements one makes, will fail to count as a form of action which the practice specifies. What one does will be described in some *other* way.

One may illustrate this point from the game of baseball. Many of the actions one performs in a game of baseball one can do by oneself or with others whether there is the game or not. For example, one can throw a ball, run, or swing a peculiarly shaped piece of wood.

But one cannot steal base, or strike out, or draw a walk, or make an error, or balk; although one can do certain things which appear to resemble these actions such as sliding into a bag, missing a grounder and so on. Striking out, stealing a base, balking, etc., are all actions which can only happen in a game. No matter what a person did, what he did would not be described as stealing a base or striking out or drawing a walk unless he could also be described as playing baseball, and for him to be doing this presupposes the rule-like practice which constitutes the game The practice is logically prior to particular cases: unless there is the practice the terms referring to actions specified by it lack a sense.[23]

2. The practice view leads to an entirely different conception of the authority which each person has to decide on the propriety of following a rule in particular cases. To engage in a practice, to perform those actions specified by a practice, means to follow the appropriate rules. If one wants to do an action which a certain practice specifies then there is no way to do it except to follow the rules which define it. Therefore, it doesn't make sense for a person to raise the question whether or not a rule of a practice correctly applies to *his* case where the action he contemplates is a form of action defined by a practice. If someone were to raise such a question, he would

[23] One might feel that it is a mistake to say that a practice is logically prior to the forms of action it specifies on the grounds that if there were never any instances of actions falling under a practice then we should be strongly inclined to say that there wasn't the practice either. Blue-prints for a practice do not make a practice. That there is a practice entails that there are instances of people having been engaged and now being engaged in it (with suitable qualifications). This is correct, but it doesn't hurt the claim that any given particular instance of a form of action specified by a practice presupposes the practice. This isn't so on the summary picture, as each instance must be "there" prior to the rules, so to speak, as something from which one gets the rule by applying the utilitarian principle to it directly.

simply show that he didn't understand the situation in which he was acting. If one wants to perform an action specified by a practice, the only legitimate question concerns the nature of the practice itself ("How do I go about making a will?").

This point is illustrated by the behavior expected of a player in games. If one wants to play a game, one doesn't treat the rules of the game as guides as to what is best in particular cases. In a game of baseball if a batter were to ask "Can I have four strikes?" it would be assumed that he was asking what the rule was; and if, when told what the rule was, he were to say that he meant that on this occasion he thought it would be best on the whole for him to have four strikes rather than three, this would be most kindly taken as a joke. One might contend that baseball would be a better game if four strikes were allowed instead of three; but one cannot picture the rules as guides to what is best on the whole in particular cases, and question their applicability to particular cases as particular cases.

3 and 4. To complete the four points of comparison with the summary conception, it is clear from what has been said that rules of practices are not guides to help one decide particular cases correctly as judged by some higher ethical principal. And neither the quasi-statistical notion of generality, nor the notion of a particular exception, can apply to the rules of practices. A more or less general rule of a practice must be a rule which according to the structure of the practice applies to more or fewer of the kinds of cases arising under it; or it must be a rule which is more or less basic to the understanding of the practice. Again, a particular case cannot be an exception to a rule of a practice. An exception is rather a qualification or a further specification of the rule.

It follows from what we have said about the practice conception of rules that if a person is engaged in a practice, and if he is asked why *he* does what *he* does, or if he is asked to defend what he does, then his explanation, or defense, lies in referring the questioner to the practice. He cannot say of *his* action, if it is an action specified by a practice, that he does it rather than some other because he thinks it is best on the whole.[24] When a man engaged in a practice is queried about his action he must assume that the questioner either doesn't know that he is engaged in it ("Why are you in a hurry to pay him?" "I promised to pay him today") or doesn't know what the practice is. One doesn't so much justify one's particular action as explain, or show, that it is in accordance with the practice. The reason for this is that it is only against the stage-setting of the practice that one's particular action is described as it is. Only by reference to the practice can one *say* what one is doing. To explain or to defend one's own action, as a particular action, one fits it into the practice which defines it. If this is not accepted it's a sign that a different question is being raised as to whether one is justified in accepting the practice, or in tolerating it. When the challenge is to the practice, citing the rules (saying what the practice is) is naturally to no avail. But when the challenge is to the particular action defined by the practice, there is nothing one can do but refer to the rules. Concerning particular actions there is only a question for one who isn't clear as to what the practice is, or who doesn't know that it is being engaged in. This is to be contrasted with the case of a maxim which may be taken as pointing to the correct decision on the case as decided on *other* grounds, and so giving a challenge on the case a sense by having it question whether these other grounds really support the decision on this case.

If one compares the two conceptions of rules I have discussed, one can see how the summary conception misses the significance of the distinction between justifying a practice and justifying actions falling under it. On this view rules are regarded as guides whose purpose it is to indicate the ideally rational decision on the given particular case which the flawless application of the utilitarian principle would yield. One has, in principle, full option to use the guides or to discard them as the situation warrants without one's moral office being altered in any way: whether one discards the rules or not, one always holds the office of a rational person seeking case by case to realize the best on the whole. But on the practice conception, if one holds an office defined by a practice then questions regarding one's actions in this office are settled by reference to the rules which define the practice. If one seeks to question these rules, then one's office undergoes a fundamental change: one then assumes the office of one empowered to change and criticize the rules, or the office of a reformer, and so on. The summary conception does away with the distinction of offices and the various forms of argument appropriate to each. On that conception there is one office and so no offices at all. It therefore obscures the fact that the utilitarian principle must, in the case of actions and offices defined by a practice, apply to the practice, so that general utilitarian arguments are not available to those who act in offices so defined.[25]

---

[24] A philosophical joke (in the mouth of Jeremy Bentham): "When I run to the other wicket after my partner has struck a good ball I do so because it is best on the whole."

[25] How do these remarks apply to the case of the promise known only to father and son? Well, at first sight the son certainly holds the office of promisor, and so he isn't allowed by the practice to weigh the particular case on general utilitarian grounds. Suppose instead that he wishes to consider himself in the office of one empowered to criticize and change the practice, leaving aside the question as to his right to move from his previously assumed office to another. Then he may consider utilitarian arguments as applied to the practice; but once he does this he will see that there are such arguments for not allowing a general utilitarian defense in the practice for this sort of case. For to do so would make it impossible to ask for and to give a kind of promise which one often wants to be able to ask for and to give. Therefore he will not want to change the practice, and so as a promisor he has no option but to keep his promise.

Some qualifications are necessary in what I have said. First, I may have talked of the summary and the practice conceptions of rules as if only one of them could be true of rules, and if true of any rules, then necessarily true of *all* rules. I do not, of course, mean this. (It is the critics of utilitarianism who make this mistake insofar as their arguments against utilitarianism presuppose a summary conception of the rules of practices.) Some rules will fit one conception, some rules the other; and so there are rules of practices (rules in the strict sense), and maxims and "rules of thumb."

Secondly, there are further distinctions that can be made in classifying rules, distinctions which should be made if one were considering other questions. The distinctions which I have drawn are those most relevant for the rather special matter I have discussed, and are not intended to be exhaustive.

Finally, there will be many borderline cases about which it will be difficult, if not impossible, to decide which conception of rules is applicable. One expects border-line cases with any concept, and they are especially likely in connection with such involved concepts as those of a practice, institution, game, rule, and so on. Wittgenstein has shown how fluid these notions are.[26] What I have done is to emphasize and sharpen two conceptions for the limited purpose of this paper.

IV

What I have tried to show by distinguishing between two conceptions of rules is that there is a way of regarding rules which allows the option to consider particular cases on general utilitarian grounds; whereas there is another conception which does not admit of such discretion except insofar as the rules themselves authorize it. I want to suggest that the tendency while doing philosophy to picture rules in accordance with the summary conception is what may

have blinded philosophers to the significance of the distinction between justifying a practice and justifying a particular action falling under it; and it does so by misrepresenting the logical force of the reference to the rules in the case of a challenge to a particular action falling under a practice, and by obscuring the fact that where there is a practice, it is the practice itself that must be the subject of the utilitarian principle.

It is surely no accident that two of the traditional test cases of utilitarianism, punishment and promises, are clear cases of practices. Under the influence of the summary conception it is natural to suppose that the officials of a penal system, and one who has made a promise, may decide what to do in particular cases on utilitarian grounds. One fails to see that a general discretion to decide particular cases on utilitarian grounds is incompatible with the concept of a practice; and that what discretion one does have is itself defined by the practice (e.g., a judge may have discretion to determine the penalty within certain limits). The traditional objections to utilitarianism which I have discussed presuppose the attribution to judges, and to those who have made promises, of a plenitude of moral authority to decide particular cases on utilitarian grounds. But once one fits utilitarianism together with the notion of a practice, and notes that punishment and promising are practices, then one sees that this attribution is logically precluded.

That punishment and promising are practices is beyond question. In the case of promising this is shown by the fact that the form of words "I promise" is a performative utterance which presupposes the stage-setting of the practice and the proprieties defined by it. Saying the words "I promise" will only be promising given the existence of the practice. It would be absurd to interpret the rules about promising in accordance with the summary conception. It is absurd to say, for example, that the rule that promises should be kept could have arisen from its being found in past cases to be best on the whole to keep one's promise; for

---

[26] *Philosophical Investigations* (Oxford, 1953), I, pars. 65–71, for example.

unless there were already the understanding that one keeps one's promises as part of the practice itself there couldn't have been any cases of promising.

It must, of course, be granted that the rules defining promising are not codified, and that one's conception of what they are necessarily depends on one's moral training. Therefore it is likely that there is considerable variation in the way people understand the practice, and room for argument as to how it is best set up. For example, differences as to how strictly various defenses are to be taken, or just what defenses are available, are likely to arise amongst persons with different backgrounds. But irrespective of these variations it belongs to the concept of the practice of promising that the general utilitarian defense is not available to the promisor. That this is so accounts for the force of the traditional objection which I have discussed. And the point I wish to make is that when one fits the utilitarian view together with the practice conception of rules, as one must in the appropriate cases, then there is nothing in that view which entails that there must be such a defense, either in the practice of promising, or in any other practice.

Punishment is also a clear case. There are many actions in the sequence of events which constitute someone's being punished which presuppose a practice. One can see this by considering the definition of punishment which I gave when discussing Carritt's criticism of utilitarianism. The definition there stated refers to such things as the normal rights of a citizen, rules of law, due process of law, trials and courts of law, statutes, etc., none of which can exist outside the elaborate stage-setting of a legal system. It is also the case that many of the actions for which people are punished presuppose practices. For example, one is punished for stealing, for trespassing, and the like, which presuppose the institution of property. It is impossible to say what punishment is, or to describe a particular instance of it, without referring to offices, actions, and offenses specified by practices. Punishment is a move in an elaborate legal game and presupposes the complex of practices which make up the legal order. The same thing is true of the less formal sorts of punishment: a parent or guardian or someone in proper authority may punish a child, but no one else can.

There is one mistaken interpretation of what I have been saying which it is worthwhile to warn against. One might think that the use I am making of the distinction between justifying a practice and justifying the particular actions falling under it involves one in a definite social and political attitude in that it leads to a kind of conservatism. It might seem that I am saying that for each person the social practices of his society provide the standard of justification for his actions; therefore let each person abide by them and his conduct will be justified.

This interpretation is entirely wrong. The point I have been making is rather a logical point. To be sure, it has consequences in matters of ethical theory; but in itself it leads to no particular social or political attitude. It is simply that where a form of action is specified by a practice there is no justification possible of the particular action of a particular person save by reference to the practice. In such cases the action is what it is in virtue of the practice and to explain it is to refer to the practice. There is no inference whatsoever to be drawn with respect to whether or not one should accept the practices of one's society. One can be as radical as one likes but in the case of actions specified by practices the objects of one's radicalism must be the social practices and people's acceptance of them.

I have tried to show that when we fit the utilitarian view together with the practice conception of rules, where this conception is appropriate,[27] we can form-

[27] As I have already stated, it is not always easy to say where the conception is appropriate. Nor do I care to discuss at this point the general sorts of cases to which it does apply except to say that one should not take it for granted that it applies to many so-called "moral rules." It is my feel-

ulate it in a way which saves it from several traditional objections. I have

---

ing that relatively few actions of the moral life are defined by practices and that the practice conception is more relevant to understanding legal and legal-like arguments than it is to the more complex sort of moral arguments. Utilitarianism must be fitted to different conceptions of rules depending on the case, and no doubt the failure to do this has been one source of difficulty in interpreting it correctly.

further tried to show how the logical force of the distinction between justifying a practice and justifying an action falling under it is connected with the practice conception of rules and cannot be understood as long as one regards the rules of practices in accordance with the summary view. Why, when doing philosophy, one may be inclined to so regard them, I have not discussed. The reasons for this are evidently very deep and would require another paper.

Rules and Consequences
ANDREW OLDENQUIST

*S*ir *David Ross* has remarked on the "clear antithesis" between ethical systems in which duty is the central theme, and those in which goods or ends are central. It is an antithesis between those philosophers who hold that 'right', 'ought', and 'duty', embodied in certain moral rules, are terms more fundamental to the judgment of what persons do than are 'good' or 'intrinsic good'; and those philosophers who hold that 'good' or 'intrinsic good', embodied in certain ethical principles is the more fundamental concept. This antithesis has also been expressed as one between deontological and teleological ethical systems. It has, among its other effects, generated the controversy betwen philosophers who believe that 'right' can be defined in terms of 'good' and those who believe that it cannot.

I shall maintain that the traditional teleological-deontological distinction does not mark two fundamentally different theories about what is relevant to the rightness of an action, but instead only distinguishes two alternative ways of saying the same thing, which I shall call the "language of ends" and the "language of rules". Hence I shall argue that the teleological-deontological distinction is a false dualism which has contributed only

confusion to moral philosophy. My point of attack is to examine the common distinction between actions, on the one hand, and the consequences of actions, on the other, with an eye to seeing how or why it is that some events count as parts of actions and others count as consequences of actions. Roughly, my first three sections attack the idea that the appeal to rules and the appeal to consequences are logically distinct and incompatible tests for the rightness of individual actions. In Section IV I argue that Stephen Toulmin's restricted utilitarianism cannot resolve the difficulties of traditional formalists and teleological (or utilitarian) theories because it reaffirms and indeed glorifies the main source of these difficulties, namely the bifurcation of moral reasoning into deontological and teleological reasoning.

I

The privilege has been claimed, for both rules of action and good or bad consequences, of being the sole or primary ground of an action's rightness. But how are we to separate an action from its consequences with clarity and finality sufficient to support the importance of this distinction? Any attempt to specify what a person did involves reference to

FROM: *Mind*, Vol. LXXV (April 1966). Reprinted by permission of editor and author.

what happened, in other words, to what could be called consequences, however direct and immediate they might be. There is a perfectly understandable sense according to which we can say that lying is the consequence of speaking in a certain way, and even speaking at all is the consequence of a certain set of intentions and bodily activities. Let us suppose that a man is "campaigning for Kennedy". If questioned about what that means, I might say that what he "actually" was doing was distributing posters, persuading Democrats to register, and the like, and that his being a campaigner is a *consequence* of this activity. If, furthermore, I was asked what he "actually did" in distributing posters, I might reply that he went to the printers, picked up the posters, walked into all the local Democratic headquarters in the city, and so on; and that a consequence of all these actions was that posters were distributed.[1] It is plain that this kind of analysis can be carried to the point where all we can say that the man "actually did" were certain trivial and individually meaningless bodily acts and, perhaps, the intending of these acts.

On the other hand, a dedicated man may say that his goal or aim is the elimination of elephantiasis in Samoa. It would be quite proper, also, to say that this man is doing something, namely, stamping out elephantiasis in Samoa. If the objection is made that this is surely not what we mean by "an action" but is really a very composite activity, one can reply that in exactly the way in which this composite activity is broken down into individual constitutive actions, each of these constitutive actions may be analyzed into simpler actions; and that apart from the dictates of convention,

we have as good grounds for calling the one as for calling the other an action. Similarly, when a person says that his moral end or goal is the greatest happiness of the greatest number of people, it also would be quite proper to say, on the appropriate occasions, that he performs or attempts to perform a certain morally significant kind of action, namely, that of increasing the happiness of the greatest number of people. In general, almost any occurrence or set of occurrences, having a conscious human source, may, at the sole cost of stretching certain conventional ways of speaking, be called either an action or the consequence of an action.

What happens when a person is said to have "done something" or "attained something" is that a whole chain or system of causally connected *events* takes place. The more remote events in this system, due to lack of perfect knowledge on our part, can be predicted only so far. It is a person's lack of knowledge of the later events in a series he has started which accounts for one of the practical reasons why he designates some of these events part of his "action" and others of them "consequences". However, when we expect an event which we nevertheless did not specifically intend, we often call this event a "consequence" or "result" of our action rather than an "action" itself. Normally we say that lying is an action because the lie is one of the intended segments of the long series of causally connected events which we produce. Yet we do not call all intended events "actions". Even when one intends to bring about a certain set of events and there are many variables involved, the causal chains extending far into the future—in this kind of case we are inclined to say that one has an aim, goal or end, the attainment of which will be a *consequence* of certain prior actions, rather than to say simply that one is "doing something". I think we are inclined to give the name "end" or "consequence" to complex patterns of events, like the actual curing of cancer and, more obviously because it is less attainable

---

[1] In this kind of case usage is flexible enough that it is often a matter of indifference whether we say that a person did X, or that he did something else which had X as its consequence. Contrast, however, the conscious breaking down of "actions" for the purpose of mitigating responsibility: '*You* ruined his career.'—'No I didn't, I merely told the truth.'

and less definite, the actual maximization of happiness, even though both are things we intend.

The theoretical continuity of a sequence of events, which we conventionally separate into "action" and "consequences", is important for ethical theory. Our ability to shift the status of morally relevant events back and forth between that of "consequence" and "component of an action" has of course been recognized for a long time. The recognition that this can be done has often been employed to solve one of the easier problems in Kant's ethics, namely that of justifying some beneficial lies without appealing to consequences. What are called the consequences of one kind of action may be made part of the specification of another kind of action and, thus interpreted, become the content of a possible moral rule. Hence it has been pointed out that Kant did not allow his maxims, and consequently his conception of a kind of action, to be sufficiently complicated: "I will allow myself to lie to a murderer who seeks a friend in my house" is not a maxim about lying simply, but nevertheless is about a kind of action. But what seems not to have been noticed by those who point this out is that they have thereby undermined whatever unique significance a deontological theory was supposed to have. They have simply shown that they can make the same points as their teleological rivals.

Solely how we decide to classify the later events in the causal series of events is what accounts for our ability to distinguish (and choose) between judging that an action is right or wrong because it has certain consequences and judging that an action is right or wrong because it is an action of a certain sort. If we are free to construe certain morally significant events as *either* specifications of the action *or* as its consequences, then we are free to say *either* that the action is right or wrong because it has certain consequences, *or* that it is right or wrong because it is of a certain sort. And if we are free to do this, then we are free to appeal to rules or consequences, as

we please. Finally if, as seems certain, it is of no moral significance whether or not we let a given event count as part of the action or instead as a consequence of a simpler version of the action, then whether we appeal to rules or to consequences to determine the rightness or wrongness of a particular action is of no moral significance. This is the skeleton of my argument, and the rest of this paper will serve to fill it out.

II

In *Five Types of Ethical Theory* (p. 207) C. D. Broad has defined deontological and teleological ethical theories as follows:

Deontological theories hold that there are ethical propositions of the form: "Such and such a kind of action would always be right (or wrong) in such and such circumstances, no matter what its consequences might be.". . .
Teleological theories hold that the rightness or wrongness of an action is always determined by its tendency to produce certain consequences which are intrinsically good or bad.

Broad's definition of a deontological theory maintains that all consequences whatever are irrelevant to the rightness or wrongness of a particular action. But there appears to be no difference, in terms of the production of morally relevant events, between *circumstances* (in Broad's phrase "in such and such circumstances") and consequences. Circumstances are what alter the outcome of actions, and are in fact often taken to *be* the altered outcomes of actions belonging to certain classes. For example, Broad's deontologist might say that lying is always wrong in circumstances which exclude those where telling the truth would reveal vital information to a war-time enemy; and that a lie falling into the above class always would be wrong "no matter what its consequences might be". Now the above claim is self-contradictory unless we interpret "consequences" to mean consequences other than those which consist in the revelation of vital information to the enemy. But on this interpretation the claim of the deontologist (". . . no matter what its consequences might be") has become trivially true. The irrelevance of consequences, which is taken by Broad and other philosophers to signal an important difference between deontologists and teleological moral philosophers, is empty of significance because all the events deemed morally relevant at the time of formulating the rule are already referred to in the content of the rule and in the specification of circumstances.

The teleological position is misleading for reasons which exactly correspond to those raised against the deontological position. The *morally relevant events*, referred to by the deontologist in his description of the nature of the action and as "such and such circumstances", are now called "consequences of the action" by the teleologist, and are thereby held to be forever separate from the action itself, and hence to comprise an external locus for the moral determinants of the action. This appears to lend support to the view that a teleological justification explains or gives a reason why an act is wrong in a way in which a deontological justification fails to do so. The teleologist claims that a kind of action is wrong because of some fact about that kind of action, namely its bad consequences, while the formalist appears merely to proclaim that a certain kind of action is wrong without appealing to some further fact about it. In other words the apparent distinctness of consequences from what they justify appears to give consequences more justificatory power. To reason this way is to be misled by the action-consequence dualism. Insofar as the formalist and teleologist each notices that certain events are "wrong-making", it makes no difference whether these events are taken to be part of or instead external to the action.

Two points need to be made against the teleologist's position: (1) The privileged position given by the teleologist to consequences, *qua* "reasons"-candidates, causes him to lose sight of the possible moral relevance of events which he allows to remain part of the action. It is a mistake to say that lying is not wrong *unless* it has bad effects, although it might help to bring around the adamant teleologist by playing the game his way, by pointing out that speaking sometimes has the bad effect of being a lie. (2) The consequences of an action, by the reverse of the process by which we broke down the deontologist's highly specified rules, may be readily incorporated within an action itself, and this more highly specified action made the content of a moral rule. Or if this procedure gives us an action that includes too much of what conventionally we are inclined to call "consequences", we may incorporate these events within the circumstances under which the rule is said to apply or not apply. Similar points need to be made about the position of the deontologist. He may, for example, be subject to a corresponding inability to see the moral significance of events which do not find themselves in *his* privileged classification.

Teleologists naturally want to determine an action by all its morally relevant effects, but have often criticized deontologists for their rigidity, *i.e.* for wanting to determine an action by a single rule ('One ought not to lie')—as if the dictum "consequences are irrelevant" somehow guaranteed that the deontologist must leave out something morally relevant. That the deontologist must do this is absurd, since it is precisely because he has adopted the "language of rules" and not the "language of ends" that whatever events he deems morally relevant get expressed in moral rules of one kind or another. If he has eccentric moral opinions he will leave out what we consider to be relevant features, but there could not possibly be anything about the nature of deontological language that required that he do so. Equally absurd is the corresponding claim of the deontologist that judging an action by its effects somehow must leave out something of moral relevance. The logic of the language of ends sets practically no limits on what can count as an end or effect, although one's moral opinions, *e.g.* those of a hedonistic utilitarian, naturally set limits on what counts as a morally relevant effect. Each of these meta-ethical theories, in so far as it purports to be saying something about the nature of moral reasons which is incompatible with what its terminological complement says, is false; and each, in so far as it neither implies such an incompatibility nor is used as vehicle for false moral opinions, is trivially true.

Kinds of morally significant events, when construed as constitutive of a kind of action, have been said to define "*prima facie* obligations", and the same events, when construed as sets of consequences, have been called "intrinsic goods". What both Ross, when he speaks of *prima facie* obligations, and G. E. Moore, when he speaks of intrinsic goods, are getting at is the role of recurring and relatively simple morally significant events or sets of events which often suffice, either by default or in combination with other morally significant events, to determine the moral quality of particular wholes which contain them. In the *Right and the Good* Ross has explained *prima facie* obligations under the double aspect of being (1) "objective facts involved in the nature of the situation, or more strictly in an element of its nature", and (2) merely presumptive moral determinants of individual actions and not "duties proper", since duty proper "depends on all the morally significant kinds it is an instance of" (pp. 20, 19). Intrinsic goods, in so far as they are used to justify duties, are explainable under the same double aspect of being (1) objective features of certain consequences, and (2) merely presumptively determinative of the individual obligations of which they are consequences, and not determinative of duty proper since duty proper depends on all the significant events involved. Moreover, whether a set of morally significant events is classified as an intrinsic good or instead as a *prima facie* obligation depends on whether we choose to classify this set of events as part of

the action or instead as consequences of a simpler version of the action.

III

It is now necessary to guard against a misunderstanding. I have argued that when we wish to back up a moral judgment of a particular action we may appeal either to rules or to consequences, since the morally significant events, which comprise our reason, can be taken to be part of the action or instead can be taken to be effects of a different, less highly specified action. I have not maintained, nor does it follow from what I have said, that we always are morally obligated to do actions which have good or the best consequences. Put quite generally, it is one thing to say that *if* an action is an obligation the significant events which make it so may be referred to in either deontological or teleological language. It is a further thing to say that all actions with good or the best effects are obligations and accordingly that good or the best effects always can be reformulated so as to define corresponding rules of obligation. There is no incompatibility in maintaining, correctly, I think, that the first of these claims is true and that the second is false. Most of us attach greater moral importance to refraining from doing public harm than to doing public good and hence, with some exceptions, we limit rules of obligation to prohibitions of certain kinds of actions just as we limit consequences which can justify obligations to bad consequences.

We can divide morally significant events into those which are "obligation-making" and those which are not. The latter might be thought to present a problem because consequences which are good, but nevertheless not "good enough" to obligate, have no obvious deontological equivalents. One way to answer this is simply to acknowledge that moral rules concern only what is obligatory and forbidden and hence that most good consequences, when made components of expanded versions of the actions (of which otherwise they would *be* consequences), do not have corresponding rules at all[2] I doubt very much if there are moral rules about actions which are right but not duties, or if there are "supererogatory rules". Nevertheless the notion of an "imperfect duty" seems to be intelligible. Hence *e.g.* the general obligation to act benevolently, where no given instance of benevolence is a duty, might serve as the formalist analogue of certain types of good consequence which imply that the actions which produce them are right but in no given instance obligatory.

Of course some philosophers have maintained that consequences which are less than extraordinarily good justify obligations and other philosophers have claimed that only bad consequences justify obligations or prohibitions. But this is a matter of philosophers' moral opinions and has nothing to do with the logic of the situation. Consider, for example, a teleological theory which maintained that one ought to do that action which, among the alternatives available, produced the best results. This is a way of saying that absolutely every action a person does is either a duty or immoral, unless, of course, more than one of the possible alternative actions produces optimum results. In so far as it is not said what kinds of results are good, the deontological equivalent to such a theory would maintain merely that every alternative possible action fell under a moral rule, where the action falling under the most stringent rule was one's duty and any of its alternatives would be an immoral action. Each theory would involve discerning and weighing countless morally significant events, con-

struing them as sets of consequences or as complicated rules, and doubtless according to each of these odd theories nearly every action that any person ever did or will do would be immoral. Thus the problem of deciding which types of consequences, among innumerable good ones, are sufficiently weighty to determine obligations is not a problem which has no formalist analogue. The problem of deciding which ostensible rules of obligation are legitimate, and which are weightier in cases of conflict, is the same problem.

There is, however, a situation in which the reciprocal translatability of a given set of events expressed in the language of rules or the language of ends does not hold. Every system of events of moral interest is one orginated by a person, and this origination is always an action, to be evaluated, if it is to be evaluated at all, by means of action-words such as 'right', 'ought', and 'duty'. That is to say, when we reach activities that are simple enough—such as depressing a pedal—we cannot easily re-describe them as ends or goals because we cannot easily think of antecedent actions which would lead to these goals. Thus we cannot help but use the language of rules and say 'You ought to step on the brake when so-and-so happens' because the achievement of stepping on the brake is very nearly at the beginning of the system of events the person starts. But we do have a choice about the effects of stepping on the brake. We can say either 'You ought to stop the car (when so-and-so happens)'; or 'Your goal (when so-and-so happens) is stopping the car' where prior actions, *e.g.* stepping on the brake, which result in the achievement of this goal are actions you ought to do.[3] Whenever we can separate the thing to be done from how it is to be done, we can let the former be a goal and the latter rules for attaining it. But what is very simple cannot easily be divided

---

[2] 'Deontology' means 'theory of duty or obligation' and this meaning still underlies a narrower and current philosophical meaning of the term, *viz.* the determination of duties by virtue of actions being of certain kinds, and not by virtue of their having certain consequences. Since I am not exclusively concerned with obligation, 'formalism' is a better name than 'deontology' for the one side of the dualism that interests me except that the former name lacks an elegant opposite ('utilitarianism' is quite inappropriate).

[3] See R. M. Hare, *The Language of Morals* (Oxford, 1952) chap. 4, for a related discussion of these types of alternatives.

in this way. Because, in the above sense, actions are irreducible in morals, so, also, are rules.

IV

So far I have discussed giving reasons in support of particular moral judgments. There are more complicated operations such as taking justified exception to moral rules or principles, resolving conflicts of rules, and challenging rules *qua* rules. It has recently been maintained that we support judgments of individual actions by appeal to rules alone, but support judgments resulting from any of the latter operations by appeal to consequences. Thus Toulmin attempts to resolve the conflict between deontological and teleological ethical theories as follows:

Consider . . . the musty old conundrum over which moral philosophers have battled for so long: namely, whether the 'real' analysis of 'X is right' is 'X is an instance of a rule of action (or maxim, or prima facie obligation)', or 'X is the alternative which of all those open to us is likely to have the best results'.

. . . The answer, with comparatively little over-simplification, is that it depends upon the nature of the 'thing'. If it is an action which is an unambiguous instance of a maxim generally accepted in the community concerned, it will be right just because it is an instance of such a maxim; but, if it is an action over which there is a 'conflict of duties', or is itself a principle (or social practice) as opposed to a particular action, it will be right or wrong according as its consequences are likely to be good or bad.

When we bear in mind the function of ethics, therefore we see that the answer to the philosophers' question is 'Either, depending on the nature of the case'. The question, in other words, falls within the logical limits set by the function of ethics —provided only that you are prepared to accept 'Either' as an answer.

As a matter of history, philosophers have not been so prepared: they have tended to demand an 'unequivocal' answer—'The first' or 'The second', and not 'Either'—and to assume that either the 'deontological' or the 'teleological' answer must be 'true', and the other 'false'* (Reason in Ethics, *pp. 154–155*).

Toulmin's answer to the "musty old conundrum" with which this paper is concerned is to bifurcate moral reasoning, such that within one delimited area of moral reasoning only the "deontological answer" is appropriate, while within another delimited area of moral reasoning only the "teleological answer" is appropriate. I shall show that when we qualify moral rules, resolve conflicts of rules, and make judgments about rules *qua* rules, it makes no significant difference whether we support such qualifications, resolutions, and judgments by appeal to rules or instead by appeal to consequences.

First, consider situations in which we believe that a moral rule, such as 'One ought not to disobey one's parents', requires qualification. One way to expose what would be over-rigid adherence to a rule, were we to follow it in certain special situations, is to point out what would be the bad consequences of following the rule in those types of situation. 'I would commit myself to working at a job I hate' and 'We would all be killed' state consequences which would be satisfactory reasons for restricting the scope of the rule in question. But the undesirable events here expressed as consequences also could have been embodied in rules: 'One ought not to commit oneself to a grossly unsuitable vocation' and 'One ought to prevent the death of persons'. If we do this, then, without change in moral significance, and without waving the red flag of "consequences" and "exceptions" before the eye of the rule user, we have a situation where one proposes to restrict or tighten the original rule by appeal to other (*ex hypothesi*) more demanding rules. The situation is thus changed from one where rules clash with consequences to one where two or more rules conflict. The possibility of reformulating our description of the situation in this way shows that restricting rules by appeal to sufficiently weighty consequences is no more revolutionary, no less feasible, than is modifying one rule because it clashes with another sufficiently weighty rule. If, in a given situation, the hypothesis is that certain events are sufficiently weighty to determine an obligation, plainly they remain so whether they be formulated in deontological or teleological language.

With regard to the second type of situation, in which moral rules conflict, I think that in practice most conflicts of rules are resolved by simply recognizing that one rule is more demanding than the other. If a decision cannot be reached in this way we may appeal to another rule which reinforces one of the two conflicting rules. Or, if we prefer, we may appeal to relevant consequences. This type of situation is merely the reverse of that described above. Any of the consequences to which Toulmin says we appeal in order to resolve conflicts of rules could be re-expressed as part of the conflict of a supplementary moral rule describing an action of expanded complexity.

Consider, thirdly, the situation where we question whether or not a rule is a good rule, as when we try to decide what moral rules to teach to children or to the imaginary citizens of an ideal society. Most persons would appeal to utilitarian criteria in such cases. We might argue that the rule is a good rule, a rule we ought to teach, if it has the effect of tending to make different persons' interests compatible, and a bad rule, a rule we ought not to teach, if it has the opposite tendency. Philosophers are not always clear about what they are appealing to when they speak of the "effect of having a rule". They may mean the effect of the rule's general promulgation, without assuming that everybody or even most persons follow it; they may mean the hypothetical collective consequences of everybody's obeying the rule; or they may mean the hypothetical collective consequence of everybody's doing what the rule forbids, with or without also assuming that the rule is promulgated. But any of the sets of events referred to above in terms of good and bad consequences could be re-expressed as the content of rules, in these cases utilitarian rules such as 'One ought to act optimifically' or 'One ought not to do harm'. 'One ought to seek optimific consequences' of course is not a utilitarian rule, but a principle, since in this case the actions one ought to do are said to be obligatory not because they are of a certain sort but because they have good consequences. To one who takes seriously the teleological-deontological dualism this principle is "logically distinct" from 'One ought to act optimifically', but if what I have been maintaining is true, utilitarian rules and utilitarian principles are not distinct in any significant respect.

Utilitarian rules *are* peculiar in the respect that they can be used to judge other rules, such as 'One ought not to lie', as well as rules of skill and prudence. By 'can be used to judge other rules' I do not mean only that they can be used to restrict or qualify another rule, for qualification of a rule must take place whenever two rules conflict with one another; rather, I mean that the decisions by which we accept or reject other rules *qua* rules fall within the scope of utilitarian rules. For example, our decision to teach our children the rule 'One ought not to lie' falls within the scope of the utilitarian rule 'One ought to act optimifically', in the sense that it either heeds or violates it. Other moral rules such as 'One ought not to lie' or 'One ought not to kill' lack this logical peculiarity: they are not such that the acceptance or rejection of other moral rules falls within their scope; viz. accepting or teaching the rule 'One ought not to kill' neither heeds nor violates the rule 'One ought not to lie'. Hence there is a distinction between rules which can be used to judge other rules *qua* rules and rules which cannot be so used.

Toulmin's restricted utilitarianism disallows the use of utilitarian criteria to test individual actions, for the reason that if we limit the application of such criteria to legislative deliberation and the justification of rules we avoid clashes between utility and certain common rules of obligation, and thus escape a traditional objection to utilitarianism. To this purpose Toulmin devised an apparatus within which appeal to rules and appeal to consequences are logically distinct modes of moral reasoning. But if we choose to appeal to utility in the form of a utilitarian rule the apparatus cannot be used to do the job for which it was designed, namely to limit our recourse to some of the moral as distinct from merely the supposed "logical" features of classical utilitarianism. Classical utilitarianism or indeed any normative utilitarian theory need not rest quietly in the teleological cast Toulmin has given it. Thus the inability of restricted utilitarianism to handle utilitarian rules is exposed by J. J. C. Smart when he says:

If 'act optimifically' is itself one of our rules then there will always be a conflict of rules whenever to keep a rule is not itself optimific. If this is so, restricted utilitarianism collapses into extreme utilitarianism.[4]

Smart's conclusion follows if we attempt to base a restriction on the applicability of *normative* utilitarian considerations upon the assumption that non-utilitarian claims, ordinary duties such as 'You ought to keep this promise', are justified invariably by appeal to deontological criteria, while typically utilitarian claims are justified invariably by appeal to teleological criteria. For the assumption is false and hence the clever "extreme utilitarian", by converting rules into ends and ends into rules, can make the restricted utilitarian, who is committed to this logical dualism, say the opposite of what he wishes to say. Philosophers who attempt to restrict utilitarianism in terms of the dualism of rules and consequences find themselves attempting to base an important moral claim on hopelessly shifting sands, and they must find another reason for restricting the application of utility.

[4] J. J. C. Smart, "Extreme and Restricted Utilitarianism," *Philosophical Quarterly*, vi (October 1956), 354.

Must an Action
Right for One
Be Right
for All?

Immanuel Kant, in the *Groundwork of the Metaphysic of Morals,* endeavors to discover the single, supreme principle of morality. This he finds in the categorical imperative, conceived not in itself as a moral principle but as a test by which genuine moral principles can be separated from spurious ones. There are several formulations of the categorical imperative, each of them being construed as necessarily connected with every other.

As a background to the formulation of the categorical imperative, Kant offers three propositions, which he sees as basic to an adequate conception of morality. There is some question as to how the first should be stated. He expresses the second and third as follows: (2) An action done from duty has its moral worth, not in the purpose to be attained by it, but in the maxim in accordance with which it is decided upon; (3) duty is the necessity to act out of reverence for the law. The first proposition is not explicitly stated, though we are told that (3) is "an inference from the two preceding" propositions. Thus (1) plus (2) will entail (3). If we ask what claim of Kant's fulfills this requirement, it would seem that this best serves the purpose: "It is precisely in this that the worth of character begins to show itself—a moral worth and beyond all comparison the highest—namely, that one does good, not from inclination, but from duty." Somewhat restated, Kant's three propositions are:

(1) An action is morally good insofar as it is done from (and not merely in accord with) duty.

(2) An action done from duty has its moral worth in the maxim (law) in accord with which it is performed.

(3) Duty is the necessity to act out of reverence for the law.

A word of explanation concerning each proposition is in order. To act merely in accord with duty is to do what is morally right for some other reason than that it is right. Thus a man may fail to cheat his customers because he is afraid of financial loss if he is discovered. To act from duty is to do what is right *because* it is right, and what makes an action right is that it is in accord with the moral law. Thus one who does the right act because it is right may be said to act out of respect for the law. This clarifies (1). Now (2) asserts that the moral worth of an action derives from its maxim. That an action is right is determined by this: does its maxim pass the test of the categorical imperative? If so, it is the right action to perform; if not, it is not the right action to perform, no matter how noble one's purposes in doing it.

So (2) says that an action is right in virtue of its maxim passing the test of the categorical imperative, and (1) says that the moral goodness of an action is determined by whether or not it is performed just because it is right. An agent who performs an action because it is right acts out of respect for the law. In accord with (3), duty is the necessity to act out of respect for what is right—to act from reverence for the moral law.

Our exposition of (1), (2), and (3) have made use of the terms "maxim" and "categorical imperative." A maxim is a description or a specification of an action, along with the statement of a resolution to perform it. Thus, "Let me now write a letter home" is a maxim, as is "Let me now read Kant." A maxim is universalized when made into an imperative involving all men (or all members of a certain class of men). Thus the universalizations of the maxims just mentioned are, respectively, "Let everyone now write a letter home" and "Let everyone now read Kant." Further, an adequate maxim will mention all the morally relevant features of an action and of its circumstances. Thus our first universalized maxim might more plausibly read, "Let everyone whose parents will otherwise be unduly worried if they receive no letter now write home." Now some maxims, duly universalized and inclusive of morally relevant features, can be stated as moral laws of the form "Everyone ought to . . .," and some cannot. "Let one aid his neighbor when his neighbor is in need" may well be transformable into a moral law stating that everyone ought to aid his neighbor when his neighbor is in need (with, no doubt, appropriate restrictions). But, "Let me kill for pleasure when I want," universalized into "Let everyone kill for pleasure when he wants," seems ill suited as raw material for a moral law; upon transformation into a moral law, it becomes "Everyone ought to kill for pleasure when he wants." How, though, does one tell which maxims one ought to follow? One ought to follow maxims that can be universalized consistently. More carefully, it is permissible to act on a maxim whose universalization is consistent and obligatory to act on those maxims that can be universalized consistently, whereas their opposites ("Let everyone *not . . .*") cannot.

The categorical imperative is put this way in Section One of the *Groundwork*: "I ought never to act except in such a way that I can also will that my maxim should become a universal law." This is, Kant believes, a principle with which "the ordinary reason of mankind also agrees completely in its practical judgments and always has the aforesaid principle before its eyes," though presumably not in this precise formulation.

In the second section (not included below), Kant offers these formulations of the one categorical imperative: (1) Act on a maxim only if you can at the same time will that it should become a universal law; (2) act as if the maxim of your action were to become through your will a universal law of nature; (3) act in such a way that you always treat humanity, whether in your own person or in that of another, never simply as a means, but always at the same time as an end; (4) act so that your will can regard itself at the same time as making universal laws through its maxims; (5) act as if through your maxims you were a law-making member of the kingdom of ends; (6) all maxims proceeding from our own making of laws ought to harmonize with a possible kingdom of ends as a kingdom of nature. While it would take many pages to deal fully with the interconnections of these formulations of the categorical imperative, a few words on this topic may be helpful. (1) says, in effect, that "if it is right for anyone to do A in circumstance C, it is right for everyone to do A in C," where A stands for the description of an action and includes all its morally relevant features and where C stands for the description of the circumstances of that action and includes all the morally relevant features of those circumstances. (Or, A could be so construed as to include C.) (1) is thus a principle of consistency in morality. The consistency in view is not simply logical consistency, though any maxim that is logically inconsistent will of course be unacceptable. (To follow such a maxim would be impossible, and something one could be morally condemned for attempting.) More significantly it is an inconsistency between a maxim and its universalization, as is clear from Kant's examples.

For one knowingly to make a promise he cannot or will not keep is to adopt, at least temporarily, a practice that universally followed would make promise-making impossible. A society where making false promises is a practice would be a society where in fact there could be no practice of promise-making—for the practice of promise-making presupposes mutual trust and so is incompatible with the practice of making false promises. The practice of making false promises is hence self-defeating, and so any individual act of false promise-making cannot consistently be universalized. This is clearly the intent of Kant's argument: the practices in question are inconsistent in the sense that both cannot be followed. But the act of making false promises, when universalized into a practice, would in fact require the existence of *both* practices. Such, at least, is Kant's contention. A world in which incompatible practices are followed is no possible world at all. Any act that, when made into a universal practice, would lead to this sort of contradiction is wrong; so says (2).

(3) states that to treat a man merely as a means is also to act in a contradictory manner; for it is a necessary truth in Kant's view that rational nature—including human nature—is an end in itself. To deny a necessary truth is to be inconsistent. To so act as to treat a nonlogically necessary moral truth as if it were not true is to act immorally; at least, this is so with respect to acting so as to deny the worth of human nature.

We are to be consistent in the above ways, and, in so doing, we can regard ourselves "at the same time as making universal law" through our maxims—compare (4)—and as if we through our "maxims [are] . . . law-making members of the kingdom of ends" in which each man treats humanity in his own person and that of every other always as an end and never as a means alone. We thus act so as to make a kingdom of ends real—compare (6)—in which we have "a systematic union of different rational beings under common laws"—compare (5). This indicates, though only in outline, some of the interconnections between the various formulations of the categorical imperative.

Two additional comments will end this brief exposition of Kant's position. In the first section, reproduced below, Kant is probing for the foundations of common morality. He believes he has found this in the categorical imperative. Thus his aim is not to found a new morality—he would regard any attempt at a "new" morality with grave suspicion—but rather to discover the principle that underlies all serious moral reflection. Nonetheless (our second point) philosophy is necessary for morals in this sense: without a clear conception of the basis of our moral reflection, we are likely to accept incompatible moral ideals and may even abandon all moral principles. Thus investigation into the basis of moral reflection—into what provides its content and justification—is in Kant's view eminently practical.

H. J. Paton defends Kant against certain misunderstandings. First, Kant's view of ethics seems so formal. But of course, the *Groundwork of the Metaphysic of Morals* is not all of Kant's ethic. It is only his discussion of the supreme principle of morality. Further, he does not direct our attention away from particular actions when he speaks of the moral law. "Paton writes: "The law is not for Kant an end to which the action is a means; it is the form or principle of the action itself." Second, Kant does not ignore consequences; he, Paton says, maintains "that the expected consequences cannot be the *determining ground* of an action if it is to have moral worth." But the "consequences" of an action are included by Kant in the maxim describing the action; by "action" Kant means "action-including-consequences." Nor does this mean that Kant after all does decide whether an action is right or wrong on the basis of consequences. His appeal is to the *consistency* of maxims, and so to the *consistency* of consequences.

R. B. Brandt offers three objections to Kant's categorical imperative as a criterion for sorting right actions from wrong. He also adds two qualifications, which will, he believes, make Kant's criterion more acceptable. It is worth comparing Brandt's first qualification (that the agent who formulates the maxim be an impartial and sympathetic person) with Kant's own "Act in such a way that you always treat humanity, whether in your own person or in the person of another, never simply as a means, but always at the same time as an end." This will presumably eliminate Brandt's slave-owner, who could accept the maxim "Let a slave-owner put a slave to death with torture if it pleases his fancy."

Brandt also contends that some maxims are such that one person can accept their universalization but another cannot. He supposes that "the reader will be able to think of maxims he would not be able to consistently accept as universal laws." Brandt makes what can be accepted "relativistic," varying from one person to another. It is extremely doubtful that Kant intended his test to be relativistic in this sense; what is inconsistent for one person to adopt will presumably be inconsistent for anyone else to adopt. One question for the reader is whether Brandt's reading of Kant is fair—not to Kant's intentions (there is, I think, no question of Kant's intending his doctrine to be, in the sense explained, relativistic) but to what his claims actually entail.

Brandt further claims that one could describe an action, or formulate a maxim, so explicitly and specifically that its universalization will be acceptable on Kantian grounds, whereas it would not be acceptable were it more generally described. It may be doubted whether the crucial issue is really the explicitness of the description. "Let anyone who wishes to do so perform a murder for pleasure of a person 5'7", male, 139.7 pounds, wearing a peppermint-striped suit at 12:01 A.M. in Times Square Station" is pretty specific, but it is hardly universalizable on Kantian grounds. But there is a question as to which features of an action *are* morally relevant and so should be included in the description of an action. Doubtless we can easily agree on a good deal of what will *not* count as morally relevant features; beyond what will count as treating a man as an end and never as a means only, the *Groundwork* does not help much in telling us what must be counted as morally relevant features. This, no doubt, was not Kant's intention in that work. But it does point to an incompleteness in the work—one that Kant was aware of, and one that the interested reader can consider for himself by examining the books referred to at the end of this section, and, of course, by his own reflection.

Right Actions Must Be Universalizable
IMMANUEL KANT

TRANSITION
FROM THE COMMON RATIONAL
KNOWLEDGE OF MORALITY
TO THE PHILOSOPHICAL

*N*othing can *possibly* be conceived in the world, or even out of it, which can be called good without qualification, except a *good will.* Intelligence, wit, judgment, and the other *talents* of the mind, however they may be named, or courage, resolution, perseverance, as qualities of temperament, are undoubtedly good and desirable in many respects; but these gifts of nature may also become extremely bad and mischievous if the will which is to make use of them, and which, therefore, con-

FROM: *Fundamental Principles of the Metaphysics of Morals*, T. K. Abbott, trans. Section I (originally published in 1783). The numbers in brackets refer to the corresponding pages of the German edition of this work edited by Rosencranz and Schubert in 1838, Vol. VIII.

stitutes what is called *character*, is not good. It is the same with the *gifts of fortune*. Power, riches, honor, even health, and the general well-being and contentment with one's condition which is called *happiness*, inspire pride, and often presumption, if there is not a good will to correct the influence of these on the mind, and with this also to rectify the whole principle of acting, and adapt it to its end. The sight of a being who is not adorned with a single feature of a pure and good will, enjoying unbroken prosperity, can never give pleasure to an impartial rational spectator. [12] Thus a good will appears to constitute the indispensable condition even of being worthy of happiness.

There are even some qualities which are of service to this good will itself, and may facilitate its action, yet which have no intrinsic unconditional value, but always presuppose a good will, and this qualifies the esteem that we justly have for them, and does not permit us to regard them as absolutely good. Moderation in the affections and passions, self-control, and calm deliberation are not only good in many respects, but even seem to constitute part of the intrinsic worth of the person; but they are far from deserving to be called good without qualification, although they have been so unconditionally praised by the ancients. For without the principles of a good will, they may become extremely bad; and the coolness of a villain not only makes him far more dangerous, but also directly makes him more abominable in our eyes than he would have been without it.

A good will is good not because of what it performs or effects, not by its aptness for the attainment of some proposed end, but simply by virtue of the volition—that is, it is good in itself, and considered by itself is to be esteemed much higher than all that can be brought about by it in favor of any inclination, nay, even of the sum-total of all inclinations. Even if it should happen that, owing to special disfavor or fortune, or the niggardly provision of a step-motherly nature, this will should wholly lack power to accomplish its purpose, if with its greatest efforts it should yet achieve nothing, and there should remain only the good will (not, to be sure, a mere wish, but the summoning of all means in our power), then, like a jewel, it would still shine by its own light, as a thing which has its whole value in itself. [13] Its usefulness or fruitlessness can neither add to nor take away anything from this value. It would be, as it were, only the setting to enable us to handle it the more conveniently in common commerce, or to attract to it the attention to those who are not yet connoisseurs, but not to recommend it to true connoisseurs, or to determine its value.

There is, however, something so strange in this idea of the absolute value of the mere will, in which no account is taken of its utility, that notwithstanding the thorough assent of even common reason to the idea, yet a suspicion must arise that it may perhaps really be the product of mere high-flown fancy, and that we may have misunderstood the purpose of nature in assigning reason as the governor of our will. Therefore we will examine this idea from this point of view.

In the physical constitution of an organized being, that is, a being adapted suitably to the purposes of life, we assume it as a fundamental principle that no organ for any purpose will be found but what is also the fittest and best adapted for that purpose. Now in a being which has reason and a will, if the proper object of nature were its *conservation,* its *welfare,* in a word, its *happiness,* then nature would have hit upon a very bad arrangement in selecting the reason of the creature to carry out this purpose. For all the actions which the creature has to perform with a view to this purpose, and the whole rule of its conduct, would be far more surely prescribed to it by instinct, and that end would have been attained thereby much more certainly than it ever can be by reason. Should reason have been communicated to this favored creature over and above, it must only have served it to contemplate the happy constitution of its nature, [14] to admire it, to congratulate itself thereon, and to feel thankful for it to the beneficent cause, but not that it should subject its desires to that weak and delusive guidance, and meddle bunglingly with the purpose of nature. In a word, nature would have taken care that reason should not break forth into *practical exercise*, nor have the presumption, with its weak insight, to think out for itself the plan of happiness and of the means of attaining it. Nature would not only have taken on herself the choice of the ends but also of the means, and with wise foresight would have entrusted both to instinct.

And, in fact, we find that the more a cultivated reason applies itself with deliberate purpose to the enjoyment of life and happiness, so much the more does the man fail of true satisfaction. And from this circumstance there arises in many, if they are candid enough to confess it, a certain degree of *misology*, that is, hatred of reason, especially in the case of those who are most experienced in the use of it, because after calculating all the advantages they derive —I do not say from the invention of all the arts of common luxury, but even from the sciences (which seem to them to be after all only a luxury of the understanding)—they find that they have, in fact, brought trouble on their shoulders rather than gained in happiness; and they end by envying rather than despising the more common stamp of men who keep closer to the guidance of mere instinct, and do not allow their reason much influence on their conduct. And this we must admit, that the judgment of those who would very much lower the lofty eulogies of the advantages which reason gives us in regard to the happiness and satisfaction of life, or who would even reduce them below zero, is by no means morose or ungrateful to the goodness with which the world is governed, but that there lies at the root of these judgments the idea [15] that our existence has a different and far nobler end, for which, and not for happiness, reason is properly

intended, and which must, therefore, be regarded as the supreme condition to which the private ends of man must, for the most part, be postponed.

For as reason is not competent to guide the will with certainty in regard to its objects and the satisfaction of all our wants (which it to some extent even multiplies), this being an end to which an implanted instinct would have led with much greater certainty; and since, nevertheless, reason is imparted to us as a practical faculty, that is, as one which is to have influence on the *will*, therefore, admitting that nature generally in the distribution of her capacities has adapted the means to the end, its true destination must be to produce a *will*, not merely good as a *means* to something else, but *good in itself*, for which reason was absolutely necessary. This will then, though not indeed the sole and complete good, must be the supreme good and the condition of every other, even of the desire of happiness. Under these circumstances, there is nothing inconsistent with the wisdom of nature in the fact that the cultivation of the reason, which is requisite for the first and unconditional purpose, does in many ways interfere, at least in this life, with the attainment of the second, which is always conditional —namely, happiness. Nay, it may even reduce it to nothing, without nature thereby failing of her purpose. For reason recognizes the establishment of a good will as its highest practical destination, and in attaining this purpose is capable only of a satisfaction of its own proper kind, namely, that from the attainment of an end, which end again is determined by reason only, notwithstanding that this may involve many a disappointment to the ends of inclination. [16]

We have then to develop the notion of a will which deserves to be highly esteemed for itself, and is good without a view to anything further, a notion which exists already in the sound natural understanding, requiring rather to be cleared up than to be taught, and which in estimating the value of our actions always takes the first place and constitutes the condition of all the rest. In order to do this, we will take the notion of duty, which includes that of a good will, although implying certain subjective restrictions and hindrances. These, however, far from concealing it or rendering it unrecognizable, rather bring it out by contrast and make it shine forth so much the brighter.

I omit here all actions which are already recognized as inconsistent with duty, although they may be useful for this or that purpose, for with these the question whether they are done *from duty* cannot arise at all, since they even conflict with it. I also set aside those actions which really conform to duty, but to which men have *no* direct *inclination*, performing them because they are impelled thereto by some other inclination. For in this case we can readily distinguish whether the action which agrees with duty is done *from duty* or from a selfish view. It is much harder to make this distinction when the action accords with duty, and the subject has besides a *direct* inclination to it. For example, it is always a matter of duty that a dealer should not overcharge an inexperienced purchaser; and wherever there is much commerce the prudent tradesman does not overcharge, but keeps a fixed price for everyone, so that a child buys of him as well as any other. Men are thus *honestly* served; but this is not enough to make us believe that the tradesman has so acted from duty and from principles of honesty; his own advantage required it; it is out of the question in this case to suppose that he might besides have a direct inclination in favor of the buyers, so that, [17] as it were, from love he should give no advantage to one over another. Accordingly the action was done neither from duty nor from direct inclination, but merely with a selfish view.

On the other hand, it is a duty to maintain one's life; and, in addition, everyone has also a direct inclination to do so. But on this account the often anxious care which most men take for it has no intrinsic worth, and their

maxim has no moral import. They preserve their life *as duty requires*, no doubt, but not *because duty requires*. On the other hand, if adversity and hopeless sorrow have completely taken away the relish for life, if the unfortunate one, strong in mind, indignant at his fate rather than desponding or dejected, wishes for death, and yet preserves his life without loving it—not from inclination or fear, but from duty—then his maxim has a moral worth.

To be beneficent when we can is a duty; and besides this, there are many minds so sympathetically constituted that, without any other motive of vanity or self-interest, they find a pleasure in spreading joy around them, and can take delight in the satisfaction of others so far as it is their own work. But I maintain that in such a case an action of this kind, however proper, however amiable it may be, has nevertheless no true moral worth, but is on a level with other inclinations, for example, the inclination to honor, which, if it is happily directed to that which is in fact of public utility and accordant with duty, and consequently honorable, deserves praise and encouragement, but not esteem. For the maxim lacks the moral import, namely, that such actions be done *from duty*, not from inclination. Put the case that the mind of that philanthropist was clouded by sorrow of his own, [18] extinguishing all sympathy with the lot of others, and that while he still has the power to benefit others in distress, he is not touched by their trouble because he is absorbed with his own; and now suppose that he tears himself out of this dead insensibility and performs the action without any inclination to it, but simply from duty, then first has his action its genuine moral worth. Further still, if nature has put little sympathy in the heart of this or that man, if he, supposed to be an upright man, is by temperament cold and indifferent to the sufferings of others, perhaps because in respect of his own he is provided with the special gift of patience and fortitude, and supposes, or even requires, that others should have the same—and such a man would certainly not be the meanest product of nature—but if nature had not specially framed him for a philanthropist, would he not still find in himself a source from whence to give himself a far higher worth than that of a good-natured temperament could be? Unquestionably. It is just in this that the moral worth of the character is brought out which is incomparably the highest of all, namely, that he is beneficent, not from inclination, but from duty.

To secure one's own happiness is a duty, at least indirectly; for discontent with one's condition, under a pressure of many anxieties and amidst unsatisfied wants, might easily become a great *temptation to transgression of duty*. But here again, without looking to duty, all men have already the strongest and most intimate inclination to happiness, because it is just in this idea that all inclinations are combined in one total. But the precept of happiness is often of such a sort that it greatly interferes with some inclinations, and yet a man cannot form any definite and certain conception of the sum of satisfaction of all of them which is called happiness. [19] It is not then to be wondered at that a single inclination, definite both as to what it promises and as to the time within which it can be gratified, is often able to overcome such a fluctuating idea, and that a gouty patient, for instance, can choose to enjoy what he likes, and to suffer what he may, since, according to his calculation, on this occasion at least, he has [only] not sacrificed the enjoyment of the present moment to a possibly mistaken expectation of a happiness which is supposed to be found in health. But even in this case, if the general desire for happiness did not influence his will, and supposing that in his particular case health was not a necessary element in this calculation, there yet remains in this, as in all other cases, this law—namely, that he should promote his happiness not from inclination but from duty, and by this would his conduct first acquire true moral worth.

It is in this manner, undoubtedly, that we are to understand those passages of Scripture also in which we are commanded to love our neighbor, even our enemy. For love, as an affection, cannot be commanded, but beneficence for duty's sake may, even though we are not impelled to it by any inclination—nay, are even repelled by a natural and unconquerable aversion. This is *practical* love, and not *pathological*—a love which is seated in the will, and not in the propensions of sense—in principles of action and not of tender sympathy; and it is this love alone which can be commanded.*

The second proposition is: That an action done from duty derives its moral worth, *not from the purpose* which is to be attained by it, but from the maxim by which it is determined, and therefore does not depend on the realization of the object of the action, but merely on the *principle of volition* by which the action has taken place, without regard to any object of desire. [20] It is clear from what precedes that the purposes which we may have in view in our actions, or their effects regarded as ends and springs of the will, cannot give to actions any unconditional or moral worth. In what, then, can their worth lie if it is not to consist in the will and in reference to its expected effect? It cannot lie anywhere but in the *principle of the will* without regard to the ends which can be attained by the action. For the will stands between its *a priori* principle, which is formal, and its *a posteriori* spring, which is material, as between two roads, and as it must be determined by something, it follows that it must be determined by the formal principle of volition when an action is done from duty, in which case every material principle has been withdrawn from it.

The third proposition, which is a consequence of the two preceding, I would express thus: *Duty is the necessity of acting from respect for the law.*

* See introduction to this section.

I may have *inclination* for an object as the effect of my proposed action, but I cannot have *respect* for it just for this reason that it is an effect and not an energy of will. Similarly, I cannot have respect for inclination, whether my own or another's; I can at most, if my own, approve it; if another's, sometimes even love it, that is, look on it as favorable to my own interest. It is only what is connected with my will as a principle, by no means as an effect—what does not subserve my inclination, but overpowers it, or at least in case of choice excludes it from its calculation—in other words, simply the law of itself, which can be an object of respect, and hence a command. Now an action done from duty must wholly exclude the influence of inclination, and with it every object of the will, so that nothing remains which can determine the will except objectively the *law*, and subjectively *pure respect* [21] for this practical law, and consequently the maxim[1] that I should follow this law even to the thwarting of all my inclinations.

Thus the moral worth of an action does not lie in the effect expected from it, nor in any principle of action which requires to borrow its motive from this expected effect. For all these effects—agreeableness of one's condition, and even the promotion of the happiness of others—could have been also brought about by other causes, so that for this there would have been no need of the will of a rational being; whereas it is in this alone that the supreme and unconditional good can be found. The preeminent good which we call moral can therefore consist in nothing else than *the conception of law* in itself, *which certainly is only possible in a rational being*, in so far as this conception, and not the expected effect, determines the will. This

is a good which is already present in the person who acts accordingly, and we have not to wait for it to appear first in the result[2] [22]

But what sort of law can that be the conception of which must determine the will, even without paying any regard to the effect expected from it, in order that this will may be called good absolutely and without qualification? As I have deprived the will of every impulse which could arise to it from obedience to any law, there remains nothing but

[1] *A maxim* is the subjective principle of volition. The objective principle (*i. e.,* that which would also serve subjectively as a practical principle to all rational beings if reason had full power over the faculty of desire) is the practical *law*.

[2] It might be here objected to me that I take refuge behind the word *respect* in an obscure feeling, instead of giving a distinct solution of the question by a concept of the reason. But although respect is a feeling, it is not a feeling *received* through influence, but is *self-wrought* by a rational concept, and, therefore, is specially distinct from all feelings of the former kind, which may be referred either to inclination or fear. What I recognize immediately as a law for me, I recognize with respect. This merely signifies the consciousness that my will is *subordinate* to a law, without the intervention of other influences on my sense. The immediate determination of the will by the law, and the consciousness of this, is called *respect*, so that this is regarded as an *effect* of the law on the subject, and not as the *cause* of it. Respect is properly the [22] conception of a worth which thwarts my self-love. Accordingly it is something which is considered neither as an object of inclination nor of fear, although it has something analogous to both. The *object* of respect is the *law* only, that is, the law which we impose on *ourselves,* and yet recognize as necessary in itself. As a law, we are subjected to it without consulting self-love; as imposed by us on ourselves, it is a result of our will. In the former aspect it has an analogy to fear, in the latter to inclination. Respect for a person is properly only respect for the law (of honesty, etc.) of which he gives us an example. Since we also look on the improvement of our talents as a duty, we consider that we see in a person of talents, as it were, the *example of a law* (viz. to become like him in this by exercise), and this constitutes our respect. All so-called moral *interest* consists simply in *respect* for the law.

the universal conformity of its actions to law in general, which alone is to serve the will as a principle, that is, I am never to act otherwise than so *that I could also will that my maxim should become a universal law*. Here, now, it is the simple conformity to law in general, without assuming any particular law applicable to certain actions, that serves the will as its principle, and must so serve it if duty is not to be a vain delusion and a chimerical notion. The common reason of men in its practical judgments perfectly coincides with this, and always has in view the principle here suggested. Let the question be, for example: May I when in distress make a promise with the intention not to keep it? I readily distinguish here between the two significations which the question may have: whether it is prudent [23] or whether it is right to make a false promise? The former may undoubtedly often be the case. I see clearly indeed that it is not enough to extricate myself from a present difficulty by means of this subterfuge, but it must be well considered whether there may not hereafter spring from this lie much greater inconvenience than that from which I now free myself, and as, with all my supposed *cunning*, the consequences cannot be so easily foreseen but that credit once lost may be much more injurious to me than any mischief which I seek to avoid at present, it should be considered whether it would not be more *prudent* to act herein according to a universal maxim, and to make it a habit to promise nothing except with the intention of keeping it. But it is soon clear to me that such a maxim will still only be based on the fear of consequences. Now it is a wholly different thing to be truthful from duty, and to be so from apprehension of injurious consequences. In the first case, the very notion of the action already implies a law for me; in the second case, I must first look about elsewhere to see what results may be combined with it which would affect myself. For to deviate from the principle of duty is beyond all doubt

wicked; but to be unfaithful to my maxim of prudence may often be very advantageous to me, although to abide by it is certainly safer. The shortest way, however, and an unerring one, to discover the answer to this question whether a lying promise is consistent with duty, is to ask myself, Should I be content that my maxim (to extricate myself from difficulty by a false promise) should hold good as a universal law, for myself as well as for others; and should I be able to say to myself, "Every one may make a deceitful promise when he finds himself in a difficulty from which he cannot otherwise extricate himself"? [24] Then I presently become aware that, while I can will the lie, I can by no means will that lying should be a universal law. For with such a law there would be no promises at all, since it would be in vain to allege my intention in regard to my future actions to those who would not believe this allegation, or if they overhastily did so, would pay me back in my own coin. Hence my maxim, as soon as it should be made a universal law, would necessarily destroy itself.

I do not, therefore, need any far-reaching penetration to discern what I have to do in order that my will may be morally good. Inexperienced in the course of the world, incapable of being prepared for all its contingencies, I only ask myself: Canst thou also will that thy maxim should be a universal law? If not, then it must be rejected, and that not because of a disadvantage accruing from it to myself or even to others, but because it cannot enter as a principle into a possible universal legislation, and reason extorts from me immediate respect for such legislation. I do not indeed as yet *discern* on what this respect is based (this the philosopher may inquire), but at least I understand this—that it is an estimation of the worth which far outweighs all worth of what is recommended by inclination, and that the necessity of acting from *pure* respect for the practical law is what constitutes duty, to which every other motive must give place because it is the condition of a will being good *in itself*, and the worth of such a will is above everything.

Thus, then, without quitting the moral knowledge of common human reason, we have arrived at its principle. And although, no doubt, common men do not conceive it in such an abstract and universal form, yet they always have it really before their eyes and use it as the standard of their decision. Here it would be easy to show how, with this compass in hand, [25] men are well able to distinguish, in every case that occurs, what is good, what bad, conformably to duty or inconsistent with it, if, without in the least teaching them anything new, we only, like Socrates, direct their attention to the principle they themselves employ; and that, therefore, we do not need science and philosophy to know what we should do to be honest and good, yea, even wise and virtuous. Indeed we might well have conjectured beforehand that the knowledge of what every man is bound to do, and therefore also to know, would be within the reach of every man, even the commonest. Here we cannot forbear admiration when we see how great an advantage the practical judgment has over the theoretical in the common understanding of men. In the latter, if common reason ventures to depart from the laws of experience and from the perceptions of the senses, it falls into mere inconceivabilities and self-contradictions, at least into a chaos of uncertainty, obscurity, and instability. But in the practical sphere it is just when the common understanding excludes all sensible springs from practical laws that its power of judgment begins to show itself to advantage. It then becomes even subtle, whether it be that it chicanes with its own conscience or with other claims respecting what is to be called right, or whether it desires for its own instruction to determine honestly the worth of actions; and, in the latter case, it may even have as good a hope of hitting the mark as any philosopher whatever can promise himself. Nay, it is almost more

sure of doing so, because the philosopher cannot have any other principle, while he may easily perplex his judgment by a multitude of considerations foreign to the matter, and so turn aside from the right way. Would it not therefore be wiser in moral concerns to acquiesce in the judgment of common reason, [26] or at most only to call in philosophy for the purpose of rendering the system of morals more complete and intelligible, and its rules more convenient for use (especially for disputation), but not so as to draw off the common understanding from its happy simplicity, or to bring it by means of philosophy into a new path of inquiry and instruction?

Innocence is indeed a glorious thing; only, on the other hand, it is very sad that it cannot well maintain itself, and is easily seduced. On this account even wisdom—which otherwise consists more in conduct than in knowledge—yet has need of science, not in order to learn from it, but to secure for its precepts admission and permanence. Against all the comands of duty which reason represents to man as so deserving of respect, he feels in himself a powerful counterpoise in his wants and inclinations, the entire satisfaction of which he sums up under the name of happiness. Now reason issues its commands unyieldingly, without promising anything to the inclinations, and, as it were, with disregard and contempt for these claims, which are so impetuous and at the same time so plausible, and which will not allow themselves to be suppressed by any command. Hence there arises a natural *dialectic,* that is, a disposition to argue against these strict laws of duty and to question their validity, or at least their purity and strictness; and, if possible, to make them more accordant with our wishes and inclinations, that is to say, to corrupt them at their very source and entirely to destroy their worth—a thing which even common practical reason cannot ultimately call good.

Thus is the *common reason of man* compelled to go out of its sphere and to take a step into the field of a *practical philosophy*, not to satisfy any speculative want (which never occurs to it as long as it is content to be mere sound reason), but even on practical grounds, [27] in order to attain in it information and clear instruction respecting the source of its principle, and the correct determination of it in opposition to the maxims which are based on wants and inclinations, so that it may escape from the perplexity of opposite claims,

and not run the risk of losing all genuine moral principles through the equivocation into which it easily falls. Thus, when practical reason cultivates itself, there insensibly arises in it a dialectic which forces it to seek aid in philosophy, just as happens to it in its theoretic use; and in this case, therefore, as well as in the other, it will find rest nowhere but in a thorough critical examination of our reason.

Some Common Misinterpretations of Kant

H. J. PATON

CRITICISMS

*I*t may be thought that Kant's doctrine is paradoxical, and that we have somehow been tricked by the subtlety and complexity of the argument. We began with a good will 'shining like a jewel for its own sake.' We end with a merely formal maxim, a mysterious reverence for empty law as such, a vague principle of law-abidingness, and an unworkable test of universality for the maxims of our actions. All this formalism and legalism may leave us cold. Furthermore, it may be said, we have been argued gradually into a manifestly ludicrous view, the view that in determining our duty no account whatever is to be taken of the results sought or attained by our action.

These criticisms can be answered only by a re-examination of our previous argument and indeed of Kant's argument as a whole, but we may attempt to make brief comments on some of the points raised.

KANT'S FORMALISM

On the theoretical side there is little justification for complaining of Kant's

formalism. We ought not to expect an abstract philosophical analysis of moral goodness to arouse the same warm emotion as may be aroused by the spectacle of a good man or a good action; nor is it the business of a moral philosopher to 'emotionalise the district'—to quote the phrase used by a disappointed American visitor to one of Professor Cook Wilson's lectures. Kant's terminology may be technical, but it was familiar in his time, if not in ours. It is well adapted to the expression of his meaning; nor is it on acquaintance more rebarbative than that of many modern philosophers.

It is hard to see why we should blame a philosopher for being too formal in dealing with the form of anything, even the form of morality. We do not blame Mr. Bertrand Russell because his logic is too formal, though some people may wish that he would write another kind of logic as well. Why should we complain that Kant's ethics is too formal, especially as he *has* written another kind of ethics, his *Metaphysics of Morals*, not to mention his *Lectures*? In the *Groundwork* Kant, as he says, is dealing with the supreme principle of morality: he is dealing with the *a priori* part of ethics

FROM: *The Categorical Imperative*, H. J. Paton. (London: Hutchinson and Co., Ltd., 1947), Ch. 7. Reprinted by permission of Hutchinson and Co., Ltd.

in abstraction and considering the form of moral action apart from the matter. When Kant sets before himself a programme of this kind he is in the habit of sticking to it. It is hard to see why he should be blamed for keeping to his subject and excluding irrelevancies. It is still harder to see why he should be charged with forgetting that moral action has a matter as well as a form, an empirical as well as an *a priori* element, and an object as well as a supreme principle. Kant does not forget. He expects his readers to remember.

KANT'S LEGALISM

It may be replied that this answer does not really meet the criticism, which is concerned more with the formalism or legalism of his moral attitude than with his method of exposition. No doubt, it may be said, good men of a certain type may take a pride in obeying the law for the sake of law, and in controlling inclinations from the standpoint of a detached and unmoved reason; but it is a great mistake to identify such a type with the moral life at its best.

It is true that a man's philosophy, and especially his moral philosophy, takes a certain colour from his own individual moral attitude. This applies to Kant as to any one else, and may help to explain certain idiosyncrasies of emphasis and perspective; but I do not think it vitiates his analysis, and it certainly does not excuse us from meeting his arguments. Kant himself was a gentle and humane man with a passion for freedom and a hatred of intolerance: there is no evidence whatever to suggest that he was either cold or domineering or ascetic. I have tried to expose, in the course of my discussion, some of the misconceptions on which this charge of legalism is based; but there is one special point which must be added in the present connexion.

The main ground for charging Kant with legalism is the belief that he bids us perform our moral actions for the sake of a vague abstraction called the law, and thereby forbids us to per-form moral actions for their own sake. Since this view is completely opposed to Kant's doctrine, and yet may easily be read into his language, I will try to make his position clear.

According to Kant every action aims at a result or end or object. In non-moral behavior we perform the action because we desire the object; we then have what Kant calls a 'pathological' interest in the object, and our interest in the action is *mediate*—that is, it depends on our interest in the object. In moral behaviour we perform the action because the action, aiming as it does at certain results, is an embodiment of the moral law; but it must not be supposed that the action is then willed only as a means to an empty abstraction called 'the law'. On the contrary, we take an *immediate* interest in the action itself 'when the universal validity of its maxim is a sufficient determining ground of the will'.[1] One of Kant's strongest convictions is that we take an *immediate* interest in moral actions. This is the reason why on his view actions done out of immediate inclinations, such as sympathy and benevolence, are more difficult to distinguish from moral actions than are actions done from self-interest, where there is no immediate inclination to the action. This immediate moral interest is indeed another name for 'reverence'.[2] which we may feel for actions, and still more for persons, in whom the law is embodied.

I do not believe that there need be any real inconsistency in Kant about this: he is entitled to say both that we take an immediate interest in a moral action and that we do the action for the sake of the law. The category of means and end is inadequate to action, and grossly inadequate to moral action. The law is not for Kant an end to which the action is a means: it is the form or principle of the action itself. Although

[1] *Groundwork* [*Fundamental Principles*], 460 n. (= 122 n.). See also 413 n. (= 38 n.).

[2] *Gr.*, 401 n. (= 17n.).

it is the condition of the action's goodness, it is nevertheless an element in the action itself.[3]

THE IGNORING
OF CONSEQUENCES

Nothing, I suppose, will ever get rid of the illusion that for Kant a good man must take no account of consequences —in some sense which means that a good man must be a perfect fool. This interpretation rests on the ambiguities of language.[4] There is a sense in which the good man will take no account of consequences in deciding what he ought to do. He will not *begin* with the consequences and say that because an action will have certain consequences which he desires, therefore he will regard the action as his duty. He knows that it may be his duty not to produce results which he may greatly desire. Kant is right in saying that the expected consequences cannot be the *determining ground* of an action if it is to have moral worth. Nevertheless the good man begins with the *maxim* of a proposed action and asks himself whether the maxim can be willed as a universal law; and the maxim is always of the form 'if I am in certain circumstances, I will perform an action likely to have certain consequences'. How could we propose to steal or to kill or to act

[3] Compare Chapter I §7, at the end. What Kant says about the highest good—in *K.p.V.*, 109–10 = 244–5 (= 196–7)— applies to any action or object. I will summarise and simplify. If our volition is determined by the thought of an action or object independently of the law, then our action is not moral. The moral law is the only determining ground of the pure will. But *it goes without saying* (*Es versteht sich von selbst*) that if the moral law is *included* in the concept of such an action or object as its supreme condition, then the concept of such an action or object and of its realisation by our will is *at the same time* the determining ground of the pure will.

[4] It is, however, also encouraged by a tendency in Kant to exaggerate the generally sound principle that in many cases remoter consequences ought to be ignored.

at all, if we ignored the fact that an action has consequences? Nevertheless we must not judge the action to be right or wrong according as we like or dislike the consequences. The test is whether the maxim of such an action is compatible with the nature of a universal law which is to hold for others as well as for myself. A good man aims at consequences because of the law: he does not obey the law merely because of the consequences.

Such is the simple and obvious truth so often caricatured. If Kant had said merely that we must not allow our desires for particular consequences to determine our judgment of what our duty is, he would have avoided a great deal of misunderstanding.

THE SOUNDNESS
OF KANT'S DOCTRINE

One of the great merits of Kant's doctrine is the sharp distinction which he makes between the *a priori* and the empirical, between duty and inclination. Since he wrote, there is no longer any excuse for the muddled thinking which confuses *my* good with *the* good and consciously or unconsciously substitutes for the moral motive mere desire for our own personal happiness either in this world or the next. A veiled and unconscious hedonism is as corrupting as it is confused. The primary aim of a good man is not to satisfy his own inclinations, however generous, but to obey a law which is the same for all, and only so does he cease to be self-centered and become moral. There is no more fundamental difference than that between a life of prudence or self-love and one of moral goodness.

We cannot give a general description of moral action by reference to its objects, both because the objects of moral action vary indefinitely and because they may be produced by action which is not moral. Moral action must be described, not by its objects, but by its motive or principle or maxim; and this principle or maxim, for the same reasons as before, cannot *merely* be one of producing certain objects. The only possibility is that it should be a maxim of obeying a law which is the same for all: in Kant's language, it must be a formal maxim.

A man who is guided by the formal maxim of morality must not be conceived as acting in a vacuum. In the light of this maxim he selects and controls his ordinary maxims of self-love and inclination. In this way he resembles the prudent man, who selects and controls his maxims of inclination in the light of the maxim of self-love. The behavior of the prudent man is familiar to us all, though we do not describe it in Kant's language; and it too is the work of practical reason. The work of reason in moral action is not very much more difficult to conceive than the work of reason in prudential action.

I will add one more point in anticipation of what is to follow. One of the reasons why Kant ascribes absolute value to a good will is that in obeying law for its own sake a good man is raised above the stream of events which we call nature: he is no longer at the mercy of his own natural instincts and desires. A good man is free in so far as he obeys the formal law which is the product of his rational will instead of being pulled about by desire, and it is this freedom which arouses Kant's veneration. Whatever be our judgment of this, we do well to note that Kant's view of the formal character of the moral law is necessary to his doctrine of freedom. So far his philosophy has at least the merit of being consistent.

A Critique of Kant
RICHARD BRANDT

We have been suggesting that a person's ethical convictions are invalid or unsatisfactory insofar as they fail to satisfy two conditions: (*a*) mutual consistency, when taken with the person's factual beliefs; and (*b*) capacity of his particular ethical judgments to be supported by general principles that make no reference to individuals. There are further conditions that valid ethical convictions must satisfy, but failure to meet either of these two is sufficient ground for concluding that something is wrong with one's system of ethical beliefs.

These two conditions of validity were not first discovered in the twentieth century. One is inclined to say that some recognition of them (of course not explicit formulation) goes back as far as the earliest debate about ethical issues. Statements of principles roughly corresponding to them have occurred sporadically, since early times, in the writings of philosophers. However, one philosopher in particular, Immanuel Kant (1724–1804), had a good deal to say about a criterion for valid ethical judgments very similar to our two conditions. It will repay us to consider his theory.

There are several facts that make Kant's theory especially interesting, aside from its great historical influence. First, there are influential philosophers today who hold views very similar to his: for instance, H. J. Paton and R. M. Hare . . . Also, Kant's proposal is sufficiently different from what we have suggested that we should consider substituting it, or some variant of it, for our two conditions. Finally, Kant claimed that his test for a valid ethical judgment was a sufficient test by itself. It is worthwhile to examine this claim.

Kant's consideration of ethical problems is concentrated on one particular type of ethical statement, state-

FROM: *Ethical Theory*, Richard B. Brandt. (Englewood Cliffs, N.J.: Prentice-Hall, Inc., 1959), pp. 27–35. Reprinted by permission of Prentice-Hall, Inc.

ments about duty or obligation. His most interesting thesis in fact is relevant only to this special case. This fact, however, hardly limits the interest of his reasoning, in view of the fact that the assessment of statements about obligation is perhaps the most important problem for ethical theory.

Let us now outline the main points of Kant's view. He begins his best-known work on ethics (*Grundlegung zur Metaphysik der Sitten*, first published in 1785),[1] by saying that there is only one thing that can be called worthwhile without any qualifications or conditions: a good character. He then asks himself: What is it that makes character good? His answer is that character is made good by just one thing, by being conscientious, which is being ready to do one's duty as one sees it, and for no other reason than just that it is one's duty. On his view, generosity and sympathy have nothing to do with goodness of character. Kant thought that if we want to know whether a particular action was fine or praiseworthy, there is exactly one thing we have to know: whether the person performed the deed because he saw that it was required by duty. Otherwise, it was morally worthless and did not show forth a good character.

The reader may well think that some of these assertions are questionable. Let us not pursue this issue now, however; . . . The important thing now is what Kant proceeds to say about the concept of duty.

In order to understand Kant's view of duty, it is best to begin with his idea that every deed somehow involves a "maxim" (his term) or policy-directive. What he means is this. Whenever a person acts, at least whenever he is acting

[1] Translations by H. J. Paton, *The Moral Law* (London: Hutchinson's University Library, 1948); by L. W. Beck (ed.), *Critique of Practical Reason* (Chicago: University of Chicago Press, 1949); and by T. K. Abbott, in *Kant's Critique of Practical Reason and other Works on the Theory of Ethics* (London: Longmans, Green, and Co., 1909).

intelligently and not simply by reflex, he is aware of what the situation is, what are the probable consequences of various lines of action he might take, and of the relation of these consequences to the desires and needs of himself and others. He will be aware of these things to some degree at least. Furthermore, the fact that a person who is so aware acts in a certain way shows that he accepts, at least for the moment, a corresponding policy-directive relevant to his circumstances. He is accepting, for the moment, a general maxim or directive of the form, "In circumstances of the kind *FGH*, let me do *A*!" Of course, a person does not normally formulate such maxims when he acts, although in principle it seems he always could do so. Kant's view, then, is that in this sense every action or decision or resolve embodies a maxim like "Let me do *A* in circumstances of the kind *FGH*!" We should notice that there is a sense in which the maxim of an act is *subjective:* the "maxim" of an act represents the kind of act the agent *thinks* it is, and the kind of situation the agent *thinks* it is. Usually, of course, the real quality of the action, and of the situation, will actually be what the agent thinks, but it need not be. There will be some divergence, in all cases, between the subject's thought of his act and his situation, and the real character of his act and situation, for his act and situation will have many properties *in addition* to those the agent thinks of.

Kant believed that certain maxims in this sense are and can be shown to be *universalizable* in a sense to be explained in a moment. Furthermore, he held that if the maxim is universalizable, then it is morally permissible to perform the act of which we think in terms of that maxim; if it is not universalizable, then that act is not morally permissible (unless we contrive to think of the same act in terms of some other maxim that is universalizable). Furthermore, if it is not morally permissible to perform a certain act, it is one's *duty* not to perform that act. On Kant's view, then, if we can decide which maxims are universalizable, we have the key to deciding what is morally permissible and what is our duty.[2]

What is meant by saying that a maxim is *universalizable?* This is a central point of Kant's theory. What Kant has in mind is essentially very old but none the less impressive. *Roughly,* a maxim is universalizable if it accords with the Golden Rule: "Do unto others as you would have them do unto you." Or, more exactly but still only roughly:

---

[2] There are some puzzles here, to which Kant's answers are not clear. (1) Suppose the maxim in terms of which one thinks of an act is not universalizable, but some other maxim (say, a more specific one) in terms of which one could equally properly think of one's situation and act as they really are, is universalizable. Is it then morally permissible to perform the act? It seems that Kant ought to say that in one sense it is not (from the point of view of the actual agent and his thinking), but that in another sense it is (from the point of view, say, of a better informed or more thoughtful agent). Perhaps he could say: Subjectively it is not permissible, but objectively it is. But he does not make the distinction. (2) Suppose an agent's maxim is universalizable, but he is mistaken in his thoughts about what his situation is or his act would be. And suppose that a person more accurately informed would think of the situation and action in terms of a maxim that could not be universalized. Is the action permissible or not? Again, Kant ought to say that in a sense it is and in a sense it isn't.

Since an agent cannot get outside himself and think of an act otherwise than as he does think of it (except in being careful to get his facts as straight as he can), from the point of view of the agent the only thing that is important is how the situation looks to him. Kant can therefore be excused for neglecting the "objective" facts, from a practical point of view. Nevertheless, the distinction is important, particularly since two agents, in identical "objective" situations, might on Kant's theory have the duty of doing opposite things, if they were differently informed and thought of the situation in different ways.

"A person's maxim is universalizable if, and only if, he can agree, as a matter of reflective policy, to everyone else also acting in accordance with it."

One might ask: "*Why* did Kant suppose that an action is morally permissible if and only if the maxim, in terms of which the agent thinks of it, is universalizable?" What Kant has to say about this is by no means as clear as one could wish, and what is clear is not very convincing. However, there are some simple considerations that undoubtedly influenced his thinking, and which we should not overlook. What do we think of a person who acts in a way in which he is well aware he does not want others to act? We think his act shows lack of respect for others; it is a selfish act. We think less of him on account of it. We tend to say that he did what he ought not to have done, that he did what it was his duty not to do. In contrast, if a person is always careful to act only in ways in which he would be willing to have others act, we are inclined to praise him. We think he has the most important part, at least, of a good character. We would be likely to say he does not fail to do his duty. Hence, Kant comes very naturally to his view about the relation of duty, or moral permissibility, and universalizability of maxim —although we shall see that his view is indefensible.

Let us now consider more carefully his view that it is one's duty to perform only morally permissible acts[3] and that an act is morally permissible if and only if its maxim (as the agent thinks of it) is universalizable.

Duty demands, Kant says, that we act *only* on universalizable maxims. More explicitly, it demands the following: "Act *only* on that maxim on which you can

---

[3] Kant's view is not at all that it is our duty to perform *all* morally permissible acts, but only that we are enjoined *not* to perform ones that are not permissible. Thus, it may be morally permissible for me to invite Miss A to marry me; but there is not necessarily an obligation to do so.

will that everyone should act."[4] Kant has another way of putting it, which we may put in our own words as follows. Suppose it were true that, whenever we acted on a certain maxim, we should have a kind of hypnotic effect on other people, so that from then on they would always act on this same maxim. In this case, we should be very careful about our actions, knowing full well their effect on the actions of others toward us. With this (approximate) thought in mind, Kant says that duty makes the following demand on us: "Act as if the maxims of your action were to become through your choice a universal law of nature." So, one is failing in his duty if his action is not one he would perform if he knew this hypnotic effect would take place.

Does Kant mean that an act is morally permissible if and only if its maxim, as the agent thinks of it, *is in fact* universalizable, or if and only if the *agent thinks* it is universalizable? Kant seems to take the former stand, but we should notice that such a view raises questions. At least, if we think that it cannot be a person's duty to do something he cannot know is his duty, it would be odd to say it is his duty to avoid acting according to a maxim that cannot be universalized, if it so happens that the agent thinks it can be, and is not in a position to know that it cannot! But let us ignore this problem.

Let us now consider more carefully what it is for a maxim to be universalizable. Kant obviously meant to ex-

clude altogether maxims that contain proper names. He seems to take for granted that we need consider, as candidates for the status of universalizable maxims, only those from which proper names can be eliminated—as we have required above that they be eliminated from "general" moral statements. What Kant is really saying, then, is that a maxim is universalizable if and only if it contains no proper names and its agent can choose . . . , and so on. Let us now examine, however, what he says explicitly about universalizability.

The question whether a maxim is universalizable is not quite as simple as it looks, as we shall see more fully when we consider some of Kant's examples. It has, in Kant's thinking, two distinct aspects or moments. First, a maxim is universalizable only if it is *possible* for *everyone* to act on it (or for it to be a universal law of nature). Thus, a maxim is disqualified if it is inconsistent. It is also disqualified if it is impossible for everyone to act on it, in the sense of "causal impossibility," that is, excluded from the range of possibility by the laws of nature. More fully, he thought that a maxim is universalizable only if it is possible (in the sense both of being logically consistent and compatible with the laws of nature) both for *one* person to follow it, and also for *everybody* to follow it. We may summarize all this by saying that one condition for the universalizability of a maxim, according to Kant, is the objective possibility of everybody acting according to it. There is a second condition, however. A maxim is universalizable only if it is *possible for the agent to choose*, as a matter of reflective policy, that everyone follow it. We might say, then, that a second condition for a maxim being universalizable is that its being universally followed is subjectively acceptable to the agent. Kant thought that some maxims will satisfy the first condition but not the second. He wrote:

Some actions are of such a nature that their maxims cannot even be conceived as

[4] In his exact words, "Handle nur nach derjenigen Maxime, durch die du zugleich wollen kannst, dass sie ein allgemeines Gesetz werde." *Immanuel Kant's Werke,* edited by A. Buchenau and E. Cassirer (Berlin: Bruno Cassirer, 1922), vol. IV, 279.

The verb "will" in English seems to have no use corresponding to the German "wollen." A better translation would therefore be like one suggested earlier: "Act only on the maxim which you can agree, as a matter of reflective policy, to have made a guiding law for the action of everyone else."

universal laws of nature without contradiction, far from it being possible that one should choose that they be so. With others there is not this inherent impossibility, but it is still impossible to choose that their maxims be evaluated to the status of universal laws of nature, since such a choice would contradict itself [weil ein solcher Wille sich selbst widersprechen würde].[5]

The second of Kant's two conditions is more puzzling than may appear at first glance. Isn't it possible that one person might be willing for a certain maxim to be universally followed, but a second person not? In this case, it would seem that the first person could say, correctly, "Action on this maxim is permissible," although the second person could also say, correctly, "Action on this maxim is not permissible." Many will think that any such result shows that something has gone seriously wrong —although perhaps not justly, for we shall see that "ethical relativists" insist that this very outcome is unavoidable (and, up to a point, we shall hold this ourselves). It seems that Kant himself was convinced that this difficulty would not arise (or at least was not aware of the fact it might arise), perhaps because of a further point, in his second test, that we have not yet emphasized. It appears that Kant intended to say not merely that it must be possible for the agent to choose that everyone act on a maxim, but that it must be possible for him so to choose "without contradicting" himself, that is, without this choice falling into conflict with stronger or more important wants or desires in himself. (This supplement to the concept of universalization is a complication, however. Now, in order to decide whether a maxim is moral, we have to ask not merely whether we can accept its being made universal law, but whether we can choose *without internal disharmony* that it be made a

universal law—a much more complex matter, so that perhaps we can seldom be quite sure whether we can or cannot.) Even with Kant's test so amended, however, it is not obvious that the original puzzle is avoided. Perhaps some people are so constructed that they can choose, without internal disharmony, that a certain maxim become a universal law of nature, whereas other people are so constructed that they cannot. Kant might deny that they are or can be so constructed, but he certainly gives no reason for thinking they are not. We need not say that this is a serious difficulty for his view, but we should be aware of the fact that his view leads to this result.

Let us now look at his examples. Kant gives separate examples to illustrate the two different parts of universalizability, two for the first part, and two for the second. Let us begin with the first part, the *possibility* (logical or causal) of everyone conforming to the maxim.[6]

Kant considers the following maxim: "When I think myself in need of money, I shall borrow and promise to repay, although I know that I can never do so." Kant argues that this maxim is not universalizable.

How would it be if my maxim were universal law? Then I see at once that it could never hold as a universal law of nature, but would necessarily contradict itself. For supposing it to be a universal law that everyone when he thinks himself in a difficulty should be able to promise whatever he pleases, with the purpose of not keeping his promise, the promise itself would become impossible,

---

[5] Cassirer, IV, 282; Abbott translation, pp. 41–42.

[6] When a maxim is disqualified by this test, Kant says we have a "perfect" obligation not to perform the corresponding act. By saying the obligation is "perfect," Kant apparently meant that it is proper to enforce it by law, and that its force can never be overridden by conflicting obligations. See H. J. Paton, *The Categorical Imperative* (London: Hutchinson's University Library, 1953), pp. 147 f.

as well as the end that one might have in view in it, since no one would consider that anything was promised to him, but would ridicule all such statements as vain pretences.[7]

It is well to notice right away that Kant's argument does not prove what he thinks it does; it does not prove that it is *impossible* for everyone to act on the maxim. What it is plausible to argue is that, were everyone to feel free to borrow money with false promises, then soon very few would lend money in response to such pleas, and the desire that usually motivates attempts to borrow would in most cases be frustrated. Such considerations perhaps do show that no intelligent person would be willing to agree to a universal policy of following the maxim; hence, Kant could fairly say that he shows the maxim does not satisfy the second condition in his test. However, he has not shown it does not satisfy the first condition; he has not shown it is *impossible* for all to adopt the maxim. It is *possible* for everyone to adopt the maxim and follow it, for everyone can perfectly well resolve that, *if and when* some gullible person is willing to lend money on the strength of a promise to repay, one may borrow from him, knowing full well one can never repay. True, such gullible souls may rarely turn up if everyone adopts this maxim, but they may occasionally, and the maxim directs how to handle them when they do.

One would like to know if there is *any* maxim that an individual could follow (in the sense that it would not be impossible for him to follow it) but that could not be followed by everyone. Kant evidently thought there are many such but he did not succeed in showing that there are. It would be rash, however, to say that there are none. For instance, a couple might plan to have a baby born in the following year, its arrival being

timed so that it would be the one baby born first that year, but not *every* couple could successfully execute such plans. If this example is well taken, then Kant's condition of possibility of universal acceptance does disqualify at least one maxim, but it is not yet clear that it disqualifies any that are of serious moral interest.

Let us now look at Kant's illustration of the second part of his test for universalizability: the subjective acceptability of a universal law. This time he is attacking a refusal to give to charity. He says:

A fourth [man], who is in prosperity, while he sees that others have to contend with great wretchedness and that he could help them, thinks: What concern is it of mine? Let everyone be as happy as Heaven pleases, or as he can make himself; I will take nothing from him nor even envy him, only I do not wish to contribute anything to his welfare or to his assistance in distress. Now no doubt if such a mode of thinking were a universal law, the human race might very well subsist. . . . But . . . it is impossible to will *that such a principle should have the universal validity of a law of nature. For a will which resolved this would contradict itself, inasmuch as many cases might occur in which one would have need of the love and sympathy of others, and in which, by such a law of nature, sprung from his own will, he would deprive himself of all hope of the aid he desires.*[8]

This second part of Kant's test clearly does what the first does not: it disqualifies many maxims, some of them important. At least, presumably the reader will be able to think of many maxims he would not be able consistently to accept as universal laws. It is more questionable whether it disqualifies many

[7] T. K. Abbott (translator), *Kant's Critique of Practical Reason and other Works on the Theory of Ethics* (London: Longmans, Green, and Co., 1909), p. 40. By permission. Cassirer edn., IV, 280.

[8] T. K. Abbott (translator), *Kant's Critique of Practical Reason and other Works on the Theory of Ethics* (London: Longmans, Green, and Co., 1909), p. 41. By permission. Cassirer edn., IV, p. 281.

important maxims *for all agents*, in view of the "relativistic" implications pointed out above. Take, for instance, his example of charitable giving. Doubtless every prudent person would hesitate at least briefly before supporting the selfish rule. However, if one's investments are well chosen, and if one also takes an optimistic view of the future of capitalist society, perhaps he could choose the selfish maxim without internal disharmony. Probably some could choose it, and some could not. This result of the application of Kant's test will go far to discredit it in the eyes of anyone who is convinced either (1) that charitable giving is the duty of everyone who can afford it, or (2) that if charitable giving is the duty of anyone it is the duty of everyone in the same situation.

Let us look at two further difficulties in Kant's test for universalizability.

Consider an example. Suppose a student has borrowed $9.81 from his roommate, and is considering whether he should repay it. He finds it impossible to universalize the maxim, "When you have borrowed money, don't repay." But there are somewhat more specific maxims, which he can equally well regard as the maxims of his act. He happens upon this one: "Whenever one student in a small coeducational college borrows exactly $9.81 from another student who is his roommate, and on the day of the loan the borrower is exactly—— years old (corresponding to his own age), and the creditor is exactly—— years old, and the borrower's weight is exactly——and his height exactly——, and the creditor's weight is exactly—— and his height exactly——, and if the borrower finds it very inconvenient to repay, then let him not repay the money." The student finds himself heartily in favor of universalizing this maxim. Hence, he concludes it is morally permissible to ignore the debt.

On Kant's theory this reasoning is perfectly legitimate. The maxim obviously fits the student's situation; he believes about it all the things mentioned in the maxim. Similar reasoning could be produced in support of any action one cared to justify. Therefore, although the second part of Kant's test will disqualify many important *maxims*, it is clear that a suitable choice of maxims will allow one to conclude properly that any *action* that one may wish to show is morally permissible, is morally permissible.

The final difficulty with the test is that its implications do not agree with what anybody can seriously believe about what is morally permissible. Consider another example. Suppose there were a slave-owner, perfectly secure in his power, and, further, that he pondered over the following maxim: "Let a slave-owner put a slave to death with torture, if it pleases his fancy." The reader will presumably agree that no such rule is acceptable, and that action in accordance with it would be immoral. But can it not survive Kant's test? It is not easy to see why it *cannot* be made a rule for everybody; indeed, very possibly there have been times in the history of the world when all slave-owners have in fact accepted it. Moreover, the slave-owner could *accept* such a maxim as universal law without suffering internal disharmony. Doubtless sensitive, thoughtful people would wish no such thing made a universal law, or rather would want no such thing to occur at all, but, it seems, some persons might.

One is inclined to suggest that two complications of Kant's proposal are called for, at the very least. First, it would be more plausible if Kant said a maxim is universalizable if the agent could accept it as universal law *even if he did not believe that he would be in some favored position, or if he were an impartial and sympathetic person.* Presumably no slave-owner who met these qualifications could accept the maxim as universal law; hence, it would not qualify as universalizable. Second, it would be more plausible if Kant said a maxim is universalizable only if the agent would accept it as universal law if he had *perfectly vivid and correct beliefs about what it would be like to have it made universal law.* This further condition would disqualify many maxims that we should agree ought to be disqualified. Conceivably, some Kantian scholars may maintain that the theory Kant in fact held already includes these amendments. We shall not attempt to decide on this point. We can agree, however, that his theory would be much more plausible than the theory we have attributed to him, if it did.

We now understand what Kant meant when he said that it is a person's duty to avoid any action that is not morally permissible, and that an act is morally permissible if and only if the maxim in terms of which the agent thinks of it is universalizable, that is, if and only if it is both objectively (causally and logically) possible, and subjectively acceptable to the agent, for everybody to adopt the maxim as a guiding rule for conduct. We can also now understand why his proposal is unacceptable at least as it stands. (1) Highly immoral maxims can be both objectively possible and subjectively acceptable to the agent, if the agent is a calloused person and is in a favorable position. (2) To many it will

be a serious objection that his theory leaves open the possibility that a maxim will be universalizable for one person, but not for another. Many people think, for strong reasons, that if an act is right at all, it is right for everybody in the same circumstances. (3) If an agent wishes to justify an act, he can choose to think of it in terms of a maxim so specific that he need have no qualms about embracing it as a guiding rule for conduct for everybody. According to Kant's theory, anybody who is eager to justify his action to himself can always succeed in doing so. . . .

Further Readings

ON THE REQUIREMENT OF GENERALITY:

R. M. Hare, "Universalizability," *Proceedings*, The Aristotelian Society, 1954–55, pp. 295–312.

M. G. Singer, "Generalization in Ethics," *Mind*, LXIV (1955), 361–75.

A. C. Ewing, "What Would Happen if Everybody Acted Like Me?" *Philosophy*, XXVIII (1953), 16–29.

C. D. Broad, "On the Function of False Hypotheses in Ethics," *Ethics*, XXVI (1916), 377–97.

Philosophy
of
Religion

he philosophy of religion consists in the attempt to answer certain questions. Among these questions are the following: (1) Can it be proved that God exists, or proved that He does not? (2) Are "God exists" and "There is evil" logically incompatible in the sense that anyone who holds that both statements are true contradicts himself? (3) Do we directly experience God so that we know that He exists not by inferring that He does but by encountering Him? (4) Does man survive his death? (5) Are such claims as "God loves us" meaningful at all—that is, do they succeed in communicating something either true or false, as opposed to being simply and only a way of expressing our own feelings or evoking feelings in others? Selections elaborating these questions are included here.

There are, of course, still other questions that are relevant to the philosophy of religion: How, if at all, are religion and morality related? Is there an essence of religion—a core of belief, acceptance of which is essential to every religion? Does religious experience provide any evidence of the truth of religious belief? And there are others as well.

The approach to these questions, insofar as it is purely philosophical, will appeal to reasons and arguments that do not depend on the authority of a divine revelation. Traditionally theology has been concerned with the explication and systematization of the statements contained in a sacred text. A philosopher, as philosopher, has no such text. He is allowed appeal only to what he can defend as true, on some other ground than that the claim in question was revealed by God, or to what hopefully is so clearly true as not to need defense. Issues concerning logical consistency, proof, evidence, and intelligibility or meaningfulness loom large here as elsewhere in philosophy. The role of such issues in attempts to answer questions in the philosophy of religion is illustrated rather fully in the essays that follow.

K. E. Y.

Can the Existence
of God
Be Proved?

The
Ontological
Argument

If the denial of a statement is contradictory, clearly the statement being denied is necessarily true. If "God does not exist" is contradictory, "God exists" is necessarily true.

St. Anselm endeavored to show that by reflecting on the meaning of the word "God," we can see that the statement "God exists" is true in just this way. His argument can be stated in this manner. The word "God" means "the being than whom no greater can be conceived." So "God exists" is identical to "The being than whom no greater can be conceived exists." Now suppose someone denies that there is such a being. He will be maintaining that this statement is true: "The being than whom no greater can be conceived does not exist." But anyone who maintains that the being than whom no greater can be conceived does not exist cannot be right. For suppose that no such being exists. The man who denies that God exists understands what the phrase "the being than whom no greater can be conceived" means, for he denies that there is any such being. Let us say, then, that when one understands what such a phrase as "the being than whom no greater, etc." means, that being exists in his understanding. Roughly, this means that he has an *idea* of this being, where an idea is conceived as a mental phenomenon. Let us say that a being exists "in reality" if it exists independently of whether anyone has an idea of it or not. Now, Anselm asserts, to exist in the understanding *and* in reality is greater than to exist in the understanding alone. If we suppose that the being than whom no greater can be conceived exists in the understanding alone, then we can in fact conceive of a greater being—one existing *both* in the understanding and in reality. So if we take (1) the being than whom no greater can be conceived does not exist (in reality) as true, we admit that (2) the being than whom no greater can be conceived exists (only) in the understanding. Since (3) it is greater to exist both in understanding and reality than to exist in the understanding alone, it follows that (4) a being can be conceived which is greater than the being than whom no greater can be conceived—namely, a being like the one described in (2) but one that exists also in reality. But (4) is contradictory. Since (1), (2), and (3) entail (4), at least one of these statements must be false. Since (2) is entailed by (1)—plus the claim that what we understand exists in the understanding—we can eliminate (2) and consider only (1) and (3). But (3) is obviously true. So (1) must be false. Hence a being than whom no greater can be conceived exists (in reality).

Put this way, Anselm's argument relies on two crucial doctrines in addition to his analysis of the word "God." These doctrines are:

(1′) When one understands the word "God," there exists something in his understanding (some mental phenomenon) in virtue of which he understands that word.

(3) To exist in the understanding and reality is greater than to exist in the understanding alone.

It is (1′) that Gregory of Rimini attacks, making these two criticisms. First, consider the phrase "the round square." We understand the phrase well enough to know that it does not, and cannot, designate any actual entity (anything which exists "in reality"). But any idea adequate to this phrase would also have to be both round and square—which is impossible. The point is not that an idea must be both round and square, for ideas are not extended entities. The point is rather that if an idea *I* is to represent an object *O*, *I* must correspond to *O*. But no idea could correspond to an entity whose description is contradictory, as ideas represent only what *can be*. So (1′) is not, as it stands, true. What concerns Gregory is how we can be sure that (1′) is true. We can be sure that (1′) is true if we can discover some general and true, principle from which (1′) follows. One such principle might be: (P_1) When one understands *any* word, there is something in his understanding (some mental phenomenon) in virtue of which he understands that word. And presumably this "something" must be such that the word in question applies to it. But there is *nothing* to which "the round square" does, or could, apply. But all that this shows is that some *other* principle than (P_1) must be used to justify (1′).

Here is such a principle: (P_2) Whenever one understands a word *W*, where it is logically possible that there is something to which W applies, there is something in his understanding (some mental phenomenon) in virtue of which he understands what W means (and, presumably, to which W applies).

Here, however, Gregory's second criticism is relevant. Consider the phrase "the number one higher than that number ever specifically thought of by any human being." Suppose the highest number that anyone has ever specifically thought of is four trillion. Then two things become evident. First, the phrase *does* designate; it designates what "four trillion and one" designates. Second, since no one has thought of this number, there is nothing (no mental phenomenon) to which this phrase applies in virtue of which one understands that phrase. So this principle (P_2) is false. So we have no reason to accept ($1'$) or (3) and hence no reason to accept Anselm's argument.

Some philosophers have suggested that we read Anselm in a quite different way. Anselm, it is suggested, was wrong to put his insights in terms of an *argument*. Accepting the view expressed in ($1'$), Nicholas Malebranche argued that since God is infinite, He cannot be represented by any idea, because any idea is finite. Since we know what the word "God" means, and since ($1'$) is true, we must be directly aware of God Himself. We do not *infer* that God exists, but rather we *encounter* Him. It looks, however, as if we *infer* that we encounter Him, and our confidence concerning the truth of this conclusion depends on the premises from which it is inferred. Among these premises, in addition to ($1'$), are these: (P_3) If an idea I represents a being B, then idea I must contain as much ideal reality (that is, capacity to represent reality external to our minds) as the being has nonideal reality, and (P_4) no idea can have an infinite amount of ideal reality. Such premises are enormously hard to state clearly enough to make appraisal of them possible.

Among the philosophers who believe that Anselm's argument misleadingly states a genuine insight, not all have held to premises such as ($1'$), (P_3) and (P_4). Rather, in the case of W. E. Hocking, the claim is made that in becoming aware of our own limitations and finitude, we also become aware of a being without limitation and so infinite. But while Hocking does not appeal to ($1'$), (P_3) or (P_4), it is quite plain that he has his own system of claims, in terms of which he interprets his experience. He thus illustrates nicely that an appeal to religious experience is also an appeal to a particular way of interpreting one's experience and is not merely a report of one's experience in purely descriptive and indisputable terms.

It Is Self-Contradictory to Deny That God Exists

ANSELM

Lord, who gives understanding to faith give to me as much as you deem suitable, that I may understand that You are as we believe You to be, and that

You are what we believe You to be. Now we believe that You are something than which nothing greater can be thought. But perhaps there is no such

FROM: Prosologian, Chapters 2 and 3; J. R. Weinberg, trans. (originally published c. 1077).

nature since 'the fool hath said in his heart: There is no God?' But surely this very same fool, when he hears what I say: 'something than which nothing greater can be thought,' understands what he hears, and what he understands is in his mind, even if he does not understand that it exists. For it is one thing for a thing to be in the mind, but something else to understand that a thing exists. For when a painter pre-thinks what is about to be made, he has it in mind but he does not yet understand that it exists because he has not yet made it. But when he has already painted it, he both has it in his mind and also understands that it exists because he has already made it. Hence, even the fool is convinced that something exists in the mind than which nothing greater can be thought, because when he hears this he understands and whatever is understood is in the mind. But surely that than which a greater cannot be thought cannot exist merely in the mind. For if it exists merely in the mind, it can be thought to exist also in reality which is greater. So if that than which a greater cannot be thought exists merely in the mind, that very same thing than which a greater cannot be thought is something than which a greater can be thought. But surely this cannot be. Hence, without doubt, something than which a greater cannot be thought exists both in the mind and in reality.

Indeed, it exists so truly that it cannot be thought not to be. For something can be thought to exist which cannot be thought not to exist, which is greater than what can be thought not to exist. So, if that than which a greater cannot be thought can be thought not to exist, that very thing than which a greater cannot be thought, is not that than which a greater cannot be thought; which is impossible. So there exists so truly something than which a greater cannot be thought that it cannot be thought not to exist.

You are that very thing, Lord our God.

A Critique of Anselm
GREGORY OF RIMINI

*W*hen it is argued: "By following natural reason it must be stated that there is really something than which a greater cannot be thought, hence something of infinite intensive power must be posited," I reply that the antecedent can be understood in two different ways. First, the word "greater" can be understood to precede the phrase "can be thought," second, it can be understood to come after the phrase "can be thought." That the second clearly differs from the first is obvious from an example. Let us suppose that it is impossible for there to be an ant bigger than an elephant. Then "no ant bigger than an elephant can be thought" is true, because its denial "some ant bigger than an elephant can be thought" is false. For there is no true singular statement from "Some ant bigger than an elephant can be thought." Indeed, any singular statement of the kind is false because it has a false implication on the point of the subject,[1] whether an existing or merely imagined ant is indicated. Nevertheless, if "bigger" is put after "can be thought," as in "no ant can be thought [to be] greater than an elephant," the statement

[1] I.e., that there is an ant bigger than an elephant.

FROM *Questions on the First Book of the Sentences* Distinctions 42–44, ed. of 1522, folio. 70ff.; J. R. Weinberg, trans.

is false, because there is nothing to prevent anyone from supposing that some or any ant is bigger than an elephant.[2]

So if the antecedent of the main argument is taken in the first way, then Aristotle or anyone else who maintains that something perfect exists which is not an infinitely powerful being could concede that antecedent, and yet deny what is supposed to follow from it. For he could say that "... a greater than anything of finite power can be thought" is false, although he could allow that "something can be thought to be greater than anything of finite power" but the implication [that something greater than anything of finite power exists] would not be proved thereby.

When he [Anselm] says that something than which a greater cannot be thought is in the intellect, but not merely in the intellect but also in reality, it is clear that if it is to serve for a proof, the word "greater" must be understood to come after "can be thought." And

[2] Thus "some ant is bigger than an elephant" can be thought as true. This will, of course, be a false thought, but that false thoughts occur is certainly the case.

taken in this sense, the antecedent could be denied.

Thus "the expression 'what does not exist' exists, so what does not exist exists" is an invalid implication, for here the antecedent is true, but the consequent implies a contradiction if its subject-term stands for an object.

For, just as it does not follow from "The expression 'what cannot be thought' can be thought," that "what cannot be thought can be thought," (since anyone hearing me say "what cannot be thought" thinks what he hears and what he thinks is thought, but the consequent implies a contradiction if its subject-term is taken to stand for an object), so also, anyone hearing the expression "a greater than that than which a greater cannot be thought" understands what he hears, yet it is not valid to infer from "the expression 'a greater than that than which a greater cannot be thought' is understood" that "a greater than that than which a greater can be thought is understood." For the antecedent of this inference is true, but the consequent is false, if its subject-term is taken to stand for an object even according to Anselm.

A Brief Comment on Gregory's Critique
J. R. WEINBERG

Gregory of Rimini's critique of the argument of Anselm is almost unique in medieval philosophical criticism. Instead of directly challenging the assumption that there is no proper concept of God on the basis of an Aristotelian theory of the sensory origin of all concepts, Gregory asks whether the assumption "If I understand a statement, something exists in my mind [that] corresponds to the grammatical subject of the statement" is generally correct. It had been assumed (for example by Aristotle and Augustine) that there are verbal elements of consciousness to which the subject-terms of sentences refer. That there are and must be exceptions to such a generalization is the point made in the selection just offered. Perhaps a modern example will make the point clearer.

It can be proved that there is no prime number whose square root equals the quotient of two integers. The proof follows: Suppose there is a prime number p whose square root equals m/n, that is, $\sqrt{p} = m/n$.

$$\text{Then } p = m^2/n^2 \text{, or}$$
$$n^2 p = m^2.$$

Now it is known that (1) every whole number has a unique set of primes as its ultimate factors, and (2) the square of any whole number will contain an even number of prime factors. Hence m^2 and n^2 each have an even number of prime factors. But pn^2 has an odd number of prime factors. So $pn^2 = m^2$ is a self-contradictory formula. Hence our supposition "There is a prime number p whose square root equals m/n" is also logically false, and its denial, "There is no prime number whose square root equals m/n," is logically true. But this means that, although we understood the statement "There is a prime number whose square root equals the quotient m/n," nothing in or outside of consciousness could possibly correspond to the subject "prime whose square root equals m/n." That is, we can understand the sentence as a whole without supposing that there is anything in the mind to which the grammatical subject refers.

Hence Anselm has not established his main initial point, namely, that if I understand the expression "that than which nothing greater can be thought exists," there must be something in my mind that corresponds to "that than which nothing greater can be thought." Gregory's several examples bring out this point very nicely.

We Can Be Directly Aware of God
NICHOLAS MALEBRANCHE

THE EXISTENCE OF GOD
WE SEE ALL THINGS IN GOD,
AND NOTHING FINITE IS CAPABLE
OF REPRESENTING HIM—
THUS IT IS SUFFICIENT TO THINK
OF HIM TO KNOW THAT HE EXISTS.

THEODORE. Well, Aristes, what do you think of that intelligible world into which I led you yesterday? Does it still startle your imagination? Does your mind advance firmly and steadily in the land of meditative spirits, in this region inaccessible to those who listen only to their senses?

ARISTES. What a beautiful spectacle is this archetype of the universe, Theodore! I have been contemplating it with much satisfaction. What an agreeable surprise it is for the soul to find itself without suffering death transported into this land of truth, where it discovers an abundance of nourishment. I am not yet, it is true, accustomed to this celestial manna, to this nourishment which is all spiritual. At certain moments it seems quite hollow and slight. But when I partake of it with proper attention I find so much savour and solidity therein that I can no longer think of feeding with the brutes in a material world.

THEODORE. Oh, my dear Aristes, what are you telling me? Are you speaking seriously?

ARISTES. Quite seriously. I wish no

FROM: *Dialogues on Metaphysics and on Religion*, Dialogue Two, Morris Ginsberg (London: George Allen & Unwin, Ltd., 1921), pp. 86–98. Reprinted by permission of George Allen & Unwin, Ltd. Originally published in 1688.

longer to listen to my senses. I wish always to enter into the innermost core of my being and to live on the abundance which I find there. My senses are adapted for leading my body to the ordinary pastures. I am willing that it should follow them. But that I should follow them, I myself! That I shall never do again. I wish to follow Reason alone, and to step by the aid of my attention into the land of truth, where I may find delicious repasts, repasts which alone are fit nourishment for intelligent beings.

THEODORE. You have, then, surely forgotten that you have a body. But you will not be long without thinking of it, or rather without thinking with reference to it. This body which you neglect now will force you soon to obtain food for it and to occupy yourself with its wants. For as yet the mind cannot free itself so readily from matter. Yet now that your mind is firm, tell me, pray, what you have discovered in this land of ideas. Do you understand, now, what this Reason is, of which we speak in the material and terrestrial world and of which we know so little? I promised you yesterday to lead you beyond all created things to the very presence of the Creator. Have you not flown there by yourself and without thinking of Theodore?

ARISTES. I confess I did think that, without lacking in the respect which I owe to you, I could go myself along the road which you had shown me. I have followed it, and I have, it seems to me, recognised clearly what you told me yesterday, namely, that the universal Reason is eternal and that it has its being in God alone. I will indicate the steps of the argument in a few words. Judge, then, and tell me if I have gone astray.

After you left me I remained for some time in hesitation and suspense. But, driven by a secret enthusiasm, I seemed to be saying to myself, I do not know how: "Reason belongs to me in common with Theodore; why then can I not consult it and follow it?" and it has led me, unless I am mistaken, up to Him who possesses it as His own, and by the necessity of His being; for it seems to lead there quite naturally. Here, then, is the argument in simple and non-figurative language:

Infinite intelligible extension is not a modification of my mind. It is immutable, eternal, necessary. I cannot doubt its reality or immensity. But nothing that is immutable, eternal, necessary, and, above all, infinite is a created thing, nor can it belong to a created thing. Hence it belongs to the Creator and can be only in God. Hence there is a God, and a Reason, a God in whom there is the archetype which I contemplate of the created world which I inhabit—a God in whom there is that Reason which illumines me by means of the purely intellectual ideas which it furnishes in abundance to my mind and to the minds of all men. For I am sure that all men are united with the same Reason as I am, and since I am certain that they see or can see what I see when I enter into myself and when I discover therein the truth or necessary relations which are contained in the intelligible substance of the universal Reason which dwells in me, or rather in which all intelligences dwell.

THEODORE. You have not been led astray, my dear Aristes. You have followed reason, and it has led you to Him who engendered it out of His own substance and who possesses it throughout all eternity. But do not imagine that it has disclosed to you the nature of that supreme Being to whom it has led you. When you contemplate intelligible extension you only see as yet the archetype of the material world which we inhabit and that of an infinity of other possible worlds. You do in truth see the divine Substance, for it alone is visible, it alone can illumine the mind. Yet you do not see it in itself or as it really is. You only see it in its relation to material creations, you only see it so far as they participate in it, or in so far as it is representative of them. Consequently it is not, strictly speaking, God Himself that you see, but only the matter which He can produce.

You certainly see, by means of the infinite intelligible extension, *that* God is. For He alone can possess all that you see, since nothing finite can contain an infinite reality. But you do not see *what* God is. For there is no limit to the Divine perfections, and that which you see when you think of immense spaces is lacking in an infinity of perfections. I say "that which you see," not the substance which represents to you what you see. For this substance, which you do not see in itself, has infinite perfections.

Assuredly, the substance which contains this intelligible extension is all-powerful. It is infinitely wise. It includes an infinity of perfections and realities. It includes, for example, an infinity of intelligible numbers. But the intelligible extension has nothing in common with all these things. There is no wisdom, power or unity in all this extension which you contemplate. For you know that all numbers are commensurable among themselves, since they have unity for a common measure. If, then, the parts of extension divided and subdivided by the mind can be reduced to unity, they will always be commensurable amongst themselves by this unity, which as you know is certainly not the case. Thus the divine Substance in that simplicity to which we cannot attain contains an infinity of quite different intelligible perfections by means of which God illumines us without allowing Himself to be seen as He is, or in His individual and absolute reality, but merely in His reality which is general and relative to possible created beings. Nevertheless, try to follow me. I will try to lead you as near as possible to the Divine.

The infinite intelligible extension is only the archetype of an infinity of possible worlds similar to our own. By means of it I only see certain determinate beings—material things. When I think of this extension I do not see the divine Substance, except in so far as it is representative of bodies and is participated in by them. But now, when I think of Being, and not of determinate beings, when I think of *the* Infinite, and not of such and such an infinite, it is certain,

in the first place, that I do not see such a vast reality in the modifications of my mind. For if I cannot find in these modifications sufficient reality to enable me to represent to myself an infinity in extension, a fortiori I cannot find in it sufficient reality for representing to myself what is infinite in every way. Thus, it is only God, the Infinite, the Unlimited, it is only the Infinite infinitely infinite who can comprise the infinitely infinite reality which I see when I think of Being, and not of such and such beings or of such and such infinities.

In the second place, it is certain that the idea of Being, of reality, of unlimited perfection, or of the infinite in every way, is not the divine substance in so far as it is representative of such and such a created thing or is participated in by such and such a created thing. For every created thing is necessarily a definite being. It is a contradiction that God should make or create a Being in general or one Infinite in every way which should not be God Himself, or should not be equal to His own principle. The Son or the Holy Spirit do not merely share in the divine Being. They receive Him in His entirety, or, to speak of things more within the reach of our minds, it is clear that our idea of a circle in general is only the idea of intelligible extension in so far as it represents a certain circle or is shared in by a certain circle. For the idea of a circle in general, or of the essence of a circle, represents infinite circles, is adapted to infinite circles. This idea comprises the idea of the infinite. For to think of a circle in general is to think of an infinite number of circles as a single circle. I do not know whether you follow what I wish to make you understand. Here it is in two words. The idea of Being without restrictions, of the infinite, of the general, is not the idea of created things, or of the essences of created things, but the idea which represents the Divine or the essence of the Divine. All particular beings participate in Being, but no particular being can equal it. Being comprises all things, but all beings created or possible, in all their manifold variety, cannot exhaust the immense extension of Being.

ARISTES. It seems to me, I can see your meaning. You define God as He defined Himself in speaking to Moses, "God is that which is."[1] Intelligible extension is the idea or archetype of bodies. But the being without restrictions, in a word, Being, is the idea of God; it is that which represents Him to our minds as we see Him in this life.

THEODORE. Very good. But above all you must note that God or the Infinite is not visible by an idea representative of Him. The Infinite is its own idea. It has no Archetype. It can be known, but it cannot be constructed. Only created things, only determinate beings, can be constructed, or can be visible through ideas which represent them even before they are produced. We can see a circle, a house, a sun, though they may not actually exist. For all that is finite can be seen in the Infinite, which comprises all intelligible ideas of the finite. The Infinite, on the other hand, can be seen only in itself, for nothing finite can represent the Infinite. If we think of God, it follows that He exists. A finite being, though known, may not exist. We can see its essence without its existence, its idea without itself. But we cannot see the essence of the Infinite without its existence, or the idea of Being without Being. For Being can have no idea representative of it. There is no archetype which could comprise all its intelligible reality. The Infinite is its own archetype, and contains within itself the archetype of all beings.

Thus, you see that the proposition, "there is a God," is in itself the clearest of all existential propositions, and that it is even as certain as the proposition, "I think, therefore I am." You see, moreover, what is meant by God, for God, Being, and the Infinite, are one and the same.

But, once more, make no mistake about this matter. You see only con-

fusedly and as from a distance what God is. You do not see Him as He is, because, though you see the Infinite or Being without restriction, you only see it in a very imperfect manner. You do not see it as a single being. You see a multiplicity of created things in the infinity of uncreated Being, but you do not see its unity distinctly. For you cannot see it so much in its absolute reality as in the reality which attaches to it in its relation to possible created things, the number of which it could increase indefinitely without their ever equalling the reality which represents them. You see it as the universal Reason which illumines all intelligences according to the measure of light necessary for their guidance, and for revealing as much of His perfections as can be shared in by limited beings. But you do not discover the property which is essential to the Infinite, that, namely, of being at the same time one and many; composed, so to speak, of an infinity of different perfections, and yet so simple that in it each perfection comprises all the others without any real distinction.[2]

God does not communicate His substance to any of His creatures; He only communicates to them His perfections; not as they are in His substance, but in so far as His substance is representative of them, and in accordance with the limitations bound up with the nature of created things. Intelligible extension, for instance, represents bodies; it is their archetype or their idea. But, although this extension occupies no place, bodies are and must be locally extended because of the limitations essential to all finite created things, and because no finite created thing can have this property or character, incomprehensible to the human mind, of being at the same time one thing and all things, of being at the same time perfectly simple and yet in possession of all sorts of perfections.

Thus, intelligible extension represents infinite spaces, but it does not fill

[1] Exod. iii. 14.

[2] Cf. *Première lettre touchant la Défense de M. Arnauld*, Note 18.

any; and although it fills, so to speak, all minds and discloses itself to them, it follows in no way that our mind is spatial. If our mind could only see infinite spaces through local conjunction with locally extended spaces, then, in order to see infinite spaces, it would itself have to be infinitely extended.[3]

The divine Substance is everywhere, without being extended locally. It has no limits. It is not contained in the universe. But it is not this Substance as expanded everywhere that we see when we think of spaces. For were this the case our mind, being finite, would never be able to think of infinite spaces.[4] Yet the intelligible extension, which we see in the divine Substance which comprises it, is this Substance only in so far as it is representative of material beings and participated in by them. This is all I can tell you. But observe, that this Being without restriction, or the Infinite in every way which we think of, is not merely the divine Substance in so far as it is representative of all possible beings; for, though we have no detailed ideas of all these beings, we are yet assured that they cannot equal or exhaust the intelligible reality of the Infinite. In a sense, then, it is the divine Substance of God that we see. But in this life we only see it in a way so confused and distant, that we see rather *that* it is than *what* it is; we see rather that it is the source and archetype of all being than its own nature or its perfections in themselves.

ARISTES. Is there not a contradiction in what you are saying? If nothing finite can have enough reality to represent the Infinite (and this appears evident), does it not necessarily follow that we see the divine Substance in itself?

THEODORE. I do not deny that we see the divine Substance in itself. We see it in itself in this sense that we do not see it through any finite thing representing it. But we do *not* see it in itself in the sense that we can reach its simplicity or discover its perfections.

[3] *Ibid.,* second and eleven following notes.

[4] *Ibid.,* and Dialogue VIII.

Since you agree that nothing finite can represent the Infinite, it is clear that if you see the Infinite you can only see it in itself. But it is certain that you do see it; for otherwise when you ask me whether there is a God or an Infinite Being, you would be asking a ridiculous question, by means of a proposition the terms of which you do not understand. It would be just as if you were to ask me whether there is a Blictri,[5] that is to say, a particular thing without knowing what thing.

Assuredly, all men have the idea of God or are thinking of the Infinite when they ask whether He exists. But they believe they could think of Him though He did not really exist, for they do not realise that nothing finite can represent Him. As they can think of several things which do not exist because created things can be seen though they do not exist, since they are not seen in themselves, but in the ideas which represent them, they imagine that it is the same in the case of the Infinite, and that He could be thought of though He does not exist. This is the reason which makes them seek, without recognising Him whom they encounter at all moments, and whom they would recognise soon enough if they entered into themselves and reflected on their ideas.

ARISTES. You convince me, Theodore, but there still remains some doubt. It seems to me that the idea which I have of Being in general or of the Infinite is an idea of my own workmanship. It seems to me that the mind can make general ideas out of several particular ideas. When one has seen several trees, an apple-tree, a pear-tree, a plum-tree, etc., one gets the general idea of a tree. In the same way, when one has seen several beings, one forms the general idea of Being. Hence this general idea of Being is only a confused assemblage of all the others. Thus I have been taught and thus I have always understood the matter.

THEODORE. Your mind, Aristes, is

[5] A nonsense word.

a marvellous worker. It can extract the Infinite from the finite, the idea of Being without restriction from the ideas of particular beings. Perhaps it finds in the wealth of its own supply sufficient reality to give to finite ideas that which they want in order to be infinite. I do not know whether this is what you have been taught, but I believe I do know that you have never comprehended it.

ARISTES. If our ideas were infinite, assuredly they would not be products of our work nor modifications of our mind. That cannot be disputed. But perhaps they are finite, though through them we can think of the Infinite. Or perhaps the Infinite which we see is not really infinite. It may be, as I have just said, a confused conglomeration of several finite things. The general idea of Being is perhaps only a confused mass of particular beings. I have some difficulty in ridding my mind of this thought.

THEODORE. Yes, Aristes, our ideas are finite, if by our ideas you understand our perceptions or the modifications of our minds. But if you understand by the idea of the Infinite that which the mind sees when it thinks of it, or that which is then the immediate object of the mind, assuredly that is infinite, for it is seen as such. Note, I say it is seen as such. The impression which the Infinite makes on the mind is finite. There is even more perception in the mind, and the idea makes a greater impression, in a word, there is more thought, when we know a small object clearly and distinctly, than when we think confusedly of a big object or even of the Infinite. But, though the mind is nearly always more affected, penetrated, modified by a finite idea than by an infinite one, there is nevertheless more reality in the infinite idea than in the finite one, more reality in Being without restriction than in any finite being you could mention.

You cannot rid your mind of the thought that general ideas are no more than a confused collection of certain particular ideas, or at least of the thought that you have the power to form them

out of this collective whole. Let us see how much truth and how much falsehood there is in this thought for which you show so strong a bias. You think, Aristes, now of a circle with a diameter of one foot, then of one whose diameter is two feet, three feet, four feet, etc., and finally you do not determine the length of the diameter at all, and you think of a circle in general. The idea of this circle in general, you would say, is the confused collection of the circles of which you have thought. This conclusion is certainly false. For the idea of a circle in general represents infinite circles and is applicable to them all, and you have only thought of a finite number of circles. What happens must rather be that you have discovered the secret of forming the idea of a circle in general out of five or six circles that you have seen, and this is true in one sense and false in another. It is false if you mean that there is enough reality in the idea of five or six circles to form the idea of a circle in general. But it is true in the sense that after having recognised that the magnitude of the circles does not change their properties, you have perhaps ceased to consider them one after another as having a determinate magnitude in order to consider in general only an indeterminate magnitude. Thus you have, so to speak, formed the idea of a circle in general by spreading the idea of generality over the confused ideas of the circles which you have imagined. Yet I submit to you that you can form general ideas at all only because you find in the idea of Infinity enough reality to give generality to your ideas. You can think of an indeterminate diameter only because you see the infinite in extension and because you can increase or diminish it *ad infinitum*. I submit to you that you could never think of the abstract forms of genera and species, if the idea of the Infinite which is inseparable from your mind did not naturally become united with the particular idea of which you are aware. You could think of a definite circle, but not of a circle in general. You could become aware of a certain definite equality between radii but not of a general equality between indeterminate radii.

The reason is that no finite and determinate idea can ever represent anything infinite or indeterminate. The mind, however, without any reflection adds to its finite ideas the idea of generality which it finds in the Infinite. For just as the mind spreads over the idea of a definite extension, though it be divisible *ad infinitum,* the idea of indivisible unity, so it spreads over certain particular ideas the general idea of perfect equality. And it is this which leads the mind into an infinite number of errors. For all the falsity of our ideas has its source in the fact that we confuse them one with another and further with our own mental modifications. But of this we shall speak on another occasion.

ARISTES. What you say is all very well, Theodore. But, are you not looking upon ideas as entirely distinct from our perceptions? It seems to me that the idea of a circle in general is only a confused perception of several circles of varied size, in other words, a collection of diverse, rather indistinct mental modifications, each of which is the idea or the perception of a certain circle.

THEODORE. Yes, without doubt,[6] I think there is a good deal of difference between our ideas and our perceptions, between ourselves who are aware and that of which we are aware. For I know that the finite cannot find within itself that whereby to represent the Infinite. I know that I do not possess within myself any intelligible reality, and that so far from finding in my own substance the idea of all things I cannot even find therein the idea of my own being. For I am entirely unintelligible to myself, and I can never see what I am except when it pleases God to disclose to me the idea or archetype of minds which is comprised in the universal Reason. But of this we shall speak on another occasion.[7]

[6] Cf. *Réponse au livre des Vraies et des Fausses Idées.*

[7] Cf. *Recherche,* Bk. III, Pt. II, Ch. VII.

Assuredly, Aristes, if your ideas were only modifications of your mind, the confused collection of thousands upon thousands of ideas would only yield a confused complex, incapable of any generality. Take twenty colours, mix them together so as to excite in you a sensation of a colour in general. At the same time produce within yourself several different feelings or sensations so as to form a sensation or feeling in general. You will soon see that this is impossible. For in mixing diverse colours you turn green, grey, blue into what is after all always some particular colour. Dizziness is but a confused agglomeration of sensations or modifications of the soul; yet it is after all a particular feeling or sensation. This is so because every modification of a particular being and of our mind cannot but be particular. It can never rise to the generality which ideas possess. It is true you can think of pain in general, but your mind could never be modified except by a particular pain. And if you can think of pain in general, it is because you can add generality to all things. But, now, you could not obtain this idea of generality from the resources of your own mind. It has too much reality. It follows, therefore, that the Infinite Mind must furnish you with it out of its own abundance.

ARISTES. I have nothing to say in reply. All that you are telling me seems to be evident, but I am surprised that these general ideas, which have infinitely more reality than particular ideas, should affect or touch me less than these latter, and should appear to me to have much less solidity.

THEODORE. That is so because they make themselves felt in a less degree, or rather because they do not make themselves felt at all. Do not judge, Aristes, of the reality of ideas in the way children judge of the reality of bodies. Children think that the space between the earth and the sky is not real because it does not make itself felt. And there are few people who discern that there is just as much matter in a cubic foot of air as in a cubic foot of lead, because lead is harder, heavier, in a word, more capable of affecting the senses than air. Do not follow their example. Judge the reality of ideas not by the feelings which you have of them, which indicate their action upon you in a confused manner, but by the light of intelligence which reveals their nature to you. Otherwise you will think that the ideas which are sensed and those which affect you, as, for example, the idea which you have of the floor which you press with your foot, have more reality than the purely intelligible ideas, though at bottom there is no difference.

ARISTES. No *difference*, Theodore? Do you mean to assert that the idea of extension of which I think is not different from the idea of the extension which I see, which I press with my foot, which offers resistance?

THEODORE. No, Aristes, there are not two kinds of extension, nor two kinds of ideas representative of them. And if this extension of which you think were to touch you or to modify your soul affectively, intelligible though it be, it would appear to you sensible. It would appear to you hard, cold, coloured, and perhaps painful, for you would perhaps attribute to it all the feelings which you would have. Once more, we must not judge of things by the feelings which we have of them. We must not think that ice has more reality than water because it exhibits a greater resistance.

If you believed that fire had more force or efficiency than earth, your mistake would have some justification. For there is some reason for judging of the magnitude of forces by that of their effects. But to believe that the idea of extension which affects you through some feeling is of another nature, or has more reality, than the extension of which you think, without having a sensible impression of it, is to take the absolute for the relative, or to judge of the nature of things as they are in themselves

through the relation in which they stand to us. Along that line we should ascribe more reality to the point of a thorn than to all the rest of the universe, or even to the infinite Being. When you get accustomed to distinguishing your feelings from your ideas, you will recognise that the same idea of extension can be known, imagined, felt, according to the various ways in which the divine Substance which comprises it applies it to your mind. Do not believe then that the Infinite, or Being in general, has less reality than the idea of a definite object which is affecting you at the moment in a very vivid and sensible fashion. Judge of things by the ideas which represent them, and do not attribute to them anything that resembles the feelings that affect you. Later you will understand more clearly what at present I am merely indicating in outline.

ARISTES. All that you have just told me, Theodore, is fearfully abstract, and I have difficulty in keeping a firm hold upon it. My mind is strangely overstrained; a little repose, if you please. I must think over all these great and sublime truths at my leisure. I will endeavour to make myself familiar with them by the difficult effort of pure attention. But at present I am not capable of such an effort. I must have rest in order to recoup my strength.

THEODORE. I knew quite well, Aristes that you could not keep your mind clear for long. Go, lead your body to the pasture ground. Refresh your imagination with a variety of reassuring and pleasing things. But try nevertheless to retain some taste for truth, and as soon as you feel yourself capable of nourishing yourself with it and of meditating upon it, leave all else for its sake. Forget even what you are as much as possible. Your needs must attend to the wants of the body, but it is a great mistake to occupy yourself with its pleasures.

The Ontological Argument Reinterpreted
WILLIAM HOCKING

Nature appears to men as their most general bond of community. Nature also appears as existence *par excellence*. When we lose sight of God, Nature becomes our standard of reality. If we have a God we should like to make his existence as sure as *that!* Hence it is that most attempts at proof of God have begun with Nature, and have tried to make his existence secure by showing him in some valid connection with this world, such as that of cause to the world as effect. God as cause of the world would be real even as the world is real. The so-called cosmological argument follows this line of connection, and finds that the world has a single conscious cause, itself uncaused, who is God.

If we wish to be assured that this cause is not only a voluntary cause but a benevolent one as well, we make a premise of the *good* which as experienced in the world is our natural type of goodness; and we find that the intender of this is good even as the result is good.

But by these means we do not find God. If we could prove a first and conscious cause, still we could prove only such cause as is equivalent to his effect; we could prove only such goodness as is equivalent to this mixture of goodness and evil that we here find. A very limited Being would this be, a God who is only as great as his world, only as good, and finally *only as real*.

By such ways we can only reach a being in whom the qualities of experience are refunded, without change or heightening. But in such case, we may as well believe in the world as we find it; and proceed with our work of mastering it, without reference to God.

Such proofs are not wholly true to the spirit of religion; for historically men have lifted their minds to God rather because the world is unsatisfactory, than because it satisfies. We wish a God who is greater than the world, also better than the world as found, and also more real.

And such more perfect being is what these proofs have in spirit sought: for in referring the world to a conscious Will, they have meant to imply that Will is greater than Nature; and in making the world dependent upon a divine Purpose they have intended to show that the Good is more real than the evil, and will vindicate itself. But clearly no such results can be gained by taking Nature as a standard and moving toward God by relations of causality or purpose: these relations can rise no higher than their source. It is the denial of that assumed starting-point that is the intellectual heart of religion.

On the other hand, we cannot dispense with the world as a point of beginning for the reasons given. What other way, then, can be found of relating this world to God? Follow the history of religion. Observe the Mind dissatisfied with its world. Note the criticism which it makes of Nature, as less than self-sufficient, less than all-good, less than real. And note that of a sudden it has claimed to possess the self-sufficient, the good, the real. What has occurred to the mind of man?

It may seem as though that with which man had been criticizing his experience, namely, his idea of a better and more real, had in a moment taken on objective shape to him. His dissatisfaction with his world has implied a conception of a world not thus defective, and this conception has been set up as sub-

FROM: *The Meaning of God in Human Experience*, William Hocking. (New Haven, Conn.: Yale University Press, 1912), pp. 304–316. Reprinted by permission of Yale University Press.

stantial fact, in his idea of God. He has turned his idea into a reality; or he has instinctively assigned a reality to his idea, yet without blurring the features of his actual world. It is *some leap from idea to reality* that constitutes the essential historic movement of the mind to God.

Now it is just this leap from idea to reality that distinguishes an ancient proof of God's existence; a proof which has become known as the "ontological argument," the argument which assigns a real or ontological value to an idea. I have an idea of God: therefore God exists.

In general, the circumstance that I have an idea of an object is the emptiest of reasons for supposing that object to exist. Whatever force such reasoning can have must depend on some peculiarities of the idea of God, not found in ideas or ideals generally. It must be shown, as we tried to show of the idea of Other Mind, that this idea has something unique about it which forbids the supposition that it is a "mere idea." This, with various degrees of success, have the thinkers who resort to the ontological argument—from Augustine and Anselm to Hegel and Royce—tried to do. It is always with some incredulity that we meet the assertion that any idea of ours carries with it its own guarantee of reality. Yet this same ontological argument is the only one which is wholly faithful to the history, the anthropology, of religion. It is the only proof of God.

Although an idea which should carry on its face an assurance of reality must have something unique about it, we are not without analogies which may help to interpret this extraordinary type of argument. The idea of God is not the only one of our ideas which seems to convey an assurance of objectivity. My idea of *space*, for example, I incline to regard as real. Of my idea of *causality*, I can hardly think that it is an idea only, a form of relating events without an objective counterpart. So also with the beauty of things, or their goodness; I know that these are ideas of mine,

and yet as I regard these qualities valid for other viewers of the same objects, I attribute these qualities to the objects. Instinctively also we project beyond ourselves, or repudiate in some way as not our own, whatever in idea is new, whatever is sublime and holy, whatever is obligatory, whatever strikes me with a consciousness of my self as a lesser thing. Even self-consciousness seems to come, at times, as a revelation from beyond myself. It is not without precedent, then, that an idea should convey with itself some apparent title to reality: it is not impossible that some idea, as perchance the idea of God, should be able to make this title good.

Let us examine this movement of thought more nearly. Nature must early have appeared to man as somewhat less than real—else those early speculations with regard to a creator or maker would hardly have occurred to him. At the root of all these awkward conceptions regarding clay-shaping or egg-laying or spewing or magic-word-pronouncing deities lies an uneasy persuasion that the things of physical existence are subject to something; and to something of the quality of human spirit. If Nature ever wore to early man that aspect which seems primary to us—the aspect of *self-sufficiency*, it must have gone hand in hand with a quite contrary aspect—that of being *illusory*, also possible to us, though with some effort.

We may find that illusory aspect by such considerations as these: The appearance of self-sufficiency belongs not more to Nature as a whole than to each thing in Nature. By that same view which shows us Nature as *there* in its own right, is also each thing there in its own right. But with regard to the several things in Nature we know that this appearance is not true. The apparent self-sufficiency of single things if real would make the World an aggregate in which every thing went its own way without regard to another: self-sufficiency of the parts is equivalent to *accidentality*. Each thing is in reality infinitely dependent on all the rest. But with the banishment of self-sufficiency in the parts, there is no retaining of it in the Whole: there is nothing in which this infinite dependence of part on part comes to rest, unless I conceive the whole thing as *dependent on my Self*, dream-fashion,—deriving its reality, so to speak, from the center outward, rather than from inaccessible infinitely distant world-borders and beginnings inward. The world is real I now say simply *as my experience*—a not-unheard-of point of view. The self-sufficient world of Nature has suddenly become an *illusion*.

Yet I cannot rest here; because I know that I am not the source of the reality of Nature. True, if I am not real, nothing is real: something in my conception of reality starts from me; and all my objects become real, as by infection from that. But true it is, likewise, that unless Nature is real, nothing is real: something in my conception of reality is borne in upon me from beyond. I am real, in part, by virtue of what is not-myself. The real must partake of the qualities of myself and of Nature; and must be other than either.

Through this experience of cognitive restlessness (or "dialectic") early man, to whom the illusory side of Nature was more familiar probably than to us, may have passed in his own readier way; he finds as his resting place the real as Creative Spirit. Nature settles into its third stage of regard: it is neither self-sufficient nor illusory; it has *derivative* reality. As over against me, it is real; as over against the Creative Spirit, it is not real. But how is this conception hit upon? May it be that this thought of Nature as dependent on Spirit is some quick embodiment of an elusive but genuine experience? This idea of a creator does indeed quickly float away from any experience it may have sprung from; becoming promptly materialized and set in the sky as part of the world-created—removed from that World, yet all too much involved in it. Yet may it be that *this idea* is one which must have reality?

Must it not be so? For one thing I cannot by any means escape: namely, that reality itself is present to me in experience; and all of this process of judging this and that thing to be unreal or less than real is made possible simply by the grasp of that reality which at any moment I have. My negations are made possible by my one secure position; and as my hold on reality is variable, so my ability to see through the various pretenders-to-reality to reality itself will vary. Nature can only appear to me as illusory in some moment of unusual clearness of perception; for ordinarily the pretence of nature to be self-sufficient is a harmless and even useful simplification of my view. So if my own existence is recognized by me in some moment as partial and dependent existence, that recognition is a moment of "illumination," which the relation of my self to what is beyond my self becomes presently distinct: and in grasping this relation, I am catching some fleeting glimpse of the *terms* between which the relation exists. I am experiencing that which is beyond myself in no wise differently than in that moment I am experiencing myself: and my judgment of dependence is made possible by a positive and present knowledge of that upon which I depend.

If, then, I discover that my world of nature and self, taken severally or together, falls short of reality, this discovery is due to what I know of reality —not abstractly, but in experience. If I judge this system of nature-and-self to be non-self-sufficient, it is by a knowledge of the self-sufficient; if I condemn, it is by virtue of something in my possession not subject to condemnation; if I criticize and correct, it is by comparison with or reference to some present object not subject to criticism and correction. When I perceive myself in this curious relation to the world of physical facts— superior and not superior, creative and unable to create—that play of unrest is due to, and is defining, a simultaneous perception of the object to which this unrest does not apply. The positive content which I give to that absolute object is a report of experience; whatever idea I make of it is an idea derived nowhere but from that experience. If I am able to frame a tenable conception of nature in dependence upon a creative spirit not myself, that conception is true; for my idea can set me outside of nature only as in experience I have already broken away from the spell of the natural world. In whatever sense, then, I am able to conceive nature as dependent upon spirit, in that sense nature is dependent upon spirit. This idea carries its reality with it.

It is impossible that my idea should be a "mere" idea, for it is only possible for me to take this standpoint, external to nature and myself, in idea in so far as I do at the same time take it in experience also. And that this experience of a more valid reality than that of nature is truly described as an experience of other mind, we have in our previous chapter sufficiently dwelt upon. The ontological argument may be regarded as a logical epitome of what we there, in our own independent research, came upon. The ontological argument, in its true form, is a report of experience.

If we wished, in briefest compass, to state the antithesis between the ontological argument and other arguments for the existence of a God, we might put the situation thus:

These other arguments reason that *because the world is God is.* The ontological argument reasons that *because the world is not, God is.* It is not from the world as a stable premise that we can proceed to God as a conclusion: it is rather when the world ceases to satisfy us as a premise, and appears as a conclusion from something more substantial, that we find God—proceeding then from the world as a conclusion to God as a premise. We have no other premise to begin with: no proof of God can be deductive. It is because neither my world nor myself can serve as a foundation for thought and action that I must grope for a deeper foundation. And what I learn in this groping is, that my consciousness of those defects will reveal, though in faintest degree, the positive object which is free therefrom. It is because we cannot infer from nature to

God along causal or other natural lines, and only because of this, that the idea of God implies existence.

It is not every historical form of the ontological argument that has expressed this experience: and not every form of it appears to me valid. It does not seem to me that any abstract idea of an "all-perfect being" must necessarily be real. Nor does it seem to me that we are justified in inferring from any idea to its reality unless that reality can be present to the idea in experience. No form of the argument can be valid which finds God at the level of thought only, and not at the level of sensation. We are only justified in attributing reality to an idea if reality is already present in the discovery of the idea. When in our search for reality we fix attention upon Nature, it is because we already know that whatever reality is, it cannot be out of connection with that world of Nature-experience: and when we judge Nature unreal, it is only as we discover at the same time in concrete way how Nature is related to the Real. I can infer from that idea by which I criticize Nature to the reality of that idea only because I know Nature (and Self) to contain some characters of reality that cannot be omitted, or left behind. My real must already be given, in order that my idea may be found real. The true idea of God is not one which can leave out either Nature or myself; if my idea of God is real, it is real in experience. Hence I have preferred to state the argument not thus: I have an idea of God, therefore God exists. But rather thus: I have an idea of God, therefore I have an experience of God.

Reality can only be proved by the ontological argument; and conversely, the ontological argument can only be applied to reality. But in so far as reality dwells in Self, or Other Mind, or Nature, an ontological argument may be stated in proof of their existence. Thus, the Cartesian certitude may with greater validity be put into this form:

I think myself, therefore I exist; or
I have an idea of Self, Self exists.

For in thinking myself I find myself in experience and thus in living relation to that reality which experience presents. So may it be with Nature:

I have an idea of physical Nature, Nature exists.

That is, in whatever sense I conceive Nature, in that sense physical nature is real. Idealism has wavered much in its judgment regarding the reality of Nature, and of "material substance." It has said that we have no idea of matter; and again it has said that matter does not exist, which implies that we have an idea of it. Some meaning, however, we do attribute to the word matter; and without enquiring what that definable meaning may be, we may say in advance that whatever idea is framable corresponds to reality as experienced. We need not fear that this realism of Nature will detach Nature from God; though if we could think it so detached it would doubtless so exist. For of independence also, in whatever sense I can think the independence of beings, in that sense independence obtains between them. That which is most independent of me, namely the Other Mind, has been the first object of our ontological findings. The object of certain knowledge has this threefold structure, Self, Nature, and Other Mind; and God, the appropriate object of ontological proof, includes these three.

And is not, after all, this same ancient ontological argument the great and timely necessity for man in all his thinking? That which permanently threatens all our thinking is the damning commentary, "mere thought"—our own commentary on our own work, especially upon our own religion. Escape from illusion is what we require, whether in dealing with God or man or nature; escape from phantasmal intercourse, from sub-jective prisons from whose walls words and prayers rebound without outer effect. *Idea* we must have if we think; but an adequate realism for our idea we must also have. We shall never be too fully assured that our idea has reached beyond ourself, and has its ground in that which is not ourself.

Any reflection that can infallibly break the walls of the Self, opens up at once an infinite World-field. Set a second to my One, and I have given all the numbers. A single point outside the circle of "*Bewusstseins-immanenz*," and I am free to open myself to all reality and to all men. It is this point that the ontological argument aims to put into our possession; the reflection which this argument embodies is the only, and wholly simple, defence against our be-setting subjectivity. "Bethink thyself of the ground whereon thou standest. *By what idea* hast thou judged thy thought to be illusion, and mere subjectivity? Is it not by an idea of something wholly actual and immediate? Is not that Reality thy own present possession?"

This present actuality of experience, "pure experience," finds me in living relation with that which is most utterly not-myself. Here, in the immediate, is my absolute escape from immediacy. Here in the given present is my escape from myself, my window opening upon infinity, my exit into God. Religion thus becomes the concrete bond between men; for he who has consciously found his way to God, has found his way to man also.

Thus it is that idea may give back the reality of which idea is forever robbing us; for while idea is the greatest enemy of the actual, it is only through idea that idea can be held firmly to its compelling and controlling object, the real as found in experience.

The
Cosmological
and Teleological
Arguments

*S*t. *Thomas Aquinas* believed that there are true statements—statements that it would be altogether unreasonable to doubt—which rationally justify the belief that God exists. Thus he offered "Five Ways" of proving that God exists. Each of these arguments is intended to prove something different about God. Other considerations were taken to show that the five conclusions were indeed true of *one* being, not five different beings. The first argument can be put in this fashion: (1) Some things are in motion; (2) nothing can move itself; (3) there cannot be an infinite series of things moved by other things. So (4) there must be a First Mover.

Several points must be made in order to understand this argument. First, being "in motion" is simply to *change*, not only in place but in any other way. Second, (1) is intended to be "evident to the senses." But (1), in the sense intended by Aquinas, can be true only if something persists or remains the same throughout perceived alterations. Critics have made it clear that this claim involves an analysis of perceptual experience and is no mere report of what is open to sensory observation. Third, there is a subproof for (2). Aquinas is not denying that one can, on one's own, walk across the room or wave one's hand. His claim is made somewhat clearer by the defense he offers of (2). Let X and Y be things capable of changing, and let Q be any quality. Aquinas argues: (2a) To move is to go from potentiality to actuality with respect to some quality—or, conversely, from actuality to potentiality (a thing is an actuality with respect to a quality Q if it has Q, and in potentiality with respect to Q if it could have Q but does not have Q). (2b) X can move Y from potentiality to actuality with respect to a quality Q only if X has Q. (2c) In order for X to change itself with respect to Q, X would have to *have* Q. (2d) In order for X to change itself with respect to Q, X would have to be able to *become* Q, and so *not* have Q. Hence (2e) in order for X to change itself with respect to any quality Q, X must at the same time both have and not have Q. But since this is impossible, X cannot change itself with respect to any quality. The crucial premise in this subproof is (2b). Many changes occur that *seem* to be counterexamples to (2b). Paint that turns a board red when applied to it must itself be red, but must a steak that satisfies my hunger have its own hunger satisfied (whatever that might be like)? I may cause surprise in someone by giving him an unexpected present, but I and my present need not have the feeling of surprise in order to cause it in the recipient. If (2b) does not apply to such cases, *why* not? And if it does, perhaps things can—contrary to (2)—change (move) themselves. Or if these cases (and many others) are not really counterexamples to (2b), this has to be shown; and it is not easy to see how this will be done. In reaction to such problems, the scope of (2) is sometimes restricted to coming into existence and ceasing to exist. Restating the argument with this restriction on (2)—and also on (3)—is left as an exercise for the interested reader.

Fourth, premise (3) requires some comment. Aquinas admits that it is in no way impossible that there has been an infinite past series of causes and effects. His denial that the world has always existed is based upon his belief that the book of *Genesis* denies this, not on any philosophical argument. How, then, can he hold (3) to be true? Because it is not a *past* infinite series that he has in mind. Basically Aquinas' view is this: In order for us to have an adequate explanation at any given time T that a contingent being (that is, a being that *could* fail to exist) exists at T, there must exist a necessary being (that is, a being that could *not* fail to exist) which also exists at T. Whether at T only two beings or a billion beings exist, *one* necessary being must exist at T or there is no sufficient explanation of the fact that something rather than nothing exists at T. And since this is true of *any* time you please, it is true at *all* times. Thus Aquinas' point is not that there must have been a temporally first member of a temporal series going back a while into the past. It is that if *right now* something exists that *could* fail to exist now, there must be something existing that could *not* fail to exist (now or any other time). And this undercuts the criticism that even if Aquinas proved that there was a First Cause, this would not prove that this First Cause still exists.

Finally, there is also a subproof for (3). It goes like this: (3a) If everything is moved by something other than itself, then there is no First Mover; (3b) if there is no First Mover, there is no subsequent mover; (3c) if there is no subsequent mover, there is no motion now; but (3d) there is motion now, so (3e) there are subsequent movers; hence (3f) there must be a First Mover. Premise (3b), however, is ambiguous. If a "subsequent mover" is simply "a mover that follows the First Mover," (3b) is true by definition, but we are left quite uninformed as to why (3c) is true. One could not, on pain of begging the question, appeal to (3) in defending (3c), for (3c) is supposedly going to provide some support for (3).

Or "subsequent mover" can be defined simply as "a mover that follows some other mover (whether First or not)." Then (3b) is not true by definition, so we must ask why it is to be accepted. On this reading, it says that nothing can move unless there is a First Mover. Why? Well, there would seem to be only one reason—that an infinite series of beings, all of which are moved by something else, is impossible. But once again this is (3), and whereas (3b) was supposed to provide support for (3), it looks as if (3) is needed if we are to have any basis for asserting (3b). The subproof, then, seems singularly unhelpful.

Substantially similar remarks can, I believe, be made about the Second Way. The Third Way, then, goes as follows: (1) There are contingent beings (that is, things that *do* exist but that could have failed to exist); (2) whatever is contingent will at some time cease to exist; (3) if everything is contingent, then at some time nothing will exist; (4) if at some past time nothing existed, since nothing can come into existence save through something that exists, there would be nothing existing now; (5) since something exists now, it is false that there was a past time when nothing existed; so (6) it is also false that everything that exists is contingent; that is, some being is necessary (noncontingent).

Once again, the argument requires interpretation due to the compressed form in which it appears. There is an obvious gap between premises (3) and (4). The time mentioned in (3) is not specified to be past; it might just as well be future. Now Aquinas is here allowing (for the sake of argument) that past time may indeed be infinite. If past time *were* infinite, then every possible occurrence would have occurred. One such possibility, if everything is contingent, is that nothing existed at some past time. And then (4) fits nicely into place. On the other hand, if past time is viewed as finite, there is no clear connection between (3) and (4).

There is evidently an inference in Aquinas' reasoning from (2) to (3); he reasons that since every contingent thing can cease to exist, at some time no contingent things will exist. The inference is plainly fallacious. (2) is analogous to (2′) every swan will die; and (3) is analogous to (3′) at some time no swan will exist. But so long as new swans are born, there will continue to be swans; (2′) does not by itself entail (3′). Nor does (2) by itself entail (3). Further, it is hardly clear that (2) is true; that something (say, the moon) *can* cease to exist does not entail that it *will* cease to exist.

In spite of the apparent temporal reference of its premises, the argument can be read in an atemporal manner. Part at any rate of the thesis of the Third Way would seem to be this: that a contingent being exists at time T (no matter whether T is past, present, or future) entails that a noncontingent being (a necessary being) exists. Otherwise there could be no contingent beings at all. In his critique of this kind of argumentation, David Hume focuses his attention on the concepts of contingency and necessity and the theses to which Aquinas appeals which make use of these notions. C. J. Ducasse, a contemporary philosopher, criticizes this argument and the first two arguments as well.

Hume's powerful critique is briefly stated. His challenge can be summarized in this manner: (a) to claim a being is *necessary* is to claim that something exists whose nonexistence is not conceivable; but "whatever we conceive as existent, we can conceive as nonexistent"; (b) waiving (a), if there is a necessary being, why can't it simply be the universe? (c) if a series of events is genuinely conceived as infinite (toward the past), then *necessarily* it has no first cause; (d) the *whole* series cannot be said to have a cause that the members taken singly do not have—to explain the existence of a causal series is not to explain the existence of its members and *also* to explain the existence of the series itself. I think that (a) is best conceived as offering this challenge: the clearest notion of necessity that we have is "logically necessary," but no being is necessary in this sense, for that would mean that its nonexistence was inconceivable; so what sense of "necessary" (if any) can be provided in which a being can be necessary in such a way as to provide explanation for the existence of other beings but itself need no explanation? And (b) is best considered as a challenge to a defender of Aquinas to show that God exists "necessarily" in a way in which the universe could not also be said to do so.

The challenges Hume makes in (a) and (b) raise absolutely central issues, and any one who wishes to defend Aquinas must meet them successfully. Ducasse raises objections similar to (c) and (d), and we will discuss these shortly.

Ducasse offers quite representative criticisms of the cosmological and teleological arguments. With respect to the cosmological argument, he objects that: (a) if there must always be, for anything we name, a further cause, then God must also have a cause; whereas if not everything need have a further cause, nothing is wrong with an infinite regress of causes; (b) there is no contradiction in the notion of an infinite series of past events—compare Hume's objection (c); (c) the phrase *causa sui* (cause of itself) is contradictory, since something would have to not exist to be caused to exist, but also would have to exist in order to cause anything; (d) if anything is either a First Cause or a Self-caused Being, the universe itself is as good a candidate as any; just because each part of the universe is contingent (that is, could fail to exist), it does not follow that the universe as a whole (that is, every part of it) could fail to exist—compare Hume's objection (d).

It is clear that (b) and (c) do not touch Aquinas' formulation of the argument. Regarding (b), Aquinas agrees that it is not contradictory to say that there has been an infinite past series. Regarding (c), nothing in his argument commits him to saying that God is self-caused. God, as First Mover, causes all motion (change) but is Himself not caused to change at all, by Himself or by something else.

But Ducasse's (a) and (d) are relevant to Aquinas' claims. Objection (d) is in effect an answer to a possible reply to objection (a). Part of what (a) says is that if there must be a First Mover, to say that the universe is that mover is as plausible as to say that God is. A possible reply is that since every part of the universe is contingent, the universe itself must be contingent. And (d) replies that: (d1) Every part of the universe is contingent, does not entail (d2) the universe itself is contingent. Of course, the fact that every part of a whole has a property does not, in general, entail that the whole has that property; that every piece of a picture puzzle is square-shaped does not entail that the puzzle as a whole is square-shaped. But sometimes the inference can be made. That every part of a machine is made only of iron entails that the machine as a whole is made only of iron. What inferences can be made from part to whole depend on the property in question. But it is hard to see exactly what principle will sort out cases like the puzzle example from cases like the iron example, and it is not easy to see on which side the inference from (d1) to (d2) falls. Still, it does seem possible (conceivable) that there be no universe at all. If so, (d2) is true whether it follows or does not follow from (d1). The important objection, then, is (a). It includes two criticisms: (a1) Why must everything have a cause? (a2) *if* everything must have a cause, how can we except God? Even if one replies to (a2) by saying that "If God exists, then He is not caused" is necessarily true, the question expressed in (a1) remains. Since "Everything must have a cause" is not true by definition, and since it cannot be shown by experiment to be true, its truth value is not easy to decide upon. The defender of Aquinas must find a way of showing it to be true.

The Fourth Way is a version of the moral argument with which the following section is concerned. The Fifth Way, however, is a version of the teleological argument, or argument from design. A teleological explanation is an explanation in terms of the activity of a purposive agent. Such explanations abound in everyday life. "She went to the store in order to buy a dress," "He bought the brush so he could paint his house," and "People bring presents to other people to show affection" are all teleological explanations. Now sometimes objects that are not purposive agents act, so to speak, *as if* they were purposive agents. Machines work as if it were their conscious goal to produce a particular product; acorns grow into oak trees as if this result were something they had intended. Machines were designed to work as they do; so, for Aquinas (and, indeed for any orthodox Christian or Jew or Moslem), were acorns.

We are now in a position to state the Fifth Way. (1) Things which are not purposive agents "act for an end, and this is evident from their acting always, or almost always, in the same way, so as to obtain the best result"; (2) that which acts without knowledge "cannot move toward an end unless it be directed" by a purposive agent; so: (3) some purposive agent exists "by whom all natural things are directed to their end," namely, God.

It is quite clear that (3) does not follow from (1) and (2) alone. That every moving arrow (to use Aquinas' example) is shot by some bowman does not show that some *one* bowman shoots every arrow that is shot. An appeal to parsimony (roughly, the explanation that postulates the least number of entities and still explains the data is best) is also necessary (and debatable). But even if one accepts the appeal to parsimony, problems arise.

Let us say that when an object, whether an artifact or a natural object, goes through an apparently purposive process, it manifests "designedness."

Since it is at least logically possible that something, so to speak, acts as if it were designed even though it was not designed by anyone (and proponents of the teleological argument admit this), the sentence "*X* manifests designedness" does not by itself entail "*X* was designed by a purposive agent." "Designedness" is in this respect a neutral concept. The teleological argument is successful only if the best explanation of the fact that natural objects manifest designedness is that they were designed by a purposive agent. Historically a severe blow was dealt to the teleological argument by the Darwinian claim that natural selection (a process involving no purposive activity) could account for the existent forms of life. The selection from F. R. Tennant offers a formulation of the teleological argument made with full awareness of Darwin's work. It appeals more to the general order and intelligibility of the world and its suitability as a human moral environment than to particular examples of objects (for example, the eye) that manifest designedness.

Concerning the teleological argument, or argument from design, Ducasse argues that (a) if the existence of designedness in the universe requires explanation, so does the existence of someone with the capacity to produce that designedness; (b) there is (as Hume noted) no reason to postulate a *perfect* Designer or only *one* designer, even if some designer or other must be postulated: (c) again as Hume noted, designedness often does not, in human experience, result from human design: (d) we could explain the designedness of, for example, an eye, in terms of "an automatic objectification of an obscure craving or felt need to see," and this explanation is no more problematic than one requiring that a designer can, without hands or tools, design and produce an eye.

Neither (b) nor (c) require extensive commentary. It is true that the argument shows, at best, that there is (or was) a powerful and very intelligent Designer, not an absolutely all-knowing, all-powerful one. (The qualification "*or was*" shows how important it is that the First Way and the Fifth be true of the same being—the designer must be a necessary being.) This much seems indisputable; if the existence of a designer *is* proved, he *may* be (but the argument gives no reason to suppose him to be) a perfect being.

It is also true that objects of ordinary experience manifest designedness but were designed by no human agent. But it is just these objects that provide the evidence to which the teleological argument appeals. In this connection Hume also appeals to explanations of designedness other than by reference to a purposive agent, as does Ducasse in (d). It remains, then, to discuss Ducasse's (a) and (d).

It seems clear that (a) is true unless it is true that (a1), the data one appeals to in making a teleological explanation, do not themselves require explanation. And (a1) will have to be true even though (at least for the purposes of the teleological argument) it is true that (a2), states of affairs manifesting designedness, always require teleological explanation. Now (a), (a1), and (a2) raise two distinct but related questions: (1) When is it appropriate to require an explanation? and (2) is any one sort of explanation, in some sense which can be made clear, more ultimate than another sort? Is, for example, teleological explanation somehow more ultimate than causal explanation which is nonteleological? Or are both equally ultimate? Or does ultimacy, in some clear sense of the term, belong to causal explanation which is nonteleological? Again, is the datum one appeals to in formulating teleological explanation—namely, the activity of a purposive being—somehow not in need of further explanation? A defender of Aquinas or Tennant would, it seems, have to hold this view; he would have to defend (a1). It is just this view that Ducasse challenges in (a).

In offering objection (d), Ducasse raises another issue. Suppose one grants (a1). He can then suggest that (a3), the data referred to in offering explanations in terms of objectifications of felt needs, are in need of no further explanation. Further, if one explains states of affairs that manifest designedness in terms of objectifications of felt needs, one offers a nonteleological explanation. So even if (a1) is true, (a3) may also be true, in which case we need some reason for preferring teleological explanations to objectification-of-felt-need explanations. This is a further point upon which the teleological arguer is, it would seem, required to offer cogent defense.

Five Arguments for God's Existence
THOMAS AQUINAS

WHETHER IT CAN BE
DEMONSTRATED
THAT GOD EXISTS?

*W*e proceed thus to the Second Article:—

OBJECTION 1. It seems that the existence of God cannot be demonstrated. For it is an article of faith that God exists. But what is of faith cannot be demonstrated, because a demonstration produces scientific knowledge, whereas faith is of the unseen, as is clear from the Apostle (*Heb*. xi. 1). Therefore it cannot be demonstrated that God exists.

OBJ. 2. Further, essence is the middle term of demonstration. But we cannot know in what God's essence consists, but solely in what it does not consist, as Damascene says.[1] Therefore we cannot demonstrate that God exists.

OBJ. 3. Further, if the existence of God were demonstrated, this could only

[1] *De Fide Orth.*, I, 4 (PG 94, 800).

be from His effects. But His effects are not proportioned to Him, since He is infinite and His effects are finite, and between the finite and infinite there is no proportion. Therefore, since a cause cannot be demonstrated by an effect not proportioned to it, it seems that the existence of God cannot be demonstrated.

On the contrary, The Apostle says: *The invisible things of Him are clearly seen, being understood by the things that are made* (*Rom*. i. 20). But this would not be unless the existence of God could be demonstrated through the things that are made; for the first thing we must know of anything is, whether it exists.

I answer that, Demonstration can be made in two ways: One is through the cause, and is called *propter quid*, and this is to argue from what is prior absolutely. The other is through the effect, and is called a demonstration *quia*; this is to argue from what is prior relatively only to us. When an effect is better known to us than its cause, from the

FROM: *Summa Theologica*, Part I, Question 2, Articles 2, 3, in *Basic Writings of St. Thomas Aquinas*, Anton C. Pegis, ed. (New York: Random House, Inc., 1948). Reprinted by permission of Random House and Burns and Oates, Ltd.

effect we proceed to the knowledge of the cause. And from every effect the existence of its proper cause can be demonstrated, so long as its effects are better known to us; because, since every effect depends upon its cause, if the effect exists, the cause must pre-exist. Hence the existence of God, in so far as it is not self-evident to us, can be demonstrated from those of His effects which are known to us.

REPLY OBJ. 1. The existence of God and other like truths about God, which can be known by natural reason, are not articles of faith, but are preambles to the articles; for faith presupposes natural knowledge, even as grace presupposes nature and perfection the perfectible. Nevertheless, there is nothing to prevent a man, who cannot grasp a proof, from accepting, as a matter of faith, something which in itself is capable of being scientifically known and demonstrated.

REPLY OBJ. 2. When the existence of a cause is demonstrated from an effect, this effect takes the place of the definition of the cause in proving the cause's existence. This is especially the case in regard to God, because, in order to prove the existence of anything, it is necessary to accept as a middle term the meaning of the name, and not its essence, for the question of its essence follows on the question of its existence. Now the names given to God are derived from His effects, as will be later shown.[2] Consequently, in demonstrating the existence of God from His effects, we may take for the middle term the meaning of the name *God*.

REPLY OBJ. 3. From effects not proportioned to the cause no perfect knowledge of that cause can be obtained. Yet from every effect the existence of the cause can be clearly demonstrated, and so we can demonstrate the existence of God from His effects; though from them we cannot know God perfectly as He is in His essence.

[2] Q. 13, a. 1.

THIRD ARTICLE

WHETHER GOD EXISTS?

We proceed thus to the Third Article:—

OBJECTION 1. It seems that God does not exist; because if one of two contraries be infinite, the other would be altogether destroyed. But the name *God* means that He is infinite goodness. If therefore, God existed, there would be no evil discoverable; but there is evil in the world. Therefore God does not exist.

OBJ. 2. Further, it is superfluous to suppose that what can be accounted for by a few principles has been produced by many. But it seems that everything we see in the world can be accounted for by other principles, supposing God did not exist. For all natural things can be reduced to one principle, which is nature; and all voluntary things can be reduced to one principle, which is human reason, or will. Therefore there is no need to suppose God's existence.

On the contrary, It is said in the person of God: *I am Who am (Exod. iii. 14).*

I answer that, The existence of God can be proved in five ways.

The first and more manifest way is the argument from motion. It is certain, and evident to our senses, that in the world some things are in motion. Now whatever is moved is moved by another, for nothing can be moved except it is in potentiality to that towards which it is moved; whereas a thing moves inasmuch as it is in act. For motion is nothing else than the reduction of something from potentiality to actuality. But nothing can be reduced from potentiality to actuality, except by something in a state of actuality. Thus that which is actually hot, as fire, makes wood, which is potentially hot, to be actually hot, and thereby moves and changes it. Now it is not possible that the same thing should be at once in actuality and potentiality in the same respect, but only in different respects. For what is actually hot cannot simultaneously be potentially hot; but it is simultaneously potentially cold.

It is therefore impossible that in the same respect and in the same way a thing should be both mover and moved, *i.e.*, that it should move itself. Therefore, whatever is moved must be moved by another. If that by which it is moved be itself moved, then this also must needs be moved by another, and that by another again. But this cannot go on to infinity, because then there would be no first mover, and, consequently, no other mover, seeing that subsequent movers move only inasmuch as they are moved by the first mover; as the staff moves only because it is moved by the hand. Therefore it is necessary to arrive at a first mover, moved by no other; and this everyone understands to be God.

The second way is from the nature of efficient cause. In the world of sensible things we find there is an order of efficient causes. There is no case known (neither is it, indeed, possible) in which a thing is found to be the efficient cause of itself; for so it would be prior to itself, which is impossible. Now in efficient causes it is not possible to go on to infinity, because in all efficient causes following in order, the first is the cause of the intermediate cause, and the intermediate is the cause of the ultimate cause, whether the intermediate cause be several, or one only. Now to take away the cause is to take away the effect. Therefore, if there be no first cause among efficient causes, there will be no ultimate, nor any intermediate, cause. But if in efficient causes it is possible to go on to infinity, there will be no first efficient cause, neither will there be an ultimate effect, nor any intermediate efficient causes; all of which is plainly false. Therefore it is necessary to admit a first efficient cause, to which everyone gives the name of God.

The third way is taken from possibility and necessity, and runs thus. We find in nature things that are possible to be and not to be, since they are found to be generated, and to be corrupted, and consequently, it is possible for them to be and not to be. But it is impossible for these always to exist, for that which can not-be at some time is not. Therefore, if everything can not-be, then at one time there was nothing in existence. Now if this were true, even now there would be nothing in existence, because that which does not exist begins to exist only through something already existing. Therefore, if at one time nothing was in existence, it would have been impossible for anything to have begun to exist; and thus even now nothing would be in existence—which is absurd. Therefore, not all beings are merely possible, but there must exist something the existence of which is necessary. But every necessary thing either has its necessity caused by another, or not. Now it is impossible to go on to infinity in necessary things which have their necessity caused by another, as has been already proved in regard to efficient causes. Therefore we cannot but admit the existence of some being having of itself its own necessity, and not receiving it from another, but rather causing in others their necessity. This all men speak of as God.

The fourth way is taken from the gradation to be found in things. Among beings there are some more and some less good, true, noble, and the like. But *more* and *less* are predicted of different things according as they resemble in their different ways something which is the maximum, as a thing is said to be hotter according as it more nearly resembles that which is hottest; so that there is something which is truest, something best, something noblest, and, consequently, something which is most being, for those things that are greatest in truth are greatest in being, as it is written in *Metaph*. ii.[3] Now the maximum in any genus is the cause of all in that genus, as fire, which is the maximum of heat, is the cause of all hot things, as is said in the same book.[4] Therefore there must also be something which is to all beings the cause of their being, goodness, and every other perfection; and this we call God.

[3] *Metaph.* Ia, 1 (993b 30).

[4] *Ibid.* (993b 25).

The fifth way is taken from the governance of the world. We see that things which lack knowledge, such as natural bodies, act for an end, and this is evident from their acting always, or nearly always, in the same way, so as to obtain the best result. Hence it is plain that they achieve their end, not fortuitously, but designedly. Now whatever lacks knowledge cannot move towards an end, unless it be directed by some being endowed with knowledge and intelligence; as the arrow is directed by the archer. Therefore some intelligent being exists by whom all natural things are directed to their end; and this being we call God.

REPLY OBJ. 1. As Augustine says: *Since God is the highest good, He would not allow any evil to exist in His works,* unless *His omnipotence and goodness were such as to bring good even out of evil.*[5] This is part of the infinite goodness of God, that He should allow evil to exist, and out of it produce good.

REPLY OBJ. 2. Since nature works for a determinate end under the direction of a higher agent, whatever is done by nature must be traced back to God as to its first cause. So likewise whatever is done voluntarily must be traced back to some higher cause other than human reason and will, since these can change and fail; for all things that are changeable and capable of defect must be traced back to an immovable and self-necessary first principle, as has been shown.

[5] *Enchir.,* XI (PL 40, 236).

The Cosmological Argument Is Not Cogent
DAVID HUME

*B*ut *if so* many difficulties attend the argument *a posteriori,* said Demea, had we not better adhere to that simple and sublime argument *a priori* which, by offering to us infallible demonstration, cuts off at once all doubt and difficulty? By this argument, too, we may prove the *infinity* of the Divine attributes, which, I am afraid, can never be ascertained with certainty from any other topic. For how can an effect which either is finite or, for aught we know, may be so—how can such an effect, I say, prove an infinite cause? The unity, too, of the Divine Nature it is very difficult, if not absolutely impossible, to deduce merely from contemplating the works of nature; nor will the uniformity alone of the plan, even were it allowed, give us any assurance of that attribute. Whereas the argument *a priori* . . .

You seem to reason, Demea, interposed Cleanthes, as if those advantages and conveniences in the abstract argument were full proofs of its solidity. But it is first proper, in my opinion, to determine what argument of this nature you choose to insist on; and we shall afterwards, from itself, better than from its *useful* consequences, endeavour to determine what value we ought to put upon it.

The argument, replied Demea, which I would insist on is the common one. Whatever exists must have a cause or reason of its existence, it being absolutely impossible for anything to produce itself or be the cause of its own existence. In mounting up, therefore, from effects to causes, we must either go on in tracing an infinite succession, without any ultimate cause at all, or must at least have recourse to some ultimate cause that is *necessarily* existent. Now that the first supposition is absurd may be thus proved. In the infinite chain or

FROM: *Dialogues Concerning Natural Religion,* David Hume. Part 9 (originally published in 1779).

succession of causes and effects, each single effect is determined to exist by the power and efficacy of that cause which immediately preceded; but the whole eternal chain or succession, taken together, is not determined or caused by anything, and yet it is evident that it requires a cause or reason, as much as any particular object which begins to exist in time. The question is still reasonable why this particular succession of causes existed from eternity, and not any other succession or no succession at all. If there be no necessarily existent being, any supposition which can be formed is equally possible; nor is there any more absurdity in nothing's having existed from eternity than there is in that succession of causes which constitutes the universe. What was it, then, which determined *something* to exist rather than *nothing*, and bestowed being on a particular possibility, exclusive of the rest? *External causes*, there are supposed to be none. *Chance* is a word without a meaning. Was it *nothing*? But that can never produce anything. We must, therefore, have recourse to a necessarily existent Being who carries the *reason* of his existence in himself, and who cannot be supposed not to exist, without an express contradiction. There is, consequently, such a Being—that is, there is a Deity.

I shall not leave it to Philo, said Cleanthes, though I know that the starting objections is his chief delight, to point out the weakness of this metaphysical reasoning. It seems to me so obviously ill-grounded, and at the same time of so little consequence to the cause of true piety and religion, that I shall myself venture to show the fallacy of it.

I shall begin with observing that there is an evident absurdity in pretending to demonstrate a matter of fact, or to prove it by any arguments *a priori*. Nothing is demonstrable unless the contrary implies a contradiction. Nothing that is distinctly conceivable implies a contradiction. Whatever we conceive as existent, we can also conceive as non-existent. There is no being, therefore, whose non-existence implies a contradic-

tion. Consequently there is no being whose existence is demonstrable. I propose this argument as entirely decisive, and am willing to rest the whole controversy upon it.

It is pretended that the Deity is a necessarily existent being; and this necessity of his existence is attempted to be explained by asserting that, if we knew his whole essence or nature, we should perceive it to be as impossible for him not to exist, as for twice two not to be four. But it is evident that this can never happen, while our faculties remain the same as at present. It will still be possible for us, at any time, to conceive the non-existence of what we formerly conceived to exist; nor can the mind ever lie under a necessity of supposing any object to remain always in being; in the same manner as we lie under a necessity of always conceiving twice two to be four. The words, therefore, *necessary existence* have no meaning or, which is the same thing, none that is consistent.

But further, why may not the material universe be the necessarily existent Being, according to this pretended explication of necessity? We dare not affirm that we know all the qualities of matter; and, for aught we can determine, it may contain some qualities which, were they known, would make its non-existence appear as great a contradiction as that twice two is five. I find only one argument employed to prove that the material world is not the necessarily existent Being; and this argument is derived from the contingency both of the matter and form of the world. "Any particle of matter," it is said, "may be *conceived* to be annihilated, and any form may be *conceived* to be altered. Such an annihilation or alteration, therefore, is not impossible."[1] But it seems a great partiality not to perceive that the same argument extends equally to the Deity, so far as we have any conception of him, and that the mind can at least imagine him to be non-existent or his attributes to be altered. It must be some unknown, inconceivable

[1] Dr. Clarke.

qualities which can make his non-existence appear impossible or his attributes unalterable; and no reason can be assigned why these qualities may not belong to matter. As they are altogether unknown and inconceivable, they can never be proved incompatible with it.

Add to this that in tracing an eternal succession of objects it seems absurd to inquire for a general cause or first author. How can anything that exists from eternity have a cause, since that relation implies a priority in time and a beginning of existence?

In such a chain, too, or succession of objects, each part is caused by that which preceded it, and causes that which succeeds it. Where then is the difficulty? But the *whole*, you say, wants a cause. I answer that the uniting of these parts into a whole, like the uniting of several distinct countries into one kingdom, or several distinct members into one body, is performed merely by an arbitrary act of the mind, and has no influence on the nature of things. Did I show you the particular causes of each individual in a collection of twenty particles of matter, I should think it very unreasonable should you afterwards ask me what was the cause of the whole twenty. This is sufficiently explained in explaining the cause of the parts.

Though the reasonings which you have urged, Cleanthes, may well excuse me, said Philo, from starting any further difficulties, yet I cannot forbear insisting still upon another topic. It is observed by arithmeticians that the products of 9 compose always either 9 or some lesser product of 9 if you add together all the characters of which any of the former products is composed. Thus, of 18, 27, 36, which are products of 9, you make 9 by adding 1 to 8, 2 to 7, 3 to 6. Thus 369 is a product also of 9; and if you add 3, 6, and 9, you make 18, a lesser product of 9.[2] To a superficial observer so wonderful a regularity may be admired as the effect either of chance or design; but a skilful algebraist immediately concludes it to be the work of necessity, and demonstrates that it must for ever result from the nature of these numbers. Is it not probable, I ask, that the whole economy of the universe is conducted by a like necessity, though no human algebra can furnish a key which solves the difficulty? And instead of admiring the order of natural beings, may it not happen that, could we penetrate into the intimate nature of bodies, we should clearly see why it was absolutely impossible they could ever admit of any other disposition? So dangerous is it to introduce this idea of necessity into the present question! and so naturally does it afford an inference directly opposite to the religious hypothesis!

But dropping all these abstractions, continued Philo, and confining ourselves to more familiar topics, I shall venture to add an observation that the argument *a priori* has seldom been found very convincing, except to people of a metaphysical head who have accustomed themselves to abstract reasoning, and who, finding from mathematics that the understanding frequently leads to truth through obscurity, and contrary to first appearances, have transferred the same habit of thinking to subjects where it ought not to have place. Other people, even of good sense and the best inclined to religion, feel always some deficiency in such arguments, though they are not perhaps able to explain distinctly where it lies—a certain proof that men ever did and ever will derive their religion from other sources than from this species of reasoning.

[2] *Republique des Lettres*, Aut 1685.

A Reinterpretation of the Teleological Argument
F. R. TENNANT

In an exposition of the significance of the moral order for theistic philosophy, the first step is to point out that man belongs to Nature, and is an essential part of it, in such a sense that the world cannot be described or explained as a whole without taking him and his moral values into account. Prof. Pringle-Pattison, especially, has elaborated the doctrine that, as he expresses it, "man is organic to the world". What precisely this, or the similar phrase "man is the child of Nature", should mean, if either is to be more than a half-truth, needs to be made clear. Insofar as man's soul, i.e. man as *noümenon*, or (in the language of spiritualistic pluralism) the dominant monad in the empirical self, is concerned, we are not authorised by known facts to regard man as organic to Nature, or as the child of Nature, in the sense that he is an emergent product of cosmic evolution. We are rather forbidden by psychology to entertain any such notion. But, this proviso being observed—it must qualify all that is further said in the present connexion—we can affirm that man's body, with all its conditioning of his mentality, his sociality, knowledge and morality, is 'of a piece' with Nature; and that, in so far as he is a phenomenal being, man is organic to Nature, or a product of the world. And this fact is as significant for our estimation of Nature as for our anthropology. If man is Nature's child, Nature is the wonderful mother of such a child. Any account of her which ignores the fact of her maternity is scientifically partial and philosophically insignificant. Her capacity to produce man must be reckoned among her potencies, explain it how we may. And man is no monstrous birth out of due time,

no freak or sport. In respect of his body and the bodily conditioning of his mentality, man is like, and has genetic continuity with, Nature's humbler and earlier-born children. In the fulness of time Nature found self-utterance in a son possessed of the intelligent and moral status. Maybe she was pregnant with him from the beginning, and the world-ages are the period of her gestation. As to this anthropocentric view of the world-process, and its co-existensiveness with teleological interpretation, more will presently be said. But in the light of man's continuity with the rest of the world we can at once dismiss the view that Nature suddenly "stumbled" or "darkly blundered" on man, while "churning the universe with mindless motion". The world-process is a *praeparatio anthropologica,* whether designedly or not, and man is the culmination, up to the present stage of the knowable history of Nature, of a gradual ascent. We cannot explain man in terms of physical Nature; conceivably Nature may be found explicable—in another sense of the word—in terms of man, and can be called 'the threshold of spirit'. Judging the genealogical tree by its roots, naturalism once preached that Darwin had put an end to the assumption that man occupies an exceptional position on our planet; apparently implying that there is no difference of status between man and the primordial slime because stages between the two are traceable. But if we judge the tree by its fruits, Darwin may rather be said to have restored man to the position from which Copernicus seemed to have ousted him, in making it possible to read the humanising of Nature in the naturalising of man, and to regard man as not only the last term and the

FROM: *Philosophical Theology*, F. R. Tennant. (New York: Cambridge University Press, 1928), Vol. II, Chapter 4, p. 99–120. Reprinted by permission of Cambridge University Press.

crown of Nature's long upward effort, but also as its end or goal.[1]

The phrase 'organic to Nature', as applied to man, may serve to sum up other relations between humanity and the world besides that of parentage or blood-affinity. It implies also a denial of the assertion that man is an excrescence upon Nature in the sense of being an alien in a world that is indifferent to his moral aims, or hostile to his ideals. The most forcible presentation of this view, that the cosmic process and human morality are antithetical, is perhaps that contained in Huxley's *Romanes Lecture*. It is therefore here selected for examination. Huxley's first point was that the world, as involving struggle for existence and extermination of the less fit, is no "school of virtue". If that statement merely meant that it is not from Nature that we are to imbibe our ethical maxims, no one would wish to dispute it. But it would then overlook the fact that in other senses Nature may fairly be called a school of virtue. In the first place, Nature is largely a cosmos ruled by uniformity or law; and if Nature's uniformity and impartiality are a main source of the trouble to which man is born, they are also a precondition of all intelligent, and therefore of all moral, life. In this respect Nature is the power that makes it possible for noümenal man to be, as phenomenal man, a moral being. Further, it is partly through his being "the plaything of hazard and the prey of hardship" that man's moral virtues are acquired. The world is thus instrumental to the emergence, maintenance, and progressiveness, of morality. The second charge which Huxley preferred against the cosmos is that the physical world works upon man solely through his lower nature, his ingrained appetites, etc., and against his higher ethical interests. Nature is thus the cause of his 'original sin', and is diabolically provocative of his diverse immoralities. This also is true; but again it presents but one

aspect of the facts. For, apart from man's bodily appetites and impulses it is inconceivable that ethical principles should gain purchase on him. Hunger and sex are the bed-rock of human morality; and the self-determination which human morality presupposes is hardly possible without the conflict between moral reason and non-moral impulse. Morality cannot be made without raw material; and in providing this raw material Nature is once more instrumental to man's acquisition of the moral status. Morality thus has its roots in Nature, however indispensable be the innate and non-inherited potentialities of the pure ego or soul. The non-moral cosmos, personified into a morally evil world by pessimistic poets for the purpose of giving it, as Mr. Chesterton has said of one of them, a piece of their mind, has nevertheless subserved the moralisation of human souls, even when soliciting to carnality. And it is an exaggeration to say that Nature fosters only tendencies that issue in vice. We have seen before that there is such a thing as 'natural virtue', or 'original rectitude', as 'instinctive' as is self-seeking; and Nature plainly appraises health and vigor, thus inciting to temperance and self-control. Lastly, Huxley maintained that the world is indifferent to man's moral aspirations, in that they along with him are destined to be extinguished before the break-up of the solar system. Here he became unwarrantably dogmatical: for, apart from the fact that science's predictions are not unconditional, speculations as to the ruin of a fragment of the universe, based on partial knowledge of a larger fragment of what, for all we know, may be possessed of a power to make all things new, are too precarious to be considered exhaustive of the possibilities even as to our terrestrial home, let alone those as to a future life.

Nature, then, has produced moral beings, is instrumental to moral life and therefore amenable to 'instrumental' moral valuation, and is relatively modifiable by operative moral ideas—or, rather, by moral agents pursuing ideals.

[1] A. Seth Pringle-Pattison, *The Idea of God*, 1917, pp. 82 f.

Nature and moral man are not at strife, but are organically one. The whole process of Nature is capable of being regarded as instrumental to the development of intelligent and moral creatures. Acquisition of the moral status is in line with the other stages of the long 'ascent of man', and is its climax—unless we reserve that name for the morality which, tinged with sentiment transcending reverence for duty, passes into religion.

The more or less separable fields of fact which have now been surveyed may each be said to admit of teleological explanation even if explanation of the causal or the descriptive type be forthcoming in every case. None of them calls for resort to final causes merely because other kinds of causality, or linkage according to law, are not assignable. Theism no longer plants its God in the gaps between the explanatory achievements of natural science, which are apt to get scientifically closed up. Causal explanation and teleological explanation are not mutually exclusive alternatives; and neither can perform the function of the other. It is rather when these several fields of fact are no longer considered one by one, but as parts of the whole or terms of a continuous series, and when for their dovetailing and interconnectedness a sufficient ground is sought, such as mechanical and proximate causation no longer seems to supply, that divine design is forcibly suggested. Paley's watch is no analogue of the human eye; but it may none the less be an approximate analogue of Nature as a whole. Thus the wider teleological argument is not comparable with a chain whose strength is precisely that of its weakest link; it is comparable rather with a piece of chain-armour. And this can the better be seen if the relevant facts be presented again so as to display especially their connexions and their gradually increasing suggestiveness.

There is no intrinsic necessity that a world, or an assemblage of existents and happenings, indefinably and unaccountably 'standing out' as against nothingness, be a cosmos, even to the extent of any one existent being comparable with another or behaving in the same way twice. Reality, or the aggregate of those determinate beings, might conceivably be a 'chaos' of disparates and inconsistencies such that if any of its members possessed consciousness or awareness and the potentiality of intelligence, they would find the world presented to them utterly unintelligible. Our world is, however, a cosmos, at least in the humblest sense of the word, and the original determinateness of its terms or *posita* is such as to make it intelligible. This, of course, constitutes a teleological proof of theism no more than does the existence of the word afford a causal or cosmological proof. The mystery of mysteries is that something exists; and if the one underived or uncaused existent be God, the creator of all things else, God is "the last irrationality", and creation is the next to the last inexplicability. To replace absolute pluralism by theism is to reduce an indefinite number of separate inexplicabilities to these two alone; and so far economy, and therefore explicability of a kind, is secured. It is of no important kind, however: for there is no more wonder about a self-subsistent plurality than about a self-subsistent individual. But when the intelligibility of a cosmos, rather than the mere existence of a world of any sort, is the fact to be considered, teleological theism evinces more conspicuously its advantage, in other respects than that of economy, over absolute pluralism. For over and above the forthcomingness, conceived as self-subsistence, of the many existents, is their adaptiveness, inherent in their primary determinateness and relations, to the requirements of intelligibility. This further particularises their determinateness and so bespeaks more of coincidence in the 'fortuitous'. For cosmos-quality, or intelligibility, in our world, which conceivably might have been a determinate 'chaos', non-theistic philosophy can assign no reason. If the world 'made itself', so to say, or is the self-subsistent Absolute, its adaptiveness to understanding has simply happened, and is part and parcel of the pluralist's last irrationality. It gives him more to explain or to refuse to explain: for why should the many arrange themselves to form an intelligible and an organic whole? If, on the other hand, this be due to an intelligent Creator designing the world to be a theatre for rational life, mystery is minimised, and a possible and sufficient reason is assigned. More than this cannot be extracted out of the initial fact that the world is intelligible, in the sense that has as yet solely been in question; but if it be merely a hint that Nature's dice may be loaded, it is to be observed that the hint becomes broader as Nature is further examined, and as the knowledge-process is analysed. For instance, the particular species of intelligibility, in which the knowledge of common sense and science consists, is mediated by the 'real' categories; and they depend for their forthcomingness on the contingency that the dominant monad in man is embodied, or associated with monads such as also constitute Nature but which, in virtue of some mysterious affinity, are not merely bits of Nature to the soul but also its windows and telephonic exchange-office mediating to it all its knowledge whatsoever, even its self-knowledge. Thus, as step by step the machinery which produces intelligibility is scientifically explored and made manifest, the richer in specialised determinateness are some of the world's constituents found to be; and therefore the more suggestive is the intricate adaptiveness, involved in knowledge of the world by man, of pre-established harmony or immanent guidance, or both, and the less reasonable or credible becomes the alternative theory of cumulative groundless coincidence. The doctrine that man is organic to Nature can now be broadened out so as to embrace the fact that it is only in so far as he is part and parcel of Nature that he can ejectively make the knowledge-venture, and only in virtue of Nature's affinity with him that his postulatory categories receive pragmatic verification, and his assimilation-drafts are honoured. When the

impossible Cartesian rationalism is exchanged for the humanism or anthropism which, implicit in Kant, is explicitly demanded by more modern empirical knowledge of the human mind, the epistemological argument for theism begins to acquire a forcibleness that was lacking to the arbitrary, if not circular, reasoning of Descartes. It is, however, but a fragment of the epistemological argument to establish the anthropocentric theory of knowledge, which is ultimately based on the fact that between the soul and the world, in so far as knowledge of the one by the other is concerned, stands the body; and the epistemological line or mesh-work is but a fragment of the teleological argument as a whole.

Turning now from Nature's knowability to her structure and history, we may revert first to the fact of adaptiveness in the organic realm, which, so far, has only been found not to yield teleological proof of the narrower kind. Here adaptiveness, unhappily described as internal teleology, is not teleological at all in so far as it is internal to the organism. There is no end present to the agent. It is from the (ps) standpoint of the biologist, not from the (ψ) standpoint of the organism, that reference to the future is involved in organic adaptedness. Again, neither the occurrence nor the progressiveness of organic adaptations, taking *singillatim*, calls for other than natural, if non-mechanical, causation. It is true that the course of living Nature is not mere change, but change that admits of valuation, of one kind or another; of valuation not only in terms of fitness for survival but also in terms of differentiation or complexity of structure and function, and of subservience to further development culminating, in man, in rationality and morality. Despite cases of stagnancy and of degeneration, which equally with progress may ensure biological fitness, the plasticity, formative power, or *élan* in organic Nature secures not only self-conservation but also progress, morphological and ultimately mental, so that within the main line of development there has been a steady advance from amoeba to man. But each step and special adaptation, each case of emergence of something new and higher, in this long process, can be sufficiently accounted for in terms of natural, non-teleological causation. So far as the foregoing facts are concerned there is no need to resort to external teleology. It is not *necessary* to invoke design in order to find a guarantee for the stability, in face of the ever-present possibility of deletion of the 'higher' by the 'fitter', of the long and gradual ascent, remarkable as that is. It is rather when the essential part played by the environment, physical and organic, in the progressive development of the organic world, is appreciated, that non-teleological explanation ceases to be plausible in this sphere, and, conspiration being precluded, external design begins to be indicated or strongly suggested. It is the environment that is the selector, though 'selection' is a figurative expression when applied to non-intelligent Nature. Subjective selection, or the Lamarckean factor, may decide what shall arise; but the environment decides what shall stand. And before discussing the alternatives of theistic teleology and naturalistic Pyrrhonism (if the doctrine of fortuitousness or ungrounded coincidence may so be called), it may be submitted that the fact just mentioned restricts our choice to the one or the other of them, in that, when taken into account, it deprives the only other forthcoming alternative, viz. the theory of 'unconscious purpose', of such plausibility as, *prima facie*, it may seem to possess.

The phrases 'unconscious will' and 'unconscious purpose' are, of course, when taken literally, contradictions in terms. That, however, is unimportant. Overlooking the poetic licence evinced in such forms of speech, we may inquire what the writers who favour them mean by them, or what are their equivalents in scientific terminology. This is not always easy to ascertain with precision; but it would seem to amount to the assertion of an *élan vital* present in Nature as a whole, an intrinsic potency to strive blindly towards, and to attain by changes

that we valuing subjects call progressive from the lower to the higher, what, from the same intelligent point of view, are relative goals: not ends of a designer, nor merely temporally later stages in a process, but 'ends' in the sense of later stages that happen to be of higher value, of one kind or another, than the earlier stages, *as if* foreseen and striven for. This kind of *Zweckmässigkeit* without *Absichtlichkeit* has a parallel in human endeavours. Men have sometimes "built more wisely than they knew", and human societies may fashion institutions, beliefs, etc., without any of their members having a preconceived definite idea of the 'end' in which their activities are destined to issue. One thing that was willed leads on to other things that were not at first willed or even imagined, and *sometimes* these other things are found desirable, or are goods to be preserved. Sometimes, however, they are of the opposite kind, so that reforms or revolutions find place in human history. And here, if the theory before us be not misunderstood, this analogy breaks down. For the theory ascribes to Nature an intrinsic potency which, if it is to succeed in the absence of that self-correction by which erring human mentality can change its own course and avoid impending catastrophes, must inevitably go, like animal instinct, straight to its mark in all essentials and on all critical occasions. Nature's 'unconscious wisdom', in other words, must vastly exceed the sapience and foresight of humanity, liable as that is to errors which, save for reasoned amendment, might prove fatal. In fact the theory requires us to believe that Nature keeps her head, which *ex hypothesi* is brainless, through all the changes and chances of cosmic history.

Further, 'unconscious purpose', which has turned out to be as fatalistic as mechanism and yet as value-realising as man, does not seem, on examination, to be one and the same thing in the different kingdoms of Nature. In that part of the organic world that is (macroscopically) psychical it is said to be exemplified in animal impulse, or the non-volitional conation of individual organisms. But this subjective selectiveness of the individual, though essential to organic development, does not of itself suffice to secure it. The organism, in filling its skin, may get itself a better skin to fill, but on the other hand it might burst its skin; and blind or random movement, such as might secure escape from the painful or displeasing, may land 'out of the frying-pan into the fire'. Natural selection can only secure the progress of species in virtue of such individual catastrophes, misfits, etc., in organisms inspired with venturesomeness and *élan*. Individual variations are mostly indefinite or in many directions, not in the straight path of progress alone; and it is the environment, as censor, that plays the larger part in determining a steady and permanent advance, as contrasted with the sporadic and evanescent experiments which make progress a possibility. Thus the environment, the preponderating part of which is inorganic, as well as its organic denizens, needs to be accredited with 'unconscious purpose'; yet it lacks even the animal conatus and the vegetable 'formative power' which, though they are Actualities, are not unconsciously *purposive*, in that, of themselves, they are not fraught with an exclusively progressive trend. A formative power lodged in the physical, as science has hitherto understood it, making as if for a goal, is not an Actuality known to science. Consequently, it here becomes impossible to find any explanatoriness, and indeed any meaning, in 'unconscious purpose'. If it but asserts that in the inorganic world there is a potency of adaptiveness, that is but a new name for the fact that the environment is adapted; it but restates the fact to be explained, the problem to be solved, and proffers no explanation or solution. An explanation, however, is offered by teleology and theism. (It is a fact that Nature, as inorganic, is as much adapted to organic life as organic life is adaptive to physical environment; and it is not a matter of indifference whether we say "God has wisely willed it so" or "Nature has wisely arranged this", simply because Nature has no wisdom wherewith to arrange anything. If Nature evinces wisdom, the wisdom is Another's.) The issue narrows to whether what we may generically call the order in Nature is to be accounted an outcome of wisdom or of undesigned coincidence. Indeed, in so far as the question is as to explicability, the issue narrows to the vanishing-point; for assertion of coincidence in the self-subsistent, wondrous in respect of its manifoldness and complex interlacingness, is, again, not explanation but statement of what calls for explanation.

The manifoldness of the coincidences on which the order in the world, including man, is conditional, has already been sufficiently illustrated, though it might be more minutely and extensively expounded. These coincidences, let it be repeated, are present in the determinate natures of the cosmic elements, the world's original existents and their primary collocations, in the adjustment of similarity to difference between them which is the ground of all the uniformity and variety, the stability and the progressiveness, of the irreversible process of becoming; in the alogical *posita*, their logico-mathematical relations, their determinate *rapport* which is such as to provide a law-making, and so a law-governed, world; a world instrumental to valuation and evocative of it, and intelligible in the peculiar anthropic sense which saturates the meaning of 'knowledge' whenever that word denotes the Actual processes in which the human mind comes to an understanding with Actuality. What is here being called coincidence is to be seen, again, in the stages of emergence of novelty which issue not, as conceivably they might and as mere mechanism suggests they perhaps should, in successive labile configurations of a cosmic dust-cloud blown by a changing cosmic wind, but in an evolutionary process in which much goes that comes, while nevertheless the unceasing flux is such that one whole world-state is, as it were, a built storey and a scaffolding for the erection of another. Emergents 'here' seem to 'take note of', or be relevant to, causally unconnected[2] emergents 'there', in both space and time, since an elaborate interlacing of contingencies is requisite to secure inorganic Nature's adaptedness to be a theatre of life. Any miscarriage in promiscuous 'naturation', such as might ruin the whole, as a puff of air may lay low the soaring house of cards, has been avoided in the making of *Natura naturata*; and though such possibilities do not suggest themselves to science contemplating Nature as a system of Lagrangean equations, the historical process conceivably might be seen to have teemed with critical moments and crucial situations by a visualising compeer of Laplace's calculator. Similarly in the organic world, erratic and venturesomely varying conative individuals may have constantly endangered, as much as they have provided for, the future of the world. Orderly progress, however, has been attained; and it has been ensured by the firm hand and the directivity of already stabilised environment. Organisms, and man in especial measure, have the world with them in their aspiringness. It is not so much the progressiveness displayed in the world-process as the intricate and harmonious interconnexion, rendering progress, intelligibility and intelligence, etc., possible, that in its marvellousness suggests intelligent art. On the other hand, it is the progressiveness which suggests that such art is directed toward an end—realisation of 'the good'.

So long as attention is paid exclusively to the universal, the logical and rational, as is necessary in the case of science but is arbitrary in the case of philosophy, the inner significance of this world, with all its particular 'thusness', will be missed. It is in the concrete or the historical, to which the universal is but incidental and of which the logical or rational is but one nexus among others, that meaning can be, and seems

2 Causally unconnected in the sense in which experimental science must use the notion of causal connexion.

to be, conveyed: and as the history, made by the mindless or by practically infinitesimal minds, is on so grand a scale intelligible to universalising intellect, there would seem to be directive intelligence behind it. It is in the characteristics of *this* world, in the particular determinateness of the collocations prescriptive of its Actual course, and—not least—in the anthropism thrust by Nature on the non-anthropic pure egos out of which she has made men, and its affinity with the world in respect of both genetic continuity and epistemic capacity, that purposiveness lets itself be read. If we thus read things, a unique significance attaches to the realm of the moral, amongst other teleologically suggestive domains of fact, in that it enables us to advance from belief that the world is a work of art to belief that it is constructed for a purpose, and worthily specifies what the purpose is, or includes. If we decline to explain things thus, it would seem that the only alternative is to regard the self-subsistent entities, of which the world is constituted, as comparable with letters of type which have shuffled themselves not only into a book or a literature but also into a reader commanding the particular tongue in which the book utters its unintentional meaning. If the inference from cumulative adaptiveness to design be non-logical, as is admitted, it at least is not unreasonable.

Even critical and iconoclastic philosophers have treated with respect forms of teleological argument such as were current in their day. Hume denied that the argument is logically coercive, but he allows Philo, in the *Dialogues*, to admit that the fitness of final causes in the universe and its parts strikes us with such irresistible force that all objections to them appear cavils and sophisms. Kant, again, speaks of it as the clearest of the 'proofs', and as the one most in harmony with the common reason of mankind. Yet the more comprehensive and synoptic design-argument that is now producible is more imposing than any contemplated in their day. Hume almost ignored man and his moral status; while

Kant, who saw in man's moral faculty the central fact about the universe, so over-emphasised its purely rational functioning as to overlook its historical development, its alogical content, and the respects in which it is 'of a piece' with Nature. The greater strength claimed for the newer argument consists in its exhibition of the interconnexion and reciprocal adaptation between systems of fact which used to be treated as if isolated. It can now be submitted that if the uniformity of Nature rests on mechanical postulates, and the 'validity' of moral principles involves a moral postulate, the evolutionary progressiveness of the world points to a teleological postulate. And if this evolution is to be explained, or to be assigned a sufficient ground, instead of being merely accepted as a brute happening, the historical and alogical aspect of the world-process must not only be regarded as the primary reality *in ordine cognoscendi* but also as our clue to the *ordo*, and the *ratio, essendi*. Mechanism and the universalisings of pure rationality are tools as useless for this purpose as a typing-machine and a book of logarithms are for landscape-painting: for the problem is reducible to the question, *cui bono?* Teleological explanation is comparable with discernment of "the signs of the times" rather than of "the face of the sky"; and although to fail to discern cosmical signs of the former kind need not be to class oneself with the "hypocrites", to be indifferent as to whether there be such signs may be said to involve venturing less than the "all that doth become a man". Perhaps all thinking being is thus indifferent, or even uninquisitive. When the teleological or theistic explanation of the world is not adopted, it is because one's explanation-craving is satiated before the limit to which the theist presses is reached in the regress, or because a seemingly better explanation has been found, or because one has become convinced that none has been found that tallies with all the facts. Whether theism satisfies this last condition will be discussed in another chapter, and more remains to be said as to certain alternatives to theism; but it has perhaps already been shewn that no *explanation* is contained in the assertion that the world is an organic whole and consequently involves adaptiveness. That is only a restatement of the occult and wondrous fact that cries for explanation. The world's 'thusness' is explained, however, if it be attributable to the design and creativeness of a Being whose purpose is, or includes, the realisation of moral values. Further back than a creative Spirit it is neither needful nor possible to go. But further back than the world we can and must go, because the notion of a non-intelligent world that produces intelligent beings and makes itself intelligible, that can have no purpose and yet abundantly seems to bespeak one, and so forth, is not the clearest and most reason-satisfying conception that our minds can build wherein to rest. Moreover, as J. Ward has observed, the alternative that the world's evolution is ultimate, or its own sufficient reason, ignores the fact that we rational beings are part of the evolution, so that our demand for a sufficient reason is "a demand that the world itself has raised".

At more than one place in this chapter stress has been laid on the intelligibilty of the world to the specifically anthropic intelligence possessed by us, and on the connexion between the conditioning of that intelligibility, on the one hand, and the constitution and process of Nature, on the other hand. Thus a close relationship is indicated between teleological explanation and an anthropocentric world-view; and this relationship may now be more explicitly described.

Anthropocentrism, in some sense, is involved in cosmic teleology. It is useless for ethical theism to argue that the world evidences design unless the only rational and moral denizen of the world, in so far as it is known to us, be assumed to afford an indication as to what the designed end of the world-process is. And, as thus stated, anthropocentrism involves no human arrogance or self-exaltation. It does not assert that man, as a zoological species or genus whose geographical distribution is presumably confined to this planet, is the highest being under God, or the final stage of progressive cosmic evolution, or the end and the whole end of the divine design. It is compatible with belief in "thrones, dominions, principalities, powers", or angels and archangels, and in the possibility that in other worlds there are rational beings akin to us in being embodied and having their specific intelligence moulded thereby.[3] It is content to allow that the divine end, in its completeness, is unfathomable. Nor does it imply that lower creatures evolved in the world-process are necessarily of but instrumental value as stages or means to ends, and, when not figuring in man's genealogical tree, are mere by-products in the making of humanity. Anthropocentrism rather means that, whereas in the realm of Nature beneath man no final purpose can be discerned, such purpose may be discerned in beings possessed of rationality, appreciation, self-

[3] It is, of course, a matter of indifference to teleology and anthropocentric interpretation whether the material heavens contain a plurality of inhabited worlds. But it is interesting to find recent astronomy, as represented by Prof. Eddington, inclined to the views that the physical universe probably does not greatly extend beyond the range of human observation, and that the number of the heavenly bodies suitable for the maintenance of life (as it is conditioned on this earth) is extremely small. It is commonly deemed absurd to suppose that, out of the immense number of worlds known to astronomy, only one is peopled with living beings; yet it is not a question of numbers but of chemical and physiological conditions. Science pronounces the globes which satisfy these conditions to be, in all probability, very few; while organic life involving only inorganic chemistry, organisms adapted to the temperature of the burning fiery furnace, and so forth, are notions that hardly lie within the sphere of scientific imagination. If anyone likes to maintain that the Creator of the starry heaven is "mindful" *only* of man, neither will science accuse him of grotesque exaggeration nor will theism need to hope that he is absolutely accurate.

determination, and morality. Man may exhibit these powers and attributes in but a limited or humble degree. But, in its essence, intelligence may be common to a hierarchy of beings; and it is in virtue of his membership in that hierarchy, if such there be, rather than in his distinctive or specific and contingent characteristics, the anthropic or human, that man shares the privilege of being a bearer of the highest values, and of being in some relative, rather than in an absolute and exhaustive, sense bound up with the otherwise ineffable divine purpose. Teleology is interpretation of beginnings by *terminus ad quem*, lower stages by higher, process by product, and temporal becoming in terms of realisation of values; and the *terminus ad quem* of the world, so far as the world-process has as yet gone, and in so far as the world is known, is man. It is not that he is the last evolute in time; indeed his parasites should be later: but that he is the highest product in respect of value, and in the light of whose emergence all Nature, to which he is akin, seems to have its *raison d'être*. Hence the necessity of his figuring pre-eminently in theistic philosophy, if that is to be based on facts rather than on preconceived ideas, and is not to transcend fact save in the inevitable way of fact-controlled and reasonable extrapolation and idealisation. That the investigation, pursued in the preceding volume and in the present chapter, of man's rational and moral status and its conditioning by his physical and social environment, has involved more emphasising of what may be called man's anthropism than of his rationality, etc., in the abstract, is a necessity dictated by facts and by the empirical method. But now that the anthropocentric view of the world has been reached, and the facts which justify it have been set forth, our attention may move on from terrestrial contingencies, creaturely limitations, and specifically human characteristics, to the generic features which, from the point of view of theism, must be common to the mind of man and the Mind of God. The anthropocentric view of the world is a necessary step to the theistic interpretation of the world and man: it need not profess to be more.

The empirical approach to theism being essentially teleological, it is now necessary to raise the question, what an end or purpose, as attributable to the Deity, consists in. The idea of purpose is derived from the sphere of human activity; and such meaning as is imported into it from that context has necessary relevance only so long as that context is not transcended: such is the empirical doctrine as to the scope and validity of ideas or ideational propositions. But when applied to God, whose activities, by definition or *ex hypothesi*, include some that are unique, and whose intelligence is necessarily different in some respects from ours, the idea may become non-significant. Theism that would use the idea, it has sometimes been urged, must be unduly anthropomorphic. That need not be so, however, if such constituents of the complex idea of purpose as involve intrinsic limitations of human mentality and activity can be eliminated from it, while others, essential to the conception of purposiveness but separable from their human manifestation, can be isolated for legitimate transference to the sphere of divine activity. What elements require to be eliminated, modified, or newly related, in such recasting of the idea, has been differently decided by different exponents of theism; and perhaps it is premature to undertake the analysis and re-synthesis until an exposition has been given of one's conception of the nature and attributes of the Deity. In the absence of such preliminary discussion it may suffice to indicate possible divergences of view, as occasion calls.

In the conception of human purpose we may distinguish the following constituent elements: (1) the pre-conceived idea of a situation to be reached, (2) desire for that situation because of its value to the agent, (3) the use—in general—of means for the attainment of it, (4) the actualisation—generally by stages—of what was contemplated in thought and striven for. Into the first

of these, and indeed into all of them, the idea of temporal succession enters: idea of the goal is previous to attainment of goal, desire to fruition, and so on. And whether the temporal form, characterising human experience, is to be carried over into the conception of God's activity and experience is a disputed question; that it has been variously answered is the chief source of divergence of view as to what exactly purpose, ascribed to the Deity, is. This question is not to be discussed for the present. It need only be remarked here that *if* it be possible to conceive of purposive activity as not necessarily involving the temporal stages which have been indicated, so that separation of ideated end and accomplished end be non-essential, and if concomitance of plan with actualised volition be as useful a notion as that of succession of the one upon the other, then the purposiveness of the world will consist in its being an organic system, or one in which the natures and interconnexions of the parts are determined by the whole, and in its being an expression of intelligence but not an actualisation of a *pre-existent plan. According to this attenuated conception of purpose the relation of means to end, generally involved in human purposefulness, also vanishes.

The element of value, of desire and satisfaction, is not eliminable from the idea of purpose. Without it the category of end would lose its distinctiveness and become identical with some other, such as cause or ground, mechanism, or non-contradiction. The tendency to minimise or cancel valuation, in this connexion, and to speak of satisfactoriness as something of logical nature, conceivable in abstraction from satisfaction, is evinced by absolute monists rather than by theists. In whatever sense the world may be said to embody divine purpose, the least that can be meant is that the world contains what is of worth to the Supreme Being.

The third factor in human purposing, adaptation of means to end, is again one which some theists have been reluctant to admit into the conception of divine purpose: partly because of its temporal implication; partly because it is thought to bespeak limited power and need to overcome difficulties; and sometimes on the ground that the divine end is the world-process, not some perfected outcome of it, and that everything that we would regard as but a stage or a means toward something else is, for God, itself an end. This last issue may be considered immediately; but whether the relation of a determinate God to a determinate world, other than Himself, admits of being conceived without ascription to Him of some kinds of limitation such as do not render the distinction between means or stages and end obviously superfluous in the case of divine activity, is a question that will receive later the discussion for which it calls. The fourth of the factors into which the idea of purpose has been resolved presents no especial problem other than that already indicated when the first was touched upon.

It has been remarked before that Nature and man, empirically studied, may strongly suggest that the world is an outcome of intelligence and purpose, while *the* purpose or divine end which the universe and the world-process subserve may remain unknowable to us. But, as we have also seen, speculation on the latter subject must be allowed to influence views as to the nature of the purposiveness that is involved in the former assertion. The forthcoming alternative views, between which facts scarcely enable us to decide, may be briefly mentioned. The divine purposing may be conceived as pre-ordination, in which every detail is foreseen. An analogy is presented in Mozart's (alleged) method of composition, who is said to have imagined a movement—its themes, development, embroidery, counterpoint and orchestration—in all its detail and as a simultaneous whole, before he wrote it. If God's composition of the cosmos be regarded as similar to this, all its purposiveness will be expressed in the initial collocations, and evolution will be preformation. On the other hand, God's activity

might be conceived as fluent, or even as "increasing", rather than as wholly static, purpose. It might then be compared, in relevant respects, with the work of a dramatist or a novelist such, perhaps, as Thackeray, who seems to have moulded his characters and plot, to some extent, as he wrote. And it would appear that the divine purposiveness must be partly thus conceived if conative creaturely activity may either co-operate or clash with the Creator's, so that providential control and adaptation to the emergent must enter into the realisation of the divine plan.

Again, though the divine end is usually construed eschatologically, there is an alternative interpretation. It may be that there is no "far off divine event" toward which creation was predestined to move: the process itself may constitute the end. Certainly progress has a unique value, incapable of the absorption or transmutation which some values undergo; and the conception of the divine end as a perfected society of ethical individuals, and a philosophy of history such as is based on that presupposition, are not free from difficulties. At any rate the securing of the consummation will need to be so conceived as not to involve sacrifice of the ethical dignity of the individual person as an end for himself, and no mere instrument to the future perfecting of others. The social good may but be good in that it ministers to the goodness of individuals, each of whom—as the Christian conception of the Fatherhood of God implies—is singly an end for God. Position in the time-series, or the progress-series of social development towards perfection, may be of no moment as compared with the individual's use of his opportunities, such as they may be: timelessness, in the sense of indifference to axiological rank as temporally circumstanced, may characterise the valuation he receives from God, who seeth not as man seeth, and may read the heart rather than 'Objectively' estimate the actual output of the will. If so, asymptotic attainment of ethical perfection, and the ideal consummation, may be contingent or conditional aspects of the divine end, while progressive becoming, throughout all reaches and domains of the universe, may be its ultimate essence. These alternative conceivabilities are here merely mentioned; their relative tenability is not to be investigated. But it may further be observed that if evolution is itself an end and not a means to an end, the hard dualism of means and end must vanish. Childhood, for instance, will not be merely a stage in the making of a man; nor will groping past generations have worked merely to provide their posterity with better opportunities for making further advance. As a rose-bud has a beauty or perfection different from but quite equal to that of the full-blown rose, so may each stage in the life of the individual or the race have, along with its appropriate work, an intrinsic value, or be an end in itself as well as a means to something beyond. The only conclusion now to be elicited from the foregoing remarks is that teleology and theism may admit of statement in terms of other than the static concepts, and the abstractions such as perfection that is of no *kind*, which dominated thought until a century or so ago, and which, within the spheres of philosophy and theology, still impose themselves on some evolutionists.

The teleological approach to theism, with which this chapter has been concerned, has been made from the fact that conformity to law is intrinsic to the world, and from the conclusion that such order belongs to the world as ontal. It has already been found not to be blocked by science or by mechanistic philosophy of Nature and its law-abidingness. Besides being a cosmos explicable, in one general sense, in terms of its structure and scientific intelligibility, the world is a bearer and a producer of values in that in our *rapport* with it we are affected by it. The world is not com-

pletely described if this aspect of it is left out: less than all the data would but then be taken account of. The Actual or historical world-process, from which mechanism is an abstraction, is characterised by irreversibility, epigenesis, progressiveness of development, and by manifold adaptations which adaptedly interlace. It evokes explanation, consequently, of a different type from that pursued by physical science; and it accords pragmatic verification to use of the category of design for this new kind of explanation, as well as to use of the causal category for scientific explanation. If reason stand to formal rationality in a relation similar to that in which philosophy stands to mechanical science, philosophical reasonableness cannot be a mere extension of scientific, or of logico-mathematical, rationality; and if existential 'knowledge' is allowed its postulates, it seems but partial to disallow to 'knowledge' concerning the value-aspect of Actuality the postulate that is similarly needful to it. *Homo* who provides the *mensura* for all and every kind of intelligibility needs not to blind himself to the fact that he is more than a logical thinker, or to the fact that he stands in other relations with the universe than that of knowing about its structure. He cannot but have other problems besides that of the relation of being to thought. Philosophy in other words, is an affair of living as well as a mode of thinking. All causal knowledge is, in the last resort, but reasonable and postulatory: teleology is therefore a development from science along its own lines, or a continuation, by extrapolation, of the plotted curve which comprehensively describes its knowledge. And this is the *apologia* of theism such as professes to be reasonable belief for the guidance of life, when arranged by science and logic—or by more pretentious theology.

A Critique of the Cosmological and Teleological Arguments

C. J. DUCASSE

THE COSMOLOGICAL ARGUMENT FOR EXISTENCE OF THE GOD OF MONOTHEISM

*F*rom time to time, articles or books are written concerning the question whether sea serpents really exist, or whether on the contrary the serious reports of a specimen's having been sighted are explicable as due to malobservation. If, when this question arises, one were to reply that of course sea serpents exist, namely the well-known *Hydrophidae*, which live in the warmer parts of the Indian and Pacific oceans, are viviparous, feed on fishes, have a flattened tail, and so on, one would immediately be told that although these reptiles are serpents and live in the sea, they are not what one means when one asks whether sea serpents exist.

This example brings out the basic fact that no question as to the existence or nonexistence of something is even theoretically capable of answer unless one understands to begin with *what kind of thing* it is, about which that question is being asked. If one were to accost a person and simply ask him: "Are there any?" he would naturally ask us at once: "Any what?" Lacking specification of this, one's question is completely insoluble because completely ambiguous.

The bearing of these considerations on the question as to whether a God exists is evident. It is capable of an answer—in principle at least, even if perhaps not at a given time—only if one understands what sort of a being is meant by the word God, which is used in the question. In the classical arguments for the existence of a God, the god meant has been that of monotheism, and conceived mainly in the cosmological role commented upon above. It has been a God conceived as a person, in the sense of possessed of will, feelings, knowledge, and power; but as superperson in the sense of being infinite instead of, like human persons, finite; and "perfect," i.e., omnipotent, omniscient, and wholly good. The characteristic of infinity is made a part of the definition not here simply, as Leupa suggests in a different connection, out of man's insatiable megalomania, but in order to entail uniqueness of the God defined, i.e., to entail monotheism; the reasoning being that if one God's power is unlimited, then there can be no other god since the power of another would automatically limit that of the former.

The first of the three classical arguments for the existence of a God as so conceived is called the Cosmological Argument and takes as its major premise that nothing can exist or occur without a sufficient cause. It is then pointed out that no man or other thing in the world caused itself, but that each was caused by something antecedent. The same thing is true, however, of that antecedent itself, and of the antecedent of it, and so on; so that, it is argued, one must come at last to a first cause, which is God, and without which nothing at all would have come to be. This argument has been put in a variety of forms, and is the most popular. It is implicit in the common reference to God as "the Creator."

Considered by daylight, however, this "proof" is at once seen to be a logical monstrosity, since it attempts to prove its conclusion, viz., that something (to wit, God) exists without a cause, by taking as premise the very contradictory of this, viz., that nothing exists without a cause. This is exactly like arguing that, since all crows are black, therefore one crow is not black. As Schopenhauer puts the point, the law of universal causation

FROM: *A Philosophical Scrutiny of Religion*, C. J. Ducasse. (New York: The Ronald Press Company, 1953), pp. 333–339 and pp. 342–346. Reprinted by permission of the Ronald Press Company.

"is not so accommodating as to let itself be used like a hired cab, which we dismiss when we have reached our destination";[1] rather, if we start riding it, we have to keep on riding, without end.

But, it is sometimes objected, the universe *must* have had a beginning. The alleged necessity of this, however, is not evident. Many of the persons who assert it seem to have no difficulty in believing that the universe, in one form or another, or at the very least, human souls, will continue existing through infinite time. And, if infinitely prolonged existence in the forward direction is conceivable without contradiction, it is equally conceivable in the backward direction. That there must have been a beginning is no more self-evident than that there will have to be an end.

As an example of the kind of logic sometimes used in attempts to save Cosmological Argument, may be mentioned the following purported demonstration that an infinite regress of causes is impossible. It is based on the assertion that nowhere in the backward series of causes can there be found an "adequately sufficient reason" for the existence of any one member, say *A*, of the series. This is supposedly proved by observing that "if the *adequately sufficient reason* for *A*'s existence could be found in any one such cause or group of causes, then all causes in the series prior to this group could be considered as nonexisting as far as their requirement for *A*'s existence is concerned. But if any cause in the series is considered as nonexisting, then all subsequent causes in the series must be considered as nonexisting and hence *A* as nonexisting. Hence the hypothesis, that any cause in the series can give an adequately sufficient reason for *A*'s existence, results in the absurd conclusion that *A* cannot be existing."[2]

Obviously, however, if this proves anything at all, it is only that any *one* cause, or *finite number* of causes, cannot be an "adequately sufficient reason" for the existence of *A*; whereas what needed to be proved was that *the whole* of an *infinite* series of prior causes is not an "adequately sufficient reason" for the existence of *A*. But nothing in the article cited contributes in the least to show this.

A few words may be added concerning the contradiction alleged by the French philosopher Renouvier to be involved in the supposition that an infinite series of events have already taken place. As summarized by Ferm,[3] it is that if the sum total of past events "is already infinite, nothing more can be added since the infinite cannot be made greater than itself. Thus no further events would be possible since the infinite is already reached and cannot be added to or increased—a *reductio ad absurdum*."

The reply, of course, is that infinite series, of which there are several kinds, have peculiar properties. For instance, in an infinite series, certain parts of it have as many items as the whole of it; for example, there are just as many even numbers—namely, an infinity—as there are numbers altogether; for the number series, and the even-number series which is only a part of it, can be put in one-to-one correspondence, as follows:

$$1, \quad 2, \quad 3, \quad 4, \quad 5, \quad 6, \quad 7, \ldots$$
$$2, \quad 4, \quad 6, \quad 8, \quad 10, \quad 12, \quad 14, \ldots$$

In doing this, one would *never* run out of even numbers in the lower line, with which to match the numbers in the upper.

Again, it can be shown that an infinite series, each member of which consists of an infinite series of whole numbers, contains no more numbers altogether than does the series of the whole numbers. But it can also be shown that there are more numerous ways of ordering the items of the series of the whole numbers than there are whole

[1] Arthur Schopenhauer, *The Fourfold Root of the Principle of Sufficient Reason,* trans. Mme Karl Hillebrand (London: Bell and Sons, 1891), pp. 42–43.

[2] "Science and True Religion," by the Rev. John S. O'Conor, *The Scientific Monthly* (February, 1941), 177.

[3] Ferm, *First Chapters in Religious Philosophy,* p. 124 n.

numbers altogether, so that certain infinite collections have more items than certain other infinite collections! Also, and more directly relevant to Renouvier's contention, some infinite series do—paradoxical as it sounds—have both a first and last term; for example, the series of fractions between and including ¼ and ½. To this infinite series, it is perfectly possible to add any finite number of other fractions we please, for instance, $1\frac{1}{16}$, ⅝ and ¾; or an infinite number of other fractions, for instance, all those between ½ and ¾. But although such addition is possible, the numerousness of the sum is exactly the same as that of the fractions between and including ¼ and ½.[4] Infinite series are queer things indeed, but if one is going to bring them into an argument for the existence of a God, one has to take them with the properties they do have, queer as these may be.

An attempt is sometimes made to evade the contradiction in terms, which as Schopenhauer points out is contained in the expression "the first cause," by introducing the notion of immanent cause, or *causa sui*, and applying it to the postulated first cause, saying that it too is indeed caused, but is *self*-caused.

Causes and effects, however, are essentially events and essentially successive, so that—unless "cause" in *causa sui* is used in some sense radically other than its common one—the expression *causa sui* too is a contradiction in terms, implying as it does that the cause concerned exists before it yet exists. The right emblem for *causa sui*, Schopenhauer pointedly remarks, "is Baron Münchhausen, sinking on horseback into the water, clinging by the legs to his horse and pulling both himself and the animal out by his own pigtail."[5]

The relation, however, which the expressions *causa sui* and "immanent cause" are intended to refer to, is not causality at all in its ordinary sense, but is the kind of relation which would obtain in the case of something whose existence would follow with *logical* necessity from its *essence*, i.e., from its nature or description. But this kind of relation, which as we shall see is the one invoked in the famous but fallacious "Ontological Proof" of the existence of God, is another monstrosity, born of confusion between, or of the dire need for one's purposes to confuse, the two distinct notions of *cause* (of the existence of something) and of *evidence* (of the truth of a proposition).[6]

In the attempt to save the Cosmological Argument's validity, it is sometimes urged that the law of universal causality applies only to things or events whose existence is "contingent," i.e., dependent on something external to themselves, and not to something, namely, God, which being *causa sui*, is "absolutely necessary." But if it were possible at all for anything to be "self-caused," then no reason appears why the world as a whole, i.e., the *entire* series of contingent things and events, might not itself be so. The expression "absolute necessity," however, is itself internally contradictory no less than is *causa sui*, for necessity is the *relation* between something necessitated and something necessitating it, and yet "absolute necessity" would mean necessity that is *not relational*.

On the other hand; if, in the expression "absolute necessity," the qualification "absolute" is not intended to negate the relational nature of necessity, then the only meaning left for "absolute" is "categorical" (as opposed to "hypothetical"). But, that existence of something B is categorically necessary means (1) that B is so related to something else A that *if* A exists, *then* necessarily B exists; *and* (2) that A *does* exist. Hence, to

---

[4] An illuminating discussion of the concept of infinity, readable without special mathematical training, is E. V. Huntington, *The Continuum as a Type of Order* (Cambridge: Harvard University Press).

[5] Schopenhauer, *op. cit.*, p. 17.

[6] That this confusion pervades Spinoza's *Ethics* is clearly shown by Schopenhauer, *op. cit.*, pp. 13–20, who calls attention to the fact that Spinoza finds himself forced to write again and again, *"ratio seu causa."*

prove that existence of B is necessary "absolutely," i.e., categorically, one must first have proved not only that if A exists then B necessarily exists, but also have somehow proved *that* A *does exist*. And, of course, the Cosmological Argument does not do this at all.

Again, it is sometimes contended that although the existence of any particular thing or event in the causal series is accounted for by reference to its immediate cause in the series, and so on backwards *ad infinitum*, nevertheless the series as a whole, i.e., the world, could conceivably have been more or less different from what it actually has been, and therefore that a cause external to the whole series (namely, God) is required to account for its being what it actually has been, rather than different. But if this argument has any force at all, it requires us then to ask in turn for the cause of that external cause, and for the cause of its cause, etc., thus leading us only to another causal series, at right angles as it were to the series constituting the universe, but like it infinitely regressive, i.e., without a first term.

Finally, if instead of taking as major premise that nothing can exist without a cause, one were to take instead that nothing except God can exist without a cause, then no use could be made of *this* premise to show that a God exists; for it would constitute only a covert declaration that, by the word "God," one *means* a being who can exist without a cause; and the question would then remain whether any such being does or does not exist.

THE ARGUMENT FROM DESIGN

Kant, Schopenhauer, and some other critics of the classical arguments for the existence of the monotheistic God have regarded the logic of the Argument from Design as somewhat more respectable than that of the other two. It has, however, been severely criticized by Hume and, as we shall see, has ultimately the same defects as that of the Cosmological Argument.

As impressive a way as any to state the argument from design would

probably be the following. Suppose that man eventually manages to reach the moon, and that when the crew of the first rocket arrives it finds not only the uninhabited and uninhabitable lifeless body astronomers had predicted they would, but also, on some rock there, a complete camera quite similar to those manufactured on earth. How could its existence there be explained?

Someone might answer that, after all, the surface of the moon has been subjected for ages to violent bombardment by meteorites, and has probably been also churned by volcanic phenomena, so that, in the billions of years of its existence, almost any imaginable arrangement of its various materials is very likely to have occurred automatically; and that the camera happens to be merely one of these chance combinations.

This explanation would of course at once be rejected as impossible on the ground that the kinds of things which the forces invoked are known to be capable of producing are radically different from the kind of thing a camera is. For example, those forces in fact do not polish but scratch and crack such pieces of glass as they may happen to work on; nor are those forces capable of cutting fine screw threads, such as exist in the lens mounting and on the lens retainer, to say nothing of them screwing the latter into the former, with the lens between. And so on.

The supposition that the camera found on the moon came into existence in this manner would therefore rightly be judged preposterous. The camera, it would be said, is an object in which every part—lens, shutter, diaphragm, focusing mechanism, shutter speed regulator, dark chamber, light-sensitive film—and the relations in space of these parts to one another, are precisely what they would have to be if a photograph is to result when the shutter release is depressed; and the only hypothesis at all plausible, to account for the existence of such a complex and special arrangement of materials, is that some intelligent being conceived the idea of photographs, desired to be able to take them, designed an apparatus which would make this possible, and constructed it.

But now it is asked, if this is the only adequate explanation of the existence of a camera, is it not then necessarily also the only adequate explanation of the existence of man's eye, which in every essential part is itself literally a camera? Man, however, neither designs nor constructs his own eye. Therefore some other intelligently purposive being —namely, God—must have done so. Hence, the argument concludes, a God must exist. The same conclusion is drawn, of course, from the existence of the numerous other specialized organs of the bodies of men and of other living beings, and is extended to the specialized conditions of temperature, moisture, composition of the atmosphere, etc., indispensable to life.[7]

Obviously, however, if such capacities as the eye possesses are explicable only as products of the intelligent activity of a purposive being, the capacities of that being himself are quite as remarkable as those of the eye he designed, and are themselves then explicable only by postulation of a purposive designer of the designer of the eye—just as a designer of men is postulated to account for the fact that men have such capacities as that of designing and constructing cameras.

But explanation thus in terms of intelligently purposive causation, instead of in terms of blind causation, still has for its major premise that nothing exists without a sufficient cause (whether blind or purposive) for its being; and from this premise, as we have seen, what follows is not that a first cause, itself uncaused, must exist, but on the contrary that none such can exist. An infinite regress—here of intelligent designer-constructors—is what the mode of explanation postulated by the Design Argument logically entails; and, as we have also seen, no logical contradiction is contained

in this entailed consequence, whatever may be its merits in other respects.

A second point is that, if indeed a designer or a series of designers needs to be postulated to account for the facts in view, then such a designer need not be an omnipotent, omniscient, and wholly good being, but one only potent, intelligent, and good enough to design and create the kind of world which actually exists—a world which indeed contains many clever adjustments and felicitous adaptions, but which also contains a vast amount of evil, waste, disease, maladjustment and frustration. For if man is assumed competent to perceive correctly that the universe contains many good things and exhibits much teleology, there is then no ground to deny him equal competence to perceive also correctly that the universe contains numerous evils and much dysteleology. The pious admonitions to distrust his competence to judge that one thing or another is really an evil, which are addressed to him by writers of theodicies, are called for equally with regard to man's judgment that this or that thing is really good, if they are called for at all.

It is well to bear in mind further that a designer is not necessarily superior in every respect to what he designs and constructs: man, for instance, designs and constructs many instruments —microscopes, electronic computers, steam shovels, etc.—whose capacities to do certain things vastly exceed his own. Indeed, even the simplest of the innumerable tools man makes is constructed by him because he himself lacks capacities the tool possesses: even a crude knife or axe has a better cutting edge than have man's teeth or nails.

At this point, however, we may return to the comparison of the eye to the camera, and ask whether it is indeed true, as the Argument from Design asserts, that only intelligent plan and construction can account for the existence of such highly adapted structures. The answer, as Hume points out, is that this is only one of the ways in which, according to experience, such structures actually come

---

[7] Wm. Paley, *Natural Theology* (New York: Harper's Family Library, 1840) is a classical instance of such a train of thought.

into being. Natural growth, vegetable and animal, is another actual way; and if, instead of starting with the camera, we should elect to start with the eye, then, if we had not observed how cameras are constructed, what the similarity of the camera to the eye would suggest to us would be that the camera too must be somehow a product of *natural growth*. To suppose it, of course, would be to speculate—to postulate that the process of coming to be, in a case, viz., the camera's, where we did not observe it, is of the same kind, viz., growth, as in the case of the eye, where we do observe it taking place—ontogenetically through cell division, and phylogenetically through mutation and automatic elimination of mutations disadvantageous to preservation of life. But the converse supposition, viz., that the eye comes into existence as does the camera, is speculation too and speculation quite as wild; for in the production of the eye we do not observe any hands, lens-polishing instruments, or other tools such as produce a camera. Nor do we observe any designer at work. Moreover, if we speculatively postulate one, we have to postulate in addition that he is capable of doing in some wholly mysterious manner without hands or tools what camera makers can do only by means of these. And further, if we proceed on the supposition that the eye comes into existence, like the camera, by design and intelligent construction, then what the supposition suggests is not one infinitely wise and potent designer-constructor, but much rather a plurality of finite designers and artisans, collaborating to turn out a generally neat but by no means perfect piece of work—indeed, sometimes one so defective that a camera maker that did no better would soon go bankrupt.

Rather than all this, however, we can suppose more economically but quite as explanatorily that the eye is, as Schopenhauer would have said, an automatic objectification of an obscure craving or felt need to see; the hand, of a craving to grasp, etc. Such craving, however, not being *purpose* since purpose implies not only a craving but in addition an idea of what would satisfy the craving; and still less being *intelligent* purpose since this implies not only a craving and an idea of what would satisfy it, but in addition knowledge, or at least beliefs, as to what actions would or might bring into existence that which would satisfy the craving. It may be objected that we do not understand *how* an obscure craving to see can generate an eye or at least the bodily variations which gradually culminate in an eye. But we do not understand in the least better *how* the craving of a designer external to man, that man shall have an eye, can generate without hands or tools that eye in man. Hence, if we suppose a craving to be somehow capable of doing the trick, it is more economical to locate it in the animal himself, who at least is known to exist, than in an external designer, whose existence is purely suppositious and not in the least more explanatory.

The considerations appealed to by the Argument from Design thus do not, when their implications are developed logically, contribute anything that would support the hypothesis of an omniscient, and perfectly good designer. Rather, they militate against it. The only sort of God compatible with, though not evidenced by, the observable facts would be, as John Stuart Mill perceived, a God possibly great but nevertheless limited in power, or knowledge, or goodness, or in any two or all three of these respects.

The
Moral
Argument

Immanuel Kant offers an argument which, in effect, attempts to base religion on morality. The conclusion can perhaps best be stated in these terms: It is reasonable to believe that there is a morally perfect Being possessed of sufficient power to guarantee justice. Often, at least, Kant uses "knowledge" in such a way that only what is empirically testable can count as knowledge; so we cannot, for Kant, *know* that God exists. The ontological, cosmological, and teleological proofs are all, in Kant's opinion, unsuccessful. But by means of his version of the moral argument, we can, he suggests, rationally justify the belief that God exists in the sense that this claim is presupposed by morality. But we must be careful in putting Kant's view even in this way, for normally "*P* presupposes *Q*" means " that *Q* is false entails that *P* is false," while Kant holds that all our moral obligations but one would remain intact even were "God exists" known to be false.

With a minimum of oversimplification, Kant's argument can be stated in these terms: (1) The highest good includes two elements—worthiness of being happy and actually possessing happiness; (2) it is possible that one possess one of the elements but not the other, for good men can be unhappy and happy men can be evil. (These claims are to be found in Kant's Introduction; hereafter we will be dealing with Section Five.) (3) Everyone is obligated to seek the highest good, in the sense that he is obligated to seek a state of affairs in which each man receives happiness proportionate to his worthiness of it. (4) Whatever everyone is obligated to seek can be attained; thus the highest good can be attained. (5) No man can guarantee that he himself or anyone else gains whatever happiness he is worthy of; so (6) unless there is a being both powerful enough to bring about this proportionment and good enough always to do so, the highest good will not be attained. Hence (7) there must be a being of this sort.

Kant does not claim that this argument shows that we have a duty to believe in God, nor (as we have mentioned) would any duty except that specified in (3) be canceled were (7) known to be false. Further, it should be mentioned that Kant develops his argument in the context of a moral and teleological system; he refers to some of the elements of this system in the selection that follows. Even if the specific argument under review should fail, it is possible that the system as a whole could be revised and defended. But that is too large an issue for consideration here. The last two sections of our selection from Kant offer further explication of the sense in which Kant believes that he has established (7) as a postulate.

However, we do not, on Kant's own terms, have the obligation specified in (3). We are, perhaps, under the obligation to do what we can to further the highest good, but—for the very reason specified in (6)—we are not obligated to seek the highest good. The difference between these obligations is not hard to understand. Consider the difference between (A) Jones is obligated to eliminate all the suffering in the world, and (B) Jones is obligated to eliminate whatever suffering he can eliminate. There is no problem in seeing how (B) could express an obligation that Jones has, while (A), being well beyond Jones's capacities, expresses no obligation that Jones has. Analogously, one could have an obligation to do what he can to further progress toward the highest good, but not have an obligation to seek or attain the highest good. One could make the same point by noting that (3) is ambiguous as between these obligations and is acceptable only on the weaker interpretation. So (3) is incorrect, and (5) is thus unsupported. Hence we have no proof of (7).

The Existence of God Is a Justified Postulate
IMMANUEL KANT

OF THE DIALECTIC
OF PURE REASON
IN DEFINING THE CONCEPTION
OF THE "SUMMUM BONUM"

The conception of the *summum* itself contains an ambiguity which might occasion needless disputes if we did not attend to it. The *summum* may mean either the supreme (*supremum*) or the perfect (*consummatum*). The former is that condition which is itself unconditioned, *i.e.* is not subordinate to any other (*originarium*); the second is that whole which is not a part of a greater whole of the same kind (*perfectissimum*). It has been shown in the Analytic that *virtue* (as worthiness to be happy) is the *supreme condition* of all that can appear to us desirable, and consequently of all our pursuit of happiness, and is therefore the *supreme* good. But it does not follow that it is the whole and perfect good as the object of the desires of rational finite beings; for this requires happiness also, and that not merely in the partial eyes of the person who makes himself an end, but even in the judgment of an impartial reason, which regards persons in general as ends in themselves. For to need happiness, to deserve it (247), and yet at the same time not to participate in it, cannot be consistent with the perfect volition of a rational being possessed at the same time of all power, if, for the sake of experiment, we conceive such a being. Now inasmuch as virtue and happiness together constitute the possession of the *summum bonum* in a person, and the distribution of happiness in exact proportion to morality (which is the worth of the per-

son, and his worthiness to be happy) constitutes the *summum bonum* of a possible world; hence this *summum bonum* expresses the whole, the perfect good, in which, however, virtue as the condition is always the supreme good, since it has no condition above it; whereas happiness, while it is pleasant to the possessor of it, is not of itself absolutely and in all respects good, but always presupposes morally right behaviour as its condition. (216)

When two elements are *necessarily* united in one concept, they must be connected as reason and consequence, and this either so that their unity is considered as *analytical* (logical connexion), or as *synthetical* (real connexion)—the former following the law of identity, the latter that of causality. The connexion of virtue and happiness may therefore be understood in two ways: either the endeavour to be virtuous and the rational pursuit of happiness are not two distinct actions, but absolutely identical, in which case no maxim need be made the principle of the former, other than what serves for the latter; or the connexion consists in this, that virtue produces happiness as something distinct from the consciousness of virtue, as a cause produces an effect.

The ancient Greek schools were, properly speaking, only two, and in determining the conception of the *summum bonum* these followed in fact one and the same method, inasmuch as they did not allow virtue and happiness to be regarded as two distinct elements of the *summum bonum*, and consequently sought (248) the unity of the principle by the rule of identity; but they differed as to which of the two was to be taken

FROM: *Kant's Critique of Practical Reason and Other Works on the Theory of Ethics*, T. K. Abbott. (Essex, England: Longmans Green and Co., Ltd.,) pp. 206–209, 220–231, 240–246. Reprinted by permission of Longmans Green and Co., Ltd. (originally published in 1788). The numbers in brackets in the text refer to the corresponding pages of the 1838 Rosencranz and Schubert edition, Vol. VIII.

as the fundamental notion. The *Epicurean* said: To be conscious that one's maxims lead to happiness is virtue; the *Stoic* said: To be conscious of one's virtue is happiness. With the former, *Prudence* was equivalent to morality; with the latter, who chose a higher designation for virtue, morality alone was true wisdom.

While we must admire the men who in such early times tried all imaginable ways of extending the domain of philosophy, we must at the same time lament that their acuteness was unfortunately misapplied in trying to trace out identity between two extremely heterogeneous notions, those of happiness and virtue. But it agrees with the dialectical spirit of their times (and subtle minds are even now sometimes misled in the same way) to get rid of irreconcilable differences in principle by seeking to change them into a mere contest about words, and thus apparently working out the identity of the notion under different names, and this usually occurs in cases where the combination of heterogeneous principles lies so deep or so high, or would require so complete a transformation of the doctrines assumed in the rest of the philosophical system, that men are afraid to penetrate deeply into the real difference, and prefer treating it as a difference in matters of form.

While both schools sought to trace out the identity of the practical principles of virtue and happiness, they were not agreed as to the way in which they tried to force this identity, but were separated infinitely from one another, the one placing its principle on the side of sense, the other on that of reason; the one in the consciousness of sensible wants, the other in the independence of practical reason (249) on all sensible grounds of determination. According to the Epicurean the notion of virtue was already involved in the maxim: To promote one's own happiness; according to the Stoics, on the other hand, the feeling of happiness was already contained in the consciousness of virtue. Now

whatever is contained in another notion is identical with part of the containing notion, but not with the whole, and moreover two wholes may be specifically distinct, although they consist of the same parts, namely, if the parts are united into a whole in totally different ways. The Stoic maintained that virtue was the *whole summum bonum*, and happiness only the consciousness of possessing it, as making part of the state of the subject. The Epicurean maintained that happiness was the *whole summum bonum*, and virtue only the form of the maxim for its pursuit, viz. the rational use of the means for attaining it.

Now it is clear from the Analytic that the maxims of virtue and those of private happiness are quite heterogeneous as to their supreme practical principle; and although they belong to one *summum bonum* which together they make possible, yet they are so far from coinciding that they restrict and check one another very much in the same subject. Thus the question, *How is the summum bonum practically possible?* still remains an unsolved problem, notwithstanding all the *attempts at coalition* that have hitherto been made. The Analytic has, however, shown what it is that makes the problem difficult to solve; namely, that happiness and morality are two specifically *distinct elements of the summum bonum*, and therefore their combination *cannot* be *analytically* cognized (as if the man that seeks his own happiness should find by mere analysis of his conception that in so acting he is virtuous, or as if the man that follows virtue should in the consciousness of such conduct find that he is already happy *ipso facto*) (250), but must be a *synthesis* of concepts. Now since this combination is recognized as *à priori*, and therefore as practically necessary, and consequently not as derived from experience, so that the possibility of the *summum bonum* does not rest on any empirical principle, it follows that the *deduction* [legitimation] of this concept must be *transcendental*. It is *à priori* (morally) necessary to *produce the summum bonum by freedom of will*: therefore the condition of its possibility must rest solely on *à priori* principles of cognition. . .

THE EXISTENCE OF GOD AS A POSTULATE OF PURE PRACTICAL REASON

In the foregoing analysis the moral law led to a practical problem which is prescribed by pure reason alone, without the aid of any sensible motives, namely, that of the necessary completeness of the first and principal element of the *summum bonum*, viz. Morality; and as this can be perfectly solved only in eternity, to the postulate of *immorality*. The same law must also lead us to affirm the possibility of the second element of the *summum bonum*, viz. Happiness proportioned to that morality, and this on grounds as disinterested as before, and solely from impartial reason; that is, it must lead to the supposition of the existence of a cause adequate to this effect; in other words, it must postulate the *existence of God*, as the necessary condition of the possibility of the *summum bonum* (an object of the will which is necessarily connected with the moral legislation of pure reason). We proceed to exhibit this connexion in a convincing manner.

Happiness is the condition of a rational being in the world with whom *everything goes according to his wish and will*; it rests, therefore, on the harmony of physical nature with his whole end, and likewise with the essential determining principle of his will. Now the moral law as a law of freedom commands by determining principles (266), which ought to be quite independent on nature and on its harmony with our faculty of desire (as springs). But the acting rational being in the world is not the cause of the world and of nature itself. There is not the least ground, therefore, in the moral law for a necessary connexion between morality and proportionate happiness in a being that belongs to the world as part of it, and therefore dependent on it, and which for that rea-son cannot by his will be a cause of this nature, nor by his own power make it thoroughly harmonize, as far as his happiness is concerned, with his practical principles. Nevertheless, in the practical problem of pure reason, *i.e.* the necessary pursuit of the *summum bonum*, such a connexion is postulated as necessary: we ought to endeavour to promote the *summum bonum*, which, therefore, must be possible. Accordingly, the existence of a cause of all nature, distinct from nature itself, and containing the principle of this connexion, namely, of the exact harmony of happiness with morality, is also *postulated*. Now, this supreme cause must contain the principle of the harmony of nature, not merely with a law of the will of rational beings, but with the conception of this *law*, in so far as they make it the *supreme determining principle of the will*, and consequently not merely with the form of morals, but with their morality as their motive, that is, with their moral character. Therefore, the *summum bonum* is possible in the world only on the supposition of a Supreme Being[1] having a causality corresponding to moral character. Now a being that is capable of acting on the conception of laws is an *intelligence* (a rational being), and the causality of such a being according to this conception of laws is his *will*; therefore the supreme cause of nature, which must be presupposed as a condition of the *summum bonum* (267) is a being which is the cause of nature by *intelligence* and *will*, consequently its author, that is God. It follows that the postulate of the possibility of the *highest derived good* (the best world) is likewise the postulate of the reality of a *highest original good*, that is to say, of the existence of God. Now it was seen to be a duty for us to promote the *summum bonum*; consequently it is not merely allowable,

[1] [The original has "a Supreme Nature." "*Natur*," however, almost invariably means "physical nature"; therefore Hartenstein supplies the words "cause of" before "nature." More probably "Nature" is a slip for "*Ursache*," "cause."]

but it is a necessity connected with duty as a requisite, that we should presuppose the possibility of this *summum bonum*; and as this is possible only on condition of the existence of God, it inseparably connects the supposition of this with duty; that is, it is morally necessary to assume the existence of God.

It must be remembered here that this moral necessity is *subjective*, that is, it is a want, and not *objective*, that is, itself a duty, for there cannot be a duty to suppose the existence of anything (since this concerns only the theoretical employment of reason). Moreover, it is not meant by this that it is necessary to suppose the existence of God *as a basis of all obligation in general* (for this rests, as has been sufficiently proved, simply on the autonomy of reason itself). What belongs to duty here is only the endeavour to realize and promote the *summum bonum* in the world, the possibility of which can therefore be postulated; and as our reason finds it not conceivable except on the supposition of a supreme intelligence, the admission of this existence is therefore connected with the consciousness of our duty, although the admission itself belongs to the domain of speculative reason. Considered in respect of this alone, as a principle of explanation, it may be called a *hypothesis*, but in reference to the intelligibility of an object given us by the moral law (the *summum bonum*), and consequently of a requirement for practical purposes, it may be called *faith*, that is to say a pure *rational faith*, since pure reason (268) (both in its theoretical and its practical use) is the sole source from which it springs.

From this *deduction* it is now intelligible why the *Greek* schools could never attain the solution of their problem of the practical possibility of the *summum bonum*, because they made the rule of the use which the will of man makes of his freedom the sole and sufficient ground of this possibility, thinking that they had no need for that purpose of the existence of God. No doubt they were so far right

that they established the principle of morals of itself independently on this postulate, from the relation of reason only to the will, and consequently made it the *supreme* practical condition of the *summum bonum*; but it was not therefore the *whole* condition of its possibility. The *Epicureans* had indeed assumed as the supreme principle of morality a wholly false one, namely, that of happiness, and had substituted for a law a maxim of arbitrary choice according to every man's inclination; they proceeded, however, *consistently* enough in this, that they degraded their *summum bonum* likewise just in proportion to the meanness of their fundamental principle, and looked for no greater happiness than can be attained by human prudence (including temperance and moderation of the inclinations), and this, as we know, would be scanty enough and would be very different according to circumstances; not to mention the exceptions that their maxims must perpetually admit and which make them incapable of being laws. The *Stoics*, on the contrary, had chosen their supreme practical principle quite rightly, making virtue the condition of the *summum bonum*; but when they represented the degree of virtue required by its pure law as fully attainable in this life, they not only strained the moral powers of the *man* whom they called *the wise* beyond all the limits of his nature, and assumed (269) a thing that contradicts all our knowledge of men, but also and principally they would not allow the second *element* of the *summum bonum*, namely, happiness, to be properly a special object of human desire, but made their *wise man*, like a divinity in his consciousness of the excellence of his person, wholly independent on nature (as regards his own contentment); they exposed him indeed to the evils of life, but made him not subject to them (at the same time representing him also as free from moral evil). They thus, in fact, left out the second element of the *summum bonum*, namely, personal happiness, placing it solely in action and satisfaction with one's own personal worth, thus including it in the consciousness of being morally minded, in which they might have been sufficiently refuted by the voice of their own nature.

The doctrine of Christianity,[2] even

[2] It is commonly held that the Christian precept of morality has no advantage in respect of purity over the moral conceptions of the Stoics; the distinction between them is, however, very obvious. The Stoic system made the consciousness of strength of mind the pivot on which all moral dispositions should turn; and although its disciples spoke of duties and even defined them very well, yet they placed the spring and proper determining principle of the will in an elevation of the mind above the lower springs of the senses, which owe their power only to weakness of mind. With them, therefore, virtue was a sort of heroism in the *wise man* who, raising himself above the animal nature of man, is sufficient for himself, and while he prescribes duties to others is himself raised above them, and is not subject to any temptation to transgress the moral law. All this, however, they could not have done if they had conceived this law in all its purity and strictness, as the precept of the Gospel does. When I give the name *idea* to a perfection to which nothing adequate can be given in experience, it does not follow that the moral ideas are something transcendent, that is something of which we could not even determine the concept adequately, or of which it is uncertain whether there is any object corresponding to it at all (270), as is the case with the ideas of speculative reason; on the contrary, being types of practical perfection, they serve as the indispensable rule of conduct and likewise as the *standard of comparison*. Now if I consider *Christian morals* on their philosophical side, then compared with the ideas of the Greek schools they would appear as follows: the ideas of the *Cynics*, the *Epicureans*, the *Stoics*, and the *Christians* are: *simplicity of nature, prudence, wisdom*, and *holiness*. In respect of the way of attaining them, the Greek schools were distinguished from one another thus, that the Cynics only required *common sense*, the others the path of *science*, but both found the mere *use of natural powers* sufficient for the purpose. Christian morality, because its precept is framed (as a moral precept must be) so pure and unyielding, takes from man all

if we do not consider it as a religious doctrine, gives, touching this point (269), a conception of the *summum bonum* (the kingdom of God), which alone satisfies the strictest demand of practical reason. The moral law is holy (unyielding) and demands holiness of morals, although all the moral perfection to which man can attain is still only virtue, that is, a rightful disposition arising from *respect* for the law, implying consciousness of a constant propensity to transgression, or at least a want of purity, that is, a mixture of many spurious (not moral) motives of obedience to the law, consequently a self-esteem combined with humility. In respect, then, of the holiness which the Christian law requires, this leaves the creature nothing but a progress in *infinitum*, but for that very reason it justifies him in hoping for an endless duration of his existence. The *worth* of a character *perfectly* accordant with the moral law is infinite, since (270) the only restriction on all possible happiness in the judgment of a wise and all-powerful distributor of it is the absence of conformity of rational beings to their duty. But the moral law of itself does not *promise* any happiness, for according to our conceptions of an order of nature in general, this is not necessarily connected with obedience to the law. Now Christian morality supplies this defect (of the second indispensable element of the *summum bonum*) by representing the world, in which rational beings devote themselves with all their soul to the moral law, as a *kingdom of God*, in which nature and morality are brought into a harmony foreign to each of itself, by a holy Author who makes the derived *summum bonum* possible. *Holiness* of life is prescribed to them as

confidence that he can be fully adequate to it, at least in this life, but again sets it up by enabling us to hope that if we act as well as it is in our *power* to do, then what is not in our power will come in to our aid from another source, whether we know how this may be or not. *Aristotle* and *Plato* differed only as to the *origin* of our moral conceptions.

a rule even in this life, while the welfare proportioned to it, namely, *bliss*, is represented as attainable only in an eternity; because the *former* must always be the pattern of their conduct in every state, and progress towards it is already possible and necessary in this life; while the *latter*, under the name of happiness, cannot be attained at all in this world (so far as our own power is concerned), and therefore is made simply an object of hope. Nevertheless, the Christian principle of *morality* itself is not theological (so as to be heteronomy), but is autonomy of pure practical reason, since it does not make the knowledge of God and His will the foundation of these laws, but only of the attainment of the *summum bonum*, on condition of following these laws, and it does not even place the proper *spring* of this obedience in the desired results, but solely in the conception of duty, as that of which the faithful observance alone constitutes the worthiness to obtain those happy consequences.

In this manner the moral laws lead through the conception of the *summum bonum* as the object and final end of pure practical reason to *religion* (271), that is, to the *recognition of all duties as divine commands, not as sanctions,*[3] *that is to say, arbitrary ordinances of a foreign will and contingent in themselves,* but as essential *laws* of every free will in itself, which, nevertheless, must be regarded as commands of the Supreme Being, because it is only from a morally perfect (holy and good) and at the same time all-powerful will, and consequently only through harmony with this will, that we can hope to attain the *summum bonum* which the moral law makes it our duty to take as the object of our endeavours. Here again, then, all remains disinterested and founded merely on duty; neither fear nor hope being made the fundamental springs, which if taken as principles would destroy the whole moral

worth of actions. The moral law commands me to make the highest possible good in a world the ultimate object of all my conduct. But I cannot hope to effect this otherwise than by the harmony of my will with that of a holy and good Author of the world; and although the conception of the *summum bonum* as a whole, in which the greatest happiness is conceived as combined in the most exact proportion with the highest degree of moral perfection (possible in creatures), includes *my own happiness*, yet it is not this that is the determining principle of the will which is enjoined to promote the *summum bonum*, but the moral law, which, on the contrary, limits by strict conditions my unbounded desire of happiness.

Hence also morality is not properly the doctrine how we should *make* ourselves happy, but how we should become *worthy* of happiness. It is only when religion is added that there also comes in the hope of participating some day in happiness in proportion as we have endeavoured to be not unworthy of it.

(272) A man is *worthy* to possess a thing or a state when his possession of it is in harmony with the *summum bonum*. We can now easily see that all worthiness depends on moral conduct, since in the conception of the *summum bonum* this constitutes the condition of the rest (which belongs to one's state), namely, the participation of happiness. Now it follows from this that *morality* should never be treated as a *doctrine of happiness*, that is, an instruction how to become happy; for it has to do simply with the rational condition (*conditio sine qua non*) of happiness, not with the means of attaining it. But when morality has been completely expounded (which merely imposes duties instead of providing rules for selfish desires), then first, after the moral desire to promote the *summum bonum* (to bring the kingdom of God to us) has been awakened, a desire founded on a law, and which could not previously arise in any selfish mind, and when for the behoof of this desire the step to religion has been taken, then

---

[3] [The word 'sanction' is here used in the technical German sense, which is familiar to students of history in connexion with the 'Pragmatic Sanction.']

this ethical doctrine may be also called a doctrine of happiness because the *hope* of happiness first begins with religion only.

We can also see from this that, when we ask what is *God's ultimate end* in creating the world, we must not name the *happiness* of the rational beings in it, but the *summum bonum*, which adds a further condition to that wish of such beings, namely, the condition of being worthy of happiness, that is, the *morality* of these same rational beings, a condition which alone contains the rule by which only they can hope to share in the former at the hand of a *wise* Author. For as *wisdom* theoretically considered signifies *the knowledge of the summum bonum*, and practically *the accordance of the will with the summum bonum*, we cannot attribute to a supreme independent wisdom an end based merely on *goodness* (273). For we cannot conceive the action of this goodness (in respect of the happiness of rational beings) as suitable to the highest original good, except under the restrictive conditions of harmony with the holiness of His will. Therefore those who placed the end of creation in the glory of God (provided that this is not conceived anthropomorphically as a desire to be praised) have perhaps hit upon the best expression. For nothing glorifies God more than that which is the most estimable thing in the world, respect for His command, the observance of the holy duty that His law imposes on us, when there is added thereto His glorious plan of crowning such a beautiful order of things with corresponding happiness. If the latter (to speak humanly) makes Him worthy of love, by the *former* He is an object of adoration. Even men can never acquire respect by benevolence alone, though they may gain love, so that the greatest beneficence only procures them honour when it is regulated by worthiness.[5]

[5] In order to make these characteristics of these conceptions clear, I add the remark that whilst we ascribe to God various attributes, the quality of which we also find applicable to creatures, only that in Him

That in the order of ends, man (and with him every rational being) is *an end in himself*, that is, that he can never be used merely as a means by any (274) (not even by God) without being at the same time an end also himself, that therefore *humanity* in our person must be *holy* to ourselves, this follows now of itself because he is the *subject*[6] *of the moral law*, in other words, of that which is holy in itself, and on account of which and in agreement with which alone can anything be termed holy. For this moral law is founded on the autonomy of his will, as a free will which by its universal laws must necessarily be able to agree with that to which it is to submit itself.

OF THE POSTULATES OF PURE PRACTICAL REASON IN GENERAL

They all proceed from the principle of morality, which is not a postulate but a law, by which reason determines the will directly, which will, because it is so determined as a pure will, requires these necessary conditions of obedience to its precept. These postulates are not theoretical dogmas but, suppositions practically necessary; while then they do [not][7] extend our speculative knowledge, they give

they are raised to the highest degree, *e.g.* power, knowledge, presence, goodness, &c., under the designations of omnipotence, omniscience, omnipresence, &c., there are three that are ascribed to God exclusively, and yet without the addition of greatness, and which are all moral. He is the *only holy*, the *only blessed*, the *only wise*, because these conceptions already imply the absence of limitation. In the order of these attributes He is also the *holy lawgiver* (and creator), the *good governor* (and preserver), and the *just judge*, three attributes which include everything by which God is the object of religion, and conformity with which the metaphysical perfections are added of themselves in the reason.

[6] [That the ambiguity of the word *subject* may not mislead the reader, it may be remarked that it is here used in the psychological sense *subjectum legis*, not *subjectus legi*.]

[7] [Absent from the original text.]

objective reality to the ideas of speculative reason in general (by means of their reference to what is practical), and give it a right to concepts, the possibility even of which it could not otherwise venture to affirm.

These postulates are those *of immortality, freedom* positively considered (as the causality of a being so far as he belongs to the intelligible world), and the *existence of God.* The *first* results from the practically necessary condition of a duration (275) adequate to the complete fulfilment of the moral law; the *second* from the necessary supposition of independence on the sensible world, and of the faculty of determining one's will according to the law of an intelligible world, that is, of freedom; the *third* from the necessary condition of the existence of the *summum bonum* in such an intelligible world, by the supposition of the supreme independent good, that is, the existence of God.

Thus the fact that respect for the moral law necessarily makes the *summum bonum* an object of our endeavours, and the supposition thence resulting of its objective reality, lead through the postulates of practical reason to conceptions which speculative reason might indeed present as problems, but could never solve. Thus it leads—1. To that one in the solution of which the latter could do nothing but commit *paralogisms* (namely, that of immortality), because it could not lay hold of the character of permanence, by which to complete the psychological conception of an ultimate subject necessarily ascribed to the soul in self-consciousness, so as to make it the real conception of a substance, a character which practical reason furnishes by the postulate of a duration required for accordance with the moral law in the *summum bonum,* which is the whole end of practical reason. 2. It leads to that of which speculative reason contained nothing but *antinomy,* the solution of which it could only found on a notion problematically conceivable indeed, but whose objective reality it could not prove or determine, namely, the *cosmological* idea of an intel-

ligible world and the consciousness of our existence in it, by means of the postulate of freedom (the reality of which it lays down by virtue of the moral law), and with it likewise the law of an intelligible world, to which speculative reason could only point, but could not define its conception. 3. What speculative reason was able to think, but was obliged to leave undetermined as a mere transcendental *ideal* (276), viz. the *theological* conception of the First Being, to this it gives significance (in a practical view, that is, as a condition of the possibility of the object of a will determined by that law), namely, as the supreme principle of the *summum bonum* in an intelligible world, by means of moral legislation in it invested with sovereign power.

Is our knowledge, however, actually extended in this way by pure practical reason, and is that *immanent* in practical reason which for the speculative was only *transcendent*? Certainly, but *only in a practical point of view.* For we do not thereby take knowledge of the nature of our souls, nor of the intelligible world, nor of the Supreme Being, with respect to what they are in themselves, but we have merely combined the conceptions of them in the *practical* concept of the *summum bonum* as the object of our will, and this altogether *à priori,* but only by means of the moral law, and merely in reference to it, in respect of the object which it commands. But how freedom is possible, and how we are to conceive this kind of causality theoretically and positively, is not thereby discovered; but only that there is such a causality is postulated by the moral law and in its behoof. It is the same with the remaining ideas, the possibility of which no human intelligence will ever fathom, but the truth of which, on the other hand, no sophistry will ever wrest from the conviction even of the commonest man.

OF BELIEF FROM A REQUIREMENT
OF PURE REASON

A want or requirement of pure reason in its speculative use leads only to a *hypothesis*; that of pure practical reason to a *postulate*; for in the former case I ascend from the result as high as I please in the series of causes, not in order to give objective reality to the result (*e.g.* the causal connexion of things and changes in the world), but in order thoroughly to satisfy my inquiring reason in respect of it. Thus I see before me order and design in nature, and need not resort to speculation to assure myself of their *reality*, but to *explain* them I have *to pre-suppose a Deity* as their cause; and then since the inference from an effect to a definite cause is always uncertain and doubtful, especially to a cause so precise and so perfectly defined as we have to conceive in God, hence the highest degree of certainty to which this pre-supposition can be brought is, that it is the most rational opinion for us men[8] (288). On the other hand, a requirement of pure *practical* reason is based on a *duty*, that of making something (the *summum bonum*) the object of my will so as to promote it with all my powers; in which case I must suppose its possibility, and consequently also the conditions necessary thereto, namely, God, freedom, and immortality; since I cannot prove these by my speculative reason, although neither can I refute them. This duty is founded on something that is indeed quite independent on these

[8] But even here we should not be able to allege a requirement *of reason*, if we had not before our eyes a problematical, but yet inevitable, conception of reason, namely, that of an absolutely necessary being. This conception now seeks to be defined, and this, in addition to the tendency to extend itself, is the objective ground of a requirement of speculative reason, namely, to have a more precise definition of the conception of a necessary being which is to serve as the first cause of other beings, so as to make these[*] latter knowable by some means. Without such antecedent necessary problems there are no *requirements*—at least not of *pure reason*—the rest are requirements of *inclination*.

[*] I read 'diese' with the ed. of 1791. Rosenkranz and Hartenstein both read 'dieses,' 'this being.'

suppositions, and is of itself apodictically certain, namely, the moral law; and so far it needs no further support by theoretical views as to the inner constitution of things, the secret final aim of the order of the world, or a presiding ruler thereof, in order to bind me in the most perfect manner to act in unconditional conformity to the law. But the subjective effect of this law, namely, the mental *disposition* conformed to it and made necessary by it, to promote the practically possible *summum bonum*, this pre-supposes at least that the latter is *possible*, for it would be practically impossible to strive after the object of a conception which at bottom was empty and had no object. Now the above-mentioned postulates concern only the physical or metaphysical conditions of the *possibility* of the *summum bonum* (289); in a word, those which lie in the nature of things; not however, for the sake of an arbitrary speculative purpose, but of a practically necessary end of a pure rational will, which in this case does not *choose*, but *obeys* an inexorable command of reason, the foundation of which is *objective*, in the constitution of things as they must be universally judged by pure reason, and is not based on *inclination*; for we are in nowise justified in assuming, on account of what we *wish* on merely *subjective* grounds, that the means thereto are possible or that its object is real. This, then, is an absolutely necessary requirement, and what it pre-supposes is not merely justified as an allowable hypothesis, but as a postulate in a practical point of view; and admitting that the pure moral law inexorably binds every man as a command (not as a rule of prudence), the righteous man may say: I *will* that there be a God, that my existence in this world be also an existence outside the chain of physical causes, and in a pure world of the understanding, and lastly, that my duration be endless; I firmly abide by this, and will not let this faith be taken from me; for in this instance alone my interest, because I *must* not relax anything of it, inevitably determines my judgment, without regarding sophistries, however unable I may be to answer them or to oppose them with others more plausible.[9]

. . . .

(290) In order to prevent misconception in the use of a notion as yet so unusual as that of a faith of pure practical reason, let me be permitted to add one more remark. It might almost seem as if this rational faith were here announced as itself a *command*, namely, that we should assume the *summum bonum* as possible. But a faith that is commanded is nonsense. Let the preceding analysis, however, be remembered of what is required to be supposed in the conception of the *summum bonum*, and it will be seen that it cannot be commanded to assume this possibility, and no practical disposition of mind is required

[9] In the *Deutsches Museum,* February, 1787, there is a dissertation by a very subtle and clear-headed man, the late *Wizenmann,* whose early death is to be lamented, in which he disputes the right to argue from a want to the objective reality of its object, and illustrates the point by the example of *a man in love,* who, having fooled himself into an idea of beauty, which is merely a chimera of his own brain, would fain conclude that such an object really exists somewhere (290). I quite agree with him in this, in all cases where the want is founded on *inclination,* which cannot necessarily postulate the existence of its object even for the man that is affected by it, much less can it contain a demand valid for everyone, and therefore it is merely a *subjective* ground of the wish. But in the present case we have a want of reason springing from an objective determining principle of the will, namely, the moral law, which necessarily binds every rational being, and therefore justifies him in assuming *à priori* in nature the conditions proper for it, and makes the latter inseparable from the complete practical use of reason. It is a duty to realize the *summum bonum* to the utmost of our power, therefore it must be possible, consequently it is unavoidable for every rational being in the world to assume what is necessary for its objective possibility. The assumption is as necessary as the moral law, in connexion with which alone it is valid.

to *admit* it; but that speculative reason must concede it without being asked, for no one can affirm that it is *impossible* in itself that rational beings in the world should at the same time be worthy of happiness in conformity with the moral law, and also possess this happiness proportionately. Now in respect of the first element of the *summum bonum,* namely, that which concerns morality, the moral law gives merely a command, and to doubt the possibility of that element would be the same as to call in question the moral law itself (291). But as regards the second element of that object, namely, happiness perfectly proportioned to that worthiness, it is true that there is no need of a command to admit its possibility in general, for theoretical reason has nothing to say against it; but *the manner* in which we have to conceive this harmony of the laws of nature with those of freedom has in it something in respect of which we have a *choice,* because theoretical reason decides nothing with apodictic certainty about it, and in respect of this there may be a moral interest which turns the scale.

I had said above that in a mere course of nature in the world an accurate correspondence between happiness and moral worth is not to be expected, and must be regarded as impossible, and that therefore the possibility of the *summum bonum* cannot be admitted from this side except on the supposition of a moral Author of the world. I purposely reserved the restriction of this judgment to the *subjective* conditions of our reason, in order not to make use of it until the manner of this belief should be defined more precisely. The fact is that the impossibility referred to is *merely subjective,* that is, our reason finds it *impossible for it* to render conceivable in the way of a mere course of nature a connexion so exactly proportioned and so thoroughly adapted to an end, between two sets of events happening according to such distinct laws; although, as with everything else in nature that is adapted to an end, it cannot prove, that is, show by sufficient objective reasons, that it is not possible by universal laws of nature.

Now, however, a deciding principle of a different kind comes into play to turn the scale in this uncertainty of speculative reason. The command to promote the *summum bonum* is established on an objective basis (in practical reason); the possibility of the same in general is likewise established on an objective basis (292) (in theoretical reason, which has nothing to say against it). But reason cannot decide objectively in what way we are to conceive this possibility; whether by universal laws of nature without a wise Author presiding over nature, or only on supposition of such an Author. Now here there comes in a *subjective* condition of reason; the only way theoretically possible for it, of conceiving the exact harmony of the kingdom of nature with the kingdom of morals, which is the condition of the possibility of the *summum bonum*; and at the same time the only one conducive to morality (which depends on an objective law of reason). Now since the promotion of this *summum bonum*, and therefore the supposition of its possibility, are *objectively* necessary (though only as a result of practical reason), while at the same time the manner in which we would conceive it rests with our own choice, and in this choice a free interest of pure practical reason decides for the assumption of a wise Author of the world; it is clear that the principle that herein determines our judgment, though as a want it is *subjective*, yet at the same time being the means of promoting what is *objectively* (practically) necessary, is the foundation of a *maxim* of belief in a moral point of view, that is, a *faith of pure practical reason*. This, then, is not commanded, but being a voluntary determination of our judgment, conducive to the moral (commanded) purpose, and moreover harmonizing with the theoretical requirement of reason, to assume that existence and to make it the foundation of our further employment of reason, it has itself sprung from the moral disposition of mind; it may there-

fore at times waver even in the well-disposed, but can never be reduced to unbelief.

OF THE WISE ADAPTATION OF MAN'S COGNITIVE FACULTIES TO HIS PRACTICAL DESTINATION

(293) If human nature is destined to endeavour after the *summum bonum*, we must suppose also that the measure of its cognitive faculties, and particularly their relation to one another, is suitable to this end. Now the Critique of Pure *Speculative* Reason proves that this is incapable of solving satisfactorily the most weighty problems that are proposed to it, although it does not ignore the natural and important hints received from the same reason, nor the great steps that it can make to approach to this great goal that is set before it, which, however, it can never reach of itself, even with the help of the greatest knowledge of nature. Nature then seems here to have provided us only in a *step-motherly* fashion with the faculty required for our end.

Suppose now that in this matter nature had conformed to our wish, and had given us that capacity of discernment or that enlightenment which we would gladly possess, or which some *imagine* they actually possess, what would in all probability be the consequence? Unless our whole nature were at the same time changed, our inclinations, which always have the first word, would first of all demand their own satisfaction, and joined with rational reflection, the greatest possible and most lasting satisfaction, under the name of happiness; the moral law (294) would afterwards speak, in order to keep them within their proper bounds, and even to subject them all to a higher end, which has no regard to inclination. But instead of the conflict that the moral disposition has now to carry on with the inclinations, in which, though after some defeats, moral strength of mind may be gradually acquired, *God* and *eternity* with their *awful majesty* would stand unceasingly *before our eyes* (for what we can prove perfectly is to us as certain as that of which we are assured by the sight of our eyes). Transgression of the law, would, no doubt, be avoided; what is commanded would be done; but the mental *disposition*, from which actions ought to proceed, cannot be infused by any command, and in this case the spur of action is ever active and *external*, so that reason has no need to exert itself in order to gather strength to resist the inclinations by a lively representation of the dignity of the law: hence most of the actions that conformed to the law would be done from fear, a few only from hope, and none at all from duty, and the moral worth of actions, on which alone in the eyes of supreme wisdom the worth of the person and even that of the world depends, would cease to exist. As long as the nature of man remains what it is, his conduct would thus be changed into mere mechanism, in which, as in a puppet-show, everything would *gesticulate* well, but there would be *no life* in the figures. Now, when it is quite otherwise with us, when with all the effort of our reason we have only a very obscure and doubtful view into the future, when the Governor of the world allows us only to conjecture His existence and His majesty, not to behold them or prove them clearly; and, on the other hand, the moral law within us, without promising or threatening anything with certainty, demands of us disinterested respect; and only when this respect has become active (295) and dominant does it allow us by means of it a prospect into the world of the supersensible, and then only with weak glances; all this being so, there is room for true moral disposition, immediately devoted to the law, and a rational creature can become worthy of sharing in the *summum bonum* that corresponds to the worth of his person and not merely to his actions. Thus what the study of nature and of man teaches us sufficiently elsewhere may well be true here also; that the unsearchable wisdom by which we exist is not less worthy of admiration in what it has denied than in what it has granted.

Does Evil
Prove
That God
Does Not Exist?

The problem of evil can be stated fairly simply. According to traditional theism, God, is all-knowing, all-powerful, and all-good. He created the world from nothing and providentially governs the course of history. Nonetheless, there is evil in the world—pain and suffering that apparently serve no good purpose, natural disasters that kill and maim and destroy, murder and malice that hurt all parties concerned. Why, if God exists and has the nature ascribed to Him (and, for traditional theism, if no being having that nature exists, then God does not exist), is there any evil, let alone so much of it?

There are at least three distinct questions here. The purpose of this introduction is to sort them out and to indicate some of the answers given in the selections that follow. The three questions are:

(I) Are the statements (1) "God (an all-knowing, all-powerful, all-good being) exists" and (2) "There is evil" logically incompatible, so that if (2) is true, then (1) is false?

558

(II) If (1) and (2) are logically compatible, does (2) nonetheless provide strong *evidence* against (1)? Two statements can be logically compatible (both *can* be true without contradiction, while the truth of one of them constitutes strong evidence against the truth of the other. For example: (3) Jones was the only man in the near vicinity of Smith when Smith was murdered, and Jones was the only man who would profit from Smith's death, and (4) Jones did not murder Smith, are compatible but (3) provides reasons relevant to showing (4) to be false. Our question is: Does (2) provide a reason relevant to showing (1) to be false?

(III) *Why* is evil permitted by God, granting that God does exist? To attempt to answer this question is to offer a *theodicy*, an explanation of the role of evil in the plans of providence.

(I) Philosophers differ greatly as to the answer to our question. J. L. Mackie takes it to be *obvious* that (1) and (2) are incompatible, so much so that any attempt to show that they are compatible *must* somehow be mistaken. In contrast, Nelson Pike categorically denies that they are incompatible and doubts that any argument to show that they are incompatible could be effective.

Mackie admits that (1) and (2) *alone* are not incompatible; he says that "we need some additional premises, or perhaps some quasi-logical rules connecting the terms 'good,' 'evil,' and 'omnipotent.' " The admission is important: even for Mackie, (1) and (2) *by themselves* are not incompatible. Pike, however, is dubious that any additional premises are available which are true and will, with (1) and (2), yield a contradiction. If (5) every evil there is serves some morally sufficient purpose (Pike offers some remarks to clarify the phrase "morally sufficient purpose") is true, then it is dubious that there are any further premises that will serve Mackie's purposes. And, Pike remarks, until (5) is proven false, Hume's argument (and Mackie's as well) "against the existence of God is not finished. And it is not at all obvious that it is *capable* of effective completion." So far as these selections go, then, the critic needs a proof of (5) to make good his case, and no proof of (5) is offered. Pike is dubious that there is any, and he may be right.

(II) But if one grants that (1) and (2) are compatible, (2) may still be evidence against (1). Many of Mackie's comments could be reinterpreted along these lines, and much of Hume's Part XI is also capable of being interpreted in this manner. Two comments will, I believe, clarify this aspect of the discussion. One is that, as Pike notes, Philo (or Hume through Philo) uses (2) in a specific way. He does not use (2), primarily at least, as evidence against (1). Rather, he argues that if (1) is inferred from data we get by observing natural phenomena and human conduct, we must use *all* the data obtained from such observation. Among these data is the existence of evil. Not only (as we noted in the section on the cosmological and teleological arguments) are we at most entitled to infer a *somewhat* knowledgeable and powerful Designer from these data, but we are *at most* entitled to infer a *somewhat* good being. Philo remarks: "I am sceptic enough to allow that the bad appearances [i.e., evil] . . . may be compatible with such attributes as you suppose, but surely they can never prove these attributes." The fact of evil prevents us from inferring from the existence and character of the natural and human environment to an all-good Deity, even if in fact God is all-good. So used, as Pike notes, (2) is not an objection to a theology that takes the existence of God as a datum of faith though it may be an objection to a theology that infers from the phenomena of nature and history to an all-good Deity.

But (2) *has* been used as evidence against (1). One important way (see Mackie's article) in which this has been done is by suggesting that God could have created a better world than our own—for example by not permitting such things as pain, fear, temptation, and the like, and by having created men so that they were morally perfect. The response has traditionally been made that these evils are justified in that they make certain virtues possible. Ninian Smart offers a fresh and powerful statement of this line of argument. His thesis is that the *meaning* of the claims that God could create morally perfect men and that it would be better for there to be no pain, fear, or temptation is unclear. As Smart puts it, "the point [is] that moral discourse is embedded in the cosmic status quo." Since our appraisal of a man as good is closely tied to how he reacts in contexts that involve fear, pain, temptation, and the like, the more we alter these contexts the less clear it is when a man should be called "good" or what would be *meant* by calling him "good." Evaluation of Smart's argument is a complex matter. Perhaps *some* alteration for the better of some kinds or degrees are consistent with our using our moral terms as we now do, but not other kinds or degrees of alteration of present conditions. However this issue is to be resolved, Smart raises a significant question as to how clear it is that claims of the form "It would obviously be better had God created the world so that . . ." are true, or even intelligible. Of course there are other ways in which (2) has been used as putative evidence against (1).

(III) There is disagreement as to how important it is for a theist to attempt some answer to our third question—that is, offer some kind of theodicy. Mackie, taking the problem of evil to be intractable, would of course deny that any theodicy could possibly succeed. Pike, however, says that for a theology that does not attempt to infer (1) from empirical and evaluative data—as opposed to accepting (1) on the basis of an a priori proof such as Anselm's or taking (1) as a datum of faith—"The problem of evil can only be the problem of discovering a *specific* theodicy which is adequate." But given (1), there must be a morally sufficient reason for whatever evils there are, and "once it is granted that there is some specific reason for evil, there is a sense in which it is no longer vital to find it."

Hume, however, raises several questions, which anyone who wishes to offer a theodicy will attempt to answer. Whether it is *necessary* for a theist to offer a theodicy is, as noted, open to question. It would seem, however, that he only strengthens his claim that (2) does not constitute evidence against (1) as he succeeds in the difficult (perhaps even presumptuous) task of writing a theodicy.

Not every issue raised in the following selections fits neatly in the above classification. Two such issues are particularly important and deserve mention. One is this: In "God is good," to what degree is "good" identical in meaning and function to the word "good" in "Jones (a particular man) is good." There is the danger that in attempting to be reverent, a theist may claim that the sense in which God is good is incomprehensible to us, that we just do not know what "God is good" means. But if this view is held, it is altogether problematic as to why God should be revered, or even respected.

The other issue is that each of the writers assumes that (2) is true— that there *is* evil in the universe in some nonarbitrary sense of "evil." This claim is not itself indubitable, as it requires that moral claims—(2) at least— be known or reasonably believed to be true. This in turn raises the question whether moral sentences *have* truth value and *can* be rationally appraised. (See *Theory of Knowledge*: "Is Moral Knowledge Possible?" and *Ethics*: "How Can Ethical Viewpoints Be Evaluated?")

The Existence of Evil Does Prove That God Does Not Exist
DAVID HUME

X

*I*t is my opinion, I own, replied Demea, that each man feels, in a manner, the truth of religion within his own breast, and, from a consciousness of his imbecility and misery rather than from any reasoning, is led to seek protection from that Being on whom he and all nature is dependent. So anxious or so tedious are even the best scenes of life that futurity is still the object of all our hopes and fears. We incessantly look forward and endeavour, by prayers, adoration, and sacrifice, to appease those unknown powers whom we find, by experience, so able to afflict and oppress us. Wretched creatures that we are! What resource for us amidst the innumerable ills of life did not religion suggest some methods of atonement, and appease those terrors with which we are incessantly agitated and tormented?

I am indeed persuaded, said Philo, that the best and indeed the only method of bringing everyone to a due sense of religion is by just representations of the misery and wickedness of men. And for that purpose a talent of eloquence and strong imagery is more requisite than that of reasoning and argument. For is it necessary to prove what everyone feels within himself? It is only necessary to make us feel it, if possible, more intimately and sensibly.

The people, indeed, replied Demea, are sufficiently convinced of this great and melancholy truth. The miseries of life, the unhappiness of man, the general corruptions of our nature, the unsatisfactory enjoyment of pleasures, riches, honours—these phrases have become almost proverbial in all languages. And who can doubt of what all men declare from their own immediate feeling and experience?

In this point, said Philo, the learned are perfectly agreed with the vulgar; and in all letters, *sacred* and *profane*, the topic of human misery has been insisted on with the most pathetic eloquence that sorrow and melancholy could inspire. The poets, who speak from sentiment, without a system, and whose testimony has therefore the more authority, abound in images of this nature. From Homer down to Dr. Young, the whole inspired tribe have ever been sensible that no other representation of things would suit the feeling and observation of each individual.

As to authorities, replied Demea, you need not seek them. Look round this library of Cleanthes. I shall venture to

FROM: *Dialogues Concerning Natural Religion*, David Hume. Parts 10 and 11 (originally published in 1779).

affirm that, except authors of particular sciences, such as chemistry or botany, who have no occasion to treat of human life, there is scarce one of those innumerable writers from whom the sense of human misery has not, in some passage or other, extorted a complaint and confession of it. At least, the chance is entirely on that side; and no one author has ever, so far as I can recollect, been so extravagant as to deny it.

There you must excuse me, said Philo: Leibniz has denied it, and is perhaps the first[1] who ventured upon so bold and paradoxical an opinion; at least, the first who made it essential to his philosophical system.

And by being the first, replied Demea, might he not have been sensible of his error? For is this a subject in which philosophers can propose to make discoveries especially in so late an age? And can any man hope by a simple denial (for the subject scarcely admits of reasoning) to bear down the united testimony of mankind, founded on sense and consciousness?

And why should man, added he, pretend to an exemption from the lot of all other animals? The whole earth, believe me, Philo, is cursed and polluted. A perpetual war is kindled amongst all living creatures. Necessity, hunger, want stimulate the strong and courageous; fear, anxiety, terror agitate the weak and infirm. The first entrance into life gives anguish to the new-born infant and to its wretched parent; weakness, impotence, distress attend each stage of that life, and it is, at last, finished in agony and horror.

Observe, too, says Philo, the curious artifices of nature in order to embitter the life of every living being. The stronger prey upon the weaker and keep them in perpetual terror and anxiety. The weaker, too, in their turn, often prey upon the stronger, and vex and molest them without relaxation. Consider that innumerable race of insects, which either are bred on the body of each animal or, flying about, infix their stings in him. These insects have others still less than themselves which torment them. And thus on each hand, before and behind, above and below, every animal is surrounded with enemies which incessantly seek his misery and destruction.

Man alone, said Demea, seems to be, in part, an exception to this rule. For by combination in society he can easily master lions, tigers, and bears, whose greater strength and agility naturally enable them to prey upon him.

On the contrary, it is here chiefly, cried Philo, that the uniform and equal maxims of nature are most apparent. Man, it is true, can, by combination, surmount all his *real* enemies and become master of the whole animal creation; but does he not immediately raise up to himself *imaginary* enemies, the demons of his fancy, who haunt him with superstitious terrors and blast every enjoyment of life? His pleasure, as he imagines, becomes in their eyes a crime; his food and repose give them umbrage and offence; his very sleep and dreams furnish new materials to anxious fear; and even death, his refuge from every other ill, presents only the dread of endless and innumerable woes. Nor does the wolf molest more the timid flock than superstition does the anxious breast of wretched mortals.

Besides, consider, Demea: This very society by which we surmount those wild beasts, our natural enemies, what new enemies does it not raise to us? What woe and misery does it not occasion? Man is the greatest enemy of man. Oppression, injustice, contempt, contumely, violence, sedition, war, calumny, treachery, fraud—by these they mutually torment each other, and they would soon dissolve that society which they had formed were it not for the dread of still greater ills which must attend their separation.

But though these external insults, said Demea, from animals, from men,

---

[1] That sentiment had been maintained by Dr. King and some few others before Leibniz, though by none of so great fame as that German philosopher.

from all the elements, which assault us form a frightful catalogue of woes, they are nothing in comparison of those which arise within ourselves, from the distempered condition of our mind and body. How many lie under the lingering torment of diseases? Hear the pathetic enumeration of the great poet.

Intestine stone and ulcer, colic-pangs,
Demoniac frenzy, moping melancholy,
And moon-struck madness, pining
*   atrophy,*
Marasmus, and wide-wasting pestilence.
Dire was the tossing, deep the groans:
*   Despair*
Tended the sick, busiest from couch to
*   couch.*
And over them triumphant Death *his dart*
Shook: but delay'd to strike, though oft
*   invok'd*
With vows, as their chief good and final
*   hope.*[2]

The disorders of the mind, continued Demea, though more secret, are not perhaps less dismal and vexatious. Remorse, shame, anguish, rage, disappointment, anxiety, fear, dejection, despair—who has ever passed through life without cruel inroads from these tormentors? How many have scarcely ever felt any better sensations? Labour and poverty, so abhorred by everyone, are the certain lot of the far greater number; and those few privileged persons who enjoy ease and opulence never reach contentment or true felicity. All the goods of life united would not make a very happy man, but all the ills united would make a wretch indeed; and any one of them almost (and who can be free from every one?), nay, often the absence of one good (and who can possess all?) is sufficient to render life ineligible.

Were a stranger to drop on a sudden into this world, I would show him, as a specimen of its ills, an hospital full of diseases, a prison crowded with malefactors and debtors, a field of battle strewed with carcases, a fleet foundering

in the ocean, a nation languishing under tyranny, famine, or pestilence. To turn the gay side of life to him and give him a notion of its pleasures—whither should I conduct him? To a ball, to an opera, to court? He might justly think that I was only showing him a diversity of distress and sorrow.

There is no evading such striking instances, said Philo, but by apologies which still further aggravate the charge. Why have all men, I ask, in all ages, complained incessantly of the miseries of life? . . . They have no just reason, says one: these complaints proceed only from their discontented, repining, anxious disposition. . . . And can there possibly, I reply, be a more certain foundation of misery than such a wretched temper?

But if they were really as unhappy as they pretend, says my antagonist, why do they remain in life? . . .

Not satisfied with life, afraid of death—this is the secret chain, say I, that holds us. We are terrified, not bribed to the continuance of our existence.

It is only a false delicacy, he may insist, which a few refined spirits indulge, and which has spread these complaints among the whole race of mankind. . . . And what is this delicacy, I ask, which you blame? Is it anything but a greater sensibility to all the pleasures and pains of life? And if the man of a delicate, refined temper, by being so much more alive than the rest of the world, is only so much more unhappy, what judgment must we form in general of human life?

Let men remain at rest, says our adversary, and they will be easy. They are willing artificers of their own misery. . . . No! reply I: an anxious languor follows their repose; disappointment, vexation, trouble, their activity and ambition.

I can observe something like what you mention in some others, replied Cleanthes, but I confess I feel little or nothing of it in myself, and hope that it is not so common as you represent it.

If you feel not human misery yourself, cried Demea, I congratulate you on so happy a singularity. Others, seemingly

[2] [Milton: *Paradise Lost*, Bk. XI.]

the most prosperous, have not been ashamed to vent their complaints in the most melancholy strains. Let us attend to the great, the fortunate emperor, Charles V, when, tired with human grandeur, he resigned all his extensive dominions into the hands of his son. In the last harangue which he made on that memorable occasion, he publicly avowed *that the greatest prosperities which he had ever enjoyed had been mixed with so many adversities that he might truly say he had never enjoyed any satisfaction or contentment.* But did the retired life in which he sought for shelter afford him any greater happiness? If we may credit his son's account, his repentance commenced the very day of his resignation.

Cicero's fortune, from small beginnings, rose to the greatest lustre and renown; yet what pathetic complaints of the ills of life do his familiar letters, as well as philosophical discourses, contain? And suitably to his own experience, he introduces Cato, the great, the fortunate Cato protesting in his old age that had he a new life in his offer he would reject the present.

Ask yourself, ask any of your acquaintance, whether they would live over again the last ten or twenty years of their life. No! but the next twenty, they say, will be better:

And from the dregs of life, hope to receive
What the first sprightly running could not give[3]

Thus, at last, they find (such is the greatness of human misery, it reconciles even contradictions) that they complain at once of the shortness of life and of its vanity and sorrow.

And is it possible, Cleanthes, said Philo, that after all these reflections, and infinitely more which might be suggested, you can still persevere in your anthropomorphism, and assert the moral at-

³ [John Dryden, *Aureng-Zebe*, Act IV, sc. 1.]

tributes of the Deity, his justice, benevolence, mercy, and rectitude, to be of the same nature with these virtues in human creatures? His power, we allow, is infinite; whatever he wills is executed; but neither man nor any other animal is happy; therefore, he does not will their happiness. His wisdom is infinite; he is never mistaken in choosing the means to any end; but the course of nature tends not to human or animal felicity; therefore, it is not established for that purpose. Through the whole compass of human knowledge there are no inferences more certain and infallible than these. In what respect, then, do his benevolence and mercy resemble the benevolence and mercy of men?

Epicurus' old questions are yet unanswered.

Is he willing to prevent evil, but not able? then is he impotent. Is he able, but not willing? then he is malevolent. Is he both able and willing? whence then is evil?

You ascribe, Cleanthes, (and I believe justly) a purpose and intention to nature. But what, I beseech you, is the object of that curious artifice and machinery which she has displayed in all animals—the preservation alone of individuals, and propagation of the species? It seems enough for her purpose if such a rank be barely upheld in the universe, without any care or concern for the happiness of the members that compose it. No resource for this purpose: no machinery in order merely to give pleasure or ease; no fund of pure joy and contentment; no indulgence without some want or necessity accompanying it. At least, the few phenomena of this nature are overbalanced by opposite phenomena of still greater importance.

Our sense of music, harmony, and indeed beauty of all kinds, gives satisfaction, without being absolutely necessary to the preservation and propagation of the species. But what racking pains, on the other hand, arise from gouts, gravels, megrims, toothaches, rheumatisms, where the injury to the animal machinery is either small or incurable?

Mirth, laughter, play, frolic seem gratuitous satisfactions which have no further tendency; spleen, melancholy, discontent, superstition are pains of the same nature. How then does the Divine benevolence display itself, in the sense of your anthropomorphites? None but we mystics, as you were pleased to call us, can account for this strange mixture of phenomena, by deriving it from attributes infinitely perfect but incomprehensible.

And have you, at last, said Cleanthes smiling, betrayed your intentions, Philo? Your long agreement with Demea did indeed a little surprise me, but I find you were all the while erecting a concealed battery against me. And I must confess that you have now fallen upon a subject worthy of your noble spirit of opposition and controversy. If you can make out the present point, and prove mankind to be unhappy or corrupted, there is an end at once of all religion. For to what purpose establish the natural attributes of the Deity, while the moral are still doubtful and uncertain?

You take umbrage very easily, replied Demea, at opinions the most innocent and the most generally received, even amongst the religious and devout themselves; and nothing can be more surprising than to find a topic like this— concerning the wickedness and misery of man—charged with no less than atheism and profaneness. Have not all pious divines and preachers who have indulged their rhetoric on so fertile a subject, have they not easily, I say, given a solution of any difficulties which may attend it? This world is but a point in comparison of the universe; this life but a moment in comparison of eternity. The present evil phenomena, therefore, are rectified in other regions, and in some future period of existence. And the eyes of men, being then opened to larger views of things, see the whole connection of general laws, and trace, with adoration, the benevolence and rectitude of the Deity through all the mazes and intricacies of his providence.

No! replied Cleanthes, no! These arbitrary suppositions can never be admitted, contrary to matter of fact, visible and uncontroverted. Whence can any cause be known but from its known effects? Whence can any hypothesis be proved but from the apparent phenomena? To establish one hypothesis upon another is building entirely in the air; and the utmost we ever attain by these conjectures and fictions is to ascertain the bare possibility of our opinion, but never can we, upon such terms, establish its reality.

The only method of supporting Divine benevolence—and it is what I willingly embrace—is to deny absolutely the misery and wickedness of man. Your representations are exaggerated; your melancholy views mostly fictitious; your inferences contrary to fact and experience. Health is more common than sickness; pleasure than pain; happiness than misery. And for one vexation which we meet with, we attain, upon computation, a hundred enjoyments.

Admitting your position, replied Philo, which yet is extremely doubtful, you must at the same time allow that, if pain be less frequent than pleasure, it is infinitely more violent and durable. One hour of it is often able to outweigh a day, a week, a month of our common insipid enjoyments; and how many days, weeks, and months are passed by several in the most acute torments? Pleasure, scarcely in one instance, is ever able to reach ecstasy and rapture; and in no one instance can it continue for any time at its highest pitch and altitude. The spirits evaporate, the nerves relax, the fabric is disordered, and the enjoyment quickly degenerates into fatigue and uneasiness. But pain often, good God, how often! rises to torture and agony; and the longer it continues, it becomes still more genuine agony and torture. Patience is exhausted, courage languishes, melancholy seizes us, and nothing terminates our misery but the removal of its cause or another event which is the sole cure of all evil, but which, from our natural folly, we regard with still greater horror and consternation.

But not to insist upon these topics, continued Philo, though most obvious, certain, and important, I must use the freedom to admonish you, Cleanthes, that you have put the controversy upon a most dangerous issue, and are unawares introducing a total scepticism into the most essential articles of natural and revealed theology. What! no method of fixing a just foundation for religion unless we allow the happiness of human life, and maintain a continued existence even in this world, with all our present pains, infirmities, vexations, and follies, to be eligible and desirable! But this is contrary to everyone's feeling and experience; it is contrary to an authority so established as nothing can subvert. No decisive proofs can ever be produced against this authority; nor is it possible for you to compute, estimate, and compare all the pains and all the pleasures in the lives of all men and of all animals; and thus, by your resting the whole system of religion on a point which, from its very nature, must for ever be uncertain, you tacitly confess that that system is equally uncertain.

But allowing you what never will be believed, at least, what you never possibly can prove, that animal or, at least, human happiness in this life exceeds its misery, you have yet done nothing; for this is not, by any means, what we expect from infinite power, infinite wisdom, and infinite goodness. Why is there any misery at all in the world? Not by chance, surely. From some cause then. Is it from the intention of the Deity? But he is perfectly benevolent. Is it contrary to his intention? But he is almighty. Nothing can shake the solidity of this reasoning, so short, so clear, so decisive, except we assert that these subjects exceed all human capacity, and that our common measures of truth and falsehood are not applicable to them—a topic which I have all along insisted on, but which you have, from the beginning, rejected with scorn and indignation.

But I will be contented to retire still from this intrenchment, for I deny that you can ever force me in it. I will

allow that pain or misery in man is *compatible* with infinite power and goodness in the Deity, even in your sense of these attributes: what are you advanced by all these concessions? A mere possible compatibility is not sufficient. You must *prove* these pure, unmixed, and uncontrollable attributes from the present mixed and confused phenomena, and from these alone. A hopeful undertaking! Were the phenomena ever so pure and unmixed, yet, being finite, they would be insufficient for that purpose. How much more, where they are also so jarring and discordant!

Here, Cleanthes, I find myself at ease in my argument. Here I triumph. Formerly, when we argued concerning the natural attributes of intelligence and design, I needed all my sceptical and metaphysical subtlety to elude your grasp. In many views of the universe and of its parts, particularly the latter, the beauty and fitness of final causes strike us with such irresistible force that all objections appear (what I believe they really are) mere cavils and sophisms; nor can we then imagine how it was ever possible for us to repose any weight on them. But there is no view of human life or of the condition of mankind from which, without the greatest violence, we can infer the moral attributes or learn that infinite benevolence, conjoined with infinite power and infinite wisdom, which we must discover by the eyes of faith alone. It is your turn now to tug the labouring oar, and to support your philosophical subtleties against the dictates of plain reason and experience.

XI

I scruple not to allow, said Cleanthes, that I have been apt to suspect the frequent repetition of the word *infinite*, which we meet with in all theological writers, to savour more of panegyric than of philosophy, and that any purposes of reasoning, and even of religion, would be better served were we to rest contented with more accurate and more modern expressions. The terms *admirable, excellent, superlatively great, wise,* and *holy*—

these sufficiently fill the imaginations of men, and anything beyond, besides that it leads into absurdities, has no influence on the affections or sentiments. Thus in the present subject, if we abandon all human analogy, as seems your intention, Demea, I am afraid we abandon all religion and retain no conception of the great object of our adoration. If we preserve human analogy, we must forever find it impossible to reconcile any mixture of evil in the universe with infinite attributes; much less can we ever prove the latter from the former. But supposing the Author of nature to be finitely perfect though far exceeding mankind, a satisfactory account may then be given of natural and moral evil, and every untoward phenomenon be explained and adjusted. A lesser evil may then be chosen in order to avoid a greater; inconveniences be submitted to in order to reach a desirable end; and, in a word, benevolence, regulated by wisdom and limited by necessity, may produce just such a world as the present. You, Philo, who are so prompt at starting views and reflections and analogies, I would gladly hear, at length, without interruption, your opinion of this new theory; and if it deserve our attention, we may afterwards, at more leisure, reduce it into form.

My sentiments, replied Philo, are not worth being made a mystery of; and, therefore, without any ceremony, I shall deliver what occurs to me with regard to the present subject. It must, I think, be allowed that, if a very limited intelligence whom we shall suppose utterly unacquainted with the universe were assured that it were the production of a very good, wise, and powerful Being, however finite, he would, from his conjectures, form *beforehand* a different notion of it from what we find it to be by experience; nor would he ever imagine, merely from these attributes of the cause of which he is informed, that the effect could be so full of vice and misery and disorder, as it appears in this life. Supposing now that this person were brought into the world, still assured that

it was the workmanship of such a sublime and benevolent Being, he might, perhaps, be surprised at the disappointment, but would never retract his former belief if founded on any very solid argument, since such a limited intelligence must be sensible of his own blindness and ignorance, and must allow that there may be many solutions of those phenomena which will for ever escape his comprehension. But supposing, which is the real case with regard to man, that this creature is not antecedently convinced of a supreme intelligence, benevolent, and powerful, but is left to gather such a belief from the appearances of things— this entirely alters the case, nor will he ever find any reason for such a conclusion. He may be fully convinced of the narrow limits of his understanding, but this will not help him in forming an inference concerning the goodness of superior powers, since he must form that inference from what he knows, not from what he is ignorant of. The more you exaggerate his weakness and ignorance, the more diffident you render him, and give him the greater suspicion that such subjects are beyond the reach of his faculties. You are obliged, therefore, to reason with him merely from the known phenomena, and to drop arbitrary supposition or conjecture.

Did I show you a house or palace where there was not one apartment convenient or agreeable, where the windows, doors, fires, passages, stairs, and the whole economy of the building were the source of noise, confusion, fatigue, darkness, and the extremes of heat and cold, you would certainly blame the contrivance, without any further examination. The architect would in vain display his subtilty, and prove to you that, if this door or that window were altered, greater ills would ensue. What he says may be strictly true: the alteration of one particular, while the other parts of the building remain, may only augment the inconveniences. But still you would assert in general that, if the architect had had skill and good intentions, he might have formed such a plan of the whole, and might have adjusted the parts in such a manner as would have remedied all or most of these inconveniences. His ignorance, or even your own ignorance of such a plan, will never convince you of the impossibility of it. If you find any inconveniences and deformities in the building, you will always, without entering into any detail, condemn the architect.

In short, I repeat the question: Is the world, considered in general and as it appears to us in this life, different from what a man or such a limited being would, *beforehand*, expect from a very powerful, wise, and benevolent Deity? It must be strange· prejudice to assert the contrary. And from thence I conclude that, however consistent the world may be, allowing certain suppositions and conjectures with the idea of such a Deity, it can never afford us an inference concerning his existence. The consistency is not absolutely denied, only the inference. Conjectures, especially where infinity is excluded from the Divine attributes, may perhaps be sufficient to prove a consistency, but can never be foundations for any inference.

There seem to be *four* circumstances on which depend all or the greatest part of the ills that molest sensible creatures; and it is not impossible but all these circumstances may be necessary and unavoidable. We know so little beyond common life, or even of common life, that, with regard to the economy of a universe, there is no conjecture, however wild, which may not be just, nor any one, however plausible, which may not be erroneous. All that belongs to human understanding, in this deep ignorance and obscurity, is to be skeptical or at least cautious, and not to admit of any hypothesis whatever, much less of any which is supported by no appearance of probability. Now this I assert to be the case with regard to all the causes of evil and the circumstances on which it depends. None of them appear to human reason in the least degree necessary or unavoidable, nor can we suppose them such, without the utmost license of imagination.

The *first* circumstance which introduces evil is that contrivance or economy of the animal creation by which pains, as well as pleasures, are employed to excite all creatures to action, and make them vigilant in the great work of self-preservation. Now pleasure alone, in its various degrees, seems to human understanding sufficient for this purpose. All animals might be constantly in a state of enjoyment; but when urged by any of the necessities of nature, such as thirst, hunger, weariness, instead of pain, they might feel a diminution of pleasure by which they might be prompted to seek that object which is necessary to their subsistence. Men pursue pleasure as eagerly as they avoid pain; at least, they might have been so constituted. It seems, therefore, plainly possible to carry on the business of life without any pain. Why then is any animal ever rendered susceptible of such a sensation? If animals can be free from it an hour, they might enjoy a perpetual exemption from it, and it required as particular a contrivance of their organs to produce that feeling as to endow them with sight, hearing, or any of the senses. Shall we conjecture that such a contrivance was necessary, without any appearance of reason, and shall we build on that conjecture as on the most certain truth?

But a capacity of pain would not alone produce pain were it not for the *second* circumstance, viz., the conducting of the world by general laws; and this seems nowise necessary to a very perfect Being. It is true, if everything were conducted by particular volitions, the course of nature would be perpetually broken, and no man could employ his reason in the conduct of life. But might not other particular volitions remedy this inconvenience? In short, might not the Deity exterminate all ill, wherever it were to be found, and produce all good, without any preparation or long progress of causes and effects?

Besides, we must consider that, according to the present economy of the world, the course of nature, though supposed exactly regular, yet to us appears not so, and many events are uncertain, and many disappoint our expectations. Health and sickness, calm and tempest, with an infinite number of other accidents whose causes are unknown and variable, have a great influence both on the fortunes of particular persons and on the prosperity of public societies; and indeed all human life, in a manner, depends on such accidents. A being, therefore, who knows the secret springs of the universe might easily, by particular volitions, turn all these accidents to the good of mankind and render the whole world happy, without discovering himself in any operation. A fleet whose purposes were salutary to society might always meet a fair wind. Good princes enjoy sound health and long life. Persons born to power and authority be framed with good tempers and virtuous dispositions. A few such events as these, regularly and wisely conducted, would change the face of the world, and yet would no more seem to disturb the course of nature or confound human conduct than the present economy of things where the causes are secret and variable and compounded. Some small touches given to Caligula's brain in his infancy might have converted him into a Trajan. One wave, a little higher than the rest, by burying Caesar and his fortune in the bottom of the ocean, might have restored liberty to a considerable part of mankind. There may, for aught we know, be good reasons why Providence interposes not in this manner, but they are unknown to us; and, though the mere supposition that such reasons exist may be sufficient to *save* the conclusion concerning the Divine attributes, yet surely it can never be sufficient to *establish* that conclusion.

If everything in the universe be conducted by general laws, and if animals be rendered susceptible of pain, it scarcely seems possible but some ill must arise in the various shocks of matter and the various concurrence and opposition of general laws; but this ill would be very rare were it not for the *third* circumstance which I proposed to mention, viz., the great frugality with which all powers and faculties are distributed to every particular being. So well adjusted are the organs and capacities of all animals, and so well fitted to their preservation, that, as far as history or tradition reaches, there appears not to be any single species which has yet been extinguished in the universe. Every animal has the requisite endowments, but these endowments are bestowed with so scrupulous an economy that any considerable diminution must entirely destroy the creature. Wherever one power is increased, there is a proportional abatement in the others. Animals which excel in swiftness are commonly defective in force. Those which possess both are either imperfect in some of their senses or are oppressed with the most craving wants. The human species, whose chief excellence is reason and sagacity, is of all others the most necessitous, and the most deficient in bodily advantages, without clothes, without arms, without food, without lodging, without any convenience of life, except what they owe to their own skill and industry. In short, nature seems to have formed an exact calculation of the necessities of her creatures, and, like a *rigid master*, has afforded them little more powers or endowments than what are strictly sufficient to supply those necessities. An *indulgent parent* would have bestowed a large stock in order to guard against accidents, and secure the happiness and welfare of the creature in the most unfortunate concurrence of circumstances. Every course of life would not have been so surrounded with precipices that the least departure from the true path, by mistake or necessity, must involve us in misery and ruin. Some reserve, some fund, would have been provided to ensure happiness, nor would the powers and the necessities have been adjusted with so rigid an economy. The Author of nature is inconceivably powerful; his force is supposed great, if not altogether inexhaustible, nor is there any reason, as far as we can judge, to make him observe this strict frugality in his dealings with his creatures. It would have been better, were his power extremely limited, to have created fewer animals, and to have endowed these with more faculties for their happiness and preservation. A builder is never esteemed prudent who undertakes a plan beyond what his stock will enable him to finish.

In order to cure most of the ills of human life, I require not that man should have the wings of the eagle, the swiftness of the stag, the force of the ox, the arms of the lion, the scales of the crocodile or rhinoceros; much less do I demand the sagacity of an angel or cherubim. I am contented to take an increase in one single power or faculty of his soul. Let him be endowed with a greater propensity to industry and labour, a more vigorous spring and activity of mind, a more constant bent to business and application. Let the whole species possess naturally an equal diligence with that which many individuals are able to attain by habit and reflection, and the most beneficial consequences, without any allay of ills, is the immediate and necessary result of this endowment. Almost all the moral as well as natural evils of human life arise from idleness; and were our species, by the original constitution of their frame, exempt from this vice or infirmity, the perfect cultivation of land, the improvement of arts and manufactures, the exact execution of every office and duty, immediately follows; and men at once may fully reach that state of society which is so imperfectly attained by the best regulated government. But as industry is a power, and the most valuable of any, nature seems determined, suitably to her usual maxims, to bestow it on men with a very sparing hand, and rather to punish him severely for his deficiency in it than to reward him for his attainments. She has so contrived his frame that nothing but the most violent necessity can oblige him to labour; and she employs all his other wants to overcome, at least in part, the want of diligence, and to endow him with some share of a faculty of which she has thought fit naturally to bereave him. Here our demands may be allowed very humble, and therefore the more reasonable. If we required the endowments of superior penetration and judgment, of a more delicate taste of beauty, of a nicer sensibility to benevolence and friendship, we might be told that we impiously pretend to break the order of nature, that we want to exalt ourselves into a higher rank of being, that the presents which we require, not being suitable to our state and condition, would only be pernicious to us. But it is hard, I dare to repeat it, it is hard that, being placed in a world so full of wants and necessities, where almost every being and element is either our foe or refuses its assistance . . . we should also have our own temper to struggle with, and should be deprived of that faculty which can alone fence against these multiplied evils.

The *fourth* circumstance whence arises the misery and ill of the universe is the inaccurate workmanship of all the springs and principles of the great machine of nature. It must be acknowledged that there are few parts of the universe which seem not to serve some purpose, and whose removal would not produce a visible defect and disorder in the whole. The parts hang all together, nor can one be touched without effecting the rest, in a greater or less degree. But at the same time, it must be observed that none of these parts or principles, however useful, are so accurately adjusted as to keep precisely within those bounds in which their utility consists; but they are, all of them, apt, on every occasion, to run into the one extreme or the other. One would imagine that this grand production had not received the last hand of the maker—so little finished is every part, and so coarse are the strokes with which it is executed. Thus the winds are requisite to convey the vapours along the surface of the globe, and to assist men in navigation; but how often, rising up to tempests and hurricanes, do they become pernicious? Rains are necessary to nourish all the plants and animals of the earth; but how often are they defective? how often excessive? Heat is requisite to all life and vegetation, but is not always found in the due proportion. On the mixture and secretion of the humours and juices of the body depend the health and prosperity of the animal; but the parts perform not regularly their proper function. What more useful than all the passions of the mind, ambition, vanity, love, anger? But how often do they break their bounds and cause the greatest convulsions in society? There is nothing so advantageous in the universe but what frequently becomes pernicious, by its excess or defect; nor has nature guarded, with the requisite accuracy, against all disorder or confusion. The irregularity is never perhaps so great as to destroy any species, but is often sufficient to involve the individuals in ruin and misery.

On the concurrence, then, of these *four* circumstances does all or the greatest part of natural evil depend. Were all living creatures incapable of pain, or were the world administered by particular volitions, evil never could have found access into the universe; and were animals endowed with a large stock of powers and faculties, beyond what strict necessity requires, or were the several springs and principles of the universe so accurately framed as to preserve always the just temperament and medium, there must have been very little ill in comparison of what we feel at present. What then shall we pronounce on this occasion? Shall we say that these circumstances are not necessary, and that they might easily have been altered in the contrivance of the universe? This decision seems too presumptuous for creatures so blind and ignorant. Let us be more modest in our conclusions. Let us allow that, if the goodness of the Deity (I mean a goodness like the human) could be established on any tolerable reasons *a priori*, these phenomena, however untoward, would not be sufficient to subvert that principle, but might easily, in some unknown manner, be reconcilable to it. But let us still assert that, as this goodness is not antecedently established but must be inferred from the phenomena, there can be no grounds for such an inference while there are so many ills in the universe, and while these ills might so easily have been remedied, as far as human understanding can be allowed to judge on such a subject. I am sceptic enough to allow that the bad appearances, notwithstanding all my reasonings, may be compatible with such attributes as you suppose, but surely they can never prove these attributes. Such a conclusion cannot result from scepticism, but must arise from the phenomena, and from our confidence in the reasonings which we deduce from these phenomena.

Look round this universe. What an immense profusion of beings animated and organized, sensible and active! You admire this prodigious variety and fecundity. But inspect a little more narrowly these living existences, the only beings worth regarding. How hostile and destructive to each other! How insufficient all of them for their own happiness! How contemptible or odious to the spectator! The whole presents nothing but the idea of a blind nature, impregnated by a great vivifying principle, and pouring forth from her lap, without discernment or parental care, her maimed and abortive children!

Here the Manichaean system occurs as a proper hypothesis to solve the difficulty; and, no doubt, in some respects it is very specious and has more probability than the common hypothesis, by giving a plausible account of the strange mixture of good and ill which appears in life. But if we consider, on the other hand, the perfect uniformity and agreement of the parts of the universe, we shall not discover in it any marks of the combat of a malevolent with a benevolent being. There is indeed an opposition of pains and pleasures in the feelings of sensible creatures; but are not all the operations of nature carried on by an opposition of principles, of hot and cold, moist and dry, light and heavy? The true conclusion is that the original Source of all things is entirely indifferent to all these principles, and has no more regard to good above ill than to heat above cold, or to drought above moisture, or to light above heavy.

There may *four* hypotheses be framed concerning the first causes of the universe: that they are endowed with perfect goodness; that they have perfect malice; that they are opposite and have both goodness and malice; that they have neither goodness nor malice. Mixed phenomena can never prove the two former unmixed principles; and the uniformity and steadiness of general laws seem to oppose the third. The fourth, therefore, seems by far the most probable.

What I have said concerning natural evil will apply to moral with little or no variation; and we have no more reason to infer that the rectitude of the Supreme Being resembles human rectitude than that his benevolence resembles the human. Nay, it will be thought that we have still greater cause to exclude from him moral sentiments, such as we feel them, since moral evil, in the opinion of many, is much more predominant above moral good than natural evil above natural good.

But even though this should not be allowed, and though the virtue which is in mankind should be acknowledged much superior to the vice, yet, so long as there is any vice at all in the universe, it will very much puzzle you anthropomorphites how to account for it. You must assign a cause for it, without having recourse to the first cause. But as every effect must have a cause, and that cause another, you must either carry on the progression in *infinitum* or rest on that original principle, who is the ultimate cause of all things. . . .

Hold! hold! cried Demea: Whither does your imagination hurry you? I joined in alliance with you in order to prove the incomprehensible nature of the Divine Being, and refute the principles of Cleanthes, who would measure everything by human rule and standard. But I now find you running into all the topics of the greatest libertines and infidels, and betraying that holy cause which you seemingly espoused. Are you secretly, then, a more dangerous enemy than Cleanthes himself?

And are you so late in perceiving it? replied Cleanthes. Believe me, Demea, your friend Philo, from the beginning, has been amusing himself at both our expense; and it must be confessed that the injudicious reasoning of our vulgar theology has given him but too just a handle of ridicule. The total infirmity of human reason, the absolute incomprehensibility of the Divine Nature, the great and universal misery, and still greater wickedness of men—these are strange topics, surely, to be so fondly cherished by orthodox divines and doctors. In ages of stupidity and ignorance, indeed, these principles may safely be espoused; and perhaps no views of things are more proper to promote superstition than such as encourage the blind amazement, the diffidence, and melancholy of mankind. But at present . . .

Blame not so much, interposed Philo, the ignorance of these reverend gentlemen. They know how to change their style with the times. Formerly, it was a most popular theological topic to maintain that human life was vanity and misery, and to exaggerate all the ills and pains which are incident to men. But of late years, divines, we find, begin to retract this position and maintain, though still with some hesitation, that there are more goods than evils, more pleasures than pains, even in this life. When religion stood entirely upon temper and education, it was thought proper to encourage melancholy, as indeed, mankind never have recourse to superior powers so readily as in that disposition. But as men have now learned to form principles and to draw consequences, it is necessary to change the batteries, and to make use of such arguments as will endure at least some scrutiny and examination. This variation is the same (and from the same causes) with that which I formerly remarked with regard to scepticism.

Thus Philo continued to the last

his spirit of opposition, and his censure of established opinions. But I could observe that Demea did not at all relish the latter part of the discourse; and he took occasion soon after, on some pretence or other, to leave the company.

A Critique of Hume
NELSON PIKE

*I*n parts *X and XI* of the *Dialogues Concerning Natural Religion*, Hume sets forth his views on the traditional theological problem of evil. Hume's remarks on this topic seem to me to contain a rich mixture of insight and oversight. It will be my purpose in this paper to disentangle these contrasting elements of his discussion.[1]

PHILO'S FIRST POSITION
(A) God, according to the traditional Christian view put forward by Cleanthes in the *Dialogues*, is all-powerful, all-knowing, and perfectly good. And it is clear that for Cleanthes, the terms "powerful," "knowing," and "good" apply to God in exactly the same sense in which these terms apply to men. Philo argues as follows. If God is to be all-powerful, all-knowing, and perfectly good (using all key terms in their ordinary sense), then to claim that God exists is to preclude the possibility of admitting that there occur instances of evil; that is, is to preclude the possibility of admitting that there occur instances of suffering, pain, superstition, wickedness, and so forth.[2] The statements "God exists" and

"There occur instances of suffering" are logically incompatible. Of course, no one could deny that there occur instances of suffering. Such a denial would plainly conflict with common experience.[3] Thus it follows from obvious fact that God (having the attributes assigned to Him by Cleanthes) does not exist.

This argument against the existence of God has enjoyed considerable popularity since Hume wrote the *Dialogues*. Concerning the traditional theological problem of evil, F. H. Bradley comments as follows:

The trouble has come from the idea that the Absolute is a moral person. If you start from that basis, then the relation of evil to the Absolute presents at once an irreducible dilemma. The problem then becomes insoluble, but not because it is obscure or in any way mysterious. To

---

[1] See preceding essay.

[2] It is clear that, for Philo, the term "evil" is used simply as a tag for the class containing all instances of suffering, pain and so on. Philo offers no analysis of "evil" nor does his challenge to Cleanthes rest in the

least on the particularities of the logic of this term. At one point in Part X, for example, Philo formulates his challenge to Cleanthes without using "evil." Here he speaks only of *misery*. In what is to follow, I shall (following Hume) make little use of "evil." Also, I shall use "suffering" as short for "suffering pain, superstition, wickedness, and so on."

[3] Had Philo been dealing with "evil" (defined in some special way) instead of "suffering," this move in the argument might not have been open to him.

FROM: *The Philosophical Review*, Vol. LXXII, No. 2 (1963). Reprinted by permission of the editors of *The Philosophical Review* and the author.

anyone who has the sense and courage to see things as they are, and is resolved not to mystify others or himself, there is really no question to discuss. The dilemma is plainly insoluble because it is based on a clear self-contradiction.[4]

John Stuart Mill,[5] J. E. McTaggart,[6] Antony Flew,[7] H. D. Aiken,[8] J. L. Mackie,[9] C. J. Ducasse,[10] and H. J. McCloskey[11] are but a few of the many others who have echoed Philo's finalistic dismissal of traditional theism after making reference to the logical incompatibility of "God exists" and "There occur instances of suffering." W. T. Stace refers to Hume's discussion of the matter as follows:

(Assuming that "good" and "powerful" are used in theology as they are used in ordinary discourse), we have to say that Hume was right. The charge has never been answered and never will be. The simultaneous attribution of all-power and all-goodness to the Creator of the whole world is logically incompatible with the existence of evil and pain in the world, for which reason the conception of a

[4] *Appearance and Reality* (London: Oxford University Press, 1930), p. 174. Italics mine.

[5] *Theism* (New York: The Liberal Arts Press, 1957), p. 40. See also *The Utility of Religion* (New York: The Liberal Arts Press, 1957), pp. 73ff.

[6] *Some Dogmas of Religion* (London: Edward Arnold, Ltd., 1906), pp. 212f.

[7] "Theology and Falsification," in *New Essays in Philosophical Theology*, A. Flew and A. MacIntyre, eds. (New York: The Macmillan Company, 1955), p. 108.

[8] "God and Evil: Some Relations Between Faith and Morals," *Ethics*, Vol. LXVIII (1958), p. 77ff.

[9] "Evil and Omnipotence," *Mind*, Vol. LXIV (1955).

[10] *A Philosophical Scrutiny of Religion* (New York: The Ronald Press Company, 1953), Chap. 16.

[11] "God and Evil," *The Philosophical Quarterly*, Vol. X (1960).

finite God, who is not all-powerful . . . has become popular in some quarters.[12]

In the first and second sections of this paper, I shall argue that the argument against the existence of God presented in Part X of the *Dialogues* is quite unconvincing. It is not clear at all that "God exists" and "There occur instances of suffering" are logically incompatible statements.

(B) Moving now to the details of the matter, we may, I think, formulate Philo's first challenge to Cleanthes as follows:

(1) The world contains instances of suffering.

(2) God exists—and is omnipotent and omniscient.

(3) God exists—and is perfectly good.

According to the view advanced by Philo, these three statements constitute an "inconsistent triad". Any two of them might be held together. But if any two of them are endorsed, the third must be denied. Philo argues that to say of God that he is omnipotent and omniscient is to say that he *could* prevent suffering if he wanted to. Unless God could prevent suffering, he would not qualify as both omnipotent and omniscient. But, Philo continues, to say of God that he is perfectly good is to say that God *would* prevent suffering if he could. A being who would not prevent suffering when it was within his power to do so would not qualify as perfectly good. Thus, to affirm propositions (2) and (3) is to affirm the existence of a being who both could prevent suffering if he wanted to and who would prevent suffering if he could. This, of course, is to deny the truth of proposition (1). By similar reasoning, Philo would insist, to affirm (1) and (2) is to deny the truth of (3). And to affirm (1) and (3) is to deny the truth of (2). But, as conceived by

[12] *Time and Eternity* (Princeton: Princeton University Press, 1952), p. 56.

Cleanthes, God is both omnipotent-omniscient and perfectly good. Thus, as understood by Cleanthes, "God exists" and "There occur instances of suffering" are logically incompatible statements. Since the latter of these statements is obviously true, the former must be false. Philo reflects: "Nothing can shake the solidity of this reasoning, so short, so clear (and) so decisive".

It seems to me that this argument is deficient. I do not think it follows from the claim that a being is perfectly good that he would prevent suffering if he could.

Consider this case. A parent forces a child to take a spoonful of bitter medicine. The parent thus brings about an instance of discomfort—suffering. The parent could have refrained from administering the medicine; and he knew that the child would suffer discomfort if he did administer it. Yet, when we are assured that the parent acted in the interest of the child's health and happiness, the fact that he knowingly caused discomfort is not sufficient to remove the parent from the class of perfectly good beings. If the parent fails to fit into this class, it is not because he caused *this* instance of suffering.

Given only that the parent knowingly caused an instance of discomfort, we are tempted to *blame* him for his action—that is, to exclude him from the class of perfectly good beings. But when the full circumstances are known, blame becomes inappropriate. In this case, there is what I shall call a "morally sufficient reason" for the parent's action. To say that there is a morally sufficient reason for his action is simply to say that there is a circumstance or condition which, when known, renders *blame* (though, of course, not *responsibility*) for the action inappropriate. As a general statement, a being who permits (or brings about) an instance of suffering might be perfectly good providing only that there is a morally sufficient reason for his action. Thus, it does not follow from the claim that God is perfectly good that he would prevent suffering if he could. God might

fail to prevent suffering or himself bring about suffering, while remaining perfectly good. It is required only that there be a morally sufficient reason for his action.

(C) In the light of these reflections, let us now attempt to put Philo's challenge to Cleanthes in sharper form.

(4) The world contains instances of suffering.

(5) God exists—and is omnipotent, omniscient, and perfectly good.

(6) An omnipotent and omniscient being would have no morally sufficient reason for allowing instances of suffering.

This sequence is logically tight. Suppose (6) and (4) true. If an omnipotent and omniscient being would have no morally sufficient reason for allowing instances of suffering, then, in a world containing such instances, either there would be no omnipotent and omniscient being or that being would be blameworthy. On either of these last alternatives, proposition (5) would be false. Thus, if (6) and (4) are true, (5) must be false. In similar fashion, suppose (6) and (5) true. If an omnipotent and omniscient being would have no morally sufficient reason for allowing suffering, then, if there existed an omnipotent and omniscient being who was also perfectly good, there would occur no suffering. Thus, if (6) and (5) are true, (4) must be false. Lastly, suppose (5) and (4) true. If there existed an omnipotent and omniscient being who was also perfectly good, then if there occurred suffering, the omnipotent and omniscient being (being also perfectly good) would have to have a morally sufficient reason for permitting it. Thus, if (5) and (4) are true, (6) must be false.

Now, according to Philo (and all others concerned), proposition (4) is surely true. And proposition (6)—well, what about proposition (6)? At this point, two observations are needed.

First, it would not serve Philo's purpose were he to argue the truth of proposition (6) by enumerating a number of reasons for permitting suffering (which might be assigned to an omnipotent and omniscient being) and then by showing that in each case the reason offered is not a morally sufficient reason (when assigned to an omnipotent and omniscient being). Philo could never claim to have explained all of the possibilities. And at any given point in the argument, Cleanthes could always claim that God's reason for permitting suffering is one which Philo has not yet considered. A retreat to unexamined reasons would remain open to Cleanthes regardless of how complete the list of examined reasons seemed to be.

Second, the position held by Philo in Part X of the *Dialogues* demands that he affirm proposition (6) as a *necessary truth*. If this is not already clear, consider the following inconsistent triad.

(7) All swans are white.
(8) Some swans are not large.
(9) All white things are large.

Suppose (9) true, but not necessarily true. Either (7) or (8) must be false. But the conjunction of (7) and (8) is not contradictory. If the conjunction of (7) and (8) were contradictory, then (9) would be necessary truth. Thus, unless (9) is a necessary truth, the conjunction of (7) and (8) is not contradictory. Note what happens to this antilogism when "colored" is substituted for "large." Now (9) becomes a necessary truth and, correspondingly, (7) and (8) become logically incompatible. The same holds for the inconsistent triad we are now considering. As already discovered, Philo holds that "There are instances of suffering" (proposition 4) and "God exists" (proposition 5) are logically incompatible. But (4) and (5) will be logically incompatible only if (6) is a necessary truth. Thus, if Philo is to argue that (4) and (5) are logically incompatible, he must be prepared to affirm (6) as a necessary truth.

We may now reconstitute Philo's challenge to the position held by Cleanthes.

Proposition (4) is obviously true. No one could deny that there occur in-

stances of suffering. But proposition (6) is a necessary truth. An omnipotent and omniscient being would have no morally sufficient reason for allowing instances of suffering—just as a bachelor would have no wife. Thus, there exists no being who is, at once, omnipotent, omniscient, and perfectly good. Proposition (5) must be false.

(D) This is a formidable challenge to Cleanthes' position. Its strength can best be exposed by reflecting on some of the circumstances or conditions which, in ordinary life, and with respect to ordinary agents, are usually counted as morally sufficient reasons for failing to prevent (or relieve) some given instance of suffering. Let me list five such reasons.

First, consider an agent who lacked physical ability to prevent some instance of suffering. Such an agent could claim to have had a morally sufficient reason for not preventing the instance in question.

Second, consider an agent who lacked knowledge of (or the means of knowing about) a given instance of suffering. Such an agent could claim to have had a morally sufficient reason for not preventing the suffering, even if (on all other counts) he had the ability to prevent it.

Third, consider an agent who knew of an instance of suffering and had the physical ability to prevent it, but did not *realize* that he had this ability. Such an agent could usually claim to have had a morally sufficient reason for not preventing the suffering. Example: if I push the button on the wall, the torment of the man in the next room will cease. I have the physical ability to push the button. I know that the man in the next room is in pain. But I do not know that pushing the button will relieve the torment. I do not push the button and thus do not relieve the suffering.

Fourth, consider an agent who had the ability to prevent an instance of suffering, knew of the suffering, knew that he had the ability to prevent it, but did not prevent it because he believed (rightly or wrongly) that to do so would be to fail to effect some future good which would outweigh the negative value of the suffering. Such an agent might well claim to have had a morally sufficient reason for not preventing the suffering. Example: go back to the case of the parent causing discomfort by administering bitter medicine to the child.

Fifth, consider an agent who had the ability to prevent an instance of suffering, knew of the suffering, knew that he had the ability to prevent it, but failed to prevent it because to do so would have involved his preventing a prior good which outweighed the negative value of the suffering. Such an agent might claim to have had a morally sufficient reason for not preventing the suffering. Example: a parent permits a child to eat some birthday cake knowing that his eating the cake will result in the child's feeling slightly ill later in the day. The parent estimates that the child's pleasure of the moment outweighs the discomfort which will result.

Up to this point, Philo would insist, we have not hit on a circumstance or condition which could be used by Cleanthes when constructing a "theodicy," that is, when attempting to identify the morally sufficient reason God has for permitting instances of suffering.

The first three entries on the list are obviously not available. Each makes explicit mention of some lack of knowledge or power on the part of the agent. Nothing more need be said about them. A theologian might, however, be tempted to use a reason for the fourth type when constructing a theodicy. He might propose that suffering *results in goods* which outweigh the negative value of the suffering. Famine (hunger) leads man to industry and progress. Disease (pain) leads man to knowledge and understanding. Philo suggests that no theodicy of this kind can be successful. An omnipotent and omniscient being could find other means of bringing about the same results. The mere fact that evils give rise to goods cannot serve as a morally sufficient reason for an omnipotent and omniscient being to permit suffering.

A theologian might also be tempted to use reasons of the fifth type when constructing a theodicy. He might propose that instances of suffering *result from goods* which outweigh the negative value of the suffering. That the world is run in accordance with natural law is good. But any such regular operation will result in suffering. That men have the ability to make free choices is good. But free choice will sometimes result in wrong choice and suffering. Philo argues that it is not at all clear that a world run in accordance with natural law is better than one not so regulated. And one might issue a similar challenge with respect to free will. But a more general argument has been offered in the contemporary literature on evil which is exactly analogous to the one suggested by Philo above. According to H. J. McCloskey, an omnipotent and omniscient being could devise a law-governed world which would not include suffering.[13] And according to J. L. Mackie, an omnipotent and omniscient being could create a world containing free agents which would include no suffering or wrong-doing.[14] The import of both of these suggestions is that an omnipotent and omniscient being could create a world containing whatever is good (regularity, free will, and so on) without allowing the suffering which (only factually) results from these goods. The mere fact that suffering results from good cannot serve as a morally sufficient reason for an omnipotent and omniscient being to allow suffering.

Though the above reflections may be far from conclusive, let us grant that, of the morally sufficient reasons so far considered, none could be assigned to an omnipotent and omniscient being. This, of course, is not to say that proposition (6) is true—let alone necessarily true. As mentioned earlier, proposition (6) will not be shown true by an enumerative procedure of the above kind. But consider the matter less rigorously.

---

[13] "God and Evil."

[14] "Evil and Omnipotence."

If none of the reasons so far considered could be assigned to an omnipotent and omniscient being, ought this not to raise a suspicion? Might there not be a principle operating in each of these reasons which guarantees that *no* morally sufficient reason for permitting suffering *could* be assigned to an omnipotent and omniscient being? Such a principle immediately suggests itself. Men are sometimes excused for allowing suffering. But in these cases, men are excused only because they lack the knowledge or power to prevent suffering, or because they lack the knowledge or power to bring about goods (which are causally related to suffering) without also bringing about suffering. In other words, men are excusable only because they are limited. Having a morally sufficient reason for permitting suffering *entails* having some lack of knowledge or power. If this principle is sound (and, indeed, it is initially plausible) then proposition (6) must surely be listed as a necessary truth.

DEMEA'S THEODICY

But the issue is not yet decided. Demea has offered a theodicy which does not fit any of the forms outlined above. And Philo must be willing to consider all proposals if he is to claim "decisiveness" for his argument against Cleanthes.

Demea reasons as follows:

This world is but a point in comparison of the universe; this life but a moment in comparison of eternity. The present evil phenomena, therefore, are rectified in other regions, and in some future period of existence. And the eyes of men, being then opened to larger views of things, see the whole connection of general laws, and trace with adoration, the benevolence and rectitude of the Deity through all mazes and intricacies of his providence.

It might be useful if we had a second statement of this theodicy, one taken from a traditional theological source. In Chapter LXXI of the *Summa Contra Gentiles*, St. Thomas argues as follows:

The good of the whole is of more account than the good of the part. Therefore, it belongs to a prudent governor to overlook a lack of goodness in a part, that there may be an increase of goodness in the whole. Thus, the builder hides the foundation of a house underground, that the whole house may stand firm. Now, if evil were taken away from certain parts of the universe, the perfection of the universe would be much diminished, since its beauty results from the ordered unity of good and evil things, seeing that evil arises from the failure of good, and yet certain goods are occasioned from those very evils through the providence of the governor, even as the silent pause gives sweetness to the chant. Therefore, evil should not be excluded from things by the divine providence.

Neither of these statements seems entirely satisfactory. Demea might be suggesting that the world is good on the whole—that the suffering we discover in our world is, as it were, made up for in other regions of creation. God here appears as the husband who beats his wife on occasion but makes up for it with favors at other times. In St. Thomas' statement, there are unmistakable hints of causal reasoning. Certain goods are "occasioned" by evils, as the foundation of the house permits the house to stand firm. But in both of these statements another theme is at least suggested. Let me state and explain it in my own way without pretense of historical accuracy.

I have a set of ten wooden blocks. There is a T-shaped block, an L-shaped block, an F-shaped block, and so on. No two blocks have the same shape. Let us assign each block a value—say an aesthetic value—making the T-shaped block most valuable and the L-shaped block least valuable. Now the blocks may be fitted together into formations. And let us suppose that the blocks are so shaped that there is one and only one subset of the blocks which will fit together into a square. The L-shaped block is a member of that subset. Further, let us stipulate that any formation of blocks (consisting of two or more blocks fitted together) will have more aesthetic value than any of the blocks taken individually or any subset of the blocks taken as a mere collection. And, as a last assumption, let us say that the square formation has greater aesthetic value than any other logically possible block formation. The L-shaped block is a necessary component of the square formation; that is, the L-shaped block is logically indispensable to the square formation. Thus the L-shaped block is a necessary component of the best of all possible block formations. Hence, the block with the least aesthetic value is logically indispensable to the best of all possible block formations. Without this very block, it would be logically impossible to create the best of all possible block formations.

Working from this model, let us understand Demea's theodicy as follows. Put aside the claim that instances of suffering are *de facto* causes or consequences of greater goods. God, being a perfectly good, omniscient, and omnipotent being, would create the best of all possible worlds. But the best of all possible worlds must contain instances of suffering: they are logically indispensable components. This is why there are instances of suffering in the world which God created.

What shall we say about this theodicy? Philo expresses no opinion on the subject.

Consider this reply to Demea's reasonings. A world containing instances of suffering as necessary components might be the best of all possible worlds. And if a world containing instances of suffering as necessary components were the best of all possible worlds, an omnipotent and omniscient being would have a morally sufficient reason for permitting instances of suffering. But how are we to know that, in fact, instances of suffering are logically indispensable components of the best of all possible worlds? There would appear to be no way of establishing this claim short of assuming that God does in fact exist and then concluding (as did Leibniz) that the world (containing suffering) which he did in fact create is the best of all possible

worlds. But, this procedure assumes that God exists. And this latter is precisely the question now at issue.

It seems to me that this reply to Demea's theodicy has considerable merit. First, my hypothetical objector is probably right in suggesting that the only way one could show that the best of all possible worlds must contain instances of suffering would be via the above argument in which the existence of God is assumed. Second, I think my objector is right in allowing that if instances of suffering were logically indispensable components of the best of all possible worlds, this would provide a morally sufficient reason for an omnipotent and omniscient being to permit instances of suffering. And, third, I think that my objector exhibits considerable discretion in not challenging the claim that the best of all possible worlds *might* contain instances of suffering as necessary components. I know of no argument which will show this claim to be true. But on the other hand, I know of no argument which will show this claim to be false. (I shall elaborate this last point directly.)

Thus, as I have said, the above evaluation of the theodicy advanced by Demea seems to have considerable merit. But this evaluation, *if correct*, seems to be sufficient to refute Philo's claim that "God exists" and "There occur instances of suffering" are logically incompatible statements. If instances of suffering were necessary components of the best of all possible worlds, then an omnipotent and omniscient being would have a morally sufficient reason for permitting instances of suffering. Thus, if it is *possible* that instances of suffering are necessary components of the best of all possible worlds, then there *might be* a morally sufficient reason for an omnipotent and omniscient being to permit instances of suffering. Thus if the statement "Instances of suffering are necessary components of the best of all possible worlds" is not contradictory, then proposition (6) is not a necessary truth. And, as we have seen, if proposition (6) is not a necessary truth, then "God exists" and "There occur instances of suffering" are not logically incompatible statements.

What shall we say? Is the statement "Instances of suffering are logically indispensable components of the best of all possible worlds" contradictory? That it is is simply assumed in Philo's first position. But, surely, this is not a trivial assumption. If it is correct, it must be shown to be so; it is not *obviously* correct. And how shall we argue that it is correct? Shall we, for example, assume that any case of suffering contained in any complex of events detracts from the value of the complex? If this principle were analytic, then a world containing an instance of suffering could not be the best of all possible worlds. But G. E. Moore has taught us to be suspicious of any such principle.[15] And John Wisdom has provided a series of counterexamples which tend to show that this very principle is, in fact, not analytic. Example: if I believe (rightly or wrongly) that you are in pain and become unhappy as a result of that belief, the resulting complex would appear to be better by virtue of my unhappiness (suffering) than it would have been had I believed you to be in pain but had not become unhappy (or had become happy) as a result.[16] Philo's argument against the existence of God is not finished. And it is not at all obvious that it is *capable* of effective completion. It is, I submit, far from clear that God and evil could not exist together in the same universe.

PHILO'S SECOND POSITION

At the end of Part X, Philo agrees to "retire" from his first position. He now concedes that "God exists" and "There occur instances of suffering" are not logically incompatible statements. (It is clear from the context that this adjustment in Philo's thinking is made only for purposes of argument and

[15] I refer here to Moore's discussion of "organic unities" in *Principia Ethica* (London: Macmillan & Co., Ltd., 1903), pp. 28ff.

[16] "God and Evil," *Mind*, Vol. XLIV (1935), 13f. I have modified Wisdom's example slightly.

not because Hume senses any inadequacy in Philo's first position.) Most contemporary philosophers think that Hume's major contribution to the literature on evil was made in Part X of the *Dialogues*. But it seems to me that what is of really lasting value in Hume's reflections on this subject is to be found not in Part X, but in the discussion in Part XI which follows Philo's "retirement" from his first position.

(A) Consider, first of all, a theology in which the existence of God is accepted on the basis of what is taken to be a conclusive (a priori) demonstration. (A theology in which the existence of God is taken as an item of faith can be considered here as well.) On this view, that God exists is a settled matter, not subject to review or challenge. It is, as it were, axiomatic to further theological debate. According to Philo, evil in the world presents no special problem for a theology of this sort:

Let us allow that, if the goodness of the Deity (I mean a goodness like the human) could be established on any tolerable reasons a priori, these (evil) phenomena, however untoward, would not be sufficient to subvert that principle, but might easily, in some unknown manner, be reconcilable to it.

This point, I think, is essentially correct, but it must be put more firmly.

Recalling the remarks advanced when discussing the inconsistent nature of propositions (4) through (6) above, a theologian who accepts the existence of God (either as an item of faith or on the basis of an a priori argument) must conclude either that there is some morally sufficient reason for God's allowing suffering in the world, or that there are no instances of suffering in the world. He will, of course, choose the first alternative. Thus, in a theology of the sort now under consideration, the theologian begins by affirming the existence of God and by acknowledging the occurrence of suffering. It follows *logically* that God has some morally sufficient reason for allowing instances of suffering. The conclusion is not, as Philo suggests, that there *might be* a morally sufficient reason for evil. The conclusion is, rather, that there *must be* such a reason. It *could not be otherwise.*

What then of the traditional theological problem of evil? Within a theology of the above type, the problem of evil can only be the problem of discovering a *specific* theodicy which is adequate —that is, of discovering which, if any, of the specific proposals which might be advanced really describes God's morally sufficient reason for allowing instances of suffering. This problem, of course, is not a major one for the theologian. If the problem of evil is simply the problem of uncovering the specific reason for evil— given assurance that there is (and must be) some such reason—it can hardly be counted as a critical problem. Once it is granted that there is some specific reason for evil, there is a sense in which it is no longer vital to find it. A theologian of the type we are now considering might never arrive at a satisfactory theodicy. (Philo's "unknown" reason might remain forever unknown.) He might condemn as erroneous all existing theodices and might despair of ever discovering the morally sufficient reason in question. A charge of incompleteness would be the worst that could be leveled at his world view.

(B) Cleanthes is not, of course, a theologian of the sort just described. He does not accept the existence of God as an item of faith, nor on the basis of an a priori argument. In the *Dialogues*, Cleanthes supports his theological position with an a posteriori argument from design. He argues that "order" in the universe provides sufficient evidence that the world was created by an omnipotent, omniscient, and perfectly good being.[17]

He proposes the existence of God as a quasi-scientific explanatory hypothesis, arguing its truth via the claim that it provides an adequate explanation for observed facts.

Philo has two comments to make regarding the relevance of suffering in the world for a theology of this kind.

The first is a comment with which Philo is obviously well pleased. It is offered at the end of Part X and is repeated no less than three times in Part XI. It is this: even if the existence of God and the occurrence of suffering in the world are logically compatible, one cannot argue from a world containing suffering to the existence of an omnipotent, omniscient, and perfectly good creator. This observation, I think all would agree, is correct. Given only a painting containing vast areas of green, one could not effectively argue that its creator disliked using green. There would be no *logical* conflict in holding that a painter who disliked using green painted a picture containing vast areas of green. But given *only* the picture (and no further information), the hypothesis that its creator disliked using green would be poorly supported indeed.

It is clear that in this first comment Philo has offered a criticism of Cleanthes' *argument* for the existence of God. He explicitly says that this complaint is against Cleanthes' *inference* from a world containing instances of suffering to the existence of an omnipotent, omniscient, and perfectly good creator. Philo's second comment, however, is more forceful than this. It is a challenge of the *truth* of Cleanthes' *hypothesis.*

Philo argues as follows:

Look round this universe. What an immense profusion of beings, animated and organized, sensible and active! You admire this prodigious variety and fecun-

---

[17] It is interesting to notice that, in many cases, theologians who have used an argument from design have not attempted to argue that "order" in the world proves the existence of a perfectly moral being. For example, in St. Thomas' "fifth way" and in William Paley's *Natural Theology*, "order" is used to show only that the creator of the world was *intelligent*. There are, however,

historical instances of the argument from design being used to prove the goodness as well as the intelligence of a creator. For example, Bishop Berkeley argues this way in the second of the *Dialogues Between Hylas and Philonous.*

dity. But inspect a little more narrowly these living existences, the only beings worth regarding. How hostile and destructive to each other! How insufficient all of them for their own happiness! . . . There is indeed an opposition of pains and pleasures in the feelings of sensible creatures; but are not all the operations of nature carried on by an opposition of principles, of hot and cold, moist and dry, light and heavy! The true conclusion is that the original Source of all things is entirely indifferent to all these principles, and has no more regard to good above ill than to heat above cold, or to drought above moisture, or to light above heavy.

Philo claims that *there is* an "original Source of all things" and that this source is indifferent with respect to matters of good and evil. He pretends to be inferring this conclusion from observed data. This represents a departure from Philo's much professed skepticism in the *Dialogues*. And, no doubt, many of the criticisms of Cleanthes' position which Philo advanced earlier in the *Dialogues* would apply with equal force to the inference Philo has just offered. But I shall not dwell on this last point. I think the center of Philo's remarks in this passage must be located in their skeptical rather than their metaphysical import. Philo has proposed a hypothesis which is counter to the one offered by Cleanthes. And he claims that his hypothesis is the "true conclusion" to be drawn from the observed data. But the point is not, I think, that Philo's new hypothesis is true, or even probable. The conclusion is, rather, that the hypothesis advanced by Cleanthes is false, or very improbable. When claiming that evil in the world *supports* a hypothesis which is counter to the one offered by Cleanthes, I think Philo simply means to be calling attention to the fact that evil in the world provides *evidence against* Cleanthes' theological position.

Consider the following analogy which, I think, will help expose this point. I am given certain astronomical data. In order to explain the data, I introduce the hypothesis that there exists a planet which has not yet been observed but will be observable at such and such a place in the sky at such and such a time. No other hypothesis seems as good. The anticipated hour arrives and the telescopes are trained on the designated area. No planet appears. Now, either one of two conclusions may be drawn. First, I might conclude that there is no planet there to be seen. This requires either that I reject the original astronomical data or that I admit that what seemed the best explanation of the data is not, in fact, the true explanation. Second, I might conclude that there is a planet there to be seen, but that something in the observational set-up went amiss. Perhaps the equipment was faulty, perhaps there were clouds, and so on. Which conclusion is correct? The answer is not straightforward. I must check both possibilities.

Suppose I find nothing in the observational set-up which is in the least out of order. My equipment is in good working condition, I find no clouds, and so on. To decide to retain the planet hypothesis in the face of the recalcitrant datum (my failure to observe the planet) is, in part, to decide that there is some circumstance (as yet unknown) which explains the datum *other* than the nonexistence of the planet in question. But a decision to retain the planet hypothesis (in the face of my failure to observe the planet and in the absence of an explicit explanation which "squares" this failure with the planet hypothesis) is made correctly *only* when the *evidence for* the planet hypothesis is such as to render its negation less plausible than would be the assumption of a (as yet unknown) circumstance which explains the observation failure. This, I think, is part of the very notion of dealing reasonably with an explanatory hypothesis.

Now Cleanthes has introduced the claim that there exists an omnipotent, omniscient, and perfectly good being as a way of explaining "order" in the world. And Philo, throughout the *Dialogues* (up to and including most of Part XI), has been concerned to show that this procedure provides very little (if any) solid evidence for the existence of God. The inference from the data to the hypothesis is extremely tenuous. Philo is now set for his final thrust at Cleanthes' position. Granting that God and evil are not logically incompatible, the existence of human suffering in the world must still be taken as a recalcitrant datum with respect to Cleanthes' hypothesis. Suffering, as Philo says, is not what we should antecedently expect in a world created by an omnipotent, omniscient, and perfectly good being. Since Cleanthes has offered nothing in the way of an explicit theodicy (that is, an explanation of the recalcitrant datum which would "square" it with his hypothesis) and since the *evidence for* his hypothesis is extremely weak and generally ineffective, there is pretty good reason for thinking that Cleanthes' hypothesis is false.

This, I think, is the skeptical import of Philo's closing remarks in Part XI. On this reading nothing is said about an "original Source of all things" which is indifferent with respect to matters of good and evil. Philo is simply making clear the negative force of the fact of evil in the world for a hypothesis such as the one offered by Cleanthes.

It ought not to go unnoticed that Philo's closing attack on Cleanthes' position has extremely limited application. Evil in the world has central negative importance for theology only when theology is approached as a quasi-scientific subject, as by Cleanthes. That it is seldom approached in this way will be evident to anyone who has studied the history of theology. Within most theological positions, the existence of God is taken as an item of faith or embraced on the basis of an a priori argument. Under these circumstances, where there is nothing to qualify as a "hypothesis" capable of having either negative or positive "evidence," the fact of evil in the world presents no special problem for theology. As Philo himself has suggested, when the existence of God is accepted prior to any rational consideration of the status of evil in the world, the traditional problem of evil reduces to a noncrucial perplexity of relatively minor importance.

On the Failure of All Philosophical Essays in Theodicy
IMMANUEL KANT

*B*y a *theodicée* is understood the defense of the supreme wisdom of the Author of the world against the accusation of that wisdom by reason, from what is contrary-to-end in the world.—This is named, defending the cause of God; though at bottom it may be nothing more than the cause of our assuming reason, mistaking its limits, which cause is not indeed the very best one, but must be so far approved, as (setting aside that self-conceit) man, as a rational being, has a right to prove all assertions, all the doctrines which reverence imposes on him, before he submits himself to them, in order that this reverence may be sincere and not hypocritical.

To this justification, now, is required that the opiniative advocate of God shall prove, either that that, which we judge in the world as contrary-to-end, is not so; or that, were it so, it must by no means be judged as a fact, but as an invariable consequence of the nature of things; or lastly, that it must at least be considered not as a fact of the Supreme

FROM: *Essays and Treatises*, W. Richardson, trans. in 1799 (originally published in 1791). Translation slightly emended.

Author of all things, but merely of mundane beings, to whom something can be imputed, that is, men (perhaps higher, good or bad, spiritual beings also).

The author of a Theodicée consents, then, that this action shall be brought before the court of reason; engages himself as counsel for the defendant, by formally refuting all the charges preferred by the plaintiff; and during the course of law must not put him off by an authoritative decision on the incompetency of the tribunal of reason (*exceptionem fori*), that is, must not dispatch the charges by imposing on the plaintiff a concession of the supreme wisdom of the Author of the world, which directly declares groundless, even without inquiry, all doubts that may be started; but must attend to the objections and as they by no means derogate from the conception of the supreme wisdom* by

* The proper conception of *wisdom* represents but the property of a will, to harmonize with the chief good, as the final end or *scope* of all things, *art* on the other hand, but the faculty in the use of the fittest means to *ends laid down at pleasure*; art, when it proves itself as such (which is adequate to ideas, whose possibility transcends all interpretation of human reason, for instance, when mean and end as in organized bodies, produce one another reciprocally) as a *divine art*, may not be improperly distinguished by the name of wisdom, yet in order not to permute the conceptions, by the name of a wisdom of art of the Author of the world, for the purpose of distinguishing it from his *moral wisdom*. Teleology (and by it physicothelogy) gives abundant proofs of the former in experience. But from it no inference to the moral wisdom of the Author of the world is valid, because law of nature and moral law require quite heterogeneous principles and the proof of the latter wisdom must be given *a priori* totally, therefore absolutely not grounded upon experience of what happens in the world. As now the conception of God, that shall be fit for religion (for we use it not for the behoof of the explanation of nature, of course in a speculative view) must be a conception of him as a moral Being; as this conception, as little can it be grounded upon experience, just as little

clearing them up and removing them, render everything comprehensible.—One thing, however, he has no occasion to enter on, namely to prove the supreme wisdom of God from what experience teaches of this world, for in this he would not succeed, as omniscience is thereto requisite, in order in a given world (as it gives to cognize itself in experience) to cognize that perfection, of which may be said with certainty that there is nowhere any greater in the creation and its government possible.

The contrary-to-end (*Das Zweckwidridge*) in the world, which may be opposed to the wisdom of its Author, is of a three-fold nature: I. The absolute contrary-to-end, which can be approved and desired by wisdom, neither as an end, nor as a mean. II. The conditional contrary-to-end, which consents with the wisdom of a will, indeed never as an end, but yet as a mean. The *first* is the moral contrary-to-end, as the proper evil (sin); the *second* the physical contrary-to-end, evil (pain).—But there is a conformity-to-end (*Zweckmässigkeit*) in the relation of the evils to the moral evil, as the latter once exists and neither can nor ought to be diminished; namely, in the conjunction of evils and pains, as punishments, with the evil, as a crime; and relatively to this conformity-to-end in the world the question is, whether in this justice be done to every one in the world. Consequently still a III. species of the contrary-to-end in the world must be conceived, namely, the disproportion of crimes and punishments in the world. [I.e., Kant suggests that moral evil (sin), physical evil (pain) and injustice are three kinds of evil, that every evil is of one of these kinds, and that one offering a theodicy must deal with each kind of evil. Ed.]

The attributes of the supreme wis-

can it be exhibited from merely transcendental conceptions of an absolutely necessary being, who is to us totally transcendent; so it is sufficiently evident that the proof of the existence of such a Being can be no more than a moral one.

dom of the Author of the world, against which those contraries-to-end appear as objections, are likewise three:

First, his HOLINESS, as LEGISLATOR (Creator), in contradistinction to the moral bad in the world.

Secondly, his GOODNESS, as GOVERNOR (Preserver), contrasted with the innumerable evils and pains of the rational mundane beings.

Thirdly, his JUSTICE, as JUDGE, in comparison with the evil state, in which the disproportion between the impunity of the vicious and their crimes seems to show itself in the world.*

---

* These three attributes, of which the one can by no means be reduced to the others, for instance justice to goodness, and so the whole to a smaller number, constitute the moral conception of God. Nor can their order be altered (as for example to make the goodness the chief condition of the creation of the world, to which the holiness of legislation is subordinated), without derogating from religion, 'which bottoms upon this very moral conception. Our own pure (practical) reason determines this order of rank, as, when the legislation confirms itself to the goodness, there is no more dignity of it and no firm conception of duties. Man wishes first of all, it is true, to be happy; but perspects, and grants (though unwillingly) that the worthiness of being happy, that is, the consension of the use of his liberty with the holy law, must in the decree of the Author be the condition of its validity and therefore necessarily precede. For the wish, which the subjective end (of self-love) has at bottom, cannot determine the objective end (of wisdom), which the law, that gives the will unconditionally the rule, prescribes—Punishment in the exercise of justice is by no means grounded as a mean, but as an end in the legislative wisdom; the transgression is combined with evils, not in order that another good may arise, but because the combination is, in itself, *id est*, morally and necessarily, good. Justice, it is true, presupposes goodness of the legislator (for if his will did not tend to the weal of his subjects, it could not oblige them to obey him), it is not, however goodness, but as justice essentially different from it, though comprehended in the universal conception of wisdom. Hence the complaint of the wont of

The answer to those three impeachments must be represented in the abovementioned threefold different manner, and proved according to their validity.

I. The first vindication of the holiness of the Divine will on account of the moral evil, which is complained of as disfiguring the world, his work, consists in this:

a. That there is by no means such an absolute contrary-to-end, as we take the transgression of the pure laws of our reason to be, but that it is only a fault in the eye of human wisdom; that the Divine judges them according to quite other rules incomprehensible to us, so that what we indeed find rejectable with reason relatively to our practical reason and its determination, may perhaps, in relation to Divine ends and supreme wisdom, be the fittest mean, as well for our particular weal, as for the good of the world in general; that the ways of the Supreme are not our ways (*sunt Superis sua jura*), and we err, when we judge that, which is a law but relatively for men in this life to be absolute, and thus hold that, which seems contrary-to-end to our contemplation of things from a station so low, to be so likewise, when contemplated from the highest station.—This apology, in which the defence is worse than the charge, requires no refutation, and may certainly be freely left to the detestation of every person, who has the smallest sentiment of morality. [I.e., Kant is asserting that to deny that actions condemned by the moral law are really wrong—or to say that they are wrong merely from our point of view but not from God's—does

---

justice, which shows itself in the lot that falls to men here in the world, is not that the good do not fare *well* here, but that the bad do not fare *ill* (though, when the former is superadded to the latter, the contrast still augments this difficulty). For in a divine government even the best man cannot ground his wish for well-being upon the divine justice, but must always [ground it] on his goodness; because he who does his duty merely, can lay no claim to the favor of God.

justice neither to morality nor to divine goodness. Eds.]

b. The second pretended vindication grants, it is true, the actuality of the moral evil in the world, but excuses the Author of the world by its not having been possible to be prevented; because it is grounded upon the limits of the nature of men, as finite beings.—But thereby that evil itself would be justified; and, as it cannot be imputed to men as their fault, one would need to cease to name it a moral evil.

c. The third vindication, that supposes that with respect to what we denominate moral evil men are actually guilty, [but] no guilt must be imputed to God; as he has from wise causes merely permitted, as a fact of men, but by no means approved and willed or prepared, that evil, [this vindication] tends (if no difficulty shall be found in the conception of the mere *permitting* of a Being, who is the sole Author of the world) to the same consequence with the foregoing apology (b), namely, that, as it was impossible for God himself to hinder this bad, without derogating from other higher and even moral ends, the ground of this evil (for it must now be properly named thus) must be unavoidably to be looked for in the essence of things, namely, the necessary limits of humanity as finite nature, and consequently cannot be imputed to it. [I.e., To accept either (b) or (c) is to deny the existence of moral evil, not to explain it. Eds.]

II. The justification of the Divine goodness for the [physical] evils, namely, pains, which are complained of in the world, consists herein.

a. That in the fates of men a preponderance of evil over the agreeable enjoyment of life is falsely supposed, because every one, however badly he may fare, chooses rather to live, than to be dead, and those few, who resolve on the latter, so long as they themselves delay it, thereby allow that preponderance still and, when they are insane enough to destroy themselves, merely pass to the state of insensibility, in which no pain can be felt.—But the answer to this

sophistry may surely be left to the decision of every man of a sound understanding, who has lived and reflected long enough on the value of life to be able to pronounce a judgment on this, when the question is proposed to him, Whether, I will not say on the same, but on any other conditions he pleases (only not of a fairy, but of this our terrestrial, world), he would not wish to act the play of life over again.

b. To the second justification, that the preponderancy of the painful feelings over the agreeable cannot be separated from the nature of an animal creature, like man, (as count Veri maintains in his book On the Nature of Pleasure)— one would reply, that, if it is so, there occurs another query. Why the Author of our existence has called us into life, when, according to our just calculation, it is not worthy of being wished for by us? Ill-humour here, as the Indian woman said to Dschingiskhan, who could neither give her satisfaction for the violence suffered, nor afford her security against the future, would answer, 'If thou will'st not protect us, why dost thou conquer us?'

c. The third solution of the knot is that for the sake of a future felicity God hath placed us out of goodness in the world, but that that beatitude which may be hoped for must be preceded by a state of thorough trouble and misery of the present life, where we must by the struggle with difficulties become worthy of that future glory.—But, that this time of probation (in which the most succumb, and the best have no proper satisfaction in their life) shall absolutely be the condition by the Supreme Wisdom of the pleasure that one day or other may be enjoyed by us, and that it was not feasible to let the creature become contented with every epoch of his life, may indeed be pretended, but absolutely cannot be perspected, and by an appeal to the Supreme Wisdom, who hath so willed it, the knot may be cut, to be sure, but not untied; to resolve which, however, the theodicée engages.

III. To the last charge preferred

against the justice of the Governour of the world,* is answered:

a. That the pretext of the impunity of the vicious in the world has no ground; because every crime, according to its nature, carries with itself here the punishment suitable to it, as the internal reproaches of conscience torment the vicious more than furies would.—But in this judgment there is evidently a misunderstanding. For the virtuous man herein lends his character of mind to the vicious, namely, conscientiousness in its whole strictness which, the more virtuous the man is, punishes the more rigorously on account of the smallest transgression, that the moral law in him disapproves. But, where this cast of mind and with it conscientiousness is wanting, there is likewise wanting the tormentor for crimes committed; and the vicious, if he can but escape the external chastisement for his crimes, laughs at the anxiety of the honest man to torment himself internally with his own rebukes; but the small reproaches, which he may sometimes make himself, he makes either not at all through conscience, or, if he has any, they are abundantly outweighed and requited by the sensual pleasure, for which only he has a taste.——If that charge shall be further refuted

b. by this, That it is indeed not to be denied that there is absolutely to be found no proportion conformable to justice between guilt and punishment in

* It is remarkable that among all the difficulties of uniting the course of the events of the world with the divinity of its Author, none forces itself so strongly on the mind, as that of the appearance of *justice* therein wanting. If it happens (though it is but seldom), that an unjust villain, especially one possessing power, does not escape out of the world unpunished, the impartial spectator, in a manner reconciled to heaven, rejoices. No other conformity-to-end in nature excites his affect to such a degree by the admiration of it, and so to speak lets the hand of God be so easily discerned. Why? It (the conformity-to-end) is here moral, and the only one of the sort, which one may hope to perceive in some measure in the world.

the world, and one must often perceive with indignation in the course of it a life led with crying injustice and yet happy to the very end; that this however lies in nature and is not intentionally prepared, consequently is not moral dissonance, because it is a property of virtue to struggle with adversity, (to which belongs the pain that the virtuous must suffer by the comparison of his own misfortune with the good fortune of the vicious, and sufferings serve but to enhance the value of virtue, therefore in the eye of reason this dissonance of the undeserved evils of life is resolved into the most glorious moral concord;—this solution is opposed by this, that, though these evils, when they, as the whetstone of virtue, either *precede* or accompany it, may, it is true, be represented as in a moral harmony with it, when at least the end of life crowns the latter and punishes vice; but that, when even this end falls out nonsensically, of which experience gives many examples, suffering seems to have fallen to the lot of the virtuous, not *in order* that his virtue shall be pure, but *because* it has been so (but on the other hand was contrary to the rules of prudent self-love): which is directly the contrary to justice, as man is able to form a conception of it to himself. For as to the possibility that the end of this terrestrial life may not perhaps be the end of all life, this possibility cannot be valid as a *vindication* of Providence, but is merely an authoritative decision of the morally faithful reason, by which the sceptic is referred to patience, but [is] not satisfied.

c. If finally the third solution of this unharmonious proportion between the moral value of men and the lot that falls to them, shall be attempted, by saying that, In this world must be judged all weal or ill, as a consequence of the use of the faculties of men merely according to laws of nature, proportioned to their applied address and prudence, at the same time to the circumstances also, into which they accidentally fall, but not according to their agreement with supersensible ends; whereas in a future world another order of things will subsist, and every one will obtain what his deeds here below are worth according to a moral judgment;—thus is this presupposition arbitrable. Reason, if it does not as a morally legislative faculty give an authoritative decision conformable to its interest, must rather find it probable according to mere rules of theoretical cognition, That the course of the world according to the order of nature, as here, so for the future, will determine our fate. For what other clue has reason for its theoretical presumption, than the law of nature? and, though it allowed itself, as was required of it (no. b.), to be referred to patience and the hope of a better future world; how can it expect that, as the course of things here according to the order of nature is of itself wise, it would according to the same laws in a future world be unwise? As, according to them, there is no comprehensible relation at all between the internal determining grounds of the will (namely, the moral cast of mind) according to laws of liberty, and between the (for the most part external) causes of our well-being independent of our will according to laws of nature; so the presumption remains, that the agreement of the fate of men with a Divine justice, according to the conceptions we form of it, is as little to be expected there as here. [I.e., if in this world punishment and evil are not proportioned, we are not entitled to infer from this fact that there will be a just proportionment of punishment and evil in a next life. This is the central idea in both (b) and (c). Eds.]

The issue of this process before the *forum* of philosophy is, that all theodicée has hitherto not performed what it promises, namely, to justify the moral wisdom in the government of the world against the doubts, which are entertained of it from what experience gives to cognise in this world; though indeed these doubts as objections, as far as our insight into the nature of our reason reaches with regard to the latter, cannot prove the contrary. But whether in progress of time more proper grounds of its vindication may not be found, not

to absolve the arraigned wisdom (as hitherto) merely *ab instantia*, remains still undetermined, if we do not succeed in shewing with certainty that our reason is absolutely unable for *the introspection of the relation, which a world, as we may always know it by experience bears to the Supreme Wisdom;* for then all farther essays of opiniative human wisdom to perspect the ways of Divine wisdom are totally rejected. That at least a negative wisdom, the insight of the necessary limitation of our pretensions with regard to what is beyond our reach, is attainable by us, must, in order to put an end *for ever* to this lawsuit, yet be proved; and this may be easily done.

We have a conception of a *wisdom of art* in the arrangement of this world, to which for our speculative faculty of reason objective reality is not wanting, for the purpose of arriving at a physico-theology. In like manner have we a conception of a *moral wisdom*, which may be placed in a world in general by a most perfect Author, in the moral idea of our own practical reason.—But of the *unity in the agreement* of that wisdom of art with the moral wisdom in a sensible world we have no conception, and can never hope to reach it, For, to be a creature, and as a being of nature, to follow the will of its Author merely; but yet, as a free agent (who has his will independent on external influence, which may be very contrary to the former), to be capable of imputation; and nevertheless to consider his own fact at the same time as the effect of a Supreme Being; are an association of conceptions, which we must conceive, it is true, in the idea of a world, as the chief good; but which he only, who penetrates to the knowledge of the supersensible (intelligible) world, and perspects the manner, in which it forms the basis of the sensible one, can introspect: upon which insight only the proof of the moral wisdom of the Author of the world can be grounded in the latter, as this presents but the phenomenon of the former world,—an insight which no mortal can attain.

All theodicée ought, properly speaking, to be an *explication* of nature, so far as God makes known by it the design of his will. Now every explication of the declared will of a legislator is either *doctrinal* or *authentic*. The former is what discovers by reasoning that will from the expressions, which it has used, in conjunction with the designs of the lawgiver otherwise known; the latter the legislator himself gives.

The world, as a work of God, may be contemplated by us as a divine publication of the *designs* of his will. In this however it is *frequently* for us a shut book; but it is *always* this, when, to conclude from it, though an object of experience, even the *final* end of God (which is always moral), is aimed at. The philosophical essays of this sort of explanation are doctrinal, and constitute the proper theodicée, which may therefore be termed the doctrinal one.—Yet the mere obviating of all objections to the Divine wisdom cannot be refused the name of a theodicée, when it is a *divine authoritative decision*, or (which in this case is to the same purpose) when it is a judgment of the same reason, by which we form to ourselves of necessity and before all experience the conception of God as a moral and wise Being. For there God is by our reason the very expounder of his own will announced by the creation; and this exposition we may denominate an *authentic* theodicée. Then, however, that is not the exposition of a *reasoning* (speculative) practical reason, but of a practical reason *possessing potency*, which, as it is without farther grounds absolutely commanding in legislating, may be considered as the immediate declaration and voice of God, by which he giveth a meaning to the letter of his creation. Such an authentic interpretation, now, I find in an ancient sacred book allegorically expressed.

Job is represented as a man, to the enjoyment of whose life every thing possible to be conceived was united, in order to render it perfect. Healthy, opulent, free, a commander of others whom he may make happy, surrounded by a happy family, among beloved friends; and above all (what is the most essential), contented with himself in a good conscience.

All these riches, the latter excepted, a hard fate hung over him for a trial suddenly tore away from him. From the astonishment at this unexpected overthrow come by degrees to recollection, he gave vent to complaints against his disaster; on which between him and his friends who are present under a pretext to console themselves is soon begun a disputation, wherein both parties, every one according to his own way of thinking (but chiefly according to his situation), set forth their particular theodicée, for the moral interpretation of that bad fate. Job's friends declare themselves for the system of the interpretation of all evil in the world from Divine *justice*, as so many *punishments* for crimes perpetrated; and, though they could not name any, with which they could charge the unfortunate man, they believed to be able to judge *à priori* that he must needs be guilty of some, else it would not be possible according to the Divine justice that he should be unhappy. Whereas Job—who protests, with emotion, that his conscience does not reproach him in the least on account of his whole life; but as to inevitable human faults, God himself knoweth that he made him as a frail creature,—declares himself for the system of the *inconditional decree of God. He is of one mind*, continues Job, *and who can turn him?*

In what both parties reason or, if I may be allowed the word, overreason there is nothing remarkable; but the character, in which they do so, merits the more attention. Job speaks as he thinks, and every man in his situation would be of the same mind; his friends, on the other hand, speak as if the Almighty, on whose affair they decide, and to gain whose favour by their judgment they have more at heart than the truth, listened to them in secret. These their tricks, for the sake of appearance to maintain things, which they must allow they do not perspect, and to feign a conviction, which in fact they have not, contrast well with Job's plain sincerity, which is so far from false flattery as almost to border on temerity, greatly to his advantage. *Will you,* says he, *speak*

*wickedly for God? and talk deceitfully
for him? Will ye accept his person?* will
ye *contend for God? He will surely re-
prove you, if ye do secretly accept persons!—for an hypocrite shall not come
before him.*

The latter actually confirms the issue of the history. For God deigned to
discover to Job the wisdom of his creation, chiefly on the side of its inscrutable-
ness. He let him view the beautiful side
of the creation where ends comprehensible to man set the wisdom and bounti-
ful care of the Author of the world in
an unambiguous light; but on the other
hand the frightful side too, by naming
to him productions of his potency and
among these even pernicious dreadful
things, every one of which, it is true,
seems to be adjusted for itself and for
its species conformably-to-end, but with
regard to others and even to men destructive, contrary-to-end, and not harmonizing with an universal plan arranged
by goodness and wisdom; whereby however he showeth the disposition and
preservation of the whole announcing the
wise Author of the world, though at the
same time his ways, inscrutable to us,
must be hidden even in the physical order
of things, how much more then in their
connexion with the moral (which is yet
more impenetrable to our reason)?—The
conclusion is, that, as Job acknowledges
to have judged, not maliciously, for he is
conscious to himself of his probity, but
only imprudently, on things, which are
too high for him, and which he does not
understand, God pronounceth the condemnation of Job's friends, because they
did not speak of him (God) so well (in
point of conscientiousness), as his servant Job. If now the theory, which every
one on both sides maintains, be contemplated, that of his friends may carry with
it rather the appearance of more speculative reason and pious humility: and Job
in all probability would have experienced
a bad fate before every tribunal of
dogmatical theologians, before a synod,
an inquisition, a reverend classis, or
every chief consistory of our time (one
only excepted). Therefore, only the
sincerity of the heart, not the preference

of knowledge, the honesty to acknowledge his doubts openly, and the aversion
to feign conviction, where it is not felt,
chiefly before God (where this craft besides is absurd), are the properties, which
in the Divine judgment have decided the
preference of the man of probity, in the
person of Job, over the religious flatterer.

But the belief, which arose to him
by so strange a solution of his doubts,
namely, merely the conviction of his
ignorance, could enter into the mind of
none but him, who in the midst of his
greatest doubts could say, *till I die I will
not remove my integrity from me,* &c.
For by this mindedness he proved that
he did not ground his morality upon the
belief, but the belief upon the morality:
in which case this belief only, however
weak it may be, is of a pure and genuine
sort, that is, of that sort, which grounds
a religion, not of courting favour, but
of the good life.

CONCLUDING OBSERVATION

The theodicée, as has been shown, has
not so much to do with a problem for the
advantage of science, as rather with an
affair of belief. From the authentic
theodicée we saw that in such things it
does not depend so much upon reasoning,
as upon sincerity in the observation of
the inability of our reason, and upon the
honesty not to falsify one's thoughts in
the utterance, let them be falsified with
ever so pious a view.—This occasions
the following short contemplation on a
rich fund of matter, namely, sincerity, as
the chief requisite in affairs of faith, in
collision with the propension to falsity
and impurity, as the principle defects
in human nature.

That what one says either to himself or to another, is *true*, he cannot
always be answerable (for he may err);
but he can and must be answerable for
his profession or his acknowledgment's
being *veracious*, for of it he is immediately conscious to himself. In the
former case he compares his assevera-
tion with the object in the logical judgment (by the understanding); but in
the latter, as he professes his holding-

true, with the subject (before conscience). Does he make the profession relating to the former, without being conscious to himself of the latter? he lies, as he gives out something else than what he is conscious of.—The observation that there is such an impurity in the human heart, is not new (for Job made it); but one would almost think that the attention to it is new to teachers of morals and religion: so little is it found, that they, notwithstanding the difficulty which a purifying of the minds of men, even if they *would* act conformably to duty, carries with it, have made sufficient use of that observation.—This veracity may be named the *formal conscientiousness*, the *material* consists in the circumspection to venture nothing on the risk of its being wrong: as on the contrary that consists in the consciousness of having employed this circumspection in the given case.—Moralists speak of an erring conscience. But an erring conscience is a nonentity; and, were there such a thing, one could never be sure to have acted right, because the judge himself in the last instance might err. I may err, it is true, in the judgment, *in which I believe* to be in the right: for that belongs to the understanding, which only judges objectively (whether true or false); but in the consciousness, *Whether in fact I believe* to be in the right (or merely pretend it), I absolutely cannot err, as this judgment or rather this position says nothing but that I thus judge the object.

In the carefulness to be conscious to one's self of this belief (or unbelief), and not to give out any holding-true, of which one is not conscious, consists just the formal conscientiousness, which is the ground of veracity. Therefore, who says to himself (and, what is the same in the confessions of religion, before God) that *he believes*, without perhaps having examined himself, whether he is in fact conscious to himself of this holding-true or even of such a degree of it,* lies not

only in the most absurd manner (before a knower of hearts), but in the most wicked, because it saps the very foundation of every virtuous resolution, sin-

---

only in the most absurd manner (before a knower of hearts), but in the most wicked, because it saps the very foundation of every virtuous resolution, sin-

temple of public justice, where the mere idea of it ought of itself to inspire the greatest reverence! But men lie with regard to conviction, which they have not, at least of the sort, or in the degree, they pretend, even in their internal professions; and, as this improbity (since it tends by little and little to actual persuasion) may also have external pernicious consequents, to, that mean of extorting veracity, the oath, (but indeed only an internal one, that is, the essay, whether the holding-true stand the test of an internal *juratory* examining of the profession) may too be very well used to make the audaciousness more daring, at last, however, if not to restrain externally violent assertions, at least to stupify.—By an human tribunal nothing more is demanded of the conscience of him that makes oath, than the engaging that, if there is a future Judge of the world (therefore a God and a life to come), he will be answerable to him for the truth of his external profession; *that there is such a Judge of the world*, is a profession not necessary to be demanded of him, because, if the former protestation cannot withhold the lie, the latter false profession would create just as little scruple. After this internal delation of an oath one would ask himself, Wouldest thou take upon thee, by all that is dear and sacred to thee, to answer for the truth of that weighty tenet of faith or another holden so? At such a demand conscience would be suddenly roused by the danger, to which one exposes himself by pretending more, than he can maintain with certainty, where the believing concerns an object that is not at all attainable by the way of knowing [theoretical introspection], but whose assuming, by its only rendering possible the connexion of the chief practical principle of reason with that of the theoretical cognition of nature in one system (and thus reason agreeing with itself), is above all recommendable, but yet always free.—But professions of faith, whose source is historical, when they are enjoined others as precepts, must still more be subjected to this proof-by-fire of veracity: because here the impurity and feigned conviction is extended to move persons, and their guilt becomes a burden on him, who in a manner answers for the conscience of others (for men are willingly passive with their conscience).

---

* The mean of extorting veracity in external deposing, *the oath* (*tortura spiritualis*) is held before a human tribunal not only allowed, but indispensable: a sad proof of the little reverence of men for truth, even in the

cerity. It is easily conceived how soon such blind and external *confessions* (which are easily united with an internal confession just as false), when they furnish *means of acquisition*, may gradually occasion a certain falsehood in the cast of mind of even the commonwealth.— While this public purifying of the way of thinking in all probability remains deferred to a distant period, till it perhaps one day becomes an universal principle of education and doctrine under the protection of the liberty of thinking; a few lines still may be here bestowed on the contemplation of that vice, which seems to be deeply rooted in human nature.

There is something touching and which moves the soul in displaying a sincere character, divested of all falsehood and positive dissimulation; as integrity, however, a mere simplicity and rectitude of the way of thinking (especially when its ingenuity is excused) is the least that is requisite to a good character, and therefore it is not to be conceived upon what is grounded that admiration, with which we are impressed by such an object: it must then be, that sincerity is the property, with which human nature is the least endowed. A melancholy observation! As by that only all the other properties, so far as they rest upon principles, can have an intrinsic true value. None but a contemplative misanthrope (who wishes ill to nobody, but is inclined to believe every thing bad of men) can be doubtful whether to find men *worthy* of *hatred* or of *contempt*. The properties, on whose account he would judge them to be qualified for the former treatment, are those, by which they designedly do harm. That property, however, which seems rather to expose them to the latter degradation, can be no other, than a propensity, which is *in itself bad*, though it hurts nobody, a propensity to what can be used as a mean to no end whatever; which is therefore objectively good for nothing. The former evil is nothing but that of *enmity* (more mildly expressed, unkindness); the latter can be nothing else than a *lying disposi-*

tion (falsehood, even without any design to do hurt). The *one* inclination has a view, which may in certain other references be allowed and good, for instance, enmity against incorrigible disturbers of the peace. The *other* propensity, however, is that to the use of a mean (the lie) that, whatever be the view, is good for nothing, because it is in itself bad and blameable. In the quality of man of the former species there is *wickedness*, yet with which there may be combined a fitness for good ends in certain external relations and it sins but in the means, which are not rejectable in every view. The evil of the latter sort is *naughtiness (Nichtswürdigkeit)*, by which all character is refused to man. Here I chiefly insist on the impurity lying deeply concealed, as man knows to falsify even the internal declaration in presence of his own conscience. The less ought to surprise the external inclination to fraud; it must then be this, that, though every one knows the falseness of the coin, with which he trades, it can maintain itself equally well in circulation.

In de-Luec's letters on the mountains, the history of the earth and of men, I remember to have read the following result of his in part anthropological journey. The philanthropic author set out with the good quality of our species, and sought the confirmation of it, where city luxury cannot have such influence to corrupt the minds, in the mountains, from Switzerland to the Harze; and, after his belief in disinterested helping (*Hülfleistende*) inclination began somewhat to stagger by an experience in the former, he at last infers this conclusion, *That man, as to benevolence, is good enough* (no wonder! for this rests upon implanted inclination, of which God is the Author); *if a bad* propensity to fine deceit were but not inherent in him*

---

* In the very intermixture of the bad with the good lie the great springs, which rouse into action the dormant powers of humanity, and necessitate men to develop all their talents and to approach towards the perfection of their destination.

(which is likewise not astonishing; for to withhold this depends upon the character, which man himself must form in himself)!—A result of the inquiry that every body, even without having travelled in the mountains, might have met with among his fellow-citizens, nay, yet nearer, in his own breast.

Evil and Omnipotence
J. L. MACKIE

The traditional arguments for the existence of God have been fairly thoroughly criticized by philosophers. But the theologian can, if he wishes, accept this criticism. He can admit that no rational proof of God's existence is possible. And he can still retain all that is essential to his position, by holding that God's existence is known in some other, nonrational way. I think, however, that a more telling criticism can be made by way of the traditional problem of evil. Here it can be shown, not that religious beliefs lack rational support, but that they are positively irrational, that the several parts of the essential theological doctrine are inconsistent with one another, so that the theologian can maintain his position as a whole only by a much more extreme rejection of reason than in the former case. He must now be prepared to believe, not merely what cannot be proved, but what can be *disproved* from other beliefs that he also holds.

The problem of evil, in the sense in which I shall be using the phrase, is a problem only for someone who believes that there is a God who is both omnipotent and wholly good. And it is a logical problem, the problem of clarifying and reconciling a number of beliefs: it is not a scientific problem that might be solved by further observations, or a practical problem that might be solved by a decision or an action. These points are obvious; I mention them only because they are sometimes ignored by theologians, who sometimes parry a statement of the problem with such remarks as

"Well, can you solve the problem yourself?" or "This is a mystery which may be revealed to us later" or "Evil is something to be faced and overcome, not to be merely discussed."

In its simplest form the problem is this: God is omnipotent; God is wholly good; and yet evil exists. There seems to be some contradiction between these three propositions, so that if any two of them were true the third would be false. But at the same time all three are essential parts of most theological positions: the theologian, it seems, at once *must* adhere and *cannot consistently* adhere to all three. (The problem does not arise only for theists, but I shall discuss it in the form in which it presents itself for ordinary theism.)

However, the contradiction does not arise immediately; to show it we need some additional premises, or perhaps some quasi-logical rules connecting the terms "good," "evil," and "omnipotent." These additional principles are that good is opposed to evil, in such a way that a good thing always eliminates evil as far as it can, and that there are no limits to what an omnipotent thing can do. From these it follows that a good omnipotent thing eliminates evil completely, and then the propositions that a good omnipotent thing exists, and that evil exists, are incompatible.

ADEQUATE SOLUTIONS

Now once the problem is fully stated it is clear that it can be solved, in the sense that the problem will not arise if

FROM: *Mind,* Vol. LXIV, No. 254 (1955). Reprinted by permission of the editor of *Mind* and the author.

one gives up at least one of the propositions that constitute it. If you are prepared to say that God is not wholly good, or not quite omnipotent, or that evil does not exist, or that good is not opposed to the kind of evil that exists, or that there are limits to what an omnipotent thing can do, then the problem of evil will not arise for you.

There are, then, quite a number of adequate solutions of the problem of evil, and some of these have been adopted, or almost adopted, by various thinkers. For example, a few have been prepared to deny God's omnipotence, and rather more have been prepared to keep the term "omnipotence" but severely to restrict its meaning, recording quite a number of things that an omnipotent being cannot do. Some have said that evil is an illusion, perhaps because they held that the whole world of temporal, changing things is an illusion, and that what we call evil belongs only to this world, or perhaps because they held that although temporal things *are* much as we see them, those that we call evil are not really evil. Some have said that what we call evil is merely the privation of good, that evil in a positive sense, evil that would really be opposed to good, does not exist. Many have agreed with Pope that disorder is harmony not understood, and that partial evil is universal good. Whether any of these views is *true* is, of course, another question But each of them gives an adequate solution of the problem of evil in the sense that if you accept it this problem does not arise for you, though you may, of course, have *other* problems to face

But often enough these adequate solutions are only *almost* adopted. The thinkers who restrict God's power, but keep the term "omnipotence," may reasonably be suspected of thinking, in other contexts, that his power is really unlimited. Those who say that evil is an illusion may also be thinking, inconsistently, that this illusion is itself an evil. Those who say that "evil" is merely privation of good may also be thinking,

inconsistently, that privation of good is an evil. (The fallacy here is akin to some forms of the "naturalistic fallacy" in ethics, where some think, for example, that "good" is just what contributes to evolutionary progress, and that evolutionary progress is itself good.) If Pope meant what he said in the first line of his couplet, that "disorder" is only harmony not understood, the "partial evil" of the second line must, for consistency, mean "that which, taken in isolation, falsely appears to be evil," but it would more naturally mean "that which, in isolation, really is evil." The second line, in fact, hesitates between two views, that "partial evil" isn't really evil, since only the universal quality is real, and that "partial evil" is really an evil, but only a little one.

In addition, therefore, to adequate solutions, we must recognize unsatisfactory inconsistent solutions, in which there is only a half-hearted or temporary rejection of one of the propositions which together constitute the problem. In these, one of the constituent propositions is explicitly rejected, but it is covertly reasserted or assumed elsewhere in the system.

FALLACIOUS SOLUTIONS

Besides these half-hearted solutions, which explicitly reject but implicitly assert one of the constituent propositions, there are definitely fallacious solutions which explicitly maintain all the constituent propositions, but implicitly reject at least one of them in the course of the argument that explains away the problem of evil.

There are, in fact, many so-called solutions which purport to remove the contradiction without abandoning any of its constituent propositions. These must be fallacious, as we can see from the very statement of the problem, but it is not so easy to see in each case precisely where the fallacy lies. I suggest that in all cases the fallacy has the general form suggested above: in order to solve the problem one (or perhaps more) of its constituent propositions is given up, but in such a way that it appears to have been retained, and can therefore be asserted without qualification in other contexts. Sometimes there is a further complication: the supposed solution moves to and fro between, say two of the constituent propositions, at one point asserting the first of these but covertly abandoning the second, at another point asserting the second but covertly abandoning the first. These fallacious solutions often turn upon some equivocation with the words "good" and "evil," or upon some vagueness about the way in which good and evil are opposed to one another, or about how much is meant by "omnipotence." I propose to examine some of these so-called solutions, and to exhibit their fallacies in detail. Incidentally, I shall also be considering whether an adequate solution could be reached by a minor modification of one or more of the constituent propositions, which would, however, still satisfy all the essential requirements of ordinary theism.

1. "Good cannot exist without evil" or "Evil is necessary as a counterpart to good."

It is sometimes suggested that evil is necessary as a counterpart to good, that if there were no evil there could be no good either, and that this solves the problem of evil. It is true that it points to an answer to the question "Why should there be evil?" But it does so only by qualifying some of the propositions that constitute the problem.

First, it sets a limit to what God can do, saying that God *cannot* create good without simultaneously creating evil, and this means either that God is not omnipotent or that there are *some* limits to what an omnipotent thing can do. It may be replied that these limits are always presupposed, that omnipotence has never meant the power to do what is logically impossible, and on the present view the existence of good without evil would be a logical impossibility. This

interpretation of omnipotence may, indeed, be accepted as a modification of our original account which does not reject anything that is essential to theism, and I shall in general assume it in the subsequent discussion. It is, perhaps, the most common theistic view, but I think that some theists at least have maintained that God can do what is logically impossible. Many theists, at any rate, have held that logic itself is created or laid down by God, that logic is the way in which God arbitrarily chooses to think. (This is, of course, parallel to the ethical view that morally right actions are those which God arbitrarily chooses to command, and the two views encounter similar difficulties.) And *this* account of logic is clearly inconsistent with the view that God is bound by logical necessities—unless it is possible for an omnipotent being to bind himself, an issue which we shall consider later, when we come to the Paradox of Omnipotence. This solution of the problem of evil cannot, therefore, be consistently adopted along with the view that logic is itself created by God.

But, secondly, this solution denies that evil is opposed to good in our original sense. If good and evil are counterparts, a good thing will not "eliminate evil as far as it can." Indeed, this view suggests that good and evil are not strictly qualities of things at all. Perhaps the suggestion is that good and evil are related in much the same way as great and small. Certainly, when the term "great" is used relatively as a condensation of "greater than so-and-so," and "small" is used correspondingly, greatness and smallness are counterparts and cannot exist without each other. But in this sense greatness is not a quality, not an intrinsic feature of anything; and it would be absurd to think of a movement in favor of greatness and against smallness in this sense. Such a movement would be self-defeating, since relative greatness can be promoted only by a simultaneous promotion of relative smallness. I feel sure that no theists would be content to regard God's goodness as analogous to this—as if what he supports were not the *good* but the *better*, and as if he had the paradoxical aim all things should be better than other things.

This point is obscured by the fact that "great" and "small" seem to have an absolute as well as a relative sense. I cannot discuss here whether there is absolute magnitude or not, but if there is, there could be an absolute sense for "great," it could mean of at least a certain size, and it would make sense to speak of all things getting bigger, of a universe that was expanding all over, and therefore it would make sense to speak of promoting greatness. But in *this* sense great and small are not logically necessary counterparts: either quality could exist without the other. There would be no logical impossibility in everything's being small or in everything's being great.

Neither in the absolute nor in the relative sense, then, of "great" and "small" do these terms provide an analogy of the sort that would be needed to support this solution of the problem of evil. In neither case are greatness and smallness *both* necessary counterparts *and* mutually opposed forces or possible objects for support and attack.

It may be replied that good and evil are necessary counterparts in the same way as any quality and its logical opposite: redness can occur, it is suggested, only if nonredness also occurs. But unless evil is merely the privation of good, they are not logical opposites, and some further argument would be needed to show that they are counterparts in the same way as genuine logical opposites. Let us assume that this could be given. There is still doubt of the correctness of the metaphysical principle that a quality must have a real opposite: I suggest that it is not really impossible that everything should be, say, red, that the truth is merely that if everything were red we should not notice redness, and so we should have no word "red"; we observe and give names to qualities only if they have real opposites. If so, the prin-

ciple that a term must have an opposite would belong only to our language or to our thought, and would not be an onto-logical principle, and, correspondingly, the rule that good cannot exist without evil would not state a logical necessity of a sort that God would just have to put up with. God might have made everything good, though *we* should not have noticed it if he had.

But, finally, even if we concede that this *is* an ontological principle, it will provide a solution for the problem of evil only if one is prepared to say, "Evil exists, but only just enough evil to serve as the counterpart of good." I doubt whether any theist will accept this. After all, the *ontological* requirement that non-redness should occur would be satisfied even if all the universe, except for a minute speck, were red, and, if there were a corresponding requirement for evil as a counterpart to good, a minute dose of evil would presumably do. But theists are not usually willing to say, in all contexts, that all the evil that occurs is a minute and necessary dose.

2. "Evil is necessary as a means to good."

It is sometimes suggested that evil is necessary for good not as a counter-part but as a means. In its simple form this has little plausibility as a solution of the problem of evil, since it obviously implies a severe restriction of God's power. It would be a *causal* law that you cannot have a certain end without a certain means, so that if God has to introduce evil as a means to good, he must be subject to at least some causal laws. This certainly conflicts with what a theist normally means by omnipotence. This view of God as limited by causal laws also conflicts with the view that causal laws are themselves made by God, which is more widely held than the corresponding view about the laws of logic. This conflict would, indeed, be resolved if it were possible for an omnipotent being to bind himself, and this possibility has still to be considered. Unless a favorable answer can be given to this question, the suggestion that evil is necessary as a means to good solves the problem of evil only by denying one of its constituent propositions, either that God is omnipotent or that "omnipotent" means what it says.

3. "The universe is better with some evil in it than it could be if there were no evil."

Much more important is a solution which at first seems to be a mere variant of the previous one, that evil may contribute to the goodness of a whole in which it is found, so that the universe as a whole is better as it is, with some evil in it, than it would be if there were no evil. This solution may be developed in either of two ways. It may be supported by an aesthetic analogy, by the fact that contrasts heighten beauty, that in a musical work, for example, there may occur discords which somehow add to the beauty of the work as a whole. Alternatively, it may be worked out in connection with the notion of progress, that the best possible organization of the universe will not be static, but progressive, that the gradual overcoming of evil by good is really a finer thing than would be the eternal unchallenged supremacy of good.

In either case, this solution usually starts from the assumption that the evil whose existence gives rise to the problem of evil is primarily what is called physical evil, that is to say, pain. In Hume's rather half-hearted presentation of the problem of evil, the evils that he stresses are pain and disease, and those who reply to him argue that the existence of pain and disease makes possible the existence of sympathy, benevolence, heroism, and the gradually successful struggle of doctors and reformers to overcome these evils. In fact, theists often seize the opportunity to accuse those who stress the problem of evil of taking a low, materialistic view of good and evil, equating these

with pleasure and pain, and of ignoring the more spiritual goods which can arise in the struggle against evils.

But let us see exactly what is being done here. Let us call pain and misery "first order evil" or "evil (1)." What contrasts with this, namely, pleasure and happiness, will be called "first order good" or "good (1)." Distinct from this is "second order good" or "good (2)" which somehow emerges in a complex situation in which evil (1) is a necessary component—logically, not merely causally, necessary. (Exactly *how* it emerges does not matter: in the crudest version of this solution good [2] is simply the heightening of happiness by the contrast with misery, in other versions it includes sympathy with suffering, heroism in facing danger, and the gradual decrease of first order evil and increase of first order good.) It is also being assumed that second order good is more important than first order good or evil, in particular that it more than outweighs the first order evil it involves.

Now this is a particularly subtle attempt to solve the problem of evil. It defends God's goodness and omnipotence on the ground that (on a sufficiently long view) this is the best of all logically possible worlds, because it includes the important second order goods, and yet it admits that real evils, namely first order evils, exist. But does it still hold that good and evil are opposed? Not, clearly, in the sense that we set out originally: good does not tend to eliminate evil in general. Instead, we have a modified, a more complex pattern. First order good (e.g., happiness) *contrasts with* first order evil (e.g., misery): these two are opposed in a fairly mechanical way; some second order goods (e.g., benevolence) try to maximize first order good and minimize first order evil; but God's goodness is not this, it is rather the will to maximize *second* order good. We might, therefore, call God's goodness an example of a third order goodness, or good (3). While this account is different from our original one, it might well be held to be an improvement on it, to give a more accurate description of the way in which good is opposed to evil, and to be consistent with the essential theist position.

There might, however, be several objections to this solution.

First, some might argue that such qualities as benevolence—and a fortiori the third order goodness which promotes benevolence—have a merely derivative value, that they are not higher sorts of good, but merely means to good (1), that is, to happiness, so that it would be absurd for God to keep misery in existence in order to make possible the virtues of benevolence, heroism, etc. The theist who adopts the present solution must, of course, deny this, but he can do so with some plausibility, so I should not press this objection.

Secondly, it follows from this solution that God is not in our sense benevolent or sympathetic: he is not concerned to minimize evil (1), but only to promote good (2); and this might be a disturbing conclusion for some theists.

But, thirdly, the fatal objection is this. Our analysis shows clearly the possibility of the existence of a *second* order evil, an evil (2) contrasting with good (2) as evil (1) contrasts with good (1). This would include malevolence, cruelty, callousness, cowardice, and states in which good (1) is decreasing and evil (1) increasing. And just as good (2) is held to be the important kind of good, the kind that God is concerned to promote, so evil (2) will, by analogy, be the important kind of evil, the kind which God, if he were wholly good and omnipotent, would eliminate. And yet evil (2) plainly exists, and indeed most theists (in other contexts) stress its existence more than that of evil (1). We should, therefore, state the problem of evil in terms of second order evil, and against this form of the problem the present solution is useless.

An attempt might be made to use this solution again, at a higher level, to explain the occurrence of evil (2): indeed the next main solution that we shall examine does just this, with the help of some new notions. Without any fresh notions, such a solution would have little plausibility: for example, we could hardly say that the really important good was a good (3), such as the increase of benevolence in proportion to cruelty, which logically required for its occurrence the occurrence of some second order evil. But even if evil (2) could be explained in this way, it is fairly clear that there would be third order evils contrasting with this third order good: and we should be well on the way to an infinite regress, where the solution of a problem of evil, stated in terms of evil (n), indicated the existence of an evil $(n + 1)$, and a further problem to be solved.

4. "Evil is due to human free will."

Perhaps the most important proposed solution of the problem of evil is that evil is not to be ascribed to God at all, but to the independent actions of human beings, supposed to have been endowed by God with freedom of the will. This solution may be combined with the preceding one: first order evil (e.g., pain) may be justified as a logically necessary component in second order good (e.g., sympathy) while second order evil (e.g., cruelty) is not *justified*, but is so ascribed to human beings that God cannot be held responsible for it. This combination evades my third criticism of the preceding solution.

The free-will solution also involves the preceding solution at a higher level. To explain why a wholly good God gave men free will although it would lead to some important evils, it must be argued that it is better on the whole that men should act freely, and sometimes err, than that they should be innocent automata, acting rightly in a wholly determined way. Freedom, that is to say, is now treated as a third order good, and as being more valuable than second order goods (such as sympathy and heroism) would be if they were deterministically produced, and it is being assumed that second order evils, such as cruelty, are logically necessary accompaniments of freedom, just as pain is a logically necessary precondition of sympathy.

I think that this solution is unsatisfactory primarily because of the incoherence of the notion of freedom of the will: but I cannot discuss this topic adequately here, although some of my criticisms will touch upon it.

First I should query the assumption that second order evils are logically necessary accompaniments of freedom. I should ask this: if God has made men such that in their free choices they sometimes prefer what is good and sometimes what is evil, why could he not have made men such that they always freely choose the good? If there is no logical impossibility in a man's freely choosing the good on one, or on several, occasions, there cannot be a logical impossibility in his freely choosing the good on every occasion. God was not, then, faced with a choice between making innocent automata and making beings who, in acting freely, would sometimes go wrong: there was open to him the obviously better possibility of making beings who would act freely but always go right. Clearly, his failure to avail himself of this possibility is inconsistent with his being both omnipotent and wholly good.

If it is replied that this objection is absurd, that the making of some wrong choices is logically necessary for freedom, it would seem that "freedom" must here mean complete randomness or indeterminacy, including randomness with regard to the alternatives good and evil, in other words that men's choices and consequent actions can be "free" only if they are not determined by their characters. Only on this assumption can God escape the responsibility for men's actions; for if he made them as they are, but did not determine their wrong choices, this can only be because the wrong choices are not determined by men as they are. But then if freedom is randomness, how can it be a characteristic of *will?* And, still more, how can it be

the most important good? What value or merit would there be in free choices if these were random actions which were not determined by the nature of the agent?

I conclude that to make this solution plausible two different senses of "freedom" must be confused, one sense which will justify the view that freedom is a third order good, more valuable than other goods would be without it, and another sense, sheer randomness, to prevent us from ascribing to God a decision to make men such that they sometimes go wrong when he might have made them such that they would always freely go right.

This criticism is sufficient to dispose of this solution. But besides this there is a fundamental difficulty in the notion of an omnipotent God creating men with free will, for if men's wills are really free this must mean that even God cannot control them, that is, that God is no longer omnipotent. It may be objected that God's gift of freedom to men does not mean that he *cannot* control their wills, but that he always *refrains* from controlling their wills. But why, we may ask, should God refrain from controlling evil wills? Why should he not leave men free to will rightly, but intervene when he sees them beginning to will wrongly? If God could do this, but does not, and if he is wholly good, the only explanation could be that even a wrong free act of will is not really evil, that its freedom is a value which outweighs its wrongness, so that there would be a loss of value if God took away the wrongness and the freedom together. But this is utterly opposed to what theists say about sin in other contexts. The present solution of the problem of evil, then, can be maintained only in the form that God has made men so free that he *cannot* control their wills.

This leads us to what I call the "Paradox of Omnipotence": can an omnipotent being make things which he cannot subsequently control? Or, what is practically equivalent to this, can an omnipotent being make rules which then bind himself? (These are practically equivalent because any such rules could be regarded as setting certain things beyond his control, and vice versa.) The second of these formulations is relevant to the suggestions that we have already met, that an omnipotent God creates the rules of logic or causal laws, and is then bound by them.

It is clear that this is a paradox: the questions cannot be answered satisfactorily either in the affirmative or in the negative. If we answer "Yes," it follows that if God actually makes things which he cannot control, or makes rules which bind himself, he is not omnipotent once he has made them: there are *then* things which he cannot do. But if we answer "No," we are immediately asserting that there are things which he cannot do, that is to say that he is already not omnipotent.

It cannot be replied that the question which sets this paradox is not a proper question. It would make perfectly good sense to say that a human mechanic has made a machine which he cannot control: if there is any difficulty about the question it lies in the notion of omnipotence itself.

This, incidentally, shows that although we have approached this paradox from the free-will theory, it is equally a problem for a theological determinist. No one thinks that machines have free will, yet they may well be beyond the control of their makers. The determinist might reply that anyone who makes anything determines its ways of acting, and so determines its subsequent behavior: even the human mechanic does this by his *choice* of materials and structure for his machine, though he does not know all about either of these: the mechanic thus determines, though he may not foresee, his machine's actions. And since God is omniscient, and since his creation of things is total, he both determines and foresees the ways in which his creatures will act. We may grant this, but it is beside the point. The question is not whether God *originally* determined the future actions of his creatures, but whether he can *subsequently* control their actions, or whether he was able in his original creation to put things beyond his subsequent control. Even on determinist principles the answers "Yes" and "No" are equally irreconcilable with God's omnipotence.

Before suggesting a solution of this paradox, I would point out that there is a parallel Paradox of Sovereignty. Can a legal sovereign make a law restricting its own future legislative power? For example, could the British parliament make a law forbidding any future parliament to socialize banking, and also forbidding the future repeal of this law itself? Or could the British parliament, which was legally sovereign in Australia in, say, 1899, pass a valid law, or series of laws, which made it no longer sovereign in 1933? Again, neither the affirmative nor the negative answer is really satisfactory. If we were to answer "Yes," we should be admitting the validity of a law which, if it were actually made, would mean that parliament was no longer sovereign. If we were to answer "No," we should be admitting that there is a law, not logically absurd, which parliament cannot validly make, that is, that parliament is not now a legal sovereign. This paradox can be solved in the following way. We should distinguish between first order laws, that is laws governing the actions of individuals and bodies other than the legislature, and second order laws, that is laws about laws, laws governing the actions of the legislature itself. Correspondingly, we should distinguish two orders of sovereignty, first order sovereignty (sovereignty [1]) which is unlimited authority to make first order laws, and second order sovereignty (sovereignty [2]) which is unlimited authority to make second order laws. If we say that parliament is sovereign we might mean that any parliament at any time has sovereignty (1), or we might mean that parliament has both sovereignty (1) and sovereignty (2) at present, but we cannot without contradiction mean both that the present parliament has sovereignty (2) and that every parliament at every time has sovereignty (1), for if the present parliament has sovereignty (2) it may use it to take away the sovereignty (1) of later parliaments. What the paradox shows is that we cannot ascribe to any continuing institution legal sovereignty in an inclusive sense.

The analogy between omnipotence and sovereignty shows that the paradox of omnipotence can be solved in a similar way. We must distinguish between first order omnipotence (omnipotence [1]), that is unlimited power to act, and second order omnipotence (omnipotence [2]), that is unlimited power to determine what powers to act things shall have. Then we could consistently say that God all the time has omnipotence (1), but if so no beings at any time have powers to act independently of God. Or we could say that God at one time had omnipotence (2), and used it to assign independent powers to act to certain things, so that God thereafter did not have omnipotence (1). But what the paradox shows is that we cannot consistently ascribe to any continuing being omnipotence in an inclusive sense.

An alternative solution of this paradox would be simply to deny that God is a continuing being, that any times can be assigned to his actions at all. But on this assumption (which also has difficulties of its own) no meaning can be given to the assertion that God made men with wills so free that he could not control them. The paradox of omnipotence can be avoided by putting God outside time, but the free-will solution of the problem of evil cannot be saved in this way, and equally it remains impossible to hold that an omnipotent God *binds himself* by causal or logical laws.

CONCLUSION

Of the proposed solutions of the problem of evil which we have examined, none has stood up to criticism. There may be other solutions which require examination, but this study strongly suggests that there is no valid solution of the problem which does not modify at least one of the constituent propositions in a way which would seriously affect the essential core of the theistic position.

Quite apart from the problem of evil, the paradox of omnipotence has shown that God's omnipotence must in any case be restricted in one way or another, that unqualified omnipotence cannot be ascribed to any being that continues through time. And if God and his actions are not in time, can omnipotence, or power of any sort, be meaningfully ascribed to him?

Omnipotence, Evil, and Supermen
NINIAN SMART

*I*t *has* in recent years been argued, by Professors Antony Flew and J. L. Mackie;[1] that God could have created men wholly good. For, causal determi-

nism being compatible with free will, men could have been made in such a way that, without loss of freedom, they would never have fallen (and would never fall) into sin. This if true would constitute a weighty antitheistic argument. And yet intuitively it seems unconvincing. I wish here to uncover the roots of this intuitive suspicion.

There are in the argument two as-

[1] See Antony Flew, "Divine Omnipotence and Human Freedom," in *New Essays in Philosophical Theology,* A. Flew and A. MacIntyre, eds. (New York: The Macmillan Company, 1955), Chap. 8, and J. L. Mackie, "Evil and Omnipotence." (See above.)

FROM: *Philosophy,* Vol. XXXVI, No. 137 (1961). Reprinted by permission of the editors of *Philosophy* and the author.

sertions to be distinguished. First, that causal determinism (i.e., the claim that all human actions are the results of prior causes) is compatible with free will.[2] I call this the Compatibility Thesis. Second, there is the assertion that God could have created men wholly good. This I shall call the Utopia Thesis. An apparent inference from the latter is that God cannot be both omnipotent and wholly good, since men are in fact wicked.

In the present discussion I shall concentrate on the Utopia Thesis. Clearly, of course, if the Compatibility Thesis is not established the Utopia Thesis loses its principal basis and becomes altogether doubtful. But I shall here merely try to show that the Utopia Thesis does not follow from the Compatibility Thesis, despite appearances. This may well indicate that there is something queer about the latter (and the Paradigm Case Argument, on which perhaps it principally rests, has lately come in for perspicacious criticism).[3] In the discussion I shall be assuming the truth of determinism; for if it is false, the Compatibility Thesis becomes irrelevant and the Utopia Thesis totters. The chief points in my reasoning are as follows:

The concept *good* as applied to humans connects with other concepts such as *temptation, courage, generosity*, etc. These concepts have no clear application if men were built wholly good. I bring this out by a piece of anthropological fiction, i.e., (1) let us conjure up a universe like ours, only where men are supposed to be wholly good; or (2) let us consider the possibility of Utopian universes quite unlike ours. Under (1), I try to show that it is unclear whether the "men" in such a universe are to be called wholly good or even good, and that it

[2] See Flew, *op. cit.*, p. 151.

[3] See the article "Farewell to the Paradigm-Case Argument" by J. W. N. Watkins, and Flew's comment and Watkins' reply to the comment, all in *Analysis*, Vol. XVIII, No. 2 (1957), and the articles by R. Harré and H. G. Alexander in *Analysis*, Vol. XVIII, Nos. 4–5 (1958), respectively.

is unclear whether they should be called men. And under (2), I try to show that we have even stronger reasons for saying that these things are unclear. Thus the abstract possibility that men might have been created wholly good has no clearly assignable content. Hence, it is rational to be quite agnostic about such a possibility. It follows that it will be quite unclear whether a Utopian universe will be superior (in respect of moral goodness) to ours. So the Utopia Thesis cannot constitute an antitheistic argument.

I

When we say that a man is good, we are liable to render an account of why we say this by giving reasons. For example, it might be because he has been heroic in resisting temptations, courageous in the fact of difficulties, generous to his friends, etc. Thus *good* normally connects with concepts like *courage* and so forth.

Let us look first at *temptation*. It is clear (at least on the determinist assumption) that if two identical twins were in otherwise similar situations but where one has a temptation not to do what is right, while no such temptation is presented to the other twin, and other things being equal, the tempted twin will be less likely to do what is right than the untempted one. It is this fact that temptations are empirically discovered to affect conduct that doubtless makes it relevant to consider them when appraising character and encouraging virtue. Moreover, unless we were built in a certain way there would be no temptations: for example, unless we were built so that sexual gratification is normally very pleasant there would be no serious temptations to commit adultery, etc. It would appear then that the only way to ensure that people were wholly good would be to build them in such a way that they were never tempted or only tempted to a negligible extent. True, there are two other peculiar possibilities, which I shall go on to deal with, namely (1) through lucky combination of circumstances men might never sin; (2)

frequent miraculous intervention might keep them on the straight and narrow path. However, for the moment, I consider the main possibility, that to ensure that *all* men were *always* good, men would have to possess a built-in resistance to all temptations.

Similar remarks apply to courage, generosity, etc., although in some cases the situation may be rather complex. It will, I think, be conceded that we credit people with courage on such grounds as that they have faced adverse situations with calm and disregard for danger. But the adversities arise because there are fears, desires for comfort, disinclinations to offend people, and so on. And it will be generally agreed, at least by determinists, that one twin faced with a situation where doing right inspires fear will be less likely to do what is right than the other twin not so faced with adversity, and similarly with regard to desires for comfort and so forth. Thus to ensure that men would never panic, never wilt, etc., it would be necessary, as the main possibility, to build them differently.

Perhaps generosity is a trickier case. But it is clear that a person is praised for generosity because very often there is a conflict of generosity and self-interest. Indeed, if there were not some such conflict, or thought to be, however remote, an action would not really count as generosity, perhaps; the slight qualification here is due to the possibility of situations where a person has so much money, say, that it makes no psychological difference whether he gives away a certain sum or not, but he does it out of sympathy—I shall deal with such cases below. And to say that generosity conflicts with self-interest is a shorthand way of saying that one's inclinations for comfort, etc., are liable to have a more restricted fulfilment than would otherwise be the case.

Then there are actions which exhibit such dispositions as pride, which seem remote from simple inclinations such as likings for certain sorts of food or for sexual gratification and from fairly simple impulses such as fear. But

though the springs of pride are hard to fathom, it is doubtless true that people would not display pride, in the ordinary sense, if they did not live in a socially competitive atmosphere, if they did not have desires to assert themselves, etc. One would not be sure quite how men would have to be rebuilt to immunize them from pride, but rebuilding would surely be necessary, on the determinist view.

As for the peculiar cases mentioned above—generosity not involving sacrifice and similar examples—I do not think that such instances are at all serious ones, inasmuch as (1) virtues are dispositions, and so there is a point in calling such nonsacrificial generosity generosity, in that it exhibits a disposition whose basic exercise involves sacrifice; (2) without the occasions for basic exercise of the disposition it is obscure as to what could be meant by calling the nonbasic instances of generosity instances of generosity.

These examples, then, are meant to indicate that the concept *goodness* is applied to beings of a certain sort, beings who are liable to temptations, possess inclinations, have fears, tend to assert themselves and so forth; and that if they were to be immunized from evil they would have to be built in a different way. But it soon becomes apparent that to rebuild them would mean that the ascription of goodness would become unintelligible, for the reasons why men are called good and bad have a connection with human nature as it is empirically discovered to be. Moral utterance is embedded in the cosmic status quo.

II

Of course, God is not bound by synthetic necessities: He is in no way shackled by the causal laws of our universe, for example. But in a backhanded way, He is confined by meaninglessness. For to say that God might do such-and-such where the "such-and-such" is meaningless or completely obscure is not to assert that God can *do* anything. I therefore hope to show that "God might have created men wholly good" is without intelligible content, and hence that this alleged possibility has no force as an antitheistic argument.

"God might have created men wholly good" *appears* to have content because at least it does not seem self-contradictory and because we think we can imagine such a situation. But I shall bring out its emptiness by in fact trying to do this, by imagining other possible universes. Now it may well be objected that in doing this I am showing nothing. For example, one will be wanting to make imaginative causal inferences like "If men are never to panic they must be built in such-and-such a way." But since God is not bound by causal principles the inferences have no legitimacy.

But this objection misses the point of my procedure. For my argument is based on the following dilemma. *Either* we can hope to assign a reasonably clear meaning to the possibility that men might have been created wholly good by imagining a Utopia—in which case the paradox arises that it would be quite unclear as to whether such "men" could reasonably be called wholly good. *Or* we can refuse to assign such a reasonably clear meaning to the possibility by simply postulating an unimaginable alternative universe—in which case there are even stronger reasons for doubting whether the possibility has content. Or, to make the matter *ad hominem* as against Flew, I am saying that alleged possibilities as well as alleged facts can die the Death by a Thousand Qualifications.*

I proceed then to imagine possible universes. In line with the above dilemma, I divide such universes into two classes. First, those which are cosmomorphic, i.e., those which are governed by physical laws at least roughly comparable to those found in our cosmos. Second, I consider noncosmomorphic universes, i.e., ones with a quite different set-up from ours.

1. *Cosmomorphic Utopia A*—The

first and main type of cosmomorphic utopia, where men are wholly good, can be described perhaps as follows, in line with the earlier remarks about temptations, etc.

Men will never be seriously tempted to harm or injure each other. For this reason: that no one has any serious desires liable to conflict with those of others. For instance, they would be so built that one and only one woman would attract any one man and conversely. Say: one would have an over-riding infatuation for the first unin-fatuated woman one met and vice versa. As for property: men might arrive in the world with an automatic supply of necessities and comforts, and the individual would have a built-in mechanism to ensure that the supplies of others were mysteriously distasteful (the other man's passion-fruit smells like dung). And what of danger? During, say, a thunderstorm no one would be so seriously perturbed that he would be likely to panic and harm others. Let us suppose that a signal would (so to speak) flash in the individual's brain, telling him to take cover. What if he was in the middle of an *al fresco* dinner? Perhaps the signal flashing would dry up the juices in his mouth. And so forth. (Admittedly this picture is not elaborated with much scientific expertize: of this I shall say more later.)

I think that none of the usual reasons for calling men good would apply in such a Utopia. Consider one of these harmless beings. He is wholly good, you say? Really? Has he been courageous? No, you reply, not exactly, for such creatures do not feel fear. Then he is generous to his friends perhaps? Not precisely, you respond, for there is no question of his being ungenerous. Has he resisted temptations? No, not really, for there are no temptations (nothing you could really *call* temptations). Then why call them good? Well, you say, these creatures never harm each other. . . . Yes, but the inhabitants of Alpha Centauri never harm *us*. Ah, you reply, Centaurians do not harm us because there

---

* For Flews' use of this phrase, see below, first essay in the section *Is Religious Language Meaningful?*

are as yet no ways for them to impinge upon us. Quite so, I say; it is causally impossible for them to harm us. Similarly the set-up of the Cosmomorphic Utopians makes it causally impossible for them to harm each other. The fact that it is distance in the one case and inner structure in the other makes no odds.

Now admittedly in such a conversation we are not brought face to face with the Death by a Thousand Qualifications in the form described by Flew in regard to such statements as "God loves His children." For there the criticism of the theologian is that when counterevidence is presented he takes refuge in increasingly recondite senses of "love." But in the present case one who claims that the inhabitants of Cosmomorphic Utopia A are wholly good is not precisely resisting counterevidence (that is, he is not resisting evidence that these creatures are not good and so possibly bad). Rather he is failing to give the usual reasons for calling them bad. And the positive moves are up to him. It is not sufficient airily and vaguely to say that in such an alternative universe men can be said to be wholly good. Similarly the traveller from Jupiter who tells us that unicorns are to be found there, though queer unicorns for they possess neither horns nor feet, leaves us at a justifiable loss.

Hence it is so far obscure as to what is meant by the possibility that men might have been created wholly good. For the usual criteria, at least in Cosmomorphic Utopia A, do not seem to apply. And so, even if the Compatibility Thesis is correct, it does not appear so far evident that men might have been created wholly good. For an unintelligible assertion cannot either be said to follow or not to follow from some other. And in any case, are the Utopians described above properly to be called *men?* Perhaps we ought to invent a new name: let us dub them "sapients." The question for the theist now becomes: "Why did God create men rather than sapients?" I shall return to this question later.

2. *Cosmomorphic Utopia B*—Cir-

cumstances here combine always to make men good. Adolf Hitler would never in fact be foul. He might have incipient impulses of hatred towards Jews, but these would luckily never overwhelm him, because circumstances would prevent this: he would fall in love with a Jewess, he would never get into anti-Semitic company, he would not meet with miseries in his youth, and so forth. Whenever on the point of falling for some temptation, his attention would be distracted. The whole thing would be a very, very long story. And everyone, not just the Führer, would be consistently lucky with regard to virtue and vice.

The trouble about this Utopia is that it is more like a dream than a fantasy. A corresponding meteorological dream would be: since circumstances occasionally combine to make the sun shine, let us suppose that the sky would never be overcast. This does not seem self-contradictory, to say "The sky might never be overcast." But what would a cosmomorphic universe have to be like for this to happen? Clearly it is not just luck that makes the sun shine sometimes: it is because the weather operates in a certain way. For the weather so to operate that it was never cloudy meteorological laws would have to be rewritten (and physics and biology too)—unless you are thinking of a place like the moon. Similarly, in a cosmomorphic utopia where circumstances forever combined in favor of virtue, the set-up would, according to the determinist, have to be different. Thus Cosmomorphic Utopia B is either a version of A (or of some other) or it is a mere dream masquerading as an alternative universe.

3. *Cosmomorphic Utopia C*— Suppose men were always virtuous, not because of the set-up (which would be as now) but because of frequent miraculous intervention.

It is hard to make sense of the supposition. But observationally in such a world we might discover situations like this. Causal factors C usually give rise to actions of a certain empirical type, type-A. But in some circumstances type-

A actions are wrong, and in these cases C will not have type-A effects. But it will not be that some other empirical factor will be present in such exceptions, for *ex hypothesi* the nonoccurrence of the type-A action is due to miraculous intervention. Hence either we have to count rightness and wrongness as empirical differences in order to formulate a causal law here or we must confess that no strict causal laws of human behavior could be formulated in this cosmos. The former alternative is baffling and unacceptable, while the latter is incompatible with determinism. Hence Cosmomorphic Utopia C provides no support for the Utopia Thesis.

4. I now turn to the thought of a *Noncosmomorphic Utopia*. As has been insisted, God is not limited to a cosmomorphic alternative. My anthropological fictions are feeble in comparison with the possibilities contained in God's thoughts. He might have produced a cosmos utterly unlike ours.

But as we have no notion what sapients in such a world would be like, it is even unclearer in this case what would be meant by calling them good. We would have to remain completely agnostic about such a world; and all the difficulties there are in knowing what is meant by calling God a person and good would recur with *extra* force when we try to understand what "wholly good men" could mean here. *Extra* force, because whereas God's nature is perhaps revealed to a limited extent in the *actual* cosmos, the nature of an alternative *possible* and *noncosmomorphic* universe can in no way be so revealed. Hence it follows that it is totally unclear what the possibility that God might have created a noncosmomorphic utopia amounts to.

It is therefore also unclear as to whether it would be superior to this universe. Moreover, it is most doubtful as to whether the sapients of Cosmomorphic Utopia A are superior to ourselves. I am not sure, of course, how one judges such matters; but if we rely on native wit, in default of some new method of evaluating alternative universes, it seems

by no means clear that such a utopia is a better place than ours here.

III

It may be complained that I have been unfair. My anthropological fiction has been crude and possibly biased. And the thing has not been worked out with any scientific expertize. But no one, so far as I know, with the requisite physiological, psychological and biological knowledge has attempted to work out such a fictional alternative anthropology, doubtless there are enough problems in the real-life biological sciences without our going off into subtle fantasies. But until someone were to do so, it remains obscure as to what a determinist cosmomorphic utopia would amount to.

Again it may be objected that writers have occasionally dreamed of utopias and described them. Surely these descriptions are not empty or self-contradictory? But first, fictions are no good guide unless systematically elaborated. For example, and notoriously, there are situations in science fiction which are revealed on reflection to be unintelligible or self-contradictory (e.g., in regard to "going back in time"). Again, fiction writers may not have any clearly formulated views about determinism. And it might turn out that what is allowable on a hard free will theory is not so on a determinist view. For example, an indeterminist may simply say that it might have been the case that men were always wholly good. But the determinist can only make sense of this possibility on the assumption that wholly good men would have a causal difference from men as they are. In order to imagine a man's always overcoming his harmful inclinations, he must surely imagine some change in the way his personality is built. But we have no assurance that some *unspecified* causal change would leave men more or less human and yet produce the consequence of complete goodness. Hence the change has to be specified. I have tried out a plausible fiction or two here, to show that so far one can assign no clear content to the possibility of men's being built wholly good. But maybe some determinist will dream up a plausible fantasy to establish his point. But let him do so: for so far the Utopia Thesis is wrapped in cloud.

Again it might be argued, from the side of theism, that this discussion works against angels just as much as it works against the possibility of wholly good men. If we cannot make sense of non-cosmomorphic worlds we cannot make sense of angelic worlds. Maybe so: though angels, qua messengers of God, could share in the intelligibility of God. But that takes us too far afield.

Conclusion — My anthropological fiction seems to bring out the point that moral discourse is embedded in the cos-

mic status quo (or even more narrowly, in the planetary status quo). For it is applied to a situation where men are beings of a certain sort. Thus the abstract possibility that men might have been created wholly good loses its clarity as soon as we begin to imagine alternative possible universes. If then the Utopia Thesis is quite unclear, it cannot assert anything intelligible about God. And so it cannot serve as part of an antitheistic argument. There remains of course many serious difficulties for the theist in regard to human evil. But the Utopia Thesis is not one of them.

Or not yet. We shall see how the science fiction goes.

Is
Man
Immortal?

Is
Personal Survival
Possible and Provable?

*I*n *the dialogue* "Phaedo," Plato offers an argument by analogy for the claim that man's soul (the principle of life in man and the source of his rational and moral capacities) is immortal. Strato, of the Peripatetic School, replies to this argument. What is the argument Plato offers, and what difficulty does Strato find with it?

Cebes, a character in the "Phaedo," is concerned that at death man's soul disperses (as dust is dispersed by the wind). In other words, he fears that man's capacity for thought, choice, inference, and the like vanishes when he dies. Socrates offers an argument intended to show that this does not occur.

Only certain *sorts* of things can disperse, or "come apart." It is "most probable that the incomposite things are those that are always constant and unchanging, while the composite ones are those that are different at different times and never constant." *If*, then, the soul is simple (incomposite, not composed of parts), then it is most probable that it does not change. But *is* the soul simple?

Socrates endeavors to answer this question by comparing the soul with "the equal itself, the beautiful itself, the being itself whatever it may be."

The reference here is to the Forms. These are unchanging, eternal entities that provide the reference for general terms and in virtue of which everyday objects possess the qualities that they have. There is, for example, the Form of the Good (the highest of the Forms). The word 'good' denotes this Form, and if Jones, Smith, and Brown are all good men, then each has the quality of being good. This quality they possess in virtue of "participating in" the Form of the Good. Exactly how "participating in" is to be explained is one of the perennial problems of Platonic interpretation, but whatever is good is so because it stands in this relation to the Form of the Good. Every Form, then, is non-physical, "real . . ., uniform and independent": Forms "remain unchanging and constant, never admitting any sort of change whatever." Suppose, for the sake of argument, that Plato has proved that there are Forms. Will this help to prove that the soul is immortal?

Consider, in contrast to Forms, everyday objects—chairs, tables, human bodies, and the like. These are composite, visible, changing, divisible. The soul is not visible, and, not being spatial, it can have no physical parts.

Further, the soul is what *knows*, and the Forms are the objects of knowledge. All genuine knowledge is certain, and we can know with certainty only that which is unchanging. There must be some resemblance between what is known and the knower.

The soul therefore is like the Forms, which do not change, in that it is invisible and has no physical parts. It is unlike objects, which do change and come into and go out of existence, because they are visible and composed of physical parts. Also the soul knows the Forms and so must be like them. This—plus the *value* of knowledge and of that which can know (compare the reference to the soul "ruling" and so being "divine")—give probability to the claim that the soul (conceived as distinguishable from the body) is unchanging and simple; and so the dispersal of the body does not entail the dispersal of the soul. While the force of the argument no doubt increases when it is put into the context of more of Plato's philosophy, the above account seems fair to Socrates' claims.

Now what objection did Strato have? To find out, let us fill out the Socratic argument a bit by noting some other premises to which he appeals. Being alive is essential to being a soul; as Strato puts it, "soul, so long as it exists, cannot be dead." Socrates had appealed to this premise (compare 103B):

(1) If having a property *P* is essential to *X* (that is, if being an *X* entails having *P*—as, for example, "being a mammal" entails "having vertebrae")—then *X* can never become not-*P*.

As an instantiation of (1), he offered:

(2) Being alive is essential to being a soul (or having a soul), so a soul can never lose life (become not-alive).

Socrates then inferred:

(3) The soul is immortal.

Strato questions this inference. He notes that another instantiation of (1) is:

(4) Being hot is essential to being a fire.

But this does not entail

(5) A fire cannot burn out.

We need to supplement (2) and (4) by adding "so long as it exists." But then neither (3) nor (5) can be inferred from their respective premises.

This issue is related to the portion of Socrates' argument contained in the selection that follows. We saw above that Socrates argued, by analogy, that we have better reason to accept than to deny:

(6) The soul is simple.

And we could perhaps add:

(7) Being simple is essential to being a soul.

Thus we could claim:

(8) The soul will always be simple.

But, as in previous cases, all we are entitled to claim is that so long as a soul exists, it is simple. This of course does not show that any soul always will exist.

Strato challenges Socrates' argument in yet another way. Why must something simple be therefore eternal? It cannot, of course, undergo a change in its parts—it has none. But it can simply cease to exist. In a passage that points out several of Socrates' theses, Strato puts the point forcefully:

May it not be that, even if we escape all the rest [of the objections], we cannot rebut the objection that soul is limited and has (only) a limited power? Let us grant that it brings us life, that it can exist as a separate substance, that it cannot admit the death that is opposite to the life which it brings up: nevertheless it will wear itself out one day, will be extinguished and perish of its own accord, without any attack from outside.

Cebes raises the same issue (at 87C) when he wonders if the soul may not be related to the body like a weaver to his coats—he outlasts many but is himself outlasted by his final coat. To put the problem in another way, the soul perhaps continues the same throughout many replacements of all of the cells of its body, and in that sense has many bodies. But when the last "body" ceases to function, the soul ceases to exist.

A crucial portion of Socrates' reply to Cebes depends not only on the likeness of the soul to the Forms but also on further applications of (1) (see

103A–105B); and the new applications seem, given Strato's objection, to be no sounder than the others we have considered.

H. H. Price approaches the question of imortality in a very different manner than Plato did. Offering no proof of immortality in his essay, he asks instead what is *meant* by "surviving one's death". He analyzes this notion by dealing with objections raised by those who suspect that the phrase in question has no meaning at all. A useful way of introducing Price's contentions is to list the most important objections and note his responses.

The first objection is that a disembodied mind will have no sense organs, so no sense experience, and so perhaps no experience at all. Price does not challenge the assumption that surviving one's death and being disembodied are necessarily connected. They are not, and in this regard John Hick's essay included under "Is religious language meaningful?" is a useful supplement to Price's essay. Nor does Price challenge the further claim, also implicit in the objection, that a logically necessary condition of having sense experience is having sense organs, although this claim is not self-evident. Instead he develops a conception of postmortem experience as *imaging*, or having visual, tactile, or auditory images. ("Images" here means, roughly, "experiences private to those who have them.") These images are mind-dependent; they have no existence independent of human experience. But they obey causal laws (more like the laws of Freud's psychology than those of physics, perhaps) and so allow prediction and retrodiction. Further, memory is a feature of the envisioned postmortem experience. An individual with such experiences would not, of course, be "alive" in any biochemical sense but would be quite alive in the psychological sense of "having experiences." Such images could even contain feelings of warmth, cold, dizziness, and the like, visual experiences similar to those one has of the surface of his own nose and cheeks, and a wide range of other quasi-sensory experiences.

Against this backdrop Price responds to other possible objections. If "persons are what you meet," how could any such center of experience be *met* and so be a person? Although it is not clear that this is a correct account of what persons are, one could meet others in the context Price describes if those who have image-experiences also have telepathic powers (that is, can produce images for others as well as for themselves), perhaps including the power to produce images in others that resemble a human body (similar, perhaps, to one's own body—the one he previously possessed). So persons can, in one sense, "meet" each other in the afterlife Price envisions or meet a person "there" whom one had known "here."

Reference to "here" and "there" raises another question. *Where* is the next world conceived as being? Price contends that the question is, strictly speaking, nonsense. I dream that I see, say, a tiger in a cage. The cage and the tiger are spatially related to one another. But neither is any number of feet from the head of my bed or any other material object. Price depends here on there being a distinction between perceptual space and physical space and (implicitly) claims that the former can exist without the latter.

Price continues by explaining in what senses his "next world" can, and cannot, be said to be (a) delusory, (b) unreal, and (c) subjective, contending that there are perfectly clear and respectable senses in which it is real and objective. He concludes by considering how the notion of a "next world," elaborated along the lines indicated, can be connected with the desires and character that men have in this life and how the concept of punishment could be applied to such a world.

Price is certainly correct in suggesting that the question as to how continued existence after death is to be conceived is logically prior to (its answer is presupposed by) the question as to whether there is any reason to suppose that such continued existence occurs. If his analysis of this notion is coherent, then survival is a meaningful or intelligible hypothesis. This is not unimportant; as Price notes, one cannot have evidence for an unintelligible thesis. There are other conceptions of continued existence after death than the one Price discusses. But his analysis is certainly interesting and seems to provide one sense in which a man could be said to have postmortem existence.

An Argument for Human Immortality
PLATO

Socrates now takes up the point raised by Cebes, that the soul may be dispersed at death. He urges that dispersal can only be suffered by composite objects, whereas the soul is not composite but of a single nature, like 'the beautiful itself', 'the equal itself' and Forms in general. Souls are akin to Forms, for both belong to the unseen order, whose attributes are changelessness and indestructibility, whereas body belongs to the visible order, whose attributes are the opposite of these. We may therefore believe that soul is 'altogether indestructible or nearly so'.

S*ocrates then* resumed: 'Now the sort of question that we ought to put to ourselves is this: what kind of thing is in fact liable to undergo this dispersal that you speak of? For what kind of thing should we fear that it may be dispersed, and for what kind should we not? And next we should consider to which kind the soul belongs, and so find

some ground for confidence or for apprehension about our own souls. Am I right?'

'Yes, you are.'

'Well now, isn't anything that has been compounded or has a composite nature liable to be split up into its component parts? Isn't it incomposite things alone that can possibly be exempt from that?'

'I agree that that is so', replied Cebes.

'And isn't it most probable that the incomposite things are those that are always constant and unchanging, while the composite ones are those that are different at different times and never constant?'

'I agree.'

'Then let us revert to those objects which we spoke of earlier. What of that very reality of whose existence we give an account when we question and answer each other?[1] Is that always un-

[1] I.e. in philosophical discussions; cf. 75 D 2.

FROM: *Plato's Phaedo*, R. Hackforth, trans. (New York: The Cambridge University Press, pp. 79–87), 78B–80C. Reprinted by permission of the Cambridge University Press.

changing and constant, or is it different at different times? Can the equal itself, the beautiful itself, the being itself whatever it may be, ever admit any sort of change? Or does each of these real beings, uniform[2] and independent, remain unchanging and constant, never admitting any sort of alteration whatever?'

'They must be unchanging and constant', Cebes replied.

'But what about the many beautiful things, beautiful human beings, say, or horses or garments or anything else you like? What about the many equal things? What about all the things that are called by the same name as those real beings? Are *they* constant, or in contrast to those is it too much to say that they are never identical with themselves nor identically related to one another?'[3]

'You are right about them too,' said Cebes, 'they are never constant.'

'Then again, you can touch them and see them or otherwise perceive them with your senses, whereas those unchanging objects cannot be apprehended save by the mind's reasoning. Things of that sort are invisible, are they not?'[4]

'That is perfectly true.'

'Then shall we say there are two kinds[5] of thing, the visible and the invisible?'

'Very well.'

'The invisible being always constant, the visible never?'

'We may agree to that too.'

'To proceed: we ourselves are partly body, partly soul, are we not?'

'Just so.'

'Well, which kind of thing shall we say the body tends to resemble and be akin to?'

'The visible kind; anyone can see that.'

'And the soul? Is that visible or invisible?'

'Not visible to the human eye, at all events, Socrates.'

'Oh well, we were speaking of what is or is not visible to mankind: or are you thinking of some other sort of being?'

'No: of a human being.'

'Then what is our decision about the soul, that it can be seen, or cannot?'

'That it cannot.'

'In fact it is invisible?'

'Yes.'

'Hence soul rather than body is like the invisible, while body rather than soul is like the visible.'

'Unquestionably, Socrates.'

'Now were we not saying some time ago that when the soul makes use of the body to investigate something through vision or hearing or some other sense—of course investigating by means of the body is the same as investigating by sense—it is dragged by the body towards objects that are never constant, and itself wanders in a sort of dizzy drunken confusion, inasmuch as it is apprehending confused objects?'

'Just so.'

'But when it investigates by itself alone, it passes to that other world of pure, everlasting, immortal, constant

---

[2] The term μονοειδές recurs at 80B in close conjunction with ἀδ ἄλυτον, and it is used of the Form of beauty at *Symp.* 211B. It has the same force as πᾶν ὅμοιον which Parmenides asserts of his ἕν ὄν, viz. the denial of internal difference or distinction of unlike parts.

[3] Of two things called beautiful one may be to-day more beautiful, to-morrow less so, than the other; of two things called equal one may come to be greater, or smaller, than the other. But it seems possible that οὔτε ἀλλήλοις may be added simply because equality involves two terms. I do not see how ἀλλήλοις can, as Burnet supposes, refer to things appearing beautiful or ugly, equal or unequal *to different people*, as they were said to do at 74B8.

[4] The pleonasm ἀιδῆ καὶ οὐχ ὁρατά, though of a sort common enough in Greek, would be intolerable in English.

[5] As Prof. Grube has pointed out, the words εἶδος and ἰδέα are not used in a technical sense until 103E, and thereafter become common. It is possible that this is due, or partly due, to the need to use εἶδος in its ordinary sense of 'class' or 'kind' here.

being, and by reason of its kinship thereto abides ever therewith, whensoever it has come to be by itself and is suffered to do so; and then it has rest from wandering and ever keeps close to that being, unchanged and constant, inasmuch as it is apprehending unchanging objects. And is not the experience which it then has called intelligence?'

'All you have said, Socrates, is true and admirably put.'

'Once again, then, on the strength of our previous arguments as well as of this last, which of the two kinds of thing do you find that soul resembles and is more akin to?'

'On the strength of our present line of inquiry, Socrates, I should think that the veriest dullard would agree that the soul has a far and away greater resemblance to everlasting, unchanging being than to its opposite.'

'And what does the body resemble?'
'The other kind.'

'Now consider a further point. When soul and body are conjoined, Nature prescribes that the latter should be slave and subject, the former master and ruler. Which of the two, in your judgement, does that suggest as being like the divine, and which like the mortal? Don't you think it naturally belongs to the divine to rule and lead,

and to the mortal to be ruled and subjected?'

'Yes, I do.'
'Then which is soul like?'
'Of course it is obvious, Socrates, that soul is like the divine, and body like the mortal.'

'Would you say then, Cebes, that the result of our whole discussion amounts to this: on the one hand we have that which is divine, immortal, indestructible, of a single form, accessible to thought, ever constant and abiding true to itself; and the soul is very like it: on the other hand we have that which is human, mortal, destructible, of many forms, inaccessible to thought,[6] never constant nor abiding true to itself; and the body is very like that. Is there anything to be said against that, dear Cebes?'

'Nothing.'

'Well then, that being so, isn't it right and proper for the body to be quickly destroyed, but for the soul to be altogether indestructible, or nearly so?'

'Certainly.'

---

[6] The word ἀνόητος usually means 'foolish', but for using it to mean 'not the object of thought' Plato has the precedent of Parmenides 8, 17 DK. Burnet speaks of a 'play on words', but it is hardly that.

A Critique of Plato
STRATO

*O*lympiodorus, the sixth-century Neo-platonist, has preserved in his commentary on the *Phaedo* some criticism made by Strato, known as ὁ φυσικός, the third head of the Peripatetic school, who succeeded Theophrastu sabout 287 B.C. These may most conveniently be found in Fritz Wehrli, *Die Schule des Aristoteles*, Heft V, *Strato von Lampsakos*

(1950). I have attempted a translation, following Wehrli's numbering of the fragments, and giving the pages of Norvin's edition of Olympiodorus. The meaning is usually clear enough; but two, viz. 123 (i) and (l), are unintelligible to me. I leave readers to decide for themselves on their cogency, but it may be remarked that W. Capelle, who gives a

FROM: *Plato's Phaedo*, R. Hackforth, trans. (New York: The Cambridge University Press, pp. 195–198). Reprinted by permission of Cambridge University Press.

good account of their general purport in Pauly-Wissowa, *RE* iv, i (1931), s.v. Strato 13, speaks of them as 'bündig'. (R. Hackforth)

OBJECTIONS TO

γένεσις ἐξ ἐναντίων OR ἀνταπόδοσις

(OBJECTIONS TO
COMING-TO-BE
FROM OPPOSITES OR
RECIPROCAL CHANGE
[OF OPPOSITES])
122 (D63, p. 221 N.):

(*a*) What has perished arises from what existed; yet inasmuch as the reverse is not true, what reason is there to believe in the cogency of an argument of this type?

(*b*) If a dead part of a body, e.g. a finger or a gouged-out eye, does not come back to life, then neither, plainly, can the whole [creature].

(*c*) It may be suggested that the identity between things arise out of one another is not numerical, but only specific.

(*d*) Flesh may come from food, but food does not come from flesh; rust may come from bronze, and charcoal from wood, but not *vice versa*.

(*e*) The old come from the young; but the reverse does not happen.

(*f*) Opposites may come from opposites if a substratum persists, but not if it is destroyed.

(*g*) It may be suggested that the continuance of coming-to-be is no more than the constant renewal of a species or type, as we find even in man-made objects.

OBJECTIONS TO THE
PRINCIPLE OF EXCLUSION
OF OPPOSITES
123 (C11 178–90, p. 183 N.):

(*a*) On this showing, is not every living creature deathless? For it cannot 'admit' death: that is to say, there could never be a dead living creature, any more than a dead soul.

(*b*) On this showing, are not even the souls of irrational creatures deathless,

inasmuch as they 'bring up' life and cannot 'admit' the opposite of that which they bring up?

(*c*) And presumably, on this showing, the souls of plants too, for they too make their bodies into living bodies.

(*d*) Is not everything that comes-to-be imperishable? For they are all, equally with souls, incapable of admitting their opposites: a thing that comes-to-be could never be a thing that has perished.

(*e*) Would not this apply to every natural object? Any such object exhibits a development according to its nature, and therefore cannot admit of development contrary thereto; and *qua* incapable of admitting that, it can never perish.

(*f*) On this showing it will be equally true that a composite object will never be broken up: for it cannot admit its opposite: that is to say, while remaining a composite it can never be a broken-up object.

(*g*) If we grant that a negation can have more senses than one, the soul may be 'undying' (ἀθάνατος) not in the sense that it is, or possesses, inextinguishable life, but in the sense that it can only admit one of a pair of opposites, and must either exist together with that opposite or not exist at all.

(*h*) Is it not too readily assumed that, if the soul is incapable of admitting death, and in that sense deathless, it is therefore indestructible? A stone is deathless in the sense of this argument, but a stone is not indestructible.

(*i*) What is the ground for saying that the soul 'brings up' life as a concomitant, with the purpose of arguing that it cannot admit the opposite of what is brought up? In some cases the soul is brought up [itself].

(*k*) May it not be that a thing is alive, yet the life it has is imported from without, so that it can one day lose it?

(*l*) May it not be that the soul, while not admitting the death that is the opposite of that life which soul brings up, nevertheless does admit another death, that namely which is opposite to the life which brings up soul?

(*m*) May it not be that just as fire, so long as it exists, cannot be cold, so soul, so long as it exists, cannot be dead? For it brings up life so long [only] as it exists.

(*n*) May it not be that, even if we escape all the rest, we cannot rebut the objection that soul is limited and has [only] a limited power? Let us grant that it brings up life, that it can exist as a separate substance, that it cannot admit the death that is opposite to the life which it brings up: nevertheless it will wear itself out one day, will be extinguished and perish of its own accord, without any attack from outside.

124 (D 78, p. 226 N):

But on this showing even life in a substrate cannot admit its opposite; for it cannot admit death and yet continue to exist, any more than cold can admit heat and yet continue to exist. Hence life in a substrate is incapable of being dead in the same sense as cold is incapable of being hot; nevertheless life does come to an end.

Secondly, the perishing of a thing is not the reception by it of death; if it were, a living creature would never perish; the fact is that a creature does not persist, having admitted death; rather it is dead because it has lost life; for death is loss of life.

[*The second part of this may be condensed as follows: to be dead is not to possess a positive attribute which the soul cannot in fact possess: it is the body's having lost an attribute, viz. life, which it previously possessed.*] (R. Hackforth)

(*Note by Olympiodorus.*) To this argument of Strato's Proclus adds that the extinction of a soul is its dying, and dying, in Strato's own words, is the losing by the substrate [or body] of life.

OBJECTIONS TO THE THEORY OF RECOLLECTION

125 (D25, p. 211 N.). Why can one not 'recollect' without demonstration?

126 (II41, p. 158 N.). If there is such a thing as 'recollection', how is it

that we do not attain scientific knowledge without demonstration? Or how is it that no one has ever become a wind-player or string-player without practice?

127 (D65, p. 223 N.). The mind's possession of scientific knowledge is either (*a*) antecedent to time, in which case it has no need of time and is unaffected by time, so that men are eternally possessed of it; or (*b*) subsequent to time, in which case either the mind possesses it without 'recollection', learning [what it learns in this life] for the first time, or else what it recollects is knowledge immanent in it before its incarnation; [I say knowledge] for its maker presumably makes it a perfect, and therefore a *knowing* mind; yet on entering into this world minds need to learn, that is to 'recollect'.

[*This seems tantamount to complaining that Plato's assumption of a loss of knowledge at birth is arbitrary.*] R. Hackforth

(*Note by Olympiodorus.*) Furthermore Strato in his division eliminates 'everlasting time'; the thing which [supposedly] has everlasting existence in time is, he argues, something that falls between that which exists before time was and that which exists at some point in time.

[*The argument seems to be that all existence must be either timeless (outside time) and external or temporal (in time) and impermanent.*] R. Hackforth

And why, he asks, cannot we *readily* employ 'recollection'? Or is it the fact that some of us can, but most need training for it?

OBJECTION TO THE REFUTATION OF THE [SOUL AS A HARMONY] ψυχὴ ἁρμονία THEORY

118 (II 134, p. 174 N.). As one attunement is sharper (ὀξυτέρα) or flatter than another, so one soul is sharper or more sluggish than another.

Survival and the Idea of "Another World"
H. H. PRICE

*A*s you all know, this year is the seventieth anniversary of the foundation of the Society for Psychical Research. From the very beginning, the problem of survival has been one of the main interests of the Society; and that is my excuse, if any excuse is needed, for discussing some aspects of the problem this evening. I shall not, however, talk about the evidence for survival. In this lecture I am concerned only with the conception of survival; with the *meaning* of the Survival Hypothesis, and not with its truth or falsity. When we consider the Survival Hypothesis, whether we believe it or disbelieve it, what is it that we have in mind? Can we form any idea, even a rough and provisional one, of what a disembodied human life might be like? Supposing we cannot, it will follow that what is called the Survival Hypothesis is a mere set of words and not a hypothesis at all. The evidence adduced in favour of it might still be evidence for something, and perhaps for something important, but we should no longer have the right to claim that it is evidence for survival. There cannot be evidence for something which is completely unintelligible to us.

Now let us consider the situation in which we find ourselves after seventy years of psychical research. A very great deal of work has been done on the problem of survival, and much of the best work by members of our Society. Yet there are the widest differences of opinion about the results. A number of intelligent persons would maintain that we now have a very large mass of evidence in favour of survival; that some of it is of very good quality indeed, and cannot be explained away unless we suppose that the supernormal cognitive powers of

some embodied human minds are vastly more extensive and more accurate than we can easily believe them to be; in short, that on the evidence available the Survival Hypothesis is more probable than not. Some people—and not all of them are silly or credulous—would even maintain that the Survival Hypothesis is proved, or as near to being so as my empirical hypothesis can be. On the other hand, there are also many intelligent persons who entirely reject these conclusions. Some of them, no doubt, have not taken the trouble to examine the evidence. But others of them have; they may even have given years of study to it. They would agree that the evidence is evidence of *something*, and very likely of something important. But, they would say, it cannot be evidence of survival; there *must* be some alternative explanation of it, however difficult it may be to find out. Why do they take this line? I think it is because they find the very conception of survival unintelligible. The very idea of a "discarnate human personality" seems to them a muddled or absurd one; indeed not an idea at all, but just a phrase—an emotionally exciting one, no doubt—to which no clear meaning can be given.

Moreover, we cannot just ignore the people who have not examined the evidence. Some of our most intelligent and most highly educated contemporaries are among them. These men are well aware, by this time, that the evidence does exist, even if their predecessors fifty years ago were not. If you asked them why they do not trouble to examine it in detail, they would be able to offer reasons for their attitude. And one of their reasons, and not the least weighty in their eyes, is the contention

FROM: "Survival and the Idea of 'Another World,'" *Proceedings of the Society for Psychical Research*, Vol. L, Part 182 (January 1953), 1–25. Reprinted by permission of editor and author.

I mentioned just now, that the very idea of survival is a muddled or absurd one. To borrow an example from Whately Carington, we know pretty well what we mean by asking whether Jones has survived a shipwreck. We are asking whether he continues to live after the shipwreck has occurred. Similarly it makes sense to ask whether he survived a railway accident, or the bombing of London. But if we substitute "his own death" for "a shipwreck," and ask whether he has survived it, our question (it will be urged) becomes unintelligible. Indeed, it *looks* self-contradictory, as if we were asking whether Jones is still alive at a time when he is no longer alive—whether Jones is both alive and not alive at the same time. We may try to escape from this logical absurdity by using phrases like "discarnate existence," "alive, but disembodied." But such phrases, it will be said, have no clear meaning. No amount of facts, however well established, can have the slightest tendency to support a meaningless hypothesis, or to answer an unintelligible question. It would therefore be a waste of time to examine such facts in detail. There are other and more important things to do.

If I am right so far, questions about the meaning of the word "survival" or of the phrase "life after death" are not quite so arid and academic as they may appear. Anyone who wants to maintain that there is empirical evidence for survival ought to consider these questions, whether he thinks the evidence strong or weak. Indeed, anyone who thinks there is a *problem* of survival at all should ask himself what his conception of survival is.

Now why should it be thought that the very idea of life after death is unintelligible? Surely it is easy enough to conceive (whether or not it is true) that experiences might occur after Jones's death which are linked with experiences which he had before his death, in such a way that his personal identity is preserved? But, it will be said, the idea of after-death *experiences* is just the difficulty. What kind of experiences could

they conceivably be? In a disembodied state, the supply of sensory stimuli is perforce cut off, because the supposed experient has no sense organs and no nervous system. There can therefore be no sense-perception. One has no means of being aware of material objects any longer; and if one has not, it is hard to see how one could have any emotions or wishes either. For all the emotions and wishes we have in this present life are concerned directly or indirectly with material objects, including of course our own organisms and other organisms, especially other human ones. In short, one could only be said to have experiences at all, if one is aware of some sort of a *world*. In this way, the idea of survival is bound up with the idea of "another world" or a "next world." Anyone who maintains that the idea of survival is after all intelligible must also be claiming that we can form some conception, however rough and provisional, of what "the next world" or "other world" might be like. The skeptics I have in mind would say that we can form no such conception at all; and this, I think, is one of the main reasons why they hold that the conception of survival itself is unintelligible. I wish to suggest, on the contrary, that we *can* form some conception, in outline at any rate, of what a "next world" or "another world" might be like, and consequently of the kind of experiences which disembodied minds, if indeed there are such, might be supposed to have.

The thoughts which I wish to put before you on this subject are not at all original. Something very like them is to be found in the chapter on survival in Whately Carington's book *Telepathy*,[1] and in the concluding chapter of Professor C. J. Ducasse's book *Nature, Mind and Death*.[2] Moreover, if I am not mistaken, the Hindu conception of *Kama*

[1] Whately Carington, *Telepathy* (London: Methuen & Co., Ltd., 1945).

[2] C. J. Ducasse, *Nature, Mind and Death* (La Salle, Ill.: Open Court Publishing Co. 1951).

Loka (literally, "the world of desire") is essentially the same as the one I wish to discuss; and something very similar is to be found in Mahayana Buddhism. In these two religions, of course, there is not just one "other world" but several different "other worlds," which we are supposed to experience in succession; not merely the next world, but the next but one, and another after that. But I think it will be quite enough for us to consider just the next world, without troubling ourselves about any additional other worlds which there might be. It is a sufficiently difficult task, for us Western people, to convince ourselves that it makes sense to speak of any sort of after-death world at all. Accordingly, with your permission, I shall use the expressions "next world" and "other world" interchangeably. If anyone thinks this is an oversimplification, it will be easy for him to make the necessary corrections.

The next world, I think, might be conceived as a kind of dream-world. When we are asleep, sensory stimuli are cut off, or at any rate are prevented from having their normal effects upon our brain-centres. But we still manage to have experiences. It is true that sense-perception no longer occurs, but something sufficiently like it does. In sleep, our image-producing powers, which are more or less inhibited in waking life by a continuous bombardment of sensory stimuli, are released from this inhibition. And then we are provided with a multitude of objects of awareness, about which we employ our thoughts and towards which we have desires and emotions. These objects which we are aware of behave in a way which seems very queer to us when we wake up. The laws of their behaviour are not the laws of physics. But however queer their behaviour is, it does not at all disconcert us at the time and our personal identity is not broken.

In other words, my suggestion is that the next world, if there is one, might be a world of mental images. Nor need such a world be so "thin and insubstantial" as you might think. Paradoxical as it may sound, there is nothing imaginary about a mental image. It is an actual entity, as real as anything can be. The seeming paradox arises from the ambiguity of the verb "to imagine." It does sometimes mean "to have mental images." But more usually it means "to entertain propositions without believing them"; and very often they are false propositions, and moreover we *dis*believe them in the act of entertaining them. This is what happens, for example, when we read Shakespeare's play *The Tempest*, and that is why we say that Prospero and Ariel are "imaginary characters." Mental images are not in this sense imaginary at all. We do actually experience them, and they are no more imaginary than sensations. To avoid the paradox, though at the cost of some pedantry, it would be well to distinguish between *imagining* and *imaging*, and to have two different adjectives "imaginary" and "imagy." In this terminology, it is imaging, and not imagining, that I wish to talk about; and the next world, as I am trying to conceive of it, is an *imagy* world, but not on that account an imaginary one.

Indeed, to those who experienced it an image-world would be just as "real" as this present world is; perhaps so like it, that they would have considerable difficulty in realizing that they were dead. We are, of course, sometimes told in mediumistic communications that quite a lot of people do find it difficult to realize that they are dead; and this is just what we should expect if the next world is an image-world. Lord Russell and other philosophers have maintained that a material object in this present physical world is nothing more nor less than a complicated system of *appearances*. So far as I can see, there might be a set of visual images related to each other perspectivally, with front views and side views and back views all fitting neatly together in the way that ordinary visual appearances do now. Such a group of images might contain tactual images too. Similarly it might contain auditory images and smell images. Such a family of interrelated images would make a pretty good object. It would be quite a satisfactory substitute for the material objects which we perceive in this present life. And a whole world composed of such families of mental images would make a perfectly good world.

It is possible, however, and indeed likely, that some of those images would be what Francis Galton called *generic* images. An image representing a dog or a tree need not necessarily be an exact replica of some individual dog or tree one has perceived. It might rather be a representation of a *typical* dog or tree. Our memories are more specific on some subjects than on others. How specific they are depends probably on the degree of interest we had in the individual objects or events at the time when we perceived them. An event which moved us deeply is likely to be remembered specifically and in detail; and so is an individual object to which we were much attached (for example, the home of our childhood). But with other objects which interested us less and were less attended to, we retain only a "general impression" of a whole class of objects collectively. Left to our own resources, as we should be in the other world, with nothing but our memories to depend on, we should probably be able to form only generic images of such objects. In this respect, an image-world would not be an exact replica of this one, not even of those parts of this one which we have actually perceived. To some extent it would be, so to speak, a generalized picture, rather than a detailed reproduction.

Let us now put our question in another way, and ask what kind of experience a disembodied human mind might be supposed to have. We can then answer that it might be an experience in which *imaging* replaces sense-perception; "replaces" it, in the sense that imaging would perform much the same function as sense-perception performs now, by providing us with objects about which we could have thoughts, emotions and wishes. There is no reason why we should not be "as much alive," or at any rate *feel* as much alive, in an image-world as

we do now in this present material world, which we perceive by means of our sense-organs and nervous systems. And so the use of the word "survival" ("life after death") would be perfectly justifiable.

It will be objected, perhaps, that one cannot be said to be alive unless one has a body. But what is meant here by "alive"? It is surely conceivable (whether or not it is true) that *experiences* should occur which are not causally connected with a physical organism. If they did, should we or should we not say that "life" was occurring. I do not think it matters much whether we answer Yes or No. It is purely a question of definition. If you define "life" in terms of certain very complicated physico-chemical processes, as some people would, then of course life after death is by definition impossible, because there is no longer anything to be alive. In that case, the problem of survival (*life* after bodily death) is misnamed. Instead, it ought to be called the problem of after-death *experiences*. And this is in fact the problem with which all investigators of the subject have been concerned. After all, what people want to know, when they ask whether we survive death, is simply whether experiences occur after death, or what likelihood, if any, there is that they do; and whether such experiences, if they do occur, are linked with each other and with *ante mortem* ones in such a way that personal identity is preserved. It is not physico-chemical processes which interest us, when we ask such questions. But there is another sense of the words "life" and "alive" which may be called the psychological sense; and in this sense "being alive" just *means* "having experiences of certain sorts." In this psychological sense of the word "life," it is perfectly intelligible to ask whether there is life after death, even though life in the physiological sense does *ex hypothesi* come to an end when someone dies. Or, if you like, the question is whether one could feel alive after bodily death, even though (by hypothesis) one would not *be* alive at the time. It will be just enough to satisfy most of us if the *feel-*

ing of being alive continues after death. It will not make a halfpennyworth of difference that one will not then *be* alive in the physiological or biochemical sense of the word.

It may be said, however, that "feeling alive" (life in the psychological sense) cannot just be equated with having experiences in general. Feeling alive, surely, consists in having experiences of a special sort, namely *organic sensations*— bodily feelings of various sorts. In our present experience, these bodily feelings are not as a rule separately attended to unless they are unusually intense or unusually painful. They are a kind of undifferentiated mass in the background of consciousness. All the same, it would be said, they constitute our feeling of being alive; and if they were absent (as surely they must be when the body is dead) the feeling of being alive could not be there.

I am not at all sure that this argument is as strong as it looks. I think we should still feel alive—or alive enough —provided we experienced emotions and wishes, even if no organic sensations accompanied these experiences, as they do now. But in case I am wrong here, I would suggest that *images* of organic sensations could perfectly well provide what is needed. We can quite well image to ourselves what it feels like to be in a warm bath, even when we are not actually in one; and a person who has been crippled can image what it felt like to climb a mountain. Moreover, I would ask whether we do not feel alive when we are dreaming. It seems to me that we obviously do—or at any rate quite alive enough to go on with.

This is not all. In an image-world, a dream-like world such as I am trying to describe, there is no reason at all why there should not be *visual* images resembling the body which one had in this present world. In this present life (for all who are not blind) visual percepts of one's own body form as it were the constant centre of one's perceptual world. It is perfectly possible that visual images of one's own body might perform the same function in the next. They might form the continuing centre or nucleus of one's image world, remaining more or less constant while other images altered. If this were so, we should have an additional reason for expecting that recently dead people would find it difficult to realize that they were dead, that is, disembodied. To all appearances they *would* have bodies just as they had before, and pretty much the same ones. But, of course, they might discover in time that these image-bodies were subject to rather peculiar causal laws. For example, it might be found that in an image-world our wishes tend *ipso facto* to fulfil themselves in a way they do not now. A wish to go to Oxford might be immediately followed by the occurrence of a vivid and detailed set of Oxford-like images; even though, at the moment before, one's images had resembled Piccadilly Circus or the palace of the Dalai Lama in Tibet. In that case, one would realize that "going somewhere"— transferring one's body from one place to another—was a rather different process from what it had been in the physical world. Reflecting on such experiences, one might come to the conclusion that one's body was not after all the same as the physical body one had before death. One might conclude perhaps that it must be a "spiritual" or "psychical" body, closely resembling the old body in appearance, but possessed of rather different causal properties. It has been said, of course, that phrases like "spiritual body" or "psychical body" are utterly unintelligible, and that no conceivable empirical meaning could be given to such expressions. But I would rather suggest that they might be a way (rather a misleading way perhaps) of referring to a set of body-like images. If our supposed dead empiricist continued his investigations, he might discover that his whole world—not only his own body, but everything else he was aware of—had different causal properties from the physical world, even though everything in it had shape, size, colour, and other qualities which material objects have now. And so eventually, by the exercise of ordinary inductive good sense, he could draw the conclusion that he was in "the next world" or "the other world" and no longer in this one. If, however, he were a very dogmatic philosopher, who distrusted inductive good sense and preferred a priori reasoning, I do not know what condition he would be in. Probably he would never discover that he was dead at all. Being persuaded, on a priori grounds, that life after death was impossible, he might insist on thinking that he must still be in this world, and refuse to pay attention to the new and strange causal laws which more empirical thinkers would notice.

I think, then, that there is no difficulty in conceiving that the experience of feeling alive could occur in the absence of a physical organism; or, if you prefer to put it so, a disembodied personality could *be* alive in the psychological sense, even though by definition it would not be alive in the physiological or biochemical sense.

Moreover, I do not see why disembodiment need involve the destruction of personal identity. It is, of course, sometimes supposed that personal identity depends on the continuance of a background of organic sensation—the "mass of bodily feeling" mentioned before. (This may be called the somato-centric analysis of personal identity.) We must notice, however, that this background of organic sensation is not literally the same from one period of time to another. The very most that can happen is that the organic sensations which form the background of my experience now should be *exactly similar* to those which were the background of my experience a minute ago. And as a matter of fact, the present ones need not *all* be exactly similar to the previous ones. I might have a twinge of toothache now which I did not have then. I may even have an overall feeling of lassitude now which I did not have a minute ago, so that the whole mass of bodily feeling, and not merely part of it, is rather different; and this would not interrupt my personal identity at all. The most that is required is only that the majority (not all) of my organic sensations should be closely (not exactly) similar to those I previously

had. And even this is only needed if the two occasions are close together in my private time series; the organic sensations I have now might well be very unlike those I used to have when I was one year old. I say "in my private times series." For when I wake up after eight hours of dreamless sleep my personal identity is not broken, though in the physical or public time series there has been a long interval between the last organic sensations I experienced before falling asleep, and the first ones I experience when I wake up. But if similarity, and not literal sameness, is all that is required of this "continuing organic background," it seems to me that the continuity of it could be perfectly well preserved if there were organic *images* after death very like the organic *sensations* which occurred before death.

As a matter of fact, this whole "somato-centric" analysis of personal identity appears to me highly disputable. I should have thought that Locke was much nearer the truth when he said that personal identity depends on memory. But I have tried to show that even if the "somato-centric" theory of personal identity is right, there is no reason why personal identity need be broken by bodily death, provided there are images after death which sufficiently resemble the organic sensations one had before; and this is very like what happens when one falls asleep and begins dreaming.

There is, however, another argument against the conceivability of a disembodied person, to which some present-day linguistic philosophers would attach great weight. It is neatly expressed by Mr. A. G. N. Flew when he says, "people are what you meet."[3] By a "per-

---

[3] *University*, Vol. II, No. 2, 38, in a symposium on "Death" with Professor D. M. Mackinnon. Mr. Flew obviously uses "people" as the plural of "person"; but if we are to be linguistic, I am inclined to think that the nuances of "people" are not quite the same as those of "person." When we used the word "person," in the singular or the plural, the notion of consciousness is more prominently before our minds than it is when we use the word "people."

son" we are supposed to mean a human organism which behaves in certain ways, and especially one which speaks and can be spoken to. And when we say, "this is the same person whom I saw yesterday," we are supposed to mean just that it is the same human organism which I saw yesterday, and also that it behaves in a recognizably similar way.

"People are what you meet." With all respect to Mr. Flew, I would suggest that he does not in this sense "meet" *himself*. He might indeed have had one of those curious out-of-body experiences which are occasionally mentioned in our records, and he might have seen his body from outside (if he has, I heartily congratulate him); but I do not think we should call this "meeting." And surely the important question is, what constitutes my personal identity *for myself*. It certainly does not consist in the fact that other people can "meet" me. It might be that I was for myself the same person as before, even at a time when it was quite impossible for others to meet me. No one can "meet" me when I am dreaming. They can, of course, come and look at my body lying in bed; but this is not "meeting," because no sort of social relations are possible between them and me. Yet, although temporarily "unmeetable," during my dreams I am still, for myself, the same person that I was. And if I went on dreaming *in perpetuum*, and could never be "met" again, this need not prevent me from continuing to be, for myself, the same person.

As a matter of fact, however, we can quite easily conceive that "meeting" of a kind might still be possible between discarnate experients. And therefore, even if we do make it part of the definition of "a person," that he is capable of being met by others, it will still make sense to speak of "discarnate persons," provided we allow that telepathy is possible between them. It is true that a special sort of telepathy would be needed; the sort which in life produces *telepathic apparitions*. It would not be sufficient that A's thoughts or emotions should be telepathically affected by B's. If such telepathy were sufficiently prolonged and

continuous, and especially if it were reciprocal, it would indeed have some of the characteristics of social intercourse; but I do not think we should call it "meeting," at any rate in Mr. Flew's sense of the word. It would be necessary, in addition, that A should be aware of something which could be called "B's body," or should have an experience not too unlike the experience of *seeing* another person in this life. This additional condition would be satisfied if A experienced a telepathic apparition of B. It would be necessary, further, that the telepathic apparition by means of which B "announces himself" (if one may put it so) should be recognizably similar on different occasions. And if it were a case of meeting some person *again* whom one had previously known in this world, the telepathic apparition would have to be recognizably similar to the physical body which that person had when he was still alive.

There is no reason why an image-world should not contain a number of images which are telepathic apparitions; and if it did, one could quite intelligently speak of "meeting other persons" in such a world. All the experiences I have when I meet another person in this present life could still occur, with only this difference, that percepts would be replaced by images. It would also be possible for another person to "meet" me in the same manner, if I, as a telepathic agent could cause him to experience a suitable telepathic apparition, sufficiently resembling the body I used to have when he formerly "met" me in this life.

I now turn to another problem which may have troubled some of you. If there be a next world, *where* is it? Surely it must be somewhere. But there does not seem to be any room for it. We can hardly suppose that it is up in the sky (i.e., outside the earth's atmosphere) or under the surface of the earth, as Homer and Vergil seemed to think. Such suggestions may have contented our ancestors, and the Ptolemaic astronomy may have made them acceptable, for some ages, even to the learned; but they will hardly content us. Surely the next world, if it exists, must be somewhere; and yet, it seems, there is nowhere for it to be.

The answer to this difficulty is easy if we conceive of the next world in the way I have suggested, as a dream-like world of mental images. Mental images, including dream images, are in a space of their own. They do have spatial properties. Visual images, for instance, have extension and shape, and they have spatial relations to one another. But they have no spatial relation to objects in the physical world. If I dream of a tiger, my tiger-image has extension and shape. The dark stripes have spatial relation to the yellow parts, and to each other; the nose has a spatial relation to the tail. Again, the tiger image as a whole may have spatial relations to another image in my dream, for example to an image resembling a palm tree. But suppose we have to ask how far it is from the foot of my bed, whether it is three inches long, or longer or shorter; is it not obvious that these questions are absurd ones? We cannot answer them, not because we lack the necessary information or find it impracticable to make the necessary measurements, but because the questions themselves have no meaning. In the space of the physical world these images are nowhere at all. But in relation to other images of mine, each of them is somewhere. Each of them is extended, and its parts are in spatial relations to one another. There is no a priori reason why all extended entities must be in physical space.

If we now apply these considerations to the next world, as I am conceiving of it, we see that the question "where is it?" simply does not arise. An image-world would have a space of its own. We could not find it anywhere in the space of the physical world, but this would not in the least prevent it from being a spatial world all the same. If you like, it would be its own "where."[4]

I am tempted to illustrate this point by referring to the fairy-tale of Jack and the Beanstalk. I am not of course suggesting that we should take the story seriously. But if we were asked to try to make sense of it, how should we set about it? Obviously the queer world which Jack found was not at the top of the beanstalk in the literal, spatial sense of the words "at the top of." Perhaps he found some very large pole rather like a beanstalk, and climbed up it. But (we shall say) when he got to the top he suffered an abrupt change of consciousness, and began to have a dream or waking vision of a strange country with a giant in it. To choose another and more respectable illustration: In Book VI of Vergil's *Aeneid*, we are told how Aeneas descended into the Cave of Avernus with the Sibyl and walked from there into the other world. If we wished to make the narrative of the illustrious poet intelligible, how should we set about it? We should suppose that Aeneas did go down into the cave, but that once he was there he suffered a change of consciousness, and all the strange experiences which happened afterwards—seeing the River Styx, the Elysian Fields and the rest—were part of a dream or vision which he had. The space he passed through in his journey was an image space, and the River Styx was not three Roman miles, or any other number of miles, from the cave in which his body was.

It follows that when we speak of "passing" from this world to the next, this passage is not to be thought of as any sort of movement in space. It should rather be thought of as a change of consciousness, analogous to the change which occurs when we "pass" from waking experience to dreaming. It would be a change from the perceptual type of consciousness to another type of consciousness in which perception ceases and

---

[4] Conceivably its geometrical structure might also be different from the geometrical structure of the physical world. In that case the space of the next world would not only be other than the space of the physical world, but would also be a different *sort* of space.

imaging replaces it, but unlike the change from waking consciousness to dreaming in being irreversible. I suppose that nearly everyone nowadays who talks of "passing" from this world to the other does think of the transition in this way, as some kind of irreversible change of consciousness, and not as a literal spatial transition in which one goes from one place to another place.

So much for the question "where the next world is," if there be one. I have tried to show that if the next world is conceived of as a world of mental images, the question simply does not arise. I now turn to another difficulty. It may be felt that an image-world is somehow a deception and a sham, not a real world at all. I have said that it would be a kind of dream-world. Now when one has a dream in this life, surely the things one is aware of in the dream are not *real* things. No doubt the dreamer really does have various mental images. These images do actually occur. But this is not all that happens. As a result of having these images, the dreamer believes, or takes for granted, that various material objects exist and various physical events occur; and these beliefs are mistaken. For example, he believes that there is a wall in front of him and that by a mere effort of will he succeeds in flying over the top of it. But the wall did not really exist, and he did not really fly over the top of it. He was in a state of delusion. Because of the images which he really did have, there *seemed* to him to be various objects and events which did not really exist at all. Similarly, you may argue, it may *seem* to discarnate minds (if indeed there are such) that there is a world in which they live, and a world not unlike this one. If they have mental images of the appropriate sort, it may even *seem* to them that they have bodies not unlike the ones they had in this life. But surely they will be mistaken. It is all very well to say, with the poet, that "dreams are real while they last"—that dream-objects are only called "unreal" when one wakes up, and normal sense-perceptions begin to occur with which

the dream experiences can be contrasted. And it is all very well to conclude from this that if one did *not* wake up, if the change from sense-perception to imaging were irreversible, one would not call one's dream-objects unreal, because there would then be nothing with which to contrast them. But would they not still *be* unreal for all that? Surely discarnate minds, according to my account of them, would be in a state of permanent delusion; whereas a dreamer in this life (fortunately for him) is only in a temporary one. And the fact that a delusion goes on for a long time, even forever and ever, does not make it any less delusive. Delusions do not turn themselves into realities just by going on and on. Nor are they turned into realities by the fact that their victim is deprived of the power of detecting their delusiveness.

Now, of course, if it were true that the next life (supposing there is one) is a condition of permanent delusion, we should just have to put up with it. We might not like it; we might think that a state of permanent delusion is a bad state to be in. But our likes and dislikes are irrelevant to the question. I would suggest, however, that this argument about the "delusiveness" or "unreality" of an image-world is based on confusion.

One may doubt whether there is any clear meaning in using the words "real" and "unreal" *tout court*, in this perfectly general and unspecified way. One may properly say, "this is real silver, and that is not," "this is a real pearl and that is not," or again "this is a real pool of water, and that is only a mirage." The point here is that something X is mistakenly believed to be something else Y, because it does resemble Y in some respects. It makes perfectly good sense, then, to say that X is not really Y. This piece of plated brass is not real silver, true enough. It only looks like silver. But for all that, it cannot be called "unreal" in the unqualified sense, in the sense of not existing at all. Even the mirage is something, though it is not the pool of water you took it to be. It is a perfectly good set of visual appearances, though it is not related to other appearances in the way you thought it was; for example, it does not have the relations to tactual appearances, or to visual appearances from other places, which you expected it to have. You may properly say that the mirage is not a real pool of water, or even that it is not a real physical object, and that anyone who thinks it is must be in a state of delusion. But there is no clear meaning in saying that it is just "unreal" *tout court*, without any further specification or explanation. In short, when the word "unreal" is applied to something, one means that it is different from something else, with which it might be mistakenly identified; what that something else is may not be explicitly stated, but it can be gathered from the context.

What, then, could people mean by saying that a next world such as I have described would be "unreal"? If they are saying anything intelligible, they must mean that it is different from something else, something else which it does resemble in some respects, and might therefore be confused with. And what is that something else? It is the present physical world in which we now live. An image-world, then, is only "unreal" in the sense that it is not really physical, though it might be mistakenly thought to be physical by some of those who experience it. But this only amounts to saying that the world I am describing would be an *other* world, other than this present physical world, which is just what it ought to be; other than this present physical world, and yet sufficiently like it to be possibly confused with it, because images do resemble percepts. And what would this otherness consist in? First, in the fact that it is a *space* which is other than physical space; secondly, and still more important, in the fact that the *causal laws* of an image-world would be different from the laws of physics. And this is also our ground for saying that the events we experience in dreams are "unreal," that is, not really physical, though mistakenly believed by the dreamer to be so. They do in some ways closely resemble physical events,

and that is why the mistake is possible. But the causal laws of their occurrence are quite different, as we recognize when we wake up; and just occasionally we recognize it even while we are still asleep.

Now let us consider the argument that the inhabitants of the other world, as I have described it, would be in a state of delusion. I admit that some of them might be. That would be the condition of the people described in the mediumistic communications already referred to—the people who "do not realize that they are dead." Because their images are so like the normal percepts they were accustomed to in this life, they believe mistakenly that they are still living in the physical world. But, as I already tried to explain, their state of delusion need not be permanent and irremediable. By attending to the relations between one image and another, and applying the ordinary inductive methods by which we ourselves have discovered the casual laws of this present world in which *we* live, they too could discover in time what the causal laws of *their* world are. These laws, we may suppose, would be more like the laws of Freudian psychology than the laws of physics. And once the discovery was made, they would be cured of their delusion. They would find out, perhaps with surprise, that the world they were experiencing was *other* than the physical world which they experienced before, even though like it in some respects.

Let us now try to explore the conception of a world of mental images a little more fully. Would it not be a *"subjective"* world? And surely there would be many *different* next worlds, not just one; and each of them would be private. Indeed, would there not be as many next worlds as there are discarnate minds, and each of them wholly private to the mind which experiences it? In short, it may seem that each of us, when dead, would have his own dream-world, and there would be no common or public next world at all.

"Subjective," perhaps, is a rather slippery word. Certainly, an image-world would have to be subjective in the sense of being mind-dependent, dependent for its existence upon mental processes of one sort or another; images, after all, are mental entities. But I do not think that such a world need be completely private, if telepathy occurs in the next life. I have already mentioned the part which telepathic apparitions might play in it in connection with Mr. Flew's contention that "people are what you meet." But there is more to be said. It is reasonable to suppose that in a disembodied state telepathy would occur more frequently than it does now. It seems likely that in this present life our telepathic powers are constantly being inhibited by our need to adjust ourselves to our physical environment. It even seems likely that many telepathic "impressions" which we receive at the unconscious level are shut out from consciousness by a kind of biologically motivated censorship. Once the pressure of biological needs is removed, we might expect that telepathy would occur continually, and manifest itself in consciousness by modifying and adding to the images which one experiences. (Even in this life, after all, some dreams are telepathic.)

If this is right, an image-world such as I am describing would not be the product of one single mind only, nor would it be purely private. It would be the joint product of a group of telepathically interacting minds and public to all of them. Nevertheless, one would not expect it to have unrestricted publicity. It is likely that there would still be *many* next worlds, a different one for each group of like-minded personalities. I admit I am not quite sure what might be meant by "like-minded" and "unlike-minded" in this connection. Perhaps we could say that two personalities are like-minded if their memories or their characters are sufficiently similar. It might be that Nero and Marcus Aurelius do not have a world in common, but Socrates and Marcus Aurelius do.

So far, we have a picture of many "semi-public" next worlds, if one may put it so; each of them composed of mental images, and yet not wholly private

for all that, but public to a limited group of telepathically interacting minds. Or, if you like, after death everyone does have his own dream, but there is still some overlap between one person's dream and another's because of telepathy.

I have said that such a world would be mind-dependent, even though dependent on a group of minds rather than a single mind. In what way would it be mind-dependent? Presumably in the same way as dreams are now. It would be dependent on the *memories* and the *desires* of the persons who experienced it. Their memories and their desires would determine what sort of images they had. If I may put it so, the "stuff" or "material" of such a world would come in the end from one's memories, and the "form" of it from one's desires. To use another analogy, memory would provide the pigments, and desire would paint the picture. One might expect, I think, that desires which had been unsatisfied in one's earthly life would play a specially important part in the process. That may seem an agreeable prospect. But there is another which is less agreeable. Desires which had been *repressed* in one's earthly life, because it was too painful or too disgraceful to admit that one had them, might also play a part, and perhaps an important part, in determining what images one would have in the next. And the same might be true of repressed memories. It may be suggested that what Freud (in one stage of his thought) called "the censor"—the force or barrier or mechanism which keeps some of our desires and memories out of consciousness, or only lets them in when they disguise themselves in symbolic and distorted forms—operates only in this present life and not in the next. However we conceive of "the censor," it does seem to be a device for enabling us to adapt ourselves to our environment. And when we no longer have an environment, one would expect that the barrier would come down.

We can now see that an after-death world of mental images can also be quite reasonably described in the terminology of the Hindu thinkers as "a world of desire" (Rama Loka). Indeed, this is just what we should expect if we assume that dreams, in this present life, are the best available clue to what the next life might be like. Such a world could also be described as "a world of memories"; because imaging, in the end, is a function of memory, one of the ways in which our memory-dispositions manifest themselves. But this description would be less apt, even though correct as far as it goes. To use the same rather inadequate language as before, the "materials" out of which an image-world is composed would have to come from the memories of the mind or group of minds whose world it is. But it would be their desires (including those repressed in earthly life) which determined the way in which these memories were used, the precise kind of dream which was built up out of them or on the basis of them.

It will, of course, be objected that memories cannot exist in the absence of a physical brain, nor yet desires, nor images either. But this proposition, however plausible, is after all just an empirical hypothesis, not a necessary truth. Certainly there is empirical evidence in favour of it. But there is also empirical evidence against it. Broadly speaking one might say, perhaps, that the "normal" evidence tends to support this materialistic or epiphenomenalist theory of memories, images, and desires, whereas the "supernormal" evidence on the whole tends to weaken the materialist or epiphenomenalist theory of human personality (of which this hypothesis about the brain-dependent character of memories, images, and desires is a part). Moreover, any evidence which directly supports the Survival Hypothesis (and there is quite a lot of evidence which does, provided we are prepared to admit that the Survival Hypothesis is intelligible at all) is *pro tanto* evidence against the materialistic conception of human personality.

In this lecture, I am not trying to argue in favour of the Survival Hypothesis. I am only concerned with the more modest task of trying to make it intelligible. All I want to maintain, then, is that there is nothing self-contradictory or logically absurd in the hypothesis that memories, desires, and images can exist in the absence of a physical brain. The hypothesis may, of course, be false. My point is only that it is not absurd; or if you like, that it is at any rate intelligible, whether true or not. To put the question in another way, when we are trying to work out for ourselves what sort of thing a discarnate life might conceivably be (if there is one) we have to ask what kind of *equipment*, so to speak, a discarnate mind might be supposed to have. It cannot have the power of sense-perception, nor the power of acting on the physical world by means of efferent nerves, muscles, and limbs. What would it have left? What could we take out with us, as it were, when we pass from this life to the next? What we take out with us, I suggest, can only be our memories and desires, and the power of constructing out of them an image world to suit us. Obviously we cannot take our material possessions out with us; but I do not think this is any great loss, for if we remember them well enough and are sufficiently attached to them, we shall be able to construct image-replicas of them which will be just as good, and perhaps better.

In this connection I should like to mention a point which has been made several times before. Both Whately Carington and Professor Ducasse have referred to it, and no doubt other writers have. But I believe it is of some importance and worth repeating. Ecclesiastically minded critics sometimes speak rather scathingly of the "materialistic" character of mediumistic communications. They are not at all edified by these descriptions of agreeable houses, beautiful landscapes, gardens, and the rest. And then, of course, there is Raymond Lodge's notorious cigar.[5] These critics

[5] See: Sir Oliver Lodge, *Raymond Revised* (London: Methuen & Co., Ltd., 1922), p. 113.

complain that the next world as described in these communications is no more than a reproduction of this one, slightly improved perhaps. And the argument apparently is that the "materialistic" character of the communications is evidence against their genuineness. On the contrary, as far as it goes, it is evidence *for* their genuineness. Most people in this life do like material objects and are deeply interested in them. This may be deplorable, but there it is. If so, the image-world they would create for themselves in the next life might be expected to have just the "materialistic" character of which these critics complain. If one had been fond of nice houses and pleasant gardens in this life, the image-world one would create for himself in the next might be expected to contain image-replicas of such objects, and one would make these replicas as like "the real thing" as one's memories permitted; with the help, perhaps, of telepathic influences from other minds whose tastes were similar. This would be all the more likely to happen if one had not been able to enjoy such things in this present life as much as one could wish.

But possibly I have misunderstood the objection which these ecclesiastical critics are making. Perhaps they are saying that if the next world is like this, life after death is not worth having. Well and good. If they would prefer a different sort of next world, and find the one described in these communications insipid and unsatisfying to their aspirations, then they can expect to get a different one—in fact, just the sort of next world they want. They have overlooked a crucial point which seems almost obvious; that if there is an after-death life at all, there must surely be many next worlds, separate from and as it were impenetrable to one another, corresponding to the *different* desires which different groups of discarnate personalities have.

The belief in life after death is often dismissed as "mere wish-fulfilment." Now it will be noticed that the next world as I have been trying to conceive of it is precisely a wish-fulfilment world, in much the same sense in which some dreams are described as wish-fulfilments. Should not this make a rational man very suspicious of the ideas I am putting before you? Surely this account of the other world is "too good to be true"? I think not. Here we must distinguish two different questions. The question whether human personality continues to exist after death is a question of fact, and wishes have nothing to do with it one way or the other. But *if* the answer to this factual question were "Yes" (and I emphasise the "if"), wishes might have a very great deal to do with the kind of world which discarnate beings would live in. Perhaps it may be helpful to consider a parallel case. It is a question of fact whether dreams occur in this present life. It has been settled by empirical investigation, and the wishes of the investigators have nothing to do with it. It is just a question of what the empirical facts are, whether one likes them or not. Nevertheless, granting that dreams do occur, a man's wishes might well have a very great deal to do with determining what the content of his dreams is to be; especially unconscious wishes on the one hand, and on the other, conscious wishes which are not satisfied in waking life. Of course the parallel is not exact. There is one very important difference between the two cases. With dreams, the question of fact is settled. It is quite certain that many people do have dreams. But in the case of survival, the question of fact is not settled, or not at present. It is still true, however, that though wishes have nothing to do with it, they have a very great deal to do with the kind of world we should live in after death, *if* we survive death at all.

But perhaps this does not altogether dispose of the objection that my account of the other world is "too good to be true." Surely a sober-minded and cautious person would be very shy of believing that there is, or even could be, a world in which all our wishes are fulfilled? How very suspicious we are about travellers' tales of Eldorado or descriptions of idyllic South Sea islands! Certainly we are, and on good empirical grounds. For they are tales about this present material world; and we know that matter is very often recalcitrant to human wishes. But in a dream-world Desire is king. This objection would only hold good if the world I am describing were supposed to be some part of the *material* world—another planet perhaps, or the Earthly Paradise of which some poets have written. But the next world as I am trying to conceive of it (or rather next worlds, for we have seen that there would be many different ones) is not of course supposed to be part of the material world at all. It is a dream-like world of mental images. True enough, some of these images might be expected to resemble some of the material objects with which we are familiar now; but only if, and to the extent that, their percipients *wanted* this resemblance to exist. There is every reason, then, for being suspicious about descriptions of this present material world, or alleged parts of it, on the ground that they are "too good to be true"; but when it is a "country of the mind" (if one may say so) which is being described, these suspicions are groundless. A purely mind-dependent world, if such a world there be, would *have* to be a wish-fulfilment world.

Nevertheless, likes and dislikes, however irrelevant they may be, do of course have a powerful psychological influence upon us when we consider the problem of survival; not only when we consider the factual evidence for or against, but also when we are merely considering the theoretical implications of the Survival Hypothesis itself, as I am doing now. It is therefore worthwhile to point out that the next world as I am conceiving of it need not necessarily be an agreeable place at all. If arguments about what is good or what is bad did have any relevance, a case could be made out for saying that this conception of the next world is "too bad to be true," rather than too good. As we have seen, we should have to reckon with

many different next worlds, not just with one. The world you experience after death would depend upon the kind of person you are. And if what I have said so far has any sense in it, we can easily conceive that some people's next worlds would be much more like purgatories than paradises—and pretty unpleasant purgatories too.

This is because there are *conflicting* desires within the same person. Few people, if any, are completely integrated personalities, though some people come nearer to it than others. And sometimes when a man's desires appear (even to himself) to be more or less harmonious with one another, the appearance is deceptive. His conscious desires do not conflict with one another or not much; but this harmony has only been achieved at the cost of repression. He has unconscious desires which conflict with the neatly organized pattern of his conscious life. If I was right in suggesting that repression is a biological phenomenon, if the "threshold" between conscious and unconscious no longer operates in a disembodied state, or operates much less effectively, this seeming harmony will vanish after the man is dead. To use scriptural language, the secrets of his heart will be revealed—at any rate to himself. These formerly repressed desires will manifest themselves by appropriate images, and these images might be exceedingly horrifying—as some dream-images are in this present life, and for the same reason. True enough, they will be "wish-fulfilment" images, like everything else that he experiences in the next world as I am conceiving it. But the wishes they fulfil will conflict with other wishes which he also has. And the emotional state which results might be worse than the worst nightmare; worse, because the dreamer cannot wake up from it. For example, in his after-death dream world he finds himself doing appallingly cruel actions. He never did them in his earthly life. Yet the desire to do them was there, even though repressed and unacknowledged. And now the lid is off, and this cruel desire fulfils itself by creating appropriate images. But unfortunately for his comfort, he has benevolent desires as well, perhaps quite strong ones; and so he is distressed and even horrified by these images, even though there is also a sense in which they are just the ones he wanted. Of course his benevolent desires too may be expected to manifest themselves by appropriate wish-fulfilment images. But because there is this conflict in his nature, they will not wholly satisfy him either. There will be something in him which rejects them as tedious and insipid. It is a question of the point of view, if one cares to put it so. Suppose a person has two conflicting desires *A* and *B*. Then from the point of view of desire *A*, the images which fulfil desire *B* will be unsatisfying, or unpleasant, or even horrifying; and vice versa from the point of view of desire *B*. And unfortunately, both points of view belong to the same person. He occupies them both at once.

This is not all. If psychoanalysts are right, there is such a thing as a desire to be punished. Most people, we are told, have guilt-feelings which are more or less repressed; we have desires, unacknowledged or only half-acknowledged, to suffer for the wrongs we have done. These desires too will have their way in the next world, if my picture of it is right, and will manifest themselves by images which fulfil them. It is not a very pleasant prospect, and I need not elaborate it. But it looks as if everyone would experience an image-purgatory which exactly suits him. It is true that his unpleasant experiences would not literally be punishments, any more than terrifying dreams are in this present life. They would not be inflicted upon him by an external judge; though, of course, if we are theists, we shall hold that the laws of nature, in other worlds as in this one, are in the end dependent on the will of a Divine Creator. Each man's purgatory would be just the automatic consequence of his own desires; if you like, he would punish himself by having just those images which his own good

feelings demand. But, if there is any consolation in it, he would have these unpleasant experiences because he *wanted* to have them; exceedingly unpleasant as they might be, there would still be something in him which was satisfied by them.

There is another aspect of the conflict of desires. Every adult person has what we call "a character"; a set of more or less settled and permanent desires, with the corresponding emotional dispositions, expressing themselves in a more or less predictable pattern of thoughts, feelings, and actions. But it is perfectly possible to desire that one's character should be different, perhaps very different, from what it is at present. This is what philosophers call a "second-order" desire, a desire that some of one's own desires should be altered. Such second-order desires are not necessarily ineffective, as New Year resolutions are supposed to be. People can within limits alter their own characters, and sometimes do; and if they succeed in doing so, it is in the end because they *want* to. But these "second-order" desires—desires to alter one's own character—are seldom effective immediately; and even when they appear to be, as in some cases of religious conversion, there has probably been a long period of subconscious or unconscious preparation first. To be effective, desires of this sort must occur again and again. I must go on wishing to be more generous or less timid, and not just wish it on New Year's day; I must train myself to act habitually—and think too—in the way that I should act and think if I possessed the altered character for which I wish. From the point of view of the present moment, however, one's character is something fixed and given. The wish I have at half-past twelve today will do nothing, or almost nothing, to alter it.

These remarks may seem very remote from the topic I am supposed to be discussing. But they have a direct bearing on a question which has been mentioned before: whether, or in what sense, the next world as I am conceiving of it should be called a "subjective" world. As I have already said, a next world such as I have described *would* be subjective, in the sense of mind-dependent. The minds which experience it would also have created it. It would just be the manifestation of their own memories and desires, even though it might be the joint creation of a number of telepathically interacting minds, and therefore not wholly private. But there is a sense in which it might have a certain objectivity all the same. One thing we mean by calling something "objective" is that it is so whether we like it or not, and even if we dislike it. This is also what we mean by talking about "hard facts" or "stubborn facts."

At first sight it may seem that in an image-world such as I have described there could be no hard facts or stubborn facts, and nothing objective in this sense of the word "objective." How could there be, if the world we experience is itself a wish-fulfilment world? But a man's character *is* in this sense "objective"; objective in the sense that he has it whether he likes it or not. And facts about his character are as "hard" or "stubborn" as any. Whether I like it or not, and even though I dislike it, it is a hard fact about me that I am timid or spiteful, that I am fond of eating oysters or averse from talking French. I may wish sometimes that these habitual desires and aversions of mine were different, but at any particular moment this wish will do little or nothing to alter them. In the short run, a man's permanent and habitual desires are something "given" which he must accept and put up with as best he can, even though in the very long run they are alterable.

Now in the next life, according to my picture of it, it would be these permanent and habitual desires which would determine the nature of the world in which a person has to live. His world would be, so to speak, the outgrowth of his character; it would be his own character represented before him in the form of dream-like images. There is therefore a sense in which he gets exactly

the sort of world he wants, whatever internal conflicts there may be between one of these wants and another. Yet he may very well dislike having the sort of character he does have. In the short run, as I have said, his character is something fixed and given, and objective in the sense that he has that character whether he likes it or not. Accordingly his image-world is also objective in the same sense. It is objective in the sense that it insists on presenting itself to him whether he likes it or not.

To look at the same point in another way: the next world as I am picturing it may be a very queer sort of world, but still it would be subject to causal laws. The laws would not, of course, be the laws of physics. As I have suggested already, they might be expected to be more like the laws of Freudian psychology. But they would be laws all the same, and objective in the sense that they hold good whether one liked it or not. And if we do dislike the image-world which our desires and memories create for us—if, when we get what we want, we are horrified to discover what things they were which we wanted—we shall have to set about altering our characters, which might be a very long and painful process.

Some people tell us, of course, that all desires, even the most permanent and habitual ones, will wear themselves out in time by the mere process of being satisfied. It may be so, and perhaps there is comfort in the thought. In that case the dream-like world of which I have been speaking would only be temporary, and we should have to ask whether after the next world there is a next but one. The problem of survival would then arise again in a new form. We should have to ask whether personal identity could still be preserved when we were no longer even dreaming. It could, I think, be preserved through the transition from this present, perceptible world to a dream-like image world of the kind I have been describing. But if even imaging were to cease, would there be anything left of human personality at all? Or would the state of existence—if any—which followed be one to which the notion of personality, at any rate our present notion, no longer had any application? I think that these are questions upon which it is unprofitable and perhaps impossible to speculate. (If anyone wishes to make the attempt, I can only advise him to consult the writings of the mystics, both Western and Oriental.) It is quite enough for us to consider what the *next* world might conceivably be like, and some of you may think that even this is too much.

Before I end, I should like to make one concluding remark. You may have noticed that the next world, according to my account of it, is not at all unlike what some metaphysicians say *this* world is. In the philosophy of Schopenhauer, this present world itself, in which we now live, is a world of "will and idea." And so it is in Berkeley's philosophy too; material objects are just collections of "ideas," though according to Berkeley the will which presents these ideas to us is the will of God, acting directly upon us in a way which is in effect telepathic. Could it be that these idealist metaphysicians have given us a substantially correct picture of the next world, though a mistaken picture of this one? The study of metaphysical theories is out of ques-

tion nowadays. But perhaps students of psychical research would do well to pay some attention to them. *If* there are other worlds than this (again I emphasize the "if") who knows whether with some stratum of our personalities we are not living in them now, as well as in this present one which conscious sense-perception discloses? Such a repressed and unconscious awareness of a world different from this one might be expected to break through into consciousness occasionally in the course of human history, very likely in a distorted form, and this might be the source of those very queer ideas which we read of with so much incredulity and astonishment in the writings of some speculative metaphysicians. Not knowing their source, they mistakenly applied these ideas to this world in which we now live, embellishing them sometimes with an elaborate façade of deductive reasoning. Viewed in cold blood and with a skeptical eye, their attempts may appear extremely unconvincing and their deductive reasoning fallacious. But perhaps, without knowing it, they may have valuable hints to give us if we are trying to form some conception, however tentative, of "another world." And this is something we must try to do if we take the problem of survival seriously.

Is Religious
Language
Meaningful?

Is Being Testable
a Condition of Being Intelligible?

Antony Flew lays down a challenge to the religious believer who accepts "God exists" as true. This statement cannot be true unless it is also meaningful. For any meaningful statement that is not true or false simply by definition, there must be some conceivable state of affairs which, if it occurred and were known, would count as evidence that the statement was false. Thus even though we have good evidence that George Washington was the first U.S. President, we can at least conceive of finding evidence that he was not. In so doing, we admit that it is conceivable that Washington was not the first President; we know what, for example, "Thomas Jefferson was the first U.S. President" *means*. But in the case of "God exists," what evidence would count against its being true? For the theist, Flew suggests, no evidence could possibly count against God's existence. Therefore "God exists" is not a genuine assertion at all and cannot possibly be false; if it cannot be false, it cannot be true either; as far as truth and falsity are concerned, it is meaningless.

R. M. Hare grants the thrust of Flew's argument and offers a flanking movement. He introduces the concept of a "blik." While not the most lucid concept ever formulated, the notion of a blik does clarify certain things about what Hare intends. Bliks are to be classified as beliefs that are not empirically verifiable or falsifiable. (Hare contrasts them to "more normal beliefs"). Though bliks are neither true nor false, they are presupposed by explanations, and at least some of them can be (in some sense) wrong (*see* Hare's example of the man who believes he is in danger from Oxford dons or instructors). Still the examples Hare gives of bliks provide a pretty mixed bag, and it seems clear that if the concept of a blik is to be of help in understanding theological statements, it must first be clarified far beyond anything that Hare offers. As it is, it provides a point of departure rather than a destination.

Basil Mitchell's response is apparently straightforward. The existence of evil counts as evidence against "God loves us," but not as conclusive evidence. Mitchell adds, however, that no believer can admit that any evidence *could* count decisively against his religious beliefs. This is altogether dubious. A man may admit the conceivability of conclusive evidence that he is not married but know perfectly well that there is in fact no such evidence. Analogously a believer may admit the conceivability of a world in which men *only* suffer and in which it would be clear that no God existed who loved them but may know that in fact there is no such evidence and (since God does love us) never will be. Nonetheless the response from Flew elicited by Mitchell's remarks is revealing and important.

Mitchell, we have seen, agrees with Flew that theological propositions must be viewed (if possible) as assertions and that one could conceive of evidence that would prove them false. Indeed, there is at least apparent evidence that "God loves us," for example, is false—namely, the fact of evil. For Mitchell the evidence is *only* an apparent disproof of God's existence. For Flew the existence of evil is incompatible with the existence of God. (Flew thus assumes a thesis that, as we saw in the section on the problem of evil, is quite complex and disputable.) In reply to Mitchell, Flew admits that he can offer only a disjunction: either "God exists" is meaningless or "God exists" is (due to the existence of evil) false. The latter half of the disjunction depends for its plausibility on an issue that is not clearly to be decided in Flew's favor. So perhaps, even on Flew's ground, "God exists" is meaningful, but not falsified by the existence of evil.

Flew's response to Hare is brief and pointed. Bliks, Hare says, are not assertions. For any view rightly called Christian (and Flew could have added "or Jewish"), "God loves us" is an assertion. So Hare's analysis works only for a quite heterodox theology. Second, bliks cannot serve as *reasons* for beliefs or actions as theological statements do, in the reflections of believers. So the analysis Hare offers is again not successful for theological statements as normally used.

John Hick also responds to Flew's challenge but in a way markedly different from Hare's and Mitchell's. He appeals to the notion of "eschatological verification"—verification in terms of events that occur after the death of the individual who experiences those events. (Hick's article is therefore also relevant to the topic dealt with by Price under the question "Is man immortal?")

Hick agrees that assertions must be empirically testable. (It is worth mentioning that not all philosophers grant this claim. He thus asks: what empirical evidence would in fact verify "God exists"? For Hick, to verify means to remove ignorance or uncertainty concerning the truth or falsity of some statement. He suggests that ignorance or uncertainty concerning whether "God exists" is true could be removed by a man's surviving his death and discovering that his new environment has certain properties. He describes these properties.

There are, I suggest, two possible developments of our experience such that, if they occurred in conjunction with one another (whether in this life or in another life to come) they would assure us beyond rational doubt of the reality of God, as conceived in the Christian faith. These are, first, an experience of the fulfillment of God's purpose for ourselves, as this has been disclosed in the Christian revelation; in conjunction, second, with an experience of God as he has revealed himself in the person of Christ.

Several remarks may help in clarifying Hick's program and appraising its chances for success. First, it might seem that one could only *verify* the claim that "God exists" along the lines Hick suggests. For if no one survived his death, no one could have the "developments of experience" Hick mentions. But of course one could survive and have other sorts of experience that might falsify the claim in question. So while there is no doubt an asymmetry between verification and falsification (see Hick's examples), it does not, on Hick's account, apply in the case of "God exists." Second, as Hick himself notes in the parenthetic comment in the quotation above, there is nothing *logically* impossible about verification occurring in *this* life. So, if Hick requires only that the claim "God exists" be, under *conceivable* conditions, empirically verified or falsified, reference to empirical evidence attained *after one's death* is superfluous. Third, perhaps only *some* people could, even after death, have the "developments of experience" which, according to Hick, would verify "God exists." Hick notes that these developments can perhaps "only be experienced by those who have . . . faith" in God now. This is not sufficient reason to discount such developments as positive evidence; that one can attain this evidence only by meeting specified conditions (making certain commitments) is also true for, as examples, "Parenthood has satisfactions that override its frustrations" and "Acting unselfishly is its own reward." Fourth, even when such phrases as "The fulfillment of God's purpose for ourselves" receive the clarification they obviously require (what exactly will *count* as fulfillment?), and if it is clear how postmortem experiences will be *less* ambiguous with respect to providing evidence of God's existence than present experience is, postmortem experiences will still be somewhat ambiguous in the sense that they can (without contradiction) be interpreted in more than one way. This is compatible with there being only one *plausible* interpretation. Finally, as Hick intends, his account of what would verify the claim that God exists is developed quite explicitly within the context of Christian theology. (One could, of course, develop a similar account in the context of other religious systems.) But this means that the plausibility of the claim that were these experiences to occur, we *would* have verification of "God exists" depends squarely on the acceptability of Christian theology as a context of thought in which such experiences can be interpreted. This raises large and important issues, which cannot be discussed here; but this point remains clear: a given interpretation of an experience verifies a claim only if the conceptual context within which the interpretation occurs is acceptable. This shifts the issue from one of empirical confirmation or disconfirmation of a single statement to a more complex one of appraising conceptual schemes. As his book *Faith and Knowledge* reveals, Hick is well aware of (and sympathetic toward) this line of reasoning (compare his comment in footnote 6). This is, perhaps, the logical development of reflection upon Flew's original challenge, even though it may seem far removed from the apparent simplicity of that challenge.

Religious Language Is Not Meaningful
ANTONY FLEW

Let us begin with a parable. It is a parable developed from a tale told by John Wisdom in his haunting and revelatory article "Gods." Once upon a time two explorers came upon a clearing in the jungle. In the clearing were growing many flowers and many weeds. One explorer says, "Some gardener must tend this plot." The other disagrees, "There is no gardener." So they pitch their tents and set a watch. No gardener is ever seen. "But perhaps he is an invisible gardener." So they set up a barbed-wire fence. They electrify it. They patrol with bloodhounds. (For they remember how H. G. Wells's *The Invisible Man* could be both smelt and touched through he could not be seen.) But no shrieks ever suggest that some intruder has received a shock. No movements of the wire ever betray an invisible climber. The bloodhounds never give cry. Yet still the Believer is not convinced. "But there is a gardener, invisible, intangible, insensible to electric shocks, a gardener who has no scent and makes no sound, a gardener who comes secretly to look after the garden which he loves." At last the Skeptic despairs, "But what remains of your original assertion? Just how does what you call an invisible, in-

tangible, eternally elusive gardener differ from an imaginary gardener or even from no gardener at all?"

In this parable we can see how what starts as an assertion, that something exists or that there is some analogy between certain complexes of phenomena, may be reduced step by step to an altogether different status, to an expression perhaps of a "picture preference."[1] The skeptic says there is no gardener. The Believer says there is a gardener (but invisible, etc.). One man talks about sexual behaviour. Another man prefers to talk of Aphrodite (but knows that there is not really a superhuman person additional to, and somehow responsible for, all sexual phenomena). The process of qualification may be checked at any point before the original assertion is completely withdrawn and something of that first assertion will remain (tautology). Mr. Wells's invisible man could not, admittedly, be seen, but in all other respects he was a man like the rest of us. But though the process of qualification may be, and of

[1] Cf. J. Wisdom, "Other Minds," *Mind* (1940), reprinted in his *Other Minds* (Oxford: Basil Blackwell, 1952).

FROM: *New Essays in Philosophical Theology*, Antony Flew and Alasdair MacIntyre, eds. (New York: The Macmillan Co.; and London: Student Christian Movement Press Limited, 1955), pp. 275–295. Reprinted by permission of the publishers and Professor R. M. Hare. This is the source of this essay and the following three, which form one symposium.

course usually is, checked in time, it is not always judiciously so halted. Someone may dissipate his assertion completely without noticing that he has done so. A fine brash hypothesis may thus be killed by inches, the death by a thousand qualifications.

And in this, it seems to me, lies the peculiar danger, the endemic evil, of theological utterance. Take such utterances as "God has a plan," "God created the world," "God loves us as a father loves his children." They look at first sight very much like assertions, vast cosmological assertions. Of course, this is no sure sign that they either are, or are intended to be, assertions. But let us confine ourselves to the cases where those who utter such sentences intend them to express assertions. (Merely remarking parenthetically that those who intend or interpret such utterances as cryptocommands, expressions of wishes, disguished ejaculations, concealed ethics, or as anything else but assertions are unlikely to succeed in making them either properly orthodox or practically effective.)

Now to assert that such and such is the case is necessarily equivalent to denying that such and such is not the case. Suppose then that we are in doubt as to what someone who gives vent to an utterance is asserting, or suppose that, more radically, we are skeptical as to whether he is really asserting anything at all, one way of trying to understand (or perhaps it will be to expose) his utterance is to attempt to find what he would regard as counting against, or as being incompatible with, its truth. For if the utterance is indeed an assertion, it will necessarily be equivalent to a denial of the negation of that assertion. And anything which would count against the assertion, or which would induce the speaker to withdraw it and to admit that it had been mistaken, must be part of (or the whole of) the meaning of the negation of that assertion. And to know

the meaning of the negation of an assertion is as near as makes no matter to know the meaning of that assertion. And if there is nothing which a putative assertion denies then there is nothing which it asserts either: and so it is not really an assertion. When the Skeptic in the parable asked the Believer, "Just how does what you call an invisible, intangible, eternally elusive gardener differ from an imaginary gardener or even from no gardener at all?" he was suggesting that the Believer's earlier statement had been so eroded by qualification that it was no longer an assertion at all.

Now it often seems to people who are not religious as if there was no conceivable event or series of events the occurrence of which would be admitted by sophisticated religious people to be a sufficient reason for conceding "There wasn't a God after all" or "God does not really love us then." Someone tells us that God loves us as a father loves his children. We are reassured. But then we see a child dying of inoperable cancer of the throat. His earthly father is driven frantic in his efforts to help, but his Heavenly Father reveals no obvious sign of concern. Some qualification is made—God's love is "not a merely human love" or it is "an inscrutable love," perhaps—and we realize that such sufferings are quite compatible with the truth of the assertion that "God loves us as a father (but, of course, . . .)." We are reassured again. But then perhaps we ask: what is this assurance of God's (appropriately qualified) love worth, what is this apparent guarantee really a guarantee against? Just what would have to happen not merely (morally and wrongly) to tempt but also (logically and rightly) to entitle us to say "God does not love us" or even "God does not exist"? I therefore put to the succeeding symposiasts the simple central questions, "What would have to occur or to have occurred to constitute for you a disproof of the love of, or of the existence of, God?"

A Reply to Flew (1)

R. M. HARE

I *wish* to make it clear that I shall not try to defend Christianity in particular, but religion in general—not because I do not believe in Christianity, but because you cannot understand what Christianity is, until you have understood what religion is.

I must begin by confessing that, on the ground marked out by Flew, he seems to me to be completely victorious. I therefore shift my ground by relating another parable. A certain lunatic is convinced that all dons want to murder him. His friends introduce him to all the mildest and most respectable dons that they can find, and after each of them has retired, they say, "You see, he doesn't really want to murder you; he spoke to you in a most cordial manner; surely you are convinced now?" But the lunatic replies "Yes, but that was only his diabolical cunning; he's really plotting against me the whole time, like the rest of them; I know it I tell you." However many kindly dons are produced, the reaction is still the same.

Now we say that such a person is deluded. But what is he deluded about? About the truth or falsity of an assertion? Let us apply Flew's test to him. There is no behaviour of dons that can be enacted which he will accept as counting against his theory; and therefore his theory, on this test, asserts nothing. But it does not follow that there is no difference between what he thinks about dons and what most of us think about them—otherwise we should not call him a lunatic and ourselves sane, and dons would have no reason to feel uneasy about his presence in Oxford.

Let us call that in which we differ from this lunatic, our respective *bliks*. He has an insane *blik* about dons; we have a sane one. It is important to realize that we save a sane one, not no *blik* at all; for there must be two sides to any argument—if he has a wrong *blik*, then those who are right about dons must have a right one. Flew has shown that a *blik* does not consist in an assertion or system of them; but nevertheless it is very important to have the right *blik*.

Let us try to imagine what it would be like to have different *bliks* about other things than dons. When I am driving my car, it sometimes occurs to me to wonder whether my movements of the steering-wheel will always continue to be followed by corresponding alterations in the direction of the car. I have never had a steering failure, though I have had skids, which must be similar. Moreover, I know enough about how the steering of my car is made to know the sort of thing that would have to go wrong for the steering to fail—steel joints would have to part, or steel rods break, or something—but how do I know that this won't happen? The truth is, I don't know; I just have a *blik* about steel and its properties, so that normally I trust the steering of my car; but I find it not at all difficult to imagine what it would be like to lose this *blik* and acquire the opposite one. People would say I was silly about steel; but there would be no mistaking the reality of the difference between our respective *bliks*—for example, I should never go in a motor-car. Yet I should hesitate to say that the difference between us was the difference between contradictory assertions. No amount of safe arrivals or bench-tests will remove my *blik* and restore the normal one; for my *blik* is compatible with any finite number of such tests.

It was Hume who taught us that our whole commerce with the world depends upon our *blik* about the world; and that differences between *bliks* about the world cannot be settled by observation of what happens in the world. That was why, having performed the interesting experiment of doubting the ordinary man's *blik* about the world, and showing that no proof could be given to make us adopt one *blik* rather than another, he turned to backgammon to take his mind off the problem. It seems, indeed, to be impossible even to formulate as an assertion the normal *blik* about the world which makes me put my confidence in the future reliability of steel joints, in the continued ability of the road to support my car, and not gape beneath it revealing nothing below; in the general non-homicidal tendencies of dons; in my own continued well-being (in some sense of that word that I may not now fully understand) if I continue to do what is right according to my lights; in the general likelihood of people like Hitler coming to a bad end. But perhaps a formulation less inadequate than most is to be found in the Psalms: "The earth is weak and all the inhabiters thereof: I bear up the pillars of it."

The mistake of the position which Flew selects for attack is to regard this kind of talk as some sort of *explanation*, as scientists are accustomed to use the word. As such, it would obviously be ludicrous. We no longer believe in God as an Atlas—*nous n'avons pas besoin de cette hypothèse* [we have no need of that hypothesis]. But it is nevertheless true to say that, as Hume saw, without a *blik* there can be no explanation; for it is by our *bliks* that we decide what is and what is not an explanation. Suppose we believed that everything that happened, happened by pure chance. This would not of course be an assertion; for it is compatible with anything happening or not happening, and so, incidentally, is its contradictory. But if we had this belief, we should not be able to explain or predict or plan anything. Thus, although we should not be *asserting* anything different from those of a more normal belief, there would be a great difference between us; and this is the sort of difference that there is between those who really believe in God and those who really disbelieve in him.

The word "really" is important, and may excite suspicion. I put it in, because when people have had a good Christian upbringing, as have most of those who now profess not to believe in any sort of religion, it is very hard to discover what they really believe. The reason why they find it so easy to think that they are not religious is that they have never got into the frame of mind of one who suffers from the doubts to which religion is the answer. Not for them the terrors of the primitive jungle. Having abandoned some of the more picturesque fringes of religion, they think that they have abandoned the whole thing—whereas in fact they still have got, and could not live without, a religion of a comfortably substantial, albeit highly sophisticated, kind, which differs from that of many "religious people" in little more than this, that "religious people" like to sing Psalms about theirs —a very natural and proper thing to do. But nevertheless there may be a big difference lying behind—the difference between two people who, though side by side, are walking in different directions. I do not know in what direction Flew is walking; perhaps he does not know either. But we have had some examples recently of various ways in which one can walk away from Christianity, and there are any number of possibilities. After all, man has not changed biologically since primitive times; it is his religion that has changed, and it can easily change again. And if you do not think that such changes make a difference, get acquainted with some Sikhs and some Mussulmans of the same Punjabi stock; you will find them quite different sorts of people.

There is an important difference between Flew's parable and my own which we have not yet noticed. The explorers do not *mind* about their garden; they discuss it with interest, but not with concern. But my lunatic, poor fellow, minds about dons; and I mind about the steering of my car; it often has people in it that I care for. It is because I mind very much about what goes on in the garden in which I find myself, that I am unable to share the explorers' detachment.

A Reply to Flew (2)
BASIL MITCHELL

Flew's article is searching and perceptive, but there is, I think, something odd about his conduct of the theologian's case. The theologian surely would not deny that the fact of pain counts against the assertion that God loves men. This very incompatibility generates the most intractable of theological problems—the problem of evil. So the theologian *does* recognize the fact of pain as counting against Christian doctrine. But it is true that he will not allow it—or anything—to count decisively against it; for he is committed by his faith to trust in God. His attitude is not that of the detached observer, but of the believer.

Perhaps this can be brought out by yet another parable. In time of war in an occupied country, a member of the resistance meets one night a stranger who deeply impresses him. They spend that night together in conversation. The Stranger tells the partisan that he himself is on the side of the resistance—indeed that he is in command of it, and urges the partisan to have faith in him no matter what happens. The partisan is utterly convinced at that meeting of the Stranger's sincerity and constancy and undertakes to trust him.

They never meet in conditions of intimacy again. But sometimes the Stranger is seen helping members of the resistance, and the partisan is grateful and says to his friends, "He is on our side."

Sometimes he is seen in the uniform of the police handing over patriots to the occupying power. On these occasions his friends murmur against him: but the partisan still says, "He is on our side." He still believes that, in spite of appearances, the Stranger did not deceive him. Sometimes he asks the Stranger for help and receives it. He is then thankful. Sometimes he asks and does not receive it. Then he says, "The Stranger knows best." Sometimes his friends, in exasperation, say "Well, what *would* he have to do for you to admit that you were wrong and that he is not on our side?" But the partisan refuses to answer. He will not consent to put the Stranger to the test. And sometimes his friends complain, "Well, if *that's* what you mean by his being on our side, the sooner he goes over to the other side the better."

The partisan of the parable does not allow anything to count decisively against the proposition "The Stranger is on our side." This is because he has committed himself to trust the Stranger. But he of course recognizes that the Stranger's ambiguous behaviour *does* count against what he believes about him. It is precisely this situation which constitutes the trial of his faith.

When the partisan asks for help and doesn't get it, what can he do? He can (*a*) conclude that the Stranger is not on our side; or (*b*) maintain that he is on our side, but that he has reasons for withholding help.

The first he will refuse to do. How long can he uphold the second position without its becoming just silly?

I don't think one can say in advance. It will depend on the nature of the impression created by the Stranger in the first place. It will depend, too, on the manner in which he takes the Stranger's behaviour. If he blandly dismisses it as of no consequence, as having no bearing upon his belief, it will be assumed that he is thoughtless or insane. And it quite obviously won't do for him to say easily, "Oh, when used of the Stranger the phrase 'is on our side' *means* ambiguous behaviour of this sort." In that case he would be like the religious man who says blandly of a terrible disaster "It is God's will." No, he will only be regarded as sane and reasonable in his belief, if he experiences in himself the full force of the conflict.

It is here that my parable differs

from Hare's. The partisan admits that many things may and do count against his belief: whereas Hare's lunatic who has a *blik* about dons doesn't admit that anything counts against his *blik*. Nothing *can* count against *bliks*. Also the partisan has a reason for having in the first instance committed himself, viz., the character of the Stranger; whereas the lunatic has no reason for his *blik* about dons—because, of course, you can't have reasons for *bliks*.

This means that I agree with Flew that theological utterances must be assertions. The partisan is making an assertion when he says, "The Stranger is on our side."

Do I want to say that the partisan's belief about the Stranger is, in any sense, an explanation? I think I do. It explains and makes sense of the Stranger's behaviour: it helps to explain also the resistance movement in the context of which he appears. In each case it differs from the interpretation which the others put upon the same facts.

"God loves men" resembles "the Stranger is on our side" (and many other significant statements, e.g., historical ones) in not being conclusively falsifiable. They can both be treated in at least three different ways: (1) as provisional hypotheses to be discarded if experience tells against them, (2) as significant articles of faith, (3) as vacuous formulae (expressing, perhaps, a desire for reassurance) to which experience makes no difference and which make no difference to life.

The Christian, once he has committed himself, is precluded by his faith from taking up the first attitude: "Thou shalt not tempt the Lord thy God." He is in constant danger, as Flew has observed, of slipping into the third. But he need not; and, if he does, it is a failure in faith as well as in logic.

A Response to Criticism
ANTONY FLEW

*I*t *has been* a good discussion; and I am glad to have helped to provoke it. But now . . . it must come to an end: and [I shall] make some concluding remarks. Since it is impossible to deal with all the issues raised or to comment separately upon each contribution, I will concentrate on Mitchell and Hare, as representative of two very different kinds of response to [my] challenge. . . .

The challenge, it will be remembered, ran like this. Some theological utterances seem to, and are intended to, provide explanations or express assertions. Now an assertion, to be an assertion at all, must claim that things stand thus and thus; *and not otherwise*. Similarly an explanation, to be an explanation at all, must explain why this particular thing occurs; *and not something else*. Those last clauses are crucial. And yet sophisticated religious people— or so it seemed to me—are apt to overlook this, and tend to refuse to allow, not merely that anything actually does occur, but that anything conceivably could occur, which would count against their theological assertions and explanations. But insofar as they do this their supposed explanations are actually bogus, and their seeming assertions are really vacuous.

Mitchell's response to this challenge is admirably direct, straightforward, and understanding. He agrees "that theological utterances must be assertions." He agrees that if they are to be assertions, there must be something that would count against their truth. He agrees, too, that believers are in constant danger of transforming their would-be assertions into "vacuous formulae." But he takes me to task for an oddity in my "conduct of the theologian's case." The theologian surely would not deny that the fact of pain counts against the assertion that God loves men. This very incompatibility generates the most intractable of theological problems, the problem of evil." I think he is right. I should have made a distinction between two very different ways of dealing with what looks like evidence against the love of God; the way I stressed was the expedient of qualifying the original assertion; the way the theologian usually takes, at first, is to admit that it looks bad but to insist that there is—there must be—some explanation which will show that, in spite of appearances, there really is a God who loves us. His difficulty, it seems to me, is that he has given God attributes which rule out all possible saving explanations. In Mitchell's parable of the Stranger it is easy for the believer to find plausible excuses for ambiguous behaviour; for the Stranger is a man. But suppose the Stranger is God. We cannot say that he would like to help but cannot; God is omnipotent. We cannot say that he would help if he only knew; God is omniscient. We cannot say that he is not responsible for the wickedness of others; God creates those others. Indeed an omnipotent, omniscient God must be an accessory before (and during) the fact to every human misdeed; as well as being responsible for every non-moral defect in the universe. So, though I entirely concede that Mitchell was absolutely right to insist against me that the theologian's first move is to look for an *explanation*, I still think that in the end, if relentlessly pursued, he will have to resort to the avoiding action of *qualification*. And there lies the danger of that death by a thousand qualifications, which would, I agree, constitute "a failure in faith as well as in logic."

Hare's approach is fresh and bold. He confesses that "on the ground marked out by Flew, he seems to me to be completely victorious." He therefore introduces the concept of *blik*. But while I think that there is room for some such concept in philosophy, and that philosophers should be grateful to Hare for

his invention, I nevertheless want to insist that any attempt to analyze Christian religious utterances as expressions or affirmations of a *blik* rather than as (at least would-be) assertions about the cosmos is fundamentally misguided. First, because thus interpreted they would be entirely unorthodox. If Hare's religion really is a *blik*, involving no cosmological assertions about the nature and activities of a supposed personal creator, then surely he is not a Christian at all? Second, because thus interpreted, they could scarcely do the job they do. If they were not even intended as assertions, then many religious activities would become fraudulent, or merely silly. If "You ought *because* it is God's will" asserts no more than "You ought," then the person who prefers the former phraseology is not really giving a reason, but a fraudulent substitute for one, a dialectical dud check. If "My soul must be immortal *because* God loves his children, etc." asserts no more than "My soul must be immortal," then the man who reassures himself with theological arguments for immortality is being as silly as the man who tries to clear his overdraft by writing his bank a check on the same account. (Of course neither of these utterances would be distinctively Christian; but this discussion never pretended to be so confined.) Religious utterances may indeed express false or even bogus assertions: but I simply do not believe that they are not both intended and interpreted to be or at any rate to presuppose assertions, at least in the context of religious practice, whatever shifts may be demanded, in another context, by the exigencies of theological apologetic.

One final suggestion. The philosophers of religion might well draw upon George Orwell's last appalling nightmare, *1984*, for the concept of *doublethink*. "*Doublethink* means the power of holding two contradictory beliefs simultaneously, and accepting both of them. The party intellectual knows that he is playing tricks with reality, but by the exercise of *doublethink* he also satisfies himself that reality is not violated." Perhaps religious intellectuals too are some- times driven to doublethink in order to retain their faith in a loving God in face of the reality of a heartless and indifferent world. But of this more another time, perhaps.

Religious Language Is Meaningful
JOHN HICK

*T*o ask "Is the existence of God veri- fiable?" is to pose a question which is too imprecise to be capable of being answered. There are many different con- cepts of God, and it may be that state- ments employing some of them are open to verification or falsification while state- ments employing others of them are not. Again, the notion of verifying is itself by no means perfectly clear and fixed; and it may be that on some views of the nature of verification the existence of God is verifiable whereas on other views it is not.

Instead of seeking to compile a list of the various different concepts of God and the various possible senses of "verify," I wish to argue with regard to one particular concept of deity, namely the Christian concept, that divine ex- istence is in principle verifiable; and as the first stage of this argument I must indicate what I mean by "verifiable."[1]

I

The central core of the concept of veri- fication, I suggest, is the removal of ignorance or uncertainty concerning the truth of some proposition. That *p* is veri- fied (whether *p* embodies a theory, hypothesis, prediction, or straightforward assertion) means that something happens which makes it clear that *p* is true. A question is settled so that there is no longer room for rational doubt concern- ing it. The way in which grounds for rational doubt are excluded varies of

[1] For the considerations that lead Hick to raise this question, see the preceding four essays.

course with the subject matter. But the general feature common to all cases of verification is the ascertaining of truth by the removal of grounds for rational doubt. Where such grounds are removed, we rightly speak of verification having taken place.

To characterize verification in this way is to raise the question whether the notion of verification is purely logical or is both logical and psychological. Is the statement that *p* is verified simply the statement that a certain state of affairs exists (or has existed), or is it the state- ment also that someone is aware that this state of affairs exists (or has existed) and notes that its existence establishes the truth of *p*? A geologist predicts that the earth's surface will be covered with ice in 15 million years time. Suppose that in 15 million years time the earth's sur- face *is* covered with ice, but that in the meantime the human race has perished, so that no one is left to observe the event or to draw any conclusion con- cerning the accuracy of the geologist's prediction. Do we now wish to say that his prediction has been verified, or shall we deny that it has been verified on the ground that there is no one left to do the verifying?

The use of "verify" and its cognates is sufficiently various to permit us to speak in either way. But the only sort of verification of theological propositions which is likely to interest us is one in which human beings participate. We may therefore, for our present purpose, treat verification as a logico-psychological rather than as a purely logical concept. I suggest then that "verify" be construed

FROM: *Theology Today*, "Eschatological Verification," April, 1960. Published by permission of editor and author.

as a verb which has its primary uses in the active voice: I verify, you verify, we verify, they verify or have verified. The impersonal passive, it is verified, now becomes logically secondary. To say that *p* has been verified is to say that (at least) someone has verified it, often with the implication that his or their report to this effect is generally accepted. But it is impossible, on this usage, for *p* to have been verified without someone having verified it. "Verification" is thus primarily the name for an event which takes place in human consciousness.[2] It refers to an experience, the experience of ascertaining that a given proposition or set of propositions is true. To this extent verification is a psychological notion. But of course it is also a logical notion. For needless to say, not *any* experience is rightly called an experience of verifying *p*. Both logical and psychological conditions must be fulfilled in order for verification to have taken place. In this respect, "verify" is like "know." Knowing is an experience which someone has or undergoes, or perhaps a dispositional state in which someone is, and it cannot take place without someone having or undergoing it or being in it; but not by any means every experience which people have, or every dispositional state in which they are, is rightly called knowing.

With regard to this logico-psychological concept of verification, such questions as the following arise. When *A*, but nobody else, has ascertained that *p* is true, can *p* be said to have been verified; or is it required that others also have undergone the same ascertainment? How public, in other words, must verification be? Is it necessary that *p* could in principle be verified by anyone without restriction even though perhaps only

A has in fact verified it? If so, what is meant here by "in principle"; does it signify, for example, that *p* must be verifiable by anyone who performs a certain operation; and does it imply that to do this is within everyone's power?

These questions cannot, I believe, be given any general answer applicable to all instances of the exclusion of rational doubt. The answers must be derived in each case from an investigation of the particular subject matter. It will be the object of subsequent sections of this article to undertake such an investigation in relation to the Christian concept of God.

Verification is often construed as the verification of a prediction. However verification, as the exclusion of grounds for rational doubt, does not necessarily consist in the proving correct of a prediction; a verifying experience does not always need to have been predicted in order to have the effect of excluding rational doubt. But when we are interested in the verifiability of propositions as the criterion for their having factual meaning, the notion of prediction becomes central. If a proposition contains or entails predictions which can be verified or falsified, its character as an assertion (though not of course its character as a true assertion) is thereby guaranteed.

Such predictions may be and often are conditional. For example, statements about the features of the dark side of the moon are rendered meaningful by the conditional predictions which they entail to the effect that if an observer comes to be in such a position in space, he will make such-and-such observations. It would in fact be more accurate to say that the prediction is always conditional, but that sometimes the conditions are so obvious and so likely to be fulfilled in any case that they require no special mention, while sometimes they require for their fulfillment some unusual expedition or operation. A prediction, for example, that the sun will rise within twenty-four hours is intended unconditionally, at least as concerns conditions to be fulfilled by the observer; he

---

[2] This suggestion is closely related to Carnap's insistence that, in contrast to "true," "confirmed" is time-dependent. To say that a statement is confirmed, or verified, is to say that it has been confirmed at a particular time—and, I would add, by a particular person. *See* Rudolf Carnap, "Truth and Confirmation," Feigl and Sellars, *Readings in Philosophical Analysis*, 1949, pp. 119 f.

is not required by the terms of the prediction to perform any special operation. Even in this case however there is an implied negative condition that he shall not put himself in a situation (such as immuring himself in the depths of a coal mine) from which a sunrise would not be perceptible. Other predictions however are explicitly conditional. In these cases it is true for any particular individual that in order to verify the statement in question he must go through some specified course of action. The prediction is to the effect that if you conduct such an experiment you will obtain such a result; for example, if you go into the next room you will have such-and-such visual experiences, and if you then touch the table which you see you will have such-and-such tactual experiences, and so on. The content of the "if" clause is always determined by the particular subject matter. The logic of "table" determines what you must do to verify statements about tables; the logic of "molecule" determines what you must do to verify statements about molecules; and the logic of "God" determines what you must do to verify statements about God.

In those cases in which the individual who is to verify a proposition must himself first perform some operation, it clearly cannot follow from the circumstances that the proposition is true that everybody has in fact verified it, or that everybody will at some future time verify it. For whether or not any particular person performs the requisite operation is a contingent matter.

II

What is the relation between verification and falsification? We are all familiar today with the phrase, "theology and falsification." Antony Flew[3] and others have raised instead of the question, "What possible experiences would verify 'God exists'?" the matching question

"What possible experiences would falsify 'God exists'? What conceivable state of affairs would be incompatible with the existence of God?" In posing the question in this way it was apparently assumed that verification and falsification are symmetrically related, and that the latter is apt to be the more accessible of the two.

In the most common cases, certainly, verification and falsification are symmetrically related. The logically simplest case of verification is provided by the crucial instance. Here it is integral to a given hypothesis that if, in specified circumstances, A occurs, the hypothesis is thereby shown to be true, whereas if B occurs the hypothesis is thereby shown to be false. Verification and falsification are also symmetrically related in the testing of such a proposition as "There is a table in the next room." The verifying experiences in this case are experiences of seeing and touching, predictions of which are entailed by the proposition in question, under the proviso that one goes into the next room; and the absence of such experience in those circumstances serves to falsify the proposition.

But it would be rash to assume, on this basis, that verification and falsification must always be related in this symmetrical fashion. They do not necessarily stand to one another as do the two sides of a coin, so that once the coin is spun it must fall on one side or the other. There are cases in which verification and falsification each correspond to a side on a different coin, so that one can fail to verify without this failure constituting falsification.

Consider, for example, the proposition that "there are three successive sevens in the decimal determination of π." So far as the value of π has been worked out, it does not contain a series of three sevens, but it will always be true that such a series may occur at a point not yet reached in anyone's calculations. Accordingly, the proposition may one day be verified if it is true, but can never be falsified if it is false.

The hypothesis of continued con-

[3] Antony Flew, "Theology and Falsification," reprinted above. On the philosophical antecedents of this change from the notion of verification to that of falsification, *see* Karl R. Popper, *The Logic of Scientific Discovery* (1934; E.T., 1959).

scious existence after bodily death provides an instance of a different kind of such asymmetry, and one which has a direct bearing upon the theistic problem. This hypothesis has built into it a prediction that one will after the date of one's bodily death have conscious experiences, including the experience of remembering that death. This is a prediction which will be verified in one's own experience if it is true, but which cannot be falsified if it is false. That is to say, it can be false, but *that* it is false can never be a fact which anyone has experientially verified. But this circumstance does not undermine the meaningfulness of the hypothesis, since it is also such that if it be true, it will be known to be true.

It is important to remember that we do not speak of verifying logically necessary truths, but only propositions concerning matters of fact. Accordingly verification is not to be identified with the concept of logical certification or proof. The exclusion of rational doubt concerning some matter of fact is not equivalent to the exclusion of the logical possibility of error or illusion. For truths concerning fact are not logically necessary. Their contrary is never self-contradictory. But at the same time the bare logical possibility of error does not constitute ground for rational doubt as to the veracity of our experience. If it did, no empirical proposition could ever be verified, and indeed the notion of empirical verification would be without use and therefore without sense. What we rightly seek, when we desire the verification of a factual proposition, is not a demonstration of the logical impossibility of the proposition being false (for this would be a self-contradictory demand), but such kind and degree of evidence as suffices, in the type of case in question, to exclude rational doubt.

III

These features of the concept of verification—that verification consists in the exclusion of grounds for rational doubt concerning the truth of some proposition; that this means its exclusion from particular minds; that the nature of the ex-

perience which serves to exclude grounds for rational doubt depends upon the particular subject matter; that verification is often related to predictions and that such predictions are often conditional; that verification and falsification may be asymmetrically related; and finally, that the verification of a factual proposition is not equivalent to logical certification— are all relevant to the verification of the central religious claim, "God exists." I wish now to apply these discriminations to the notion of eschatological verification, which has been briefly employed by Ian Crombie in his contribution to *New Essays in Philosophical Theology*,[4] and by myself in *Faith and Knowledge*.[5] This suggestion has on each occasion been greeted with disapproval by both philosophers and theologians. I am, however, still of the opinion that the notion of eschatological verification is sound; and further, that no viable alternative to it has been offered to establish the factual character of theism.

The strength of the notion of eschatological verification is that it is not an *ad hoc* invention but is based upon an actually operative religious concept of God. In the language of Christian faith, the word "God" stands at the center of a system of terms, such as Spirit, grace, Logos, incarnation, Kingdom of God, and many more; and the distinctly Christian conception of God can only be fully grasped in its connection with these related terms.[6] It belongs to a complex of notions which together constitute a picture of the universe in which we live, of man's place therein, of a comprehensive

[4] *Op. cit.*, p. 126.

[5] Ithaca: Cornell University Press and London: Oxford University Press. 1957, pp. 150–62.

[6] Its clear recognition of this fact, with regard not only to Christianity but to any religion, is one of the valuable features of Ninian Smart's *Reasons and Faiths* (1958). He remarks, for example, that "the claim that God exists can only be understood by reference to many, if not all, other propositions in the doctrinal scheme from which it is extrapolated" (p. 12).

divine purpose interacting with human purposes, and of the general nature of the eventual fulfillment of that divine purpose. This Christian picture of the universe, entailing as it does certain distinctive expectations concerning the future, is a very different picture from any that can be accepted by one who does not believe that the God of the New Testament exists. Further, these differences are such as to show themselves in human experience. The possibility of experiential confirmation is thus built into the Christian concept of God; and the notion of eschatological verification seeks to relate this fact to the problem of theological meaning.

Let me first give a general theological indication of this suggestion, by repeating a parable which I have related elsewhere,[7] and then try to make it more precise and eligible for discussion. Here, first, is the parable.

Two men are travelling together along a road. One of them believes that it leads to a Celestial City, the other that it leads nowhere; but since this is the only road there is, both must travel it. Neither has been this way before, and therefore neither is able to say what they will find around each next corner. During their journey they meet both with moments of refreshment and delight, and with moments of hardship and danger. All the time one of them thinks of his journey as a pilgrimage to the Celestial City and interprets the pleasant parts as encouragements and the obstacles as trials of his purpose and lessons in endurance, prepared by the king of that city and designed to make of him a worthy citizen of the place when at last he arrives there. The other, however, believes none of this and sees their journey as an unavoidable and aimless ramble. Since he has no choice in the matter, he enjoys the good and endures the bad. But for him there is no Celestial City to be reached, no all-encompassing purpose ordaining their journey; only the road itself and the luck of the road in good weather and in bad.

During the course of the journey the issue between them is not an experimental one. They do not entertain different expectations about the coming details of the road, but only about its ultimate destination. And yet when they do turn the last corner it will be apparent that one of them has been right all the time and the other wrong. Thus although the issue between them has not been experimental, it has nevertheless from the start been a real issue. They have not merely felt differently about the road; for one was feeling appropriately and the other inappropriately in relation to the actual state of affairs. Their opposed interpretations of the road constituted genuinely rival assertions, though assertions whose assertion-status has the peculiar characteristic of being guaranteed retrospectively by a future crux.

This parable has of course (like all parables) strict limitations. It is designed to make only one point: that Christian doctrine postulates an ultimate unambiguous state of existence *in patria* as well as our present ambiguous existence *in via*. There is a state of having arrived as well as a state of journeying, an eternal heavenly life as well as an earthly pilgrimage. The alleged future experience of this state cannot, of course, be appealed to as evidence for theism as a present interpretation of our experience; but it does suffice to render the choice between theism and atheism a real and not a merely empty or verbal choice. And although this does not affect the logic of the situation, it should be added that the alternative interpretations are more than theoretical, for they render different practical plans and policies appropriate now.

The universe as envisaged by the theist, then, differs as a totality from the universe as envisaged by the atheist. This difference does not, however, from our present standpoint within the universe, involve a difference in the objective content of each or even any of its passing moments. The theist and the atheist do not (or need not) expect different events to occur in the successive details of the temporal process. They do not (or need

[7] *Faith and Knowledge*, pp. 150f.

not) entertain divergent expectations of the course of history viewed from within. But the theist does and the atheist does not expect that when history is completed it will seem to have led to a particular end-state and to have fulfilled a specific purpose, namely that of creating "children of God."

IV

The idea of an eschatological verification of theism can make sense, however, only if the logically prior idea of continued personal existence after death is intelligible. A desultory debate on this topic has been going on for several years in some of the philosophical periodicals. C. I. Lewis has contended that the hypothesis of immortality "is an hypothesis about our own future experience. And our understanding of what would verify it has no lack of clarity."[8] And Morris Schlick agreed, adding. "We must conclude that immortality, in the sense defined [i.e. 'survival after death,' rather than 'never-ending life'], should not be regarded as a 'metaphysical problem,' but is an empirical hypothesis, because it possesses logical verifiability. It could be verified by following the prescription: 'Wait until you die!' "[9] However, others have challenged this conclusion, either on the ground that the phrase "surviving death" is self-contradictory in ordinary language or, more substantially, on the ground that the traditional distinction between soul and body cannot be sustained.[10] I should like to address myself to this latter view. The only self of which we know, it is said, is the empirical self, the walking, talking, acting, sleeping individual who lives, it may be, for some

sixty to eighty years and then dies. Mental events and mental characteristics are analyzed into the modes of behavior and behavioral dispositions of this empirical self. The human being is described as an organism capable of acting in the "high-level" ways which we characterize as intelligent, thoughtful, humorous, calculating, and the like. The concept of mind or soul is thus not the concept of a "ghost in the machine" (to use Gilbert Ryle's loaded phrase[11]) but of the more flexible and sophisticated ways in which human beings behave and have it in them to behave. On this view there is no room for the notion of soul in distinction from body; and if there is no soul in distinction from body there can be no question of the soul surviving the death of the body. Against this philosophical background the specifically Christian (and also Jewish) belief in the resurrection of the flesh or body, in contrast to the Hellenic notion of the survival of a disembodied soul, might be expected to have attracted more attention than it has. For it is consonant with the conception of man as an indissoluble psychophysical unity, and yet it also offers the possibility of an empirical meaning for the idea of "life after death."

Paul is the chief Biblical expositor of the idea of the resurrection of the body.[12] His view, as I understand it, is this. When someone has died he is, apart from any special divine action, extinct. A human being is by nature mortal and subject to annihilation by death. But in fact God, by an act of sovereign power, either sometimes or always resurrects or (better) reconstitutes or recreates him—not, however, as the identical physical organism that he was before death, but as a *soma pneumatikon* ("spiritual body") embodying the dispositional characteristics and memory traces of the deceased physical organism, and inhabiting an environment with which the *soma pneu-*

---

[8] "Experience and Meaning," *Philosophical Review*, 1934, reprinted in Feigl and Sellars, *Readings in Philosophical Analysis,* 1949, p. 142.

[9] "Meaning and Verification," *Philosophical Review*, 1936, reprinted in Feigl and Sellars, *op. cit.*, p. 160.

[10] *See* e.g., A. G. N. Flew, "Death," *New Essays in Philosophical Theology*; "Can a Man Witness his own Funeral?" *Hibbert Journal*, 1956.

[11] *The Concept of Mind*, 1949, which contains an important exposition of the interpretation of "mental" qualities as characteristics of behavior.

[12] I Cor. 15.

matikon is continuous as the ante-mortem body was continuous with our present world. In discussing this notion we may well abandon the word "spiritual," as lacking today any precise established usage, and speak of "resurrection bodies" and of "the resurrection world." The principal questions to be asked concern the relation between the physical world and the resurrection world, and the criteria of personal identity which are operating when it is alleged that a certain inhabitant of the resurrection world is the same person as an individual who once inhabited this present world. The first of these questions turns out on investigation to be the more difficult of the two, and I shall take the easier one first.

Let me sketch a very odd possibility (concerning which, however, I wish to emphasize not so much its oddness as its possibility!), and then see how far it can be stretched in the direction of the notion of the resurrection body. In the process of stretching it will become even more odd than it was before; but my aim will be to show that, however odd, it remains within the bounds of the logically possible. This progression will be presented in three pictures, arranged in a self-explanatory order.

First picture: Suppose that at some learned gathering in this country one of the company were suddenly and inexplicably to disappear, and that at the same moment an exact replica of him were suddenly and inexplicably to appear at some comparable meeting in Australia. The person who appears in Australia is exactly similar, as to both bodily and mental characteristics, with the person who disappears in America. There is continuity of memory, complete similarity of bodily features, including even fingerprints, hair and eye coloration and stomach contents, and also of beliefs, habits, and mental propensities. In fact there is everything that would lead us to identify the one who appeared with the one who disappeared, except continuity of occupancy of space. We may suppose, for example, that a deputation of the colleagues of the man who

disappeared fly to Australia to interview the replica of him which is reported there, and find that he is in all respects but one exactly as though he had traveled from say, Princeton to Melbourne, by conventional means. The only difference is that he describes how, as he was sitting listening to Dr. Z. reading a paper, on blinking his eye he suddenly found himself sitting in a different room listening to a different paper by an Australian scholar. He asks his colleagues how the meeting had gone after he ceased to be there, and what they had made of his disappearance, and so on. He clearly thinks of himself as the one who was present with them at their meeting in the United States. I suggest that faced with all these circumstances his colleagues would soon, if not immediately, find themselves thinking of him and treating him as the individual who had so inexplicably disappeared from their midst. We should be extending our normal use of "same person" in a way which the postulated facts would both demand and justify if we said that the one who appears in Australia is the same person as the one who disappears in America. The factors inclining us to identify them would far outweigh the factors disinclining us to do this. We should have no reasonable alternative but to extend our usage of "the same person" to cover the strange new case.

Second picture: Now let us suppose that the event in America is not a sudden and inexplicable disappearance, and indeed not a disappearance at all but a sudden death. Only, at the moment when the individual dies, a replica of him as he was at the moment before his death, complete with memory up to that instant, appears in Australia. Even with the corpse on our hands, it would still, I suggest, be an extension of "same person" required and warranted by the postulated facts, to say that the same person who died has been miraculously re-created in Australia. The case would be considerably odder than in the previous picture, because of the existence of the corpse in America contemporaneously with the existence of the living person in Australia. But I submit that, although the oddness of this circumstance may be stated as strongly as you please, and can indeed hardly be overstated, yet it does not exceed the bounds of the logically possible. Once again we must imagine some of the deceased's colleagues going to Australia to interview the person who has suddenly appeared there. He would perfectly remember them and their meeting, be interested in what had happened, and be as amazed and dumbfounded about it as anyone else; and he would perhaps be worried about the possible legal complications if he should return to America to claim his property; and so on. Once again, I believe, they would soon find themselves thinking of him and treating him as the same person as the dead Princetonian. Once again the factors inclining us to say that the one who died and the one who appeared are the same person would outweigh the factors inclining us to say that they are different people. Once again we should have to extend our usage of "the same person" to cover this new case.

Third picture: My third supposal is that the replica, complete with memory, etc., appears, not in Australia, but as a resurrection replica in a different world altogether, a resurrection world inhabited by resurrected persons. This world occupies its own space, distinct from the space with which we are now familiar.[13] That is to say, an object in the resurrection world is not situated at any distance or in any direction from an object in our present world, although each object in either world is spatially related to each other object in the same world.

Mr. X, then, dies. A Mr. X replica, complete with the set of memory traces which Mr. X had at the last moment before his death, comes into existence. It is composed of other material than physical matter, and is located in a resurrection world which does not stand in any spatial relationship with the physical world. Let us leave out of consideration St. Paul's hint that the resurrection body may be as unlike the physical body as is a full grain of wheat from the wheat seed, and consider the simpler picture in which the resurrection body has the same shape as the physical body.[14]

In these circumstances, how does Mr. X know that he has been resurrected or recreated? He remembers dying; or rather he remembers being on what he took to be his death-bed, and becoming progressively weaker until, presumably, he lost consciousness. But how does he know that (to put it Irishly) his "dying" proved fatal; and that he did not, after losing consciousness, begin to recover strength, and has now simply waked up?

The picture is readily enough elaborated to answer this question. Mr. X meets and recognizes a number of relatives and friends and historical personages whom he knows to have died; and from the fact of their presence, and also from their testimony that he has only just now appeared in their world, he is convinced that he has died. Evidences of this kind could mount up to the point at which they are quite as strong as the evidence which, in pictures one and two, convince the individual in question that he has been miraculously translated to Australia. Resurrected persons would be individually no more in doubt about their own identity than we are now, and would be able to identify one another in the same kinds of ways, and with a like degree of assurance, as we do now.

If it be granted that resurrected persons might be able to arrive at a rationally founded conviction that their existence is *post-mortem*, how could they know that the world in which they find themselves is in a different space from that in which their physical bodies were? How could such a one know that he is not in a like situation with the person in picture number two, who dies in America

---

[13] On this possibility, *see* Anthony Quinton, "Spaces and Times," *Philosophy*, XXXVII, No. 140 (April, 1962).

[14] As would seem to be assumed, for example, by Irenaeus (*Adversus Haereses*, Bk. II, Ch. 34, Sec. 1).

and appears as a full-blooded replica in Australia, leaving his corpse in the U.S.A. —except that now the replica is situated, not in Australia, but on a planet of some other star?

It is of course conceivable that the space of the resurrection world should have properties which are manifestly incompatible with its being a region of physical space. But on the other hand, it is not of the essence of the notion of a resurrection world that its space should have properties different from those of physical space. And supposing it not to have different properties, it is not evident that a resurrected individual could learn from any direct observations that he was not on a planet of some sun which is at so great a distance from our own sun that the stellar scenery visible from it is quite unlike that which we can now see. The grounds that a resurrected person would have for believing that he is in a different space from physical space (supposing there to be no discernible difference in spatial properties) would be the same as the grounds that any of us may have now for believing this concerning resurrected individuals. These grounds are indirect and consist in all those considerations (*e.g.*, Luke 16:26) which lead most of those who consider the question to reject as absurd the possibility of, for example, radio communication or rocket travel between earth and heaven.

V

In the present context my only concern is to claim that this doctrine of the divine creation of bodies, composed of a material other than that of physical matter, which bodies are endowed with sufficient correspondence of characteristics with our present bodies, and sufficient continuity of memory with our present consciousness, for us to speak of the same person being raised up again to life in a new environment, is not self-contradictory. If, then, it cannot be ruled out *ab initio* as meaningless, we may go on to consider whether and how it is related to the possible verification of Christian theism.

So far I have argued that a survival prediction such as is contained in the *corpus* of Christian belief is in principle subject to future verification. But this does not take the argument by any means as far as it must go if it is to succeed. For survival, simply as such, would not serve to verify theism. It would not necessarily be a state of affairs which is manifestly incompatible with the non-existence of God. It might be taken just as a surprising natural fact. The atheist, in his resurrection body, and able to remember his life on earth, might say that the universe has turned out to be more complex, and perhaps more to be approved of, than he had realized. But the mere fact of survival, with a new body in a new environment, would not demonstrate to him that there is a God. It is fully compatible with the notion of survival that the life to come be, so far as the theistic problem is concerned, essentially a continuation of the present life, and religiously no less ambiguous. And in this event, survival after bodily death would not in the least constitute a final verification of theistic faith.

I shall not spend time in trying to draw a picture of a resurrection existence which would merely prolong the religious ambiguity of our present life. The important question, for our purpose, is not whether one can conceive of after-life experiences which would *not* verify theism (and in point of fact one can fairly easily conceive them), but whether one can conceive of after-life experiences which *would* serve to verify theism.

I think that we can. In trying to do so I shall not appeal to the traditional doctrine, which figures especially in Catholic and mystical theology, of the Beatific Vision of God. The difficulty presented by this doctrine is not so much that of deciding whether there are grounds for believing it, as of deciding what it means. I shall not, however, elaborate this difficulty, but pass directly to the investigation of a different and, as it seems to me, more intelligible possibility. This is the possibility not of a direct vision of God, whatever that might mean, but of a *situation* which points unambiguously to the existence of a loving God. This would be a situation which, so far as its religious significance is concerned, contrasts in a certain important respect with our present situation. Our present situation is one which in some ways seems to confirm and in other ways to contradict the truth of theism. Some events around us suggest the presence of an unseen benevolent intelligence and others suggest that no such intelligence is at work. Our situation is religiously ambiguous. But in order for us to be aware of this fact we must already have some idea, however vague, of what it would be for our situation to be not ambiguous, but on the contrary wholly evidential of God. I therefore want to try to make clearer this presupposed concept of a religiously unambiguous situation.

There are, I suggest, two possible developments of our experience such that, if they occurred in conjunction with one another (whether in this life or in another life to come), they would assure us beyond rational doubt of the reality of God, as conceived in the Christian faith. These are, *first*, an experience of the fulfillment of God's purpose for ourselves, as this has been disclosed in the Christian revelation; in conjunction, *second*, with an experience of communion with God as he has revealed himself in the person of Christ.

The divine purpose for human lfie, as this is depicted in the New Testament documents, is the bringing of the human person, in society with his fellows, to enjoy a certain valuable quality of personal life, the content of which is given in the character of Christ—which quality of life (*i.e.* life in relationship with God, described in the Fourth Gospel as eternal life) is said to be the proper destiny of human nature and the source of man's final self-fulfillment and happiness. The verification situation with regard to such a fulfillment is asymmetrical. On the one hand, so long as the divine purpose remains unfulfilled, we cannot know that it never will be fulfilled in the future; hence no final falsification is possible of the claim that this fulfillment will occur —unless, of course, the prediction contains a specific time clause which, in Christian teaching, it does not. But on the other hand, if and when the divine purpose *is* fulfilled in our own experience, we must be able to recognize and rejoice in that fulfillment. For the fulfillment would not be for us the promised fulfillment without our own conscious participation in it.

It is important to note that one can say this much without being cognizant in advance of the concrete form which such fulfillment will take. The before-and-after situation is analogous to that of a small child looking forward to adult life and then, having grown to adulthood, looking back upon childhood. The child possesses and can use correctly in various contexts the concept of "being grown-up," although he does not know, concretely, what it is like to be grown-up. But when he reaches adulthood he is nevertheless able to know that he has reached it; he is able to recognize the experience of living a grown-up life even though he did not know in advance just what to expect. For his understanding of adult maturity grows as he himself matures. Something similar may be supposed to happen in the case of the fulfillment of the divine purpose for human life. That fulfillment may be as far removed from our present condition as is mature adulthood from the mind of a little child; nevertheless, we possess already a comparatively vague notion of this final fulfillment, and as we move towards it our concept will itself become more adequate; and if and when we finally reach that fulfillment, the problem of recognizing it will have disappeared in the process.

The other feature that must, I suggest, be present in a state of affairs that would verify theism, is that the fulfillment of God's purpose be apprehended *as* the fulfillment of God's purpose and not simply as a natural state of affairs. To this end it must be accompanied by an experience of communion with God as he has made himself known to men in Christ.

The specifically Christian clause, "as he has made himself known to men in Christ," is essential, for it provides a solution to the problem of recognition in the awareness of God. Several writers have pointed out the logical difficulty involved in any claim to have encountered God.[15] How could one know that it was *God* whom one had encountered? God is described in Christian theology in terms of various absolute qualities, such as omnipotence, omnipresence, perfect goodness, infinite love, etc., which cannot as such be observed by us, as can their finite analogues, limited power, local presence, finite goodness, and human love. One can recognize that a being whom one "encounters" has a given finite degree of power, but how does one recognize that he has *un*limited power? How does one observe that an encountered being is *omni*present? How does one perceive that his goodness and love, which one can perhaps see to exceed any human goodness and love, are actually infinite? Such qualities cannot be given in human experience. One might claim, then, to have encountered a Being whom one presumes, or trusts, or hopes to be God; but one cannot claim to have encountered a Being whom one recognized to be the infinite, almighty, eternal Creator.

This difficulty is met in Christianity by the doctrine of the Incarnation—although this was not among the considerations which led to the formulation of that doctrine. The idea of incarnation provides answers to the two related questions: "How do we know that God has certain absolute qualities which, by their very nature, transcend human experience?" and "How can there be an eschatological verification of theism which is based upon a recognition of the presence of God in his Kingdom?"

In Christianity God is known as "the God and Father of our Lord Jesus Christ."[16] God is the Being about whom

Jesus taught; the Being in relation to whom Jesus lived, and into a relationship with whom he brought his disciples; the Being whose *agape* [self-giving love] toward men was seen on earth in the life of Jesus. In short, God is the transcendent Creator who has revealed himself in Christ. Now Jesus' teaching about the Father is a part of that self-disclosure, and it is from this teaching (together with that of the prophets who preceded him) that the Christian knowledge of God's transcendent being is derived. Only God himself knows his own infinite nature; and our human belief about that nature is based upon his self-revelation to men in Christ. As Karl Barth expresses it, "Jesus Christ is the knowability of God."[17] Our beliefs about God's infinite being are not capable of observational verification, being beyond the scope of human experience, but they are susceptible of indirect verification by the removal of rational doubt concerning the authority of Christ. An experience of the reign of the Son in the Kingdom of the Father would confirm that authority, and therewith, indirectly, the validity of Jesus' teaching concerning the character of God in his infinite transcendent nature.

The further question as to how an eschatological experience of the Kingdom of God could be known to be such has already been answered by implication. It is God's union with man in Christ that makes possible man's recognition of the fulfillment of God's purpose for man as being indeed the fulfillment of *God's* purpose for him. The presence of Christ in his Kingdom marks this as being beyond doubt the Kingdom of the God and Father of the Lord Jesus Christ.

It is true that even the experience of the realization of the promised Kingdom of God, with Christ reigning as Lord of the New Aeon, would not constitute a logical certification of his claims nor, accordingly, of the reality of God. But this will not seem remarkable to any philosopher in the empiricist tradition,

[15] For example, H. W. Hepburn, *Christianity and Paradox*, 1958, pp. 56f.

[16] II Cor. 11:31.

[17] *Church Dogmatics*, Vol. II, Pt. I, p. 150.

who knows that it is only a confusion to demand that a factual proposition be an analytic truth. A set of expectations based upon faith in the historic Jesus as the incarnation of God, and in his teaching as being divinely authoritative, could be so fully confirmed in *post-mortem* experience as to leave no grounds for rational doubt as to the validity of that faith.

VI

There remains of course the problem (which falls to the New Testament scholar rather than to the philosopher) whether Christian tradition, and in particular the New Trestament, provides a sufficiently authentic "picture" of the mind and character of Christ to make such recognition possible. I cannot here attempt to enter into the vast field of Biblical criticism, and shall confine myself to the logical point, which only emphasizes the importance of the historical question, that a verification of theism made possible by the Incarnation is dependent upon the Christian's having a genuine contact with the person of Christ, even though this is mediated through the life and tradition of the Church.

One further point remains to be considered. When we ask the question, "*To whom* is theism verified?" one is initially inclined to assume that the answer must be, "To everyone." We are inclined to assume that, as in my parable of the journey, the believer must be confirmed in his belief, and the unbeliever converted from his unbelief. But this assumption is neither demanded by the nature of verification nor by any means unequivocally supported by our Christian sources.

We have already noted that a verifiable prediction may be conditional. "There is a table in the next room" entails conditional predictions of the form: if someone goes into the next room he will see, etc. But no one is compelled to go into the next room. Now it may be that the predictions concerning human experience which are entailed by the proposition that God exists are conditional predictions and that no one is compelled to fulfill those conditions. Indeed we stress in much of our theology that the manner of the divine self-disclosure to men is such that our human status as free and responsible beings is respected, and an awareness of God is never forced upon us. It may then be a condition of *post-mortem* verification that we be already in some degree conscious of God by an uncompelled response to his modes of revelation in this world. It may be that such a voluntary consciousness of God is an essential element in the fulfillment of the divine purpose for human nature, so that the verification of theism which consists in an experience of the final fulfillment of that purpose can only be experienced by those who have already entered upon an awareness of God by the religious mode of apperception which we call faith.

If this be so, it has the consequence that only the theistic believer can find the vindication of his belief. This circumstance would not of course set any restriction upon who can become a believer, but it would involve that while theistic faith can be verified—found by one who holds it to be beyond rational doubt—yet it cannot be proved to the nonbeliever. Such an asymmetry would connect with that strand of New Testament teaching which speaks of a division of mankind even in the world to come.

Having noted this possibility I will only express my personal opinion that the logic of the New Testament as a whole, though admittedly not always its explicit content, leads to a belief in ultimate universal salvation. However, my concern here is not to seek to establish the religious facts, but rather to establish that there are such things as religious facts, and in particular that the existence or nonexistence of the God of the New Testament is a matter of fact, and claims as such eventual experiential verification.

Bibliography

THEORY OF KNOWLEDGE

Alexander, P. *Sensationalism and Scientific Explanation*. London: Routledge and Kegan Paul Ltd., 1963.

Armstrong, D. *Bodily Sensations*. London: Routledge and Kegan Paul Ltd., 1962.

———. *Perception and the Physical World*. London: Routledge and Kegan Paul Ltd., 1961.

Ayer, A. J. *The Foundations of Empirical Knowledge*. New York: The Macmillan Company, 1940.

Beck, L. *The Metaphysics of Descartes*. New York: Oxford University Press, Inc., 1969.

Dretske, F. *Seeing and Knowing*. London: Routledge and Kegan Paul Ltd., 1969.

Casteñeda, H. *Intentionality, Minds and Perception*. Detroit, Mich.: Wayne State University Press, 1966.

Chisholm, R. *Realism and the Background to Phenomenology*. New York: The Free Press, 1960.

———. *Theory of Knowledge*. Englewood Cliffs, N.J.: Prenctice-Hall, Inc., 1966.

Ewing, A. C. *The Idealist Tradition from Berkeley to Bradley*. New York: The Free Press, 1957.

Flew, A. *Logic and Language*. Series I and II. Oxford: Basil Blackwell & Mott Ltd., 1961, 1963.

———. *Essays in Conceptual Analysis*. New York: The Macmillan Company, 1960.

Griffiths, A. P., ed. *Knowledge and Belief*. New York: Oxford University Press, Inc., 1967.

Hamlyn, D. M. *Sensation and Perception*. London: George Allen and Unwin Ltd., 1959.

Hall, E. *Categorial Analysis*. Edited by E. M. Adams. Chapel Hill, N.C.: University of North Carolina Press, 1964.

Hill, T. E. *Contemporary Theories of Knowledge*. New York: The Ronald Press Company, 1961.

Hicks, G. Dawes. *Berkeley*. New York: Russell and Russell Publishers, 1968.

Hirst, R. J., ed. *Perception and the External World*. New York: The Macmillan Company, 1965.

Lewis, C. I. *An Analysis of Knowledge and Valuation*. LaSalle, Ill.: Open Court Publishing Co., 1946.

Joske, W. *Material Objects*. New York: St. Martin's Press, Inc., 1967.

Kenny, A. *Descartes*. New York: Random House, Inc., 1968.

Kneale, W. and M. *The Development of Logic*. Oxford: The Clarendon Press, 1962.

Lovejoy, A. *The Revolt Against Dualism*. LaSalle, Ill.: Open Court Publishing Co., 1930.

Moore, G. E. *Some Main Problems of Philosophy*. London: George Allen and Unwin Ltd., 1953.

Price, H. H. *Perception*. London: Methuen Publishers, 1932.

―――. *Hume's Theory of the External World*. New York: Oxford University Press, Inc., 1940.

―――. *Thinking and Experience*. London: Hutchinson & Co., Ltd., 1933.

Quine, W. *Word and Object*. Cambridge, Mass.: The M.I.T. Press, 1960.

Rorty, R., ed. *The Linguistic Turn*. Chicago, Ill.: University of Chicago Press, 1967.

Russell, B. *Human Knowledge and Its Scope and Limits*. New York: Simon and Schuster, Inc., 1948.

―――. *Our Knowledge of the External World*. London: George Allen and Unwin Ltd., 1926.

Sellars, W. *Science, Perception and Reality*. London: Routledge and Kegan Paul Ltd., 1963.

Smart, J. *Philosophy and Scientific Realism*. London: Routledge and Kegan Paul Ltd., 1963.

Swartz, R. J. *Perceiving, Sensing and Knowing*. New York: Doubleday and Company, Inc., 1965.

Vendler, Z. *Linguistics in Philosophy*. Ithaca, N.Y.: Cornell University Press, 1967.

Weinberg, J. R. *Abstraction, Relations and Induction*. Madison, Wis.: University of Wisconsin Press, 1965.

―――. *An Examination of Logical Positivism*. London: Routledge and Kegan Paul Ltd., 1936.

Wiggins, D. *Identity and Spatio-Temporal Continuity*. Oxford: Basil Blackwell & Mott Ltd., 1967.

METAPHYSICS

Anscombe, E. and Geach, P. *Three Philosophers*. Ithaca, N.Y.: Cornell University Press, 1961.

Ayer, A. J. *The Concept of Person and Other Essays*. New York: St. Martin's Press, Inc., 1963.

Berofsky, B. *Free Will and Determinism*. New York: Harper and Row, Publishers, 1966.

Black, Max. *Philosophical Analysis*. Englewood Cliffs, N.J.: Prentice-Hall, Inc., 1963.

Blanshard, B. *Reason and Analysis*. LaSalle, Ill.: Open Court Publishing Co., 1962.

Broad, C. D. *The Mind and Its Place in Nature*. London: Routledge and Kegan Paul Ltd., 1925.

Chappell, Vere. *The Philosophy of Mind*. Englewood Cliffs, N.J.: Prentice-Hall, Inc., 1962.

Cornman, J. and Lehrer, K. *An Introduction to Philosophical Arguments*. New York: The Macmillan Company, 1968.

DeGeorge, Richard T. *Classical and Contemporary Metaphysics*. New York: Holt, Rinehart and Winston, Inc., 1962.

Drennen, D. A. *A Modern Introduction to Metaphysics*. New York: The Free Press, 1962.

Ducasse, C. J. *Nature, Mind and Death*. LaSalle, Ill.: Open Court Publishing Co., 1951.

Dworkin, G. *Determinism, Free Will and Moral Responsibility*. Englewood Cliffs, N.J.: Prentice-Hall, Inc., 1970.

Emmet, Dorothy. *The Nature of Metaphysical Thinking*. New York: The Macmillan Company, 1946.

Feigl, H. and Sellars, W. *Readings in Philosophical Analysis*. New York: Appleton-Century-Crofts, 1949.

Flew, A. *Body, Mind and Death*. New York: The Macmillan Company, 1964.

Hall, E. *Philosophical Systems*. Chicago, Ill.: University of Chicago Press, 1960.

Hampshire, S. *Philosophy of Mind*. New York: Harper and Row, Publishers, 1966.

Hook, Sidney. *Dimensions of Mind*. New York: The Macmillan Company, 1960.

Hospers, John. *An Introduction to Philosophical Analysis*. 2d ed. Englewood Cliffs, N.J.: Prentice-Hall, Inc., 1967.

Kennick, W. E. and Lazerowitz, Morris. *Metaphysics: Readings and Reappraisals*. Englewood Cliffs, N.J.: Prentice-Hall, Inc., 1966.

Lehrer, Keith. *Freedom and Determinism*. New York: Random House, Inc., 1966.

Locke, D. *Myself and Others*. New York: Oxford University Press, Inc., 1968.

Mandelbaum, M. *Philosophy, Science and Sense Perception*. Baltimore, Md.: The Johns Hopkins Press, 1964.

Nagel, E. *The Structure of Science*. New York: Harcourt, Brace and World, Inc., 1961.

Pears, D. F. *The Nature of Metaphysics*. New York: The Macmillan Company, 1957.

———. *Freedom and the Will*. New York: St. Martin's Press, Inc., 1963.

Pepper, Stephen. *World Hypotheses*. Berkeley, Calif.: University of California Press, 1942.

Shoemaker, S. *Self-Knowledge and Self-Identity*. Ithaca, N.Y.: Cornell University Press, 1963.

Strawson, P. F. *Individuals: An Essay in Descriptive Metaphysics*. London: Methuen Publishers, 1959.

Taylor, A. E. *Elements of Metaphysics*. London: Methuen Publishers, 1903.

Taylor, Richard. *Action and Purpose*. Englewood Cliffs, N.J.: Prentice-Hall, Inc., 1966.

Vesey, G. *Body and Mind*. London: George Allen and Unwin Ltd., 1964.

———. *The Embodied Mind*. London: George Allen and Unwin Ltd., 1965.

Walsh, W. H. *Metaphysics*. London: Hutchinson & Co., Ltd., 1963.

White, A. R. *The Philosophy of Mind*. Englewood Cliffs, N.J.: Prentice-Hall, Inc., 1967.

Wisdom, John. *Problems of Mind and Matter*. New York: Cambridge University Press, 1934.

———. *Other Minds*. Oxford: Basil Blackwell & Mott Ltd., 1962.

ETHICS

Adams, E. M. *Ethical Naturalism and the Modern World-View*. Chapel Hill, N.C.: University of North Carolina Press, 1961.

Baier, K. *The Moral Point of View*. Ithaca, N.Y.: Cornell University Press, 1958.

Blanshard, B. *Reason and Goodness*. LaSalle, Ill.: Open Court Publishing Co., 1961.

Bradley, F. H. *Ethical Studies*. New York: Oxford University Press, Inc., 1962.

Brandt, R. B. *Ethical Theory*. Englewood Cliffs, N.J.: Prentice-Hall, Inc., 1959.

Broad, C. D. *Five Types of Ethical Theory*. New York: Harcourt, Brace and World, Inc., 1934.

Brunner, Emil. *The Divine Imperative*. Philadelphia: The Westminster Press, 1947.

Carritt, E. F. *The Theory of Morals*. New York: Oxford University Press, Inc., 1928.

Casteñeda, H. and Nakhnikian, G. *Morality and the Language of Conduct*. Detroit, Mich.: Wayne State University Press, 1963.

Edwards, Paul. *The Logic of Moral Discourse*. New York: The Free Press, 1955.

Ekman, R. *Readings in the Problems of Ethics*. New York: Charles Scribner's Sons, 1965.

Foot, P. *Theories of Ethics*. New York: Oxford University Press, Inc., 1966.

Frankena, W. *Ethics*. Englewood Cliffs, N.J.: Prentice-Hall, Inc., 1963.

Hall, E. W. *Our Knowledge of Fact and Value*. Chapel Hill, N.C.: University of North Carolina Press, 1961.

———. *What Is Value*. New York: Humanities Press, Inc., 1952.

Hare, R. M. *Freedom and Reason*. Oxford: The Clarendon Press, 1963.

———. *The Language of Morals*. Oxford: The Clarendon Press, 1952.

Hospers, J. *Human Conduct*. New York: Harcourt, Brace and World, Inc., 1961.

Jones, Sontag, Beckner, and Fogelin. *Approaches to Ethics*. New York: McGraw-Hill Book Company, 1962.

Lyons, David. *The Forms and Limits of Utilitarianism*. Oxford: The Clarendon Press, 1969.

Melden, A. I. *Readings in Ethical Theory*. Englewood Cliffs, N.J.: Prentice-Hall, Inc., 1955.

Moore, G. E. *Principia Ethica*. New York: Cambridge University Press, 1929.

Nowell-Smith, P. *Ethics*. London: Penguin Books Ltd., 1954.

Oldenquist, A. *Readings in Moral Philosophy*. Boston: Houghton Mifflin Company, 1969.

Pritchard, H. A. *Moral Obligation*. Oxford: The Clarendon Press, 1949.

Ross, W. D. *The Foundations of Ethics*. Oxford: The Clarendon Press, 1939.

———. *The Right and the Good*. Oxford: The Clarendon Press, 1930.

Sellars, W. and Hospers, J. *Readings in Ethical Theory*. New York: Appleton-Century-Crofts, 1952.

Sidgwick. *Methods of Ethics*. New York: The Macmillan Company, 1922.

Singer, Marcus. *Generalization in Ethics*. New York: Alfred A. Knopf, Inc., 1961.

Smart, J. J. C. *An Outline of a System of Utilitarian Ethics*. Melbourne: Melbourne University Press, 1961.

Stace, W. T. *The Concept of Morals*. New York: The Macmillan Company, 1937.

Stevenson, C. L. *Ethics and Language*. New Haven, Conn.: Yale University Press, 1944.

———. *Facts and Values*. New Haven, Conn.: Yale University Press, 1944.

Taylor, Paul. *Normative Discourse*. Englewood Cliffs, N.J.: Prentice-Hall, Inc., 1961.

Thomas, G. *Christian Ethics and Moral Philosophy*. New York: Charles Scribner's Sons, 1955.

Von Wright, G. *The Varieties of Goodness*. London: Routledge and Kegan Paul Ltd., 1963.

Westermarck, E. *The Origin and Development of Moral Ideas*. 2 vols. New York: The Macmillan Company, 1906.

PHILOSOPHY OF RELIGION

Abernathy, G. and Langford, T. *Philosophy of Religion*. 2d ed. New York: The Macmillan Company, 1968.

Alston, William. *Religious Belief and Philosophical Thought*. New York: Harcourt, Brace and World, Inc., 1963.

Baillie, John. *Our Knowledge of God*. New York: Charles Scribner's Sons, 1939.

Bevan, E. *Symbolism and Belief*. Boston: Beacon Press, 1957.

Cahn, Stephen. *Philosophy of Religion*. New York: Harper and Row, Publishers, 1970.

Campbell, C. A. *Selfhood and Godhood*. London: George Allen and Unwin Ltd., 1957.

Carnell, E. J. *Christian Commitment*. New York: The Macmillan Company, 1962.

Cullmann, Oscar. *Immortality of the Soul or Resurrection of the Body*. London: Epworth Press, 1958.

Farrar, A. *Finite and Infinite*. London: Dacre Press, 1943.

———. *The Glass of Vision*. London: Dacre Press, 1948.

Ferre, F. *Logic, Language and God*. New York: Harper and Row, Publishers, 1961.

Flew, A. *God and Philosophy*. New York: Harcourt, Brace and World, Inc., 1966.

Frank, E. *Philosophical Understanding and Religious Truth*. New York: Oxford University Press, Inc., 1945.

Hick, John. *Classical and Contemporary Readings in the Philosophy of Religion*. 2d ed. Englewood Cliffs, N.J.: Prentice-Hall, Inc., 1970.

———. *Faith and Knowledge*. 2d. ed. Ithaca, N.Y.: Cornell University Press, 1966.

———, ed. *Faith and the Philosophers*. New York: St. Martin's Press, Inc., 1964.

———. *Philosophy of Religion*. Englewood Cliffs, N.J.: Prentice-Hall, Inc., 1963.

Hook, S., ed. *Religious Experience and Truth*. London: Oliver and Boyd Ltd., 1962.

James, William. *Essays on Faith and Morals*. New York: The World Publishing Company, 1962.

———. *The Varieties of Religious Experience*. New York: The New American Library, Inc., 1958.

———. *The Will To Believe*. New York: Dover Publications, Inc., 1956.

Kant, Immanuel. *Religion Within the Limits of Reason Alone*. New York: Harper and Row, Publishers, 1960.

Lewis, C. S. *Mere Christianity*. New York: The Macmillan Company, 1956.

———. *Miracles*. New York: The Macmillan Company, 1955.

———. *Screwtape Letters*. London: William Collins Sons and Company, 1943.

Lewis, H. D. *Our Experience of God*. London: George Allen and Unwin Ltd., 1959.
MacGregor, G. and Robb, J. *Readings in Religious Philosophy*. Boston: Houghton Mifflin Company, 1963.
Martin, C. B. *Religious Belief*. Ithaca, N.Y.: Cornell University Press, 1959.
Mavrodes, G. *Belief in God*. New York: Random House, Inc., 1970.
———— and Hackett, S. *Problems and Perspectives in the Philosophy of Religion*. Boston: Allyn and Bacon, Inc., 1967.
McIntyre, A. C. *Metaphysical Beliefs*. London: SCM Press Ltd., 1957.
Mitchell, Basil. *Faith and Logic*. London: George Allen and Unwin Ltd., 1957.
Niebuhr, H. R. *The Meaning of Revelation*. New York: The Macmillan Company, 1941.
Niebuhr, R. *The Nature and Destiny of Man*. New York: Charles Scribner's Sons, 1941.
Pike, Nelson. *God and Timelessness*. New York: Schocken Books, Inc., 1970.
Plantinga, Alvin, ed. *Faith and Philosophy*. Grand Rapids, Mich.: Eerdmans Publishing Company, 1964.
————. *God and Other Minds*. Ithaca, N.Y.: Cornell University Press, 1967.
Ramsey, Ian, ed. *The Prospect for Metaphysics*. New York: Philosophical Library, Inc., 1961.
————. *Religious Language*. New York: The Macmillan Company, 1963.
Smart, Ninian. *Philosophers and Religious Truth*. London: SCM Press Ltd., 1964.
————. *Reasons and Faiths*. London: Routledge and Kegan Paul Ltd., 1958.
Smith, John. *Experience and God*. New York: Oxford University Press, Inc., 1968.
Stace, W. T. *Time and Eternity*. Princeton, N.J.: Princeton University Press, 1952.
Taylor, A. E. *The Faith of a Moralist*. New York: The Macmillan Company, 1932.
Temple, William. *Nature, Man and God*. New York: The Macmillan Company, 1956.
von Hugel, Baron. *Essays and Addresses*. 2 vols. London: J. M. Dent and Sons Ltd., 1921.
Yandell, Keith. *Basic Issues in the Philosophy of Religion*. Boston: Allyn and Bacon, Inc., 1971.
————. *God, Man and Religion*. New York: McGraw-Hill Book Company, 1972.